The HUTCHINSON
FACTFINDER

Helicon

© Helicon Publishing Ltd 1998
Maps copyright © Helicon Publishing Ltd 1998

All rights reserved

First Published 1992
Second Edition 1994
Reissued with corrections 1998
Reprinted 1999

Helicon Publishing Ltd
42 Hythe Bridge Street Oxford OX1 2EP

Set in Helvetica and Times

Printed and bound in Great Britain by
The Bath Press Ltd, Bath, Somerset

ISBN 1-85986-000-1

British Library Cataloguing in Publication Data
A catalogue record for this book is available from
the British Library

Project Editor
Denise Dresner

Assistant Editor
Helen Maxey

Text Editors
Jane Anson, Lionel and Janet Browne,
Ingrid von Essen, Edith Harkness

Researcher
Anna Farkas

Index
Ann Barrett

Page Make-up
Roger Walker

Production
Tony Ballsdon

Contributors
Paul Bahn, Ian Derbyshire, J D Derbyshire, Michael
Dewar, Dougal Dixon, Nigel Dudley, Robert Dyer,
Ingrid von Essen, Eric Farge, Wendy Grossman,
Peter Lafferty, Robin Maconie, Tom McArthur,
David Munro, Joanna O'Brien, Maureen O'Connor,
Robert Paisley, Martin Palmer, Paulette Pratt,
Tim Pulleine, John Pym, Chris Rhys, Ian Ridpath,
Julian Rowe, Emma Shackleton, Jack Schofield,
Steve Smyth, Joe Staines, Calum Storrie

The HUTCHINSON
FACTFINDER

CONTENTS

SCIENCE AND TECHNOLOGY

Time and Measurement

Imperial units 1 • Metric units 1 • Conversion tables for weights and measurements 2 • Temperature scales 3 • SI units 4 • Decibels 5 • Miscellaneous measures 6 • International paper sizes 9 • Book publishing papers 9 • International time zones 10 • Calendars 11 • Islamic calendar 11 • Jewish calendar 12 • Chinese calendar 13 • Year equivalents between calendars 14 • Perpetual calendar 15 • Names of the months and days 19 • Wedding anniversaries 19 • Birthstones 19 • Signs of the zodiac 20

Archaeology

Terms and techniques 21 • Chronological chart 24 • Archaeology chronology 26

Astronomy

Space exploration 29 • Space flight chronology 30 • Space probe chronology 32 • Main launches 1992–1993 33 • The solar system 34 • Major comets 35 • Solar and lunar eclipses 36 • Largest meteorites 37 • Planets 38 • Largest planetary satellites 39 • Stars, galaxies, and the Universe 40 • Constellations 41 • Brightest stars 42 • Technical terms 43 • Astronomy chronology 45 • Telescopes and observatories 47 • Large ground-based telescopes 48 • Astronomers and astronauts 49 • Astronomers Royal 50

Chemistry

Divisions 53 • Biochemistry 53 • Biochemistry chronology 54 • Inorganic chemistry 56 • Chemical elements 57 • Transuranic elements 59 • Discovery of the elements 60 • Periodic table of the elements 62 • Organic chemistry 62 • Terms 65 • Chemistry chronology 66 • pH scale 70 • Great chemists 72 • Nobel Prize for Chemistry 74

Computing and Electronics

How computers work 77 • Uses of computers 77 • Computing chronology 78 • Computer hardware 80 • Computing terms 81 • Binary code 82 • Programming languages 84 • Electronics terms 85 • Electronics chronology 87

Earth Science

The developing earth 90 • Geological time chart 91 • Major ice ages 91 • Earth science chronology 92 • The interior of the earth 94 • Major 20th-century earthquakes 94 • Richter scale 95 • Mercalli scale 95 • Volcanic eruptions 96 • The surface of the earth 96 • Largest deserts 97 • Major islands 97 • Largest lakes 98 • Highest mountains 99 • Longest rivers 100 Major waterfalls 101 • Atmosphere and ocean 101 • Floods and cyclones 103 • The world's oceans and seas 104

Energy

Terms 105 • Nuclear energy chronology 106 • Nuclear power accidents 107 • Nuclear reactors worldwide 107 • UK energy production and consumption 108 • Energy demands worldwide 109

Engineering and Building

Terms 111 • Remarkable bridges 111 • Longest bridges 112 • Highest railway bridges 112 • Longest ship canals 113 • Highest dams 113 • Tallest buildings 114 • Longest railway tunnels 114 • Channel tunnel chronology 115

Environment and Conservation

The natural world 116 • Water-scarce countries 118 • Environmental issues and pollutants 119 • Air pollution 119 • Deforestation 120 • Endangered species, global 121 • Endangered species, European red list 122 • Major oil spills 124 • The wildlife trade 126 • Environmental groups and initiatives 127 • National parks 128 • UK blue-flag beaches 130 • Hunting statistics 132

Food, Nutrition, and Agriculture

Food and drink 133 • Composition of cheeses 133 • Composition of milks 135 • Main types of vitamins 136 • Main trace minerals 137 • Daily dietary requirements 138 • Cooking methods 140 • Food technology 141 • E numbers 142 • Agriculture 143 • Agriculture chronology 147

Life Sciences

Evolutionary biology 149 • Numbers of species 150 • Reproduction 150 • Biology chronology 151 • The life cycle 151 • The maintenance of life 154 • The macroscopic world 155 • Animal lifespans 155 • The animal kingdom 156 • Insect classification 157 • Mollusc classification 158 • Mammal classification 158 • Fish classification 159 • Animal speeds 161 • Collective names of animals 160 • The plant kingdom 162 • The microscopic world 163 • The new synthesis 164 • New techniques 166

Mathematics

Terms 168 • Calculating common areas 168 • Bases 169 •
Mathematics chronology 170 • Prime numbers 175 • Great
mathematicians 178 • Fields medalists 178 • Large numbers 180 •
Roman numerals 181 • Playing-cards and dice odds 181

Physics

Terms 182 • Fundamental constants 183 • Physics chronology 186 •
Particle physics 189 • Subatomic particles 190 •
Great physicists 191 • Nobel Prize for Physics 194

Telecommunications and Video Technology

Terms 196 • Telecommunications chronology 198 • Television
chronology 200

BUSINESS AND ECONOMICS

Business

Business terms 202

International Economics

Terms 210 • GNP statistics 212 • Institutions and organizations 215 •
Nobel Prize for Economics 218 • World currency exchange rates 219

THE ARTS

Architecture

History 221 • Terms 222 • Biographies 224

Art

Ancient art 229 • Classical art 229 • Medieval art 231 • The Italian
Renaissance 232 • The 15th and 16th centuries 233 • Major Western
artists 234 • The 17th century 235 • The 18th century 236 • The
19th century 237 • The 20th century 238 • Eastern art 241

Cinema

Great directors 243 • Cinema chronology 245 • Film-festival awards
248 • Academy Awards 249

Dance

Genres 251 • Avant-garde dance repertory 251 • Ballet repertory 252
• Dance chronology 254 • Great 20th-century choreographers 256

Literature and Language

Great writers 257 • Nobel Prize for Literature 265 • Booker Prize 266 • Pulitzer Prize 267 • Goncourt Prize 267 • Poets laureate 267 • Grammar and usage 267 • Common spelling errors 270 • Language roots 271 • Word borrowings 271 • Main language groups 275 • Proofreading marks 276 • British and American sign language 278 • Abbreviations and acronyms 279 • Foreign words and phrases 287

Music

Terms 293 • Major operas 295 • Great composers 296 • Musical expressions 299 • Popular music and jazz 300 • UK best-selling singles 306

Photography

Terms 308 • Photography chronology 309 • Biographies 311

Theatre

Genres 315 • Theatre chronology 316 • Recent theatre award winners 319 • Biographies 319 • Shakespeare's plays 324

SOCIETY

Clothes and Fashion

Designers of today 327

Education

Terms 330

Health and Medicine

Medical terms 334 • The human body 336 • Composition of blood 337 • Bones of the human body 338 • Chronology of Western medicine 341 • Psychological disorders 341 • Phobias 343 • Chronology of psychology 345 •Diseases and disorders 346 • Types of drugs 353 • Plant-derived drugs 354 • Alternative therapies 354 • Nobel Prize for Physiology or Medicine 357

International Organizations

International organizations 360 • The European Community 363 • European Community Commission posts 364 • European Community Commission presidents 364 • The United Nations 365 • United Nations secretary generals 366 • United Nations members 368 • United Nations peacekeeping operations 1993 370 •

The British Commonwealth 370 • Human-rights and relief
organizations 372

Law

Terms 373 • Legal and penal institutions 381

Media

Television and radio networks 384 • International news agencies 386 •
International newspapers 388 • Advertising restrictions on European
television 391

Politics

Political ideologies 392 • Political terms 394 • UK central
government 397 • Major political thinkers 400 • Nobel Prize
for Peace 401

Religion

Major religious traditions 403 • Religious movements 409 •
Rites of passage 410 • Holy books 411 • Books of the Bible 412 •
Religious figures 413 • Popes 414 • Holy places 414 •
Religious festivals 415 • Christian festivals 418 • Hindu
festivals 419 • Buddhist festivals 419 • Patron saints 420 •
Saints' days 421

Sport

Events and records 424 • Biographies 445 • Sites of summer Olympic
Games 460 • Sites of Commonwealth Games 460

Transport

Air transport 461 • Flight chronology 462 • Rail transport 463 •
Rail transport chronology 463 • Road transport 464 •
Car chronology 465 • Countries with left-hand driving 466 •
Sea transport 466 • Sea transport chronology 467 • Road distances
between UK towns 468 • Road distances between European
cities 468 • Air distances between international cities 470 • Worst
railway disasters 472

Warfare

Military terms 473 • Treaties and conferences 478 • Wars and
leaders 479 • World War I chronology 482 • Notable naval
battles 483 • World War II chronology 484 • Civil wars and related
battles 485 • Weapons and equipment 486 • The arms trade 488 •
Armed forces ranks 489

THE WORLD

History

The Seven Wonders of the World 490 • Ancient Egypt 490 •
Ancient Greece 491 • Ancient Rome 492 • Roman emperors 493 •
Ottoman emperors 493 • Holy Roman emperors 494 • Ming and Qing
dynasty 494 • Emperors of India 495 • Inca emperors 495 • Aztec
emperors 495 • Emperors of Japan 496 • Kings of France 498 •
Rulers of Spain 498 • Kings of Italy 498 • House of Habsburg 498 •
Tsars of Russia 499 • Kings and queens of Scotland 499 • English
sovereigns 500 • The end of colonialism 501 • Revolutions 502 •
World chronology 506

World Leaders

Leaders of the modern world 530 • Prime ministers of the UK 543 •
Presidents of the USA 544 • Prime ministers of Australia 544 • Prime
ministers of Canada 545 • Prime ministers of New Zealand 545 •
Prime ministers of India 545 • Prime ministers of Japan 545 •
Presidents and Communist Party leaders of the USSR 546 • Prime
ministers and Communist Party leaders of China 546 • Prime ministers
and presidents of South Africa 546

Continents

Africa 547 • Antarctica 548 • Asia 550 • Europe 552 • North
America 553 • Oceania 554 • South America 555

Countries and Population

Countries of the world 557 • Largest countries by area 673 • Largest
countries by population 674 • The world's largest cities 674 • Urban
population growth 675 • Worldwide population growth 676 • World
literacy rates 677 • World life expectancy 678 • Human development
index 679 • States of the USA 680 • National holidays worldwide
682 • Indigenous populations and land rights 688 • Ethnic groups and
languages 689

Index

697

SCIENCE AND TECHNOLOGY

TIME AND MEASUREMENT

Imperial units

Length

1 foot	=	12 inches		
1 yard	=	3 feet		
1 rod	=	5$\frac{1}{2}$ yards		
1 chain	=	4 rods	=	22 yards
1 furlong	=	10 chain	=	220 yards
1 mile	=	5,280 feet		
1 mile	=	1,760 yards		
1 mile	=	8 furlongs		

Nautical

1 fathom	=	6 feet
1 cable length	=	100 fathoms
1 nautical mile	=	6,080 feet

Area

1 square foot	=	144 square inches
1 square yard	=	9 square feet
1 square rod	=	304$\frac{1}{4}$ square yards
1 rood	=	40 square rods
1 acre	=	4 roods
1 acre	=	4,840 square yards
1 square mile	=	640 acres

Volume

1 cubic foot	=	1,728 cubic inches
1 cubic yard	=	27 cubic feet
1 bulk barrel	=	5.8 cubic feet

Shipping

1 register ton	=	100 cubic feet

Capacity

1 fluid ounce	=	8 fluid drams
1 gill	=	5 fluid ounces
1 pint	=	4 gills
1 quart	=	2 pints
1 gallon	=	4 quarts
1 peck	=	2 gallons
1 bushel	=	4 pecks
1 quarter	=	8 bushels
1 bulk barrel	=	36 gallons

Weight (avoirdupois)

1 ounce	=	437$\frac{1}{2}$ grains
1 ounce	=	16 drams
1 pound	=	16 ounces
1 stone	=	14 pounds
1 quarter	=	28 pounds
1 hundredweight	=	4 quarters
1 ton	=	20 hundredweight

Metric units

Length

1 centimetre (cm)	= 10 millimetres (mm)	
1 decimetre (dm)	= 10 centimetres	= 100 millimetres
1 metre (m)	= 10 decimetres	= 1,000 millimetres
1 decametre (dam)	= 10 metres	
1 hectometre (hm)	= 10 decametres	= 100 metres
1 kilometre (km)	= 10 hectometres	= 1,000 metres

Area

1 square centimetre (cm^2)	= 100 square millimetres (mm^2)	
1 square metre (m^2)	= 10,000 square centimetres	
	= 1,000,000 square millimetres	
1 are (a)	= 100 square metres	
1 hectare (ha)	= 100 ares	
	= 10,000 square metres	
1 square kilometre (km^2)	= 100 hectares	
	= 1,000,000 square metres	

Weight (avoirdupois)

1 centigram (cg)	= 10 milligrams (mg)	
1 decigram (dg)	= 10 centigram	
	= 100 milligrams	
1 gram (g)	= 10 decigrams	
	= 1,000 milligrams	
1 decagram (dag)	= 10 grams	
1 hectogram (hg)	= 10 decagrams	= 100 grams
1 kilogram (kg)	= 10 hectograms	= 1,000 grams
1 tonne or metric ton (t)	= 1,000 kilograms	

Volume

1 cubic centimetre (cm^3)	= 1,000 cubic millimetres (mm^3)	
1 cubic decimetre (dm^3)	= 1,000 cubic centimetres	
	= 1,000,000 cubic millimetres	
1 cubic metre (m^3)	= 1,000 cubic decimetres	
	= 1,000,000 cubic centimetres	
	= 1,000,000,000 cubic millimetres	

Capacity

1 centilitre (cl)	= 10 millilitres (ml)	
1 decilitre (dl)	= 10 centilitres	= 100 millilitres
1 litre (l)	= 10 decilitres	= 1,000 millilitres
1 decalitre (dal)	= 10 litres	
1 hectolitre (hl)	= 10 decalitres	= 100 litres
1 kilolitre (kl)	= 10 hectolitres	= 1,000 litres

Conversion tables

To convert from imperial to metric	Multiply by	To convert from metric to imperial	Multiply by
Length			
inches	25.4	millimetres	0.039,37
feet	0.3048	metres	3.2808
yards	0.9144	metres	1.0936
furlongs	0.201	kilometres	4.971
miles	1.6093	kilometres	0.6214
Area			
square inches	6.4516	square centimetres	0.1550
square feet	0.0929	square metres	10.7639
square yards	0.8361	square metres	1.1960
square miles	2.5900	square kilometres	0.3861
acres	4046.86	square metres	0.000,247
acres	0.4047	hectares	2.47105
hectares	0.001	square kilometres	1,000
Volume, capacity			
cubic inches	16.3871	cubic centimetres	0.0610
cubic feet	0.02832	cubic metres	35.3134
cubic yards	0.7646	cubic metres	1.3079
fluid ounces	28.4131	millilitres	0.0352
pints	0.5683	litres	1.760
quarts	1.1365	litres	0.88
imperial gallons	4.54609	litres	0.21997
US gallons	3.7854	litres	0.2642
Mass/weight			
ounces	28.3495	grams	0.03527
pounds	0.4536	kilograms	2.2046
stone (14 lb)	6.3503	kilograms	0.1575
tons (imperial)	1016.05	kilograms	0.00098
tons (US)	907.2	kilograms	0.001
tons (imperial)	0.9842	tonnes	1.0161
tons (US)	0.9072	tonnes	1.102
Speed			
miles per hour	1.6093	kilometres per hour	0.6214
feet per second	0.3048	metres per second	3.2808
Force			
pound force	4.448	newton	0.2248
kilogram force	9.8096	newton	0.1019
Pressure			
pounds per square inch	6.894,76	kilopascals	0.1450
tons per square inch	15.4443	megapascals	0.0647
atmospheres	101,325	newtons per square metre	0.000,009,86
atmospheres	14.69	pounds per square inch	0.068
Energy			
calorie	4.186	joule	0.238
kilowatt hour	3,600,000	joule	0.000,000,277
Power			
horsepower	0.7457	kilowatts	1.341
Fuel consumption			
miles per gallon	0.3540	kilometres per litre	2.825
miles per US gallon	0.4251	kilometres per litre	2.3521
gallons per mile	2.8248	litres per kilometre	0.3540
US gallons per mile	2.3521	litres per kilometre	0.4251

Temperature scales

The freezing point and boiling point of water are 0 °C and 100 °C on the Celsius (centigrade) scale (100 degrees), and 32 °F and 212 °F on the Fahrenheit scale (180 degrees). So Celsius and Fahrenheit temperatures can be converted as follows:

$$C = (F - 32) \times {}^{100}/_{180}$$

$$F = (C \times {}^{180}/_{100}) + 32$$

Table of equivalent temperatures

°C	°F	°C	°F	°C	°F	°C	°F
100	212.0	70	158.0	40	104.0	10	50.0
99	210.2	69	156.2	39	102.2	9	48.2
98	208.4	68	154.4	38	100.4	8	46.4
97	206.6	67	152.6	37	98.6	7	44.6
96	204.8	66	150.8	36	96.8	6	42.8
95	203.0	65	149.0	35	95.0	5	41.0
94	201.2	64	147.2	34	93.2	4	39.2
93	199.4	63	145.4	33	91.4	3	37.4
92	197.6	62	143.6	32	89.6	2	35.6
91	195.8	61	141.8	31	87.8	1	33.8
90	194.0	60	140.0	30	86.0	0	32.0
89	192.2	59	138.2	29	84.2	−1	30.2
88	190.4	58	136.4	28	82.4	−2	28.4
87	188.6	57	134.6	27	80.6	−3	26.6
86	186.8	56	132.8	26	78.8	−4	24.8
85	185.0	55	131.0	25	77.0	−5	23.0
84	183.2	54	129.2	24	75.2	−6	21.2
83	181.4	53	127.4	23	73.4	−7	19.4
82	179.6	52	125.6	22	71.6	−8	17.6
81	177.8	51	123.8	21	69.8	−9	15.8
80	176.0	50	122.0	20	68.0	−10	14.0
79	174.2	49	120.2	19	66.2	−11	12.2
78	172.4	48	118.4	18	64.4	−12	10.4
77	170.6	47	116.6	17	62.6	−13	8.6
76	168.8	46	114.8	16	60.8	−14	6.8
75	167.0	45	113.0	15	59.0	−15	5.0
74	165.2	44	111.2	14	57.2	−16	3.2
73	163.4	43	109.4	13	55.4	−17	1.4
72	161.6	42	107.6	12	53.6	−18	−0.4
71	159.8	41	105.8	11	51.8	−19	−2.2

SI units

Base units

Quantity	Unit name	Unit symbol	Definition
length	metre	m	length of the path travelled by light in vacuum during a time interval of 1/299,792,458 of a second
mass	kilogram	kg	mass of the international prototype of the kilogram, in the Bureau International des Poids et Mésures at Sèvres, near Paris, France
time	second	s	duration of 9,129,631,770 periods of the radiation corresponding to the transition between the two hyperfine levels of the ground state of the caesium-133 atom electric
current	ampere	A	that constant current which, if maintained in two straight parallel conductors of negligible circular cross-section, and placed 1 metre apart in vacuum, would produce between these conductors a force equal to 2×10^{-7} newton per metre of length thermodynamic
temperature	kelvin	K	the fraction 1/273.15 of the thermodynamic temperature of the triple point of water, where water, ice and water vapour are in equilibrium
luminous intensity	candela	cd	the luminous intensity, in a given direction, of a source that emits monochromatic radiation of frequency 540×10^{12} Hz and has a radiant intensity in that direction of 1/683 watts per steradian
amount of substance	mole	mol	the amount of substance of a system which contains as many elementary entities as there are atoms in 0.012 kilograms of carbon-12

Supplementary and derived units

Quantity	Unit name	Unit symbol
plane angle	radian	rad
solid angle	steradian	sr
area	square metre	m^2
volume	cubic metre	m^3
velocity, speed	metre per second	$m\ s^{-1}$
angular velocity	radian per second	$rad\ s^{-1}$
acceleration	metre per second squared	$m\ s^{-2}$
angular acceleration	radian per second squared	$rad\ s^{-2}$
frequency	hertz (= cycle per second)	Hz
rotational frequency	reciprocal second	s^{-1}
density, mass density	kilogram per cubic metre	$kg\ m^3$
momentum	kilogram metre per second	$kg\ m\ s^{-1}$
angular momentum	kilogram metre squared per second	$kg\ m^{-2}\ s^{-1}$
moment of inertia	kilogram metre squared kg	m^{-2}
force	newton	$N\ (kg\ m\ s^{-2})$
moment of force (torque)	newton metre	$N\ m$
pressure, stress	pascal	$Pa\ (N\ m^{-2})$
viscosity (kinematic)	metre squared per second	$m^{-2}\ s^{-1}$
viscosity (dynamic)	pascal second	$Pa\ s\ (N\ s\ m^{-2})$
surface tension	newton per metre	$N\ m^{-1}$
energy, work, quantity of heat	joule	$J\ (N\ m)$
power, radiant flux	watt	$W\ (J\ s^{-1})$
temperature	degree Celsius	°C
thermal coefficient of linear expansion	reciprocal kelvin	K^{-1}
heat flux density, irradiance	watt per square metre	$W\ m^{-2}$
thermal conductivity	watt per metre kelvin	$W\ m^{-1}\ K^{-1}$
coefficient of heat transfer	watt per square metre kelvin	$W\ m^{-2}\ K^{-1}$
heat capacity	joule per kelvin	$J\ K^{-1}$
specific heat capacity	joule per kilogram kelvin	$J\ kg^{-1}\ K^{-1}$
entropy	joule per kelvin	$J\ K^{-1}$
specific entropy	joule per kilogram kelvin	$J\ kg^{-1}\ K^{-1}$
specific energy, specific latent heat	joule per kilogram	$J\ kg^{-1}$
quantity of electricity, electric charge	coulomb	$(A\ s)$
electric potential, potential difference, electromotive force	volt	$V\ (W\ A^{-1})$
electric field strength	volt per metre	$V\ m^{-1}$
electric resistance	ohm	$\Omega\ (V\ A^{-1})$
electric conductance	siemens	$S\ (A\ V^{-1})$
electric capacitance	farad	$F\ (A\ s\ V^{-1})$

SI units (cont.)

Quantity	Unit name	Unit symbol
magnetic flux	weber	Wb (V s)
inductance	henry	H (V s A⁻¹)
magnetic flux density	tesla	T (Wb m⁻²)
magnetic field strength	ampere per metre	A m⁻¹
luminous flux	lumen	lm (cd sr)
luminance	candela per square metre	(cd m⁻²)
illuminance	lux	lx (lm m⁻²)
radiation activity	becquerel	Bq (s⁻¹)
radiation absorbed dose	gray	Gy (J kg⁻¹)

SI multiplying prefixes multiple	Prefix	Symbol	Example
1,000,000,000,000,000,000 (10^{18})	exa-	E	Eg (exagram)
1,000,000,000,000,000 (10^{15})	peta-	P	PJ (petajoule)
1,000,000,000,000 (10^{12})	tera-	T	TV (teravolt)
1,000,000,000 (10^{9})	giga-	G	GW (gigawatt)
1,000,000 (10^{6})	mega-	M	MHz (megahertz)
1,000 (10^{3})	kilo-	k	kg (kilogram)
100 (10^{2})	hecto-	h	hm (hectometre)
10	deca-	da-	daN (decanewton)
0.1 (10^{-1})	deci-	d	dC (decicoulomb)
0.01 (10^{-2})	centi-	c	cm (centimetre)
0.001 (10^{-3})	milli-	m	mA (milliampere)
0.000,001 (10^{-6})	micro-	μ	μF (microfarad)
0.000,000,001 (10^{-9})	nano-	n	nm (nanometre)
0.000,000,000,001 (10^{-12})	pico-	p	ps (picosecond)
0.000,000,000,000,001 (10^{-15})	femto-	f	frad (femtoradian)
0.000,000,000,000,000,001 (10^{-18})	atto-	a	aT (attotesla)

Decibels

Decibels (dB) measure the relative intensity or loudness of sound. A difference of 10 dB between two sounds means that the intensity of one sound is ten times louder than that of the other. Because of the way the ear responds to such differences in sound intensity, this tenfold difference results in one sound's being perceived to be twice as loud as the other. So, for example, a 20 dB sound is twice as loud as a 10 dB sound; 30 dB is four times louder; 40 dB is eight times louder; and so on. One decibel is the smallest difference that the ear can detect between sounds. Sounds of 120 dB and upwards cause physical pain.

Decibels	Typical sound
0	threshold of hearing
10	rustle of leaves in gentle breeze
10	quiet whisper
20	average whisper
20–50	quiet conversation
40–45	hotel; theatre (between performances)
50–65	loud conversation
65–70	traffic on busy street
65–90	train
75–80	factory (light/medium work)
90	heavy traffic
90–100	thunder
110–140	jet aircraft on take-off
130	threshold of pain
140–190	space rocket at take-off

Miscellaneous measures

acoustic ohm	c.g.s. unit of acoustic impedance (the ratio of sound pressure on a surface to sound flux through the surface)
acre	traditional English land measure equal to 4,480 square yards (4,047 sq m/0.405 ha)
acre-foot	unit sometimes used to measure large volumes of water such as reservoirs; 1 acre-foot = 1,233.5 cu m/43,560 cu ft
astronomical unit	unit (symbol AU) equal to the mean distance of the Earth from the Sun: 149,597,870 km/92,955,800 mi
atmosphere	unit of pressure (abbreviation atm); 1 standard atmosphere = 101,325 pascals
barn	unit of area, especially the cross-sectional area of an atomic nucleus; 1 barn = 10^{-28} sq m
barrel	unit of liquid capacity; volume depends on liquid being measured. One barrel of oil = 159 litres/35 imperial gallons; one barrel of alcohol = 189 litres/41.5 imperial gallons
base box	imperial unit of area used in metal plating; 1 base box = 31,360 sq in/20.232 sq m
baud	unit of electrical signalling speed equal to one pulse per second; 300 baud = approximately 300 words per minute
brewster	unit (symbol B) for measuring reaction of optical materials to stress
British thermal unit	imperial unit of heat (symbol Btu); 1 Btu = approximately 1,055 joules
bushel	dry or liquid measure equal to 8 gallons or 4 pecks (2,219.36 cu in/36.37 litres) in the UK
cable	unit of length used on ships, taken as one-tenth of a nautical mile (185.3 m/608 ft)
calorie	c.g.s. unit of heat, now replaced by the joule; 1 calorie = approximately 4.2 joules
carat	unit for measuring mass of precious stones; 1 carat = 0.2 g/0.00705 oz
carat	unit of purity in gold; pure gold is 24-carat
carcel	obsolete unit of luminous intensity
cental	name for the short hundredweight; 1 cental = 100 lb/45.4 kg
chaldron	obsolete unit measuring capacity; 1 UK chaldron = 288 gallons or 1.309 cu m
clausius	in engineering, a unit of entropy; defined as the ratio of energy to temperature above absolute zero
cleanliness unit	unit for measuring air pollution, equal to the number of particles greater than 0.5 micrometres in diameter per cubic foot of air
clo	unit of thermal insulation of clothing; standard clothes have insulation of about 1 clo, the warmest is about 4 clo per 2.5 cm/1 in of thickness
clusec	unit for measuring the power of a vacuum pump
condensation number	in physics, the ratio of the number of molecules condensing on a surface to the number of molecules touching that surface
cord	unit for measuring the volume of wood cut for fuel; 1 cord = 128 cu ft/3,456 cu m, or a stack 8 ft/2.4 m long, 4 ft/1.2 m wide and 4 ft high
crith	unit of mass for weighing gases; 1 crith = the mass of 1 litre of hydrogen gas at standard temperature and pressure
cubit	earliest known unit of length; 1 cubit = approximately 50.5 cm/20.6 in, the length of the human forearm from tip of the middle finger to the elbow
curie	former unit of radioactivity (symbol Ci); 1 curie = 37×10^9 becquerels
cwt	symbol for hundredweight, unit of weight equal to 112 pounds/50.802 kg; 100 lb/45.36 in the USA
dalton	international atomic mass unit, equivalent to $\frac{1}{12}$ of the mass of a neutral carbon-12 atom
darcy	c.g.s. unit (symbol D) of permeability, used mainly in geology to describe the permeability of rock
darwin	unit of measurement of evolutionary rate of change
decontamination factor	unit measuring the effectiveness of radiological decontamination; ratio of original contamination to the radiation remaining
demal	unit measuring concentration; 1 demal = 1 gram-equivalent of solute in 1 cubic decimetre of solvent
denier	unit used to measure the fineness of yarns; 9,000 metres of 15 denier nylon weighs 15 g/0.5 oz
dioptre	optical unit measuring the power of a lens; the reciprocal of the focal length in metres
drachm	unit of apothecaries' measure; 1 drachm = 60 grains = 3.887 grams
dyne	c.g.s. unit of force; 10^5 dynes = 1 newton
einstein unit	unit for measuring photoenergy in atomic physics
eotvos unit	unit (symbol E) for measuring small changes in intensity of the Earth's gravity with horizontal distance
erg	c.g.s. unit of work, equal to the work done by a force of 1 dyne moving through 1 cm
erlang	unit for measuring telephone traffic intensity
fathom	unit of depth measurement in mining, seafaring and handling timber; 1 fathom = 1.83 m/6 ft
finsen unit	unit (symbol FU) for measuring intensity of ultraviolet light; UV light of 2 FU causes sunburn in 15 minutes
fluid ounce	measure of capacity, equivalent in the USA to $\frac{1}{16}$ of a pint; in the UK and Canada, equals $\frac{1}{20}$ of a pint

Miscellaneous measures *(cont.)*

foot	imperial unit of length (symbol ft), equivalent to 0.3048 m
foot-candela	unit of illuminance, replaced by the lux; 1 foot-candle = 10.674 lux
foot-pound	imperial unit of energy (symbol ft-lb); 1 ft-lb = 1.356 joule
frigorie	unit (symbol fg) used in refrigeration engineering to measure heat energy; 1 frigorie = 1,000 calories = 4,185 joules
furlong	unit of measurement, originating in Anglo-Saxon England, equivalent to 220 yd/201.168 m
galileo	unit (symbol Gal) of acceleration, used in geological surveying; 1 galileo = 10^{-2} metres per second per second
gallon	imperial liquid or dry measure, equal to 4.546 litres, and subdivided into 4 quarts or 8 pints; US gallon = 3.785 litres
gauss	c.g.s. unit (symbol) of magnetic flux density, replaced by the tesla
gill	imperial unit of volume for liquid measure, equal to $1/_4$ of a pint or 5 fluid ounces (0.142 litre)
grain	smallest unit of mass in the three English systems (avoirdupois, troy, apothecaries' weights) used in the UK and USA; 1 grain = 0.0648 g
hand	unit used in measuring the height of a horse from front hoof to shoulder (withers); 1 hand = 10.2 cm/4 in
hardness number	unit measuring hardness of materials. There are three different hardness scales: Brinell, Rockwell, and Vickers
hartree	atomic unit of energy, equivalent to atomic unit of charge divided by atomic unit of length; 1 hartree = 4.850 x 10^{-18} joule
haze factor	unit of visibility in mist or fog; the ratio of brightness of mist compared with that of the object
Hehner number	unit measuring concentration of fatty acids in oils; a Hehner number of 1 = 1 kg of fatty acid in 100 kg of oil or fat
hide	unit of measurement used in the 12th century to measure the extent of arable land; 1 hide = 256 acres (104 hectares)
horsepower	imperial unit (abbreviation hp) of power, now replaced by the watt
hundredweight	imperial unit (abbreviation cwt) of mass; 1 cwt = 112 lb/50.8 kg
inch	imperial unit (abbreviation in) of linear measure, a twelfth of a foot; 1 in = 2.54 cm
inferno	unit used in astrophysics for describing the temperature inside a star; 1 inferno = 1 billion K
iodine number	unit measuring percentage of iodine absorbed in a substance
jansky	unit used in radio astronomy to measure radiation received from space; 1 jansky = 10^{-26} watts per square metre per hertz
kayser	unit used in spectroscopy to measure wave number (number of waves in a unit length; a wavelength of 1.0 cm has a wave number of 10 kaysers
knot	unit used in navigation to measure a ship's speed; 1 knot = 1 nautical mile per hour, or about 1.15 miles per hour
league	obsolete imperial unit of length; 1 league = 3 miles = 4,828 metres
light year	unit used in astronomy to measure distance; the distance travelled by light in a year, approximately
mache	obsolete unit of radioactive concentration; 1 mache is a concentration of 3.7 x 10^{-7} curies of radioactive material in one cubic metre of a medium
maxwell	c.g.s. unit (symbol Mx) of magnetic flux
megaton	measurement of the explosive power of a nuclear weapon; 1 megaton = one million tons of trinitrotoluene (TNT)
mil	(a) thousandth of a litre; contraction of the word millilitre. (b) imperial measure of length, equal to 10^{-3} inch; also known as the thou
mile	imperial unit of linear measure; a statute mile = 1.760 yards/1.60934 km, and an international nautical mile = 2,226 yards/1,852 km
millimetre of mercury	unit of pressure (symbol mmHg) used in medicine for measuring blood pressure
morgan	arbitrary unit used in genetics; 1 morgan is the distance along the chromosome in a gene that gives a recombination frequency of 1%
nautical mile	unit of distance used in navigation, equal to the average length of one minute of arc on a great circle of the earth, or 1,852 m/6,076.12 ft
neper	unit used in telecommunications; gives the attenuation of amplitudes of currents or powers as the natural logarithm of the ratio
oersted	c.g.s. unit (symbol Oe) of magnetic field strength, now replaced by amperes per metre
ounce	unit of mass, $1/_{16}$ of a pound avoirdupois, equal to 437.5 grains (28.35 g; also $1/_{12}$ of a pound troy, equal to 480 grains
parsec	unit (symbol pc) used in astronomy for distances to stars and galaxies; 1 parsec = 3.216 light years, 2.063 x astronomical units and 3.086 x 10^{13} km
peck	obsolete unit of dry measure, equal to 8 quarts or a quarter bushel (9.002 litres)
pennyweight	imperial unit of mass; 1 dwt = 24 grains = 1.555 x 10^{-3} kg
perch	obsolete imperial unit of length; 1 perch = $5^1/_2$ yards = 5.029 metres. Also called the rod or pole

Miscellaneous measures *(cont.)*

pint	imperial unit of liquid or dry measure, equal to 20 fluid ounces, half a quart, $\frac{1}{8}$ of a gallon, or 0.568 litre; in the USA, a liquid pint = 0.473 litre, while a dry pint = 0.550 litre
point	metric unit of mass used in relation to gemstones; 1 point = 0.01 metric carat = 2×10^{-6} kg
poise	c.g.s. unit of dynamic viscosity; 1 poise = 1 dyne-second per square centimetre
pound	imperial unit (abbreviation lb) of mass; the avoirdupois pound or imperial standard pound = 7,000 grains/0.45 kg, while the pound troy (used for weighing precious metals) = 5,760 grains/0.37 kg
poundal	imperial unit (abbreviation pdl) of force; 1 poundal = 0.1383 newtons
quart	imperial liquid or dry measure, equal to 2 pints or 1.136 litres; in the USA a liquid quart = 0.946 litre, while a dry quart = 1.101 litres
rad	unit of absorbed radiation dose, replaced in the SI system by the gray; 1 rad = 0.01 joule of radiation absorbed by 1 kg of matter
relative biological effectiveness	relative damage caused to living tissue by different types of radiation
rood	imperial unit of area; 1 rood = $\frac{1}{4}$ acre = 1,011.7 sq m
roentgen	unit (symbol R) of radiation exposure, used for X- and gamma ray
rydberg	atomic unit of energy, equivalent to atomic unit of charge divided by twice atomic unit of length; 1 rydberg = 2.425×10^{-18} joule
sabin	unit of sound absorption, used in acoustical engineering; 1 sabin = absorption of 1 sq ft (0.093 sq m) of a perfectly absorbing surface
scruple	imperial unit of apothecaries measure; 1 scruple = 20 grains = 1.3×10^{-4} kg
shackle	unit of length used at sea for measuring cable or chain; 1 shackle = 15 fathoms (90 ft/27 m)
slug	obsolete imperial unit of mass, equal to 14.6 kg/32.17 lb
snellen	unit expressing the visual power of the eye
sone	unit of subjective loudness
standard volume	in physics, the volume occupied by 1 kilogram molecule (molecular mass in kilograms) of any gas at standard temperature and pressure; approximately 22.414 cu m
stokes	c.g.s. unit (symbol St) of kinematic viscosity
stone	imperial unit (abbreviation st) of mass; 1 stone = 14 lb/6.35 kg
strontium unit	measures concentration of strontium-90 in organic medium relative to concentration of calcium
tex	metric unit of line density; 1 tex is the line density of a thread with a mass of 1 gram and a length of 1 kilometre
tog	measure of thermal insulation, used in textile trade; a light summer suit = 1 tog
ton	imperial unit of mass. The long ton (UK) is 1,016 kg/2,240 lb; the short ton (USA) is 907 kg/2,000 lb
yard	imperial unit (symbol yd) of length, equivalent to 3 ft/0.9144 m

International paper sizes

	Millimetres	Inches
Large Post	419.1 × 533.4	$16^1/_2 × 21$
Demy	444.5 × 571.5	$17^1/_2 × 22^1/_2$
Medium	457.2 × 584.2	$18 × 23$
Royal	508 × 635	$20 × 25$
Double Crown	508 × 762	$20 × 30$

A series (books, magazines, stationery)

A0	841 × 1189	$33^1/_8 × 46^3/_4$
A1	594 × 841	$23^3/_8 × 33^1/_8$
A2	420 × 594	$16^1/_2 × 23^3/_8$
A3	297 × 420	$11^3/_4 × 16^1/_2$
A4	210 × 297	$8^1/_4 × 11^3/_4$
A5	148 × 210	$5^7/_8 × 8^1/_4$

B series (posters etc)

B0	1414 × 1000	$55^5/_8 × 39^3/_8$
B1	1000 × 707	$39^3/_8 × 27^7/_8$
B2	707 × 500	$27^7/_8 × 19^5/_8$
B3	500 × 353	$19^5/_8 × 13^7/_8$
B4	353 × 250	$13^7/_8 × 9^7/_8$
B5	250 × 176	$9^7/_8 × 7$

C series (envelopes)

C4	324 × 229	$12^3/_4 × 9$
C5	229 × 162	$9 × 6^3/_8$
C6	162 × 114	$6^3/_8 × 3^1/_4$
DL	220 × 110	$8^5/_8 × 4^3/_8$

Metric range of book publishing papers

Name	Trimmed page (mm)	Untrimmed page (mm)	Quad sheet (mm)	Pages to view	Pages from sheet
Metric Crown 8vo	186 × 123	192 × 126	768 × 1008	32	64
Metric Crown 4to	246 × 189	252 × 192	768 × 1008	16	32
Metric Large Crown 8vo	198 × 129	204 × 132	816 × 1056	32	64
Metric Demy 8vo	216 × 138	222 × 141	888 × 1128	32	64
Metric Demy 4to	276 × 219	282 × 222	888 × 1128	16	32
Metric Royal 8vo	234 × 156	240 × 159	960 × 1272	32	64
Metric Royal 4to	312 × 237	318 × 240	960 × 1272	16	32

Time zones and relative times *

At 12.00 noon, Greenwich Mean Time (GMT), the standard time elsewhere around the world is as follows:

Abu Dhabi	16.00	Dublin	12.00	Oslo	13.00
Accra	12.00	Florence	13.00	Ottawa	07.00
Addis Ababa	15.00	Frankfurt	13.00	Panama City	07.00
Adelaide	21.30	Gdansk	13.00	Paris	13.00
Alexandria	14.00	Geneva	13.00	Perth	20.00
Algiers	13.00	Gibraltar	13.00	Port Said	14.00
Amman	14.00	Hague, The	13.00	Prague	13.00
Amsterdam	13.00	Harare	14.00	Quebec	07.00
Anchorage	02.00	Havana	07.00	Rangoon	18.30
Ankara	14.00	Helsinki	14.00	Rawalpindi	17.00
Athens	14.00	Ho Chi Minh City	19.00	Reykjavik	12.00
Auckland	24.00	Hobart	22.00	Rio de Janeiro	09.00
Baghdad	15.00	Hong Kong	20.00	Riyadh	15.00
Bahrain	15.00	Istanbul	14.00	Rome	13.00
Bangkok	19.00	Jakarta	19.00	San Francisco	04.00
Barcelona	13.00	Jerusalem	14.00	Santiago	08.00
Beijing	20.00	Johannesburg	14.00	Seoul	21.00
Beirut	14.00	Karachi	17.00	Shanghai	20.00
Belgrade	13.00	Kiev	15.00	Singapore	20.00
Berlin	13.00	Kuala Lumpur	20.00	Sofia	14.00
Berne	13.00	Kuwait	15.00	St Petersburg	15.00
Bogota	07.00	Kyoto	21.00	Stockholm	13.00
Bombay	17.30	Lagos	13.00	Sydney	22.00
Bonn	13.00	Le Havre	13.00	Taipei	20.00
Brazzaville	13.00	Lima	07.00	Tashkent	18.00
Brisbane	22.00	Lisbon	12.00	Tehran	15.30
Brussels	13.00	Los Angeles	04.00	Tel Aviv	14.00
Bucharest	14.00	Luanda	13.00	Tenerife	12.00
Budapest	13.00	Luxembourg	13.00	Tokyo	21.00
Buenos Aires	09.00	Lyon	13.00	Toronto	07.00
Cairo	14.00	Madras	17.30	Tripoli	13.00
Calcutta	17.30	Madrid	13.00	Tunis	13.00
Canberra	22.00	Manila	20.00	Valparaiso	08.00
Cape Town	14.00	Marseille	13.00	Vancouver	04.00
Caracas	08.00	Mecca	15.00	Vatican City	13.00
Casablanca	12.00	Melbourne	22.00	Venice	13.00
Chicago	06.00	Mexico City	06.00	Vienna	13.00
Cologne	13.00	Milan	13.00	Vladivostok	22.00
Colombo	17.30	Minsk	15.00	Volgograd	16.00
Copenhagen	13.00	Monrovia	11.00	Warsaw	13.00
Dacca	18.00	Montevideo	09.00	Washington	07.00
Damascus	14.00	Montreal	07.00	Wellington	24.00
Dar es Salaam	15.00	Moscow	15.00	Winnipeg	06.00
Darwin	21.30	Munich	13.00	Yokohama	21.00
Delhi	17.30	Nairobi	15.00	Zagreb	13.00
Denver	05.00	New Orleans	06.00	Zurich	13.00
Djakarta	20.00	New York	07.00		
Dubai	16.00	Nicosia	14.00		

The surface of the earth is divided into 24 time zones. Each zone represents 15° of longitude or 1 hour of time. Countries to the east of London and the Greenwich meridian are ahead of Greenwich Mean Time (GMT) and countries to the west are behind. The time indicated in the table above is fixed by law and is called standard time. Use of daylight saving time (such as British Summer Time) varies widely.

Calendars

The calendar is the division of the year into months, weeks and days, and the method of ordering the years. All early calendars except the ancient Egyptian were lunar. The word 'calendar' comes from the Latin *kalendae* or *calendae*, the first day of the month on which, in Ancient Rome, solemn proclamation was made of the appearance of the new moon. The Western or Gregorian calendar derives from the *Julian calendar* instituted by Julius Caesar 46 BC. From year one, an assumed date of the birth of Jesus, dates are calculated backwards (BC 'before Christ' or BCE 'before common era' and forwards (ad Latin anno Domini 'in the year of the Lord' or CE 'common era'). The lunar month (period between one new moon and the next) naturally averages 29.5 days, but the Western calendar uses for convenience a calendar month with a complete number of days, 30 or 31 (Feb has 28). For adjustments, since there are slightly fewer than six extra hours a year left over, they are added to Feb as a 29th day every fourth year (leap year), century years being excepted unless they are divisible by 400. For example, 1896 was a leap year; 1900 was not, but 2000 will be. The next leap year is 1996.

Gregorian calendar

The Julian calendar was adjusted by Pope Gregory XIII 1582, who eliminated the accumulated error caused by the faulty calculation of the length of a year and avoided its recurrence by restricting century leap years to those divisible by 400. Other states only gradually changed from Old Style to New Style; Britain and its colonies adopted the Gregorian calendar 1752, when the error amounted to 11 days, and 3 Sept 1752 became 14 Sept (at the same time the beginning of the year was put back from 25 March to 1 Jan). Russia did not adopt it until the October Revolution of 1917, so that the event (then 25 Oct) is currently celebrated 7 Nov.

Islamic calendar

The Islamic calendar is reckoned from the year of the *hijra*, or flight of Muhammad from Mecca to Medina. The corresponding date in the Julian calendar is 16 July AD 622. The years are purely lunar, and consist of 12 months with alternately 29 or 30 days, plus one extra day at the end of the 12th month (Dhul- Hijja) in leap years, which occur at stated intervals in each cycle of 30 years.

Islamic calendar 1414 and 1415 (June 1993–June 1995)

The beginning of the month in the Islamic calendar depends on the visibility of the new moon; therefore dates may differ from those stated here

Hijrah month	1414 AH	1415 AH
1 Muharram	20 June 1993	9 June 1994
1 Safar	20 July 1993	9 July 1994
1 Rabi'a I	18 Aug 1993	7 Aug 1994
1 Rabi'a II	17 Sept 1993	6 Sept 1994
1 Jumada I	16 Oct 1993	5 Oct 1994
1 Jumada II	15 Nov 1993	4 Nov 1994
1 Rajab	14 Dec 1993	4 Dec 1994
1 Sha'ban	13 Jan 1994	2 Jan 1995
1 Ramadan	11 Feb 1994	31 Jan 1995
1 Shawwal	13 March 1994	2 March 1995
1 Dhul-Qi'da	11 April 1994	31 March 1995
1 Dhul-Hijja	11 May 1994	30 April 1995

Important days	1414 AH	1415 AH
Hijrah New Year	20 June 1993	9 June 1994
Ashura'	29 June 1993	18 June 1994
Birthday of the prophet Muhammad	29 Aug 1993	18 Aug 1994
Lailat-ul-Isra'wal Mi'raj	8 Jan 1994	29 Dec 1994
Lailat-ul-Bara'h	26 Jan 1994	15 Jan 1995
Ramadan	11 Feb 1994	31 Jan 1995
Lailat-ul-Qadr	8 March 1994	25 Feb 1995
Eid-ul-Fitr	13 March 1994	2 March 1995
Arafat	19 May 1994	8 May 1995
Eid-ul-Adha	20 May 1994	9 May 1995

AH – *anno Hegirae*, the Muslim era

Jewish calendar

The Jewish calendar is a complex combination of lunar and solar cycles, varied by considerations of religious observance. A year may have 12 or 13 months, each of which normally alternates between 29 and 30 days; the New Year (Rosh Hashanah) falls between 5 Sept and 5 Oct. The calendar dates from the hypothetical creation of the world (taken as 7 Oct 3761 BC). Some say that the Jewish calendar as used today was formalized in AD 358 by Rabbi Hillel II;

others that this occurred later. A Jewish year is one of the following six types:

Minimal Common	353 days
Regular Common	354 days
Full Common	355 days
Minimal Leap	383 days
Regular Leap	384 days
Full Leap	385 days

Jewish calendar 5754 and 5755 (Sept 1993–Sept 1995)

Jewish month	AM 5754	AM 5755
1 Tishri	16 Sept 1993	6–7 Sept 1994
1 Marcheshvan	16 Oct 1993	5–6 Oct 1994
1 Kislev	15 Nov 1993	4 Nov 1994
1 Tebet	15 Dec 1993	3–4 Dec 1994
1 Shebat	13 Jan 1994	2 Jan 1995
1 Adar*	12 Feb 1994	1 Feb/3 March 1995
1 Nisan	13 March 1994	1 April 1995
1 Iyar	12 April 1994	1 May 1995
1 Sivan	11 May 1994	30 May 1995
1 Tammuz	10 June 1994	10 June 1995
1 Av	9 July 1994	28 July 1995
1 Elul	8 Aug 1994	27 Aug 1995

Jewish fasts and festivals

Date in Jewish calendar	Fast/festival	Date in 1994/1995
1–2 Tishri	Rosh Hashanah (New Year)	6–7 Sept
3 Tishri	Fast of Gedaliah*	8 Sept
10 Tishri	Yom Kippur (Day of Atonement)	15 Sept
15–21 Tishri	Succot (Feast of Tabernacles)	20–26 Sept
22 Tishri	Shemini Atzeret	27 Sept
23 Tishri	Simchat Torah	28 Sept
25 Kislev	Hanukkah (Dedication of the Temple) begins	28 Nov–5 Dec
10 Tebet	Fast of Tevet	13 Dec
13 Adar	Fast of Esther†	24 Feb
14 Adar	Purim	25 Feb
15 Adar	Shushan Purim	26 Feb
14 Nisan	Taanit Behorim (Fast of the Firstborn)	24 March
15–22 Nisan	Pesach (Passover)	27 March–3 April
27 Nisan	Yom Ha-Shoah (Holocaust Day)	8 April
4 Lyar	Yom Ha'Zikharon (Remembrance Day)	13 April
5 Lyar	Yom Ha'Atzmaut (Independence Day)	14 April
18 Lyar	33rd Day of Counting the Omer	29 April
28 Lyar	Yom Yerushalayim (Jerusalem Day)	9 May
6–7 Sivan	Shavuot (Festival of Weeks)	16–17 May
17 Tammuz	Fast of 17 Tammuz**	26 June
9 Av	Fast of 9 Av**	17 July

*   Ve-Adar in leap years.

** If these dates fall on the sabbath the fast is kept on the following day.

† This fast is observed on 11 Adar (or 11 Ve-Adar in leap years) if 13 Adar falls on a sabbath.

AM – anno mundi, in the year of the world

Chinese calendar

Chinese calendar

The Chinese calendar is lunar, with a cycle of 60 years. A year consists of 12 alternating 29- and 30-day months, totalling 354 days. The 12 animal names attached to years and hours in the Chinese calendar are sometimes given to the months as well. Both the traditional and, from 1911, the Western calendar are in use in China.

Year equivalents between Gregorian, Jewish, Islamic, and Hindu calendars*

Jewish (AM)[1]	*Islamic (AH)*[2]	*Hindu (SE)*[3]
5752 (9 Sept 1991–27 Sept 1992)	**1412** (13 July 1991–1 July 1992)	**1913** (22March 1991–20 March 1992)
5753 (28 Sept 1992–15 Sept 1993)	**1413** (2 July 1992–20 June 1993)	**1914** (21 March 1992–21 March 1993)
5754 (16 Sept 1993–5 Sept 1994)	**1414** (21 June 1993–9 June 1994)	**1915** (22 March 1993–21 March 1994)
5755 (6 Sept 1994–24 Sept 1995)	**1415** (10 June 1994–30 May 1995)	**1916** (22 March 1994–21 March 1995)
5756 (25 Sept 1995–13 Sept 1996)	**1416** (31 May 1995–18 May 1996)	**1917** (22 March 1995–20 March 1996)
5757 (14 Sept 1996–1 Oct 1997)	**1417** (19 May 1996–8 May 1997)	**1918** (21 March 1996–21 March 1997)
5758 (2 Oct 1997–20 Sept 1998)	**1418** (9 May 1997–27 April 1998)	**1919** (22 March 1997–21 March 1998)
5759 (21 Sept 1998–10 Sept 1999)	**1419** (28 April–16 April 1999)	**1920** (22 March 1998–21 March 1999)
5760 (11 Sept 1999–29 Sept 2000)	**1420** (17 April 1999–5 April 2000)	**1921** (22 March 1999–21 March 2000)

* Gregorian equivalents appear in brackets
[1] Anno Mundi - calculated from 3761 BC (year attributed to the creation of the world)
[2] Anno Hegirae - calculated from AD 622, the year of Muhammad's flight from Mecca to Medina.
[3] Saka era - calculated from AD 78, the beginning of the Saka era.

Perpetual Calendar

The number shown for each year indicates which Gregorian calendar to use.

1821 — 2	1847 — 6	1873 — 4	1899 — 1	1925 — 5	1951 — 2	1977 — 7	2003 — 4	2029 — 2	2055 — 6
1822 — 3	1848 —14	1874 — 5	1900 — 2	1926 — 6	1952 —10	1978 — 1	2004 —12	2030 — 3	2056 —14
1823 — 4	1849 — 2	1875 — 6	1901 — 3	1927 — 7	1953 — 5	1979 — 2	2005 — 7	2031 — 4	2057 — 2
1824 —12	1850 — 3	1876 —14	1902 — 4	1928 — 8	1954 — 6	1980 —10	2006 — 1	2032 —12	2058 — 3
1825 — 7	1851 — 4	1877 — 2	1903 — 5	1929 — 3	1955 — 7	1981 — 5	2007 — 2	2033 — 7	2059 — 4
1826 — 1	1852 —12	1878 — 3	1904 —13	1930 — 4	1956 — 8	1982 — 6	2008 —10	2034 — 1	2060 —12
1827 — 2	1853 — 7	1879 — 4	1905 — 1	1931 — 5	1957 — 3	1983 — 7	2009 — 5	2035 — 2	2061 — 7
1828 —10	1854 — 1	1880 —12	1906 — 2	1932 —13	1958 — 4	1984 — 8	2010 — 6	2036 —10	2062 — 1
1829 — 5	1855 — 2	1881 — 7	1907 — 3	1933 — 1	1959 — 5	1985 — 3	2011 — 7	2037 — 5	2063 — 2
1830 — 6	1856 —10	1882 — 1	1908 —11	1934 — 2	1960 —13	1986 — 4	2012 — 8	2038 — 6	2064 —10
1831 — 7	1857 — 5	1883 — 2	1909 — 6	1935 — 3	1961 — 1	1987 — 5	2013 — 3	2039 — 7	2065 — 5
1832 — 8	1858 — 6	1884 —10	1910 — 7	1936 —11	1962 — 2	1988 —13	2014 — 4	2040 — 8	2066 — 6
1833 — 3	1859 — 7	1885 — 5	1911 — 1	1937 — 6	1963 — 3	1989 — 1	2015 — 5	2041 — 3	2067 — 7
1834 — 4	1860 — 8	1886 — 6	1912 — 9	1938 — 7	1964 —11	1990 — 2	2016 —13	2042 — 4	2068 — 8
1835 — 5	1861 — 3	1887 — 7	1913 — 4	1939 — 1	1965 — 6	1991 — 3	2017 — 1	2043 — 5	2069 — 3
1836 —13	1862 — 4	1888 — 8	1914 — 5	1940 — 9	1966 — 7	1992 —11	2018 — 2	2044 —13	2070 — 4
1837 — 1	1863 — 5	1889 — 3	1915 — 6	1941 — 4	1967 — 1	1993 — 6	2019 — 3	2045 — 1	2071 — 5
1838 — 2	1864 —13	1890 — 4	1916 —14	1942 — 5	1968 — 9	1994 — 7	2020 —11	2046 — 2	2072 —13
1839 — 3	1865 — 1	1891 — 5	1917 — 2	1943 — 6	1969 — 4	1995 — 1	2021 — 6	2047 — 3	2073 — 1
1840 —11	1866 — 2	1892 —13	1918 — 3	1944 —14	1970 — 5	1996 — 9	2022 — 7	2048 —11	2074 — 2
1841 — 6	1867 — 3	1893 — 1	1919 — 4	1945 — 2	1971 — 6	1997 — 4	2023 — 1	2049 — 6	2075 — 3
1842 — 7	1868 —11	1894 — 2	1920 —12	1946 — 3	1972 —14	1998 — 5	2024 — 9	2050 — 7	2076 —11
1843 — 1	1869 — 6	1895 — 3	1921 — 7	1947 — 4	1973 — 2	1999 — 6	2025 — 4	2051 — 1	2077 — 6
1844 — 9	1870 — 7	1896 —11	1922 — 1	1948 —12	1974 — 3	2000 —14	2026 — 5	2052 — 9	2078 — 7
1845 — 4	1871 — 1	1897 — 6	1923 — 2	1949 — 7	1975 — 4	2001 — 2	2027 — 6	2053 — 4	2079 — 1
1846 — 5	1872 — 9	1898 — 7	1924 —10	1950 — 1	1976 —12	2002 — 3	2028 —14	2054 — 5	2080 — 9

1

JANUARY
S	M	T	W	T	F	S
1	2	3	4	5	6	7
8	9	10	11	12	13	14
15	16	17	18	19	20	21
22	23	24	25	26	27	28
29	30	31				

MAY
S	M	T	W	T	F	S
1	2	3	4	5	6	
7	8	9	10	11	12	13
14	15	16	17	18	19	20
21	22	23	24	25	26	27
28	29	30	31			

SEPTEMBER
S	M	T	W	T	F	S
					1	2
3	4	5	6	7	8	9
10	11	12	13	14	15	16
17	18	19	20	21	22	23
24	25	26	27	28	29	30

FEBRUARY
S	M	T	W	T	F	S
			1	2	3	4
5	6	7	8	9	10	11
12	13	14	15	16	17	18
19	20	21	22	23	24	25
26	27	28				

JUNE
S	M	T	W	T	F	S
				1	2	3
4	5	6	7	8	9	10
11	12	13	14	15	16	17
18	19	20	21	22	23	24
25	26	27	28	29	30	

OCTOBER
S	M	T	W	T	F	S
1	2	3	4	5	6	7
8	9	10	11	12	13	14
15	16	17	18	19	20	21
22	23	24	25	26	27	28
29	30	31				

MARCH
S	M	T	W	T	F	S
			1	2	3	4
5	6	7	8	9	10	11
12	13	14	15	16	17	18
19	20	21	22	23	24	25
26	27	28	29	30	31	

JULY
S	M	T	W	T	F	S
						1
2	3	4	5	6	7	8
9	10	11	12	13	14	15
16	17	18	19	20	21	22
23	24	25	26	27	28	29
30	31					

NOVEMBER
S	M	T	W	T	F	S
			1	2	3	4
5	6	7	8	9	10	11
12	13	14	15	16	17	18
19	20	21	22	23	24	25
26	27	28	29	30		

APRIL
S	M	T	W	T	F	S
						1
2	3	4	5	6	7	8
9	10	11	12	13	14	15
16	17	18	19	20	21	22
23	24	25	26	27	28	29
30						

AUGUST
S	M	T	W	T	F	S
		1	2	3	4	5
6	7	8	9	10	11	12
13	14	15	16	17	18	19
20	21	22	23	24	25	26
27	28	29	30	31		

DECEMBER
S	M	T	W	T	F	S
					1	2
3	4	5	6	7	8	9
10	11	12	13	14	15	16
17	18	19	20	21	22	23
24	25	26	27	28	29	30
31						

2

JANUARY
S	M	T	W	T	F	S
	1	2	3	4	5	6
7	8	9	10	11	12	13
14	15	16	17	18	19	20
21	22	23	24	25	26	27
28	29	30	31			

MAY
S	M	T	W	T	F	S
		1	2	3	4	5
6	7	8	9	10	11	12
13	14	15	16	17	18	19
20	21	22	23	24	25	26
27	28	29	30	31		

SEPTEMBER
S	M	T	W	T	F	S
						1
2	3	4	5	6	7	8
9	10	11	12	13	14	15
16	17	18	19	20	21	22
23	24	25	26	27	28	29
30						

FEBRUARY
S	M	T	W	T	F	S
				1	2	3
4	5	6	7	8	9	10
11	12	13	14	15	16	17
18	19	20	21	22	23	24
25	26	27	28			

JUNE
S	M	T	W	T	F	S
					1	2
3	4	5	6	7	8	9
10	11	12	13	14	15	16
17	18	19	20	21	22	23
24	25	26	27	28	29	30

OCTOBER
S	M	T	W	T	F	S
	1	2	3	4	5	6
7	8	9	10	11	12	13
14	15	16	17	18	19	20
21	22	23	24	25	26	27
28	29	30	31			

MARCH
S	M	T	W	T	F	S
				1	2	3
4	5	6	7	8	9	10
11	12	13	14	15	16	17
18	19	20	21	22	23	24
25	26	27	28	29	30	31

JULY
S	M	T	W	T	F	S
1	2	3	4	5	6	7
8	9	10	11	12	13	14
15	16	17	18	19	20	21
22	23	24	25	26	27	28
29	30	31				

NOVEMBER
S	M	T	W	T	F	S
				1	2	3
4	5	6	7	8	9	10
11	12	13	14	15	16	17
18	19	20	21	22	23	24
25	26	27	28	29	30	

APRIL
S	M	T	W	T	F	S
1	2	3	4	5	6	7
8	9	10	11	12	13	14
15	16	17	18	19	20	21
22	23	24	25	26	27	28
29	30					

AUGUST
S	M	T	W	T	F	S
			1	2	3	4
5	6	7	8	9	10	11
12	13	14	15	16	17	18
19	20	21	22	23	24	25
26	27	28	29	30	31	

DECEMBER
S	M	T	W	T	F	S
						1
2	3	4	5	6	7	8
9	10	11	12	13	14	15
16	17	18	19	20	21	22
23	24	25	26	27	28	29
30	31					

3

JANUARY
S	M	T	W	T	F	S
		1	2	3	4	5
6	7	8	9	10	11	12
13	14	15	16	17	18	19
20	21	22	23	24	25	26
27	28	29	30	31		

MAY
S	M	T	W	T	F	S
			1	2	3	4
5	6	7	8	9	10	11
12	13	14	15	16	17	18
19	20	21	22	23	24	25
26	27	28	29	30	31	

SEPTEMBER
S	M	T	W	T	F	S
1	2	3	4	5	6	7
8	9	10	11	12	13	14
15	16	17	18	19	20	21
22	23	24	25	26	27	28
29	30					

FEBRUARY
S	M	T	W	T	F	S
					1	2
3	4	5	6	7	8	9
10	11	12	13	14	15	16
17	18	19	20	21	22	23
24	25	26	27	28		

JUNE
S	M	T	W	T	F	S
						1
2	3	4	5	6	7	8
9	10	11	12	13	14	15
16	17	18	19	20	21	22
23	24	25	26	27	28	29
30						

OCTOBER
S	M	T	W	T	F	S
		1	2	3	4	5
6	7	8	9	10	11	12
13	14	15	16	17	18	19
20	21	22	23	24	25	26
27	28	29	30	31		

MARCH
S	M	T	W	T	F	S
					1	2
3	4	5	6	7	8	9
10	11	12	13	14	15	16
17	18	19	20	21	22	23
24	25	26	27	28	29	30
31						

JULY
S	M	T	W	T	F	S
	1	2	3	4	5	6
7	8	9	10	11	12	13
14	15	16	17	18	19	20
21	22	23	24	25	26	27
28	29	30	31			

NOVEMBER
S	M	T	W	T	F	S
					1	2
3	4	5	6	7	8	9
10	11	12	13	14	15	16
17	18	19	20	21	22	23
24	25	26	27	28	29	30

APRIL
S	M	T	W	T	F	S
	1	2	3	4	5	6
7	8	9	10	11	12	13
14	15	16	17	18	19	20
21	22	23	24	25	26	27
28	29	30				

AUGUST
S	M	T	W	T	F	S
				1	2	3
4	5	6	7	8	9	10
11	12	13	14	15	16	17
18	19	20	21	22	23	24
25	26	27	28	29	30	31

DECEMBER
S	M	T	W	T	F	S
1	2	3	4	5	6	7
8	9	10	11	12	13	14
15	16	17	18	19	20	21
22	23	24	25	26	27	28
29	30	31				

4

JANUARY
S	M	T	W	T	F	S
			1	2	3	4
5	6	7	8	9	10	11
12	13	14	15	16	17	18
19	20	21	22	23	24	25
26	27	28	29	30	31	

MAY
S	M	T	W	T	F	S
				1	2	3
4	5	6	7	8	9	10
11	12	13	14	15	16	17
18	19	20	21	22	23	24
25	26	27	28	29	30	31

SEPTEMBER
S	M	T	W	T	F	S
	1	2	3	4	5	6
7	8	9	10	11	12	13
14	15	16	17	18	19	20
21	22	23	24	25	26	27
28	29	30				

FEBRUARY
S	M	T	W	T	F	S
						1
2	3	4	5	6	7	8
9	10	11	12	13	14	15
16	17	18	19	20	21	22
23	24	25	26	27	28	

JUNE
S	M	T	W	T	F	S
1	2	3	4	5	6	7
8	9	10	11	12	13	14
15	16	17	18	19	20	21
22	23	24	25	26	27	28
29	30					

OCTOBER
S	M	T	W	T	F	S
			1	2	3	4
5	6	7	8	9	10	11
12	13	14	15	16	17	18
19	20	21	22	23	24	25
26	27	28	29	30	31	

MARCH
S	M	T	W	T	F	S
						1
2	3	4	5	6	7	8
9	10	11	12	13	14	15
16	17	18	19	20	21	22
23	24	25	26	27	28	29
30	31					

JULY
S	M	T	W	T	F	S
		1	2	3	4	5
6	7	8	9	10	11	12
13	14	15	16	17	18	19
20	21	22	23	24	25	26
27	28	29	30	31		

NOVEMBER
S	M	T	W	T	F	S
						1
2	3	4	5	6	7	8
9	10	11	12	13	14	15
16	17	18	19	20	21	22
23	24	25	26	27	28	29
30						

APRIL
S	M	T	W	T	F	S
		1	2	3	4	5
6	7	8	9	10	11	12
13	14	15	16	17	18	19
20	21	22	23	24	25	26
27	28	29	30			

AUGUST
S	M	T	W	T	F	S
					1	2
3	4	5	6	7	8	9
10	11	12	13	14	15	16
17	18	19	20	21	22	23
24	25	26	27	28	29	30
31						

DECEMBER
S	M	T	W	T	F	S
	1	2	3	4	5	6
7	8	9	10	11	12	13
14	15	16	17	18	19	20
21	22	23	24	25	26	27
28	29	30	31			

5

JANUARY
S	M	T	W	T	F	S
				1	2	3
4	5	6	7	8	9	10
11	12	13	14	15	16	17
18	19	20	21	22	23	24
25	26	27	28	29	30	31

MAY
S	M	T	W	T	F	S
					1	2
3	4	5	6	7	8	9
10	11	12	13	14	15	16
17	18	19	20	21	22	23
24	25	26	27	28	29	30
31						

SEPTEMBER
S	M	T	W	T	F	S
		1	2	3	4	5
6	7	8	9	10	11	12
13	14	15	16	17	18	19
20	21	22	23	24	25	26
27	28	29	30			

FEBRUARY
S	M	T	W	T	F	S
1	2	3	4	5	6	7
8	9	10	11	12	13	14
15	16	17	18	19	20	21
22	23	24	25	26	27	28

JUNE
S	M	T	W	T	F	S
	1	2	3	4	5	6
7	8	9	10	11	12	13
14	15	16	17	18	19	20
21	22	23	24	25	26	27
28	29	30				

OCTOBER
S	M	T	W	T	F	S
				1	2	3
4	5	6	7	8	9	10
11	12	13	14	15	16	17
18	19	20	21	22	23	24
25	26	27	28	29	30	31

MARCH
S	M	T	W	T	F	S
1	2	3	4	5	6	7
8	9	10	11	12	13	14
15	16	17	18	19	20	21
22	23	24	25	26	27	28
29	30	31				

JULY
S	M	T	W	T	F	S
			1	2	3	4
5	6	7	8	9	10	11
12	13	14	15	16	17	18
19	20	21	22	23	24	25
26	27	28	29	30	31	

NOVEMBER
S	M	T	W	T	F	S
1	2	3	4	5	6	7
8	9	10	11	12	13	14
15	16	17	18	19	20	21
22	23	24	25	26	27	28
29	30					

APRIL
S	M	T	W	T	F	S
			1	2	3	4
5	6	7	8	9	10	11
12	13	14	15	16	17	18
19	20	21	22	23	24	25
26	27	28	29	30		

AUGUST
S	M	T	W	T	F	S
						1
2	3	4	5	6	7	8
9	10	11	12	13	14	15
16	17	18	19	20	21	22
23	24	25	26	27	28	29
30	31					

DECEMBER
S	M	T	W	T	F	S
		1	2	3	4	5
6	7	8	9	10	11	12
13	14	15	16	17	18	19
20	21	22	23	24	25	26
27	28	29	30	31		

6

JANUARY
S	M	T	W	T	F	S
					1	2
3	4	5	6	7	8	9
10	11	12	13	14	15	16
17	18	19	20	21	22	23
24	25	26	27	28	29	30
31						

MAY
S	M	T	W	T	F	S
						1
2	3	4	5	6	7	8
9	10	11	12	13	14	15
16	17	18	19	20	21	22
23	24	25	26	27	28	29
30	31					

SEPTEMBER
S	M	T	W	T	F	S
			1	2	3	4
5	6	7	8	9	10	11
12	13	14	15	16	17	18
19	20	21	22	23	24	25
26	27	28	29	30		

FEBRUARY
S	M	T	W	T	F	S
	1	2	3	4	5	6
7	8	9	10	11	12	13
14	15	16	17	18	19	20
21	22	23	24	25	26	27
28						

JUNE
S	M	T	W	T	F	S
		1	2	3	4	5
6	7	8	9	10	11	12
13	14	15	16	17	18	19
20	21	22	23	24	25	26
27	28	29	30			

OCTOBER
S	M	T	W	T	F	S
					1	2
3	4	5	6	7	8	9
10	11	12	13	14	15	16
17	18	19	20	21	22	23
24	25	26	27	28	29	30
31						

MARCH
S	M	T	W	T	F	S
	1	2	3	4	5	6
7	8	9	10	11	12	13
14	15	16	17	18	19	20
21	22	23	24	25	26	27
28	29	30	31			

JULY
S	M	T	W	T	F	S
				1	2	3
4	5	6	7	8	9	10
11	12	13	14	15	16	17
18	19	20	21	22	23	24
25	26	27	28	29	30	31

NOVEMBER
S	M	T	W	T	F	S
	1	2	3	4	5	6
7	8	9	10	11	12	13
14	15	16	17	18	19	20
21	22	23	24	25	26	27
28	29	30				

APRIL
S	M	T	W	T	F	S
				1	2	3
4	5	6	7	8	9	10
11	12	13	14	15	16	17
18	19	20	21	22	23	24
25	26	27	28	29	30	

AUGUST
S	M	T	W	T	F	S
1	2	3	4	5	6	7
8	9	10	11	12	13	14
15	16	17	18	19	20	21
22	23	24	25	26	27	28
29	30	31				

DECEMBER
S	M	T	W	T	F	S
			1	2	3	4
5	6	7	8	9	10	11
12	13	14	15	16	17	18
19	20	21	22	23	24	25
26	27	28	29	30	31	

7

JANUARY
S	M	T	W	T	F	S
						1
2	3	4	5	6	7	8
9	10	11	12	13	14	15
16	17	18	19	20	21	22
23	24	25	26	27	28	29
30	31					

FEBRUARY
S	M	T	W	T	F	S
		1	2	3	4	5
6	7	8	9	10	11	12
13	14	15	16	17	18	19
20	21	22	23	24	25	26
27	28					

MARCH
S	M	T	W	T	F	S
		1	2	3	4	5
6	7	8	9	10	11	12
13	14	15	16	17	18	19
20	21	22	23	24	25	26
27	28	29	30	31		

APRIL
S	M	T	W	T	F	S
					1	2
3	4	5	6	7	8	9
10	11	12	13	14	15	16
17	18	19	20	21	22	23
24	25	26	27	28	29	30

MAY
S	M	T	W	T	F	S
1	2	3	4	5	6	7
8	9	10	11	12	13	14
15	16	17	18	19	20	21
22	23	24	25	26	27	28
29	30	31				

JUNE
S	M	T	W	T	F	S
			1	2	3	4
5	6	7	8	9	10	11
12	13	14	15	16	17	18
19	20	21	22	23	24	25
26	27	28	29	30		

JULY
S	M	T	W	T	F	S
					1	2
3	4	5	6	7	8	9
10	11	12	13	14	15	16
17	18	19	20	21	22	23
24	25	26	27	28	29	30
31						

AUGUST
S	M	T	W	T	F	S
	1	2	3	4	5	6
7	8	9	10	11	12	13
14	15	16	17	18	19	20
21	22	23	24	25	26	27
28	29	30	31			

SEPTEMBER
S	M	T	W	T	F	S
				1	2	3
4	5	6	7	8	9	10
11	12	13	14	15	16	17
18	19	20	21	22	23	24
25	26	27	28	29	30	

OCTOBER
S	M	T	W	T	F	S
						1
2	3	4	5	6	7	8
9	10	11	12	13	14	15
16	17	18	19	20	21	22
23	24	25	26	27	28	29
30	31					

NOVEMBER
S	M	T	W	T	F	S
		1	2	3	4	5
6	7	8	9	10	11	12
13	14	15	16	17	18	19
20	21	22	23	24	25	26
27	28	29	30			

DECEMBER
S	M	T	W	T	F	S
				1	2	3
4	5	6	7	8	9	10
11	12	13	14	15	16	17
18	19	20	21	22	23	24
25	26	27	28	29	30	31

8

JANUARY
S	M	T	W	T	F	S
1	2	3	4	5	6	7
8	9	10	11	12	13	14
15	16	17	18	19	20	21
22	23	24	25	26	27	28
29	30	31				

FEBRUARY
S	M	T	W	T	F	S
			1	2	3	4
5	6	7	8	9	10	11
12	13	14	15	16	17	18
19	20	21	22	23	24	25
26	27	28	29			

MARCH
S	M	T	W	T	F	S
				1	2	3
4	5	6	7	8	9	10
11	12	13	14	15	16	17
18	19	20	21	22	23	24
25	26	27	28	29	30	31

APRIL
S	M	T	W	T	F	S
1	2	3	4	5	6	7
8	9	10	11	12	13	14
15	16	17	18	19	20	21
22	23	24	25	26	27	28
29	30					

MAY
S	M	T	W	T	F	S
		1	2	3	4	5
6	7	8	9	10	11	12
13	14	15	16	17	18	19
20	21	22	23	24	25	26
27	28	29	30	31		

JUNE
S	M	T	W	T	F	S
					1	2
3	4	5	6	7	8	9
10	11	12	13	14	15	16
17	18	19	20	21	22	23
24	25	26	27	28	29	30

JULY
S	M	T	W	T	F	S
1	2	3	4	5	6	7
8	9	10	11	12	13	14
15	16	17	18	19	20	21
22	23	24	25	26	27	28
29	30	31				

AUGUST
S	M	T	W	T	F	S
			1	2	3	4
5	6	7	8	9	10	11
12	13	14	15	16	17	18
19	20	21	22	23	24	25
26	27	28	29	30	31	

SEPTEMBER
S	M	T	W	T	F	S
						1
2	3	4	5	6	7	8
9	10	11	12	13	14	15
16	17	18	19	20	21	22
23	24	25	26	27	28	29
30						

OCTOBER
S	M	T	W	T	F	S
	1	2	3	4	5	6
7	8	9	10	11	12	13
14	15	16	17	18	19	20
21	22	23	24	25	26	27
28	29	30	31			

NOVEMBER
S	M	T	W	T	F	S
				1	2	3
4	5	6	7	8	9	10
11	12	13	14	15	16	17
18	19	20	21	22	23	24
25	26	27	28	29	30	

DECEMBER
S	M	T	W	T	F	S
						1
2	3	4	5	6	7	8
9	10	11	12	13	14	15
16	17	18	19	20	21	22
23	24	25	26	27	28	29
30	31					

9

JANUARY
S	M	T	W	T	F	S
	1	2	3	4	5	6
7	8	9	10	11	12	13
14	15	16	17	18	19	20
21	22	23	24	25	26	27
28	29	30	31			

FEBRUARY
S	M	T	W	T	F	S
				1	2	3
4	5	6	7	8	9	10
11	12	13	14	15	16	17
18	19	20	21	22	23	24
25	26	27	28	29		

MARCH
S	M	T	W	T	F	S
					1	2
3	4	5	6	7	8	9
10	11	12	13	14	15	16
17	18	19	20	21	22	23
24	25	26	27	28	29	30
31						

APRIL
S	M	T	W	T	F	S
	1	2	3	4	5	6
7	8	9	10	11	12	13
14	15	16	17	18	19	20
21	22	23	24	25	26	27
28	29	30				

MAY
S	M	T	W	T	F	S
			1	2	3	4
5	6	7	8	9	10	11
12	13	14	15	16	17	18
19	20	21	22	23	24	25
26	27	28	29	30	31	

JUNE
S	M	T	W	T	F	S
						1
2	3	4	5	6	7	8
9	10	11	12	13	14	15
16	17	18	19	20	21	22
23	24	25	26	27	28	29
30						

JULY
S	M	T	W	T	F	S
	1	2	3	4	5	6
7	8	9	10	11	12	13
14	15	16	17	18	19	20
21	22	23	24	25	26	27
28	29	30	31			

AUGUST
S	M	T	W	T	F	S
				1	2	3
4	5	6	7	8	9	10
11	12	13	14	15	16	17
18	19	20	21	22	23	24
25	26	27	28	29	30	31

SEPTEMBER
S	M	T	W	T	F	S
1	2	3	4	5	6	7
8	9	10	11	12	13	14
15	16	17	18	19	20	21
22	23	24	25	26	27	28
29	30					

OCTOBER
S	M	T	W	T	F	S
		1	2	3	4	5
6	7	8	9	10	11	12
13	14	15	16	17	18	19
20	21	22	23	24	25	26
27	28	29	30	31		

NOVEMBER
S	M	T	W	T	F	S
					1	2
3	4	5	6	7	8	9
10	11	12	13	14	15	16
17	18	19	20	21	22	23
24	25	26	27	28	29	30

DECEMBER
S	M	T	W	T	F	S
1	2	3	4	5	6	7
8	9	10	11	12	13	14
15	16	17	18	19	20	21
22	23	24	25	26	27	28
29	30	31				

10

JANUARY
S	M	T	W	T	F	S
		1	2	3	4	5
6	7	8	9	10	11	12
13	14	15	16	17	18	19
20	21	22	23	24	25	26
27	28	29	30	31		

FEBRUARY
S	M	T	W	T	F	S
					1	2
3	4	5	6	7	8	9
10	11	12	13	14	15	16
17	18	19	20	21	22	23
24	25	26	27	28	29	

MARCH
S	M	T	W	T	F	S
						1
2	3	4	5	6	7	8
9	10	11	12	13	14	15
16	17	18	19	20	21	22
23	24	25	26	27	28	29
30	31					

APRIL
S	M	T	W	T	F	S
		1	2	3	4	5
6	7	8	9	10	11	12
13	14	15	16	17	18	19
20	21	22	23	24	25	26
27	28	29	30			

MAY
S	M	T	W	T	F	S
				1	2	3
4	5	6	7	8	9	10
11	12	13	14	15	16	17
18	19	20	21	22	23	24
25	26	27	28	29	30	31

JUNE
S	M	T	W	T	F	S
1	2	3	4	5	6	7
8	9	10	11	12	13	14
15	16	17	18	19	20	21
22	23	24	25	26	27	28
29	30					

JULY
S	M	T	W	T	F	S
		1	2	3	4	5
6	7	8	9	10	11	12
13	14	15	16	17	18	19
20	21	22	23	24	25	26
27	28	29	30	31		

AUGUST
S	M	T	W	T	F	S
					1	2
3	4	5	6	7	8	9
10	11	12	13	14	15	16
17	18	19	20	21	22	23
24	25	26	27	28	29	30
31						

SEPTEMBER
S	M	T	W	T	F	S
	1	2	3	4	5	6
7	8	9	10	11	12	13
14	15	16	17	18	19	20
21	22	23	24	25	26	27
28	29	30				

OCTOBER
S	M	T	W	T	F	S
			1	2	3	4
5	6	7	8	9	10	11
12	13	14	15	16	17	18
19	20	21	22	23	24	25
26	27	28	29	30	31	

NOVEMBER
S	M	T	W	T	F	S
						1
2	3	4	5	6	7	8
9	10	11	12	13	14	15
16	17	18	19	20	21	22
23	24	25	26	27	28	29
30						

DECEMBER
S	M	T	W	T	F	S
	1	2	3	4	5	6
7	8	9	10	11	12	13
14	15	16	17	18	19	20
21	22	23	24	25	26	27
28	29	30	31			

11

JANUARY
```
 S  M  T  W  T  F  S
             1  2  3  4
 5  6  7  8  9 10 11
12 13 14 15 16 17 18
19 20 21 22 23 24 25
26 27 28 29 30 31
```

FEBRUARY
```
 S  M  T  W  T  F  S
                   1
 2  3  4  5  6  7  8
 9 10 11 12 13 14 15
16 17 18 19 20 21 22
23 24 25 26 27 28 29
```

MARCH
```
 S  M  T  W  T  F  S
 1  2  3  4  5  6  7
 8  9 10 11 12 13 14
15 16 17 18 19 20 21
22 23 24 25 26 27 28
29 30 31
```

APRIL
```
 S  M  T  W  T  F  S
             1  2  3  4
 5  6  7  8  9 10 11
12 13 14 15 16 17 18
19 20 21 22 23 24 25
26 27 28 29 30
```

MAY
```
 S  M  T  W  T  F  S
                1  2
 3  4  5  6  7  8  9
10 11 12 13 14 15 16
17 18 19 20 21 22 23
24 25 26 27 28 29 30
31
```

JUNE
```
 S  M  T  W  T  F  S
    1  2  3  4  5  6
 7  8  9 10 11 12 13
14 15 16 17 18 19 20
21 22 23 24 25 26 27
28 29 30
```

JULY
```
 S  M  T  W  T  F  S
             1  2  3  4
 5  6  7  8  9 10 11
12 13 14 15 16 17 18
19 20 21 22 23 24 25
26 27 28 29 30 31
```

AUGUST
```
 S  M  T  W  T  F  S
                      1
 2  3  4  5  6  7  8
 9 10 11 12 13 14 15
16 17 18 19 20 21 22
23 24 25 26 27 28 29
30 31
```

SEPTEMBER
```
 S  M  T  W  T  F  S
    1  2  3  4  5
 6  7  8  9 10 11 12
13 14 15 16 17 18 19
20 21 22 23 24 25 26
27 28 29 30
```

OCTOBER
```
 S  M  T  W  T  F  S
                1  2  3
 4  5  6  7  8  9 10
11 12 13 14 15 16 17
18 19 20 21 22 23 24
25 26 27 28 29 30 31
```

NOVEMBER
```
 S  M  T  W  T  F  S
 1  2  3  4  5  6  7
 8  9 10 11 12 13 14
15 16 17 18 19 20 21
22 23 24 25 26 27 28
29 30
```

DECEMBER
```
 S  M  T  W  T  F  S
       1  2  3  4  5
 6  7  8  9 10 11 12
13 14 15 16 17 18 19
20 21 22 23 24 25 26
27 28 29 30 31
```

12

JANUARY
```
 S  M  T  W  T  F  S
                1  2  3
 4  5  6  7  8  9 10
11 12 13 14 15 16 17
18 19 20 21 22 23 24
25 26 27 28 29 30 31
```

FEBRUARY
```
 S  M  T  W  T  F  S
 1  2  3  4  5  6  7
 8  9 10 11 12 13 14
15 16 17 18 19 20 21
22 23 24 25 26 27 28
29
```

MARCH
```
 S  M  T  W  T  F  S
    1  2  3  4  5  6
 7  8  9 10 11 12 13
14 15 16 17 18 19 20
21 22 23 24 25 26 27
28 29 30 31
```

APRIL
```
 S  M  T  W  T  F  S
             1  2  3
 4  5  6  7  8  9 10
11 12 13 14 15 16 17
18 19 20 21 22 23 24
25 26 27 28 29 30
```

MAY
```
 S  M  T  W  T  F  S
                   1
 2  3  4  5  6  7  8
 9 10 11 12 13 14 15
16 17 18 19 20 21 22
23 24 25 26 27 28 29
30 31
```

JUNE
```
 S  M  T  W  T  F  S
       1  2  3  4  5
 6  7  8  9 10 11 12
13 14 15 16 17 18 19
20 21 22 23 24 25 26
27 28 29 30
```

JULY
```
 S  M  T  W  T  F  S
             1  2  3
 4  5  6  7  8  9 10
11 12 13 14 15 16 17
18 19 20 21 22 23 24
25 26 27 28 29 30 31
```

AUGUST
```
 S  M  T  W  T  F  S
 1  2  3  4  5  6  7
 8  9 10 11 12 13 14
15 16 17 18 19 20 21
22 23 24 25 26 27 28
29 30 31
```

SEPTEMBER
```
 S  M  T  W  T  F  S
          1  2  3  4
 5  6  7  8  9 10 11
12 13 14 15 16 17 18
19 20 21 22 23 24 25
26 27 28 29 30
```

OCTOBER
```
 S  M  T  W  T  F  S
                1  2
 3  4  5  6  7  8  9
10 11 12 13 14 15 16
17 18 19 20 21 22 23
24 25 26 27 28 29 30
31
```

NOVEMBER
```
 S  M  T  W  T  F  S
    1  2  3  4  5  6
 7  8  9 10 11 12 13
14 15 16 17 18 19 20
21 22 23 24 25 26 27
28 29 30
```

DECEMBER
```
 S  M  T  W  T  F  S
          1  2  3  4
 5  6  7  8  9 10 11
12 13 14 15 16 17 18
19 20 21 22 23 24 25
26 27 28 29 30 31
```

13

JANUARY
```
 S  M  T  W  T  F  S
                   1  2
 3  4  5  6  7  8  9
10 11 12 13 14 15 16
17 18 19 20 21 22 23
24 25 26 27 28 29 30
31
```

FEBRUARY
```
 S  M  T  W  T  F  S
    1  2  3  4  5  6
 7  8  9 10 11 12 13
14 15 16 17 18 19 20
21 22 23 24 25 26 27
28 29
```

MARCH
```
 S  M  T  W  T  F  S
       1  2  3  4  5
 6  7  8  9 10 11 12
13 14 15 16 17 18 19
20 21 22 23 24 25 26
27 28 29 30 31
```

APRIL
```
 S  M  T  W  T  F  S
                   1  2
 3  4  5  6  7  8  9
10 11 12 13 14 15 16
17 18 19 20 21 22 23
24 25 26 27 28 29 30
```

MAY
```
 S  M  T  W  T  F  S
 1  2  3  4  5  6  7
 8  9 10 11 12 13 14
15 16 17 18 19 20 21
22 23 24 25 26 27 28
29 30 31
```

JUNE
```
 S  M  T  W  T  F  S
          1  2  3  4
 5  6  7  8  9 10 11
12 13 14 15 16 17 18
19 20 21 22 23 24 25
26 27 28 29 30
```

JULY
```
 S  M  T  W  T  F  S
                   1  2
 3  4  5  6  7  8  9
10 11 12 13 14 15 16
17 18 19 20 21 22 23
24 25 26 27 28 29 30
31
```

AUGUST
```
 S  M  T  W  T  F  S
    1  2  3  4  5  6
 7  8  9 10 11 12 13
14 15 16 17 18 19 20
21 22 23 24 25 26 27
28 29 30 31
```

SEPTEMBER
```
 S  M  T  W  T  F  S
             1  2  3
 4  5  6  7  8  9 10
11 12 13 14 15 16 17
18 19 20 21 22 23 24
25 26 27 28 29 30
```

OCTOBER
```
 S  M  T  W  T  F  S
                      1
 2  3  4  5  6  7  8
 9 10 11 12 13 14 15
16 17 18 19 20 21 22
23 24 25 26 27 28 29
30 31
```

NOVEMBER
```
 S  M  T  W  T  F  S
       1  2  3  4  5
 6  7  8  9 10 11 12
13 14 15 16 17 18 19
20 21 22 23 24 25 26
27 28 29 30
```

DECEMBER
```
 S  M  T  W  T  F  S
             1  2  3
 4  5  6  7  8  9 10
11 12 13 14 15 16 17
18 19 20 21 22 23 24
25 26 27 28 29 30 31
```

14

JANUARY
```
 S  M  T  W  T  F  S
                      1
 2  3  4  5  6  7  8
 9 10 11 12 13 14 15
16 17 18 19 20 21 22
23 24 25 26 27 28 29
30 31
```

FEBRUARY
```
 S  M  T  W  T  F  S
       1  2  3  4  5
 6  7  8  9 10 11 12
13 14 15 16 17 18 19
20 21 22 23 24 25 26
27 28 29
```

MARCH
```
 S  M  T  W  T  F  S
          1  2  3  4
 5  6  7  8  9 10 11
12 13 14 15 16 17 18
19 20 21 22 23 24 25
26 27 28 29 30 31
```

APRIL
```
 S  M  T  W  T  F  S
                      1
 2  3  4  5  6  7  8
 9 10 11 12 13 14 15
16 17 18 19 20 21 22
23 24 25 26 27 28 29
30
```

MAY
```
 S  M  T  W  T  F  S
    1  2  3  4  5  6
 7  8  9 10 11 12 13
14 15 16 17 18 19 20
21 22 23 24 25 26 27
28 29 30 31
```

JUNE
```
 S  M  T  W  T  F  S
             1  2  3
 4  5  6  7  8  9 10
11 12 13 14 15 16 17
18 19 20 21 22 23 24
25 26 27 28 29 30
```

JULY
```
 S  M  T  W  T  F  S
                      1
 2  3  4  5  6  7  8
 9 10 11 12 13 14 15
16 17 18 19 20 21 22
23 24 25 26 27 28 29
30 31
```

AUGUST
```
 S  M  T  W  T  F  S
       1  2  3  4  5
 6  7  8  9 10 11 12
13 14 15 16 17 18 19
20 21 22 23 24 25 26
27 28 29 30 31
```

SEPTEMBER
```
 S  M  T  W  T  F  S
                   1  2
 3  4  5  6  7  8  9
10 11 12 13 14 15 16
17 18 19 20 21 22 23
24 25 26 27 28 29 30
```

OCTOBER
```
 S  M  T  W  T  F  S
 1  2  3  4  5  6  7
 8  9 10 11 12 13 14
15 16 17 18 19 20 21
22 23 24 25 26 27 28
29 30 31
```

NOVEMBER
```
 S  M  T  W  T  F  S
             1  2  3  4
 5  6  7  8  9 10 11
12 13 14 15 16 17 18
19 20 21 22 23 24 25
26 27 28 29 30
```

DECEMBER
```
 S  M  T  W  T  F  S
                   1  2
 3  4  5  6  7  8  9
10 11 12 13 14 15 16
17 18 19 20 21 22 23
24 25 26 27 28 29 30
31
```

Months

The month names in most European languages were probably derived as follows:

January	Janus, Roman god
February	Februar, Roman festival of purification
March	Mars, Roman god
April	Latin *aperire*, 'to open'
May	Maia, Roman goddess
June	Juno, Roman goddess
July	Julius Caesar, Roman general
August	Augustus, Roman emperor
September	Latin *septem*, 'seven'
October	Latin *octo*, 'eight'
November	Latin *novem*, 'nine'
December	Latin *decem*, 'ten'

Wedding anniversaries

In many Western countries, different wedding anniversaries have become associated with gifts of different materials. There is variation between countries.

Anniversary	Material
1st	cotton
2nd	paper
3rd	leather
4th	fruit, flowers
5th	wood
6th	sugar
7th	copper, wool
8th	bronze, pottery
9th	pottery, willow
10th	tin
11th	steel
12th	silk, linen
13th	lace
14th	ivory
15th	crystal
20th	china
25th	silver
30th	pearl
35th	coral
40th	ruby
45th	sapphire
50th	gold
55th	emerald
60th	diamond
70th	platinum

Days of the week

The names of the days are derived as follows:

English	Latin	Saxon
Sunday	Dies Solis	Sun's Day
Monday	Dies Lunae	Moon's Day
Tuesday	Dies Martis	Tiu's Day
Wednesday	Dies Mercurii	Woden's Day
Thursday	Dies Jovis	Thor's Day
Friday	Dies Veneris	Frigg's Day
Saturday	Dies Saturni	Saeternes' Day

Tiu Anglo-Saxon counterpart of Nordic Tyr, son of Odin, God of War, closest to Mars (Greek Ares), son of Roman God Jupiter (Greek Zeus); *Woden* Anglo-Saxon counterpart of Odin, Nordic dispenser of victory, closest to Mercury (Greek Hermes), Roman messenger of victory; *Thor* Nordic God of Thunder, eldest son of Odin, closest to Roman Jupiter (Greek Zeus); *Frigg* (or *Freyja*) wife of Odin, the Nordic Goddess of Love, equivalent to Venus (Greek Aphrodite)

Birthstones

Month	Stone	Quality
January	garnet	constancy
February	amethyst	sincerity
March	bloodstone	courage
April	diamond	innocence and lasting love
May	emerald	success and hope
June	pearl	health and purity
July	ruby	love and contentment
August	agate	married happiness
September	sapphire	wisdom
October	opal	hope
November	topaz	fidelity
December	turquoise	harmony

Signs of the zodiac

Spring signs

Aries, the Ram
(Mar 21 – Apr 19)

Taurus, the Bull
(Apr 20 – May 20)

Gemini, the Twins
(May 21 – Jun 20)

Summer signs

Cancer, the Crab
(Jun 21 – Jul 22)

Leo, the Lion
(Jul 23 – Aug 22)

Virgo, the Virgin
(Aug 23 – Sep 22)

Autumn signs

Libra, the Balance
(Sep 23 – Oct 22)

Scorpio, the Scorpion
(Oct 23 – Nov 21)

Sagittarius, the Archer
(Nov 22 – Dec 21)

Winter signs

Capricorn, the Goat
(Dec 22 – Jan 19)

Aquarius, the Water Bearer
(Jan 20 – Feb 18)

Pisces, the Fishes
(Feb 19 – Mar 20)

ARCHAEOLOGY

Terms and Techniques

absolute dating the determination of age in calendar years by reference to a fixed time scale. Also called chronometric dating, it usually incorporates a measure of uncertainty, expressed as a standard deviation.

accelerator mass spectrometry (AMS) a new radiocarbon dating method that determines the actual number of carbon-14 atoms in a sample rather than the small numbers of carbon-14 atoms that decay radioactively during the measurement time of the conventional method. This method requires only a tiny sample, and its measurement time is only about one hour (as opposed to days for radiocarbon dating), but it is expensive.

aerial photography or *aerial archaeology* taking photographs from a high level, a technique used in archaeology to detect surface features (such as crop marks, soil marks, shadow marks) that are not clearly visible from ground level and which indicate the presence of ancient features; for example, crops will show differences in growth and colour if they are growing over a buried wall foundation or other stone feature.

aerial reconnaissance technique used primarily for the recording and interpretation of archaeological sites from the air, though at times it can also be useful in discovering new sites. *Thermal prospection* (also called thermography) is an expensive remote-sensing method that uses heat sensors in aircraft which scan the varying temperatures of remains below ground. Images produced from LANDSAT satellites have been used to discover ancient sites and landscapes (in particular Mayan sites in Mesoamerica); SLAR (sideways looking aerial radar) from NASA aircraft has also been used to reveal ancient sites and field systems.

anthropology the study of humanity's physical characteristics and culture, generally divided into the three subdisciplines of physical (biological) anthropology, social (cultural) anthropology, and archaeology.

archaeology the study of the human past through the systematic recovery and analysis of material remains. Its aims are to recover, describe, and classify this material, to describe the form and behaviour of past societies, and to understand the reasons for this behaviour. A truly inter-disciplinary subject, it has borrowed many of its major theoretical and methodological concepts and approaches from history and anthropology.

methods Principal activities include preliminary field (or site) surveys, excavation (where necessary), and the classification, dating, and interpretation of finds. Related disciplines that have been useful in archaeological reconstruction include stratigraphy (the study of geological strata), dendrochronology (the establishment of chronological sequences through the study of tree rings), palaeobotany (the study of ancient pollens, seeds, and grains), epigraphy (the study of inscriptions), and numismatics (the study of coins).

Since 1958 radiocarbon dating has been used and refined to establish the age of archaeological strata and associated materials.

archaeomagnetic dating dating technique based on the palaeomagnetism of archaeological materials such as baked clay structures (hearths, kilns, ovens). When originally heated, their magnetic particles realigned with the Earth's magnetic field at the time, and since that field changes over time, local and regional chronologies of field-direction can be built up and independently dated. In England for example such curves have been established for the last 2000 years, allowing for any sample to be dated within that span to within approximately 50 years.

archaeozoology or *zooarchaeology* branch of archaeology involving the analysis of animal remains for information on physiology and ecology; for the interpretation of these remains in association with artefacts and people; and for data on subsistence, dietary and butchering patterns, animal domestication, and palaeoenvironment.

artefact any movable object that has been used, modified, or manufactured by humans, such as a tool, weapon, or vessel.

assemblage a collection of artefacts that can be considered a single analytic unit, occurring together at a particular time and place. Frequently repeated assemblages that represent a broad range of human activity are termed an archaeological culture.

atomic absorption spectrometry technique used to determine quantitatively the chemical composition of artefactual metals, minerals, and rocks, in order to identify raw material sources, to relate artefacts of the same material, or to trace trade routes. A sample of the material is atomized in a flame, and its light intensity measured. The method is slow and destructive.

attribute characteristic element of a particular archaeological culture or group; or a specific element of an individual artefact, such as the rim of a pot or the base of a projectile point, or a type of decoration, raw material, or colour.

auger tool used to collect sediment and soil samples below ground without hand excavation, or to determine the depth and type of archaeological deposits. The auger may be hand- or machine-powered.

bosing locating buried pits or ditches by striking the surface of the ground with a heavy wooden mallet; a duller sound is produced over any disturbance.

Bronze Age stage of prehistory and early history when copper and bronze became the first metals worked extensively and used for tools and weapons. It developed out of the Stone Age, preceded the Iron Age, and may be dated 5000–1200 BC in the Middle East and about 2000–500 BC in Europe. Mining and metalworking were the first specialized industries, and the invention of the wheel during this time revolutionized transport. Agricultural productivity (which began during the Neolithic period, about 10,000 BC), and hence the size of the population that could be supported, was transformed by the ox-drawn plough.

Recent discoveries in Thailand suggest that the Far East, rather than the Middle East, was the cradle of the Bronze Age.

cognitive archaeology the study of past ways of thought from material remains, and of the meanings evoked by the symbolic nature of material culture.

computerized axial tomography (CAT) a technique for looking inside bodies or mummies without disturbing them. X-ray scans made at intervals produce a series of cross-sectional 'slices' that the computer can reformat to create images from any angle.

context an artefact's matrix (the sediment or material surrounding it), its provenance (its three- dimensional position within that matrix), and its association with other artefacts in the matrix.

contract archaeology archaeological survey and/ or excavation undertaken under the aegis of state legislation, most often in advance of highway construction or urban development.

core solid cylinder of sediment or soil collected with a coring device and used to evaluate the geological context and stratigraphy of archaeological material or to obtain palaeobotanical samples. Core can also mean the tool used to extract a core sample from the ground, or a stone blank from which flakes or blades are removed.

cross-dating demonstrating the degree to which cultural groups were contemporary by establishing links between them. For example, objects produced by one group might be found in the remains of another.

cultural anthropology or *social anthropology* subdiscipline of anthropology that analyses human culture and society, the nonbiological and behavioural aspects of humanity. Two principal branches are ethnography (the study at first hand of living cultures) and ethnology (the comparison of cultures using ethnographic evidence).

cultural resource management the legally mandated protection of archaeological sites located on public lands that are threatened by destruction, usually through development. The term is mainly used in the USA.

dating means employed to establish a chronological ordering of past cultures and events, and a timescale against which to set that sequence. Dating is an integral part of the discipline, and the success of much archaeological analysis depends on the precision of dating that can be achieved.

Relative dating methods – such as stratigraphy and seriation – are used to order archaeological material into sequences, placing earlier before later, but without linking these sequences to dates in calendar years. *Absolute dating* methods – such as radiocarbon dating, thermoluminescence, potassium-argon dating, electron spin resonance, fission track dating, archaeomagnetism, dendrochronology – are those that determine age in calendar years by reference to a fixed time scale, but often incorporate a degree of uncertainty, expressed as a standard deviation.

Archaeological dating is at its most reliable when relative and absolute methods are used together, for example when the relative sequence assigned to layers in an excavation can be confirmed by absolute dates for each layer. Where circumstances permit, results from one absolute method should be cross-checked by those from another, for example radiocarbon by dendrochronology or by thermoluminescence.

dendrochronology dating technique that uses tree-ring sequences to date timbers and other logs from archaeological structures and sites. This technique is based on the principle that every year trees add a ring of growth, and by counting these rings their age can be determined. An unbroken series of rings can be built up and extended back for centuries by 'overlapping' identical sequences preserved on modern and ancient timbers; subsequently, any piece of wood found in the area can have its rings checked against the master sequence and its precise age established. 'Floating' chronologies, which do not extend to the present day, have been built up in many regions worldwide and allow for relative dating between structures and sites.

In North America, sequences of tree rings extending back over 8,000 years have been obtained by using cores from the bristle-cone pine (*Pinus aristata*), which can live for over 4,000 years. Such sequences have proved very useful for calibrating, or correcting, radiocarbon dates, which were found to have serious discrepancies due to a differences in the atmosphere's carbon-14 content over time.

diffusion the spread of ideas, objects or cultural traits from one culture or society to another, rather than their independent invention; for example a diffusionist school of thought held that Egypt was the source of metallurgy and megalithic building, whereas it is now accepted that these traits arose independently in different areas.

dowsing unconventional and controversial method for locating subsurface features by holding out a twig, rod, or pendulum and waiting for it to move. Although used at times in archaeology, it is not taken seriously by most archaeologists.

electrolysis a cleaning process in archaeological conservation, especially of material from underwater archaeology, involving immersing the object in a chemical solution, and passing a weak current between it and a surrounding metal grill. Corrosive salts move slowly from the object (cathode) to the grill (anode), leaving the artifact clean.

electron spin resonance (ESR) is a non-destructive dating method applicable to teeth, bone, heat-treated flint, ceramics, sediments and stalagmitic concretions. It enables electrons, displaced by natural radiation and then trapped in the structure, to be measured; their number indicate the age of the specimen.

environmental archaeology a subfield of archaeology aimed at identifying processes, factors and conditions of past biological and physical environmental systems and how they relate to cultural systems. It is an eminently inter-disciplinary field, where archaeologists and natural scientists combine to reconstruct the human uses of plants and animals and how societies adapted to changing environmental conditions.

eolith naturally shaped or fractured stone found in Lower Pleistocene deposits and once believed by some scholars to be the oldest known artefact type, dating to the pre-Palaeolithic era. They are now recognized as not having been made by humans.

ethnoarchaeology the study of human behaviour and the material culture of living societies, in order to see how materials enter the archaeological record, and that way to provide hypotheses explaining the production, use, and disposal patterns of ancient material culture.

ethnography study of living cultures, using anthropological techniques, like participant observation (where the anthropologist lives in the society being studied) and a reliance on informants. Ethnography has provided many data of use to archaeologists as analogies.

ethnology study of contemporary peoples, concentrating on their geography and culture, as distinct from their social systems. Ethnologists make a comparative analysis of data from different cultures to understand how cultures work and why they change, with a view to deriving general principles about human society.

excavation or *dig* the systematic recovery of data through the exposure of buried sites and artefacts. Excavation is destructive, and is therefore accompanied by a comprehensive recording of all material found and its three-dimensional locations (its context). As much material and information as possible must be recovered from any dig. A full record of all the techniques employed in the excavation itself must also be made, so that future archaeologists will be able to evaluate the results of the work accurately.

Besides being destructive, excavation is also costly. For both these reasons, it should be used only as a last resort. It can be partial, with only a sample of the site investigated, or total. Samples are chosen either intuitively, in which case excavators investigate those areas they feel will be most productive, or statistically, in which case the sample is drawn using various statistical techniques, so as to ensure that it is representative. An important goal of excavation is a full understanding of a site's stratigraphy; that is, the vertical layering of a site. These layers or levels can be defined naturally (for example, soil changes), culturally (for example, different occupation levels), or arbitrarily (for example, 10 cm levels). Excavation can also be done horizontally, to uncover larger areas of a particular layer and reveal the spatial relationships between artefacts and features in that layer. This is known as open-area excavation and is used especially where single-period deposits lie close to the surface, and the time dimension is represented by lateral movement rather than by the placing of one building on top of the preceding one.

Most excavators employ a flexible combination of vertical and horizontal digging, adapting to the nature of their site and the questions they are seeking to answer.

experimental archaeology the controlled replication of ancient technologies and behaviour in order to provide hypotheses that can be tested by actual archaeological data. Experiments can range in size from the reproduction of ancient tools in order to learn about their processes of manufacture and use, and their effectiveness, to the construction of whole villages and ancient subsistence practices in long-term experiments.

faunal dating imprecise method of relative dating based on evolutionary changes in particular species of animals so as to form a chronological sequence.

feature nonportable element of a site, such as a hearth, wall, post-hole, or activity area. Some are constructed (e.g. houses, storerooms, burial features), while others simply form over time, such as heaps of shells, or quarry areas.

field survey the examination of the surface of the earth for evidence of archaeological remains, without recourse to excavation. Surveys can be carried out unsystematically, where *field walking* takes place over areas suspected of having archaeological material, and the location of any finds or surface features encountered is plotted; or systematically, where the area is divided into a grid and a sample of its sectors is walked, making the survey more representative of the whole and hence more accurate.

fission-track dating dating method based on the natural and spontaneous nuclear fission of uranium-238 and its physical product, linear atomic displacements (tracks) created along the trajectory of released energized fission fragments. Knowing the rate of fission (a constant), the uranium content of the material, and by counting the number of fission tracks, the age of the material can be determined. The method is most widely used to date volcanic deposits adjacent to archaeological material.

grid system excavation technique that aims to include both the vertical and horizontal dimensions by retaining intact baulks (standing sections) of earth between the excavated squares of the grid so that different layers can be traced and correlated across the site of the vertical profiles.

historical archaeology the archaeological study of historically documented cultures, especially in America and Australia, where it is directed at colonial and post-colonial settlements. The European equivalent is medieval and post-medieval archaeology.

hoard valuables or prized possessions that have been deliberately buried, often in times of conflict or war, and never reclaimed. Coins, objects in precious metals, and scrap metal are the most common objects found in hoards. In July 1991 the largest hoard found in Britain was discovered, consisting of 7,000 15th-century coins; it was declared a treasure trove.

Iron Age developmental stage of human technology when weapons and tools were made from iron. Iron was produced in Thailand by about 1600 BC but was considered inferior in strength to bronze until about 1000 BC when metallurgical techniques improved and the alloy steel was produced by adding carbon during the smelting process. In Europe, it begins around 1100 BC, and early Iron Age cultures are represented by the Villanovans in Italy and Hallstatt in La Téne in central and western Europe; it is also the time when Celtic art flourished. The end of the period overlaps with the expansion of imperial Rome around the 1st century BC, but beyond the borders of the Empire it is generally taken to end much later, around the 4th-6th centuries AD.

CHRONOLOGICAL CHART SHOWING MAJOR CULTURAL DEVELOPMENTS WORLDWIDE

Years AD/BC	North Europe	Mediterranean	Near East	Egypt and Africa
1,500				Great Zimbabwe
1,000	Medieval states	BYZANTINE EMPIRE		
500			ISLAM	
AD	ROMAN EMPIRE	ROMAN EMPIRE		Towns (Africa) AXUM
BC				
500	IRON AGE	CLASSICAL GREECE	PERSIA BABYLON ASSYRIA	LATE PERIOD
1,000				
1,500		Iron	HITITES	NEW KINGDOM
2,000	BRONZE AGE (Stonehenge)	MYCENAE	Iron	MIDDLE KINGDOM
2,500		MINOAN		OLD KINGDOM (Pyramids)
3,000			SUMER	EARLY DYNASTIC
3,500			Writing Cities Wheeled vehicles	Towns (Egypt)
4,000				
4,500	Megaliths	Copper (Balkans)		
5,000	Farming, pottery			
5,500			Irrigation	
6,000				
6,500		Farming, pottery	Copper	Cattle (North Africa)
7,000			Pottery	Pottery (Sudan)
7,500			Wheat, rye etc	
8,000				
8,500				
9,000			Sheep	
9,500				
10,000				

Information supplied by Paul Bahn

isotopic analysis the analysis of ratios of the principal isotopes preserved in human bone in order to reconstruct ancient diet, based on the principle that different food categories (for example, marine resources) leave specific chemical signatures in the body.

landscape archaeology the study of human occupation and activities on landscapes, in particular the patterning of settlements and sites within that broad perspective through time.

magnetometer device for measuring the intensity of the Earth's magnetic field; distortions in this field occur when archaeological structures such as kilns and hearths are present, or pits and ditches. The technique allows for such features to be located without disturbing the ground, and for excavation to be focused on the most likely area.

material culture the physical, human-made remains of past societies (tools, buildings, and so on) which constitute the major source of evidence for archaeology.

matrix the physical material within which cultural debris or fossils are contained or embedded.

Mesolithic the Middle Stone Age developmental stage of human technology and of ◊prehistory, following the Paleolithic and preceding the Neolithic.

India	East Asia and Pacific	North America	Meso-America	South America	Years AD/BC
				INCA	1,500
			AZTEC		1,000
	New Zealand settled States (*Japan*)	Cahokia Chaco HOPEWELL	"TOLTEC"	CHIMU	500
		PUEBLOS	MAYA		AD
	Great Wall (*China*)		TEOTIHUACAN	MOCHE	BC
MAURYAN Iron	Cast iron (*China*)				500
	Lapita (*Polynesia*) SHANG (*China*)	Maize (*Southwest*)	OLMEC	CHAVIN	1,000
					1,500
INDUS					2,000
	Walled villages (*China*)				2,500
				Temple-mounds	3,000
				Maize, llama cotton	3,500
					4,000
					4,500
					5,000
	Rice-millet (*China*)		Maize	Manioc	5,500
				Pottery (*Amazonia*)	6,000
			Beans, squash, peppers	Beans, squash peppers	6,500
Farming	Gardens (*New Guinea*)				7,000
					7,500
					8,000
					8,500
					9,000
	Pottery (*Japan*)				9,500
					10,000

While the environment changed with the withdrawal of the Pleistocene ice sheets around 10,000 years ago, the old Palaeolithic hunting and gathering way of life continued during the Mesolithic; changes in the tool assemblages however reflect adaptations to environmental changes, with the flint industries of this period characterized by microliths (very small flint tools) in great number. With the introduction of farming and stock-rearing the Mesolithic gave way to the Neolithic (occurring in Britain around 4000 BC).

metal detector electronic device for detecting metal on or beneath the surface of the ground. It is used to survey areas for buried metallic objects, occasionally by archaeologists. However, their indiscriminate use by treasure hunters has led to their being banned on recognized archaeological sites in some countries; in Britain the law forbids the use of metal detectors on 'scheduled' (that is, nationally important) sites.

metallographic examination method of analysing the manufacturing techniques of metal artefacts. A cross-sectional slice of an artefact is polished, etched to highlight internal structures, and examined under a metallurgical microscope. The reflected light of the microscope enhances uneven surfaces, revealing grain size, shape, and boundaries, inclusions, fabric, defects, and other detail.

Archaeology: chronology

14th–16th centuries	The Renaissance revived interest in Classical Greek and Roman art and architecture, including ruins and buried art and artefacts.
1748	The buried Roman city of Pompeii was discovered under lava from Vesuvius.
1784	Thomas Jefferson excavated an Indian burial mound on the Rivanna River in Virginia and wrote a report on his finds.
1790	John Frere identified Old Stone Age (Palaeolithic) tools together with large extinct animals.
1822	Jean François Champollion deciphered Egyptian hieroglyphics.
1836	Christian Thomsen devised the Stone, Bronze, and Iron Age classification.
1840s	Austen Layard excavated the Assyrian capital of Nineveh.
1868	The Great Zimbabwe ruins in E Africa were first seen by Europeans.
1871	Heinrich Schliemann began excavations at Troy.
1879	Stone Age paintings were first discovered at Altamira, Spain.
1880s	Augustus Pitt-Rivers developed the concept of stratigraphy (identification of successive layers of soil within a site with successive archaeological stages; the most recent at the top).
1891	Flinders Petrie began excavating Akhetaton in Egypt.
1899–1935	Arthur Evans excavated Minoan Knossos in Crete.
1900–44	Max Uhle began the systematic study of the civilizations of Peru.
1911	The Inca city of Machu Picchu was discovered by Hiram Bingham in the Andes.
1911–12	The Piltdown skull was 'discovered'; it was proved to be a fake 1949.
1914–18	Osbert Crawford developed the technique of aerial survey of sites.
1917–27	John Eric Thompson (1898-1975) discovered the great Mayan sites in Yucatán, Mexico.
1922	Tutankhamen's tomb in Egypt was opened by Howard Carter.
1926	A kill site in Folsom, New Mexico, was found with human-made spearpoints in association with ancient bison.
1935	Dendrochronology (dating events in the distant past by counting tree rings) was developed by A E Douglas.
1939	An Anglo-Saxon ship-burial treasure was found at Sutton Hoo, England.
1947	The first of the Dead Sea Scrolls was discovered.
1948	The *Proconsul* prehistoric ape was discovered by Mary Leakey in Kenya.
1950s–1970s	Several early hominid fossils were found by Louis Leakey in Olduvai Gorge.
1953	Michael Ventris deciphered Minoan Linear B.
1960s	Radiocarbon and thermoluminescence measurement techniques were developed as aids for dating remains.
1961	The Swedish warship *Wasa* was raised at Stockholm.
1963	Walter Emery pioneered rescue archaeology at Abu Simbel before the site was flooded by the Aswan Dam.
1969	Human remains found at Lake Mungo, Australia, were dated at 26,000 years; earliest evidence of ritual cremation.
1974	The Tomb of Shi Huangdi was discovered in China. The footprints of a hominid called 'Lucy', 3 to 3.7 million years old, were found at Laetoli in Ethiopia.
1978	The tomb of Philip II of Macedon (Alexander the Great's father) was discovered in Greece.
1979	The Aztec capital Tenochtitlán was excavated beneath a zone of Mexico City.
1982	The English king Henry VIII's warship *Mary Rose* of 1545 was raised and studied with new techniques in underwater archaeology.
1985	The tomb of Maya, Tutankhamen's treasurer, was discovered at Saqqara, Egypt.
1988	The Turin Shroud was established as being of medieval origin by radiocarbon dating.
1989	The remains of the Globe and Rose Theatres, where many of Shakespeare's plays were originally performed, were discovered in London.
1991	Body of man from 5,300 years ago, with clothing, bow, arrows, a copper axe, and other implements, found preserved in Italian Alps.
1992	The world's oldest surviving wooden structure, a well 15 m/49 ft deep made of huge oak timbers at Kückhoven, Germany, was dated by tree-rings to 5,300 BC.
1993	Drawings done in charcoal on the walls of the Cosquer Cave (whose underwater entrance near Marseilles, France, was discovered in 1991), were dated by radiocarbon to 27,110 years ago, making this the oldest directly dated cave art in the world.

microwear analysis or *usewear analysis* the examination of the surface and working edge of an artefact for signs of use (such as damage or residue), often by means of a high-powered microscope. The technique is principally used in the study of stone tools, which suffer diagnostic damage or polishing when used to cut, saw, or pierce other materials.

Neolithic last period of the ◊Stone Age, characterized by settled communities based on agriculture and domesticated animals, and identified by sophisticated, finely honed stone tools, and ceramic wares. The earliest Neolithic communities appeared about 9000 BC in the Middle East, followed by Egypt, India, and China. In Europe farming began in about 6500 BC in the Balkans and Aegean, spreading north and east by 1000 BC. Sometimes called the Neolithic Revolution, the period marks the most important single development of humanity as it brought with it sedentarism, which in turn encouraged growth and greater specialization.

New Archaeology development in the 1960s aimed at making archaeology more scientific, now more often referred to as Processual Archaeology. It proposed that archaeology should openly state its assumptions and use specific scientific procedures derived from Positivism. Some adherents of New Archaeology believed that laws of human behaviour were obtainable by using the correct methodologies.

palaeobotany or *palaeoethnobotany* or *archaeobotany* the recovery and identification of plant remains from archaeological contexts, and their use in the reconstruction of past environments and economies.

Palaeolithic earliest stage of human technology and development of the Stone Age, beginning with the emergence of hominids and the production of the earliest stone tools (approximately three million years ago), and lasting till the retreat of the ice sheets about 10,000 years ago. Its subdivisions are the Lower Palaeolithic, in which the earliest hominids appear (*Australopithecus* and *Homo erectus*; the Middle Palaeolithic, the age of Neanderthals; and the Upper Paleolithic, marked by the appearance of *Homo sapiens* and the remarkable cave art of western Europe (for example the caves at Lascaux). The final stage also saw the colonization of the New World and Australia.

palaeontology the study of ancient life that encompasses the structure of ancient organisms and their environment, evolution, and ecology, as revealed by their fossils.

phosphate analysis the regular sampling and chemical analysis of phosphorus levels in the soil around archaeological sites in order to locate concentrations of human bone and excrement, and hence areas of human activity, settlements, and burial grounds.

physical anthropology or *biological anthropology* subdiscipline of anthropology that studies human biological or physical characteristics and how they evolved.

pollen analysis or *palynology* the study of fossil and living pollen and spores, utilized in palaeoenvironmental and palaeoclimatic reconstruction, identifying natural and humanly induced vegetation changes, and developing relative chronologies.

potassium-argon dating an isotopic dating method based on the radioactive decay of potassium-40 to the stable isotope argon-40. The method is used primarily to date volcanic layers in stratigraphic sequences with archaeological deposits, and the palaeomagnetic reversal timescale. Ages are based on the known half-life of 40K, and the ratio of 40K/40Ar. The method is routinely applied from about 100,000 to 30 million years ago.

prehistory human cultures before the use of writing. It constitutes the longest segment of the human past, and is the major object of study of archaeology. A classification system was devised 1816 by Danish archaeologist Christian Thomsen, based on the predominant materials used by early hu:nans for tools and weapons: Stone Age, Bronze Age, Iron Age. Prehistory and history can overlap in time – for example, prehistoric Iron Age cultures existed at the same time as the historic Roman culture; and in our own age, 'prehistoric' societies have existed contemporaneously with modern ones, for example the Kung Bushmen or the Australian aborigines.

protohistory period following prehistory but prior to the appearance of history as documented in written records.

radiocarbon dating or *carbon dating* a radiometric dating technique used for determining the age of carbon-bearing materials including wood and plant remains, bone, peat, and shell. It is based on the radioactive decay of the carbon-14 isotope in the sample to nitrogen, with the release of (beta) particles that is initiated when an organism dies and ceases to exchange carbon-14 with the atmosphere. After death the carbon-14 content is a function of time and is determined by counting (beta) particles with either a proportional gas or a liquid scintillation counter for a period of time.

The method yields reliable ages back to *c.* 30,000 years, but its results require correction since the atmospheric production rate of carbon-14 has not been constant through time. Radiocarbon dates from tree rings showed that material before 1000 BC had been exposed to greater concentrations of carbon-14. Now radiocarbon dates are calibrated against calendar dates obtained from tree rings, or, for earlier periods, against uranium/thorium dates obtained from coral. A new advance, AMS (accelerator mass spectrometry) requires only tiny samples of the material being dated, and counts the atoms of carbon-14 directly, disregarding their decay.

relative dating dating methods that measure differences in age utilizing an ordinal scale. For example, they include sequencing of events or objects relative to one another but without linkage to ages in calendar years.

remote sensing gathering and recording information from a distance. Space probes have sent back photographs and data about planets as distant as Neptune. In archaeology, surface survey techniques provide information without disturbing subsurface deposits.

rescue archaeology or *salvage archaeology* the location and recording (usually by rapid excavation) of archaeological sites before they are destroyed by contemporary construction or other developments. Salvage archaeology is also concerned with the various laws enacted to mitigate the threat.

resistivity survey geophysical survey method used to locate buried features and structures with a resistivity meter. An electrical current is passed through the soil between electrodes and the resistance (normally a consequence of moisture content) is recorded. In this way buried features can be detected through their differential retention of groundwater – so, for example, a stone feature will show greater resistance than the soil around it, and a damp pit will show less.

seriation relative dating technique in which artefacts are temporally organized, according to their relative popularity. Evolutionary seriation is based on changes that represent essentially technological improvements, while stylistic seriation is based on gradual changes in the frequencies of stylistic attributes, so that the greater the similarity in style, the closer in age artefacts are to each other.

site any location where there is evidence for past human behaviour. A site can be as small as an isolated find, which is either a single artefact or a small number of artefacts, or as large as an ancient city. Sites are classified according to function: major types include domestic/habitation sites, kill sites, and processing/butchering sites.

site catchment analysis (SCA) the definition of the site catchment, the total area from which the site's contents have been derived (i.e. the full inventory of its artefactual and non-artefactual remains, and their sources), and an assessment of the catchment's economic potential.

site exploitation territory the territory surrounding a site that was habitually exploited by the site's inhabitants. Territories are normally seen as having a radius of one hour's walking distance for farmers, and a two-hour distance for hunter-gatherers.

sondage deep test-pit used to investigate a site's stratigraphy (layered arrangement of deposits) before carrying out larger-scale excavation.

spectrographic analysis technique used to analyse the component elements of a chemical compound; it is based on the principle that the light given off when the compound is vaporized will break up into a distinctive pattern when split into a spectrum by a prism. By analyzing the pattern of lines in the spectrum the elements present in the compound can be determined. The technique has been especially useful in metal analysis, but is also applied to pottery, obsidian, and glass.

step-trenching excavation technique used on very deep sites such as Middle Eastern 'tells' (mounds) where a large area opened at the top gradually narrows as the dig descends in a series of large steps.

Stone Age the developmental stage of humans in prehistory before the use of metals, when tools and weapons were made chiefly of stone, especially flint. The Stone Age is subdivided into the Old or Palaeolithic, the Middle or Mesolithic, and the New or Neolithic. The people of the Old Stone Age were hunters and gatherers, whereas the Neolithic people took the first steps in agriculture, the domestication of animals, weaving, and pottery.

stratigraphy the study of the formation, composition, sequence, and correlation of stratified sediment, soils, and rocks. Stratigraphy is the principal means by which the context of archaeological deposits is evaluated, chronologies are constructed, and events are sequenced. It is invaluable for interpreting the sequence of deposition of the site and thereby the relative age of artefacts, features, and other phenomena in the site.

thermoluminescence (TL) is used to date fired archaeological material such as pottery and burned flint tools. When the material was originally fired, any electrons trapped in it by radiation escaped, emitting light known as thermoluminescence, and thereby setting the TL clock to zero. By measuring the amount of TL emitted when the material is reheated, and know-

ing its radioactive content, one can calculate the lapse of time since the original firing.

thin-section analysis technique using a sample chip – ground down to a paper-thin sheet and mounted on a glass slide – that is utilized in petrological analysis of the mineralogical composition of ceramics, stone artefacts, and soils.

Three Age System scheme first formulated by Christian Thomsen (1788–1865) in 1816–19 to divide prehistory into a Stone Age, Bronze Age, and Iron Age. Further subdivisions followed, with the Stone Age being divided into the Old and the New (the Palaeolithic and Neolithic), a Middle (Mesolithic) Stone Age added later, and the Copper Age added between the New Stone Age and Bronze Age. While providing a valuable and valid classification system for prehistoric material, it did not provide dates but only a sequence of developmental stages, which, furthermore, were not necessarily followed in that order by different societies.

trace element analysis the study (e.g. by neutron activation analysis or X-ray fluorescence) of elements that occur naturally in minor amounts in minerals in soil and sediment. Trace elements can be identified by various analyses and may serve as 'fingerprints' for some artifact raw material sources.

typology the systematic organization of artifacts into types on the basis of their shared attributes. The two objectives are classification, i.e. grouping objects according to their shape, leading to a type series; and, through the comparison of different types, to discover how these types relate to each other. The latter process can lead to seriation, which demonstrates the development of a type of artifact (the development may be related to function, technological advance, fashion, etc.). Such information requires an independent dating source for at least several examples in the series in order to establish the rate of change.

underwater reconnaissance geophysical methods of underwater survey including the proton magnetometer, towed behind a survey vessel to detect iron and steel objects that distort the earth's magnetic field; side-scan sonar, that transmits sound waves in a fan-shaped beam to produce a graphic image of subsurface features on the sea-bed; and a sub-bottom profiler that emits sound pulses that bounce back from features and objects buried under the sea-floor.

X-ray diffraction analysis a physical technique used to identify the mineralogy of material such as ceramics, stone, sediments and weathering products on metals. The sample is ground to powder, and exposed to X-rays at various angles; the diffraction patterns produced are compared with reference standards for identification.

X-ray fluorescence spectrometry (XRF) a physical technique used to determine the major and trace elements in the chemical composition of materials such as ceramics, obsidian and glass that may help in identifying the material source. The sample is bombarded with X-rays, and the wavelengths of the released energy, or fluorescent X-rays, are detected and measured. Different elements have unique wavelengths, while their concentrations can be estimated from the intensity of the released X-rays.

ASTRONOMY

Space Exploration

Ames Research Center US space-research (NASA) installation at Mountain View, California, USA, for the study of aeronautics and life sciences. It has managed the Pioneer series of planetary probes and is involved in the search for extraterrestrial life.

Apollo project US space project to land a person on the Moon, achieved 20 July 1969, when Neil Armstrong was the first to set foot there. He was accompanied on the Moon's surface by Col Edwin E Aldrin Jr; Michael Collins remained in the orbiting command module.

Apollo–Soyuz test project joint US-Soviet space mission in which an Apollo and a Soyuz craft docked while in orbit around the Earth on 17 July 1975. The craft remained attached for two days and crew members were able to move from one craft to the other through an airlock attached to the nose of the Apollo. The mission was designed to test rescue procedures as well as having political significance.

Ariane launch vehicle built in a series by the European Space Agency (first flight 1979). The launch site is at Kourou in French Guiana. Ariane is a three-stage rocket using liquid fuels. Since 1984 it has been operated commercially by Arianespace, a private company financed by European banks and aerospace industries.

Ariel series of six UK satellites launched by the USA 1962–79, the most significant of which was *Ariel 5*, 1974, which made a pioneering survey of the sky at X-ray wavelengths.

astronaut person making flights into space; the term *cosmonaut* is used in the West for any astronaut from the former Soviet Union.

astronautics the science of space travel.

astronomy the science of the celestial bodies: the Sun, the Moon, and the planets; the stars and galaxies; and all other objects in the universe. It is concerned with their positions, motions, distances, and physical conditions; and with their origins and evolution. Astronomy thus divides into fields such as astrophysics, celestial mechanics, and cosmology.

Cape Canaveral promontory on the Atlantic coast of Florida, USA, 367 km/228 mi N of Miami, used as a rocket launch site by NASA. It was known as Cape Kennedy 1963–73. The Kennedy Space Center is nearby.

Cassini joint space probe of NASA and the European Space Agency to the planet Saturn. *Cassini* is scheduled to be launched in Oct 1997 and will go into orbit around Saturn in June 2004, dropping off a subprobe, *Huygens*, to land on Saturn's largest moon, Titan.

communications satellite relay station in space for sending telephone, television, telex, and other messages around the world. Messages are sent to and from the satellites via ground stations. Most communications satellites are in geostationary orbit, appearing to hang fixed over one point on the Earth's surface. The first satellite to carry TV signals across the Atlantic Ocean was *Telstar* 1962.

Cosmos name used from the early 1960s for nearly all Soviet artificial satellites. Over 2,200 Cosmos satellites had been launched by the end of 1992.

Delta rocket US rocket used to launch many scientific and communications satellites since 1960, based on the Thor ballistic missile. Several increasingly powerful versions, produced as satellites, became larger and heavier. Solid-fuel boosters were attached to the first stage to increase lifting power.

Edwards Air Force Base military USAF centre in California, situated on a dry lake bed, often used as a landing site by the space shuttle.

Energiya the most powerful Soviet space rocket, capable, with the use of strap-on boosters, of launching payloads of up to 190 tonnes into Earth orbit. It was first launched 15 May 1987.

European Space Agency (ESA) organization of European countries (Austria, Belgium, Denmark, France, Germany, Ireland, Italy, the Netherlands, Norway, Spain, Sweden, Switzerland, and the UK) that engages in space research and technology. It was founded 1975, with headquarters in Paris. ESA is working on its own space-shuttle project, Hermes.

Explorer series of US scientific satellites. *Explorer 1*, launched Jan 1958, was the first US satellite in orbit and discovered the Van Allen radiation belts around the Earth.

Galileo spacecraft launched from the space shuttle *Atlantis* Oct 1989, on a six-year journey to Jupiter. It flew past Venus in Feb 1990 and passed within 970 km/600 mi of Earth in Dec 1990, using the gravitational fields of these two planets to increase its velocity. The craft flew past Earth again 1992 to receive its final boost towards Jupiter. It flew past the asteroid Gaspra in Oct 1991, taking close-up photographs.

Gemini project US space programme (1965–66) in which astronauts practised rendezvous and docking of spacecraft, and working outside their spacecraft, in preparation for the Apollo Moon landings.

Giotto space probe built by the European Space Agency to study Halley's comet. Launched by an Ariane rocket in July 1985, *Giotto* passed within 600 km/375 mi of the comet's nucleus on 13 March 1986. On 2 July 1990 it flew 23,000 km/14,300 mi from Earth, which – by means of the phenomenon known as gravity assist – diverted its path to encounter another comet, Grigg-Skjellerup, on 10 July 1992.

Goddard Space Flight Center NASA installation at Greenbelt, Maryland, USA, responsible for the operation of NASA's crewless scientific satellites, including the Hubble Space Telescope. It is also home of the National Space Science Data Center, a repository of data collected by satellites.

Hipparcos (acronym for *high-precision parallax collecting satellite*) satellite launched by the European Space Agency Aug 1989. It is the world's first astrometry satellite and is providing precise positions, distances, colours, brightnesses, and apparent

Space flight: chronology

1926	US engineer Robert Goddard launched the first liquid-fuel rocket.
1937–45	In Germany, Wernher von Braun developed the V2 rocket.
1957	4 Oct: The first space satellite, *Sputnik 1* (USSR, Russian *fellow-traveller*), orbited the Earth at a height of 229–898 km/142–558 mi in 96.2 min. 3 Nov: *Sputnik 2* was launched carrying a dog, *Laika*; it died on board seven days later.
1958	31 Jan: *Explorer 1*, the first US satellite, discovered the Van Allen radiation belts.
1961	12 April: the first crewed spaceship, *Vostok 1* (USSR), with Yuri Gagarin on board, was recovered after a single orbit of 89.1 min at a height of 142–175 km/88–109 mi.
1962	20 Feb: John Glenn in *Friendship 7* (USA) became the first American to orbit the Earth. *Telstar* (USA), a communications satellite, sent the first live television transmission between the USA and Europe.
1963	16–19 June: Valentina Tereshkova in *Vostok 1* (USSR) became the first woman in space.
1967	24 April: Vladimir Komarov was the first person to be killed in space research, when his ship, *Soyuz 1* (USSR), crash-landed on the Earth.
1969	20 July: Neil Armstrong of *Apollo 11* (USA) was the first person to walk on the Moon.
1970	10 Nov: *Luna 17* (USSR) was launched; its space probe, *Lunokhod*, took photographs and made soil analyses of the Moon's surface.
1971	19 April: *Salyut 1* (USSR), the first orbital space station, was established; it was later visited by the *Soyuz 11* crewed spacecraft.
1973	*Skylab 2*, the first US orbital space station, was established.
1975	15–24 July: *Apollo 18* (USA) and *Soyuz 19* (USSR) made a joint flight and linked up in space.
1979	The European Space Agency's satellite launcher, *Ariane 1*, was launched.
1981	12 April: The first reusable crewed spacecraft, the space shuttle *Columbia* (USA), was launched.
1986	Space shuttle *Challenger* (USA) exploded shortly after take-off, killing all seven crew members.
1988	US shuttle programme resumed with launch of *Discovery*. Soviet shuttle *Buran* was launched from the rocket *Energiya*. Soviet cosmonauts Musa Manarov and Vladimir Titov in space station *Mir* spent a record 365 days 59 min in space.
1990	April: Hubble Space Telescope (USA) was launched from Cape Canaveral. 1 June: X-ray and ultraviolet astronomy satellite *ROSAT* (USA/Germany/UK) was launched from Cape Canaveral. 2 Dec: *Astro-1* ultraviolet observatory and the Broad Band X-ray Telescope were launched from the space shuttle *Columbia*. Japanese television journalist Toyohiro Akiyama was launched with Viktor Afanasyev and Musa Manarov to the space station *Mir*.
1991	5 April: The Gamma Ray Observatory was launched from the space shuttle *Atlantis* to survey the sky at gamma-ray wavelengths. 18 May: Astronaut Helen Sharman, the first Briton in space, was launched with Anatoli Artsebarsky and Sergei Krikalek to *Mir* space station, returning to Earth 26 May in *Soyuz TM-11* with Viktor Afanasyev and Musa Manarov. Manarov set a record for the longest time spent in space, 541 days, having also spent a year aboard *Mir* 1988.
1992	European satellite *Hipparcos*, launched 1989 to measure the position of 120,000 stars, failed to reach geostationary orbit and went into a highly elliptical orbit, swooping to within 500 km/308 mi of the Earth every ten hours. The mission was later retrieved. 16 May: Space shuttle *Endeavour* returned to Earth after its maiden voyage. During its mission, it circled the Earth 141 times and travelled 4 million km/2.5 million mi. 23 Oct: *LAGEOS II* (Laser Geodynamics Satellite) was released from the space shuttle *Columbia* into an orbit so stable that it will still be circling the Earth in billions of years.
1993	Dec: Space shuttle *Endeavour* successfully carried out mission to replace the Hubble Space Telescope.
1994	Feb: Japan's heavy-lifting H-2 rocket successfully launched, carrying a crewless shuttle craft.

motions for over 100,000 stars. It is named after the Greek astronomer Hipparchus.

Hubble Space Telescope (HST) telescope placed into orbit around the Earth, at an altitude of 610 km/380 mi, by the space shuttle *Discovery* in April 1990. The telescope's position in space means that light from distant galaxies is not obscured by the atmosphere, and it therefore performs many times better than any ground-based instrument. Soon after its launch, it was found that the main mirror suffered from spherical aberration and so could not be focused properly. A successful repair mission in Dec 1993 (costing $360 million, and involving 30 hours of spacewalks by five astronauts) corrected the fault.

Intelsat International Telecommunications Satellite Organization, established 1964 to operate a worldwide system of communications satellites. More than 100 countries are members of Intelsat. Intelsat satellites are stationed in geostationary orbit (maintaining their positions relative to the Earth) over the Atlantic, Pacific, and Indian Oceans. The first Intelsat satellite was *Early Bird*, launched 1965.

IRAS Infrared Astronomy Satellite, a joint US-UK-Dutch satellite launched 1983 to survey the sky at infrared wavelengths, studying areas of star formation, distant galaxies, possible embryo planetary systems around other stars; it discovered five new comets in our own Solar System.

Jet Propulsion Laboratory NASA installation in Pasadena, California, operated by the California Institute of Technology. It is the command centre for NASA's deep-space probes such as the Voyager, Magellan, and Galileo missions, with which it communicates via the Deep Space Network of radio telescopes in Goldstone, California; Madrid, Spain; and Canberra, Australia.

Johnson Space Center NASA installation in Houston, Texas, home of mission control for crewed space missions. It is the main centre for the selection and training of astronauts.

Kennedy Space Center NASA launch site on Merritt Island, near Cape Canaveral, Florida, used for Apollo and space-shuttle launches. The first flight to land on the Moon (1969) and *Skylab*, the first orbiting laboratory (1973), were launched here.

Kourou town in French Guiana, NW of Cayenne, site of the *Guiana Space Centre* of the European Space Agency. Situated near the equator, it is an ideal site for launching satellites into geostationary orbit.

Landsat series of satellites used for monitoring Earth resources. The first was launched in 1972.

Magellan NASA space probe to Venus, launched May 1989. It went into orbit around Venus in Aug 1990 to make a detailed map of the planet by radar. It revealed volcanoes, meteorite craters, and fold mountains on the planet's surface.

Mariner spacecraft series of US space probes that explored the planets Mercury, Venus, and Mars 1962–75. *Mariner 9* 1971 mapped the entire Martian surface, and photographed Mars' moons. *Mariner 10* 1974–75 took close-up photographs of Mercury and Venus, and measured temperature, radiation, and magnetic fields.

Marshall Space Flight Center NASA installation at Huntsville, Alabama, where the series of Saturn rockets and the space-shuttle engines were developed. It also manages various payloads for the space shuttle, including the *Spacelab* space station.

Mars Observer NASA space probe launched 1992 to orbit Mars and survey the planet, its atmosphere, and the polar caps. It was also scheduled to communicate information from the robot vehicles delivered by Russia's Mars 94 mission. The $1 billion project miscarried, however, when the probe unaccountably stopped transmitting Aug 1993, three days before it was due to drop into orbit

Mir Soviet space station, the core of which was launched 20 Feb 1986. It has been enlarged by adding extra sections to it. Cosmonauts have spent up to a year at a time aboard *Mir*, with visits from other crews.

Moon probe crewless spacecraft used to investigate the Moon. Early probes flew past the Moon or crash-landed on it, but later ones achieved soft landings or went into orbit. Soviet probes included the Luna/Lunik series. US probes (Ranger, Surveyor, Lunar Orbiter) prepared the way for the Apollo crewed flights. The first space probe to hit the Moon was the Soviet *Luna 2*, on 13 Sept 1959.

NASA *National Aeronautics and Space Administration* US government agency, founded 1958, for space-flight and aeronautical research. Its main installation is at the Kennedy Space Center in Florida. NASA's Apollo project took the first people to the Moon 1969.

Pioneer probe any of a series of US Solar-System space probes 1958–78. *Pioneer 5*, launched 1960, was the first of a series to study the solar wind between the planets. *Pioneer 10*, launched 1972, was the first probe to reach Jupiter 1973 and to leave the Solar System 1983. *Pioneer 11*, launched 1973, passed Jupiter 1974, and was the first probe to reach Saturn 1979, before also leaving the Solar System.

Plesetsk rocket-launching site 170 km/105 mi S of Archangel, Russia. From 1966 the USSR launched artificial satellites from here, mostly military.

Proton rocket Soviet space rocket introduced 1965, used to launch heavy satellites, space probes, and the Salyut and *Mir* space stations.

Redstone rocket short-range US military missile, modified for use as a space launcher. Redstone rockets launched the first two flights of the Mercury project. A modified Redstone, *Juno 1*, launched the first US satellite, *Explorer 1*, in 1958.

rocket projectile driven by the reaction of gases produced by a fast-burning fuel. Unlike jet engines, which are also reaction engines, modern rockets carry their own oxygen supply to burn their fuel and do not require any surrounding atmosphere. Being the only form of propulsion available that can function in a vacuum, rockets are essential to exploration in outer space. Multistage rockets have to be used, consisting of a number of rockets joined together.

ROSAT joint US-German-UK satellite launched 1990 to study cosmic sources of X-rays and extremely short ultraviolet wavelengths.

Salyut series of seven space stations launched by the USSR 1971–82. Salyut was cylindrical in shape, 15 m/50 ft long, and weighed 19 tonnes/21 tons. It housed two or three cosmonauts at a time, for missions lasting up to eight months.

satellite any small body that orbits a larger one, either natural or artificial. Natural satellites that orbit planets are called moons. The first *artificial satellite*, *Sputnik 1*, was launched into orbit around the Earth by the USSR 1957. Artificial satellites are used for scientific purposes, communications, weather forecasting, and military applications. The largest artificial satellites can be seen by the naked eye.

At any time, there are several thousand artificial satellites orbiting the Earth, including active satellites, satellites that have ended their working lives, and discarded sections of rockets.

Saturn rocket family of large US rockets, developed by Wernher von Braun (1912–1977) for the Apollo project. The two-stage *Saturn IB* was used for launching Apollo spacecraft into orbit around the Earth. The three-stage *Saturn V* sent Apollo spacecraft to the Moon and launched the *Skylab* space station. The liftoff thrust of a *Saturn V* was 3,500 tonnes. After Apollo and *Skylab*, the Saturn rockets were retired in favour of the space shuttle.

Skylab US space station, in orbit 1973–79, made from the adapted upper stage of a *Saturn V* rocket. At 75 tonnes/82.5 tons, it was the heaviest object ever put into space, and was 25.6 m/84 ft long. *Skylab* contained a workshop for carrying out experiments in weightlessness, an observatory for monitoring the Sun, and cameras for photographing the Earth's surface.

Space probe: chronology

1959	13 Sept: *Luna 2* (USSR) hit the Moon, the first craft to do so.
	10 Oct: *Luna 3* photographed the far side of the Moon.
1962	14 Dec: *Mariner 2* (USA) flew past Venus; launch date 26 Aug 1962.
1964	31 July: *Ranger 7* (USA) hit the Moon, having sent back 4,316 pictures before impact.
1965	14 July: *Mariner 4* flew past Mars; launch date 28 Nov 1964.
1966	3 Feb: *Luna 9* achieved the first soft landing on the Moon, having transmitted 27 close-up panoramic photographs; launch date 31 Jan 1966.
	2 June: *Surveyor 1* (USA) landed softly on the Moon and returned 11,150 pictures; launch date 30 May 1965.
1971	13 Nov: *Mariner 9* entered orbit of Mars; launch date 30 May 1971.
1973	3 Dec: *Pioneer 10* (USA) flew past Jupiter; launch date 3 March 1972.
1974	29 March: *Mariner 10* flew past Mercury; launch date 3 Nov 1973.
1975	22 Oct: *Venera 9* (USSR) landed softly on Venus and returned its first pictures; launch date 8 June 1975.
1976	20 July: *Viking 1* (USA) first landed on Mars; launch date 20 Aug 1975.
	3 Sept: *Viking 2* transmitted data from the surface of Mars.
1977	20 Aug: *Voyager 2* (USA) launched.
	5 Sept: *Voyager 1* launched.
1978	4 Dec: *Pioneer-Venus 1* (USA) orbited Venus; launch date 20 May 1978.
1979	5 March and 9 July: *Voyager 1* and *Voyager 2* encountered Jupiter, respectively.
1980	12 Nov: *Voyager 1* reached Saturn.
1981	25 Aug: *Voyager 2* flew past Saturn.
1982	1 March: *Venera 13* transmitted its first colour pictures of the surface of Venus; launch date 30 Oct 1981.
1983	10 Oct: *Venera 15* mapped the surface of Venus from orbit; launch date 2 June 1983.
1985	2 July: *Giotto* (European Space Agency) launched to Halley's comet.
1986	24 Jan: *Voyager 2* encountered Uranus. 13—14 March: *Giotto* met Halley's comet, closest approach 596 km/370 mi, at a speed 50 times faster than that of a bullet.
1989	4 May: *Magellan* (USA) launched from space shuttle *Atlantis* on a 15-month cruise to Venus across 15 million km/ 9 million mi of space.
	25 Aug: *Voyager 2* reached Neptune (4,400 million km/2,700 million mi from Earth), approaching it to within 4,850 km/3,010 mi. 18 Oct: *Galileo* (USA) launched from space shuttle *Atlantis* for six-year journey to Jupiter.
1990	10 Aug: *Magellan* arrived at Venus and transmitted its first pictures 16 Aug 1990.
	6 Oct: *Ulysses* (European Space Agency) launched from space shuttle *Discovery*, to study the Sun.
1991	29 Oct: *Galileo* made the closest-ever approach to an asteroid, Gaspra, flying within 1,600 km/990 mi.
1992	8 Feb: *Ulysses* flew past Jupiter at a distance of 380,000 km/236,000 mi from the surface, just inside the orbit of Io and closer than 11 of Jupiter's 16 moons.
	10 July: *Giotto* (USA) flew at a speed of 14 kms/8.5 mps to within 200 km/124 mi of comet Grigg-Skellerup, 12 light years (240 million km/150 mi) away from Earth.
	25 Sept: *Mars Observer* (USA) launched from Cape Canaveral, the first US mission to Mars for 17 years. 10 Oct: *Pioneer-Venus 1* burned up in the atmosphere of Venus.
1993	21 Aug: *Mars Observer* disappeared three days before it was due to drop into orbit around Mars.
	28 Aug: *Galileo* passed 1000 km/621 mi from asteroid Ida.

Soyuz Soviet series of spacecraft, capable of carrying up to three cosmonauts. Soyuz spacecraft consist of three parts: a rear section containing engines; the central crew compartment; and a forward compartment that gives additional room for working and living space. They are now used for ferrying crews up to space stations, though they were originally used for independent space flight.

Spacelab small space station built by the European Space Agency, carried in the cargo bay of the US space shuttle, in which it remains throughout each flight, returning to Earth with the shuttle. The first *Spacelab* mission lasted ten days Nov–Dec 1983. *Spacelab* consists of a pressurized module in which astronauts can work, and a series of pallets, open to the vacuum of space, on which equipment is mounted.

space probe any instrumented object sent beyond Earth to collect data from other parts of the solar system and from deep space. The first probe was the Soviet *Lunik 1*, which flew past the Moon 1959. The first successful planetary probe was the US *Mariner*

2, which flew past Venus 1962, using transfer orbit. The first space probe to leave the Solar System was *Pioneer 10* 1983. Space probes include *Galileo*, *Giotto*, *Magellan*, *Mars Observer*, *Ulysses*, the Moon probes, and the Mariner, Pioneer, Viking, and Voyager series. Japan launched its first space probe 1990.

space shuttle reusable crewed spacecraft. The first was launched 12 April 1981 by the USA. It was developed by NASA to reduce the cost of using space for commercial, scientific, and military purposes. After leaving its payload in space, the space-shuttle orbiter can be flown back to Earth to land on a runway, and is then available for reuse.

The first Soviet shuttle, *Buran*, was launched without a crew by the *Energiya* rocket 15 Nov 1988. In Japan, development of a crewless shuttle began 1986.

space sickness or *space adaptation syndrome* feeling of nausea, sometimes accompanied by vomiting, experienced by about 40% of all astronauts during their first few days in space. It is akin to travel sickness, and is thought to be caused by confusion of the body's balancing mechanism, located in the inner

Main launches June 1992 – December 1993

Launch date	Flight	Remarks
1992		
7 June	EUVE	Extreme Ultraviolet Explorer scientific satellite launched from Cape Canaveral to study the sky at ultra-violet wavelengths
25 June	STS 50	Space Shuttle Columbia carried US Microgravity Laboratory on the longest shuttle flight to date, 13 days. Crew: Richard Richards, Kenneth Bowersox, Carl Meade, Ellen Baker, Bonnie Dunbar, Lawrence Delucas, Eugene Trinh. Landed at Kennedy Space Center 9 July
27 July	Soyuz TM-15	Michel Tognini of France launched with Anatoli Solovyov and Sergey Avdeyev to Mir space station. Tognini returned 10 August in Soyuz TM-14 with Aleksandr Viktorenko and Aleksandr Kalery. Solovyov and Avdeyev remained aboard Mir until 1 Feb 1993
31 July	STS 46	Space Shuttle Atlantis launched Eureca (European recoverable carrier) and Tethered Satellite. Crew: Loren Shriver, Andrew Allen, Franklin Chang-Diaz, Jeffrey Hoffman, Claude Nicollier (ESA), Marsha Ivins, Franco Malerba (Italy). Landed at Kennedy Space Center 8 August
12 Sept	STS 47	Space Shuttle Endeavour launches Japanese Spacelab mission. Crew: Robert Gibson, Curtis Brown, Jan Davis, Jerome Apt, Mae Jemison, Mark Lee, Mamoru Mohri (Japan). Landed at Kennedy Space Center 20 September
25 Sept	Mars Observer	Mars probe launched by Titan rocket from Cape Canaveral. Contact was lost in Aug 1993 shortly before it was due to go into orbit around Mars
22 Oct	STS 52	Space Shuttle Columbia launched Lageos 2 geology satellite and carried US materials processing experiments and Canadian experiments. Crew: James Wetherbee, Michael Baker, William Shepherd, Tamara Jernigan, Charles Veach, Steven MacLean (Canada). Landed at Kennedy Space Center 1 Nov
2 Dec	STS 53	Space Shuttle Discovery launched Department of Defense satellite. Crew: David Walker, Robert Cabana, Guion Bluford, James Voss, Michael Clifford. Landed at Edwards Air Force Base 9 Dec
1993		
13 Jan	STS 54	Space Shuttle Endeavour launched TDRS-F communications satellite. Crew: John Casper, Donald McMonagle, Gregory Harbaugh, Mario Runco, Susan Helms. Landed at Kennedy Space Center 19 Jan
24 Jan	Soyuz TM-16	Gennady Manakov and Aleksandr Poleshchuk launched to Mir space station
8 April	STS 56	Space Shuttle Discovery carried ATLAS 2 atmospheric science laboratory. Crew: Kenneth Cameron, Stephen Oswald, Michael Foale, Kenneth Cockrell, Ellen Ochoa. Landed at Kennedy Space Center 17 April
26 April	STS 55	Space Shuttle Columbia carried second German Spacelab mission. Crew: Steven Nagel, Tom Henricks, Jerry Ross, Charles Precourt, Bernard Harris, Ulrich Walter (Germany), Hans Schlegel (Germany). Landed at Edwards Air Force Base 6 May
21 June	STS 57	Space Shuttle Endeavour carried Spacelab 1 pressurized module and retrieved the Eureca satellite. Crew: Ronald Grabe, Brian Duffy, David Low, Nancy Sherlock, Jeff Wisoff, Janice Voss. Landed at Kennedy Space Center 1 July
1 July	Soyuz TM-17	Jean-Pierre Haigneré of France launched with Vasily Tsibylev and Aleksandr Serebrov to Mir space station. Haigneré returned 22 July with Gennady Manakov and Aleksandr Poleshchuk in Soyuz TM-16
12 Sept	STS 51	Space Shuttle Discovery launched Advanced Communications Technology Satellite. Crew: Frank Culbertson, William Readdy, James Newman, Daniel Bursch, Carl Walz. Walz and Newman made 6-hour EVA to test techniques for Hubble Space Telescope repair mission. Landed at Kennedy Space Center 22 Sept
18 Oct	STS 58	Space Shuttle Columbia carried second Spacelab Life Sciences mission. Crew: John Blaha, Richard Searfoss, Rhea Seddon, William McArthur, David Wolf, Shannon Lucid, Martin Fettman. Landed at Edwards Air Force Base 2 Nov after the longest shuttle mission to date
2 Dec	STS 61	Space Shuttle Endeavour mission to repair the Hubble Space Telescope. Crew: Richard Covey, Kenneth Bowersox, Story Musgrave, Jeffrey Hoffman, Tom Akers, Kathryn Thornton, Claude Nicollier. Landed at Kennedy Space Center 13 Dec

ear, by weightlessness. The sensation passes after a few days as the body adapts.

space station any large structure designed for human occupation in space for extended periods of time. Space stations are used for carrying out astronomical observations and surveys of Earth, as well as for biological studies and the processing of materials in weightlessness. The first space stations were the Soviet *Salyut 1* 1971 and the US *Skylab* 1973–79.

NASA plans to build a larger space station, to be called *Freedom*, and place it in orbit during the 1990s, in cooperation with other countries, including the European Space Agency, which is building a module called *Columbus*, and Japan, also building a module.

space suit protective suit worn by astronauts and cosmonauts in space. It provides an insulated, air-conditioned cocoon in which people can live and work for hours at a time outside the spacecraft. Inside the suit is a cooling garment that keeps the body at a comfortable temperature even during vigorous work. The suit provides air to breathe, and removes exhaled carbon dioxide and moisture. The suit's outer layers insulate the occupant from the extremes of hot and cold in space (–150°C/–240°F in the shade to +180°C/+350°F in sunlight) and from the impact of small meteorites. Some space suits have a jet-propelled backpack, which the wearer can use to move about.

Sputnik series of ten Soviet Earth-orbiting satellites. *Sputnik 1* was the first artificial satellite, launched 4 Oct 1957. It weighed 84 kg/185 lb, with a 58 cm/23 in diameter, and carried only a simple radio transmitter which allowed scientists to track it as it orbited Earth. It burned up in the atmosphere 92 days later. Sputniks were superseded in the early 1960s by the Cosmos series.

Telstar US communications satellite, launched 10 July 1962, which relayed the first live television transmissions between the USA and Europe. *Telstar* orbited the Earth in 158 minutes, and so had to be tracked by ground stations, unlike the geostationary satellites of today.

Titan rocket family of US space rockets, developed from the Titan intercontinental missile. Two-stage Titan rockets launched the Gemini crewed missions. More powerful Titans, with additional stages and strap-on boosters, were used to launch spy satellites and space probes, including the *Viking* and *Voyager* probes and *Mars Observer*.

Ulysses space probe to study the Sun's poles, launched 1990 by a US space shuttle. It is a joint project by NASA and the European Space Agency. In Feb 1992, the gravity of Jupiter swung *Ulysses* on to a path that loops it first under the Sun's south pole in 1994 and then over the north pole in 1995 to study the Sun and solar wind at latitudes not observable from the Earth.

Vanguard early series of US Earth-orbiting satellites and their associated rocket launcher. *Vanguard 1* was the second US satellite, launched 17 March 1958 by the three-stage Vanguard rocket. Tracking of its orbit revealed that Earth is slightly pear-shaped. The series ended Sept 1959 with *Vanguard 3*.

Viking probes two US space probes to Mars, each one consisting of an orbiter and a lander. They were launched 20 Aug and 9 Sept 1975 and touched down about a year later. They transmitted colour pictures and analysed the soil. No definite signs of life were found.

Voskhod Soviet spacecraft used in the mid-1960s; it was modified from the single-seat *Vostok*, and was the first spacecraft capable of carrying two or three cosmonauts. During *Voskhod 2*'s flight 1965, Aleksi Leonov made the first space walk.

Vostok first Soviet spacecraft, used 1961–63. Vostok was a metal sphere 2.3 m/7.5 ft in diameter,

capable of carrying one cosmonaut. It made flights lasting up to five days. *Vostok 1* carried the first person into space, Yuri Gagarin (1934–1968).

Voyager probes two US space probes, originally Mariners. *Voyager 1*, launched 5 Sept 1977, passed Jupiter March 1979, and reached Saturn Nov 1980. *Voyager 2* was launched earlier, 20 Aug 1977, on a slower trajectory that took it past Jupiter July 1979, Saturn Aug 1981, Uranus Jan 1986, and Neptune Aug 1989. Like the Pioneer probes, the Voyagers are on their way out of the Solar System. As of mid-1993 *Voyager 1* was 8 billion km/5 billion mi from the Sun, and *Voyager 2* over 6 billion km/3.8 billion mi from the Sun. Their tasks now include helping scientists to locate the position of the heliopause, the boundary at which the influence of the Sun gives way to the forces exerted by other stars.

weightlessness condition in which there is no gravitational force acting on a body, either because gravitational force is cancelled out by equal and opposite acceleration, or because the body is so far outside a planet's gravitational field that it no force is exerted upon it. Astronauts in space, though seemingly 'weightless', do not experience zero gravity because of the motion of their spacecraft.

The Solar System

Apollo asteroid member of a group of asteroids whose orbits cross that of the Earth. They are named after the first of their kind, Apollo, discovered 1932 and then lost until 1973. Apollo asteroids are so small and faint that they are difficult to see except when close to Earth (Apollo is about 2 km/1.2 mi across).

asteroid or *minor planet* any of many thousands of small bodies, composed of rock and iron, that orbit the Sun. Most lie in a belt between the orbits of Mars and Jupiter, and are thought to be fragments left over from the formation of the Solar System. About 100,000 may exist, but their total mass is only a few hundredths the mass of the Moon.

aurora coloured light in the night sky near the Earth's magnetic poles, called *aurora borealis*, 'northern lights', in the northern hemisphere and *aurora australis* in the southern hemisphere. An aurora is usually in the form of a luminous arch with its apex towards the magnetic pole followed by arcs, bands, rays, curtains, and coronas, usually green but often showing shades of blue and red, and sometimes yellow or white. Auroras are caused at heights of over 100 km/60 mi by a fast stream of charged particles from solar flares and low-density 'holes' in the Sun's corona. These are guided by the Earth's magnetic field towards the north and south magnetic poles, where they enter the upper atmosphere and bombard the gases in the atmosphere, causing them to emit visible light.

Baily's beads bright spots of sunlight seen around the edge of the Moon for a few seconds immediately before and after a total eclipse of the Sun, caused by sunlight shining between mountains at the Moon's edge. Sometimes one bead is much brighter than the others, producing the so-called *diamond ring* effect. The effect was described 1836 by English astronomer Francis Baily (1774–1844).

Callisto the second largest moon of Jupiter, 4,800 km/3,000 mi in diameter, orbiting every 16.7 days at a distance of 1.9 million km/1.2 million mi from the planet. Its surface is covered with large craters.

Ceres the largest asteroid, 940 km/584 mi in diameter, and the first to be discovered (by Italian astronomer Giuseppe Piazzi 1801). Ceres orbits the Sun every 4.6 years at an average distance of 414 million km/257 million mi. Its mass is about one-seventieth of that of the Moon.

Chiron unusual Solar-System object orbiting between Saturn and Uranus, discovered 1977 by US astronomer Charles T Kowal (1940–   ). Initially classified as an asteroid, it is now believed to be a giant cometary nucleus about 200 km/120 mi across, composed of ice with a dark crust of carbon dust.

chromosphere layer of mostly hydrogen gas about 10,000 km/6,000 mi deep above the visible surface of the Sun (the photosphere). It appears pinkish red during eclipses of the Sun.

comet small, icy body orbiting the Sun, usually on a highly elliptical path. A comet consists of a central nucleus a few kilometres across, and has been likened to a dirty snowball because it consists mostly of ice mixed with dust. As the comet approaches the Sun the nucleus heats up, releasing gas and dust which form a tenuous coma, up to 100,000 km/60,000 mi wide, around the nucleus. Gas and dust stream away from the coma to form one or more tails, which may extend for millions of kilometres. A dozen or more comets are discovered every year.

corona faint halo of hot (about 2,000,000°C/3,600,000°F) and tenuous gas around the Sun, which boils from the surface. It is visible at solar eclipses or through a *coronagraph*, an instrument that blocks light from the Sun's brilliant disc. Gas flows away from the corona to form the solar wind.

crater bowl-shaped depression, usually round and with steep sides. Craters are formed by explosive events such as the eruption of a volcano or by the impact of a meteorite. The Moon has more than 300,000 craters over 1 km/6 mi in diameter, formed by meteorite bombardment.

crescent curved shape of the Moon when it appears less than half-illuminated.

Deimos one of the two moons of Mars. It is irregularly shaped, 15 × 12 × 11 km/9 × 7.5 × 7 mi, orbits at a height of 24,000 km/15,000 mi every 1.26 days, and is not as heavily cratered as the other moon, Phobos. Deimos was discovered 1877 by US astronomer Asaph Hall (1829–1907), and is thought to be an asteroid captured by Mars's gravity.

Earth the third planet from the Sun. It is almost spherical, flattened slightly at the poles, and is composed of three concentric layers: the core, the mantle, and the crust. 70% of the surface (including the north and south polar icecaps) is covered with water. The Earth is surrounded by a life-supporting atmosphere and is the only planet on which life is known to exist.

mean distance from the Sun 149,500,000 km/92,860,000 mi.

equatorial diameter 12,756 km/7,923 mi.

circumference 40,070 km/24,900 mi.

rotation period 23 hr 56 min 4.1 sec.

year (complete orbit, or sidereal period) 365 days 5 hr 48 min 46 sec. Earth's average speed around the Sun is 30 kps/18.5 mps; the plane of its orbit is inclined to its equatorial plane at an angle of 23.5°, the reason for the changing seasons.

atmosphere nitrogen 78.09%; oxygen 20.95%; argon 0.93%; carbon dioxide 0.03%; and less than 0.0001% neon, helium, krypton, hydrogen, xenon, ozone, radon.

Major comets

Name	First recorded sighting	Orbital period (years)	Interesting facts
Halley's comet	240 BC	76	Parent of Eta Aquarid and Orionid meteor showers
Comet Tempel-Tuttle	AD 1366	33	Parent of Leonid meteors
Biela's comet	1772	6.6	Broke in half 1846; not seen since 1852
Encke's comet	1786	3.3	Parent of Taurid meteors
Comet Swift-Tuttle	1862	130	Parent of Perseid meteors; reappeared 1992
Comet Ikeya-Seki	1965	880	So-called 'Sun-grazing' comet, passed 500, 000 km/300,000 mi above surface of Sun on 21 Oct 1965
Comet Kohoutek	1973		Observed from space by *Skylab* astronauts; period too long to calculate accurately
Comet West	1975	500,000	Nucleus broke into four parts
Comet Bowell	1980		Ejected from Solar System after close encounter with Jupiter
Comet IRAS-Araki-Alcock	1983		Passed only 4.5 million km/2.8 million mi from Earth on 11 May 1983; period too long to calculate accurately
Comet Austin	1989		Passed 32 million km/20 million mi from Earth 1990

Solar and lunar eclipses until 2000*

Date	Type of eclipse	Time of maximum eclipse (UT)	Main area of visibility
1994			
10 May	Sun annular	17h 12m	North and Central America
3 November	Sun total	13h 40m	South America, southern Africa
1995			
29 April	Sun annular	17h 33m	South and Central America
24 October	Sun total	04h 33m	India, SE Asia, Oceania, northern Australia
1996			
3/4 April	Moon total	00h 10m	Eastern North America, Central and South America, Europe, Africa, western Asia
17 April	Sun partial	22h 38m	New Zealand, southern Pacific Ocean
27 September	Moon total	02h 54m	The Americas, Europe, Africa, western Asia
12 October	Sun partial	14h 03m	NE Canada, Greenland, western Europe, North Africa
1997			
9 March	Sun total	01h 25m	E Asia, Japan
1/2 September	Sun partial	00h 05m	Australia, New Zealand
16 September	Moon total	18h 47m	Europe, Africa, Asia, Australasia
1998			
26 February	Sun total	17h 29m	S and E USA, Central America, northern South America
22 August	Sun annular	02h 07m	SE Asia, Oceania, Australasia
1999			
16 February	Sun annular	06h 35m	Southern Indian Ocean, Antarctica, Australia
11 August	Sun total	11h 04m	Europe, North Africa, Arabia, western Asia
2000			
21 January	Moon total	04h 44m	The Americas, Europe, Africa, western Asia
5 February	Sun partial	12h 50m	Antarctica
1 July	Sun partial	19h 34m	SE Pacific Ocean
16 July	Moon total	13h 56m	SE Asia, Australasia
31 July	Sun partial	02h 14m	Arctic regions
25 December	Sun partial	17h 36m	USA, eastern Canada, Central America, Caribbean

* Except partial eclipses of the Moon

surface land surface 150,000,000 sq km/57,500,000 sq mi (greatest height above sea level 8,872 m/29,118 ft Mount Everest); water surface 361,000,000 sq km/139,400,000 sq mi (greatest depth 11,034 m/36,201 ft Mariana Trench in the Pacific). The interior is thought to be an inner core about 2,600 km/1,600 mi in diameter, of solid iron and nickel; an outer core about 2,250 km/1,400 mi thick, of molten iron and nickel; and a mantle of mostly solid rock about 2,900 km/1,800 mi thick, separated by the Mohorovičič discontinuity from the Earth's crust. The crust and the topmost layer of the mantle form about 12 major moving plates, some of which carry the continents. The plates are in constant, slow motion, called tectonic drift.

satellite the Moon.

age 4.6 billion years. The Earth was formed with the rest of the Solar System by consolidation of interstellar dust. Life began about 3.5 billion years ago.

eclipse passage of an astronomical body through the shadow of another. The term is usually employed for solar and lunar eclipses, which may be either partial or total, but also, for example, for eclipses by Jupiter of its satellites. An eclipse of a star by a body in the Solar System is called an occultation. A *solar eclipse* occurs when the Moon passes in front of the Sun as seen from Earth, and can happen only at new Moon. A total solar eclipse can last up to 7.5 minutes. Between two and five solar eclipses occur each year. A *lunar eclipse* occurs when the Moon passes into the shadow of the Earth, becoming dim until emerging from the shadow. Lunar eclipses may be partial or total, and they can happen only at full Moon. Total lunar eclipses last for up to 100 minutes; the maximum number each year is three.

Encke's comet comet with the shortest known orbital period, 3.3 years. It is named after German mathematician and astronomer Johann Franz Encke (1791–1865), who calculated its orbit in 1819 from earlier sightings.

Eros the first asteroid to be discovered (1898) that has an orbit coming within that of Mars. It can pass 22 million km/14 million mi from the Earth, as observed in 1975. It measures about 36 × 12 km/22 × 7 mi and orbits the Sun every 1.8 years.

Europa the fourth largest moon of the planet Jupiter, diameter 3,140 km/1,950 mi, orbiting 671,000 km/417,000 mi from the planet every 3.55 days. It is covered by ice and criss-crossed by thousands of thin cracks, each some 50,000 km/30,000 mi long.

Ganymede the largest moon of the planet Jupiter, and the largest moon in the Solar System, 5,260 km/3,270 mi in diameter (larger than the planet Mercury). It orbits Jupiter every 7.2 days at a distance of

1.1 million km/700,000 mi. Its surface is a mixture of cratered and grooved terrain.

Halley's comet comet that orbits the Sun about every 76 years, named after English scientist Edmund Halley (1656–1742), who calculated its orbit. It is the brightest and most conspicuous of the periodic comets. Recorded sightings go back over 2,000 years. It travels around the Sun in the opposite direction to the planets. Its orbit is inclined at almost 20° to the main plane of the Solar System and ranges between the orbits of Venus and Neptune. It will next reappear 2061.

heliosphere region of space through which the solar wind flows outwards from the Sun. The *heliopause* is the boundary of this region, believed to lie about 100 astronomical units from the Sun, where the flow of the solar wind merges with the interstellar gas.

Icarus Apollo asteroid 1.5 km/1 mi in diameter, discovered 1949. It orbits the Sun every 409 days at a distance of 28–300 million km/18–186 million mi (0.19–2.0 astronomical units). It was the first asteroid known to approach the Sun closer than does the planet Mercury. In 1968 it passed 6 million km/4 million mi from the Earth.

inferior planet planet (Mercury or Venus) whose orbit lies within that of the Earth, best observed when at its greatest elongation from the Sun, either at eastern elongation in the evening (setting after the Sun) or at western elongation in the morning (rising before the Sun).

interplanetary matter gas and dust thinly spread through the Solar System. The gas flows outwards from the Sun as the solar wind. Fine dust lies in the plane of the Solar System, scattering sunlight to cause the zodiacal light. Swarms of dust shed by comets enter the Earth's atmosphere to cause meteor showers.

Io the third largest moon of the planet Jupiter, 3,630 km/2,260 mi in diameter, orbiting in 1.77 days at a distance of 422,000 km/262,000 mi. It is the most volcanically active body in the Solar System, covered by hundreds of vents that erupt not lava but sulphur, giving Io an orange-coloured surface.

Jupiter the fifth planet from the Sun, and the largest in the Solar System (equatorial diameter 142,800 km/88,700 mi), with a mass more than twice that of all the other planets combined, 318 times that of the Earth's. It takes 11.86 years to orbit the Sun, at an average distance of 778 million km/484 million mi, and has at least 16 moons. It is largely composed of hydrogen and helium, liquefied by pressure in its interior, and probably with a rocky core larger than the Earth. Its main feature is the Great Red Spot, a cloud of rising gases, revolving anticlockwise, 14,000 km/8,500 mi wide and some 30,000 km/20,000 mi long.

Kuiper belt a ring of small, icy bodies orbiting the Sun beyond the outermost planet. The Kuiper belt, named after the American astronomer Gerard Kuiper who proposed its existence in 1951, is thought to be the source of comets that orbit the Sun with periods of less than 200 years.

The first member of the Kuiper belt was seen in 1992.

Lagrangian points five locations in space where the centrifugal and gravitational forces of two bodies neutralize each other; a third, less massive body located at any one of these points will be held in equilibrium with respect to the other two. Three of the points, L1–L3, lie on a line joining the two large bodies. The other two points, L4 and L5, which are the most stable, lie on either side of this line. Their existence was predicted in 1772 by French mathematician Joseph Louis Lagrange (1736–1813).

magnetosphere volume of space surrounding a planet, controlled by the planet's magnetic field and acting as a magnetic 'shell'. The Earth's magnetosphere extends 64,000 km/40,000 mi towards the Sun, but many times this distance on the side away from the Sun.

mare (plural *maria*) dark lowland plain on the Moon. The name comes from Latin 'sea', because these areas were once wrongly thought to be water.

Mars the fourth planet from the Sun, average distance 227.9 million km/141.6 million mi. It revolves around the Sun in 687 Earth days, and has a rotation period of 24 hr 37 min. It is much smaller than Venus or Earth, with a diameter 6,780 km/4,210 mi, and mass 0.11 that of Earth. Mars is slightly pearshaped, with a low, level northern hemisphere, which is comparatively uncratered and geologically 'young', and a heavily cratered 'ancient' southern hemisphere.

Mercury the closest planet to the Sun, at an average distance of 58 million km/36 million mi. Its diameter is 4,880 km/3,030 mi, its mass 0.056 that of Earth. Mercury orbits the Sun every 88 days, and spins on its axis every 59 days. On its sunward side the surface temperature reaches over 400°C/752°F, but on the 'night' side it falls to –170°C/–274°F. Mercury has an atmosphere with minute traces of argon and helium; it has no moons.

meteor flash of light in the sky, popularly known as a *shooting* or *falling star*, caused by a particle of dust, a *meteoroid*, entering the atmosphere at speeds up to 70 kps/45 mps and burning up by friction at a height of around 100 km/60 mi. On any clear night, several *sporadic meteors* can be seen each hour; more than 500,000 meteors visible to the naked eye burn up in Earth's atmosphere every day.

meteorite piece of rock or metal from space that reaches the surface of the Earth, Moon, or other body. Most meteorites are thought to be fragments from

The 11 largest meteorites

Name and location	Weight (tonnes)
Hoba West, Grootfontein, Namibia	60
Ahnighito, Greenland	30
Bacuberito, Mexico	27
Mbosi, Tanzania	26
Agpalik, Greenland	20
Armanty, Mongolia	20
Chupaderos, Mexico	14
Willamette, Oregon, USA	14
Campo del Cielo, Argentina	13
Mundrabilla, W Australia	12
Morito, Mexico	11

Planets

Planet	Main constituents	Atmosphere	Average distance from Sun in millions of km	Time for one orbit in Earth-years	Diameter in thousands of km	Average density if density of water is 1 unit
Mercury	rocky, ferrous	–	58	0.241	4.88	5.4
Venus	rocky, ferrous	carbon dioxide	108	0.615	12.10	5.2
Earth	rocky, ferrous	nitrogen, oxygen	150	1.00	12.76	5.5
Mars	rocky	carbon dioxide	228	1.88	6.78	3.9
Jupiter	liquid hydrogen, helium	–	778	11.86	142.80	1.3
Saturn	hydrogen, helium	–	1,427	29.46	120.00	0.7
Uranus	icy, hydrogen, helium	hydrogen, helium	2,870	84.00	50.80	1.3
Neptune	icy, hydrogen, helium	hydrogen, helium	4,497	164.80	48.60	1.8
Pluto	icy, rocky	methane	5,900	248.50	2.25	about 2

asteroids, although some may be pieces from the heads of comets. Most are stony, although some are made of iron and a few have a mixed rock-iron composition. Meteorites provide evidence for the nature of the Solar System and may be similar to the Earth's core and mantle, neither of which can be observed directly. The Earth sweeps up an estimated 16,000 tonnes of meteoric material every year.

moon any natural satellite that orbits a planet. Mercury and Venus are the only planets in the Solar System that do not have moons.

Moon the natural satellite of Earth, 3,476 km/2,160 mi in diameter, with a mass 0.012 (approximately one-eightieth) that of Earth. Its surface gravity is only 0.16 (one-sixth) that of Earth. Its average distance from Earth is 384,400 km/238,855 mi, and it orbits in a west-to-east direction every 27.32 days (the *sidereal month*). It spins on its axis with one side permanently turned towards Earth. The Moon has no atmosphere or water.

Neptune the eighth planet in average distance from the Sun. Neptune orbits the Sun every 164.8 years at an average distance of 4.497 billion km/2.794 billion mi. It is a giant gas (hydrogen, helium, methane) planet, with a diameter of 48,600 km/30,200 mi and a mass 17.2 times that of Earth. Its rotation period is 16 hours 7 minutes. The methane in its atmosphere absorbs red light and gives the planet a blue colouring. It is believed to have a central rocky core covered by a layer of ice. Neptune has eight known moons.

occultation temporary obscuring of a star by a body in the Solar System. Occultations are used to provide information about changes in an orbit, and the structure of objects in space, such as radio sources.

Oort cloud spherical cloud of comets beyond Pluto, extending out to about 100,000 astronomical units (1.5 light years) from the Sun. The gravitational effect of passing stars and the rest of our Galaxy disturbs comets from the cloud so that they fall in towards the Sun on highly elongated orbits, becoming visible from Earth. As many as 10 trillion comets may reside in the Oort cloud, named after Dutch astronomer Jan Oort (1900–1992) who postulated it 1950.

Phobos one of the two moons of Mars, discovered 1877 by US astronomer Asaph Hall (1829–1907). It is an irregularly shaped lump of rock, cratered by meteorite impacts. Phobos is 27 × 22 × 19 km/17 × 13 × 12 mi across, and orbits Mars every 0.32 days at a distance of 9,400 km/5,840 mi from the planet's centre. It is thought to be an asteroid captured by Mars's gravity.

photosphere visible surface of the Sun, which emits light and heat. About 300 km/200 mi deep, it consists of incandescent gas at a temperature of 5,800K (5,530°C/9,980°F).

planet large celestial body in orbit around a star, composed of rock, metal, or gas. There are nine planets in the solar system: Mercury, Venus, Earth, Mars, Jupiter, Saturn, Neptune, Uranus, and Pluto. The inner four, called the *terrestrial planets*, are small and rocky, and include the planet Earth. The outer planets, with the exception of Pluto, are called the giant planets, large balls of rock, liquid, and gas; the largest is Jupiter, which contains more than twice as much mass as all the other planets combined. Planets do not produce light, but reflect the light of their parent star.

Pluto the smallest and, usually, outermost planet of the Solar System. The existence of Pluto was predicted by calculation by Percival Lowell and the planet was located by Clyde Tombaugh in 1930. It orbits the Sun every 248.5 years at an average distance of 5.8 billion km/3.6 billion mi. Its highly elliptical orbit occasionally takes it within the orbit of Neptune, as in 1979–99. Pluto has a diameter of about 2,300 km/1,400 mi, and a mass about 0.002 that of Earth. It is of low density, composed of rock and ice, with frozen methane on its surface and a thin atmosphere. It has one moon, Charon, half its own diameter.

prominence bright cloud of gas projecting from the Sun into space 100,000 km/60,000 mi or more. *Quiescent prominences* last for months, and are held in place by magnetic fields in the Sun's corona. *Surge prominences* shoot gas into space at speeds of 1,000 kps/600 mps. *Loop prominences* are gases falling back to the Sun's surface after a solar flare.

satellite any small body that orbits a larger one, either natural or artificial. Natural satellites that orbit planets are called moons. The first *artificial satellite*, *Sputnik 1*, was launched into orbit around the Earth by the USSR 1957. Artificial satellites are used for scientific purposes, communications, weather forecasting, and military applications. The largest artificial satellites can be seen by the naked eye.

Saturn the second-largest planet in the Solar System, sixth from the Sun, and encircled by bright and easily visible equatorial rings. Viewed through a telescope it is ochre. Saturn orbits the Sun every 29.46 years at an average distance of 1,427,000,000 km/886,700,000 mi. Its equatorial diameter is 120,000 km/ 75,000 mi, but its polar diameter is 12,000 km/7,450 mi smaller, a result of its fast rotation and low density, the lowest of any planet. Saturn spins on its axis every 10 hours 14 minutes at its equator, slowing to 10 hours 40 minutes at high latitudes. Its mass is 95 times that of Earth, and its magnetic field 1,000 times stronger. Saturn is believed to have a small core of rock and iron, encased in ice and topped by a deep layer of liquid hydrogen. There are 18 known moons, its largest being Titan. The rings visible from Earth begin about 14,000 km/ 9,000 mi from the planet's cloudtops and extend out to about 76,000 km/47,000 mi. Made of small chunks of ice and rock (averaging 1 m/3 ft across), they are 275,000 km/170,000 mi rim to rim, but only 100 m/ 300 ft thick. The Voyager probes showed that the rings actually consist of thousands of closely spaced ringlets, looking like the grooves in a gramophone record.

Solar System the Sun (a star) and all the bodies orbiting it: the nine planets (Mercury, Venus, Earth, Mars, Jupiter, Saturn, Uranus, Neptune, and Pluto), their moons, the asteroids, and the comets. It is thought to have formed from a cloud of gas and dust in space about 4.6 billion years ago. The Sun contains 99% of the mass of the Solar System.

solar flare brilliant eruption on the Sun above a sunspot, thought to be caused by release of magnetic energy. Flares reach maximum brightness within a few minutes, then fade away over about an hour. They eject a burst of atomic particles into space at up to 1,000 kps/600 mps. When these particles reach Earth they can cause radio blackouts, disruptions of the Earth's magnetic field, and auroras.

solar spicules short-lived jets of hot gas in the upper chromosphere of the Sun. Spiky in appearance, they move at high velocities along lines of magnetic force to which they owe their shape, and last for a few minutes each. Spicules appear to disperse material into the corona.

solar wind stream of atomic particles, mostly protons and electrons, from the Sun's corona, flowing outwards at speeds of between 300 kps/200 mps and 1,000 kps/600 mps.

Sun the star at the centre of the Solar System. Its diameter is 1,392,000 km/865,000 mi; its temperature at the surface is about 5,800K (5,530°C/9,980°F), and at the centre 15,000,000K (15,000,000°C/27,000,000°F). It is composed of about 70% hydrogen and 30% helium, with other elements making up less than 1%. The Sun's energy is generated by nuclear fusion reactions that turn hydrogen into helium at its centre. The gas core is far denser than mercury or lead on Earth. The Sun is about 4.7 billion years old, with a predicted lifetime of 10 billion years.

sunspot dark patch on the surface of the Sun, actually an area of cooler gas, thought to be caused by strong magnetic fields that block the outward flow of heat to the Sun's surface. Sunspots consist of a dark central *umbra*, about 4,000K (3,700°C/6,700°F), and a lighter surrounding *penumbra*, about 5,500K (5,200°C/9,400°F). They last from several days to over a month, ranging in size from 2,000 km/ 1,250 mi to groups stretching for over 100,000 km/ 62,000 mi. The number of sunspots visible at a given time varies from none to over 100 in a cycle averaging 11 years.

superior planet planet that is farther away from the Sun than the Earth is; that is, Mars, Jupiter, Saturn, Uranus, Neptune, and Pluto.

tektite small, rounded, glassy stone, found in certain regions of the Earth, such as Australasia. Tektites are probably the scattered drops of molten rock thrown out by the impact of a large meteorite.

Titan the largest moon of the planet Saturn, with a diameter of 5,150 km/3,200 mi and a mean distance from Saturn of 1,222,000 km/759,000 mi. It is the second largest moon in the Solar System (Ganymede, of Jupiter, is larger), and the only moon in the Solar System with a substantial atmosphere (mostly nitrogen).

Uranus the seventh planet from the Sun, discovered by William Herschel 1781. It is twice as far out as the sixth planet, Saturn. Uranus has a diameter of 50,800 km/31,600 mi and a mass 14.5 times that of Earth. It orbits the Sun in 84 years at an average distance of 2.9 billion km/1.8 billion mi. The spin axis of Uranus is tilted at 98°, so that one pole points towards the Sun, giving extreme seasons. It has 15 moons, and thin rings around its equator.

Venus the second planet from the Sun. It orbits the Sun every 225 days at an average distance of 108.2 million km/67.2 million mi and can approach the Earth to within 38 million km/24 million mi, closer than any other planet. Its diameter is 12,100 km/7,500 mi and its mass is 0.82 that of Earth. Venus rotates on

Largest natural planetary satellites

Planet	Satellite	Diameter in km	Mean distance from centre of primary in km	Orbital period in days	Reciprocal mass (planet = 1)
Jupiter	Ganymede	5,262	1,070,000	7.16	12,800
Saturn	Titan	5,150	1,221,800	15.95	4,200
Jupiter	Callisto	4,800	1,883,000	16.69	17,700
Jupiter	Io	3,630	421,600	1.77	21,400
Earth	Moon	3,476	384,400	27.32	81.3
Jupiter	Europa	3,138	670,900	3.55	39,700
Neptune	Triton	2,700	354,300	5.88	770

its axis more slowly than any other planet, once every 243 days and from east to west, the opposite direction to the other planets (except Uranus and possibly Pluto). Venus is shrouded by clouds of sulphuric acid droplets that sweep across the planet from east to west every four days. The atmosphere is almost entirely carbon dioxide, which traps the Sun's heat by the greenhouse effect and raises the planet's surface temperature to 480°C/900°F, with an atmospheric pressure of 90 times that at the surface of the Earth.

zodiacal light cone-shaped light sometimes seen extending from the Sun along the ecliptic, visible after sunset or before sunrise. It is due to thinly spread dust particles in the central plane of the Solar System. It is very faint, and requires a dark, clear sky to be seen.

Stars, Galaxies, and the Universe

Algol or ***Beta Persei*** eclipsing binary, a pair of rotating stars in the constellation Perseus, one of which eclipses the other every 69 hours, causing its brightness to drop by two-thirds.

Alpha Centauri or ***Rigil Kent*** brightest star in the constellation Centaurus and the third brightest star in the sky. It is actually a triple star: three stars orbiting round their common centre of mass. The two brighter stars orbit each other every 80 years, and the third, Proxima Centauri, is the closest star to the Sun, 4.2 light years away, 0.1 light years closer than the other two.

Andromeda galaxy galaxy 2.2 million light years away from Earth in the constellation Andromeda, and the most distant object visible to the naked eye. It is the largest member of the Local Group of galaxies. Like the Milky Way, it is a spiral orbited by several companion galaxies but contains about twice as many stars. It is about 200,000 light years across.

Barnard's star second closest star to the Sun, six light years away in the constellation Ophiuchus. It is a faint red dwarf of 10th magnitude, visible only through a telescope. It is named after US astronomer Edward E Barnard (1857–1923), who discovered 1916 that it has the fastest proper motion of any star, crossing 1 degree of sky every 350 years.

Big Bang the hypothetical 'explosive' event that marked the origin of the universe as we know it. At the time of the Big Bang, the entire universe was squeezed into a hot, superdense state. The Big Bang explosion threw this compacted material outwards, producing the expanding universe. The cause of the Big Bang is unknown; observations of the current rate of expansion of the universe suggest that it took place about 10 to 20 billion years ago. The Big Bang theory began modern cosmology.

binary star pair of stars moving in orbit around their common centre of mass. Observations show that most stars are binary, or even multiple; for example, the nearest star system to the Sun, Alpha Centauri.

black hole object in space whose gravity is so great that nothing can escape from it, not even light. Thought to form when massive stars shrink at the ends of their lives, a black hole sucks in more matter, including other stars, from the space around it. Matter that falls into a black hole is squeezed to infinite density at the centre of the hole. Black holes can be detected because gas falling towards them becomes so hot that it emits X-rays. Four have been identified in our Galaxy.

brown dwarf hypothetical object less massive than a star, but heavier than a planet. Brown dwarfs would not have enough mass to ignite nuclear reactions at their centres, but would shine by heat released during their contraction from a gas cloud. Because of the difficulty of detection, no brown dwarfs have been spotted with certainty, but some astronomers believe that vast numbers of them may exist throughout the Galaxy.

Cepheid variable yellow supergiant star that varies regularly in brightness every few days or weeks as a result of pulsations. The time that a Cepheid variable takes to pulsate is directly related to its average brightness; the longer the pulsation period, the brighter the star.

constellation one of the 88 areas into which the sky is divided for the purposes of identifying and naming celestial objects. The first constellations were simple, arbitrary patterns of stars in which early civilizations visualized gods, sacred beasts, and mythical heroes. (See table opposite.)

cosmic background radiation or *3° radiation* electromagnetic radiation left over from the original formation of the universe in the Big Bang around 15 billion years ago. It corresponds to an overall background temperature of 3K (–270°C/–454°F), or 3°C above absolute zero. In 1992 the Cosmic Background Explorer satellite, COBE, detected slight ripples in the strength of the background radiation that are believed to mark the first stage in the formation of galaxies.

dark matter hypothetical matter that, according to current theories of cosmology, makes up 90–99% of the mass of the universe but so far remains undetected.

double star two stars that appear close together. Most double stars attract each other through gravity, and orbit each other, forming a genuine binary star, but other double stars are at different distances from Earth, and lie in the same line of sight only by chance.

eclipsing binary binary (double) star in which the two stars periodically pass in front of each other as seen from Earth.

galaxy congregation of millions or billions of stars, held together by gravity. *Spiral galaxies*, such as the Milky Way, are flattened in shape, with a central bulge of old stars surrounded by a disc of younger stars, arranged in spiral arms like a Catherine wheel. *Barred spirals* are spiral galaxies that have a straight bar of stars across their centre, from the ends of which the spiral arms emerge. The arms of spiral galaxies contain gas and dust from which new stars are still forming. *Elliptical galaxies* contain old stars and very little gas. They include the most massive galaxies known, containing a trillion stars. At least some elliptical galaxies are thought to be formed by mergers between spiral galaxies. There are also irregular galaxies. Most galaxies occur in clusters, containing anything from a few to thousands of members.

Constellations

Constellation	Popular name	Constellation	Popular name
Andromeda	–	Lacerta	Lizard
Antilla	Airpump	Leo	Lion
Apus	Bird of Paradise	Leo Minor	Little Lion
Aquarius	Water-bearer	Lepus	Hare
Aquila	Eagle	Libra	Balance
Ara	Altar	Lupus	Wolf
Aries	Ram	Lynx	–
Auriga	Charioteer	Lyra	Lyre
		Mensa	Table
Boötes	Herdsman	Microscopium	Microscope
Caelum	Chisel	Monoceros	Unicorn
Camelopadalis	Giraffe	Musca	Southern Fly
Cancer	Crab	Norma	Rule
Canes Venatici	Hunting Dogs	Octans	Octant
Canis Major	Great Dog	Ophiuchus	Serpent-bearer
Canis Minor	Little Dog	Orion	–
Capricornus	Sea-goat	Pavo	Peacock
Carina	Keel	Pegasus	Flying Horse
Cassiopeia	–	Perseus	–
Centaurus	Centaur	Phoenix	–
Cepheus	–	Pictor	Painter
Cetus	Whale	Pisces	Fishes
Chamaeleon	Chameleon	Piscis Austrinus	Southern Fish
Circinus	Compasses	Puppis	Poop
Columba	Dove	Pyxis	Compass
Coma Berenices	Berenice's Hair	Reticulum	Net
Corona Australis	Southern Crown	Sagitta	Arrow
Corona Borealis	Northern Crown	Sagittarius	Archer
Corvus	Crow	Scorpius	Scorpion
Crater	Cup	Sculptor	–
Crux	Southern Cross	Scutum	Shield
Cygnus	Swan	Serpens	Serpent
Delphinus	Dolphin	Sextans	Sextant
Dorado	Goldfish	Taurus	Bull
Draco	Dragon	Telescopium	Telescope
Equuleus	Foal	Triangulum	Triangle
Eridanus	River	Triangulum Australe	Southern Triangle
Fornax	Furnace	Tuscana	Toucan
Gemini	Twins	Ursa Major	Great Bear
Grus	Crane	Ursa Minor	Little Bear
Hercules	–	Vela	Sails
Horologium	Clock	Virgo	Virgin
Hydra	Watersnake	Volans	Flying Fish
Hydrus	Little Snake	Vulpecula	Fox
Indus	Indian		

globular cluster spherical or near–spherical star cluster containing from approximately 10,000 to millions of stars. More than a hundred globular clusters are distributed in a spherical halo around our Galaxy. They consist of old stars, formed early in the Galaxy's history. Globular clusters are also found around other galaxies.

interstellar molecules over 50 different types of molecule existing in gas clouds in our Galaxy. Most have been detected by their radio emissions, but some have been found by the absorption lines they produce in the spectra of starlight. The most complex molecules, many of them based on carbon, are found in the dense clouds where stars are forming. They may be significant for the origin of life elsewhere in space.

Local Group cluster of about 30 galaxies that includes our own, the Milky Way. Like other groups of galaxies, the Local Group is held together by the gravitational attraction among its members, and does not expand with the expanding universe. Its two largest galaxies are the Milky Way and the Andromeda galaxy; most of the others are small and faint.

Magellanic Clouds the two galaxies nearest to our own Galaxy. They are irregularly shaped, and appear as detached parts of the Milky Way, in the southern constellations Dorado and Tucana.

Milky Way faint band of light crossing the night sky, consisting of stars in the plane of our Galaxy. The name Milky Way is often used for the Galaxy itself. It is a spiral galaxy, about 100,000 light years in diameter, containing at least 100 billion stars. The Sun is in one of its spiral arms, about 25,000 light years from the centre.

Mira or ***Omicron Ceti*** the brightest long-period pulsating variable star, located in the constellation Cetus. Mira was the first star discovered to vary periodically in brightness.

nebula (plural ***nebulae***) cloud of gas and dust in space. Nebulae are the birthplaces of stars, but some (planetary) nebulae are produced by gas thrown off from dying stars. Nebulae are classified depending on whether they emit, reflect, or absorb light.

An ***emission nebula***, such as the Orion nebula, glows brightly because its gas is energized by stars that have formed within it. In a ***reflection nebula***, starlight reflects off grains of dust in the nebula, such as surround the stars of the Pleiades cluster. A ***dark nebula*** is a dense cloud, composed of molecular hydrogen, which partially or completely absorbs light behind it. Examples include the Coalsack nebula in Crux and the Horsehead nebula in Orion.

neutron star very small, superdense star composed mostly of neutrons. They are thought to form when massive stars explode as supernovae, during which the protons and electrons of the star's atoms merge, owing to intense gravitational collapse, to make neutrons. A neutron star may have the mass of up to three Suns, compressed into a globe only 20 km/12 mi in diameter. If its mass is any greater, its gravity will be so strong that it will shrink even further to become a black hole. Being so small, neutron stars can spin very quickly. The rapidly flashing radio stars called pulsars are believed to be neutron stars. The flashing is caused by a rotating beam of radio energy similar in behaviour to a lighthouse beam of light.

nova (plural ***novae***) faint star that suddenly erupts in brightness by 10,000 times or more. Novae are believed to occur in close binary star systems, where gas from one star flows to a companion white dwarf. The gas ignites and is thrown off in an explosion at speeds of 1,500 kps/930 mps or more. Unlike a supernova, the star is not completely disrupted by the outburst. After a few weeks or months it subsides to its previous state; it may erupt many more times.

Olbers' paradox question put forward 1826 by German astronomer Heinrich Olbers (1758–1840), who asked: If the universe is infinite in extent and filled with stars, why is the sky dark at night? The answer is that the stars do not live infinitely long, so there is not enough starlight to fill the universe. A wrong answer, frequently given, is that the expansion of the universe weakens the starlight.

oscillating universe theory that states that the gravitational attraction of the mass within the universe will eventually slow down and stop the expansion of the universe. The outward motions of the galaxies will then be reversed, eventually resulting in a 'Big Crunch' where all the matter in the universe would be contracted into a small volume of high density. This could undergo a further Big Bang, thereby creating another expansion phase. The theory suggests that the universe would alternately expand and collapse through alternate Big Bangs and Big Crunches.

planetary nebula shell of gas thrown off by a star at the end of its life. Planetary nebulae have nothing to do with planets. They were named by William Herschel, who thought their rounded shape resembled the disc of a planet. After a star such as the Sun has expanded to become a red giant, its outer layers are ejected into space to form a planetary nebula, leaving the core as a white dwarf at the centre.

Plaskett's Star the most massive binary star known, consisting of two supergiants of about 40 and 50 solar masses, orbiting each other every 14.4 days. Plaskett's star lies in the constellation Monoceros and is named after Canadian astronomer John S Plaskett (1865–1941), who identified it as a binary star and discovered its massive nature in 1922.

Polaris or ***Pole Star*** or ***North Star*** the bright star closest to the north celestial pole, and the brightest star in the constellation Ursa Minor. Its position is indicated by the 'pointers' in Ursa Major. Polaris is a yellow supergiant about 500 light years away.

Proxima Centauri the closest star to the Sun, 4.2 light years away. It is a faint red dwarf, visible only with a telescope, and is a member of the Alpha Centauri triple-star system.

pulsar celestial source that emits pulses of energy at regular intervals, ranging from a few seconds to a few thousandths of a second. Pulsars are thought to be rapidly rotating neutron stars, which flash at radio and other wavelengths as they spin. They were discovered in 1967. Over 500 radio pulsars are now known in our Galaxy, although a million or so may exist.

quasar (from *quasi*-stell*ar* object or QSO) starlike object emitting more energy than 100 giant galaxies. Quasars are the most distant extragalactic objects known (up to 10 billion light years away), and were discovered 1964–65. They are thought to be at the centre of galaxies, their brilliance emanating from the stars and gas falling towards an immense black hole

Stars: the top twenty brightest stars

Common name	Scientific name	Apparent magnitude
Sirius	α Canis Majoris	−1.46
Canopus	α Carinae	−0.72
Rigil Kent	α Centauri	−0.27*
Arcturus	α Boötis	−0.4
Vega	α Lyrae	+0.03
Capella	α Aurigae	0.08
Rigel	β Orionis	0.12
Procyon	α Canis Minoris	0.38
Achernar	α Eridani	0.46
Betelgeuse	α Orionis	0.50**
Hadar	β Centauri	0.61
Altair	α Aquilae	0.77
Acrux	α Crucis	0.79*
Aldebaran	α Tauri	0.85**
Antares	α Scorpii	0.96**
Spica	α Virginis	0.98
Pollux	β Geminorum	1.14
Fomalhaut	α Piscis Austrini	1.16
Deneb	α Cygni	1.25
Mimosa	β Crucis	1.25

* combined magnitude of double star
** variable

at their nucleus. Quasar light shows a large red shift, indicating that they are very distant. Some quasars emit radio waves but most are radio-quiet.

radio galaxy galaxy that is a strong source of electromagnetic waves of radio wavelengths. All galaxies, including our own, emit some radio waves, but radio galaxies are up to a million times more powerful.

red dwarf any star that is cool, faint, and small (about one-tenth the mass and diameter of the Sun). Red dwarfs burn slowly, and have estimated lifetimes of 100 billion years. They may be the most abundant type of star, but are difficult to see because they are so faint. Two of the closest stars to the Sun, Proxima Centauri and Barnard's Star, are red dwarfs.

red giant any large bright star with a cool surface. It is thought to represent a late stage in the evolution of a star like the Sun, as it runs out of hydrogen fuel at its centre. Red giants have diameters between 10 and 100 million times that of the Sun. They are very bright because they are so large, although their surface temperature is lower than that of the Sun, about 2,000–3,000K (1,700–2,700°C/3,000°–5,000°F).

Seyfert galaxy galaxy whose small, bright centre is caused by hot gas moving at high speed around a massive central object, possibly a black hole. Almost all Seyferts are spiral galaxies. They seem to be closely related to quasars, but are about 100 times fainter. They are named after their discoverer Carl Seyfert (1911–1960).

star luminous globe of gas, mainly hydrogen and helium, which produces its own heat and light by nuclear reactions. The surface temperatures of stars range from 2,000°C/3,600°F to 200,000°C/360,000°F and the corresponding colours range from red to blue-white. When, after billions of years, all the hydrogen at the core has been converted into helium, the star swells to become a *red giant*, its core collapses in on itself to form a small and very dense body called a *white dwarf*, which eventually fades away.

Some very large stars do not end their lives as white dwarfs. They pass through their cycle quickly, becoming red supergiants that eventually explode into brilliant supernovae. Part of the core remaining after such an explosion may collapse to form a small superdense neutron star.

star cluster group of related stars, usually held together by gravity. Members of a star cluster are thought to form together from one large cloud of gas in space. *Open clusters* such as the Pleiades contain from a dozen to many hundreds of young stars, loosely scattered over several light years. Globular clusters are larger and much more densely packed, containing perhaps 100,000 old stars.

steady-state theory theory that claims that the universe has no origin but is expanding because new matter is being created continuously throughout the universe. The theory was proposed 1948 by Hermann Bondi (1919–), Thomas Gold (1920–), and Fred Hoyle (1915–), but was dealt a severe blow in 1965 by the discovery of cosmic background radiation (radiation left over from the formation of the universe) and - is now largely rejected in favour of the Big Bang theory.

supernova the explosive death of a star, which temporarily attains a brightness of 100 million Suns or more, so that it can shine as brilliantly as a small galaxy for a few days or weeks. Astronomers have catalogued about 150 supernovae in our galaxy.

universe all of space and its contents, the study of which is called cosmology. The universe is thought to be between 10 billion and 20 billion years old, and is mostly empty space, dotted with galaxies for as far as telescopes can see. The most distant detected galaxies and quasars lie 10 billion light years or more from Earth, and are moving farther apart as the universe expands. The most widely accepted explanation of how the universe came into being and evolved is the Big Bang theory of an expanding universe.

variable star star whose brightness changes, either regularly or irregularly, over a period ranging from a few hours to months or even years. The Cepheid variables regularly expand and contract in size every few days or weeks.

white dwarf small, hot star, the last stage in the life of a star such as the Sun. White dwarfs have a mass similar to that of the Sun, but only 1% of the Sun's diameter, similar in size to the Earth. Most have surface temperatures of 8,000°C/14,400°F or more, hotter than the Sun. Yet, being so small, their overall luminosities may be less than 1% of that of the Sun. The Milky Way contains an estimated 50 billion white dwarfs.

Technical Terms

aberration of starlight apparent displacement of a star from its true position, due to the combined effects of the speed of light and the speed of the Earth in orbit around the Sun (about 30 km per second/18.5 mi per second).

albedo the fraction of the incoming light reflected by a body such as a planet. A body with a high albedo, near 1, is very bright, while a body with a low albedo, near 0, is dark. The Moon has an average albedo of 0.12, Venus 0.65, Earth 0.37.

aphelion the point at which an object, travelling in an elliptical orbit around the Sun, is at its farthest from the Sun.

apogee the point at which an object, travelling in an elliptical orbit around the Earth, is at its farthest from the Earth.

arc minute, arc second units for measuring small angles, used in geometry, surveying, map-making, and astronomy. An arc minute (symbol ') is one-sixtieth of a degree, and an arc second (symbol ") is one-sixtieth of an arc minute. Small distances in the sky, as between two close stars or the apparent width of a planet's disc, are expressed in minutes and seconds of arc.

astrometry measurement of the precise positions of stars, planets, and other bodies in space. Such information is needed for practical purposes including accurate timekeeping, surveying and navigation, and calculating orbits and measuring distances in space.

astronomical unit unit (symbol AU) equal to the mean distance of the Earth from the Sun: 149,597,870 km/92,955,800 mi. It is used to describe planetary distances. Light travels this distance in approximately 8.3 minutes.

astrophotography use of photography in astronomical research. The first successful photograph of a celestial object was the daguerreotype plate of the Moon taken by John W Draper (1811–1882) of the USA in March 1840. The first photograph of a star, Vega, was taken by US astronomer William C Bond (1789–1859) in 1850.

celestial mechanics the branch of astronomy that deals with the calculation of the orbits of celestial bodies, their gravitational attractions (such as those that produce the Earth's tides), and also the orbits of artificial satellites and space probes. It is based on the laws of motion and gravity laid down by Isaac Newton (1642–1727).

celestial sphere imaginary sphere surrounding the Earth, on which the celestial bodies seem to lie. The positions of bodies such as stars, planets, and galaxies are specified by their coordinates on the celestial sphere. The equivalents of latitude and longitude on the celestial sphere are called declination and right ascension (which is measured in hours from 0 to 24). The *celestial poles* lie directly above the Earth's poles, and the *celestial equator* lies over the Earth's equator. The celestial sphere appears to rotate once around the Earth each day, actually a result of the rotation of the Earth on its axis.

charge-coupled device (CCD) device for forming images electronically, using a layer of silicon that releases electrons when struck by incoming light. The electrons are stored in pixels and read off into a computer at the end of the exposure. CCDs have now almost entirely replaced photographic film in astrophotography because they are 30 times more sensitive to light than a photographic plate and can reveal objects millions of times fainter than can be seen with the naked eye.

conjunction the alignment of two celestial bodies as seen from Earth. A superior planet (or other object) is in conjunction when it lies behind the Sun. An inferior planet (or other object) comes to *inferior conjunction* when it passes between the Earth and the Sun; it is at *superior conjunction* when it passes behind the Sun. *Planetary conjunction* takes place when a planet is closely aligned with another celestial object, such as the Moon, a star, or another planet.

cosmology study of the structure of the universe. Modern cosmology began in the 1920s with the discovery that the universe is expanding, which suggested that it began in an explosion, the Big Bang. An alternative view, now discarded, the steady-state theory, claimed that the universe has no origin, but is expanding because new matter is being continually created.

declination the coordinate on the celestial sphere (imaginary sphere surrounding the Earth) that corresponds to latitude on the Earth's surface. Declination runs from 0° at the celestial equator to 90° at the north and south celestial poles.

ecliptic the path, against the background of stars, that the Sun appears to follow each year as the Earth orbits the Sun. It can be thought of as the plane of the Earth's orbit projected on to the celestial sphere (imaginary sphere around the Earth).

elongation the angular distance between the Sun and a planet or other Solar-System object. This angle is 0° at conjunction, 90° at quadrature, and 180° at opposition.

equinox the points in spring and autumn at which the Sun's path, the ecliptic, crosses the celestial equator, so that the day and night are of approximately equal length. The *vernal equinox* occurs about 21 March and the *autumnal equinox*, 23 Sept.

escape velocity minimum velocity with which an object must be projected for it to escape from the gravitational pull of a planetary body. In the case of the Earth, the escape velocity is 11.2 kps/6.9 mps; the Moon 2.4 kps/1.5 mps; Mars 5 kps/3.1 mps; and Jupiter 59.6 kps/37 mps.

exobiology study of life forms that may possibly exist elsewhere in the universe, and of the effects of extraterrestrial environments on Earth organisms.

geostationary orbit circular path 35,900 km/22,300 mi above the Earth's equator on which a satellite takes 24 hours, moving from west to east, to complete an orbit, thus appearing to hang stationary over one place on the Earth's surface. Geostationary orbits are particularly used for communications satellites and weather satellites. They were first thought of by the author Arthur C Clarke. A *geosynchronous orbit* lies at the same distance from Earth but is inclined to the equator.

gravitational lensing bending of light by a gravitational field, predicted by Albert Einstein's general theory of relativity. The effect was first detected 1917 when the light from stars was found to be bent as it passed the totally eclipsed Sun. More remarkable is the splitting of light from distant quasars into two or more images by intervening galaxies. In 1979 the first double image of a quasar produced by gravitational lensing was discovered and a quadruple image of another quasar was later found.

gravity force of attraction that arises between objects by virtue of their masses. On Earth, gravity is the force of attraction between any object in the Earth's gravitational field and the Earth itself. It is regarded as one of the four fundamental forces of nature, the other three being the electromagnetic force, the strong nuclear force, and the weak nuclear force. The gravitational force is the weakest of the four forces, but it acts over great distances. The particle that is postulated as the carrier of the gravitational force is the graviton.

Greenwich Mean Time (GMT) local time on the zero line of longitude (the *Greenwich meridian*), which passes through the Old Royal Observatory in Greenwich, London. It was replaced 1986 by coordinated universal time (UTC), but continued to be used to measure longitudes and the world's standard time zones.

Hertzsprung–Russell diagram graph on which the surface temperatures of stars are plotted against their luminosities. Most stars, including the Sun, fall into a narrow band called the *main sequence*. When a star grows old it moves from the main sequence to the upper right part of the graph, into the area of the giants and supergiants. At the end of its life, as the star shrinks to become a white dwarf, it moves again,

Astronomy: chronology

2300 BC	Chinese astronomers made their earliest observations.
2000	Babylonian priests made their first observational records.
1900	Stonehenge was constructed: first phase.
365	The Chinese observed the satellites of Jupiter with the naked eye.
3rd century	Aristarchus argued that the Sun is the centre of the Solar System.
2nd century AD	Ptolemy's complicated Earth-centred system was promulgated, which dominated the astronomy of the Middle Ages.
1543	Copernicus revived the ideas of Aristarchus in *De Revolutionibus*.
1608	Hans Lippershey invented the telescope, which was first used by Galileo 1609.
1609	Johannes Kepler's first two laws of planetary motion were published (the third appeared 1619).
1632	The world's first official observatory was established in Leiden in the Netherlands.
1633	Galileo's theories were condemned by the Inquisition.
1675	The Royal Greenwich Observatory was founded in England.
1687	Isaac Newton's *Principia* was published, including his 'law of universal gravitation'.
1705	Edmond Halley correctly predicted that the comet that had passed the Earth in 1682 would return in 1758; the comet was later to be known by his name.
1781	William Herschel discovered Uranus and recognized stellar systems beyond our Galaxy.
1796	Pierre Laplace elaborated his theory of the origin of the Solar System.
1801	Giuseppe Piazzi discovered the first asteroid, Ceres.
1814	Joseph von Fraunhofer first studied absorption lines in the solar spectrum.
1846	Neptune was identified by Johann Galle, following predictions by John Adams and Urbain Leverrier.
1859	Gustav Kirchhoff explained dark lines in the Sun's spectrum.
1887	The earliest photographic star charts were produced.
1889	Edward Barnard took the first photographs of the Milky Way.
1908	Fragment of comet fell at Tunguska, Siberia.
1920	Arthur Eddington began the study of interstellar matter.
1923	Edwin Hubble proved that the galaxies are systems independent of the Milky Way, and by 1930 had confirmed the concept of an expanding universe.
1930	The planet Pluto was discovered by Clyde Tombaugh at the Lowell Observatory, Arizona, USA.
1931	Karl Jansky founded radio astronomy.
1945	Radar contact with the Moon was established by Z Bay of Hungary and the US Army Signal Corps Laboratory.
1948	The 5-m/200-in Hale reflector telescope was installed at Mount Palomar, California, USA.
1957	The Jodrell Bank telescope dish in England was completed.
1957	The first Sputnik satellite (USSR) opened the age of space observation.
1962	The first X-ray source was discovered in Scorpius.
1963	The first quasar was discovered.
1967	The first pulsar was discovered by Jocelyn Bell and Antony Hewish.
1969	The first crewed Moon landing was made by US astronauts.
1976	A 6-m/240-in reflector telescope was installed at Mount Semirodniki, USSR.
1977	Uranus was discovered to have rings.
1977	The spacecraft *Voyager 1* and *2* were launched, passing Jupiter and Saturn 1979–81.
1978	The spacecraft *Pioneer Venus 1* and *2* reached Venus.
1978	A satellite of Pluto, Charon, was discovered by James Christy of the US Naval Observatory.
1986	Halley's comet returned. *Voyager 2* flew past Uranus and discovered six new moons.
1987	Supernova SN1987A flared up, becoming the first supernova to be visible to the naked eye since 1604. The 4.2-m/165-in William Herschel Telescope on La Palma, Canary Islands, and the James Clerk Maxwell Telescope on Mauna Kea, Hawaii, began operation.
1988	The most distant individual star was recorded – a supernova, 5 billion light years away, in the AC118 cluster of galaxies.
1989	*Voyager 2* flew by Neptune and discovered eight moons and three rings.
1990	Hubble Space Telescope was launched into orbit by the US space shuttle.
1991	The space probe *Galileo* flew past the asteroid Gaspra, approaching it to within 26,000 km/16,200 mi.
1992	COBE satellite detected ripples from the Big Bang that mark the first stage in the formation of galaxies. NASA began 10-year search for radio signals from extraterrestrial beings.

to the bottom left area. It is named after the Dane Ejnar Hertzsprung (1873–1967) and the American Henry Norris Russell (1877–1957), who independently devised in the years 1911–13.

Hubble's constant measure of the rate at which the universe is expanding, named after US astronomer Edwin Hubble (1889–1953). Observations suggest that galaxies are moving apart at a rate of 50–100 kps/

30–60 mps for every million parsecs of distance. This means that the universe, which began at one point according to the Big Bang theory, is between 10 billion and 20 billion years old (probably closer to 20).

Hubble's law law that relates a galaxy's distance from us to its speed of recession as the universe expands, announced in 1929 by Edwin Hubble. He found that galaxies are moving apart at speeds that increase in direct proportion to their distance apart. The rate of expansion is known as Hubble's constant.

inclination the angle between the ecliptic and the plane of the orbit of a planet, asteroid, or comet. In the case of satellites orbiting a planet, it is the angle between the plane of orbit of the satellite and the equator of the planet.

light year the distance travelled by a beam of light in a vacuum in one year, approximately 9.46 trillion (million million) km/5.88 trillion mi.

luminosity or *brightness* the amount of light emitted by a star, measured in magnitudes. The apparent brightness of an object decreases in proportion to the square of its distance from the observer. The luminosity of a star or other body can be expressed in relation to that of the Sun.

magnitude measure of the brightness of a star or other celestial object. The larger the number denoting the magnitude, the fainter the object. Zero or first magnitude indicates some of the brightest stars. Still brighter are those of negative magnitude, such as Sirius, whose magnitude is –1.46. *Apparent magnitude* is the brightness of an object as seen from Earth; *absolute magnitude* is the brightness at a standard distance of 10 parsecs (32.6 light years).

nadir the point on the celestial sphere vertically below the observer and hence diametrically opposite the *zenith*.

nutation slight 'nodding' of the Earth in space, caused by the varying gravitational pulls of the Sun and Moon. Nutation changes the angle of the Earth's axial tilt (average 23.5°) by about 9 seconds of arc to either side of its mean position, a complete cycle taking just over 18.5 years.

opposition the moment at which a body in the Solar System lies opposite the Sun in the sky as seen from the Earth and crosses the meridian at about midnight.

orbit path of one body in space around another, such as the orbit of Earth around the Sun, or the Moon around Earth. When the two bodies are similar in mass, as in a binary star, both bodies move around their common centre of mass. The movement of objects in orbit follows the laws of German astronomer Johann Kepler (1571–1630), which apply to artificial satellites as well as to natural bodies.

parallax the change in the apparent position of an object against its background when viewed from two different positions. In astronomy, nearby stars show a shift owing to parallax when viewed from different positions on the Earth's orbit around the Sun. A star's parallax is used to deduce its distance.

parsec unit (symbol pc) used for distances to stars and galaxies. One parsec is equal to 3.2616 light years, 2.063 × 10^5 astronomical units, and 3.086 x 10^{13} km.

perigee the point at which an object, travelling in an elliptical orbit around the Earth, is at its closest to the Earth. The point at which it is farthest from the Earth is the apogee.

perihelion the point at which an object, travelling in an elliptical orbit around the Sun, is at its closest to the Sun. The point at which it is farthest from the Sun is the aphelion.

phase the apparent shape of the Moon or a planet when all or part of its illuminated hemisphere is facing Earth. The Moon undergoes a full cycle of phases from new (when between Earth and the Sun) through first quarter (when at 90° eastern elongation from the Sun), full (when opposite the Sun), and last quarter (when at 90° western elongation from the Sun).

precession slow wobble of the Earth on its axis, like that of a spinning top. The gravitational pulls of the Sun and Moon on the Earth's equatorial bulge cause the Earth's axis to trace out a circle on the sky every 25,800 years. The position of the celestial poles (see celestial sphere) is constantly changing owing to precession, as are the positions of the equinoxes (the points at which the celestial equator intersects the Sun's path around the sky). The *precession of the equinoxes* means that there is a gradual westward drift in the ecliptic – the path that the Sun appears to follow – and in the coordinates of objects on the celestial sphere.

proper motion gradual change in the position of a star that results from its motion in orbit around our Galaxy, the Milky Way. Proper motions are slight and undetectable to the naked eye, but can be accurately measured on telescopic photographs taken many years apart.

red shift the lengthening of the wavelengths of light from an object as a result of its motion away from us. It is an example of the Doppler effect. The red shift in light from galaxies is evidence that the universe is expanding. A strong gravitational field can also produce a red shift in light; this is termed *gravitational red shift*.

right ascension the coordinate on the celestial sphere that corresponds to longitude on the surface of the Earth. It is measured in hours, minutes, and seconds eastwards from the point where the Sun's path, the ecliptic, once a year intersects the celestial equator; this point is called the *vernal equinox*.

sidereal period the orbital period of a planet around the Sun, or a moon around a planet, with reference to a background star. The sidereal period of a planet is in effect a 'year'. A synodic period is a full circle as seen from Earth.

singularity the point at the centre of a black hole at which it is predicted that the infinite gravitational forces will compress the infalling mass of the collapsing star to infinite density. It is a point in spacetime at which the known laws of physics break down. In the Big Bang theory, it is the point from which the expansion of the universe began.

solstice either of the points at which the Sun is farthest north or south of the celestial equator each year. The *summer solstice*, when the Sun is farthest north, occurs around June 21; the *winter solstice* around Dec 22.

speckle interferometry technique whereby large telescopes can achieve high resolution of astronomical objects despite the adverse effects of the atmosphere through which light from the object under study must pass. It involves the taking of large numbers of images, each under high magnification and with short exposure times. The pictures are then combined to form the final picture.

synodic period the time taken for a planet or moon to return to the same position in its orbit as seen from the Earth; that is, from one opposition to the next. It differs from the sidereal period because the Earth is moving in orbit around the Sun.

transfer orbit elliptical path followed by a spacecraft moving from one orbit to another, designed to save fuel although making the journey time longer.

transit the passage of a smaller object across the visible disc of a larger one. Transits of the inferior planets occur when they pass directly between the Earth and the Sun, and are seen as tiny dark spots against the Sun's disc.

universal time (UT) another name for Greenwich Mean Time. It is based on the rotation of the Earth, which is not quite constant. Since 1972, UT has been replaced by *coordinated universal time* (UTC), which is based on uniform atomic time.

zenith uppermost point of the celestial horizon, immediately above the observer; the nadir is below, diametrically opposite.

zodiac zone of the heavens containing the paths of the Sun, Moon, and planets. When this was devised by the ancient Greeks, only five planets were known, making the zodiac about 16° wide. In astrology, the zodiac is divided into 12 signs, each 30° in extent: Aries, Taurus, Gemini, Cancer, Leo, Virgo, Libra, Scorpio, Sagittarius, Capricorn, Aquarius, and Pisces. These do not cover the same areas of sky as the astronomical constellations.

Telescopes and Observatories

Algonquin Radio Observatory site in Ontario, Canada, of the radio telescope, 46 m/150 ft in diameter, of the National Research Council of Canada, opened 1966.

Arecibo site in Puerto Rico of the world's largest single-dish radio telescope, 305 m/1,000 ft in diameter. It is built in a natural hollow and uses the rotation of the Earth to scan the sky. It has been used both for radar work on the planets and for conventional radio astronomy, and is operated by Cornell University, USA.

Australia Telescope giant radio telescope in New South Wales, Australia, operated by the Commonwealth Scientific and Industrial Research Organization (CSIRO). It consists of six 22-m/72-ft antennae at Culgoora, a similar antenna at Siding Spring Mountain, and the 64-m/210-ft Parkes radio telescope – the whole simulating a dish 300 m/186 mi across.

David Dunlap Observatory Canadian observatory at Richmond Hill, Ontario, operated by the University of Toronto, with a 1.88-m/74-in reflector, the largest optical telescope in Canada, opened 1935.

Dominion Astrophysical Observatory Canadian observatory near Victoria, British Columbia, the site of a 1.85-m/73-in reflector opened 1918, operated by the National Research Council of Canada. The associated Dominion Radio Astrophysical Observatory at Penticton, British Columbia, operates a 26-m/84-ft radio dish and an aperture synthesis radio telescope.

Effelsberg site near Bonn, Germany, of the world's largest fully steerable radio telescope, the 100-m/328-ft radio dish of the Max Planck Institute for Radio Astronomy, opened 1971.

European Southern Observatory observatory operated jointly by Belgium, Denmark, France, Germany, Italy, the Netherlands, Sweden, and Switzerland. Its telescopes, located at La Silla, Chile, include a 3.6-m/142-in reflector opened 1976 and the 3.58-m/141-in New Technology Telescope opened 1990. By 1988 work began on the Very Large Telescope, consisting of four 8-m/315-in reflectors mounted independently but capable of working in combination.

Jodrell Bank site in Cheshire, England, of the Nuffield Radio Astronomy Laboratories of the University of Manchester. Its largest instrument is the 76-m/250-ft radio dish (the Lovell Telescope), completed 1957 and modified 1970. A 38 × 25 m/125 × 82 ft elliptical radio dish was introduced 1964, capable of working at shorter wavelengths. These radio telescopes are used in conjunction with six smaller dishes up to 230 km/143 mi apart in an array called MERLIN (*m*ulti-*e*lement *r*adio-*l*inked *i*nterferometer *n*etwork) to produce detailed maps of radio sources.

Keck Telescope world's largest optical telescope, situated on Mauna Kea, Hawaii, USA. It has a primary mirror 10 m/33 ft in diameter, unique in that it consists of 36 hexagonal sections, each controlled and adjusted by a computer to generate single images of the objects observed. It received its first images Nov 1990. An identical telescope, to be named Keck II, is under construction next to it and is due for completion 1996. Both telescopes are jointly owned by the California Institute of Technology and the University of California.

Kitt Peak National Observatory US observatory in the Quinlan Mountains near Tucson, Arizona, operated by AURA (Association of Universities for Research into Astronomy). Its main telescopes are the 4-m/158-in Mayall reflector, opened 1973, and the McMath Solar Telescope, opened 1962, the world's largest of its type. Among numerous other telescopes on the site is a 2.3-m/90-in reflector owned by the Steward Observatory of the University of Arizona.

Las Campanas Observatory site in Chile of the 2.5-m/100-in Du Pont telescope of the Carnegie Institution of Washington, opened 1977.

Lick Observatory observatory of the University of California on Mount Hamilton, California, USA. Its main instruments are the 3.04-m/120-in Shane reflector, opened 1959, and a 91-cm/36-in refractor, opened 1888, the second-largest refractor in the world.

Lowell Observatory US observatory in Flagstaff, Arizona, with a 61-cm/24-in refractor opened in 1896. The observatory now operates other telescopes at a nearby site on Anderson Mesa, including the 1.83-m/72-in Perkins reflector of Ohio State and Ohio Wesleyan universities.

McDonald Observatory observatory of the University of Texas on Mount Locke, Texas, USA. It is the site of a 2.72-m/107-in reflector opened 1969 and a 2.08-m/82-in reflector opened 1939.

Mauna Kea observatory in Hawaii, USA, built on a dormant volcano at 4,200 m/13,784 ft above sea level. Because of its elevation high above clouds, atmospheric moisture, and artificial lighting, Mauna Kea is ideal for infrared astronomy. The first telescope on the site was installed 1970. Several countries now operate telescopes there, and the world's largest optical telescope, the Keck Telescope, is also situated on Mauna Kea.

Mills Cross type of radio telescope consisting of two rows of aerials at right angles to each other, invented 1953 by the Australian radio astronomer Bernard Mills (1920–   ). The cross-shape produces a narrow beam useful for pinpointing the positions of radio sources.

Mount Palomar US observatory 80 km/50 mi NE of San Diego, California. It has a 5-m/200-in diameter reflector called the Hale. Completed 1948, it was the world's premier observatory during the 1950s.

Mount Wilson site near Los Angeles, California, of the 2.5-m/100-in Hooker telescope, opened 1917, with which Edwin Hubble discovered the expansion of the universe. It was closed in 1985 when the Carnegie Institution withdrew its support. Two solar telescopes in towers 18.3 m/60 ft and 45.7 m/150 ft tall, and a 1.5-m/60-in reflector opened 1908, still operate there.

Mullard Radio Astronomy Observatory radio observatory of the University of Cambridge, England. Its main instrument is the Ryle Telescope, eight dishes 12.8 m/42 ft wide in a line 5 km/3 mi long, opened 1972.

Multiple Mirror Telescope telescope on Mount Hopkins, Arizona, USA, opened 1979, consisting of six 1.83-m/72-in mirrors mounted in a hexagon, the light-collecting area of which equals that of a single mirror of 4.5 m/176 in diameter. It is planned to replace the six mirrors with a single mirror 6.5 m/256 in wide.

New Technology Telescope optical telescope that forms part of the European Southern Observatory, La Silla, Chile; it came into operation 1991. It has a thin, lightweight mirror, 3.38 m/141 in across, which is kept in shape by computer-adjustable supports to produce a sharper image than is possible with conventional mirrors. Such a system is termed *active optics*.

observatory site or facility for observing astronomical or meteorological phenomena. The earliest recorded observatory was in Alexandria, N Africa, built by Ptolemy Soter in about 300 BC. The modern observatory dates from the invention of the telescope. Observatories may be ground-based, carried on aircraft, or sent into orbit as satellites, in space stations, and on the space shuttle.

The most powerful optical telescopes covering the sky are at Mauna Kea, Hawaii; Mount Palomar, California; Kitt Peak National Observatory, Arizona; La Palma, Canary Islands; Cerro Tololo Inter-American Observatory, and the European Southern Observatory, Chile; Siding Spring Mountain, Australia; and Zelenchukskaya in the Caucasus. Radio astronomy observatories include Jodrell Bank, Cheshire, England; the Mullard Radio Astronomy Observatory, Cambridge, England; Arecibo, Puerto Rico; Effelsberg, Germany; and Parkes, Australia. The Hubble Space Telescope was launched into orbit April 1990. The Very Large Telescope is under construction by the European Southern Observatory in the mountains of N Chile, for completion by 1999.

Parkes site in New South Wales of the Australian National Radio Astronomy Observatory, featuring a radio telescope of 64-m/210-ft aperture, run by the Commonwealth Scientific and Industrial Research Organization.

planetarium optical projection device by means of which the motions of stars and planets are reproduced on a domed ceiling representing the sky.

radio telescope instrument for detecting radio waves from the universe in radio astronomy. Radio telescopes usually consist of a metal bowl that collects and focuses radio waves the way a concave mirror col-

Large ground-based telescopes worldwide (1991–2000)

Telescope	Description	Cost $m	Ready	Location
Keck I	10m segmented optical mirror	91	1993	Mauna Kea, Hawaii
Keck II	10m segmented optical mirror	85	1996	Mauna Kea, Hawaii
Columbus	2 × 8.4m honeycomb-back optical mirrors	60*	1997	To be announced
Gemini Northern	8m thin meniscus optical mirror	{ 176†	1999	Mauna Kea, Hawaii
Gemini Southern	8m thin meniscus optical mirror		2001	Cerro Pachon, Chile
Subaru ('Pleiades')	8m thin meniscus optical mirror	200	1999	Mauna Kea, Hawaii
Magellan	6.5m honeycomb-back optical mirror	30	1997	Las Campanas, Chile
Very Large Telescope (VLT)	4 × 8m optical array	315	1999	Cerro Paranal, Chile
Big Optical Array (BOA)	6 × 0.5m optical array, 70m max. baseline	20	1993	Flagstaff, Arizona
CHARA Array	7 × 1m optical array, 400m max. baseline	10‡	1996	To be announced
Millimetre Array (MMA)	40 × 8m radio array, 3km max. baseline	120	1997	To be announced
Very Long Baseline Array (VLBA)	10 × 25m radio array, 8,000km max. baseline	85	1993	From Hawaii to St Croix
Multiple Mirror Telescope conversion	6.5m honeycomb-back optical mirror	20	1996	Tucson, Arizona

*66% promised †90% promised ‡50% promised

Source: The Economist research

lects and focuses light waves. Radio telescopes are much larger than optical telescopes, because the wavelengths they are detecting are much longer than the wavelength of light. The largest single dish is 305 m/1,000 ft across, at Arecibo, Puerto Rico.

Royal Greenwich Observatory the national astronomical observatory of the UK, founded 1675 at Greenwich, E London, England, to provide navigational information for sailors. After World War II it was moved to Herstmonceux Castle, Sussex; in 1990 it was transferred to Cambridge. It also operates telescopes on La Palma in the Canary Islands, including the 4.2-m/165-in William Herschel Telescope, commissioned 1987.

Schmidt Telescope reflecting telescope used for taking wide-angle photographs of the sky. It was invented 1930 by Estonian astronomer Bernhard Schmidt (1879–1935), and has an added corrector lens to help focus the incoming light. Examples are the 1.2-m/48-in Schmidt telescope on Mount Palomar and the UK Schmidt telescope, of the same size, at Siding Spring.

Siding Spring Mountain peak 400 km/250 mi NW of Sydney, site of the UK Schmidt Telescope, opened 1973, and the 3.9-m/154-in Anglo-Australian Telescope, opened 1975, which was the first big telescope to be fully computer-controlled. It is one of the most powerful telescopes in the southern hemisphere.

South African Astronomical Observatory national observatory of South Africa at Sutherland, founded 1973 after the merger of the Royal Observatory, Cape Town, and the Republic Observatory, Johannesburg, and operated by the Council for Scientific and Industrial Research of South Africa. Its main telescope is a 1.88-m/74-in reflector formerly at the Radcliffe Observatory, Pretoria.

telescope optical instrument that magnifies images of faint and distant objects; any device for collecting and focusing light and other forms of electromagnetic radiation. It is a major research tool in astronomy and is used to sight over land and sea; small telescopes can be attached to cameras and rifles. A telescope with a large aperture, or opening, can distinguish finer detail and fainter objects than one with a small aperture. The *refracting telescope* uses lenses, and the *reflecting telescope* uses mirrors. A third type, the *catadioptric telescope*, with a combination of lenses and mirrors, is used increasingly.

United Kingdom Infrared Telescope (UKIRT) 3.8-m/150-in reflecting telescope for observing at infrared wavelengths, opened in 1978 on Mauna Kea, Hawaii, USA, and operated by the Royal Observatory, Edinburgh, Scotland.

US Naval Observatory US government observatory in Washington DC, which provides the nation's time service and publishes almanacs for navigators, surveyors, and astronomers. It contains a 66-cm/26-in refracting telescope opened 1873. A 1.55-m/61-in reflector for measuring positions of celestial objects was opened 1964 at Flagstaff, Arizona.

Very Large Array (VLA) largest and most complex single-site radio telescope in the world. It is located on the Plains of San Augustine, 80 km/50 mi W of Socorro, New Mexico, USA. It consists of 27 dish antennae, each 25 m/82 ft in diameter, arranged along three equally spaced arms forming a Y-shaped array. Two of the arms are 21 km/13 mi long, and the third, to the north, is 19 km/11.8 mi long. The dishes are mounted on railway tracks, enabling the configuration and size of the array to be altered as required.

Yerkes Observatory astronomical centre in Wisconsin, USA, founded 1897. It houses the world's largest refracting optical telescope, with a lens of 102 cm/40 in diameter.

Zelenchukskaya site of the world's largest single-mirror optical telescope, with a mirror of 6 m/236 in diameter, in the Caucasus Mountains of Russia. At the same site is the RATAN 600 radio telescope, consisting of radio reflectors in a circle of 600 m/2,000 ft diameter. Both instruments are operated by the Academy of Sciences in St Petersburg.

Astronomers and Astronauts

Adams John Couch 1819–1892. English astronomer who mathematically deduced the existence of the planet Neptune 1845 from the effects of its gravitational pull on the motion of Uranus, although it was not found until 1846 by J G Galle. Adams also studied the Moon's motion, the Leonid meteors, and terrestrial magnetism.

Airy George Biddell 1801–1892. English astronomer who installed a transit telescope at the Royal Observatory at Greenwich, England, and accurately measured Greenwich Mean Time by the stars as they crossed the meridian.

Aldrin Edwin (Eugene 'Buzz') 1930– . US astronaut who landed on the Moon with Neil Armstrong during the *Apollo 11* mission in July 1969, becoming the second person to set foot on the Moon.

Anaximander c. 610–c. 546 BC. Greek astronomer and philosopher. He claimed that the Earth was a cylinder three times wider than it is deep, motionless at the centre of the universe, and the celestial bodies were fire seen through holes in the hollow rims of wheels encircling the Earth. He is thought to have been the first to determine solstices and equinoxes.

Aristarchus of Samos c. 320–c. 250 BC. Greek astronomer. The first to argue that the Earth moves around the Sun, he was ridiculed for his beliefs. He was also the first astronomer to estimate the sizes of the Sun and Moon and their distances from the Earth.

Armstrong Neil Alden 1930– . US astronaut. In 1969, he became the first person to set foot on the Moon, and said, 'That's one small step for a man, one giant leap for mankind.' The Moon landing was part of the Apollo project.

Baade Walter 1893–1960. German-born US astronomer who made observations that doubled the scale and age of the universe. Baade worked at Mount Wilson Observatory, USA, and discovered that stars are in two distinct populations according to their age, known as Population I (the younger) and Population II (the older). Later, he found that Cepheid variable stars of Population I are brighter than had been supposed, and hence farther away.

Bessel Friedrich Wilhelm 1784–1846. German astronomer and mathematician, the first person to find the approximate distance to a star by direct methods when he measured the parallax (annual displacement) of the star 61 Cygni in 1838.

Bode Johann Elert 1747–1826. German astronomer who published the first atlas of all stars visible to the naked eye, *Uranographia* 1801. He devised Bode's law, a numerical sequence that gives the approximate distance of the planets from the Sun.

Bradley James 1693–1762. English astronomer who in 1728 discovered the aberration of starlight. From the amount of aberration in star positions, he was able to calculate the speed of light. In 1748, he announced the discovery of nutation (variation in the Earth's axial tilt).

Brahe Tycho 1546–1601. Danish astronomer who made accurate observations of the planets from which German astronomer and mathematician Johannes Kepler proved that planets orbit the Sun in ellipses. His discovery and report of the 1572 supernova brought him recognition, and his observations of the comet of 1577 proved that it moved on an orbit among the planets, thus disproving the Greek view that comets were in the Earth's atmosphere.

Cannon Annie Jump 1863–1941. US astronomer who, from 1896, worked at Harvard College Observatory and carried out revolutionary work on the classification of stars by examining their spectra. Her system, still used today, has spectra arranged according to temperature and runs from O through B, A, F, G, K, and M. O-type stars are the hottest, with surface temperatures of over 25,000 K.

Cassini Giovanni Domenico 1625–1712. Italian-French astronomer who discovered four moons of Saturn and the gap in the rings of Saturn now called the *Cassini division*.

Chandrasekhar Subrahmanyan 1910–1995. Indian-born US astrophysicist who made pioneering studies of the structure and evolution of stars. The *Chandrasekhar limit* of 1.4 Suns is the maximum mass of a white dwarf before it turns into a neutron star. Nobel Prize for Physics 1983.

Copernicus Nicolaus 1473–1543. Polish astronomer who believed that the Sun, not the Earth, is at the centre of the Solar System, thus defying the

Christian church doctrine of the time. For 30 years he worked on the hypothesis that the rotation and the orbital motion of the Earth were responsible for the apparent movement of the heavenly bodies. His great work *De Revolutionibus Orbium Coelestium/About the Revolutions of the Heavenly Spheres* was not published until the year of his death.

Eddington Arthur Stanley 1882–1944. British astrophysicist who studied the motions, equilibrium, luminosity, and atomic structure of the stars. In 1919 his observation of stars during an eclipse confirmed Einstein's prediction that light is bent when passing near the Sun. In *The Expanding Universe* 1933 he expressed the theory that in the spherical universe the outer galaxies or spiral nebulae are receding from one another.

Flamsteed John 1646–1719. English astronomer who began systematic observations of the positions of the stars, Moon, and planets at the Royal Observatory he founded at Greenwich, London, 1676. His observations were published 1725.

Gagarin Yuri (Alexeyevich) 1934–1968. Soviet cosmonaut who in 1961 became the first human in space, aboard the spacecraft *Vostok 1*, completing one orbit of the Earth.

Galle Johann Gottfried 1812–1910. German astronomer who located the planet Neptune 1846, close to the position predicted by French astronomer Urbain Leverrier.

Glenn John (Herschel), Jr 1921– . US astronaut and politician. On 20 Feb 1962, he became the first American to orbit the Earth, doing so three times in the Mercury spacecraft *Friendship 7*, in a flight lasting 4 hr 55 min. After retiring from NASA, he was elected to the US Senate as a Democrat from Ohio 1974.

Hale George Ellery 1868–1938. US astronomer who made pioneer studies of the Sun and founded three major observatories. In 1889 he invented the spectroheliograph, a device for photographing the Sun at particular wavelengths. In 1897 he founded the Yerkes Observatory in Wisconsin, and in 1917 he established on Mount Wilson, California, a 2.5-m/100-in reflector, the world's largest telescope until superseded 1948 by the 5-m/200-in reflector on Mount Palomar, which Hale had planned just before he died.

Halley Edmond 1656–1742. English atronomer who not only identified 1705 the comet that was later to be known by his name, but also compiled a star catalogue, detected the proper motion of stars using historical records, and began a line of research that – after his death – resulted in a reasonably accurate calculation of the astronomical unit.

Herschel John Frederick William 1792–1871. English scientist and astronomer, son of William Herschel. He discovered thousands of close double stars, clusters, and nebulae, reported 1847. His inventions include astronomical instruments.

Herschel William 1738–1822. German-born English astronomer. He was a skilled telescope maker, and pioneered the study of binary stars and nebulae. He discovered the planet Uranus 1781 and infrared solar rays 1801. He catalogued over 800 double stars, and found over 2,500 nebulae, catalogued by his

Astronomers Royal

John Flamsteed	1675–1719
Edmond Halley	1720–1742
James Bradley	1742–1762
Nathaniel Bliss	1762–1764
Nevil Maskelyne	1765–1811
John Pond	1811–1835
George Airy	1835–1881
William Christie	1881–1910
Frank Dyson	1910–1933
Harold Spencer Jones	1933–1955
Richard Woolley	1956–1971
Martin Ryle	1972–1982
F Graham Smith	1982–1990
Arnold Wolfendale	1991–

sister *Caroline Herschel* (1750–1848); this work was continued by his son John Herschel. By studying the distribution of stars, William established the basic form of our Galaxy, the Milky Way.

Hewish Antony 1924– . British radio astronomer who was awarded, with Martin Ryle, the Nobel Prize for Physics 1974 for his work on pulsars, rapidly rotating neutron stars that emit pulses of energy.

Hipparchus *c.* 190–*c.* 120 BC. Greek astronomer who invented trigonometry, calculated the lengths of the solar year and the lunar month, discovered the precession of the equinoxes, made a catalogue of 800 fixed stars, and advanced Eratosthenes' method of determining the situation of places on the Earth's surface by lines of latitude and longitude.

Hoyle Fred(erick) 1915– . English astronomer and writer. In 1948 he joined with Hermann Bondi (1919–) and Thomas Gold (1920–) in developing the steady-state theory. In 1957, with Geoffrey and Margaret Burbidge (1925– and 1919–) and William Fowler (1911–), he showed that chemical elements heavier than hydrogen and helium are built up by nuclear reactions inside stars. He has suggested that life originates in the gas clouds of space and is delivered to the Earth by passing comets.

Hubble Edwin Powell 1889–1953. US astronomer who discovered the existence of other galaxies outside our own, and classified them according to their shape. In 1929 he announced *Hubble's law*, which states that the galaxies are moving apart at a rate that increases with their distance.

Jansky Karl Guthe 1905–1950. US radio engineer who discovered that the Milky Way Galaxy emanates radio waves; he did not follow up his discovery, but it marked the birth of radioastronomy.

Kepler Johannes 1571–1630. German mathematician and astronomer. He formulated what are now called *Kepler's laws* of planetary motion: (1) the orbit of each planet is an ellipse with the Sun at one of the foci; (2) the radius vector of each planet sweeps out equal areas in equal times; (3) the squares of the periods of the planets are proportional to the cubes of their mean distances from the Sun.

Laplace Pierre Simon, Marquis de Laplace 1749–1827. French astronomer and mathematician. In 1796, he theorized that the Solar System originated from a cloud of gas (the nebular hypothesis). He studied the motion of the Moon and planets, and published a five-volume survey of celestial mechanics, *Traité de méchanique céleste* 1799–1825. Among his mathematical achievements was the development of probability theory.

Leavitt Henrietta Swan 1868–1921. US astronomer who in 1912 discovered the *period–luminosity law* that links the brightness of a Cepheid variable star to its period of variation. This law allows astronomers to use Cepheid variables as 'standard candles' for measuring distances in space.

Lemaître Georges Edouard 1894–1966. Belgian cosmologist who in 1927 proposed the Big Bang theory of the origin of the universe. He predicted that the entire universe was expanding, which the US astronomer Edwin Hubble confirmed. Lemaître suggested that the expansion had been started by an initial explosion, the Big Bang, a theory that is now generally accepted.

Leonov Aleksei Arkhipovich 1934– . Soviet cosmonaut. In 1965 he was the first person to walk in space, from the spacecraft *Voskhod 2*.

Leverrier Urbain Jean Joseph 1811–1877. French astronomer who predicted the existence and position of the planet Neptune, discovered in 1846.

Lovell Bernard 1913– . British radio astronomer, director until 1981 of Jodrell Bank Experimental Station (now Nuffield Radio Astronomy Laboratories).

Lowell Percival 1855–1916. US astronomer who predicted the existence of a 'Planet X' beyond Neptune, and started the search that led to the discovery of Pluto in 1930. In 1894 he founded the Lowell Observatory at Flagstaff, Arizona, where he reported seeing the apparent 'canals' on Mars previously reported by Giovanni Schiaparelli.

Messier Charles 1730–1817. French astronomer who discovered 15 comets and in 1781 published a list of 103 star clusters and nebulae. Objects on this list are given M (for Messier) numbers, which astronomers still use today, such as M1 (the Crab nebula) and M31 (the Andromeda galaxy).

Olbers Heinrich 1758–1840. German astronomer, a founder member of the *Celestial Police*, a group of astronomers who attempted to locate a supposed 'missing planet' between Mars and Jupiter. During his search he discovered two asteroids, Pallas 1802 and Vesta 1807. Also credited to Olbers are a number of comet discoveries and a new method of calculating cometary orbits.

Oort Jan Hendrik 1900–1992. Dutch astronomer. In 1927, he calculated the mass and size of our Galaxy, the Milky Way, and the Sun's distance from its centre, from the observed movements of stars around the Galaxy's centre. In 1950 Oort proposed that comets exist in a vast swarm, now called the *Oort cloud*, at the edge of the Solar System.

Piazzi Giuseppe 1746–1826. Italian astronomer who in 1801 identified the first asteroid, which he named Ceres. He was director of Palermo Observatory.

Ptolemy (Claudius Ptolemaeus) *c.* 100–170. Egyptian astronomer and geographer who worked in Alexandria. His *Almagest* developed the theory that Earth is the centre of the universe, with the Sun, Moon, and stars revolving around it. In 1543 the Polish astronomer Copernicus proposed an alternative to the *Ptolemaic system*.

Ryle Martin 1918–1984. English radioastronomer. At the Mullard Radio Astronomy Observatory, Cambridge, he developed the technique of sky-mapping using 'aperture synthesis', combining smaller dish aerials to give the characteristics of one large one. His work on the distribution of radio sources in the universe brought confirmation of the Big Bang theory. He won, with Antony Hewish, the Nobel Prize for Physics 1974.

Schiaparelli Giovanni (Virginio) 1835–1910. Italian astronomer who thought he discovered canals on Mars. He studied ancient and medieval astronomy, discovered the asteroid 69 (Hesperia) April 1861, observed double stars, and revealed the connection between comets and meteors. In 1877 he was the first to draw attention to apparent linear markings on Mars, which gave rise to a controversy over whether they could be canals. These markings are now known to be optical effects and not real lines.

Shapley Harlow 1885–1972. US astronomer whose study of globular clusters showed that they were arranged in a halo around the Galaxy, and that the Galaxy was much larger than previously thought. He realized that the Sun was not at the centre of the Galaxy as then assumed, but two-thirds of the way out to the rim.

Shepard Alan (Bartlett) 1923– . US astronaut, the fifth person to walk on the Moon. He was the first American in space, as pilot of the suborbital *Mercury-Redstone 3* mission on board the *Freedom 7* capsule May 1961, and commanded the *Apollo 14* lunar landing mission 1971.

Struve Friedrich Georg Wilhelm 1793–1864. German-born Russian astronomer, a pioneer in the observation of double stars. The founder and first director (from 1839) of Pulkovo Observatory near St Petersburg, he was succeeded by his son *Otto Wilhelm Struve* (1819–1905). His great-grandson *Otto Struve* (1897–1963) left the USSR in 1921 for the USA, where he became joint director of the Yerkes and McDonald observatories 1932 and championed the notion that planetary systems were common around stars.

Tereshkova Valentina Vladimirovna 1937– . Soviet cosmonaut, the first woman to fly in space. In June 1963 she made a three-day flight in *Vostok 6*, orbiting the Earth 48 times.

Tombaugh Clyde (William) 1906– . US astronomer who discovered the planet Pluto 1930. He was an assistant at the Lowell Observatory in Flagstaff, Arizona.

Van Allen James (Alfred) 1914– . US physicist whose instruments aboard the first US satellite *Explorer 1* 1958 led to the discovery of the Van Allen belts, two zones of intense radiation around the Earth. He pioneered high-altitude research with rockets after World War II.

CHEMISTRY

Divisions

analytical chemistry branch of chemistry that deals with the determination of the chemical composition of substances. *Qualitative analysis* determines the identities of the substances in a given sample; *quantitative analysis* determines how much of a particular substance is present.

biochemistry science concerned with the chemistry of living organisms: the structure and reactions of proteins (such as enzymes), nucleic acids, carbohydrates, and lipids. Its study has led to an increased understanding of life processes, such as those by which organisms synthesize essential chemicals from food materials, store and generate energy, and pass on their characteristics through their genetic material. A great deal of medical research is concerned with the ways in which these processes are disrupted. Biochemistry also has applications in agriculture and in the food industry (for instance, in the use of enzymes).

inorganic chemistry branch of chemistry dealing with the chemical properties of the elements and their compounds, excluding the more complex covalent compounds of carbon, which are considered in organic chemistry.

organic chemistry branch of chemistry that deals with carbon compounds. Organic compounds form the chemical basis of life and are more abundant than inorganic compounds. In a typical organic compound, each carbon atom forms bonds covalently with each of its neighbouring carbon atoms in a chain or ring, and additionally with other atoms, commonly hydrogen, oxygen, nitrogen, or sulphur. Compounds containing only carbon and hydrogen are known as *hydrocarbons*.

physical chemistry branch of chemistry concerned with examining the relationships between the chemical compositions of substances and the physical properties that they display. Most chemical reactions exhibit some physical phenomenon (change of state, temperature, pressure, or volume, or the use or production of electricity), and the measurement and study of such phenomena has led to many chemical theories and laws.

Biochemistry

amino acid water-soluble organic molecule, mainly composed of carbon, oxygen, hydrogen, and nitrogen, containing both a basic amino group (NH_2) and an acidic carboxyl (COOH) group. When two or more amino acids are joined together, they are known as peptides; proteins are made up of interacting polypeptides (peptide chains consisting of more than three amino acids) and are folded or twisted in characteristic shapes.

Many different proteins are found in the cells of living organisms, but they are all made up of the same 20 amino acids, joined together in varying combinations (although other types of amino acid do occur infrequently in nature). Eight of these, the *essential amino acids*, cannot be synthesized by humans and must be obtained from the diet. Children need a further two amino acids that are not essential for adults. Other animals also need some preformed amino acids in their diet, but green plants can manufacture all the amino acids they need from simpler molecules, relying on energy from the Sun and minerals (including nitrates) from the soil.

ATP abbreviation for *adenosine triphosphate*, a nucleotide molecule found in all cells. It can yield large amounts of energy, and is used to drive the thousands of biological processes needed to sustain life, growth, movement, and reproduction. Green plants use light energy to manufacture ATP as part of the process of photosynthesis. In animals, ATP is formed by the breakdown of glucose molecules, usually obtained from the carbohydrate component of a diet, in a series of reactions termed respiration. It is the driving force behind muscle contraction and the synthesis of complex molecules needed by individual cells.

carbohydrate chemical compound composed of carbon, hydrogen, and oxygen, with the basic formula $C_m(H_2O)_n$, and related compounds with the same basic structure but modified functional groups. As sugar and starch, carbohydrates form a major energy-providing part of the human diet. The simplest carbohydrates are sugars (*monosaccharides*, such as glucose and fructose, and *disaccharides*, such as sucrose), which are soluble compounds, some with a sweet taste. When these basic sugar units are joined together in long chains or branching structures they form *polysaccharides*, such as starch and glycogen, which often serve as food stores in living organisms. Even more complex carbohydrates are known, including chitin, which is found in the cell walls of fungi and the hard outer skeletons of insects, and cellulose, which makes up the cell walls of plants. Carbohydrates form the chief foodstuffs of herbivorous animals.

disaccharide sugar made up of two monosaccharides or simple sugars, such as glucose or fructose. Sucrose, $C_{12}H_{22}O_{11}$, or table sugar, is a disaccharide.

DNA (*deoxyribonucleic acid*) complex giant molecule that contains, in chemically coded form, all the information needed to build, control, and maintain a living organism. DNA is a ladderlike double-stranded nucleic acid that forms the basis of genetic inheritance in all organisms, except for a few viruses that have only RNA. In organisms other than bacteria it is organized into chromosomes and contained in the cell nucleus.

DNA is made up of two chains of nucleotide subunits, with each nucleotide containing either a purine (adenine or guanine) or pyrimidine (cytosine or thymine) base. The bases link up with each other (adenine linking with thymine, and cytosine with guanine) to form base pairs that connect the two strands of the DNA molecule like the rungs of a twisted ladder. The specific way in which the pairs form means that the base sequence is preserved from generation to generation.

Biochemistry: chronology

c. 1830	Johannes Müller discovered proteins.
1833	Anselme Payen and J F Persoz first isolated an enzyme.
1862	Haemoglobin was first crystallized.
1869	The genetic material DNA (deoxyribonucleic acid) was discovered by Friedrich Mieschler
1899	Emil Fischer postulated the 'lock-and-key' hypothesis to explain the specificity of enzyme action.
1913	Leonor Michaelis and M L Menten developed a mathematical equation describing the rate of enzyme-catalysed reactions
1915	The hormone thyroxine was first isolated from thyroid-gland tissue.
1920	The chromosome theory of heredity was postulated by Thomas H Morgan; growth hormone was discovered by Herbert McLean Evans and J A Long.
1921	Insulin was first isolated from the pancreas by Frederick Banting and Charles Best.
1926	Insulin was obtained in pure crystalline form.
1927	Thyroxine was first synthesized.
1928	Alexander Fleming discovered penicillin.
1931	Paul Karrer deduced the structure of retinol (vitamin A); vitamin D compounds were obtained in crystalline form by Adolf Windaus and Askew, independently of each other.
1932	Charles Glen King isolated ascorbic acid (vitamin C).
1933	Tadeus Reichstein synthesized ascorbic acid.
1935	Richard Kuhn and Karrer established the structure of riboflavin (vitamin B_2).
1936	Robert Williams established the structure of thiamine (vitamin B_1); biotin was isolated by Kogl and Tonnis.
1937	Niacin was isolated and identified by Conrad Arnold Elvehjem.
1938	Pyridoxine (vitamin B_6) was isolated in pure crystalline form.
1939	The structure of pyridoxine was determined by Kuhn.
1940	Hans Krebs proposed the citric acid (Krebs) cycle; Hickman isolated retinol in pure crystalline form; Williams established the structure of pantothenic acid; biotin was identified by Albert Szent-Györgyi, Vincent Du Vigneaud, and co-workers.
1941	Penicillin was isolated and characterized by Howard Florey and Ernst Chain.
1943	The role of DNA in genetic inheritance was first demonstrated by Oswald Avery, Colin MacLeod, and Maclyn McCarty.
1950	The basic components of DNA were established by Erwin Chargaff; the alpha-helical structure of proteins was established by Linus Pauling and R B Corey.
1953	James Watson and Francis Crick determined the molecular structure of DNA.
1956	Mahlon Hoagland and Paul Zamecnick discovered transfer RNA (ribonucleic acid); mechanisms for the biosynthesis of RNA and DNA were discovered by Arthur Kornberg and Severo Ochoa.
1957	Interferon was discovered by Alick Isaacs and Jean Lindemann.
1958	The structure of RNA was determined.
1960	Messenger RNA was discovered by Sydney Brenner and François Jacob.
1961	Marshall Nirenberg and Severo Ochoa determined the chemical nature of the genetic code.
1965	Insulin was first synthesized.
1966	The immobilization of enzymes was achieved by Chibata.
1968	Brain hormones were discovered by Roger Guillemin and Andrew Schally.
1975	J Hughes and Hans Kosterlitz discovered encephalins.
1976	Guillemin discovered endorphins.
1977	J Baxter determined the genetic code for human growth hormone.
1978	Human insulin was first produced by genetic engineering.
1979	The biosynthetic production of human growth hormone was announced by Howard Goodman and J Baxter of the University of California, and by D V Goeddel and Seeburg of Genentech.
1982	Louis Chedid and Michael Sela developed the first synthesized vaccine.
1983	The first commercially available product of genetic engineering (Humulin) was launched.
1985	Alec Jeffreys devised genetic fingerprinting.
1993	UK researchers introduced a healthy version of the gene for cystic fibrosis into the lungs of mice with induced cystic fibrosis, restoring normal function.

enzyme biological catalyst produced in cells, and capable of speeding up the chemical reactions necessary for life by converting one molecule (substrate) into another. Enzymes are not themselves destroyed by this process. They are large, complex proteins, and are highly specific, each chemical reaction requiring its own particular enzyme. The enzyme fits into a 'slot' (active site) in the substrate molecule, forming an enzyme–substrate complex that lasts until the substrate is altered or split, after which the enzyme can fall away. The substrate may therefore be compared to a lock, and the enzyme to the key required to open it. (See *Life Sciences* for more on enzymes.)

fat in the broadest sense, a mixture of lipids – chiefly triglycerides (lipids containing three fatty acid molecules linked to a molecule of glycerol). More specifically, the term refers to a lipid mixture that is solid at room temperature (20°C); lipid mixtures that are liquid at room temperature are called *oils*. The higher the proportion of saturated fatty acids in a mixture, the harder the fat. Fats are essential constituents of food for many animals, with a calorific value twice that of carbohydrates; however, eating too much fat, especially fat of animal origin, has been linked with heart disease in humans. In many animals and plants, excess carbohydrates and proteins are converted into fats for storage. Mammals and other vertebrates store fats in specialized connective tissues (adipose tissues), which not only act as energy reserves but also insulate the body and cushion its organs.

glucose or *dextrose* or *grape-sugar* $C_6H_{12}O_6$ sugar present in the blood, and found also in honey and fruit juices. It is a source of energy for the body, being produced from other sugars and starches to form the 'energy currency' of many biochemical reactions also involving ATP. Glucose is prepared in syrup form by the hydrolysis of cane sugar or starch, and may be purified to a white crystalline powder. Glucose is a monosaccharide sugar (made up of a single sugar unit), unlike the more familiar sucrose (cane or beet sugar), which is a disaccharide (made up of two sugar units: glucose and fructose).

immunoglobulin human globulin protein that can be separated from blood and administered to confer immediate immunity on the recipient. It participates in the immune reaction as the antibody for a specific antigen (disease-causing agent). Normal immunoglobulin (gamma globulin) is the fraction of the blood serum that, in general, contains the most antibodies, and is obtained from plasma pooled from about a thousand donors. It is given for short-term (two to three months) protection when a person is at risk, mainly from hepatitis A (infectious hepatitis), or when a pregnant woman, not immunized against German measles, is exposed to the rubella virus. Specific immunoglobulins are injected when a nonimmunized person is at risk of infection from a potentially fatal disease, such as hepatitis B (serum hepatitis), rabies, or tetanus. These immunoglobulins are prepared from blood pooled from donors convalescing from the disease.

isoenzyme or *isozyme* one of a number of enzymes (biological catalysts) that act within the same organism on the same substrate but differ from each other in their affinity for that substrate or in their regulatory properties. Different isoenzymes are usually coded by different genes and can be separated from each other by such methods as electrophoresis.

Krebs cycle or *citric acid cycle* or *tricarboxylic acid cycle* final part of the chain of biochemical reactions by which organisms break down food using oxygen to release energy (respiration). It takes place within structures called mitochondria in the body's cells, and breaks down food molecules in a series of small steps, producing energy-rich molecules of ATP.

lipid any of a large number of esters of fatty acids, commonly formed by the reaction of a fatty acid with glycerol. They are soluble in alcohol but not in water. Lipids are the chief constituents of plant and animal waxes, fats, and oils. Phospholipids are lipids that also contain a phosphate group, usually linked to an organic base; they are major components of biological cell membranes.

metabolism the chemical processes of living organisms: a constant alternation of building up (*anabolism*) and breaking down (*catabolism*). For

example, green plants build up complex organic substances from water, carbon dioxide, and mineral salts (photosynthesis); by digestion animals partially break down complex organic substances, ingested as food, and subsequently resynthesize them in their own bodies.

monosaccharide or *simple sugar* carbohydrate that cannot be hydrolysed (split) into smaller carbohydrate units. Examples are glucose and fructose, both of which have the molecular formula $C_6H_{12}O_6$.

nucleic acid complex organic acid made up of a long chain of nucleotides. The two types, known as DNA (deoxyribonucleic acid) and RNA (ribonucleic acid), form the basis of heredity. The nucleotides are made up of a sugar (deoxyribose or ribose), a phosphate group, and one of four purine or pyrimidine bases. The order of the bases along the nucleic acid strand contains the genetic code.

nucleotide organic compound consisting of a purine (adenine or guanine) or a pyrimidine (thymine, uracil, or cytosine) base linked to a sugar (deoxyribose or ribose) and a phosphate group. DNA and RNA are made up of long chains of nucleotides.

peptide molecule comprising two or more amino acid molecules (not necessarily different) joined by *peptide bonds*, whereby the acid group of one acid is linked to the amino group of the other (–CO.NH). The number of amino acid molecules in the peptide is indicated by referring to it as a di-, tri-, or polypeptide (two, three, or many amino acids). Proteins are built up of interacting polypeptide chains with various types of bonds occurring between the chains. Incomplete hydrolysis (splitting up) of a protein yields a mixture of peptides, examination of which helps to determine the sequence in which the amino acids occur within the protein.

polysaccharide long-chain carbohydrate made up of hundreds or thousands of linked simple sugars (monosaccharides) such as glucose and closely related molecules. The polysaccharides are natural polymers. They either act as energy-rich food stores in plants (starch) and animals (glycogen), or have structural roles in the plant cell wall (cellulose, pectin) or the tough outer skeleton of insects and similar creatures (chitin).

protein complex, biologically important substance composed of amino acids joined by peptide bonds. Other types of bond, such as sulphur–sulphur bonds, hydrogen bonds, and cation bridges between acid sites, are responsible for creating the protein's characteristic three-dimensional structure, which may be fibrous, globular, or pleated. (See *Life Sciences* for more on protein.)

recombinant DNA in genetic engineering, DNA formed by splicing together genes from different sources into new combinations.

respiration biochemical process whereby food molecules are progressively broken down (oxidized) to release energy in the form of ATP. In most organisms this requires oxygen, but in some bacteria the oxidant is the nitrate or sulphate ion instead. In all higher organisms, respiration occurs in the mitochondria. Respiration is also used to mean breathing, although this is more accurately described as a form of gas exchange.

RNA *ribonucleic acid* nucleic acid involved in the process of translating the genetic material DNA into proteins. It is usually single-stranded, unlike the double-stranded DNA, and consists of a large number of nucleotides strung together, each of which comprises the sugar ribose, a phosphate group, and one of four bases (uracil, cytosine, adenine, or guanine). RNA is copied from DNA by the formation of base pairs, with uracil taking the place of thymine.

RNA occurs in three major forms, each with a different function in the synthesis of protein molecules. *Messenger RNA* (mRNA) acts as the template for protein synthesis. Each codon (a set of three bases) on the RNA molecule is matched up with the corresponding amino acid, in accordance with the genetic code. This process (translation) takes place in the ribosomes, which are made up of proteins and *ribosomal RNA* (rRNA). *Transfer RNA* (tRNA) is responsible for combining with specific amino acids, and then matching up a special 'anticodon' sequence of its own with a codon on the mRNA. This is how the genetic code is translated.

Although RNA is normally associated only with the process of protein synthesis, it makes up the hereditary material itself in some viruses, such as retroviruses.

steroid any of a group of cyclic, unsaturated alcohols (lipids without fatty acid components), which, like sterols, have a complex molecular structure consisting of four carbon rings. Steroids include the sex hormones, such as testosterone, the corticosteroid hormones produced by the adrenal gland, bile acids, and cholesterol. The term is commonly used to refer to anabolic steroid.

sterol any of a group of solid, cyclic, unsaturated alcohols, with a complex structure that includes four carbon rings; cholesterol is an example. Steroids are derived from sterols.

substrate a compound or mixture of compounds acted on by an enzyme. The term also refers to a substance such as agar that provides the nutrients for the metabolism of microorganisms. Since the enzyme systems of microorganisms regulate their metabolism, the essential meaning is the same.

sugar or *sucrose* sweet, soluble crystalline carbohydrate found in the pith of sugar cane and in sugar beet. It is a *disaccharide* sugar, each of its molecules being made up of two simple-sugar (*monosaccharide*) units: glucose and fructose. Sugar is easily digested and forms a major source of energy in humans, being used in cooking and in the food industry as a sweetener and, in high concentrations, as a preservative.

urea $CO(NH_2)_2$ waste product formed in the mammalian liver when nitrogen compounds are broken down. It is excreted in urine. When purified, it is a white, crystalline solid. In industry it is used to make urea-formaldehyde plastics (or resins), pharmaceuticals, and fertilizers.

vitamin any of various chemically unrelated organic compounds that are necessary in small quantities for the normal functioning of the body. Many act as coenzymes, small molecules that enable enzymes to function effectively. They are normally present in adequate amounts in a balanced diet. Deficiency of a vitamin will normally lead to a metabolic disorder ('deficiency disease'), which can be remedied by sufficient intake of the vitamin. They are generally classified as *water-soluble* (B and C) or *fat-soluble* (A, D, E, and K).

Inorganic Chemistry

ammonia NH_3 colourless, pungent-smelling gas, lighter than air and very soluble in water. It is made on an industrial scale by the Haber process, and is used mainly to produce nitrogenous fertilizers, some explosives, and nitric acid.

aqua regia mixture of three parts concentrated hydrochloric acid and one part concentrated nitric acid, which dissolves all metals except silver.

bauxite principal ore of aluminium, consisting of a mixture of hydrated aluminium oxides and hydroxides, generally contaminated with compounds of iron, which give it a red colour. To produce aluminium the ore is processed into a white powder (alumina), which is then smelted by passing a large electric current through it.

carbon nonmetallic element, symbol C, atomic number 6, relative atomic mass 12.011. It is one of the most widely distributed elements, both inorganically and organically, and occurs in combination with other elements in all plants and animals. The atoms of carbon can link with one another in rings or chains, giving rise to innumerable complex compounds. It occurs in nature (1) in the pure state in three crystalline forms of graphite, diamond, and various fullerenes; (2) as calcium carbonate ($CaCO_3$) in carbonaceous rocks such as chalk and limestone; (3) as carbon dioxide (CO_2) in the atmosphere; and (4) as hydrocarbons in the fossil fuels petroleum, coal, and natural gas. Noncrystalline forms of pure carbon include charcoal and coal. When added to steel, carbon forms a wide range of alloys. In its elemental form, it is widely used as a moderator in nuclear reactors; as colloidal graphite it is a good lubricant, which, when deposited on a surface in a vacuum, obviates photoelectric and secondary emission of electrons. The radioactive isotope C-14 (half-life 5,730 years) is widely used in archaeological dating and as a tracer in biological research. Analysis of interstellar dust has led to the discovery of discrete carbon molecules, each containing 60 carbon atoms. These C_{60} molecules have been named buckminsterfullerenes.

ferrite ceramic ferrimagnetic material. Ferrites are iron oxides to which small quantities of transition metal oxides (such as cobalt and nickel oxides) have been added. They are used in transformer cores, radio antenna, and, formerly, in computer memories.

gallium arsenide GaAs compound of gallium and arsenic that has been proposed as a rival to silicon as a semiconductor material for microprocessors. Chips made from gallium arsenide require less electric power and process data faster than those made from silicon.

gold heavy, precious, yellow, metallic element; symbol Au, atomic number 79, relative atomic mass 197.0. It is unaffected by temperature changes and is highly resistant to acids. For manufacture, gold is

Chemical elements

Symbol	Name	Atomic number	Atomic mass[1]	Melting or fusing point (°C)	Relative density
Ac	Actinium	89	(227)	–	–
Ag	Silver	47	107.868	10.5	960
Al	Aluminium	13	26.9815	2.58	658
Am	Americium	95	(243)	–	–
Ar	Argon	18	39.948	gas	–188
As	Arsenic	33	74.9216	5.73	Volatile, 450
At	Astatine	85	(210)	–	–
Au	Gold	79	196.9665	19.3	1,062
B	Boron	5	10.81	2.5	2,300
Ba	Barium	56	137.34	3.75	850
Be	Beryllium	4	9.0122	1.93	1,281
Bi	Bismuth	83	208.9806	9.80	268
Bk	Berkelium	97	(249)	–	–
Br	Bromine	35	79.904	3.19	–7.3
C	Carbon	6	12.011	3.52	Infusible
Ca	Calcium	20	40.08	1.58	851
Cd	Cadmium	48	112.40	8.64	320
Ce	Cerium	58	140.12	6.68	623
Cf	Californium	98	(251)	–	–
Cl	Chlorine	17	35.453	gas	–102
Cm	Curium	96	(247)	–	–
Co	Cobalt	27	58.9332	8.6	1,490
Cr	Chromium	24	51.996	6.5	1,510
Cs	Caesium	55	132.9055	1.88	26
Cu	Copper	29	63.546	8.9	1,083
Dy	Dysprosium	66	162.50	–	–
Er	Erbium	68	167.26	4.8	–
Es	Einsteinium	99	(254)	–	–
Eu	Europium	63	151.96	–	–
F	Fluorine	9	18.9984	gas	–223
Fe	Iron	26	55.847	7.86	1,525
Fm	Fermium	100	(253)	–	–
Ga	Gallium	31	69.72	5.95	30
Gd	Gadolinium	64	157.25	–	–
Ge	Germanium	32	72.59	5.47	958
H	Hydrogen	1	1.0080	gas	–258
Ha	Hafnium	72	178.49	12.1	2,500
He	Helium	2	4.0026	gas	–272
Hg	Mercury	80	200.59	13.596	–38.9
Ho	Holmium	67	164.9303	–	–
I	Iodine	53	126.9045	4.95	114
In	Indium	49	114.82	7.4	155
Ir	Iridium	77	192.22	22.4	2,375
K	Potassium	19	39.102	0.87	63
Kr	Krypton	36	83.80	gas	–169
La	Lanthanum	57	138.9055	6.1	810
Li	Lithium	3	6.941	0.585	186
Lu	Lutetium	71	174.97	–	–
Lr	Lawrencium	103	–	–	–
Md	Mendelevium	101	(256)	–	–
Mg	Magnesium	12	24.305	1.74	651
Mn	Manganese	25	54.9380	7.39	1,220
Mo	Molybdenum	42	95.94	10.2	2,500
N	Nitrogen	7	14.0067	gas	–211
Na	Sodium	11	22.9898	0.978	97
Nb	Niobium	41	92.9064	8.4	1,950
Nd	Neodymium	60	144.24	6.96	840
Ne	Neon	10	20.179	gas	–248.6
Ni	Nickel	28	58.71	8.9	1,452
No	Nobelium	102	(254)	–	–
Np	Neptunium	93	(237)	–	–
O	Oxygen	8	15.9994	gas	–227

Chemical elements (cont.)

Symbol	Name	Atomic number	Atomic mass	Melting or fusing point (°C)	Relative density
Os	Osmium	76	190.2	22.48	2,700
P	Phosphorus	15	30.9738	1.8–2.3	44
Pa	Protactinium	91	231.0359	–	–
Pb	Lead	82	207.2	11.37	327
Pd	Palladium	46	106.4	11.4	1,549
Pm	Promethium	61	(145)	–	–
Po	Polonium	84	(210)	–	–
Pr	Praseodymium	59	140.9077	6.48	940
Pt	Platinum	78	195.09	21.5	1,755
Pu	Plutonium	94	(242)	–	–
Ra	Radium	88	226.0254	6.0	700
Rb	Rubidium	37	85.4678	1.52	39
Re	Rhenium	75	186.2	21	3,000
Rh	Rhodium	45	102.9055	12.1	1,950
Rn	Radon	86	(222)	gas	–150
Ru	Ruthenium	44	101.07	12.26	2,400
S	Sulfur	16	32.06	2.07	115–119
Sb	Antimony	51	121.75	6.62	629
Sc	Scandium	21	44.9559	–	–
Se	Selenium	34	78.96	4.5	170–220
Si	Silicon	14	28.086	2.0–2.4	1,370
Sm	Samarium	62	150.4	7.7	1,350
Sn	Tin	50	118.69	7.3	232
Sr	Strontium	38	87.62	2.54	800
Ta	Tantalum	73	180.9479	16.6	2,900
Tb	Terbium	65	158.9254	–	–
Tc	Technetium	43	(99)	–	–
Te	Tellurium	52	127.60	6.0	446
Th	Thorium	90	232.0381	11.00	1,750
Ti	Titanium	22	47.90	4.54	1,850
Tl	Thallium	81	204.37	11.85	302
Tm	Thulium	69	168.9342	–	–
U	Uranium	92	238.029	18.7	–
Une	Unnilennium[2]	109	266	–	–
Unh	Unnilhexium[2]	106	263	–	–
Uno	Unniloctium[2]	108	265	–	–
Unp	Unnilpentium[2]	105	262	–	–
Unq	Unnilquadium[2]	104	262	–	–
Uns	Unnilseptium[2]	107	262	–	–
V	Vanadium	23	50.9414	5.5	1,710
W	Tungsten	74	183.85	19.1	2,900–3,000
Xe	Xenon	54	131.30	gas	–140
Y	Yttrium	39	88.9059	3.8	–
Yb	Ytterbium	70	173.04	–	–
Zn	Zinc	30	65.37	7.12	418
Zr	Zirconium	40	91.22	4.15	2,130

[1] the number in brackets refers to the most stable isotope of that element.
[2] elements as yet unnamed; temporary identification assigned until a name is approved by the International Union of Pure and Applied Chemistry. Names proposed for unnilpentium are nielsbohrium and hahnium, and for unnilquadium are kurchatovium and rutherfordium.

alloyed with another strengthening metal (such as copper or silver), its purity being measured in carats on a scale of 24. Like silver, gold is used in printed circuits and for electrical contacts because of its excellent electrical conductivity.

halogen any of a group of five nonmetallic elements with similar chemical bonding properties: fluorine, chlorine, bromine, iodine, and astatine. They form a linked group in the periodic table of the elements, descending from fluorine, the most reactive, to astatine, the least reactive. They combine directly with most metals to form salts, such as common salt (NaCl). Each halogen has seven electrons in its valence shell, which accounts for the chemical similarities displayed by the group.

hydrochloric acid HCl solution of hydrogen chloride (a colourless, acidic gas) in water. The concentrated acid is about 35% hydrogen chloride and is corrosive. The acid is a typical strong, monobasic acid forming only one series of salts, the chlorides. It has many industrial uses, including recovery of zinc from galvanized scrap iron and the production of chlorine. It is also produced in the stomachs of animals for the purposes of digestion.

hydrogen colourless, odourless, gaseous, nonmetallic element, symbol H, atomic number 1, relative atomic mass 1.00797. It is the lightest of all the elements and occurs on Earth chiefly in combination with oxygen as water. Hydrogen is the most abundant element in the universe, where it accounts for 93% of the total number of atoms and 76% of the total mass. It is a component of most stars, including the Sun, whose heat and light are produced through the nuclear-fusion process that converts hydrogen into helium. Its isotopes deuterium and tritium (half-life 12.5 years) are used in nuclear weapons, and deuterons (deuterium nuclei) are used in synthesizing elements.

metal any of a class of chemical elements with certain chemical characteristics (metallic character) and physical properties: they are good conductors of heat and electricity; opaque, but reflect light well; malleable, which enables them to be cold-worked and rolled into sheets; and ductile, which permits them to be drawn into thin wires. Metallic elements compose about 75% of the 109 elements shown in the periodic table of the elements. They form alloys with each other, bases with the hydroxyl radical (OH), and replace the hydrogen in an acid to form a salt. The majority are found in nature in the combined form only, as compounds or mineral ores; about 16 of them also occur in the elemental form, as native metals. Their chemical properties are largely determined by

Transuranic elements

Atomic number	Name	Symbol	Year discovered	Source of first preparation identified	Isotope	Half-life of first isotope identified
Actinide series						
93	neptunium	Np	1940	irradiation of uranium-238 with neutrons	Np-239	2.35 days
94	plutonium	Pu	1941	bombardment of uranium-238 with deuterons	Pu-238	86.4 years
95	americium	Am	1944	irradiation of plutonium-239 with neutrons	Am-241	458 years
96	curium	Cm	1944	bombardment of plutonium-239 with helium nuclei	Cm-242	162.5 days
97	berkelium	Bk	1949	bombardment of americium-241 with helium nuclei	Bk-243	4.5 hours
98	californium	Cf	1950	bombardment of curium-242 with helium nuclei	Cf-245	44 minutes
99	einsteinium	Es	1952	irradiation of uranium-238 with neutrons in first thermonuclear explosion	Es-253	20 days
100	fermium	Fm	1953	irradiation of uranium-238 with neutrons in first thermonuclear explosion	Fm-235	20 hours
101	mendelevium	Md	1955	bombardment of einsteinium-253 with helium nuclei	Md-256	76 minutes
102	nobelium	No	1958	bombardment of curium-246 with carbon nuclei	No-255	2.3 secs
103	lawrencium	Lr	1961	bombardment of californium-252 with boron nuclei	Lr-257	4.3 secs
Transactinide elements						
104	unnilquadium* (also called rutherfordium or kurchatovium)	Unq	1969	bombardment of californium-249 with carbon-12 nuclei	Unq-257	3.4 secs
105	unnilpentium* (also called hahnium or nielsbohrium)	Unp	1970	bombardment of californium-249 with nitrogen-15 nuclei	Unp-260	1.6 secs
106	unnilhexium*	Unh	1974	bombardment of californium-249 with oxygen-18 nuclei	Unh-263	0.9 secs
107	unnilseptium*	Uns	1977	bombardment of bismuth-209 with nuclei of chromium-54	Uns	102 m/secs†
108	unniloctium*	Uno	1984	bombardment of lead-208 with nuclei of iron-58	Uno-265	1.8 m/secs
109	unnilennium*	Une	1982	bombardment of bismuth-209 with nuclei of iron-58	Une	3.4 m/secs

* names for elements 104–109 are as proposed by the International Union for Pure and Applied Chemistry 1980
† m/secs = milliseconds

Discovery of the elements

Date	Element (symbol)	Discoverer	Date	Element (symbol)	Discoverer
prehistoric knowledge	antimony (Sb) arsenic (As) bismuth (Bi) carbon (C) copper (Cu) gold (Au) iron (Fe) lead (Pb) mercury (Hg) silver (Ag) sulphur (S) tin (Sn) zinc (Zn)		1798	beryllium (Be)	Louis-Nicolas Vauquelin (isolated by Friedrich Wöhler and Antoine-Alexandre-Brutus Bussy 1828)
1557	platinum (Pt)	Julius Scaliger	1801	vanadium (V)	Andrés del Rio (disputed), or Nils Sefström 1830
1669	phosphorus (P)	Hennig Brand	1801	niobium (Nb)	Charles Hatchett
1702	boron (B)	Wilhelm Homberg	1802	tantalum (Ta)	Anders Ekeberg
1735	cobalt (Co)	Georg Brandt	1803	cerium (Ce)	Jöns Berzelius and Wilhelm Hisinger, and independently by Martin Klaproth
1751	nickel (Ni)	Axel Cronstedt			
1755	magnesium (Mg)	Joseph Black (isolated by Humphry Davy 1808)		iridium (Ir)	Smithson Tennant
				osmium (Os)	Smithson Tennant
				palladium (Pd)	William Wollaston
				rhodium (Rh)	William Wollaston
1766	hydrogen (H)	Henry Cavendish	1807	potassium (K)	Humphry Davy
1771	fluorine (F)	Karl Scheele (isolated by Henri Moissan 1886)		sodium (Na)	Humphry Davy
			1808	barium (Ba)	Humphry Davy
1772	nitrogen (N)	Daniel Rutherford		boron (B)	Humphry Davy, and independently by Joseph Gay-Lussac and Louis-Jacques Thénard
1774	chlorine (Cl)	Karl Scheele			
	manganese (Mn)	Johann Gottlieb Gahn		calcium (Ca)	Humphry Davy
	oxygen (O)	Joseph Priestley and Karl Scheele, independently of each other		strontium (Sr)	Humphry Davy
			1811	iodine (I)	Bernard Courtois
			1817	cadmium (Cd)	Friedrich Strohmeyer
1778	molybdenum (Mo)	detected by Karl Scheele (isolated by Peter Jacob Hjelm 1782)		lithium (Li)	Johan Arfwedson
				selenium (Se)	Jöns Berzelius
			1823	silicon (Si)	Jöns Berzelius
			1824	aluminium (Al)	Hans Oersted (also attributed to Friedrich Wöhler 1827)
1782	tellurium (Te)	Franz Müller			
1783	tungsten (W)	Juan José Elhuyar and Fausto Elhuyar	1826	bromine (Br)	Antoine-Jérôme Balard
1789	uranium (U)	Martin Klaproth (isolated by Eugène Péligot 1841)	1827	ruthenium (Ru)	G W Osann (isolated by Karl Klaus 1844)
			1828	thorium (Th)	Jöns Berzelius
	zirconium (Zr)	Martin Klaproth	1839	lanthanum (La)	Carl Mosander
1790	titanium (Ti)	William Gregor	1842	erbium (Er)	Carl Mosander
1794	yttrium (Y)	Johan Gadolin	1843	terbium (Tb)	Carl Mosander
1797	chromium (Cr)	Louis-Nicolas Vauquelin	1860	caesium (Cs)	Robert Bunsen and Gustav Kirchoff

the extent to which their atoms can lose one or more electrons and form positive ions (cations).

nitric acid or *aqua fortis* HNO_3 fuming acid obtained by the oxidation of ammonia or the action of sulphuric acid on potassium nitrate. It is a highly corrosive acid, dissolving most metals, and a strong oxidizing agent. It is used in the nitration and esterification of organic substances, and in the making of sulphuric acid, nitrates, explosives, plastics, and dyes.

nitrogen colourless, odourless, tasteless, gaseous, nonmetallic element, symbol N, atomic number 7, relative atomic mass 14.0067. It forms almost 80% of the Earth's atmosphere by volume and is a constituent of all plant and animal tissues (in proteins and nucleic acids). Nitrogen is obtained for industrial use by the liquefaction and fractional distillation of air. It is used in the Haber process to make ammonia, NH_3, and to provide an inert atmosphere for certain chemical reactions. Its compounds are used in the manufacture of foods, drugs, fertilizers, dyes, and explosives.

nonmetal one of a set of elements (around 20 in total) with certain physical and chemical properties opposite to those of metals. Nonmetals accept electrons and are sometimes called electronegative elements.

oxygen colourless, odourless, tasteless, nonmetallic, gaseous element, symbol O, atomic number 8, relative atomic mass 15.9994. It is the most abundant element in the Earth's crust (almost 50% by mass),

Date	Element (symbol)	Discoverer
1861	rubidium (Rb)	Robert Bunsen and Gustav Kirchoff
	thallium (Tl)	William Crookes (isolated by William Crookes and Claude August Lamy, independently of each other 1862)
1863	indium (In)	Ferdinand Reich and Hieronymus Richter
1868	helium (He)	Pierre Janssen
1875	gallium (Ga)	Paul Lecoq de Boisbaudran
1876	scandium (Sc)	Lars Nilson
1878	ytterbium (Yb)	Jean Charles de Marignac
1879	holmium (Ho)	Per Cleve
	samarium (Sm)	Paul Lecoq de Boisbaudran
	thulium (Tm)	Per Cleve
1885	neodymium (Nd)	Carl von Welsbach
	praseodymium (Pr)	Carl von Welsbach
1886	dysprosium (Dy)	Paul Lecoq de Boisbaudran
	gadolinium (Gd)	Paul Lecoq de Boisbaudran
	germanium (Ge)	Clemens Winkler
1894	argon (Ar)	John Rayleigh and William Ramsay
1898	krypton (Kr)	William Ramsay and Morris Travers
	neon (Ne)	William Ramsay and Morris Travers
	polonium (Po)	Marie and Pierre Curie
	radium (Ra)	Marie Curie
	xenon (Xe)	William Ramsay and Morris Travers
1899	actinium (Ac)	André Debierne
1900	radon (Rn)	Friedrich Dorn
1901	europium (Eu)	Eugène Demarçay
1907	lutetium (Lu)	Georges Urbain and Carl von Welsbach independently of each other

forms about 21% by volume of the atmosphere, and is present in combined form in water and many other substances. In nature it exists as a molecule composed of two atoms (O_2); single atoms of oxygen are very short-lived owing to their reactivity. Life on Earth evolved using oxygen, which is a by-product of photosynthesis and the basis for respiration in plants and animals. Oxygen is essential for combustion, and is used with ethyne (acetylene) in high-temperature oxyacetylene welding and cutting torches.

ozone O_3 highly reactive pale-blue gas with a penetrating odour. Ozone is an allotrope of oxygen, made up of three atoms of oxygen. It is formed when the molecule of the stable form of oxygen (O_2) is split by ultraviolet radiation or electrical discharge. It forms a thin layer in the upper atmosphere, which protects life on Earth from ultraviolet rays, a cause of skin cancer. At lower atmospheric levels it is an air pollutant and contributes to the greenhouse effect. (See *Environment* for more.)

phosphate salt or ester of phosphoric acid. Incomplete neutralization of phosphoric acid gives rise to acid phosphates. Phosphates are used as fertilizers, and are required for the development of healthy root systems. They are involved in many biochemical processes, often as part of complex molecules, such as adenosine triphosphate (ATP).

plutonium silvery-white, radioactive, metallic element of the actinide series, symbol Pu, atomic number 94, relative atomic mass 239.13. It occurs in nature in minute quantities in pitchblende and other ores, but is produced in quantity only synthetically. It is one of three fissile elements (elements capable of splitting into other elements – the others are thorium and uranium), and is used as a fuel in fast-breeder reactors and in making nuclear weapons. It has a long half-life (24,000 years) during which time it remains highly toxic, and poses considerable disposal problems.

silicon brittle, nonmetallic element, symbol Si, atomic number 14, relative atomic mass 28.086. It is the second most abundant element (after oxygen) in the Earth's crust and occurs in amorphous and crystalline forms. In nature it is found only in combination with other elements, chiefly with oxygen in silica (silicon dioxide, SiO_2) and the silicates. These form the mineral quartz, which makes up most sands, gravels, and beaches. The crystalline form of silicon is used as a deoxidizing and hardening agent in steel, and has become the basis of the electronics industry because of its semiconductor properties, being used to make 'silicon chips' for microprocessors.

silver white, lustrous, precious, extremely malleable and ductile, metallic element, symbol Ag, atomic number 47, relative atomic mass 107.868. It occurs in nature in ores and as a free metal; the chief ores are sulphides, from which the metal is extracted by smelting with lead. It is one of the best metallic conductors of both heat and electricity; its most useful compounds are the chloride and bromide, which darken on exposure to light and are the basis of photographic emulsions.

sulphur brittle, pale-yellow, nonmetallic element, symbol S, atomic number 16, relative atomic mass 32.064. It occurs in three forms: two crystalline (called rhombic and monoclinic, following the arrangements of the atoms within the crystals) and one amorphous. It burns in air with a blue flame and a stifling odour. Sulphur is widely used in the manufacture of sulphuric acid (used to treat phosphate rock to make fertilizers) and in making paper, matches, gunpowder and fireworks, in vulcanizing rubber, and in medicines and insecticides. It is also a good electrical insulator.

sulphuric acid or *oil of vitriol* H_2SO_4 dense, viscous, colourless liquid that is extremely corrosive. It gives out heat when added to water and can cause severe burns. Sulphuric acid is used extensively in the chemical industry, in the refining of petrol, and in the manufacture of fertilizers, detergents, explosives, and dyes. It forms the acid component of car batteries.

periodic table of the elements

| 1 Hydrogen **H** 1.00794 | atomic number — name — symbol — relative atomic mass |

element

superphosphate phosphate fertilizer made by treating apatite with sulphuric or phosphoric acid. The commercial mixture contains largely monocalcium phosphate. Single-superphosphate obtained from apatite and sulphuric acid contains 16-20% available phosphorus, as P_2O_5; triple-superphosphate contains 45-50% phosphorus.

transuranic element or *transuranium element* chemical element with an atomic number of 93 or more – that is, with a greater number of protons in the nucleus than uranium. All transuranic elements are radioactive. Neptunium and plutonium are found in nature; the others are synthesized in nuclear reactions. (See table on page 59.)

uranium hard, lustrous, silver-white, malleable and ductile, radioactive, metallic element of the actinide series, symbol U, atomic number 92, relative atomic mass 238.029. It is the most abundant radioactive element in the Earth's crust, its decay giving rise to essentially all radioactive elements in nature; its final decay

product is the stable element lead. Uranium is one of three fissile elements (elements capable of splitting into other elements; the others are plutonium and thorium); the isotope uranium-235 is used as a fuel in nuclear reactors and in making nuclear weapons.

water H_2O liquid without colour, taste, or odour, an oxide of hydrogen. It is the most abundant substance on Earth, and is essential to all forms of life. Water begins to freeze at 0°C or 32°F, and to boil at 100°C or 212°F. When liquid, it is virtually incompressible; frozen, it expands by $1/_{11}$ of its volume. It has the highest known specific heat, and acts as an efficient solvent, particularly when hot.

Organic Chemistry

alcohol any member of a group of organic chemical compounds characterized by the presence of one or more aliphatic OH (hydroxyl) groups in the mole-

			III	IV	V	VI	VII	0
								2 Helium **He** 4.00260
			5 Boron **B** 10.81	6 Carbon **C** 12.011	7 Nitrogen **N** 14.0067	8 Oxygen **O** 15.9994	9 Fluorine **F** 18.99840	10 Neon **Ne** 20.179
			13 Aluminium **Al** 26.98154	14 Silicon **Si** 28.086	15 Phosphorus **P** 30.97376P	16 Sulphur **S** 32.06	17 Chlorine **Cl** 35.453	18 Argon **Ar** 39.948
28 Nickel **Ni** 58.70	29 Copper **Cu** 63.546	30 Zinc **Zn** 65.38	31 Gallium **Ga** 69.72	32 Germanium **Ge** 72.59	33 Arsenic **As** 74.9216	34 Selenium **Se** 78.96	35 Bromine **Br** 79.904	36 Krypton **Kr** 83.80
46 Palladium **Pd** 106.4	47 Silver **Ag** 107.868	48 Cadmium **Cd** 112.40	49 Indium **In** 114.82	50 Tin **Sn** 118.69	51 Antimony **Sb** 121.75	52 Tellurium **Te** 127.75	53 Iodine **I** 126.9045	54 Xenon **Xe** 131.30
78 Platinum **Pt** 195.09	79 Gold **Au** 196.9665	80 Mercury **Hg** 200.59	81 Thallium **Tl** 204.37	82 Lead **Pb** 207.37	83 Bismuth **Bi** 207.2	84 Polonium **Po** 210	85 Astatine **At** 211	86 Radon **Rn** 222.0176

63 Europium **Eu** 151.96	64 Gadolinium **Gd** 157.25	65 Terbium **Tb** 158.9254	66 Dysprosium **Dy** 162.50	67 Holmium **Ho** 164.9304	68 Erbium **Er** 167.26	69 Thulium **Tm** 168.9342	70 Ytterbium **Yb** 173.04	71 Lutetium **Lu** 174.97
95 Americium **Am** 243.0614	96 Curium **Cm** 247.0703	97 Berkelium **Bk** 247.0703	98 Californium **Cf** 251.0786	99 Einsteinium **Es** 252.0828	100 Fermium **Fm** 257.0951	101 Mendelevium **Me** 258.0986	102 Nobelium **No** 259.1009	103 Lawrencium **Lr** 260.1054

cule, and which form esters with acids. The main uses of alcohols are as solvents for gums, resins, lacquers, and varnishes; in the making of dyes; for essential oils in perfumery; and for medical substances in pharmacy. Alcohol (ethanol) is produced naturally in the fermentation process and is consumed as part of alcoholic beverages.

aldehyde any of a group of organic chemical compounds prepared by oxidation of primary alcohols, so that the OH (hydroxyl) group loses its hydrogen to give an oxygen joined by a double bond to a carbon atom (the aldehyde group, with the formula CHO).

aliphatic compound any organic chemical compound in which the carbon atoms are joined in straight chains, as in hexane (C_6H_{14}), or in branched chains, as in 2-methylpentane ($CH_3CH(CH_3)$ $CH_2CH_2CH_3$). Aliphatic compounds have bonding electrons localized within the vicinity of the bonded atoms. Cyclic compounds that do not have delocalized electrons are also aliphatic, as in the alicyclic compound cyclo-

hexane (C_6H_{12}) or the heterocyclic piperidine ($C_5H_{11}N$).

alkane member of a group of hydrocarbons having the general formula C_nH_{2n+2}, commonly known as *paraffins*. Lighter alkanes, such as methane, ethane, propane, and butane, are colourless gases; heavier ones are liquids or solids. In nature they are found in natural gas and petroleum. As alkanes contain only single covalent bonds, they are said to be saturated.

alkene member of the group of hydrocarbons having the general formula C_nH_{2n+2}, formerly known as *olefins*. Lighter alkenes, such as ethene and propene, are gases, obtained from the cracking of oil fractions. Alkenes are unsaturated compounds, characterized by one or more double bonds between adjacent carbon atoms. They react by addition, and many useful compounds, such as poly(ethene) and bromoethane, are made from them.

alkyne member of the group of hydrocarbons with the general formula C_nH_{2n-2}, formerly known as the *acetylenes*. They are unsaturated compounds, characterized by one or more triple bonds between adjacent carbon atoms. Lighter alkynes, such as ethyne, are gases; heavier ones are liquids or solids. The best-known alkyne is ethyne (acetylene), used in oxyacetylene cutting and welding torches.

amino acid water-soluble organic molecule, mainly composed of carbon, oxygen, hydrogen, and nitrogen, containing both a basic amine group (NH_2) and an acidic carboxyl (COOH) group. When two or more amino acids are joined together, they are known as peptides; proteins are made up of interacting polypeptides (peptide chains consisting of more than three amino acids) and are folded or twisted in characteristic shapes.

aromatic compound organic chemical compound in which some of the bonding electrons are delocalized (shared among several atoms within the molecule and not localized in the vicinity of the atoms involved in bonding). The commonest aromatic compounds have ring structures, the atoms comprising the ring being either all carbon or containing one or more different atoms (usually nitrogen, sulphur, or oxygen). Typical examples are benzene (C_6H_6) and pyridine (C_6H_5N).

buckminsterfullerene form of carbon, made up of molecules (buckyballs) consisting of 60 carbon atoms arranged in 12 pentagons and 20 hexagons to form a perfect sphere. It was named after the US architect and engineer Richard Buckminster Fuller because of its structural similarity to the geodesic dome that he designed. Buckminsterfullerene can be made into stable polymers using palladium. (See feature on buckyballs in this section.)

carboxyl group –COOH the acidic functional group that determines the properties of fatty acids (carboxylic acids) and amino acids.

ester organic compound formed by the reaction between an alcohol and an acid, with the elimination of water. Unlike salts, esters are covalent compounds.

ethanoic acid common name *acetic acid* CH_3CO_2H one of the simplest fatty acids (a series of organic acids). In the pure state it is a colourless liquid with an unpleasant pungent odour; it solidifies to an icelike mass of crystals at 16.7°C/62.4°F, and hence is often called glacial ethanoic acid. Vinegar contains 5% or more ethanoic acid, produced by fermentation.

ether any of a series of organic chemical compounds having an oxygen atom linking the carbon atoms of two hydrocarbon radical groups (general formula R-O-R'); also the common name for ethoxyethane $C_2H_5OC_2H_5$ (also called diethyl ether). Ethoxyethane is a colourless, volatile, inflammable liquid, slightly soluble in water, and miscible with ethanol. It is prepared by treatment of ethanol with excess concentrated sulphuric acid at 140°C/284°F. It is used as an anaesthetic by vapour inhalation and as an external cleansing agent before surgical operations. It is also used as a solvent, and in the extraction of oils, fats, waxes, resins, and alkaloids.

fatty acid or *carboxylic acid* organic compound consisting of a hydrocarbon chain, up to 24 carbon atoms long, with a carboxyl group (–COOH) at one end. The covalent bonds between the carbon atoms may be single or double; where a double bond occurs the carbon atoms concerned carry one instead of two hydrogen atoms. Chains with only single bonds have all the hydrogen they can carry, so they are said to be *saturated* with hydrogen. Chains with one or more double bonds are said to be *unsaturated*.

functional group a small number of atoms in an arrangement that determines the chemical properties of the group and of the molecule to which it is attached (for example, the carboxyl group –COOH, or the amine group NH_2). Organic compounds can be considered as structural skeletons, with a high carbon content, with functional groups attached.

homologous series any of a number of series of organic chemicals with similar chemical properties in which members differ by a constant relative molecular mass. Alkanes (paraffins), alkenes (olefins), and alkynes (acetylenes) form such series in which members differ in mass by 14, 12, and 10 atomic mass units respectively.

hydrocarbon any of a class of chemical compounds containing only hydrogen and carbon (for example, the alkanes and alkenes). Hydrocarbons are obtained industrially, principally from petroleum and coal tar.

isomer chemical compound having the same molecular composition and mass as another, but with different physical or chemical properties owing to the different structural arrangement of its constituent atoms. For example, the organic compounds butane ($CH_3(CH_2)_2CH_3$) and methyl propane ($CH_3CH(CH_3)CH_3$) are isomers, each possessing four carbon atoms and ten hydrogen atoms but differing in the way that these are arranged with respect to each other.

ketone member of the group of organic compounds containing the carbonyl group (C=O) bonded to two atoms of carbon (instead of one carbon and one hydrogen as in aldehydes). Ketones are liquids or low-melting-point solids, slightly soluble in water. An example is propanone (acetone, CH_3COCH_3), used as a solvent.

lipid any of a large number of esters of fatty acids, commonly formed by the reaction of a fatty acid with glycerol. They are soluble in alcohol but not in water. Lipids are the chief constituents of plant and animal waxes, fats, and oils.

phenol member of a group of aromatic chemical compounds with weakly acidic properties, which are characterized by a hydroxyl (OH) group attached directly to an aromatic ring. The simplest of the phenols, derived from benzene, is also known as phenol and has the formula C_6H_5OH. It is sometimes called *carbolic acid* and can be extracted from coal tar. Pure phenol consists of colourless, needle-shaped crystals, which take up moisture from the atmosphere. It has a strong and characteristic smell and was once used as an antiseptic. It is, however, toxic by absorption through the skin.

plastic any of the stable synthetic materials that are fluid at some stage in their manufacture, when they can be shaped, and that later set to rigid or semi-rigid solids. Plastics today are chiefly derived from petroleum. Most are polymers, made up of long chains of molecules.

Processed by extrusion, injection-moulding, vacuum-forming and compression, plastics emerge in consistencies ranging from hard and inflexible to soft and rubbery. They replace an increasing number of natural substances, being lightweight, easy to clean, durable, and capable of being rendered very strong – for example, by the addition of carbon fibres – for building aircraft and other engineering projects.

polymer compound made up of a large long-chain or branching matrix composed of many repeated simple units (*monomers*). There are many polymers, both natural (cellulose, chitin, lignin) and synthetic (polyethylene and nylon, types of plastic). Synthetic polymers belong to two groups: thermosoftening and thermosetting.

polyunsaturate type of fat or oil containing a high proportion of triglyceride molecules whose fatty-acid chains contain several double bonds. By contrast, the fatty-acid chains of the triglycerides in saturated fats (such as lard) contain only single bonds. Medical evidence suggests that polyunsaturated fats, used widely in margarines and cooking fats, are less likely to contribute to cardiovascular disease than saturated fats, but there is also some evidence that they may have adverse effects on health.

saturated compound organic compound, such as propane, that contains only single covalent bonds. Saturated organic compounds can only undergo further reaction by substitution reactions, as in the production of chloropropane from propane.

tetrachloromethane or *carbon tetrachloride* CCl_4 chlorinated organic compound that is a very efficient solvent for fats and greases, and was at one time the main constituent of household dry-cleaning fluids and of fire extinguishers used with electrical and petrol fires. Its use became restricted after it was discovered to be carcinogenic and it has now been largely removed from educational and industrial laboratories.

unsaturated compound chemical compound in which two adjacent atoms are bonded by a double or triple covalent bond. Examples are alkenes and alkynes, where the two adjacent atoms are both carbon, and ketones, where the unsaturation exists between atoms of different elements.

Terms

absorption spectroscopy or *absorptiometry* technique for determining the identity or amount present of a chemical substance by measuring the amount of electromagnetic radiation the substance absorbs at specific wavelengths.

acid compound that, in solution in an ionizing solvent (usually water), gives rise to hydrogen ions (H^+ or protons). In modern chemistry, acids are defined as substances that are proton donors and accept electrons to form ionic bonds. Acids react with bases to form salts, and they act as solvents. Strong acids are corrosive; dilute acids have a sour or sharp taste, although in some organic acids this may be partially masked by other flavour characteristics. Acids are classified as monobasic, dibasic, tribasic, and so forth, according to the number of hydrogen atoms, replaceable by bases, in a molecule.

activation analysis technique used to reveal the presence and amount of minute impurities in a substance or element. A sample of a material that may contain traces of a certain element is irradiated with neutrons, as in a reactor. The gamma rays emitted by the material's radioisotope have unique energies and relative intensities, similar to the spectral lines from a luminous gas. Measurements and interpretation of the gamma-ray spectrum, using data from standard samples for comparison, provide information on the amount of impurities present.

activation energy the energy required in order to start a chemical reaction. Some elements and compounds will react together merely by bringing them into contact (spontaneous reaction). For others it is necessary to supply energy in order to start the reaction, even if there is ultimately a net output of energy. This initial energy is the activation energy.

aerogel light, transparent, highly porous material composed of more than 90% air. Such materials are formed from silica, metal oxides, and organic chemicals, and are produced by drying gels – networks of linked molecules suspended in a liquid – so that air fills the spaces previously occupied by the liquid. They are excellent heat insulators and have unusual optical, electrical, and acoustic properties.

alkali chemical compound classed as a base that is soluble in water. Alkalis neutralize acids and are soapy to the touch. The hydroxides of metals are alkalis; those of sodium (sodium hydroxide, NaOH) and of potassium (potassium hydroxide, KOH) being chemically powerful.

assay the determination of the quantity of a given substance present in a sample. Usually it refers to determining the purity of precious metals. The assay may be carried out by 'wet' methods, when the sample is wholly or partially dissolved in some reagent (often an acid), or by 'dry' or 'fire' methods, in which the compounds present in the sample are combined with other substances.

atom the smallest unit of matter that can take part in a chemical reaction, and which cannot be broken down chemically into anything simpler. An atom is made up of protons and neutrons in a central nucleus surrounded by electrons. The atoms of the various elements differ in atomic number, relative atomic mass, and chemical behaviour. There are 109 different types of atom, corresponding with the 109 known elements as listed in the periodic table of the elements.

atomic number or *proton number* the number (symbol Z) of protons in the nucleus of an atom. It is equal to the positive charge on the nucleus. In a neutral atom, it is also equal to the number of electrons surrounding the nucleus. The 109 elements are arranged in the periodic table of the elements according to their atomic number.

atomic orbital region around the nucleus of an atom (or, in a molecule, around several nuclei) in which an electron is most likely to be found. According to quantum theory, the position of an electron is uncertain; it may be found at any point. However, it is more likely to be found in some places than in others, and it is

Chemistry: chronology

c. 3000 BC	Egyptians were producing bronze, an alloy of copper and tin.
c. 450 BC	Greek philosopher Empedocles proposed that all substances are made up of a combination of four elements – earth, air, fire, and water – an idea that was developed by Plato and Aristotle and persisted for over 2,000 years.
c. 400 BC	Greek philosopher Democritus theorized that matter consists ultimately of tiny, indivisible particles, *atomos.*
AD 1	Gold, silver, copper, lead, iron, tin, and mercury were known.
200	The techniques of solution, filtration, and distillation were known.
7th–17th centuries	Chemistry was dominated by alchemy, the attempt to transform nonprecious metals such as lead and copper into gold. Though misguided, it led to the discovery of many new chemicals and techniques, such as sublimation and distillation.
12th century	Alcohol was first distilled in Europe.
1242	Gunpowder introduced to Europe from the Far East.
1620	Scientific method of reasoning expounded by Francis Bacon in his *Novum Organum.*
1650	Leyden University in the Netherlands set up the first chemistry laboratory.
1661	Robert Boyle defined an element as any substance that cannot be broken down into still simpler substances and asserted that matter is composed of 'corpuscles' (atoms) of various sorts and sizes, capable of arranging themselves into groups, each of which constitutes a chemical substance.
1662	Boyle described the inverse relationship between the volume and pressure of a fixed mass of gas (Boyle's law).
1697	Georg Stahl proposed the erroneous theory that substances burn because they are rich in a certain substance, called phlogiston.
1755	Joseph Black discovered carbon dioxide.
1774	Joseph Priestley discovered oxygen, which he called 'dephlogisticated air'. Antoine Lavoisier demonstrated his law of conservation of mass.
1777	Lavoisier showed air to be made up of a mixture of gases, and showed that one of these - oxygen - is the substance necessary for combustion (burning) and rusting to take place.
1781	Henry Cavendish showed water to be a compound.
1792	Alessandra Volta demonstrated the electrochemical series.
1807	Humphry Davy passed electric current through molten compounds (the process of electrolysis) in order to isolate elements, such as potassium, that had never been separated by chemical means. Jöns Berzelius proposed that chemicals produced by living creatures should be termed 'organic'.
1808	John Dalton published his atomic theory, which states that every element consists of similar indivisible particles – called atoms – which differ from the atoms of other elements in their mass; he also drew up a list of relative atomic masses. Joseph Gay-Lussac announced that the volumes of gases that combine chemically with one another are in simple ratios.
1811	Publication of Amedeo Avogadro's hypothesis on the relation between the volume and number of molecules of a gas, and its temperature and pressure.
1813–14	Berzelius devised the chemical symbols and formulae still used to represent elements and compounds.
1828	Franz Wöhler converted ammonium cyanate into urea – the first synthesis of an organic compound from an inorganic substance.
1832–33	Michael Faraday expounded the laws of electrolysis, and adopted the term 'ion' for the particles believed to be responsible for carrying current.
1846	Thomas Graham expounded his law of diffusion.
1853	Robert Bunsen invented the Bunsen burner.
1858	Stanislao Cannizzaro differentiated between atomic and molecular weights (masses).
1861	Organic chemistry was defined by German chemist Friedrich Kekulé as the chemistry of carbon compounds.
1864	John Newlands devised the first periodic table of the elements.
1869	Dmitri Mendeleyev expounded his periodic table of the elements (based on atomic weight), leaving gaps for elements that had not yet been discovered.
1874	Jacobus van't Hoff suggested that the four bonds of carbon are arranged tetrahedrally, and that carbon compounds can therefore be three-dimensional and asymmetric.
1884	Swedish chemist Svante Arrhenius suggested that electrolytes (solutions or molten compounds that conduct electricity) dissociate into ions, atoms or groups of atoms that carry a positive or negative charge.
1894	William Ramsey and Lord Rayleigh discovered the first inert gases, argon.
1897	The electron was discovered by J J Thomson.
1901	Mikhail Tsvet invented paper chromatography as a means of separating pigments.
1909	Sören Sörensen devised the pH scale of acidity.
1912	Max von Laue showed crystals to be composed of regular, repeating arrays of atoms by studying the patterns in which they diffract X-rays.
1913–14	Henry Moseley equated the atomic number of an element with the positive charge on its nuclei, and drew up the periodic table, based on atomic number, that is used today.

Chemistry: chronology (cont.)

1916	Gilbert Newton Lewis explained covalent bonding between atoms as a sharing of electrons.
1927	Nevil Sidgwick published his theory of valency, based on the numbers of electrons in the outer shells of the reacting atoms.
1930	Electrophoresis, which separates particles in suspension in an electric field, invented by Arne Tiselius.
1932	Deuterium (heavy hydrogen), an isotope of hydrogen, was discovered by Harold Urey.
1940	Edwin McMillan and Philip Abelson showed that new elements with a higher atomic number than uranium can be formed by bombarding uranium with neutrons, and synthesized the first transuranic element, neptunium.
1942	Plutonium was first synthesized by Glenn T Seaborg and Edwin McMillan.
1950	Derek Barton deduced that some properties of organic compounds are affected by the orientation of their functional groups (the study of which became known as conformational analysis).
1954	Einsteinium and fermium were synthesized.
1962	Neil Bartlett prepared the first compound of an inert gas, xenon hexafluoroplatinate; it was previously believed that inert gases could not take part in a chemical reaction.
1965	Robert B Woodward synthesized complex organic compounds .
1981	Quantum mechanics applied to predict course of chemical reactions by US chemist Roald Hoffmann and Kenichi Fukui of Japan.
1982	Element 109, unnilennium, synthesized.
1985	Fullerenes, a new class of carbon solids made up of closed cages of carbon atoms, were discovered by Harold Kroto and David Walton at the University of Sussex, England.
1987	US chemists Donald Cram and Charles Pederson, and Jean-Marie Lehn of France created artificial molecules that mimic the vital chemical reactions of life processes.
1990	Jean-Marie Lehn, Ulrich Koert, and Margaret Harding reported the synthesis of a new class of compounds, called nucleohelicates, that mimic the double helical structure of DNA, turned inside out.
1993	US chemists at the University of California and the Scripps Institute synthesized rapamycin, one of a group of complex, naturally occurring antibiotics and immunosuppressants being tested as anticancer agents.

these that make up the orbital. An atom or molecule has numerous orbitals, each of which has a fixed size and shape.

base a substance that accepts protons, such as the hydroxide ion (OH^-) and ammonia (NH_3). Bases react with acids to give a salt. Those that dissolve in water are called alkalis. Inorganic bases are usually oxides or hydroxides of metals, which react with dilute acids to form a salt and water. A number of carbonates also react with dilute acids, additionally giving off carbon dioxide. Many organic compounds that contain nitrogen are bases.

boiling point for any given liquid, the temperature at which any further application of heat does not raise the temperature of the liquid, but converts it into vapour.

bond the result of the forces of attraction that hold together atoms of an element or elements to form a molecule. The principal types of bonding are ionic, covalent, metallic, and intermolecular (such as hydrogen bonding). The type of bond formed depends on the elements concerned and their electronic structure.

buffer mixture of chemical compounds chosen to maintain a steady pH. The commonest buffers consist of a mixture of a weak organic acid and one of its salts or a mixture of acid salts of phosphoric acid. The addition of either an acid or a base causes a shift in the chemical equilibrium, thus keeping the pH constant.

catalyst substance that alters the speed of, or makes possible, a chemical or biochemical reaction but remains unchanged at the end of the reaction. Enzymes are natural biochemical catalysts. In practice most catalysts are used to speed up reactions.

centrifuge apparatus that rotates at high speeds, causing substances inside it to be thrown outwards. One use is for separating mixtures of substances of different densities. A common example is the separation of the lighter plasma from the heavier blood corpuscles in certain blood tests.

chain reaction mechanism that produces very fast, exothermic reactions, as in the formation of flames and explosions. The reaction begins with the formation of a single reactive molecule. This combines with an inactive molecule to form two reactive molecules. These two produce four (or more) reactive molecules; very quickly, very many reactive molecules are produced, so the reaction rate accelerates dramatically.

chemical equation method of indicating the reactants and products of a chemical reaction by using chemical symbols and formulae. A chemical equation gives two basic pieces of information: (1) the reactants (on the left-hand side) and products (right-hand side); and (2) the reacting proportions (stoichiometry) – that is, how many units of each reactant and product are involved. The equation must balance; that is, the total number of atoms of a particular element on the left-hand side must be the same as the number of atoms of that element on the right-hand side.

chemical equilibrium condition in which the products of a reversible chemical reaction are formed at the same rate at which they decompose back into the reactants, so that the concentration of each reactant and product remains constant.

chlorination treatment of water with chlorine in order to disinfect it; also, any chemical reaction in which a chlorine atom is introduced into a chemical compound.

chromatography technique for separating or analysing a mixture of gases, liquids, or dissolved substances. This is brought about by means of two immiscible substances, one of which (*the mobile phase*) transports the sample mixture through the other (*the stationary phase*). The mobile phase may be a gas or a liquid; the stationary phase may be a liquid or a solid, and may be in a column, on paper, or in a thin layer on a glass or plastic support. The components of the mixture are absorbed or impeded by the stationary phase to different extents and therefore become separated.

colligative property property that depends on the concentration of particles in a solution. Such properties include osmotic pressure, elevation of boiling point, depression of freezing point, and lowering of vapour pressure.

colloid substance composed of extremely small particles of one material (the dispersed phase) evenly and stably distributed in another material (the continuous phase). The size of the dispersed particles (1–1,000 nanometres across) is less than that of particles in suspension but greater than that of molecules in true solution. Colloids involving gases include *aerosols* (dispersions of liquid or solid particles in a gas, as in fog or smoke) and *foams* (dispersions of gases in liquids). Those involving liquids include *emulsions* (in which both the dispersed and the continuous phases are liquids) and *sols* (solid particles dispersed in a liquid). Sols in which both phases contribute to a molecular three-dimensional network have a jellylike form and are known as *gels*; gelatin, starch *solution*, and silica gel are common examples.

compound chemical substance made up of two or more elements bonded together, so that they cannot be separated by physical means. Compounds are held together by ionic or covalent bonds.

An estimated 10 million chemical compounds have been discovered; 400,000 new compounds are discovered each year.

configuration the arrangement of atoms in a molecule or of electrons in atomic orbitals.

covalent bond chemical bond produced when two atoms share one or more pairs of electrons (usually each atom contributes an electron). The bond is often represented by a single line drawn between the two atoms. Covalently bonded substances include hydrogen (H_2), water (H_2O), and most organic substances. Double bonds, seen, for example, in the alkenes, are formed when two atoms share two pairs of electrons (the atoms usually contribute a pair each); triple bonds, seen in the alkynes, are formed when atoms share three pairs of electrons. Such bonds are represented by a double or triple line, respectively, between the atoms concerned.

cracking reaction in which a large alkane molecule is broken down by heat into a smaller alkane and a small alkene molecule. The reaction is carried out at a high temperature (600°C or higher) and often in the presence of a catalyst. It is the main method of preparation of alkenes and is also used to manufacture petrol from the higher-boiling-point fractions that are obtained by fractional distillation (fractionation) of crude oil.

decomposition process whereby a chemical compound is reduced to its component substances.

detergent surface-active cleansing agent. The common detergents are made from fats (hydrocarbons) and sulphuric acid, and their long-chain molecules have a type of structure similar to that of soap molecules: a salt group at one end attached to a long hydrocarbon 'tail'. They have the advantage over soap in that they do not produce scum by forming insoluble salts with the calcium and magnesium ions present in hard water.

diffusion spontaneous and random movement of molecules or particles in a fluid (gas or liquid) from a region in which they are at a high concentration to a region in which they are at a low concentration, until a uniform concentration is achieved throughout. No mechanical mixing or stirring is involved. For instance, if a drop of ink is added to water, its molecules will diffuse until their colour becomes evenly distributed throughout. One application of diffusion is the separation of isotopes, particularly those of uranium. When uranium hexafluoride diffuses through a porous plate, the ratio of the 235 and 238 isotopes is changed slightly. With sufficient number of passages, the separation is almost complete.

dipole the uneven distribution of magnetic or electrical characteristics within a molecule or substance so that it behaves as though it possesses two equal but opposite poles or charges, a finite distance apart. The uneven distribution of electrons within a molecule composed of atoms of different electronegativities may result in an apparent concentration of electrons towards one end of the molecule and a deficiency towards the other, so that it forms a dipole consisting of apparently separated but equal positive and negative charges. A bar magnet behaves as though its magnetism were concentrated in separate north and south magnetic poles because of the uneven distribution of its magnetic field.

dissociation the process whereby a single compound splits into two or more smaller products, which may be capable of recombining to form the reactant.

distillation technique used to purify liquids or to separate mixtures of liquids possessing different boiling points. *Simple distillation* is used in the purification of liquids (or the separation of substances in solution from their solvents) – for example, in the production of pure water from a salt solution. The solution is boiled and the vapours of the solvent rise into a separate piece of apparatus (the condenser) where they are cooled and condensed. The liquid produced (the distillate) is the pure solvent; the non-volatile solutes (now in solid form) remain in the distillation vessel to be discarded as impurities or recovered as required. Mixtures of liquids (such as petroleum or aqueous ethanol) are separated by *fractional distillation*, or fractionation.

elastomer any material with rubbery properties, which stretches easily and then quickly returns to its original length when released. Natural and synthetic rubbers and such materials as polychloroprene and butadiene copolymers are elastomers. The convoluted molecular chains making up these materials are uncoiled by a stretching force, but return to their original position when released because there are relatively few crosslinks between the chains.

electron stable, negatively charged elementary particle, a constituent of all atoms, and the basic particle of electricity. The electrons in each atom surround the nucleus in groupings called shells; in a neutral atom the number of electrons is equal to the number of protons in the nucleus. This electron structure is responsible for the chemical properties of the atom. A beam of electrons will undergo diffraction (scattering) and produce interference patterns in the same way as electromagnetic waves such as light; hence they may also be regarded as waves.

electronegativity the ease with which an atom can attract electrons to itself. Electronegative elements attract electrons, forming negative ions. Nonmetals such as fluorine and chlorine have the highest values of electronegativity; metals have low values.

electrophoresis powerful technique used to separate and identify chemical compounds in a mixture. By applying an electric field to a mixture of chemicals in solution, they are made to migrate at different speeds within a plastic gel or piece of filter paper. Genetic fingerprinting depends on this technique.

element substance that cannot be split chemically into simpler substances. The atoms of a particular element all have the same number of protons in their nuclei (their atomic number). Of the 109 known elements, 95 are known to occur in nature (those with atomic numbers 1–95). Those from 96 to 109 do not occur in nature and are synthesized only, produced in particle accelerators. Eighty-one of the elements are stable; all the others, which include atomic numbers 43, 61, and from 84 up, are radioactive. The elements are classified in the periodic table.

Symbols are used to denote the elements; the symbol is usually the first letter or letters of the English or Latin name (for example, C for carbon, Ca for calcium, Fe for iron, *ferrum*). The symbol represents one atom of the element.

elution washing out of an adsorbed substance from the adsorbing material; it is used, for example, in the separation processes of chromatography and electrophoresis.

emulsion a stable dispersion of a liquid in another liquid – for example, oil and water in some cosmetic lotions.

energy of reaction energy released or absorbed during a chemical reaction, also called *enthalpy of reaction* or *heat of reaction*. In a chemical reaction, the energy stored in the reacting molecules is rarely the same as that stored in the product molecules. Depending on which is the greater, energy is either released (an *exothermic reaction*) or absorbed (an *endothermic reaction*) from the surroundings. The amount of energy released or absorbed by the quantities of substances represented by the chemical equation is the energy of reaction.

formula a representation of a molecule, radical, or ion, in which the component chemical elements are represented by their symbols. An *empirical formula* indicates the simplest ratio of the elements in a compound, without indicating how many of them there are or how they are combined. A *molecular formula* gives the number of each type of element present in one molecule. A *structural formula* shows the relative positions of the atoms and the bonds between them. For example, for ethanoic acid, the empirical formula is CH_2O, the molecular formula is $C_2H_4O_2$, and the structural formula is CH_3COOH.

fractional distillation or *fractionation* form of distillation used in industry to separate the components of a liquid mixture, for example petroleum. When the mixture is boiled, the vapours of its most volatile component rise into a vertical fractionating column where they condense to liquid form. However, as this liquid runs back down the column it is reheated to boiling point by the hot rising vapours of the next-most-volatile component and so its vapours ascend the column once more. This boiling-condensing process occurs repeatedly inside the column, eventually bringing about a temperature gradient along its length. The vapours of the more volatile components therefore reach the top of the column and enter the condenser for collection before those of the less volatile components. In the fractional distillation of petroleum, groups of compounds (fractions) possessing similar relative molecular masses and boiling points are tapped off at different points on the column.

free radical an atom or molecule that has an unpaired electron and is therefore highly reactive. Most free radicals are very short-lived. If free radicals are produced in living organisms they can be very damaging.

freezing point for any given liquid, the temperature at which any further removal of heat will convert the liquid into the solid state. The temperature remains at this point until all the liquid has solidified. It is invariable under similar conditions of pressure – for example, the freezing point of water under standard atmospheric pressure is 0°C/32°F.

immiscible term describing liquids that will not mix with each other, such as oil and water. When two immiscible liquids are shaken together, a turbid mixture is produced. This normally forms separate layers when it is left to stand.

indicator chemical compound that changes its structure and colour in response to its environment. The commonest chemical indicators detect changes in pH (for example, litmus), or in the oxidation state of a system (redox indicators).

ion atom, or group of atoms, that is either positively charged (*cation*) or negatively charged (*anion*), as a result of the loss or gain of electrons during chemical reactions or exposure to certain forms of radiation.

ion exchange process whereby an ion in one compound is replaced by a different ion, of the same charge, from another compound. It is the basis of a type of chromatography in which the components of a mixture of ions in solution are separated according to the ease with which they will replace the ions on the polymer matrix through which they flow. Ion-exchange is used in commercial water softeners to exchange the dissolved ions responsible for the water's hardness with others that do not have this effect.

ionic bond or *electrovalent bond* bond produced when atoms of one element donate electrons to atoms of another element, forming positively and negatively charged ions respectively. The electrostatic attraction between the oppositely charged ions constitutes the bond. Sodium chloride (Na^+Cl^-) is a typical ionic compound.

isotope one of two or more atoms that have the same atomic number (same number of protons), but which contain a different number of neutrons, thus differing in their atomic masses. They may be stable or radioactive, naturally occurring or synthesized.

litmus dye obtained from various lichens and used in chemistry as an indicator to test the acidic or alkaline nature of aqueous solutions; it turns red in the presence of acid, and blue in the presence of alkali.

lone pair a pair of electrons in the outermost shell of an atom that are not used in bonding. In certain circumstances, they will allow the atom to bond with atoms, ions, or molecules (such as boron trifluoride, BF_3) that are deficient in electrons, forming coordinate covalent (dative) bonds in which they provide both of the bonding electrons.

mass action, law of law stating that at a given temperature the rate at which a chemical reaction takes place is proportional to the product of the active masses of the reactants. The active mass is taken to be the molar concentration of the each reactant.

methylated spirit alcohol that has been rendered undrinkable, and is used for industrial purposes, as a fuel for spirit burners or a solvent.

mixture a substance containing two or more compounds that still retain their separate physical and chemical properties. There is no chemical bonding between them and they can be separated from each other by physical means.

molecule group of two or more atoms bonded together. A molecule of an element consists of one or more like atoms; a molecule of a compound consists of two or more different atoms bonded together. Molecules vary in size and complexity from the hydrogen molecule (H_2) to the large macromolecules of proteins. They are held together by ionic bonds, in which the atoms gain or lose electrons to form ions, or by covalent bonds, where electrons from each atom are shared in a new molecular orbital.

Most molecules are made up of small numbers of atoms but some contain rather more. For example, a molecule of aspirin contains 21 atoms. A molecule of haemoglobin, a substance found in blood, contains 758 carbon atoms, 1,203 hydrogen atoms, 195 oxygen atoms, 218 nitrogen atoms, one iron atom, and three sulphur atoms. Rubber molecules may have up to 65,000 atoms.

neutralization a process occurring when the excess acid (or excess base) in a substance is reacted with added base (or added acid) so that the resulting substance is neither acidic nor basic. In theory neutralization involves adding acid or base as required to achieve pH 7.0.

neutral solution solution of pH 7, in which the concentrations of $H^+_{(aq)}$ and $OH^-_{(aq)}$ ions are equal.

pH

0
1
2 — battery acid
3
— lemon juice
4
5 — acid rain
— human skin
6
7 — distilled water
8
9
— soap
10
11 — milk of magnesia
12
13 — caustic soda
14

increasing acidity

increasing alkalinity

neutron one of the three chief subatomic particles (the others being the proton and the electron). Neutrons have about the same mass as protons but no electric charge, and occur in the nuclei of all atoms except hydrogen. They contribute to the mass of atoms but do not affect their chemistry, which depends on the proton or electron numbers. For instance, isotopes of a single element (with different masses) differ only in the number of neutrons in their nuclei and have identical chemical properties.

oxidation the loss of electrons, gain of oxygen, or loss of hydrogen by an atom, ion, or molecule during a chemical reaction.

paraffin common name for alkane, any member of the series of hydrocarbons with the general formula C_nH_{2n+2}.

PCB abbreviation for *polychlorinated biphenyl*.

periodic table of the elements a table of classification of the elements arranged in order by their atomic numbers. The table summarizes the major properties of the elements, which are a direct consequence of the electronic (and nuclear) structure of their atoms, and enables predictions to be made about their behaviour. There are striking similarities in the chemical properties of the elements in each of the vertical columns (called *groups*), which are numbered I–VII and then 0 (from left to right) to reflect the number of electrons in the outermost unfilled shell and hence the maximum valency. A gradation of properties may be traced along the horizontal rows (called *periods*). Metallic character increases across a period from right to left, and down a group. A large block of elements, between groups II and III, contains the transition elements, characterized by displaying more than one valency state.

The first periodic table was devised by Russian chemist Dmitri Mendeleyev 1869; the elements being arranged by atomic mass (rather than by atomic number in today's table) in accordance with Mendeleyev's statement 'the properties of elements are in periodic dependence upon their atomic weight'. (See table on pp 62–63.)

pH scale from 0 to 14 for measuring acidity or alkalinity. A pH of 7.0 indicates neutrality, below 7 is acid, while above 7 is alkaline. The pH of a solution can be measured by using a broad-range indicator, either in solution or as a paper strip. The colour produced by the indicator is compared with a colour code related to the pH value. An alternative method is to use a pH meter fitted with a glass electrode.

photolysis chemical reaction that is driven by light or ultraviolet radiation. For example, the light reaction of photosynthesis (the process by which green plants manufacture carbohydrates from carbon dioxide and water) is a photolytic reaction.

polychlorinated biphenyl (PCB) any of a group of chlorinated isomers of biphenyl (C_6H_5)$_2$. They are dangerous industrial chemicals, valuable for their fire-resisting qualities. They constitute an environmental hazard because of their persistent toxicity. Since 1973 their use has been limited by international agreement.

precipitation the formation of an insoluble solid in a liquid as a result of a reaction within the liquid between two or more soluble substances. If the solid settles, it forms a *precipitate*; if the particles of solid are very small, they will remain in suspension, forming a *colloidal precipitate*.

proton positively charged subatomic particle, a fundamental constituent of any atomic nucleus. Its lifespan is effectively infinite. A proton carries a unit positive charge equal to the negative charge of an electron. The number of protons in the atom of an element is equal to its atomic, or proton, number.

radioactivity spontaneous alteration of the nuclei of radioactive atoms, accompanied by the emission of radiation. It is the property exhibited by the radioactive isotopes of stable elements and all isotopes of radioactive elements, and can be either natural or induced.

rate of reaction the speed at which a chemical reaction proceeds. It is usually expressed in terms of the concentration (usually in moles per litre) of a reactant consumed, or product formed, in unit time; so the units would be moles per litre per second (mol l^{-1} s^{-1}). The rate of a reaction may be affected by the concentration of the reactants, the temperature of the reactants, and the presence of a catalyst. If the reaction is entirely in the gas state, the rate is affected by pressure, and, for solids, it is affected by the particle size.

reaction the coming together of two or more atoms, ions, or molecules with the result that a chemical change takes place. The nature of the reaction is portrayed by a chemical equation.

reactivity series chemical series produced by arranging the metals in order of their ease of reaction with reagents such as oxygen, water, and acids. This arrangement aids the understanding of the properties of metals, helps to explain differences between them, and enables predictions to be made about a metal's behaviour, based on a knowledge of its position or properties.

redox reaction chemical change where one reactant is reduced and the other reactant oxidized. The reaction can only occur if both reactants are present and each changes simultaneously. For example, hydrogen reduces copper(II) oxide to copper while it is itself oxidized to water. The corrosion of iron and the reactions taking place in electric and electrolytic cells are just a few instances of redox reactions.

reduction the gain of electrons, loss of oxygen, or gain of hydrogen by an atom, ion, or molecule during a chemical reaction.

relative atomic mass the mass of an atom relative to one-twelfth the mass of an atom of carbon-12. It depends on the number of protons and neutrons in the atom, the electrons having negligible mass. If more than one isotope of the element is present, the relative atomic mass is calculated by taking an average that takes account of the relative proportions of each isotope, resulting in values that are not whole numbers. The term *atomic weight*, although commonly used, is strictly speaking incorrect.

repellent anything of which the smell, taste, or other properties discourages nearby creatures. *Insect repellent* is usually a chemical substance that keeps, for example, mosquitoes at bay; natural substances include citronella, lavender oil, and eucalyptus oils. A device that emits ultrasound waves is also claimed to repel insects and small mammals. The bitter-tasting denatonium saccharide may be added to medicines to prevent consumption by children, and to plastic garbage bags to repel foraging animals.

salt any member of a group of compounds containing a positive ion (cation) derived from a metal or ammonia and a negative ion (anion) derived from an acid or nonmetal. If the negative ion has a replaceable hydrogen atom it is an *acid salt* (for example sodium hydrogensulphate, $NaHSO_4$; potassium phosphonate, KH_2PO_4; sodium hydrogencarbonate, $NaHCO_3$); if not, it is classed as a *normal salt* (for example sodium chloride, NaCl; potassium sulphate, K_2SO_4; magnesium nitrate, $Mg(NO_3)_2$). *Common salt* is sodium chloride. Salts have the properties typical of ionic compounds.

Crystals of common salt (NaCl) are made up of small cubes of atoms. A crystal of rock salt contains 40,000 million million million atoms in each cubic centimetre.

solute substance that is dissolved in another substance.

solution two or more substances mixed to form a single, homogenous phase. One of the substances is the *solvent* and the others (*solutes*) are said to be dissolved in it. The constituents of a solution may be solid, liquid, or gaseous. The solvent is normally the substance that is present in greatest quantity; however, if one of the constituents is a liquid this is considered to be the solvent even if it is not the major substance.

solvent substance, usually a liquid, that will dissolve another substance. Although the commonest solvent is water, in popular use the term refers to low-boiling-point organic liquids, which are harmful if used in a confined space. They can give rise to respiratory problems, liver damage, and neurological complaints. Typical organic solvents are petroleum distillates (in glues), xylol (in paints), alcohols (for synthetic and natural resins such as shellac), esters (in lacquers, including nail varnish), ketones (in cellulose lacquers and resins), and chlorinated hydrocarbons (as paint stripper and dry-cleaning fluids).

standard temperature and pressure (STP) a standard set of conditions for experimental measurements, to enable comparisons to be made between sets of results. Standard temperature is 0°C and standard pressure 1 atmosphere (101,325 Pa).

strength of acids and bases the ability of acids and bases to dissociate in solution with water, and hence to produce a low or high pH respectively. A strong acid is fully dissociated in aqueous solution and has a low pH, whereas a weak acid is only partly dissociated and has a higher pH. A strong base will have a high pH, whereas a weaker base will not dissociate completely and will have a pH of nearer 7.

sublimation the conversion of a solid to vapour without passing through the liquid phase. Some substances that do not sublime at atmospheric pressure can be made to do so at low pressures. This is the principle of freeze-drying, during which ice sublimes at low pressure.

surfactant (contraction of *surface-active agent*) substance added to a liquid in order to increase its wetting or spreading properties. Detergents are examples.

tautomerism form of isomerism (when substances have the same molecular formula) in which two interconvertible isomers are in equilibrium. It is often specifically applied to an equilibrium between the keto (–C–C=O) and enol (–C=C–OH) forms of carbonyl compounds.

triple bond three covalent bonds between adjacent atoms, as in the alkynes ($-C\equiv C-$).

universal indicator a mixture of pH indicators, used to gauge the acidity or alkalinity of a solution. Each component changes colour at a different pH value, and so the indicator is capable of displaying a range of colours, according to the pH of the test solution, from red (at pH 1) to purple (at pH 13).

valency the measure of an element's ability to combine with other elements, expressed as the number of atoms of hydrogen (or any other standard univalent element) capable of uniting with (or replacing) its atoms. The number of electrons in the outermost shell of the atom dictates the combining ability of an element.

zwitterion ion that has both a positive and a negative charge, such as an amino acid in neutral solution. For example, glycine contains both a basic amino group (NH^2) and an acidic carboxyl group (–COOH); when both these are ionized in aqueous solution, the acid

group loses a proton to the amino group, and the molecule is positively charged at one end and negatively charged at the other.

Great Chemists

Arrhenius Svante August 1859–1927. Swedish scientist, the founder of physical chemistry. Born near Uppsala, he became a professor at Stockholm in 1895, and made a special study of electrolysis. He wrote *Worlds in the Making* and *Destinies of the Stars*, and in 1903 received the Nobel Prize for Chemistry. In 1905 he predicted global warming as a result of carbon dioxide emission from burning fossil fuels.

Berzelius Jöns Jakob 1779–1848. Swedish chemist who accurately determined more than 2,000 relative atomic and molecular masses. He devised (1813–14) the system of chemical symbols and formulae now in use and proposed oxygen as a reference standard for atomic masses. His discoveries include the elements cerium (1804), selenium (1817), and thorium (1828); he was the first to prepare silicon in its amorphous form and to isolate zirconium. The words *isomerism*, *allotropy*, and *protein* were coined by him.

Cannizzaro Stanislao 1826–1910. Italian chemist who revived interest in the work of Avogadro that had, in 1811, revealed the difference between atoms and molecules, and so established atomic and molecular weights as the basis of chemical calculations.

Curie Marie (born Sklodovska) 1867–1934. Polish scientist. In 1898 she reported the possible existence of a new, powerfully radioactive element in pitchblende ores. Her husband, Pierre (1859–1906) abandoned his own researches to assist her, and in the same year they announced the existence of polonium and radium. They isolated the pure elements 1902. Both scientists refused to take out a patent on their discovery and were jointly awarded the Davy Medal 1903 and the Nobel Prize for Physics 1903, with Antoine Becquerel. Marie Curie wrote a *Treatise on Radioactivity* 1910, and was awarded the Nobel Prize for Chemistry 1911.

Dalton John 1766–1844. English chemist who proposed the theory of atoms, which he considered to be the smallest parts of matter. He produced the first list of relative atomic masses in *Absorption of Gases* 1805 and put forward the law of partial pressures of gases (Dalton's law).

Davy Humphry 1778–1829. English chemist. He discovered, by electrolysis, the metallic elements sodium and potassium in 1807, and calcium, boron, magnesium, strontium, and barium in 1808. In addition, he established that chlorine is an element and proposed that hydrogen is present in all acids. He invented the 'safety lamp' for use in mines where methane was present, enabling miners to work in previously unsafe conditions.

Domagk Gerhard 1895–1964. German pathologist, discoverer of antibacterial sulphonamide drugs. He found in 1932 that a coal-tar dye called Prontosil red contains chemicals with powerful antibacterial properties. Sulphanilamide became the first of the sulphonamide drugs, used before antibiotics were discovered to treat a wide range of conditions, including pneumonia and septic wounds. Domagk was awarded the 1939 Nobel Prize for Physiology and Medicine (which, because of Nazi opposition, he had to wait until 1947 to claim).

Faraday Michael 1791–1867. English chemist and physicist. In 1821 he began experimenting with electromagnetism, and ten years later discovered the induction of electric currents and made the first dynamo. He subsequently found that a magnetic field will rotate the plane of polarization of light. Faraday also investigated electrolysis.

Fischer Emil Hermann 1852–1919. German chemist who produced synthetic sugars and from these various enzymes. His descriptions of the chemistry of the carbohydrates and peptides laid the foundations for the science of biochemistry. Nobel prize 1902.

Gibbs Josiah Willard 1839–1903. US theoretical physicist and chemist who developed a mathematical approach to thermodynamics. His book *Vector Analysis* 1881 established vector methods in physics.

Grignard François Auguste-Victor 1871–1935. French chemist. In 1900 he discovered a series of organic compounds, the *Grignard reagents*, that found applications as some of the most versatile reagents in organic synthesis. Members of the class contain a hydrocarbon radical, magnesium, and a halogen such as chlorine. He shared the 1912 Nobel Prize for Chemistry.

Haber Fritz 1868–1934. German chemist whose conversion of atmospheric nitrogen to ammonia opened the way for the synthetic fertilizer industry. His study of the combustion of hydrocarbons led to the commercial 'cracking' or fractional distillation of natural oil (petroleum) into its components (for example, diesel, petrol, and paraffin). In electrochemistry, he was the first to demonstrate that oxidation and reduction take place at the electrodes; from this he developed a general electrochemical theory.

Haworth Norman 1883–1950. English organic chemist who was the first to synthesize a vitamin (ascorbic acid, vitamin C) 1933, for which he shared a Nobel prize 1937.

Helmont Jean Baptiste van 1577–1644. Belgian doctor who was the first to realize that there are gases other than air, and claimed to have coined the word 'gas' (from Greek *cháos*).

Hodgkin Dorothy Crowfoot 1910–1994. English biochemist who analysed the structure of penicillin, insulin, and vitamin B_{12}. Hodgkin was the first to use a computer to analyse the molecular structure of complex chemicals, and this enabled her to produce three-dimensional models. She was awarded the Nobel Prize for Chemistry 1964.

Hofmann August Wilhelm von 1818–1892. German chemist who studied the extraction and exploitation of coal tar derivatives. Hofmann taught chemistry in London from 1845 until his return to Berlin in 1865.

Kekulé von Stradonitz Friedrich August 1829–1896. German chemist whose theory 1858 of molecular structure revolutionized organic chemistry. He proposed two resonant forms of the benzene ring.

Kendall Edward 1886–1972. US biochemist. In 1914 he isolated the hormone thyroxine, the active compound of the thyroid gland. He went on to work on secretions from the adrenal gland, among which he discovered a compound E, which was in fact the steroid cortisone. For this Kendall shared the 1950 Nobel Prize for Medicine with Philip Hench (1896–1965) and Tadeus Reichstein.

Kendrew John 1917–1997. English biochemist who determined the structure of the muscle protein myoglobin. For this work Kendrew shared the 1962 Nobel Prize for Chemistry with his colleague Max Perutz. Knighted in 1974.

Kornberg Arthur 1918– . US biochemist. In 1956, Kornberg discovered the enzyme DNA-polymerase, which enabled molecules of DNA to be synthesized for the first time. For this work Kornberg shared the 1959 Nobel Prize for Medicine with Severo Ochoa.

Kuhn Richard 1900–1967. Austrian chemist. Working at Heidelberg University in the 1930s, Kuhn succeeded in determining the structures of vitamins A, B_2, and B_6. He was awarded the 1938 Nobel Prize for Chemistry, but was unable to receive it until after World War II.

Langmuir Irving 1881–1957. US scientist who invented the mercury vapour pump for producing a high vacuum, and the atomic hydrogen welding process; he was also a pioneer of the thermionic valve. In 1932 he was awarded a Nobel prize for his work on surface chemistry.

Lavoisier Antoine Laurent 1743–1794. French chemist. He proved that combustion needed only a part of the air, which he called oxygen, thereby destroying the theory of phlogiston (an imaginary 'fire element' released during combustion). With Pierre de Laplace, the astronomer and mathematician, he showed that water was a compound of oxygen and hydrogen. In this way he established the basic rules of chemical combination.

Liebig Justus, Baron von 1803–1873. German chemist, a major contributor to agricultural chemistry. He introduced the theory of radicals and discovered chloroform and chloral.

Martin Archer John Porter 1910– . British biochemist who received the 1952 Nobel Prize for Chemistry for work with Richard Synge on paper chromatography in 1944.

Mendeleyev Dmitri Ivanovich 1834–1907. Russian chemist who framed the periodic law in chemistry 1869, which states that the chemical properties of the elements depend on their relative atomic masses. This law is the basis of the periodic table of elements, in which the elements are arranged by atomic number and organized by their related groups. For this work, Mendeleyev and Lothar Meyer (who presented a similar but independent classification of the elements) received the Davy medal in 1882. From his table Mendeleyev predicted the properties of elements then unknown (gallium, scandium, and germanium).

Mitchell Peter 1920–1992. British chemist. He received a Nobel prize in 1978 for work on the con-

Nobel Prize for Chemistry

1901	Jacobus van't Hoff (Netherlands): laws of chemical dynamics and osmotic pressure
1902	Emil Fischer (Germany): sugar and purine syntheses
1903	Svante Arrhenius (Sweden): electrolytic theory of dissociation
1904	William Ramsay (UK): inert gases in air and their locations in the periodic table
1905	Adolf von Baeyer (Germany): organic dyes and hydroaromatic compounds
1906	Henri Moissan (France): isolation of fluorine and adoption of electric furnace
1907	Eduard Buchner (Germany): biochemical researches and discovery of cell-free fermentation
1908	Ernest Rutherford (New Zealand): atomic disintegration, and the chemistry of radioactive substances
1909	Wilhelm Ostwald (Germany): catalysis, and principles of equilibria and rates of reaction
1910	Otto Wallach (Germany): alicyclic compounds
1911	Marie Curie (Poland): discovery of radium and polonium, and the isolation and study of radium
1912	Victor Grignard (France): discovery of Grignard reagent. Paul Sabatier (France): catalytic hydrogenation of organic compounds
1913	Alfred Werner (Switzerland): bonding of atoms within molecules
1914	Theodore Richards (USA): accurate determination of the atomic masses of many elements
1915	Richard Willstäter (Germany): research into plant pigments, especially chlorophyll
1916–17	no prizes awarded
1918	Fritz Haber (Germany): synthesis of ammonia from its elements
1919	no prizes awarded
1920	Walther Nernst (Germany): work on thermochemistry
1921	Frederick Soddy (UK): work on radioactive substances, especially isotopes
1922	Francis Aston (UK): mass spectrometry of isotopes of radioactive elements, and enunciation of the whole-number rule
1923	Fritz Pregl (Austria): microanalysis of organic substances
1924	no prizes awarded
1925	Richard Zsigmondy (Austria): heterogeneity of colloids
1926	Theodor Svedberg (Sweden): investigation of dispersed systems
1927	Heinrich Wieland (Germany): constitution of bile acids and related substances
1928	Adolf Windaus (Germany): constitution of sterols and related vitamins
1929	Arthur Harden (UK) and Hans von Euler- Chelpin (Germany): fermentation of sugar, and fermentative enzymes
1930	Hans Fischer (Germany): analysis of haem (the iron-bearing group in haemoglobin) and chlorophyll, and the synthesis of haemin (a compound of haem)
1931	Carl Bosch (Germany) and Friedrich Bergius (Germany): invention and development of chemical high-pressure methods
1932	Irving Langmuir (USA): surface chemistry
1933	no prizes awarded
1934	Harold Urey (USA): discovery of deuterium (heavy hydrogen)
1935	Irène and Frédéric Joliot-Curie (France): synthesis of new radioactive elements
1936	Peter Debye (Netherlands): work on molecular structures by investigation of dipole moments and the diffraction of X-rays and electrons in gases
1937	Norman Haworth (UK): work on carbohydrates and ascorbic acid (vitamin C). Paul Karrer (Switzerland): work on carotenoids, flavins, retinol (vitamin A) and riboflavin (vitamin B!2!)
1938	Richard Kuhn (Austria): carotenoids and vitamins
1939	Adolf Butenandt (Germany): work on sex hormones. Leopold Ružička (Switzerland) polymethylenes and higher terpenes
1940–42	no prizes awarded
1943	Georg von Hevesy (Sweden): use of isotopes as tracers in chemical processes
1944	Otto Hahn (Germany): discovery of nuclear fission
1945	Artturi Virtanen (Finland): agriculture and nutrition, especially fodder preservation
1946	James Sumner (USA): crystallization of enzymes. John Northrop (USA) and Wendell Stanley (USA): preparation of pure enzymes and virus proteins
1947	Robert Robinson (UK): biologically important plant products, especially alkaloids
1948	Arne Tiselius (Sweden): electrophoresis and adsorption analysis, and discoveries concerning serum proteins
1949	William Giauque (USA): chemical thermodynamics, especially at very low temperatures
1950	Otto Diels (Germany) and Kurt Alder (Germany): discovery and development of diene synthesis
1951	Edwin McMillan (USA) and Glenn Seaborg (USA): chemistry of transuranic elements
1952	Archer Martin (UK) and Richard Synge (UK): invention of partition chromatography
1953	Hermann Staudinger (West Germany): discoveries in macromolecular chemistry
1954	Linus Pauling (USA): nature of chemical bonds, especially in complex substances
1955	Vincent Du Vigneaud (USA): investigations into biochemically important sulphur compounds, and the first synthesis of a polypeptide hormone
1956	Cyril Hinshelwood (UK) and Nikoly Semenov (USSR): mechanism of chemical reactions

Nobel Prize for Chemistry *(cont.)*

1957	Alexander Todd (UK): nucleotides and nucleotide coenzymes
1958	Frederick Sanger (UK): structure of proteins, especially insulin
1959	Jaroslav Heyrovský (Czechoslovakia): polarographic methods of chemical analysis
1960	Willard Libby (USA): radiocarbon dating in archaeology, geology, and geography
1961	Melvin Calvin (USA): assimilation of carbon dioxide by plants
1962	Max Perutz (UK) and John Kendrew (UK): structures of globular proteins
1963	Karl Ziegler (West Germany) and Giulio Natta (Italy): chemistry and technology of high polymers
1964	Dorothy Crowfoot Hodgkin (UK): crystallographic determination of the structures of biochemical compounds, notably penicillin and cyanocobalamin (vitamin B!12!)
1965	Robert Woodward (USA): organic synthesis
1966	Robert Mulliken (USA): molecular orbital theory of chemical bonds and structures
1967	Manfred Eigen (West Germany), Ronald Norrish (UK), and George Porter (UK): investigation of rapid chemical reactions by means of very short pulses of energy
1968	Lars Onsager (USA): discovery of reciprocal relations, fundamental for the thermodynamics of irreversible processes
1969	Derek Barton (UK) and Odd Hassel (Norway): concept and applications of conformation
1970	Luis Federico Leloir (Argentina): discovery of sugar nucleotides and their role in carbohydrate biosynthesis
1971	Gerhard Herzberg (Canada): electronic structure and geometry of molecules, particularly free radicals
1972	Christian Anfinsen (USA), Stanford Moore (USA), and William Stein (USA): amino-acid structure and biological activity of the enzyme ribonuclease
1973	Ernst Fischer (West Germany) and Geoffrey Wilkinson (UK): chemistry of organometallic sandwich compounds
1974	Paul Flory (USA): physical chemistry of macromolecules
1975	John Cornforth (Australia): stereochemistry of enzyme-catalysed reactions. Vladimir Prelog (Yugoslavia): stereochemistry of organic molecules and their reactions
1976	William N Lipscomb (USA): structure and chemical bonding of boranes (compounds of boron and hydrogen)
1977	Ilya Prigogine (USSR): thermodynamics of irreversible and dissipative processes
1978	Peter Mitchell (UK): biological energy transfer and chemiosmotic theory
1979	Herbert Brown (USA) and Georg Wittig (West Germany): use of boron and phosphorus compounds, respectively, in organic syntheses
1980	Paul Berg (USA): biochemistry of nucleic acids, especially recombinant-DNA. Walter Gilbert (USA) and Frederick Sanger (UK): base sequences in nucleic acids
1981	Kenichi Fukui (Japan) and Roald Hoffmann (USA): theories concerning chemical reactions
1982	Aaron Klug (UK): crystallographic electron microscopy: structure of biologically important nucleic-acid-protein complexes
1983	Henry Taube (USA): electron-transfer reactions in inorganic chemical reactions
1984	Bruce Merrifield (USA): chemical syntheses on a solid matrix
1985	Herbert A Hauptman (USA) and Jerome Karle (USA): methods of determining crystal structures
1986	Dudley Herschbach (USA), Yuan Lee (USA), and John Polanyi (Canada): dynamics of chemical elementary processes
1987	Donald Cram (USA), Jean-Marie Lehn (France), and Charles Pedersen (USA): molecules with highly selective structure-specific interactions
1988	Johann Deisenhofer (West Germany), Robert Huber (West Germany), and Hartmut Michel (West Germany): three-dimensional structure of the reaction centre of photosynthesis
1989	Sydney Altman (USA) and Thomas Cech (USA): discovery of catalytic function of RNA
1990	Elias James Corey (USA): new methods of synthesizing chemical compounds
1991	Richard R Ernst (Switzerland): improvements in the technology of nuclear magnetic resonance (NMR) imaging
1992	Rudolph A Marcus (USA): theoretical discoveries relating to reduction and oxidation reactions.
1993	Kary Mullis (USA): invention of polymerase chain reaction. Michael Smith (Canada): development of technique for splicing foreign genetic segments into an organism's DNA in order to modify the proteins produced.

servation of energy by plants during respiration and photosynthesis.

Nernst (Walther) Hermann 1864–1941. German physical chemist. His investigations, for which he won the 1920 Nobel Prize for Chemistry, were concerned with heat changes in chemical reactions. He proposed in 1906 the principle known as the *Nernst heat theorem* or the third law of thermodynamics: the law states that chemical changes at the temperature of absolute zero involve no change of entropy (disorder).

Nobel Alfred Bernhard 1833–1896. Swedish chemist and engineer. He invented dynamite in 1867 and ballistite, a smokeless gunpowder, in 1889. He amassed a large fortune from the manufacture of explosives and the exploitation of the Baku oilfields in Azerbaijan, near the Caspian Sea. He left this fortune in trust for the endowment of five Nobel prizes.

Ochoa Severo 1905– . Spanish-born US biochemist. He discovered an enzyme able to assemble units of the nucleic acid RNA in 1955, while working at New York University. For his work towards the synthesis of RNA, Ochoa shared the 1959 Nobel Prize for Medicine with Arthur Kornberg.

Ostwald Wilhelm 1853–1932. German chemist who devised the Ostwald process (the oxidation of ammonia over a platinum catalyst to give nitric acid). His work on catalysts laid the foundations of the petrochemical industry. He won the Nobel Prize for Chemistry 1909.

Pauling Linus Carl 1901–1994. US theoretical chemist and biologist. His ideas on chemical bonding are fundamental to modern theories of molecular structure. He also investigated the properties and uses of vitamin C as related to human health. He won the Nobel Prize for Chemistry 1954 and the Nobel Peace Prize 1962, having campaigned for a nuclear-test ban.

Perkin William Henry 1838–1907. British chemist. In 1856 he discovered the mauve dye that originated the aniline dye industry.

Perutz Max 1914– . Austrian-born British biochemist who shared the 1962 Nobel Prize for Chemistry with John Kendrew for work on the structure of the haemoglobin molecule.

Porter George 1920– . English chemist. From 1949 he and Ronald Norrish (1897–1978) developed the technique by which flashes of high energy are used to bring about and study extremely fast chemical reactions. He shared the 1967 Nobel Prize for Chemistry with Norrish and German chemist Manfred Eigen.

Priestley Joseph 1733–1804. English chemist and Presbyterian minister. He identified the gas oxygen 1774. In 1791 his chapel and house were sacked by a mob because of his support for the French Revolution. He emigrated to the USA 1794.

Ramsay William 1852–1916. Scottish chemist who, with Lord Rayleigh, discovered argon 1894. In 1895 Ramsay produced helium and in 1898, in cooperation with Morris Travers (1872–1961), identified neon, krypton, and xenon. In 1903, with Frederick Soddy, he noted the transmutation of radium into helium, which led to the discovery of the density and relative atomic mass of radium. Nobel prize 1904.

Raoult François 1830–1901. French chemist. In 1882, while working at the University of Grenoble, Raoult formulated one of the basic laws of chemistry. *Raoult's law* enables the relative molecular mass of a substance to be determined by noting how much of it is required to depress the freezing point of a solvent by a certain amount.

Scheele Karl Wilhelm 1742–1786. Swedish chemist and pharmacist. In the book *Experiments on Air and Fire* 1777, he argued that the atmosphere was composed of two gases. One, which supported combustion (oxygen), he called 'fire air', and the other, which inhibited combustion (nitrogen), he called 'vitiated air'. He thus anticipated Joseph Priestley's discovery of oxygen by two years.

Seaborg Glenn Theodore 1912– . US nuclear chemist. He was awarded a Nobel prize in 1951 for his discoveries of transuranic elements (with atomic numbers greater than that of uranium), and for production of the radio-isotope uranium-233.

Soddy Frederick 1877–1956. English physical chemist who pioneered research into atomic disintegration and coined the term isotope. He was awarded a Nobel prize 1921 for investigating the origin and nature of isotopes.

Sumner James 1887–1955. US biochemist. In 1926 he succeeded in crystallizing the enzyme urease and demonstrating its protein nature. For this work Sumner shared the 1946 Nobel Prize for Chemistry with John Northrop and Wendell Stanley.

Svedberg Theodor 1884–1971. Swedish chemist. In 1924 he constructed the first ultracentrifuge, a machine that allowed the rapid separation of particles by mass. He was awarded the Nobel Prize for Chemistry 1926.

Szent-Györgyi Albert 1893–1986. Hungarian-born US biochemist who isolated vitamin C and studied the chemistry of muscular activity. He was awarded the Nobel Prize for Medicine 1937.

Tiselius Arne 1902–1971. Swedish chemist who developed a powerful method of chemical analysis known as electrophoresis. He applied his new techniques to the analysis of animal proteins. Nobel prize 1948.

Todd Alexander, Baron Todd 1907– . British organic chemist who won a Nobel prize 1957 for his work on the role of nucleic acids in genetics. He also synthesized vitamins B_1, B_{12}, and E.

Urey Harold Clayton 1893–1981. US chemist. In 1932 he isolated heavy water and discovered deuterium, for which he was awarded the 1934 Nobel Prize for Chemistry.

Vane John 1927– . British pharmacologist who discovered the wide role of prostaglandins in the human body, produced in response to illness and stress. He shared the 1982 Nobel Prize for Medicine with Sune Bergström (1916–) and Bengt Samuelson (1934–) of Sweden.

Wöhler Friedrich 1800–1882. German chemist, a student of Jöns Berzelius, who in 1828 was the first person to synthesize an organic compound (urea) from an inorganic compound (ammonium cyanate). He also devised a method 1827 that isolated the metals aluminum, beryllium, yttrium, and titanium from their ores.

Ziegler Karl 1898–1973. German organic chemist. In 1963 he shared the Nobel Prize for Chemistry with Giulio Natta (1903–1979) of Italy for his work on the chemistry and technology of large polymers. He combined simple molecules of the gas ethylene (ethene) into the long-chain plastic polyethylene (polyethene).

COMPUTING AND ELECTRONICS

How Computers Work

Despite their impressive capabilities, computers are really only able to perform the simplest of tasks: adding or multiplying two numbers together; determining whether one number is greater than another; and so on. It is their ability to perform these tasks extremely quickly and in a predefined sequence that gives them their apparent power.

At the heart of the computer is a *central processing unit* (CPU). The CPU is built around an *arithmetic and logic unit* (ALU), which performs all the basic computations. It includes a set of *registers* that provide limited storage for immediate data and results. The whole thing is coordinated by an internal *clock*.

The CPU is supported by *memory*. This is used to store large amounts of data, as well as programs (instructions). There are two main types of memory. *Internal memory* (or *immediate-access memory*) is readily available to the CPU. It can be accessed very quickly, but its contents are lost when the power is removed. *External memory* (or *backing storage*) is used for longer-term storage. It is provided by such devices as magnetic discs (floppy and hard discs), optical discs (such as CD-ROM), and magnetic tape. These generally provide a higher capacity than internal memory, but are considerably slower. The CPU cannot access external memory directly, so data has to be transferred to internal memory before it can be used.

The CPU communicates with external devices by means of a *bus*. This carries data between the various types of memory, and also to and from the *ports*, to which peripherals such as keyboards, screens, and printers are attached.

Programming

Computers have no intelligence of their own. They work by carrying out the detailed instructions provided by a programmer. The programmer's job is to break down the required task into a series of simple steps.

Programs are written in a *programming language*, designed for the convenience of the programmer. They are then translated into *machine code*, which the computer can execute. The translation is itself done by the computer, using a special program called a *compiler* (which performs the translation before the program is run) or an *interpreter* (which translates each part of the program as it is being executed).

Types of computer

There are four main classes of computer, corresponding roughly to their size and intended use. *Microcomputers* (also called *personal computers* or *PCs*) are the smallest and most common, used in small businesses, at home, and in schools. They are usually single-user machines but can also be linked together to form networks so that users can share data and programs. *Mainframes*, which can often service several hundred users simultaneously, are found in large organizations, such as national companies and government departments. *Minicomputers* were originally developed as smaller, cheaper, less well-equipped alternatives to mainframe computers. They may support from 10 to 200 or so users at once. The dividing line between minicomputers and mainframes has never been well defined and the advent of more powerful microcomputer-based systems that rival minicomputers has made the term even less clear. *Supercomputers* are capable of very high computing speeds and are used for highly complex scientific tasks, such as analysing the results of nuclear physics experiments and weather forecasting.

Computers are also classified by *generation*. Computers of the first generation were developed in the 1940s and 1950s, and made from valves and wire circuits. Second-generation computers, emerging in the early 1960s, incorporated transistors and printed circuits. The third generation, from the late 1960s, used integrated circuits and were often sold as families of computers, such as the IBM 360 series. Fourth-generation computers are the most commonly used in the 1990s, and are based on microprocessors, large-scale integration (LSI), and sophisticated programming languages. Finally, a fifth generation is emerging, using very large-scale integration (VLSI) and parallel processors.

Uses of Computers

artificial intelligence (AI) branch of science concerned with creating computer programs that can perform actions comparable with those of an intelligent human. Current AI research covers such areas as planning (for robot behaviour), language understanding, pattern recognition, and knowledge representation.

Early AI programs, developed in the 1960s, attempted simulations of human intelligence or were aimed at general problem-solving techniques. It is now thought that intelligent behaviour depends as much on the knowledge a system possesses as on its reasoning power. Present emphasis is on knowledge-based systems, such as expert systems. Britain's largest AI laboratory is at the Turing Institute, University of Strathclyde, Glasgow. In May 1990 the first International Robot Olympics was held there, including table-tennis matches between robots of the UK and the USA.

CAD (acronym for *computer-aided design*) the use of computers in creating and editing design drawings. CAD also allows such things as automatic testing of designs and multiple or animated three-dimensional views of designs. CAD systems are widely used in architecture, electronics, and engineering, for example in the motor-vehicle industry, where cars designed with the assistance of computers are now commonplace. A related development is CAM (computer-assisted manufacturing).

CAL (acronym for *computer-assisted learning*) the use of computers in education and training: the computer displays instructional material to a student and asks questions about the information given; the student's answers determine the sequence of the lessons.

Computing: chronology

1614	John Napier invented logarithms.
1615	William Oughtred invented the slide rule.
1623	Wilhelm Schickard (1592–1635) invented the mechanical calculating machine.
1645	Blaise Pascal produced a calculator.
1672–74	Gottfried Leibniz built his first calculator, the Stepped Reckoner.
1801	Joseph-Marie Jacquard developed an automatic loom controlled by punch cards.
1820	The first mass-produced calculator, the Arithometer, was developed by Charles Thomas de Colmar (1785–1870).
1822	Charles Babbage completed his first model for the difference engine.
1830s	Babbage created the first design for the analytical engine.
1890	Herman Hollerith developed the punched-card ruler for the US census.
1936	Alan Turing published the mathematical theory of computing.
1938	Konrad Zuse constructed the first binary calculator, using Boolean algebra.
1939	US mathematician and physicist J V Atanasoff (1903–) became the first to use electronic means for mechanizing arithmetical operations.
1943	The Colossus electronic code-breaker was developed at Bletchley Park, England. The Harvard University Mark I or Automatic Sequence Controlled Calculator (partly financed by IBM) became the first program-controlled calculator.
1946	ENIAC (acronym for electronic numerator, integrator, analyser, and computer), the first general purpose, fully electronic digital computer, was completed at the University of Pennsylvania, USA.
1948	Manchester University (England) Mark I, the first stored-program computer, was completed. William Shockley of Bell Laboratories invented the transistor.
1951	Launch of Ferranti Mark I, the first commercially produced computer. Whirlwind, the first real- time computer, was built for the US air-defence system. Grace Murray Hopper of Remington Rand invented the compiler computer program.
1952	EDVAC (acronym for electronic discrete variable computer) was completed at the Institute for Advanced Study, Princeton, USA (by John Von Neumann and others).
1953	Magnetic core memory was developed.
1958	The first integrated circuit was constructed.
1963	The first minicomputer was built by Digital Equipment (DEC). The first electronic calculator was built by Bell Punch Company.
1964	Launch of IBM System/360, the first compatible family of computers. John Kemeny and Thomas Kurtz of Dartmouth College invented BASIC (Beginner's All-purpose Symbolic Instruction Code), a computer language similar to FORTRAN.
1965	The first supercomputer, the Control Data CD6600, was developed.
1971	The first microprocessor, the Intel 4004, was announced.
1974	CLIP–4, the first computer with a parallel architecture, was developed by John Backus at IBM.
1975	Altair 8800, the first personal computer (PC), or microcomputer, was launched.
1981	The Xerox Star system, the first WIMP system (acronym for windows, icons, menus, and pointing devices), was developed. IBM launched the IBM PC.
1984	Apple launched the Macintosh computer.
1985	The Inmos T414 transputer, the first 'off-the-shelf' microprocessor for building parallel computers, was announced.
1988	The first optical microprocessor, which uses light instead of electricity, was developed.
1989	Wafer-scale silicon memory chips, able to store 200 million characters, were launched.
1990	Microsoft released Windows 3, a popular windowing environment for PCs.
1992	Philips launched the CD-I (compact disc-interactive) player, based on CD audio technology, to provide interactive multimedia programs for the home user.
1993	The Personal Digital Assistant went on sale, using a stylus for input; the PDA recognizes handwriting, which is turned into text for storage, fax transmission, or printout.

CAM (acronym for *computer–aided manufacturing*) the use of computers to control production processes; in particular, the control of machine tools and robots in factories. In some factories, the whole design and production system has been automated by linking CAD (computer-aided design) to CAM.

computer game or *video game* any computer-controlled game in which the computer (sometimes) opposes the human player. Computer games typically employ fast, animated graphics on a VDU (visual display unit), and synthesized sound.

computer graphics use of computers to display and manipulate information in pictorial form. The output may be as simple as a pie chart, or as complex as an animated sequence in a science-fiction film, or a seemingly three-dimensional engineering blueprint. Input may be achieved by scanning an image, by drawing with a mouse or stylus on a graphics tablet, or by drawing directly on the screen with a light pen. The drawing is stored in the computer as raster graphics or vector graphics. Computer graphics are increasingly used in computer-aided design (CAD), and to generate models and simulations in engineering, meteorology, medicine and surgery, and other fields of science.

Recent developments in software mean that designers on opposite sides of the world will soon be able to work on complex three-dimensional computer models using ordinary PCs linked by telephone lines rather then powerful graphics workstations.

computer simulation representation of a real-life situation in a computer program. For example, the program might simulate the flow of customers arriving at a bank. The user can alter variables, such as the number of cashiers on duty, and see the effect. More complex simulations can model the behaviour of chemical reactions or even nuclear explosions. Computers also control the actions of machines – for example, a flight simulator models the behaviour of real aircraft and allows training to take place in safety. Computer simulations are very useful when it is too dangerous, time consuming, or simply impossible to carry out a real experiment or test.

database a structured collection of data, which may be manipulated to select and sort desired items of information. For example, an accounting system might be built around a database containing details of customers and suppliers. In larger computers, the database makes data available to the various programs that need it, without the need for those programs to be aware of how the data are stored. The term is also sometimes used for simple record-keeping systems, such as mailing lists, in which there are facilities for searching, sorting, and producing records. A collection of databases is known as a *databank*. A database-management system (DBMS) program ensures that the integrity of the data is maintained by controlling the degree of access of the applications programs using the data.

desktop publishing (DTP) use of microcomputers for small-scale typesetting and page make-up. DTP systems are capable of producing camera-ready pages (pages ready for photographing and printing), made up of text and graphics, with text set in different typefaces and sizes. The page can be previewed on the screen before final printing on a laser printer.

electronic mail or *E-mail* system that enables the users of a computer network to send messages to other users. The messages are usually placed in a reserved area of backing store on a central computer until they are retrieved by the receiving user. Passwords are frequently used to prevent unauthorized access to stored messages.

expert system computer program for giving advice (such as diagnosing an illness or interpreting the law) that incorporates knowledge derived from human expertise. It is a kind of knowledge-based system containing rules that can be applied to find the solution to a problem. It is a form of artificial intelligence.

hypertext system for viewing information (both text and pictures) on a computer screen in such a way that related items of information can easily be reached. For example, the program might display a map of a country; if the user clicks (with a mouse) on a particular city, the program will display some information about that city.

information technology (IT) use of computers to produce, store, handle, and retrieve information. The machines used today are mostly microcomputers

rather than mainframe computers. Word processing, databases, and spreadsheets are just some of the software packages which have revolutionized work in the office environment.

multimedia computer system that combines audio and video components to create an interactive application that uses text, sound, and graphics (still, animated, and video sequences). For example, a multimedia database of musical instruments may allow a user not only to search and retrieve text about a particular instrument but also to see pictures of it and hear it play a piece of music. Multimedia PCs are frequently fitted with CD drives because of the high storage capacity of CD-ROM discs.

point of sale in business premises, the point where a sale is transacted, for example, a supermarket checkout. In conjunction with electronic funds transfer, point of sale is part of the terminology of 'cashless shopping', enabling buyers to transfer funds directly from their bank accounts to the shop's.

simulation short for computer simulation.

speech recognition or *voice input* in computing, any technique by which a computer can understand ordinary speech. Spoken words are divided into 'frames', each lasting about one-thirtieth of a second, which are converted to a wave form. These are then compared with a series of stored frames to determine the most likely word. Research into speech recognition started in 1938, but the technology did not become sufficiently developed for commercial applications until the late 1980s.

spreadsheet a program that mimics a sheet of ruled paper, divided into columns and rows. The user enters values in the sheet, then instructs the program to perform some operation on them, such as totalling a column or finding the average of a series of numbers. Highly complex numerical analyses may be built up from these simple steps. Spreadsheets are widely used in business for forecasting and financial control. The first spreadsheet program, Software Arts' VisiCalc, appeared 1979. The best known include Lotus 1–2–3 and Microsoft Excel.

virtual reality advanced form of computer simulation, in which a participant has the illusion of being part of an artificial environment. The participant views the environment through two tiny television screens (one for each eye) built into a visor. Sensors detect movements of the participant's head or body, causing the apparent viewing position to change. Gloves (datagloves) fitted with sensors may be worn, which allow the participant seemingly to pick up and move objects in the environment. The technology is still under development but is expected to have widespread applications; for example, in military and surgical training, architecture, and home entertainment.

word processing storage and retrieval of written text by computer. Word-processing software packages enable the writer to key in text and amend it in a number of ways. A print-out can be obtained or the text can be sent to another person or organization on disc or via electronic mail. Word-processing packages can be used with databases or graphics packages, and desk-top publishing packages are available too.

workstation high-performance desktop computer with strong graphics capabilities, traditionally used for engineering (CAD and CAM), scientific research, and desktop publishing. Frequently based on fast RISC (reduced instruction-set computer) chips, workstations generally offer more processing power than microcomputers (although the distinction between workstations and the more powerful microcomputer models is becoming increasingly blurred). Most workstations use Unix as their operating system, and have good networking facilities.

Computer Hardware

CD-ROM (abbreviation for *compact-disc read-only memory*) computer storage device developed from the technology of the audio compact disc. It consists of a plastic-coated metal disc, on which binary digital information is etched in the form of microscopic pits. This can then be read optically by passing a light beam over the disc. CD-ROMs typically hold about 550 megabytes of data, and are used in distributing large amounts of text and graphics, such as encyclopedias, catalogues, and technical manuals.

Standard CD-ROMs cannot have information written onto them by computer, but must be manufactured from a master. A compact disc that can be overwritten repeatedly by a computer has also been developed.

CD-I (or *compact-disc interactive*) is a form of CD-ROM used with a computerized reader, which responds intelligently to the user's instructions

digitizer a device that converts an analogue video signal into a digital format so that video images can be input, stored, displayed, and manipulated by a computer. The term is sometimes used to refer to a graphics tablet.

disc or *disk* a common medium for storing large volumes of data (an alternative is magnetic tape). A *magnetic disc* is rotated at high speed in a disc-drive unit as a read/write (playback or record) head passes over its surfaces to record or read the magnetic variations that encode the data. Recently, *optical discs*, such as CD-ROM (compact-disc read-only memory) and WORM (write once, read many times), have been used to store computer data. Data are recorded on the disc surface as etched microscopic pits and are read by a laser-scanning device. Optical discs have an enormous capacity – about 550 megabytes (million bytes) on a compact disc, and thousands of megabytes on a full-size optical disc.

Magnetic discs come in several forms: *fixed hard discs* are built into the disc-drive unit, occasionally stacked on top of one another. A fixed disc cannot be removed: once it is full, data must be deleted in order to free space or a complete new disc drive must be added to the computer system in order to increase storage capacity. Large fixed discs, used with mainframe and minicomputers, provide up to 3,000 megabytes. Small fixed discs for use with microcomputers typically hold 40–400 megabytes. *Removable hard discs* are common in minicomputer systems. The discs are contained, individually or as stacks, in a protective plastic case, and can be taken out of the drive unit and kept for later use. By swapping such discs around, a single hard-disc drive can be made to provide a potentially infinite storage capacity. However, access speeds and capacities tend to be lower that those associated with large fixed hard discs. A *floppy disc* (or diskette) is the most common form of backing store for microcomputers. It is much smaller in size and capacity than a hard disc, normally holding 0.5–2 megabytes of data. The floppy disc is so called because it is manufactured from thin flexible plastic coated with a magnetic material. The earliest form of floppy disc was packaged in a card case and was easily damaged; more recent versions are contained in a smaller, rigid plastic case and are much more robust. All floppy discs can be removed from the drive unit.

graphics tablet or *bit pad* an input device in which a stylus or cursor is moved, by hand, over a flat surface. The computer can keep track of the position of the stylus, so enabling the operator to input drawings or diagrams into the computer.

joystick an input device that signals to a computer the direction and extent of displacement of a hand-held lever. It is similar to the joystick used to control the flight of an aircraft. Joysticks are sometimes used to control the movement of a cursor across a display screen, but are much more frequently used to provide fast and direct input for moving the characters and symbols that feature in computer games. Unlike a mouse, which can move a pointer in any direction, simple games joysticks are often only capable of moving an object in one of eight different directions.

keyboard an input device resembling a typewriter keyboard, used to enter instructions and data. There are many variations on the layout and labelling of keys. Extra numeric keys may be added, as may special-purpose function keys, whose effects can be defined by programs in the computer.

light pen a device resembling an ordinary pen, used to indicate locations on a computer screen. With certain computer-aided design (CAD) programs, the light pen can be used to instruct the computer to change the shape, size, position, and colours of sections of a screen image. The pen has a photoreceptor at its tip that emits signals when light from the screen passes beneath it. From the timing of this signal and a gridlike representation of the screen in the computer memory, a computer program can calculate the position of the light pen.

memory the part of a system used to store data and programs either permanently or temporarily. There are two main types: immediate access memory and backing storage. Memory capacity is measured in bytes or, more conveniently, in kilobytes (units of 1,024 bytes) or megabytes (units of 1,024 kilobytes).

Immediate access memory, or *internal memory*, describes the memory locations that can be addressed directly and individually by the central processing unit. It is either read-only (stored in ROM, PROM, and EPROM chips) or read/write (stored in RAM chips). Read-only memory stores information that must be constantly available and is unlikely to be changed. It is nonvolatile – that is, it is not lost when the computer is switched off. Read/write memory is volatile – it stores programs and data only while the computer is switched on.

Backing storage, or **external memory**, is non-volatile memory, located outside the central processing unit, used to store programs and data that are not in current use. Backing storage is provided by such devices as magnetic discs (floppy and hard discs), magnetic tape (tape streamers and cassettes), optical discs (such as CD-ROM), and bubble memory. By rapidly switching blocks of information between the backing storage and the immediate-access memory, the limited size of the immediate-access memory may be increased artificially. When this technique is used to give the appearance of a larger internal memory than physically exists, the additional capacity is referred to as virtual memory.

modem (acronym for **modulator/demodulator**) device for transmitting computer data over telephone lines. Such a device is necessary because the digital signals produced by computers cannot, at present, be transmitted directly over the telephone network, which uses analogue signals. The modem converts the digital signals to analogue, and back again. Modems are used for linking remote terminals to central computers and enable computers to communicate with each other anywhere in the world.

mouse an input device used to control a pointer on a computer screen. It is a feature of graphical user-interface (GUI) systems. The mouse is about the size of a pack of playing cards, is connected to the computer by a wire, and incorporates one or more buttons that can be pressed. Moving the mouse across a flat surface causes a corresponding movement of the pointer. In this way, the operator can manipulate objects on the screen and make menu selections. Mice work either mechanically (with electrical contacts to sense the movement in two planes of a ball on a level surface), or optically (photoelectric cells detecting movement by recording light reflected from a grid on which the mouse is moved).

plotter or **graph plotter** device that draws pictures or diagrams under computer control. Plotters are often used for producing business charts, architectural plans, and engineering drawings. **Flatbed plotters** move a pen up and down across a flat drawing surface, whereas **roller plotters** roll the drawing paper past the pen as it moves from side to side.

printer an output device for producing printed copies of text or graphics. Types include the **daisy-wheel printer**, which produces good-quality text but no graphics; the **dot-matrix printer**, which produces text and graphics by printing a pattern of small dots; the **ink-jet printer**, which creates text and graphics by spraying a fine jet of quick-drying ink onto the paper; and the **laser printer**, which uses electrostatic technology very similar to that used by a photocopier to produce high-quality text and graphics.

screen or **monitor** output device on which the computer displays information for the benefit of the operator. The commonest type is the cathode-ray tube (CRT), which is similar to a television screen. Portable computers often use liquid crystal display (LCD) screens. These are harder to read than CRTs, but require less power, making them suitable for battery operation.

touch screen an input device allowing the user to communicate with the computer by touching a display screen with a finger. In this way, the user can point to a required menu option or item of data. Typically, the screen is able to detect the touch either because the finger presses against a sensitive membrane or because it interrupts a grid of light beams crossing the screen surface. Touch screens are used less widely than other pointing devices such as the mouse or joystick.

VDU abbreviation for **visual display unit** computer terminal consisting of a keyboard for input data and a screen for displaying output. The oldest and the most popular type of VDU screen is the cathode-ray tube (CRT), which uses essentially the same technology as a television screen. Other types use plasma display technology and liquid-crystal displays.

Terms

ASCII (acronym for **American standard code for information interchange**) a coding system in which numbers are assigned to letters, digits, and punctuation symbols. Although computers work in binary number code, ASCII numbers are usually quoted as decimal or hexadecimal numbers. For example, the decimal number 45 (binary 0101101) represents a hyphen, and 65 (binary 1000001) a capital A. The first 32 codes are used for control functions, such as carriage return and backspace.

binary number system or **binary number code** system of numbers to base two, using combinations of the digits 1 and 0. Codes based on binary numbers are used to represent instructions and data in all modern digital computers, the values of the binary digits (contracted to 'bits') being represented as the on/off states of switches and high/low voltages in circuits. (See table on next page.)

bit (contraction of **bi**nary digi**t**) a single binary digit, either 0 or 1. A bit is the smallest unit of data stored in a computer; all other data must be coded into a pattern of individual bits. A byte represents sufficient computer memory to store a single character of data, and usually contains eight bits. For example, in the ASCII code system used by most microcomputers the capital letter A would be stored in a single byte of memory as the bit pattern 01000001.

boot or **bootstrap** the process of starting up a computer. Most computers have a small, built-in boot program that starts automatically when the computer is switched on – its only task is to load a slightly larger program, usually from a disc, which in turn loads the main operating system. In microcomputers the operating system is often held in the permanent ROM memory and the boot program simply triggers its operation.

buffer a part of the memory used to store data temporarily while it is waiting to be used. For example, a program might store data in a printer buffer until the printer is ready to print it.

byte sufficient computer memory to store a single character of data. The character is stored in the byte of memory as a pattern of bits (binary digits), using a code such as ASCII. A byte usually contains eight bits – for example, the capital letter F can be stored as

Binary number system

Character	Binary code
A	1000001
B	1000010
C	1000011
D	1000100
E	1000101
F	1000110
G	1000111
H	1001000
I	1001001
J	1001010
K	1001011
L	1001100
M	1001101
N	1001110
O	1001111
P	1010000
Q	1010001
R	1010010
S	1010011
T	1010100
U	1010101
V	1010110
W	1010111
X	1011000
Y	1011001
Z	1011010

the bit pattern 01000110. A single byte can specify 256 values, such as the decimal numbers from 0 to 255; in the case of a single-byte pixel (picture element), it can specify 256 different colours. Three bytes (24 bits) can specify 16,777,216 values. Computer memory size is measured in *kilobytes* (1,024 bytes) or *megabytes* (1,024 kilobytes).

chip or *silicon chip* another name for an *integrated circuit*, a complete electronic circuit on a slice of silicon (or other semiconductor) crystal only a few millimetres square.

client-server architecture a system in which the mechanics of looking after data are separated from the programs that use the data. For example, the 'server' might be a central database, typically located on a large computer that is reserved for this purpose. The 'client' would be an ordinary program that requests data from the server as needed.

data facts, figures, and symbols, especially as stored in computers. The term is often used to mean raw, unprocessed facts, as distinct from information, to which a meaning or interpretation has been applied.

data compression techniques for reducing the amount of storage needed for a given amount of data. They include word tokenization (in which frequently used words are stored as shorter codes), variable bit lengths (in which common characters are represented by fewer bits than less common ones), and run-length encoding (in which a repeated value is stored once along with a count).

dedicated computer computer built into another device for the purpose of controlling or supplying information to it. Its use has increased dramatically since the advent of the microprocessor: washing machines, digital watches, cars, and video recorders all now have their own processors.

directory a list of file names, together with information that enables a computer to retrieve those files from backing storage. The computer operating system will usually store and update a directory on the backing storage to which it refers. So, for example, on each disc used by a computer a directory file will be created listing the disc's contents.

DOS (acronym for *disc operating system*) computer operating system specifically designed for use with disc storage; also used as an alternative name for a particular operating system, MS-DOS.

emulator an item of software or firmware that allows one device to imitate the functioning of another. Emulator software is commonly used to allow one make of computer to run programs written for a different make of computer. This allows a user to select from a wider range of applications programs, and perhaps to save money by running programs designed for an expensive computer on a cheaper model.

function a small part of a program that supplies a specific value – for example, the square root of a specified number, or the current date. Most programming languages incorporate a number of built-in functions; some allow programmers to write their own. A function may have one or more arguments (the values on which the function operates). A *function key* on a keyboard is one that, when pressed, performs a designated task, such as ending a program.

fuzzy logic a form of knowledge representation suitable for notions (such as 'hot' or 'loud') that cannot be defined precisely but which depend on their context. For example, a jug of water may be described as too hot or too cold, depending on whether it is to be used to wash one's face or to make tea. The central idea of fuzzy logic is *probability of set membership*. For instance, referring to someone 5 ft 9 in tall, the statement 'this person is tall' (or 'this person is a member of the set of tall people') might be about 70% true if that person is a man, and about 85% true if that person is a woman. Fuzzy logic enables computerized devices to reason more like humans, responding effectively to complex messages from their control panels and sensors. For example, a vacuum cleaner launched in 1992 by Matsushita uses fuzzy logic to adjust its sucking power in response to messages from its sensors about the type of dirt on the floor, its distribution, and its depth.

gigabyte a measure of memory capacity, equal to 1,024 megabytes. It is also used, less precisely, to mean 1,000 billion bytes.

graphical user interface (GUI) or *WIMP* a type of user interface in which programs and files appear as icons (small pictures), user options are selected from pull-down menus, and data are displayed in windows (rectangular areas), which the operator can manipulate in various ways. The operator uses a pointing device, typically a mouse, to make selections and initiate actions.

The concept of the graphical user interface was developed by the Xerox Corporation in the 1970s, was popularized with the Apple Macintosh computers in the 1980s, and is now available on many types of computer – most notably as Windows, an operating system for IBM PC-compatible microcomputers developed by the software company Microsoft.

hacking unauthorized access to a computer, either for fun or for malicious or fraudulent purposes. Hackers generally use microcomputers and telephone lines to obtain access. In computing, the term is used in a wider sense to mean using software for enjoyment or self-education, not necessarily involving unauthorized access.

hardware the mechanical, electrical, and electronic components of a computer system, as opposed to the various programs, which constitute software. Hardware associated with a microcomputer might include the power supply and housing of its processor unit, its circuit boards, VDU (screen), disc drive, keyboard, and printer.

hexadecimal number system number system to the base 16, used in computing. In hex (as it is commonly known) the decimal numbers 0–15 are represented by the characters 0, 1, 2, 3, 4, 5, 6, 7, 8, 9, A, B, C, D, E, F. Hexadecimal numbers are easy to convert to the computer's internal binary code and are more compact than binary numbers.

image compression one of a number of methods used to reduce the amount of information required to represent an image, so that it takes up less computer memory and can be transmitted more rapidly and economically via telecommunications systems. It plays a major role in fax transmission and in videophone and multimedia systems.

integrated circuit (IC), popularly called *silicon chip*, a miniaturized electronic circuit produced on a single crystal, or chip, of a semiconducting material – usually silicon. It may contain many thousands of components and yet measure only 5 mm/0.2 in square and 1 mm/0.04 in thick. The IC is encapsulated within a plastic or ceramic case, and linked via gold wires to metal pins with which it is connected to a printed circuit board and the other components that make up such electronic devices as computers and calculators.

interface the point of contact between two programs or pieces of equipment. The term is most often used for the physical connection between the computer and a peripheral device, which is used to compensate for differences in such operating characteristics as speed, data coding, voltage, and power consumption. For example, a *printer interface* is the cabling and circuitry used to transfer data from a computer to a printer, and to compensate for differences in speed and coding.

kilobyte (K or KB) a unit of memory equal to 1,024 bytes. It is sometimes used, less precisely, to mean 1,000 bytes.

laptop computer portable microcomputer, small enough to be used on the operator's lap. It consists of a single unit, incorporating a keyboard, floppy disc or hard disc drives, and a screen. The screen often forms a lid that folds back in use. It uses a liquid-crystal or gas-plasma display, rather than the bulkier and heavier cathode-ray tubes found in most display terminals. A typical laptop computer measures about 210

× 297 mm/8.3 × 11.7 in (A4), is 5 cm/2 in thick, and weighs less than 3 kg/6 lb 9 oz.

local area network (LAN) a network restricted to a single room or building. Local area networks enable around 500 devices to be connected together.

Macintosh range of microcomputers produced by Apple Computers. The Apple Macintosh, introduced in 1984, was the first popular microcomputer with a graphical user interface. The success of the Macintosh prompted other manufacturers and software companies to create their own graphical user interfaces. Most notable of these are Microsoft Windows, which runs on IBM PC-compatible microcomputers, and OSF/Motif, from the Open Software Foundation, which is used with many Unix systems.

macro in programming, a new command created by combining a number of existing ones. For example, if a programming language has separate commands for obtaining data from the keyboard and for displaying data on the screen, the programmer might create a macro that performs both these tasks with one command. A *macro key* on the keyboard combines the effects of pressing several individual keys.

megabyte (Mb) a unit of memory equal to 1,024 kilobytes. It is sometimes used, less precisely, to mean 1 million bytes.

menu a list of options, displayed on screen, from which the user may make a choice – for example, the choice of services offered to the customer by a bank cash dispenser: withdrawal, deposit, balance, or statement. Menus are used extensively in graphical user-interface (GUI) systems, where the menu options are often selected using a pointing device called a mouse.

microprocessor complete computer central processing unit (CPU) contained on a single integrated circuit, or chip. The appearance of the first microprocessor 1971 designed by Intel for a pocket calculator manufacturer heralded the introduction of the microcomputer. The microprocessor has led to a dramatic fall in the size and cost of computers, and dedicated computers can now be found in washing machines, cars, and so on. Examples of microprocessors are the Intel 8086 family and the Motorola 68000 family.

MIDI (acronym for *musical instruments digital interface*) standard interface that enables electronic musical instruments to be connected to a computer. A computer with a MIDI interface can input and store the sounds produced by the connected instruments, and can then manipulate these sounds in many different ways. For example, a single keystroke may change the key of an entire composition. Even a full written score for the composition may be automatically produced.

morphing the metamorphosis of one shape or object into another by computer-generated animation. First used in film-making in 1990, it has transformed cinema special effects. Conventional animation is limited to two dimensions; morphing enables the creation of three dimensional transformations. To create such effects, the start and end of the transformation must be specified on screen using a wire-frame model that mathematically defines the object. To make the object three-dimensional, the

Programming languages: a selection

Language	Main uses	Description
assembler languages	jobs needing detailed control of the hardware, fast execution, and small program sizes	fast and efficient but require considerable effort and skill
BASIC (*b*eginner's *a*ll-purpose *s*ymbolic *i*nstruction *co*de)	in education and the home, and among nonprofessional programmers, such as engineers	easy to learn; early versions (derived from FORTRAN) lacked the features of other languages
C	systems programming; general programming	fast and efficient; widely used as a general-purpose language; especially popular among professional programmers
COBOL (*co*mmon *b*usiness-*o*riented *l*anguage)	business programming	strongly oriented towards data processing work; easy to learn but very verbose; widely used on mainframes
FORTRAN (*for*mula *tran*slation)	scientific and computational work	based on mathematical formulae; popular among engineers, scientists, and mathematicians
LISP (*lis*t *p*rocessing)	artificial intelligence	symbolic language with a reputation for being hard to learn; popular in the academic and research communities
Modula-2	systems and real-time programming; general programming	highly structured; intended to replace Pascal for 'real-world' applications
PASCAL	general-purpose language	highly structured; widely used for teaching programming in universities
PROLOG (*pro*gramming in *log*ic)	artificial intelligence	symbolic-logic programming system, originally intended for theorem solving but now used more generally in artificial intelligence

wire can be extruded from a cross-section or turned as on a lathe to produce and evenly turned surface. This is then rendered, or filled in and shaded. Once the beginning and end objects have been created the computer can calculate the morphing process.

Morphing has many scientific uses, for example, it can be used by a palaeontologist to reconstruct a skull from a handful of teeth.

MS-DOS (abbreviation for *Microsoft Disc Operating System*) computer operating system produced by Microsoft Corporation, widely used on microcomputers with Intel x 86 family microprocessors. A version called PC-DOS is sold by IBM specifically for its personal computers. MS-DOS and PC-DOS are usually referred to as DOS. MS-DOS first appeared 1981, and was similar to an earlier system from Digital Research called CP/M.

multitasking or *multiprogramming* a system in which one processor appears to run several different programs (or different parts of the same program) at the same time. All the programs are held in memory together and each is allowed to run for a certain period. For example, one program may run while other programs are waiting for a peripheral device to work or for input from an operator. The ability to multitask depends on the operating system rather than the type of computer. Unix is one of the commonest.

neural network artificial network of processors that attempts to mimic the structure of nerve cells (neurons) in the human brain. Neural networks may be electronic, optical, or simulated by computer soft-

ware. A basic network has three layers of processors: an input layer, an output layer, and a 'hidden' layer in between. Each processor is connected to every other in the network by a system of 'synapses'; every processor in the top layer connects to every one in the hidden layer, and each of these connects to every processor in the output layer. This means that each nerve cell in the middle and bottom layers receives input from several different sources; only when the amount of input exceeds a critical level does the cell fire an output signal.

The chief characteristic of neural networks is their ability to sum up large amounts of imprecise data and decide whether they match a pattern or not. Networks of this type may be used in developing robot vision, matching fingerprints, and analysing fluctuations in stock-market prices. However, it is thought unlikely by scientists that such networks will ever be able accurately to imitate the human brain, which is very much more complicated; it contains around 10 billion nerve cells, whereas current artificial networks contain only a few hundred processors.

notebook computer small laptop computer. Notebook computers became available in the early 1990s and, even complete with screen and hard-disc drive, are no larger than a standard A4 notebook.

operating system (OS) a program that controls the basic operation of a computer. A typical OS controls the peripheral devices, organizes the filing system, provides a means of communicating with the operator, and runs other programs. Some operating systems were written for specific computers, but some are accepted standards. These include CP/M (by Digital Research) and MS-DOS (by Microsoft) for microcomputers. Unix (developed at AT&T's Bell Laboratories) is the standard on workstations, minicomputers, and super computers; it is also used on desktop PCs and mainframes.

pixel (acronym for *picture element*) single dot on a computer screen. All screen images are made up of a collection of pixels, with each pixel being either off (dark) or on (illuminated, possibly in colour). The number of pixels available determines the screen's resolution. Typical resolutions of microcomputer screens vary from 320×200 pixels to 640×480 pixels, but screens with 1024×768 pixels are now quite common for high-quality graphic (pictorial) displays.

procedure a small part of a computer program that performs a specific task, such as clearing the screen or sorting a file. A *procedural language*, such as BASIC, is one in which the programmer describes a task in terms of how it is to be done, as opposed to a *declarative language*, such as PROLOG, in which it is described in terms of the required result.

RISC (acronym for *reduced instruction-set computer*) a microprocessor (processor on a single chip) that carries out fewer instructions than other (CISC) microprocessors in common use in the 1990s. Because of the low number of machine-code instructions, the processor carries out those instructions very quickly.

software a collection of programs and procedures for making a computer perform a specific task, as opposed to hardware, the physical components of a computer system. Software is created by programmers and is either distributed on a suitable medium, such as the floppy disc, or built into the computer in the form of firmware. Examples of software include operating systems, compilers, and applications programs, such as payrolls. No computer can function without some form of software.

Unix multiuser operating system designed for minicomputers but becoming increasingly popular on large microcomputers, workstations, mainframes, and supercomputers. It was developed by AT&T's Bell Laboratories in the USA during the late 1960s, using the programming language C. It could therefore run on any machine with a C compiler, so ensuring its wide portability. Its wide range of functions and flexibility have made it widely used by universities and in commercial software.

user interface the procedures and methods through which the user operates a program. These might include menus, input forms, error messages, and keyboard procedures. A graphical user interface (GUI or WIMP) is one that makes use of icons (small pictures) and allows the user to make menu selections with a mouse.

virtual memory a technique whereby a portion of the computer backing storage, or external, memory is used as an extension of its immediate-access, or internal, memory. The contents of an area of the immediate-access memory are stored on, say, a hard disc while they are not needed, and brought back into main memory when required.

virus a piece of software that can replicate itself and transfer itself from one computer to another, without the user being aware of it. Some viruses are relatively harmless, but others can damage or destroy data. They are written by anonymous programmers, often maliciously, and are spread along telephone lines or on floppy discs. Antivirus software can be used to detect and destroy well-known viruses, but new viruses continually appear and these may bypass existing antivirus programs.

wide area network a network that connects computers distributed over a wide geographical area.

window a rectangular area on the screen of a graphical user interface. A window is used to display data and can be manipulated in various ways by the computer user.

word a group of bits (binary digits) that a computer's central processing unit treats as a single working unit. The size of a word varies from one computer to another and, in general, increasing the word length leads to a faster and more powerful computer. In the late 1970s and early 1980s, most microcomputers were 8-bit machines. During the 1980s 16-bit microcomputers were introduced and 32-bit microcomputers are now available. Mainframe computers may be 32-bit or 64-bit machines.

WYSIWYG (acronym for *what you see is what you get*) a program that attempts to display on the screen a faithful representation of the final printed output. For example, a WYSIWYG word processor would show actual page layout – line widths, page breaks, and the sizes and styles of type.

Electronics

Electronics is the branch of science that deals with the emission of electrons from conductors and semiconductors, with the subsequent manipulation of these electrons, and with the construction of electronic devices. The first electronic device was the thermionic valve, or vacuum tube, in which electrons moved in a vacuum, and led to such inventions as radio, television, radar, and the digital computer.

Replacement of valves with the comparatively tiny and reliable transistor in 1948 revolutionized electronic development. Modern electronic devices are based on minute integrated circuits (silicon chips), wafer-thin crystal slices holding tens of thousands of electronic components.

By using solid-state devices such as integrated circuits, extremely complex electronic circuits can be constructed, leading to the development of digital watches, pocket calculators, powerful microcomputers, and word processors.

adder electronic circuit in a computer or calculator that carries out the process of adding two binary numbers. A separate adder is needed for each pair of binary bits to be added. Such circuits are essential components of a computer's arithmetic and logic unit (ALU).

amplifier electronic device that magnifies the strength of a signal, such as a radio signal. The ratio of output signal strength to input signal strength is called the *gain* of the amplifier. As well as achieving high gain, an amplifier should be free from distortion and able to operate over a range of frequencies. Practical amplifiers are usually complex circuits, although simple amplifiers can be built from single transistors or valves.

analogue signal current or voltage that conveys or stores information, and varies continuously in the same way as the information it represents. Analogue signals are prone to interference and distortion. The bumps in the grooves of an LP (gramophone) record form a mechanical analogue of the sound information stored, which is then is converted into an electrical analogue signal by the record player's pick-up device.

analogue-to-digital converter (ADC) electronic circuit that converts an analogue signal into a digital one. Such a circuit is needed to convert the signal from an analogue device into a digital signal for input into a computer. For example, many sensors designed to measure physical quantities, such as temperature and pressure, produce an analogue signal in the form of voltage and this must be passed through an ADC before computer input and processing. A digital-to-analogue converter performs the opposite process.

bistable circuit or *flip-flop* simple electronic circuit that remains in one of two stable states until it receives a pulse through one of its inputs, upon which it switches, or 'flips', over to the other state. Because it is a two-state device, it can be used to store binary digits and is widely used in the integrated circuits used to build computers.

capacitor or *condenser* device for storing electric charge, used in electronic circuits; it consists of two or more metal plates separated by an insulating layer called a dielectric. Its *capacitance* is the ratio of the charge stored on either plate to the potential difference between the plates. The SI unit of capacitance is the farad, but most capacitors have much smaller capacitances, and the microfarad (a millionth of a farad) is the commonly used practical unit.

cathode the part of an electronic device in which electrons are generated. In a thermionic valve, electrons are produced by the heating effect of an applied current; in a photoelectric cell, they are produced by the interaction of light and a semiconducting material. The cathode is kept at a negative potential relative to the device's other electrodes (anodes) in order to ensure that the liberated electrons stream away from the cathode and towards the anodes.

complementary metal-oxide semiconductor (CMOS) a particular way of manufacturing integrated circuits (chips). The main advantage of CMOS chips is their low power requirement and heat dissipation, which enables them to be used in electronic watches and portable microcomputers. However, CMOS circuits are expensive to manufacture and have lower operating speeds than have circuits of the transistor–transistor logic (TTL) family.

digital a term meaning 'coded as numbers'. A digital system uses two-state, either on/off or high/low voltage pulses, to encode, receive, and transmit information. A *digital display* shows discrete values as numbers (as opposed to an analogue signal, such as the continuous sweep of a pointer on a dial). *Digital electronics* is the technology that underlies digital

techniques. Low-power, miniature, integrated circuits (chips) provide the means for the coding, storage, transmission, processing, and reconstruction of information of all kinds.

digital-to-analogue converter electronic circuit that converts a digital signal into an analogue (continuously varying) signal. Such a circuit is used to convert the digital output from a computer into the analogue voltage required to produce sound from a conventional loudspeaker.

diode combination of a cold anode and a heated cathode (or the semiconductor equivalent, which incorporates a *p–n* junction). Either device allows the passage of direct current in one direction only, and so is commonly used in a rectifier to convert alternating current (AC) to direct current (DC).

DRAM (acronym for *dynamic random-access memory*) computer memory device in the form of a silicon chip commonly used to provide the immediate-access memory of microcomputers. DRAM loses its contents unless they are read and rewritten every 2 milliseconds or so. This process is called *refreshing* the memory. DRAM is slower but cheaper than SRAM, an alternative form of silicon-chip memory.

EEPROM (acronym for *electrically erasable programmable read-only memory*) computer memory that can record data and retain it indefinitely. The data can be erased with an electrical charge and new data recorded. Some EEPROM must be removed from the computer and erased and reprogrammed using a special device. Other EEPROM, called *flash memory*, can be erased and reprogrammed without removal from the computer.

electron stable, negatively charged elementary particle; it is a constituent of all atoms, and a member of the class of particles known as leptons.

The electrons in each atom surround the nucleus in groupings called shells; in a neutral atom the number of electrons is equal to the number of protons in the nucleus. This electron structure is responsible for the chemical properties of the atom.

Electrons are the basic particles of electricity. Each carries a charge of 1.602192×10^{-19} coulomb, and all electrical charges are multiples of this quantity. A beam of electrons will undergo diffraction (scattering) and produce interference patterns in the same way as electromagnetic waves such as light; hence they may also be regarded as waves.

filter a circuit that transmits a signal of some frequencies better than others. A low-pass filter transmits signals of low frequency and direct current; a high-pass filter transmits high-frequency signals; a band-pass filter transmits signals in a band of frequencies.

gain the ratio of the amplitude of the output signal produced by an amplifier to that of the input signal. In a voltage amplifier the voltage gain is the ratio of the output voltage to the input voltage; in an inverting operational amplifier (op-amp) it is equal to the ratio of the resistance of the feedback resistor to that of the input resistor.

integrated circuit (IC), popularly called *silicon chip*, a miniaturized electronic circuit produced on a single crystal, or chip, of a semiconducting material – usually silicon. It may contain many thousands of

Electronics: chronology

1897	The electron was discovered by English physicist John Joseph Thomson.
1904	English physicist Ambrose Fleming invented the diode valve, which allows flow of electricity in one direction only.
1906	The triode electron valve, the first device to control an electric current, was invented by US physicist Lee De Forest.
1947	John Bardeen, William Shockley, and Walter Brattain invented the junction germanium transistor at the Bell Laboratories, New Jersey, USA.
1952	British physicist G W A Dunner proposed the integrated circuit.
1953	Jay Forrester of the Massachusetts Institute of Technology, USA, built a magnetic memory smaller than existing vacuum-tube memories.
1954	The silicon transistor was developed by Gordon Teal of Texas Instruments, USA.
1958	The first integrated circuit, containing five components, was built by US electrical physicist Jack Kilby.
1959	The planar transistor, which is built up in layers, or planes, was designed by Robert Noyce of Fairchild Semiconductor Corporation, USA.
1961	Steven Hofstein designed the field-effect transistor used in integrated circuits.
1971	The first microprocessor, the Intel 4004, was designed by Ted Hoff in the USA; it contained 2,250 components and could add two four-bit numbers in 11-millionths of a second.
1974	The Intel 8080 microprocessor was launched; it contained 4,500 components and could add two eight-bit numbers in 2.5-millionths of a second.
1979	The Motorola 68000 microprocessor was introduced; it contained 70,000 components and could multiply two 16-bit numbers in 3.2-millionths of a second.
1981	The Hewlett-Packard Superchip was introduced; it contained 450,000 components and could multiply two 32-bit numbers in 1.8-millionths of a second.
1985	The Inmos T414 transputer, the first microprocessor designed for use in parallel computers, was launched.
1988	The first optical microprocessor, which uses light instead of electricity, was developed.
1989	Wafer-scale silicon memory chips were introduced: the size of a beer mat, they are able to store 200 million characters.
1990	Memory chips capable of holding 4 million bits of information began to be mass-produced in Japan. The chips can store the equivalent of 520,000 characters, or the contents of a 16-page newspaper. Each chip contains 9 million components packed on a piece of silicon less than 15 mm long by 5 mm wide.
1992	Transistors made from high-temperature superconducting ceramics rather than semiconductors produced in Japan by Sanyo Electric. The new transistors are 10 times faster than semiconductor transistors.
1993	Intel launched the Pentium 64-bit processor with two separate integer processing units that can run in parallel, promising to be up to 10 times faster than earlier processors.

components and yet measure only 5 mm/0.2 in square and 1 mm/0.04 in thick. The IC is encapsulated within a plastic or ceramic case, and linked via gold wires to metal pins with which it is connected to a printed circuit board and the other components that make up such electronic devices as computers and calculators.

logic gate or *logic circuit* in electronics, one of the basic components used in building integrated circuits. The five basic types of gate make logical decisions based on the functions NOT, AND, OR, NAND (NOT AND), and NOR (NOT OR). With the exception of the NOT gate, each has two or more inputs.

Information is fed to a gate in the form of binary-coded input signals (logic value 0 stands for 'off' or 'low-voltage pulse', logic 1 for 'on' or 'high-voltage'), and each combination of input signals yields a specific output (logic 0 or 1). An *OR* gate will give a logic 1 output if one or more of its inputs receives a logic 1 signal; however, an *AND* gate will yield a logic 1 output only if it receives a logic 1 signal through both its inputs. The output of a *NOT* or *inverter* gate is the opposite of the signal received through its single input, and a *NOR* or *NAND* gate produces an output signal that is the opposite of the signal that would have been produced by an OR or AND gate respectively. The properties of a logic gate, or of a combination of gates, may be defined and presented in the form of a diagram called a *truth table*, which lists the output that will be triggered by each of the possible combinations of input signals. The process has close parallels in computer pro-gramming, where it forms the basis of binary logic.

LSI (abbreviation for *large-scale integration*) the technology that enables whole electrical circuits to be etched into a piece of semiconducting material just a few millimetres square. By the late 1960s a complete computer processor could be integrated on a single chip, or integrated circuit, and in 1971 the US electronics company Intel produced the first commercially available microprocessor. Very large-scale integration (VLSI) results in even smaller chips.

microprocessor complete computer central processing unit contained on a single integrated circuit, or chip. The appearance of the first microprocessor 1971 designed by Intel for a pocket-calculator manufacturer heralded the introduction of the microcomputer. The microprocessor has led to a dramatic fall in the size and cost of computers, and dedicated computers can now be found in washing machines, cars, and so on. Examples of microprocessors are the Intel 8086 family and the Motorola 68000 family.

operational amplifier (op-amp) type of electronic circuit that is used to increase the size of an alternating voltage signal without distorting it. Operational amplifiers are used in a wide range of electronic measuring instruments. The name arose because they were originally designed to carry out mathematical operations and solve equations.

optoelectronics branch of electronics concerned with the development of devices (based on the semiconductor gallium arsenide) that respond not only to the electrons of electronic data transmission, but also to photons.

In 1989, scientists at IBM in the USA built a gallium arsenide microprocessor ('chip') containing 8,000 transistors and four photodetectors. The densest optoelectronic chip yet produced, this can detect and process data at a speed of 1 billion bits per second.

oscillator any device producing a desired oscillation (vibration). There are many types of oscillator for different purposes, involving various arrangements of thermionic valves or components such as transistors, inductors, capacitors, and resistors. An oscillator is an essential part of a radio transmitter, generating the high-frequency carrier signal necessary for radio communication. The frequency is often controlled by the vibrations set up in a crystal (such as quartz).

p–n junction diode a two-terminal semiconductor device that allows electric current to flow in only one direction, the *forward-bias* direction. A very high resistance prevents current flow in the opposite, or *reverse-bias*, direction. It is used as a rectifier, converting alternating current (AC) to direct current (DC).

semiconductor crystalline material with an electrical conductivity between that of metals (good) and insulators (poor). The conductivity of semiconductors can usually be improved by minute additions of different substances or by other factors. Silicon, for example, has poor conductivity at low temperatures, but this is improved by the application of light, heat, or voltage; hence silicon is used in transistors, rectifiers, and integrated circuits (silicon chips).

solid-state circuit electronic circuit where all the components (resistors, capacitors, transistors, and diodes) and interconnections are made at the same time, and by the same processes, in or on one piece of single-crystal silicon. The small size of this construction accounts for its use in electronics for space vehicles and aircraft.

SRAM (acronym for *static random-access memory*) computer memory device in the form of a silicon chip used to provide immediate-access memory. SRAM is faster but more expensive than DRAM (dynamic random-access memory). DRAM loses its contents unless they are read and rewritten every 2 milliseconds or so. This process is called *refreshing* the memory. SRAM does not require such frequent refreshing.

thermionics branch of electronics dealing with the emission of electrons from matter under the influence of heat. The *thermionic valve* (electron tube), used in telegraphy and telephony and in radio and radar, is a device using space conduction by thermionically emitted electrons from an electrically heated cathode. In most applications valves have been replaced by transistors.

thyristor type of rectifier, an electronic device that conducts electricity in one direction only. The thyristor is composed of layers of semiconductor material sandwiched between two electrodes called the anode and cathode. The current can be switched on by using a third electrode called the gate. Thyristors are used to control mains-driven motors and in lighting dimmer controls.

transistor solid-state electronic component, made of semiconductor material, with three or more electrodes, that can regulate a current passing through it. A transistor can act as an amplifier, oscillator, photocell, or switch, and (unlike earlier thermionic valves) usually operates on a very small amount of power. Transistors commonly consist of a tiny sandwich of germanium or silicon, alternate layers having different electrical properties because they are impregnated with minute amounts of different impurities.

Transistors have had a great impact on the electronics industry, and thousands of millions are now made each year. They perform many of the functions of the thermionic valve, but have the advantages of greater reliability, long life, compactness, and instantaneous action, no warming-up period being necessary. They are widely used in most electronic equipment, including portable radios and televisions, computers, and satellites, and are the basis of the integrated circuit (silicon chip). They were invented at Bell Telephone Laboratories in the USA in 1948 by John Bardeen and Walter Brattain, developing the work of William Shockley.

transistor-transistor logic (TTL) the type of integrated circuit most commonly used in building electronic products. In TTL chips, the bipolar transistors are directly connected (usually collector to base). In mass-produced items, large numbers of TTL chips are commonly replaced by a small number of uncommitted logic arrays (ULAs), or logic gate arrays.

transputer a member of a family of microprocessors designed for parallel processing, developed in the UK by Inmos. In the circuits of a standard computer the processing of data takes place in sequence; in a transputer's circuits processing takes place in parallel, greatly reducing computing time for those programs that have been specifically written for it. The transputer implements a special programming language called OCCAM, which Inmos based on CSP (communicating sequential processes), developed by C A R Hoare of Oxford University Computing Laboratory.

triode three-electrode thermionic valve containing an anode and a cathode (as does a diode) with an additional negatively biased control grid. Small variations in voltage on the grid bias result in large variations in the current. The triode was commonly used in amplifiers but has now been almost entirely superseded by the transistor.

truth table in electronics, a diagram showing the effect of a particular logic gate on every combination of inputs.

uncommitted logic array (ULA) or *gate array* a type of semicustomized integrated circuit in which the logic gates are laid down to a general-purpose design but are not connected to each other. The interconnections can then be set in place according to the requirements of individual manufacturers. Producing ULAs may be cheaper than using a large number of TTL (transistor–transistor logic) chips or commissioning a fully customized chip.

valve or *electron tube* a glass tube containing gas at low pressure, which is used to control the flow of electricity in a circuit. Three or more metal electrodes are inset into the tube. By varying the voltage on one of them, called the *grid electrode*, the current through the valve can be controlled, and the valve can act as an amplifier. Valves have been replaced for most applications by transistors. However, they are still used in high-power transmitters and amplifiers, and in some hi-fi systems.

VLSI (abbreviation for *very large-scale integration*) in electronics, the early-1990s level of advanced technology in the microminiaturization of integrated circuits, and an order of magnitude smaller than LSI (large-scale integration).

voltage amplifier electronic device that increases an input signal in the form of a voltage or potential difference, delivering an output signal that is larger than the input by a specified ratio.

EARTH SCIENCE

The Developing Earth

Archaean or *Archaeozoic* the earliest eon of geological time; the first part of the Precambrian, from the formation of Earth up to about 2,500 million years ago. It was a time when no life existed, and with every new discovery of ancient life, its upper boundary is being pushed further back.

Cambrian period of geological time 570–510 million years ago; the first period of the Palaeozoic era. All invertebrate animal life appeared and marine algae were widespread. The earliest fossils with hard shells, such as trilobites, date from this period.

Carboniferous period of geological time 363–290 million years ago, the fifth period of the Palaeozoic era. In the USA, it is divided into two periods: the Mississippian (lower) and the Pennsylvanian (upper). Typical of the lower-Carboniferous rocks are shallow-water limestones, while upper-Carboniferous rocks have delta deposits with coal (hence the name). Amphibians were abundant and reptiles evolved during this period.

continental drift the theory that, about 250–200 million years ago, the Earth consisted of a single large continent (Pangaea), which subsequently broke apart to form the continents known today. The theory was proposed 1912 by German meteorologist Alfred Wegener, but such vast continental movements could not be satisfactorily explained until the study of plate tectonics in the 1960s.

continental drift

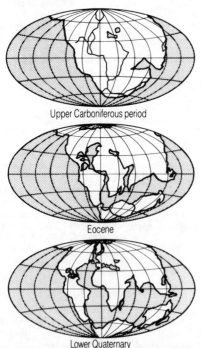

Upper Carboniferous period

Eocene

Lower Quaternary

Cretaceous period of geological time 146–65 million years ago. It is the last period of the Mesozoic era, during which angiosperm (seed-bearing) plants evolved, and dinosaurs reached a peak before their almost complete extinction at the end of the period. Chalk is a typical rock type of the second half of the period.

dating science of determining the age of geological structures, rocks, and fossils, and placing them in the context of geological time. The techniques are of two types: relative dating and absolute dating. *Relative dating* can be carried out by identifying fossils of creatures that lived only at certain times (marker fossils), and by looking at the physical relationships of rocks to other rocks of a known age. *Absolute dating* is achieved by measuring how much of a rock's radioactive elements have changed since the rock was formed, using the process of radiometric dating.

Devonian period of geological time 408–360 million years ago, the fourth period of the Palaeozoic era. Many desert sandstones from North America and Europe date from this time. The first land plants flourished in the Devonian period, corals were abundant in the seas, amphibians evolved from air-breathing fish, and insects developed on land.

epoch subdivision of a geological period in the geological time scale. Epochs are sometimes given their own names (such as the Palaeocene, Eocene, Oligocene, Miocene, and Pliocene epochs comprising the Tertiary period), or they are referred to as the late, early, or middle portions of a given period (as the Late Cretaceous or the Middle Triassic epoch).

era any of the major divisions of geological time, each including several periods, but smaller than an eon. The currently recognized eras all fall within the Phanerozoic eon – or the vast span of time, starting about 570 million years ago, when fossils are found to become abundant. The eras in ascending order are the Palaeozoic, Mesozoic, and Cenozoic. We are living in the Recent epoch of the Quaternary period of the Cenozoic era.

geological time time scale embracing the history of the Earth from its physical origin to the present day. Geological time is traditionally divided into eons (Phanerozoic, Proterozoic, and Archaean), which in turn are divided into eras, periods, epochs, ages, and finally chrons.

Gondwanaland or *Gondwana* southern land mass formed 200 million years ago by the splitting of the single world continent Pangaea. (The northern land mass was Laurasia.) It later fragmented into the continents of South America, Africa, Australia, and Antarctica, which then drifted slowly to their present positions. The baobab tree found in both Africa and Australia is a relic of this ancient land mass.

A database of the entire geology of Gondwanaland has been constructed by geologists in South Africa. The database, known as Gondwana Geoscientific Indexing Database (GO-GEOID), displays informa-

Geological time chart

Eon	Era	Period	Epoch	Millions of years ago	Life forms
Phanerozoic	Cenozoic	Quaternary	Holocene	0.01	
			Pleistocene	1.64	humans appeared
		Tertiary	Pliocene	5.2	
			Miocene	23.5	
			Oligocene	35.5	
			Eocene	56.5	
			Palaeocene	65	mammals flourished
	Mesozoic	Cretaceous		146	heyday of dinosaurs
		Jurassic		208	first birds
		Triassic		245	first mammals and dinosaurs
	Palaeozoic	Permian		290	reptiles expanded
		Carboniferous		363	first reptiles
		Devonian		409	first amphibians
		Silurian		439	first land plants
		Ordovician		510	first fish
		Cambrian		570	first fossils
(Precambrian) Proterozoic				3,500	earliest living things
Archaean				4,600	

tion as a map of Gondwana 155 million years ago, before the continents drifted apart.

Holocene epoch of geological time that began 10,000 years ago, the second and current epoch of the Quaternary period. The glaciers retreated, the climate became warmer, and humans developed significantly.

Iapetus Ocean or *Proto-Atlantic* sea that existed in early Palaeozoic times between the continent that was to become Europe and that which was to become North America. The continents moved together in the late Palaeozoic, obliterating the ocean. When they moved apart once more, they formed the Atlantic.

ice age any period of glaciation occurring in the Earth's history, but particularly that in the Pleistocene epoch, immediately preceding historic times. On the North American continent, glaciers reached as far south as the Great Lakes, and an ice sheet spread over N Europe, leaving its remains as far south as Switzerland. There were several glacial advances separated by interglacial stages during which the ice melted and temperatures were higher than today. Formerly there were thought to have been only three or four glacial advances, but recent research has shown about 20 major incidences. There is a possibility that the Pleistocene ice age is not yet over.

Major ice ages

Name	Date (years ago)
Pleistocene	1.64 million–10,000
Permo-Carboniferous	330–250 million
Ordovician	440–430 million
Verangian	615–570 million
Sturtian	820–770 million
Gnejso	940–880 million
Huronian	2,700–1,800 million

K-T boundary geologists' shorthand for the boundary between the rocks of the Cretaceous and the Tertiary periods 65 million years ago. It marks the extinction of the dinosaurs and in many places reveals a layer of iridium, possibly deposited by a meteorite that may have caused their extinction by its impact.

Laurasia northern land mass formed 200 million years ago by the splitting of the single world continent Pangaea. (The southern land mass was Gondwanaland.) It consisted of what was to become North America, Greenland, Europe, and Asia, and is believed to have broken up about 100 million years ago with the separation of North America from Europe.

mass extinction an event that produced the extinction of many species at about the same time. One notable example is the boundary between the Cretaceous and Tertiary periods (known as the K-T boundary) that saw the extinction of the dinosaurs and other big reptiles, and many of the marine invertebrates as well. Mass extinctions have taken place several times during Earth's history. The Age of Man may eventually be regarded as another.

Mesozoic era of geological time 245–65 million years ago, consisting of the Triassic, Jurassic, and Cretaceous periods. At the beginning of the era, the continents were joined together as Pangaea; dinosaurs and other giant reptiles dominated the sea and air; and ferns, horsetails, and cycads thrived in a warm climate worldwide. By the end of the Mesozoic era, the continents had begun to assume their present positions, flowering plants were dominant, and many of the large reptiles and marine fauna were becoming extinct.

Ordovician period of geological time 510–439 million years ago; the second period of the Palaeozoic era. Animal life was confined to the sea: reef-building algae and the first jawless fish are characteristic.

Earth science: chronology

1735 English lawyer George Hadley described the circulation of the atmosphere as large-scale convection currents centred on the equator.

1746 A French expedition to Lapland proved the Earth to be flattened at the poles.

1743 Christopher Packe produced the first geological map, of S England.

1744 The first map produced on modern surveying principles was produced by César-François Cassini in France.

1745 In Russia, Mikhail Vasilievich Lomonosov published a catalogue of over 3,000 minerals.

1760 Lomonosov explained the formation of icebergs. John Mitchell proposed that earthquakes are produced when one layer of rock rubs against another.

1776 James Keir suggested that some rocks, such as those making up the Giant's Causeway in Ireland, may have formed as molten material that cooled and then crystallized.

1779 French naturalist Comte George de Buffon speculated that the Earth may be much older than the 6,000 years suggested by the Bible.

1785 Scottish geologist James Hutton proposed the theory of uniformitarianism: all geological features are the result of processes that are at work today, acting over long periods of time.

1786 German–Swiss Johann von Carpentier described the European ice age.

1793 Jean Baptiste Lamarck argued that fossils are the remains of once-living animals and plants.

1794 William Smith produced the first large-scale geological maps of England.

1804 French physicists Jean Biot and Joseph Gay-Lussac studied the atmosphere from a hot-air balloon.

1809 The first geological survey of the eastern USA was produced by William Maclure.

1815 In England, William Smith showed how rock strata (layers) can be identified by the fossils found in them.

1822 Mary Ann Mantell discovered on the English coast the first fossil to be recognized as that of a dinosaur (an iguanodon). In Germany, Friedrich Mohs introduced a scale for specifying mineral hardness.

1830 Scottish geologist Charles Lyell published the first volume of *The Principles of Geology*, which described the Earth as being several hundred million years old.

1839 In the USA, Louis Agassiz described the motion and laying down of glaciers, confirming the reality of the ice ages.

1846 Irish physicist William Thomson (Lord Kelvin) estimated, using the temperature of the Earth, that the Earth is 100 million years old.

1850 US naval officer Matthew Fontaine Maury mapped the Atlantic Ocean, noting that it is deeper near its edges than at the centre.

1852 Edward Sabine in Ireland showed a link between sunspot activity and changes in the Earth's magnetic field.

1854 English astronomer George Airy calculated the mass of the Earth by measuring gravity in a coal mine.

1872 The beginning of the world's first major oceanographic expedition, the four-year voyage of the *Challenger*.

1882 Scottish physicist Balfour Stewart postulated the existence of the ionosphere (the ionized layer of the outer atmosphere) to account for differences in the Earth's magnetic field.

1884 German meteorologist Vladimir Köppen introduced a classification of the world's temperature zones.

1890 English geologist Arthur Holmes used radioactivity to date rocks, establishing the Earth to be 4.6 billion old.

1895 In the USA, Jeanette Picard launched the first balloon to be used for stratospheric research.

1896 Swedish chemist Svante Arrhenius discovered a link between the amount of carbon dioxide in the atmosphere and the global temperature.

1897 Norwegian-US meteorologist Jacob Bjerknes and his father Vilhelm developed the mathematical theory of weather forecasting.

1902 British physicist Oliver Heaviside and US engineer Arthur Edwin Kennelly predicted the existence of an electrified layer in the atmosphere that reflects radio waves. In France, Léon Teisserenc discovered layers of different temperatures in the atmosphere, which he called the troposphere and stratosphere.

1906 Richard Dixon Oldham proved the Earth to have a molten core by studying seismic waves.

1909 Yugoslav physicist Andrija Mohorovic ić discovered a discontinuity in the Earth's crust, about 30 km/18 mi below the surface, that forms the boundary between the crust and the mantle.

1912 In Germany, Alfred Wegener proposed the theory of continental drift and the existence of a supercontinent, Pangaea, in the distant past.

1913 French physicist Charles Fabry discovered the ozone layer in the upper atmosphere.

1914 German-US geologist Beno Gutenberg discovered the discontinuity that marks the boundary between the Earth's mantle and the outer core.

1922 British meteorologist Lewis Fry Richardson developed a method of numerical weather forecasting.

1925 A German expedition discovered the Mid-Atlantic ridge by means of sonar. Edward Appleton discovered a layer of the atmosphere that reflects radio waves; it was later named after him.

1929 By studying the magnetism of rocks, Japanese geologist Motonori Matuyama showed that the Earth's magnetic field reverses direction from time to time.

1935 US seismologist Charles Francis Richter established a scale for measuring the magnitude of earthquakes.

1936 Danish seismologist Inge Lehmann postulated the existence of a solid inner core of the Earth from the study of seismic waves.

1939 In Germany, Walter Maurice Elsasser proposed that eddy currents in the molten iron core cause the Earth's magnetism.

1950 Hungarian-US mathematician John Von Neumann made the first 24-hour weather forecast by computer.

1956 US geologists Bruce Charles Heezen and Maurice Ewing discovered a global network of oceanic ridges and rifts that divide the Earth's surface into plates.

1958 Using rockets, US physicist James Van Allen discovered a belt of radiation around the Earth.

1960 The world's first weather satellite, *TIROS 1*, was launched.

1963 British geophysicists Fred Vine and Drummond Matthews analysed the magnetism of rocks in the Atlantic Ocean floor and found conclusive proof of seafloor spreading.

1985 A British expedition to the Antarctic discovered a hole in the ozone layer above the South Pole.

1991 A borehole in the Kola Peninsula in Arctic Russia, begun in the 1970s, reached a depth of 12,261 m/40,240 ft (where the temperature was found to be 210°C/410°F). It is expected to reach a depth of 15,000 m/49,000 ft by 1995.

palaeomagnetism science of the reconstruction of the Earth's ancient magnetic field and the former positions of the continents from the evidence of *remanent magnetization* in ancient rocks; that is, traces left by the Earth's magnetic field in igneous rocks before they cool. Palaeomagnetism shows that the Earth's magnetic field has reversed itself – the magnetic north pole becoming the magnetic south pole, and vice versa – at approximate half-million-year intervals, with shorter reversal periods in between the major spans.

palaeontology the study of ancient life that encompasses the structure of ancient organisms and their environment, evolution, and ecology, as revealed by their fossils. The practical aspects of palaeontology are based on using the presence of different fossils to date particular rock strata and to identify rocks that were laid down under particular conditions, for instance giving rise to the formation of oil.

Palaeozoic era of geological time 570–245 million years ago. It comprises the Cambrian, Ordovician, Silurian, Devonian, Carboniferous, and Permian periods. The Cambrian, Ordovician, and Silurian constitute the Lower or Early Palaeozoic; the Devonian, Carboniferous, and Permian make up the Upper or Late Palaeozoic. The era includes the evolution of hard-shelled multicellular life forms in the sea; the invasion of land by plants and animals; and the evolution of fish, amphibians, and early reptiles. The earliest identifiable fossils date from this era.

Pangaea or *Pangea* single land mass, made up of all the present continents, believed to have existed between 250 and 200 million years ago; the rest of the Earth was covered by the Panthalassa ocean. Pangaea split into two land masses – Laurasia in the north and Gondwanaland in the south – which subsequently broke up into several continents. These then drifted slowly to their present positions.

Panthalassa ocean that covered the surface of the Earth not occupied by the world continent Pangaea between 250 and 200 million years ago.

Permian period of geological time 290–245 million years ago, the last period of the Palaeozoic era. Its end was marked by a significant change in marine life, including the extinction of many corals and trilobites. Deserts were widespread, and terrestrial amphibians and mammal-like reptiles flourished. Cone-bearing plants (gymnosperms) came to prominence.

Phanerozoic eon in Earth history, consisting of the most recent 570 million years. It comprises the Palaeozoic, Mesozoic, and Cenozoic eras. The vast majority of fossils come from this eon, owing to the evolution of hard shells and internal skeletons. The name means 'interval of well-displayed life'.

plate tectonics theory formulated in the 1960s to explain the phenomena of continental drift and seafloor spreading, and the formation of the major physical features of the Earth's surface. The Earth's outermost layer is regarded as a jigsaw of rigid major and minor plates up to 100 km/62 mi thick, which move relative to each other, probably under the influence of convection currents in the mantle beneath. Major landforms occur at the margins of the plates, where plates are colliding or moving apart – for

example, volcanoes, fold mountains, ocean trenches, and ocean ridges.

Since plate tectonics started 2,000 million years ago, the continents have travelled at about 6 cm/2.5 in per year, circling the globe at least four times, a journey of 160,000 km/100,000 mi.

Precambrian the time from the formation of Earth (4.6 billion years ago) up to 570 million years ago. Its boundary with the succeeding Cambrian period marks the time when animals first developed hard outer parts (exoskeletons) and so left abundant fossil remains. It comprises about 85% of geological time and is divided into two periods: the Archaean, in which no life existed, and the Proterozoic, in which there was life in some form.

Proterozoic eon of geological time, possible 3.5 billion to 570 million years ago, the second division of the Precambrian. It is defined as the time of simple life, since many rocks dating from this eon show traces of biological activity, and some contain the fossils of bacteria and algae.

Quaternary period of geological time that began 1.64 million years ago and is still in process. It is divided into the Pleistocene and Holocene epochs.

seafloor spreading growth of the ocean crust outwards (sideways) from ocean ridges. The concept of seafloor spreading has been combined with that of continental drift and incorporated into plate tectonics.

stratigraphy branch of geology that deals with the sequence of formation of sedimentary rock layers and the conditions under which they were formed. Its basis was developed by William Smith, a British canal engineer.

stromatolite mound produced in shallow water by mats of algae that trap mud particles. Another mat grows on the trapped mud layer and this traps another layer of mud and so on. The stromatolite grows to heights of a metre or so. They are uncommon today but their fossils are among the earliest evidence for living things — over 2,000 million years old.

tectonics the study of the movements of rocks on the Earth's surface. On a small scale tectonics involves the formation of folds and faults, but on a large scale plate tectonics deals with the movement of the Earth's surface as a whole.

Tertiary period of geological time 65–1.64 million years ago, divided into five epochs: Palaeocene, Eocene, Oligocene, Miocene, and Pliocene. During the Tertiary, mammals took over all the ecological niches left vacant by the extinction of the dinosaurs, and became the prevalent land animals. The continents took on their present positions, and climatic and vegetation zones as we know them became established. Within the geological time column the Tertiary follows the Cretaceous period and is succeeded by the Quaternary period.

Triassic period of geological time 245–208 million years ago, the first period of the Mesozoic era. The continents were fused together to form the world continent Pangaea. Triassic sediments contain remains of early dinosaurs and other reptiles now extinct. By late Triassic times, the first mammals had evolved.

The Interior of the Earth

asthenosphere division of the Earth's structure lying beneath the lithosphere, at a depth of approximately 70 km/45 mi to 260 km/160 mi. It is thought to be the soft, partially molten layer of the mantle on which the rigid plates of the Earth's surface move to produce the motions of plate tectonics.

bed single sedimentary rock unit with a distinct set of physical characteristics or contained fossils, readily distinguishable from those of beds above and below. Well-defined partings called *bedding planes* separate successive beds or strata.

continent any one of the seven large land masses of the Earth, as distinct from the oceans. They are Asia, Africa, North America, South America, Europe, Australia, and Antarctica. Continents are constantly moving and evolving. A continent does not end at the coastline; its boundary is the edge of the shallow continental shelf, which may extend several hundred kilometres or miles out to sea.

core the innermost part of the Earth. It is divided into an inner core, the upper boundary of which is 1,700 km/1,060 mi from the centre, and an outer core, 1,820 km/1,130 mi thick. Both parts are thought to consist of iron-nickel alloy, with the inner core being solid and the outer core being semisolid. The temperature may be 3,000°C/5,400°F.

craton or *shield* core of a continent, a vast tract of highly deformed metamorphic rock around which the continent has been built. Intense mountain-building periods shook these shield areas in Precambrian times before stable conditions set in.

crust the outermost part of the structure of Earth, consisting of two distinct parts, the oceanic crust and the continental crust. The *oceanic* crust is on average about 10 km/6.2 mi thick and consists mostly of basaltic types of rock. By contrast, the *continental* crust is largely made of granite and is more complex in its structure. Because of the movements of plate tectonics, the oceanic crust is in no place older than about 200 million years. However, parts of the continental crust are over 3 billion years old.

diagenesis or *lithification* the physical and chemical changes by which a sediment becomes a sedimentary rock. The main processes involved include compaction of the grains, and the cementing together of the grains by the growth of new minerals deposited by percolating groundwater.

earthquake shaking of the Earth's surface as a result of the sudden release of stresses built up in the Earth's crust. The study of earthquakes is called seismology. Most earthquakes occur along faults (fractures or breaks) in the crust. Plate tectonic movements generate the major proportion: as two plates move past each other they can become jammed and deformed, and a series of shock waves (seismic waves) occur when they spring free. Their force (magnitude) is measured on the Richter scale, and their effect (intensity) on the Mercalli scale. The point at which an earthquake originates is the *seismic focus*; the point on the Earth's surface directly above this is the *epicentre*.

Major 20th-century earthquakes

Date	Place	Magnitude (Richter scale)	Number of deaths
1906	San Francisco, USA	8.3	450
1908	Messina, Italy	7.5	83,000
1915	Avezzano, Italy	7.5	29,980
1920	Gansu, China	8.6	100,000
1923	Tokyo, Japan	8.3	99,330
1927	Nan-Shan, China	8.3	200,000
1932	Gansu, China	7.6	70,000
1935	Quetta, India	7.5	30,000
1939	Erzincan, Turkey	7.9	30,000
1939	Chillán, Chile	8.3	28,000
1948	USSR	7.3	110,000
1970	N Peru	7.7	66,794
1976	Tangshan, China	8.2	242,000
1978	NE Iran	7.7	25,000
1980	El Asnam, Algeria	7.3	20,000
1985	Mexico	8.1	25,000
1988	Armenia, USSR	6.9	25,000
1989	San Francisco, USA	7.1	300
1990	NW Iran	7.7	50,000

epicentre the point on the Earth's surface immediately above the seismic focus of an earthquake. Most damage usually takes place at an earthquake's epicentre. The term sometimes refers to a point directly above or below a nuclear explosion ('at ground zero').

fault fracture in the Earth's crust along which the two sides have moved as a result of differing strains in the adjacent rock bodies. Displacement of rock masses horizontally or vertically along a fault may be microscopic, or it may be massive, causing major earthquakes.

fold bend in beds or layers of rock. If the bend is arched in the middle it is called an *anticline*; if it sags downwards in the middle it is called a *syncline*. The line along which a bed of rock folds is called its axis. The axial plane is the plane joining the axes of successive beds.

geochemistry science of chemistry as it applies to geology. It deals with the relative and absolute abundances of the chemical elements and their isotopes in the Earth, and also with the chemical changes that accompany geologic processes.

geophysics branch of earth science using physics to study the Earth's surface, interior, and atmosphere. Studies also include winds, weather, tides, earthquakes, volcanoes, and their effects.

geothermal energy energy extracted for heating and electricity generation from natural steam, hot water, or hot dry rocks in the Earth's crust. Water is pumped down through an injection well where it passes through joints in the hot rocks. It rises to the surface through a recovery well and may be converted to steam or run through a heat exchanger. Dry steam may be directed through turbines to produce electricity. It is a important source of energy in volcanically active areas such as Iceland and New Zealand.

geyser natural spring that intermittently discharges an explosive column of steam and hot water into the air due to the build-up of steam in underground chambers.

One of the most remarkable geysers is Old Faithful, in Yellowstone National Park, Wyoming, USA. Geysers also occur in New Zealand and Iceland.

intrusion mass of igneous rock that has formed by 'injection' of molten rock, or magma, into existing cracks beneath the surface of the Earth, as distinct from a volcanic rock mass which has erupted from the surface. Intrusion features include vertical cylindrical structures such as stocks, pipes, and necks; sheet structures such as dykes that cut across the strata and sills that push between them; laccoliths, which are blisters that push up the overlying rock; and batholiths, which represent chambers of solidified magma and contain vast volumes of rock.

lava molten rock that erupts from a volcano and cools to form extrusive igneous rock. It differs from magma in that it is molten rock on the surface; magma is molten rock below the surface. Lava that is high in silica is viscous and sticky and does not flow far; it forms a steep-sided conical volcano, for example Mount Fuji, Japan. Low-silica lava can flow for long distances and forms a broad flat volcano, such as Kilauea, Hawaii.

lithosphere topmost layer of the Earth's structure, forming the jigsaw of plates that take part in the movements of plate tectonics. The lithosphere comprises the crust and a portion of the upper mantle. It is regarded as being rigid and moves about on the semi-molten asthenosphere. The lithosphere is about 75 km/47 mi thick.

magma molten rock material beneath the Earth's surface from which igneous rocks are formed. Lava is magma that has reached the surface and solidified, losing some of its components on the way.

mantle intermediate zone of the Earth between the crust and the core, accounting for 82% of the Earth's volume. It is thought to consist of silicate minerals such as olivine.

Mercalli scale scale used to measure the intensity of an earthquake. It differs from the Richter scale, which measures *magnitude*. It is named after the Italian seismologist Giuseppe Mercalli (1850–1914). Intensity is a subjective value, based on observed phenomena, and varies from place to place with the same earthquake.

Richter scale

Magnitude	Relative amount of energy released	Examples
1		
2		
3		
4	1	Carlisle, England, 1979
5	30	San Francisco and New England, USA, 1979
		Wrexham, Wales, 1990
6	100	San Fernando, California, 1971
7	30,000	Chimbote, Peru, 1970
		San Francisco, 1989
8	1,000,000	Tangshan, China, 1976
		San Francisco, 1906
		Lisbon, Portugal, 1755
		Alaska, 1964
		Gansu, China, 1920

metamorphism geological term referring to the changes in rocks of the Earth's crust caused by increasing pressure and temperature. The resulting rocks are metamorphic rocks. All metamorphic changes take place in solid rocks. If the rocks melt and then harden, they become igneous rocks.

Mohorovičič discontinuity also *Moho* or *M-discontinuity* boundary that separates the Earth's crust and mantle, marked by a rapid increase in the speed of earthquake waves. It follows the variations in the thickness of the crust and is found approximately 32 km/20 mi below the continents and about 10 km/6 mi below the oceans. It is named after the Yugoslav geophysicist Andrija Mohorovičič (1857–1936) who suspected its presence after analysing seismic waves from the Kulpa Valley earthquake 1909.

petrology branch of geology that deals with the study of rocks, their mineral compositions, and their origins.

Richter scale scale based on measurement of seismic waves, used to determine the magnitude of an earthquake at its epicentre. The magnitude of an earthquake differs from its intensity, measured by the Mercalli scale, which is subjective and varies from place

Mercalli scale

Intensity value	Description
I	Only detected by instrument.
II	Felt by people resting.
III	Felt indoors; hanging objects swing; feels like passing traffic.
IV	Feels like passing heavy traffic; standing cars rock; windows, dishes, and doors rattle; wooden frames creak.
V	Felt outdoors; sleepers are woken; liquids spill; doors swing open.
VI	Felt by everybody; people stagger; windows break; trees and bushes rustle; weak plaster cracks.
VII	Difficult to stand upright; noticed by vehicle drivers; plaster, loose bricks, tiles, and chimneys fall; bells ring.
VIII	Car steering affected; some collapse of masonry; chimney stacks and towers fall; branches break from trees; cracks in wet ground.
IX	General panic; serious damage to buildings; underground pipes break; cracks and subsidence in ground.
X	Most buildings destroyed; landslides; water thrown out of canals.
XI	Rails bent; underground pipes totally destroyed.
XII	Damage nearly total; rocks displaced; objects thrown into the air.

The ten most serious recorded volcanic eruptions in history

Date	Volcano/country	Est. death toll
26 Aug 1883	Krakatoa (Indonesia)	36,000
8 May 1902	Mont Pelée (Martinique)	30,000
13 Nov 1985	Nevada del Ruiz (Colombia)	23,000
25 March 1669	Etna (Sicily)	20,000
24 Aug 1979	Vesuvius (Italy)	16,000
1169	Etna (Sicily)	15,000
5 April 1815	Tambora (Java)	12,000
1792	Unzen-Dake (Japan)	10,000
June–Aug 1783	Skaptar (Iceland)	10,000
May 1919	Kelud (Indonesia)	5,000

to place for the same earthquake. The scale is named after US seismologist Charles Richter.

sial the substance of the Earth's continental crust, as distinct from the sima of the ocean crust. The name, now used rarely, is derived from *si*lica and *al*umina, its two main chemical constituents.

sima the substance of the Earth's oceanic crust, as distinct from the sial of the continental crust. The name, now used rarely, is derived from *si*lica and *ma*gnesia, its two main chemical constituents.

volcano crack in the Earth's crust through which hot magma (molten rock) and gases well up. The magma becomes known as lava when it reaches the surface. A volcanic mountain, usually cone shaped with a crater on top, is formed around the opening, or vent, by the build-up of solidified lava and ashes (rock fragments). Most volcanoes arise on plate margins, where the movements of plates generate magma or allow it to rise from the mantle beneath. However, a number are found far from plate-margin activity, on 'hot spots' where the Earth's crust is thin.

The explosion of Krakatoa, an island between Java and Sumatra in the Pacific Ocean, in 1883, was equivalent to 26 of the most powerful H-bombs ever exploded. The dense cloud of dust produced reduced the Sun's heating effect by 20%. The dust circled the world within a month, producing blazing red sunsets as far afield as London.

The Surface of the Earth

abyssal zone dark ocean region 2,000-6,000 m/ 6,500-19,500 ft deep; temperature 4°C/39°F. Three-quarters of the area of the deep ocean floor lies in the abyssal zone, which is too far from the surface for photosynthesis to take place. Some fish and crustaceans living there are blind or have their own light sources. The region above is the bathyal zone; the region below, the hadal zone.

alluvial deposit layer of broken rocky matter, or sediment, formed from material that has been carried in suspension by a river or stream and dropped as the velocity of the current changes. River plains and deltas are made entirely of alluvial deposits, but smaller pockets can be found in the beds of upland torrents.

Antarctic Circle imaginary line that encircles the South Pole at latitude 66° 32' S. The line encompasses the continent of Antarctica and the Antarctic Ocean.

anticline fold in the rocks of the Earth's crust in which the layers or beds bulge upwards to form an arch (seldom preserved intact).

aquifer any rock formation containing water. The rock of an aquifer must be porous and permeable (full of interconnected holes) so that it can absorb water. Aquifers supply artesian wells, and are actively sought in arid areas as sources of drinking and irrigation water.

archipelago group of islands, or an area of sea containing a group of islands. The islands of an archipelago are usually volcanic in origin, and they sometimes represent the tops of peaks in areas around continental margins flooded by the sea.

Arctic Circle imaginary line that encircles the North Pole at latitude 66° 32' N. Within this line there is at least one day in the summer during which the Sun never sets, and at least one day in the winter during which the Sun never rises.

artesian well well that is supplied with water rising from an underground water-saturated rock layer (aquifer). The water rises from the aquifer under its own pressure. Such a well may be drilled into an aquifer that is confined by impermeable rocks both above and below. If the water table (the top of the region of water saturation) in that aquifer is above the level of the well head, hydrostatic pressure will force the water to the surface.

badlands barren landscape cut by erosion into a maze of ravines, pinnacles, gullies and sharp-edged ridges. Areas in South Dakota and Nebraska, USA, are examples.

caldera very large basin-shaped crater. Calderas are found at the tops of volcanoes, where the original peak has collapsed into an empty chamber beneath. The basin, many times larger than the original volcanic vent, may be flooded, producing a crater lake, or the flat floor may contain a number of small volcanic cones, produced by volcanic activity after the collapse.

crater bowl-shaped depression, usually round and with steep sides. Craters are formed by explosive events such as the eruption of a volcano or by the impact of a meteorite. A caldera is a much larger feature.

delta tract of land at a river's mouth, composed of silt deposited as the water slows on entering the sea. Familiar examples of large deltas are those of the Mississippi, Ganges and Brahmaputra, Rhîne, Po, Danube, and Nile; the shape of the Nile delta is like the Greek letter *delta* Δ, and thus gave rise to the name.

desert arid area without sufficient rainfall and, consequently, vegetation to support human life. The term includes the ice areas of the polar regions (known as cold deserts). Almost 33% of the Earth's land surface is desert, and this proportion is increasing.

dune mound or ridge of wind-drifted sand. Loose sand is blown and bounced along by the wind, up the windward side of a dune. The sand particles then fall to rest on the lee side, while more are blown up from the windward side. In this way, a dune moves gradually downwind.

equator the *terrestrial equator* is the great circle whose plane is perpendicular to the Earth's axis (the line joining the poles). Its length is 40,092 km/24,901.8

Largest deserts

Name and location	Area*	
	Sq km	Sq m
Sahara, N Africa	8,600,000	3,320,000
Arabian, SW Asia	2,330,000	900,000
Gobi, Mongolia and NE China	1,166,000	450,000
Patagonian, Argentina	673,000	260,000
Great Victoria, SW Australia	647,000	250,000
Great Basin, SW USA	492,000	190,000
Chihuahuan, Mexico	450,000	175,000
Great Sandy, NW Australia	400,000	150,000
Sonoran, SW USA	310,000	120,000
Kyzyl Kum, SW USSR	300,000	115,000
Takla Makan, N China	270,000	105,000
Kalahari, SW Africa	260,000	100,000

* desert areas are very approximate, because clear physical boundaries may not occur

mi, divided into 360 degrees of longitude. The equator encircles the broadest part of the Earth, and represents 0° latitude. It divides the Earth into two halves, called the northern and the southern hemispheres.

erosion wearing away of the Earth's surface, caused by the breakdown and transportation of particles of rock or soil (by contrast, weathering does not involve transportation). Agents of erosion include the sea, rivers, glaciers, and wind. Water, consisting of sea waves and currents, rivers, and rain; ice, in the form of glaciers; and wind, hurling sand fragments against exposed rocks and moving dunes along, are the most potent forces of erosion. People also contribute to erosion by bad farming practices and the cutting down of forests, which can lead to the formation of dust bowls.

fjord or *fiord* narrow sea inlet enclosed by high cliffs. Fjords are found in Norway, New Zealand, and western parts of Scotland. They are formed when an overdeepened U-shaped glacial valley is drowned by a rise in sea-level. At the mouth of the fjord there is a characteristic lip causing a shallowing of the water. This is due to reduced glacial erosion and the deposition of moraine at this point.

flood plain area of periodic flooding along the course of river valleys. When river discharge exceeds the capacity of the channel, water rises over the channel banks and floods the adjacent low-lying lands. As water spills out of the channel, some alluvium (silty material) will be deposited on the banks to form levees (raised river banks). This water will slowly seep into the flood plain, depositing a new layer of rich fertile alluvium as it does so. Many important floodplains, such as the inner Niger delta in Mali, occur in arid areas where their exceptional productivity has great importance for the local economy.

glacier tongue of ice, originating in mountains in snowfields above the snowline, which moves slowly downhill and is constantly replenished from its source. The scenery produced by the erosive action of glaciers is characteristic and includes glacial troughs (U-shaped valleys), corries, and arêtes. In lowlands, the laying down of moraine (rocky debris once carried by glaciers) produces a variety of landscape features.

The longest glacier in the world is the Lambert Glacier in Australian Antarctic Territory. It is up to 64 km/40 mi wide and at least 400 km/250 mi long.

ground water water collected underground in porous rock strata and soils; it emerges at the surface as springs and streams. The groundwater's upper level

Major islands

Name and location	Sq km	Sq mi
Greenland (North Atlantic)	2,175,600	840,000
New Guinea (SW Pacific)	800,000	309,000
Borneo (SW Pacific)	744,100	287,300
Madagascar (Indian Ocean)	587,000	227,000
Baffin (Canadian Arctic)	507,258	195,928
Sumatra (Indian Ocean)	473,600	182,860
Honshu (NW Pacific)	230,966	89,176
Great Britain (N Atlantic)	229,978	88,795
Victoria (Canadian Arctic)	217,206	83,896
Ellesmere (Canadian Arctic)	196,160	75,767
Sulawesi (Indian Ocean)	189,216	73,057
South Island, New Zealand (SW Pacific)	149,883	57,870
Java (Indian Ocean)	126,602	48,900
North Island, New Zealand (SW Pacific)	114,669	44,274
Cuba (Caribbean Sea)	110,800	44,800
Newfoundland (NW Atlantic)	108,860	42,030
Luzon (W Pacific)	104,688	40,420
Iceland (N Atlantic)	103,000	39,800
Mindanao (W Pacific)	94,630	36,537
Ireland -- N and the Republic (N Atlantic)	84,400	32,600
Hokkaido (NW Pacific)	83,515	32,245
Sakhalin (NW Pacific)	76,400	29,500
Hispaniola -- Dominican Republic and Haiti (Caribbean Sea)	76,000	29,300
Banks (Canadian Arctic)	70,000	27,038
Tasmania (SW Pacific)	67,800	26,200
Sri Lanka (Indian Ocean)	64,600	24,900
Devon (Canadian Arctic)	55,247	21,331

Major lakes

Name and location	Sq km	Sq mi
Caspian Sea (Azerbaijan/Russia/Kazakhstan/Turkmenistan/Iran)	370,990	143,240
Superior (USA/Canada)	82,071	31,700
Victoria (Tanzania/Kenya/Uganda)	69,463	26,820
Aral Sea (Kazakhstan/Uzbekistan)	64,500	24,904
Huron (USA/Canada)	59,547	23,000
Michigan (USA)	57,735	22,300
Tanganyika (Malawi/Zaire/Zambia/Burundi)	32,880	12,700
Baikal (Russia)	31,456	12,150
Great Bear (Canada)	31,316	12,096
Malawi (Tanzania/Malawi/Mozambique)	28,867	11,150
Great Slave (Canada)	28,560	11,031
Erie (USA/Canada)	25,657	9,910
Winnipeg (Canada)	25,380	9,417
Ontario (USA/Canada)	19,547	7,550
Balkhash (Kazakhstan)	18,421	7,115
Ladoga (Russia)	17,695	6,835
Chad (Chad/Niger/Nigeria)	16,310	6,300
Maracaibo (Venezuela)	13,507	5,217

is called the *water table*. Sandy or other kinds of beds that are filled with groundwater are called *aquifers*. Recent estimates are that usable ground water amounts to more than 90% of all the fresh water on Earth; however, keeping such supplies free of pollutants entering the recharge areas is a critical environmental concern.

International Date Line (IDL) imaginary line that approximately follows the 180° line of longitude. The date is put forward a day when crossing the line going west, and back a day when going east. The IDL was chosen at the International Meridian Conference 1884.

island area of land surrounded entirely by water. Islands can be formed in many ways. *Continental islands* were once part of the mainland, but became isolated (by tectonic movement, erosion, or a rise in sea level, for example). *Volcanic islands*, such as Japan, were formed by the explosion of underwater volcanoes. *Coral islands* consist mainly of coral, built up over many years. An *atoll* is a circular coral reef surrounding a lagoon; atolls were formed when a coral reef grew up around a volcanic island that subsequently sank or was submerged by a rise in sea level. *Barrier islands* are found by the shore in shallow water, and are formed by the deposition of sediment eroded from the shoreline. (See table on previous page.)

lake body of still water lying in depressed ground without direct communication with the sea. Lakes are common in formerly glaciated regions, along the courses of slow rivers, and in low land near the sea. The main classifications are by origin: *glacial lakes*, formed by glacial scouring; *barrier lakes*, formed by landslides and glacial moraines; *crater lakes*, found in volcanoes; and *tectonic lakes*, in natural fissures.

Most lakes are freshwater, such as the Great Lakes in North America, but in hot regions where evaporation is excessive they may contain many salts, the Dead Sea is an example. In the 20th century large artificial lakes have been created in connection with hydroelectric and other works. Some lakes have become polluted as a result of human activity. Sometimes *eutrophication* (a state of overnourishment)

occurs, when agricultural fertilizers leaching into lakes cause an explosion of aquatic life, which then depletes the lake's oxygen supply until it is no longer able to support life.

landslide sudden downward movement of a mass of soil or rocks from a cliff or steep slope. Landslides happen when a slope becomes unstable, usually because the base has been undercut or materials within the mass have become wet and slippery.

latitude and longitude imaginary lines used to locate position on the globe. Lines of latitude are drawn parallel to the equator, with 0° at the equator and 90° at the north and south poles. Lines of longitude are drawn at right angles to these, with 0° (the Prime Meridian) passing through Greenwich, England.

meander loop-shaped curve in a river flowing across flat country. As a river flows, any curve in its course is accentuated by the current. The current is fastest on the outside of the curve where it cuts into the bank; on the curve's inside the current is slow and deposits any transported material. In this way the river changes its course across the flood plain.

meridian half a great circle drawn on the Earth's surface passing through both poles and thus through all places with the same longitude. Terrestrial longitudes are usually measured from the Greenwich Meridian.

moraine rocky debris or till carried along and deposited by a glacier. Material eroded from the side of a glaciated valley and carried along the glacier's edge is called lateral moraine; that worn from the valley floor and carried along the base of the glacier is called ground moraine. Rubble dropped at the foot of a melting glacier is called terminal moraine.

mountain natural upward projection of the Earth's surface, higher and steeper than a hill. The process of mountain building (orogeny) consists of volcanism, folding, faulting, and thrusting, resulting from the collision and welding together of two tectonic plates. This process deforms the rock and compresses the sediment between the two plates into mountain chains. (See table on following page.)

latitude and longitude

Point X lies on longitude 60°W

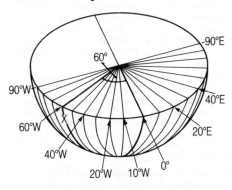

Point X lies on latitude 20°S

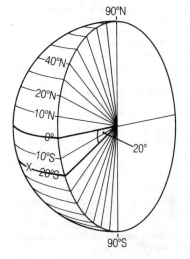

Together longitude 60°W latitude 20°S places point X on a precise position on the globe.

peat fibrous organic substance found in bogs and formed by the incomplete decomposition of plants such as sphagnum moss. N Asia, Canada, Finland, Ireland, and other places have large deposits, which have been dried and used as fuel from ancient times. Peat can also be used as a soil additive.

permafrost condition in which a deep layer of soil does not thaw out during the summer. Permafrost occurs under periglacial conditions. It is claimed that 26% of the world's land surface is permafrost.

plain or *grassland* land, usually flat, upon which grass predominates. The plains cover large areas of the Earth's surface, especially between the deserts of the tropics and the rainforests of the equator, and have rain in one season only. In such regions the climate belts move north and south during the year, bringing rainforest conditions at one time and desert conditions at another. Temperate plains include the North Euro-

Highest mountains

Name	Height		Location
	m	*ft*	
Everest	8,850	29,030	China–Nepal
K2	8,610	28,250	Kashmir–Jammu
Kangchenjunga	8,590	28,170	India–Nepal
Lhotse	8,500	27,890	China–Nepal
Kangchenjunga S Peak	8,470	27,800	India–Nepal
Makalu I	8,470	27,800	China–Nepal
Kangchenjunga W Peak	8,420	27,620	India–Nepal
Llotse E Peak	8,380	27,500	China–Nepal
Dhaulagiri	8,170	26,810	Nepal
Cho Oyu	8,150	26,750	China–Nepal
Manaslu	8,130	26,660	Nepal
Nanga Parbat	8,130	26,660	Kashmir–Jammu
Annapurna I	8,080	26,500	Nepal
Gasherbrum I	8,070	26,470	Kashmir–Jammu
Broad-highest	8,050	26,400	Kashmir–Jammu
Gasherbrum II	8,030	26,360	Kashmir–Jammu
Gosainthan	8,010	26,290	China
Broad-middle	8,000	26,250	Kashmir–Jammu
Gasherbrum III	7,950	26,090	Kashmir–Jammu
Annapurna II	7,940	26,040	Nepal
Nanda Devi	7,820	25,660	India
Rakaposhi	7,790	25,560	Kashmir
Kamet	7,760	25,450	India
Ulugh Muztagh	7,720	25,340	Tibet
Tirich Mir	7,690	25,230	Pakistan

* Heights are given to the nearest 10m/ft.

pean Plain, the High Plains of the USA and Canada, and the Russian Plain also known as the steppe.

plateau elevated area of fairly flat land, or a mountainous region in which the peaks are at the same height. An *intermontane plateau* is one surrounded by mountains. A *piedmont plateau* is one that lies between the mountains and low-lying land. A *continental plateau* rises abruptly from low-lying lands or the sea. Examples are the Tibetan Plateau and the Massif Central in France.

polder area of flat reclaimed land that used to be covered by a river, lake, or the sea. Polders have been artificially drained and protected from flooding by building dykes. They are common in the Netherlands, where the total land area has been increased by nearly one-fifth since AD 1200. Such schemes as the Zuider Zee project have provided some of the best agricultural land in the country.

pole either of the geographic north and south points of the axis about which the Earth rotates. The geographic poles differ from the magnetic poles, which are the points towards which a freely suspended magnetic needle will point.

In 1985, the magnetic north pole was some 350 km/ 218 mi NW of Resolute Bay, Northwest Territories, Canada. It moves northwards about 10 km/6 mi each year, although it can vary in a day about 80 km/ 50 mi from its average position. It is relocated every decade in order to update navigational charts.

It is thought that periodic changes in the Earth's core cause a reversal of the magnetic poles. Many animals, including migrating birds and fish, are believed to orientate themselves partly using the

Major rivers

Name and location	Km	Mi
Nile (NE Africa)	6,695	4,160
Amazon (South America)	6,570	4,080
Chang Jiang (China)	6,300	3,900
Mississippi–Missouri (USA)	6,020	3,740
Ob–Irtysh (China/Kazakhstan/Russia)	5,600	3,480
Huang He (China)	5,464	3,395
Paraná (Brazil)	4,500	2,800
Zaïre (Africa)	4,500	2,800
Mekong (Asia)	4,425	2,750
Amur (Asia)	4,416	2,744
Lena (Russia)	4,400	2,730
Mackenzie (Canada)	4,241	2,635
Niger (Africa)	4,185	2,600
Yenisei (Russia)	4,100	2,550
Mississippi (USA)	3,780	2,350
Murray–Darling (Australia)	3,750	2,330
Missouri (USA)	3,725	2,328
Volga (Russia)	3,685	2,290
Euphrates (Iraq)	3,600	2,240
Madeira (Brazil)	3,240	2,013
São Francisco (Brazil)	3,199	1,988
Yukon (USA/Canada)	3,185	1,979
Indus (Tibet/Pakistan)	3,180	1,975
Syrdar'ya (Kazakhstan)	3,078	1,913
Rio Grande (USA/Mexico)	3,050	1,900
Purus (Brazil)	2,993	1,860
Danube (Europe)	2,858	1,776
Brahmaputra (Asia)	2,850	1,770
Japurá (Brazil)	2,816	1,750
Salween (Myanmar/China)	2,800	1,740
Tocantins (Brazil)	2,699	1,677
Zambezi (Africa)	2,650	1,650
Paraguay (Paraguay)	2,591	1,610
Nelson–Saskatchewan (Canada)	2,570	1,600
Orinoco (Venezuela)	2,600	1,600
Amu Darya (Tajikistan/Turkmenistan/Uzbekistan)	2,540	1,578
Ural (Russia/Kazakhstan)	2,534	1,575
Kolyma (Russia)	2,513	1,562
Ganges (India/Bangladesh)	2,510	1,560
Orinoco (Venezuela)	2,400	1,490

Earth's magnetic field. A permanent scientific base collects data at the South Pole.

rift valley valley formed by the subsidence of a block of the Earth's crust between two or more parallel faults. Rift valleys are steep-sided and form where the crust is being pulled apart, as at ocean ridges, or in the Great Rift Valley of E Africa.

river long water course that flows down a slope along a channel. It originates at a point called its *source*, and enters a sea or lake at its *mouth*. Along its length it may be joined by smaller rivers called *tributaries*. A river and its tributaries are contained within a *drainage basin*.

sand loose grains of rock, sized 0.0625–2.00 mm/ 0.0025–0.08 in in diameter, consisting chiefly of quartz, but owing their varying colour to mixtures of other minerals. Sand is used in cement-making, as an abrasive, in glass-making, and for other purposes.

scarp and dip the two slopes formed when a sedimentary bed outcrops as a landscape feature. The scarp is the slope that cuts across the bedding plane; the dip is the opposite slope which follows the bedding plane. The scarp is usually steep, while the dip is a gentle slope.

sediment any loose material that has 'settled' – deposited from suspension in water, ice, or air, generally as the water current or wind speed decreases. Typical sediments are, in order of increasing coarseness, clay, mud, silt, sand, gravel, pebbles, cobbles, and boulders.

soil loose covering of broken rocky material and decaying organic matter overlying the bedrock of the Earth's surface. Various types of soil develop under different conditions: deep soils form in warm wet climates and in valleys; shallow soils form in cool dry areas and on slopes. *Pedology*, the study of soil, is significant because of the relative importance of different soil types to agriculture.

stalactite and stalagmite cave structures formed by the deposition of calcite dissolved in ground water. *Stalactites* grow downwards from the roofs or walls and can be icicle-shaped, straw-shaped, curtain-shaped, or formed as terraces. *Stalagmites* grow upwards from the cave floor and can be conical, fircone-shaped, or resemble a stack of saucers. Growing stalactites and stalagmites may meet to form a continuous column from floor to ceiling.

syncline geological term for a fold in the rocks of the Earth's crust in which the layers or beds dip inwards, thus forming a trough-like structure with a sag in the middle. The opposite structure, with the beds arching upwards, is an anticline.

topography the surface shape and aspect of the land, and its study. Topography deals with relief and contours, the distribution of mountains and valleys, the patterns of rivers, and all other features, natural and artificial, that produce the landscape.

tropics the area between the tropics of Cancer and Capricorn, defined by the parallels of latitude approximately 23°30' N and S of the equator. They are the limits of the area of Earth's surface in which the Sun can be directly overhead. The mean monthly temperature is over 20°C/68°F.

waterfall cascade of water in a river or stream. It occurs when a river flows over a bed of rock that resists erosion; weaker rocks downstream are worn away, creating a steep, vertical drop and a plunge pool into which the water falls. As the river ages, continuing erosion causes the waterfall to retreat upstream forming a deep valley, or gorge. (See table on following page.)

water table the upper level of ground water (water collected underground in porous rocks). Water that is above the water table will drain downwards; a spring forms where the water table cuts the surface of the ground. The water table rises and falls in response to rainfall and the rate at which water is extracted, for example, for irrigation and industry.

In many irrigated areas the water table is falling due to the extraction of water. That below N China, for example, is sinking at a rate of 1 m/3 ft a year. Regions with high water tables and dense industrialization have problems with pollution of the water table. In the USA, New Jersey, Florida, and Louisiana have water tables contaminated by both industrial wastes and saline seepage from the ocean.

Major waterfalls

Name and location	Total drop	
	Metres	Feet
Angel Falls (Venezuela)	979	3,212
Yosemite Falls (USA)	739	2,425
Mardalsfossen – South (Norway)	655	2,149
Tugela Falls (South Africa)	614	2,014
Cuquenan (Venezuela)	610	2,000
Sutherland (South Island, New Zealand)	580	1,903
Takkakaw Falls (Canada)	503	1,650
Ribbon Fall, Yosemite (USA)	491	1,612
Great Karamang River Falls (Guyana)	488	1,600
Mardalsfossen – North (Norway)	468	1,535
Della Falls (Canada)	440	1,443
Gavarnie (France)	422	1,385
Skjeggedal (Norway)	420	1,378
Glass Falls (Brazil)	404	1,325
Krimml (Austria)	400	1,312
Trummelbach (Switzerland)	400	1,312
Silver Strand Falls, Yosemite (USA)	357	1,170
Wallaman, Stony Creek (Australia)	346	1,137
Wollomombi (Australia)	335	1,100
Cusiana River Falls (Colombia)	300	984
Giessbach (Switzerland)	300	984
Skykkjedalsfossen (Norway)	300	984
Staubbach (Switzerland)	300	984

weathering process by which exposed rocks are broken down on the spot by the action of rain, frost, wind, and other elements of the weather. It differs from erosion in that no movement or transportation of the broken-down material takes place. Two types of weathering are recognized: physical (or mechanical) and chemical. They usually occur together.

Atmosphere and Ocean

barometer instrument that measures atmospheric pressure as an indication of weather. Most often used are the *mercury barometer* and the *aneroid barometer*.

bathyal zone upper part of the ocean, which lies on the continental shelf at a depth of between 200 m/650 ft and 2,000 m/6,500 ft.

beach strip of land bordering the sea, normally consisting of boulders and pebbles on exposed coasts or sand on sheltered coasts. It is usually defined by the high- and low-water marks. A berm, a ridge of sand and pebbles, may be found at the farthest point that the water reaches.

Beaufort scale system of recording wind velocity, devised by Francis Beaufort 1806. It is a numerical scale ranging from 0 to 17, calm being indicated by 0 and a hurricane by 12; 13–17 indicate degrees of hurricane force.

Coriolis effect the effect of the Earth's rotation on the atmosphere and on all objects on the Earth's surface. In the northern hemisphere it causes moving objects and currents to be deflected to the right; in the southern hemisphere it causes deflection to the left. The effect is named after its discoverer, French mathematician Gaspard Coriolis (1792–1843).

Weathering

Physical weathering

temperature changes	weakening rocks by expansion and contraction
frost	wedging rocks apart by the expansion of water on freezing
unloading	the loosening of rock layers by release of pressure after the erosion and removal of those layers above

Chemical weathering

carbonation	the breakdown of calcite by reaction with carbonic acid in rainwater
hydrolysis	the breakdown of feldspar into china clay by reaction with carbonic acid in rainwater
oxidation	the breakdown of iron-rich minerals due to rusting
hydration	the expansion of certain minerals due to the uptake of water

cloud water vapour condensed into minute water particles that float in masses in the atmosphere. Clouds, like fogs or mists, which occur at lower levels, are formed by the cooling of air containing water vapour, which generally condenses around tiny dust particles.

Clouds are classified according to the height at which they occur and their shape. *Cirrus* and *cirrostratus* clouds occur at around 10 km/33,000 ft. Three types of cloud are found at 3–7 km/10,000–23,000 ft: cirrocumulus, altocumulus, and altostratus. *Cirrocumulus* clouds occur in small or large rounded tufts, sometimes arranged in the pattern called mackerel sky. *Altocumulus* clouds are similar, but larger, white clouds, also arranged in lines. *Altostratus* clouds are like heavy cirrostratus clouds and may stretch across the sky as a grey sheet. *Stratocumulus* clouds are generally lower, occurring at 2–6 km/6,500–20,000 ft. They are dull grey clouds that give rise to a leaden sky that may not yield rain. Two types of clouds, *cumulus* and *cumulonimbus*, are placed in a special category because they are produced by daily ascending air currents, which take moisture into the cooler regions of the atmosphere.

current flow of a body of water or air, or of heat, moving in a definite direction. Ocean currents are fast-flowing currents of seawater generated by the wind or by variations in water density between two areas. They are partly responsible for transferring heat from the equator to the poles and thereby evening out the global heat imbalance. There are three basic types of ocean current: *drift currents* are broad and slow-moving; *stream currents* are narrow and swift-moving; and *upwelling currents* bring cold, nutrient-rich water from the ocean bottom.

cyclone alternative name for a *depression*, an area of low atmospheric pressure. A severe cyclone that forms in the tropics is called a tropical cyclone or *hurricane*. (See table on page 103.)

doldrums area of low atmospheric pressure along the equator, in the intertropical convergence zone where the NE and SE trade winds converge. The dol-

Cloud

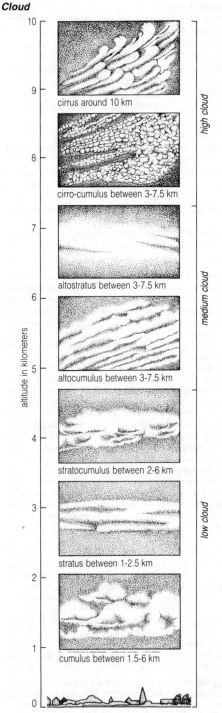

cirrus around 10 km — *high cloud*

cirro-cumulus between 3-7.5 km

altostratus between 3-7.5 km — *medium cloud*

altocumulus between 3-7.5 km

stratocumulus between 2-6 km

stratus between 1-2.5 km — *low cloud*

cumulus between 1.5-6 km

altitude in kilometers

drums are characterized by calm or very light winds, during which there may be sudden squalls and stormy weather. For this reason the areas are avoided as far as possible by sailing ships.

drought period of prolonged dry weather. The area of the world subject to serious droughts, such as the Sahara, is increasing because of destruction of forests, overgrazing, and poor agricultural practices. In the UK, drought is defined as the passing of 15 days with less than 0.2 mm of rain.

estuary river mouth widening into the sea, where fresh water mixes with salt water and tidal effects are felt.

exosphere the uppermost layer of the atmosphere. It is an ill-defined zone above the thermosphere, beginning at about 700 km/435 mi and fading off into the vacuum of space. The gases are extremely thin, with hydrogen as the main constituent.

fog cloud that collects at the surface of the Earth, composed of water vapour that has condensed on particles of dust in the atmosphere. Cloud and fog are both caused by the air temperature falling below dew point. The thickness of fog depends on the number of water particles it contains.

front the boundary between two air masses of different temperature or humidity. A *cold front* marks the line of advance of a cold air mass from below, as it displaces a warm air mass; a *warm front* marks the advance of a warm air mass as it rises up over a cold one. Frontal systems define the weather of the mid-latitudes, where warm tropical air is constantly meeting cold air from the poles.

frost condition of the weather that occurs when the air temperature is below freezing, 0°C/32°F. Water in the atmosphere is deposited as ice crystals on the ground or exposed objects. As cold air is heavier than warm, ground frost is more common than hoar frost, which is formed by the condensation of water particles in the same way that dew collects.

greenhouse effect phenomenon of the Earth's atmosphere by which solar radiation, trapped by the Earth and re-emitted from the surface, is prevented from escaping by various gases in the air. (See *Environment* for more.)

gyre circular surface rotation of ocean water in each major sea (a type of current). Gyres are large and permanent, and occupy the N and S halves of the three major oceans. Their movements are dictated by the prevailing winds and the Coriolis effect. Gyres move clockwise in the northern hemisphere and anticlockwise in the southern hemisphere.

hail precipitation in the form of pellets of ice (hailstones). It is caused by the circulation of moisture in strong convection currents, usually within cumulonimbus clouds. Water droplets freeze as they are carried upwards. As the circulation continues, layers of ice are deposited around the droplets until they become too heavy to be supported by the currents and they fall as a hailstorm.

hurricane revolving storm in tropical regions, called *typhoon* in the N Pacific. It originates between 5° and 20° N or S of the equator, when the surface temperature of the ocean is above 27°C/80°F. A central calm area, called the eye, is surrounded by inwardly spiralling winds (anticlockwise in the northern hemisphere) of up to 320 kph/200 mph. A hurricane is accompanied by lightning and torrential

The ten worst recorded cyclones and floods in history

Date	Flood/cyclone	Region affected	Est. death toll
Aug 1931	flood	China (Huang He/Yellow River)	3,700,000
Sept 1887	flood	China (Huang He/Yellow River)	900,000
13 Nov 1970	cyclone	East Pakistan (Bangladesh)	500,000
1939	flood	China (north)	400,000
1642	flood	China (Kaifeng)	300,000
7 Oct 1737	cyclone	India (Bengal)	300,000
1881	cyclone	Vietnam (Haiphong)	300,000
23 April 1969	flood	China (Shandong peninsula)	200,000
30 April 1991	cyclone	Bangladesh	126,000
1228	flood	Netherlands	100,000

rain, and can cause extensive damage. In meteorology, a hurricane is a wind of force 12 or more on the Beaufort scale.

isobar line drawn on maps and weather charts linking all places with the same atmospheric pressure (usually measured in millibars). When used in weather forecasting, the distance between the isobars is an indication of the barometric gradient.

jet stream narrow band of very fast wind (velocities of over 150 kph/95 mph) found at altitudes of 10–16 km/6–10 mi in the upper troposphere or lower stratosphere. Jet streams usually occur about the latitudes of the Westerlies (35°–60°).

lagoon coastal body of shallow salt water, usually with limited access to the sea. The term is normally used to describe the shallow sea area cut off by a coral reef or barrier islands.

lightning high-voltage electrical discharge between two charged rainclouds or between a cloud and the Earth, caused by the build-up of electrical charges. Air in the path of lightning ionizes (becomes conducting), and expands; the accompanying noise is heard as thunder. Currents of 20,000 amperes and temperatures of 30,000°C/54,000°F are common.

magnetic storm a sudden disturbance affecting the Earth's magnetic field, causing anomalies in radio transmissions and magnetic compasses. It is probably caused by sunspot activity.

Mediterranean climate climate characterized by hot dry summers and warm wet winters. Mediterranean zones are situated in either hemisphere on the western side of continents, between latitudes of 30° and 60°.

mesosphere layer in the Earth's atmosphere above the stratosphere and below the thermosphere. It lies between about 50 km/31 mi and 80 km/50 mi above the ground.

meteorology scientific observation and study of the atmosphere, so that weather can be accurately forecast. Data from meteorological stations and weather satellites are collated by computer at central agencies, and forecast and weather maps based on current readings are issued at regular intervals. Modern analysis can give useful forecasts for up to six days ahead.

monsoon wind pattern that brings seasonally heavy rain to S Asia; it blows towards the sea in winter and towards the land in summer. The monsoon may cause destructive flooding all over India and SE Asia from April to Sept. Thousands of people are rendered homeless each year.

ocean great mass of salt water. Strictly speaking three oceans exist – the Atlantic, Indian, and Pacific – to which the Arctic is often added. They cover approximately 70% or 363,000,000 sq km/ 140,000,000 sq mi of the total surface area of the Earth. Water levels recorded in the world's oceans have shown an increase of 10–15 cm/4–6 in over the past 100 years.

depth (average) 3,660 m/12,000 ft, but shallow ledges 180 m/600 ft run out from the continents, beyond which the continental slope reaches down to the *abyssal zone*, the largest area, ranging from 2,000–6,000 m/6,500–19,500 ft. Only the *deep-sea trenches* go deeper, the deepest recorded being 11,034 m/36,201 ft (by the *Vityaz*, USSR) in the Mariana Trench of the W Pacific 1957.

features deep trenches (off E and SE Asia, and western South America), volcanic belts (in the W Pacific and E Indian Ocean), and ocean ridges (in the mid-Atlantic, E Pacific, and Indian Ocean).

temperature varies on the surface with latitude (–2°C to +29°C); decreases rapidly to 370 m/1,200 ft, then more slowly to 2,200 m/7,200 ft; and hardly at all beyond that.

water contents salinity averages about 3%; minerals commercially extracted include bromine, magnesium, potassium, salt; those potentially recoverable include aluminium, calcium, copper, gold, manganese, silver. (See table on following page.)

ocean ridge mountain range on the seabed indicating the presence of a constructive plate margin (where tectonic plates are moving apart and magma rises to the surface). Ocean ridges, such as the Mid-Atlantic Ridge, consist of many segments offset along faults, and can rise thousands of metres above the surrounding seabed.

ocean trench deep trench in the seabed indicating the presence of a destructive margin (produced by the movements of plate tectonics). The subduction or dragging downwards of one plate of the lithosphere beneath another means that the ocean floor is pulled down. Ocean trenches are found around the edge of the Pacific Ocean and the NE Indian Ocean; minor ones occur in the Caribbean and near the Falkland Islands.

ooze sediment of fine texture consisting mainly of organic matter found on the ocean floor at depths greater than 2,000 m/6,600 ft. Several kinds of ooze exist, each named after its constituents.

Oceans and seas

	Area		Average depth	
	Sq km	*Sq mi*	*M*	*Ft*
Pacific Ocean	166,242,000	64,186,300	3,939	12,925
Atlantic Ocean	86,557,000	33,420,000	3,575	11,730
Indian Ocean	73,427,500	28,350,500	3,840	12,598
Arctic Ocean	13,224,000	5,105,700	1,038	3,407
South China Sea	2,975,000	1,148,500	1,464	4,802
Caribbean Sea	2,516,000	971,400	2,575	8,448
Mediterranean Sea	2,510,000	969,100	1,501	4,926
Bering Sea	2,261,061	873,000	1,491	4,893
Gulf of Mexico	1,508,000	582,100	1,614	5,297
Sea of Okhotsk	1,392,000	537,500	973	3,192
Sea of Japan	1,013,000	391,100	1,667	5,468
Hudson Bay	730,000	281,900	93	305
East China Sea	665,000	256,600	189	620
Andaman Sea	565,000	218,100	1,118	3,667
Black Sea	508,000	196,100	1,190	3,906
Red Sea	453,000	174,900	538	1,764
North Sea	427,000	164,900	94	308
Baltic Sea	382,000	147,500	55	180
Yellow Sea	294,000	113,500	37	121
Persian Gulf	230,000	88,800	100	328
Gulf of St Lawrence	162,000	62,530	810	2,660
Gulf of California	153,000	59,100	724	2,375
English Channel	89,900	34,700	54	177
Irish Sea	88,550	34,200	60	197
Bass Strait	75,000	28,950	70	230

rain form of precipitation in which separate drops of water fall to the Earth's surface from clouds. The drops are formed by the accumulation of fine droplets that condense from water vapour in the air. The condensation is usually brought about by rising and subsequent cooling of air.

thunderstorm severe storm of very heavy rain, thunder, and lightning. Thunderstorms are usually caused by the intense heating of the ground surface during summer. The warm air rises rapidly to form tall cumulonimbus clouds with a characteristic anvil-shaped top. Electrical charges accumulate in the clouds and are discharged to the ground as flashes of lightning. Air in the path of lightning becomes heated and expands rapidly, creating shock waves that are heard as a crash or rumble of thunder. The rough distance between an observer and a lightning flash can be calculated by timing the number of seconds between the flash and the thunder. A gap of 3 seconds represents about a kilometre; 5 seconds represents about a mile.

tornado extremely violent revolving storm with swirling, funnel-shaped clouds, caused by a rising column of warm air propelled by strong wind. A tornado can rise to a great height, but with a diameter of only a few hundred metres or yards or less. Tornadoes move with wind speeds of 160–480 kph/100–300 mph, destroying everything in their path. They are common in central USA and Australia.

trade wind prevailing wind that blows towards the equator from the northeast and southeast. Trade winds are caused by hot air rising at the equator and the consequent movement of air from north and south to take its place. The winds are deflected towards the west because of the Earth's west-to-east rotation. The unpredictable calms known as the doldrums lie at their convergence.

troposphere lower part of the Earth's atmosphere extending about 10.5 km/6.5 mi from the Earth's surface, in which temperature decreases with height to about –60°C/–76°F except in local layers of temperature inversion. The *tropopause* is the upper boundary of the troposphere, above which the temperature increases slowly with height within the atmosphere. All of the Earth's weather takes place within the troposphere.

tsunami (Japanese 'harbour wave') wave generated by an undersea earthquake or volcanic eruption. In the open ocean it may take the form of several successive waves, rarely in excess of a metre in height but travelling at speeds of 650–800 kph/400-500 mph. In the coastal shallows tsunamis slow down and build up, producing towering waves that can sweep inland and cause great loss of life and property.

wind the lateral movement of the Earth's atmosphere from high-pressure areas (anticyclones) to low-pressure areas (depression). Its speed is measured using an anemometer or by studying its effects on, for example, trees by using the Beaufort Scale. Although modified by features such as land and water, there is a basic worldwide system of trade winds, Westerlies, monsoons, and others.

ENERGY

Terms

The chief direct sources of energy are oil, coal, wood, and natural gas, and indirectly, electricity produced by the use of such fuels or derived from water power or nuclear fission. Increasing costs, and the prospect of the exhaustion of nonrenewable resources, led in the 1980s to consideration of alternative, renewable sources. These included solar power, which provides completely 'clean' energy; wind and wave power; tidal power (which, like geothermal power, is geographically limited in application); utilization of organic waste, such as chicken manure; photosynthetic power, produced by use of simple, fast-reproducing plants as fuel; and nuclear power, by fusion rather than fission.

Burning fossil fuels causes acid rain and is gradually increasing the carbon dioxide content in the atmosphere, with unknown consequences for future generations. Coal-fired power stations also release significant amounts of radioactive material, and the potential dangers of nuclear power stations are greater still. The ultimate nonrenewable but almost inexhaustible energy source would be nuclear fusion (the way in which energy is generated in the Sun), but controlled fusion is a long way off. Harnessing resources generally implies converting their energy into electrical form, because electrical energy is easy to convert to other forms and to transmit from place to place, though not to store.

biofuel any solid, liquid, or gaseous fuel produced from organic (once living) matter, either directly from plants or indirectly from industrial, commercial, domestic, or agricultural wastes. There are three main ways for the development of biofuels: the burning of dry organic wastes (such as household refuse, industrial and agricultural wastes, straw, wood, and peat); the fermentation of wet wastes (such as animal dung) in the absence of oxygen to produce biogas (containing up to 60% methane), or the fermentation of sugar cane or corn to produce alcohol; and energy forestry (producing fast-growing wood for fuel).

combined cycle generation system of electricity generation that makes use of both a gas turbine and a steam turbine. Combined cycle plants are more efficient than conventional generating plants, with an efficiency of energy conversion of around 40% (compared with under 38% for conventional plants). In combined cycle generation, the gas turbine is powered by burning gas fuel, and turns an electric generator. The exhaust gases are then used to heat water to produce steam. The steam powers a steam turbine attached to an electric generator, producing additional electricity.

combined heat and power generation (CHP generation) simultaneous production of electricity and useful heat in a power station. The heat is often in the form of hot water or steam, which can be used for local district heating or in industry. The electricity output from a CHP plant is lower than from a conventional station, but the overall efficiency of energy conversion is higher.

electricity generation and supply electricity is the most useful and most convenient form of energy, readily convertible into heat and light and used to power machines. Because electricity readily flows through wires, it can be made, or generated, in one place and distributed to anywhere it is needed. It is generated at power stations where a suitable energy source is harnessed to drive turbines that spin electricity generators. The generators produce alternating current (AC), and the producing units are generally called turboalternators. The main energy sources for electricity generation are coal, oil, water power (hydroelectricity), natural gas, and nuclear power, with limited contributions from wind, tidal, and geo-thermal power. Nuclear fuel provides the cheapest form of electricity generation in Britain, but environmental considerations may limit its future development.

Electricity is generated at power stations at about 25,000 volts, which is not a suitable voltage for long-distance transmission. For minimal power loss, transmission must take place at very high voltage (400,000 volts or more). The generated voltage is therefore increased, or stepped-up, by a transformer. The resulting high-voltage electricity is then fed into the main arteries of the grid system, an interconnected network of power stations and distribution centres covering a large area, sometimes (as in the UK) countrywide, even (as in Europe) from country to country. After transmission to a local substation, the line voltage is reduced by a step-down transformer and distributed to consumers.

fossil fuel fuel, such as coal, oil, and natural gas, formed from the fossilized remains of plants that lived hundreds of millions of years ago. Fossil fuels are a nonrenewable resource and will eventually run out. Extraction of coal and oil causes considerable environmental pollution, and burning coal contributes to problems of acid rain and the greenhouse effect.

geothermal energy energy extracted for heating and electricity generation from natural steam, hot water, or hot dry rocks in the Earth's crust. Water is pumped down through an injection well where it passes through joints in the hot rocks. It rises to the surface through a recovery well and may be converted to steam or run through a heat exchanger. Dry steam may be directed through turbines to produce electricity. It is a important source of energy in volcanically active areas such as Iceland and New Zealand.

heat pump machine, run by electricity or another power source, that cools the interior of a building by removing heat from interior air and pumping it out or, conversely, heats the inside by extracting energy from the atmosphere or from a hot-water source and pumping it in.

heat storage any means of storing heat for release later. It is usually achieved by using materials that undergo phase changes, for example, Glauber's salt and sodium pyrophosphate, which melts at 70°C/158°F. The latter is used to store off-peak heat in the home: the salt is liquefied by cheap heat during the night and then freezes to give off heat during the day. Other developments include the use of plastic crystals, which change their structure rather than melting when they are heated. They could be incorporated in curtains or clothing.

hydroelectric power (HEP) electricity generated by moving water. In a typical HEP scheme, water stored in a reservoir, often created by damming a river, is piped into water turbines, coupled to electricity generators. In pumped storage plants, water flowing through the turbines is recycled. A tidal power station exploits the rise and fall of the tides. About one-fifth of the world's electricity comes from HEP. HEP plants have prodigious generating capacities. The Grand Coulee plant in Washington State, USA, has a power output of some 10,000 megawatts. The Itaipu power station on the Paraná River (Brazil/Paraguay) has a potential capacity of 12,000 megawatts.

natural gas mixture of flammable gases found in the Earth's crust (often in association with petroleum), now one of the world's three main fossil fuels (with coal and oil). Natural gas is a mixture of hydrocarbons, chiefly methane, with ethane, butane, and propane. Before the gas is piped to storage tanks and on to consumers, butane and propane are removed and liquefied to form 'bottled gas'. Natural gas is liquefied for transport and storage, and is therefore often used where other fuels are scarce and expensive.

nuclear energy energy from the inner core or nucleus of the atom, as opposed to energy released in chemical processes, which is derived from the electrons surrounding the nucleus. *Nuclear fission*, as in an atom bomb, is achieved by allowing a neutron to strike the nucleus of an atom of fissile material (such as uranium-235 or plutonium-239), which then splits apart to release two or three other neutrons. If the uranium-235 is pure, a chain reaction is set up when these neutrons in turn strike other nuclei. This happens very quickly, resulting in the tremendous release of energy seen in nuclear weapons. The process is controlled inside the reactor of a nuclear power plant by absorbing excess neutrons in control rods and slowing down their speed. *Nuclear fusion* is the process whereby hydrogen nuclei fuse to helium

nuclei with an accompanying release of energy. It is a continuing reaction in the Sun and other stars. Nuclear fusion is the principle behind thermonuclear weapons (the hydrogen bomb). Attempts to harness fusion for commercial power production have so far been unsuccessful, although the Joint European Torus (or JET) laboratory at Culham, Oxfordshire, England, achieved fusion 1991.

nuclear reactor device for producing nuclear energy in a controlled manner. There are various types of reactor in use, all using nuclear fission.

In a *gas-cooled reactor*, a circulating gas under pressure (such as carbon dioxide) removes heat from the core of the reactor, which usually contains natural uranium. The efficiency of the fission process is increased by slowing neutrons in the core by using a moderator such as carbon. The reaction is controlled with neutron-absorbing rods made of boron. An *advanced gas-cooled reactor* (AGR) generally has enriched uranium as its fuel. A *water-cooled reactor*, such as the steam-generating heavy water (deuterium oxide) reactor, has water circulating through the hot core. The water is converted to steam, which drives turbo-alternators for generating electricity. The most widely used reactor is the *pressurized-water reactor* (PWR), which contains a sealed system of pressurized water that is heated to form steam in heat exchangers in an external circuit. The *fast reactor* has no moderator and uses fast neutrons to bring about fission. It uses a mixture of plutonium and uranium oxide as fuel. When operating, uranium is converted to plutonium, which can be extracted and used later as fuel. The fast breeder is so called because it produces more plutonium than it consumes. Heat is removed from the reactor by a coolant of liquid sodium.

Public concern over the safety of nuclear reactors has been intensified by explosions and accidental release of radioactive materials. The safest system allows for the emergency cooling of a reactor by automatically flooding an overheated core with water. Other concerns about nuclear power centre on the difficulties of reprocessing nuclear fuel and disposing safely of nuclear waste, and the cost of main-

---

Nuclear energy: chronology

1896   French physicist Henri Becquerel discovered radioactivity.
1905   In Switzerland, Albert Einstein showed that mass can be converted into energy.
1911   New Zealand physicist Ernest Rutherford proposed the nuclear model of the atom.
1919   Rutherford split the atom, by bombarding a nitrogen nucleus with alpha particles.
1939   Otto Hahn, Fritz Strassman, and Lise Meitner announced the discovery of nuclear fission.
1942   Enrico Fermi built the first nuclear reactor, in a squash court at the University of Chicago, USA.
1946   The first fast reactor, called Clementine, was built at Los Alamos, New Mexico.
1951   The Experimental Breeder Reactor, Idaho, USA, produced the first electricity to be generated by nuclear energy.
1954   The first reactor for generating electricity was built in the USSR, at Obninsk.
1956   The world's first commercial nuclear power station, Calder Hall, came into operation in the UK.
1957   The release of radiation from Windscale (now Sellafield) nuclear power station, Cumbria, England, caused 39 deaths to 1977. In Kyshym, USSR, the venting of plutonium waste caused high but undisclosed casualties (30 small communities were deleted from maps produced in 1958).
1959   Experimental fast reactor built in Dounreay, N Scotland.
1979   Nuclear-reactor accident at Three Mile Island, Pennsylvania, USA.
1986   An explosive leak from a reactor at Chernobyl, the Ukraine, resulted in clouds of radioactive material spreading as far as Sweden; 31 people were killed and thousands of square kilometres were contaminated.
1991   The first controlled and substantial production of nuclear-fusion energy (a two-second pulse of 1.7 MW) was achieved at JET, the Joint European Torus, at Culham, Oxfordshire, England.

Worst known nuclear-power accidents

Year	Power station	Type of accident
1957	Windscale (UK)	radioactive leak after fire destroyed the reactor's core
1976	Greifswald (East Germany)	near meltdown of the reactor
1979	Three Mile Island (USA)	release of thousands of gallons of radioactive water and a plume of radioactive gas after the near meltdown of a pressurized-water reactor
1979	Church Rock (USA)	leak of 100 million gallons of radioactive water
1986	Chernobyl (Ukraine)	explosion spread radioactive pollution and contamination across central, northern, and western Europe
1992	St Petersburg (Russia)	leak of radioactive iodine from a Chernobyl-type reactor

taining nuclear power stations and of decommissioning them at the end of their lives.

In 1989, the UK government decided to postpone the construction of new nuclear power stations; in the USA, no new stations have been commissioned in over a decade. Rancho Seco, near Sacramento, California, was the first nuclear power station to be closed, by popular vote, in 1989. Sweden is committed to decommissioning its reactors. Some countries, such as France, are pressing ahead with their nuclear programmes. (See also *nuclear safety* and *nuclear waste* in *Environment and Conservation*.)

Nuclear reactors, worldwide

Reactors and percentage share of electricity generation, 1992

Country	Reactors in operation	Reactors being built	Nuclear electricity (% of total)
Argentina	2	1	19.1
Belgium	7		59.3
Brazil	1	1	0.6
Bulgaria	6		34.0
Canada	20	2	16.4
China	1	2	
Cuba		2	
CSFR	8	6	28.6
Finland	4		33.3
France	56	5	72.7
Germany	21		27.6
Hungary	4		48.4
India	7	7	1.8
Iran		2	
Japan	42	10	23.8
Korea	9	3	47.5
Mexico	1	1	3.6
Netherlands	2		4.9
Pakistan	1		0.8
Romania		5	
South Africa	2		5.9
Spain	9		35.9
Sweden	12		51.6
Switzerland	5		40.0
Taiwan	6		37.8
UK	37	1	20.6
USA	111	3	21.7
Ex-USSR	45	25	12.6
Ex-Yugoslavia	1		6.3
Total	420	76	

Source: Nuclear Forum

petroleum or *crude oil* natural mineral oil, a thick greenish-brown flammable liquid found underground in permeable rocks. Petroleum consists of hydrocarbons mixed with oxygen, sulphur, nitrogen, and other elements in varying proportions. It is thought to be derived from ancient organic material that has been converted by, first, bacterial action, then heat and pressure (but its origin may be chemical also). From crude petroleum, various products are made by distillation and other processes; for example, fuel oil, petrol, kerosene, diesel, lubricating oil, paraffin wax, and petroleum jelly.

The organic material in petroleum was laid down millions of years ago (hence it is known as a fossil fuel). Petroleum is found trapped in porous reservoir rocks, such as sandstone or limestone, in anticlines and other traps below impervious rock layers. Oil may flow from wells under natural pressure, causing it to rise up the borehole, but many oil wells require pumping to bring the oil to the surface.

The exploitation of oilfields began with the first commercial well in Pennsylvania 1859. The USA led in production until the 1960s, when the Middle East outproduced other areas, their immense reserves leading to a worldwide dependence on cheap oil for transport and industry. In 1961 the Organization of the Petroleum Exporting Countries (OPEC) was established to avoid exploitation of member countries; after OPEC's price rises 1973, the International Energy Agency (IEA) was established 1974 to protect the interests of oil-consuming countries. New technologies were introduced to pump oil from offshore and from the Arctic (the Alaska pipeline) in an effort to avoid a monopoly by OPEC. Petroleum products and chemicals are used in large quantities in the manufacture of detergents, artificial fibres, plastics, insecticides, fertilizers, pharmaceuticals, toiletries, and synthetic rubber. Aviation fuel is a volatile form of petrol.

The burning of petroleum fuel is one cause of air pollution. The transport of oil can lead to catastrophes – for example, the *Torrey Canyon* tanker lost off SW England 1967, which led to an agreement by the international oil companies 1968 to pay compensation for massive shore pollution. The 1989 oil spill in Alaska from the *Exxon Valdez* damaged the area's fragile environment, despite clean-up efforts. Drilling for oil involves the risks of accidental spillage and drilling-rig accidents. The problems associated with oil have led to the various alternative energy technologies. A new kind of bacterium was developed during the 1970s in the USA, capable of 'eating' oil as a means of countering oil spills. Its cre-

Energy in the UK

Production and consumption of primary fuels, 1988-92 (m tonnes of oil or oil equivalent)

Year	Total	Coal	Petroleum	Natural gas[1]	Primary electricity		
					Nuclear	Natural flow hydro[2]	
Energy production							
1988	229.7	61.1	114.5	39.3	13.45	1.42	
1989	206.4	59.5	91.8	38.3	15.35	1.38	
1990	205.3	55.5	91.6	42.5	14.19	1.55	
1991	211.7	56.6	91.3	47.3	15.17	1.37	
1992 (p)	211.6	51.4	94.2	47.7	16.68	1.62	
% change	–	–9.1	+3.3	+0.8	+9.9	+18.0	
Energy consumption (seasonally adjusted)							Net imports
1988	201.9	65.9	68.3	49.7	13.45	1.42	3.08
1989	204.9	64.5	70.2	50.5	15.35	1.38	3.03
1990	209.3	65.0	73.3	52.4	14.19	1.55	2.87
1991	207.0	63.1	70.8	52.7	15.17	1.37	3.94
1992 (p)	207.4	60.0	70.9	54.2	16.68	1.62	4.01
% change	+0.2	–5.0	+0.1	+3.0	+9.9	+18.2	+1.8

[1] Including non-energy use and excluding gas flared or re-injected.
[2] Excludes generation from pumped storage stations. Including generation at wind stations.
(p) provisional

Source: Energy Trends/DTI

ation gave rise to the so-called Frankenstein law (a ruling that allowed new forms of life created in laboratories to be patented).

renewable resource natural resource that is replaced by natural processes in a reasonable amount of time. Soil, water, forests, plants, and animals are all renewable resources as long as they are properly conserved. Solar, wind, wave, and geothermal energies are based on renewable resources.

solar energy energy derived from the Sun's radiation. The amount of energy falling on just 1 sq km/0.3861 sq mi is about 4,000 megawatts, enough to heat and light a small town. In one second the Sun gives off 13 million times more energy than all the electricity used in the USA in one year. *Solar heaters* have industrial or domestic uses. They usually consist of a black (heat-absorbing) panel containing pipes through which air or water, heated by the Sun, is circulated, either by thermal convection or by a pump.

Solar energy may also be harnessed indirectly using *solar cells* (photovoltaic cells) made of panels of semiconductor material (usually silicon), which generate electricity when illuminated by sunlight. Although it is difficult to generate a high output from solar energy compared to sources such as nuclear or fossil fuels, it is a major nonpolluting and renewable energy source used as far north as Scandinavia as well as in the SW USA and in Mediterranean countries.

A solar furnace, such as that built 1970 at Odeillo in the French Pyrénées, has thousands of mirrors to focus the Sun's rays; it produces uncontaminated intensive heat (up to 3,000°C/5,400°F) for industrial and scientific or experimental purposes. The world's first solar power station connected to a national grid opened 1991 at Adrano in Sicily. Scores of giant mirrors move to follow the Sun throughout the day,

focusing the rays into a boiler. Steam from the boiler drives a conventional turbine. The plant generates up to 1 megawatt. A similar system, called Solar 1, has been built in the Mojave desert near Daggett, California, USA. It consists of 1,818 computer-controlled mirrors arranged in circles around a 91 m/300 ft central boiler tower. Advanced schemes have been proposed that would use giant solar reflectors in space to harness solar energy and beam it down to Earth in the form of microwaves. Despite their low running costs, their high installation cost and low power output have meant that solar cells have found few applications outside space probes and artificial satellites. Solar heating is, however, widely used for domestic purposes in many parts of the world.

tidal power station hydroelectric power plant that uses the 'head' of water created by the rise and fall of the ocean tides to spin the water turbines. An example is located on the estuary of the river Rance in the Gulf of St Malo, Brittany, France, which has been in use since 1966.

turbine engine in which steam, water, gas, or air is made to spin a rotating shaft by pushing on angled blades, like a fan. Turbines are among the most powerful machines. Steam turbines are used to drive generators in power stations and ships' propellers; water turbines spin the generators in hydroelectric power plants; and gas turbines (as jet engines; see jet propulsion) power most aircraft and drive machines in industry.

The high-temperature, high-pressure steam for *steam turbines* is raised in boilers heated by furnaces burning coal, oil, or gas, or by nuclear energy. A steam turbine consists of a shaft, or rotor, which rotates inside a fixed casing (stator). The rotor carries 'wheels' consisting of blades, or vanes. The stator

Energy demands worldwide

Primary energy* consumption by fuel, 1991 (m tonnes oil equivalent)

	Oil	Natural gas	Coal	Nuclear energy	Hydro-electric	Total
North America						
USA	774.4	507.7	477.9	165.9	26.1	1,952.0
Canada	74.8	57.2	25.3	22.1	26.4	205.8
Latin America						
Argentina	20.1	19.0	1.4	2.2	1.2	43.9
Brazil	63.3	3.7	9.7	0.4	18.5	95.6
Mexico	72.6	33.4	6.6	1.1	8.1	121.8
Venezuela	17.3	18.6	0.3	—	3.7	39.9
Others	79.0	9.6	6.7	—	6.8	102.1
OECD Europe						
Austria	11.2	5.7	3.8	—	2.8	23.5
Belgium & Luxembourg	25.9	8.6	10.9	10.4	†	55.8
Denmark	9.1	2.0	6.5	—	—	17.6
Finland	10.6	2.4	3.6	4.8	1.1	22.5
France	94.4	27.6	20.3	65.0	4.2	211.5
Germany	133.4	56.8	112.4	38.0	1.3	341.9
Greece	15.5	0.2	8.2	—	0.2	24.1
Iceland	0.6	0.0	0.1	—	0.4	1.1
Republic of Ireland	4.6	1.4	4.3	—	0.1	10.4
Italy	91.7	41.4	14.2	—	3.5	150.8
Netherlands	35.4	33.5	9.2	1.0	—	79.1
Norway	8.9	0.0	0.5	—	8.3	17.7
Portugal	11.4	0.0	0.8	—	0.3	12.5
Spain	46.1	5.5	18.7	13.0	2.2	85.5
Sweden	14.6	0.7	2.0	18.6	5.3	41.2
Switzerland	13.0	1.5	0.3	5.6	2.8	23.2
Turkey	22.0	3.8	22.5	—	1.4	49.7
UK	82.9	54.2	63.4	15.5	0.3	216.3
Non–OECD Europe						
Ex-USSR	420.1	560.0	253.4	54.7	20.2	1,308.4
Czechoslovakia	13.2	10.2	31.7	5.9	0.4	61.4
Hungary	7.4	9.2	5.8	3.4	†	25.8
Poland	13.5	8.1	79.7	—	0.1	101.4
Others	33.0	32.4	35.2	5.4	4.1	110.1
Middle East	153.1	79.9	2.7	—	0.9	236.6
Africa	97.4	32.9	78.3	2.5	6.7	217.8
Asia & Australasia						
Australia	31.1	16.5	39.9	—	1.3	88.8
China	117.9	13.4	543.8	—	10.6	685.7
India	58.0	12.8	106.0	1.4	5.7	183.9
Indonesia	32.4	8.1	3.9	—	0.6	45.0
Japan	247.3	49.5	78.7	54.1	8.6	438.2
Malaysia	11.3	8.1	0.5	—	0.3	20.2
New Zealand	4.7	4.1	1.3	—	2.1	12.2
Philippines	11.1	—	1.2	—	0.4	12.7
Singapore	19.9	—	—	—	—	19.9
South Korea	56.1	3.5	24.1	14.1	0.4	98.2
Taiwan	27.9	1.9	14.0	9.2	0.3	53.3
Thailand	21.1	6.8	4.7	—	0.3	32.9
Others	32.1	17.8	51.7	0.1	7.9	109.6
Total World	3,141.1	1,769.7	2,186.2	514.4	195.9	7,807.6

* *comprises commercially traded fuels only. Excluded therefore are fuels such as wood, peat, and animal waste, which, though important in many countries, are unreliably documented in terms of consumption statistics.*
† *less than 0.05*

Source: BP Statistical Review of World Energy 1992

has vanes set between the vanes of the rotor, which direct the steam through the rotor vanes at the optimum angle. When steam expands through the turbine, it spins the rotor by reaction. Less widely used than the reaction turbine is the *impulse turbine*, which works by directing a jet of steam at blades on a rotor. Similarly there are reaction and impulse water turbines: impulse turbines work on the same principle as the water wheel and consist of sets of buckets arranged around the edge of a wheel; reaction turbines look much like propellers and are fully immersed in the water.

In a *gas turbine* a compressed mixture of air and gas, or vaporized fuel, is ignited, and the hot gases produced expand through the turbine blades, spinning the rotor. In the industrial gas turbine, the rotor shaft drives machines. In the jet engine, the turbine drives the compressor, which supplies the compressed air to the engine, but most of the power developed comes from the jet exhaust in the form of propulsive thrust.

water mill machine that harnesses the energy in flowing water to produce mechanical power, typically for milling (grinding) grain. Water from a stream is directed against the paddles of a water wheel to make it turn. Simple gearing transfers this motion to the millstones. The modern equivalent of the water wheel is the water turbine, used in hydroelectric power plants.

wave power power obtained by harnessing the energy of water waves. Various schemes have been advanced since 1973, when oil prices rose dramatically and an energy shortage threatened. In 1974 the British engineer Stephen Salter developed the duck – a floating boom whose segments nod up and down with the waves. The nodding motion can be used to drive pumps and spin generators. Another device, developed in Japan, uses an oscillating water column to harness wave power. However, a major break-

through will be required if wave power is ever to contribute significantly to the world's energy needs.

windmill mill with sails or vanes that, by the action of wind upon them, drive machinery for grinding corn or pumping water, for example. Wind turbines, designed to use wind power on a large scale, usually have a propeller-type rotor mounted on a tall shell tower. The turbine drives a generator for producing electricity. The main types of traditional windmill are the *post mill*, which is turned around a post when the direction of the wind changes, and the *tower mill*, which has a revolving turret on top. It usually has a device (fantail) that keeps the sails pointing into the wind.

wind turbine windmill of advanced aerodynamic design connected to an electricity generator and used in wind-power installations. Wind turbines can be either large propeller-type rotors mounted on a tall tower, or flexible metal strips fixed to a vertical axle at top and bottom. In 1990, over 20,000 wind turbines were in use throughout the world, generating 1,600 megawatts of power.

The world's largest wind turbine is on Hawaii, in the Pacific Ocean. It has two blades 50 m/160 ft long on top of a tower 20 storeys high. An example of a propeller turbine is found at Tvind in Denmark and has an output of some 2 megawatts. Other machines use novel rotors, such as the 'egg-beater' design developed at Sandia Laboratories in New Mexico, USA. The largest wind turbine on mainland Britain is at Richborough on the Kent coast. The three-bladed turbine, which is 35 m/115 ft across, produces 1 megawatt of power. Britain's largest vertical-axis wind turbine has two 24 m/80 ft blades and began operating in Dyfed, Wales, 1990.

Worldwide, wind turbines on land produce only the energy equivalent of a single nuclear power station (such as the Sizewell nuclear station). In Britain, 300 turbines, mainly in Cornwall, the northwest, and Wales, provide enough power for 60,000 homes.

ENGINEERING AND BUILDING

Terms

adobe Spanish name for sun-baked earth bricks, or buildings made with them. The material commonly consists of sandy clay or loam mixed with straw or grass. Another less common form of adobe is made from dampened earth which is pressed within moulds (*pisé de terre*). The techniques are commonly found in Spain, Latin America, and the southwestern USA – areas where the climate is warm and dry. Modern adobe houses are covered with stucco, a type of plaster.

brick common building material, rectangular in shape, made of clay that has been fired in a kiln. Bricks are made by kneading a mixture of crushed clay and other materials into a stiff mud and extruding it into a ribbon. The ribbon is cut into individual bricks, which are fired at a temperature of up to about 1,000°C/1,800°F. In wall building, bricks are either laid out as stretchers (long side facing out) or as headers (short side facing out). The two principle patterns of brickwork are **English bond**, in which alternate courses, or layers, are made up of stretchers or headers only; and **Flemish bond**, in which stretchers and headers alternate within courses.

bridge structure that provides a continuous path or road over water, valleys, ravines, or above other roads. The basic designs and composites of these are based on the way they bear the weight of the structure and its load. Bridges may be classified into the following main groups: **arch** bridges, thrusting outwards but downwards at their ends, in compression (Sydney Harbour bridge, Australia, for example); **beam**, or **girder** bridges, supported at each end by the ground with the weight thrusting downwards (Rio Niterói bridge, Guanabara Bay, Brazil); **cable-stayed** bridges, relying on diagonal cables connected directly between the bridge deck and supporting towers at each end (Alex Fraser bridge, Fraser River, British Columbia) – sometimes having movable parts, like swing and draw bridges, to allow traffic to pass beneath; **cantilever** bridges, a complex form of girder bridge (Quebec bridge, St Lawrence River, Canada); **suspension** bridges, using cables under tension to pull inwards against anchorages on either side of the span, so that the roadway hangs from the main cables by a network of vertical cables (Golden Gate Bridge, San Francisco, USA).

canal artificial waterway constructed for drainage, irrigation, or navigation. *Irrigation canals* carry water for irrigation from rivers, reservoirs, or wells, and are designed to maintain an even flow of water over the whole length. *Navigation and ship canals* are constructed at one level between *locks*, and frequently link with rivers or sea inlets to form a waterway system. The Suez Canal 1869 and the Panama Canal 1914 eliminated long trips around continents and dramatically shortened shipping routes. (See table on page 113.)

cement any bonding agent used to unite particles in a single mass or to cause one surface to adhere to another. *Portland cement* is a powder obtained from burning together a mixture of lime (or chalk)

The world's most remarkable bridges

Name	Location	Type and length
Angostura	Cuidad Bolivar, Venezuela	suspension-type bridge; span 712 m/2,336 ft; total length 1,678 m/5,507 ft
Bendorf Bridge	Coblenz, Germany	three-span cement girder bridge; main span 208 m/682 ft; total length 1,030 m/3,378 ft
Bosphorous Bridge	Istanbul, Turkey (linking Europe to Asia)	suspension bridge; total length 1,074 m/ 3,524 ft
Gladsville Bridge	Sydney Australia	concrete arch bridge; 305 m/1,000 ft – world's longest concrete arch
Humber Bridge	Kingston upon Hull, England	suspension bridge; total span 1,410 m/4,628 ft – world's longest suspension bridge
Ikuchi Bridge	Honshu/Shikoku, Japan	cable-stayed bridge; 490 m/1,608 ft span
Lake Pontchartrain Bridge	New Orleans, USA	multiple-span; 38,421 m/126,055 ft – world's longest multiple span
Oosterscelderbrug	Flushing/Rotterdam, The Netherlands	traffic causeway over Zeeland sea arm total length 19 km/31.25 mi
Rio-Niteroi	Guanabara Bay, Brazil	continuous box and plate girder bridge; 14 km/8.7 mi – world's longest box girder bridge
Tagus River Bridge	Lisbon, Portugal	main span 1,013 m/3,323 ft
Zoo Bridge	Cologne, Germany	steel box girder bridge; main span 259 m/850 ft

Longest bridges, by span

Name	Location	Date	Length m/ft
Suspension spans			
Humber Estuary	Hull-Grimsby, England	1973–81	1,410/4,626
Verrazono Narrows	Brooklyn-Staten Island, New York Harbour, USA	1959–64	1,298/4,260
Golden Gate	San Francisco, California, USA	1937	1,280/4,200
Mackinac Straits	Michigan, USA	1957	1,158/3,800
Bosporus	Golden Horn, Istanbul, Turkey	1973	1,074/3,524
George Washington	Hudson River, New York, USA	1927–31	1,067/3,500
Ponte 25 Abril, (Salazar)	Tagus River, Lisbon, Portugal	1966	1,013/3,323
Firth of Forth (road)	South Queensferry, Scotland	1958–64	1,006/3,300
Severn River	Beachley, England	1961–66	988/3,240
Cantilever spans			
Pont de Quebec (railroad)	St Lawrence, Canada	1918	549/1,800
Ravenswood	West Virginia, USA	1981	525/1,723
Firth of Forth (rail)	South Queensferry, Scotland	1882–90	521/1,710
Commodore Barry	Chester, Pennsylvania, USA	1974	494/1,622
Greater New Orleans	Mississippi River Louisiana, USA	1958	480/1,575
Howrah (railroad)	Hooghly River, Calcutta, India	1936–43	988/3,240
Steel arch spans			
New River Gorge	Fayetteville, West Virginia, USA	1977	518.2/1,700
Bayonne (Killvan Kull)	New Jersey-Staten Island, USA	1932	504/1,652
Sydney Harbour	Sydney, Australia	1923–32	503/1,500

Railway bridges over 100 m/328 ft high

Bridge	Railway	Position	Height m/ft	Date opened
Mala Rijeka Viaduct	Yugoslav Railways (JZ)	Kolasin on Belgrade–Bar line	198/650	1976
Vresk	Iranian State	220 km (137 miles) from Bandar Shah on Caspian Sea Trans Iranian line	152/500	1938
Fades Viaduct	French National	Clermont-Ferrand–Montluçon line	132.5/435	1909
Khotur	Iranian State	Khotur River near Khoi	131/430	1973
Victoria Falls	Rhodesia Railways	Livingstone	128/420	1904
Pfaffenberg-Zwenberg	Austrian Federal	Mallnitz-Spittal	120/394	1971
Viaur	French National	Tanus, Rodez–Albi	116/381	1902
Garabit Viaduct	French National	Neussargues–Mallnitz	112/367	1884
Müngstner	German Federal	Mügsten, over River Wupper	107/350	1897
Rio Grande	Costa Rica	Near San José	105/346	
Vance Creek	Simpson Timber Co	Shelton, west of Tacoma, Washington, USA	105/346	1928
Tramo Sobre	Former Buenos Aires Great Southern, Argentina	Rio Negro	104/344	
Viaduct No. 2	Turkish State	Between Konakler and Günaykoy on Izmir–Afyonkarahisar line, 199.3 km from Izmir	103/338	1900
Faux-Mau-Ti	Chinese Peoples Republic	Yunnan section	102/335	1910
Rio Chinipas	Chihuahua–Pacific Mexico	On Ojinago–Topolobampo line	101/330	
Corte	Corsica	Corte	100/328	1894
Lindischgraben	Austrian Federal	Tauern Railway Obervellach–Penk	100/328	1977
Ten Tze	Chinese Peoples Republic	Yunnan section	*c* 100/*c* 328	1910

and clay, and when mixed with water and sand or gravel, turns into mortar or concrete. In geology, a chemically precipitated material such as carbonate that occupies the interstices of clastic rocks is called cement.

cladding thin layer of external covering on a building; for example, tiles, wood, stone, concrete.

concrete building material composed of cement, stone, sand, and water. It has been used since Egyptian and Roman times. During the 20th century, it has been increasingly employed as an economical alternative to materials such as brick and wood. From the 1980s, however, there has been a move away from concrete in house-building due to its comparatively short life span.

Longest ship canals

Canal, year opened	Route	Length Km/mi
Baltic-White Sea (formerly Stalin), 1933	Canalized river	235/146
Suez*, 1869	Red Sea to Mediterranean Sea	166/103
V I Lenin Volga Don, 1952	Black Sea to Caspian Sea	100/62.2
Kiel (or North Sea), 1895	North Sea to Baltic Sea	98/61
Houston*, 1940	Houston to Gulf of Mexico	91/56.7
Alfonso XIII, 1926	Seville to Gulf of Cadiz	85/53
Panama, 1914	Pacific Ocean to Caribbean Sea	81/50.5
Manchester Ship, 1894	Manchester to Mersey estuary	57/35.5
Welland, 1929	Lake Ontario to Lake Erie	45/28
Brussels (Willebroeck), 1922	Brussels to North Sea	32/19.8

Has no locks

dam a structure built to hold back water in order to prevent flooding, provide water for irrigation and storage, and to provide hydroelectric power. The biggest dams are of the earth- and rock-fill type, also called *embankment dams*. Such dams are generally built on broad val-ley sites. Deep, narrow gorges dictate a *concrete dam*, where the strength of reinforced concrete can withstand the water pressures involved. Many concrete dams are triangular in cross-section, with their vertical face pointing upstream. Their sheer weight holds them in position, and they are called *gravity dams*. Other concrete dams, however, are more slight and are built in the shape of an arch, with the curve facing upstream: the *arch dam* derives its strength from the arch shape, just as an arch bridge does. A valuable development in arid regions, as in parts of Brazil, is the *underground dam*, where water is stored on a solid rock base, with a wall to ground level, so avoiding rapid evaporation.

masonry the craft of constructing stonework walls. The various styles of masonry include *random rubblework*, irregular stones arranged according to fit; *coursed rubblework*, irregular stones arranged in broad horizontal bands, or courses; *ashlar masonry*, smooth square-cut stones arranged in courses; *Cyclopean masonry*, large polygonal stones cut to fit eachother; *rustification*, large stones separated by deep joints and chiselled or hammered into a variety of styles. Rustification is usually employed at the base of buildings, on top of an ashlar base, to give an appearance of added strength.

module a standard or unit that governs the form of the rest: for example, Japanese room sizes are traditionally governed by multiples of standard tatami floor mats; today prefabricated buildings are mass-produced in a similar way. The components of a spacecraft are designed in coordination; for example, for the Apollo Moon landings the craft comprised a command module (for working, eating, sleeping), service module (electricity generators, oxygen supplies, manoeuvring rocket), and lunar module (to land and return the astronauts).

prefabricated building the use of large elements, such as walls, floors, and roofs, that are factory produced and subsequently assembled on site.

prestressed concrete reinforced concrete in which ducts enclose mechanically tensioned steel cables. This allows the most efficient use of the tensile strength of steel with the compressive strength of concrete.

pylon steel lattice tower that supports high-tension electrical cables. In ancient Egyptian architecture, a pylon is one of a pair of inward-sloping towers that flank an entrance.

space-frame lightweight, triangulated, structural framework, designed to be of uniform load resistance and used principally in large-span constructions, such as exhibition halls, stadia, and aircraft hangars. The Eiffel Tower, Paris 1899, is of space-frame constructoin. A contemporary development is Buckminster Fuller's *geodesic dome*, a shell-like space-frame covered in plastic, plywood, or metal sheeting.

tunnel passageway through a mountain, under a body of water, or under ground. Tunnelling is an increasingly important branch of civil engineering in

The world's highest dams

Name	Country	Height above lowest formation
Rogun*	Tajikistan	335 m/1,099 ft
Nurek	Tajikistan	300 m/984 ft
Grand Dixence	Switzerland	285 m/935 ft
Inguri	Georgia	272 m/892 ft
Boruca*	Costa Rica	267 m/875 ft
Chicoasen	Mexico	261 m/856 ft
Tehri*	India	261 m/856 ft
Kambaratinsk*	Kyrgyzstan	255 m/836 ft
Kishau*	India	253 m/830 ft
Sayano-Shushensk*	Russia	245 m/804 ft
Guavio	Colombia	243 m/797 ft
Mica	Canada	242 m/794 ft
Ertan*	China	240 m/787 ft
Mauvoisin	Switzerland	237 m/778 ft
Chivor	Colombia	237 m/778 ft
Kishau*	India	236 m/774 ft
El Cajon	Honduras	234 m/768 ft
Chirkey	Russian Federation	233 m/765 ft
Oroville	USA	230 m/754 ft
Bekhme*	Iraq	230 m/754 ft
Bhakra	India	226 m/741 ft
Hoover	USA	221 m/738 ft
Contra	Switzerland	220 m/772 ft
Mratinje	Yugoslavia	220 m/772 ft

under construction

World's tallest buildings and structures

Tallest inhabited buildings and tallest structures

Building and location	Year completed	Height m/ft	Storeys
Sears Tower, Chicago	1974	443/1,454*	110
World Trade Centre (twin towers), New York	1972	417/1,368*	110
Empire State Building, New York	1931	381/1,250*	102
Bank of China, Hong Kong	1989	368/1,209	72
Amoco Building, Chicago	1971	346/1,136	80
John Hancock Centre, Chicago	1967	344/1,127	100
Chrysler Building, New York	1930	319/1,046	77
First Interstate World Center, Los Angeles	1989	310/1,017	73
Texas Commerce Tower, Houston	1981	305/1,002	75
Allied Bank Plaza, Houston	1983	302/992	71
Messe Turin Building, Frankfurt	1991	256/841	70
Canary Wharf Tower, London	1990	244/800	56

* excluding TV antennae

Tallest structures

Structure and location	Height m/ft
Warszawa Radio Mast,** Konstantynow, Poland	646/2,120
KTHI-TV Mast, Fargo, North Dakota	629/2,063
CN Tower, Metro Center, Toronto	555/1,822

** collapsed during renovation, Aug 1991

mining, transport and other areas. In the 19th century there were two major advances: the use of compressed air within underwater tunnels to balance the external pressure of water, and, on land, the development of the tunnel shield to support the rockface and assist excavation. In recent years there have been notable developments in linings, such as concrete segments and steel liner plates, and in the use of rotary diggers and cutters, and explosives.

Major tunnels include: *Orange–Fish River* (South Africa) 1975, longest irrigation tunnel, 82 km/51 mi; *Chesapeake Bay Bridge–Tunnel* (USA) 1963, combined bridge, causeway, and tunnel structure, 28 km/17.5 mi; *St Gotthard* (Switzerland–Italy) 1980, longest road tunnel, 16.3 km/10.1 mi; *Seikan* (Japan) 1964–85, longest rail tunnel, Honshu–Hokkaido, under Tsugaru Strait, 53.9 km/33.5 mi, 23.3 km/14.5 mi undersea (however, a bullet-train service is no longer economical); *Simplon* (Switzerland–Italy) 1906, longest rail tunnel on land, 19.8 km/12.3 mi; *Rogers Pass* (Canada) 1989, longest tunnel in the western hemisphere, 35 km/22 mi long, through the Selkirk Mountains, British Columbia. Plans for the *Channel tunnel* linking England and France were approved by the French and British governments in 1986, and work is under way with a schedule for completion in early 1994.

World's longest railway tunnels

Tunnel	Location	Date	Km/mi
Seikan*	Japan	1985	54/33.5
Channel Tunnel	UK – France	1994	50/31
Dai-shimizu	Japan	1979	23/14
Simplon No. 1 and 2	Switzerland – Italy	1906, 1922	19/12
Kanmon	Japan	1975	19/12
Apennine	Italy	1934	18/11
Rokko	Japan	1972	16/10
Mt MacDonald	Canada	1989	15/9.1
Gotthard	Switzerland	1882	14/9
Lotschberg	Switzerland	1913	14/9
Hokuriku	Japan	1962	14/9
Mont Canis (Frejus)	France – Italy	1871	13/8
Shin-Shimizu	Japan	1961	13/8
Aki	Japan	1975	13/8
Cascade	USA	1929	13/8
Flathead	USA	1970	13/8
Keijo	Japan	1970	11/7
Lierasen	Norway	1973	11/7
Santa Lucia	Italy	1977	10/6
Arlberg	Austria	1884	10/6
Moffat	USA	1928	10/6

* Longest sub-aqueous rail

Channel Tunnel: chronology

1751	French farmer Nicolas Desmaret suggested a fixed link across the English Channel.
1802	French mining engineer Albert Mathieu-Favier proposed to Napoleon I a Channel tunnel through which horse-drawn carriages might travel. Discussions with British politicians ceased 1803 when war broke out between the two countries.
1834	Aim de Gamond of France suggested the construction of a submerged tube across the Channel.
1842	De la Haye of Liverpool designed an underwater tube, the sections of which would be bolted together underwater by workers without diving apparatus.
1851	Hector Horeau proposed a tunnel that would slope down towards the middle of the Channel and up thereafter, so that the carriages would be propelled downhill by their own weight and for a short distance uphill, after which compressed air would take over as the motive power.
1857	A joint committee of British and French scientists approved the aim of constructing a Channel tunnel.
1875	Channel-tunnel bills were passed by the British and French parliaments.
1876	An Anglo-French protocol was signed laying down the basis of a treaty governing construction of a tunnel.
1878	Borings began from the French and British sides of the Channel.
1882	British government forced abandonment of the project after public opinion, fearing invasion by the French, turned against the tunnel.
1904	Signing of the Entente Cordiale between France and the UK enabled plans to be reconsidered. Albert Sartiaux and Francis Fox proposed a twin-tunnel scheme.
1907	A new Channel-tunnel bill was defeated in the British parliament.
1930	A Channel-tunnel bill narrowly failed in British parliament.
1930–40	British prime minister Winston Churchill and the French government supported the digging of a tunnel.
1955	Defence objections to a tunnel were lifted in the UK by prime minister Harold Macmillan.
1957	Channel Tunnel Study Group established.
1961	Study Group plans for a double-bore tunnel presented to British government.
1964	Ernest Marples, Minister of Transport, and his French counterpart gave go-ahead for construction.
1967	British government invited tunnel-building proposals from private interests.
1973	Anglo-French treaty on trial borings signed.
1974	New tunnel bill introduced in British parliament but was not passed before election called by Harold Wilson.
1975	British government cancelled project because of escalating costs.
1981	Anglo-French summit agreed to investigation of possible tunnel.
1982	Intergovernmental study group on tunnel established.
1984	Construction of tunnel agreed in principle at Anglo-French summit.
1986	Anglo-French treaty signed; design submitted by a consortium called the Channel Tunnel Group accepted.
1987	Legislation completed, Anglo-French treaty ratified; construction started in Nov.
1990	First breakthrough of service tunnel took place Dec.
1991	Breakthrough of first rail tunnel in May; the second rail tunnel was completed in June.
1994	The Queen and President Mitterrand officially inaugurated the Channel Tunnel. Limited commercial Eurostar services (for foot passengers) commenced and commercial shuttle services (for cars).
1995	Eurotunnel chairman Alistair Morton warned of the risk of financial collapse. Cost of project reported at £8 billion. Complete service for cars started. Eurotunnel suspended interest payments on its £8 billion debt. The millionth car was carried through the tunnel.
1996	A fire broke out in a freight train injuring 34 people, and resulting in the tunnel being closed for repair.

ENVIRONMENT AND CONSERVATION

The Natural World

balance of nature the idea that there is an inherent equilibrium in most ecosystems, with plants and animals interacting so as to produce a stable, continuing system of life on Earth. Organisms in the ecosystem are adapted to each other – for example, waste products produced by one species are used by another and resources used by some are replenished by others; the oxygen needed by animals is produced by plants while the waste product of animal respiration, carbon dioxide, is used by plants as a raw material in photosynthesis. The nitrogen cycle, the water cycle, and the control of animal populations by natural predators are other examples. The activities of human beings can, and frequently do, disrupt the balance of nature.

biodiversity (contraction of *biological diversity*) measure of the variety of the Earth's animal, plant, and microbial species; of genetic differences within species; and of the ecosystems that support those species. Its maintenance is important for ecological stability and as a resource for research into, for example, new drugs and crops. Research suggests that biodiversity is far greater than previously realized, especially among smaller organisms – for instance, it is thought that only 1–10% of the world's bacterial species have been identified. Tropical rainforest is particularly rich in biodiversity. In the 20th century, however, the destruction of habitats is believed to have resulted in the most severe and rapid loss of diversity in the history of the planet. An international convention for the preservation of biodiversity was signed by over 100 world leaders 1992.

biological oxygen demand (BOD) the amount of dissolved oxygen taken up by microorganisms in a sample of water. Since these microorganisms live by decomposing organic matter, and the amount of oxygen used is proportional to their number and metabolic rate, BOD can be used as a measure of the extent to which the water is polluted with organic compounds.

biome broad natural assemblage of plants and animals shaped by common patterns of vegetation and climate. Examples include the tundra biome and the desert biome.

biosphere the narrow zone that supports life on our planet. It is limited to the waters of the Earth, a fraction of its crust, and the lower regions of the atmosphere.

carbon cycle sequence by which carbon circulates and is recycled through the natural world. The carbon element from carbon dioxide, released into the atmosphere by living things as a result of respiration, is taken up by plants during photosynthesis and converted into carbohydrates; the oxygen component is released back into the atmosphere. The simplest link in the carbon cycle occurs when an animal eats a plant and carbon is transferred from, say, a leaf cell to the animal body. Today, the carbon cycle is in danger of being disrupted by the increased consumption and

burning of fossil fuels, and the burning of large tracts of tropical forests, as a result of which levels of carbon dioxide are building up in the atmosphere and probably contributing to the greenhouse effect.

carrying capacity the maximum number of animals of a given species that a particular area can support. When the carrying capacity is exceeded, there is insufficient food (or other resources) for the members of the population. The population may then be reduced by emigration, reproductive failure, or death through starvation.

chemical oxygen demand (COD) measure of water and effluent quality, expressed as the amount of oxygen (in parts per million) required to oxidize the reducing substances present.

climate weather conditions at a particular place over a period of time. Climate encompasses all the meteorological elements and the factors that influence them. The primary factors that determine the variations of climate over the surface of the Earth are: (a) the effect of latitude and the tilt of the Earth's axis to the plane of the orbit about the Sun (66.5°); (b) the large-scale movements of different wind belts over the Earth's surface; (c) the temperature difference between land and sea; (d) contours of the ground; and (e) location of the area in relation to ocean currents. Catastrophic variations to climate may be caused by the impact of another planetary body, or by clouds resulting from volcanic activity. The most important local or global meteorological changes brought about by human activity are those linked with ozone depleters and the greenhouse effect.

colonization the spread of species into a new habitat, such as a freshly cleared field, a new motorway verge, or a recently flooded valley. The first species to move in are called *pioneers*, and may establish conditions that allow other animals and plants to move in (for example, by improving the condition of the soil or by providing shade). Over time a range of

---

Coral reef biological diversity, 1992

Location	Coral species	Fish species (number)
Philippines	400	1,500
Great Barrier Reef (Australia)	350	1,500
New Caledonia	300	1,000
French Polynesia	168	800
Aqaba	150	400
Toliara (Madagascar)	147	552
Society Islands	120	633
St Gilles (Réunion)	120	258
Tadjoura (Djibouti)	65	180
Baie Possession (Réunion)	54	109
Tutia Reef (Tanzania)	52	192
Hermitage (Réunion)	30	81
Kuwait	23	85

Source: State of the World 1993/Worldwatch Institute

species arrives and the habitat matures; early colonizers will probably be replaced, so that the variety of animal and plant life present changes. This is known as succession.

community any assemblage of plants, animals, and other organisms living within a circumscribed area. Communities are usually named by reference to a dominant feature such as characteristic plant species (for example, beech-wood community), or a prominent physical feature (for example, a freshwater-pond community).

ecology study of the relationship among organisms and the environments in which they live, including all living and nonliving components. The term was coined by German biologist Ernst Haeckel (1834–1919) 1866.

Ecology may be concerned with individual organisms (for example, behavioural ecology, feeding strategies), with populations (for example, population dynamics), or with entire communities (for example, competition between species for access to resources in an ecosystem, or predator–prey relationships). Applied ecology is concerned with the management and conservation of habitats and the consequences and control of pollution.

ecosystem integrated unit consisting of the community of living organisms and the physical environment in a particular area. The relationships among species in an ecosystem are usually complex and finely balanced, and removal of any one species may be disastrous. The removal of a major predator, for example, can result in the destruction of the ecosystem through overgrazing by herbivores.

habitat localized environment in which an organism lives, and which provides for all (or almost all) of its needs. The diversity of habitats found within the Earth's ecosystem is enormous, and they are changing all the time. Many can be considered inorganic or physical; for example, the Arctic icecap, a cave, or a cliff face. Others are more complex; for instance, a woodland or a forest floor. Some habitats are so precise that they are called *microhabitats*, such as the area under a stone where a particular type of insect lives. Most habitats provide a home for many species.

hedge or *hedgerow* row of closely planted shrubs or low trees, generally acting as a land division and windbreak. Hedges also serve as a source of food and as a refuge for wildlife, and provide a habitat not unlike the understorey of a natural forest.

mangrove any of several shrubs and trees, especially of the mangrove family Rhizophoraceae, found in the muddy swamps of tropical and subtropical coasts and estuaries. By sending down aerial roots from their branches, they rapidly form close-growing mangrove thickets. Their timber is impervious to water and resists marine worms. Mangrove swamps are important for stabilizing coastlines and are provide rich spawning grounds for fish and shellfish. These habitats are being destroyed in many countries.

national park land set aside and conserved for public enjoyment. The first was Yellowstone National Park, USA, established 1872. National parks include not only the most scenic places, but

also places distinguished for their historic, prehistoric, or scientific interest, or for their superior recreational assets. They range from areas the size of small countries to pockets of just a few hectares.

In England and Wales under the National Park Act 1949 the Peak District, Lake District, Snowdonia, and other areas of natural beauty were designated national parks. In the UK, national parks are not wholly wilderness or conservation areas, but merely places where planning controls on development are stricter than elsewhere. They are run by National Park Authorities and financed by national government (75%) and local government (25%).

nature reserve area set aside to protect a habitat and the wildlife that lives within it, with only restricted admission for the public. A nature reserve often provides a sanctuary for rare species. The world's largest is Etosha Reserve, Namibia; area 99,520 sq km/38,415 sq mi.

niche the 'place' occupied by a species in its habitat, including all chemical, physical, and biological components, such as what it eats, the time of day at which the species feeds, temperature, moisture, the parts of the habitat that it uses (for example, trees or open grassland), the way it reproduces, and how it behaves.

It is believed that no two species can occupy exactly the same niche, because they would be in direct competition for the same resources at every stage of their life cycle.

nonrenewable resource natural resource, such as coal or oil, that takes thousands or millions of years to form naturally and can therefore not be replaced once it is consumed. The main energy sources used by humans are nonrenewable; renewable sources, such as solar, tidal, and geothermal power, have so far been less exploited.

oceanography study of the oceans, their origin, composition, structure, history, and wildlife (seabirds, fish, plankton, and other organisms). Much oceanography uses computer simulations to plot the possible movements of the waters, and many studies are carried out by remote sensing.

Oceanography involves the study of water movements – currents, waves, and tides – and the chemical and physical properties of the seawater. It deals with the origin and topography of the ocean floor – ocean trenches and ridges formed by plate tectonics, and continental shelves from the submerged portions of the continents.

The World Ocean Circulation Experiment, a seven-year project begun 1990, involves researchers from 44 countries examining the physics of the ocean and its role in the climate of the Earth. It is based at Southampton University, England.

rainforest dense forest usually found on or near the equator where the climate is hot and wet. Heavy rainfall results as the moist air brought by the converging tradewinds rises because of the heat. Over half the tropical rainforests are in Central and South America, the rest in SE Asia and Africa. They provide the bulk of the oxygen needed for plant and animal respiration. Tropical rainforest once covered 14% of the Earth's land surface, but are now being destroyed at an increasing rate as their valuable timber is harvested

Facing water scarcity

Water-scarce countries, 1992, with projections for 2010[1]

| Region/Country | Per capita renewable water supplies | | |
	1992	2010	Change
	(cubic meters per person)		(%)
Africa			
Algeria	730	500	–32
Botswana	710	420	–41
Burundi	620	360	–42
Cape Verde	500	290	–42
Djibouti	750	430	–43
Egypt	30	20	–33
Kenya	560	330	–41
Libya	160	100	–38
Mauritania	190	110	–42
Rwanda	820	440	–46
Tunisia	450	330	–27
Middle East			
Bahrain	0	0	0
Israel	330	250	–24
Jordan	190	110	–42
Kuwait	0	0	0
Qatar	40	30	–25
Saudi Arabia	140	70	–50
Syria	550	300	–45
United Arab Emirates	120	60	–50
Yemen	240	130	–46
Other			
Barbados	170	170	0
Belgium	840	870	+4
Hungary	580	570	–2
Malta	80	80	0
Netherlands	660	600	–9
Singapore	210	190	–10
Additional Countries by 2010			
Malawi	1,030	600	–42
Sudan	1,130	710	–37
Morocco	1,150	830	–28
South Africa	1,200	760	–37
Oman	1,250	670	–46
Somalia	1,390	830	–40
Lebanon	1,410	980	–30
Niger	1,690	930	–45

[1] Countries with per capita renewable water supplies of less than 1,000 cubic meters per year. Does not include water flowing in from neighbouring countries.

and the land cleared for agriculture, causing problems of deforestation. By 1991 over 50% of the world's rainforest had been removed, though they still comprise about 50% of all growing wood on the planet, and harbour at least 40% of the Earth's species (plants and animals). If clearance continues at the present rate, all of the world's primary (undisturbed) rainforest will disappear or be damaged within the next 30 years.

Tropical rainforests are characterized by a great diversity of species, usually of tall broad-leafed evergreen trees, with many climbing vines and ferns, some of which are a main source of raw materials for medicines. A tropical forest, if properly preserved, can yield medicinal plants, oils (from cedar, juniper, cinnamon, sandalwood), spices, gums, resins (used in inks, lacquers, linoleum), tanning and dyeing materials, forage for animals, beverages, poisons, green manure, rubber, and animal products (feathers, hides, honey).

Other rainforests include montane, upper montane or cloud, mangrove, and subtropical. Rainforests comprise some of the most complex and diverse ecosystems on the planet and help to regulate global weather patterns. When deforestation occurs, the microclimate of the mature forest disappears; soil erosion and flooding become major problems since rainforests protect the shallow tropical soils. Clearing of the rainforests may lead to a global warming of the atmosphere, and contribute to the greenhouse effect.

renewable resource natural resource that is replaced by natural processes in a reasonable amount of time. Soil, water, forests, plants, and animals are all renewable resources as long as they are properly conserved. Solar, wind, wave, and geothermal energies are based on renewable resources.

water water covers 70% of the Earth's surface and supports all forms of Earth's life. The *water cycle* or *hydrological cycle* is the natural circulation of water through the biosphere. Water is lost from the Earth's surface to the atmosphere either by evaporation from the surface of lakes, rivers, and oceans, or through the transpiration of plants. This atmospheric water forms clouds that condense to deposit moisture on the land and sea as rain or snow. The water that collects on land flows to the ocean in streams and rivers.

Water supply in sparsely populated regions usually comes from underground water rising to the surface in natural springs, supplemented by pumps and wells. Urban sources are deep artesian wells, rivers, and reservoirs, usually formed from enlarged lakes or dammed and flooded valleys, from which water is conveyed by pipes, conduits, and aqueducts to filter beds. As water seeps through layers of shingle, gravel, and sand, harmful organisms are removed and the water is then distributed by pumping or gravitation through mains and pipes. Often other substances are added to the water, such as chlorine and fluorine; aluminium sulphate is the most widely used chemical in water treatment. In coastal desert areas, such as the Arabian peninsula, desalination plants remove salt from sea water. The Earth's water, both fresh and saline, have been polluted by industrial and domestic chemicals, many of which are toxic and others radioactive.

wetland permanently wet land area or habitat. Wetlands include areas of marsh, fen, bog, flood plain, and shallow coastal areas. Wetlands are extremely fertile. They provide warm, sheltered waters for fisheries, lush vegetation for grazing livestock, and an abundance of wildlife. Estuaries and seaweed beds are more than 16 times as productive as the open ocean.

Loss of wetlands is a worldwide environmental problem as a result of drainage for agriculture, plantation forestry, pollution, and urban expansion. There have been a number of attempts to protect wetlands through international treaties, but drainage schemes continue in many countries. Creation of new wetland areas is taking place on some nature reserves.

wilderness area of uninhabited land that has never been disturbed by humans. In the USA wilderness areas are specially designated by Congress and protected by federal agencies.

Environmental Issues and Pollutants

acid rain acidic precipitation (rain, snow, or mist), thought to be caused principally by the release into the atmosphere of sulphur dioxide (SO_2) and oxides of nitrogen. Sulphur dioxide is formed by the burning of fossil fuels, such as coal, that contain high quantities of sulphur; nitrogen oxides are contributed from various industrial activities and from car exhaust fumes.

Acid rain is linked with damage to and the death of forests and lake organisms in Scandinavia, Europe, and eastern North America. It also results in damage to buildings and statues. US and European power stations that burn fossil fuels release some 8 g/0.3 oz of sulphur dioxide and 3 g/0.1 oz of nitrogen oxides per kilowatt-hour. According to the UK Department of the Environment figures, emissions of sulphur dioxide from power stations would have to be decreased by 81% in order to arrest damage.

aerosol particles of liquid or solid suspended in a gas. Aerosol cans contain a substance such as scent or cleaner packed under pressure with a device for releasing it as a fine spray. Most aerosols used chlorofluorocarbons (CFCs) as propellants until these were found to cause destruction of the ozone layer in the stratosphere. Most so-called 'ozone-friendly' aerosols also use ozone-depleting chemicals, although they are not as destructive as CFCs.

air pollution contamination of the atmosphere caused by the discharge, accidental or deliberate, of a wide range of toxic airborne substances. Often the amount of the released substance is relatively high in a certain locality, so the harmful effects become more noticeable. The cost of preventing any discharge of pollutants into the air is prohibitive, so attempts are more usually made to reduce gradually the amount of discharge and to disperse this as quickly as possible by using a very tall chimney, or by intermittent release.

antiknock substance added to petrol to reduce knocking in car engines. It is a mixture of dibromoethane and tetraethyl lead. Its use in leaded petrol has resulted in atmospheric pollution by lead compounds. Children exposed to this form of pollution over long periods of time can suffer impaired learning ability. Unleaded petrol has been used in the USA for some years, and is increasingly popular in the UK. Leaded petrol cannot be used in cars fitted with catalytic converters.

biodegradable capable of being broken down by living organisms, principally bacteria and fungi. In biodegradable substances, such as food and sewage, the natural processes of decay lead to compaction and liquefaction, and to the release of nutrients that are then recycled by the ecosystem. Nonbiodegradable substances, such as glass, heavy metals, and most types of plastic, present serious problems of disposal.

carbon dioxide CO_2 colourless, odourless gas, slightly soluble in water and denser than air. It is produced by living things during the processes of respiration and the decay of organic matter, and plays a vital role in the carbon cycle. It is used as a coolant in its solid form (known as 'dry ice'), and in the chemical industry. Its increasing density contributes to the greenhouse effect and global warming. Britain has 1% of the world's population, yet it produces 3% of CO_2 emissions; the USA has 5% of the world's population and produces 25% of CO_2 emissions.

carbon monoxide CO colourless, odourless gas formed when carbon is oxidized in a limited supply of air. It is a poisonous constituent of car exhaust fumes, forming a stable compound with haemoglobin in the blood, thus preventing the haemoglobin from transporting oxygen to the body tissues.

catalytic converter device fitted to the exhaust system of a motor vehicle in order to reduce toxic emissions from the engine. It converts harmful exhaust products to relatively harmless ones by passing the exhaust gases over a mixture of catalysts. *Oxidation catalysts* (small amounts of precious palladium and platinum metals) convert hydrocarbons (unburnt fuel) and carbon monoxide into carbon dioxide and water, while *three-way catalysts* (platinum and rhodium metals) convert nitrogen oxide gases into nitrogen and oxygen.

Over the lifetime of a vehicle, a catalytic converter can reduce hydrocarbon emissions by 87%, carbon monoxide emissions by 85%, and nitrogen oxide emissions by 62%, but will cause a slight increase in the amount of carbon dioxide emitted. Catalytic converters are standard in the USA, where a 90% reduction in pollution from cars was achieved without loss of engine performance or fuel economy.

Air pollution

Pollutant	Sources	Effects
sulphur dioxide SO_2	oil, coal combustion in power stations	acid rain formed, which damages plants, trees, buildings, and lakes
oxides of nitrogen NO, NO_2	high-temperature combustion in cars, and to some extent power stations	acid rain formed
lead compounds	from leaded petrol used by cars	nerve poison
carbon dioxide CO_2	oil, coal, petrol, diesel combustion	greenhouse effect
carbon monoxide CO	limited combustion of oil, coal, petrol, diesel fuels	poisonous, leads to photochemical smog in some areas
nuclear waste	nuclear power plants, nuclear weapon testing, war	radioactivity, contamination of locality, cancers, mutations, death

chlorofluorocarbon (CFC) synthetic chemical that is odourless, nontoxic, nonflammable, and chemically inert. CFCs have been used as propellants in aerosol cans, as refrigerants in refrigerators and air conditioners, and in the manufacture of foam packaging. They are partly responsible for the destruction of the ozone layer. In June 1990 representatives of 93 nations, including the UK and the USA, agreed to phase out production of CFCs by the end of the 20th century.

When CFCs are released into the atmosphere, they drift up slowly into the stratosphere, where, under the influence of ultraviolet radiation from the Sun, they break down into chlorine atoms which destroy the ozone layer and allow harmful radiation from the Sun to reach the Earth's surface. CFCs can remain in the atmosphere for more than 100 years. Replacements for CFCs are being developed, and research into safe methods of destroying existing CFCs is being carried out. The European Community has agreed to ban by the end of 1995 a range of CFCs.

compost organic material decomposed by bacteria under controlled conditions to make a nutrient-rich natural fertilizer for use in gardening or farming. A well-made compost heap reaches a high temperature during the composting process, killing most weed seeds that might be present.

conservation action taken to protect and preserve the natural world, usually from pollution, overexploitation, and other harmful features of human activity. The late 1980s saw a great increase in public concern for the environment, with membership of conservation groups, such as Friends of the Earth, rising sharply. Globally the most important issues include the depletion of atmospheric ozone by the action of chlorofluorocarbons (CFCs), the build-up of carbon dioxide in the atmosphere (thought to contribute to an intensification of the greenhouse effect), and the destruction of the tropical rainforests.

In the UK the conservation debate has centred on water quality, road-building schemes, the safety of nuclear power, and animal rights.

DDT abbreviation for *dichloro- diphenyl-trichloroethane* ($ClC_6H_5)_2CHCHCl_2$), an insecticide discovered 1939 by Swiss chemist Paul Müller. It is useful in the control of insects that spread malaria, but resistant strains develop. DDT is highly toxic and persists in the environment and in living tissue. Its use is now banned in most countries, but it continues to be used on food plants in Latin America.

deforestation destruction of forest for timber, fuel, charcoal burning, and clearing for agriculture and extractive industries, such as mining, without planting new trees to replace those lost (reafforestation) or

Tropical deforestation

Tropical moist forests: status in select countries, 1991

Country	Area (sq km)	Original extent of forest cover (sq km)	Present extent of forest cover (sq km)	Current amount of annual deforestation (sq km per year; with percentage)
Bolivia	1,098,581	90,000	70,000	1,500 (2.1%)
Brazil	8,511,960	2,860,000	2,200,000	50,000 (2.3%)
Burma	696,500	500,000	245,000	8,000 (3.3%)
Cameroon	475,442	220,000	164,000	2,000 (1.2%)
C America	522,915	500,000	90,000	3,300 (3.7%)
Colombia	1,138,891	700,000	278,500	6,500 (2.3%)
Congo	342,000	100,000	90,000	700 (0.8%)
Ecuador	270,670	132,000	76,000	3,000 (4.0%)
Gabon	267,670	240,000	200,000	600 (0.3%)
Guyanas (French Guiana, Guyana, and Surinam)	469,790	500,000	410,000	500 (0.12%)
India	3,287,000	1,600,000	165,000	4,000 (2.4%)
Indonesia	1,919,300	1,220,000	860,000	12,000 (1.4%)
Cote D'Ivoire	322,463	160,000	16,000	2,500 (15.6%)
Kampuchea	181,035	120,000	67,000	500 (0.75%)
Laos	236,800	110,000	68,000	1,000 (1.5%)
Madagascar	590,992	62,000	24,000	2,000 (8.3%)
Malaysia	329,079	305,000	157,000	4,800 (3.1%)
Mexico	1,967,180	400,000	166,000	7,000 (4.2%)
Nigeria	924,000	72,000	28,000	4,000 (14.3%)
Papua New Guinea	461,700	425,000	360,000	3,500 (1.0%)
Peru	1,285,220	700,000	515,000	3,500 (0.7%)
Philippines	299,400	250,000	50,000	2,700 (5.4%)
Thailand	513,517	435,000	74,000	6,000 (8.4%)
Venezuela	912,050	420,000	350,000	1,500 (0.4%)
Vietnam	334,331	260,000	60,000	3,500 (5.8%)
Zaire	2,344,886	1,245,000	1,000,000	4,000 (0.4%)
Total		*13,626,000*	*7,783,500*	*138,600 (1.8%)*

Source: Friends of the Earth

working on a cycle that allows the natural forest to regenerate. Deforestation causes fertile soil to be blown away or washed into rivers, leading to soil erosion, drought, flooding, and loss of wildlife. Deforestation is taking place in both tropical rainforests and temperate forests.

desertification creation of deserts by changes in climate, or by human-aided processes. The processes leading to desertification include overgrazing, destruction of forest belts, and exhaustion of the soil by intensive cultivation without restoration of fertility – all of which may be prompted by the pressures of an expanding population, by concentration in land ownership, or by other political conditions forcing people onto unsuitable land. About 135 million people are directly affected by desertification, mainly in Africa, the Indian subcontinent, and South America.

dioxin any of a family of over 200 organic chemicals, but especially 2,3,7,8-tetrachlorodibenzo-dioxin (2,3,7,8-TCDD), a highly toxic chemical that occurs, for example, as an impurity in the defoliant Agent Orange, used in the Vietnam War, and sometimes in the weedkiller 2,4,5-T. It has been associated with a disfiguring skin complaint (chloracne), birth defects, miscarriages, and cancer. UK government figures released in 1989 showed dioxin levels in breast milk 100 times higher than guidelines set for environmental dioxin.

Disasters involving accidental release of large amounts of dioxin into the environment have occurred at Seveso, Italy, and Times Beach, Missouri, USA. Small amounts of dioxins are released by the burning of a wide range of chlorinated materials (treated wood, exhaust fumes from fuels treated with chlorinated additives, and plastics) and as a side effect of some techniques of papermaking. The possibility of food becoming contaminated by dioxins in the environment has led the EC to decrease significantly the allowed levels of dioxin emissions from incinerators.

endangered species plant or animal species whose numbers are so few that it is at risk of becoming extinct. Officially designated endangered species are listed by the International Union for the Conservation of Nature (IUCN).

An example of an endangered species is the Javan rhinoceros. There are only about 50 alive today and, unless active steps are taken to promote this species' survival, it will probably be extinct within a few decades.

energy conservation methods of reducing energy use through insulation, increasing energy efficiency, and changes in patterns of use. Profligate energy use by industrialized countries contributes greatly to air pollution and the greenhouse effect when it draws on nonrenewable energy sources.

It has been calculated that increasing energy efficiency alone could reduce carbon dioxide emissions in several high-income countries by 1–2% a year. By applying existing conservation methods, UK electricity use could be reduced by 4 gigawatts by the year 2000 – the equivalent of four Sizewell nuclear power stations – according to a study by the Open University. The average annual decrease in energy consumption in relation to gross national product 1973–87 was 1.2% in France, 2% in the UK, 2.1% in the USA, and 2.8% in Japan.

eutrophication excessive enrichment of rivers, lakes, and shallow sea areas, primarily by nitrate fertilizers washed from the soil by rain, by phosphates from fertilizers and detergents in municipal sewage, and by nutrients in sewage itself. These encourage the growth of algae and bacteria, which use up the oxygen in the water, thereby making it uninhabitable for fishes and other animal life.

extinction the complete disappearance of a species. In the past, extinctions are believed to have occurred because species were unable to adapt quickly enough to a naturally changing environment. Today, most extinctions are due to human activity. Some species, such as the dodo of Mauritius, the moas of New Zealand, and the passenger pigeon of North America, were exterminated by hunting. Others became extinct when their habitat was destroyed.

Mass extinctions are episodes during which whole groups of species have become extinct, the best known being that of the dinosaurs, other large reptiles, and various marine invertebrates about 65 million years ago. Another mass extinction occurred about 10,000 years ago when many giant species of mammal died out. This is known as the 'Pleistocene overkill' because their disappearance was probably hastened by the hunting activities of prehistoric humans. The greatest mass extinction occurred about 250 million years ago marking the Permian-Triassic boundary, when up to 96% of all living species

---

Endangered species

Species	Observation
plants	one-quarter of the world's plants are threatened with extinction by the year 2010
amphibians	worldwide decline in numbers; half of New Zealand's frog species are now extinct
birds	three-quarters of all bird species are declining or threatened with extinction
carnivores	almost all species of cats and bears are declining in numbers
fish	one-third of North American freshwater fish are rare or endangered; half the fish species in Lake Victoria, Africa's largest lake, are close to extinction due to predation by the introduced Nile perch
invertebrates	about 100 species are lost each day due to deforestation; half the freshwater snails in the southeastern USA are now extinct or threatened; over one-quarter of Germany's invertebrates are threatened
mammals	half of Australia's mammals are threatened; 40% of mammals in France, the Netherlands, Germany, and Portugal are threatened
primates	two-thirds of primate species are threatened
reptiles	over 40% of reptile species are threatened

Species under threat

Number of threatened species by species group in the European red list of globally threatened animals and plants, 1992

Country	Mammals[1]	Birds	Reptiles and amphibians	Fresh-water fishes	Invertebrates
Albania	9	6	2	1	8
Austria	6	5	1	4	59
Belgium	6	3	0	0	27
Bulgaria	19	15	2	5	35
Ex-Czechoslovakia	11	7	1	5	37
Denmark	6	3	0	1	29
Finland	8	3	0	1	33
France	15	7	9	2	111
Germany	7	5	0	4	65
Greece	16	13	6	6	19
Hungary	12	9	1	3	36
Italy	16	7	17	2	42
Netherlands	6	3	0	0	25
Norway	10	3	0	1	28
Poland	12	5	0	3	35
Portugal	15	11	3	4	24
Romania	14	13	2	4	15
Spain	23	16	10	4	55
Sweden	10	4	0	1	44
Switzerland	9	3	2	2	52
Turkey	19	17	17	18	20
Ukraine	17	13	1	6	18
Ex-USSR	28	17	9	9	30
UK	7	4	0	2	31
Ex-Yugoslavia	13	12	5	5	21

[1]Whales, dolphins, and porpoises are not included

Source: Economic Commission for Europe

became extinct. It was proposed 1982 that mass extinctions occur periodically, at approximately 26-million-year intervals.

The current mass extinction is largely due to human destruction of habitats, as in the tropical forests and coral reefs; it is far more serious and damaging than mass extinctions of the past because of the speed at which it occurs. Man-made climatic changes and pollution also make it less likely that the biosphere can recover and evolve new species to suit a changed environment. The rate of extinction is difficult to estimate, since most losses occur in the rich environment of the tropical rainforest, where the total number of existent species is not known. Conservative estimates put the rate of loss due to deforestation alone at 4,000 to 6,000 species a year. Overall, the rate could be as high as one species an hour, with the loss of one species putting those dependent on it at risk. Australia has the worst record for extinction: 18 mammals have disappeared since Europeans settled there, and 40 more are threatened.

The last mouse-eared bat (*Myotis myotis*) in the UK died 1990. This is the first mammal to have become extinct in the UK for 250 years, since the last wolf was exterminated.

firewood the principal fuel for some 2 billion people, mainly in the Third World. In principle a renewable energy source, firewood is being cut far faster than the trees can regenerate in many areas of Africa and Asia, leading to deforestation. In Mali, for example, wood provides 97% of total energy consumption, and deforestation is running at an estimated 9,000 hectares a year. The heat efficiency of firewood can be increased by use of stoves, but many people cannot afford to buy these.

fossil fuel fuel, such as coal, oil, and natural gas, formed from the fossilized remains of plants that lived hundreds of millions of years ago. Fossil fuels are a nonrenewable resource and will eventually run out. Extraction of coal and oil causes considerable environmental pollution, and burning coal contributes to problems of acid rain and the greenhouse effect.

Gaia hypothesis theory that the Earth's living and nonliving systems form an inseparable whole that is regulated and kept adapted for life by living organisms themselves. The planet therefore functions as a single organism, or a giant cell. Since life and environment are so closely linked, there is a need for humans to understand and maintain the physical environment and living things around them. The Gaia hypothesis was elaborated by British scientist James Lovelock (1919–) in the 1970s.

global warming projected imminent climate change attributed to the greenhouse effect.

green audit inspection of a company to assess the total environmental impact of its activities or of a particular product or process.

greenhouse effect phenomenon of the Earth's atmosphere by which solar radiation, trapped by the Earth and re-emitted from the surface, is prevented from escaping by various gases in the air. The result is a rise in the Earth's temperature. The main greenhouse gases are carbon dioxide, methane, and chlorofluorocarbons (CFCs). Fossil-fuel consumption and forest fires are the main causes of carbon-dioxide build-up; methane is a byproduct of agriculture (rice, cattle, sheep). Water vapour is another greenhouse gas.

The United Nations Environment Programme estimates that by 2025 average world temperatures will have risen by 1.5°C with a consequent rise of 20 cm in sea level. Low-lying areas and entire countries would be threatened by flooding and crops would be affected by the change in climate. A computer model from the British Meteorological Office predicts a warming of 2.7°C for a doubling of carbon dioxide. The concentration of carbon dioxide in the atmosphere is estimated to have risen by 25% since the Industrial Revolution, and 10% since 1950; the rate of increase is now 0.5% a year. However, predictions about global warming and its possible climatic effects are tentative and often conflict with each other.

Dubbed the 'greenhouse effect' by Swedish scientist Svante Arrhenius (1859–1927), it was first predicted 1827 by French mathematician Joseph Fourier (1768–1830).

halon organic chemical compound containing one or two carbon atoms, together with bromine and other halogens. The halons are gases and are widely used in fire extinguishers. As destroyers of the ozone layer, they are up to ten times more effective than chlorofluorocarbons (CFCs), to which they are chemically related. Levels in the atmosphere are rising by about 25% each year, mainly through the testing of fire-fighting equipment.

insulation process or material that prevents or reduces the flow of electricity, heat, or sound from one place to another. *U thermal* or *heat insulation* makes use of insulating materials such as fibreglass to reduce the loss of heat through the roof and walls of buildings. The U-value of a material is a measure of its ability to conduct heat – a material chosen as an insulator should therefore have a low U-value. Air trapped between the fibres of clothes acts as a thermal insulator, preventing loss of body warmth.

leaching process by which substances are washed out of the soil. Fertilizers leached out of the soil drain into rivers, lakes, and ponds and cause water pollution. In tropical areas, leaching of the soil after the destruction of forests removes scarce nutrients and can lead to a dramatic loss of soil fertility. The leaching of soluble minerals in soils can lead to the formation of distinct soil horizons as different minerals are deposited at successively lower levels.

lead heavy, soft, malleable, grey, metallic element, symbol Pb (from Latin *plumbum*). As a cumulative poison, lead enters the body from lead water pipes, lead-based paints, and leaded petrol. In humans, exposure to lead shortly after birth is associated with impaired mental health between the ages of two and four.

mercury or *quicksilver* heavy, silver-grey, metallic element, symbol Hg (from Latin *hydrargyrum*). Mercury is a cumulative poison that can contaminate the food chain and cause intestinal disturbance, kidney and brain damage, and birth defects in humans. (The World Health Organization's 'safe' limit for mercury is 0.5 milligrams of mercury per kilogram of muscle tissue.) The discharge into the sea by industry of organic mercury compounds such as dimethylmercury is the chief cause of mercury poisoning in the latter half of the 20th century.

nitrate any salt of nitric acid, containing the NO_3^- ion. Nitrates of various kinds are used in explosives, in the chemical industry, in curing meat, and as inorganic fertilizers. Being soluble in water, nitrate is leached out by rain into streams and reservoirs. High levels are now found in drinking water in arable areas. These may be harmful to newborn babies, and have been tentatively linked with stomach cancer. The UK current standard is 100 milligrams per litre, double the EC limits to be implemented by 1993.

nuclear safety measures to avoid accidents in the operation of nuclear reactors and in the production and disposal of nuclear weapons and of nuclear waste. There are no guarantees of the safety of any of the various methods of disposal.

nuclear accidents
1957 At Windscale (now Sellafield), Cumbria, England, fire destroyed the core of a reactor, releasing large quantities of radioactive fumes into the atmosphere.

1965 130 km/80 mi off the coast of Japan, a US Navy Skyhawk jet bomber fell off the deck of the ship *Ticonderoga*, sinking in 4,900 m/16,000 ft of water. It carried a one-megaton hydrogen bomb. The accident was only revealed in 1989.

1979 In Three Mile Island, Harrisburg, Pennsylvania, USA, a combination of mechanical and electrical failure, as well as operator error, caused a pressurized water reactor to leak radioactive matter.

1979 In Church Rock, New Mexico, USA, 380 million litres/100 million gallons of radioactive water containing uranium leaked from a pond into the Rio Purco, causing the water to become over 6,500 times as radioactive as safety standards allow for drinking water.

1986 In Chernobyl, Ukraine, there was an explosive leak, caused by overheating, from a nonpressurized boiling-water reactor, one of the largest in Europe. The resulting clouds of radioactive material spread as far as the UK; 31 people were killed in the explosion (many more are expected to die or become ill because of the long-term effects of radiation), and thousands of square kilometres of land were contaminated by fallout.

1993 In Tomsk, Siberia, Russian Federation, a tank exploded at a uranium reprocessing plant, sending a cloud of radioactive particles into the air.

nuclear waste the radioactive and toxic by-products of the nuclear-energy and nuclear-weapons industries. Nuclear waste may have an active life of several thousand years. Reactor waste is of three types: *high-level* spent fuel, or the residue when nuclear fuel has been removed from a reactor and reprocessed; *intermediate*, which may be long- or short-lived; and *low-level*, but bulky, waste from reactors, which has only short-lived radioactivity. Disposal, by burial on land or at sea, has raised problems of safety, environmental pollution, and security. In absolute terms, nuclear waste cannot be safely relocated or disposed of.

About one-third of the fuel from nuclear reactors becomes spent each year. It is removed to a *reprocessing* plant where radioactive waste products are chemically separated from remaining uranium and plutonium, in an expensive and dangerous process.

This practice increases the volume of radioactive waste more than a hundred times.

The dumping of nuclear waste at sea officially stopped 1983, when a moratorium was agreed by the members of the London Dumping Convention (a United Nations body that controls disposal of wastes at sea). Covertly, the USSR continued dumping, and deposited thousands of tonnes of nuclear waste and three faulty reactors in the sea 1964–86.

In 1990, a scientific study revealed an increased risk of leukaemia in children whose fathers had worked at Sellafield, Cumbria, England, between 1950 and 1985. Sellafield is the world's greatest discharger of radioactive waste, followed by Hanford, Washington (USA). (See feature in this section.)

oil spill oil released by damage to or discharge from a tanker or oil installation. An oil spill kills all shore life, clogging up the feathers of birds and suffocating other creatures. At sea, toxic chemicals leach into the water below, poisoning sea life. Mixed with dust, the oil forms globules that sink to the seabed, poisoning sea life there as well.

In March 1989, the *Exxon Valdez* (belonging to the Exxon Corporation) spilled oil in Alaska's Prince William Sound, covering 12,400 sq km/4,800 sq mi and killing at least 34,400 sea birds, 10,000 sea otters, and up to 16 whales. The incident led to the US Oil Pollution Act of 1990, which requires tankers operating in US waters to have double hulls. The world's largest oil spill was in the Persian Gulf in Feb 1991 as a direct result of hostilities during the Gulf War. Around 6–8 million barrels of oil were spilled, polluting 675 km/ 420 mi of Saudi coastline. In some places, the oil was 30 cm/12 in deep in the sand. In Jan 1993, the *Braer* oil tanker went aground near the Shetland Islands, discharging its 85,000-tonne cargo into the surrounding waters.

Oil spills around Britain's coasts in 1990 numbered around 791. There were 135 clean-up operations, at a cost of £2 million.

organic farming farming without the use of synthetic fertilizers (such as nitrates and phosphates), pesticides (herbicides, insecticides, and fungicides), or other agrochemicals (such as hormones, growth stimulants, or fruit regulators). (For more, see *Food and Agriculture*.)

overfishing fishing at rates that exceed the sustained-yield cropping of fish species, resulting in a net population decline. For example, in the North Atlantic, herring has been fished to the verge of extinction and the cod and haddock populations are severely depleted. In the Third World, use of huge factory ships, often by fisheries from industrialized countries, has depleted stocks for local people who cannot obtain protein in any other way.

ozone O_3 highly reactive pale-blue gas with a penetrating odour. Ozone forms a thin layer in the upper atmosphere, which protects life on Earth from ultra-violet rays, a cause of skin cancer. At lower atmospheric levels it is an air pollutant.

Ground-level ozone can cause asthma attacks, stunted growth in plants, and corrosion of certain materials. It is produced by the action of sunlight on air pollutants, including car exhaust fumes, and is so dangerous that the US Environment Protection Agency recommends people should not be exposed for more than one hour a day to ozone levels of 120 parts per billion (ppb), while the World Health Organization recommends a lower 76–100 ppb. It is known that even at levels of 60 ppb ozone causes respiratory problems, and may cause the yields of some crops to fall.

ozone hole a continent-sized hole in the ozone layer has formed over Antarctica. It is believed that the ozone layer is depleting at a rate of about 5% every 10 years over N Europe, with depletion extending south to the Mediterranean and southern USA. However, ozone depletion over the polar regions – 50% over the Antarctic compared with 3% over the Arctic 1989 – is the most dramatic manifestation of a general global effect. This has been caused by chemicals collectively known as ozone depleters.

ozone depleter any chemical that destroys the ozone in the stratosphere. Most ozone depleters are chemically stable compounds containing chlorine or bromine, which remain unchanged for long enough to drift up to the upper atmosphere. The best known are chlorofluorocarbons (CFCs), but many other ozone depleters are known, including halons, used in some fire extinguishers; methyl chloroform and carbon tetrachloride, both solvents; some CFC substitutes; and the pesticide methyl bromide.

Major oil spills

Year	Place	Source	Quantity (tonnes)	(litres)
1967	off Cornwall, England	*Torrey Canyon*	107,100	
1968	off South Africa	*World Glory*		51,194,000
1972	Gulf of Oman	*Sea Star*	103,500	
1977	North Sea	Ekofisk oilfield		31,040,000
1978	off France	*Amoco Cadiz*	200,000	
1979	Gulf of Mexico	Ixtoc 1 oil well	535,000	
1979	off Trinidad and Tobago	collision of *Atlantic Empress* and *Aegean Captain*	270,000	
1983	Persian Gulf	Nowruz oilfield	540,000	
1983	off South Africa	*Castillo de Beliver*	225,000	
1989	off Alaska	*Exxon Valdez*		40,504,000
1991	Persian Gulf	oil wells in Kuwait and Iraq		130–585,000,000
1993	Shetland Islands, Scotland	*Braer*	85,000	

packaging material, usually of metal, paper, plastic, or glass, used to protect products, make them easier to display, and as a form of advertising. Environmentalists have criticized packaging materials as being wasteful of energy and resources. In Germany from 1993, shops are obliged to take back surplus paper and plastic packaging, empty cans, toothpaste tubes, and yoghurt cartons, and a compulsory deposit is levied on certain types of packaging.

pesticide any chemical used in farming, gardening, or indoors to combat pests. Pesticides are of three main types: *insecticides* (to kill insects), *fungicides* (to kill fungal diseases), and *herbicides* (to kill plants, mainly those considered weeds). Pesticides cause a number of pollution problems through spray drift onto surrounding areas, direct contamination of users or the public, and as residues on food. The safest pesticides include those made from plants, such as the insecticides pyrethrum and derris.

More potent are synthetic products, such as chlorinated hydrocarbons. These products, including DDT and dieldrin, are highly toxic to wildlife and often to human beings, so their use is now restricted by law in some areas and is declining. Safer pesticides, such as malathion, are based on organic phosphorus compounds, but they still present hazards to health. The aid organization Oxfam estimates that pesticides cause about 10,000 deaths worldwide every year. There are around 4,000 cases of acute pesticide poisoning a year in the UK.

polluter-pays principle the idea that whoever causes pollution is responsible for the cost of repairing any damage. The principle is accepted in British law but has in practice often been ignored; for example, farmers causing the death of fish through slurry pollution have not been fined the full costs of restocking the river.

pollution the harmful effect on the environment of by-products of human activity, principally industrial and agricultural processes – for example, noise, smoke, car emissions, chemical and radioactive effluents in air, seas, and rivers, pesticides, radiation, sewage, and household waste. Pollution contributes to the greenhouse effect.

In the UK in 1987, air pollution caused by carbon monoxide emission from road transport was measured at 5.26 million tonnes. California passed a law in 1990 stating that 2% of all new cars sold by 1998 must be emission free. In Feb 1990, the UK had failed to apply 21 European Community Laws on air and water pollution and faced prosecution before the European Court of Justice on 31 of the 160 EC directives in force. The existence of 1,300 toxic waste tips in the UK in 1990 posed a considerable threat for increased water pollution.

radon colourless, odourless, gaseous, radioactive, nonmetallic element, symbol Rn. Radon is the densest gas known and occurs in small amounts in spring water, streams, and the air, being formed from the natural radioactive decay of radium. The average radon radiation level found in a study of 40 British limestone caves was 2,900 becquerels per cubic metre. This compares with the National Radiological Protection Board's set level of 200 Bq per cubic metre at which removal of radon from homes is recommended.

recycling processing of industrial and household waste (such as paper, glass, and some metals and plastics) so that it can be reused. This saves expenditure on scarce raw materials, slows down the depletion of nonrenewable resources, and helps to reduce pollution.

The USA recycles only around 13% of its waste, compared to around 33% in Japan. However, all US states encourage or require local recycling programmes to be set up. By 1992, around 33% of newspapers, 22% of office paper, 64% of aluminium cans, 3% of plastic containers, and 20% of all glass bottles and jars were recycled.

Most British recycling schemes are voluntary, and rely on people taking waste items to a central collection point. However, some local authorities, such as Leeds, now ask householders to separate waste before collection, making recycling possible on a much larger scale.

reuse multiple use of a product (often a form of packaging), by returning it to the retailer, manufacturer, or processor each time. Many such returnable items are sold with a deposit which is reimbursed if the item is returned. Reuse is usually more energy- and resource-efficient than recycling unless there are large transport or cleaning costs.

sewage disposal the disposal of human excreta and other waterborne waste products from houses, streets, and factories. Conveyed through sewers to sewage works, sewage has to undergo a series of treatments to be acceptable for discharge into rivers or the sea, according to various local laws and ordinances. Raw sewage, or sewage that has not been treated adequately, is one serious source of water pollution and a cause of eutrophication.

In the industrialized countries of the West, most industries are responsible for disposing of their own wastes. Government agencies establish industrial waste-disposal standards. In most countries, sewage works for residential areas are the responsibility of local authorities. The solid waste (sludge) may be spread over fields as a fertilizer or, in a few countries, dumped at sea. A significant proportion of bathing beaches in densely populated regions have unacceptably high bacterial content, largely as a result of untreated sewage being discharged into rivers and the sea. This can, for example, cause stomach upsets in swimmers.

The use of raw sewage as a fertilizer (long practised in China) has the drawback that disease-causing microorganisms can survive in the soil and be transferred to people or animals by consumption of subsequent crops. Sewage sludge is safer, but may contain dangerous levels of heavy metals and other industrial contaminants.

slash and burn simple agricultural method whereby natural vegetation is cut and burned, and the clearing then farmed for a few years until the soil loses its fertility, whereupon farmers move on and leave the area to regrow. Although this is possible with a small, widely dispersed population, it becomes unsustainable with more people and is now a form of deforestation.

slurry form of manure composed mainly of liquids. Slurry is collected and stored on many farms, especially when large numbers of animals are kept in factory units. When slurry tanks are accidentally or deliberately breached, large amounts can spill into rivers, killing fish and causing eutrophication. Some slurry is spread on fields as a fertilizer.

Slurry spills in the UK increased enormously in the 1980s and were by 1991 running at rates of over 4,000 a year. Tighter regulations were being introduced to curb this pollution.

soil erosion the wearing away and redistribution of the Earth's soil layer. It is caused by the action of water, wind, and ice, and also by improper methods of agriculture. If unchecked, soil erosion results in the formation of deserts (desertification). It has been estimated that 20% of the world's cultivated topsoil was lost between 1950 and 1990.

If the rate of erosion exceeds the rate of soil formation (from rock and decomposing organic matter), then the land will decline and eventually become infertile. The removal of forests or other vegetation often leads to serious soil erosion, because plant roots bind soil, and without them the soil is free to wash or blow away, as in the American dust bowl. The effect is worse on hillsides, and there has been devastating loss of soil where forests have been cleared from mountainsides, as in Madagascar. Improved agricultural practices such as contour ploughing are needed to combat soil erosion. Windbreaks, such as hedges or strips planted with coarse grass, are valuable, and organic farming can reduce soil erosion by as much as 75%.

sustained-yield cropping the removal of surplus individuals from a population of organisms so that the population maintains a constant size. This usually requires selective removal of animals of all ages and both sexes to ensure a balanced population structure. Taking too many individuals can result in a population decline, as in overfishing.

unleaded petrol petrol manufactured without the addition of antiknock. It has a slightly lower octane rating than leaded petrol but has the advantage of not polluting the atmosphere with lead compounds. Many cars can be converted to running on unleaded petrol by altering the timing of the engine, and most new cars are designed to do so. Cars fitted with a catalytic converter must use unleaded fuel. The use of unleaded petrol has been standard in the USA for some years and is increasing in the UK (encouraged by a lower rate of tax than that levied on leaded petrol).

Waldsterben (German 'forest death') tree decline related to air pollution, common throughout the industrialized world. It appears to be caused by a mixture of pollutants; the precise chemical mix varies between locations, but it includes acid rain, ozone, sulphur dioxide, and nitrogen oxides. Britain's trees are among the most badly affected in Europe.

waste materials that are no longer needed and are discarded. Examples are household waste, industrial waste (which often contains toxic chemicals), medical waste (which may contain organisms that cause disease), and nuclear waste (which is radioactive). By recycling, some materials in waste can be reclaimed for further use. In 1990, the industrialized nations generated 2 billion tonnes of waste. In the USA, 40 tonnes of solid waste are generated annually per person. In Britain, the average person throws away about ten times their own body weight in household refuse each year. Collectively, the country generates about 50 million tonnes of waste per year.

waste disposal depositing waste. Methods of waste disposal vary according to the materials in the waste and include incineration, burial at designated sites, and dumping at sea. Organic waste can be treated and reused as fertilizer. Nuclear waste and toxic waste are usually buried or dumped at sea, although this does not negate the danger.

The wildlife trade

Reported trade in wildlife and wildlife products, 1992 (imports and exports, in thousands)

Wildlife		Africa	Asia	Europe	North & Central America	South America	World
Mammals							
Live primates	I	–	7	15	17	–	42
	E	7.8	22	3	5	3.8	43
Cat skins	I	6.7	7	116	43	1.0	175
	E	7.7	60	15	87	3.4	179
Raw ivory *(kg)*	I	14.2	505	133	26	0.1	679
	E	303.7	280	134	2	–	720
Birds							
Live parrots	I	13.2	67	196	322	6.2	606
	E	160.3	89	55	36	265.3	607
Reptiles							
Reptile skins	I	3.4	2,480	3,908	2,436	80.7	8,910
	E	359.7	4,198	1,539	930	1,900.3	8,953

I = imports
E = exports

Source: World Resources Institute

Waste disposal is an increasing problem in the late 20th century. Environmental groups, such as Greenpeace and Friends of the Earth, are campaigning for more recycling, a change in lifestyle so that less waste (from packaging and containers to nuclear materials) is produced, and safer methods of disposal.

The industrial waste dumped every year by the UK in the North Sea includes 550,000 tonnes of fly ash from coal-fired power stations. The British government stopped North Sea dumping 1993, but dumping in the heavily polluted Irish Sea will continue. Industrial pollution is suspected of causing ecological problems, including an epidemic that killed hundreds of seals 1989. The Irish Sea receives 80 tonnes of uranium a year from phosphate rock processing, and 300 million gallons of sewage every day, 80% of it untreated or merely screened. In 1988, 80,000 tonnes of hazardous waste were imported into the UK for processing, including 6,000 tonnes of polychlorinated biphenyls.

water pollution any addition to fresh or sea water that disrupts biological processes or causes a health hazard. Common pollutants include nitrate, pesticides, and sewage, though a huge range of industrial contaminants, such as chemical by-products and residues created in the manufacture of various goods, also enter water – legally, accidentally, and through illegal dumping.

weedkiller or **herbicide** chemical that kills some or all plants. Selective herbicides are effective with cereal crops because they kill all broad-leaved plants without affecting grasslike leaves. Those that kill all plants include sodium chlorate, paraquat, and Agent Orange. The widespread use of weedkillers in agriculture has led to an increase in crop yield but also to pollution of soil and water supplies and killing of birds and small animals, as well as creating a health hazard for humans.

whaling the hunting of whales, largely discontinued 1986. Whales are killed for whale oil (made from the thick layer of fat under the skin called 'blubber'), used for food and cosmetics; for the large reserve of oil in the head of the sperm whale, used in the leather industry; and for ambergris, a waxlike substance from the intestines, used in making perfumes. There are synthetic substitutes for all these products. Whales are also killed for their meat, which is eaten by the Japanese and was used as pet food in the USA and Europe.

The International Whaling Commission (IWC), established 1946, failed to enforce quotas on whale killing until world concern about the possible extinction of the whale mounted in the 1970s. By the end of the 1980s, 90% of blue, fin, humpback, and sperm whales had been wiped out. Low reproduction rates mean that protected species are slow to recover. After 1986 only Iceland, Japan, Norway, and the USSR continued with limited whaling for 'scientific purposes', but Japan has been repeatedly implicated in commercial whaling, and pirates also operate. In 1990, the IWC rejected every proposal from Japan, Norway, and the USSR for further scientific whaling. Norway, Greenland, the Faroes, and Iceland formed a breakaway whaling club. In 1991, Japan held a 'final' whale feast before conforming to the regulations of the IWC. In 1993, Norway decided to flout the moratorium and resume commercial hunting of minke whales.

wildlife trade international trade in live plants and animals, and in wildlife products such as skins, horns, shells, and feathers. The trade has made some species virtually extinct, and whole ecosystems (for example, coral reefs) are threatened. Wildlife trade is to some extent regulated by CITES (the Convention on International Trade in Endangered Species).

Species almost eradicated by trade in their products include many of the largest whales, crocodiles, marine turtles, and some wild cats. Until recently, some 2 million snake skins were exported from India every year. Populations of black rhino and African elephant have collapsed because of hunting for their horns and tusks (ivory), and poaching remains a problem in cases where trade is prohibited.

Environmental Groups and Initiatives

CITES (acronym for *Convention on International Trade in Endangered Species*) international agreement under the auspices of the IUCN with the aim of regulating trade in endangered species of animals and plants. The agreement came into force 1975 and by 1991 had been signed by 110 states. It prohibits any trade in a category of 8,000 highly endangered species and controls trade in a further 30,000 species.

Council for the Protection of Rural England countryside conservation group founded 1926 with a brief that extends from planning controls to energy policy. A central organization campaigns on national issues and 42 local groups lobby on regional matters. The *Campaign for the Preservation of Rural Wales* is the Welsh equivalent.

Countryside Council for Wales Welsh nature conservation body formed 1991 by the fusion of the former Nature Conservancy Council and the Welsh Countryside Commission. It is government-funded and administers conservation and land-use policies within Wales.

English Nature agency created 1991 from the division of the Nature Conservancy Council into English, Scottish, and Welsh sections. It is government-funded and responsible for designating and managing national nature reserves and other conservation areas, advising government ministers on policies, providing advice and information, and commissioning or undertaking relevant scientific research.

Environmentally Sensitive Area (ESA) scheme introduced by the UK Ministry of Agriculture 1984, as a result of EC legislation, to protect some of the most beautiful areas of the British countryside from the loss and damage caused by agricultural change. The first areas to be designated ESAs are in the Pennine Dales, the North Peak District, the Norfolk Broads, the Breckland, the Suffolk River Valleys, the Test Valley, the South Downs, the Somerset Levels and Moors, West Penwith, Cornwall, the Shropshire Borders, the Cambrian Mountains, and the Lleyn Peninsula.

Major national parks (Europe and the Americas)

Name	Location	Area sq km	sq mi
Europe			
Hohe Tauern	Austria	2,589	1,000
Lake District	England, UK	2,292	885
Snowdonia	Wales, UK	2,142	827
Sarek	Sweden	1,940	749
Pfälzerwald	Germany	1,793	692
Yorkshire Dales	England, UK	1,769	683
Peak District	England, UK	1,438	555
North York Moors	England, UK	1,436	554
Brecon Beacons	Wales, UK	1,351	522
Northumberland	England, UK	1,049	405
Dartmoor	England, UK	954	368
Bialowieski/ Belovezhskaya	Poland/Belarus	928	358
Cévennes	France	844	326
Gran Paradiso	Italy	700	270
Exmoor	England, UK	693	268
Pembrokeshire Coast	Wales, UK	584	225
Rondane	Norway	572	221
Vanoise	France	528	204
Hortobágyi	Hungary	520	201
Pallas-Ounastunturi	Finland	500	193
Skaftafell	Iceland	500	193
Abruzzi	Italy	392	151
USA			
Wrangell–St Elias	SE Alaska	32,970	12,730
Gates of the Arctic	N Alaska	28,540	11,019
Katmai	SW Alaska	17,928	6,922
Denali	S Alaska	16,452	6,352
Glacier Bay	SE Alaska	15,695	6,060
Lake Clark	S Alaska	9,870	3,811
Yellowstone	Idaho/Montana/ Wyoming	8,984	3,469
Death Valley	California/ Nevada	8,368	3,231
Kobuk Valley	N Alaska	6,920	2,672
Everglades	S Florida	5,661	2,186
Grand Canyon	NW Arizona	4,931	1,904
Glacier	NW Montana	4,102	1,584
Olympic	NW Washington	3,703	1,430
Yosemite	E California	3,079	1,189
Big Bend	W Texas	2,866	1,106
Isle Royale	NW Michigan	2,314	893
Kenai Fjords	S Alaska	2,295	886
Great Smoky Mountains	N Tennessee	2,106	813

Name	Location	Area sq km	sq mi
North Cascades	N Washington	2,043	789
Kings Canyon	E California	1,862	719
Sequoia	E California	1,629	629
Canyonlands	SE Utah	1,366	527
Grand Teton	NW Wyoming	1,257	485
Rocky Mountain	Central Colorado	1,068	412
Channel Islands	S California	1,009	390
Badlands	SW South Dakota	985	380
Capitol Reef	S Utah	979	378
Mount Rainier	SW Washington	953	368
Hawaii Volcanoes	Hawaii	927	358
Voyageurs	N Minnesota	887	342
Shenandoah	Virginia	788	304
Biscayne	SE Florida	729	281
Crater Lake	SW Oregon	649	250
Zion	SW Utah	593	229
Redwood	NW California	443	171
Lassen Volcanic	N California	430	166
Petrified Forest	E Arizona	378	146
Guadalupe Mountains	W Texas	309	119
Arches	E Utah	297	115
Theodore Roosevelt	W North Dakota	285	110
Mammoth Cave	Central Kentucky	212	82
Mesa Verde	SW Colorado	211	81
Carlsbad Caverns	SE New Mexico	189	73
Arcadia	SE Maine	158	61
Bryce Canyon	SW Utah	145	56
Haleakala	Hawaii	120	46
Wind Cave	SW South Dakota	114	44
Virgin Islands	Virgin Islands	59	23
Hot Springs	Central Arkansas	24	9
Canada			
Banff	Alberta	6,641	2,564
Jasper	Alberta	10,878	4,200
Wood Buffalo	Alberta/ Northwest Territories	44,800	17,297
South America			
Canaima	Venezuela	30,000	11,583
Manu	Peru	15,328	5,918
Amazonia	Brazil	10,000	3,861
Galápagos	Ecuador	6,790	2,622

In these ESAs, farmers are encouraged to use traditional methods to preserve the value of the land as a wildlife habitat. A farmer who joins the scheme agrees to manage the land in this way for at least five years. In return for this agreement, the Ministry of Agriculture pays the farmer a sum that reflects the financial losses incurred as a result of reconciling conservation with commercial farming. Further ESAs were in 1993 under threat from budget cuts.

Environmental Protection Agency (EPA) US agency set up 1970 to control water and air quality, industrial and commercial wastes, pesticides, noise,

and radiation. In its own words, it aims to protect 'the country from being degraded, and its health threatened, by a multitude of human activities initiated without regard to long-ranging effects upon the life-supporting properties, the economic uses, and the recreational value of air, land, and water'.

Friends of the Earth (FoE or FOE) environmental pressure group, established in the UK 1971, that aims to protect the environment and to promote rational and sustainable use of the Earth's resources. It campaigns on issues such as acid rain; air, sea, river, and land pollution; recycling; disposal of toxic wastes;

nuclear power and renewable energy; the destruction of rainforests; pesticides; and agriculture. FoE has branches in 30 countries.

Green Party political party aiming to 'preserve the planet and its people', based on the premise that incessant economic growth is unsustainable. The leaderless party structure reflects a general commitment to decentralization. Green parties sprang up in W Europe in the 1970s and in E Europe from 1988. Parties in different countries are linked to one another but unaffiliated with any pressure group.

Greenpeace international environmental pressure group, founded 1971, with a policy of nonviolent direct action backed by scientific research. During a protest against French atmospheric nuclear testing in the S Pacific 1985, its ship *Rainbow Warrior* was sunk by French intelligence agents, killing a crew member.

Henry Doubleday Research Association British gardening group founded 1954 to investigate organic growing techniques. It runs the *National Centre for Organic Gardening*, a 1-hectare/22-acre demonstration site, at Ryton-on-Dunsmore near Coventry, England. The association is named after the person who first imported Russian comfrey, a popular green-manuring crop.

International Union for Conservation of Nature (IUCN) organization established by the United Nations to promote the conservation of wildlife and habitats as part of the national policies of member states. It has formulated guidelines and established research programmes (for example, the International Biological Programme) and set up advisory bodies (such as Survival Commissions). In 1980, it launched the *World Conservation Strategy* to highlight particular problems, designating a small number of areas *World Heritage Sites* to ensure their survival as unspoiled habitats (for example, Yosemite National Park in the USA, and the Simen Mountains in Ethiopia).

Montréal Protocol international agreement, signed 1987 and reviewed 1992, to stop the production of ozone-depleting chemicals by the year 2000. A controversial amendment concerns a fund established to pay for the transfer of ozone-safe technology to poor countries.

National Rivers Authority (NRA) UK government agency launched 1989. It is responsible for managing water resources, investigating and regulating pollution, and taking over flood controls and land drainage from the former ten regional water authorities of England and Wales.

National Trust British trust founded 1895 for the preservation of land and buildings of historic interest or beauty, incorporated by act of Parliament 1907. It is the largest private landowner in Britain. The National Trust for Scotland was established 1931.

Natural Environment Research Council (NERC) UK organization established by royal charter 1965 to undertake and support research in the earth sciences, to give advice both on exploiting natural resources and on protecting the environment, and to support education and training of scientists in these

fields of study. Research areas include geothermal energy, industrial pollution, waste disposal, satellite surveying, acid rain, biotechnology, atmospheric circulation, and climate. Research is carried out principally within the UK but also in Antarctica and in many Third World countries. It comprises 13 research bodies.

Nature Conservancy Council (NCC) former name of UK government agency divided 1991 into English Nature, Scottish Natural Heritage, and the Countryside Council for Wales.

Scottish Natural Heritage Scottish nature conservation body formed 1991 after the break up of the national Nature Conservancy Council. It is government-funded.

Single European Act 1986 update of the Treaty of Rome (signed in 1957) that provides a legal basis for action by the European Community in matters relating to the environment. The act requires that environmental protection shall be a part of all other Community policies. Also, it allows for agreement by a qualified majority on some legislation, whereas before such decisions had to be unanimous.

site of special scientific interest (SSSI) in the UK, land that has been identified as having animals, plants, or geological features that need to be protected and conserved. From 1991, these sites were designated and administered by English Nature, Scottish Natural Heritage, and the Countryside Council for Wales.

Numbers fluctuate, but there were over 5,000 SSSIs in 1991, covering about 6% of Britain. Although SSSIs enjoy some legal protection, this does not in practice always prevent damage or destruction; during 1989, for example, 44 SSSIs were so badly damaged that they were no longer worth protecting.

Soil Association pioneer British ecological organization founded 1946, which campaigns against pesticides and promotes organic farming. It also sets the Standards for Organic Agriculture; administers and monitors the Symbol Scheme (the Symbol is a quality mark for organically grown food); researches and publishes findings on organic issues; lobbies the government for changes in agriculture; and promotes educational programmes for the general public on organic farming.

World Conservation Monitoring Centre organization established 1983, to support international programmes for conservation and sustainable development through the provision of information on the world's biological diversity. It provides information to the World Wide Fund for Nature, the World Conservation Union (IUCN), and the United Nations Environment Programme (UNEP) (*not* direct to the general public).

World Wide Fund for Nature (WWF, formerly the *World Wildlife Fund*) international organization established 1961 to raise funds for conservation by public appeal. Projects include conservation of particular species, for example, the tiger and giant panda, and special areas, such as the Simen Mountains, Ethiopia.

Seaside bathing: the best and the worst

Beaches listed in the 1993 Good Beach Guide, judged by their concurrence with mandatory EC bathing-water standards

Recommended beaches:

England

Cornwall	Sandy Mouth, Bude; Widemouth Sands; Polzeath; Constantine Bay; Treyarnon; Crantock; The Towans, Hayle, St Ives; Porthmeor, St Ives; Whitesand Bay, Sennan Cove; Poldhu Cove, Mullion; Kynance Cove, The Lizard Kennack Sands, Kuggar; Towan Beach; Pendowar Beach, Veryan; Whitesand Bay,Freathy
Devon	Woolacombe; Shipload Bay, Hartland Quay; Wembury; Bigbury-on-Sea; Slapton Sands; Blackpool Sands; Watcombe to Maidencombe; Sidmouth-Jacobs Ladder
Dorset	Seaton, Bridport; West Bay; Burton Bradstock; Durdle Door; Sandbanks, Poole; Highcliffe
Hampshire	Lee-on-Solent; Stokes Bay
Kent	Botany Bay
Norfolk	Hunstanton; Sea Palling
Northumberland	Druridge; Warkworth; Alnmouth; Low Newton; Beadnell; Bamburgh
Suffolk	Aldeburgh; Southwold, The Denes; South Beach, Lowestoft
Sussex	Cuckmere Haven
Isle of Wight	Compton Bay

Scotland

Borders	Pease Sands
Highlands	Duncansby Head; Sandside Bay; Scourie; Clashnessie; Clachtoll; Balnakiel Bay; Colbackie; Achmelvich; Achnahaird; Achiltibnie; Gruinard Bay; Applecross; The Coral Beaches; Morar; Carmusdarrach; Traigh; Sanna Bay; Calgary Bay; Erraid
Lothian	Thortonloch

Wales

Cardigan	Mwnt
Dyfed	Abereiddy; Whitesand Bay; Barafundle Bay; Pembrey
Gwynedd	Porth Oer
West Glamorgan	Rhosili; Port Eynon; Oxwich

Northern Ireland

Co Antrim	West Bay Strand; Port Rush
Co Down	Crawfordsburn; Tyrella; Cranfield
Co Londonderry	Benone

Guernsey

Pembroke Bay; Petit Bot Bay; L'Eree Beach; Vazon Beach; Cobo Beach; Port Soif

Jersey

Archirondel; St Brelade; Portelet; St Ouens; Plemont

The following beaches failed to meet EC minimum mandatory bathing-water standards and were considered a health risk:

England

Cornwall	Crackington Haven
Dorset	Eastbourne (east of pier)

Wales

Dyfed	New Quay; Cwmtudu, New Quay
West Glamorgan	Caswell Bay

The following beaches were dropped from the guide because of sewage solids, excessive litter, or other debris:

England

Cornwall	Praa Sands (sewage-related debris)
North Yorkshire	Whitby (dog faeces, litter)

Scotland

Fife	Tentsmuir Point, Tayport (sewage-related debris, litter)
Grampian	Strathbeg (litter); Burghead Bay (litter);
Highlands	Dornoch (litter); Gairloch (sewage)
Strathclyde	Blackwaterfoot (sewage)

Wales

Dyfed	Borth (sewage)

Seaside bathing: the best and the worst *(cont.)*

The following beaches were dropped because they did not meet strict EC standards:

England

Cornwall	Trebarwith Strand; Harlyn Bay; Treyarnon Bay; Padstow; Holywell Bay; Bow or Vault; Gorran Haven; Cawsand Bay
Devon	Teignmouth; Budleigh Salterton
Dorset	Weymouth; Ringstead Bay; Lulworth Cove; Kimmeridge; Studland Beach; Bournemouth
Humberside	Hornsea; Bridlington
Kent	Whitstable
Norfolk	Wells
North Yorkshire	Filey Sands; Cayton Bay; Robin Hood's Bay; Runswick Bay
Suffolk	Dunwich
Sussex	Bexhill
Isle of Wight	Sandown

Scotland

Grampian	Stonehaven; Sandend; Cullen Sands
Lothian	Gullane
Strathclyde	Troon
Tayside	Montrose Links

Wales

Anglesey	Aberffaw
Gwynedd	Aberdaron; Harlech; Tal-y-bont
West Glamorgan	Langland Bay

Northern Ireland

Co Antrim	Brown's Bay
Co Down	Helen's Bay
Co Londonderry	Portstewart

The following beaches were not monitored by the National Rivers Authority, River Purification Boards, or the Department of the Environment, and so could not be recommended:

England

Cornwall	Priest's Cove, St Just; Polperro Cove; Lantic Bay; Lansallos Bay
Devon	Branscombe
Northumberland	Embleton Bay; Cocklawburn

Wales

Anglesey	Traeth Lligy, Moelfre; Llanddwyn, Newborough
Gwynedd	Dinas Dinlle; Traeth Penllech, Llangwnnadl

Northern Ireland

Co Antrim	White Park Bay

Ten ways to reduce damage to the environment

1 Minimize use of your car, and travel by bike, bus or train instead.
2 Avoid aerosols where possible, and if you do use them, only choose those clearly marked 'ozone friendly'.
3 Do not buy tropical hardwood products, unless they are certified as coming from sustainably managed forests by an independent body.
4 Select the most energy-efficient electrical appliances you can find.
5 Save energy by draught-stripping and insulating your home.
6 Recycle waste paper, bottles, and aluminium cans, and compost all vegetable and garden waste.
7 Choose recycled paper products wherever possible.
8 Save water by having a shower instead of a bath, installing a dual flush toilet, and using a water butt for the garden.
9 Always buy organically grown food where it is available.
10 Avoid over-consumption.

Hunting of selected species, numbers killed

	Period	Roe deer	Wild boar	Hare	Pheasant	Partridge	Fallow deer	Wild reindeer	Moose	Fox
Austria	1970	143,883	2,993	342,870	409,767	105,203	81	-	-	37,197
	1985	211,975	6,154	246,831	300,736	10,135	108	-	-	29,916
	1989	237,922	10,058	205,279	7,976	264		-	1,699	
Belarus	1985	90	5,317	83,029	-			-	2,998	1,221
	1989	617	6,405	86,344		87		-	3,952	841
Bulgaria	1985	14,120	17,210	100,273	122,060	38,210		-	-	54,636
	1988	15,950	19,140	73,500	136,900	84,150		-	-	32,300
Canada*	1983	-	-	-	-	-	-	-	67,238	105,568
Cyprus	1986		-	50,000	-	250,000		-	-	-
	1989		-	56,000	-	209,000		-	-	-
CSFR	1970	66,610	8,351	1,054,674	1,112,503	8,261	1,925	-	-	30,684
	1985	99,694	47,896	288,315	597,710	-	3,781	-	-	46,602
	1988	89,959	65,330	187,415	673,934	119	4,481	-	-	54,703
Denmark	1985	51,000	-	187,000	655,000	53,000		-	-	45,000
	1988	54,000	-	151,000	633,000	50,000		-	-	50,000
Finland	1972	290	-	34,000	5,400	3,000	-	-	3,400	21,000
	1985	3,000	-	54,000	6,000	1,900	-	-	55,000	28,000
	1988	3,450	-	36,000	7,700	1,200	28	-	53,370	35,000
France	1986	108,556	-	-	-	-	279	-	-	-
	1989	143,800	-	-	-	-	117	-	-	-
West Germany	1985	169,860	126,820	16,656	13,407	-	12,831	-	-	90,883
	1989	155,700	150,000	15,757	12,246	7	18,400	-	-	101,003
East Germany*	1989	757,157	89,023	619,929	449,509	31,239	13,960	-	-	250,060
Greece*	1988	-	-	-	-	-	-	-	-	50,000
Hungary	1970	19,700	9,000	295,200	487,000	74,900	700	-	-	28,000
	1985	41,800	35,900	223,400	714,500	600	4,100	-	-	31,638
	1989	36,300	40,900	129,500	888,100	2,700	3,400	-	-	31,697
Luxembourg	1970	4,655	356	7,531	5,271	3,515	-	-	-	957
	1985	5,566	1,155	2,858	1,511	0	-	-	-	992
	1989	6,500	1,500	3,500	650	-	-	-	-	3,500
Netherlands	1975	5,383	805	-	-	55,000	-	-	-	-
	1985	7,000	1,200	200,000	280,000	18,000	-	-	-	-
	1988	7,600	925	-	-	-	-	-	-	-
Norway	1977	6,660	-	50,000	-	-	-	7,290	12,900	29,000
	1985	-	-	127,000	-	-	-	10,371	25,372	30,000
	1988	28,000	-	124,000	-	-	-	8,739	24,972	18,000
Poland	1970	19,000	2,400	386,000	82,000	121,000	-	-	-	-
	1985	128,475	76,804	252,791	80,489	103,426	1,070	-	1,290	26,161
	1988	108,865	74,830	223,715	95,778	120,307	1,100	-	1,307	31,162
Romania	1988	1,180	10,700	65,800	48,000	200	520	-	-	17,900
Sweden	1971	44,000	-	210,000	42,700	3,600	1,200	-	36,000	77,000
	1988	142,000	-	320,000	10,000	1,500	2,400	-	135,000	23,000
Switzerland	1989	36,317	621	8,546	-	-	-	-	-	26,602
Turkey*	1990	-	50,000	-	-	500,000	-	-	-	120,000
Ukraine	1985	3,372	6,504	325,656	12,278	16,303	-	-	8,712	862
	1989	6,851	8,231	400,298	-	40,286	-	-	13,143	1,497
USSR	1985	30,864	76,822	1,304,958	30,382	281,946	-	129,256	70,184	88,410
	1989	53,321	106,094	1,511,242	-	644,925	-	104,442	97,235	92,542
UK*	1988	-	-	350,000	13,000,000	330,000	-	-	-	200,000
Yugoslavia	1970	20,866	4,384	415,022	415,022	436,806	293,009	385	-	75,090
	1985	62,396	13,776	292,317	620,109	59,527	299	-	-	72,661
	1988	57,972	16,445	243,031	530,930	58,046	365	-	-	61,471

Comments on countries marked with *: Canada: In 1983, 204,541 deer and 37,874 caribou were killed. East Germany, Figures for roe, and fallow deer include accidental kills. Greece: Roe and European deer are protected species. Turkey: In 1990, European deer, hare, pheasant, fallow deer and mouflon were fully protected. UK: Figures are very rough estimates. Data are retrieved from a survey made in more than 700 estates with an average size of over 1,000 acres. On the basis of the survey results, the average number killed per 100 hectares was calculated on a national basis. In 1988, the number of hares killed per 100 ha was 17, 1,229 for pheasant, 21 for partridge and 22 for fox.

Source: IEDS

FOOD, NUTRITION, AND AGRICULTURE

Food and Drink

beer alcoholic drink made from water and malt (fermented barley or other grain), flavoured with hops. Beer contains between 1% and 6% alcohol. The medieval distinction between beer (containing hops) and *ale* (without hops) has now fallen into disuse and beer has come to be used strictly as a generic term including ale, stout, and lager. *Stout* is top fermented, but is sweet and strongly flavoured with roasted grain; *lager* is a light beer, bottom fermented and matured over a longer period.

biscuit small, flat, brittle cake of baked dough. The basic components of biscuit dough are weak flour and fat; other ingredients, such as eggs, sugar, chocolate, and spices, may be added to vary the flavour and texture. Originally made from slices of unleavened bread baked until hard and dry, biscuits could be stored for several years, and were a useful, though dull, source of carbohydrate on long sea voyages and military campaigns. The first biscuit factory opened in Carlisle, N England, 1815 and the UK is now Europe's largest producer and consumer of factory-made biscuits.

bread food baked from a kneaded dough or batter made with ground cereals, usually wheat, and water; many other ingredients may be added. The dough may be unleavened or raised (usually with yeast).

Leavened bread was first made in the ancient Middle East and Egypt in brick ovens similar to ceramic kilns. The yeast creates gas, making the dough rise. Traditionally bread has been made from whole grains: wheat, barley, rye and oats, ground into a meal which varied in quality. Modern manufacturing processes have changed this to optimize the profit and shorten the manufacturing time. Fermentation is speeded up using ascorbic acid and potassium bromide with fast-acting flour improvers. White bread was developed by the end of the 19th century by roller-milling, which removed the wheat germ to satisfy fashionable consumer demand, but lacking in important fibre and nutrient content. Today, some of the nutrients, such as vitamins, are removed in the processing of bread are synthetically replaced.

bulghur wheat or *bulgar* or *burghul* cracked wholewheat, made by cooking the grains, then drying and cracking them. It is widely eaten in the Middle East. Coarser bulghur may be cooked in the same way as rice; more finely ground bulghur is mixed with minced meat to make a paste that may be eaten as a dip with salad, or shaped and stuffed before being grilled or fried.

butter solid, edible yellowish fat made from whole milk. Usually by machine, the cream is churned, the buttermilk drawn off, and the butter washed, salted, and worked, to achieve an even consistency. Colour and flavouring may be added. British butter typically contains 1,300 micrograms vitamin A per 100g in summer and 500 micrograms per 100g in winter; it contains about 82% fat, 0.4% protein, and up to 16% water.

cake baked food item made from a mixture of weak flour, sugar, eggs, and fat (usually butter or margarine). Other ingredients, such as dried fruits, can be added, and pastry is sometimes used as a base. Cakes may be eaten to celebrate special occasions. The UK is Europe's biggest producer of factory-made cakes.

cereal, breakfast food prepared from the seeds of cereal crops. Some cereals require cooking (porridge oats), but most are ready to eat. Mass-marketed cereals include refined and sweetened varieties as well as whole cereals such as muesli. Whole cereals are more nutritious and provide more fibre than the refined cereals, which often have vitamins and flavourings added to replace those lost in the refining process.

cheese food made from the *curds* (solids) of soured milk from cows, sheep, or goats, separated from the *whey* (liquid), then salted, put into moulds, and pressed into firm blocks. Cheese is ripened with bacteria or surface fungi, and kept for a time to mature before eating.

There are six main types of cheese. *Soft cheeses* may be ripe or unripe, and include cottage cheese and high-fat soft cheeses such as Bel Paese, Camembert, and Neufchatel. *Semi-hard cheeses* are ripened by bacteria (Munster) or by bacteria and surface fungi (Port Salut, Gouda, St Paulin); they may also have penicillin moulds injected into them (Roquefort, Gorgonzola, blue Stilton, Wensleydale). *Hard cheeses* are ripened by bacteria, and include Cheddar, Cheshire, and Cucciocavallo; some have large cavities within them, such as Swiss Emmental and Gruyère. *Very hard cheeses*, such as Parmesan and Spalen, are made with skimmed milk. *Processed cheese* is made with dried skim-milk powder and additives, and *whey cheese* is made by heat coagulation of the proteins from whey; examples are Mysost and Primost.

cider fermented drink made from the juice of the apple; in the USA, the term usually refers to unfermented (nonalcoholic) apple juice. Cider has been

Composition of cheeses

Cheese	Fat (%)	Protein (%)	Calcium (mg)	Salt (mg)	Calories (per 100 g)
Cheddar	32.2	25	750	700	398
Roquefort	31.5	21.5	315	–	368
Camembert	min 26	17.5	105	–	299
Emmental	28	27.5	925	710	370
processed	28	25	850	1,1150	360
cottage	0.3	17	90	290	86

made for more than 2,000 years, and for many centuries has been a popular drink in France and England, which are now its main centres of production.

cocoa and chocolate food products made from the cacao (or cocoa) bean, fruit of a tropical tree *Theobroma cacao*, now cultivated mainly in Africa. Chocolate as a drink was introduced to Europe from the New World by the Spanish in the 16th century; eating chocolate was first produced in the late 18th century.

Preparation takes place in the importing country and consists chiefly of roasting, winnowing, and grinding the nib (the edible portion of the bean). If *cocoa* for drinking is required, a proportion of the cocoa butter is removed by hydraulic pressure and the remaining cocoa is reduced by further grinding and sieving to a fine powder. *Plain chocolate* is made by removing some of the cocoa butter and adding a little sugar. It is dark and has a slightly bitter flavour. *Milk chocolate* a sweeter variety, made by adding condensed or powdered milk and a larger amount of sugar. In the UK, cheaper vegetable fats are widely substituted for milk, and chocolate need contain only 20% cocoa solids. *White chocolate* contains cocoa butter but no cocoa solids, and is flavoured with sugar and vanilla.

coffee drink made from the roasted and ground beanlike seeds found inside the red berries of any of several species of shrubs of the genus *Coffea*. It contains a stimulant, caffeine. Coffee drinking began in Arab regions in the 14th century but did not become common in Europe until 300 years later, when the first coffee houses were opened in Vienna, and soon after in Paris and London. The world's largest producers are Brazil, Colombia, and Côte d'Ivoire.

The flavour of coffee beans depends on the variety grown, the location of the plantation, and the manner in which the beans were processed; for example, Arabica beans, grown at high altitudes, are considered finer than the cheaper Robusta and Liberian varieties. Manufacturers, therefore, blend beans from a number of sources in order to achieve a consistent product.

cream the part of milk that has the highest fat content; it can be separated by centrifugation or gravity (if milk is left to stand, the upper layer will be cream, the lower layer skimmed milk). To whip cream, that is, process it to trap air bubbles, it must contain at least 30% fat. *Clotted cream* is made from heating double cream over a bain marie, or by floating milk and skimming off the clotted upper layer. It should contain 55% fat and 4% protein.

drink, soft drink that provides water and often sugar, in a flavoured form. Soft drinks include all kinds of carbonated drinks, such as variously flavoured colas and sodas, ginger ale, and soda water. Many fruit-flavoured drinks contain no fruit but consist of water, sugar or artificial sweetener, and synthetic flavourings.

egg the shell-covered egg of a domestic chicken, duck, or goose, or of a game bird such as quail. It is a highly nutritious food: the albumin, or egg white, of a chicken's egg is 10% protein; the yolk is 33% fat and 15% protein, and contains vitamins A, B, and D. The yolk also contains cholesterol, a fatty substance associated with heart disease.

Eggs have many uses in cooking. They can be used for thickening sauces, binding and coating crumbly foods, and raising batters and cakes; whisked egg white gives a foamy texture to soufflés and desserts; and yolk acts as an emulsifier, keeping oil in suspension in mixtures such as mayonnaise.

fibre, dietary or *roughage* plant material that cannot be digested by human digestive enzymes; it consists largely of cellulose, a carbohydrate found in plant cell walls. Fibre adds bulk to the gut contents, assisting the muscular contractions that force food along the intestine. A diet low in fibre causes constipation and is believed to increase the risk of developing diverticulitis, diabetes, gall-bladder disease, and cancer of the large bowel – conditions that are rare in countries where the diet contains a high proportion of unrefined cereals.

Soluble fibre consists of indigestible plant carbohydrates (such as pectins, hemicelluloses, and gums) that dissolve in water. A high proportion of the fibre in such foods as oat bran, pulses, and vegetables is of this sort.

fish flesh or roe of freshwater or saltwater fish. The nutrient composition of fish is similar to that of meat, except that there are no obvious deposits of fat. Examples of fish comparatively high in fat are salmon, mackerel, and herring. White fish such as cod, haddock, and whiting contain only 0.4–4% fat. Fish are good sources of B vitamins and iodine, and the fatty fish livers are good sources of A and D vitamins. Calcium can be obtained from fish with soft skeletons, such as sardines. Roe and caviar have a high protein content (20–25%).

flour foodstuff made by grinding starchy vegetable materials, usually cereal grains, into a fine powder. Flour may also be made from root vegetables such as potato and cassava, and from pulses such as soya beans and chick peas. The most commonly used cereal flour is wheat flour.

The properties of wheat flour depend on the strain of wheat used. Bread requires strong ('hard') flour, with a high gluten content. *Durum flour* also has a high gluten content, and is used for pasta. Cakes and biscuits are made from weak ('soft') flour, containing less gluten. *Granary flour* contains malted flakes of wheat. Wheat flour may contain varying proportions of bran (husk) and wheatgerm (embryo), ranging from 100% *wholemeal flour* to refined white flour, which has less than 75% of the whole grain. Much of the flour available now is bleached to whiten it; bleaching also destroys some of its vitamin content, so synthetic vitamins are added instead.

fruit in ordinary usage, any sweet, fleshy plant item, such as an orange, strawberry, or rhubarb stalk. When eaten they provide vitamins, minerals, and enzymes, but little protein.

Fruits are divided into three agricultural categories on the basis of the climate in which they grow. *Temperate fruits* require a cold season for satisfactory growth; the principal temperate fruits are apples, pears, plums, peaches, apricots, cherries, and soft fruits, such as strawberries. *Subtropical fruits* require warm conditions but can survive light frosts; they include oranges and other citrus fruits, dates, pomegranates, and avocados. *Tropical fruits* cannot tolerate temperatures that drop close to freezing point; they include bananas, mangoes, pineapples, papayas, and litchis.

fruit juice juice extracted from fruits, either by pressing (citrus fruits) or by spinning at high speed in a centrifuge (other fruits). Although fruit juice provides no fibre, its nutritional value is close to that of the whole fruit. Most fruit juices are transported in concentrated form, and are diluted and pasteurized before being packaged. Concentrated juices may be used as sweeteners in cooking.

herb any plant (usually a flowering plant) tasting sweet, bitter, aromatic, or pungent, used in cooking, medicine, or perfumery. Most herbs are temperate plants; they include bay, thyme, borage, mint, chives, and tarragon. Their leaves and stems release aromatic oils on being crushed, chopped, or heated, and may be used fresh, dried, or freeze-dried.

honey sweet syrup produced by honey bees from the nectar of flowers. It is stored in honeycombs and made in excess of their needs as food for the winter. Honey comprises various sugars, mainly laevulose and dextrose, with enzymes, colouring matter, acids, and pollen grains. It has antibacterial properties and was widely used in ancient Egypt, Greece, and Rome as a wound salve. It is still popular for sore throats, in hot drinks or in lozenges.

ice cream rich, creamy, frozen confectionery, made commercially from the early 20th century from various milk products, sugar, and fruit and nut flavourings, usually with additives to improve keeping qualities and ease of serving.

In the UK, the sale of ice cream made with 'non-milk' animal or vegetable fat, and with chemical additives to give colour and flavour, is permitted. Water ices and sorbets are frozen fruit juices and do not contain milk or cream. **Sherbet** is a frozen dessert of watered fruit juice, egg white, and sugar, like an ice, but with gelatin and milk added.

lard clarified edible pig fat. It is used in cooking and in the manufacture of margarine, soaps, and ointments. It can be heated to very high temperatures without burning.

liqueur alcoholic liquor made by infusing flavouring substances (fruits, herbs, spices) in alcohol. Specific recipes are closely guarded commercial secrets. Originally liqueurs were used as medicines and are still thought of as digestives.

macrobiotics dietary system of organically grown wholefoods. It originates in Zen Buddhism, and attempts to balance the principles of yin and yang, thought to be present in foods in different proportions.

margarine butter substitute made from animal fats and/or vegetable oils. French chemist Hippolyte Mège-Mouries invented margarine 1889. Today, margarines are usually made with vegetable oils, such as soy, corn (maize), or sunflower oil, giving a product low in saturated fats and fortified with vitamins A and D.

meat flesh of animals taken as food, in Western countries chiefly the muscle tissue of domestic cattle (beef and veal), sheep (lamb and mutton), pigs (pork), and poultry. The practice of cooking meat is at least 600,000 years old.

Beef, lamb, and mutton are termed **red meats**; poultry, pork, and veal are termed **white meats**. Meat has a high protein content and is a good source of B vitamins and iron; its fat tends to have a high proportion of saturated fatty acids. **Game** is meat obtained from wild animals and birds, such as deer, hare, grouse, pheasant, and wild duck. It has a stronger flavour than that of farm-reared animals, and is thought to be less easy to digest. Before being cooked, therefore, it is stored suspended ('hung') in a cool place to make it more tender, generally for two to eight days. **Offal** comprises the edible internal organs of an animal, and also its head, feet, tail, tongue, and bone marrow. It is generally cheaper than muscle tissue.

Meat is wasteful in production (the same area of grazing land would produce far greater food value in cereal crops). The main exporters are Argentina, Australia, New Zealand, Canada, the USA, and Denmark (chiefly bacon). The consumption of meat in 1989 was 111 kg/244 lb per person in the USA, 68 kg/150 lb in the UK, 30 kg/66 lb in Japan, 6 kg/13 lb in Nigeria, and 1 kg/2.2 lb in India. Research suggests that, in a healthy diet, consumption of meat (especially with a high fat content) should not exceed the Japanese level.

milk secretion of the mammary glands of female mammals, with which they suckle their young. Over 85% is water, the remainder comprising protein, fat, lactose (a sugar), calcium, phosphorus, iron, and vitamins. The milk of cows, goats, and sheep is often consumed by humans, but regular drinking of milk after infancy is principally a Western practice; for people in most of the world, milk causes flatulence and diarrhoea.

Milk composition varies among species, depending on the nutritional requirements of the young; human milk contains less protein and more lactose than that of cows. **Skimmed milk** is what remains when the cream has been separated from milk. It is readily dried and is available in large quantities at low prices, so it is often sent as food aid to Third World countries. **Evaporated milk** is milk reduced by heat until it reaches about half its volume. **Condensed milk** is concentrated to about a third of its original volume with added sugar.

Composition of milks

Source	Protein (g/100ml)	Fat (g/100 ml)	Carbohydrate (g/100ml)	Energy Kcal/100ml
cow	3.5	3.5	5.0	65
buffalo	4.3	7.5	4.5	105
camel	3.7	4.2	4.0	70
ewe	6.5	7.0	5.0	110
goat	3.7	5.0	4.5	75
mare	1.3	1.2	5.5	30
reindeer	10.5	22.5	2.5	250
human	1.1	6.2	7.5	70

mineral water water with mineral constituents gathered from the rocks with which it comes in contact, and classified by these into earthy, brine, and oil mineral waters; also water with artificially added minerals and, sometimes, carbon dioxide.

Main types of vitamins

Vitamin/chemical name	Source	Established benefit	Deficiency symptoms
A retinol beta carotene (converts to A in the body)	liver, egg yolks, whole milk, butter, dark green vegetables, yellow and orange vegetables, and yellow/red fruits	prevents night blindness and xerophthalmia (a common cause of blindness among children in developing countries); helps keep the skin and mucous membranes resistant to infection	night blindness; rough skin impaired bone growth
B₁ thiamin	germ and bran of seeds, grains; yeast	prevents beri-beri; essential to carbohydrate metabolism and health of nervous system	beri-beri, Korsakov's syndrome
B₂ riboflavin	liver, milk, meat, poultry, broccoli, mushrooms	protects skin, mouth, eyes, eyelids, mucous membranes	skin disorders; failure to thrive
B₆ pyridoxine/ pantothenic acid/biotin	meat, poultry, fish, fruits, nuts, whole grains, leafy vegetables, yeast extract	helps prevent anaemia, skin lesions, nerve damage; important in the regulation of the central nervous system and in protein metabolism	dermatitis; neurological disorders
B₁₂ cyanocobalamin	liver, meat, fish, eggs, dairy products, soybeans	needed to form red blood cells; helps prevent pernicious anaemia	anaemia, neurological disturbance
folic acid	green leafy vegetables, liver, peanuts; cooking and processing can cause serious losses in food	helps protect against cervical dysplasia (precancerous changes in the cells of the uterine cervix)	anaemia
C ascorbic acid	citrus fruit, green peppers, blackcurrants, strawberries, other fruits, fresh leafy vegetables, potatoes; losses occur during storage and cooking	prevents scurvy, loose teeth; fights haemorrhage; maintains collagen, a protein necessary for the formation of skin, ligaments, and bones; helps heal wounds and mend fractures, and aids in resisting some types of virus and bacterial infections	scurvy
D cholecalciferol	liver, butter, fatty fish, egg yolks, fortified milk; also produced when skin is exposed to sunlight	important for bone development; prevents rickets	rickets; osteomalacia (bone malformation)
E tocopherols	nuts, seeds, whole grains, vegetable and fish-liver oils	helps prevent retrolental fibroplasia (an eye disorder in premature infants), anaemia; helps protect red blood cells	multiple diseases produced in laboratory animals; humans, multiple symptoms follow impaired fat absorption
K phytomenadione	leafy vegetables, corn and soybean oils, liver, meat, cereals, dairy products, fruits	helps prevent haemorrhage (necessary for the formation of prothrombin, which helps blood to clot)	haemorrhagic problems
niacin	grains, meat, nuts, offal, fish	maintains the health of skin, tongue, and digestive system	pellagra

Main trace minerals

Trace minerals	Source	Deficiency symptoms
calcium	milk and dairy products, blackstrap molasses, sardines, citrus fruits, leafy vegetables	rickets in children; osteoporosis in adults
chromium	liver, wholemeal bread, black pepper, beer, brewer's yeast	adult-onset diabetes
copper	green vegetables, liver, fish, oysters	anaemia; Menkes's syndrome
fluorine	tea, seafood, fluoridated drinking water	tooth decay; possibly osteoporosis
iodine	iodized salt, table salt, seafood, salt-water fish, seaweed	cretinism in new-born children; goitre
iron	offal, beans, green leafy vegetables, shell-fish, egg yolk, potatoes, molasses, dried fruit	anaemia
magnesium	nuts, whole grains, green leafy vegetables (eaten raw)	muscular weakness; insomnia; irregular heart beat
manganese	green leafy vegetables, legumes, cereal grains, tea	not known in humans
molybolenum	cereal grains, liver, kidney, legumes, some dark green vegetables	not known in humans
phosphorus	milk and dairy products, bread and other cereal products, meat, poultry, fish, eggs, dried beans, and peas	bone pain; loss of appetite; muscular weakness
potassium	vegetables, meat, milk, bran, bananas, orange juice	fatigue; muscular weakness; kidney and lung failure; irregular heart beat; in severe cases of depletion, heart failure
selenium	meat, fish, cereal products, garlic, egg yolk	not known in humans
sodium	table salt, bread and cereal products, meat products including bacon and ham, milk	impaired acid–base balance in body fluids (very rare)
zinc	meat and meat products, milk, bread and other cereal products, oysters, legumes	loss of appetite; impaired wound healing; impaired sexual development; stunting

The most widely sold mineral water is Perrier, from the French village of Vergèze in W Provence. It is naturally carbonated, but the gas is removed at source and then used to recarbonate the water during bottling. Evian water comes from Haute-Savoie *département*, France, and Malvern water from Hereford and Worcester, England. Some mineral waters contain relatively high bacterial contaminants.

mushroom fruiting body of certain fungi, consisting of an upright stem and a spore-producing cap with radiating gills on the undersurface. Many species are inedible or even poisonous. Cultivated edible mushrooms are usually species of the genus *Agaricus*. Edible wild, or field, mushrooms include the cep *Boletus edulis*, the chanterelle *Cantharellus cibarius*, and the horn of plenty *Cratellus cornicupoides*, all woodland species; and the horse mushroom *Agaricus arvensis* and shaggy ink cap *Corpinus comatus*, found in grassland. The most prized mushrooms are truffles (various species of *Tuber*), which fruit underground, and morels (species of *Morchella*).

mustard strong-tasting condiment made from the whole, crushed, or ground seeds of the black, brown, or white mustard plants. Table mustard is most often used as an accompaniment to meat, although it can also be used in sauces and dressings, and with fish.

English mustard is made from finely milled brown and white mustard seed to which turmeric is added as a colorant. French *Dijon mustard* contains brown mustard seed, verjuice (the juice of unripe grapes), oil, and white wine. Other varieties are made with vinegar, and may be flavoured with herbs or garlic.

nut commonly, any edible seed or fruit with a woody shell, such as a coconut, almond, walnut, peanut (groundnut), Brazil nut, or hazelnut. The edible parts of most nuts provide a concentrated, nutritious food, containing vitamins, minerals, and enzymes, about 50% fat, and 10–20% protein, although a few, such as chestnuts, are high in carbohydrates and have only a moderate protein content of 5%. Nuts also provide edible oils.

Most nuts are produced by perennial trees and shrubs. Whereas the majority of nuts are obtained from plantations, considerable quantities of pecans and brazil nuts are still collected from the wild.

oil, cooking any fat that is liquid at room temperature, extracted from the seeds or fruits of certain plants, and used for frying, salad dressings, and sauces and condiments such as mayonnaise and mustard. Plants used for cooking oil include sunflower, olive, maize (corn), soya, peanut, and rape. Vegetable oil is a blend of more than one type of oil. Most oils are hot-pressed and refined, a process that leaves them without smell or flavour. Cold-pressed, unrefined oils keep their flavour. Oils are generally low in cholesterol and contain a high proportion of polyunsaturated or monounsaturated fatty acids, although all except soya and corn oil become saturated when heated.

Recommended daily amounts of nutrients for population groups

Age ranges	Energy		Protein	Calcium	Iron	Vitamin A	Thiamin (retinol equivalent)	Riboflavin	Niacin	Vitamin C	Vitamin D[1]
years	MJ	kcal	g	mg	mg	µg	mg	mg	mg	mg	µg
Boys											
Under 1	3.25	780	19	600	6	450	0.3	0.4	5	20	7.5
1	5.0	1,200	30	600	7	300	0.5	0.6	7	20	10
2	5.75	1,400	35	600	7	300	0.6	0.7	8	20	10
3–4	6.5	1,560	39	600	8	300	0.6	0.8	9	20	10
5–6	7.25	1,740	43	600	10	300	0.7	0.9	10	20	–
7–8	8.25	1,980	49	600	10	400	0.8	1.0	11	20	–
9–11	9.5	2,280	56	700	12	575	0.9	1.2	14	25	–
12–14	11.0	2,640	66	700	12	725	1.1	1.4	16	25	–
15–17	12.0	2,880	72	600	12	750	1.2	1.7	19	30	–
Girls											
Under 1	3.0	720	18	600	6	450	0.3	0.4	5	20	7.5
1	4.5	1,100	27	600	7	300	0.4	0.6	7	20	10
2	5.5	1,300	32	600	7	300	0.5	0.7	8	20	10
3–4	6.25	1,500	37	600	8	300	0.6	0.8	9	20	10
5–6	7.0	1,680	42	600	10	300	0.7	0.9	10	20	–
7–8	8.0	1,900	48	600	10	400	0.8	1.0	11	20	–
9–11	8.5	2,050	51	700	12[2]	575	0.8	1.2	14	25	–
12–14	9.0	2,150	53	700	12[2]	725	0.9	1.4	16	25	–
15–17	9.0	2,150	53	600	12[2]	750	0.9	1.7	19	30	–
Men											
18–34											
Sedentary	10.5	2,510	62	500	10	750	1.0	1.6	18	30	–
Moderately active	12.0	2,900	72	500	10	750	1.2	1.6	18	30	–
Very active	14.0	3,350	84	500	10	750	1.3	1.6	18	30	–
35–64											
Sedentary	10.0	2,400	60	500	10	750	1.0	1.6	18	30	–
Moderately active	11.5	2,750	69	500	10	750	1.1	1.6	18	30	–
Very active	14.0	3,350	84	500	10	750	1.3	1.6	18	30	–
65–74	10.0	2,400	60	500	10	750	1.0	1.6	18	30	–
75 and over	9.0	2,150	54	500	10	750	0.9	1.6	18	30	–
Women											
18–54											
Most occupations	9.0	2,150	54	500	12[2]	750	0.9	1.3	15	30	–
Very active	10.5	2,500	62	500	12[2]	750	1.0	1.3	15	30	–
55–74	8.0	1,900	47	500	10	750	0.8	1.3	15	30	–
75 and over	7.0	1,680	42	500	10	750	0.7	1.3	15	30	–
Pregnant	10.0	2,400	60	1,200	13	750	1.0	1.6	18	60	10
Lactating	11.5	2,750	69	1,200	15	1,200	1.1	1.8	21	60	10

[1] Most people who go out in the sun need no dietary source of vitamin D, but children and adolescents in winter, and housebound adults, are recommended to take 10 g vitamin D daily.

[2] These iron recommendations may not cover heavy menstrual losses.

Source: Department of Health and Social Security

pasta food made from a dough of durum-wheat flour or semolina, water, and sometimes egg, and cooked in boiling water. Some types of Far Eastern pasta (noodles) are made from buckwheat. It is usually served with a sauce. Pasta is available either fresh or dried, and comes in a wide variety of shapes. It may be creamy yellow or coloured green with spinach or red with tomato. Pasta has been used in Italian cooking since the Middle Ages, and is now popular in many other countries.

pastry baked dough made from flour, fat, water, and salt. It makes a useful base or container for soft, moist fillings, and is widely used for tarts, pies, quiches, and pasties. Richer pastries may include eggs, yeast, or sugar, or may use ground nuts instead of flour. Types include short pastry, flaky pastry, suet crust, filo, and choux. **Puff pastry** is made with a higher proportion of fat. Its preparation involves repeated folding, which, with the fat, makes it flaky.

pepper aromatic spice derived from the berry of the climbing plant *Piper nigrum* native to the E Indies. The dried berries (peppercorns) may be crushed or ground to release their flavour, or may be used whole. Green peppercorns are berries that have been harvested while unripe, and dried or canned; black peppercorns are unripe berries that have been left to darken and shrivel in the sun; and white peppercorns are dried ripe berries that have had their outer husks removed. Black peppercorns are hotter but less aromatic than white peppercorns.

The mild pink peppercorns that became fashionable in the 1980s are the fruits of a different plant, a member of the poison ivy family. Chilli pepper, cayenne or red pepper and the sweet peppers used as a vegetable come from capsicums native to the New World.

potato tuberous root of the perennial plant *Solanum tuberosum*, native to the Andes of South America. One of the most versatile of foods, the potato is cultivated in many varieties, particularly in temperate regions. It is a good source of carbohydrate, fibre, and vitamin C, and also contains some protein, phosphates, and iron.

Potato varieties can be grouped according to when their tubers mature: *new* or *early potatoes* are gathered in the spring and summer, are generally small and waxy, and are suitable for boiling in their skins and canning; the larger *maincrop potatoes* are lifted in the autumn, are more floury in texture, and are suitable for mashing and baking, and for commercial processing into such products as frozen chips, crisps and snacks, and potato flour.

The unrelated *sweet potato*, native to tropical America, has a sweet orange or yellow flesh and is rich in vitamin A.

pulse dried seed, such as a pea, bean, or lentil, gathered from the pod of a leguminous plant. Pulses provide a concentrated source of vegetable protein, and make a vital contribution to human diets in countries where meat is scarce, and among vegetarians.

Soya beans are the major temperate protein crop in the West; most are used for oil production or for animal feed. In Asia, most are processed into soya milk and bean curd (tofu). *Miso* is soya beans fermented with cereal grains, water, and salt, used in soups and sauces; *soya sauce* is beans fermented with salt; *tamari* is similar to soya sauce but stronger, having been matured for up to two years. *Peanuts* (groundnuts), which are not true nuts but pulses grown in underground pods, dominate pulse production in the tropical world. They yield a valuable oil and form the basis for numerous processed foods, such as peanut butter. Canned *baked beans* are usually a variety of haricot bean.

rice grain of *Oryza sativa*, principal cereal of the wet regions of the tropics and grown also in the Po valley of Italy and in the USA. Boiled or ground into flour, it forms the staple food of one-third of the world's population. It is rich in carbohydrate and contains 8–9% protein. Brown, or unhusked, rice has valuable B-vitamins that are lost in husking or polishing. Most of the the rice eaten in the world is, however, sold in polished form.

salt, common or *sodium chloride* NaCl white crystalline solid, found dissolved in sea water and as rock salt (halite) in large deposits and salt domes. Common salt is used extensively in the food industry as a preservative and for flavouring. While common salt is an essential part of our diet, some medical experts believe that excess salt can lead to high blood pressure and increased risk of heart attacks.

sauce food preparation that usually is liquid or soft, taken as a relish. Sauces may be thick or thin, hot or cold, sweet or savoury. There are sauces suitable for serving with almost any dish, ranging from the simplest vinaigrette – a cold mixture of oil, vinegar, and seasonings – to cooked sauces containing cream, wine, egg yolks, or herbs. Nutritionally sauces add little to the diet unless used in large quantities. Sugar is a major ingredient in chutney, french dressing, and tomato ketchup.

shellfish any mollusc or crustacean. Many species are eaten, including the whelk, mussel, oyster, lobster, crab, and shrimp. Shellfish are high in protein and minerals. They do not keep well, and should only be used if known to be fresh. They become tough if overcooked; some are eaten raw.

spice any aromatic vegetable substance used as a condiment and for flavouring food. Spices are mostly obtained from tropical plants, and include pepper, nutmeg, ginger, and cinnamon. They have little food value but increase the appetite and may facilitate digestion.

spirit strong alcoholic liquor, distilled from the fruit, seeds, roots, or stems of certain plants. Fruit-based spirits include Calvados (apples) and brandy (grapes); grain-based spirits include whisky (malted barley, with other grains sometimes added), gin (barley, maize, or rye), sake (rice); others include rum (sugar cane) and tequila (agave). Spirits are usually matured for several years before use; they may be drunk on their own, diluted, or iced. Sake, from Japan, is usually heated before serving.

stock liquid used as a base for soups, stews, or sauces. *White stock* is made from poultry or veal, and vegetables boiled together in water. *Brown stock* is made from red meat or bones, and vegetables, browned in fat before being boiled in water.

sugar or *sucrose* sweet, soluble crystalline carbohydrate, such as sucrose, glucose, fructose, maltose, and lactose. Sugar is easily digested and forms a major source of energy in humans, being used in cooking and in the food industry as a sweetener and, in high concentrations, as a preservative. A high consumption is associated with obesity and tooth decay. In the UK, sucrose may not be used in baby foods.

The main sources of sucrose sugar are tropical sugar cane *Saccharum officinarum*, which accounts for two-thirds of production, and temperate sugar beet *Beta vulgaris*. Minor quantities are produced from the sap of maple trees, and from sorghum and date palms. Raw sugar crystals obtained by heating the juice of sugar canes are processed to form brown sugars, such as Muscovado and Demerara, or refined and sifted to produce white sugars, such as granulated, caster, and icing. The syrup that is drained away from the raw sugar is molasses; it may be processed to form golden syrup or treacle, or fermented to form rum. Molasses obtained from sugar beet juice is too bitter for human consumption.

sweetener any chemical that gives sweetness to food. Caloric sweeteners are various forms of sugar;

noncaloric, or artificial, sweeteners are used by dieters and diabetics and provide neither energy nor bulk. Sweeteners are used to make highly processed foods attractive, whether sweet or savoury. Most of the noncaloric sweeteners do not have E numbers. Questions have been raised about the long-term health effects of several artificial sweeteners. Some are banned for baby foods and for young children: thaumatin, aspartame, acesulfame-K, sorbitol, and mannitol. Cyclamate is banned in the UK and the USA; acesulfame-K is banned in the USA.

sweets confectionery made mainly from sucrose sugar. Other ingredients include glucose, milk, nuts, fat (animal and vegetable), and fruit. Boiled-sugar sweets contain sugar, glucose, colour, and flavouring, and are boiled, cooled, and shaped. *Chewing gum* consists of synthetic or vegetable gum with colour, flavouring, and sometimes sweetener added. *Toffee* and *caramel* are made from sugar, glucose, animal fat, milk, and cream or vegetable fat, heated and shaped. The USA is the biggest producer of sweets, though the UK has the highest consumption, with millions of pounds spent each year on advertising.

tea beverage made by infusing the dried leaves of the evergreen shrub *Camellia sinensis*. Known in China as early as 2737 BC, tea was first brought to Europe AD 1610 and rapidly became a fashionable drink. In 1823, it was found growing wild in N India, and plantations were later established in Assam and Sri Lanka; producers today include Africa, South America, Georgia, Azerbaijan, Indonesia, and Iran.

The young leaves and shoots of the tea plant are picked every five years; once plucked, the young leaves are spread out on shelves, and allowed to wither in a current of air for 4–18 hours. *Green teas* (from China, Taiwan, and Japan) are steamed or heated and then rolled, dried and finally graded. *Black teas* (from Ceylon and India) are macerated in rolling machines, allowed to ferment and then dried and graded. Grading is carried out according to the size of leaf. For example, some Ceylon tea grades are orange pekoe, flowery pekoe, broken orange pekoe, broken pekoe, and fannings. The latter grades dominate the black teas sold in tea bags. Black tea make up 75% of the world's trade in tea. Some teas are scented with plant oils: Earl Grey, for example, is flavoured with oil of bergamot.

Many other plants are used in herbal teas; if leaves are used fresh the infusion is called a *tisane*.

vegetable any food plant, especially leafy plants (cabbage and lettuce), roots and tubers (carrots, parsnips, and potatoes), legumes (peas, lentils, and beans), and even flowers (cauliflower, broccoli, and artichoke). Tomatoes, peppers, aubergines, and cucumbers are generally regarded as vegetables but are technically fruits. Green leafy vegetables and potatoes are good sources of vitamin C, though much is lost in cooking, and legumes are a main source of protein. Cooking softens vegetables by dissolving pectins and hemicellulose and gelatininzing starch.

vinegar sour liquid consisting of a 4% solution of acetic acid produced by the oxidation of alcohol, used to flavour food and as a preservative in pickling. *Malt vinegar* is brown and made from malted cereals; *white vinegar* is distilled from it. Other sources of vinegar include cider, wine, and honey. *Balsamic vinegar* is wine vinegar aged in wooden barrels.

wine alcoholic beverage, usually made from fermented grape pulp, although wines have also traditionally been made from many other fruits such as damsons and elderberries. *Red wine* is the product of the grape with the skin; *white wine* of the inner pulp of the grape. The sugar content is converted to ethyl alcohol by the yeast *Saccharomyces ellipsoideus*, which lives on the skin of the grape. The largest wine-producing countries are Italy, France, Russia, Georgia, Moldova, Armenia, and Spain.

For *dry wine* the fermentation is allowed to go on longer than for *sweet* or *medium*; champagne (sparkling wine from the Champagne region of France) is bottled while still fermenting, but other sparkling wines are artificially carbonated. Some wines are fortified with additional alcohol obtained from various sources, and most wines contain preservatives, some of which may cause dangerous side effects. For this reason, organic wines, containing no preservatives, have recently become popular.

Cooking methods

Cooking method	Description
moist heat	
broiling	direct heat over flame
pan broiling	heat through hot dry metal
sautéing	pan broiling with fat
deep frying	food is immersed in hot fat
shallow frying	fat is used to stop sticking
simmering	in pan with water below
boiling point	
stewing	prolonged simmering
fricaséeing	sauté and stewing
devilling	grilling or frying after
coating food	
steaming	
cooking by steam	
pressure cooking	by steam at above 100°C
under pressure	
dry heat	
baking	cooked in an oven, often with raising agent added
roasting	cooked in an oven
grilling	direct heat onto food
microwave	
microwaving	microwaves cause oscillation of food molecules, which produces heat

Nutrient loss during cooking

Cooking method	Nutrients lost
steaming	40–70% vitamin C, some vitamin B and phosphorus pressure cooking
roasting	10–30% thiamin
baking	a little vitamins B and C
microwaving	some vitamins B and C
dry heat	20–30% vitamin B

A *vintage wine* is produced during a good year (as regards quality of wine, produced by favourable weather conditions) in recognized vineyards of a particular area; France has a guarantee of origin (*appellation controlée*), as do Italy (*Denominazione di Origine Controllata*), Spain (*Denominación Controllata*), and Germany (a series of graded qualities running from *Qualitätswein* to *Beerenauslese*).

The greatest alcohol concentration that yeasts can tolerate is 16%; most wines have an alcohol content of 10–12%. Tannin in the skin imparts a bitter taste to the wine.

wine, fortified wine that has extra alcohol added to raise its alcohol content to about 20%. Fortified wines keep well because the alcohol kills the microorganisms that spoil natural wines. Port, which originates from Oporto in Portugal, is made by adding brandy to wine before fermentation is complete; sherry, originally made in Jerez in Spain, is a dry wine fortified after fermentation and later blended with sugar for sweet sherry; vermouth is flavoured with bitter herbs. Marsala, from Sicily, is fortified after fermentation and then heated gradually.

yoghurt or *yogurt* or *yoghourt* semi-solid curdlike dairy product made from milk fermented with bacteria. It was originally made by nomadic tribes of Central Asia from mare's milk in leather pouches attached to their saddles. It is drunk plain throughout the Asian and Mediterranean region, to which it spread, but honey, sugar, and fruit were added in Europe and the USA, and the product made solid and creamy, to be eaten with a spoon.

Heat-treated, homogenized milk is inoculated with a culture of *Streptococcus lactis* and *Lactobacillus bulgaricus* in equal amounts, which change the lactose in the milk to lactic acid. Acetaldehyde gives yoghurt its characteristic flavour. Commercially, fruit, flavourings, and colouring and thickening agents are added to the fermented yoghurt.

Food Technology

Food technology is the commercial processing of foodstuffs in order to render them more palatable or digestible, or to preserve them from spoilage. Food spoils because of the action of enzymes within the food that change its chemical composition, or because of the growth of bacteria, moulds, yeasts, and other microorganisms. Fatty or oily foods also suffer oxidation of the fats, giving them an unpleasant rancid flavour. Traditional forms of processing include boiling, frying, flour-milling, bread-making, yoghurt- and cheese-making, brewing, and various methods of *food preservation*, such as salting, smoking, pickling, drying, bottling, and preserving in sugar. Modern food technology still employs traditional methods, but also uses many novel processes and additives, which allow a wider range of foodstuffs to be preserved.

additive any natural or artificial chemical added to prolong the shelf life of processed foods, alter the colour or flavour of food, or improve its nutritional value. Many additives are used and they are subject to regulation, since individuals may be affected by constant exposure even to traces of certain chemicals,

and may suffer side effects ranging from headaches and hyperactivity to cancer. Additives approved for use throughout the European Community are given an official E number. (See table on following page.)

flavours are used to alter or intensify a food's taste. They may be natural or artificial, and include artificial sweeteners. They are more numerous and less controlled than other additives.

enhancers heighten the flavour or smell of foods without imparting their own taste – for example, monosodium glutamate (MSG).

colourings enhance the visual appeal of foods.

nutrients enhance food value or replace nutrients lost in processing.

preservatives slow down the rate of spoilage by controlling the growth of bacteria and fungi.

antioxidants prevent fatty foods from going rancid by inhibiting their natural oxidation.

emulsifiers and *stabilizers* modify the texture and consistency of food, and prevent the ingredients of a mixture from separating out.

leavening agents are substances other than yeast that lighten the texture of baked products – for example, sodium bicarbonate.

acidulants sharpen the taste of foods but may also perform a buffering function in the control of acidity.

bleaching agents whiten flours.

anticaking agents prevent powdered products from coagulating into solid lumps.

humectants control the humidity of foods by absorbing and retaining moisture.

clarifying agents are used in fruit juices, vinegars, and other fermented liquids. Gelatin is the most common.

firming agents restore the texture of vegetables that may be damaged during processing.

foam regulators may be used in beer to provide a controlled 'head' on top of the poured product.

canning preservation of food in hermetically sealed steel, aluminium, or plastic containers (cans) by the application of heat. The high temperature destroys microorganisms and enzymes, and the can's seal prevents recontamination. Beverages may also be canned to preserve the carbon dioxide that makes drinks fizzy.

curing method of preserving meat by soaking it in salt (sodium chloride) solution, with saltpetre (sodium nitrate) added to give the meat its pink colour and characteristic taste. The nitrates in cured meats are converted to nitrites and nitrosamines by bacteria, and these are potentially carcinogenic to humans.

deep freezing method of preserving food by lowering its temperature to –18°C/0°F or below. It stops almost all spoilage processes, although there may be some residual enzyme activity in uncooked vegetables, which is why these are blanched (dipped in hot water to destroy the enzymes) before freezing. Microorganisms cannot grow or divide while frozen, but most remain alive and can resume activity once defrosted. Commercial techniques freeze foods rapidly in order to prevent the growth of large ice crystals, which would damage the food tissue on thawing.

E numbers

A selection of food additives authorized by the European Commission

Number	Name	Typical use
Colours		
E102	tartrazine	soft drinks
E104	quinoline yellow	
E110	sunset yellow	biscuits
E120	cochineal	alcoholic drinks
E122	carmoisine	jams and preserves
E123	amaranth	
E124	ponceau 4R	dessert mixes
E127	erythrosine	glacé cherries
E131	patent blue V	
E132	indigo carmine	
E142	green S	pastilles
E150	caramel	beers, soft drinks, sauces, gravy browning
E151	black PN	
E160 (b)	annatto; bixin; norbixin	crisps
E180	pigment rubine (lithol rubine BK)	

Antioxidants

E310	propyl gallate	vegetable oils; chewing gum
E311	octyl gallate	
E312	dodecyl gallate	
E320	butylated hydroxynisole (BHA)	beef stock cubes; cheese spread
E321	butylated hydroxytoluene (BHT)	chewing gum

Emulsifiers and Stabilizers

E407	carageenan	quick-setting jelly mixes; milk shakes
E413	tragacanth	salad dressings; processed cheese

Preservatives

E210	benzoic acid	
E211	sodium benzoate	beer, jam, salad cream, soft drinks, fruit pulp
E212	potassium benzoate	fruit-based pie fillings, marinated herring and mackerel
E213	calcium benzoate	
E214	ethyl para-hydroxy-benzoate	
E215	sodium ethyl para-hydroxy-benzoate	
E216	propyl para-hydroxy-benzoate	
E217	sodium propyl para-hydroxy-benzoate	
E218	methyl para-hydroxy-benzoate	
E220	sulphur dioxide	
E221	sodium sulphate	dried fruit, dehydrated vegetables, fruit juices and syrups,
E222	sodium bisulphite	sausages, fruit-based dairy desserts, cider, beer,
E223	sodium metabisulphite	and wine; also used to prevent browning of
E224	potassium metabisulphite	peeled potatoes and to condition biscuit doughs
E226	calcium sulphite	
E227	calcium bisulphite	
E249	potassium nitrite	
E250	sodium nitrite	bacon, ham, cured meats, corned beef and some cheeses
E251	sodium nitrate	
E252	potassium nitrate	

Others

E450 (a)	disodium dihydrogen diphosphate	butters, sequestrants,
	trisodium diphosphate	emulsifying salts,
	tetrasodium diphosphate	stabilizers, texturizers
	tetrapotassium diphosphate	raising agents, used in whipping cream, fish and meat
E450 (b)	pentasodium triphosphate	products, bread, processed cheese, canned vegetables
	pentapotassium triphosphate	

dehydration preservation of food by reducing its moisture content by 80% or more. It inhibits the activity of moulds and bacteria, and reduces the mass and volume of foods, thereby lowering distribution costs. Products such as dried milk and instant coffee are made by spraying the liquid into a rising column of dry, heated air.

freeze-drying method of preserving food by freezing it and then placing it in a vacuum chamber so that the ice is forced out as water vapour. Many of the substances that give products such as coffee their typical flavour are volatile, and would be lost in a normal drying process because they would evaporate along with the water. In the freeze-drying process these volatile compounds do not pass into the ice that is to be sublimed, and are therefore largely retained.

hydrogenation method by which liquid oils are transformed into solid products, such as margarine. Vegetable oils contain double carbon-to-carbon bonds and are therefore examples of unsaturated compounds. When hydrogen is added to these double bonds, the oils become saturated and more solid in consistency.

irradiation method of preserving food by subjecting it to low-level gamma radiation in order to kill microorganisms. Although the process is now legal in several countries, uncertainty remains about possible long-term effects on consumers from irradiated food. The process does not make the food radioactive, but some vitamins, such as vitamin C, are destroyed and many molecular changes take place including the initiation of free radicals, which may be further changed into a range of unknown and unstable chemicals. Irradiation also eradicates the smell, taste, and poor appearance of bad or ageing food products.

pasteurization treatment of food to reduce the number of microorganisms it contains and so protect consumers from disease. Harmful bacteria are killed and the development of others is delayed. For milk, the method involves heating it to 72°C/161°F for 15 seconds followed by rapid cooling to 10°C/50°F or lower. However, the process also kills beneficial bacteria and reduces the nutritive property of milk.

pickling method of preserving food by soaking it in acetic acid (found in vinegar), which stops the growth of moulds. In sauerkraut, lactic acid, produced by bacteria, has the same effect.

puffing method of processing cereal grains. The grains are first subjected to high pressures, and then suddenly ejected into a normal atmospheric pressure, causing each grain to expand sharply. This type of process is used to make puffed wheat cereals and puffed rice cakes.

refrigeration method of preserving food by lowering its temperature to below 5°C/41°F (or below 3°C/37°F for cooked foods). It slows the processes of spoilage, but is less effective for foods with a high water content. Although a convenient form of preservation, this process cannot kill microorganisms, nor stop their growth completely, and a failure to realize its limitations causes many cases of food poisoning. Refrigerator temperatures should be checked as the efficiency of the machinery can decline with age.

smoking method of preserving fresh oily meats (such as pork and goose) or fish (such as herring and salmon). Before being smoked, the food is first salted or soaked in brine, then hung to dry. Meat is hot-smoked over a fast-burning wood fire, which is covered with sawdust, producing thick smoke and partly cooking the meat. Fish may be hot-smoked or cold-smoked over a slow-burning wood fire, which does not cook it. Modern refrigeration techniques mean that food does not need to be smoked to help it keep, so factory-smoked foods tend to be smoked just enough to give them a smoky flavour, with colours added to give them the appearance of traditionally smoked food. The smoke itself may contain harmful substances.

ultra-heat treatment (UHT) preservation of milk by raising its temperature to 132°C/269°F or more. It uses higher temperatures than pasteurization, and kills all bacteria present, giving the milk a long shelf life but altering the flavour.

Agriculture

agriculture the practice of farming, including the cultivation of the soil (for raising crops) and the raising of domesticated animals. Crops are for human nourishment, animal fodder, or commodities such as cotton and sisal. Animals are raised for wool, milk, leather, dung (as fuel), or meat. The units for managing agricultural production vary from smallholdings and individually owned farms to corporate-run farms and collective farms run by entire communities.

Agriculture developed in the Middle East and Egypt at least 10,000 years ago. Farming communities soon became the base for society in China, India, Europe, Mexico, and Peru, then spread throughout the world. Reorganization along more scientific and productive lines took place in Europe in the 18th century in response to dramatic population growth.

Mechanization made considerable progress in the USA and Europe during the 19th century. After World War II, there was an explosive growth in the use of agricultural chemicals: herbicides, insecticides, fungicides, and fertilizers. In the 1960s there was development of high-yielding species, especially in the *green revolution* of the Third World, and the industrialized countries began intensive farming of cattle, poultry, and pigs. In the 1980s, hybridization by genetic engineering methods and pest control by the use of chemicals and pheromones were developed. However, there was also a reaction against some forms of intensive agriculture because of the pollution and habitat destruction caused. One result of this was a growth of alternative methods, including organic farming.

overproduction The greater efficiency in agriculture achieved since the 19th century, coupled with government subsidies for domestic production in the USA and the European Community (EC), have led to the development of high stocks, nicknamed 'lakes' (wine, milk) and 'mountains' (butter, beef, grain). The overall cost of bulk transport and the potential destabilization of other economies has acted against high producers exporting their excess on a regular basis to needy countries.

agricultural revolution sweeping changes that took place in British agriculture over the period

1750–1850 in response to the increased demand for food from a rapidly expanding population. Changes of the latter half of the 18th century included the enclosure of open fields, the introduction of four-course rotation together with new fodder crops such as turnips, and the development of improved breeds of livestock.

agrochemical artificially produced chemical used in modern, intensive agricultural systems. Agro-chemicals include nitrate and phosphate fertilizers, pesticides, some animal-feed additives, and pharmaceuticals. Many are responsible for pollution and almost all are avoided by organic farmers.

agronomy study of crops and soils, a branch of agricultural science. Agronomy includes such topics as selective breeding (of plants and animals), irrigation, pest control, and soil analysis and modification.

aquaculture or *fish farming* raising fish and shellfish (molluscs and crustaceans) under controlled conditions in tanks and ponds, sometimes in offshore pens. It has been practised for centuries in the Far East, where Japan alone produces some 100,000 tonnes of fish a year. In the 1980s, one-tenth of the world's consumption of fish and shellfish was farmed, notably carp, catfish, trout, salmon, turbot, eel, mussels, clams, oysters, and shrimp.

artificial insemination (AI) fertilization of animals by means of introducing (by instrument) semen from a sperm bank or donor into the female reproductive tract to bring about fertilization. AI is used by animal breeders to improve stock with sperm from high-quality males.

bovine spongiform encephalopathy (BSE) or *mad cow disease* disease of cattle, allied to scrapie, that renders the brain spongy and may drive an animal mad. It has been identified only in the UK, where it was first diagnosed in Nov 1986 and 12,900 cases were confirmed between June 1992 and June 1993. The organism causing it is unknown, but the source of the disease has been traced to manufactured protein feed incorporating the rendered brains of scrapie-infected sheep. BSE is very similar to, and may be related to, Creutzfeld-Jakob disease and kuru, which affect humans.

cash crop crop grown solely for sale rather than for the farmer's own use; for example, coffee, cotton, and sugar beet. Many Third World countries grow cash crops to meet their debt repayments rather than grow food for their own people. The price for these crops depends on financial interests, such as those of the multinational companies and the International Monetary Fund.

cattle any large, ruminant, even-toed, hoofed mammal of the genus *Bos*, family Bovidae. Cattle are bred for meat (beef cattle) or milk (dairy cattle). Fermentation in the four-chambered stomach allows cattle to make good use of the grass that is normally the main part of the diet. There are two main types of domesticated cattle: the European breeds and the various breeds of zebu *Bos indicus*, the humped cattle of India.

The old-established beef breeds are mostly British in origin. The Hereford, for example, is the premier English breed; ideally suited to rich lowland pastures,

it will also thrive on poorer land such as that found in the US Midwest and the Argentine pampas. Of the Scottish beef breeds, the Aberdeen Angus, a black and hornless variety, produces high-quality meat through intensive feeding methods. Other British breeds include the Devon, a hardy early-maturing type, and the Beef Shorthorn. Other European breeds tend to have less fat and are more suited to modern tastes. Examples include the Charolais and the Limousin from central France, and the Simmental, originally from Switzerland.

For dairying purposes, a breed raised in many countries is variously known as the Friesian, Holstein, or Black and White. It can give enormous milk yields, up to 13,000 l/3,450 gal in a single lactation, and will produce calves ideally suited for intensive beef production. Other dairying types include the Jersey and Guernsey, whose milk has a high butterfat content, and the Ayrshire, a smaller breed capable of staying outside all year.

cereal grass grown for its edible, nutrient-rich, starchy seeds. The term refers primarily to wheat, oats, rye, and barley, but may also refer to corn, millet, and rice. Cereals contain about 75% complex carbohydrates and 10% protein, plus fats and fibre (roughage). They store well. If all the world's cereal crop were consumed as whole-grain products directly by humans, everyone could obtain adequate protein and carbohydrate; however, a large proportion of cereal production in affluent nations is used as animal feed to boost the production of meat, dairy products, and eggs.

collective farm farm in which a group of farmers pool their land, domestic animals, and agricultural implements, retaining as private property enough only for the members' own requirements. The profits of the farm are divided among its members. In *cooperative farming*, farmers retain private ownership of the land.

combine harvester or *combine* machine used for harvesting cereals and other crops, so called because it combines the actions of reaping (cutting the crop) and threshing (beating the ears so that the grain separates).

Common Agricultural Policy (CAP) system that allows the member countries of the European Community (EC) jointly to organize and control agricultural production within their boundaries. The objectives of the CAP were outlined in the Treaty of Rome: to increase agricultural productivity, to provide a fair standard of living for farmers and their employees, to stabilize markets, and to assure the availability of supply at a price that was reasonable to the consumer. The CAP is increasingly criticized for its role in creating overproduction, and consequent environmental damage, and for the high price of food subsidies.

crop rotation system of regularly changing the crops grown on a piece of land. The crops are grown in a particular order to utilize and add to the nutrients in the soil and to prevent the build-up of insect and fungal pests. Including a legume crop, such as peas or beans, in the rotation helps build up nitrate in the soil because the roots contain bacteria capable of fixing nitrogen from the air.

dairying the business of producing milk and milk products. It is now usual for dairy farms to concentrate on the production of milk and for factories to take over the handling, processing, and distribution of milk as well as the manufacture of dairy products. In Britain, the Milk Marketing Board (1933), to which all producers must sell their milk, forms a connecting link between farms and factories.

deer farming method of producing venison through the controlled breeding and rearing of deer on farms rather than hunting them in the wild. British deer-farming enterprises have been growing in number as more farmers seek to diversify into new sources of income. The meat is sold largely to the restaurant trade, and there is a market for the antlers and skin.

factory farming intensive rearing of poultry or animals for food, usually on high-protein foodstuffs in confined quarters. Chickens for eggs and meat, and calves for veal are commonly factory farmed. Some countries restrict the use of antibiotics and growth hormones as aids to factory farming, because they can persist in the flesh of the animals after they are slaughtered. Many people object to factory farming for moral as well as health reasons.

fallow land ploughed and tilled, but left unsown for a season to allow it to recuperate. In Europe, it is associated with the medieval three-field system. It is used in some modern crop rotations.

fertilizer substance containing some or all of a range of about 20 chemical elements necessary for healthy plant growth, used to compensate for the deficiencies of poor or depleted soil. Fertilizers may be *organic*, for example farmyard manure, composts, bonemeal, blood, and fishmeal; or *inorganic*, in the form of compounds, mainly of nitrogen, phosphate, and potash.

fibre crop plant that is grown for the fibres that can be extracted from its tissues. Temperate areas produce flax and hemp; tropical and subtropical areas produce cotton, jute, and sisal. Cotton dominates fibre-crop production.

field enclosed area of land used for farming. Twentieth-century developments in agricultural science and technology have encouraged farmers to amalgamate and enlarge their fields, often to as much as 40 hectares/100 acres.

fish farming aquaculture; the cultivation of fish and shellfish for human consumption.

foot-and-mouth disease contagious eruptive viral disease of cloven-hoofed mammals, characterized by blisters in the mouth and around the hooves. In cattle it causes deterioration of milk yield and abortions. The virus is airborne, which makes its eradication extremely difficult.

In the UK, affected herds are destroyed; inoculation is practised in Europe, and in the USA, a vaccine was developed in the 1980s.

forage crop plant that is grown to feed livestock; for example, grass, clover, and kale (a form of cabbage). Forage crops cover a greater area of the world than food crops, and grass, which dominates this group, is the world's most abundant crop, though much of it is still in an unimproved state.

game farming protected rearing of gamebirds such as pheasants, partridges, and grouse for subsequent shooting. Game farms provide plenty of woodland and brush, which the birds require for cover, and may also plant special crops for them to feed on.

green revolution popular term for the change in methods of arable farming in Third World countries. The intent is to provide more and better food for their populations, by use of crop varieties (especially wheat and rice) giving higher yields, albeit with a heavy reliance on chemicals and machinery. It was instigated in the 1940s and 1950s, but abandoned by some countries in the 1980s. Much of the food produced is exported as cash crops, so that local diet does not always improve.

harrow agricultural implement used to break up the furrows left by the plough and reduce the soil to a fine consistency or tilth, and to cover the seeds after sowing. The traditional harrow consists of spikes set in a frame; modern harrows use sets of discs.

hay preserved grass used for winter livestock feed. The grass is cut and allowed to dry in the field before being removed for storage in a barn. The optimum period for cutting is when the grass has just come into flower and contains most feed value. One hectare/2.47 acres of grass can produce up to 7.5 tonnes/7.3 tons of hay.

herbicide weedkiller; any chemical used to destroy plants or check their growth.

horticulture art and science of growing flowers, fruit, and vegetables. The growth of industrial towns in the 19th century led to the development of commercial horticulture in the form of nurseries and market gardens, pioneering methods such as glasshouses, artificial heat, herbicides, and pesticides, synthetic fertilizers, and machinery. In Britain, over 500,000 acres/200,000 hectares are devoted to commercial horticulture; vegetables account for almost three-quarters of the produce.

hydroponics cultivation of plants without soil, using specially prepared solutions of mineral salts. Beginning in the 1930s, large crops were grown by hydroponic methods, at first in California but since then in many other parts of the world.

insecticide any chemical pesticide used to kill insects. Among the most effective insecticides are synthetic organic chemicals such as DDT and dieldrin, which are chlorinated hydrocarbons. These chemicals, however, have proved persistent in the environment and are also poisonous to all animal life, including humans, and are consequently banned in many countries. Other synthetic insecticides include organic phosphorus compounds such as malathion. Insecticides prepared from plants, such as derris and pyrethrum, are safer to use but need to be applied frequently and carefully.

irrigation artificial water supply for dry agricultural areas by means of dams and channels. Drawbacks are that it tends to concentrate salts, ultimately causing infertility, and that rich river silt is retained at dams, to the impoverishment of the land and fisheries below them.

legume plant of the family Leguminosae, which has a pod containing dry seeds. The family includes peas, beans, lentils, clover, and alfalfa (lucerne). Legumes are important in agriculture because of their specialized roots, which have nodules containing bacteria capable of fixing nitrogen from the air and increasing the fertility of the soil. The edible seeds of legumes are called *pulses*.

ley area of temporary grassland, sown to produce grazing and hay or silage for a period of one to ten years before being ploughed and cropped. Short-term leys are often incorporated in systems of crop rotation.

milking machine machine that uses suction to milk cows. The first milking machine was invented in the USA by L O Colvin in 1860. Later it was improved so that the suction was regularly released by a pulsating device, since it was found that continuous suction is harmful to cows.

monoculture farming system where only one crop is grown. In Third World countries this is often a cash crop, grown on plantations. Cereal crops in the industrialized world are also frequently grown on a monoculture basis; for example, wheat in the Canadian prairies.

oil crop plant from which vegetable oils are pressed from the seeds. Cool temperate areas grow rapeseed and linseed; warm temperate regions produce sunflowers, olives, and soya beans; tropical regions produce groundnuts (peanuts), palm oil, and coconuts. Some of the major vegetable oils, such as soya bean oil, peanut oil, and cottonseed oil, are derived from crops grown primarily for other purposes. Most vegetable oils are used as both edible oils and as ingredients in industrial products such as soaps, varnishes, printing inks, and paints.

organic farming farming without the use of synthetic fertilizers (such as nitrates and phosphates) or pesticides (herbicides, insecticides, and fungicides) or other agrochemicals (such as hormones, growth stimulants, or fruit regulators). In place of artificial fertilizers, compost, manure, seaweed, or other substances derived from living things are used (hence the name 'organic'). Growing a crop of a nitrogen-fixing plant such as lucerne, then ploughing it back into the soil, also fertilizes the ground. Pest-control methods include removal by hand, intercropping (planting with companion plants which deter pests), mechanical barriers to infestation, crop rotation, better cultivation methods, and biological control. Weeds can be controlled by hoeing, mulching (covering with manure, straw, or black plastic), or burning off. Organic farming methods produce food with minimal pesticide residues and greatly reduce pollution of the environment. They are more labour-intensive, and therefore more expensive, but use less fossil fuel. Soil structure is greatly improved by organic methods.

pesticide any chemical used in farming, gardening or indoors to combat pests. Pesticides are of three main types: *insecticides* (to kill insects), *fungicides* (to kill fungal diseases), and *herbicides* (to kill plants, mainly those considered weeds). Pesticides cause a number of pollution problems through spray drift onto surrounding areas, direct contamination of users or the public, and as residues on food. The safest pesticides are those made from plants, such as the insecticides pyrethrum and derris.

pig even-toed hoofed mammal of the family Suidae. Pigs are omnivorous, and have simple, non-ruminating stomachs and thick hides. More than 400 varieties have been bred over the centuries, many of which have all but disappeared with the development of intensive rearing systems.

The Berkshire, Chester White, Poland, China, Saddleback, Yorkshire, Duroc, and Razorback are the main surviving breeds. Modern indoor rearing methods favour the large white breeds, such as the Chester White and the originally Swedish Landrace, over coloured varieties, which tend to be hardier and can survive better outdoors. Since 1960, hybrid pigs, produced by crossing two or more breeds, have become popular for their heavy but lean carcasses.

plough agricultural implement used for tilling the soil. The plough dates from about 3500 BC, when oxen were used to pull a simple wooden blade. The modern plough consists of many 'bottoms', each comprising a curved ploughshare and angled mouldboard. The bottom is designed so that it slices into the ground and turns the soil over.

poultry domestic birds such as chickens, turkeys, ducks, and geese. Good egg-laying breeds of chicken are Leghorns, Minorcas, and Anconas; varieties most suitable for eating are Dorkings, Australorps, Brahmas, and Cornish; those useful for both purposes are Orpingtons, Rhode Island Reds, Wyandottes, Plymouth Rocks, and Jersey White Giants. Most farm poultry are hybrids, selectively crossbred for certain characteristics, including feathers and down.

Factory farming has doubled egg yields and increased the availability of poultry meat. The birds are often kept constantly in small cages, have their beaks and claws removed to prevent them from pecking their neighbours, and are given feed containing growth hormones and antibacterial drugs, which eventually make their way up the food chain to humans. Deep-litter and free-range systems account for only a small percentage of total production.

root crop plant cultivated for its swollen edible root (which may or may not be a true root). Potatoes are the major temperate root crop; the major tropical root crops are cassava, yams, and sweet potatoes. Root crops are second in importance only to cereals as human food. Roots have a high carbohydrate content, but their protein content rarely exceeds 2%. Consequently, communities relying almost exclusively upon roots may suffer from protein deficiency. Food production for a given area from roots is greater than from cereals.

scrapie fatal disease of sheep and goats that attacks the central nervous system, causing deterioration of the brain cells. It is believed to be caused by a submicroscopic organism known as a prion and may be related to bovine spongiform encephalopathy (mad cow disease).

scythe harvesting tool with long wooden handle and sharp, curving blade. It is similar to a sickle. The scythe was in common use in the Middle East and Europe from the dawn of agriculture until the early 20th century, by which time it had generally been replaced by machinery.

seed drill machine for sowing cereals and other seeds, developed by Jethro Tull (1674–1741) in Eng-

Agriculture: chronology

10,000–8000BC	Holocene (post-glacial) period of hunters and gatherers. Harvesting and storage of wild grains in SW Asia. Herding of reindeer in N Eurasia. Domestic sheep in N Iraq.
8000	Neolithic revolution with cultivation of domesticated wheats and barleys, sheep, and goats in SW Asia. Domestication of pigs in New Guinea.
7000–6000	Domestic goats, sheep, and cattle in Anatolia, Greece, Persia, and the Caspian basin. Planting and harvesting techniques transferred from Asia Minor to Europe.
5000	Beginning of Nile valley civilization. Millet cultivated in China.
3400	Flax used for textiles in Egypt. Widespread corn production in the Americas.
3200	Records of ploughing, raking, and manuring, by Egyptians.
c. 3100	River Nile dammed during the rule of King Menes.
3000	First record of asses used as beasts of burden in Egypt. Sumerian civilization used barley as main crop with wheat, dates, flax, apples, plums, and grapes.
2900	Domestication of pigs in E Asia.
2640	Reputed start of Chinese silk industry.
2500	Domestic elephants in the Indus valley. Potatoes a staple crop in Peru.
2350	Wine-making in Egypt.
2250	First known irrigation dam.
1600	Important advances in the cultivation of vines and olives in Crete.
1500	*Shadoof* (mechanism for raising water) used for irrigation in Egypt.
1400	Iron ploughshares in use in India.
1300	Aqueducts and reservoirs used for irrigation in Egypt.
1200	Domestic camels in Arabia.
1000–500	Evidence of crop rotation, manuring and irrigation in India.
600	First windmills used for corn grinding in Persia.
350	Rice cultivation well established in parts of W Africa. Hunting and gathering in the E, central, and S parts of the continent.
c. 200	Use of gears to create ox-driven water wheel for irrigation. Archimedes screw used for irrigation.
100	Cattle drawn iron ploughs in use in China.
AD 65	*De Re Rustica/On Rural Things*, Latin treatise on agriculture and irrigation.
500	'Three fields in two years' rotation used in China.
630	Cotton introduced into Arabia.
800	Origins of the 'open field' system in N Europe.
900	Wheeled ploughs in use in W Europe. Horse collar, originating in China, allowed horses to be used for ploughing as well as carrying.
1000	Frisians (NW Netherlanders) began to build dykes and reclaim land. Chinese began to introduce Champa rice which cropped much more quickly than other varieties.
11th century	Three field system replaced the two field system in W Europe. Concentration on crop growing.
1126	First artesian wells, at Artois, France.
12th century	Increasing use of water mills and windmills. Horses replaced oxen for pulling work in many areas.
12th–14th centuries	Expansion of European population brought more land into cultivation. Crop rotations, manuring, and new crops such as beans and peas helped increase productivity. Feudal system at its height.
13th–14th centuries	Agricultural recession in W Europe with a series of bad harvests, famines, and pestilence.
1347	Black Death killed about a third of the European population.
16th century	Decline of the feudal system in W Europe. More specialist forms of production were now possible with urban markets. Manorial estates and serfdom remained in E Europe. Chinese began cultivation of non-indigenous crops such as corn, sweet potatoes, potatoes, and peanuts.
17th century	Potato introduced into Europe. Norfolk crop rotation became widespread in England, involving wheat, turnips, barley and then ryegrass/clover.
1700–1845	Agricultural revolution began in Britain. Two million hectares of farmland in England enclosed. Removal of open fields in other parts of Europe followed.
c. 1701	Jethro Tull developed the seed drill and the horse-drawn hoe.
1747	First sugar extracted from sugar beet in Prussia.
1762	Veterinary school founded in Lyon, France.
1783	First plough factory in England.
1785	Cast-iron ploughshare patented.
1793	Invention of the cotton gin.
1800	Early threshing machines developed in England.
1820s	First nitrates for fertilizer imported from S America.
1830	Reaping machines developed in Scotland and the US. Steel plough made by John Deere in Illinois, US.

Agriculture: chronology *(cont.)*

1840s	Extensive potato blight in Europe.
1850s	Use of clay pipes for drainage well established throughout Europe.
1862	First steam plough used in the Netherlands.
1850–1890s	Major developments in transport and refrigeration technology altered the nature of agricultural markets with crops, dairy products, and wheat being shipped internationally.
1890s	Development of stationary engines for ploughing.
1892	First petrol-driven tractor in the USA.
1921	First attempt at crop dusting with pesticides from an aeroplane near Dayton, Ohio, US.
1938	First self-propelled grain combine harvester used in the USA.
1942–62	Huge increase in the uses of pesticides, later curbed by disquiet about their effects and increasing resistance of pests to standard controls such as DDT.
1945 onwards	Increasing use of scientific techniques, crop specialization, and larger scale of farm enterprises throughout N America and W Europe.

land 1701. The seed is stored in a hopper and delivered by tubes into furrows in the ground. The furrows are made by a set of blades, or coulters, attached to the front of the drill. A harrow is drawn behind the drill to cover up the seeds.

sheep ruminant, even-toed, hoofed mammal of the family Bovidae. The domesticated breeds are all classified as *Ovis aries*. Various breeds of sheep are reared worldwide for meat, wool, milk, and cheese, and for rotation on arable land to maintain its fertility.

Over 50 varieties of sheep were bred in the UK, but only a small proportion are still in full commercial use. They are grouped into three principal categories. The hardy *upland* breeds, such as the Scottish Blackface and Welsh Mountain, are able to survive in a bleak, rugged environment. The *shortwool* varieties, such as the Down breeds of Hampshire and Suffolk, are well adapted to thrive on the lush grassland of lowland areas. *Longwool* breeds, such as the Leicesters and Border Leicesters, were originally bred for their coarse, heavy fleeces, but are now crossed with hill-sheep flocks to produce fat lambs. In 1989, there were 41 million sheep in Britain, making Britain the main producer of lambs in Europe.

silage fodder preserved through controlled fermentation in a silo, an airtight structure that presses green crops. It is used as a winter feed for livestock. The term also refers to stacked crops that may be preserved indefinitely.

subsistence farming farming when the produce is enough to feed only the farmer and family and there is no surplus to sell.

tenant farming system whereby farmers rent their holdings from a landowner in return for the use of agricultural land.

threshing agricultural process of separating cereal grains from the plant. Traditionally, the work was carried out by hand in winter months using the flail, a jointed beating stick. Today, threshing is done automatically inside the combine harvester at the time of cutting.

topsoil the upper, cultivated layer of soil, which may vary in depth from 8 to 45 cm/3 to 18 in. It contains organic matter – the decayed remains of vegetation, which plants need for active growth – along with a variety of soil organisms, including earthworms.

tractor powerful motor vehicle, commonly having large rear wheels or caterpillar tracks, used for pulling farm machinery and loads. It is usually powered by a diesel engine and has a power-takeoff mechanism for driving machinery, and a hydraulic lift for raising and lowering implements.

LIFE SCIENCES

Evolutionary Biology

adaptation any change in the structure or function of an organism that allows it to survive and reproduce more effectively in its environment. In evolution, adaptation is thought to occur as a result of random variation in the genetic make-up of organisms (produced by mutation and recombination) coupled with natural selection.

artificial selection selective breeding of individuals that exhibit the particular characteristics that a plant or animal breeder wishes to develop. In plants, desirable features might include resistance to disease, high yield (in crop plants), or attractive appearance. In animal breeding, selection has led to the development of particular breeds of cattle for improved meat production (such as the Aberdeen Angus) or milk production (such as Jerseys).

cladistics method of biological classification (taxonomy) that uses a formal step-by-step procedure for objectively assessing the extent to which organisms share particular characters, and for assigning them to taxonomic groups. Taxonomic groups (for example, species, genus, family) are termed *clades*.

competition interaction between two or more organisms, or groups of organisms (for example, species), that use a common resource which is in short supply. Competition invariably results in a reduction in the numbers of one or both competitors, and in evolution, contributes both to the decline of certain species and to the evolution of adaptations.

convergent evolution independent evolution of similar structures in species (or other taxonomic groups) that are not closely related, as a result of living in a similar way. Thus, birds and bats have wings, not because they are descended from a common winged ancestor, but because their respective ancestors independently evolved flight.

evolution slow process of change from one form to another, as in the evolution of the universe from its formation in the Big Bang to its present state, or in the evolution of life on Earth. The current theory of the latter is called neo-Darwinism.

extinction the complete disappearance of a species. In the past, extinctions are believed to have occurred because species were unable to adapt quickly enough to a naturally changing environment. Today, most extinctions are due to human activity – hunting and habitat destruction. Conservative estimates put the rate of loss due to deforestation alone at 4,000 to 6,000 species a year. Overall, the rate could be as high as one species an hour. Those known to be at risk are called endangered species. (See *Environment* for more.)

human species, origins of evolution of humans from ancestral primates. Molecular studies put the date of the split between the human and African ape lines at 5–10 million years ago. The oldest known fossils of hominids (creatures of the human group), *Australopithecus afarensis*, found in Ethiopia and Tanzania, date from 3.5 to 4 million years ago. They may have been the ancestors of *Homo habilis*, probably the first to use stone tools. Over 1.5 million years ago, *Homo erectus*, believed by some to be descended from *H. habilis*, appeared. They were probably the first to use fire and the first to move out of Africa. Modern humans *Homo sapiens sapiens* evolved from *H. erectus* about 200,000 years ago, either in Africa or in different parts of the world at around the same time.

Lamarckism theory of evolution, now discredited, advocated during the early 19th century by French naturalist Jean Baptiste Lamarck. He believed that acquired characteristics were inherited; for example, that giraffes had lengthened their necks by stretching and passed this characteristic on to their offspring.

mutation change in the genes produced by a change in the DNA that makes up the hereditary material of all living organisms. Mutations, the raw material of evolution, result from mistakes during replication (copying) of DNA molecules. Only a few improve the organism's performance and are therefore favoured by natural selection. Mutation rates are increased by certain chemicals and by radiation.

natural selection the process whereby gene frequencies in a population change through certain individuals producing more descendants than others because they are better able to survive and reproduce in their environment. The accumulated effect of natural selection is to produce adaptations such as the insulating coat of a polar bear or the spadelike forelimbs of a mole. The process is slow, relying firstly on random variation in the genes of an organism being produced by mutation and secondly on the genetic recombination of sexual reproduction. It was recognized by English naturalists Charles Darwin and Alfred Russel Wallace as the main process driving evolution.

neo-Darwinism the modern theory of evolution, built up since the 1930s by integrating 19th-century English scientist Charles Darwin's theory of evolution through natural selection with the theory of genetic inheritance founded on the work of Austrian biologist Gregor Mendel.

phylogeny historical sequence of changes that occurs in a given species during the course of its evolution. It was once erroneously associated with ontogeny (the process of development of a living organism).

punctuated equilibrium model evolutionary theory developed by Niles Eldridge and US palaeontologist Stephen Jay Gould 1972 to explain discontinuities in the fossil record. It claims that periods of rapid change alternate with periods of relative stability (stasis), and that the appearance of new lineages is a separate process from the gradual evolution of adaptive changes within a species.

saltation the idea that an abrupt genetic change can occur in an individual, which then gives rise to a new species. The idea has now been largely discredited, although the appearance of polyploid individuals

Biological diversity

Estimated number of species worldwide

	Number identified	% of estimated total number of species
Micro-organisms	5,800 }	3–27%
Invertebrates	1,021,000 }	
Plants	322,500	67–100%
Fish	19,100	83–100%
Birds	9,100	94–100%
Reptiles and amphibians	12,000 }	90–95%
Mammals	4,000 }	
Total	**1,393,500**	
	Number of species	% identified
Low estimate of all species	4.4 million	31%
High estimate of all species	80 million	2%

This table shows the probable number of species and the extent of unidentified biological diversity worldwide. Estimates of the number of species vary widely because many species-rich ecosystems, such as tropical forests, contain unexplored and unstudied habitats, and the probable number of habitats may have been underestimated. The figures provided above are the most recent and widely accepted. The percentage values are based on the averages of a number of estimates and are intended as a guide only.

Source: WWF

(possessing three or more sets of chromosomes) can be considered an example.

species distinguishable group of organisms that resemble each other or consist of a few distinctive types, and that can all interbreed to produce fertile offspring. Species are the lowest level in the system of biological classification. Around 1.4 million species have been identified so far, of which 750,000 are insects, 250,000 are plants, and 41,000 are vertebrates.

variation difference between individuals of the same species, found in any sexually reproducing population. Variations may be almost unnoticeable in some cases, obvious in others, and can concern many aspects of the organism. Typically, variation in size, behaviour, biochemistry, or colouring may be found. The cause of the variation is genetic (that is, inherited), environmental, or usually a combination of the two. The origins of variation can be traced to the recombination of the genetic material during the formation of the gametes, and, more rarely, to mutation.

Reproduction

Reproduction is any process by which a living organism produces other organisms similar to itself. There are two kinds: asexual reproduction and sexual reproduction.

asexual reproduction reproduction that does not involve the manufacture and fusion of sex cells, nor the necessity for two parents. Asexual processes include binary fission, in which the parent organism splits into two or more new organisms, and budding, in which a new organism is formed initially as an outgrowth of the parent organism. The asexual reproduction of spores, as in ferns and mosses, is also common and many plants reproduce asexually by means of runners, rhizomes, bulbs, and corms.

Asexual reproduction carries a clear advantage in that there is no need to search for a mate nor to develop complex pollinating mechanisms; every asexual organism can reproduce on its own. Asexual reproduction can therefore lead to a rapid population build-up.

In evolutionary terms, the disadvantage of asexual reproduction is that only identical individuals, or clones, are produced – there is no variation. In the field of horticulture, where standardized production is needed, this is useful, but in the wild, a population that cannot adapt to a changing environment or evolve defences against a new disease is at risk of extinction. Many asexually reproducing organisms are therefore capable of reproducing sexually as well.

binary fission asexual reproduction whereby a single-celled organism, such as the amoeba, divides into two smaller 'daughter' cells. It can also occur in a few simple multicellular organisms, such as sea anemones, producing two smaller sea anemones of equal size.

budding asexual reproduction in which an outgrowth develops from a cell to form a new individual. Most yeasts reproduce in this way. Simple invertebrates, such as hydra, can also reproduce by budding.

In horticulture, the term is used for a technique of plant propagation whereby a bud (or scion) and a sliver of bark from one plant are transferred to an incision made in the bark of another plant (the stock). This method of grafting is often used for roses.

parthenogenesis development of an ovum (egg) without any genetic contribution from a male. Parthenogenesis is the normal means of reproduction in a few plants (for example, dandelions) and animals (for example, certain fish). Some sexually reproducing species, such as aphids, show parthenogenesis at some stage in their life cycle.

In most cases, there is no fertilization at all, but in a few, the stimulus of being fertilized by a sperm is needed to initiate development, although the male's chromosomes are not absorbed into the nucleus of the ovum. Parthenogenesis can be artificially induced in many animals (such as rabbits) by cooling, pricking, or applying acid to an egg.

sexual reproduction reproductive process in organisms that requires the union, or fertilization, of gametes (such as eggs and sperm). These are usually produced by two different individuals, although self-fertilization occurs in a few hermaphrodites such as tapeworms. Most organisms other than bacteria and cyanobacteria (blue-green algae) show some sort of sexual process. Except in some lower organisms, the gametes are of two distinct types called eggs and sperm. The organisms producing the eggs are called females, and those producing the sperm, males. The fusion of a male and a female gamete produces a *zygote*, from which a new individual develops.

Biology: chronology

c. **500 BC**	First studies of the structure and behaviour of animals, by the Greek Alcmaeon of Creton.
c. **450**	Hippocrates of Cos undertook the first detailed studies of human anatomy.
c. **350**	Aristotle laid down the basic philosophy of the biological sciences and outlined a theory of evolution.
c. **300**	Theophrastus carried out the first detailed studies of plants.
c. **AD 175**	Galen established the basic principles of anatomy and physiology.
1628	William Harvey described the circulation of the blood and the function of the heart as a pump.
1665	Robert Hooke used a microscope to describe the cellular structure of plants.
1672	Marcello Malpighi undertook the first studies in embryology by describing the development of a chicken egg.
1677	Anthony van Leeuwenhoek greatly improved the microscope and used it to describe spermatozoa as well as many microorganisms.
1682	Nehemiah Grew published the first textbook on botany.
1736	Carolus (Carl) Linnaeus published his systematic classification of plants, so establishing taxonomy.
1768–79	James Cook's voyages of discovery in the Pacific revealed an undreamed-of diversity of living species, prompting the development of theories to explain their origin.
1796	Edward Jenner established the practice of vaccination against smallpox, laying the foundations for theories of antibodies and immune reactions.
1809	Jean-Baptiste Lamarck advocated a theory of evolution through inheritance of acquired characters.
1839	Theodor Schwann proposed that all living matter is made up of cells.
1857	Louis Pasteur established that microorganisms are responsible for fermentation, creating the discipline of microbiology.
1859	Charles Darwin published *On the Origin of Species*, expounding his theory of the evolution of species by natural selection.
1866	Gregor Mendel pioneered the study of inheritance with his experiments on peas, but achieved little recognition.
1883	August Weismann proposed his theory of the continuity of the germ plasm.
1900	Mendel's work was rediscovered and the science of genetics founded.
1935	Konrad Lorenz published the first of many major studies of animal behaviour, which founded the discipline of ethology.
1953	James Watson and Francis Crick described the molecular structure of the genetic material, DNA.
1964	William Hamilton recognized the importance of inclusive fitness, so paving the way for the development of sociobiology.
1975	Discovery of endogenous opiates (the brain's own painkillers) opened up a new phase in the study of brain chemistry.
1976	Har Gobind Khorana and his colleagues constructed the first artificial gene to function naturally when inserted into a bacterial cell, a major step in genetic engineering.
1982	Gene databases were established at Heidelberg, Germany, for the European Molecular Biology Laboratory, and at Los Alamos, USA, for the US National Laboratories.
1985	The first human cancer gene, retinoblastoma, was isolated by researchers at the Massachusetts Eye and Ear Infirmary and the Whitehead Institute, Massachusetts.
1988	The Human Genome Organization (HUGO) was established in Washington DC with the aim of mapping the complete sequence of DNA.
1991	Biosphere 2, an experiment that attempts to reproduce the world's biosphere in miniature within a sealed glass dome, was launched in Arizona, USA.
1992	Researchers at the University of California, USA, stimulated the multiplication of isolated brain cells of mice, overturning the axiom that mammalian brains cannot produce replacement cells once birth has taken place. The world's largest organism, a honey fungus with underground hyphae (filaments) spreading across 600 hectares/1,480 acres, was discovered in Washington State, USA.
1994	Scientists from Pakistan and the USA unearthed a 50-million-year-old fossil whale with hind legs that would have enabled it to walk on land.

The Life Cycle

The life cycle is the sequence of developmental stages through which members of a given species pass. Most vertebrates have a simple life cycle consisting of fertilization of sex cells or gametes, a period of development as an embryo, a period of juvenile growth after hatching or birth, an adulthood including sexual reproduction, and finally death. Invertebrate life cycles are generally more complex and may involve major reconstitution of the individual's appearance (metamorphosis) and completely different styles of life. Thus dragonflies live an aquatic life as larvae and an aerial life during the adult phase. In many invertebrates and protozoa there is a sequence of stages in the life cycle, and in parasites different stages often occur in different host organisms. Plants have a special type of life cycle with two distinct phases, known as alternation of generations.

ageing the period of deterioration of the physical condition of a living organism that leads to death; in biological terms, the entire life process. Three current theories attempt to account for ageing. The first suggests that the process is genetically determined, to remove individuals that can no longer reproduce. The second suggests that it is due to the accumulation of mistakes during the replication of DNA at cell division. The third suggests that it is actively induced by pieces of DNA that move between cells, or by cancer-causing viruses; these may become abundant in old cells and induce them to produce unwanted proteins or interfere with the control functions of their DNA.

allele one of two or more alternative forms of a gene at a given position (locus) on a chromosome, caused by a difference in the DNA. Blue and brown eyes in humans are determined by different alleles of the gene for eye colour. Organisms with two sets of chromo-somes (diploids) will have two copies of each gene. If the two alleles are identical, the individual is said to be homozygous at that locus; if different, heterozygous. Some alleles show dominance over others. These mask the effect of other alleles, which are known as recessive.

alternation of generations typical life cycle of terrestrial plants and some seaweeds, in which there are two distinct forms occurring alternately: *diploid* (having two sets of chromosomes) and *haploid* (one set of chromosomes). The diploid generation produces haploid spores by meiosis (reduction cell division) and is called the sporophyte, whereas the haploid generation produces gametes (sex cells) and is called the gametophyte. The gametes fuse to form a diploid zygote which develops into a new sporophyte; thus the sporophyte and gametophyte alternate.

birth the act of producing live young from within the body of female animals. Both viviparous and ovoviviparous animals give birth to young. In viviparous animals, embryos obtain nourishment from the mother via a placenta or other means during pregnancy. In ovoviviparous animals, fertilized eggs develop and hatch in the oviduct of the mother and gain little or no nourishment from maternal tissues.

chromosome structure in a cell nucleus that carries the genes. Each chromosome consists of one very long strand of DNA, coiled and folded to produce a compact body. The point on a chromosome where a particular gene occurs is known as its locus. Most higher organisms have two copies of each chromosome (they are diploid) but some have only one (they are haploid). There are 46 chromosomes in a normal human cell.

death the cessation of all life functions, so that the molecules and structures associated with living things become disorganized and indistinguishable from similar molecules found in non-living things. When the energy for repair and replacement of complex molecules and whole cells is no longer available, large molecules such as proteins break down into simpler, soluble components. Eventually the organism partly dissolves into the soil or evaporates into the air, leaving behind skeletal material. The purpose of death may be evolutionary: individual organisms must die in order to make way for new ones, which, by virtue of sexual reproduction, may vary slightly in relation to the previous generation. Without this variation, organisms would be unable to adapt to environmental changes.

In human beings, death used to be pronounced when a person's breathing and heartbeat stopped. The advent of mechanical aids has made this point sometimes difficult to determine, and in controversial cases a person is now pronounced dead when the brain ceases to control the vital functions.

diploid having two sets of chromosomes in each cell. In sexually reproducing species, one set is derived from each parent, the gametes, or sex cells, of each parent being haploid (having only one set of chromosomes) owing to meiosis (reduction cell division).

embryo early development stage of an animal or a plant following fertilization of an ovum (egg cell) or activation of an ovum by parthenogenesis. In animals the embryo exists either within an egg (where it is nourished by food contained in the yolk) or, in mammals, in the uterus of the mother. In mammals (except marsupials), the embryo is fed through the placenta. In humans, the term 'embryo' describes the fertilized egg during its first seven weeks of existence; from the eighth week onwards it is referred to as a fetus. The plant embryo is found within the seed in higher plants.

fetus or *foetus* stage in mammalian embryo development. The human embryo is usually termed a fetus after the eighth week of development, when the limbs and external features of the head are recognizable.

fertilization in sexual reproduction, the union of two gametes (sex cells, often called egg and sperm) to produce a zygote, which combines the genetic material contributed by each parent. In self-fertilization the male and female gametes come from the same plant; in cross-fertilization they come from different plants. Self-fertilization rarely occurs in animals; usually even hermaphrodite animals cross-fertilize each other.

gamete cell that functions in sexual reproduction by merging with another gamete to form a zygote. Examples of gametes include sperm and egg cells. In most organisms, the gametes are haploid (they contain half the number of chromosomes of the parent), owing to reduction division, or meiosis.

gene unit of inherited material, encoded by a strand of DNA, and transcribed by RNA. In higher organisms, genes are located on the chromosomes. A gene is the inherited factor that consistently affects a particular character in an individual – for example, the gene for eye colour. It occurs at a particular point or locus on a particular chromosome and may have several variants or alleles, each specifying a particular form of that character – for example, blue or brown eyes. Genes do this by controlling the structure of proteins via the genetic code, as well as the amounts produced and the timing of production.

genome the full complement of genes carried by a single (haploid) set of chromosomes. The term may be applied to the genetic information carried by an individual or to the range of genes found in a given species.

genotype the particular set of alleles (variants of genes) possessed by a given organism. The term is usually used in conjunction with phenotype (physical appearance), which is the product of the genotype and all environmental effects.

germination the initial stages of growth in a seed, spore, or pollen grain. Seeds germinate when they are exposed to favourable external conditions of moisture, light, and temperature, and when any factors causing dormancy have been removed. The process begins with the uptake of water by the seed. The embryonic root, or radicle, is normally the first organ to emerge, followed by the embryonic shoot, or plumule. Food reserves, either within the endo-sperm (the nutritive tissue in the seeds of most flowering plants) or from the cotyledons (the seed leaves), are broken down to nourish the rapidly growing seedling. Germination is considered to have ended with the production of the first true leaves.

gestation in all mammals except the monotremes (duck-billed platypus and spiny anteaters), the period from the time of implantation of the embryo in the uterus to birth. This period varies among species; in humans it is about 266 days, in elephants 18–22 months, in cats about 60 days, and in some species of marsupial (such as opossum) as short as 12 days.

haploid having a single set of chromosomes in each cell. Most higher organisms are diploid – that is, they have two sets – but their gametes (sex cells) are haploid. Some plants, such as mosses, liverworts, and many seaweeds, are haploid, and male honey bees are haploid because they develop from eggs that have not been fertilized.

hermaphrodite organism that has both male and female sex organs. Hermaphroditism is the norm in species such as earthworms and snails, and is common in flowering plants. Cross-fertilization is the rule among hermaphrodites, with the parents functioning as male and female simultaneously, or as one or the other sex at different stages in their development.

heterozygous in a living organism, having two different alleles for a given trait. In homozygous organisms, by contrast, both chromosomes carry the same allele. In an outbreeding population (one that seeks mates from outside the family, tribe, or group), an individual organism will generally be heterozygous for some genes but homozygous for others.

homozygous in a living organism, having two identical alleles for a given trait. Individuals homozygous for a trait always breed true; that is, they produce offspring that resemble them in appearance when bred with a genetically similar individual; inbred varieties or species are homozygous for almost all traits. Recessive alleles are only expressed in the homozygous condition.

karyotype the set of chromosomes characteristic of a given species. It is described as the number, shape, and size of the chromosomes in a single cell of an organism. In humans, for example, the karyotype consists of 46 chromosomes, in mice 40, in crayfish 200, and in fruit flies 8.

larva stage between hatching and adulthood in those species in which the young have a different appearance and way of life from the adults. Examples include tadpoles (frogs) and caterpillars (butterflies and moths). Larvae are typical of the invertebrates, some of which (for example, shrimps) have two or more distinct larval stages. Among vertebrates, it is only the amphibians and some fishes that have a larval stage. The process whereby the larva changes

into another stage, such as a pupa (chrysalis) or adult, is known as metamorphosis.

meiosis process of cell division in which the number of chromosomes in the cell is halved. It only occurs in eukaryotic cells (that is, not in bacteria), and is part of a life cycle that involves sexual reproduction because it allows the genes of two parents to be combined without the total number of chromosomes increasing.

metamorphosis period during the life cycle of many invertebrates, most amphibians, and some fish, during which the individual's body changes from one form to another through a major reconstitution of its tissues. For example, adult frogs are produced by metamorphosis from tadpoles, and butterflies are produced from caterpillars following metamorphosis within a pupa.

mitosis the process of cell division. The genetic material of eukaryotic cells is carried on a number of chromosomes. To control their movements during cell division so that both new cells get a full complement, a system of protein tubules, known as the spindle, organizes the chromosomes into position in the middle of the cell before they replicate. The spindle then controls the movement of chromosomes as the cell goes through the stages of division: *interphase*, *prophase*, *metaphase*, *anaphase*, and *telophase*.

ovum (plural *ova*) female gamete (sex cell) before fertilization. In animals it is called an egg, and is produced in the ovaries. In plants, where it is also known as an egg cell or oosphere, the ovum is produced in an ovule. The ovum is nonmotile. It must be fertilized by a male gamete before it can develop further, except in cases of parthenogenesis.

phenotype visible traits, those actually displayed by an organism. The phenotype is not a direct reflection of the genotype because some alleles are masked by the presence of other, dominant alleles. The phenotype is further modified by the effects of the environment (for example, poor nutrition stunts growth).

pollen the grains of seed plants that contain the male gametes. In angiosperms (flowering plants) pollen is produced within anthers; in most gymnosperms (cone-bearing plants) it is produced in male cones. A pollen grain is typically yellow and, when mature, has a hard outer wall. Individual species or genera of plants can be recognized from their pollen. Pollen of insect-pollinated plants is often sticky and spiny and larger than the smooth, light grains produced by wind-pollinated species.

pregnancy in humans, the period during which an embryo grows within the womb. It begins at conception and ends at birth, and the normal length is 40 weeks. Menstruation usually stops on conception. About one in five pregnancies fails, but most of these failures occur very early on, so the woman may notice only that her period is late. After the second month, the breasts become tense and tender, and the areas round the nipples become darker. Enlargement of the uterus can be felt at about the end of the third month, and thereafter the abdomen enlarges progressively. Pregnancy in animals is called gestation.

puberty stage in human development when the individual becomes sexually mature. It may occur from the age of ten upwards. The sexual organs take on their adult form and pubic hair grows. In girls, menstruation begins, and the breasts develop; in boys, the voice breaks and becomes deeper, and facial hair develops.

pupa non-feeding, largely immobile stage of some insect life cycles, in which larval tissues are broken down and adult tissues and structures are formed. In many insects, the pupa is *exarate*, with the appendages (legs, antennae, wings) visible outside the pupal case; in butterflies and moths, it is called a chrysalis, and is *obtect*, with the appendages developing inside the case.

replication production of copies of the genetic material DNA; it occurs during cell division. Most mutations are caused by mistakes during replication.

seed the reproductive structure of higher plants (angiosperms and gymnosperms). It develops from a fertilized ovule and consists of an embryo and a food store, surrounded and protected by an outer seed coat, called the testa. The food store is contained either in a specialized nutritive tissue, the endo sperm, or in the cotyledons of the embryo itself. In angiosperms, the seed is enclosed within a fruit, whereas in gymnosperms it is usually naked and unprotected, once shed from the female cone. After germination the seed develops into a new plant.

sperm or *spermatozoon* the male gamete of animals. Each sperm cell has a head capsule containing a nucleus, a middle portion containing mitochondria (which provide energy), and a long tail (flagellum).

spore small reproductive or resting body, usually consisting of just one cell. Unlike a gamete, it does not need to fuse with another cell in order to develop into a new organism. Spores are produced by the lower plants, most fungi, some bacteria, and certain protozoa. They are generally light and easily dispersed by wind movements.

The Maintenance of Life

aerobic requiring oxygen (usually dissolved in water) for the efficient release of energy contained in food molecules, such as glucose. Almost all living organisms are aerobic, plants as well as animals, except certain (anaerobic) bacteria. Aerobic reactions occur inside every cell, and most aerobic organisms die in the absence of oxygen, but certain organisms and cells, such as those found in muscle tissue, can function for short periods anaerobically.

anaerobic not requiring oxygen for the release of energy from food molecules such as glucose. Anaerobic organisms include many bacteria, yeasts, and internal parasites. *Obligate anaerobes*, such as certain primitive bacteria, cannot function in the presence of oxygen; but *facultative anaerobes*, like the fermenting yeasts and most bacteria, can function with or without oxygen.

autotroph any living organism that synthesizes organic substances from inorganic molecules by using light or chemical energy. Autotrophs are the *primary producers* in all food chains since the materials they synthesize and store are the energy sources of all other organisms. All green plants and many planktonic organisms are autotrophs, using sunlight to convert carbon dioxide and water into sugars by photosynthesis.

basal metabolic rate (BMR) amount of energy needed by an animal just to stay alive. It is measured when the animal is awake but resting, and includes the energy required to keep the heart beating, sustain breathing, repair tissues, and keep the brain and nerves functioning. Measuring the animal's con-sumption of oxygen gives an accurate value for BMR, because oxygen is needed to release energy from food.

BMR varies from one species to another, and from males to females. In humans, it is highest in children and declines with age. Disease, including mental illness, can make it rise or fall. Hormones from the thyroid gland control the BMR.

biosynthesis synthesis of organic chemicals from simple inorganic ones by living cells; for example, the conversion of carbon dioxide and water to glucose by plants during photosynthesis. Other biosynthetic reactions produce cell constituents including proteins and fats.

carnivore animal that eats other animals. Although the term is sometimes confined to those that eat the flesh of vertebrate prey, it is often used more broadly to include any animal that eats other animals, even microscopic ones. Carrion-eaters may or may not be included.

chemosynthesis method of making protoplasm (contents of a cell) using the energy from chemical reactions, in contrast to the use of light energy employed for the same purpose in photosynthesis. The process is used by certain bacteria, which can synthesize organic compounds from carbon dioxide and water using the energy from special methods of respiration.

decomposer any organism that breaks down dead matter. Decomposers play a vital role in the ecosystem by freeing important chemical substances, such as nitrogen compounds, locked up in dead organisms or excrement. They feed on some of the released organic matter, but leave the rest to filter back into the soil or pass in gas form into the atmosphere. The principal decomposers are bacteria and fungi, but earthworms and many other invertebrates are often included in this group. The nitrogen cycle relies on the actions of decomposers.

food chain sequence showing the feeding relationships between organisms in a particular ecosystem. Each organism depends on the next lowest member of the chain for its food.

Energy in the form of food is shown to be transferred from autotrophs, or producers, which are principally plants and photosynthetic microorganisms, to a series of heterotrophs, or consumers. The heterotrophs comprise the herbivores, which feed on the producers; carnivores, which feed on the herbivores; and decomposers, which break down the dead bodies and waste products of all four groups (including their own), ready for recycling.

gas exchange exchange of gases between living organisms and the atmosphere, principally oxygen and carbon dioxide.

herbivore animal that feeds on green plants (or photosynthetic single-celled organisms) or their products, including seeds, fruit, and nectar. The most numerous type of herbivore is thought to be the zooplankton, tiny invertebrates in the surface waters of the oceans that feed on small photosynthetic algae. Herbivores are more numerous than other animals because their food is the most abundant. They form a vital link in the food chain between plants and carnivores.

heterotroph any living organism that obtains its energy from organic substances produced by other organisms. All animals and fungi are heterotrophs, and they include herbivores, carnivores, and saprotrophs (those that feed on dead animal and plant material).

nitrogen cycle the process of nitrogen passing through the ecosystem. Nitrogen, in the form of inorganic compounds (such as nitrates) in the soil, is absorbed by plants and turned into organic compounds (such as proteins) in plant tissue. A proportion of this nitrogen is eaten by herbivores, with some of this in turn being passed on to the carnivores, which feed on the herbivores. The nitrogen is ultimately returned to the soil as excrement and when organisms die and are converted back to inorganic form by decomposers.

omnivore animal that feeds on both plant and animal material. Omnivores have digestive adaptations intermediate between those of herbivores and carnivores, with relatively unspecialized digestive systems and gut microorganisms that can digest a variety of foodstuffs.

photosynthesis process by which green plants trap light energy and use it to drive a series of chemical reactions, leading to the formation of carbohydrates. All animals ultimately depend on photosynthesis because it is the method by which the basic food (sugar) is created. For photosynthesis to occur, the plant must possess chlorophyll and must have a supply of carbon dioxide and water.

Photosynthesis by cyanobacteria was responsible for the appearance of oxygen in the Earth's atmosphere 2 billion years ago, and photosynthesis by plants maintains the oxygen level today.

respiration biochemical process whereby food molecules are progressively broken down (oxidized) to release energy in the form of ATP (the nucleotide that powers cellular reactions). In most organisms this requires oxygen, but in some bacteria the oxidant is the nitrate or sulphate ion instead. In all higher organisms, respiration occurs in the mitochondria. Respiration is also used to mean breathing, although this is more accurately described as a form of gas exchange.

The Macroscopic World

ANIMAL

or *metazoan* member of the kingdom Animalia, one of the major categories of living things, the science of which is *zoology*. Animals are all heterotrophs (they obtain their energy from organic substances produced by other organisms); they have eukaryotic cells (the genetic material is contained within a distinct nucleus) bounded by a thin cell membrane rather than

the thick cell wall of plants. Most animals are capable of moving around for at least part of their life cycle.

Types

Invertebrate

animal without a backbone. The invertebrates comprise over 95% of the million or so existing animal

Animal lifespans and gestation periods

Animal	Gestation	Average longevity/ maximum longevity*
	days	years
Ass	365	12/35.8
Baboon	187	20/35.5
Bear: black	219	18/36.8
grizzly	225	25/–
polar	240	20/34.7
Beaver	122	5/20.5
Buffalo (American)	278	15/–
Camel, Bactrian	406	12/29.5
Cat (domestic)	63	12/28
Chimpanzee	231	20/44.5
Chipmunk	31	6/8
Cow	284	15/30
Deer (white-tailed)	201	8/17.5
Dog (domestic)	61	12/20
Elephant (African)	–	35/60
Elephant (Asian)	645	40/70
Elk	250	15/26.5
Fox (red)	52	7/14
Giraffe	425	10/33.5
Goat (domestic)	151	8/18
Gorilla	257	20/39.3
Guinea pig	68	4/7.5
Hippopotamus	238	25/–
Horse	330	20/46
Kangaroo	42	7/–
Leopard	98	12/19.3
Lion	100	15/25
Monkey (rhesus)	164	15/–
Moose	240	12/–
Mouse (meadow)	21	3/–
Mouse (dom. white)	19	3/3.5
Opossum (American)	14–17	1/–
Pig (domestic)	112	10/27
Puma	90	12/19
Rabbit (domestic)	31	5/13
Rhinoceros (black)	450	15/–
Rhinoceros (white)	–	20/–
Sea lion (California)	350	12/28
Sheep (domestic)	154	12/20
Squirrel (grey)	44	10/–
Tiger	105	16/26.3
Wolf (maned)	63	5/–
Zebra (Grant's)	365	15/–

Incubation time (days)	
Chicken	21
Duck	30
Goose	30
Pigeon	18
Turkey	26

*Longevity figures refer to animals in captivity; an animal's potential life span is rarely attained in nature.

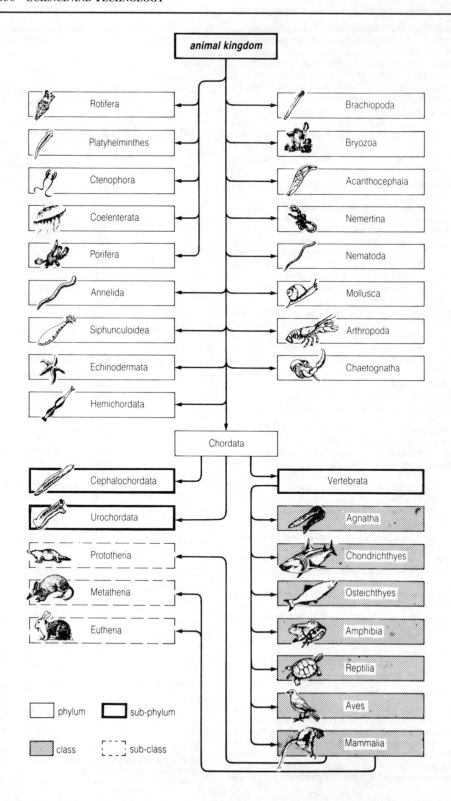

Insect classification

Class Insecta

Subclass	Order	Number of species	Common names
Apterygota (wingless insects)			
	Thysanura	350	three-pronged bristletails, silverfish
	Diplura	400	two-pronged bristletails, campodeids, japygids
	Protura	50	minute insects living in soil
	Collembola	1500	springtails
Pterygota (winged insects or forms secondarily wingless)			
Exopterygota (young resemble adults but have externally developing wings)	Ephemeroptera	1,000	mayflies
	Odonata	5,000	dragonflies, damselflies
	Plecoptera	3,000	stoneflies insects of North America
	Grylloblattodea	12	wingless soil-living
	Orthoptera	20,000	crickets, grasshoppers, locusts, mantids, roaches
	Phasmida	2,000	stick insects, leaf insects
	Dermaptera	1,000	earwigs
	Embioptera	150	web-spinners
	Dictyoptera	5,000	cockroaches, praying mantises
	Isoptera	2,000	termites
	Zoraptera	16	tiny insects living in decaying plants
	Psocoptera	1,600	booklice, barklice, psocids
	Mallophaga	2,500	biting lice, mainly parasitic on birds
	Anoplura	250	sucking lice, mainly parasitic on mammals true bugs, including aphids,
	Hemiptera	55,000	shield- and bedbugs, froghoppers, pond skaters, water boatmen
	Thysanoptera	5,000	thrips
Endopterygota (young unlike adults, undergo sudden metamorphosis)	Neuroptera	4,500	lacewings, alder flies, snake flies, ant lions
	Mecoptera	300	scorpion flies
	Lepidoptera	165,000	butterflies, moths
	Trichoptera	3,000	caddis flies
	Diptera	70,000	true flies, including bluebottles, mosquitoes, leatherjackets, midges
	Siphonaptera	1,400	fleas
	Hymenoptera	100,000	bees, wasps, ants, sawflies
	Coloeoptera	350,000	beetles, including weevils, ladybirds, glow-worms, woodworms, chafers

species and include sponges, coelenterates, flatworms, nematodes, annelid worms, arthropods, molluscs, echinoderms, and primitive aquatic chordates, such as sea squirts and lancelets.

annelid any segmented worm of the phylum Annelida. Annelids include earthworms, leeches, and marine worms such as lugworms. They have a distinct head and a soft body divided into segments shut off from one another by membranous partitions.

arachnid or *arachnoid* type of arthropod, including spiders, scorpions, and mites. They differ from insects in possessing only two main body regions, the cephalothorax and the abdomen.

arthropod member of the phylum Arthropoda; an invertebrate animal with jointed legs and a segmented body with a horny or chitinous casing (exoskeleton), which is shed periodically and replaced as the animal grows. Included are arachnids such as spiders and

mites, as well as crustaceans, millipedes, centipedes, and insects.

crustacean one of the class of arthropods that includes crabs, lobsters, shrimps, woodlice, and barnacles. The external skeleton is made of protein and chitin hardened with lime. Each segment bears a pair of appendages that may be modified as sensory feelers (antennae), as mouthparts, or as swimming, walking, or grasping structures.

echinoderm marine invertebrate of the phylum Echinodermata ('spiny-skinned'), characterized by five-radial symmetry. Echinoderms include starfishes (or sea stars), brittlestars, sea lilies, sea urchins, and sea cucumbers. The skeleton is external, made of a series of limy plates, and echinoderms generally move by using tube feet, small water-filled sacs that can be protruded or pulled back to the body.

Molluscs: classification

Phylum Mollusca

Class	
Monoplacophora	primitive marine forms, including Neopilina (2 species)

Class	
Amphineura	(1,150 species)
1 Aplacophora	wormlike marine forms
2 Polyplacophora	chitons, coat-of-mail shells

Class	
Gastropoda	snail-like molluscs, with single or no shell (9,000 species)
1 Prosobranchia	limpets, winkles, whelks
2 Opisthobranchia	seaslugs
3 Pulmonata	land and freshwater snails, slugs

Class	
Scaphopoda	tusk shells, marine burrowers (350 species)

Class	
Bivalvia	molluscs with a double (two-valved) shell (15,000 species): mussels, oysters, clams, cockles, scallops, tellins, razor shells, shipworms

Class	
Cephalopoda	molluscs with shell generally reduced, arms to capture prey, and beaklike mouth; body bilaterally symmetrical and nervous system well developed (750 species): squids, cuttlefish, octopuses, pearly nautilus, argonaut

flatworm invertebrate of the phylum Platyhelminthes. Some are free-living, but many are parasitic (for example, tapeworms and flukes). The body is simple and bilaterally symmetrical, with one opening to the intestine. Many are hermaphroditic (with both male and female sex organs), and practise self-fertilization.

insect any member of the class Insecta among the arthropods or jointed-legged animals. An insect's body is divided into head, thorax, and abdomen. The head bears a pair of feelers or antennae, and attached to the thorax are three pairs of legs and usually two pairs of wings. The skeleton is external and is composed of chitin. It is membranous at the joints, but elsewhere is hard. The life cycle of insects includes metamorphosis. More than 1 million species are known. Insects vary in size from 0.02 cm/0.007 in to 35 cm/13.5 in in length.

jellyfish marine invertebrate of the phylum Cnidaria (coelenterates) with an umbrella-shaped body composed of a semitransparent gelatinous substance, with a fringe of stinging tentacles. Most adult jellyfishes move freely, but during parts of their life cycle many are polyplike and attached. They feed on small animals that are paralysed by stinging cells in the jellyfishes' tentacles.

mollusc any invertebrate of the phylum Mollusca with a body divided into three parts, a head, a foot, and a visceral mass. The majority of molluscs are marine animals, but some inhabit fresh water, and a few are terrestrial. They include bivalves, mussels, octopuses, oysters, snails, slugs, and squids. The body is soft, limbless, and cold-blooded. There is no internal skeleton, but many species have a hard shell covering the body.

nematode unsegmented worm of the phylum Nematoda. Nematodes are pointed at both ends, with a tough, smooth outer skin. They include many free-living species found in soil and water, including the sea, but a large number are parasites, such as the roundworms and pinworms that live in humans, or the eelworms that attack plant roots. They differ from flatworms in that they have two openings to the gut (a mouth and an anus).

Vertebrate

any animal with a backbone. The 41,000 species of vertebrates include mammals, birds, reptiles, amphibians, and fishes. They include most of the larger animals, but in terms of numbers of species are only a tiny proportion of the world's animals. The zoological taxonomic group Vertebrata is a subgroup of the phylum Chordata.

amphibian member of the vertebrate class Amphibia, which generally spend their larval (tadpole) stage in fresh water, transferring to land at maturity (after metamorphosis) and generally returning to water to breed. Like fish and reptiles, they continue to grow throughout life, and cannot maintain a temperature greatly differing from that of their environment. The class includes caecilians (wormlike in appearance), salamanders, frogs, and toads.

bird backboned animal of the class Aves, the biggest group of land vertebrates, characterized by warm blood, feathers, wings, breathing through lungs, and egg-laying by the female. There are nearly 8,500 species of birds.

fish aquatic vertebrate that uses gills for obtaining oxygen from fresh or sea water. There are three main groups, not closely related: the bony fishes or Osteichthyes (goldfish, cod, tuna); the cartilaginous fishes

Mammals: classification

Order	*Typical species*
Monotremata	echidna, platypus
placental mammals:	
Marsupiala	kangaroo, koala, opossum
Insectivora	shrew, hedgehog, mole
Chiroptera	bat
Primates	lemur, monkey, ape, human
Edentata	anteater, armadillo, sloth
Pholidota	pangolin
Dermoptera	flying lemur
Rodentia	rat, mouse, squirrel, porcupine
Lagomorpha	rabbit, hare, pika
Cetacea	whale, dolphin
Carnivora	cat, dog, weasel, bear
Pinnipedia	seal, walrus
Artiodactyla	pig, deer, cattle, camel, giraffe
Perissodactyla	horse, rhinoceros, tapir
Sirenia	dugong, manatee
Tubulidentata	aardvark
Hyracoidea	hyrax
Proboscidea	elephant

Fish classification

Superclass Agnatha (jawless fishes)

Order	No of species	Examples
Petromyzoniformes	30	lamprey
Myxiniformes	15	hagfish

Superclass Gnathostomata (jawed fishes) class Chondrichthyes (cartilaginous fishes) subclass Elasmobranchii (sharks and rays)

Hexanchiformes	6	frilled shark, comb-toothed shark
Heterodontiformes	10	Port Jackson shark
Lamniformes	200	*typical* shark
Rajiformes	300	skate, ray

Subclass Holocephali (rabbitfishes)

Chimaeriformes	20	chimaera, rabbitfish

Class Osteichthyes (bony fishes) subclass Sarcopterygii (fleshy-finned fishes)

Coelacanthiformes	1	coelacanth
Ceratodiformes	1	Australian lungfish
Lepidosireniformes	4	South American and African lungfish

Subclass Actinopterygii (ray-finned fishes) superorder Chondrostei

Polypteriformes	11	bichir, reedfish
Acipensiformes	25	paddlefish, sturgeon

Superorder Holostei

Amiiformes	8	bowfin, garpike

Superorder Teleostei

Elopiformes	12	tarpon, tenpounder
Anguilliformes	300	eel
Notacanthiformes	20	spiny eel
Clupeiformes	350	herring, anchovy
Osteoglossiformes	16	arapaima, African butterfly fish
Mormyriformes	150	elephant-trunk fish, featherback
Salmoniformes	500	salmon, trout, smelt, pike
Gonorhynchiformes	15	milkfish
Cypriniformes	350	carp, barb, characin, loache
Siluriformes	200	catfish
Myctophiformes	300	deep-sea lantern fish, Bombay duck
Percopsiformes	10	pirate perch, cave-dwelling amblyopsid
Batrachoidiformes	10	toadfish
Gobiesociformes	100	clingfish, dragonets
Lophiiformes	150	anglerfish
Gadiformes	450	cod, pollack, pearlfish, eelpout
Atheriniformes	600	flying fish, toothcarp, halfbeak
Lampridiformes	50	opah, ribbonfish
Beryciformes	150	squirrelfish
Zeiformes	60	John Dory, boarfish
Gasterosteiformes	150	stickleback, pipefish, seahorse
Channiformes	5	snakeshead
Synbranchiformes	7	cuchia
Scorpaeniformes	700	gurnard, miller's thumb, stonefish
Dactylopteriformes	6	flying gurnard
Pegasiformes	4	sea-moth
Pleuronectiformes	500	flatfish
Tetraodontiformes	250	puffer fish, triggerfish, sunfish
Perciformes	6,500	perch, cichlid, damsel fish, gobie, wrass, parrotfish, gourami, marlin, mackerel, tuna, swordfish, spiny eel, mullet, barracuda, sea bream, croaker, ice fish, butterfish

Collective nouns for animals

ants	colony
bears	sleuth
bees	grist, swarm
birds	flight, volery
cats	clowder, clutter
chicks	brood, clutch
clams	bed
crows	murder
ducks	brace, team
elephants	herd
elks	gang
fish	school, shoal
foxes	leash, skulk
geese	flock, gaggle, skein
gnats	cloud, horde
goats	tribe, trip
goldfinches	charm
gorillas	band
greyhounds	leash
hares	down, husk
horses	pair, team
hounds	pack, cry, mute
kangaroos	mob, troop
larks	exaltation
leopards	leap
lions	pride
monkeys	troop
nightingales	watch
oxen	yoke
oysters	bed
partridge	covey
peacocks	muster
pheasants	nest, nide
pigs	litter
quail	bevy, covey
rhinoceri	crash
seals	pod
sheep	drove, flock
swans	bevy
toads	knot
turtles	bale
vipers	nest
whales	gam, pod
wolves	pack

or Chondrichthyes (sharks, rays); and the jawless fishes or Agnatha (hagfishes, lampreys). Most lay eggs, sometimes in vast numbers. The bony fishes constitute the majority of living fishes (about 20,000 species). The skeleton is bone, movement is controlled by mobile fins, and the body is usually covered with scales.

mammal animal characterized by having mammary glands in the female, used for suckling the young, and hair (very reduced in some species, such as whales). Mammals are divided into three groups: *placental mammals*, where the young develop inside the uterus, receiving nourishment from the blood of the mother via the placenta; *marsupials*, where the young are born at an early stage of development and develop further in a pouch on the mother's body; and *monotremes*, where the young hatch from an egg outside the mother's body and are then nourished with milk. There are over 4,000 species of mammals.

reptile any member of a class (Reptilia) of vertebrates. They include snakes, lizards, crocodiles, turtles, and tortoises. Unlike amphibians, reptiles have hard-shelled, yolk-filled eggs that are laid on land and from which fully formed young are born. Some snakes and lizards retain their eggs and give birth to live young. Reptiles are cold-blooded, and the skin is usually covered with scales. The metabolism is slow, and in some cases (certain large snakes) intervals between meals may be months.

Systems

alimentary canal in animals, the tube through which food passes; it extends from the mouth to the anus. It is a complex organ, adapted for digestion. In human adults, it is about 9 m/30 ft long, consisting of the mouth cavity, pharynx, oesophagus, stomach, and the small and large intestines.

bone hard connective tissue comprising the skeleton of most vertebrate animals. It consists of a network of collagen fibres impregnated with mineral salts, a combination that gives the bone great strength, comparable in some cases with that of reinforced concrete. Enclosed within this solid matrix are bone cells, blood vessels, and nerves. The interior of the long bones of the limbs consists of a spongy matrix filled with a soft marrow that produces blood cells.

brain in higher animals, a mass of interconnected nerve cells, forming the anterior part of the central nervous system, whose activities it coordinates and controls. In vertebrates, the brain is contained by the skull. An enlarged portion of the upper spinal cord, the *medulla oblongata*, contains centres for the control of respiration, heartbeat rate and strength, and blood pressure. Overlying this is the *cerebellum*, which is concerned with coordinating complex muscular processes such as maintaining posture and moving limbs. The cerebral hemispheres (*cerebrum*) are paired outgrowths of the front end of the forebrain, in early vertebrates mainly concerned with the senses, but in higher vertebrates greatly developed and involved in the integration of all sensory input and motor output, and in intelligent behaviour. In the brain, nerve impulses are passed across synapses by neurotransmitters, in the same way as in other parts of the nervous system.

In mammals, the cerebrum is the largest part of the brain, carrying the *cerebral cortex*. This consists of a thick surface layer of cell bodies (grey matter), below which fibre tracts (white matter) connect various parts of the cortex to each other and to other points in the central nervous system. As cerebral complexity grows, the surface of the brain becomes convoluted into deep folds.

circulatory system system of vessels in an animal's body that transports essential substances (blood or other circulatory fluid) to and from the different parts of the body. Except for simple animals such as sponges and coelenterates (jellyfishes, sea anemones, corals), all animals have a circulatory system. Although most animals have a heart or hearts to pump the blood, normal body movements circulate the fluid in some small invertebrates.

muscle contractile animal tissue that produces locomotion and maintains the movement of body substances. Muscle is made of long cells that can contract to between one-half and one-third of their relaxed length. *Striped* muscles are activated by motor nerves under voluntary control; their ends are usually attached via tendons to bones. *Involuntary* or *smooth* muscles are controlled by motor nerves of the autonomic nervous system, and are located in the gut, blood vessels, iris, and various ducts. *Cardiac* muscle occurs only in the heart, and is also controlled by the autonomic nervous system.

nervous system the system of interconnected nerve cells of most invertebrates and all vertebrates. It is composed of the central and autonomic nervous systems. It may be as simple as the nerve net of coelenterates (for example, jellyfishes) or as complex as the mammalian nervous system, with a central nervous system comprising brain and spinal cord, and a peripheral nervous system connecting up with sensory organs, muscles, and glands.

skeleton the rigid or semirigid framework that supports an animal's body, protects its internal organs, and provides anchorage points for its muscles. The skeleton may be composed of bone and cartilage (vertebrates), chitin (arthropods), calcium carbonate (molluscs and other invertebrates), or silica (many protists).

Animal speeds

Maximum speeds for a selection of animals

Animal	mph
Cheetah	70
Wildebeest	50
Lion	50
Quarterhorse	47.5
Elk	45
Cape hunting dog	45
Coyote	43
Grey fox	42
Hyena	40
Zebra	40
Greyhound	39.35
Whippet	35.50
Rabbit (domestic)	35
Jackal	35
Reindeer	32
Giraffe	32
White-tailed deer	30
Wart hog	30
Grizzly bear	30
Cat (domestic)	30
Human	27.89
Elephant	25
Black mamba snake	20
Wild turkey	15
Squirrel	12
Pig (domestic)	11
Chicken	9
Spider (Tegenaria atrica)	1.17
Giant tortoise	0.17
Three-toed sloth	0.15
Garden snail	0.03

Most of these measurements refer to the maximum speed registered for approximately quarter-mile distances.

Source: Natural History

It may be internal, forming an *endoskeleton*, or external, forming an *exoskeleton*. Another type of skeleton, found in invertebrates such as earthworms, is the *hydrostatic skeleton*. This gains partial rigidity from fluid enclosed within a body cavity. Because the fluid cannot be compressed, contraction of one part of the body results in extension of another part, giving peristaltic motion.

PLANT

an organism that carries out photosynthesis, has cellulose cell walls and complex cells, and is immobile. A few parasitic plants have lost the ability to photosynthesize but are still considered to be plants. Plants are autotrophs, that is, they make carbohydrates from water and carbon dioxide, and are the primary producers in all food chains, so that all animal life is dependent on them. They play a vital part in the carbon cycle, removing carbon dioxide from the atmosphere and generating oxygen.

algae (singular *alga*) diverse group of plants that shows great variety of form, ranging from single-celled forms to multicellular seaweeds of considerable size and complexity. Algae can be classified into 12 divisions, largely to be distinguished by their pigmentation, including the *green algae* Chlorophyta, freshwater or terrestrial; *stoneworts* Charophyta; *golden-brown algae* Chrysophyta; *brown algae* Phaeophyta, mainly marine and including the *kelps* Laminaria and allies, the largest of all algae; *red algae* Rhodophyta, mainly marine and often living parasitically or as epiphytes on other algae; *diatoms* Bacillariophyta; *yellow-green algae* Xanthophyta, mostly freshwater and terrestrial; and *blue-green algae* Cyanophyta, of simple cell structure and without sexual reproduction, mostly freshwater or terrestrial.

angiosperm flowering plant in which the seeds are enclosed within an ovary, which ripens to a fruit. Angiosperms are divided into monocotyledons (single seed leaf in the embryo) and dicotyledons (two seed leaves in the embryo). They include the majority of flowers, herbs, grasses, and trees except conifers.

bryophyte member of the Bryophyta, a division of the plant kingdom containing three classes: the Hepaticae (liverwort), Musci (moss), and Anthocerotae (hornwort). Bryophytes are generally small, low-growing, terrestrial plants with no vascular (water-conducting) system as in higher plants. Their life cycle shows a marked alternation of generations. Bryophytes chiefly occur in damp habitats and require water for the dispersal of the male gametes (antherozoids).

gymnosperm any plant whose seeds are exposed, as opposed to the structurally more advanced angiosperms, where they are inside an ovary. The group includes conifers and related plants such as cycads and ginkgos, whose seeds develop in cones.

pteridophyte simple type of vascular plant. The pteridophytes comprise four classes: the Psilosida, including the most primitive vascular plants, found mainly in the tropics; the Lycopsida, including the club mosses; the Sphenopsida, including the horsetails; and the Pteropsida, including the ferns. They are mainly terrestrial, non-flowering plants characterized by alternation of generations. They do not produce seeds.

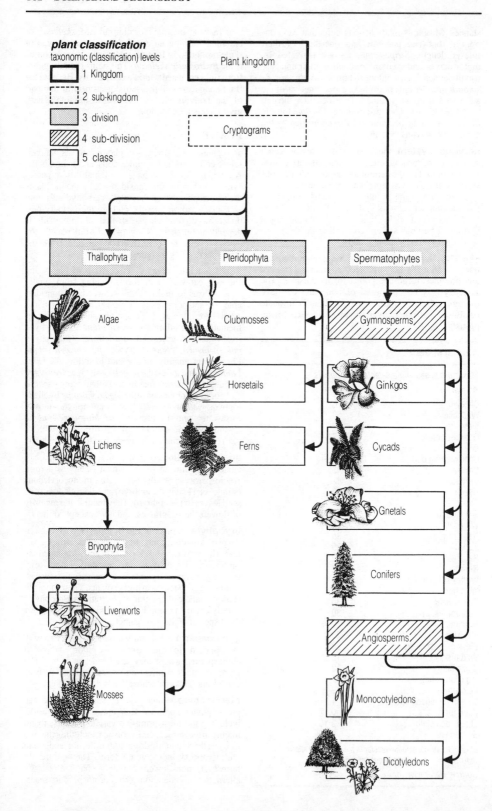

plant classification

taxonomic (classification) levels

1 Kingdom

2 sub-kingdom

3 division

4 sub-division

5 class

Plant kingdom

Cryptograms

Thallophyta

Algae

Lichens

Pteridophyta

Clubmosses

Horsetails

Ferns

Spermatophytes

Gymnosperms

Ginkgos

Cycads

Gnetals

Conifers

Bryophyta

Liverworts

Mosses

Angiosperms

Monocotyledons

Dicotyledons

Systems

chlorophyll green pigment present in most plants; it is responsible for the absorption of light energy during photosynthesis. The pigment absorbs the red and blue-violet parts of sunlight but reflects the green, thus giving plants their characteristic colour.

chloroplast structure (organelle) within a plant cell containing the green pigment chlorophyll. Chloroplasts occur in most cells of the green plant that are exposed to light, often in large numbers. Typically, they are flattened and disclike, with a double membrane enclosing the stroma, a gel-like matrix. Within the stroma are stacks of fluid-containing cavities, or vesicles, where photosynthesis occurs.

flower the reproductive unit of an angiosperm or flowering plant, typically consisting of four whorls of modified leaves: sepals, petals, stamens, and carpels. These are borne on a central axis or receptacle. The many variations in size, colour, number, and arrangement of parts are closely related to the method of pollination. Flowers adapted for wind pollination typically have reduced or absent petals and sepals and long, feathery stigmas that hang outside the flower to trap airborne pollen. The petals of insect-pollinated flowers are usually conspicuous and brightly coloured.

leaf lateral outgrowth on the stem of a plant, and in most species the primary organ of photosynthesis. The chief leaf types are cotyledons (seed leaves), scale leaves (on underground stems), foliage leaves, and bracts (in the axil of which a flower is produced). Structurally the leaf is made up of mesophyll cells surrounded by the epidermis and usually, in addition, a waxy layer, termed the cuticle, which prevents excessive evaporation of water from the leaf tissues by transpiration. The epidermis is interrupted by small pores, or stomata, through which gas exchange between the plant and the atmosphere occurs.

root the part of a plant that is usually underground, and whose primary functions are anchorage and the absorption of water and dissolved mineral salts. Roots usually grow downwards and towards water (that is, they are positively geotropic and hydrotropic). Plants such as epiphytic orchids, which grow above ground, produce aerial roots that absorb moisture from the atmosphere. Others, such as ivy, have climbing roots arising from the stems, which serve to attach the plant to trees and walls.

The Microscopic World

archaebacteria three groups of bacteria whose DNA differs significantly from that of other bacteria (called the 'eubacteria'). All are strict anaerobes; that is, they are killed by oxygen. This is thought to indicate that the archaebacteria are related to the earliest life forms, which appeared about 4 billion years ago, when there was little oxygen in the Earth's atmosphere. Archaebacteria are found in undersea vents, hot springs, the Dead Sea, and salt pans, and have adapted to refuse dumps.

bacillus member of a group of rodlike bacteria that occur everywhere in the soil and air. Some are responsible for diseases, such as anthrax, or for causing food spoilage.

bacteria (singular *bacterium*) microscopic unicellular organisms with prokaryotic cells (lacking true nuclei). They usually reproduce by binary fission (dividing into two equal parts), and since this may occur approximately every 20 minutes, a single bacterium is potentially capable of producing 16 million copies of itself in a day. It is thought that 1–10% of the world's bacteria have been identified. Many bacteria cause disease, but certain types of bacteria are vital in many food and industrial processes, while others play an essential role in the nitrogen cycle, which maintains soil fertility.

blue-green algae or *cyanobacteria* single-celled, primitive organisms that resemble bacteria in their internal cell organization, sometimes joined together in colonies or filaments. Blue-green algae are among the oldest known living organisms and, with bacteria, belong to the kingdom Monera; remains have been found in rocks up to 3.5 billion years old. They are widely distributed in aquatic habitats, on the damp surfaces of rocks and trees, and in the soil. Some can fix nitrogen and thus are necessary to the nitrogen cycle, while others follow a symbiotic existence; for example, living in association with fungi to form lichens.

cell discrete, membrane-bound portion of living matter, the smallest unit capable of an independent existence. All living organisms consist of one or more cells, with the exception of viruses. Bacteria, protozoa, and many other microorganisms consist of single cells, whereas a human is made up of billions of cells. Essential features of a cell are the membrane, which encloses it and restricts the flow of substances in and out; the jellylike material within, often known as protoplasm; the ribosomes, which carry out protein synthesis; and the DNA, which forms the hereditary material.

coccus (plural *cocci*) member of a group of globular bacteria, some of which are harmful to humans. The cocci contain the subgroups *streptococci*, where the bacteria associate in straight chains, and *staphylococci*, where the bacteria associate in branched chains.

cytoplasm the part of the cell outside the nucleus. Strictly speaking, this includes all the organelles (mitochondria, chloroplasts, and so on), but often cytoplasm refers to the jellylike matter in which the organelles are embedded (correctly termed the cytosol).

eukaryote one of the two major groupings into which all organisms are divided. Included are all organisms, except bacteria and cyanobacteria (blue-green algae), which belong to the prokaryote grouping. The cells of eukaryotes possess a clearly defined nucleus, bounded by a membrane, within which DNA is formed into distinct chromosomes. Eukaryotic cells also contain mitochondria, chloroplasts, and other structures (organelles) that, together with a defined nucleus, are lacking in the cells of prokaryotes.

methanogenic bacteria one of a group of primitive bacteria (archaebacteria). They give off methane gas as a by-product of their metabolism, and are common in sewage treatment plants and hot springs, where the temperature is high and oxygen is absent.

microorganism or *microbe* living organism invisible to the naked eye but visible under a microscope. Microorganisms include viruses and single-celled organisms such as bacteria, protozoa, yeasts, and some algae. The term has no taxonomic significance in biology. The study of microorganisms is known as microbiology.

nucleus the central, membrane-enclosed part of a eukaryotic cell, containing the chromosomes.

prokaryote organism whose cells lack organelles (specialized segregated structures such as nuclei, mitochondria, and chloroplasts). Prokaryote DNA is not arranged in chromosomes but forms a coiled structure called a *nucleoid*. The prokaryotes comprise only the *bacteria* and *cyanobacteria* (blue-green algae); all other organisms are eukaryotes.

protist single-celled organism that has a eukaryotic cell but is not a member of the plant, fungal, or animal kingdoms. The main protists are protozoa.

protozoa group of single-celled organisms without rigid cell walls. Some, such as amoeba, ingest other cells, but most are saprotrophs or parasites. The group is polyphyletic (containing organisms which have different evolutionary origins).

virus infectious particle consisting of a core of nucleic acid (DNA or RNA) enclosed in a protein shell. Viruses are acellular and able to function and reproduce only if they can invade a living cell to use the cell's system to replicate themselves. In the process, they may disrupt or alter the host cell's own DNA. The healthy human body reacts by producing an antiviral protein, interferon, which prevents the infection spreading to adjacent cells.

Viroids are even smaller than viruses; they consist of a single strand of nucleic acid with no protein coat.

Viruses are abundant in seas and lakes, with between 5 million and 250 million per millilitre of water, rising with the degree of pollution. Among diseases caused by viruses are chickenpox, common cold, herpes, influenza, rabies, smallpox, AIDS, and many plant diseases.

The New Synthesis

amino acid water-soluble organic molecule, mainly composed of carbon, oxygen, hydrogen, and nitrogen, containing both a basic amino group (NH_2) and an acidic carboxyl (COOH) group. When two or more amino acids are joined together, they are known as peptides; proteins are made up of interacting polypeptides (peptide chains consisting of more than three amino acids) and are folded or twisted in characteristic shapes.

Many different proteins are found in the cells of living organisms, but they are all made up of the same 20 amino acids, joined together in varying combinations (although other types of amino acid do occur infrequently in nature). Eight of these, the *essential amino acids*, cannot be synthesized by humans and must be obtained from the diet. Children

need a further two amino acids that are not essential for adults. Other animals also need some preformed amino acids in their diet, but green plants can manufacture all the amino acids they need from simpler molecules, relying on energy from the Sun and minerals (including nitrates) from the soil.

amylase one of a group of enzymes that break down starches into their component molecules (sugars) for use in the body. It occurs widely in both plants and animals. In humans, it is found in saliva and in pancreatic juices.

ATP abbreviation for *adenosine triphosphate*, a nucleotide molecule found in all cells. It can yield large amounts of energy, and is used to drive the thousands of biological processes needed to sustain life, growth, movement, and reproduction. Green plants use light energy to manufacture ATP as part of the process of photosynthesis. In animals, ATP is formed by the breakdown of glucose molecules, usually obtained from the carbohydrate component of a diet, in a series of reactions termed respiration. It is the driving force behind muscle contraction and the synthesis of complex molecules needed by individual cells.

base pair the linkage of two base (purine or pyrimidine) molecules in DNA. They are found in nucleotides, and form the basis of the genetic code. One base lies on one strand of the DNA double helix, and one on the other, so that the base pairs link the two strands like the rungs of a ladder. In DNA, there are four bases: adenine and guanine (purines) and cytosine and thymine (pyrimidines). Adenine always pairs with thymine, and cytosine with guanine.

codon triplet of bases in a molecule of DNA or RNA that directs the placement of a particular amino acid during the process of protein (polypeptide) synthesis. There are 64 codons in the genetic code.

cytochrome protein responsible for part of the process of respiration by which food molecules are broken down in aerobic organisms. Cytochromes are part of the electron transport chain, which uses energized electrons to reduce molecular oxygen (O_2) to oxygen ions (O_2-). These combine with hydrogen ions (H+) to form water (H_2O), the end product of aerobic respiration. As electrons are passed from one cytochrome to another, energy is released and used to make ATP (nucleotide that powers cellular reactions).

DNA *deoxyribonucleic acid* complex giant molecule that contains, in chemically coded form, all the information needed to build, control, and maintain a living organism. DNA is a ladderlike double-stranded nucleic acid that forms the basis of genetic inheritance in all organisms, except for a few viruses that have only RNA. In organisms other than bacteria it is organized into chromosomes and contained in the cell nucleus.

enzyme biological catalyst produced in cells, and capable of speeding up the chemical reactions necessary for life by converting one molecule (substrate) into another. Enzymes are not themselves destroyed by this process. They are large, complex proteins, and are highly specific, each chemical reaction requiring its own particular enzyme. The enzyme fits into a 'slot' (active site) in the substrate molecule, forming an enzyme-substrate complex that lasts until the substrate is altered or split, after which the enzyme can fall away. The substrate may therefore be compared to a lock, and the enzyme to the key required to open it.

Digestive enzymes include amylases (which digest starch), lipases (which digest fats), and proteases (which digest protein). Other enzymes play a part in the conversion of food energy into ATP; the manufacture of all the molecular components of the body; the replication of DNA when a cell divides;

DNA

how a cell divides

1 — original double helix

2 — forms ladder

3 — unzips

4 — new bases join onto opened zip teeth

5 — two identical double strands

Key
S sugars   G guanine
P phosphates   A adenine
C cytosine   T thymine

the production of hormones; and the control of movement of substances into and out of cells. Enzymes have many medical and industrial uses, from washing powders to drug production, and as research tools in molecular biology. They can be extracted from bacteria and moulds, and genetic engineering now makes it possible to tailor an enzyme for a specific purpose.

genetic code the way in which instructions for building proteins, the basic structural molecules of living matter, are 'written' in the genetic material DNA. This relationship between the sequence of bases (the subunits in a DNA molecule) and the sequence of amino acids (the subunits of a protein molecule) is the basis of heredity. The code employs codons of three bases each; it is the same in almost all organisms, except for a few minor differences recently discovered in some protozoa.

mitochondria (singular *mitochondrion*) membrane-enclosed organelles within eukaryotic cells, containing enzymes responsible for energy production during aerobic respiration. These rodlike or spherical bodies are thought to be derived from free-living bacteria that, at a very early stage in the history of life, invaded larger cells and took up a symbiotic way of life inside. Each still contains its own small loop of DNA called mitochondrial DNA, and new mitochondria arise by division of existing ones.

molecular biology study of the molecular basis of life, including the biochemistry of molecules such as DNA, RNA, and proteins, and the molecular structure and function of the various parts of living cells.

nucleotide organic compound consisting of a purine (adenine or guanine) or a pyrimidine (thymine, uracil, or cytosine) base linked to a sugar (deoxyribose or ribose) and a phosphate group. DNA and RNA are made up of long chains of nucleotides.

operon group of genes that are found next to each other on a chromosome, and are turned on and off as an integrated unit. They usually produce enzymes that control different steps in the same biochemical pathway. Operons are found in bacteria; they are less common in higher organisms, where the control of metabolism is a more complex process.

peptide molecule comprising two or more amino acid molecules (not necessarily different) joined by *peptide bonds*, whereby the acid group of one acid is linked to the amino group of the other (–CO.NH). The number of amino acid molecules in the peptide is indicated by referring to it as a di-, tri-, or polypeptide (two, three, or many amino acids).

protein complex, biologically important substance composed of amino acids joined by peptide bonds. Other types of bond, such as sulphur–sulphur bonds, hydrogen bonds, and cation bridges between acid sites, are responsible for creating the protein's characteristic three-dimensional structure, which may be fibrous, globular, or pleated.

Proteins are essential to all living organisms. As *enzymes* they regulate all aspects of metabolism. Structural proteins such as *keratin* and *collagen* make up the skin, claws, bones, tendons, and ligaments; *muscle* proteins produce movement; *haemo-*

globin transports oxygen; and *membrane* proteins regulate the movement of substances into and out of cells.

ribosome the protein-making machinery of the cell. Ribosomes are located on the endoplasmic reticulum of eukaryotic cells, and are made of proteins and a special type of RNA, ribosomal RNA. They receive messenger RNA (copied from the DNA) and amino acids, and 'translate' the messenger RNA by using its chemically coded instructions to link amino acids in a specific order, to make a strand of a particular protein.

RNA *ribonucleic acid* nucleic acid involved in the process of translating the genetic material DNA into proteins. It is usually single-stranded, unlike the double-stranded DNA, and consists of a large number of nucleotides strung together, each of which comprises the sugar ribose, a phosphate group, and one of four bases (uracil, cytosine, adenine, or guanine). RNA is copied from DNA by the formation of base pairs, with uracil taking the place of thymine. Although RNA is normally associated only with the process of protein synthesis, it makes up the hereditary material itself in some viruses, such as retroviruses.

transcription in living cells, the process by which the information for the synthesis of a protein is transferred from the DNA strand on which it is carried to the messenger RNA strand involved in the actual synthesis. It occurs by the formation of base pairs when a single strand of unwound DNA serves as a template for assembling the complementary nucleotides that make up the new RNA strand.

translation the process by which proteins are synthesized in living cells. During translation, the information coded as a sequence of nucleotides in messenger RNA is transformed into a sequence of amino acids in a peptide chain. The process involves the 'translation' of the genetic code.

New Techniques

abzyme artificially created antibody that can be used like an enzyme to accelerate reactions.

autoradiography technique for following the movement of molecules within an organism, especially a plant, by labelling with a radioactive isotope that can be traced on photographs. It is used to study photosynthesis, where the pathway of radioactive carbon dioxide can be traced as it moves through the various chemical stages.

bacteriophage virus that attacks bacteria. Such viruses are of use in genetic engineering.

biosensor device based on microelectronic circuits that can directly measure medically significant variables for the purpose of diagnosis or monitoring treatment. One such device measures the blood-sugar level using a single drop of blood, and shows the result on a liquid-crystal display within a few minutes.

biotechnology industrial use of living organisms to manufacture food, drugs, or other products. The brewing and baking industries have long relied on the yeast microorganism for fermentation purposes, while the dairy industry employs a range of bacteria and fungi to convert milk into cheeses and yoghurts. In genetic engineering, single-celled organisms with modified DNA are used to produce insulin and other drugs. Enzymes, whether extracted from cells or produced artificially, are central to most biotechnological applications.

clone group of cells or organisms arising by asexual reproduction from a single 'parent' individual. Clones therefore have exactly the same genetic make-up as the parent cell. Traditional methods of cloning have been used on plant material throughout history; they include such techniques as leaf and stem cuttings. Recent advances in biotechnology have allowed the cloning of animals.

cosmid fragment of DNA from the human genome inserted into a bacterial cell. The bacterium replicates the fragment along with its own DNA. In this way the fragments are copied for a gene library. Cosmids are characteristically 40,000 base pairs in length. The most commonly used bacterium is *Escherichia coli.* A yeast artificial chromosome works in the same way.

electron microscope instrument that produces a magnified image by using a beam of electrons instead of light rays, as in an optical microscope. An *electron lens* is an arrangement of electromagnetic coils that control and focus the beam. There is a fluorescent screen or a photographic plate on which the electrons form an image. The wavelength of the electron beam is much shorter than that of light, so much greater magnification and resolution (ability to distinguish detail) can be achieved. The development of the electron microscope has made possible the observation of very minute organisms, viruses, and even large molecules.

A transmission electron microscope passes the electron beam through a very thin slice of a specimen. A scanning electron microscope looks at the exterior of a specimen. A scanning transition electron microscope (STEM) can produce a magnification of 90 million times.

electroporation technique of introducing foreign DNA into pollen with a strong burst of electricity, used in creating genetically engineered plants.

fluorescence microscopy technique for examining samples under a microscope without slicing them into thin sections. Instead, fluorescent dyes are introduced into the tissue and used as a light source for imaging purposes. Fluorescent dyes can also be bonded to monoclonal antibodies and used to highlight areas where particular cell proteins occur.

gene bank collection of seeds or other forms of genetic material, such as tubers, spores, bacterial or yeast cultures, live animals and plants, frozen sperm and eggs, or frozen embryos. These are stored for possible future use in agriculture, plant and animal breeding, or in medicine, genetic engineering, or the restocking of wild habitats where species have become extinct. Gene banks will be increasingly used as the rate of extinction increases, depleting the Earth's genetic variety (biodiversity).

gene therapy curing or alleviating inherited diseases or defects by altering the DNA of some of the patient's cells by genetic engineering in a laboratory, and reintroducing the functioning cells into the body. In 1990, an engineered gene was used for the first time to treat a patient.

genetic engineering manipulation of genetic material by biochemical techniques. It is often achieved by the introduction of new DNA, usually by means of a virus or plasmid. This can be for pure research or to breed functionally specific plants, animals, or bacteria. These organisms with a foreign gene added are said to be transgenic.

In genetic engineering, the splicing and reconciliation of genes is used to increase knowledge of cell function and reproduction, but it can also achieve practical ends. For example, plants grown for food could be given the ability to fix nitrogen, found in some bacteria, and so reduce the need for expensive fertilizers, or simple bacteria could be modified to produce rare drugs. Developments in genetic engineering have led to the production of human insulin, human growth hormone, and a number of other bone-marrow stimulating hormones. New strains of animals have also been produced; a new strain of mouse was patented in the USA 1989 (the application was rejected in the European patent office). A vaccine against a sheep parasite (a larval tapeworm) has been developed by genetic engineering; most existing vaccines protect against bacteria and viruses. There is a risk that when transplanting genes between different types of bacteria (*Escherichia coli*, which lives in the human intestine, is often used) new and harmful strains might be produced. For this reason strict safety precautions are observed, and the altered bacteria are disabled in some way so they are unable to exist outside the laboratory.

genetic fingerprinting (or *DNA fingerprinting* or *DNA profiling*) technique used for determining the pattern of certain parts of the genetic material DNA that is unique to each individual. Like skin fingerprinting, it can accurately distinguish humans from one another, with the exception of identical siblings from multiple births. It can be applied to as little material as a single cell.

The technique involves isolating DNA from cells, then comparing and contrasting the sequences of component chemicals between individuals. The DNA pattern can be ascertained from a sample of skin, hair, or semen. Although differences are minimal (only 0.1% between unrelated people), certain regions of DNA, known as *hypervariable regions*, are unique to individuals.

Genetic fingerprinting is now allowed as a means of legal identification. It is used in paternity testing, forensic medicine, and inbreeding studies. A new method that makes it possible to express the individuals' information in digital code will mean that genetic fingerprinting will now be much more accurate than before.

molecular clock use of rates of mutation in genetic material to calculate the length of time elapsed since two related species diverged from each other during evolution. The method can be based on comparisons of the DNA or of widely occurring proteins, such as haemoglobin.

Since mutations are thought to occur at a constant rate, the length of time that must have elapsed in order to produce the difference between two species can be estimated. This information can be compared with the evidence obtained from palaeontology to reconstruct evolutionary events.

protein engineering the creation of synthetic proteins designed to carry out specific tasks. For example, an enzyme may be designed to remove grease from soiled clothes and remain stable at the high temperatures in a washing machine.

restriction enzyme bacterial enzyme that breaks a chain of DNA into two pieces at a specific point; used in genetic engineering. The point along the DNA chain at which the enzyme can work is restricted to places where a specific sequence of base pairs occurs. Different restriction enzymes will break a DNA chain at different points. The overlap between the fragments is used in determining the sequence of base pairs in the DNA chain.

sequencing determining the sequence of chemical subunits within a large molecule. Techniques for sequencing amino acids in proteins were established in the 1950s, insulin being the first for which the sequence was completed. Efforts are now being made to determine the sequence of base pairs within DNA.

transgenic organism plant, animal, bacterium, or other living organism that has had a foreign gene added to it by means of genetic engineering.

The onco-mouse is one of many transgenic organisms. It carries a human oncogene, a gene that causes the mouse to develop cancer. The gene is implanted in the mouse, having been identified and cut from its original DNA, and then joined into new, mouse DNA. Much genetic engineering is carried out with bacteria because their cells have no nucleus, making the DNA easier to separate. But as techniques and knowledge progress, larger organisms are being used. Mice are fast-breeding mammals, so they can be used to model and study human disease processes.

yeast artificial chromosome (YAC) fragment of DNA from the human genome inserted into a yeast cell. The yeast replicates the fragment along with its own DNA. In this way the fragments are copied to be preserved in a gene library. YACs are characteristically between 250,000 and 1 million base pairs in length. A cosmid works in the same way.

MATHEMATICS

Terms

abacus method of calculating with a handful of stones on 'a flat surface' (Latin *abacus*), familiar to the Greeks and Romans, and used by earlier peoples, possibly even in ancient Babylon; it still survives in the more sophisticated bead-frame form of the Russian *schoty* and the Japanese *soroban*. The abacus has been superseded by the electronic calculator.

abscissa in coordinate geometry, the *x*-coordinate of a point – that is, the horizontal distance of that point from the vertical or *y*-axis. For example, a point with the coordinates (4, 3) has an abscissa of 3. The *y*-coordinate of a point is known as the ordinate.

algebra system of arithmetic applying to any set of non-numerical symbols (usually letters), and the axioms and rules by which they are combined or operated upon; sometimes known as *generalized arithmetic*. It is used in many branches of mathematics, for example, matrix algebra and Boolean algebra (the latter method was first devised in the 19th century by the British mathematician George Boole and used in working out the logic for computers).

alternate angles a pair of angles that lie on opposite sides and at opposite ends of a transversal (a line that cuts two or more lines in the same plane). The alternate angles formed by a transversal of two parallel lines are equal.

altitude in geometry, the perpendicular distance from a vertex (corner) of a figure, such as a triangle, to the base (the side opposite the vertex).

angle in mathematics, the amount of turn or rotation; it may be defined by a pair of rays (half-lines) that share a common endpoint but do not lie on the same line. Angles are measured in degrees (°) or radians (rads) – a complete turn or circle being 360° or 2π rads. Angles are classified generally by their degree measures: *acute angles* are less than 90°; *right angles* are exactly 90° (a quarter turn); *obtuse angles* are greater than 90° but less than 180°; *reflex angles* are greater than 180° but less than 360°.

apex the highest point of a triangle, cone, or pyramid – that is, the vertex (corner) opposite a given base.

Arabic numerals or *Hindu-Arabic numerals* the symbols 0, 1, 2, 3, 4, 5, 6, 7, 8, 9, early forms of which were in use among the Arabs before being adopted by the peoples of Europe during the Middle Ages in place of Roman numerals. The symbols appear to have originated in India and probably reached Europe by way of Spain.

arc a section of a curved line or circle. A circle has three types of arc: a *semicircle*, which is exactly half of the circle; *minor arcs*, which are less than the semicircle; and *major arcs*, which are greater than the semicircle.

area the size of a surface. It is measured in square units, usually square centimetres (cm^2), square metres (m^2), or square kilometres (km^2). Surface area is the area of the outer surface of a solid.

Common areas

Figure	Rule for calculating area
rectangle	length × breadth
triangle	half base length × height
parallelogram	base length × height
trapezium	average length of parallel sides × perpendicular distance between them
circle	πr^2, where *r* is the radius sector $\dfrac{x\pi r^2}{360}$ where *x* is the angle of the sector

arithmetic branch of mathematics concerned with the study of numbers and their properties. The fundamental operations of arithmetic are addition, subtraction, multiplication, and division. Raising to powers (for example, squaring or cubing a number), the extraction of roots (for example, square roots), percentages, fractions, and ratios are developed from these operations.

associative operation mathematical operation in which the outcome is independent of the grouping of the numbers or symbols concerned. For example, multiplication is associative, as $4 \times (3 \times 2) = (4 \times 3) \times 2 = 24$; however, division is not, as $12 \div (4 \div 2) = 6$, but $(12 \div 4) \div 2 = 1.5$. Compare commutative operation and distributive operation.

axis (plural *axes*) one of the reference lines by which a point on a graph may be located. The horizontal axis is usually referred to as the *x*-axis, and the vertical axis as the *y*-axis. The term is also used to refer to the imaginary line about which an object may be said to be symmetrical (*axis of symmetry*) – for example, the diagonal of a square – or the line about which an object may revolve (*axis of rotation*).

base in mathematics, the number of different single-digit symbols used in a particular number system. In our usual (decimal) counting system of numbers (with symbols 0, 1, 2, 3, 4, 5, 6, 7, 8, 9) the base is 10. In the binary number system, which has only the symbols 1 and 0, the base is two. A base is also a number that, when raised to a particular power (that is, when multiplied by itself a particular number of times as in $10^2 = 10 \times 10 = 100$), has a logarithm equal to the power. For example, the logarithm of 100 to the base ten is 2.

In geometry, the term is used to denote the line or area on which a polygon or solid stands. (See table opposite.)

bearing the direction of a fixed point, or the path of a moving object, from a point of observation on the Earth's surface, expressed as an angle from the north. Bearings are taken by compass and are measured in degrees (°), given as three-digit numbers increasing clockwise. For instance, north is 000°, northeast is 045°, south is 180°, and southwest is 225°. True north differs slightly from magnetic north (the direction in which a compass needle points), hence NE may be denoted as 045M or 045T, depending on whether the reference line is magnetic (M) or true (T) north.

True north also differs slightly from grid north since it is impossible to show a spherical Earth on a flat map.

binomial in mathematics, an expression consisting of two terms, such as $a + b$ or $a - b$.

calculus branch of mathematics that permits the manipulation of continuously varying quantities, used in practical problems involving such matters as changing speeds, problems of flight, varying stresses in the framework of a bridge, and alternating current theory. *Integral calculus* deals with the method of summation or adding together the effects of continuously varying quantities. *Differential calculus* deals in a similar way with rates of change. Many of its applications arose from the study of the gradients of the tangents to curves.

cardinal number one of the series of numbers 0, 1, 2, 3, 4, ... Cardinal numbers relate to quantity, whereas ordinal numbers (first, second, third, fourth, ...) relate to order.

chord in geometry, a straight line joining any two points on a curve. The chord that passes through the centre of a circle (its longest chord) is the diameter. The longest and shortest chords of an ellipse (a regular oval) are called the major and minor axes respectively.

circle perfectly round shape, the path of a point that moves so as to keep a constant distance from a fixed point (the centre). Each circle has a *radius* (the distance from any point on the circle to the centre), a *circumference* (the boundary of the circle), *diameters* (straight lines crossing the circle through the centre), *chords* (lines joining two points on the circumference), *tangents* (lines that touch the circumference at one point only), *sectors* (regions inside the circle between two radii), and *segments* (regions between a chord and the circumference).

circumference the curved line that encloses a curved plane figure, for example a circle or an ellipse. Its length varies according to the nature of the curve, and may be ascertained by the appropriate formula. The circumference of a circle is πd or $2\pi r$, where d is the diameter of the circle, r is its radius and π is the constant pi, approximately equal to 3.1416.

coefficient the number part in front of an algebraic term, signifying multiplication. For example, in the expression $4x^2 + 2xy - x$, the coefficient of x^2 is 4 (because $4x^2$ means $4 \times x^2$), that of xy is 2, and that of x is -1 (because $-1 \times x = -x$).

commutative operation an operation that is independent of the order of the numbers or symbols concerned. For example, addition is commutative: the result of adding $4 + 2$ is the same as that of adding $2 + 4$; subtraction is not as $4 - 2 = 2$, but $2 - 4 = -2$. Compare associative operation and distributive operation.

complement the set of the elements within the universal set that are not contained in the designated set. For example, if the universal set is the set of all positive whole numbers and the designated set S is the set of all even numbers, then the complement of S (denoted S') is the set of all odd numbers.

concave of a surface, curving inwards, or away from the eye. For example, a bowl appears concave when viewed from above. In geometry, a concave polygon is one that has an interior angle greater than 180°. Concave is the opposite of convex.

concentric circles two or more circles that share the same centre.

cone a solid or surface consisting of the set of all straight lines passing through a fixed point (the vertex) and the points of a circle or ellipse whose plane does not contain the vertex. A circular cone of perpendicular height, with its apex above the centre of the circle, is known as a *right circular cone*; it is generated by rotating an isosceles triangle or framework about its line of symmetry. A right circular cone of perpendicular height h and base of radius r has a volume $V = \frac{1}{3}\pi r^2 h$. The distance from the edge of the base of a cone to the vertex is called the slant height. In a right circular cone of slant height l, the curved surface area is $\pi r l$, and the area of the base is πr^2. Therefore the total surface area $A = \pi r l + \pi r^2 = \pi r(l + r)$.

congruent having the same shape and size, as applied to two-dimensional or solid figures. With plane congruent figures, one figure will fit on top of the other exactly, though this may first require rotation and/or rotation of one of the figures.

conic section curve obtained when a conical surface is intersected by a plane. If the intersecting plane cuts both extensions of the cone, it yields a hyperbola; if it is parallel to the side of the cone, it produces a parabola. Other intersecting planes produce circles or ellipses.

constant a fixed quantity or one that does not change its value in relation to variables. For example, in the algebraic expression $y^2 = 5x - 3$, the numbers 3 and 5 are constants. In physics, certain quantities are regarded as universal constants, such as the speed of light in a vacuum.

converse the reversed order of a conditional statement; the converse of the statement 'if a, then b' is 'if b, then a'. The converse does not always hold true; for

Base

binary (base 2)	octal (base 8)	decimal (base 10)	hexadecimal (base 16)
0	0	0	0
1	1	1	1
10	2	2	2
11	3	3	3
100	4	4	4
101	5	5	5
110	6	6	6
111	7	7	7
1000	10	8	8
1001	11	9	9
1010	12	10	A
1011	13	11	B
1100	14	12	C
1101	15	13	D
1110	16	14	E
1111	17	15	F
10000	20	16	10
11111111	377	255	FF
1111010001	3721	2001	7D1

Mathematics: chronology

c. 2500 BC	The people of Mesopotamia (now Iraq) developed a positional numbering (place-value) system, in which the value of a digit depends in its position in a number.
c. 2000 BC	Mesopotamian mathematicians solved quadratic equations (algebraic equations in which the highest power of a variable is 2).
876 BC	A symbol for zero was used for the first time, in India.
c. 550 BC	Greek mathematician Pythagoras formulated a theorem relating the lengths of the sides of a right-angled triangle. The theorem was already known by earlier mathematicians in China, Mesopotamia, and Egypt.
c. 450 BC	Hipparcos of Metapontum discovered that some numbers are irrational (cannot be expressed as the ratio of two integers).
300 BC	Euclid laid out the laws of geometry in his book Elements, which was to remain a standard text for 2,000 years.
c. 230 BC	Eratosthenes developed a method for finding all prime numbers.
c. 100 BC	Chinese mathematicians began using negative numbers.
c. 190 BC	Chinese mathematicians used powers of 10 to express magnitudes.
c. AD 210	Diophantus of Alexandria wrote the first book on algebra.
c. 600	A decimal number system was developed in India.
829	Persian mathematician Muhammad ibn-Mūsā al-Khwārizmī published a work on algebra that made use of the decimal number system.
1202	Italian mathematician Leonardo Fibonacci studied the sequence of numbers (1, 1, 2, 3, 5, 8, 13, 21, ...) in which each number is the sum of the two preceding ones.
1550	In Germany, Rheticus published trigonometrical tables that simplified calculations involving triangles.
1614	Scottish mathematician John Napier invented logarithms, which enable lengthy calculations involving multiplication and division to be carried out by addition and subtraction.
1623	Wilhelm Schickard invented the mechanical calculating machine.
1637	French mathematician and philosopher René Descartes introduced coordinate geometry.
1654	In France, Blaise Pascal and Pierre de Fermat developed probability theory.
1666	Isaac Newton developed differential calculus, a method of calculating rates of change.
1675	German mathematician Gottfried Wilhelm Leibniz introduced the modern notation for integral calculus, a method of calculating volumes.
1679	Leibniz introduced binary arithmetic, in which only two symbols are used to represent all numbers.
1684	Leibniz published the first account of differential calculus.
1718	Jakob Bernoulli in Switzerland published his work on the calculus of variations (the study of functions that are close to their minimum or maximum values.
1746	In France, Jean le Rond d'Alembert developed the theory of complex numbers.
1747	D'Alembert used partial differential equations in mathematical physics.
1798	Norwegian mathematician Caspar Wessel introduced the vector representation of complex numbers.
1799	Karl Friedrich Gauss of Germany proved the fundamental theorem of algebra: the number of solutions of an algebraic equation is the same as the exponent of the highest term.
1810	In France, Jean Baptiste Joseph Fourier published his method of representing functions by a series of trigonometric functions.
1812	French mathematician Pierre Simon Laplace published the first complete account of probability theory.
1822	In the UK, Charles Babbage began construction of the first mechanical computer, the difference machine, a device for calculating logarithms and trigonometric functions.
1827	Gauss introduced differential geometry, in which small features of curves are described by analytical methods.
1829	In Russia, Nikolai Ivanonvich Lobachevsky developed hyperbolic geometry, in which a plane is regarded as part of a hyperbolic surface, shaped like a saddle. In France, Evariste Galois introduced the theory of groups (collections whose members obey certain simple rules of addition and multiplication).
1844	French mathematician Joseph Liouville found the first transcendental number, which cannot be expressed as an algebraic equation with rational coefficients. In Germany, Hermann Grassmann studied vectors with more than three dimensions.
1854	George Boole in the UK published his system of symbolic logic, now called Boolean algebra.
1858	English mathematician Arthur Cayley developed calculations using ordered tables called matrices.
1865	August Ferdinand Möbius in Germany described how a strip of paper can have only one side and one edge.
1892	German mathematician Georg Cantor showed that there are different kinds of infinity and studied transfinite numbers.
1895	Jules Henri Poincaré published the first paper on topology, often called 'the geometry of rubber sheets'.
1931	In the USA, Austrian-born mathematician Kurt Gödel proved that any formal system strong enough to include the laws of arithmetic is either incomplete or inconsistent.
1937	English mathematician Alan Turing published the mathematical theory of computing.
1944	John Von Neumann and Oscar Morgenstern developed game theory in the USA.
1945	The first general purpose, fully electronic digital computer, ENIAC (electronic numerator, integrator, analyser, and computer), was built at the University of Pennsylvania, USA.
1961	Meteorologist Edward Lorenz at the Massachusetts Institute of Technology, USA, discovered a mathematical system with chaotic behaviour, leading to a new branch of mathematics - chaos theory.

Mathematics: chronology *(cont.)*

1962	Benit Mandelbrot in the USA invented fractal images, using a computer that repeats the same mathematical pattern over and over again.
1975	US mathematician Mitchell Feigenbaum discovered a new fundamental constant (approximately 4.669201609103), which plays an important role in chaos theory.
1980	Mathematicians worldwide completed the classification of all finite and simple groups, a task that took over a hundred mathematicians more than 35 years to complete and whose results took up more than 14,000 pages in mathematical journals.
1989	A team of US computer mathematicians at Amdahl Corporation, California, discovered the highest known prime number (it contains 65,087 digits).
1993	Andrew Wiles proved Fermat's last theorem, one of the most baffling challenges of mathematics.

example, the converse of 'if $x = 3$, then $x^2 = 9$' is 'if $x^2 = 9$, then $x = 3$', which is not true, as x could also be -3.

convex of a surface, curving outwards, or towards the eye. For example, the outer surface of a ball appears convex. In geometry, the term is used to describe any polygon possessing no interior angle greater than 180°. Convex is the opposite of concave.

coordinate geometry or *analytical geometry* system of geometry in which points, lines, shapes, and surfaces are represented by algebraic expressions. In plane (two-dimensional) coordinate geometry, the plane is usually defined by two axes at right angles to each other, the horizontal x-axis and the vertical y-axis, meeting at O, the origin. A point on the plane can be represented by a pair of Cartesian coordinates, which define its position in terms of its distance along the x-axis and along the y-axis from O. These distances are respectively the x and y coordinates of the point.

Lines are represented as equations; for example, $y = 2x + 1$ gives a straight line, and $y = 3x^2 + 2x$ gives a parabola (a curve). The graphs of varying equations can be drawn by plotting the coordinates of points that satisfy their equations, and joining up the points. One of the advantages of coordinate geometry is that geometrical solutions can be obtained without drawing but by manipulating algebraic expressions. For example, the coordinates of the point of intersection of two straight lines can be determined by finding the unique values of x and y that satisfy both of the equations for the lines, that is, by solving them as a pair of simultaneous equations. The curves studied in simple coordinate geometry are the conic sections (circle, ellipse, parabola, and hyperbola), each of which has a characteristic equation.

cosine in trigonometry, a function of an angle in a right-angled triangle found by dividing the length of the side adjacent to the angle by the length of the hypotenuse (the longest side). It is usually shortened to *cos*.

cube in geometry, a regular solid figure whose faces are all squares. It has six equal-area faces and 12 equal-length edges. If the length of one edge is l, the volume V of the cube is given by $V = l^3$ and its surface area A by $A = 6l^2$.

cuboid six-sided three-dimensional prism whose faces are all rectangles. A brick is a cuboid.

curve in geometry, the locus of a point moving according to specified conditions. The circle is the locus of all points equidistant from a given point (the

centre). Other common geometrical curves are the ellipse, parabola, and hyperbola, which are also produced when a cone is cut by a plane at different angles. Many curves have been invented for the solution of special problems in geometry and mechanics — for example, the cissoid (the inverse of a parabola) and the cycloid.

cybernetics science concerned with how systems organize, regulate, and reproduce themselves, and also how they evolve and learn. In the laboratory, inanimate objects are created that behave like living systems. Applications range from the creation of electronic artificial limbs to the running of the fully automated factory where decision-making machines operate up to managerial level. Cybernetics was founded and named in 1947 by US mathematician Norbert Wiener.

cycloid in geometry, a curve resembling a series of arches traced out by a point on the circumference of a circle that rolls along a straight line. Its applications include the study of the motion of wheeled vehicles along roads and tracks.

cylinder in geometry, a tubular solid figure with a circular base. In everyday use, the term applies to a *right cylinder*, the curved surface of which is at right angles to the base. The volume V of a cylinder is given by the formula $V = \pi r^2 h$, where r is the radius of the base and h is the height of the cylinder. Its total surface area A has the formula $A = 2\pi r(h + r)$, where $2\pi rh$ is the curved surface area, and $2\pi r^2$ is the area of both circular ends.

decimal fraction a fraction in which the denominator is any higher power of 10. Thus $^3/_{10}$, $^{51}/_{100}$, and $^{23}/_{1,000}$ are decimal fractions and are normally expressed as 0.3, 0.51, 0.023. The use of decimals greatly simplifies addition and multiplication of fractions, though not all fractions can be expressed exactly as decimal fractions. The regular use of the decimal point appears to have been introduced about 1585, but the occasional use of decimal fractions can be traced back as far as the 12th century.

degree a unit (symbol °) of measurement of an angle or arc. A circle or complete rotation is divided into 360°. A degree may be subdivided into 60 minutes (symbol '), and each minute may be subdivided in turn into 60 seconds (symbol "). *Temperature* is also measured in degrees, which are divided on a decimal scale.

denominator the bottom number of a fraction, so called because it *names* the family of the fraction. The top number, or numerator, specifies how many unit fractions are to be taken.

determinant an array of elements written as a square, and denoted by two vertical lines enclosing the array. For a 2×2 matrix, the determinant is given by the difference between the products of the diagonal terms. For example, the determinant of the matrix

$$\begin{matrix} (a\ b) \\ (c\ d) \end{matrix} = \begin{vmatrix} a & b \\ c & d \end{vmatrix} = ad - bc$$

Determinants are used to solve sets of simultaneous equations by matrix methods.

differentiation a procedure for determining the gradient of the tangent to a curve $f(x)$ at any point x.

directed number an integer with a positive (+) or negative (–) sign attached, for example +5 or –5. On a graph, a positive sign shows a movement to the right or upwards; a negative sign indicates movement downwards or to the left.

distributive operation an operation, such as multiplication, that bears a relationship to another operation, such as addition, such that $a \times (b + c) = (a \times b) + (a \times c)$. For example, $3 \times (2 + 4) = (3 \times 2) + (3 \times 4) = 18$. Multiplication may be said to be distributive over addition. Addition is not, however, distributive over multiplication because $3 + (2 \times 4) \neq (3 + 2) \times (3 + 4)$.

dodecahedron regular solid with 12 pentagonal faces and 12 vertices. It is one of the five regular polyhedra, or Platonic solids.

ellipse curve joining all points (loci) around two fixed points (foci) such that the sum of the distances from those points is always constant. The diameter passing through the foci is the major axis, and the diameter bisecting this at right angles is the minor axis. An ellipse is one of a series of curves known as conic sections. A slice across a cone that is not made parallel to, and does not pass through, the base will produce an ellipse.

epicycloid a curve resembling a series of arches traced out by a point on the circumference of a circle that rolls around another circle of a different diameter. If the two circles have the same diameter, the curve is a cardioid.

equation in mathematics, expression that represents the equality of two expressions involving constants and/or variables, and thus usually includes an equals sign (=). For example, the equation $A = \pi r^2$ equates the area A of a circle of radius r to the product πr^2. The algebraic equation $y = mx + c$ is the general one in coordinate geometry for a straight line.

If a mathematical equation is true for all variables in a given domain, it is sometimes called an identity and denoted by $\equiv$.

equilateral of a geometrical figure, having all sides of equal length. An equilateral triangle, to which the term is most often applied, has all three sides equal and all three angles equal (at 60°).

exponent or *index* in mathematics, a number that indicates the number of times a term is multiplied by itself; for example $x^2 = x \times x$, $4^3 = 4 \times 4 \times 4$. Exponents obey certain rules. Terms that contain them are multiplied together by adding the exponents; for example, $x^2 \times x^5 = x^7$. Division of such terms is done by subtracting the exponents; for example, $y^5 \div y^3 =$ y^2. Any number with the exponent 0 is equal to 1; for example, $x^0 = 1$ and $99^0 = 1$.

exponential descriptive of a function in which the variable quantity is an exponent (a number indicating the power to which another number or expression is raised). Exponential functions and series involve the constant $e = 2.71828...$. Scottish mathematician John Napier devised natural logarithms in 1614 with e as the base.

Exponential functions are basic mathematical functions, written as e^x or exp x. *Exponential growth* is not constant. It applies, for example, to population growth, where the population doubles in a short time period. A graph of population number against time produces a curve that is characteristically rather flat at first but then shoots almost directly upwards.

factor a number that divides into another number exactly. For example, the factors of 64 are 1, 2, 4, 8, 16, 32, and 64. In algebra, certain kinds of polynomials (expressions consisting of several or many terms) can be factorized. For example, the factors of $x^2 + 3x + 2$ are $x + 1$ and $x + 2$, since $x^2 + 3x + 2 = (x + 1)(x + 2)$. This is called factorization.

factorial of a positive number, the product of all the whole numbers (integers) inclusive between 1 and the number itself. A factorial is indicated by the symbol '!'. Thus $6! = 1 \times 2 \times 3 \times 4 \times 5 \times 6 = 720$. Factorial zero, 0!, is defined as 1.

fractal an irregular shape or surface produced by a procedure of repeated subdivision. Generated on a computer screen, fractals are used in creating models for geographical or biological processes (for example, the creation of a coastline by erosion or accretion, or the growth of plants). The name was coined by the French mathematician Benoit Mandelbrot. Fractals are also used for computer art.

fraction a number that indicates one or more equal parts of a whole. Usually, the number of equal parts into which the unit is divided (denominator) is written below a horizontal line, and the number of parts comprising the fraction (numerator) is written above; thus $^2/_3$ or $^3/_4$. Such fractions are called *vulgar* or *simple* fractions. The denominator can never be zero.

A *proper fraction* is one in which the numerator is less than the denominator. An *improper fraction* has a numerator that is larger than the denominator, for example $^3/_2$. It can therefore be expressed as a mixed number, for example, $1^1/_2$. A *decimal fraction* has as its denominator a power of 10, and these are omitted by use of the decimal point and notation, for example 0.04, which is $^4/_{100}$. Fractions are also known as the *rational numbers*, that is numbers formed by a ratio. *Integers* may be expressed as fractions with a denominator of 1.

function a function f is a non-empty set of ordered pairs $(x, f(x))$ of which no two can have the same first element. Hence, if $f(x) = x^2$, two ordered pairs are $(-2, 4)$ and $(2, 4)$. The set of all first elements in a function's ordered pairs is called the *domain*; the set of all second elements is the *range*. In the algebraic expression $y = 4x^3 + 2$, the dependent variable y is a function of the independent variable x, generally written as $f(x)$.

geometry branch of mathematics concerned with the properties of space, usually in terms of plane (two-dimensional) and solid (three-dimensional) figures. The subject is usually divided into *pure geometry*, which embraces roughly the plane and solid geometry dealt with in Euclid's *Elements*, and *analytical* or *coordinate geometry*, in which problems are solved using algebraic methods. A third, quite distinct, type includes the non-Euclidean geometries.

group a finite or infinite set of elements that can be combined by an operation; formally, a group must satisfy certain conditions. For example, the set of all integers (positive or negative whole numbers) forms a group with regard to addition because: (1) addition is associative, that is, the sum of two or more integers is the same regardless of the order in which the integers are added; (2) adding two integers gives another integer; (3) the set includes an identity element 0, which has no effect on any integer to which it is added (for example, $0 + 3 = 3$); and (4) each integer has an inverse (for instance, 7 has the inverse -7), such that the sum of an integer and its inverse   is 0. *Group theory* is the study of the properties of groups.

helix a three-dimensional curve resembling a spring, corkscrew, or screw thread. It is generated by a line that encircles a cylinder or cone at a constant angle.

hyperbola a curve formed by cutting a right circular cone with a plane so that the angle between the plane and the base is greater than the angle between the base and the side of the cone. All hyperbolae are bounded by two asymptotes (straight lines which the hyperbola moves closer and closer to but never reaches). A hyperbola is a member of the family of curves known as conic sections.

hypotenuse the longest side of a right-angled triangle, opposite the right angle. It is of particular application in Pythagoras's theorem (the square of the hypotenuse equals the sum of the squares of the other two sides), and in trigonometry where the ratios sine and cosine are defined as the ratios opposite/hypotenuse and adjacent/hypotenuse respectively.

icosahedron (plural *icosahedra*) regular solid with 20 equilateral (equal-sided) triangular faces. It is one of the five regular polyhedra, or Platonic solids.

infinity mathematical quantity that is larger than any fixed assignable quantity; symbol ∞. By convention, the result of dividing any number by zero is regarded as infinity.

integer any whole number. Integers may be positive or negative; 0 is an integer, and is often considered positive. Formally, integers are members of the set Z = {... $-3, -2, -1, 0, 1, 2, 3,...$ }. Fractions, such as $^1/_2$ and 0.35, are known as non-integral numbers ('not integers').

integration a method in calculus of determining the solutions of definite or indefinite integrals. An example of a definite integral can be thought of as finding the area under a curve (as represented by an algebraic expression or function) between particular values of the function's variable. In practice, integral calculus provides scientists with a powerful tool for doing calculations that involve a continually varying quantity (such as determining the position at any given instant of a space rocket that is accelerating away from

Earth). Its basic principles were discovered in the late 1660s independently by the German philosopher Leibniz and the British scientist Newton.

linear equation a relationship between two variables that, when plotted on Cartesian axes produces a straight-line graph; the equation has the general form $y = mx + c$, where m is the slope of the line represented by the equation and c is the y-intercept, or the value of y where the line crosses the y-axis in the Cartesian coordinate system. Sets of linear equations can be used to describe the behaviour of buildings, bridges, trusses, and other static structures.

locus (Latin 'place') traditionally the path traced out by a moving point, but now defined as the set of all points on a curve satisfying given conditions. For example, the locus of a point that moves so that it is always at the same distance from another fixed point is a circle; the locus of a point that is always at the same distance from two fixed points is a straight line that perpendicularly bisects the line joining them.

logarithm or *log* the exponent or index of a number to a specified base – usually 10. For example, the logarithm to the base 10 of 1,000 is 3 because $10^3 = 1,000$; the logarithm of 2 is 0.3010 because $2 = 10^{0.3010}$. Before the advent of cheap electronic calculators, multiplication and division could be simplified by being replaced with the addition and subtraction of logarithms.

For any two numbers x and y (where $x = b^a$ and $y = b^c$) $x \times y = b^a \times b^c = b^{a + c}$; hence we would add the logarithms of x and y, and look up this answer in antilogarithm tables. Tables of logarithms and antilogarithms are available that show conversions of numbers into logarithms, and vice versa. For example, to multiply 6,560 by 980, one looks up their logarithms (3.8169 and 2.9912), adds them together (6.8081), then looks up the antilogarithm of this to get the answer (6,428,800). *Natural* or *Napierian logarithms* are to the base e, an irrational number equal to approximately 2.7183.

magic square in mathematics, a square array of different numbers in which the rows, columns, and diagonals add up to the same total. A simple example employing the numbers 1 to 9, with a total of 15, is:

6	7	2
1	5	9
8	3	4

matrix a square ($n \times n$) or rectangular ($m \times n$) array of elements (numbers or algebraic variables). They are a means of condensing information about mathematical systems and can be used for, among other things, solving simultaneous linear equations and transformations.

maximum and minimum in coordinate geometry, points at which the slope of a curve representing a function changes from positive to negative (maximum), or from negative to positive (minimum). A tangent to the curve at a maximum or minimum has zero gradient. Maxima and minima can be found by differentiating the function for the curve and setting the differential to zero (the value of the slope at the turning point). For example, differentiating the function for the parabola $y = 2x^2 - 8x$ gives dy/dx =

$4x - 8$. Setting this equal to zero gives $x = 2$, so that $y = -8$ (found by substituting $x = 2$ into the parabola equation). Thus the function has a minimum at the point $(2, -8)$.

mean a measure of the average of a number of terms or quantities. The simple *arithmetic mean* is the average value of the quantities, that is, the sum of the quantities divided by their number. The *weighted mean* takes into account the frequency of the terms that are summed; it is calculated by multiplying each term by the number of times it occurs, summing the results and dividing this total by the total number of occurrences. The *geometric mean* of n quantities is the nth root of their product. In statistics, it is a measure of central tendency of a set of data.

modulus a number that divides exactly into the difference between two given numbers. Also, the multiplication factor used to convert a logarithm of one base to a logarithm of another base. Also, another name for absolute value.

number symbol used in counting or measuring. In mathematics, there are various kinds of numbers. The everyday number system is the decimal ('proceeding by tens') system, using the base ten. *Real numbers* include all rational numbers (integers, or whole numbers, and fractions) and irrational numbers (those not expressible as fractions). *Complex numbers* include the real and unreal numbers (real-number multiples of the square root of -1). The binary number system, used in computers, has two as its base.

The ordinary numerals, 0, 1, 2, 3, 4, 5, 6, 7, 8, and 9, give a counting system that, in the decimal system, continues 10, 11, 12, 13, and so on. These are whole numbers (integers), with fractions represented as, for example, $\frac{1}{4}$, $\frac{1}{2}$, $\frac{3}{4}$, or as decimal fractions (0.25, 0.5, 0.75). They are also *rational numbers*. *Irrational numbers* cannot be represented in this way and require symbols, such as $\sqrt{2}$, π, and e. They can be expressed numerically only as the (inexact) approximations 1.414, 3.142 and 2.718 (to three places of decimals) respectively. The symbols π and e are also examples of *transcendental numbers*, because they (unlike $\sqrt{2}$) cannot be derived by solving a polynomial equation (an equation with one variable quantity) with rational coefficients (multiplying factors). Complex numbers, which include the real numbers as well as unreal numbers, take the general form $a + bi$, where $i = \sqrt{-1}$ (that is, $i^2 = -1$), and a is the real part and bi the unreal part.

number theory the abstract study of the structure of number systems and the properties of positive integers (whole numbers). For example, the theories of factors and prime numbers fall within this area as do the work of mathematicians Giuseppe Peano (1858–1932), Pierre de Fermat, and Karl Gauss.

numerator the number or symbol that appears above the line in a vulgar fraction. For example, the numerator of 5/6 is 5. The numerator represents the fraction's dividend and indicates how many of the equal parts indicated by the denominator (number or symbol below the line) comprise the fraction.

octahedron (regular) one of the five platonic solids with eight faces each of whichis an equilateral triangle. The figure made by joining the midpoints of the faces is a perfect cube and the vertices of theoctahe-dron are themselves the mid points of the faces of asurrounding cube. For this reason cube and octahedron are calleddual solids.

ordinal number one of the series first, second, third, fourth, ... Ordinal numbers relate to order, whereas cardinal numbers (1, 2, 3, 4, ...) relate to quantity, or count.

ordinate in coordinate geometry, the y coordinate of a point; that is, the vertical distance of the point from the horizontal or x-axis. For example, a point with the coordinates (3,4) has an ordinate of 4.

origin the point where the x axis meets the y axis. The coordinates of the origin are (0,0).

parabola a curve formed by cutting a right circular cone with a plane parallel to the sloping side of the cone. A parabola is one of the family of curves known as conic sections. The graph of $y = x^2$ is a parabola. The corresponding solid figure, the paraboloid, is formed by rotating a parabola about its axis. It is a common shape for headlight reflectors, dish-shaped microwave and radar aerials, and radiotele-scopes, since a source of radiation placed at the focus of a paraboloidal reflector is propagated as a parallel beam.

parallel lines and parallel planes straight lines or planes that always remain a constant distance from one another no matter how far they are extended. This is a principle of Euclidean geometry. Some non-Euclidean geometries, such as elliptical and hyperbolic geometry, however, reject Euclid's parallel axiom.

parallelogram a quadrilateral (four-sided plane figure) with opposite pairs of sides equal in length and parallel, and opposite angles equal. The diagonals of a parallelogram bisect each other. Its area is the product of the length of one side and the perpendicular distance between this and the opposite side. In the special case when all four sides are equal in length, the parallelogram is known as a rhombus, and when the internal angles are right angles, it is a rectangle or square.

percentage way of representing a number as a fraction of 100. Thus 45 percent (45%) equals $\frac{45}{100}$, and 45% of 20 is $\frac{45}{100} \times 20 = 9$. In general, if a quantity x changes to y, the percentage change is $100(x - y)/x$. Thus, if the number of people in a room changes from 40 to 50, the percentage increase is $(100 \times 10)/40 = 25\%$. To express a fraction as a percentage, its denominator must first be converted to 100 – for example, $\frac{1}{8} = 12.5/100 = 12.5\%$. The use of percentages often makes it easier to compare fractions that do not have a common denominator.

perimeter or *boundary* line drawn around the edge of an area or shape. For example, the perimeter of a rectangle is the sum of its four sides; the perimeter of a circle is known as its *circumference*.

permutation a specified arrangement of a group of objects. It is the arrangement of a distinct objects taken b at a time in all possible orders. It is given by $a!/(a - b)!$, where '!' stands for factorial. For example, the number of permutations of four letters taken from any group of six different letters is $6!/2! = (1 \times 2 \times 3 \times 4 \times 5 \times 6)/(1 \times 2) = 360$. The theoretical number of four-letter 'words' that can be made from an alphabet of 26 letters is $26!/22! = 358,800$.

perpendicular at a right angle; also, a line at right angles to another or to a plane. For a pair of skew lines (lines in three dimensions that do not meet), there is just one common perpendicular, which is at right angles to both lines; the nearest points on the two lines are the feet of this perpendicular.

polygon a plane (two-dimensional) figure with three or more straight-line sides. Common polygons have names which define the number of sides (for example, triangle, quadrilateral, pentagon). These are all convex polygons, having no interior angle greater than 180°. The sum of the internal angles of a polygon having n sides is given by the formula $(2n - 4) \times 90°$; therefore, the more sides a polygon has, the larger the sum of its internal angles and, in the case of a convex polygon, the more closely it approximates to a circle.

polyhedron a solid figure with four or more plane faces. The more faces there are on a polyhedron, the more closely it approximates to a sphere. Knowledge of the properties of polyhedra is needed in crystallography and stereochemistry to determine the shapes of crystals and molecules. There are only five types of regular polyhedron (with all faces the same size and shape): the tetrahedron (four equilateral triangular faces), cube (six square faces), octahedron (eight equilateral triangles), dodecahedron (12 regular pentagons) and icosahedron (20 equilateral triangles).

prime number number that can be divided only by 1 or itself, that is, having no other factors. There is an infinite number of primes, the first ten of which are 2, 3, 5, 7, 11, 13, 17, 19, 23, and 29 (by definition, the number 1 is excluded from the set of prime numbers). The number 2 is the only even prime because all other even numbers have 2 as a factor.

In 1989, researchers at Amdahl Corporation, Sunnyvale, California, calculated the largest known prime number. It has 65,087 digits, and is more than a trillion trillion trillion times as large as the previous record holder. It took over a year of computation to locate the number and prove it was a prime.

prism a solid figure whose cross section is constant in planes drawn perpendicular to its axis. A cube, for example, is a rectangular prism with all faces (bases and sides) the same shape and size. A cylinder is a prism with a circular cross section.

probability likelihood, or chance, that an event will occur, often expressed as odds, or in mathematics, numerically as a fraction or decimal. In general, the probability that n particular events will happen out of a total of m possible events is n/m. A certainty has a probability of 1; an impossibility has a probability of 0. Empirical probability is defined as the number of successful events divided by the total possible number of events.

In tossing a coin, the chance that it will land 'heads' is the same as the chance that it will land 'tails', that is, 1 to 1 or even; mathematically, this probability is expressed as $^1/_2$ or 0.5. The odds against any chosen number coming up on the roll of a fair die are 5 to 1; the probability is $^1/_6$ or 0.1666... Probability theory was developed by the French mathematicians Blaise Pascal and Pierre de Fermat in the 17th century, initially in response to a request to calculate the odds of being dealt various hands at cards. Today, probability plays a major part in the mathematics of atomic theory and finds application in insurance and statistical studies.

progression sequence of numbers each formed by a specific relationship to its predecessor. An *arithmetic progression* has numbers that increase or decrease by a common sum or difference (for example, 2, 4, 6, 8); a *geometric progression* has numbers each bearing a fixed ratio to its predecessor (for example, 3, 6, 12, 24); and a *harmonic progression* has numbers whose reciprocals are in arithmetical progression, for example 1, $^1/_2$, $^1/_3$, $^1/_4$.

proportion two variable quantities x and y are proportional if, for all values of x, $y = kx$, where k is a constant. This means that if x increases, y increases in a linear fashion. A graph of x against y would be a straight line passing through the origin (the point $x = 0$, $y = 0$). y is inversely proportional to x if the graph of y against $1/x$ is a straight line through the origin. The corresponding equation is $y = k/x$. Many laws of science relate quantities that are proportional.

pyramid a three-dimensional figure with triangular side-faces meeting at a common vertex (point) and with a polygon as its base. The volume V of a pyramid is given by $V = ^1/_3 Bh$, where B is the area of the base and h is the perpendicular height. Pyramids are generally classified by their bases. For example, the Egyptian pyramids have square bases, and are therefore called square pyramids. Triangular pyramids are also known as tetrahedra ('four sides').

Pythagoras' theorem in geometry, a theorem stating that in a right-angled triangle, the area of the square on the hypotenuse (the longest side) is equal to the sum of the areas of the squares drawn on the other two sides. If the hypotenuse is h units long and the lengths of the other sides are a and b, then $h^2 = a^2 + b^2$. The theorem provides a way of calculating the length of any side of a right-angled triangle if the lengths of the other two sides are known.

Prime numbers

A prime number is a natural number other than 1, which can only be divided by itself and 1. The table below lists all the prime numbers between 1 and 1,000.

2	3	5	7	11	13	17	19	23
29	31	37	41	43	47	53	59	61
67	71	73	79	83	89	97	101	103
107	109	113	127	131	137	139	149	151
157	163	167	173	179	181	191	193	197
199	211	223	227	229	233	239	241	251
257	263	269	271	277	281	283	293	307
311	313	317	331	337	347	349	353	359
367	373	379	383	389	397	401	409	419
421	431	433	439	443	449	457	461	463
467	479	487	491	499	503	509	521	523
541	547	557	563	569	571	577	587	593
599	601	607	613	617	619	631	641	643
647	653	659	661	673	677	683	691	701
709	719	727	733	739	743	751	757	761
769	773	787	797	809	811	821	823	827
829	839	853	857	859	863	877	881	883
887	907	911	919	929	937	941	947	953
967	971	977	983	991	997			

quadratic equation a polynomial equation of second degree (that is, an equation containing as its highest power the square of a variable, such as x^2). The general formula of such equations is $ax^2 + bx + c = 0$, in which a, b, and c are real numbers, and only the coefficient a cannot equal 0. In coordinate geometry, a quadratic function represents a parabola.

Some quadratic equations can be solved by factorization, or the values of x can be found by using the formula for the general solution

$$x = [-b \pm \sqrt{(b^2 - 4ac)}]/2a.$$

Depending on the value of the discriminant $b^2 - 4ac$, a quadratic equation has two real, two equal, or two complex roots (solutions). When $b^2 - 4ac < 0$, there are two distinct real roots. When $b^2 - 4ac = 0$, there are two equal real roots. When $b^2 - 4ac > 0$, there are two distinct complex roots.

radian SI unit (symbol rad) of plane angles, an alternative unit to the degree. It is the angle at the centre of a circle when the centre is joined to the two ends of an arc (part of the circumference) equal in length to the radius of the circle. There are 2π (approximately 6.284) radians in a full circle (360°). One radian is approximately 57°, and 1° is $\pi/180$ or approximately 0.0175 radians. Radians are commonly used to specify angles in polar coordinates

ratio measure of the relative size of two quantities or of two measurements (in similar units), expressed as a proportion. For example, the ratio of vowels to consonants in the alphabet is 5:21; the ratio of 500 m to 2 km is 500:2,000, or 1:4.

reciprocal the result of dividing a given quantity into 1. Thus the reciprocal of 2 is $^1/_2$; of $^2/_3$ is $^3/_2$; of x^2 is $^1/_{x^2}$ or x^{-2}.

rectangle quadrilateral (four-sided plane figure) with opposite sides equal and parallel and with each interior angle a right angle (90°). Its area A is the product of the length l and height h; that is, $A = l \times h$. A rectangle with all four sides equal is a square.

rhombus an equilateral (all sides equal) parallelogram. Its diagonals bisect each other at right angles, and its area is half the product of the lengths of the two diagonals. A rhombus whose internal angles are 90° is called a square.

right-angled triangle triangle in which one of the angles is a right angle (90°). It is the basic form of triangle for defining trigonometrical ratios (for example, sine, cosine, and tangent) and for which Pythagoras' theorem holds true. The longest side of a right-angled triangle is called the hypotenuse; its area is equal to half the product of the lengths of the two shorter sides. Any triangle constructed with its hypotenuse as the diameter of a circle, with its opposite vertex (corner) on the circumference, is a right-angled triangle. This is a fundamental theorem in geometry, first credited to the Greek mathematician Thales about 580 BC.

Roman numerals ancient European number system using symbols different from Arabic numerals (the ordinary numbers 1, 2, 3, 4, 5, and so on). The seven key symbols in Roman numerals, as represented today, are I (1), V (5), X (10), L (50), C (100),

D (500) and M (1,000). There is no zero, and therefore no place-value as is fundamental to the Arabic system. The first ten Roman numerals are I, II, III, IV (or IIII), V, VI, VII, VIII, IX, and X. When a Roman symbol is preceded by a symbol of equal or greater value, the values of the symbols are added (XVI = 16). When a symbol is preceded by a symbol of less value, the values are subtracted (XL = 40). A horizontal bar over a symbol indicates a multiple of 1,000 ($\bar{X}$ = 10,000). Although addition and subtraction are fairly straightforward using Roman numerals, the absence of a zero makes other arithmetic calculations (such as multiplication) clumsy and difficult.

scalar quantity a quantity that has magnitude but no direction, as distinct from a vector quantity, which has a direction as well as a magnitude. Temperature, mass, and volume are scalar quantities.

set or *class* any collection of defined things (elements), provided the elements are distinct and that there is a rule to decide whether an element is a member of a set. It is usually denoted by a capital letter and indicated by curly brackets { }. For example, L may represent the set that consists of all the letters of the alphabet. The symbol ϵ stands for 'is a member of'; thus $p \in L$ means that p belongs to the set consisting of all letters, and $4 \notin L$ means that 4 does not belong to the set consisting of all letters.

A *finite set* has a limited number of members, such as the letters of the alphabet; an *infinite set* has an unlimited number of members, such as all whole numbers; an *empty* or *null set* has no members, such as the number of people who have swum across the Atlantic Ocean, written as { } or $\varnothing$; a *single-element set* has only one member, such as days of the week beginning with M, written as {Monday}. *Equal sets* have the same members; for example, if W = {days of the week} and S = {Sunday, Monday, Tuesday, Wednesday, Thursday, Friday, Saturday}, it can be said that $W = S$. Sets with the same number of members are *equivalent sets*. Sets with some members in common are *intersecting sets*; for example, if R = {red playing cards} and F = {face cards}, then R and F share the members that are red face cards. Sets with no members in common are *disjoint sets*. Sets contained within others are *subsets*; for example, V = {vowels} is a subset of L = {letters of the alphabet}. Sets and their interrelationships are often illustrated by a Venn diagram.

significant figures the figures in a number that, by virtue of their place value, express the magnitude of that number to a specified degree of accuracy. The final significant figure is rounded up if the following digit is greater than 5. For example, 5,463,254 to three significant figures is 5,460,000; 3.462891 to four significant figures is 3.463; 0.00347 to two significant figures is 0.0035.

simultaneous equations one of two or more algebraic equations that contain two or more unknown quantities that may have a unique solution. For example, in the case of two linear equations with two unknown variables, such as (i) $x + 3y = 6$ and (ii) $3y - 2x = 4$, the solution will be those unique values of x and y that are valid for both equations. Linear simultaneous equations can be solved by using algebraic manipulation to eliminate one of the variables, coordinate geometry, or matrices.

sine in trigonometry, a function of an angle in a right-angled triangle which is defined as the ratio of the length of the side opposite the angle to the length of the hypotenuse (the longest side). Various properties in physics vary sinusoidally; that is, they can be represented diagrammatically by a sine wave (a graph obtained by plotting values of angles against the values of their sines). Examples include simple harmonic motion, such as the way alternating current (AC) electricity varies with time.

speed the rate at which an object moves. The average speed v of an object may be calculated by dividing the distance s it has travelled by the time t taken to do so, and may be expressed as:

$$v = s/t$$

The usual units of speed are metres per second or kilometres per hour. Speed is a scalar quantity in which direction of motion is unimportant (unlike the vector quantity velocity, in which both magnitude and direction must be taken into consideration).

sphere a perfectly round object with all points on its surface the same distance from the centre. This distance is the radius of the sphere. For a sphere of radius r, the volume $V = \frac{4}{3}\pi r^3$ and the surface area $A = 4\pi^2$.

square root a number that when squared (multiplied by itself) equals a given number. For example, the square root of 25 (written $\sqrt{25}$) is ± 5, because $5 \times 5 = 25$, and $(-5) \times (-5) = 25$. As an exponent, a square root is represented by $^1/_2$, for example, $16^{1/2} = \pm 4$. Negative numbers (less than 0) do not have square roots that are real numbers. Their roots are represented by complex numbers, in which the square root of -1 is given the symbol i (that is, $\pm i^2 = -1$). Thus the square root of -4 is $\sqrt{[(-1) \times 4]} = \sqrt{-1} \times \sqrt{4} = 2i$.

standard deviation in statistics, a measure (symbol Σ or s) of the spread of data. The deviation (difference) of each of the data items from the mean is found, and their values squared. The mean value of these squares is then calculated. The standard deviation is the square root of this mean.

statistics branch of mathematics concerned with the collection and interpretation of data. For example, to determine the mean age of the children in a school, a statistically acceptable answer might be obtained by calculating an average based on the ages of a representative sample, consisting, for example, of a random tenth of the pupils from each class. Probability is the branch of statistics dealing with predictions of events.

tangent a straight line that touches a curve and gives the gradient of the curve at the point of contact. At a maximum, minimum, or point of inflection, the tangent to a curve has zero gradient. Also, in trigonometry, a function of an acute angle in a right-angled triangle, defined as the ratio of the length of the side opposite the angle to the length of the side adjacent to it; a way of expressing the gradient of a line.

tetrahedron (plural *tetrahedra*) a polyhedron with four triangular faces; that is, a pyramid on a triangular base. A regular tetrahedron has equilateral triangles as its faces. In chemistry and crystallography, tetrahedra describe the shapes of some molecules and

topology

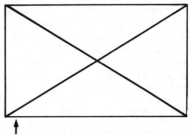

this figure is topologically equivalent to this one

crystals; for example, the carbon atoms in a crystal of diamond are arranged in space as a set of interconnected regular tetrahedra.

topology branch of geometry that deals with those properties of a figure that remain unchanged even when the figure is transformed (bent, stretched) – for example, when a square painted on a rubber sheet is deformed by distorting the sheet. Topology has scientific applications, as in the study of turbulence in flowing fluids. The map of a subway system is an example of the topological representation of a network; connectivity (the way the lines join together) is preserved, but shape and size are not. The topological theory, proposed 1880, that only four colors are required in order to produce a map in which no two adjoining countries have the same color, inspired extensive research, and was proved 1972 by Kenneth Appel and Wolfgang Haken.

trapezium a four-sided plane figure (quadrilateral) with no two sides parallel.

triangle a three-sided plane figure, the sum of whose interior angles is 180°. Triangles can be classified by the relative lengths of their sides. A *scalene triangle* has no sides of equal length; an *isosceles triangle* has at least two equal sides; an *equilateral triangle* has three equal sides (and three equal angles of 60°). A *right-angled triangle* has one angle of 90°.

trigonometry branch of mathematics that solves problems relating to plane and spherical triangles. Its principles are based on the fixed proportions of sides for a particular angle in a right-angled triangle, the simplest of which are known as the sine, cosine, and tangent (so-called trigonometrical ratios). It is of practical importance in navigation, surveying, and simple harmonic motion in physics.

variable a changing quantity (one that can take various values), as opposed to a constant. For example, in the algebraic expression $y = 4x^3 + 2$, the variables are x and y, whereas 4 and 2 are constants.

variance in statistics, the square of the standard deviation, the measure of spread of data. Population and sample variance are denoted by Σ^2 or s^2, respectively.

vector quantity any physical quantity that has both magnitude and direction (such as the velocity or acceleration of an object) as distinct from scalar quantity (such as speed, density, or mass), which has magnitude but no direction. A vector is represented either geometrically by an arrow whose length corresponds to its magnitude and points in an appropriate direction, or by a pair of numbers written vertically and placed within brackets (xy). Vectors can be added graphically by constructing a parallelogram of vectors (such as the parallelogram of forces commonly employed in physics and engineering). In technical writing, a vector is denoted by **bold** type, underlined AB, or overlined AB.

velocity speed of an object in a given direction. Velocity is a vector quantity, since its direction is important as well as its magnitude (or speed).

Venn diagram a diagram representing a set or sets and the logical relationships between them. The sets are drawn as circles. An area of overlap between two circles (sets) contains elements that are common to both sets, and thus represents a third set. Circles that do not overlap represent sets with no elements in common (disjoint sets).

vertex (plural **vertices**) a point shared by three or more sides of a solid figure; the point farthest from a figure's base; or the point of intersection of two sides of a plane figure or the two rays of an angle.

volume the space occupied by a three-dimensional solid object. A prism (such as a cube) or a cylinder has a volume equal to the area of the base multiplied by the height. For a pyramid or cone, the volume is equal to one-third of the area of the base multiplied by the perpendicular height. The volume of a sphere is equal to $^4/_3\pi r^3$, where r is the radius. Volumes of irregular solids may be calculated by the technique of integration.

Great Mathematicians

Archimedes $c.$ 287–212 BC. Greek mathematician who made major discoveries in geometry, hydro-statics, and mechanics. He formulated a law of fluid displacement (Archimedes' principle), and is credited with the invention of the Archimedes screw, a cylindrical device for raising water. This device is still used to raise water in the Nile delta.

Bernoulli Swiss family that produced many mathematicians and scientists in the 17th, 18th, and 19th centuries, in particular the brothers **Jakob** (1654–1705) and **Johann** (1667–1748). Jakob and Johann were pioneers of Leibniz's calculus. Jakob used calculus to study the forms of many curves arising in practical situations, and studied mathematical probability; **Bernoulli numbers** are named after him.

Johann developed exponential calculus and contributed to many areas of applied mathematics, including the problem of a particle moving in a gravitational field. His son, **Daniel** (1700–1782) worked on calculus and probability, and in physics proposed **Bernoulli's principle**.

Boole George 1815–1864. English mathematician whose work *The Mathematical Analysis of Logic* 1847 established the basis of modern mathematical logic, and whose **Boolean algebra** can be used in designing computers.

Cantor Georg 1845–1918. German mathematician who followed his work on number theory and trigonometry by considering the foundations of mathematics. He defined real numbers and produced a treatment of irrational numbers using a series of transfinite numbers. Cantor's set theory has been used in the development of topology and real function theory.

Cauchy Augustin Louis 1789–1857. French mathematician who employed rigorous methods of analysis. His prolific output included work on complex functions, determinants, and probability, and on the convergence of infinite series. In calculus, he refined the concepts of the limit and the definite integral.

Fields medals

Awarded every four years by the International Congress of Mathematicians

	Fields medalists:
1936	Lars Ahlfors, Finland
	Jesse Douglas, USA
1950	Atle Selberg, USA
	Laurent Schwartz, France
1954	Kunihiko Kodaira, USA
	Jean-Pierre Serre, France
1958	Klaus Roth, UK
	René Thom, France
1962	Lars Hörmander, Sweden
	John Milnor, USA
1966	Michael Atiyah, UK
	Paul J Cohen, USA
	Alexander Grothendieck, France
	Stephen Smale, USA
1970	Alan Baker, UK
	Heisuke Hironaka, USA
	Sergei Novikov, USSR
	John G Thompson, USA
1974	Enrico Bombieri, Italy
	David Mumford, USA
1978	Pierre Deligne, Belgium
	Charles Fefferman, USA
	G A Margulis, USSR
	Daniel Quillen, USA
1982	Alain Connes, France
	William Thurston, USA
	S T Yau, USA
1986	Simon Donaldson, UK
	Gerd Faltings, FRG
	Michael Freedman, USA
1990	Vladimir Drinfeld, USSR
	Vaughan F R Jones, USA
	Shigefumi Mori, Japan
	Edward Witten, USA

Descartes René 1596–1650. French philosopher and mathematician. He believed that commonly accepted knowledge was doubtful because of the subjective nature of the senses, and attempted to rebuild human knowledge using as his foundation *cogito ergo sum* ('I think, therefore I am'). He also believed that the entire material universe could be explained in terms of mathematical physics, and founded coordinate geometry as a way of defining and manipulating geometrical shapes by means of algebraic expressions. Cartesian coordinates, the means by which points are represented in this system, are named after him. Descartes also established the science of optics, and helped to shape contemporary theories of astronomy and animal behaviour.

Eratosthenes *c.* 276–194 BC. Greek geographer and mathematician whose map of the ancient world was the first to contain lines of latitude and longitude, and who calculated the Earth's circumference with an error of about 10%. His mathematical achievements include a method for duplicating the cube, and for finding prime numbers (Eratosthenes' sieve).

Euclid *c.* 330–*c.* 260 BC. Greek mathematician, who lived in Alexandria and wrote the *Stoicheia/Elements* in 13 books, of which nine deal with plane and solid geometry and four with number theory. His great achievement lay in the systematic arrangement of previous discoveries, based on axioms, definitions, and theorems.

Euler Leonhard 1707–1783. Swiss mathematician. He developed the theory of differential equations and the calculus of variations, and worked in astronomy and optics. He was a pupil of Johann Bernoulli.

Fermat Pierre de 1601–1665. French mathematician, who with Blaise Pascal founded the theory of probability and the modern theory of numbers and who made contributions to analytical geometry. *Fermat's last theorem* states that equations of the form $xn + yn = zn$ where x, y, z, and n are all integers have no solutions if $n < 2$. The theorem still remains unproven (and therefore, strictly speaking, constitutes a conjecture rather than a theorem).

Fibonacci Leonardo, also known as *Leonardo of Pisa c.* 1175–*c.* 1250. Italian mathematician. He published *Liber abaci* in Pisa 1202, which was instrumental in the introduction of Arabic notation into Europe. From 1960, interest increased in *Fibonacci numbers*, in their simplest form a sequence in which each number is the sum of its two predecessors (1, 1, 2, 3, 5, 8, 13, ..). They have unusual characteristics with possible applications in botany, psychology, and astronomy (for example, a more exact correspondence than is given by Bode's law to the distances between the planets and the Sun).

Galois Evariste 1811–1832. French mathematician who originated the theory of groups. His attempts to gain recognition for his work were largely thwarted by the French mathematical establishment, critical of his lack of formal qualifications. Galois was killed in a duel before he was 21. The night before, he had hurriedly written out his unpublished discoveries on group theory, the importance of which would come to be appreciated more and more as the 19th century progressed.

Gauss Karl Friedrich 1777–1855. German mathematician who worked on the theory of numbers, non-Euclidean geometry, and the mathematical development of electric and magnetic theory. A method of neutralizing a magnetic field, used to protect ships from magnetic mines, is called 'degaussing'.

Gödel Kurt 1906–1978. Austrian-born US mathematician and philosopher. He proved that a mathematical system always contains statements that can be neither proved nor disproved within the system; in other words, as a science, mathematics can never be totally consistent and totally complete. He worked on relativity, constructing a mathematical model of the universe that made travel back through time theoretically possible.

Hilbert David 1862–1943. German mathematician who founded the formalist school with the publication of *Grundlagen der Geometrie/Foundations of Geometry* 1899, which was based on his idea of postulates. He attempted to put mathematics on a logical foundation through defining it in terms of a number of basic principles, which Gödel later showed to be impossible; nonetheless, his attempt greatly influenced 20th-century mathematicians.

Khwārizmī, al- Muhammad ibn- Mūsā *c.* 780–*c.* 850. Persian mathematician from Khwarizm (now Khiva, Uzbekistan), who lived and worked in Baghdad. He wrote a book on algebra, from part of whose title (*al-jabr*) comes the word 'algebra', and a book in which he introduced to the West the Hindu-Arabic decimal number system. The word 'algorithm' is a corruption of his name. He also compiled astronomical tables and was responsible for introducing the concept of zero into Arab mathematics.

Lagrange Joseph Louis 1736–1813. French mathematician. His *Mécanique analytique* 1788 applied mathematical analysis, using principles established by Newton, to such problems as the movements of planets when affected by each other's gravitational force. He presided over the commission that introduced the metric system in 1793.

Leibniz Gottfried Wilhelm 1646–1716. German mathematician and philosopher. Independently of, but concurrently with, the British scientist Isaac Newton he developed the branch of mathematics known as calculus. In his metaphysical works, such as *The Monadology* 1714, he argued that everything consisted of innumerable units, *monads*, the individual properties of which determined each thing's past, present, and future. Monads, although independent of each other, interacted predictably; this meant that Christian faith and scientific reason need not be in conflict and that 'this is the best of all possible worlds'. His optimism is satirized in Voltaire's *Candide*.

Lobachevsky Nikolai Ivanovich 1792–1856. Russian mathematician who concurrently with, but independently of, Karl Gauss and the Hungarian János Bolyai (1802–1860), founded non-Euclidean geometry. Lobachevsky published the first account of the subject in 1829, but his work went unrecognized until Georg Riemann's system was published.

Lorenz Ludwig Valentine 1829–1891. Danish mathematician and physicist. He developed mathematical formulae to describe phenomena such as the relation

Large numbers

Nomenclature for large numbers varies in different countries. In the USA and France, numbers advance by increments of a thousand:

billion	1,000,000,000	1×10^9
trillion	1,000,000,000,000	1×10^{12}
quadrillion	1,000,000,000,000,000	1×10^{15}

However, in the UK and Germany numbers have traditionally advanced by increments of a million:

million	1,000,000	1×10^6
billion	1,000,000,000,000	1×10^{12}
trillion	1,000,000,000,000,000,000	1×10^{18}
quadrillion	1,000,000,000,000,000,000,000,000	1×10^{24}

This has a certain amount of logic on its side, particularly for classical scholars:

billion = million^2	(bi-)
trillion = million^3	(tri-)
quadrillion = million^4	(quadr-)

The US usage is starting to prevail in the UK as well, particularly as it is now universally used by economists and statisticians. The higher numbers, in both styles, are as follows:

Number	USA	UK
quintillion	1×10^{18}	1×10^{30}
sextillion	1×10^{21}	1×10^{36}
septillion	1×10^{24}	1×10^{42}
octillion	1×10^{27}	1×10^{48}
nonillion	1×10^{30}	1×10^{54}
decillion	1×10^{33}	1×10^{60}
vigintillion	1×10^{63}	1×10^{120}
centillion	1×10^{303}	1×10^{600}

between the refraction of light and the density of a pure transparent substance, and the relation between a metal's electrical and thermal conductivity and temperature.

Mandelbrot Benoit B 1924– .Polish born US scientist who coined the term *fractal geometry* to describe 'self-similar' shape, a motif that repeats indefinitely, each time smaller.

Markov Andrei 1856–1922. Russian mathematician, formulator of the Markov chain, an example of a stochastic (random) process.

Möbius August Ferdinand 1790–1868. German mathematician, discoverer of the Möbius strip and considered one of the founders of topology.

Napier John 1550–1617. Scottish mathematician who invented logarithms 1614 and 'Napier's bones', an early mechanical calculating device for multi-plication and division.

Newton Isaac 1642–1727. English physicist and mathematician who laid the foundations of physics as a modern discipline. He discovered the law of gravity, created calculus, discovered that white light is composed of many colours, and developed the three standard laws of motion still in use today. In 1685, he expounded his universal law of gravitation. His *Philosophiae naturalis principia mathematica*, usually referred to as *Principia*, was published in 1687, with the aid of Edmond Halley.

Pascal Blaise 1623–1662. French philosopher and mathematician. He contributed to the development of hydraulics, the calculus, and the mathematical theory of probability. *Pascal's triangle* is a triangular array of numbers in which each number is the sum of the pair of numbers above it. Plotted at equal distances along a horizontal axis, the numbers in the rows give the binomial probability distribution with equal probability of success and failure, such as when tossing fair coins.

Poincaré Jules Henri 1854–1912. French mathematician who developed the theory of differential equations and was a pioneer in relativity theory. He suggested that Isaac Newton's laws for the behaviour of the universe could be the exception rather than the rule. However, the calculation was so complex and time-consuming that he never managed to realize its full implication.

Pythagoras *c.* 580–500 BC. Greek mathematician and philosopher who formulated the Pythagorean theorem. Much of his work concerned numbers, to which he assigned mystical properties. For example, he classified numbers into triangular ones (1, 3, 6, 10,...), which can be represented as a triangular array, and square ones (1, 4, 9, 16,...), which form squares. He also observed that any two adjacent triangular numbers add to a square number (for example, 1 + 3 = 4; 3 + 6 = 9; 6 + 10 = 16;...).

Riemann Georg Friedrich Bernhard 1826–1866. German mathematician whose system of non-Euclidean geometry, thought at the time to be a mere mathematical curiosity, was used by Einstein to develop his general theory of relativity.

Rubik Erno 1944– . Hungarian architect who invented the *Rubik cube*, a multicoloured puzzle that can be manipulated and rearranged in only one correct way, but about 43 trillion wrong ones. Intended to help his students understand three-dimensional design, it became a fad that swept around the world.

Roman numerals

The basic Roman numerals are:

I	1
V	5
X	10
L	50
C	100
D	500
M	1,000

Other numbers are formed from these by adding or subtracting. The value of a symbol following another of the same or greater value is added: II = 2; III = 3; CC = 200. The value of a symbol preceding one of greater value is subtracted: IX = 9; CM = 900. The value of a symbol standing between two of greater value is subtracted from that of the second, the remainder being added to the first: XIX = 19.

The first twelve numbers are best known from the clock face:

I	1
II	2
III	3
IV	4
V	5
VI	6
VII	7
VIII	8
IX	9
X	10
XI	11
XII	12

Roman numerals are usually written in capital letters, but may be written in lower case, as in numbering subdivisions (Act I scene iv), or the preliminary pages of a book.

A bar over a symbol indicates multiplication by 1,000:

D̄	500,000

Thales 640–546 BC. Greek philosopher and scientist. He made advances in geometry, predicted an eclipse of the Sun 585 BC, and, as a philosophical materialist, theorized that water was the first principle of all things, that the Earth floated on water, and so proposed an explanation for earthquakes. He lived in Miletus in Asia Minor.

Turing Alan Mathison 1912–1954. English mathematician and logician. In 1936 he described a 'universal computing machine' that could theoretically be programmed to solve any problem capable of solution by a specially designed machine. This concept, now called the *Turing machine*, foreshadowed the digital computer.

Von Neumann John 1903–1957. Hungarian-born US scientist and mathematician, known for his pioneering work on computer design. He invented his 'rings of operators' (called Von Neumann algebras) in the late 1930s, and also contributed to set theory, games theory, cybernetics (with his theory of self-reproduc-

Playing cards and dice odds

Poker hands

Hand	No. possible	Odds against
Royal flush	4	649,739 to 1
Other straight flush	36	72,192 to 1
Four of a kind	624	4,164 to 1
Full house	3,744	693 to 1
Flush	5,108	508 to 1
Straight	10,200	254 to 1
Three of a kind	54,912	46 to 1
Two pairs	123,552	20 to 1
One pair	1,098,240	4 to 3
Nothing	1,302,540	1 to 1
Total	2,598,960	

Dice *(probabilities of total count from two dice on a single throw)*

Total count	Odds against
2	35 to 1
3	17 to 1
4	11 to 1
5	8 to 1
6	31 to 5
7	5 to 1
8	31 to 5
9	8 to 1
10	11 to 1
11	17 to 1
12	35 to 1

Dice *(probabilities of consecutive winning plays)*

No. of consecutive wins	By 7, 11 or point
1	244 in 495
2	6 in 25
3	3 in 25
4	1 in 17
5	1 in 34
6	1 in 70
7	1 in 141
8	1 in 287
9	1 in 582

Bridge *(odds against suit distribution in a hand)*

Suit distribution in a hand	Odds against
4-4-3-2	4 to 1
5-4-2-2	8 to 1
6-4-2-1	20 to 1
7-4-1-1	254 to 1
8-4-1-0	2,211 to 1
13-0-0-0	158,753,389,899 to 1

ing automata, called *Von Neumann mach-ines*), and the development of the atomic and hydrogen bombs.

Wiener Norbert 1894–1964. US mathematician. Best known for his book *Cybernetics* 1948, he laid the theoretical groundwork for information feedback systems. He laid the foundation of the study of stochastic processes (those dependent on random events), including Brownian movement (evidence of constant random motion of molecules).

PHYSICS

Terms

absolute zero lowest temperature theoretically possible, zero degrees Kelvin (0K), equivalent to −273.15°C/−459.67°F, at which molecules are motionless. Although the third law of thermodynamics indicates the impossibility of reaching absolute zero exactly, a temperature of seven-millionths of a degree above absolute zero was achieved by a team of scientists at Lancaster University, England, in June 1993. Near absolute zero, the physical properties of some materials change substantially; for example, some metals lose their electrical resistance and become superconductive.

acoustics in general, the experimental and theoretical science of sound and its transmission; in particular, that branch of the science that has to do with the phenomena of sound in a particular space such as a room or theatre.

analogue signal electric current or voltage that conveys or stores information, and varies continuously in the same way as the information it represents (unlike a digital signal). Analogue signals are prone to interference and distortion.

centre of mass or *centre of gravity* point in or near an object from which its total weight appears to originate and can be assumed to act. A symmetrical homogeneous object such as a sphere or cube has its centre of mass at its physical centre; a hollow shape (such as a cup) may have its centre of mass in space inside the hollow.

chain reaction nuclear fission reaction that is maintained because neutrons released by the splitting of some atomic nuclei themselves go on to split others, releasing even more neutrons. Such a reaction can be controlled (as in a nuclear reactor) by using moderators to absorb excess neutrons. Uncontrolled, a chain reaction produces a nuclear explosion (as in an atom bomb).

critical mass in nuclear physics, the minimum mass of fissile material that can undergo a continuous chain reaction. Below this mass, too many neutrons escape from the surface for a chain reaction to carry on; above the critical mass, the reaction may accelerate into a nuclear explosion.

cryogenics the science of very low temperatures (approaching absolute zero), including the production of very low temperatures and the exploitation of special properties associated with them, such as the disappearance of electrical resistance (superconductivity).

density measure of the compactness of a substance; it is equal to its mass per unit volume and is measured in kg per cubic metre/lb per cubic foot. Density is a scalar quantity. The density D of a mass m occupying a volume V is given by the formula:

$$D = m/V.$$

Relative density is the ratio of the density of a substance to that of water at 4°C.

diffraction the slight spreading of a light beam into a pattern of light and dark bands when it passes through a narrow slit or past the edge of an obstruction. A *diffraction grating* is a plate of glass or metal ruled with close, equidistant parallel lines used for separating a wave train such as a beam of incident light into its component frequencies (white light results in a spectrum).

digital in electronics and computing, a term meaning 'coded as numbers'. A digital system uses two- state, either on/off or high/low voltage pulses, to encode, receive, and transmit information. A *digital display* shows discrete values as numbers (as opposed to an analogue signal, such as the continuous sweep of a pointer on a dial). *Digital electronics* is the technology that underlies digital techniques. Low-power, miniature, integrated circuits (chips) provide the means for the coding, storage, transmission, processing, and reconstruction of information of all kinds.

dynamics or *kinetics* in mechanics, the mathematical and physical study of the behaviour of bodies under the action of forces that produce changes of motion in them.

efficiency the output of a machine (work done by the machine) divided by the input (work put into the machine), usually expressed as a percentage. Because of losses caused by friction, efficiency is always less than 100%, although it can approach this for electrical machines with no moving parts (such as a transformer).

elasticity the ability of a solid to recover its shape once deforming forces (stresses modifying its dimensions or shape) are removed. An elastic material obeys Hooke's law: that is, its deformation is proportional to the applied stress up to a certain point, called the *elastic limit*, beyond which additional stress will deform it permanently. Elastic materials include metals and rubber; however, all materials have some degree of elasticity.

electric current the flow of electrically charged particles through a conducting circuit due to the presence of a potential difference. The current at any point in a circuit is the amount of charge flowing per second; its SI unit is the ampere (coulomb per second). Current carries electrical energy from a power supply, such as a battery of electrical cells, to the components of the circuit, where it is converted into other forms of energy, such as heat, light, or motion. It may be either direct current or alternating current.

electricity all phenomena caused by electric charge, whether static or in motion. Electric charge is caused by an excess or deficit of electrons in the charged substance, and an electric current by the movement of electrons around a circuit. Substances may be electrical conductors, such as metals, which allow the passage of electricity through them, or insulators, such as rubber, which are extremely poor conductors. Substances with relatively poor conductivities that can be improved by the addition of heat or light are known as semiconductors.

electrodynamics the branch of physics dealing with electric currents and associated magnetic forces. Quantum electrodynamics (QED) studies the interaction between charged particles and their emission and absorption of electromagnetic radiation. This field combines quantum theory and relativity theory, making accurate predictions about subatomic processes involving charged particles such as electrons and protons.

electromagnetic waves oscillating electric and magnetic fields travelling together through space at a speed of nearly 300,000 km/186,000 mi per second. The (limitless) range of possible wavelengths or frequencies of electromagnetic waves, which can be thought of as making up the *electromagnetic spectrum*, includes radio waves, infrared radiation, visible light, ultraviolet radiation, X-rays, and gamma rays.

energy the capacity for doing work. Potential energy (PE) is energy deriving from position; thus a stretched spring has elastic PE, and an object raised to a height above the Earth's surface, or the water in an elevated reservoir, has gravitational PE. A lump of coal and a tank of petrol, together with the oxygen needed for their combustion, have chemical energy. Other sorts of energy include electrical and nuclear energy, and light and sound. Moving bodies possess kinetic energy (KE). Energy can be converted from one form to another, but the total quantity stays the same (in accordance with the conservation of energy principle). For example, as an apple falls, it loses gravitational PE but gains KE.

engine device for converting stored energy into useful work or movement. Most engines use a fuel as their energy store. The fuel is burned to produce heat energy – hence the name 'heat engine' – which is then converted into movement. Heat engines can be classified according to the fuel they use (petrol engine or diesel engine), or according to whether the fuel is burnt inside (internal combustion engine) or outside (steam engine) the engine, or according to whether they produce a reciprocating or rotary motion (turbine or Wankel engine).

entropy in thermodynamics, a parameter representing the state of disorder of a system at the atomic, ionic, or molecular level; the greater the disorder, the higher the entropy. Thus the fast-moving disordered molecules of water vapour have higher entropy than those of more ordered liquid water, which in turn have more entropy than the molecules in solid crystalline ice.

equilibrium unchanging condition in which the forces acting on a particle or system of particles (a body) cancel out, or in which energy is distributed among the particles of a system in the most probable way; or the state in which a body is at rest or moving at constant velocity. A body is in *thermal equilibrium* with its surroundings if no heat enters or leaves it, so that all its parts are at the same temperature as the surroundings.

field region of space in which an object exerts a force on another separate object because of certain properties they both possess. For example, there is a force of attraction between any two objects that have mass when one is in the gravitational field of the other. Other fields of force include electric fields (caused by electric charges) and magnetic fields (caused by magnetic poles), either of which can involve attractive or repulsive forces.

force any influence that tends to change the state of rest or the uniform motion in a straight line of a body. The action of an unbalanced or resultant force results in the acceleration of a body in the direction of action of the force or it may, if the body is unable to move freely, result in its deformation. Force is a vector quantity, possessing both magnitude and direction; its SI unit is the newton.

frequency the number of periodic oscillations, vibrations, or waves occurring per unit of time. The unit of frequency is the hertz (Hz), one hertz being equivalent to one cycle per second. Human beings can hear sounds from objects vibrating in the range 20–15,000 Hz. Ultrasonic frequencies are those above 15,000 Hz; infrasound is low-frequency sound.

friction the force that opposes the relative motion of two bodies in contact. The *coefficient of friction* is the ratio of the force required to achieve this relative motion to the force pressing the two bodies together.

fundamental constant physical quantity that is constant in all circumstances throughout the whole universe. Examples are the electric charge of an electron, the speed of light, Planck's constant, and the gravitational constant.

Fundamental constants

Constant	Symbol	Value in SI units
acceleration of free fall	g	9.80665 m s^{-2}
Avogadro's constant	N_A	6.02252×10^{23} mol^{-1}
Boltzmann's constant	$k = R/N_A$	1.380622×10^{-23} J K^{-1}
electronic charge	e	1.602192×10^{-19} C
electronic rest mass	m_e	9.109558×10^{-31} kg
Faraday's constant	F	9.648670×10^4 C mol^{-1}
gas constant	R	8.31434 J K^{-1} mol^{-1}
gravitational constant	G	6.664×10^{-11} N m^2 kg^{-2}
Loschmidt's number	N_L	2.68719×10^{25} m^{-3}
neutron rest mass	m_n	1.67492×10^{-27} kg
Planck's constant	h	6.626196×10^{-34} J s
proton rest mass	m_p	1.672614×10^{-27} kg
speed of light	c	2.99792458×10^8 m s^{-1}
standard atmospheric pressure	P	1.01325×10^5 Pa
Stefan–Boltzmann constant	Σ	5.6697×10^{-8} W m^{-2} K^{-4}

grand unified theory (GUT) sought-for theory that would combine the theory of the strong nuclear force (called quantum chromodynamics) with the theory of the weak nuclear and electromagnetic forces. The search for the grand unified theory is part of a larger programme seeking a unified field theory, which would combine all the forces of nature (including gravity) within one framework.

gravity force of attraction that arises between objects by virtue of their masses. On Earth, gravity is the force of attraction between any object in the Earth's gravitational field and the Earth itself. It is regarded as one of the four fundamental forces of nature. The gravitational force is the weakest of the four forces, but it acts over great distances. The particle that is postulated as the carrier of the gravitational force is the graviton.

half-life during radioactive decay, the time in which the strength of a radioactive source decays to half its original value. In theory, the decay process is never complete and there is always some residual radioactivity. For this reason, the half-life (the time taken for 50% of the isotope to decay) is measured, rather than the total decay time. It may vary from millionths of a second to billions of years. Plutonium-239, one of the most toxic of all radioactive substances, has a half-life of about 24,000 years.

heat form of internal energy possessed by a substance by virtue of the kinetic energy in the motion of its molecules or atoms. Heat energy is transferred by conduction, convection, and radiation. It always flows from a region of higher temperature (heat intensity) to one of lower temperature. Its effect on a substance may be simply to raise its temperature, or to cause it to expand, melt (if a solid), vaporize (if a liquid), or increase its pressure (if a confined gas). Quantities of heat are usually measured in units of energy, such as joules (J) or calories (C).

hydrodynamics the science of nonviscous fluids (such as water, alcohol, and ether) in motion.

hydrostatics the branch of statics dealing with the mechanical problems of fluids in equilibrium – that is, in a static condition. Practical applications include shipbuilding and dam design.

inertia the tendency of an object to remain in a state of rest or uniform motion until an external force is applied, as stated by Isaac Newton's first law of motion.

interference the phenomenon of two or more wave motions interacting and combining to produce a resultant wave of larger or smaller amplitude (depending on whether the combining waves are in or out of phase with each other).

Interference of white light (multiwavelength) results in spectral coloured fringes; for example, the iridescent colours of oil films seen on water or soap bubbles. With monochromatic light (of a single wavelength), interference produces patterns of light and dark bands. This is the basis of holography, for example. Interference of sound waves of similar frequency produces the phenomenon of beats, often used by musicians when tuning an instrument. Interferometry can also be applied to radio waves, and is a powerful tool in modern astronomy.

kinetic theory theory describing the physical properties of matter in terms of the behaviour – principally movement – of its component atoms or molecules. The temperature of a substance is dependent on the velocity of movement of its constituent particles, increased temperature being accompanied by increased movement. A gas consists of rapidly moving atoms or molecules and, according to kinetic theory, it is their continual impact on the walls of the containing vessel that accounts for the pressure of the gas. The slowing of molecular motion as temperature falls, according to kinetic theory, accounts for the physical properties of liquids and solids, culminating in the concept of no molecular motion at absolute zero (0K/–273°C). By making various assumptions about the nature of gas molecules, it is possible to derive from the kinetic theory the various gas laws (such as Avogadro's hypothesis, Boyle's law, and Charles's law).

laser (acronym for *light amplification by stimulated emission of radiation*) device for producing a narrow beam of light, capable of travelling over vast distances without dispersion, and of being focused to give enormous power densities (10^8 watts per cm^2 for high-energy lasers). The uses of lasers include communications (a laser beam can carry much more information than can radio waves), cutting, drilling, welding, satellite tracking, medical and biological research, and surgery.

A gallium arsenide microchip, produced by IBM in 1989, contains the world's smallest lasers in the form of cylinders of semiconductor roughly one tenth of the thickness of a human hair; a million lasers can fit on a chip 1 cm/2.5 in square.

lens in optics, a piece of a transparent material, such as glass, with two polished surfaces – one concave or convex, and the other plane, concave, or convex – that modifies rays of light. A convex lens brings rays of light together; a concave lens makes the rays diverge. Lenses are essential to spectacles, microscopes, telescopes, cameras, and almost all optical instruments.

lever simple machine consisting of a rigid rod pivoted at a fixed point called the fulcrum, used for shifting or raising a heavy load or applying force in a similar way. Levers are classified into orders according to where the effort is applied, and the load-moving force developed, in relation to the position of the fulcrum.

A *first-order* lever has the load and the effort on opposite sides of the fulcrum; for example, a see-saw or pair of scissors. A *second-order* lever has the load and the effort on the same side of the fulcrum, with the load nearer the fulcrum; for example, nutcrackers or a wheelbarrow. A *third-order* lever has the effort nearer the fulcrum than the load, with both on the same side of it; for example, a pair of tweezers or tongs.

light electromagnetic waves in the visible range, having a wavelength from about 400 nanometres in the extreme violet to about 770 nanometres in the extreme red. Light is considered to exhibit particle and wave properties, and the fundamental particle, or quantum, of light is called the photon. The speed of light (and of all electromagnetic radiation) in a vacuum is approximately 300,000 km/186,000 mi per second, and is a universal constant denoted by c.

luminescence emission of light from a body when its atoms are excited by means other than raising its temperature. Short-lived luminescence is called fluorescence; longer-lived luminescence is called phosphorescence.

magnetism phenomena associated with magnetic fields. Magnetic fields are produced by moving charged particles: in electromagnets, electrons flow through a coil of wire connected to a battery; in permanent magnets, spinning electrons within the atoms generate the field.

mass the quantity of matter in a body as measured by its inertia. Mass determines the acceleration produced in a body by a given force acting on it, the acceleration being inversely proportional to the mass of the body. The mass also determines the force exerted on a body by gravity on Earth, although this attraction varies slightly from place to place. In the SI system, the base unit of mass is the kilogram.

mechanics branch of physics dealing with the motions of bodies and the forces causing these motions, and also with the forces acting on bodies in equilibrium. It is usually divided into dynamics and statics.

mirror any polished surface that reflects light; often made from 'silvered' glass (in practice, a mercury-alloy coating of glass). A plane (flat) mirror produces a same-size, erect 'virtual' image located behind the mirror at the same distance from it as the object is in front of it. A spherical concave mirror produces a reduced, inverted real image in front or an enlarged, erect virtual image behind it (as in a shaving mirror), depending on how close the object is to the mirror. A spherical convex mirror produces a reduced, erect virtual image behind it (as in a car's rear-view mirror).

Newton's laws of motion three laws that form the basis of Newtonian mechanics. (1) Unless acted upon by a net force, a body at rest stays at rest, and a moving body continues moving at the same speed in the same straight line. (2) A net force applied to a body gives it a rate of change of momentum proportional to the force and in the direction of the force. (3) When a body A exerts a force on a body B, B exerts an equal and opposite force on A; that is, to every action there is an equal and opposite reaction.

nuclear fission process whereby an atomic nucleus breaks up into two or more major fragments with the emission of two or three neutrons. It is accompanied by the release of energy in the form of gamma radiation and the kinetic energy of the emitted particles. Fission occurs spontaneously in nuclei of uranium-235, the main fuel used in nuclear reactors. However, the process can also be induced by bombarding nuclei with neutrons.

nuclear fusion process whereby two atomic nuclei are fused, with the release of a large amount of energy. Very high temperatures and pressures are thought to be required in order for the process to happen. Under these conditions the atoms involved are stripped of all their electrons so that the remaining particles, which together make up plasma, can come close together at very high speeds and overcome the mutual repulsion of the positive charges on the atomic nuclei. At very close range another nuclear force will come into play, fusing the particles together to form a larger nucleus. Because fusion is accompanied by the release of large amounts of energy, methods of achieving controlled fusion are the subject of research around the world.

optics branch of physics that deals with the study of light and vision – for example, shadows and mirror images, lenses, microscopes, telescopes, and cameras. For all practical purposes light rays travel in straight lines, although Albert Einstein demonstrated that they may be 'bent' by a gravitational field. On striking a surface they are reflected or refracted with some absorption of energy, and the study of this is known as geometrical optics.

potential, electric the relative electrical state of an object. A charged conductor, for example, has a higher potential than the Earth, whose potential is taken by convention to be zero. An electric cell (battery) has a potential in relation to emf (electromotive force), which can make current flow in an external circuit. The difference in potential between two points – the potential difference – is expressed in volts; that is, a 12 V battery has a potential difference of 12 volts between its negative and positive terminals.

power the rate of doing work or consuming energy. It is measured in watts (joules per second) or other units of work per unit time.

pressure the force acting normally (at right angles) to a body per unit surface area. The SI unit of pressure is the pascal (newton per square metre), equal to 0.01 millibars. In a fluid (liquid or gas), pressure increases with depth. At the edge of Earth's atmosphere, pressure is zero, whereas at sea level atmospheric pressure due to the weight of the air above is about 100 kilopascals (1,013 millibars or 1 atmosphere). Pressure is commonly measured by means of a barometer, manometer, or Bourdon gauge.

quantum theory or *quantum mechanics* the theory that energy does not have a continuous range of values, but is, instead, absorbed or radiated discontinuously, in multiples of definite, indivisible units called quanta. Just as earlier theory showed how light, generally seen as a wave motion, could also in some ways be seen as composed of discrete particles (photons), quantum theory shows how atomic particles such as electrons may also be seen as having wavelike properties. Quantum theory is the basis of particle physics, modern theoretical chemistry, and the solid-state physics that describes the behaviour of the silicon chips used in computers.

radiation emission of radiant energy as particles or waves; for example, heat, light, alpha particles, and beta particles.

radioactivity spontaneous alteration of the nuclei of radioactive atoms, accompanied by the emission of radiation. It is the property exhibited by the radioactive isotopes of stable elements and all isotopes of radioactive elements, and can be either natural or induced.

radioisotope (contraction of *radioactive isotope*) naturally occurring or synthetic radioactive form of an element. Most radioisotopes are made by bombarding a stable element with neutrons in the core of a nuclear reactor. The radiations given off by radioisotopes are easy to detect (hence their use as

Physics: chronology

c. 400 BC	The first 'atomic' theory was put forward by Democritus.
c. 250	Archimedes' principle of buoyancy was established.
AD 1600	Magnetism was described by William Gilbert.
1608	Hans Lippershey invented the refracting telescope.
c. 1610	The principle of falling bodies descending to earth at the same speed was established by Galileo.
1642	The principles of hydraulics were put forward by Blaise Pascal.
1643	The mercury barometer was invented by Evangelista Torricelli.
1656	The pendulum clock was invented by Christiaan Huygens.
1662	Boyle's law concerning the behaviour of gases was established by Robert Boyle.
c. 1665	Isaac Newton put forward the law of gravity, stating that the Earth exerts a constant force on falling bodies.
1690	The wave theory of light was propounded by Christiaan Huygens.
1704	The corpuscular theory of light was put forward by Isaac Newton.
1714	The mercury thermometer was invented by Daniel Fahrenheit.
1764	Specific and latent heats were described by Joseph Black.
1771	The link between nerve action and electricity was discovered by Luigi Galvani.
c. 1787	Charles's law relating the pressure, volume, and temperature of a gas was established by Jacques Charles.
1795	The metric system was adopted in France.
1798	The link between heat and friction was discovered by Benjamin Rumford.
1800	Alessandro Volta invented the Voltaic cell.
1801	Interference of light was discovered by Thomas Young.
1808	The 'modern' atomic theory was propounded by John Dalton.
1811	Avogadro's hypothesis relating volumes and numbers of molecules of gases was proposed by Amedeo Avogadro.
1814	Fraunhofer lines in the solar spectrum were mapped by Joseph von Fraunhofer.
1815	Refraction of light was explained by Augustin Fresnel.
1819	The discovery of electromagnetism was made by Hans Oersted.
1821	The dynamo principle was described by Michael Faraday; the thermocouple was discovered by Thomas Seebeck.
1822	The laws of electrodynamics were established by André Ampère.
1824	Thermodynamics as a branch of physics was proposed by Sadi Carnot.
1827	Ohm's law of electrical resistance was established by Georg Ohm; Brownian motion resulting from molecular vibrations was observed by Robert Brown.
1829	The law of gaseous diffusion was established by Thomas Graham.
1831	Electromagnetic induction was discovered by Faraday.
1834	Faraday discovered self-induction.
1842	The principle of conservation of energy was observed by Julius von Mayer.
c. 1847	The mechanical equivalent of heat was described by James Joule.
1849	A measurement of speed of light was put forward by French physicist Armand Fizeau (1819–1896).
1851	The rotation of the Earth was demonstrated by Jean Foucault.
1858	The mirror galvanometer, an instrument for measuring small electric currents, was invented by William Thomson (Lord Kelvin).
1859	Spectrographic analysis was made by Robert Bunsen and Gustav Kirchhoff.
1861	Osmosis was discovered.
1873	Light was conceived as electromagnetic radiation by James Maxwell.
1877	A theory of sound as vibrations in an elastic medium was propounded by John Rayleigh.
1880	Piezoelectricity was discovered by Pierre Curie.
1887	The existence of radio waves was predicted by Heinrich Hertz.
1895	X-rays were discovered by Wilhelm Röntgen.
1896	The discovery of radioactivity was made by Antoine Becquerel.
1897	Joseph Thomson discovered the electron.
1899	Ernest Rutherford discovered alpha and beta rays.
1900	Quantum theory was propounded by Max Planck; the discovery of gamma rays was made by French physicist Paul-Ulrich Villard (1860–1934).
1902	Oliver Heaviside discovered the ionosphere.
1904	The theory of radioactivity was put forward by Rutherford and Frederick Soddy.
1905	Albert Einstein propounded his special theory of relativity.
1908	The Geiger counter was invented by Hans Geiger and Rutherford.
1911	The discovery of the atomic nucleus was made by Rutherford.
1913	The orbiting electron atomic theory was propounded by Danish physicist Niels Bohr.
1915	X-ray crystallography was discovered by William and Lawrence Bragg.
1916	Einstein put forward his general theory of relativity; mass spectrography was discovered by William Aston.
1924	Edward Appleton made his study of the Heaviside layer.
1926	Wave mechanics was introduced by Erwin Schrödinger.
1927	The uncertainty principle of atomic physics was established by Werner Heisenberg.

Physics: chronology *(cont.)*

1931   The cyclotron was developed by Ernest Lawrence.
1932   The discovery of the neutron was made by James Chadwick; the electron microscope was developed by Vladimir Zworykin.
1933   The positron, the antiparticle of the electron, was discovered by Carl Anderson.
1934   Artificial radioactivity was developed by Frédéric and Irène Joliot-Curie.
1939   The discovery of nuclear fission was made by Otto Hahn and Fritz Strassmann.
1942   The first controlled nuclear chain reaction was achieved by Enrico Fermi.
1956   The neutrino, an elementary particle, was discovered by Clyde Cowan and Fred Reines.
1960   The Mössbauer effect of atom emissions was discovered by Rudolf Mössbauer; the first maser was developed by US physicist Theodore Maiman (1927–).
1963   Maiman developed the first laser.
1964   Murray Gell-Mann and George Zweig discovered the quark.
1967   Jocelyn Bell (now Burnell) and Antony Hewish discovered pulsars (rapidly rotating neutron stars that emit pulses of energy).
1971   The theory of superconductivity was announced, where electrical resistance in some metals vanishes above absolute zero.
1979   The discovery of the asymmetry of elementary particles was made by US physicists James W Cronin and Val L Fitch.
1982   The discovery of processes involved in the evolution of stars was made by Subrahmanyan Chandrasekhar and William Fowler.
1983   Evidence of the existence of weakons (W and Z particles) was confirmed at CERN, validating the link between the weak nuclear force and the electromagnetic force.
1986   The first high-temperature superconductor was discovered, able to conduct electricity without resistance at a temperature of $-238°C/-396°F$.
1989   CERN's Large Electron Positron Collider (LEP), a particle accelerator with a circumference of 27 km/16.8 mi, came into operation.
1991   LEP experiments demonstrated the existence of three generations of elementary particles, each with two quarks and two leptons.
1992   Japanese researchers developed a material that becomes superconducting at $-103°C/-153°F$ (about 45°C/80°F warmer than the previous record).
1993   Top quark discovered at Fermilab, the US particle physics laboratory near Chicago, USA.

tracers), can in some instances penetrate substantial thicknesses of materials, and have profound effects (such as genetic mutation) on living matter. Although dangerous, radioisotopes are used in the fields of medicine, industry, agriculture, and research.

reflection the throwing back or deflection of waves, such as light or sound waves, when they hit a surface. The *law of reflection* states that the angle of incidence (the angle between the ray and a perpendicular line drawn to the surface) is equal to the angle of reflection (the angle between the reflected ray and a perpendicular to the surface).

refraction the bending of a wave of light, heat, or sound when it passes from one medium to another. Refraction occurs because waves travel at different velocities in different media.

relativity the theory of the relative rather than absolute character of motion and mass, and the interdependence of matter, time, and space, as developed by German physicist Albert Einstein in two phases:

special theory (1905) Starting with the premises that (1) the laws of nature are the same for all observers in unaccelerated motion, and (2) the speed of light is independent of the motion of its source, Einstein postulated that the time interval between two events was longer for an observer in whose frame of reference the events occur in different places than for the observer for whom they occur at the same place.

general theory of relativity (1915) The geometrical properties of space-time were to be conceived as modified locally by the presence of a body with mass. A planet's orbit around the Sun (as observed in three-dimensional space) arises from its natural trajectory in modified space-time; there is no need to invoke, as Isaac Newton did, a force of gravity coming from the Sun and acting on the planet. Einstein's theory predicted slight differences in the orbits of the planets from Newton's theory, which were observable in the case of Mercury. The new theory also said light rays should bend when they pass by a massive object, owing to the object's effect on local space-time. The predicted bending of starlight was observed during the eclipse of the Sun 1919, when light from distant stars passing close to the Sun was not masked by sunlight.

resistance that property of a substance that restricts the flow of electricity through it, associated with the conversion of electrical energy to heat; also the magnitude of this property. Resistance depends on many factors, such as the nature of the material, its temperature, dimensions, and thermal properties; degree of impurity; the nature and state of illumination of the surface; and the frequency and magnitude of the current. The SI unit of resistance is the ohm.

resonance rapid and uncontrolled increase in the size of a vibration when the vibrating object is subject to a force varying at its natural frequency. In a trombone, for example, the length of the air column in the instrument is adjusted until it resonates with the note being sounded. Resonance effects are also produced by many electrical circuits. Tuning a radio, for example, is done by adjusting the natural frequency of the receiver circuit until it coincides with the frequency of the radio waves falling on the aerial.

semiconductor crystalline material with an electrical conductivity between that of metals (good) and insulators (poor). The conductivity of semiconductors can usually be improved by minute additions of different substances or by other factors. Silicon, for example, has poor conductivity at low temperatures, but this is improved by the application of light, heat, or voltage; hence silicon is used in transistors, rectifiers, and integrated circuits (silicon chips).

SI units (French *Système International d'Unités*) standard system of scientific units used by scientists worldwide. Originally proposed in 1960, it replaces the m.k.s., c.g.s., and f.p.s. systems. It is based on seven basic units: the metre (m) for length, kilogram (kg) for mass, second (s) for time, ampere (A) for electrical current, kelvin (K) for temperature, mole (mol) for amount of substance, and candela (cd) for luminosity. (See tables in *Time and Measurement* section.)

sound physiological sensation received by the ear, originating in a vibration (pressure variation in the air) that communicates itself to the air, and travels in every direction, spreading out as an expanding sphere. All sound waves in air travel with a speed dependent on the temperature; under ordinary conditions, this is about 330 m/1,070 ft per second. The pitch of the sound depends on the number of vibrations imposed on the air per second, but the speed is unaffected. The loudness of a sound is dependent primarily on the amplitude of the vibration of the air.

spectroscopy study of spectra associated with atoms or molecules in solid, liquid, or gaseous phase. Spectroscopy can be used to identify unknown compounds and is an invaluable tool in science, medicine, and industry (for example, in checking the purity of drugs).

spectrum (plural *spectra*) arrangement of frequencies or wavelengths when electromagnetic radiations are separated into their constituent parts. Visible light is part of the electromagnetic spectrum and most sources emit waves over a range of wavelengths that can be broken up or 'dispersed'; white light can be separated into red, orange, yellow, green, blue, indigo, and violet. The visible spectrum was first studied by Isaac Newton, who showed in 1672 how white light could be broken up into different colours.

states of matter forms (solid, liquid, or gas) in which material can exist. Whether a material is solid, liquid, or gas depends on its temperature and the pressure on it. The transition between states takes place at definite temperatures, called melting point and boiling point.

statics branch of mechanics concerned with the behaviour of bodies at rest and forces in equilibrium.

stress and strain in the science of materials, measures of the deforming force applied to a body (stress) and of the resulting change in its shape (strain). For a perfectly elastic material, stress is proportional to strain (Hooke's law).

surface tension the property that causes the surface of a liquid to behave as if it were covered with a weak elastic skin; this is why a needle can float on water. It is caused by the exposed surface's tendency to contract to the smallest possible area because of unequal cohesive forces between molecules at the surface. Allied phenomena include the formation of droplets, the concave profile of a meniscus, and the capillary action by which water soaks into a sponge.

temperature the state of hotness or coldness of a body, and the condition that determines whether or not it will transfer heat to, or receive heat from, another body according to the laws of thermodynamics. It is measured in degrees Celsius (before 1948 called centigrade), kelvin, or Fahrenheit.

tension reaction force set up in a body that is subjected to stress. In a stretched string or wire it exerts a pull that is equal in magnitude but opposite in direction to the stress being applied at its ends. Tension originates in the net attractive intermolecular force created when a stress causes the mean distance separating a material's molecules to become greater than the equilibrium distance. It is measured in newtons.

thermodynamics branch of physics dealing with the transformation of heat into and from other forms of energy. It is the basis of the study of the efficient working of engines, such as the steam and internal-combustion engines. The three laws of thermodynamics are (1) energy can be neither created nor destroyed, heat and mechanical work being mutually convertible; (2) it is impossible for an unaided self-acting machine to convey heat from one body to another at a higher temperature; and (3) it is impossible by any procedure, no matter how idealized, to reduce any system to the absolute zero of temperature (0K/−273°C) in a finite number of operations. Put into mathematical form, these laws have widespread applications in physics and chemistry.

ultrasound pressure waves similar in nature to sound waves but occurring at frequencies above 20,000 Hz (cycles per second), the approximate upper limit of human hearing (15–16 Hz is the lower limit). Ultrasonics is concerned with the study and practical application of these phenomena.

viscosity the resistance of a fluid to flow, caused by its internal friction, which makes it resist flowing past a solid surface or other layers of the fluid. It applies to the motion of an object moving through a fluid as well as the motion of a fluid passing by an object.

wave disturbance consisting of a series of oscillations that propagate through a medium (or space). There are two types: in a *longitudinal wave* (such as a sound wave) the disturbance is parallel to the wave's direction of travel; in a *transverse wave* (such as an electromagnetic wave) it is perpendicular. The medium only vibrates as the wave passes; it does not travel outward from the source with the waves.

weight the force exerted on an object by gravity. The weight of an object depends on its mass – the amount of material in it – and the strength of the Earth's gravitational pull, which decreases with height. Consequently, an object weighs less at the top of a mountain than at sea level. On the Moon, an object has only one-sixth of its weight on Earth, because the pull of the Moon's gravity is one-sixth that of the Earth.

work measure of the result of transferring energy from one system to another to cause an object to move. Work should not be confused with energy (the capacity to do work, which is also measured in joules) or with power (the rate of doing work, measured in joules per second).

Particle Physics

antimatter matter in which most of the attributes (such as electrical charge, magnetic moment, and spin) of elementary particles are reversed. Such particles (antiparticles) can be created in particle accelerators, such as those at CERN in Geneva, Switzerland, and at Fermilab in the USA.

baryon heavy subatomic particle made up of three indivisible elementary particles called quarks. The baryons form a subclass of the hadrons, and comprise the nucleons (protons and neutrons) and hyperons.

boson elementary particle whose spin can only take values that are whole numbers or zero. Bosons may be classified as gauge bosons (carriers of the four fundamental forces) or mesons. All elementary particles are either bosons or fermions.

electron stable, negatively charged elementary particle; it is a constituent of all atoms, and a member of the class of particles known as leptons. The electrons in each atom surround the nucleus in groupings called shells; in a neutral atom the number of electrons is equal to the number of protons in the nucleus. This electron structure is responsible for the chemical properties of the atom.

fermion subatomic particle whose spin can only take values that are half-integers, such as $1/2$ or $3/2$. Fermions may be classified as leptons, such as the electron, and baryons, such as the proton and neutron. All elementary particles are either fermions or bosons.

forces, fundamental the four fundamental interactions believed to be at work in the physical universe. There are two long-range forces: *gravity*, which keeps the planets in orbit around the Sun, and acts between all particles that have mass; and the *electromagnetic force*, which stops solids from falling apart, and acts between all particles with electric charge. There are two very short-range forces which operate only inside the atomic nucleus: the *weak nuclear force*, responsible for the reactions that fuel the Sun and for the emission of beta particles from certain nuclei; and the *strong nuclear force*, which binds together the protons and neutrons in the nuclei of atoms. The relative strengths of the four forces are: strong, 1; electromagnetic, 10^{-2}; weak, 10^{-6}; gravitational, 10^{-40}.

gauge boson or *field particle* any of the particles that carry the four fundamental forces of nature. Gauge bosons are elementary particles that cannot be subdivided, and include the photon, the graviton, the gluons, and the weakons.

gluon gauge boson that carries the strong nuclear force, responsible for binding quarks together to form the strongly interacting subatomic particles known as hadrons. There are eight kinds of gluon.

graviton gauge boson that is the postulated carrier of gravity.

hadron subatomic particle that experiences the strong nuclear force. Each is made up of two or three indivisible particles called quarks. The hadrons are grouped into the baryons (protons, neutrons, and hyperons) and the mesons (particles with masses between those of electrons and protons).

Higgs particle or *Higgs boson* postulated elementary particle whose existence would explain why particles, such as the intermediate vector boson, have mass. The current theory of elementary particles, called the standard model, cannot explain how mass arises. To overcome this difficulty, Peter Higgs (1929–) of the University of Edinburgh, Scotland, and Thomas Kibble (1932–) of Imperial College, London, England, proposed in 1964 a new particle that binds to other particles and gives them their mass. The Higgs particle has not yet been detected experimentally.

hyperon type of hadron; any of a group of highly unstable elementary particles that includes all the baryons with a mass greater than the neutron. They are all composed of three quarks. The lambda, xi, sigma, and omega particles are hyperons.

lepton any of a class of light elementary particles that are not affected by the strong nuclear force; they do not interact strongly with other particles or nuclei. The leptons are comprised of the electron, muon, and tau, and their neutrinos (the electron neutrino, muon neutrino, and tau neutrino), plus their six antiparticles.

meson unstable subatomic particle made up of two indivisible elementary particles called quarks. It has a mass intermediate between that of the electron and that of the proton, is found in cosmic radiation, and is emitted by nuclei under bombardment by very high-energy particles.

muon elementary particle similar to the electron except for its mass, which is 207 times greater than that of the electron. It has a half-life of 2 millionths of a second, decaying into electrons and neutrinos. The muon was originally thought to be a meson and is thus sometimes called a mu meson, although current opinion is that it is a lepton.

neutrino any of three uncharged elementary particles (and their antiparticles) of the lepton class, having a mass too close to zero to be measured. The most familiar type, the antiparticle of the electron neutrino, is emitted in the beta decay of a nucleus. The other two are the muon neutrino and the tau neutrino.

neutron one of the three main subatomic particles, the others being the proton and the electron. The neutron is a composite particle, being made up of three quarks, and therefore belongs to the baryon group of the hadrons. Neutrons have about the same mass as protons but no electric charge, and occur in the nuclei of all atoms except hydrogen. They contribute to the mass of atoms but do not affect their chemistry.

nucleus the positively charged central part of an atom, which constitutes almost all its mass. Except for hydrogen nuclei, which have only protons, nuclei are composed of both protons and neutrons. Surrounding the nuclei are electrons, which contain a negative charge equal to the protons, thus giving the atom a neutral charge.

photon elementary particle or 'package' (quantum) of energy in which light and other forms of electromagnetic radiation are emitted. The photon has both particle and wave properties; it has no charge, is considered massless but possesses momentum and energy. It is one of the gauge bosons, a particle that

PRINCIPAL SUBATOMIC PARTICLES

	Group	Particle	Symbol	Charge	Mass (MeV)	Spin	Lifetime (sec)
elementary particle	quark	up	u	$\frac{2}{3}$	336	$\frac{1}{2}$	?
		down	d	$-\frac{1}{3}$	336	$\frac{1}{2}$	?
		(top)	t	$(\frac{2}{3})$	(<600,000)	$(\frac{1}{2})$	?
		bottom	b	$-\frac{1}{3}$	4,700	$\frac{1}{2}$	?
		strange	s	$-\frac{1}{3}$	540	$\frac{1}{2}$	?
		charm	c	$\frac{2}{3}$	1,500	$\frac{1}{2}$	?
	lepton	electron	e^-	-1	0·511	$\frac{1}{2}$	stable
		electron neutrino	ν_e	0	(0)	$\frac{1}{2}$	stable
		muon	μ^-	-1	105·66	$\frac{1}{2}$	$2\cdot2 \times 10^{-6}$
		muon neutrino	ν_μ	0	(0)	$\frac{1}{2}$	stable
		tau	τ^-	-1	1,784	$\frac{1}{2}$	$3\cdot4 \times 10^{-13}$
		tau neutrino	ν_τ	0	(0)	$\frac{1}{2}$	?
	gauge boson	photon	γ	0	0	1	stable
		graviton	g	0	(0)	2	stable
		gluon	g	0	0	1	?
		weakon	$W^\pm$	±1	81,000	1	?
			Z	0	94,000	1	?
hadron	meson	pion	π^+	1	139·57	0	$2\cdot6 \times 10^{-8}$
			π^0	0	134·96	0	$8\cdot3 \times 10^{-17}$
		kaon	K^+	1	493·67	0	$1\cdot2 \times 10^{-8}$
			K^0_s	0	497·67	0	$8\cdot9 \times 10^{-11}$
			K^0_L	0	497·67	0	$5\cdot18 \times 10^{-8}$
		psi	Ψ	0	3,100	1	$6\cdot3 \times 10^{-2}$
		upsilon	Y	0	9,460	1	$\sim 1 \times 10^{-20}$
	baryon	nucleon					
		proton	p	1	938·28	$\frac{1}{2}$	stable
		nucleon	n	0	939·57	$\frac{1}{2}$	920
		hyperon					
		lambda	Λ	0	1,115·6	$\frac{1}{2}$	$2\cdot63 \times 10^{-10}$
		sigma	Σ^+	1	1,189·4	$\frac{1}{2}$	$8\cdot0 \times 10^{-11}$
			Σ^-	-1	1,197·3	$\frac{1}{2}$	$1\cdot5 \times 10^{-10}$
			Σ^0	0	1,192·5	$\frac{1}{2}$	$5\cdot8 \times 10^{-20}$
		xi	Ξ^-	-1	1,321·3	$\frac{1}{2}$	$1\cdot64 \times 10^{-10}$
			Ξ^0	0	1,314·9	$\frac{1}{2}$	$2\cdot9 \times 10^{-10}$
		omega	Ω	-1	1,672·4	$\frac{3}{2}$	$8\cdot2 \times 10^{-11}$

? indicates that the particle's lifetime has yet to be determined
( ) indicates that the property has been deduced but not confirmed
MeV = million electron volts

cannot be subdivided, and is the carrier of the electromagnetic force, one of the fundamental forces of nature.

proton positively charged subatomic particle, a constituent of the nucleus of all atoms. It belongs to the baryon subclass of the hadrons. A proton is extremely long-lived, with a lifespan of at least 10^{32} years. It carries a unit positive charge equal to the negative charge of an electron. Its mass is almost 1,836 times that of an electron, or 1.67×10^{-24} g. The number of protons in the atom of an element is equal to the atomic number of that element.

quantum chromodynamics (QCD) theory describing the interactions of quarks, the elementary particles that make up all hadrons (subatomic particles such as protons and neutrons). In quantum chromodynamics, quarks are considered to interact by exchanging particles called gluons, which carry the strong nuclear force, and whose role is to 'glue' quarks together. The mathematics involved in the theory is complex, and although a number of successful predictions have been made, the theory does not yet compare in accuracy with quantum electrodynamics, upon which it is modelled.

quantum electrodynamics (QED) theory describing the interaction of charged subatomic particles within electric and magnetic fields. It combines quantum theory and relativity, and considers charged particles to interact by the exchange of photons. QED is remarkable for the accuracy of its predictions – for example, it has been used to calculate the value of some physical quantities to an accuracy of ten decimal places, a feat equivalent to calculating the distance between New York and Los Angeles to within the thickness of a hair. The theory was developed by US physicists Richard Feynman and Julian Schwinger, and by Japanese physicist Sin-Itiro Tomonaga 1948.

quark elementary particle that is the fundamental constituent of all hadrons (baryons, such as neutrons and protons, and mesons). There are six types, or 'flavours': up, down, top, bottom, strange, and charm, each of which has three varieties, or 'colours': red, yellow, and blue (visual colour is not meant, although the analogy is useful in many ways). To each quark there is an antiparticle, called an antiquark.

spin the intrinsic angular momentum of a subatomic particle, nucleus, atom, or molecule, which continues even when the particle comes to rest. A particle in a specific energy state has a particular spin, just as it has a particular electric charge and mass. According to quantum theory, this is restricted to discrete and indivisible values, specified by a spin quantum number. Because of its spin, a charged particle acts as a small magnet and is affected by magnetic fields.

standard model the modern theory of elementary particles and their interactions. According to the standard model, elementary particles are classified as leptons (light particles, such as electrons), hadrons (particles, such as neutrons and protons, that are formed from quarks), and gauge bosons. Leptons and hadrons interact by exchanging gauge bosons, each of which is responsible for a different fundamental force: photons mediate the electromagnetic force, which affects all charged particles; gluons mediate the strong nuclear force, which affects quarks; gravitons mediate the force of gravity; and the weakons (intermediate vector bosons) mediate the weak nuclear force.

superstring theory mathematical theory developed in the 1980s to explain the properties of elementary particles and the forces between them (in particular, gravity and the nuclear forces) in a way that combines relativity and quantum theory. In string theory, the fundamental objects in the universe are not pointlike particles but extremely small stringlike objects. These objects exist in a universe of ten dimensions, although, for reasons not yet understood, only three space dimensions and one dimension of time are discernible.

supersymmetry theory that relates the two classes of elementary particle, the fermions and the bosons. According to supersymmetry, each fermion particle has a boson partner particle, and vice versa. It has not been possible to marry up all the known fermions with the known bosons, and so the theory postulates the existence of other, as yet undiscovered fermions, such as the photinos (partners of the photons), gluinos (partners of the gluons), and gravitinos (partners of the gravitons). Using these ideas, it has become possible to develop a theory of gravity – called supergravity – that extends Albert Einstein's work and considers the gravitational, nuclear, and electromagnetic forces to be manifestations of an underlying superforce. Supersymmetry has been incorporated into the superstring theory, and appears to be a crucial ingredient in the 'theory of everything' sought by scientists.

tau elementary particle with the same electric charge as the electron but a mass nearly double that of a proton. It has a lifetime of around 3×10^{-13} seconds and belongs to the lepton family of particles: those that interact via the electromagnetic, weak nuclear, and gravitational forces, but not the strong nuclear force.

uncertainty principle or *indeterminacy principle* the principle that it is meaningless to speak of a particle's position, momentum, or other parameters, except as results of measurements; measuring, however, involves an interaction (such as a photon of light bouncing off the particle under scrutiny), which must disturb the particle, though the disturbance is noticeable only at an atomic scale. The principle implies that one cannot, even in theory, predict the moment-to-moment behaviour of such a system.

weakon or *intermediate vector boson* gauge boson that carries the weak nuclear force, one of the fundamental forces of nature. There are three types of weakon: the positive and negative W particle and the neutral Z particle.

Z particle elementary particle, one of the weakons responsible for carrying the weak nuclear force.

Great Physicists

Ampère André Marie 1775–1836. French physicist and mathematician who made many discoveries in electromagnetism and electrodynamics. He followed up the work of Danish physicist Hans Oersted (1777–1851) on the interaction between magnets and electric currents, developing a rule for determining the direction of the magnetic field associated with an electric current. The ampere is named after him.

Bohr Niels (Henrik David) 1885–1962. Danish physicist. His theoretic work produced a new model of atomic structure, now called the Bohr model, and helped establish the validity of quantum theory.

Boyle Robert 1627–1691. Irish physicist and chemist who published the seminal *The Sceptical Chymist* 1661. He formulated *Boyle's law* 1662.

Broglie Louis de, 7th Duc de Broglie 1892–1987. French theoretical physicist who established that all subatomic particles can be described either by particle equations or by wave equations, thus laying the foundations of wave mechanics. Nobel Prize for Physics 1929.

Carnot (Nicolas Leonard) Sadi 1796–1832. French scientist and military engineer who founded the science of thermodynamics; his pioneering work was *Reflexions sur la puissance motrice du feu/On the Motive Power of Fire*, which considered the changes that would take place in an idealized, frictionless steam engine.

Cavendish Henry 1731–1810. English physicist who discovered hydrogen (which he called 'inflammable air') 1766, and determined the compositions of water and of nitric acid.

Chadwick James 1891–1974. British physicist. In 1932, he discovered the particle in the nucleus of an atom that became known as the neutron because it has no electric charge. Nobel Prize for Physics 1935.

Curie Marie (born Sklodovska) 1867–1934. Polish scientist. In 1898 she reported the possible existence of a new, powerfully radioactive element in pitchblende ores.

Her husband, *Pierre Curie* (1859-1906), abandoned his own researches to assist her, and in the same year they announced the existence of polonium and radium. They isolated the pure elements 1902. They shared the Nobel Prize for Physics 1903 with

Antoine Becquerel (1852–1908); Marie Curie wrote a *Treatise on Radioactivity* 1910, and was awarded the Nobel Prize for Chemistry 1911.

Dirac Paul Adrien Maurice 1902–1984. British physicist who worked out a version of quantum mechanics consistent with special relativity. The existence of the positron (positive electron) was one of its predictions. He shared the Nobel Prize for Physics 1933 with Erwin Schrödinger.

Einstein Albert 1879–1955. German-born US physicist who formulated the *theories of relativity*, and worked on radiation physics and thermodynamics. In 1905 he published the special theory of relativity, and in 1915 issued his general theory of relativity. He received the Nobel Prize for Physics 1921.

His last conception of the basic laws governing the universe was outlined in his unified field theory, made public 1953.

Faraday Michael 1791–1867. English chemist and physicist. In 1821 he began experimenting with electromagnetism, and ten years later discovered the induction of electric currents and made the first dynamo. He subsequently found that a magnetic field will rotate the plane of polarization of light. Faraday also investigated electrolysis.

Fermi Enrico 1901–1954. Italian-born US physicist who proved the existence of new radioactive elements produced by bombardment with neutrons, and discovered nuclear reactions produced by low-energy neutrons. His theoretical work included study of the weak nuclear force, one of the fundamental forces of nature, and (with Paul Dirac) of the quantum statistics of fermion particles. Nobel prize 1938.

Feynman Richard P(hillips) 1918–1988. US physicist whose work laid the foundations of quantum electrodynamics. As a member of the committee investigating the *Challenger* space-shuttle disaster 1986, he demonstrated the lethal faults in rubber seals on the shuttle's booster rocket. For his work on the theory of radiation he shared the Nobel Prize for Physics 1965.

Foucault Jean Bernard Léon 1819–1868. French physicist who used a pendulum to demonstrate the rotation of the Earth on its axis, and invented the gyroscope.

Gabor Dennis 1900–1979. Hungarian-born British physicist. In 1947 he invented the holographic method of three-dimensional photography. Nobel prize 1971.

Galileo properly Galileo Galilei 1564–1642. Italian mathematician, astronomer, and physicist. He developed the astronomical telescope and was the first to see sunspots, the four main satellites of Jupiter, mountains and craters on the Moon, and the appearance of Venus going through 'phases', thus proving it was orbiting the Sun. In mechanics, Galileo discovered that freely falling bodies, heavy or light, had the same, constant acceleration (although the story of his dropping cannonballs from the Leaning Tower of Pisa is questionable) and that a body moving on a perfectly smooth horizontal surface would neither speed up nor slow down.

Gell-Mann Murray 1929– . US physicist. In 1964, he formulated the theory of the quark as one of the fundamental constituents of matter. In 1969, he was awarded a Nobel prize for his work on elementary particles and their interaction.

Glashow Sheldon Lee 1932– . US particle physicist. In 1964, he proposed the existence of a fourth 'charmed' quark, and later argued that quarks must be coloured. Insights gained from these theoretical studies enabled Glashow to consider ways in which the weak nuclear force and the electromagnetic force (two of the fundamental forces of nature) could be unified as a single force now called the electroweak force. For this work he shared the Nobel Prize for Physics 1979 with Abdus Salam and Steven Weinberg.

Hawking Stephen 1942– . English physicist who has researched black holes and gravitational field theory. His books include *A Brief History of Time* 1988, in which he argues that our universe is only one small part of a 'super-universe' that has existed for ever and comprises an infinite number of universes like our own.

Heisenberg Werner Carl 1901–1976. German physicist who developed quantum theory and formulated the *uncertainty principle*, which concerns matter, radiation, and their reactions, and places absolute limits on the achievable accuracy of measurement. Nobel prize 1932.

Hertz Heinrich 1857–1894. German physicist who studied electromagnetic waves, showing that their behaviour resembles that of light and heat waves.

Hooke Robert 1635–1703. English scientist and inventor, originator of *Hooke's law*, and considered the foremost mechanic of his time. His inventions included a telegraph system, the spirit level, marine barometer, and sea gauge. He coined the term 'cell' in biology.

Josephson Brian 1940– . British physicist, a leading authority on superconductivity. In 1973, he shared a Nobel prize for his theoretical predictions of the properties of a supercurrent through a tunnel barrier (the Josephson effect), which led to the development of the Josephson junction.

Joule James Prescott 1818–1889. English physicist whose work on the relations between electrical, mechanical, and chemical effects led to the discovery of the first law of thermodynamics.

Kelvin William Thomson, 1st Baron Kelvin 1824–1907. Irish physicist who introduced the *kelvin scale*, the absolute scale of temperature. His work on the conservation of energy 1851 led to the second law of thermodynamics.

Lawrence Ernest O(rlando) 1901–1958. US physicist whose invention of the cyclotron particle accelerator pioneered the production of artificial radioisotopes.

Michelson Albert Abraham 1852–1931. German-born US physicist. In conjunction with Edward Morley, he performed in 1887 the *Michelson–Morley experiment* to detect the motion of the Earth through the postulated ether (a medium believed to be necessary for the propagation of light). The failure of the experiment indicated the nonexistence of the ether, and led Albert Einstein to his theory of relativity. Michelson was the first American to be awarded a Nobel prize, in 1907.

Newton Isaac 1642–1727. English physicist and mathematician who laid the foundations of physics as a modern discipline. He discovered the law of gravity, created calculus, discovered that white light is composed of many colours, and developed the three standard laws of motion still in use today. During 1665–66, he discovered the binomial theorem, and differential and integral calculus, and also began to investigate the phenomenon of gravitation. In 1685, he expounded his universal law of gravitation. His *Philosophiae naturalis principia mathematica*, usually referred to as *Principia*, was published in 1687.

Ohm Georg Simon 1787–1854. German physicist who studied electricity and discovered the fundamental law that bears his name. The SI unit of electrical resistance is named after him.

Pauli Wolfgang 1900–1958. Austrian physicist who originated the *exclusion principle*: in a given system no two fermions (electrons, protons, neutrons, or other elementary particles of half-integral spin) can be characterized by the same set of quantum numbers. He also predicted the existence of neutrinos. He was awarded a Nobel prize 1945 for his work on atomic structure.

Planck Max 1858–1947. German physicist who framed the quantum theory 1900. His research into the manner in which heated bodies radiate energy led him to report that energy is emitted only in indivisible amounts, called quanta, the magnitudes of which are proportional to the frequency of the radiation. His discovery ran counter to classical physics and is held to have marked the commencement of the modern science. Nobel Prize for Physics 1918.

Powell Cecil Frank 1903–1969. English physicist. From the 1930s he and his team at Bristol University investigated the charged subatomic particles in cosmic radiation by using photographic emulsions carried in weather balloons. This led to his discovery of the pion (pi meson) 1946, a particle whose existence had been predicted by the Japanese physicist Hideki Yukawa (1907–1981) 1935. Powell received a Nobel prize 1950.

Rutherford Ernest 1871–1937. New Zealand physicist, a pioneer of modern atomic science. His main research was in the field of radioactivity, and he dis-

covered alpha, beta, and gamma rays. He named the nucleus, and was the first to recognize the nuclear nature of the atom. Nobel prize 1908.

Salam Abdus 1926–   . Pakistani physicist. In 1967, he proposed a theory linking the electromagnetic and weak nuclear forces, also arrived at independently by Steven Weinberg. In 1979, he was the first person from his country to receive a Nobel prize, which he shared with Weinberg and Sheldon Glashow.

Schrödinger Erwin 1887–1961. Austrian physicist who advanced the study of wave mechanics (an aspect of quantum theory). He became senior professor at the Dublin Institute for Advanced Studies 1940. He shared (with Paul Dirac) a Nobel prize 1933.

Shockley William 1910–1989. US physicist and amateur geneticist who worked with John Bardeen (1908–   ) and Walter Brattain (1902–1987) on the invention of the transistor. They were jointly awarded a Nobel prize 1956. During the 1970s, Shockley was criticized for his claim that blacks were genetically inferior to whites in terms of intelligence.

Thomson J(oseph) J(ohn) 1856–1940. English physicist who discovered the electron. He was responsible for organizing the Cavendish atomic research laboratory at Cambridge University. His work inaugurated the electrical theory of the atom, and his elucidation of positive rays and their application to an analysis of neon led to Francis Aston's (1877–1945) discovery of isotopes. Nobel prize 1906.

Volta Alessandro 1745–1827. Italian physicist who invented the first electric cell (the voltaic pile), the electrophorus (an early electrostatic generator), and an electroscope.

Watt James 1736–1819. Scottish engineer who developed the steam engine. He made the steam engine developed by Thomas Newcomen (1663–1729) vastly more efficient by cooling the used steam in a condenser separate from the main cylinder.

Weinberg Steven 1933–   . US physicist who in 1967 demonstrated, together with Abdus Salam, that the weak nuclear force and the electromagnetic force (two of the fundamental forces of nature) are variations of a single underlying force, now called the electroweak force. Weinberg and Salam shared a Nobel prize with Sheldon Glashow in 1979.

Nobel prize for physics

1901	Wilhelm Röntgen (Germany): discovery of X-rays
1902	Hendrik Lorentz (Netherlands) and Pieter Zeeman (Netherlands): influence of magnetism on radiation phenomena
1903	Antoine Becquerel (France): discovery of spontaneous radioactivity. Pierre Curie (France) and Marie Curie (Poland): researches on radiation phenomena
1904	John Strutt (Lord Rayleigh, UK): densities of gases and discovery of argon
1905	Philipp von Lenard (Germany): work on cathode rays
1906	Joseph J Thomson (UK): theoretical and experimental work on the conduction of electricity by gases
1907	Albert Michelson (USA): measurement of the speed of light through the design and application of precise optical instruments such as the interferometer
1908	Gabriel Lippmann (France): photographic reproduction of colours by interference
1909	Guglielmo Marconi (Italy) and Karl Braun (Germany): development of wireless telegraphy
1910	Johannes van der Waals (Netherlands): equation describing the physical behaviour of gases and liquids
1911	Wilhelm Wien (Germany): laws governing radiation of heat
1912	Nils Dalen (Sweden): invention of light-controlled valves, which allow lighthouses and buoys to operate automatically
1913	Heike Kamerlingh-Onnes (Netherlands): studies of properties of matter at low temperatures
1914	Max von Laue (Germany): discovery of diffraction of X-rays by crystals
1915	William Bragg (UK) and Lawrence Bragg (UK): X-ray analysis of crystal structures
1916	no prizes awarded
1917	Charles Barkla (UK): discovery of characteristic X-ray emission of the elements
1918	Max Planck (Germany): formulation of quantum theory
1919	Johannes Stark (Germany): discovery of Doppler effect in rays of positive ions, and splitting of spectral lines in electric fields
1920	Charles Guillaume (Switzerland): precision measurements through anomalies in nickel--steel alloys
1921	Albert Einstein (Switzerland): theoretical physics, especially law of photoelectric effect
1922	Niels Bohr (Denmark): structure of atoms and radiation emanating from them
1923	Robert Millikan (USA): discovery of the electric charge of an electron, and study of the photoelectric effect
1924	Karl Siegbahn (Sweden): X-ray spectroscopy
1925	James Franck (USA) and Gustav Hertz (Germany): laws governing the impact of an electron upon an atom
1926	Jean Perrin (France): confirmation of the discontinuous structure of matter
1927	Arthur Compton (USA): transfer of energy from electromagnetic radiation to a particle. Charles Wilson (UK): invention of the Wilson cloud chamber, by which the movement of electrically charged particles may be tracked
1928	Owen Richardson (UK): thermionic phenomena and associated law
1929	Louis-Victor de Broglie (France): discovery of wavelike nature of electrons
1930	Venkata Raman (India): discovery of the scattering of single-wavelength light when it is passed through a transparent substance
1931	no prizes awarded
1932	Werner Heisenberg (Germany): creation of quantum mechanics
1933	Erwin Schrödinger (Austria) and Paul Dirac (UK): development of quantum mechanics
1934	no prizes awarded
1935	James Chadwick (UK): discovery of the neutron
1936	Victor Hess (Austria): discovery of cosmic radiation. Carl Anderson (USA): discovery of the positron
1937	Clinton Davisson (USA) and George Thomson (UK): diffraction of electrons by crystals
1938	Enrico Fermi (USA): use of neutron irradiation to produce new elements, and discovery of nuclear reactions induced by slow neutrons
1939	Ernest O Lawrence (USA): invention and development of cyclotron, and production of artificial radioactive elements
1940–42	no prizes awarded
1943	Otto Stern (Germany): molecular-ray method of investigating elementary particles, and discovery of magnetic moment of proton
1944	Isidor Isaac Rabi (USA): resonance method of recording the magnetic properties of atomic nuclei
1945	Wolfgang Pauli (Austria): discovery of the exclusion principle
1946	Percy Bridgman (USA): development of high-pressure physics
1947	Edward Appleton (UK): physics of the upper atmosphere
1948	Patrick Blackett (UK): application of the Wilson cloud chamber to nuclear physics and cosmic radiation
1949	Yukawa Hideki (Japan): theoretical work predicting existence of mesons
1950	Cecil Powell (UK): use of photographic emulsion to study nuclear processes, and discovery of pions (pi mesons)
1951	John Cockcroft (UK) and Ernest Walton (Ireland): transmutation of atomic nuclei by means of accelerated subatomic particles
1952	Felix Bloch (USA) and Edward Purcell (USA): precise nuclear-magnetic measurements
1953	Frits Zernike (Netherlands): invention of phase-contrast microscope
1954	Max Born (Germany): statistical interpretation of wave function in quantum mechanics. Walther Bothe (Germany): coincidence method of detecting the emission of electrons

Nobel prize for physics (cont.)

1955 Willis Lamb (USA): structure of hydrogen spectrum. Polykarp Kusch (USA): determination of magnetic moment of the electron

1956 William Shockley (USA), John Bardeen (USA), and Walter Houser Brattain (USA): study of semiconductors, and discovery of transistor effect

1957 Yang Chen Ning (USA) and Lee Tsung-Dao (China): investigations of weak interactions between elementary particles

1958 Pavel Cherenkov (USSR), Ilya Frank (USSR), and Igor Tamm (USA): discovery and interpretation of Cherenkov radiation

1959 Emilio Segrè (Italy) and Owen Chamberlain (USA): discovery of the antiproton

1960 Donald Glaser (USA): invention of the bubble chamber

1961 Robert Hofstadter (USA): scattering of electrons in atomic nuclei, and structure of protons and neutrons. Rudolf Mössbauer (Germany): resonance absorption of gamma radiation

1962 Lev Landau (USSR): theories of condensed matter, especially liquid helium

1963 Eugene Wigner (USA): discovery and application of symmetry principles in atomic physics. Maria Goeppert-Mayer (USA) and Hans Jensen (Germany): discovery of the shell-like structure of atomic nuclei

1964 Charles Townes (USA), Nikolai Basov (USSR), and Aleksandr Prokhorov (USSR): quantum electronics leading to construction of oscillators and amplifiers based on maser--laser principle

1965 Sin-Itiro Tomonaga (Japan), Julian Schwinger (USA), and Richard Feynman (USA): quantum electrodynamics

1966 Alfred Kastler (France): development of optical pumping, whereby atoms are raised to higher energy levels by illumination

1967 Hans Bethe (USA): theory of nuclear reactions, and discoveries concerning production of energy in stars

1968 Luis Alvarez (USA): elementary-particle physics, and discovery of resonance states, using hydrogen bubble chamber and data analysis

1969 Murray Gell-Mann (USA): classification of elementary particles, and study of their interactions

1970 Hannes Alfvén (Sweden): magnetohydrodynamics and its applications in plasma physics. Louis Néel (France): antiferromagnetism and ferromagnetism in solid-state physics

1971 Dennis Gabor (UK): invention and development of holography

1972 John Bardeen (USA), Leon Cooper (USA), and John Robert Schrieffer (USA): theory of superconductivity

1973 Leo Eskai (Japan) and Ivar Giaver (USA): tunnelling phenomena in semiconductors and superconductors. Brian Josephson (UK): theoretical predictions of the properties of a supercurrent through a tunnel barrier

1974 Martin Ryle (UK) and Antony Hewish (UK): development of radioastronomy, particularly aperture-synthesis technique, and the discovery of pulsars

1975 Aage Bohr (Denmark), Ben Mottelson (Denmark), and James Rainwater (USA): discovery of connection between collective motion and particle motion in atomic nuclei, and development of theory of nuclear structure

1976 Burton Richter (USA) and Samuel Ting (USA): discovery of the psi meson

1977 Philip Anderson (USA), Nevill Mott (UK), and John Van Vleck (USA): electronic structure of magnetic and disordered systems

1978 Pyotr Kapitza (USSR): low-temperature physics. Arno Penzias (Germany), and Robert Wilson (USA): discovery of cosmic background radiation

1979 Sheldon Glashow (USA), Abdus Salam (Pakistan), and Steven Weinberg (USA): unified theory of weak and electromagnetic fundamental forces, and prediction of the existence of the weak neutral current

1980 James W Cronin (USA) and Val Fitch (USA): violations of fundamental symmetry principles in the decay of neutral kaon mesons

1981 Nicolaas Bloemergen (USA) and Arthur Schawlow (USA): development of laser spectroscopy. Kai Siegbahn (Sweden): high- resolution electron spectroscopy

1982 Kenneth Wilson (USA): theory for critical phenomena in connection with phase transitions

1983 Subrahmanyan Chandrasekhar (USA): theoretical studies of physical processes in connection with structure and evolution of stars. William Fowler (USA): nuclear reactions involved in the formation of chemical elements in the universe

1984 Carlo Rubbia (Italy) and Simon van der Meer (Netherlands): contributions to the discovery of the W and Z particles (weakons)

1985 Klaus von Klitzing (Germany): discovery of the quantized Hall effect

1986 Erns Ruska (Germany): electron optics, and design of the first electron microscope. Gerd Binnig (Germany) and Heinrich Rohrer (Switzerland): design of scanning tunnelling microscope

1987 Georg Bednorz (Germany) and Alex Mu#4ller (Switzerland): superconductivity in ceramic materials

1988 Leon M Lederman (USA), Melvin Schwartz (USA), and Jack Steinberger (Germany): neutrino-beam method, and demonstration of the doublet structure of leptons through discovery of muon neutrino

1989 Norman Ramsey (USA): measurement techniques leading to discovery of caesium atomic clock. Hans Dehmelt (USA) and Wolfgang Paul (Germany): ion-trap method for isolating single atoms

1990 Jerome Friedman (USA), Henry Kendall (USA), and Richard Taylor (Canada): experiments demonstrating that protons and neutrons are made up of quarks

1991 Pierre-Gilles de Gennes (France): work on disordered systems including polymers and liquid crystals; development of mathematical methods for studying the behaviour of molecules in a liquid on the verge of solidifying

1992 Georges Charpak (Poland): invention and development of detectors used in high-energy physics

1993 Joseph Taylor (USA) and Russell Hulse (USA): discovery of the first binary pulsar

TELECOMMUNICATIONS AND VIDEO TECHNOLOGY

Telecommunications are communications over a distance, generally by electronic means. Long-distance voice communication was pioneered 1876 by Scottish–US inventor Alexander Graham Bell (1847–1922), when he invented the telephone as a result of English chemist and physicist Michael Faraday's (1791–1867) discovery of electromagnetism. Today it is possible to communicate with most countries by telephone cable, or by satellite or microwave link, with more than 100,000 simultaneous conversations and several television channels being carried by the latest satellites. Integrated Services Digital Network (ISDN) makes videophones and high-quality fax possible; the world's first large-scale centre of ISDN began operating in Japan 1988. ISDN is a system that transmits voice and image data on a single transmission line by changing them into digital signals. The chief method of relaying long-distance calls on land is microwave radio transmission.

The first mechanical telecommunications systems were the semaphore and heliograph (using flashes of sunlight), invented in the mid-19th century, but the forerunner of the present telecommunications age was the electric telegraph. The earliest practicable telegraph instrument was invented by William Cooke (1806–1879) and Charles Wheatstone (1802–1875) in Britain 1837 and used by railway companies. In the USA, Samuel Morse (1791–1872) invented a signalling code, Morse code, which is still used, and a recording telegraph, first used commercially between England and France 1851. As a result of German physicist Heinrich Hertz's (1857–1894) discoveries using electromagnetic waves, Italian inventor Guglielmo Marconi (1874–1937) pioneered a 'wireless' telegraph, ancestor of the radio. He established wireless communication between England and France 1899 and across the Atlantic 1901. The modern telegraph uses teleprinters to send coded messages along telecommunications lines. Telegraphs are keyboard-operated machines that transmit a five-unit Baudot code. The receiving teleprinter automatically prints the received message.

The drawback to long-distance voice communication via microwave radio transmission is that the transmissions follow a straight line from tower to tower, so that over the sea the system becomes impracticable. A solution was put forward 1945 by US science-fiction writer Arthur C Clarke, when he proposed a system of communications satellites in an orbit 35,900 km/22,300 mi above the equator, where they would circle the Earth in exactly 24 hours, and thus appear fixed in the sky. Such a system is now in operation internationally, by Intelsat. The satellites are called geostationary satellites (syncoms). The first to be successfully launched, by Delta rocket from Cape Canaveral, was *Syncom 2* in July 1963. Many such satellites are now in use, concentrated over heavy traffic areas such as the Atlantic, Indian, and Pacific oceans. Telegraphy, telephony, and television transmissions are carried simultaneously by high-frequency radio waves. They are beamed to the satellites from large dish antennae or Earth stations, which connect with international networks. Recent advances include the use of fibre-optic cables consisting of fine glass fibres for telephone lines instead of the usual copper cables. The telecommunications signals are transmitted along the fibres on pulses of laser light.

The first public telegraph line was laid in England between Paddington (London) and Slough 1843. In 1980, the Post Office opened its first System X (all-electronic, digital) telephone exchange in London, a method already adopted in North America. In the UK, Goonhilly (Cornwall) and Madley are the main Earth stations for satellite transmissions.

Terms

aerial or *antenna* conducting device that radiates or receives electromagnetic waves. The design of an aerial depends principally on the wavelength of the signal. Long waves (hundreds of metres in wavelength) may employ long wire aerials; short waves (several centimetres in wavelength) may employ rods and dipoles; microwaves may also use dipoles – often with reflectors arranged like a toast rack – or highly directional parabolic dish aerials. Because microwaves travel in straight lines, giving line-of-sight communication, microwave aerials are usually located at the tops of tall masts or towers.

amplifier electronic device that magnifies the strength of a signal, such as a radio signal. The ratio of output signal strength to input signal strength is called the *gain* of the amplifier. As well as achieving high gain, an amplifier should be free from distortion and able to operate over a range of frequencies. Practical amplifiers are usually complex circuits, although simple amplifiers can be built from single transistors or valves.

baud unit of electrical signalling speed equal to one pulse (one bit) per second, used in data transmission, measuring the rate at which signals are sent between electronic devices such as telegraphs and computers; 300 baud is about 300 words a minute.

cable television distribution of broadcast signals through cable relay systems. Narrow-band systems were originally used to deliver services to areas with poor regular reception; systems with wider bands, using coaxial and fibreoptic cable, are increasingly used for distribution and development of home-based interactive services.

cellular phone or *cellphone* mobile radio telephone, one of a network connected to the telephone system by a computer-controlled communication system. Service areas are divided into small 'cells', about 5 km/3 mi across, each with a separate low-power transmitter.

citizens' band (CB) short-range radio communication facility (around 27 MHz) used by members of the public in the USA and many European countries to talk to one another or call for emergency assistance. Use of a form of citizens' band called Open Channel (above 928 MHz) was legalized in the UK 1980.

coaxial cable electric cable that consists of a solid or stranded central conductor insulated from and surrounded by a solid or braided conducting tube or sheath. It can transmit the high-frequency signals used in television, telephone, and other telecommunications transmissions.

communications satellite relay station in space for sending telephone, television, telex, and other messages around the world. Messages are sent to and from the satellites via ground stations. Most communications satellites are in geostationary orbit, appearing to hang fixed over one point on the Earth's surface. A new generation of satellites, called *direct broadcast satellites*, are powerful enough to transmit direct to small domestic aerials. The power for such satellites is produced by solar cells.

data communications sending and receiving data via any communications medium, such as a telephone line. The term usually implies that the data are digital (such as computer data) rather than analogue (such as voice messages). However, in the ISDN (Integrated Services Digital Network) system, all data – including voices and video images – are transmitted digitally.

data compression techniques for reducing the amount of storage needed for a given amount of data. They include word tokenization (in which frequently used words are stored as shorter codes), variable bit lengths (in which common characters are represented by fewer bits than less common ones), and run-length encoding (in which a repeated value is stored once along with a count).

digital coded as numbers. A digital system uses two-state, either on/off or high/low voltage pulses, to encode, receive, and transmit information. A *digital display* shows discrete values as numbers (as opposed to an analogue signal, such as the continuous sweep of a pointer on a dial).

Digital electronics is the technology that underlies digital techniques. Low-power, miniature, integrated circuits (chips) provide the means for the coding, storage, transmission, processing, and reconstruction of information of all kinds.

digital data transmission way of sending data by converting all signals (whether pictures, sounds, or words) into numeric (normally binary) codes before transmission, then reconverting them on receipt. This virtually eliminates any distortion or degradation of the signal during transmission, storage, or processing.

digital sampling electronic process used in telecommunications for transforming a constantly varying (analogue) signal into one composed of discrete units, a digital signal.

digital television any system of transmitting television programmes in digital codes. A fully digital high-definition system was demonstrated in the USA 1992.

Until the late 1980s, it was considered impossible to convert a TV signal into digital code because of the sheer amount of information needed to represent a visual image – the current British PAL system needs about 6 million bits of information each second; HDTV needs about 30 million bits each second. However, data-compression techniques have been developed to reduce the number of bits that need to be transmitted each second. As a result, digital technology is being developed that will offer sharper pictures on wider screens, and HDTV with image quality comparable to a cinema. A common world standard for digital TV was agreed in 1993 at a meeting of engineers representing manufacturers and broadcasters from 18 countries.

eidophor television projection system that produces pictures up to 10 m/33 ft square at sports events and rock concerts, for example. The system uses three coloured beams of light, one of each primary colour (red, blue, and green), which scan the screen. The intensity of each beam is controlled by the strength of the corresponding colour in the television picture.

electronic mail or *E-mail* telecommunications system that enables the users of a computer to send written messages to other users. A modem connects the computer to the telephone network, through which the signals are sent from terminal to terminal.

fax (common name for *facsimile transmission* or *telefax*) the transmission of images over a telecommunications link, usually the telephone network. When placed on a fax machine, the original image is scanned by a transmitting device and converted into coded signals, which travel via the telephone lines to the receiving fax machine, where an image is created that is a copy of the original. Photographs as well as printed text and drawings can be sent. The standard transmission takes place at 4,800 or 9,600 bits of information per second.

high-definition television (HDTV) television system offering a significantly greater number of scanning lines, and therefore a clearer picture, than that provided by conventional systems. The Japanese HDTV system, or Vision as it is trade-named in Japan, uses 1,125 scanning lines and an aspect ratio of 16:9 instead of the squarish 4:3 which conventional television uses. A European HDTV system, called HD-MAC, using 1,250 lines, is under development. In the USA, fractal mathematics may be used to encode and broadcast HDTV, following a 1992 decision by the National Institute for Standards and Technology to fund a new chip to decode digitized pictures.

Integrated Services Digital Network (ISDN) internationally developed telecommunications system for sending signals in digital format along optical fibres and coaxial cable. It involves converting the 'local loop' – the link between the user's telephone (or private automatic branch exchange) and the digital telephone exchange – from an analogue system into a digital system, thereby greatly increasing the amount of information that can be carried. The first large-scale use of ISDN began in Japan 1988.

British Telecom began offering ISDN to businesses 1991, with some 47,000 ISDN-equipped lines. Its adoption in the UK is expected to stimulate the use of data-communications services such as faxing, teleshopping, and home banking. New services may include computer conferencing, where both voice and

Telecommunications: chronology

1794	Claude Chappe in France built a long-distance signalling system using semaphore.
1839	Charles Wheatstone and William Cooke devised an electric telegraph in England.
1843	Samuel Morse transmitted the first message along a telegraph line in the USA, using his Morse code of signals – short (dots) and long (dashes).
1858	The first transatlantic telegraph cable was laid.
1876	Alexander Graham Bell invented the telephone.
1877	Thomas Edison invented the carbon transmitter for the telephone.
1878	The first telephone exchange was opened at New Haven, Connecticut.
1884	The first long-distance telephone line was installed, between Boston and New York.
1891	A telephone cable was laid between England and France.
1892	The first automatic telephone exchange was opened, at La Porte, Indiana, USA.
1894	Guglielmo Marconi pioneered wireless telegraphy in Italy, later moving to England.
1900	Reginald Fessenden in the USA first broadcast voice by radio.
1901	Marconi transmitted the first radio signals across the Atlantic.
1904	John Ambrose Fleming invented the thermionic valve.
1907	Charles Krumm introduced the forerunner of the teleprinter.
1920	Stations in Detroit and Pittsburgh, USA, began regular radio broadcasts.
1922	The BBC began its first radio transmissions, for the London station 2LO.
1932	The Post Office introduced the Telex in Britain.
1956	The first transatlantic telephone cable was laid.
1962	*Telstar* pioneered transatlantic satellite communications, transmitting live TV pictures.
1966	Charles Kao in England advanced the idea of using optical fibres for telecommunications transmissions.
1969	Live TV pictures were sent from astronauts on the Moon back to Earth.
1975	The Post Office announced Prestel, the world's first viewdata system, using the telephone lines to link a computer data bank with the TV screen.
1977	The first optical-fibre cable was installed in California.
1984	First commercial cellphone service started in Chicago, USA.
1988	International Services Digital Network (ISDN), an international system for sending signals in digital format along optical fibres and coaxial cable, launched in Japan.
1989	The first transoceanic optical-fibre cable, capable of carrying 40,000 simultaneous telephone conversations, was laid between Europe and the USA.
1991	ISDN introduced in the UK.
1992	Videophones, made possible by advances in image compression and the development of ISDN, introduced in the UK.
1993	Electronic version of the *Guardian* newspaper, for those with impaired vision, launched in the UK. The newspaper is transmitted to the user's home and printed out in braille or spoken by a speech synthesizer.

computer communications take place simultaneously, and videophones.

interactive video (IV) computer-mediated system that enables the user to interact with and control information (including text, recorded speech, or moving images) stored on video disc. IV is most commonly used for training purposes, using analogue video discs, but has wider applications with digital video systems such as CD-I (Compact Disc Interactive, from Philips and Sony) which are based on the CD-ROM format derived from audio compact discs.

loudspeaker electromechanical device that converts electrical signals into sound waves, which are radiated into the air. The most common type of loudspeaker is the *moving-coil speaker*. Electrical signals from, for example, a radio are fed to a coil of fine wire wound around the top of a cone. The coil is surrounded by a magnet. When signals pass through it, the coil becomes an electromagnet, which by moving causes the cone to vibrate, setting up sound waves.

microphone primary component in a sound-reproducing system, whereby the mechanical energy of sound waves is converted into electrical signals by means of a transducer. One of the simplest is the telephone receiver mouthpiece, invented by Scottish-US inventor Alexander Graham Bell in 1876; other types of microphone are used with broadcasting and sound-film apparatus.

modulation the intermittent change of frequency, or amplitude, of a carrier wave, in accordance with the audio characteristics of the speaking voice, music, or other signal being transmitted. Microwave or light waves can carry digital information in pulse-code modulation; radio waves are altered for transmission with AM (amplitude modulation) or FM (frequency modulation).

multiplexing sending several messages simultaneously along the same telephone or telegraph wire. In *frequency-division multiplexing*, signals of different frequency, each carrying a different message, are transmitted. Electrical frequency filters separate the message at the receiving station. In *time-division multiplexing*, the messages are broken into sections and the sections of several messages interleaved during transmission. *Pulse-code modulation* allows hundreds of messages to be sent simultaneously over a single link.

optical fibre very fine, optically pure glass fibre through which light can be reflected to transmit an image or information from one end to the other. Optical fibres are increasingly being used to replace copper wire in telephone cables, the messages being coded as pulses of light rather than a fluctuating electric current.

oscillator any device producing a desired oscillation (vibration). There are many types of oscillator for different purposes, involving various arrangements of thermionic valves or components such as transistors, inductors, capacitors, and resistors. An oscillator is an essential part of a radio transmitter, generating the high-frequency carrier signal necessary for radio communication. The frequency is often controlled by the vibrations set up in a crystal (such as quartz).

pulse-code modulation (PCM) form of digital modulation in which microwaves or light waves (the carrier waves) are switched on and off in pulses of varying length according to a binary code. It is a relatively simple matter to transmit data that are already in binary code, such as those used by computer, by these means. An analogue audio signal can be converted into a *pulse-amplitude modulated* signal (PAM) by regular sampling of its amplitude. The value of the amplitude is then converted into a binary code for transmission on the carrier wave.

radio transmission and reception of radio waves. In radio *transmission* a microphone converts sound waves (pressure variations in the air) into electromagnetic waves; these are picked up by a receiving aerial and fed to a loudspeaker, which converts them back into sound waves.

To carry the transmitted electrical signal, an oscillator produces a carrier wave of high frequency; different stations are allocated different transmitting carrier frequencies. A modulator superimposes the audiofrequency signal on the carrier. There are two main ways of doing this: *amplitude modulation* (AM), used for long- and medium-wave broadcasts, in which the strength of the carrier is made to fluctuate in time with the audio signal; and *frequency modulation* (FM), as used for VHF (very high frequency) broadcasts, in which the frequency of the carrier is made to fluctuate. The transmitting aerial emits the modulated electromagnetic waves, which travel outwards from it.

In radio *reception*, a receiving aerial picks up minute voltages in response to the waves sent out by a transmitter. A tuned circuit selects a particular frequency, usually by means of a variable capacitor connected across a coil of wire. A demodulator disentangles the audio signal from the carrier, which is now discarded, having served its purpose. An amplifier boosts the audio signal for feeding to the loudspeaker. In a superheterodyne receiver, the incoming signal is mixed with an internally generated signal of fixed frequency so that the amplifier circuits can operate near their optimum frequncy.

receiver, radio component of a radio communication system that receives and processes radio waves. It detects and selects modulated radio waves by means of an aerial and tuned circuit, and then separates the transmitted information from the carrier wave by a process that involves rectification. The receiver device will usually also include the amplifiers that produce the audio signals.

scrambling circuit in radiotelephony, a transmitting circuit that renders signals unintelligible unless received by the corresponding unscrambling circuit.

signal-to-noise ratio ratio of the power of an electrical signal to that of the unwanted noise accompanying the signal. It is expressed in decibels. In general, the higher the signal-to-noise ratio, the better. For a telephone, an acceptable ratio is 40 decibels; for television, the acceptable ratio is 50 decibels.

single-sideband transmission radio-wave transmission using either the frequency band above the carrier wave frequency, or below, instead of both (as now).

superheterodyne receiver the most widely used type of radio receiver, in which the incoming signal is mixed with a signal of fixed frequency generated within the receiver circuits. The resulting signal, called the intermediate-frequency (i.f.) signal, has a frequency between that of the incoming signal and the internal signal. The intermediate frequency is near the optimum frequency of the amplifier to which the i.f. signal is passed. This arrangement ensures greater gain and selectivity. The superheterodyne system is also used in basic television receivers.

System X modular, computer-controlled, digital switching system used in telephone exchanges from 1980.

telephone instrument for communicating by voice over long distances, invented by Scottish–US inventor Alexander Graham Bell 1876. The transmitter (mouthpiece) consists of a carbon microphone, with a diaphragm that vibrates when a person speaks into it. The diaphragm vibrations compress grains of carbon to a greater or lesser extent, altering their resistance to an electric current passing through them. This sets up variable electrical signals, which travel along the telephone lines to the receiver of the person being called. There they cause the magnetism of an electromagnet to vary, making a diaphragm above the electromagnet vibrate and give out sound waves, which mirror those that entered the mouthpiece originally.

A cordless telephone is connected to a base unit by radio. It can be used at distances up to about 100 m/330 ft from the base unit.

teletext broadcast system of displaying information on a television screen. The information – typically about news items, entertainment, sport, and finance – is constantly updated. Teletext is a form of videotext, pioneered in Britain by the British Broadcasting Corporation (BBC) with Ceefax and by Independent Television with Teletext.

television (TV) reproduction at a distance by radio waves of visual images. For transmission, a TV camera converts the pattern of light it takes in into a pattern of electrical charges. This is scanned line by line by a beam of electrons from an electron gun, resulting in variable electrical signals that represent the picture. These signals are combined with a radio carrier wave and broadcast as electromagnetic waves. The TV aerial picks up the wave and feeds it to the receiver (TV set). This separates out the vision signals, which pass to a cathode-ray tube where a beam of electrons is made to scan across the screen line by line, mirroring the action of the electron gun in the TV camera. The result is a recreation of the pattern of light that entered the camera. Twenty-five pictures are built up each second with interlaced scanning in Europe (30 in North America), with a total of 625 lines in Europe (525 lines in North America and Japan); high-definition television (HDTV) offers a significantly greater number of scanning lines.

television channels In addition to transmissions received by all viewers, the 1970s and 1980s saw the growth of pay-television cable networks, which are received only by subscribers, and of devices, such as those used in the Qube system (USA), which allow the viewers' opinions to be transmitted instantaneously to the studio via a response button, so that, for example, a home viewing audience can vote in a talent competition. The number of programme channels continues to increase, following the introduction of satellite-beamed TV signals.

history In 1873 it was realized that, since the electrical properties of the nonmetallic chemical element selenium vary according to the amount of light to which it is exposed, light could be converted into electrical impulses, making it possible to transmit such impulses over a distance and then reconvert them into light. The chief difficulty was seen to be the 'splitting of the picture' so that the infinite variety of light and shade values might be transmitted and reproduced. Mechanical devices were used at the first practical demonstration of television, given by Scottish electrical engineer John Logie Baird (1888–1946) in London 27 Jan 1926, and cathode-ray tubes

were used experimentally in the UK from 1934. The world's first public television service was started from the BBC station at Alexandra Palace in N London, 2 Nov 1936. In 1990 in the UK, the average viewing time per person was 25.5 hours each week.

colour television Baird gave a demonstration of colour TV in London 1928, but it was not until Dec 1953 that the first successful system was adopted for broadcasting, in the USA. This is called the NTSC system, since it was developed by the National Television System Committee, and variations of it were developed in Europe; for example, SECAM (sequential and memory) in France and Eastern Europe, and PAL (phase alternation by line) in most of Western Europe. The three differ only in the way colour signals are prepared for transmission, the scanning rate, and the number of lines used. When there was no agreement on a universal European system 1964, in 1967 the UK, West Germany, the Netherlands, and Switzerland adopted PAL while France and the USSR adopted SECAM. In 1989, the European Community agreed to harmonize TV channels from 1991, allowing any station to show programmes anywhere in the EC.

The method of colour reproduction is related to that used in colour photography and printing. It uses the principle that any colours can be made by mixing the primary colours red, green, and blue in appropriate proportions. In colour television, the receiver reproduces only three basic colours: red, green, and blue. The effect of yellow, for example, is reproduced by combining equal amounts of red and green light,

Television: chronology

1878	William Crookes in England invented the Crookes tube, which produced cathode rays.
1884	Paul Nipkow in Germany built a mechanical scanning device, the Nipkow disc, a rotating disc with a spiral pattern of holes in it.
1897	Karl Ferdinand Braun, also in Germany, modified the Crookes tube to produce the ancestor of the TV receiver picture tube.
1906	Boris Rosing in Russia began experimenting with the Nipkow disc and cathode-ray tube, eventually succeeding in transmitting some crude TV pictures.
1923	Vladimir Zworykin in the USA invented the first electronic camera tube, the iconoscope.
1926	John Logie Baird demonstrated a workable TV system, using mechanical scanning by Nipkow disc.
1928	Baird demonstrated colour TV.
1929	The BBC began broadcasting experimental TV programmes using Baird's system.
1936	The BBC began regular broadcasting using Baird's system from Alexandra Palace, London.
1940	Experimental colour TV transmission began in the USA, using the present-day system of colour reproduction.
1953	Successful colour TV transmissions began in the USA.
1956	The first video tape recorder was produced in California by the Ampex Corporation.
1962	TV signals were transmitted across the Atlantic via the *Telstar* satellite.
1970	The first videodisc system was announced by Decca in Britain and AEG-Telefunken in Germany, but it was not perfected until the 1980s, when laser scanning was used for playback.
1973	The BBC and Independent Television in the UK introduced the world's first teletext systems, Ceefax and Oracle, respectively.
1975	Sony introduced their videocassette tape-recorder system, Betamax, for domestic viewers, six years after their professional U-Matic system. The UK Post Office (now British Telecom) announced their Prestel viewdata system.
1979	Matsushita in Japan developed a pocket-sized, flat-screen TV set, using a liquid-crystal display.
1986	Data broadcasting using digital techniques was developed; an enhancement of teletext was produced.
1989	The Japanese began broadcasting high-definition television; satellite television was introduced in the UK.
1990	The BBC introduced a digital stereo sound system (NICAM); MAC, a European system allowing greater picture definition, more data, and sound tracks, was introduced.
1992	All-digital high-definition television demonstrated in the USA.
1993	A worldwide standard for digital television was agreed by manufacturers and broadcasters.

while white is formed by a mixture of all three basic colours. Signals indicate the amounts of red, green, and blue light to be generated at the receiver.

To transmit each of these three signals in the same way as the single brightness signal in black and white television would need three times the normal band width and reduce the number of possible stations and programmes to one-third of that possible with monochrome television. The three signals are therefore coded into one complex signal, which is transmitted as a more or less normal black and white signal and produces a satisfactory – or compatible – picture on black and white receivers. A fraction of each primary red, green, and blue signal is added together to produce the normal brightness, or luminance, signal. The minimum of extra colouring information is then sent by a special subcarrier signal, which is superimposed on the brightness signal. This extra colouring information corresponds to the hue and saturation of the transmitted colour, but without any of the fine detail of the picture. The impression of sharpness is conveyed only by the brightness signal, the colouring being added as a broad colour wash. The various colour systems differ only in the way in which the colouring information is sent on the subcarrier signal. The colour receiver has to amplify the complex signal and decode it back to the basic red, green, and blue signals; these primary signals are then applied to a colour cathode-ray tube.

The colour display tube is the heart of any colour receiver. Many designs of colour picture tubes have been invented; the most successful of these is known as the 'shadow mask tube'. It operates on similar electronic principles to the black and white television picture tube, but the screen is composed of a fine mosaic of over one million dots arranged in an orderly fashion. One-third of the dots glow red when bombarded by electrons, one-third glow green, and one-third blue. There are three sources of electrons, respectively modulated by the red, green, and blue signals. The tube is arranged so that the shadow mask allows only the red signals to hit red dots, the green signals to hit green dots, and the blue signals to hit blue dots. The glowing dots are so small that from a normal viewing distance the colours merge into one another and a picture with a full range of colours is seen.

video camera or *camcorder* portable television camera that takes moving pictures electronically on magnetic tape. It produces an electrical output signal corresponding to rapid line-by-line scanning of the field of view. The output is recorded on video cassette and is played back on a television screen via a video tape recorder.

video disc disc with pictures and sounds recorded on it, played back by laser. The video disc is a type of compact disc.

The video disc was originated by Scottish inventor John Logie Baird 1928, and became commercially available 1978. It is chiefly used to provide commercial films for private viewing. Most systems use a 30-cm/12-in rotating vinyl disc coated with a reflective material. Laser scanning recovers picture and sound signals from the surface where they are recorded as a spiral of microscopic pits.

video tape recorder (VTR) device for recording pictures and sound on cassettes or spools of magnetic tape. The first commercial VTR was launched 1956 for the television broadcasting industry, but from the late 1970s cheaper models developed for home use, to record broadcast programmes for future viewing and to view rented or owned video cassettes of commercial films.

Video recording works in the same way as audio tape recording: the picture information is stored as a line of varying magnetism, or track, on a plastic tape covered with magnetic material. The main difficulty – the huge amount of information needed to reproduce a picture – is overcome by arranging the video track diagonally across the tape. During recording, the tape is wrapped around a drum in a spiral fashion. The recording head rotates inside the drum. The combination of the forward motion of the tape and the rotation of the head produces a diagonal track. The audio signal accompanying the video signal is recorded as a separate track along the edge of the tape.

Two video cassette systems were introduced by Japanese firms in the 1970s. The Sony Betamax was technically superior, but Matsushita's VHS had larger marketing resources behind it and after some years became the sole system on the market. Super-VHS is an improved version of the VHS system, launched 1989, with higher picture definition and colour quality.

videotext system in which information (text and simple pictures) is displayed on a television (video) screen. There are two basic systems, known as teletext and viewdata; both require the use of a television receiver with a special decoder.

viewdata system of displaying information on a television screen in which the information is extracted from a computer data bank and transmitted via the telephone lines. It is one form of videotext. The British Post Office (now British Telecom) developed the world's first viewdata system, Prestel, 1975, and similar systems are now in widespread use in other countries. Viewdata users have access to an almost unlimited store of information, presented on the screen in the form of 'pages'.

Since viewdata uses telephone lines, it can become a two-way interactive information system, making possible, for example, home banking and shopping. In contrast, the only user input allowed by the teletext system is to select the information to be displayed.

BUSINESS AND ECONOMICS

BUSINESS

Business Terms

added value or **value added** the sales revenue from selling a firm's products less the cost of the materials or purchases used in those products. An increasingly used indicator of relative efficiency within and between firms, although in the latter case open to distortion where mark-up varies between standard and premium-priced segments of a market.

adverse variance a difference between actual and budgeted spending or income that results in the organization having less money than planned.

alpha share on the stock market, a share in any of the companies most commonly traded – that is, the larger companies.

amortization the ending of a debt by paying it off gradually, over a period of time. The term is used to describe either the paying-off of a cash debt or the accounting procedure by which the value of an asset is progressively reduced ('depreciated') over a number of years.

annual accounts summary of the records of a company's financial activities, prepared by an accountant and in most countries made available for public inspection. Annual accounts include a balance sheet and a profit/loss or income/expenditure account.

annual general meeting (AGM) yearly meeting of the shareholders of a company or the members of an organization, at which business including consideration of the annual report and accounts, the election of officers, and the appointment of auditors is normally carried out.

annual percentage rate (APR) charge (including interest) for granting consumer credit, expressed as an equivalent once-a-year percentage figure of the amount of the credit granted. It is usually approximately double the flat rate of interest, or simple interest. In the UK, lenders are legally required to state the APR when advertising loans.

arbitrageur person who buys securities (such as currency or commodities) in one country or market for immediate resale in another market, to take advantage of different prices. Arbitrage became widespread during the 1970s and 1980s with the increasing deregulation of financial markets. The effect of arbitrage is to lessen or eliminate the price differentials among the markets. The term took on additional meaning with the increase in corporate buy-outs in the deregulated atmosphere of the late 1980s. Arbitrageurs speculated on target companies, buying stock and reselling it at the higher buy-out price.

articles of association in the UK, the rules governing the relationship between a registered company, its members (the shareholders), and its directors. The articles of association are deposited with the Registrar of Companies along with the memorandum of association.

asset in business accounting, a term that covers the land or property of a company or individual, payments due from bills, investments, and anything else owned that can be turned into cash. On a company's balance sheet, total assets must be equal to liabilities (money and services owed). An *intangible asset* is one that is not physical, for example a brand name or a list of business contacts. A *fixed asset* is a possession or valuable that is used over a long period of time. Examples of physical fixed assets include factories, offices, machinery, lorries, company cars, and office equipment.

asset stripping sale or exploitation by other means of the assets of a business, often one that has been taken over for that very purpose. The parts of the business may be potentially more valuable separately than together. Asset stripping is a major force for the more efficient use of assets.

audit official inspection of a company's accounts by a qualified accountant as required by law each year to ensure that the company balance sheet reflects the true state of its affairs.

bad debt bill or debt that has not been paid and is most unlikely to be paid. Bad debts eventually have to be 'written off' on the profit and loss account. They are counted as a provision and are deducted from the account.

balance sheet statement of the financial position of a company or individual on a specific date, showing both assets and liabilities.

bankruptcy process by which the property of a person (in legal terms, an individual or corporation) unable to pay debts is taken away under a court order and divided fairly among the person's creditors, after preferential payments such as taxes and wages. Proceedings may be instituted either by the debtor (voluntary bankruptcy) or by any creditor for a substantial sum (involuntary bankruptcy). Until 'discharged', a bankrupt is severely restricted in financial activities.

base rate the rate of interest to which most bank lending is linked, the actual rate depending on the status of the borrower. A prestigious company might command a rate only 1% above base rate, while an individual would be charged several points above.

bear speculator who sells stocks or shares on the stock exchange expecting a fall in the price in order to buy them back at a profit; the opposite of a bull. In a bear market, prices fall and bears prosper.

beta share on the stock exchange, a share traded less actively than an alpha share.

bill of exchange form of commercial credit instrument, or IOU, used in international trade. In Britain, a bill of exchange is defined by the Bills of Exchange

Act 1882 as an unconditional order in writing addressed by one person to another, signed by the person giving it, requiring the person to whom it is addressed to pay on demand or at a fixed or determinable future time a certain sum in money to or to the order of a specified person, or to the bearer.

bill of lading document giving proof of particular goods having been loaded on a ship. The person to whom the goods are being sent normally needs to show the bill of lading in order to obtain the release of the goods. For air freight, there is an *airway bill*.

blue chip stock that is considered strong and reliable in terms of the dividend yield and capital value. Blue-chip companies are favoured by stock-market investors more interested in security than risk taking.

bond security issued by a government, local authority, company, bank, or other institution on fixed interest. Usually a long-term security, a bond may be irredeemable (with no date of redemption), secured (giving the investor a claim on the company's property or on a part of its assets), or unsecured (not protected by a lien). Property bonds are non-fixed securities with the yield fixed to property investment.

brand named good that in the perception of the buyer is different from other similar goods in the market; its name and logo, or *trademark*. A *brand leader* is a branded product that has the largest share of the market for all products of that type.

breakeven the level of output where costs equal revenue and no profit or loss is made.

broker intermediary who arranges the sale of financial products (shares, insurance, mortgages, and so on) to the public for a commission or brokerage fee.

budget estimate of income and expenditure for some future period, used in financial planning.

bull speculator who buys stocks or shares on the stock exchange expecting a rise in the price in order to sell them later at a profit; the opposite of a bear. In a bull market, prices rise and bulls profit.

business plan key management tool that focuses on business objectives, the products or services involved, estimated market potential, expertise in the firm, projected financial results, the money required from investors, and the likely investment return.

call demand for money, especially instalments of part-paid securities.

capacity the maximum amount that can be produced when all the resources in an economy, industry, or firm are employed as fully as possible. Capacity constraints can be caused by lack of investment and skills shortages, and spare capacity can be caused by lack of demand.

capital employed the total assets of a company (excluding intangibles, such as good will) less its current liabilities (including overdrafts, short-term loans, trade and other creditors).

capital expenditure spending on fixed assets such as plant and equipment, trade investments, or the purchase of other businesses.

capital flight transfer of funds from a particular national economy or out of a particular currency in anticipation of less attractive investment conditions.

cartel agreement among national or international firms to fix prices for their products. A cartel may restrict supply (output) to raise prices in order to increase member profits. It therefore represents a form of oligopoly.

cash flow input of cash required to cover all expenses of a business, whether revenue or capital. Alternatively, the actual or prospective balance between the various outgoing and incoming movements which are designated in total, positive or negative according to which is greater.

commodity something produced for sale. Commodities may be consumer goods, such as radios, or producer goods, such as copper bars. *Commodity markets* deal in raw or semi-raw materials that are amenable to grading and that can be stored for considerable periods without deterioration.

company a number of people grouped together as a business enterprise. Types of company include public limited companies, partnerships, joint ventures, sole proprietorships, and branches of foreign companies. Most companies are private and, unlike public companies, cannot offer their shares to the general public.

consumer person who purchases goods and services. Consumers demand goods which businesses provide, and they need to be protected by law from unfair traders; hence the need for consumer protection acts and the work of consumer bodies such as the Consumers' Association.

consumer durable any commodity for personal use that has a long life, such as furniture and electrical goods, as opposed to food and drink, which are *perishables* and have to be replaced frequently.

consumer sovereignty a situation where consumers decide what is to be produced by producers. In a market economy, this is achieved through companies being forced to compete to attract the spending of consumers. The opposite of consumer sovereignty is producer sovereignty, the situation where producers decide what consumers can buy. In a market economy, this could be the result of monopoly power, or the use of advertising which manipulates the desires of consumers for products.

convertible loan stock stock or bond (paying a fixed interest) that may be converted into a stated number of shares at a specific date.

corporate strategy the way an organization intends to meet its objectives. This may be set out in a document of its principles, its situation, and the environment in which it expects to operate.

cost for a business, the amount of money it has to spend in order to produce goods and services for sale. *Direct costs* are costs that vary directly with output, such as raw material inputs. *Indirect costs* are costs that change as output changes but not in direct proportion. *Overhead costs* are the costs of running the business, which do not change as output changes. In economics, these three cost concepts are called variable, semi-variable, and fixed costs. *Total cost* is the sum of all costs incurred in producing a given level of output.

cost–benefit analysis process whereby a project is assessed for its social and welfare benefits in addition to considering the financial return on investment. For example, this might take into account the environmental impact of an industrial plant or convenience for users of a new railway. A major difficulty is finding a way to quantify net social costs and benefits.

cost of sales the cost incurred directly by a business in making sales. This may include the cost of raw materials or goods bought for resale and labour costs incurred in producing goods. It does not include overhead costs.

creditor individual or business organization that is owed money by another individual or business. Money owed to creditors by a company is a current liability on the company's balance sheet.

critical-path analysis procedure used in the management of complex projects to minimize the amount of time taken. The analysis shows which subprojects can run in parallel with each other, and which have to be completed, in which order, before other subprojects can follow on. Complex projects may involve hundreds of subprojects, and computer applications packages for critical-path analysis are widely used to help reduce the time and effort involved in their analysis.

cumulative preference share preference share whose entitlement to dividend is carried forward to a subsequent year whenever a dividend is not paid.

current asset or *circulating* or *floating asset* any asset of a business that could be turned into cash in a limited period of time, generally less than a year. Current assets include stocks, accounts receivable or billings, short-term investments, and cash.

current liability any debt of a business that falls due within one year. Current liabilities include creditors (including employees), bank overdrafts, and interest.

current ratio or *working capital ratio* in a company, the ratio of current assets to current liabilities. It is a general indication of the solvency of a company, the adequacy of its working capital and its ability to meet day-to-day calls upon it.

dawn raid sudden and unexpected buying of a significant proportion of a company's shares, usually as a prelude to a takeover bid. The aim is to prevent the target company from having time to organize opposition to the takeover.

debenture or *company stock* long-term loan raised by a company through the issue of debenture certificates, using its assets as security for repayment.

debt something that is owed by a person, organization, or country, usually money, goods, or services. Debt usually occurs as a result of borrowing credit. *Debt servicing* is the payment of interest on a debt. A *debtor* is an individual, business organization, or government that owes money to another. (For *international debt*, see *International Economics*.)

deferred share on the stock market, a share that typically warrants a dividend only after a specified dividend has been paid on the ordinary shares; it may, however, be entitled to a dividend on all the profits after that point.

depreciation the decline of a currency's value in relation to other currencies. Depreciation also describes the fall in value of an asset (such as factory machinery) resulting from age, wear and tear, or other circumstances. It is an important factor in assessing company profits and tax liabilities.

director person who is elected to the board of directors of a company by shareholders at the annual general meeting of the company. Directors are by law responsible for protecting the interests of shareholders in a company. They appoint managers to run the company on a day-to-day basis.

diseconomies of scale increase in the average cost of production as output increases in the long run. Diseconomies of scale are said to arise because larger businesses find it more difficult to manage their resources, particularly their workers, than small firms. For example, a large firm may employ too many managers, which pushes up their average costs.

diversification corporate strategy of entering distinctly new products or markets, as opposed to simply adding to an existing product range. A company may diversify in order to spread its risks or because its original area of operation is becoming less profitable.

dividend the amount of money that company directors decide should be taken out of net profits for distribution to shareholders. It is usually declared as a percentage or fixed amount per share.

earnings pay including basic pay plus any additional payments such as overtime pay or bonus payments. *Gross earnings* are earnings before deductions such as income tax and national insurance contributions have been taken away. *Net earnings* are earnings after deductions.

economies of scale increase in production capacity at a financial cost that is more than compensated for by the greater volume of output. For example, there would be economies of scale present if a car manufacturer could manufacture cars at £5,000 per car if it produced 100,000 cars per year, but at £4,000 per car if it produced 200,000 cars per year.

EFTPOS (acronym for *electronic funds transfer at point of sale*) transfer of funds from one bank account to another by electronic means. For example, a customer inserts a plastic card into a point-of-sale computer terminal in a supermarket, and telephone lines are used to make an automatic debit from the customer's bank account to settle the bill.

end-use certificate in shipping, a document intended to assure authorities of the eventual application (generally also the final customer and destination) of a particular actual or intended shipment. End-use certificates are needed in cases where there are political controls on exports, such as advanced military weapons.

equal-opportunity policy plan of action that spells out what constitutes unfair discrimination in order to guide employment practices and to ensure that the organization is working within the legislation on equal pay, sex and race discrimination.

equity a company's assets, less its liabilities, which are the property of the owner or shareholders. Popularly, equities are stocks and shares which do not pay interest at fixed rates but pay dividends based on the company's performance. The value of equities tends to rise over the long term, but in the short term they are a risk investment because prices can fall as well as rise. Equity is also used to refer to the paid value of mortgaged real property, most commonly a house.

Eurobond bond underwritten by an international syndicate and sold in countries other than the country of the currency in which the issue is denominated. It provides longer-term financing than is possible with loans in Eurodollars.

executive director company director who is also an employee of the company.

experience curve observed effect of improved performance of individuals and organizations as experience of a repeated task increases.

external economies of scale fall in the average cost of production for a firm arising from the growth of the industry in which the firm operates. For example, growth in an industry might lead to an increase in the number of component supply firms for that industry, which might lead to a fall in the price of components.

factoring lending money to a company on the security of money owed to that company; this is often done on the basis of collecting those debts. The lender is known as the factor. Factoring may also describe acting as a commission agent for the sale of goods.

favourable variance difference between actual and budgeted spending or income that results in an organization having more money than planned.

Financial Times indices scales for measuring aspects of the stock market, published by the *Financial Times* of London. They are: FT ordinary, FT- SE 100, FT-Actuaries All Share, FT Government Securities, FT Fixed Interest, FT-SE Eurotrack 200, FT-Actuaries World Index and Indices of National and Regional Markets.

financial year in the UK, from 6 April one year to 5 April the following year. The financial year of a company (its accounting year) may differ from this. A company can choose any 12-month period for its accounting year.

fixed cost or *overhead cost* cost that does not vary directly with output, but remains constant as output increases. For example, a company may increase its output by one third; variable costs will increase in proportion with this but fixed costs will stay the same.

Fordism mass production characterized by a high degree of job specialization, as typified by Ford motor company's early use of assembly lines. *Post-Fordism* management theory and practice emphasizes flexibility and autonomy of decision-making for nonmanagerial staff. It is concerned more with facilitating and coordinating tasks than with control.

franchise the right given by one company to another to manufacture, distribute, or provide its products. Examples of franchise operations in the UK include Benetton and the Body Shop. Many US companies use franchises to distribute their products.

future contract to buy or sell a specific quantity of a particular commodity or currency (or even a purely notional sum, such as the value of a particular stock index) at a particular date in the future. There is usually no physical exchange between buyer and seller. It is only the difference between the ground value and the market value that changes. Such transactions are a function of the *futures market*.

gearing ratio ratio of a company's permanent loan capital (preference shares and long-term loans) to its equity (ordinary shares plus reserves). If the gearing ratio is above 100%, then the company is considered to be highly geared. It has more long-term debt than equity, so if the company goes through bad trading conditions, it will face more difficulties than a company with a lower gearing ratio; this is because the company with the higher gearing ratio will have to carry on paying interest on its loans, whereas a company with a lower gearing but the same amount of loans plus equity can cut the dividends paid to shareholders. The burden of the higher interest payments could push the company into bankruptcy.

GmbH abbreviation for *Gesellshaft mit beschrankter Haftung* (German 'limited liability company').

golden share share, often with overriding voting powers, issued by governments to control privatized companies.

greenmail payment made by a target company to avoid a takeover; for example, buying back a portion of its own shares from a potential predator (either a person or a company) at an inflated price.

grey market dealing in shares using methods that are legal but perhaps officially frowned upon – for example, before issue and flotation.

gross a particular figure or price, calculated before the deduction of specific items such as commission, discounts, interest, and taxes. The opposite is net.

gross profit the difference between sales revenue and the direct cost of production for a business. It does not take account of the overheads of the business. The gross profit is usually shown in the profit and loss account of the company.

human-resource management or *personnel management* recruitment, selection, and training of staff, and efforts to involve them in the company. Japanese firms, in particular, invest heavily in human-resource management.

indirect cost or *semi-variable cost* cost that changes as output changes, but not in direct proportion. For example, the costs of running an office are indirect costs for a manufacturing company. Day-to-day changes in output in the factory will not affect office costs. However, a permanent 20% increase in output may lead to a need for more office staff and hence higher indirect costs.

indirect tax tax on products or services. VAT (value-added tax) and excise duties are examples of indirect taxes. The opposite of an indirect tax is a direct tax, a tax on income.

industrial tribunal independent panel which decides on legal cases brought before it including employment issues such as unfair dismissal, redundancy, equal opportunities, and discrimination at work.

inflation accounting method of accounting that allows for the changing purchasing power of money due to inflation.

insider trading or *insider dealing* illegal use of privileged information in dealing on a stock exchange; for example, when a company takeover bid is imminent. Insider trading is in theory detected by the Securities and Investment Board (SIB) in the UK, and the Securities and Exchange Commission (SEC) in the USA. Neither agency, however, has any legal powers other than public disclosure and they do not bring prosecutions themselves.

insolvency inability to pay debts, which may lead to bankruptcy.

internal economies of scale fall in the average cost of production for a firm arising from a change in the scale of production by that firm.

inventory list of goods owned. The owner of a furnished house that is rented out is likely to have an inventory of all the furniture, fixtures, and fittings in the house. In business studies, an inventory usually refers to the stocks of goods held by a company.

investment the purchase of any asset with the potential to yield future financial benefit to the purchaser (such as a house, a work of art, stocks and shares, or even a private education).

investment trust public company that makes investments in other companies on behalf of its shareholders. It may issue shares to raise capital and issue fixed interest securities.

issued capital the nominal value of those shares in a company that have been allotted. The issued capital is equivalent to the amount invested, provided the issue has not been at a premium price.

job enrichment initiative or incentive that makes a job more satisfying to perform. For example, giving workers more control over how a task is to be completed often leads to job enrichment because workers can think out their own way of tackling the task, change their pattern of working when they want, and feel more responsible for achieving the end product.

joint venture undertaking in which an individual or legal entity of one country forms a company with those of another country, with risks being shared.

junk bond derogatory term for a security officially rated as 'below investment grade'. It is issued in order to raise capital quickly, typically to finance a takeover to be paid for by the sale of assets once the company is acquired. Junk bonds have a high yield, but are a high-risk investment.

just-in-time (JIT) production management practice requiring that incoming supplies arrive at the time when they are needed by the customer, most typically in a manufacturer's assembly operations. JIT requires considerable cooperation between supplier and customer, but can reduce expenses and improve efficiency, for example by reducing stock levels and by increasing the quality of goods supplied.

key-results analysis management procedure involving the identification of performance components critical to a particular process or event, the nec-essary level of performance required from them, and the methods of monitoring to be used.

learning curve graphical representation of the improvement in performance of a person executing a new task.

leveraged buyout purchase of a controlling proportion of the shares of a company by its own management, financed almost exclusively by borrowing. It is so called because the ratio of a company's long-term debt to its equity (capital assets) is known as its 'leverage'.

limited company company for whose debts the members are liable only to a limited extent. The capital of a limited company is divided into small units, and profits are distributed according to shareholding. It is the usual type of company formation in the UK.

limited liability legal safeguard that allows shareholders to be liable for their company's debts only up to and including the value of their shareholding. For example, if a limited liability company goes bankrupt with debts of 1 million, the shareholders are not liable for any of that debt, although the value of their shares in the company would be worthless.

liquidation the winding-up of a company by converting all its assets into money to pay off its liabilities.

loan form of borrowing by individuals, businesses, and governments. Individuals and companies usually obtain loans from banks. The loan with interest is typically paid back in fixed monthly instalments over a period of between one and five years in the UK, although longer-term loans and different repayment conditions may be negotiated. Debentures and mortgages are specific forms of loan. In business, loans are the second most important way (after retained profit) in which firms finance their expansion.

loss the opposite of profit, when revenues are less than costs.

management accounting the use of financial accounts in the process of decision-making within a business organization. Examples would include finding out which business activities were least profitable and then making a decision about whether to continue with these activities.

management buyout purchase of control of a company by its management, generally with debt funding, making it a leveraged buyout.

management information system computer system used for converting company data from internal and external sources into appropriate information, and then communicating it to managers at all levels, enabling them to carry out their work.

managing director the director of a company who is also its most senior manager. The managing director is therefore responsible for the day-to-day running of the company and has a seat on the board. The managing director may also be the chair of the company, but in large companies the role of chair is likely to be separate from that of managing director.

market capitalization market value of a company, based on the market price of all its issued securities – a price that would be unlikely to apply, however, if a bid were actually made for control of them.

marketing mix the factors that help a firm to sell its products. Four elements – the *four Ps* – are normally distinguished: getting the right *product* to the market, at the right *price*; ensuring that the *promotion* in terms of advertising and marketing for the product is right; and ensuring that the product is distributed to the most convenient *place* for customers to buy it.

market maker in the UK, a stockbroker entitled to deal directly on the stock exchange. The role was created in Oct 1986, when the jobber (intermediary) disappeared from the stock exchange. Market makers trade in the dual capacity of broker and jobber.

market segment portion of a market characterized by such similarity of customers, their requirements and/or buying behaviour, that those who sell the products or services bought by these customers can aim their marketing effort specifically at this segment.

market share the proportion of a market taken by one producer. Market share can be measured in terms of volume of sales; for example, company X sold 40% of all the cars sold last month in the UK market. Or it can be measured as the value of sales; for example, company X sold 30% of the total value of all cars sold in the UK market last month. Or it could be measured in terms of output by volume or value; for example, company X could have produced 50% of all the cars made in the UK even though its UK market share was 30% because it exported cars to other markets while some cars sold in the UK were produced in other countries.

memorandum of association document that defines the purpose of a company and the amount and different classes of share capital. In the UK, the memorandum is drawn up on formation of the company, together with the articles of association.

merger linking of two or more companies, either by creating a new organization by consolidating the original companies or by absorption by one company of the others. Unlike a takeover, which is not always a voluntary fusion of the parties, a merger is the result of an agreement.

minority interest item in the consolidated accounts of a holding company that represents the value of any shares in its subsidiaries that it does not itself own.

multinational corporation company or enterprise operating in several countries, usually defined as one that has 25% or more of its output capacity located outside its country of origin.

In 1992, the world's 500 largest companies, generally multinationals, controlled at least 70% of world trade, 80% of foreign investment, and 30% of global GDP.

national insurance in the UK, state social-security scheme that provides child allowances, maternity benefits, and payments to the unemployed, sick, and retired, and also covers medical treatment. It is paid for by weekly or monthly contributions from employees and employers.

net of a particular figure or price, calculated after the deduction of specific items such as commission, discounts, interest, and taxes. The opposite is gross.

net assets either the total assets of a company less its current liabilities (that is, the capital employed) or the total assets less current liabilities, debt capital, long-term loans and provisions, which would form the amount available to ordinary shareholders if the company were to be wound up.

net current assets current assets minus current liabilities. A company is only solvent if its net current assets are positive.

net worth the total assets of a company less its total liabilities, equivalent to the interest of the ordinary shareholders in the company.

nonexecutive director member of the board of a company who is not an employee of the company. A nonexecutive director can provide a wider perspective to the outlook of the board, but may be limited by not having access to informal sources of information.

nonvoting share ordinary share in a company that is without entitlement to vote at shareholders' meetings. Shares are often distinguished as A-shares (voting) and B-shares (nonvoting).

option contract giving the owner the right (as opposed to the obligation, as with futures contracts) to buy or sell a specific quantity of a particular commodity or currency at a future date and at an agreed price, in return for a premium. The buyer or seller can decide not to exercise the option if it would prove disadvantageous.

ordinary share type of share in a company. Ordinary shareholders receive a variable rate of dividend. When company profits are high, the dividends will be high also. If the company is doing badly, it may well reduce or even stop paying any dividend to ordinary shareholders. Ordinary shareholders have only second claim on dividends after preference shareholders.

overhead any of the fixed costs in a business that do not vary in the short term. These might include property rental, heating and lighting, insurance, and administration costs.

patent certificate issued by the government through the Patent Office giving a person or business organization the exclusive right to make, use, or sell a newly invented product. The patent normally lasts 25 years from the day it is granted. Patents are important because they enable a business organization to generate profits from its research and development by preventing other companies from copying the process or product.

PAYE abbreviation for *Pay-As-You- Earn* in the UK, a system of tax collection in which income tax is deducted on a regular basis by the employer before wages are paid. PAYE tax deductions are calculated so that when added up they will approximately equal the total amount of tax likely to be due in that year. In the USA it is called *withholding tax*.

performance-related pay the element of a wage or salary that is linked to the working performance of an individual or working group, according to a prior arrangement.

piggyback export scheme firm already established in the export field making its services available without charge to a small firm just entering the market.

The small firm thus obtains the assistance of the large firm's good will, experience, and know-how, and is saved the trouble and expense of setting up its own export department.

poison pill tactic to avoid hostile business takeover by making the target unattractive. For example, a company may give a certain class of shareholders the right to have their shares redeemed at a very good price in the event of the company being taken over, thus involving the potential predator in considerable extra cost.

preference share share in a company with rights in various ways superior to those of ordinary shares; for example, priority to a fixed dividend and priority over ordinary shares in the event of the company being wound up.

premium price difference between the current market price of a security and its issue price (where the current price is the greater).

price/earnings ratio or *p/e ratio* a company's share price divided by its earnings per share after tax.

price elasticity of demand responsiveness of changes in quantity demanded to a change in the price of a product. It is measured by the formula: percentage change in quantity demanded/percentage change in price. For example, if the price of butter is reduced by 10% and the demand increases by 20%, the price elasticity of demand is 2.

pricing strategy the decision a business organization has to make about the price at which it will sell its products. Pricing strategies include creaming, penetration pricing, profit maximization, price capturing, price discrimination, range pricing, and loss leading.

prime rate the interest rate charged by commercial banks to their best customers. It is the lowest interest or base rate on which other rates are calculated according to the risk involved. Only borrowers who have the highest credit rating qualify for the prime rate.

profit amount by which total revenue exceeds total cost. It is the reward for risk-taking for shareholders in a business organization. *Gross profit* is the difference between sales revenue and the direct cost of production. *Net profit* is total revenue minus total direct and indirect cost (for example, overheads, the cost of running the business).

profit and loss account in a set of accounts, the account that compares all revenues and all costs of a business organization in order to arrive at a figure for net profit (or loss). The credit side of the account starts with a figure for gross profit – the difference between turnover and cost of products sold. Other revenues added to gross profit might include interest on investments and rent from let properties. All costs other than the cost of new stock purchased (already taken into account when calculating gross profit) are placed on the debit side of the account. The costs include overhead costs.

profit-sharing scheme in a company, arrangements for some or all the employees to receive cash or shares related to the profits of the company.

public relations (PR) promotion of a positive image about itself to the general public by a business or other organization. Public relations departments deal with critical letters from the public about the business. They also attempt to get free media publicity; for example, by providing stories or photographs to the press.

put option on the stock market, the right to sell a specific number of shares at a specific price on or before a specific date.

quality circle small group of production workers concerned with problems relating to the quality, safety, and efficiency of their product. Key characteristics of quality circles are size (8–12 members); voluntary membership; natural work groups, rather than artificially created ones; autonomy in setting their own agenda; access to senior managers; and a relatively permanent existence. Quality circles were popularized in Japan.

quality control steps taken to ensure that products are of a minimum acceptable standard for buyers of the product. In manufacturing, quality control should be achieved through inspection of products at each stage of the manufacturing process. In services, quality control is just as important but quality of service is often more difficult to define and measure. Quality control can cost money if products are poorly made and end up being rejected. Poor quality also leads to a poor image for a business organization and lower sales.

rate of return the income from an investment expressed as a percentage of the cost of that investment.

receiver in law, a person appointed by a court to collect and manage the assets of an individual, company, or partnership in serious financial difficulties. In the case of bankruptcy, the assets may be sold and distributed by a receiver to creditors.

redeemable preference share share in a company that the company has a right to buy back at a specific price.

research and development (R&D) process undertaken by a business organization before the launch of a product. Research is usually scientific research into materials and production processes. Product development is application of that research to the development of existing or new products.

Large companies may have a research and development department with its own budget and staff. Smaller companies are less likely to be able to afford R&D. The relatively low expenditure on R&D by UK civilian manufacturing companies compared to their competitors abroad is one possible reason for the low rate of economic growth of the UK economy and for deindustrialization in the UK.

revenue money received from the sale of a product. *Total revenue* can be calculated by multiplying the average price received by the total quantity sold. *Average revenue* is the average price received and is calculated by dividing total revenue by total quantity sold. *Marginal revenue* is the revenue gained from the sale of an additional unit of output.

reverse takeover a company selling itself to another (a white knight) to avoid being the target of a purchase by an unwelcome predator.

rights issue new shares offered to existing shareholders to raise new capital. Shareholders receive a discount on the market price while the company benefits from not having the costs of a relaunch of the new issue.

risk capital or *venture capital* finance provided by venture capital companies, individuals, and merchant banks for medium- or long-term business ventures that are not their own and in which there is a strong element of risk.

sales promotion selling technique used by a business organization to persuade customers to buy its products in the short term. *Below-the-line promotion*, or merchandising, includes special offers such as gifts, discounts, competitions, better-value offers (for example, 500 grams for the price of 400 grams), and trade-ins. *Above-the-line promotion* is advertising.

scrip issue or *subscription certificate* UK term for bonus issue.

sequestrator person or organization appointed by a court of law to control the assets of another person or organization within the jurisdiction of that court.

shareholder owner of part of the share capital of a company. Shareholders own shares in order to make a return on them. They do this partly by receiving dividends, a share of any profit made by the company, and partly by seeing the price of their shares rise over time if the value of the company increases.

solvency state of a business when its current assets exceed its current liabilities, in other words, when it has positive net current assets or positive working capital. This means that it has enough liquid assets to pay off its debts in the short term.

spreadsheet software package that enables the user to analyse data because it will perform calculations and routine mathematical operations. A cash-flow forecast could be prepared on a spreadsheet.

stag subscriber for new share issues who expects to profit from a rise in price on early trading in the shares.

stakeholder any person or group that has a stake in an organization: primarily, shareholders, employees, management, customers, and suppliers.

Standard and Poor's Stock Price Index or *S & P 500* index of the US stock market covering 500 stocks broken down into sectors.

stocks and shares investment holdings (securities) in private or public undertakings. Although distinctions have become blurred, in the UK stock usually means fixed-interest securities – for example, those issued by central and local government – while shares represent a stake in the ownership of a trading company which, if they are ordinary shares, yield to the owner dividends reflecting the success of the company. In the USA the term 'stock' generally signifies what in the UK is an ordinary share.

supply curve diagrammatic illustration of the relationship between the price of a good and the quantity that producers will supply at that price. It is said to be upward-sloping because the higher the price, the more profitable existing production becomes, attracting new companies into the industry and thus increasing the quantity supplied.

SWOT analysis breakdown of an organization into its *s*trengths and *w*eaknesses (the internal analysis), with an assessment of the *o*pportunities open to it and the *t*hreats confronting it. SWOT analysis is commonly used in marketing and strategic studies.

takeover acquisition by one company of a sufficient number of shares in another company to have effective control of that company – usually 51%, although a controlling stake may be as little as 30%.

Takeovers may be agreed or contested; methods employed include the *dawn raid*, and methods of avoiding an unwelcome takeover include *reverse takeover*, *poison pills*, or inviting a *white knight* to make a takeover bid.

TESSA (acronym for *tax-exempt special savings account*) UK scheme, introduced 1991, to encourage longer-term savings by making interest tax-free on deposits of up to £9,000 over five years.

trading account in a set of accounts, the account that deals with turnover (the value of sales) and the cost of new stock purchased. The trading account enables a business organization to calculate gross profit, the difference between the value of sales and the cost of new stock.

turnover the value of sales of a business organization over a period of time. For example, if a shop sells 10,000 items in a week at an average price of 2 each, then its weekly turnover is 20,000. Profit of a company is not only affected by the total turnover but also by the rate of turnover.

unit trust company that invests its clients' funds in other companies. The units it issues represent holdings of shares, which means unit shareholders have a wider spread of capital than if they bought shares on the stock market.

venture capital or *risk capital* money put up by investors such as merchant banks to fund a new company or expansion of an established company. The organization providing the money receives a share of the company's equity and seeks to make a profit by rapid growth in the value of its stake, as a result of expansion by the start-up company or 'venture'.

white knight company invited by the target of a takeover bid to make a rival bid. The company invited to bid is usually one that is already on good terms with the target company.

working capital current assets minus current liabilities of a business organization. It is the assets that are left free, after liabilities have been covered, for the business to use or put to work if it feels that it should take that risk.

yield the annual percentage return from an investment; on ordinary shares it is the dividend expressed as a percentage.

zero-based budgeting management technique requiring that no resources for a new period of a programme are approved and/or released unless their justification can be demonstrated against alternative options.

INTERNATIONAL ECONOMICS

Terms

aid, development money given or lent on concessional terms to developing countries or spent on maintaining agencies for this purpose. In the late 1980s official aid from governments of richer nations amounted to $45–60 billion annually, whereas voluntary organizations in the West received about $2.4 billion a year for the Third World. The World Bank is the largest dispenser of aid. In 1992 it transferred $49.7 million to developing countries. All industrialized United Nations (UN) member countries devote a proportion of their gross national product to aid, ranging from 0.20% of GNP (Ireland) to 1.10% (Norway) (1988 figures). Each country spends more than half this contribution on direct bilateral assistance to countries with which they have historical or military links or hope to encourage trade. The rest goes to international organizations such as UN and World Bank agencies, which distribute aid multilaterally.

balance of payments account of a country's debit and credit transactions with other countries. Items are divided into the *current account*, which includes both visible trade (imports and exports of goods) and invisible trade (services such as transport, tourism, interest, and dividends), and the *capital account*, which includes investment in and out of the country, international grants, and loans. Deficits or surpluses on these accounts are brought into balance by buying and selling reserves of foreign currencies.

A *balance of payments crisis* arises when a country's current account deteriorates because the cost of imports exceeds income from exports. Persistent trade deficits often result in heavy government borrowing overseas, which in turn leads to a debt crisis.

bank financial institution that uses funds deposited with it to lend money to companies or individuals, and also provides financial services to its customers. A *central bank* (in the UK, the Bank of England) issues currency for the government, in order to provide cash for circulation and exchange.

Big Bang popular term for the changes instituted in late 1986 to the organization and practices of the City of London as Britain's financial centre, including the liberalization of the London Stock Exchange. This involved merging the functions of jobber (dealer in stocks and shares) and broker (who mediates between the jobber and the public), introducing negotiated commission rates, and allowing foreign banks and financial companies to own British brokers/jobbers, or themselves to join the London Stock Exchange.

capital accumulated or inherited wealth held in the form of assets (such as stocks and shares, property, and bank deposits). In stricter terms, capital is defined as the stock of goods used in the production of other goods, and may be *fixed capital* (such as buildings, plant, and machinery) that is durable, or *circulating capital* (raw materials and components) that is used up quickly.

collective bargaining process whereby management, representing an employer, and a trade union, representing employees, agree to negotiate jointly terms and conditions of employment. Agreements can be company-based or industry-wide.

comparative advantage law of international trade first elaborated by English economist David Ricardo (1772–1823) showing that trade becomes worthwhile if the cost of production of particular items differs between one country and another.

consumption the purchase of goods and services for final use, as opposed to spending by firms on capital goods, known as capital formation.

cost of living cost of goods and services needed for an average standard of living. In Britain the cost-of-living index was introduced 1914 and based on the expenditure of a working-class family of a man, woman, and three children; the standard is 100. Known from 1947 as the Retail Price Index (RPI), it is revised to allow for inflation.

cost-push inflation theory stating that inflation is caused by increases in the costs of production. A rise in wages, profit levels, or product inputs to the firm will push up its costs. It responds by increasing its prices. This then contributes to inflation in the economy.

credit means by which goods or services are obtained without immediate payment, usually by agreeing to pay interest. The three main forms are *consumer credit* (usually extended to individuals by retailers), *bank credit* (such as overdrafts or personal loans), and *trade credit* (common in the commercial world both within countries and internationally). Consumer credit is increasingly used to pay for goods. In the USA in 1991 it amounted to $756 billion, with about 18% of disposable income expended on hire-purchase and credit card payments.

In the UK in 1992, net lending to consumers amounted to approximately £35 billion.

crowding out situation in which an increase in government expenditure results in a fall in private-sector investment, either because it causes inflation or a rise in interest rates (as a result of increased government borrowing) or because it reduces the efficiency of production as a result of government intervention. Crowding out has been used in recent years as a justification of supply-side economics such as the privatization of state-owned industries and services.

currency the type of money in use in a country; for example, the US dollar, the Australian dollar, the UK pound sterling, the German Deutschmark, and the Japanese yen.

debt, international money owed by one country to another. It began on a large scale with the investment in foreign countries by newly industrialized countries in the late 19th to early 20th centuries. International debt became a global problem as a result of the oil crisis of the 1970s.

The World Bank was established 1945 as an agency of the United Nations to finance international development, by providing loans where private capital was not forthcoming. Loans were made largely at prevailing market rates ('hard loans') and therefore generally to the developed countries, who could afford them. In 1960 the International Development Association

(IDA) was set up as an offshoot of the World Bank to provide interest-free ('soft') loans over a long period to finance the economies of developing countries and assist their long-term development. The cash surpluses of Middle Eastern oil-producing countries were channelled by Western banks to Third World countries. However, a slump in the world economy, and increases in interest rates, resulted in the debtor countries paying an ever-increasing share of their national output in debt servicing (paying off the interest on a debt, rather than paying off the debt itself). As a result, many loans had to be *rescheduled* (renegotiated so that repayments were made over a longer term).

The debtor countries paid more than $1,300 billion 1982–90, yet their debt increased by 61%. Africa transferred $10 billion a year (1993) to the rich countries in debt repayments. Banks in the creditor countries had received $44–$50 billion in tax relief on bad debts by 1993.

In 1980–81 Poland ceased making repayments on international debts. Today, the countries most at risk include Mexico and Brazil, both of which have a *debt-servicing ratio* (proportion of export earnings which is required to pay off the debt) of more than 50%. In May 1987 the world's largest bank, Citibank of New York, announced that it was writing off $3 billion of international loans, mainly due to Brazil's repeated rescheduling of debt repayments. The dangers of the current scale of international debt (the so-called *debt crisis*) is that the debtor country can only continue to repay its existing debts by means of further loans; for the Western countries, there is the possibility of a confidence crisis causing panic withdrawals of deposits and consequent collapse of the banking system.

deficit financing planned excess of expenditure over income, dictated by government policy, creating a shortfall of public revenue which is met by borrowing. The decision to create a deficit is made to stimulate an economy by increasing consumer purchasing and at the same time to create more jobs.

demand-pull inflation rise in prices (inflation) caused by excess aggregate demand (total demand for goods and services) in the economy. For example, when the economy is in boom, aggregate demand tends to be rising quickly, but inflation also rises quickly.

deregulation US term for freeing markets from protection, with the aim of improving competitiveness. It often results in greater monopoly control. An example is the deregulation of the US airline industry 1978, after which 14 new companies began flying. By 1991 only one was left. In Britain, the major changes in the City of London 1986 (the Big Bang) were in part deregulation.

devaluation lowering of the official value of a currency against other currencies, so that exports become cheaper and imports more expensive. Used when a country is badly in deficit in its balance of trade, it results in the goods the country produces being cheaper abroad, so that the economy is stimulated by increased foreign demand. *Revaluation* is the opposite process.

Devaluation of important currencies upsets the balance of the world's money markets and encourages speculation. The increased cost of imported food, raw materials, and manufactured goods as a consequence of devaluation may stimulate an acceleration in inflation, especially when commodities are rising in price because of increased world demand.

disinvestment withdrawal of investments in a country for political reasons. The term is also used to describe non-replacement of stock as it wears out.

It is generally applied to the removal of funds from South Africa in recent years by some multinational companies, and to the withdrawal of private investment funds (by universities, pension funds, and other organizations) from portfolios doing business in South Africa. Disinvestment may be motivated by fear of loss of business in the home market caused by adverse publicity or by fear of loss of foreign resources if the local government changes.

Dow Jones Index (*Dow Jones Industrial 30 Share Index*) scale for measuring the average share price and percentage change of 30 major US industrial companies. It has been calculated and published since 1897 by the financial news publisher Dow Jones and Co.

economic growth rate of growth of output of all goods and services in an economy, usually measured as the percentage increase in gross domestic product or gross national product from one year to the next. It is regarded as an indicator of the rate of increase or decrease in the standard of living; it is negative in a recession, as it was in the UK in 1991 and 1992, when economic growth was –2.5% and –0.4% respectively.

exchange rate the price at which one currency is bought or sold in terms of other currencies, gold, or accounting units such as the special drawing right of the International Monetary Fund. Exchange rates may be fixed by international agreement or by government policy; or they may be wholly or partly allowed to 'float' (that is, find their own level) in world currency markets.

Central banks, as large holders of foreign currency, often intervene to buy or sell particular currencies in an effort to maintain some stability in exchange   rates.

exchange-rate policy policy of government towards the level of the exchange rate of its currency. It may want to influence the exchange rate by using its gold and foreign currency reserves held by its central bank to buy and sell its currency. It can also use interest rates (monetary policy) to alter the value of the currency.

excise duty indirect tax levied on certain goods produced within a country, such as petrol, alcohol, and tobacco. It is collected by the government's Customs and Excise department.

export goods or service produced in one country and sold to another. Exports may be visible (goods physically exported) or invisible (services provided in the exporting country but paid for by residents of another country).

Financial Times Index (FT Index) indicator measuring the daily movement of 30 major industrial share prices on the London Stock Exchange (1935 = 100), issued by the UK *Financial Times* newspaper. Other FT indices cover government securities, fixed-interest securities, gold mine shares, and Stock Exchange activity.

Gross national product *

Countries with the highest GNP per head:

Country	GNP per head (US $)
Switzerland	35,500
Japan	32,018
Luxembourg	31,080
Sweden	29,600
Denmark	28,200
Norway	28,200
Finland	24,400
Belgium	22,600
Iceland	22,580
USA	22,520
Canada	21,170
Netherlands	21,400
Liechtenstein	21,020
Italy	20,200
United Arab Emirates	19,680
Singapore	18,143
Australia	17,320
UK	17,300

Countries with the lowest GNP per head:

Country	GNP per head (US $)
Bhutan	190
Chad	190
Guinea-Bissau	180
Nepal	170
Somalia	150
Tanzania	120
Ethiopia	120
Mozambique	80

* based on 1990-92 estimates

fiscal policy that part of government policy devoted to raising revenue, notably through taxation, and deciding on government borrowing (the public sector borrowing requirement), and the priorities and purposes governing its expenditure.

Fiscal policy can also be used to direct the economy. For example, value-added tax (VAT) and excise duty on tobacco discourages cigarette smoking; mortgage tax relief encourages people to buy their own home. At a macroeconomic level, more public spending and less taxation will stimulate total spending in the economy, leading probably to a fall in unemployment but a rise in inflation.

free-enterprise economy another term for free-market economy.

free-market economy or *free-enterprise economy* economic system where the factors of production are mainly owned by private individuals or organizations, and where resource allocation takes place through the market mechanism. Government plays a relatively small role in providing goods and services, but it is responsible for upholding laws which protect rights to own property, and for maintaining a stable currency.

gilt-edged securities stocks and shares issued and guaranteed by the British government to raise funds and traded on the Stock Exchange. A relatively risk-free investment, gilts bear fixed interest and are usually redeemable on a specified date. The term is now used generally to describe securities of the highest value.

gross national product (GNP) the most commonly used measurement of the wealth of a country. GNP is defined as the total value of all goods and services produced by firms owned by the country concerned. It is measured as the gross domestic product plus income from abroad, minus income earned during the same period by foreign investors within the country.

hyperinflation rapid and uncontrolled inflation, or increases in prices, usually associated with political and/or social instability (as in Germany in the 1920s).

import product or service that one country purchases from another for domestic consumption, or for processing and re-exporting (Hong Kong, for example, is heavily dependent on imports for its export business). Imports may be visible (goods) or invisible (services). If an importing country does not have a counterbalancing value of exports, it may experience balance-of-payments difficulties and accordingly consider restricting imports by some form of protectionism (such as an import tariff or import quotas).

import control control that limits the number of imports entering the country. One type of import control is an import quota.

incomes policy government-initiated exercise to curb inflation by restraining rises in incomes, on either a voluntary or a compulsory basis; often linked with action to control prices, in which case it becomes a prices and incomes policy.

income tax direct tax levied on personal income, mainly wages and salaries, but which may include the value of receipts other than in cash. It is one of the main instruments for achieving a government's income redistribution objectives. In contrast, *indirect taxes* are duties payable whenever a specific product is purchased; examples include VAT and customs duties.

inflation rise in the general level of prices. The many causes include increased production costs (*cost-push inflation*); *demand-pull inflation* results when overall demand exceeds supply. Suppressed inflation occurs in controlled economies and is reflected in rationing, shortages, and black-market prices. Deflation, a fall in the general level of prices, is the reverse of inflation.

interest sum of money paid by a borrower to a lender in return for the loan, usually expressed as a percentage per annum. *Simple interest* is interest calculated as a straight percentage of the amount loaned or invested. In *compound interest*, the interest earned over a period of time (for example, per annum) is added to the investment, so that at the end of the next period interest is paid on that total.

invisible trade international trade in services. In a balance of payments account, invisible exports are exports of services and invisible imports are imports of services.

laissez faire theory that the state should not intervene in economic affairs, except to break up a monopoly. The degree to which intervention should take place is one of the chief problems of economics.

Scottish economist Adam Smith (1723–1790) justified the theory in *The Wealth of Nations* 1776.

The 20th century has seen an increasing degree of state intervention to promote social benefits, which after World War II in Europe was extended into the field of nationalization of leading industries and services. However, from the 1970s, laissez-faire policies were again pursued in the UK and the USA.

market any situation where buyers and sellers are in contact with each other. This could be a street market or a world market where buyers and sellers communicate via letters, faxes, telephones, and representatives. In a perfect or *free market*, there are many buyers and sellers, so that no single buyer or seller is able to influence the price of the product; there is therefore perfect competition in the market. In an *imperfect market* either a few buyers or sellers (or even just one) dominates the market.

market economy free-market economy where most resources are allocated through markets rather than through state planning.

market forces the forces of demand (a want backed by the ability to pay) and supply (the willingness and ability to supply).

Some economists argue that resources are allocated most efficiently when producers are able to respond to consumer demand without intervention from 'distortions' such as governments and trade unions, and that profits and competition between firms and individuals provide sufficient incentives to produce efficiently (monetarism). Critics of this view suggest that market forces alone may not be efficient because they fail to consider social costs and benefits, and may also fail to provide for the needs of the less well off, since private firms aiming to make a profit respond to the ability to pay.

monetarism economic policy, advocated by the economist Milton Friedman (1912–   ) and the Chicago school of economists, that proposes control of a country's money supply to keep it in step with the country's ability to produce goods, with the aim of curbing inflation. Cutting government spending is advocated, and the long-term aim is to return as much of the economy as possible to the private sector, allegedly in the interests of efficiency.

Central banks use the discount rate and other tools to restrict or expand the supply of money to the economy. Additionally, credit is restricted by high interest rates, and industry is not cushioned against internal market forces or overseas competition (with the aim of preventing 'overstaffing', 'restrictive' union practices, and 'excessive' wage demands). Unemployment may result from some efforts to withdraw government safety nets, but monetarists claim it is less than eventually occurs if the methods of Keynesian economics are adopted. Monetarist policies were widely adopted in the 1980s in response to the inflation problems caused by spiralling oil prices in 1979.

monetary policy economic policy aimed at controlling the amount of money in circulation, usually through controlling the level of lending or credit. Increasing interest rates is an example of a contractionary monetary policy, which aims to reduce inflation by reducing the rate of growth of spending in the economy.

money any common medium of exchange acceptable in payment for goods or services or for the settlement of debts; legal tender. Money is usually coinage (invented by the Chinese in the second millennium BC) and paper notes (used by the Chinese from about AD 800). Developments such as the cheque and credit card fulfil many of the traditional functions of money.

money supply quantity of money in circulation in an economy at any given time. It can include notes, coins, and clearing-bank and other deposits used for everyday payments. Changes in the quantity of lending are a major determinant of changes in the money supply. One of the main principles of monetarism is that increases in the money supply in excess of the rate of economic growth are the chief cause of inflation.

In Britain there are several definitions of money supply. M0 was defined as notes and coins in circulation, together with the operational balance of clearing banks with the Bank of England. M1 encompasses M0 plus current-account deposits; M2, now rarely used, covers the M1 items plus deposit accounts; M3 covers M2 items plus all other deposits held by UK citizens and companies in the UK banking sector. In May 1987 the Bank of England introduced M4 (M3 plus building-society deposits) and M5 (M4 plus Treasury bills and local-authority deposits).

monopoly the domination of a market for a particular product or service by a single company, which can therefore restrict competition and keep prices high. In practice, a company can be said to have a monopoly when it controls a significant proportion of the market (technically an oligopoly).

multiplier theoretical concept, formulated by John Maynard Keynes (1883–1946), of the effect on national income or employment by an adjustment in overall demand. For example, investment by a company in a new plant will stimulate new income and expenditure, which will in turn generate new investment, and so on, so that the actual increase in national income may be several times greater than the original investment.

national debt debt incurred by the central government of a country to its own people and institutions and also to overseas creditors. A government can borrow from the public by means of selling interest-bearing bonds, for example, or from abroad. Traditionally, a major cause of national debt was the cost of war but in recent decades governments have borrowed heavily in order to finance development or nationalization, to support an ailing currency, or to avoid raising taxes.

At the end of the financial year 1992–93, the UK national debt was approximately £127 billion. This represented a rise in the national debt since 1991–92, caused by a budget deficit, or public sector borrowing requirement (PSBR) of £35 billion in the year 1992–93.

newly industrialized country (NIC) country that has in recent decades experienced a breakthrough into manufacturing and rapid export-led economic growth. The prime examples are Taiwan, Hong Kong, Singapore, and South Korea. Their economic development during the 1970s and 1980s was partly due to a rapid increase of manufactured goods in their exports.

oligopoly situation in which a few companies control the major part of a particular market and concert their actions to perpetuate such control. This may include an agreement to fix prices (a cartel).

poll tax tax levied on every individual, without reference to income or property. Being simple to administer, it was among the earliest sorts of tax (introduced in England 1377), but because it is a regressive tax, in that it falls proportionately more on poorer people, it has often proved unpopular. The *community charge*, a type of poll tax, was introduced in the UK 1989–90 but replaced by a 'council tax' 1993–94. The combined cost of its collection and abolition was estimated at £4 billion.

privatization policy or process of selling or transferring state-owned or public assets and services (notably nationalized industries) to private investors. Privatization of services involves the government contracting private firms to supply services previously supplied by public authorities.

Supporters of privatization argue that the public benefits from theoretically greater efficiency from firms already in the competitive market, and the release of resources for more appropriate use by government. Those against privatization believe that it transfers a country's assets from all the people to a controlling minority, that public utilities such as gas and water become private monopolies, and that a profit-making state-owned company raises revenue for the government.

In many cases the trend towards privatization has been prompted by dissatisfaction with the high level of subsidies being given to often inefficient state enterprise. The term 'privatization' is used even when the state retains a majority share of an enterprise.

The policy has been pursued by the post-1979 Conservative administration in the UK, and by recent governments in France, Japan, Italy, New Zealand and elsewhere. By 1988 the practice had spread worldwide, with communist countries such as China and Cuba selling off housing to private tenants.

productivity the output produced by a given quantity of labour, usually measured as output per person employed in the firm, industry, sector, or economy concerned. Productivity is determined by the quality and quantity of the fixed capital used by labour, and the effort of the workers concerned.

profit-sharing system whereby an employer pays the workers a fixed share of the company's profits. It originated in France in the early 19th century and was widely practised for a time within the cooperative movement.

public-sector borrowing requirement (PSBR) the amount of money needed by a government to cover any deficit in financing its own activities.

The PSBR includes loans to local authorities and public corporations, and also the funds raised by local authorities and public corporations from other sources. It is financed chiefly by sales of debt to the public outside the banking system (gilt-edged stocks, national savings, and local-authority stocks and bonds), by external transactions with other countries, and by borrowing from the banking system. In the UK, after the 1986 budget, this measure was changed

to the *public-sector financial deficit (PSFD)*, which is net of the asset sales due to privatization, which are thought to distort the PSBR.

public-sector debt repayment (PSDR) the amount of money left over when government expenditure (public spending) is subtracted from government receipts. This occurs only when government spending is less than government receipts. A PSDR enables a government to repay some of the national debt.

quantity theory of money economic theory claiming that an increase in the amount of money in circulation causes a proportionate increase in prices. The theory dates from the 17th century and was elaborated by US economist Irving Fisher (1867–1947). Supported and developed by US economist Milton Friedman (1912–), it forms the theoretical basis of monetarism.

recession fall in business activity lasting more than a few months, causing stagnation in a country's output. A serious recession is called a *slump*.

reserve currency a country's holding of internationally acceptable means of payment (major foreign currencies or gold); central banks also hold the ultimate reserve of money for their domestic banking sector. On the asset side of company balance sheets, undistributed profits are listed as reserves.

retail price index (RPI) indicator of variations in the cost of living.

savings unspent income, after deduction of tax. In economics a distinction is made between investment, involving the purchase of capital goods, such as buying a house, and saving (where capital goods are not directly purchased; for example, buying shares).

Say's law the 'law of markets' formulated by Jean-Baptiste Say (1767–1832) to the effect that supply creates its own demand and that resources can never be underused.

self-sufficiency situation where no trade takes place between an individual or a group and others. If an economy were self-sufficient, it would not export or import. In a modern economy, there is very little self-sufficiency because specialization enables individuals to enjoy a much higher standard of living then if they were self-sufficient.

slump in the business or trade cycle, the period of time when the economy is in depression, unemployment is very high, and national income is well below its full employment level. In the UK, the economy experienced a slump in the 1930s (the Great Depression), in 1980–81, and 1990–92.

social costs and benefits the costs and benefits to society as a whole that result from economic decisions. These include private costs (the financial cost of production incurred by firms) and benefits (the profits made by firms and the value to people of consuming goods and services) and external costs and benefits (affecting those not directly involved in production or consumption); pollution is one of the external costs.

Transport policy provides a clear example of the need to take external costs and benefits into account, where increases in the demand for private road transport generate considerable external costs in the form of pollution, road repairs, and extra costs to firms using transport networks and to medical services as a result of traffic congestion.

stagflation economic condition (experienced in Europe in the 1970s) in which rapid inflation is accompanied by stagnating, even declining, output and by increasing unemployment. Its cause is often sharp increases in costs of raw materials and/or labour.

stock exchange institution for the buying and selling of stocks and shares (securities). The world's largest stock exchanges are London, New York (Wall Street), and Tokyo. The oldest stock exchanges are Antwerp 1460, Hamburg 1558, Amsterdam 1602, New York 1790, and London 1801.

trade cycle or *business cycle* period of time that includes a peak and trough of economic activity, as measured by a country's national income. In Keynesian economics, one of the main roles of the government is to smooth out the peaks and troughs of the trade cycle by intervening in the economy, thus minimizing 'overheating' and 'stagnation'. This is accomplished by regulating interest rates and government spending.

Treasury bill in Britain, borrowing by the government in the form of a promissory note to repay the bearer 91 days from the date of issue; such bills represent a flexible and relatively cheap way for the government to borrow money for immediate needs.

unemployment lack of paid employment. The unemployed are usually defined as those out of work who are available for and actively seeking work. Unemployment is measured either as a total or as a percentage of those who are available for work, known as the working population or labour force. Periods of widespread unemployment in Europe and the USA in the 20th century include 1929–1930s and the years since the mid-1970s.

Unemployment is, generally, subdivided into *frictional unemployment*, the inevitable temporary unemployment of those moving from one job to another; *cyclical unemployment*, caused by a downswing in the business cycle; *seasonal unemployment*, in an area where there is high demand only during holiday periods, for example; and *structural unemployment*, where changing technology or other long-term change in the economy results in large numbers without work.

Many Third World countries suffer from severe unemployment and underemployment; the problem is exacerbated by rapid growth of population and lack of skills. In industrialized countries, unemployment has been a phenomenon since the mid-1970s, when the rise in world oil prices caused a downturn in economic activity, and greater use of high technology has improved output without the need for more jobs. The average unemployment rate in industrialized countries (the members of the OECD) was 8% in 1993 compared with only 3% in 1970, with some countries, such as Spain and Ireland, suffering over 15%. In the USA, the unemployment rate was 7% in 1993. In China, nearly a quarter of the urban labour force is unemployed.

unlisted securities market market for the shares of companies that are not included in the official list of the main market of the stock exchange. These lower-tier markets are less stringently regulated than the main markets and provide an intermediate step for new or small companies trying to reach the main markets.

visible trade international trade in goods. Trade in visibles is put on the current account of the balance of payments. Visible exports minus visible imports gives the balance of trade.

Institutions and Organizations

African Development Bank (ADB) international organization founded 1963 to promote and finance economic development across the continent. Members include 51 African and 25 non-African countries. Its headquarters are in Abidja'n, Cote d'Ivoire.

Arab Common Market organization providing for the abolition of customs duties on agricultural products, and reductions on other items, between the member states: Egypt, Iraq, Jordan, and Syria. It was founded 1965.

Arab Monetary Fund (AMF) money reserve established 1976 by 20 Arab states plus the Palestine Liberation Organization to provide a mechanism for promoting greater stability in exchange rates and to coordinate Arab economic and monetary policies. It operates mainly by regulating petrodollars within the Arab community to make member countries less dependent on the West for the handling of their surplus money. The fund's headquarters are in Abu Dhabi in the United Arab Emirates.

Asian Development Bank (ADB) bank founded 1966 to stimulate growth in Asia and the Far East by administering direct loans and technical assistance. Members include 30 countries within the region and 14 countries of W Europe and North America. The headquarters are in Manila, Philippines.

Bank for International Settlements (BIS) bank established 1930 to handle German reparations settlements from World War I. The BIS (based in Basel, Switzerland) is today a centre for economic and monetary research and assists cooperation of central banks. It also has important trustee duties. Its place in the international financial world was superseded from 1944 by the International Monetary Fund.

Bank of England UK central bank founded by act of Parliament 1694. It was entrusted with issuing bank notes 1844 and nationalized 1946. It is banker to the clearing banks and the UK government.

As the government's bank, it manages and arranges the financing of the public sector borrowing requirement and the national debt, implements monetary policy and exchange-rate policy by intervening in foreign-exchange markets, and supervises the UK banking system.

Central American Common Market CACM (*Mercado Común Centroamericana* MCCA) economic alliance established 1960 by El Salvador, Guatemala, Honduras (seceded 1970), and Nicaragua; Costa Rica joined 1962. Formed to encourage economic development and cooperation between the smaller Central American nations and to attract industrial capital, CACM failed to live up to early expectations: nationalist interests remained strong and by the mid-1980s political instability in the region and border conflicts between members were hindering its activities.

Colombo Plan plan for cooperative economic and social development in Asia and the Pacific, established 1950. The 26 member countries are Afghanistan, Australia, Bangladesh, Bhutan, Cambodia, Canada, Fiji, India, Indonesia, Iran, Japan, South Korea, Laos, Malaysia, Maldives, Myanmar (Burma), Nepal, New Zealand, Pakistan, Papua New Guinea, Philippines, Singapore, Sri Lanka, Thailand, UK, and USA. They meet annually to discuss economic and development plans such as irrigation, hydroelectric schemes, and technical training.

Comecon (acronym for *Council for Mutual Economic Assistance*, or *CMEA*) economic organization 1949–91, linking the USSR with Bulgaria, Czechoslovakia, Hungary, Poland, Romania, East Germany (1950–90), Mongolia (from 1962), Cuba (from 1972), and Vietnam (from 1978), with Yugoslavia as an associated member. Albania also belonged 1949–61. Its establishment was prompted by the Marshall Plan.

In Jan 1991 it was agreed that Comecon should be effectively disbanded and replaced by a new body, the Organization for International Economic Cooperation (OIEC), to be based probably in Budapest. The OIEC would act as a 'clearing house' for mutual E European trade, and would coordinate E European policy towards the European Community.

European Bank for Reconstruction and Development (EBRD) international organization founded 1990 to assist the economic reconstruction of E Europe by financing industrial and economic expansion, using loan guarantees, equity investment, and underwriting, to promote the transition to free-market capitalist systems. The bank was originally proposed by French president François Mitterand, and his former adviser Jacques Attali became its first president in 1990; he resigned in 1993. Its headquarters are in London.

Members include Albania, Armenia, Australia, Austria, Azerbaijan, Belarus, Belgium, Bulgaria, Canada, Cyprus, the Czech Republic, Denmark, Egypt, Estonia, Finland, France, Georgia, Germany, Greece, Hungary, Iceland, Ireland, Israel, Italy, Japan, Kazakhstan, South Korea, Kyrgyzstan, Latvia, Liechtenstein, Lithuania, Luxembourg, Malta, Mexico, Moldova, Morocco, the Netherlands, New Zealand, Norway, Poland, Portugal, Romania, Russia, Slovakia, Spain, Sweden, Switzerland, Tajikistan, Turkey, Turkmenistan, Ukraine, the UK, the USA, Uzbekistan, Yugoslavia, the Commission of the European Community, and the European Investment Bank.

European Free Trade Association (EFTA) organization established 1960 consisting of Austria, Finland, Iceland, Norway, Sweden, Switzerland, and (from 1991) Liechtenstein, previously a nonvoting associate member. There are no import duties between members.

In 1973 the EC signed agreements with EFTA members, setting up a free-trade area of over 300 million consumers. Trade between the two groups amounted to over half of total EFTA trade. A further pact signed 1991 between the EC and EFTA provided for a European Economic Area to be set up, allowing EFTA greater access to the EC market by ending many of the restrictions. The area would span 19 nations and 380 million people.

European Monetary System (EMS) attempt by the European Community to bring financial cooperation and monetary stability to Europe. It was established 1979 in the wake of the 1974 oil crisis, which brought growing economic disruption to European economies because of floating exchange rates. Central to the EMS is the *Exchange Rate Mechanism* (ERM), a voluntary system of semi-fixed exchange rates based on the European Currency Unit (ECU).

Each currency has a central rate with every other currency and with the ECU which is maintained within a band of fluctuation. The UK entered the ERM in Oct 1990, and left in Sept 1992, when doubts about the prospects for movement towards a single European currency caused speculators to sell the weaker ERM currencies, particularly sterling. This forced sterling out of its ERM band. Between Oct 1990 and Sept 1992, sterling's central rate with the Deutschmark was £1 = DM2.95 and the central rate with the ECU was £1 = 1.43 ECU.

In August 1993, the ERM band was allowed to fluctuate by 15% on either side for all ERM currencies except the Deutschmark and guilder; this move was necessitated by the weakening of many European currencies, including the French franc, against the Deutschmark. The widening of the ERM band put back the timetable for a single European currency, as one of the conditions for a single currency was that all of the ERM currencies had to fall within the original narrow band of 2.5%.

Federal Reserve System (the 'Fed') US central banking system and note-issuing authority, established 1913 to regulate the country's credit and monetary policy. The Fed consists of the 12 federal reserve banks, their 25 branches and other facilities throughout the country; it is headed by a board of governors in Washington DC, appointed by the president with Senate approval.

The Fed plays a major role in the formulation and implementation of US monetary policy. Inflation, interest rates, and overall economic activity can be governed by the Fed's decision to expand or restrict the supply of money to the economy.

General Agreement on Tariffs and Trade (GATT) organization within the United Nations founded 1948 with the aim of encouraging free trade between nations through low tariffs, abolitions of quotas, and curbs on subsidies.

The latest rounds of talks, begun in Uruguay in 1986, intended to cut restrictions on trade of manufactured goods, agriculture, textiles, and services. The Uruguay round was scheduled to end in 1990, but reached a deadlock in Dec 1990 after negotiators failed to agree on a plan to reduce farm subsidies. However, in Nov 1992, the EC negotiator agreed to a scaled-down reduction in agricultural subsidies, but without the support of the French government. Farmers in France and other EC countries demonstrated against these cuts.

Inter-American Development Bank (IADB) bank founded 1959, at the instigation of the Organization of American States, to finance economic and social development, particularly in the less wealthy regions of the Americas. Its membership includes the states of Central and Southern America, the Caribbean, and the USA, as well as Austria, Belgium, Canada, Denmark, Finland, France, Germany, Israel, Italy, Japan, the Netherlands, Spain, Sweden, Switzerland, and the UK. Its headquarters are in Washington DC.

International Monetary Fund (IMF) specialized agency of the United Nations, headquarters Washington DC, established under the 1944 Bretton Woods agreement and operational since 1947. It seeks to promote international monetary cooperation and the growth of world trade, and to smooth multilateral payment arrangements among member states. IMF standby loans are available to members in balance-of-payments difficulties (the amount being governed by the member's quota), usually on the basis that the country must agree to take certain corrective measures.

The Fund also operates other drawing facilities, including several designed to provide preferential credit to developing countries with liquidity problems. Having previously operated in US dollars linked to gold, since 1972 the IMF has used the special drawing right (SDR) as its standard unit of account, valued in terms of a weighted 'basket' of major currencies. Since the 1971 Smithsonian agreement permitting wider fluctuations from specified currency parities, IMF rules have been progressively adapted to the increasing prevalence of fully floating exchange rates.

LIFFE (acronym for *London International Financial Futures Exchange*) one of the exchanges in London where futures contracts are traded. It opened 1982 and began options trading in 1985.

Monopolies and Mergers Commission (MMC) UK government body re-established 1973 under the Fair Trading Act and, since 1980, embracing the Competition Act. Its role is to investigate and report when there is a risk of creating a monopoly by a company merger or takeover, or when a newspaper or newspaper assets are transferred. It also investigates companies, nationalized industries, or local authorities that are suspected of operating in a noncompetitive way. The US equivalent is the *Federal Trade Commission* (FTC).

Organization for Economic Cooperation and Development (OECD) international organization of 24 industrialized countries that provides a forum for discussion and coordination of member states' economic and social policies. Founded 1961, with its headquarters in Paris, the OECD superseded the Organization for European Economic Cooperation (established 1948 to implement the Marshall Plan) when the USA and Canada became members and its scope was extended to include development aid.

The OECD members are: Australia, Austria, Belgium, Canada, Denmark, Finland, France, Germany, Greece, Iceland, Ireland, Italy, Japan, Luxembourg, Netherlands, New Zealand, Norway, Portugal, Spain, Sweden, Switzerland, Turkey, UK, and USA.

Organization of Petroleum-Exporting Countries (OPEC) body established 1960 to coordinate price and supply policies of oil-producing states. Its concerted action in raising prices in the 1970s triggered worldwide recession but also lessened demand so that its influence was reduced by the mid-1980s. OPEC members in 1991 were: Algeria, Ecuador, Gabon, Indonesia, Iran, Iraq, Kuwait, Libya, Nigeria, Qatar, Saudi Arabia, the United Arab Emirates, and Venezuela.

OPEC's importance in the world market was reflected in its ability to implement oil price increases from $3 a barrel 1973 to $30 a barrel 1980. In the 1980s, OPEC's dominant position was undermined by reduced demand for oil in industrialized countries, increased non-OPEC oil supplies, and production of alternative energy. These factors contributed to the dramatic fall in world oil prices to $10 a barrel in July 1986 from $28 at the beginning of the year. OPEC's efforts to stabilize oil prices through mandatory reduced production have been resisted by various members.

Securities and Exchange Commission (*SEC*) official US agency created 1934 to ensure full disclosure to the investing public and protection against malpractice in the securities (stocks and bonds) and financial markets (such as insider trading). The SEC is also an impartial adviser to federal courts in bankruptcy cases involving publicly held corporations. Since 1988, the SEC has been authorized to pay bounties for information leading to conviction of inside traders.

Securities and Investment Board UK body with the overall responsibility for policing financial dealings in the City of London. Introduced in 1987 following the deregulation process of the so-called Big Bang, it acts as an umbrella organization to such self-regulating bodies as the Stock Exchange.

World Bank popular name for the *International Bank for Reconstruction and Development* specialized agency of the United Nations that borrows in the commercial market and lends on commercial terms. It was established 1945 under the 1944 Bretton Woods agreement, which also created the International Monetary Fund. The *International Development Association* is an arm of the World Bank.

The World Bank now earns almost as much money from interest and loan repayments as it hands out in new loans every year. Over 60% of the bank's loans go to suppliers outside the borrower countries for such things as consultancy services, oil, and machinery. Control of the bank is vested in a board of executives representing national governments, whose votes are apportioned according to the amount they have funded the bank. Thus the USA has nearly 20% of the vote and always appoints the board's president.

In 1992 the World Bank made a net transfer of $49.7 million to developing countries.

Nobel Prize for Economics

1969 Ragnar Frisch (Norway) and Jan Tinbergen (Netherlands): work in econometrics
1970 Paul A Samuelson (USA): scientific analysis of economic theory
1971 Simon Kuznets (USA): research on the economic growth of nations
1972 Sir John Hicks (UK) and Kenneth J Arrow (USA): contributions to general economic equilibrium theory
1973 Wassily Leontief (USA): work on input analysis
1974 Gunnar Myrdal (Sweden) and Friedrich von Hayek (UK): analysis of the interdependence of economic, social, and institutional phenomena
1975 Leonid V Kantorovich (Russia) and Tjalling C Koopmans (USA): contributions to the theory of optimum allocation of resources
1976 Milton Friedman (USA): consumption analysis, monetary theory and economic stabilization
1977 Bertil Ohlin (Sweden) and James Meade (UK): contributions to theory of international trade
1978 Herbert A Simon (USA): decision-making processes in economic organization
1979 W Arthur Lewis (UK) and Theodore W Schultz (USA): analysis of economic processes in developing nations
1980 Lawrence R Klein (USA): development and analysis of empirical models of business fluctuations
1981 James Tobin (USA): empirical macro economic theories
1982 George Stigler (USA): work on the economic effects of governmental regulation
1983 Gerard Debrau (USA): mathematical proof of supply and demand theory
1984 Sir Richard Stone (UK): development of a national income accounting system
1985 Franco Modigliani (USA): analysis of household savings and financial markets
1986 James McGill Buchanan (USA): political theories advocating limited government role in the economy
1987 Robert M Solow (USA): contributions to the theory of economic growth
1988 Maurice Allais (France): contributions to the theory of markets and efficient use of resources
1989 Trygve Haavelmo (Norway): testing fundamental econometric theories
1990 Harry Markowitz, Merton Miller and William Sharpe (USA): pioneering theories on managing investment portfolios and corporate finances
1991 Ronald H Coase (USA): work on value and social problems of companies
1992 Gary S Becker (USA): work linking economic theory to aspects of human behaviour, drawing on other social sciences
1993 Robert Fogel and Douglass North (USA): creating a new method of studying economic history (cliometrics)

World currency exchange rates

Country	Currency	£ sterling	Country	Currency	£ sterling
Afghanistan	afgháni	1576.05	Falkland Islands	Falkland pound	2.25
Albania	lek	165.11	Fiji Islands	Fiji dollar	2.28
Algeria	dinar	29.73	Finland	markka	8.69
Andorra	French franc	8.92	French Pacific	CFP Franc	162.12
	Spanish peseta	209.54	Islands		
Angola	kwanza	6004.30	France	French franc	8.92
Antigua	East Caribbean dollar	4.05	French Guiana	French franc	8.92
Argentina	austral	1.50	Gabon	CFA franc	445.83
Aruba	florin	2.69	Gambia	dalasi	13.57
Australia	Australian dollar	2.20	Germany	Deutschmark	2.56
Austria	schilling	18.06	Ghana	cedi	975.65
Azores	port escudo	260.00	Gibraltar	Gibraltar pound	2.25
Bahamas	Bahamian dollar	1.50	Greece	drachma	358.36
Bahrain	Bahrain dinar	0.57	Greenland	Danish krone	10.18
Bangladesh	taka	59.53	Grenada	East Caribbean dollar	4.05
Barbados	Barbados dollar	3.02	Guadaloupe	local franc	8.92
Belgium	Belgian franc	54.26	Guam	US dollar	1.50
Belize	Belize dollar	3.00	Guatemala	quetzal	8.61
Benin	CFA franc	445.83	Guinea	Guinea franc	1219.25
Bermuda	Bermudian dollar	1.50	Guinea-Bissau	Guinea-Bissau peso	7505.00
Bhutan	ngultrum	47.10	Guyana	Guyanese dollar	189.13
Bolivia	boliviano	6.45	Haiti	gourde	18.01
Botswana	pula	3.72	Honduras	lempira	10.24
Bouvet Island	Norwegian krone	11.10	Hong Kong	Hong Kong dollar	11.64
Brazil	cruzeiro	112.39	Hungary	forint	143.60
Brunei	Brunei dollar	2.42	Iceland	Icelandic krona	107.89
Bulgaria	lev	40.96	India	Indian rupee	47.10
Burkina Faso	CFA franc	445.83	Indonesia	rupiah	3143.39
Burundi	Burundi franc	349.23	Iran	Iranian riyal	2377.58
Cambodia	Cambodian riel	5253.50	Iraq	Iraqi dinar	0.47
Cameroon	CFA franc	445.83	Irish Republic	punt	2.10
Canada	Canadian dollar	1.94	Israel	shekel	4.19
Cape Verde	Cape Verde escudo	111.37	Italy	lira	2394.09
Cayman Islands	Cayman Island dollar	1.28	Jamaica	Jamaican dollar	36.02
Central African	CFA franc	445.83	Japan	yen	156.73
Republic			Jordan	Jordanian dinar	1.04
Chad	CFA franc	445.83	Kenya	Kenyan shilling	98.43
Chile	Chilean peso (m)	609.51	Kiribati	Australian dollar	2.20
	Chilean peso (o)	643.04	Korea, North	won	3.23
China	Renminbi yuan	8.65	Korea, South	won	1210.56
Colombia	Colombian peso	1203.53	Kuwait	Kuwaiti dinar	0.45
Commonwealth	rouble	1478.48	Laos	new kip	1080.72
of Ind States			Lebanon	Lebanese pound	2593.72
Comoros	CFA franc	445.83	Lesotho	maluti	5.06
Congo	CFA franc	445.83	Liberia	Liberian dollar	1.50
Costa Rica	colón	213.52	Libya	Libyan dinar	0.45
Côte d'Ivoire	CFA franc	445.83	Liechtenstein	Swiss franc	2.25
Cuba	Cuban peso	1.98	Lithuania	Lita	6.00
Cyprus	Cyprus pound	2.90	Luxembourg	Luxembourg franc	54.26
Czech Republic	koruna	44.73	Macao	pataca	12.02
Denmark	Danish kroner	10.18	Madagascar	Malagasy franc	2922.82
Djibouti	Djibouti franc	267.42	Malawi	kwacha	6.66
Dominica	East Caribbean dollar	4.05	Malaysia	ringgit	3.83
Dominican	Dominican peso	19.51	Maldive Islands	rufiya	17.97
Republic			Mali Republic	CFA franc	445.83
Ecuador	sucre(d)	2919.44	Malta	Maltese lira	3.83
	sucre(o)	2776.85	Martinique	local franc	8.92
Egypt	Egyptian pound	5.01	Mauritania	ougiya	170.83
El Salvador	colón	13.11	Mauritius	Mauritius rupee	27.27
Equatorial Guinea	CFA franc	445.83	Mexico	Mexican peso	12.17
Estonia	kroon	20.40	Monaco	French franc	8.92
Ethiopia	Ethiopian birr	4.50	Mongolia	tugrik	600.40
Faeroe Islands	Danish kroner	10.18	Montserrat	East Caribbean dollar	4.05

World currency exchange rates *(cont.)*

Country	Currency	£ sterling	Country	Currency	£ sterling
Morocco	dirham	14.03	South Africa	rand(c)	5.06
Mozambique	metical	5905.90		rand(g)	6.96
Myanmar	kyat	9.21	Spain	peseta	209.54
Namibia	South African rand	5.06	Sri Lanka	Sri Lanka rupee	73.17
Nauru Island	Australian dollar	2.20	Sudan Republic	Sudanese pound	195.13
Nepal	Nepalese rupee	68.84		diner	19.51
Netherlands	guilder	2.88	Surinam	Surinam guilder	2.68
Netherlands Antilles	Antillian guilder	2.69	Swaziland	lilangeni	5.06
			Sweden	krona	12.04
New Zealand	New Zealand dollar	2.72	Switzerland	Swiss franc	2.25
Nicaragua	gold cordoba	9.26	Syria	Syrian pound	32.27
Niger Republic	CFA franc	445.83	Taiwan	New Taiwan dollar	40.42
Nigeria	naira	37.52	Tanzania	Tanzanian shilling	688.15
Norway	Norwegian krone	11.10	Thailand	baht	37.82
Oman	Omani rial	0.58	Togo Republic	CFA franc	445.83
Pakistan	Pakistan rupee	44.73	Tonga Islands	pa'anga	2.20
Panama	balboa	1.50	Trinidad and Tobago	Trinidad and Tobago dollar	8.31
Papua New Guinea	kina	1.46			
Paraguay	guaraní	2619.24	Tunisia	Tunisian dinar	1.52
Peru	new sol	3.09	Turkey	Turkish lira	17455.34
Philippines	peso	41.88	Turks and Caicos Islands	US dollar	1.50
Pitcairn Islands	New Zealand dollar	2.72			
Poland	zloty	27403.76	Tuvalu	Australian dollar	2.20
Portugal	escudo	260.00	Uganda	new shilling	1794.16
Puerto Rico	US dollar	1.50	Ukraine	karbovanets	8645.76
Qatar	Qatar riyal	5.51	United Arab Emirates	UAE dirham	5.51
Réunion Islands	French franc	8.92			
Romania	leu	1205.30	United Kingdom	pound sterling	1
Rwanda	Rwandan franc	173.01	United States	US dollar	1.50
St Christopher	East Caribbean dollar	4.05	Uruguay	nuevo peso	6.00
St Helena	pound sterling	2.25			
St Lucia	East Caribbean dollar	4.05	Vanuatu	vatu	181.62
St Pierre	French franc	8.92	Vatican City State	lira	2394.09
St Vincent	East Caribbean dollar	4.05	Venezuela	bolívar	139.22
San Marino	Italian lira	2394.09	Vietnam	dong	15933.11
São Tomé e Principe	dobra	360.24	Virgin Islands, British	US dollar	1.50
Saudi Arabia	Saudi riyal	5.63	Virgin Islands, US	US dollar	1.50
Senegal	CFA franc	445.83	Western Samoa	taia	3.86
Seychelles	Seychelles rupee	7.83	Yemen, Republic of	Yemini dinar	0.69
Sierra Leone	leone	825.55		Yemini riyal	24.77
Singapore	dollar	2.42	Yugoslavia	New Yugoslav dinar	20.41
Solomon Islands	Solomon Island dollar	4.77	Zaire Republic	zaire	6906101.00
Somali Republic	Somali shilling	3932.62	Zambia	kwacha	108.35
			Zimbabwe	Zimbabwe dollar	9.94

Abbreviations: (c) commercial rate; (d) controlled rate; (g) financial rate; (m) market rate; (o) official rate.

Data supplied by Bank of America, Economics Department, London Trading Centre (as of August 1993)

THE ARTS

ARCHITECTURE

History

Architecture is the art of designing structures. The term covers the design of the visual appearance of structures; their internal arrangements of space; selection of external and internal building materials; design or selection of natural and artificial lighting systems, as well as mechanical, electrical, and plumbing systems; and design or selection of decorations and furnishings. Architectural style may emerge from evolution of techniques and styles particular to a culture in a given time period with or without identifiable individuals as architects, or may be attributed to specific individuals or groups of architects working together on a project.

early architecture little remains of the earliest forms of architecture, but archaeologists have examined remains of prehistoric sites and documented Stone Age villages of wooden post buildings with above-ground construction of organic materials such as mud or wattle and daub from the Upper Paleolithic, Mesolithic, and Neolithic periods in Asia, the Middle East, Europe, and the Americas. More extensive remains of stone-built structures have given clues to later Neolithic farming communities as well as habitations, storehouses, and religious and civic structures of early civilizations. The best documented are those of ancient Egypt, where exhaustive work in the 19th and 20th centuries revealed much about ordinary buildings, the monumental structures such as the pyramid tombs near modern Cairo, and the temple and tomb complexes concentrated at Luxor and Thebes.

Classical this architecture evolved its basic forms in Greece between the 16th and 2nd centuries BC. Its hallmark characteristic is its post-and-lintel construction of temples and public structures, classified into the Doric, Ionic, and Corinthian orders, defined by simple, scrolled, and acanthus-leaf capitals for support columns, respectively. The Romans copied and expanded on Greek Classical forms, notably introducing bricks and concrete and inventing the vault, arch, and dome for public buildings and aqueducts.

Byzantine this architecture developed primarily in the E Roman Empire from the 4th century, with its centre at Byzantium (later named Constantinople, now Istanbul). Its most notable feature was construction of churches, some very large, based on the Greek cross plan (Hagia Sophia, Istanbul; St Mark's, Venice), with formalized painted and mosaic decoration.

Islamic this architecture developed from the 8th century, when the Islamic religion spread from its centre in the Middle East west to Spain and E to China and parts of the Philippine Islands. Notable features are the development of the tower with dome and the pointed arch. Islamic architecture, chiefly through Spanish examples such as the Great Mosque at Córdoba and the Alhambra in Granada, profoundly influenced Christian church architecture – for example, by adoption of the pointed arch into the Gothic arch.

Romanesque this architecture is associated with Western European Christianity from the 8th to the 12th centuries. It is marked by churches with massive walls for structural integrity, rounded arches, small windows, and resulting dark volumes of interior space. In England this style is generally referred to as Norman architecture (Durham Cathedral). The style enjoyed a renewal of interest in Europe and the USA in the late 19th and early 20th centuries.

Gothic this architecture emerged out of Romanesque, since the pointed arch and flying buttress made it possible to change from thick supporting walls to lighter curtain walls with extensive expansion of window areas (and stained-glass artwork) and resulting increases in interior light. Gothic architecture was developed particularly in France from the 12th to 16th centuries. The style is divided into Early Gothic (Sens Cathedral), High Gothic (Chartres Cathedral), and Late or Flamboyant Gothic. In England the corresponding divisions are Early English (Salisbury Cathedral), Decorated (Wells Cathedral), and Perpendicular (Kings College Chapel, Cambridge). Gothic was also developed extensively in Germany and neighbouring countries and in Italy.

Renaissance this architecture of 15th- and 16th-century Europe saw the rebirth of Classical form and motifs in the Italian Neo-Classical movement. A major source of inspiration was the work of the 1st-century BC Roman engineer Vitruvius for Palladio, Alberti, Brunelleschi, Bramante, and Michelangelo – the major Renaissance architects. The Palladian style was extensively used later in England by Inigo Jones and the Classical idiom by Christopher Wren. Classical or Neo-Classical style and its elements have been popular in the USA from the 18th century, as evidenced in much of the civic and commercial architecture since the time of the early republic (the US Capitol and Supreme Court buildings in Washington; many state capitols).

Baroque European architecture of the 17th and 18th centuries elaborated on Classical models with exuberant and extravagant decoration. In large-scale public buildings, the style is best seen in the innovative work of Giovanni Bernini and Francesco Borromini in Italy and later by John Vanbrugh, Nicholas Hawksmoor, and Christopher Wren in England. There were numerous practitioners in France and the German-speaking countries; Vienna is rich in Baroque work.

Rococo this architecture extends the Baroque style with an even greater extravagance of design motifs, using a new lightness of detail and naturalistic elements, such as shells, flowers, and trees.

Neo-Classical European architecture of the 18th and 19th centuries again focused on the more severe Classical idiom (inspired by archaeological finds), producing, for example, the large-scale rebuilding of London by Robert Adam and John Nash and later of Paris by Georges Haussman.

Neo-Gothic the later part of the 19th century saw a Gothic revival in Europe and the USA, most evident in churches and public buildings (such as the Houses of Parliament in London, designed by Charles Barry).

Art Nouveau was a new movement arising at the end of the 19th century, characterized by sinuous, flowing shapes, informal room plans, and particular attention to interior as well as architectural design. The style is best seen in England in the work of Charles Rennie Mackintosh (Glasgow Art School), in Paris at the entrances to the Metro and in Spain by the work of Antonio Gaudí.

Modernism an increasing emphasis on rationalism and reduction of ornament led to Modernism (also known as Functionalism or the International Style) in the 1930s. Seeking to exclude everything that did not have a purpose, the latest technological advances in glass, steel, and concrete were used to full advantage. Major architects included Frank Lloyd Wright, Mies van der Rohe, Le Corbusier, and Alvar Aalto.

Brutalism architectural style of the 1950s and 1960s that evolved from the work of Le Corbusier and Mies van der Rohe. It stressed functionalism and honesty to materials; steel and concrete were favoured. In the UK the style was developed by Alison and Peter Smithson.

Post-Modernism in the 1980s a Post-Modernist movement emerged, which split into two camps:

High Tech, represented in Britain by architects such as Norman Foster, Richard Rogers, and James Stirling (Hong Kong and Shanghai Bank, Hong Kong, Lloyd's, London, *Staatsgalerie Stuttgart* respectively); and architects using elements from the architecture of previous times, either following certain tenets of the Classical orders – Neo-Classicism yet again – such as Quinlan Terry, or using such elements at whim, such as Michael Graves.

Deconstruction a style that fragments forms and space by taking the usual building elements of floors, walls, and ceilings and sliding them apart to create a sense of disorientation and movement. Its proponents include Zaha Hadid (1950–) in the UK, Frank Gehry (1929–) and Peter Eisenman (1932–) in the USA, and Co-op Himmelbau in Austria.

Terms

arch curved structure of masonry that supports the weight of material over an open space, as in a bridge or doorway. It originally consisted of several wedge-shaped stones supported by their mutual pressure. The term is also applied to any curved structure that is an arch in form only.

atrium an inner, open courtyard. Originally the central court or main room of an ancient Roman house, open to the sky, often with a shallow pool to catch water.

bailey open space or court of a stone-built castle.

basilica type of Roman public building; a large roofed hall flanked by columns, generally with an aisle on each side, used for judicial or other public business. The earliest known basilica, at Pompeii, dates from the 2nd century BC. This architectural form was adopted by the early Christians for their churches.

buttress reinforcement in brick or masonry, built against a wall to give it strength. A *flying buttress* is an arc transmitting the force of the wall to be supported to an outer buttress, common in Gothic architecture.

cantilever beam or structure that is fixed at one end only, though it may be supported at some point along its length; for example, a diving board. The cantilever principle, widely used in construction engineering, eliminates the need for a second main support at the free end of the beam, allowing for more elegant structures and reducing the amount of materials required. Many large-span bridges have been built on the cantilever principle.

caryatid building support or pillar in the shape of a woman, the name deriving from the Karyatides, who were priestesses at the temple of Artemis at Karyai; the male equivalent is a *telamon* or *atlas*.

castle private fortress of a king or noble during the Middle Ages. At first a building on a mound surrounded by a wooden fence, this was later copied in stone. The earliest castles in Britain were built following the Norman Conquest, and the art of castle building reached a peak in the 13th century. By the 15th century, the need for castles for domestic defence had largely disappeared, and the advent of gunpowder made them largely useless against attack.

cathedral Christian church containing the throne of a bishop or archbishop, which is usually situated on the south side of the choir. There are cathedrals in most of the chief cities of Europe; UK cathedrals include Canterbury Cathedral (spanning the Norman to Perpendicular periods), Exeter Cathedral (13th-century Gothic), and Coventry Cathedral (rebuilt after World War II, consecrated 1962).

château term originally applied to a French medieval castle, but now used to describe a country house or important residence in France. The château was first used as a domestic building in the late 15th century; by the reign of Louis XIII (1610–43) fortifications such as moats and keeps were no longer used for defensive purposes, but merely as decorative features. The Loire valley contains some fine examples of châteaux.

church building designed as a Christian place of worship. Churches were first built in the 3rd century, when persecution ceased under the Holy Roman emperor Constantine. The original church design was based on the Roman basilica, with a central nave, aisles either side, and an apse at one end.

cloister a covered walk within a convent or monastery, often opening onto a courtyard.

colonnade row of columns supporting arches or an entablature.

column a structure, round or polygonal in plan, erected vertically as a support for some part of a building. Cretan paintings reveal the existence of wooden columns in Aegean architecture, about 1500 BC. The Hittites, Assyrians, and Egyptians also used wooden columns, and they are a feature of the monumental architecture of China and Japan. In Classical architecture there are five principal types (or orders) of column: Doric, Ionic, Corinthian, Tuscan, and Composite.

community architecture movement enabling people to work directly with architects in the design and building of their own homes and neighbourhoods. It is an approach strongly encouraged by the Prince of Wales.

conservation, architectural attempts to maintain the character of buildings and historical areas. In England this is subject to a growing body of legislation that has designated more listed buildings. There are now over 6,000 conservation areas throughout England alone.

curtain wall in buildings, a light-weight wall of glass or aluminium that is not load-bearing and is hung from a metal frame rather than built up from the ground like a brick wall. Curtain walls are typically used in high-rise blocks.

garden city in the UK, a town built in a rural area and designed to combine town and country advantages, with its own industries, controlled developments, private and public gardens, and cultural centre. The idea was proposed by Sir Ebenezer Howard (1850–1928), who in 1899 founded the Garden City Association, which established the first garden city, Letchworth (in Hertfordshire).

gargoyle spout projecting from the roof gutter of a building with the purpose of directing water away from the wall. The term is usually applied to the ornamental forms found in Gothic architecture; these were carved in stone in the form of fantastic animals, angels, or human heads.

geodesic dome spherical dome whose surface is formed by an arrangement of short rods arranged in triangles. The rods lie on geodesics (the shortest lines joining two points on a curved surface). This dome allows large spaces to be enclosed using the minimum of materials, and was patented by US engineer Buckminster Fuller 1954.

green belt area surrounding a large city, officially designated not to be built on but preserved where possible as open space (for agricultural and recreational use). In the UK the first green belts were established from 1938 around conurbations such as London in order to prevent urban sprawl. New towns were set up to take the overspill population.

ha-ha in landscape gardening, a sunken boundary wall permitting an unobstructed view beyond a garden; a device much used by Capability Brown in the 18th century.

listed building in Britain, a building officially recognized as having historical or architectural interest and therefore legally protected from alteration or demolition. In England the listing is drawn up by the Secretary of State for the Environment under the advice of the English Heritage organization, which provides various resources for architectural conservation.

mezzanine architectural term for a storey with a lower ceiling placed between two main storeys, usually between the ground and first floors of a building.

minaret slender turret or tower attached to a Muslim mosque or to buildings designed in that style. It has one or more balconies, from which the *muezzin* calls the people to prayer five times a day.

misericord or *miserere* in church architecture, a projection on the underside of a hinged seat of the choir stalls, used as a rest for a priest when standing during long services. Misericords are often decorated with carvings.

obelisk tall, tapering column of stone, much used in ancient Egyptian and Roman architecture. Examples are Cleopatra's Needles 1475 BC, one of which is in London, the other in New York.

order in classical architecture, the column (including capital, shaft, and base) and the entablature, considered as an architectural whole. The five orders are Doric, Ionic, Corinthian, Tuscan, and Composite.

pantheon originally a temple for worshipping all the gods, such as that in ancient Rome, rebuilt by the emperor Hadrian and still used as a church. In more recent times, the name has been used for a building where famous people are buried (Panthéon, Paris).

pediment the triangular part crowning the fronts of buildings in Classical styles. The pediment was a distinctive feature of Greek temples.

peristyle range of columns surrounding a building or open courtyard.

piano nobile the main floor of a house, containing the main reception room.

portico porch with a pediment and columns.

pyramid four-sided building with triangular sides used in ancient Egypt to enclose a royal tomb; for example, the Great Pyramid of Khufu/Cheops at Gîza, near Cairo, 230 m/755 ft square and 147 m/481 ft high. In Babylon and Assyria broadly stepped pyramids (ziggurats) were used as the base for a shrine to a god: the Tower of Babel was probably one of these.

satellite town new town planned and built to serve a particular local industry, or as a dormitory or overspill town for people who work in a nearby metropolis. New towns in Britain include Port Sunlight near Birkenhead (Cheshire), built to house workers at Lever Brothers soap factories. More recent examples include Welwyn Garden City (1948), Cumbernauld (1955), and Milton Keynes (1967).

sick building syndrome malaise diagnosed in the early 1980s among office workers and thought to be caused by such pollutants as formaldehyde (from furniture and insulating materials), benzene (from paint), and the solvent trichloroethene, concentrated in air-conditioned buildings. Symptoms include headache, sore throat, tiredness, colds, and flu. Studies have found that it can cause a 40% drop in productivity and a 30% rise in absenteeism.

skyscraper building so tall that it appears to 'scrape the sky', developed 1868 in New York, USA, where land prices were high and the geology allowed such methods of construction. Skyscrapers are now found in cities throughout the world. The world's tallest free-standing structure is the CN (Canadian National) Tower, Toronto, 555 m/1,821 ft.

town planning the design of buildings or groups of buildings in a physical and social context, concentrating on the relationship between various buildings and their environment, as well as on their uses.

urban renewal the adaptation of existing buildings and neighbourhoods in towns and cities to meet changes in economic, social, and environmental requirements, rather than demolishing them. Since the early 1970s, when it became less expensive to renew than to build, urban renewal has increased.

vault arched ceiling or roof built mainly of stone or bricks.

Biographies

Aalto Alvar 1898–1976. Finnish architect and designer. One of Finland's first Modernists, he had a unique architectural style, characterized by asymmetry, curved walls, and contrast of natural materials. His buildings include the Hall of Residence at the Massachusetts Institute of Technology, Cambridge, Massachusetts, 1947–49; Technical High School, Otaniemi, 1962–65; and Finlandia Hall, Helsinki, 1972. He invented a new form of laminated bent-plywood furniture 1932 and won many design awards for household and industrial items.

Adam family of Scottish architects and designers. *William Adam* (1689–1748) was the leading Scottish architect of his day, and his son *Robert Adam* (1728–1792) is considered one of the greatest British architects of the late 18th century, who transformed the prevailing Palladian fashion in architecture to a Neo-Classical style. He designed interiors for many great country houses and earned a considerable reputation as a furniture designer.

Alberti Leon Battista 1404–1472. Italian Renaissance architect and theorist who recognized the principles of Classical architecture and their modification for Renaissance practice in *On Architecture* 1452.

Archigram London-based group of English architects in the 1960s whose work was experimental and polemical; architecture was to be technological and flexible. The group included Peter Cook (1936–), Dennis Crompton (1935–), David Greene (1937–), Ron Herron (1930–), and Mike Webb (1937–).

Barry Charles 1795–1860. English architect of the Neo-Gothic Houses of Parliament at Westminster, London, 1840–60, in collaboration with Augustus Pugin.

Berlage Hendrikus 1856–1934. Dutch architect of the Amsterdam Stock Exchange 1897–1903. His individualist style marked a move away from 19th-century historicism and towards Dutch Expressionism.

Bernini Giovanni Lorenzo 1598–1680. Italian sculptor, architect, and painter, a leading figure in the development of the Baroque style. His work in Rome includes the colonnaded piazza in front of St Peter's Basilica (1656), fountains (as in the Piazza Navona), and papal monuments. His sculpture includes *The*

Ecstasy of St Theresa 1645–52 (Sta Maria della Vittoria, Rome) and numerous portrait busts.

Borromini Francesco 1599–1667. Italian Baroque architect, one of the two most important (with Bernini, his main rival) in 17th-century Rome. Whereas Bernini designed in a florid, expansive style, his pupil Borromini developed a highly idiosyncratic and austere use of the Classical language of architecture. His genius may be seen in the cathedrals of San Carlo 1641 and San Ivo 1660, and the oratorio of St Filippo Neri 1650.

Bramante Donato c. 1444–1514. Italian Renaissance architect and artist. Inspired by Classical designs, he was employed by Pope Julius II in rebuilding part of the Vatican and St Peter's in Rome.

Breuer Marcel 1902–1981. Hungarian-born architect and designer who studied and taught at the Bauhaus school in Germany. His tubular steel chair 1925 was the first of its kind. He moved to England, then to the USA, where he was in partnership with Walter Gropius 1937–40. His buildings show an affinity with natural materials; the best known is the Bijenkorf, Rotterdam, the Netherlands 1953.

Brunelleschi Filippo 1377–1446. Italian Renaissance architect. One of the earliest and greatest Renaissance architects, he pioneered the scientific use of perspective. He was responsible for the construction of the dome of Florence Cathedral (completed 1438), a feat deemed impossible by many of his contemporaries.

Burlington Richard Boyle, 3rd Earl of Burlington 1694–1753. British architectural patron and architect; one of the premier exponents of the Palladian style in Britain. His buildings, such as Chiswick House, London, 1725–29, are characterized by absolute adherence to the Classical rules. His major protégé was William Kent.

Butterfield William 1814–1900. English Gothic Revival architect. His work is characterized by vigorous, aggressive forms and multicoloured striped and patterned brickwork, as in the church of All Saints, Margaret Street, London 1850–59, and Keble College, Oxford 1867–83.

Casson Hugh 1910– . British architect, professor at the Royal College of Art 1953–75, and president of the Royal Academy 1976–84. His books include *Victorian Architecture* 1948. He was director of architecture for the Festival of Britain 1948–51.

Chambers William 1726–1796. British architect and popularizer of Chinese influence (for example, the pagoda in Kew Gardens, London) and designer of Somerset House, London.

Coates Nigel 1949– . British architect. While teaching at the Architectural Association in London in the early 1980s, Coates and a group of students founded NATO (Narrative Architecture Today) and produced an influential series of manifestos and drawings on the theme of the imaginative regeneration of derelict areas of London.

Eyck Aldo van 1918– . Dutch architect with a strong commitment to social architecture. His works include an Orphans' Home 1957–60, and a refuge for single mothers, Mothers' House 1978; both are in Amsterdam.

Farrell Terry 1938– . British architect working in a Post-Modern idiom, largely for corporate clients seeking an alternative to the rigours of High Tech or Modernist office blocks. His Embankment Place scheme 1991 sits theatrically on top of Charing Cross station in Westminster, London, and has been likened to a giant jukebox.

Foster Norman 1935– . English architect of the high-tech school. His buildings include the Willis Faber office, Ipswich, 1978, the Sainsbury Centre for Visual Arts at the University of East Anglia 1974 (opened 1978), the headquarters of the Hong Kong and Shanghai Bank, Hong Kong, 1986, and Stansted Airport, Essex, 1991.

Fuller (Richard) Buckminster 1895–1983. US architect, engineer, and futurist social philosopher who embarked on an unorthodox career in an attempt to maximize energy resources through improved technology. In 1947 he invented the lightweight geodesic dome, a half-sphere of triangular components independent of buttress or vault.

Gaudí Antonio 1852–1926. Spanish architect distinguished for his flamboyant Art Nouveau style. Gaudí worked almost exclusively in Barcelona, designing both domestic and industrial buildings. He introduced colour, unusual materials, and audacious technical innovations. His spectacular Church of the Holy Family, Barcelona, begun 1883, is still under construction.

Gehry Frank 1929– . US architect, based in Los Angeles. His architecture approaches abstract art in its use of collage and montage techniques.

Gibbs James 1682–1754. Scottish Neo-Classical architect whose works include St Martin-in-the-Fields, London, 1722–26, Radcliffe Camera, Oxford, 1737–49, and Bank Hall, Warrington, Cheshire, 1750.

Gilbert Cass 1859–1934. US architect, major developer of the skyscraper. His designed the Woolworth Building, New York, 1913, the highest building in America (868 ft/265 m) when built and famous for its use of Gothic decorative detail.

Grimshaw Nicholas 1939– . English architect whose work has developed along distinctly High Tech lines, diverging sharply from that of his former partner, Terry Farrell. His Financial Times printing works, London 1988, is an uncompromising industrial building, exposing machinery to view through a glass outer wall. He created the British Pavilion for Expo'92 in Seville in similar vein, but also addressed problems of climatic control, incorporating a huge wall of water in its façade and sail-like mechanisms on the roof.

Gropius Walter Adolf 1883–1969. German architect who lived in the USA from 1937. He was an early exponent of the international modern style defined by glass curtain walls, cubic blocks, and unsupported corners – for example, the model factory and office building at the 1914 Cologne Werkbund exhibition. A founder-director of the Bauhaus school in Weimar 1919–28, he advocated teamwork in design and artistic standards in industrial production.

Haussmann Georges Eugène, Baron Haussmann 1809–1891. French administrator who replanned medieval Paris 1853–70 to achieve the current city plan, with wide boulevards and parks. The cost of his scheme and his authoritarianism caused opposition, and he was made to resign.

Hawksmoor Nicholas 1661–1736. English architect, assistant to Christopher Wren in designing London churches and St Paul's Cathedral; joint architect with John Vanbrugh of Castle Howard and Blenheim Palace. His genius is displayed in a quirky and uncompromising style incorporating elements from both Gothic and Classical sources. The original west towers of Westminster Abbey, long attributed to Wren, were designed by Hawksmoor.

Howard Ebenezer 1850–1928. English town planner and founder of the ideal of the garden city, through his book *Tomorrow* 1898 (republished as *Garden Cities of Tomorrow* 1902).

Isozaki Arata 1931– . Japanese architect. One of Kenzo Tange's team 1954–63, his Post-Modernist works include Ochanomizu Square, Tokyo (retaining the existing facades), and buildings for the 1992 Barcelona Olympics.

Jellicoe Geoffrey 1900– . English architect, landscape architect, and historian. His contribution to 20th-century thinking on landscapes and gardens has been mainly through his writings, notably *Landscape of Man* 1975. However, he has also made an impact as a designer, working in a comtemplative and poetic vein and frequently incorporating water and sculptures. Representative of his work are the Kennedy Memorial at Runnymede, Berkshire 1965, and the gardens at Sutton Place, Sussex, 1980–84.

Jencks Charles 1939– . US architectural theorist and furniture designer. He coined the term 'Post-Modern architecture' and wrote *The Language of Post-Modern Architecture* 1984.

Johnson Philip (Cortelyou) 1906– . US architect who coined the term 'international style'. Originally designing in the style of Mies van der Rohe, he later became an exponent of Post-Modernism. He designed the giant AT&T building in New York 1978, a pink skyscraper with a Chippendale-style cabinet top. He was director of architecture and design at the Museum of Modern Art, New York 1932–54, where he built the annexe and sculpture court.

Jones Inigo 1573–c. 1652. English classical architect. Born in London, he studied in Italy and was influenced by the works of Palladio. He was employed by James I to design scenery for Ben Jonson's masques. He designed the Queen's House, Greenwich, 1616–35 and his English Renaissance masterpiece, the Banquet House in Whitehall, London, 1619–22.

Kahn Louis 1901–1974. US architect, born in Estonia. A follower of Mies van de Rohe, he developed a classically romantic style, in which functional 'servant' areas, such as stairwells and air ducts, featured prominently, often as towerlike structures surrounding the main living and working, or 'served', areas. His projects are characterized by an imaginative use of concrete and brick and include the Salk Institute for Biological Studies, La Jolla, California, and the British Art Center at Yale University.

Lasdun Denys 1914– . British architect. He designed the Royal College of Surgeons in Regent's Park, London 1960–64, some of the buildings at the University of East Anglia, Norwich, and the National Theatre 1976–77 on London's South Bank. He was knighted 1976.

Le Corbusier assumed name of Charles-Édouard Jeanneret 1887–1965. Swiss architect. His functionalist approach to town planning in industrial society was based on the interrelationship between machine forms and the techniques of modern architecture. His concept, *La Ville radieuse*, developed in Marseille, France (1945–50) and Chandigarh, India, placed buildings and open spaces with related functions in a circular formation, with buildings based on standard-sized units mathematically calculated according to the proportions of the human figure.

Ledoux Claude-Nicolas 1736–1806. French Neo-Classical architect, stylistically comparable to E L Boullée in his use of austere, geometric forms, exemplified in his toll houses for Paris; for instance, the Barrière de la Villette in the Place de Stalingrad.

Lethaby William Richard 1857–1931. English architect. An assistant to Norman Shaw, he embraced the principles of William Morris and Philip Webb in the Arts and Crafts movement, and was cofounder and first director of the Central School of Arts and Crafts from 1894. He wrote a collection of essays entitled *Form in Civilization* 1922.

Lutyens Edwin Landseer 1869–1944. English architect. His designs ranged from picturesque to Renaissance-style country houses and ultimately evolved into a Classical style as in the Cenotaph, London, and the Viceroy's House, New Delhi.

Mackintosh Charles Rennie 1868–1928. Scottish architect, designer, and painter, whose chief work includes the Glasgow School of Art 1896, various Glasgow tea rooms 1897 to about 1911, and Hill House, Helensburgh, 1902–03. His early work is Art Nouveau; he subsequently developed a unique style, both rational and expressive. Influenced by the Arts and Crafts Movement, he designed furniture and fittings, cutlery, and lighting to go with his interiors. Although initially influential, Mackintosh was not successful in his lifetime and has only recently come to be regarded as a pioneeer of modern design.

Meier Richard 1934– . US architect whose white designs spring from the poetic modernism of the Le Corbusier villas of the 1920s. His abstract style is at its most mature in the Museum für Kunsthandwerk (Museum of Arts and Crafts), Frankfurt, Germany, which was completed 1984. He is the architect for the Getty Museum, Los Angeles.

Mendelsohn Erich 1887–1953. German Expressionist architect who designed the Einstein Tower, Potsdam, 1919–20. His later work fused Modernist and Expressionist styles; in Britain he built the de la Warr Pavilion 1935–36 in Bexhill-on-Sea, East Sussex. In 1941 he settled in the USA, where he built the Maimonides Hospital, San Francisco, 1946–50.

Mies van der Rohe Ludwig 1886–1969. German architect who practised in the USA from 1937. He succeeded Walter Gropius as director of the Bauhaus 1929–33. He designed the bronze-and-glass Seagram building in New York City 1956–59 and numerous apartment buildings.

Moore Charles 1925– . US architect with an eclectic approach to design. He was an early exponent of Post-Modernism in, for example, his students' housing for Kresge College, University of California at Santa Cruz, 1973–74, and the Piazza d'Italia in New Orleans, 1975–78, which is one of the key monuments of Post-Modernism.

Nash John 1752–1835. English architect. He laid out Regent's Park, London, and its approaches. Between 1813 and 1820 he planned Regent Street (later rebuilt), repaired and enlarged Buckingham Palace (for which he designed Marble Arch), and rebuilt Brighton Pavilion in flamboyant oriental style.

Nervi Pier Luigi 1891–1979. Italian architect who used soft steel mesh within concrete to give it flowing form. For example, the Turin exhibition hall 1949, the UNESCO building in Paris 1952, and the cathedral at New Norcia, near Perth, Australia, 1960.

Neutra Richard Joseph 1892–1970. Austrian-born architect who became a US citizen 1929. His works, often in impressive landscape settings, include Lovell Health House, Los Angeles (1929), and Mathematics Park, Princeton, New Jersey.

Niemeyer Oscar 1907– . Brazilian architect, joint designer of the United Nations headquarters in New York and of many buildings in Brasília, capital of Brazil.

Olbrich Joseph Maria 1867–1908. Viennese architect who worked under Otto Wagner and was opposed to the overornamentation of Art Nouveau. His major buildings, however, remain Art Nouveau in spirit: the Vienna Sezession 1897–98, the Hochzeitsturm 1907, and the Tietz department store in Düsseldorf, Germany.

Palladio Andrea 1518–1580. Italian Renaissance architect noted for his harmonious and balanced classical structures. He designed numerous country houses in and around Vicenza, Italy, making use of Roman classical forms, symmetry, and proportion. The Villa Malcontenta and the Villa Rotonda are examples of houses designed from 1540 for patrician families of the Venetian Republic; he also designed churches in Venice. His ideas were revived in England in the early 17th century by Inigo Jones and in the 18th century by Lord Burlington and later by architects in Italy, Holland, Germany, Russia, and the USA. Examples of Neo-Classical architecture influenced by 'Palladian' buildings include Washington's home at Mount Vernon, USA, the palace of Tsarskoe Selo in Russia, and Prior Park, England.

Paxton Joseph 1801–1865. English architect, garden superintendent to the Duke of Devonshire from 1826 and designer of the Great Exhibition building 1851 (the Crystal Palace), which was revolutionary in its structural use of glass and iron.

Pei Ieoh Ming 1917– . Chinese-born US Modernist/High Tech architect, noted for the use of glass walls. His buildings include the Bank of China Tower, Hong Kong, 1987; the glass pyramid in front of the Louvre, Paris, 1989; East Building, National Gallery of Art, Washington DC, 1978; and the John Hancock Tower, Boston 1979.

Piranesi Giambattista 1720–1778. Italian architect, most significant for his powerful etchings of Roman antiquities and as a theorist of architecture, advocating imaginative use of Roman models. Only one of his designs was built, Sta Maria del Priorato, Rome.

Pugin Augustus Welby Northmore 1812–1852. English architect, collaborator with Charles Barry in the detailed design of the Houses of Parliament. He did much to revive Gothic architecture in England.

Rogers Richard 1933– . British architect. His works include the Centre Pompidou in Paris 1977 (jointly with Renzo Piano) and the Lloyd's building in London 1986.

Saarinen Eero 1910–1961. Finnish-born US architect distinguished for a wide range of innovative modern designs using a variety of creative shapes for buildings. His works include the US embassy, London, the TWA terminal, New York, and Dulles Airport, Washington DC. He collaborated on a number of projects with his father, Eliel Saarinen.

Saarinen Eliel 1873–1950. Finnish architect and town planner, founder of the Finnish Romantic school. In 1923 he emigrated to the USA, where he contributed to US skyscraper design by his work in Chicago, and later turned to functionalism.

Sant'Elia Antonio 1888–1916. Italian architect. His drawings convey a Futurist vision of a metropolis with skyscrapers, traffic lanes, and streamlined factories.

Schinkel Karl Friedrich 1781–1841. Prussian Neo-Classical architect. Major works include the Old Museum, Berlin, 1823–30, the Nikolaikirche in Potsdam 1830–37, and the Roman Bath 1833 in the park of Potsdam.

Scott (George) Gilbert 1811–1878. English architect. As the leading practical architect in the mid-19th-century Gothic revival in England, Scott was responsible for the building or restoration of many public buildings, including the Albert Memorial, the Foreign Office, and St Pancras Station, all in London.

Serlio Sebastiano 1475–1554. Italian architect and painter, author of *L'Architettura* 1537–51, which set down practical rules for the use of the Classical orders, and was used by architects of the Neo-Classical style throughout Europe.

Shaw (Richard) Norman 1831–1912. British architect. He was the leader of the trend away from Gothic and Tudor styles back to Georgian lines. His buildings include Swan House, Chelsea, 1876.

Sinan 1489–1588. Ottoman architect, chief architect from 1538 to Suleiman the Magnificent. Among the hundreds of buildings he designed are the Suleimaniye in Istanbul, a mosque complex, and the Topkapi Saray, palace of the sultan (now a museum).

Smirke Robert 1780–1867. English Classical architect, designer of the British Museum, London (1823–47).

Smithson Alison 1928– and Peter 1923– . British architects, teachers, and theorists, best known for their development in the 1950s and 1960s of the style known as Brutalism, for example in Hunstanton School, Norfolk, 1954; the Economist Building, London, 1964; and Robin Hood Gardens, London, 1968–72.

Soane John 1753–1837. English architect whose individual Neo-Classical designs anticipated contemporary taste. He designed his own house in Lincoln's Inn Fields, London, now the *Soane Museum*. Little remains of his extensive work at the Bank of England, London.

Speer Albert 1905–1981. German architect and minister in the Nazi government during World War II. Commissioned by Hitler, Speer, like his counterparts in Fascist Italy, chose an overblown Classicism to glorify the state, as, for example, in his plan for the Berlin and Nuremberg Party Congress Grounds 1934.

Stirling James 1926–1992. British architect, associated with collegiate and museum architecture. His works include the engineering building at Leicester University, and the Clore Gallery (the extension to house the Turner collection) at the Tate Gallery, London, opened in 1987.

Sullivan Louis Henry 1856–1924. US architect, a leader of the Chicago school of architects and an early developer of the skyscraper. His skyscrapers include the Wainwright Building, St Louis, 1890 and the Guaranty Building, Buffalo, 1894. He was the teacher of Frank Lloyd Wright.

Tange Kenzo 1913– . Japanese architect. His works include the National Gymnasium, Tokyo, for the 1964 Olympics, and the city of Abuja, planned to replace Lagos as the capital of Nigeria.

Terry (John) Quinlan 1937– . British Neo-Classical architect. His work includes country houses, for example Merks Hall, Great Dunmow, Essex, 1982, and the larger-scale Richmond, London, riverside project, commissioned 1984.

Vanbrugh John 1664–1726. English Baroque architect and dramatist. He designed Blenheim Palace, Oxfordshire, and Castle Howard, Yorkshire, and wrote the comic dramas *The Relapse* 1696 and *The Provok'd Wife* 1697.

Venturi Robert 1925– . US architect. He pioneered Post-Modernism through his books *Complexity and Contradiction in Architecture* 1967 (Pulitzer Prize 1991) and *Learning from Las Vegas* 1972. In 1986 he was commissioned to design the extension to the National Gallery, London, opened 1991.

Vitruvius (Marcus Vitruvius Pollio) 1st century BC. Roman architect whose ten-volume interpretation of Roman architecture *De architectura* influenced Leon Battista Alberti and Andrea Palladio.

Voysey Charles Francis Annesley 1857–1941. English architect and designer. He designed country houses which were characteristically asymmetrical with massive buttresses, long sloping roofs, and rough-cast walls. He also designed textiles and wallpaper.

Wagner Otto 1841–1918. Viennese architect. Initially designing in the Art Nouveau style, for example

Vienna Stadtbahn 1894–97, he later rejected ornament for rationalism, as in the Post Office Savings Bank, Vienna, 1904–06. He influenced such Viennese architects as Josef Hoffmann, Adolf Loos, and Joseph Olbrich.

Waterhouse Alfred 1830–1905. English architect. He was a leading exponent of Victorian Neo-Gothic using, typically, multicoloured tiles and bricks. His works include the Natural History Museum in London 1868.

Webb Philip (Speakman) 1831–1915. English architect. He mostly designed private houses, including the Red House, Bexley Heath, Sussex, for William Morris, and was one of the leading figures, with Richard Norman Shaw and C F A Voysey, in the revival of domestic English architecture in the late 19th century.

Wren Christopher 1632–1723. English architect, designer of St Paul's Cathedral, London, built 1675–1710; many London churches including St Bride's, Fleet Street, and St Mary-le-Bow, Cheapside; the Royal Exchange; Marlborough House; and the Sheldonian Theatre, Oxford. After the Great Fire of London 1666, he prepared a plan for rebuilding the city, but it was not adopted. Instead, Wren was commissioned to rebuild 51 City churches and St Paul's Cathedral. The west towers of Westminster Abbey, often attributed to him, were the design of his pupil Hawksmoor.

Wright Frank Lloyd 1869–1959. US architect who rejected Neo-Classicist styles for 'organic architecture', in which buildings reflected their natural surroundings. Among his buildings are his Wisconsin home Taliesin East 1925; Falling Water, near Pittsburgh, Pennsylvania, 1936, a house built straddling a waterfall; and the Guggenheim Museum, New York, 1959. Wright also designed buildings in Japan from 1915 to 1922, most notably the Imperial Hotel in Tokyo 1922.

ART

History of Western Art

In the visual arts of Western civilization, painting and sculpture have been the dominant forms for many centuries. This has not always been the case in other cultures. Islamic art, for example, is one of ornament, as artists were forbidden to portray living creatures. In some cultures masks, tattoos, pottery, and metalwork have been the main forms of visual art. In the recent past technology has made new art forms possible, such as photography and cinema, and today electronic media – computer graphics, computer-aided animation and 'painting', and other imaging techniques – have led to entirely new ways of creating and presenting visual images.

ANCIENT ART

prehistoric art 25,000–1000 BC. The history of the fine arts, painting and sculpture, begins about 21,000 BC in the Paleolithic, or Old Stone Age. Vivid, lifelike images of animals and humans have been found incised, painted or sculpted on the walls deep inside the caves where our ancestors sheltered, mostly in Spain and in southwestern France, but also in Portugal, Sicily, and Russia. The images of reindeer, mammoth, horses and bison are most common, varying from very small to almost lifesize. It is thought that they served as part of a 'magic' ritual to ensure a successful hunt. Paintings such as those at the caves of *Lascaux* in France show great skill in drawing, with vigorous and sweepingly graceful outlines. Stone Age people also used flint tools to carve small figurines in bone, horn, or stone. The most famous of these is the so-called *Venus of Willendorf*, a limestone statuette 4.5 in high, found in lower Austria and dating from about 21,000 BC. Her exaggeratedly bulbous form makes clear her magic significance as a fertility figure.

art of early civilizations 14,000–300 BC. Architecture became the new art form when people began to settle in communities as farmers rather than as hunters. They decorated their buildings with sculpture, imposing a sense of pattern and order on them, although Stonehenge in Britain (1800–1400 BC) had not achieved this sophistication. In Europe, *Celtic art* ornamented tombs, crosses, metalwork and pottery with stylized animal and plant forms in swirling curvilinear patterns. Pottery had reached Europe from the Near East where it began as early as 5500 BC in Mesopotamia, where sign pictures also grew into cuneiform (wedge-shaped) writing. The Near and Middle East produced many highly developed urban civilizations, including the *Sumerian* (4000 BC), and the *Persian* (550 BC). In these cultures, sculptures and reliefs of people, gods, and animals decorated palaces, temples, and tombs telling stories or praising their gods and rulers. A fine example is the grand stairway of the *Persian royal palace*, Persepolis, from 518–6 BC. Outstanding examples of precious metalwork, glassware, and pottery also survive, of which there are splendid collections in the British Museum and the Louvre.

Egyptian art 3000–200 BC. *The Great Sphinx at Giza* (2680–2565 BC), a gigantic human-headed lion carved from an outcropping of natural rock, is the supreme example of Egyptian sculpture. 185 ft long and 63 ft high, it was meant to guard for eternity the god-king's pyramid tomb nearby. Most Egyptian art is funerary, largely consisting of sculptured relief panels painted in bright, lifelike colours covering the walls of tombs and temples. They depend on strong, simple outlines, the main aim being clarity: to portray the dead in their idealized prime, their servants and families, and the objects, animals, foods and activities they enjoyed in life, so that these could be magically transported into the afterworld to be enjoyed forever.

Human forms are recomposed almost diagrammatically to show the whole of a person, face and legs in profile, upper torso in front view, hips three-quarters and with the eye magnified. If anything needed further description a hieroglyphic label would be added. Statues, whether of wood or stone, were also generally painted. They retain a strong cubic sense of the block from which they were hewn, with the figures facing straight ahead, the arms in a single unit with the body. The serene vision of eternity found in all Egyptian art is epitomized in the beautiful portrait head of *Queen Nefertiti* in the Staatlich Museum, Berlin, dating from about 1360 BC.

art of Aegean civilizations 2800–100 BC. The *Minoan* and *Mycenean* civilizations flourished in the area of the Aegean Sea from about 2800 BC. Based on the island of Crete, Minoan society was pleasure-loving and open, and its major monument, the new *palace at Knossos* (1700 BC), was decorated with cheerful frescoes of scenes from daily life, plants, birds, and leaping fish and dolphins. Their pottery was painted in the same fresh, spontaneous style with plant and animal motifs curving to suit the form of the vases. In 1400 they were conquered by the Myceneans from the Peloponnese, whose art reflected its more warlike society. Instead of airy palaces, they constructed fortified citadels such as Mycenae itself, which was entered through the *Lion Gate* (1330), named for the remarkable monumental sculpture that adorns it. In the nearby Cyclades Islands a unique art form emerged about 2800: the small marble *Cycladic figures* much admired today, which represent the Great Mother Goddess in such streamlined simplicity that her face is simply an elongated oval with a triangular nose.

Many of the ideas and art forms of these early seafaring civilizations were to be adapted by the Greeks who came from Central Asia between 2000–1000 BC to establish their own splendid culture that was to dominate Western taste and thought for many centuries.

CLASSICAL ART

Greek art 1000–400 BC. Greek temples are almost sculptures in themselves, designed not to be entered but to be looked at. The sculptured reliefs which decorated them, such as the *Elgin Marbles* (now in the British Museum) which came from the Parthenon in

Athens, show perfectly the Greek artistic ideal: the human form at its most beautiful.

The major periods of Greek art can be divided into the Archaic (late 8th century–480 BC), Classical (480–323 BC), and Hellenistic (323–27 BC). No large-scale painting survives, although colour was very important, and even the white marble sculptures we admire today were originally brightly painted.

In the *Archaic* period the statues of naked standing men *kouroi* and draped females *korai* show an Egyptian influence in their rigid frontality. By about 500 BC the figure was allowed to relax its weight onto one leg and immediately seemed to come alive. The archaic smile which gave these early figures a certain cheerful sameness vanished in the *Classical* period when expressions assumed a dignified serenity. Further movement was introduced in new poses such as in Myron's bronze *Diskobolus/The Discus Thrower* (460–50 BC), and in the rhythmic Parthenon reliefs of men and horses supervised by Phidias. Artists were no longer anonymous and among sculptors whose work is known are **Praxiteles**, **Scopas**, **Lysippus**, and **Polykleitos**, whose *Doryphoros/The Spear Carrier* (450–440) was of such harmony and poise that it set a standard for beautiful proportions which is still in use today. Praxiteles introduced the female nude into the sculptural repertory with the graceful *Aphrodite of Knidos*, (c. 350 BC). It was easier to express movement in bronze, hollow-cast by the lost wax method, but few bronze sculptures survive and many are known only through Roman copies in marble.

The *Hellenistic* period, when the Greek Empire under Alexander the Great spread to Egypt and beyond Iraq, produced such sculptures as the *Winged Victory of Samothrace* with its dramatic drapery, the expressive *Dying Gaul* and the tortured *Laocoon*, which explored the effects of movement and of deeply-felt emotion.

Vase painting is the one form of Greek painting which has survived the centuries. Good, even great, artists worked as both potters and painters until the 5th century BC and the works they signed were exported throughout the Empire. Made in several standard shapes and sizes, the pottery served as functional containers for wine, water, and oil. The first decoration took the form of simple lines and circles, from which the *'Geometric style'* emerged near Athens in the 10th century BC. It consisted of precisely drawn patterns, the most characteristic being the key meander. Gradually the bands of decoration multiplied and the human figure, geometrically stylized, was added.

About 700 BC the potters of Corinth invented the *black figure* technique in which the unglazed red clay was painted in black with mythological scenes, gods and battles in a narrative frieze. About 530 BC Athenian potters reversed the process and developed the more sophisticated *red figure* pottery, which allowed for more detailed and elaborate painting of the figures in red against a black background. This grew increasingly naturalistic, with lively scenes of daily life. The finest examples date from the mid-6th century–mid-5th century BC at Athens. Later painters tried to follow major art trends and represent spatial depth, dissipating the unique quality of their fine linear technique.

The ancient Greeks excelled in carving gems and cameos, and in jewellery and metalwork. They also invented the pictorial mosaic and from the 5th century BC onwards floors were paved with coloured pebbles depicting mythological subjects. Later, specially cut cubes of stone and glass called *tesserae* were used, and Greek craftsmen working for the Romans reproduced famous paintings such as that of *Alexander at the Battle of Issus* from Pompeii, giving us some idea of these lost masterpieces.

Roman art 753 BC–410 AD. During the 8th century BC the Etruscans appeared as the first native Italian civilization, north and west of the river Tiber. Their art shows influences of archaic Greece and the Near East. Their coffins (*sarcophagi*), carved with reliefs and topped with portraits of the dead, reclining on one elbow as if at an eternal banquet, were to influence the later Romans and early Christians.

Under Julius Caesar's successor Augustus (27 BC–14 AD) the Roman Empire was established. Art and architecture played an important role in unifying the European nations under Roman rule. The Romans greatly admired Greek art and became the first collectors, importing vast quantities of marbles and bronzes, and even some Greek craftsmen to make copies. Realistic portrait sculpture was an important original development by the Romans. A cult of heroes began and in public places official statues were erected of generals, rulers and philosophers. The portrait bust developed as a new art form from about 75 BC; these were serious, factual portraits of a rugged race of patriarchs to whose wisdom and authority their subject nations should reasonably submit.

Narrative relief sculpture also flourished in Rome, again linked to the need to commemorate publicly the glorious victories of their heroes. These appeared on monumental altars, triumphal arches and giant columns such as *Trajan's Column* 106–113 AD which records his historic battles like a strip cartoon, winding its way around the column for 656 ft. Strict realism in portraiture gave way to a certain amount of Greek-style idealization in the propaganda statues of the emperors, befitting their semi-divine status. Gods and allegorical figures feature with Rome's heroes on such narrative relief sculptures as those on Augustus's giant altar to peace, the *Ara Pacis* 13–9 BC.

Very little **Roman painting** has survived, and much of what is has due to the volcanic eruption of Mount Vesuvius in AD 79 which buried the southern Italian seaside towns of Pompeii and Herculaneum under ash, thus preserving the lively and impressionistic wall paintings (frescoes) which decorated the holiday villas of an art-loving elite. Favourite motifs were illusionistic and still-life. A type of interior decoration known as *Grotesque*, rediscovered in Rome during the Renaissance, combined swirling plant motifs, strange animals and tiny fanciful scenes. Grotesque was much used in later decorative schemes whenever it was fashionable to quote the Classical period.

The art of *mosaic* was universally popular throughout the Roman Empire. It was introduced from Greece and used for floors as well as walls and vaults, in *trompe l'oeil* effects, geometric patterns and scenes from daily life and mythology.

MEDIEVAL ART

early Christian and Byzantine art 330–1453 AD.

In 312 the Emperor Constantine was converted to Christianity and made it one of the official religions of the Roman State. Churches were built, and artistic traditions adapted to the portrayal of the new Christian saints and symbols. Roman burial chests *(sarcophagi)* were adopted by the Christians and their imagery of pagan myths gradually changed into biblical themes.

Byzantine style developed in the East in Constantinople which in 330 became the headquarters of the Roman Empire, and an Eastern Christian tradition was maintained there until 1453 when Constantinople was conquered by the Turks. The use of mosaic came to be associated with both Byzantine art and early Christian church decoration in the West. Ravenna became the Western imperial capital in the 5th century, and the ecclesiastical buildings there, built in the 5th and 6th centuries, are a glorious tribute to the art of mosaic, presenting powerful religious images on walls and vaults in brilliant, glittering colour. Byzantine art moved away from the natural portrayal of people and became highly stylized, symbolizing the divine. Ornament became flattened into intricate lacework patterns. Oriental, highly decorative, and unchanging, the Byzantine style can be seen in the icons – often thought to be capable of working miracles – which have remained for centuries the main religious art of Greece and Russia.

art of the Dark Ages 400–800 AD.

The 400 years between the fall of the Roman Empire and the establishment of Charlemagne's new Holy Roman Empire in 800 are traditionally known as the Dark Ages, and the art of that period as belonging to the Migration Period. Through a time of turmoil and invasion, with the northern 'barbarians' overrunning the old Mediterranean civilizations, the Christian church maintained its stability and the interchange of artistic traditions fostered creativity.

The art of the migrant peoples consisted mainly of portable objects, articles of personal use or adornment. They excelled in metalwork and jewellery, often in gold with garnet or enamel inlays and ornamented with highly stylized, animal-based interlace patterns. This type of ornament was translated into manuscript illumination such as the decorated pages of the *Lindisfarne Gospel* (British Museum, London) which dates from the 7th century, or the 8th century *Book of Kells* (Trinity College, Dublin). With Charlemagne's Christian Empire modelled on that of ancient Rome, a cultural renaissance ensued, drawing its inspiration from the late Classical artistic traditions of the early Christians. At Charlemagne's capital, Aachen, the human figure was re-introduced into art and continuous narrative was rediscovered in the *Tours Bibles* produced there. They in turn influenced the sculptured reliefs on the bronze doors at St Michael's Church, Hildesheim, Germany, dating from 1015, the first doors cast in one piece in the West since Roman times.

art of the Middle Ages 800–1300 AD.

Under the unifying force of the Latin Church, a new civilization spread across Europe which during the 10th century produced a style in art called *Romanesque*, and, in England, *Norman*. Chiefly evident in relief sculpture surrounding church portals, on capitals and corbels, it translated manuscript illuminations into stone, combining naturalistic elements from the antique Roman style with the fantastic, poetical, and pattern-loving Celtic and Germanic tradition. Imaginary beasts, monsters, saints, and sinners mingle with humour and innocence in an enchanted world of biblical themes. Fine examples remain in Burgundy and southwest France, extending down into Spain on the pilgrimage route to Santiago de Compostela.

Gothic during the late 12th and 13th centuries European cities began to raise great cathedrals, and sculptural decoration became more monumental. The cathedrals of Chartres and Reims in France had such extensive sculptural programmes that many artists came from far afield to work and learn there. A new interest in the natural world is shown in such examples as the strikingly life-like founder figures of Naumberg Cathedral, East Germany, (c. 1245) or in the naturalistic foliage on the capitals at Southwell in England.

With the increased height of the cathedrals, stained glass windows became their new glory. Chartres, where an entire set of stained glass is preserved, awesomely illustrates the magical effect of coloured light seemingly suspended within its dark interior. Both windows and sculpture, by depicting the lives of the saints and texts from the bible, gave the faithful an encyclopedic view of the Christian history of the world.

Art patronage, although still mainly concerned with religious imagery, now burgeoned in the many small courts of Europe and under this influence art became more stylized, delicate and refined. Even the Virgin Mary was portrayed as an elegant young queen. In her most characteristic pose, holding the Christ child in her arms, her weight shifts gracefully onto one hip causing her body to form an S-curve and her drapery to fall into elegant folds. This figure stance, the 'Gothic sway', became a hallmark of the period. Court patronage produced exquisite small ivories, precious goldsmith's work, devotional books illustrated with miniatures, and tapestries which warmed cold castle walls, depicting romantic tales or the joys of springtime.

In Italy, the monumentality of the antique Roman past subdued the spread of northern Gothic ideas. A type of *Gothic Classicism* was developed by the sculptors Nicola and Giovanni **Pisano** (working 1258–1314) whose four great pulpits carved in relief (Siena, Pisa, Pistoia) show the influence of antique sarcophagi but also that of French Gothic in the dramatic expressiveness of their figures.

An innovative group of painters brought the art of *fresco painting*, always important in Italy, to a new height. **Giotto**'s (1267–1337) cycle of the lives of Mary and Christ in the Arena Chapel, Padua (c. 1300) set a new standard for figural naturalism, seen as proto-Renaissance, and in the Town Hall of Siena Ambrogio **Lorenzetti** (c. 1306–1345) illustrated the effects of *Good and Bad Government* (1337) in panoramic townscapes and landscapes.

Panel painting, in jewel-like colours on a gold background, developed from Byzantine models, and the Sienese painter **Duccio**'s (c. 1255/60–c. 1318) *Maestá* for the High Altar of Siena Cathedral

(1308–11) achieved a peak of expressive power of line and colour. Simone **Martini** (c. 1284–1344) developed this into courtly refinement in both frescoes (for example Assisi, Siena) and panel paintings, and became a major influence on the *International Gothic* style which in the years around 1400 achieved the perfect mix of French courtliness and the Italian command of form, together with a delight in the observed details of nature. A magnificent example of this moment in art can be seen in the miniatures painted for the devotional book, the *Très Riches Heures du Duc de Berry*, by the Flemish **Limbourg** brothers in about 1415.

THE ITALIAN RENAISSANCE

Florence the rebirth or 'Renaissance' of Classical art and learning began in Florence in the early 15th century. The self-made men of Florence, merchants and bankers, saw themselves as direct descendants of the great men of ancient Rome and, led by the Medici family, vied with each other in patronage of all the arts, building palaces and churches filled with sculptured and painted monuments to themselves. In this new age of humanism, people – and the aesthetic delights of the world they lived in – were suddenly important.

The most far-reaching artistic innovation of the period, which was one of continual discovery and rediscovery, was that of scientific *perspective* by Filippo **Brunelleschi** (1377–1446), the architect who later built the dome of Florence Cathedral. Perspective allowed artists to create an authentic three-dimensional space, correctly sized to the figures within their paintings. **Masaccio** (1401–28) used this new style to superb effect in his frescoes in the Brancacci Chapel, Santa Maria del Carmine, in which the apostles look like Roman gods. The sculptor **Donatello** (c. 1386–1466) used perspective in his relief sculptures. His bronze statues, like the youthful *David* (1430–2), the first free-standing nude since antiquity, or his equestrian statue of the mercenary General Gattamelata (1443, Padua) look back to Classical prototypes but have the alert liveliness of all early Renaissance art. In his later work, such as his wood-carving of the aged Mary Magdalene (1445), he sought dramatic expression through distortion, even ugliness. His only real rival was the goldsmith and bronze sculptor Lorenzo **Ghiberti** (1378–1455), who only gradually adapted his graceful **International Gothic** style to Renaissance ideals in such works as the gilt-bronze Baptistery doors which Michelangelo called 'The Gates of Paradise'.

Paolo **Uccello**'s (1397–1475) decorative paintings reflect an obsessive interest in mathematical perspective. **Fra Angelico** (c. 1400–55) used delicate colours and a simple style to express his religious feeling. Andrea del **Castagno**'s (c. 1421–1457) style was fiercely linear. The antithesis of his violent suffering figures are Piero **della Francesca**'s (c. 1420–1492) strangely silent ones. Solidly rounded in pale light, immobile within perfect perspective spaces, they express an enigmatic timelessness. His mastery of geometry, proportion, form, and colour is breathtakingly evident in his frescoes of *The Legend of the True Cross* in San Francesco in Arezzo (1452–66).

Many sculptors produced public statues, grandiose tombs, Roman-style portrait busts and innumerable versions of the Madonna and Child. The Florentines enjoyed seeing themselves in religious paintings and they appear in crowd scenes in many magnificent frescoes in the churches of their city, such as those by Domenico del **Ghirlandaio** (c. 1449–1494). He was the most popular painter in Florence in the latter part of the 15th century, respected for his honesty, which is epitomized in his portrait of *An Old Man with a Child* (c. 1480) in the Louvre. His contemporaries included Antonio **Pollaiuolo** (c. 1432–1498), whose interest centres on the nude in action; Andrea del **Verrocchio** (1435–1488), famous for the equestrian statue of Bartolomeo Colleoni in Venice (1481–96); and **Botticelli** (1445–1510), whose poetic, gracefully linear paintings of Madonnas and mythological subjects such as *The Birth of Venus* (1482) show the Florentine ideal of female beauty. Almost every art work produced included some reference to antiquity, either in form or content.

Leonardo da Vinci 1452–1519. Through his genius, the art of the early 16th century became the *High Renaissance*, attaining a grandeur that appealed particularly to the popes, who now became the leading art patrons in their attempt to build the 'New Rome'. Leonardo's enquiring scientific mind led him to investigate every aspect of the natural world from anatomy to aerodynamics. His notebooks and drawings remain his finest legacy, but his experiments also revolutionized painting style. Instead of a white background, he used a dark one to allow the overlying colour a more three-dimensional existence. He invented 'aerial perspective' whereby the misty atmosphere (*sfumato*) blurs and changes the colours of the landscape as it dissolves into the distance. His principle of grouping figures within an imaginary pyramid, linked by their gestures and emotions, became a High Renaissance compositional rule. His *Madonna of the Rocks* (Louvre) exemplifies all these ideas.

Michelangelo Buonarroti 1475–1564. His giant talent dominated the High Renaissance and led his contemporaries to label him 'Divine'. No other artist could escape his influence. He said of his stone carvings, such as the monumental *David* in Florence (1501–4), that he was simply revealing the figure hidden within the block. His massive figure style was translated into paint in the *Sistine Chapel frescoes* (Vatican, Rome) covering the ceiling with human figures, mostly nude, all grandly Classical, telling the Old Testament story from Genesis to the Deluge (1508–11) and finishing on the altar wall with a titanic *Last Judgement* (1541).

Raphael (Raffaello Sanzio) 1483–1520. He quickly mastered the innovations of Leonardo and Michelangelo and in 1509 was commissioned to fresco the *Stanza della Segnature* in the Vatican, where his classicist *School of Athens* is his masterpiece. Immensely prolific and popular, he combined both delicacy and grandeur in his work.

Mannerism Giulio **Romano** (c. 1499–1546), Raphael's principal follower, exaggerated his style into an individual one of his own, heralding the next major art movement, Mannerism. This flouted the 'rules' of Renaissance order and harmony by striving for idiosyncratic, sometimes alarming, effects. The Florentine Andrea **del Sarto** (1486–1531) and his assistants **Pontormo** (1494–1556) and **Rosso** Fiorentino (1494–1540) each pursued self-consciously mannered styles, as did Giorgio **Vasari** (1511–1574), who is chiefly remembered for his book *The Lives of the Most Excellent Architects, Painters and Sculptors* (1550), in which he coined the term 'Mannerist' and laid down the chronology of the history of art which is still in use today. Mannerism appealed particularly to courtly patrons and it became increasingly effete. The Medici, now grand dukes, employed such artists as the sculptor Benvenuto **Cellini** (1500–71), as famous for his racy autobiography as for the gilt salt cellar he made for the King of France; Agnolo **Bronzino** (1503–1572), whose patrician portraits display a stony hauteur; and Giovanni da **Bologna** (Giambologna) (1529–1608), whose elegant small bronze statuettes were widely reproduced.

Venice the Venetian Renaissance was slow in coming because of the city's traditional links with the East. Two non-Venetians were influential: Antonello **da Messina** (*c.* 1430–79), who in 1475 brought to Venice the new Flemish technique of oil painting, and Andrea **Mantegna** (*c.* 1431–1506), an archaeologically-minded painter whose figures looked like antique sculptures. Giovanni **Bellini** (*c.* 1430–1516) specialized in devotional pictures of the Madonna, but his sensitive appreciation of light and colour introduced that element of sensuality to Venetian talent which later made **Titian** (Tiziano Vecellio) (1487–1576) the preferred painter of Emperor Charles V and his son Philip II of Spain. His fellow-painter **Giorgione** (*c.* 1478–1510) died young, leaving only a few securely attributed works, but who nevertheless made an innovative mark with his small, intimate, easel paintings and a new treatment of figures in a landscape. **Veronese** (*c.* 1528–88) and Jacopo **Tintoretto** (1518–94) worked on a much larger scale, Veronese excelling in sumptuous *trompe l'oeil* interior decorations and Tintoretto in dramatic religious paintings, spectacularly lit and composed with daring foreshortening. His paintings for the Venetian Scuola di San Rocco (1566–88) foreshadow, in their exciting exuberance, the next major movement, the **Baroque**.

THE 15TH AND 16TH CENTURIES

Northern European artists took their inspiration from Gothic sources, but shared with the Italians an insatiable interest in realistic portrayals of themselves and their world.

Netherlands one of the first examples of the new *humanism* was the work of Claus **Sluter** (*c.* 1380–1406). His mourning figures on the tomb of Philip the Bold, Duke of Burgundy, their faces hidden by the hoods of their robes, are poignantly mute but solidly real people.

In Flanders where the patrons were wealthy merchants, Robert **Campin** (1378–1444) put his *Madonna and Child before a Firescreen* (1420–30, National Gallery, London) into an ordinary living room and through its open window showed a Flemish town. Mary's halo is replaced by the circular fire-screen behind her, an example of disguised symbolism, making the supernatural seem real.

Among Campin's followers, all marvellous draughtsmen, was Jan **van Eyck** (d.1441) whose strength lay in his detailed analysis of the beauty of the world around him. His innovative recipe for oil painting makes his colours glow like precious jewels. In his *Arnolfini Wedding* (1434, National Gallery, London) the bride and groom appear in a domestic interior crammed with disguised symbols, in a kind of pictorial marriage certificate. Flemish realism reached Italy with the Portinari Altarpiece, an *Adoration of the Shepherds* by Hugo **van der Goes** (d. 1481). Commissioned by the Medici agent in Bruges, it was sent to Florence where it had a considerable effect on Italian artists. The quietly contemplative portraits of Hans **Memlinc** (d. 1481) sum up the achievement of 15th-century Netherlands painters.

Individual styles proliferated in the 16th century. Hieronymous **Bosch** (*c.* 1450–1516) painted nightmarish scenes filled with diminutive human figures caught in a surrealist demonic world. Pieter **Brueghel** the Elder (1525/30–69) treated biblical subjects as contemporary events, viewing with compassion a miserable humanity. In his paintings of the seasons (1565) he brilliantly evokes both winter's icy silence and the golden warmth of summer.

Germany the giant among German artists was Albrecht **Dürer** (1471–1528). His intellectual powers put him in line with the great Italian masters and their influence introduced a new solidity of form into his basically Gothic style. Particularly important as a graphic artist, he was widely influential through woodcuts and engravings. Mathias **Grünewald** (*c.* 1460–1528), a tragic visionary, used colour symbolically in the *Isenheim Altar* (1512–15, Colmar), painted for hospital patients to see the crucified Christ, covered with festering wounds, sharing their suffering. Lucas **Cranach** the Elder (1473–1538) painted self-conscious courtly nudes, and Albrecht **Altdorfer** (*c.*1489–1538) painted landscapes in which tiny human figures are dwarfed by nature's immensity.

Spain Philip II did not care for the work of **El Greco** (1541–1614), the painter who really established Spain as an artistic centre. Trained in Venice, and particularly influenced by Tintoretto, he developed his hallucinatory style in Toledo, where his patrons were ecclesiastics and the intelligentsia. In his *Burial of Count Orgaz* (1586) the flame-like figures and unearthly colours blend mystic vision and reality.

England Renaissance ideas arrived with the German Hans Holbein the Younger (1497–1543), who was by 1536 court painter to Henry VIII. His piercing portraits of the king and his wives, and his delicate portrait drawings, give a superb pictorial record of the Tudor court. The court of Elizabeth I comes to life for us through the art of the miniature. Nicholas **Hilliard** (*c.* 1547–1619) developed an unparalleled technique, delicate, refined and often lyrically poetic as in his *Young Man amid Roses* (*c.* 1590, Victoria and Albert Museum, London).

France Jean **Fouquet** (*c.* 1420–81) painted miniatures as well as altarpieces in which Italian influences take tangible shape. Jean **Clouet** (d. 1541) and his son François (d. 1572) were court painters to King

Major western artists

Period	Painters	Sculptors
Classical		Myron 5th century BC Phidias 5th century BC Polykleitos 5th century BC Praxiteles 4th century BC Lysippus 4th century BC
Medieval	Limbourg brothers early 15th century Duccio c. 1255/60–c. 1318 Giotto c. 1266–1337 Lorenzetti c. 1306–1345	Nicola and Giovanni Pisano working c. 1258–1314 Claus Sluter c. 1380–1406
Italian Renaissance	Masaccio 1401–1428 Leonardo da Vinci 1452–1519 Bellini c. 1430–1516 Mantegna c. 1431–1506 Raphael 1483–1520 Titian 1487–1576	Ghiberti 1378–1455 Donatello 1386–1466 Michelangelo 1475–1564
Mannerism	Rosso Fiorentino 1494–1540 Pontormo 1494–1556 Giulio Romano 1499–1546 Bronzino 1503–1572 Vasari 1511–1574	Cellini 1500–1571 Giambologna 1529–1608
15th and 16th centuries outside Italy	van Eyck c. 1390–1441 Bosch c. 1450–1516 Dürer 1471–1528 Brueghel the Elder 1525/30–1569 Holbein the Younger c. 1497–1543 El Greco 1541–1614	
17th century	Carracci 1560–1609 Caravaggio 1573–1610 Rubens 1577–1640 Poussin 1594–1665 Velázquez 1599–1660 Claude Lorrain 1600–1682 Rembrandt 1606–1669	Bernini 1598–1680
18th century	Watteau 1684–1721 Tiepolo 1696–1770 Gainsborough 1727–1788 Goya 1746–1828 David 1748–1825	Canova 1757–1822
19th century	Friedrich 1774–1840 Turner 1775–1851 Ingres 1780–1867 Delacroix 1798–1863 Courbet 1819–1877 Manet 1832–1883 Monet 1840–1926 Cézanne 1839–1906 van Gogh 1853–1890	Rodin 1840–1917
20th century	Kandinsky 1866–1944 Matisse 1869–1954 Mondrian 1872–1944 Picasso 1881–1973 Malevich 1878–1935 Duchamp 1887–1968 Pollock 1912–1956 Warhol 1928–1987 Bacon 1909–1992 Braque 1882–1963 Klee 1879–1940 Rothko 1903–1970	Brancusi 1876–1957 Giacometti 1901–1966 Moore 1898–1986 David Smith 1906–1965 Hepworth 1903–1975 Calder, Alexander 1898–1976 Gabo 1890–1977

Francis I. Jean's portrait of the king splendidly expresses the king's concern with elegance and decoration, and François' half-nude portrait of Diane de Poitiers, *The Lady in Her Bath*, is a piece of refined eroticism. His style reflects Italian Mannerist ideas as developed by the so-called *School of Fontainebleau* founded by Rosso and **Primaticcio** (1504/5–1570) who came to decorate the royal hunting lodge in the 1530s. They devised a unique type of stucco decoration combining figures in high relief with decorative swags, cartouches and strapwork. These Mannerist motifs were copied all over northern Europe, where they were called 'Renaissance'.

THE 17TH CENTURY

Italy in Rome, the Counter-Reformation of the Catholic church against Protestantism launched an exciting, emotionally appealing new style, the *Baroque*. The sculptor and architect Gianlorenzo **Bernini** (1598–1680) was its principal exponent, revitalizing Rome with his exuberantly dramatic masterpieces. His *Ecstasy of St Teresa* at Santa Maria della Vittoria is a theatrical set-piece in which supernatural light pours from a hidden window to illuminate the rapturous saint, whose body seems to shudder as an angel prepares to pierce her heart with the arrow of divine love.

Large-scale illusionistic fresco painting transformed ceilings into heavens, thronged with flying saints and angels. A spectacular example is Pietro **da Cortona**'s colossal *Allegory of Divine Providence* (1629–37) in the Barberini Palace, glorifying the pope and his family. Hundreds of figures are drawn upwards toward God's golden light, aswarm with bees, the Barberini family emblem.

Balancing this flamboyant artistic stream were the *Classicists*, who even in religious commissions looked back to the concepts of harmony and order of antiquity. Annibale **Carracci** (1560–1609) in the years around 1600 decorated Cardinal Farnese's gallery of antique sculpture in the Farnese Palace, turning the walls and ceiling into a *trompe l'oeil* classical picture gallery. He also introduced the landscape as a new category of art with his *Flight into Egypt* (1603), which has as its real subject an idealized vision of the classical Roman countryside, harmonious and calm.

Among Carracci's assistants who became famous in their own right were the consistently classicizing **Domenichino** (1581–1641) and Guido **Reni** (1575–1642) who often succumbed to popular taste with emotive paintings of repentant sinners rolling tearful eyes toward heaven. The work of Michelangelo Merisi da **Caravaggio** (1573–1619) introduced something totally different and unique, a harsh realism in which ordinary folk with dirty feet appear as saints and apostles, lit by a raking spotlight as if God's piercing eye had picked them out from the surrounding blackness of sin. One of his most striking followers was Georges **de la Tour** (1593–1652), a French artist whose simplified figures assume a spiritual purity, modelled by God's light in the form of a single candle shining in the darkness.

France art was used to establish the splendour of Louis XIV's centralized authority and divine kingship. Although grandiose in the extreme, the decorative schemes, portraits, and history paintings produced by the members of the new artists' Academy (formed 1648) were based on Classical rules, rigidly controlled by Charles **Lebrun** (1619–90), who was appointed First Painter to the King in 1662. He was the first Director of the Academy and of the Gobelins Manufactory, which employed its members to produce the art, tapestries, and furnishings for Louis's new Palace of Versailles.

The two major French artists of the century lived in Rome, escaping the constricting grip of the Academy. Claude **Lorrain** (1600–82) was the first painter to specialize entirely in landscapes, reducing the storytelling elements to small foreground figures. The romantic suggestiveness of the Classical past appealed to him, and he created an enchanting idyllic world, luminous and poetic. The intellectual Nicolas **Poussin** (1594–1665) composed his classical landscapes with mathematical precision but his people remained important, noble and heroic. Not even his religious works escape the pervasive influence of antiquity. In his *Last Supper* (1647, Edinburgh), Christ and the disciples lounge on couches as if at a Roman banquet.

Spain as in Rome, art in Spain aimed to excite Counter-Reformation zeal. José **Ribera** (1591–1652) carried a Caravaggesque style to brutal extremes to shock people into identifying with the sufferings inherent in Christian history. Francisco **Zurbarán** (1598–1664) expressed religious feeling in the opposite way, with solemn, silent monks and saints lost in a private world of meditation. Bartolomé Esteban **Murillo** (1617–82) painted sentimental *Holy Families* and sugar-sweet *Madonnas* fluently, cheerfully, and with a feather-light touch and lovely colours.

Diego Rodriguez de Silva **Velázquez** (1599–1660) was the giant of Spanish painting, reflecting many aspects of the 17th-century Spanish world. By 1623 he was court painter to Philip IV in Madrid, where he was influenced by Philip's collection of 16th century Venetian paintings. The most fascinating of his lifelike portraits of the Spanish court is *Las Meninas/The Ladies-in-Waiting* (1655, Prado, Madrid), a complex group portrait which includes Velázquez himself at his easel, and the king and queen as pale reflections in a mirror.

Netherlands Peter Paul **Rubens** (1577–1640) brought the sensual exuberance of the Italian Baroque to the Netherlands. A many-sided genius, artist, scholar and diplomat, he used his powerful pictorial imagination to create, with an army of assistants, innumerable religious and allegorical paintings for the churches and palaces of Catholic Europe. His largest commission was the cycle of 21 enormous canvases allegorizing the life of Marie de Medici, Queen of France (Louvre, Paris). His sheer delight in life can be seen in his magnificent colours, opulent nudes, and expansive landscapes.

Rubens's Grand Baroque style did not suit the Protestant merchants of the new Dutch Republic, who wanted small paintings reflecting their own lives and interests. Among the artists who responded to this demand, the towering genius was **Rembrandt** van Rijn (1606–69), all of whose paintings hint at some inner drama. In his portraits and biblical scenes he saw light as a spiritual mystery which momentarily allows his characters to loom out of the surrounding shadows.

His self-portraits (nearly 100 in number) touchingly trace the drama of his own passage through life and even the large group portrait, *The Night Watch* (1642) becomes a suspense story. A master draughtsman and printmaker, over 1,000 drawings survive.

The greatest of the straightforward portraitists was Frans **Hals** (c. 1581–1666), whose free brushstrokes caught fleeting moments brilliantly in such paintings as the so-called *Laughing Cavalier* (1624, Wallace Collection, London).

Genre pictures, scenes of daily life, merrymakers and peasants – often uncouth, comic, or satirical – were the speciality of such painters as Jan **Steen** (1626–79), in whose anecdotal scenes of traditional festivals or slovenly households the pleasures of drink, gluttony, and wantonness hold sway.

During the 1650s genre painters took a different view of their society. Instead of depicting boisterous low-life, painters like Pieter de **Hooch** (1629–84) chose scenes of domestic virtue, well-ordered households where families live in harmony in quiet sunlit rooms. Jan **Vermeer** (1632–75) was the greatest master of these scenes of peaceful prosperity, arranging domestic interiors as if they were abstract forms and enclosing his characters within an enamelled world of pearly light. *A Young Woman Standing at a Virginal* (c. 1670, National Gallery, London) is a superb example of the small group of paintings he produced, each one a masterpiece.

The Dutch specialities of seascape and landscape made giant strides during the century, based on low horizons with emphasis on a great expanse of sky. Experts in this were Aelbert **Cuyp** (1620–91) who bathed his views in a golden light, and Jacob van **Ruisdael** (1638/9–1709), who painted in many moods, responding to the shifting patterns of light and shade in nature.

Still-life painting also burgeoned: fruit, flowers, fish, banquets, breakfasts, groaning boards of every kind, in which the artist displayed skill in painting inanimate objects, often with a hidden religious significance.

England Charles I had employed Rubens to paint the ceiling of the Banqueting House at Whitehall 1629–30. Rubens's assistant Anthony **van Dyck** (1599–1641) became Court Painter in 1632 and created magnificent portraits of the aristocracy, cool and elegant in shimmering silks. The German Peter **Lely** (1618–80) succeeded him under the Restoration to depict a society that exudes an air of well-fed decadence. By contrast, the English-born Samuel **Cooper** (1609–72), painter to the Parliamentarians and most famous for his portraits of Oliver Cromwell ('warts and all'), was a miniaturist whose serious, objective portraits raised the status of his art to that of oil painting.

THE 18TH CENTURY

France the beginning of the 18th century saw the start of a frivolous new style in art, the *Rococo*. Jean-Antoine **Watteau** (1684–1721) devised for his aristocratic patrons the *Fête Gallante*, a type of painting in which amorous couples in poetic landscapes contemplate the transience of life and love.

The more overtly sensual work of François **Boucher** (1703–70), First Painter to Louis XV,

included voluptuous scenes of naked gods and goddesses. Painting at the same time, but completely against the mainstream, was Jean-Baptiste-Siméon **Chardin** (1699–1779), whose still-lifes and genre scenes have a masterful dignity. Jean-Honoré **Fragonard** (1732–1806) continued with the Rococo theme under Louis XVI, light-heartedly reflecting the licentiousness of courtly life. But all this changed with the Revolution and in 1789 Neo-Classicism became the dominant style under the Republic. Its artistic dictator, Jacques-Louis **David** (1748–1825) in his *Death of Marat* (1793) turned a political murder into a classical tragedy. Later, under Napoleon's Empire, David painted heroic portraits and scenes celebrating its glory.

Italy Antonio **Canova** (1757–1822), the sculptor, also exalted Napoleon and his family in classicizing portraits, and the vogue for this style dominated most English and European sculpture right through the Victorian era. Rococo illusionistic fresco-painting in Italy was the special province of Giovanni-Battista **Tiepolo** (1696–1770), a Venetian who decorated palaces and churches there and elsewhere in Europe. His painted ceilings became vast, airy regions whose delicate colour shadings made the sky seem endless.

The *vedutisti* (view-painters) produced souvenir views for young English gentlemen making the Grand Tour to complete their education with first-hand viewing of Renaissance and Classical art. In Venice, Francesco **Guardi** (1712–93) painted atmospheric visions of the floating city, pulsating with life. The views of (Giovanni) Antonio **Canaletto** (1697–1768), though faithfully observed, are static in comparison.

In Rome, Giovanni Battista **Piranesi** (1720–78) produced etchings inspired by his feelings for the evocative quality of ruins. His most original work, however, was a series which turned the ruins into images of terrifying imaginary prisons, fantasies of architectural madness.

Spain produced one artist of enormous talent and versatility, Francisco de **Goya** y Lucientes (1746–1828), whose work expresses a wide range of feeling and emotion and explores a variety of themes. Court Painter to Charles IV and later to Joseph Bonaparte under the French occupation of Spain, his portraits were acutely perceptive, his war scenes savagely dramatic, his religious paintings believable and his strange late fantasies powerfully imaginative. He is often seen as the source of 20th century art.

England produced a memorable group of fine artists, each expressing the varied interests of the age. Joseph **Wright** of Derby (1734–97), scientifically-minded, painted such scenes as *Experiment with an Air Pump* (1768). George **Stubbs** (1724–1806) specialized in horse paintings, based on painstaking scientific investigation. Sir Joshua **Reynolds** (1723–92), first President of the Royal Academy (founded 1768), wanted to introduce the European Grand Manner into English painting with history paintings on exalted themes of heroism, but the demand was for portraits; his were confident but lacking in spontaneity, based more on theory than on inspiration.

Thomas **Gainsborough** (1727–88) was also a popular portraitist, although he would have preferred to paint landscapes and made much of them in the backgrounds of his pictures. William **Hogarth** (1697–1764) is best known through engravings of his satirical series of paintings, such as *The Rake's Progress* (1735).

Reacting against the academic theorizing of Reynolds, the poet William **Blake** (1757–1827) illustrated his writings with mystical visions, and the imaginative Henry **Fuseli** (1741–1825) plumbed the depths of his subconscious for grotesque and fantastic dream images in such paintings as *The Nightmare* (1782).

THE 19TH CENTURY

France vast historical, religious, and mythological pictures were no longer greatly in demand, and after the fall of Napoleon in 1814 French artists trained in the Academic Grand Manner had to seek new dramatic themes. They looked to the world around them; Theodore **Géricault** (1791–1824) found his subject in the gruesome sufferings of the survivors of a recent shipwreck, which he portrayed in his huge *Raft of the Medusa* (1816, Louvre, Paris). His desire to express and evoke emotion put Géricault among the *Romantics*, whose art sought to speak passionately to the heart in contrast to the *Classicists* who appealed to the intellect. These two opposing approaches dominated much of the art of the century.

Eugène **Delacroix** (1798–1863) became the best-known Romantic painter. His *Massacre of Chios* (1824, Louvre) shows Greeks enslaved by wild Turkish horsemen, a contemporary atrocity. Admired as a colourist, he used a technique of divided brushwork – adjacent brush marks of contrasting colour which the eye mixes as it scans – that anticipates the Impressionists. He learned this from seeing Constable's *Hay Wain*, when it was exhibited in Paris in 1824.

By contrast, the brushwork is invisible in the enamelled paintings of Jean-Auguste-Dominique **Ingres** (1780–1867), the leading exponent of French Neo-Classicism. Drawing was the foundation of his style, emphasizing line and control at the expense of colour and expression.

Gustave **Courbet** (1819–77), reacting against both Classicists and Romantics, set out to establish a new *Realism*, based solely on direct observation of the things around him. His *Burial at Ornans* (1850) showed ordinary working people gathered round a village grave, and shocked the Establishment art world with its 'vulgarity' and 'coarseness'. Another Realist was Honoré **Daumier** (1808–79) whose lithographs of the 1830s dissected Parisian society with a surgeon's scalpel.

Throughout Europe, 19th-century artists found their ideal subject matter in the landscape. In France, Jean-Baptiste-Camille **Corot** (1796–1875) made it acceptable by recomposing his open-air studies into a harmonious, classical whole, although a romantic mood pervades his later misty confections. Theodore **Rousseau** (1812–67) led a group of artists who in 1844 sought refuge from the Industrial Revolution in the woods of Barbizon, near Paris. Their close observation of nature produced a new awareness of its changing moods. Jean-François **Millet** (1814–75) also settled at Barbizon but his romantic landscapes, such as *The Angelus* (1857–9, Louvre), introduce idealized peasants who manage to commune with nature while toiling to wrest from it their daily bread.

Germany a different, more melancholy Romantic sensibility invaded the landscapes of a small group of painters working in Germany. Seeking to express the mystery of God in nature and people's oneness with it, the evocative paintings of Caspar David **Friedrich** (1774–1840) usually include a small poetic figure contemplating distant mountain peaks or moonlit seashores.

England the two greatest artists of the century were landscapists – Joseph Mallord William **Turner** (1775–1851) and John **Constable** (1776–1837), both finding inspiration in the thriving English water-colour school. Turner was the master painter of English Romanticism.

Not concerned with the human figure, it was always through nature itself that he could express human feeling, as in the poignant last voyage of the ship *The Fighting Temeraire* (1839, Tate Gallery, London). His increasing obsession with light and its deep emotional significance turned his late pictures into misty abstract visions. Reputedly his dying words were 'The sun is God'.

Constable too was fascinated with the effects of light. He made innumerable painted sketches of the changing windy sky and in his *Hay Wain* used white marks like snowflakes to express the way light gave the landscape its freshness and sparkle.

Although primarily interested in romantic literary or biblical themes, the *Pre-Raphaelites* led by Dante Gabriel **Rossetti** (1828–82) in the 1840s and 50s took a detailed look at nature, in their claim to a realistic vision; from this influence the medievalist designer-artist William **Morris** (1834–96) developed his stylized patterns of leaves and flowers for fabrics and wallpapers.

The opposition to the Pre-Raphaelites was led by two Establishment artists, Frederic, Lord **Leighton** (1830–96) and Sir Lawrence **Alma-Tadema** (1836–1912), whose equally romantic view pretended to Classicism by centring on pseudo-genre scenes of daily life in ancient Greece and Rome. This pleased their educated patrons enough to earn knighthoods for them both.

Impressionism in the second half of the century France took an innovative look at nature. A direct precursor was Edouard **Manet** (1832–83), who carried on Courbet's scientific spirit of realism, making the eye the sole judge of reality. Stylistically, he gave up modelling forms in volume in favour of *suggesting* them by juxtaposed colours and gradations of tones, and, like Courbet, the subject matter of his pictures was always modern life. His *Déjeuner sur l'herbe/Luncheon on the Grass* (Louvre) updated a Renaissance prototype to 1862.

The Impressionists delighted in painting real life but the scenes and objects they painted became increasingly less important than the way they were affected by the ever-changing play of light. Evolving in the 1860s, the Impressionist group painted out of doors, capturing the immediacy and freshness of light on rippling water or on moving leaves. To catch these fleeting moments they broke up the forms they painted into fragments of pure colour laid side by side directly on the canvas, rather than mixing them on a palette. The members of the group were Alfred **Sisley** (1839–99), Camille **Pissarro** (1831–1903), Claude **Monet** (1840–1926) whose *Impression, Sunrise* of 1872 (Musée Marmottan, Paris) gave the movement its name, Pierre-Auguste **Renoir** (1841–1919), and Edgar **Degas** (1834–1917).

By the late 1870s they had each gone on to pursue individual interests, and the acceptance of a common purpose had had its day. Sisley and Pissarro continued painting landscapes, but Renoir became more interested in the female nude and Degas in 'snapshot' studies of dancers and jockeys. Degas hardly ever painted landscapes but instead concentrated on the spectacle of the racetrack and the ballet in oddly angled compositions influenced by snapshot photography. Monet remained obsessed with the optical effects of light on colour and carried his original fragmented technique to the final extreme in series of paintings such as those of the façade of Rouen Cathedral (1894) or his famous water lilies, showing the changing colour effects at different times of day. With these variations on a theme the actual subject did not matter at all, and in this he anticipated the abstract art of the 20th century.

Post-Impressionism other artists of the same generation who used the innovations of the Impressionists as a basis for developing their own styles are called the Post-Impressionists. They include Paul **Cézanne** (1839–1906), who infused something more permanent into their spontaneous vision by using geometrical shapes to form a solid scaffolding for his pictorial compositions; and Georges **Seurat** (1859–91), who achieved greater structure in his landscapes through the technique of *pointillism* (also known as Neo-Impressionism) which turns the Impressionist's separate brush-strokes into minute points of pure colour. The eye then mixes these for itself. Green grass, for instance, is made up of closely packed points of blue and yellow. In this painstaking method any idea of spontaneity vanishes, and the effect is stable and serene.

Henri de **Toulouse-Lautrec** (1864–1901) portrayed the low-life of Parisian bars and music halls without sentiment or judgement. Like Degas, he recorded contemporary life in informal poses from odd angles and his bold, colourful posters show the influence of Japanese colour prints.

The great Dutch individualist Vincent **van Gogh** (1853–90) longed to give visible form to every emotion and used violent rhythmic brushwork and brilliant unnatural colours to express his inner passions, even in something as simple as a pot of sunflowers. Paul **Gauguin** (1848–1903) also went beyond the Impressionists' notion of reality, seeking a more direct experience of life in the magical rites of so-called primitive peoples in his colourful works from the South Seas.

Symbolism was a movement initiated by poets as a reaction to materialist values, and their 1886 Manifesto sought to re-establish the imagination in art. Their most admired painter was Gustave **Moreau** (1826–98) whose paintings of biblical and mythological subjects contain psychological overtones expressed through exotic settings, strange colours and eerie light. Odilon **Redon** (1840–1916) trans-

lated dreams into bizarre and striking visual images. In the paintings of the Norwegian Edvard **Munch** (1863–1944), a particularly northern sense of fear and alienation is given extreme expression in such painings as *The Scream* (1893).

The Nabis (from Hebrew 'prophet') were followers of Gauguin who used simple forms and flat colours as he did for emotional effect, in a new style called *synthetisme*. Among the Nabis, Pierre **Bonnard** (1867–1947) and Edouard **Vuillard** (1868–1940) were less concerned with mystical ideas and found that with contemporary domestic interiors they could develop their interest in sumptuously coloured and patterned surfaces. Their work was dubbed *intimisme*.

sculpture the work of the Parisian Auguste **Rodin** (1840–1917) shows an extraordinary technical facility and a deep understanding of the human form. A romantic realist who infused his forms with passion, such famous sculptures as *The Thinker* and *The Kiss* were originally designed for a never-completed giant set of bronze doors, *The Gates of Hell*, with themes taken from Dante's *Divine Comedy*. The Musée Rodin in Paris houses many examples of his work and their preparatory drawings.

THE 2OTH CENTURY

The 20th century has been an age of experimentation, with the boundaries of art being continually stretched by a succession of avant-garde movements. The antinaturalism of the Symbolists and the Post-Impressionists, which attempted to reveal the essential reality behind the mere appearance of things, was continued in the first decade by Picasso, Matisse, and other artists before finally developing into complete abstraction.

Fauvism, a short-lived movement, began in France around 1905 and ended just three years later. The painters were nicknamed *Les Fauves* ('wild beasts') because of the extreme brilliance of the colours, which were often applied in jarring combinations to heighten the emotional impact. Henri **Matisse** (1869–1954), the major figure of the movement, spent his life refining this expressive use of pure colour partially influenced by the pattern-making of North African decorative art. André **Derain** (1880–1954) at this time enlarged the brushstrokes of Neo-Impressionism to produce a vibrant mosaic of colour, whereas Maurice **de Vlaminck** (1876–1958) was more influenced by the violent intensity of van Gogh. Georges **Rouault** (1871–1958), though associated with the group, employed more sombre colours enclosed by thick dark outlines reminiscent of stained glass.

Cubism was invented by Pablo **Picasso** (1881–1973) and the former Fauvist Georges **Braque** (1882–1963). By fragmenting the objects they depicted, then reconstructing them as a series of almost geometric facets that overlap and interlock with each other, they attempted to explode the harmonious and unified perspective of the Renaissance. In its place is an image of multiple viewpoints seen simultaneously. Initially the work grew out of Picasso's fascination with African sculpture as in his

Les Demoiselles d'Avignon (1907, MOMA, New York). The influence of Cézanne can also be found in the simplification of forms and the ambiguity of the picture space. Emotion and narrative were avoided, colours were muted, and anti-illusionistic devices such as stencilled writing and collage were introduced. The two artists worked closely together from 1907 to 1914 but neither believed in theorizing about their work. This was done by later followers Juan Gris, Albert Gleizes, Jean Metzinger, Fernand Léger, and Robert **Delaunay** (1885–1941), the last named forming his own, more sensual and poetic variant of Cubism known as *Orphism*.

Futurism The Italian poet Filippo **Marinetti** (1876–1944) published the *Futurist Manifesto* in 1909, which demanded a new art to celebrate the age of the machine. He called for the destruction of the museums and eulogized the modern world and the 'beauty of speed and energy'. The most talented of the artists inspired by his ideas was the painter and sculptor Umberto **Boccioni** (1882–1916), who wrote his own *Technical Manifesto of Painting* the following year. But it was not until a trip to Paris and contact with Cubism that the Futurist artists managed to create a sufficiently dynamic style to match their rhetoric. Giacomo **Balla** (1871–1958) produced the painting *Dog on a Leash* which attempted to convey sequential movement in the manner of the photographers Muybridge and Marey. Gino **Severini** (1883–1966) painted a topsy-turvy landscape as if seen from the moving window of a *Suburban Train Arriving at Paris* (1915, Tate Gallery, London). Boccioni's sculpture *Unique Forms of Continuity in Space* (1913, Tate Gallery) shows the dynamic interaction between a striding figure and its surrounding space.

Expressionism Germany was the scene of two successive Expressionist groups. In 1905 a group of artists in Dresden, with obvious parallels to the Fauves, founded *Die Brücke* ('the bridge'). Led by Ernst Ludwig **Kirchner** (1880–1938), they sought to express their 'inner convictions ... with spontaneity and sincerity'. This raw subjectivity is best seen in Kirchner's vivid scenes of the Berlin streets and in the prints of Karl **Schmidt-Rotluff** (1884–1976). The woodcut was a favourite medium of the group because of its primitive simplicity. In Munich *Der Blaue Reiter* ('the blue rider') group was set up in 1911 by Wassily **Kandinsky** (1866–1944). Influenced by the spiritual ideas of the Theosophists, Kandinsky believed that precise emotional and spiritual ideas could be conveyed by form and colour. He evolved a highly subjective style which finally became purely abstract. His colleague Franc **Marc** (1880–1916), partially inspired by Orphism, produced pantheistic celebrations of nature in which animals, particularly horses, dominate.

Suprematism After working in a manner that fused Cubism and Futurism with Russian folk styles, Kasimir **Malevich** (1878–1935) developed an abstract language of simple geometrical forms which he called Suprematism. In 1913, he painted a black square on a white ground as a rejection of 'ordinary objective life'. A white square on a white ground represented the ultimate in spiritual enlightenment, uniting the viewer with the infinite.

Constructivism was another Russian movement that also employed a nonobjective visual language, but in the service of the Revolution rather than the spiritual. *Beat the Whites with the Red Wedge* (1919) by El **Lissitsky** (1890–1941) (a student of Malevich) has an easily understandable and overtly political message. Vladimir **Tatlin** (1885–1953) designed a *Monument to the Third International* as a vast, skeletal, rotating tower, symbolic of technical endeavour and aspiration – it was never built. Naum **Gabo** (1890–1977) was less political than Tatlin but as important in pioneering the new 'constructed' architectural sculpture that employed materials like plastic to reveal the structural logic of the form. Stalin denounced these artists as bourgeois formalists and instead favoured a highly academic, official style known as Socialist Realism.

Neo-Plasticism Dutch painter Piet **Mondrian** (1872–1944), like Malevich, tried to express the 'truths of the universe' through pure aesthetics. Using primary colours, black, white, and grey, he painted parallel horizontal lines that intersected vertical ones. The perfection described by the parallel lines, the right-angle intersections, and the rectangles of pure colour were meant to mirror the ultimate perfection of the universe. In 1917 he headed a group called *De Stijl* ('the style') which included Theo **van Doesburg** (1883–1931) and the furniture designer Gerrit **Rietveld** (1888–1964). Like the Constructivists, with whom they had links, they believed in the artist as 'designer' with responsibilities to enhance every aspect of modern life by their work.

Many of the ideas of these seemingly disparate Modern groups were propagated at the *Bauhaus*, an influential German school of art and design, where several major artists, including Kandinsky, taught.

Dada, so called for its infantile associations, was considerably less positive and utopian in its aims. Born at the Cabaret Voltaire, Zürich, Switzerland, in 1916, it was an anarchic series of gestures that aimed to shock by undermining the sanctity of art with all its rules and values. Tristan **Tzara** 'created' poems by tearing out words from newspapers, then drawing them out of a hat. Similarly, Hans **Arp** (1887–1966) made collages by randomly dropping pieces of paper, then fixing them where they landed. Chance was more valid than choice. At the same time in New York, Marcel **Duchamp** (1887–1968) exhibited 'ready-made' art works: a snow shovel bought in a hardware store, a bicycle wheel mounted on a stool, a urinal.

Surrealism succeeded Dada. In 1922 the French writer André **Breton** (1896–1966) made it a coherent and organized group, precisely what Dada rejected. Freud's investigations into the unconscious were an inspiration, as were the strange empty townscapes of the Italian painter Giorgio **de Chirico** (1888–1978). Some Surrealist artists, like André **Masson** (1896–   ) and Joan **Miro** (1893–1983), attempted to connect with the unconscious through automatic drawing. Others, like Salvador **Dali** (1904–1989) and René **Magritte** (1898–1967), used a more realistic style to create an imagery of dreams. In both cases, thought and creativity were liberated by the absence of reason. Even Picasso was regarded as a Surrealist by Breton and certainly his work of the late 1920s and the 1930s explored the destructive human impulses. This is most dramatically seen in **Guernica** (1936, Prado, Madrid), in which his horrified reaction to the German Luftwaffe's bombing of a Basque town during the Spanish Civil War has the quality of an epic nightmare.

The impact of Surrealism was widespread. In Britain the landscapes of Paul **Nash** (1889–1946) became even more haunted and mysterious. The Swiss painter Paul **Klee** (1879–1940) painted quirky semiabstract pictures and Marc **Chagall** (1881–1955) evoked the memories of his Jewish-Russian childhood. Both artist delved into the imagination for their visions in a way that paralleled Surrealism.

Abstract Expressionism Many European artists moved to the USA in the years around World War II. New York became the centre of world art and Abstract Expressionism its first major movement. Influenced by Mondrian as well as by Surrealism, US avant-garde painting divided into two groups: the Gesture painters (or Action painters) and the Colour Field painters. Jackson **Pollock** (1912–1956) led the Gesture painters. By putting his canvas on the floor and swirling paint on it, he created a complex web of multicoloured trails which spectators could retrace with their eyes, thereby reliving the artist's dynamic act of creation. The Colour Field painter Mark **Rothko** (1903–1970) filled large canvases with shimmering blocks of solid colour, the contemplation of which offered the spectator a transcendent experience.

Pop art was to some extent a reaction against the anguished soul-searching of Abstract Expressionism as well as being a celebration of consumerism and popular culture. Pop artists plundered the mass media, employing the imagery of advertising, comic strips, and the movies. Jasper **Johns** (1930–) gave us paintings of targets and the American flag in endless permutations. Andy **Warhol** (1928–1987), through the medium of the screen print, transformed celebrities and events, from Marilyn Monroe to the electric chair, into contemporary icons. Roy **Lichtenstein** (1923–), in paintings like *Whaam!* (1963, Tate Gallery, London) presents a comic-strip moment in a wittily depersonalized parody of its original style. In the UK, artists like Richard **Hamilton** (1922–) and Eduoardo **Paolozzi** (1924–)had a similar disregard for the division between high and low culture. In Paolozzi's case this meant using almost any material that came to hand, making his collages and sculptures almost archaeological concentrates of the late 20th century.

Op art The paintings of Victor **Vasarely** (1908–) and Bridget **Riley** (1931–) use abstraction to create optical illusions, confusing the spectator's eye with coloured lines and dots that appear to jump, blend, and waver.

In sculpture the influence of Rodin dominated the early years of the century. Matisse, Émile-Antoine **Bourdelle** (1861–1929), and the Cubist sculptors extended Rodin's liberated attitude to the human form as a complex and dynamic surface. The raw directness of African sculpture affected the work of Jacob **Epstein** (1880–1959), Henri **Gaudier-Brzeska** (1891–1915), and Amedeo **Modigliani** (1884–1920), while in Germany Ernst **Barlach**

(1870–1938) derived similar inspiration from late Gothic sculpture. Constantin **Brancusi** (1876–1957) in his carvings gradually refined and simplified his work into pure, almost abstract forms, like the ovoid *Prometheus* (1911). Henry **Moore** (1898–1957) created a more rugged reduction of the human form which reflects the full and flowing contours of nature. At the other extreme, the elongated and emaciated figures of Alberto **Giacometti** (1901–1966) emit a sense of spiritual and existential isolation. Both Dada and Cubist collage encouraged a more varied and untraditional choice and use of materials, evident in the work of the Russian Constructivists. In the 1930s Picasso and Julio **Gonzalez** (1876–1972) made highly linear 'drawings in space' by welding sheets and strips of metal together. This direction was pursued in a more dramatic and monumental way by David **Smith** (1906–1965) and his fellow American Alexander **Calder** (1989–1976), who invented mobiles, flat shapes attached in patterns to rods that hang from the ceiling and move gently in the air. More recently Jean **Tinguely** (1925–) has employed electricity to create movement in his elaborate, whimsical machine constructions.

contemporary trends Since the freethinking 1960s, a bewildering number of new trends and movements have appeared, many of which stress the intellectual and material processes behind an art work's creation.

Minimalism reacted to the promiscuity of Pop art by reducing the art object to a bare and essential purity, devoid of any exterior reference or meaning. *Equivalent VIII* (1966) by Carl **Andre** (1935–), two layers of bricks laid on the floor, caused great controversy when purchased by the Tate Gallery, London.

Super Realism or *Photo Realism* imitates reality through exact, illusionistic copies of colour photographs in the work of Richard **Estes** (1932–)and waxworklike sculptures in the work of Duane **Hanson** (1925–). Meaning and intention are obscured by the clinical detachment of the execution and the banality of the subject matter.

Conceptualism Here the actual art object is challenged and sometimes replaced by the ideas behind it. Documentation in the form of statements and photographs may be presented on gallery walls.

Performance art is the staging of events by artists. It may be theatrical but it differs from theatre in its emphasis on visual complexity rather than on a text. In *Body art* the artist uses his or her own body as a vehicle for often confrontational ideas. *Land art* or *Earth art* involves the direct interaction of the artist with the environment. It is usually ephemeral and so preserved only in documentation. **Christo** Javacheff (1935–) has wrapped up part of the Australian coastline (1979), erected a curtain in a Colorado valley (1981), and a long running fence across California (1986). Richard **Long** (1945–) maps and photographs his landscape journeys, displaying them in galleries with works made from natural materials collected en route.

Although these developments undermined the conventional notion of the art work as permanent and unique, traditional forms like figurative oil painting have, even so, continued to thrive since World War II, albeit in increasingly extreme manifestations. In the work of the painter Francis **Bacon** (1909-1992), scenes of horror and brutality are presented as the typical condition of modern humans. Since the 1970s, other painters, the so-called *Neo-Expressionists* or *Bad painters*, like Julian **Schnabel** (1951–), Anselm **Kiefer** (1945–), Georg **Baselitz** (1938–), and Francesco **Clemente** (1952–), have created an equally direct and lurid visual language in order to explore issues of personal and national history and mythology.

Eastern Art

Chinese art From the Bronze Age to the Cultural Revolution, Chinese art shows a stylistic unity unparalleled in any other culture. From about the 1st century AD Buddhism inspired much sculpture and painting. The *Han dynasty* (206 BC–AD 220) produced outstanding metalwork, ceramics, and sculpture. The *Song dynasty* (960–1278) established standards of idyllic landscape and nature painting in a delicate calligraphic style.

Neolithic Period Accomplished pottery dates back to about 2500 BC, already showing a distinctive Chinese approach to form.

Bronze Age Rich burial goods, with bronzes and jade carvings, survive from the second millennium BC, decorated with hieroglyphs and simple stylized animal forms. Astonishing life-size terracotta figures from the Qin period (about 221–206 BC) guard the tomb of Emperor Shi Huangdi in the old capital of Xian. Bronze horses, naturalistic but displaying the soft curving lines of the Chinese style, are a feature of the Han dynasty.

Early Buddhism Once Buddhism was established in China it inspired a monumental art, with huge rock-cut Buddhas and graceful linear relief sculptures at the monasteries of Yungang, about 460–535, and Longmen. Bronze images show the same curving lines and rounded forms.

Tang dynasty (618–907) Art during the Tang dynasty shows increasing sophistication in idealized images and naturalistic portraits, such as the carved figures of Buddhist monks (Luohan). This period also produced brilliant metalwork and delicate ceramics. It is known that the aims and, broadly speaking, the style of Chinese painting were already well established, but few paintings survive, with the exception of some Tang scrolls and silk paintings.

Song dynasty The golden age of painting was during the Song dynasty (960–1278). The imperial court created its own workshop, fostering a fine calligraphic art, mainly devoted to natural subjects – landscape, mountains, trees, flowers, birds, and horses – though genre scenes of court beauties were also popular. Scrolls, albums, and fans of silk or paper were painted with watercolours and ink, using soft brushes that produced many different textures. Painting was associated with literature, and painters added poems or quotations to their work to intensify the effect. Ma Yuan (*c.* 1190–1224) and Xia Gui (active *c.* 1180–1230) are among the painters; Muqi (1180–*c.* 1270) was a monk known for exquisite brushwork. The Song dynasty also produced the first true porcelain, achieving a classic simplicity and delicacy in colouring and form.

Ming dynasty (1368–1644) Painters of this period continued the landscape tradition, setting new standards in idealized visions. The painter Dong Qichang wrote a history and theory of Chinese painting. The Song style of porcelain gradually gave way to increasingly elaborate decorative work, and pale shades were superseded by rich colours, as in Ming blue-and- white patterned ware.

Qing dynasty (1644–1911) During the Qing dynasty the so-called Individualist Spirits emerged, painters who developed bolder, personal styles of brushwork.

20th century The strong spirit that supported traditional art began to fade in the 19th and 20th centuries, but attempts to incorporate modernist ideas have been frowned on by the authorities. Not directly concerned with the representation of political events, Chinese art took some years before responding to the political upheavals of this century. Subsequently, response to offical directives produced a period of Soviet-style realism followed by a reversion to a peasant school of painting, which was the officially favoured direction for art during the Cultural Revolution. Mao Zedong was a calligrapher and calligraphy remains, perhaps, the most flourishing art form in China.

Influence Chinese art had a great impact on surrounding countries. The art of Korea was almost wholly inspired by Chinese example for many centuries. Along with Buddhism, Chinese styles of art were established in Japan in the 6th–7th centuries BC and continued to exert a profound influence, though Japanese culture soon developed an independent style.

Indian art Indian art dates back to the ancient Indus Valley civilization of about 3000 BC. Sophisticated artistic styles emerged from the 1st century AD. Buddhist art includes sculptures and murals. Hindu artists created sculptural schemes in caves and huge temple complexes; the Hindu style is lively, with voluptuous nude figures. The Islamic Mogul Empire of the 16th-17th centuries created an exquisite style of miniature painting, inspired by Persian examples.

Buddhist art In NW India the Gandhara kingdom produced the first known images of the Buddha in a monumental soft and rounded style that was exported, with the Buddhist religion, to China, Korea, and Japan. The Kusana and Andhra periods (1st-4th centuries AD) led to the mature and voluptuous art of the Gupta period, which spread widely over SE Asia. The Gupta kingdom emerged around the 4th century AD in the Ganges plain; Mathura, Sarnath, Ajanta, and Aurangabad were centres of Buddhist sculpture. The caves of Ajanta have extensive remains of murals of the 5th and 6th centuries as well as sculpture. The same tradition led in the 6th and 7th centuries to the painting of frescoes, usually depicting incidents in the legends of the Buddhist, Hindu, and Jain religions.

Hindu art Hinduism advanced further in central and S India. Influenced by Buddhist art, Hindu artists created brilliant sculptural schemes in rock-cut caves at Mamallapuram, and huge temple complexes: for example, in Orissa, Konarak, and Khajuraho. The caves at Ellora are known for their ensemble of religious art (Buddhist, Hindu, and Jain) dating from the 6th and 7th centuries. By the 13th century Hinduism became the major religion. The figures of its many exotic deities are rounded and sensuous, their poses based on religious dance movements. Eroticism enters with exuberantly amorous couples symbolizing the unity of the divine. Sculpture was generally of a religious character, but the Gujarat school also excelled in decorating dwelling houses.

Mogul art dates from the Muslim invasion of NW India in the Middle Ages. The invaders destroyed Buddhist and Hindu temple art and introduced their own styles. An early example of their work is the Q'utb mosque of about 1200 in Delhi. They introduced a school of painting based on Persian forms; Indian artists absorbed and expanded this art with great technical virtuosity. Court artists excelled in miniature painting, particularly in the reigns of Jehangir and Shah Jahan (*c.* 1566-1658). Their subjects ranged from portraiture and histories to birds, animals, and flowers. After a period of decline, Indian art has enjoyed a renaissance in modern times, for example the work of Abanindranath Tagore, Amrita Sher-Gil, Jamini Roy, and Sailoz Mookherjee.

Japanese art Early Japanese art was influenced by China. Painting later developed a distinct Japanese character, bolder and more angular, with the spread of Zen Buddhism in the 12th century. Ink painting and calligraphy flourished, followed by book illustration and decorative screens. Japanese prints developed in the 17th century, with multicolour prints invented around 1765. Buddhist sculpture proliferated from 580, and Japanese sculptors excelled at portraits. Japanese pottery stresses simplicity.

The *Jōmon* period (10,000–300 BC) was characterized by cord-marked pottery. In the *Yayoi* period (300 BC–AD 300) elegant pottery with geometric designs and *dōtaku*, bronze bells decorated with engravings, were the dominant *objets d'art*. During the *Kofun* period (300–552) burial mounds held *haniwa*, clay figures, some of which show Chinese influence. The *Asuka* period (552–646) is characterized by Buddhist art, introduced from Korea 552, which flourished in sculpture, metalwork, and embroidered silk banners. Painters' guilds were formed. During the *Nara* period (646–794) religious and portrait sculptures were made of bronze, clay, or dry lacquer. A few painted scrolls, screens, and murals survive. Textiles were decorated with batik, tie-dye, stencils, embroidery, and brocade. In the *Heian* period (794–1185) Buddhist statues became formalized and were usually made of wood. Shinto images emerged. A native style of secular painting (*Yamato-e*) developed, especially in scroll painting, with a strong emphasis on surface design. Lacquerware was also decoratively stylized. In the *Kamakura* period (1185–1392) sculpture and painting became vigorously realistic. Portraits were important, as were landscapes and religious, narrative, and humorous picture scrolls. During the *Ashikaga* or *Muromachi* period (1392–1568) the rapid ink sketch in line and wash introduced by Zen priests from China became popular. Pottery gained in importance from the spread of the tea ceremony. Masks and costumes were made for Nō theatre. Artists of the *Momoyama* period (1568–1615) produced beautiful screens to decorate palaces and castles. The arrival of Korean potters also inspired new styles. The *Tokugawa* or *Edo* period (1615–1867) is characterized by the print (*ukiyo-e*) which originated in genre paintings of 16th- and 17th-century kabuki actors and teahouse women. It developed into the woodcut and after 1740 the true colour print, while its range of subject matter expanded. *Ukiyo-e* artists include Utamaro and Hokusai. Lacquer and textiles became more sumptuous. Tiny *netsuke* figures were mostly carved from ivory or wood. In the *Meiji* period (1868–1912) painting was influenced by styles of Western art, for example Impressionism. Most recently, in the *Shōwa* period (1926–89), attempts were made to revive the traditional Japanese painting style and to combine traditional and foreign styles.

CINEMA

Great Directors

Allen Woody. Adopted name of Allen Stewart Konigsberg 1935– . US film writer, director, and actor, known for his cynical, witty, often self-deprecating parody and offbeat humor.

His films include *Sleeper* 1973, *Annie Hall* 1977 (for which he won three Academy Awards), *Manhattan* 1979, and *Hannah and Her Sisters* 1986, all of which he directed, wrote, and appeared in. From the late 1970s, Allen has mixed his output of comedies with straight dramas, such as *Interiors* 1978 and *Another Woman* 1988, but *Crimes and Misdemeanors* 1990 broke with tradition by combining humour and straight drama. Other films include *Take the Money and Run* 1969, *Sleeper* 1973, *Love and Death* 1975, *Stardust Memories* 1982, *Zelig* 1983, *Purple Rose of Cairo* 1985, *Night and Fog* 1991 and *Manhattan Murder Mystery* 1993.

Altman Robert 1925– . US maverick film director. His antiwar comedy *M.A.S.H.* 1970 was a critical and commercial success; subsequent films include *McCabe and Mrs Miller* 1971, *The Long Goodbye* 1973, *Nashville* 1975, and *Popeye* 1980.

Antonioni Michelangelo 1912– . Italian film director, whose work evinces both formal innovation and an acute power to analyse the effects of affluence and technology on contemporary sensibility. He began as a maker of documentaries and directed his first feature film, *Cronaca di un Amore* in 1950, gradually developing the elliptical approach to narrative seen in *L'Avventura* 1960 and its successors. His other films include *Blow Up* 1966, filmed in England, the US-made *Zabriskie Point* 1970, *The Passenger* 1974, and *Identification of a Woman* 1982.

Bergman Ingmar 1918– . Swedish stage producer (from the 1930s) and film director (from the 1950s). His work deals with complex moral, psychological, and metaphysical problems and is tinged with pessimism. His films include *Wild Strawberries* 1957, *The Seventh Seal* 1957, *Persona* 1966, *Cries and Whispers* 1972, *The Serpent's Egg* and *Autumn Sonata* both 1978, and *Fanny and Alexander* 1982. He is one of the greatest directors of acting performances.

Buñuel Luis 1900–1983. Spanish Surrealist film director. He collaborated with Salvador Dali on *Un Chien andalou* 1928 and *L'Age d'or/The Golden Age* 1930, and established his solo career in Mexico with *Los olvidados/The Young and the Damned* 1950. His works are often anticlerical, with black humour and erotic imagery.

Later, he worked in France with higher budgets on such films as *Le Charme discret de la bourgeoisie/The Discreet Charm of the Bourgeoisie* 1972 (Academy Award winner) and *Cet Obscur Objet du désir/That Obscure Object of Desire* 1977.

Capra Frank 1897–1991. Italian-born US film director. His satirical, populist comedies, which often have idealistic heroes, were hugely successful in the 1930s, and he won Academy Awards for *It Happened One Night* 1934, *Mr Deeds Goes to Town* 1936, and *Mr Smith Goes to Washington* 1939.

Capra began as a gagman for silent comedies, then directed several films with Harry Langdon (1884–1944). An instinctive craftsman, his popular success continued after World War II with the sentimental and imaginative *It's a Wonderful Life* 1946, but subsequently waned. His later work included *A Hole in the Head* 1959 and *A Pocketful of Miracles* 1961.

Carné Marcel 1909– . French director known for the romantic fatalism of such films as *Drôle de Drame* 1936, *Hôtel du Nord* 1938, *Le Quai des brumes/Port of Shadows* 1938, and *Le Jour se lève/Daybreak* 1939. His masterpiece, *Les Enfants du paradis/The Children of Paradise* 1943–45, was made with his longtime collaborator, the poet and screenwriter Jacques Prévert (1900-1977).

Chaplin Charlie (Charles Spencer) 1889–1977. English film actor and director. He made his reputation as a tramp with a smudge moustache, bowler hat, and twirling cane in silent comedies from the mid-1910s, including *The Rink* 1916, *The Kid* 1920, and *The Gold Rush* 1925. His work often contrasts buffoonery with pathos, and his later films combine dialogue with mime and music, as in *The Great Dictator* 1940 and *Limelight* 1952 (the latter won an Oscar for Chaplin's musical theme). His other films include *City Lights* 1931, *Modern Times* 1936, and *Monsieur Verdoux* 1947. He was one of cinema's most popular and greatest stars, and his "Little Tramp' character became recognized and loved the world over.

Chaplin was born in south London and first appeared on the stage at the age of five. In 1913 he joined Mack Sennett's Keystone Company in Los Angeles, and from 1915 he took artistic control of all his films. When accused of communist sympathies during the McCarthy witchhunt, he left the USA 1952 and moved to Switzerland. He received special Oscars 1928 and 1972.

Coppola Francis Ford 1939– . US film director and screenwriter. He directed *The Godfather* 1972, which became one of the biggest money-making films of all time, and its sequels *The Godfather Part II* 1974, which garnered seven Academy Awards, and *The Godfather Part III* 1990. His other films include *Apocalypse Now* 1979, *One From the Heart* 1982, *Rumblefish* 1983, *The Outsiders* 1983, and *Tucker: The Man and His Dream* 1988.

After working on horror B-films, his first successes were *Finian's Rainbow* 1968 and *Patton* 1969, for which his screenplay won an Academy Award. Among his other films are *The Conversation* 1972, *The Cotton Club* 1984, and *Gardens of Stone* 1987.

De Mille Cecil B(lount) 1881–1959. US film director and producer. He entered films 1913 with Jesse L Lasky (with whom he later established Paramount Pictures), and was one of the founders of Hollywood. He specialized in biblical epics, such as *The Sign of the Cross* 1932 and *The Ten Commandments* 1923; remade 1956. He also made the 1952 Academy Award-winning circus movie *The Greatest Show on Earth*.

De Sica Vittorio 1902–1974. Italian director and actor. He won his first Oscar with *Bicycle Thieves* 1948, a film of subtle realism. Later films included *Umberto D* 1952, *Two Women* 1960, and *The Garden of the Finzi-Continis* 1971. His considerable acting credits include *Madame de ...* 1953 and *The Millionaires* 1960.

Disney Walt(er Elias) 1901–1966. US filmmaker and animator, a pioneer of family entertainment. He established his own studio in Hollywood 1923, and his first Mickey Mouse cartoons (*Plane Crazy*, which was silent, and *Steamboat Willie*, which had sound) appeared 1928. In addition to short cartoons, the studio made feature-length animated films, including *Snow White and the Seven Dwarfs* 1938, *Pinocchio* 1940, *Fantasia* 1940, *Dumbo* 1941, *Bambi* 1942, *Cinderella* 1950, *Alice in Wonderland* 1952, and *Peter Pan* 1953. Disney's cartoon figures also appeared in comic books, magazines, books, and records, which helped make his animated characters loved throughout the world.

The Disney studio also made nature-study films such as *The Living Desert* 1953, which have been criticized for their fictionalization of nature: wild animals were placed in unnatural situations to create "drama'. Feature films with human casts were made from 1946, such as *Davy Crockett* 1955, *The Swiss Family Robinson* 1960, and *Mary Poppins* 1964.

Disney produced the first television series in colour in 1961. He also conceived the idea of theme parks, of which Disneyland, California was the first (1955). Walt Disney World, near Orlando, Florida, 1971, included the Epcot (Experimental Prototype Community of Tomorrow) Center 1982, a cross between a science museum and a theme park. There is also a park in Tokyo, Japan, and – opened in 1992 – the EuroDisney park in Paris, France.

Dreyer Carl Theodor 1889–1968. Danish film director. His wide range of films include the austere silent classic *La Passion de Jeanne d'Arc/The Passion of Joan of Arc* 1928 and the Expressionist horror film *Vampyr* 1932, after the failure of which Dreyer made no full-length films until *Vredens Dag/Day of Wrath* 1943. His two late masterpieces are *Ordet/The Word* 1955 and *Gertrud* 1964.

Eisenstein Sergei Mikhailovich 1898–1948. Latvian film director who pioneered film theory and introduced the use of montage (the juxtaposition of shots to create a particular effect) as a means of propaganda, as in *The Battleship Potemkin* 1925.

The Soviet dictator Stalin banned the second part of Eisenstein's projected trilogy *Ivan the Terrible* 1944–46. The last part was never made. His other films include *Strike* 1925, *October* 1928, *Que Viva Mexico!* 1931–32, and *Alexander Nevsky* 1938.

Fellini Federico 1920–1993. Italian film director whose films combine dream and fantasy sequences with satire and autobiographical details. His films include *I vitelloni/The Young and the Passionate* 1953, *La Strada* 1954 (Academy Award 1956), *Le notti di Cabiria/The Nights of Cabiria* 1956, *La dolce vita* 1960, *Otto e mezzo/8 ¹/₂* 1963, *Giulietta degli spiriti/Juliet of the Spirits* 1965, *Satyricon* 1969, *Roma/Fellini's Roma* 1972, *Amarcord* 1974, *Casanova* 1976, and *La città delle donne/City of Women* 1980.

Ford John. Adopted name of Sean O'Feeney 1895–1973. US film director. Active from the silent film era, he was one of the early creators of the 'Western', directing *The Iron Horse* 1924; *Stagecoach* 1939 became his masterpiece. But he also worked in many other genres, and won Academy Awards for *The Informer* 1935, *The Grapes of Wrath* 1940, *How Green Was My Valley* 1941, and *The Quiet Man* 1952.

Other films include *They Were Expendable* 1945, *She Wore a Yellow Ribbon* 1949, *Rio Grande* 1950, *The Last Hurrah* 1958, and *The Man Who Shot Liberty Valance* 1962.

Gance Abel 1889–1981. French film director who was one of the great innovators of the French silent cinema. His romantic epic *Napoléon* 1927 (restored in 1980 and subsequently widely shown) was the high point of his career. One of the most ambitious silent epic films, it features colour and triple-screen sequences, as well as multiple-exposure shots.

An actor in films from 1909 and a director from 1912, Gance showed his inclination for experiment in films such as *J'Accuse* 1919 and *La Roue* 1922. The process culminated in *Napoléon*, with its extravagant use of hand-held cameras, rapid cutting, and superimpositions. The arrival of sound seemed to stifle his creative output, though he continued to work, mainly on historical films, until the 1960s. Later films included *Lucreze Borgia* 1935 and *Austerlitz* 1960.

Godard Jean-Luc 1930– . French film director, one of the leaders of New Wave cinema. His works are often characterized by experimental techniques and an unconventional dramatic form, as well as by political allusions. His films include *A bout de souffle* 1959, *Vivre sa Vie* 1962, *Pierrot le fou* 1965, *Weekend* 1968, and *Je vous salue, Marie* 1985.

Griffith D(avid) W(ark) 1875–1948. US film director, one of the most influential figures in the development of cinema as an art. He made hundreds of "one-reelers' 1908–13, in which he pioneered the techniques of masking, fade-out, flashback, crosscut, close-up, and long shot. After much experimentation, his masterpiece as a director emerged, *The Birth of a Nation* 1915, about the aftermath of the Civil War, later criticized as degrading to blacks.

Other films include the epic *Intolerance* 1916, *Broken Blossoms* 1919, *Way Down East* 1920, *Orphans of the Storm* 1921, and *The Struggle* 1931. He was a cofounder of United Artists 1919. With the advent of sound, his reputation was eclipsed, and he lived forgotten in Hollywood until his death.

Hawks Howard 1896–1977. US director and producer. In a career spanning over four decades, Hawks worked in virtually all the popular American genres – westerns, thrillers, screwball comedies, among others – and brought to them a skill and professionalism that made him the arch-exponent of Hollywood filmmaking.

Hawks had been an aviator and racing driver before entering the cinema, and films as varied as *Scarface* 1932, *The Big Sleep* 1946, and *Rio Bravo* 1959 are concerned with both danger and the need for functional expertise. At the same time, uniquely fast-talking comedies like *His Girl Friday* 1940 turned the preoccupations of his action movies on their head by dramatising the lure of irresponsibility. His other films

Cinema: chronology

1826–34	Various machines invented to show moving images: the stroboscope, zoetrope, and thaumatrope.
1872	Eadweard Muybridge demonstrated movement of horses' legs by using 24 cameras.
1877	Invention of Praxinoscope; developed as a projector of successive images on screen 1879 in France.
1878–95	Marey, a French physiologist, developed various types of camera for recording human and animal movements.
1887	Augustin le Prince produced the first series of images on a perforated film; Thomas A Edison, having developed the phonograph, took the first steps in developing a motion-picture recording and reproducing device to accompany recorded sound.
1888	William Friese-Greene (1855-1921) showed the first celluloid film and patented a movie camera.
1889	Edison invented 35-mm film.
1890–94	Edison, using perforated film, developed his Kinetograph camera and Kinetoscope individual viewer; developed commercially in New York, London, and Paris.
1895	The Lumière brothers projected, to a paying audience, a film of an oncoming train arriving at a station. Some of the audience fled in terror.
1896	Charles Pathé introduced the Berliner gramophone, using discs in synchronization with film. Lack of amplification, however, made the performances ineffective.
1900	Attempts to synchronize film and disc were made by Leon Gaumont (1863–1946) in France and Goldschmidt in Germany, leading later to the Vitaphone system of the USA.
1902	Georges Méliès made *Le Voyage dans la Lune/A Trip to the Moon*.
1903	The first Western was made in the USA: *The Great Train Robbery* by Edwin Porter.
1906	The earliest colour film (Kinemacolor) was patented in Britain by George Albert Smith (1864–1959).
1907–11	The first films shot in the Los Angeles area called Hollywood. In France, Emile Cohl (1857–1938) experimented with film animation.
1911	The first Hollywood studio, Horsley's Centaur Film Company, was established, followed in 1915 by Carl Laemmle's Universal City and Thomas Ince's studio.
1912	In Britain, Eugene Lauste designed experimental 'sound on film' systems.
1914–18	Full newsreel coverage of World War I.
1915	*The Birth of a Nation*, D W Griffith's epic on the American Civil War, was released in the USA.
1917	35 mm was officially adopted as the standard format for motion picture film by the Society of Motion Picture Engineers of America.
1918–19	A sound system called Tri-Ergon was developed in Germany, which led to sound being recorded on film photographically. Photography with sound was also developed in the USA by Lee De Forest in his Phonofilm system.
1923	First sound film (as Phonofilm) demonstrated.
1926	*Don Juan*, a silent film with a synchronized music score, was released.
1927	Release of the first major sound film, *The Jazz Singer*, consisting of some songs and a few moments of dialogue, by Warner Brothers, New York City. The first Academy Awards (Oscars) were presented.
1928	Walt Disney released his first Mickey Mouse cartoon, *Steamboat Willie*. The first all-talking film, *Lights of New York*, was released.
1930	*The Big Trail*, a Western filmed and shown in 70-mm rather than the standard 35-mm format, was released. 70 mm is still used, mainly for big-budget epics such as *Lawrence of Arabia*.
1932	Technicolor (three-colour) process introduced and used for a Walt Disney cartoon film.
1935	*Becky Sharp*, the first film in three-colour Technicolor was released.
1937	Walt Disney released the first feature-length (82 minutes) cartoon, *Snow White and the Seven Dwarfs*.
1939	*Gone With the Wind*, regarded as one of Hollywood's greatest achievements, was released.
1952	Cinerama, a wide-screen presentation using three cameras and three projectors, was introduced in New York.
1953	Commercial 3-D (three-dimensional) cinema and wide-screen CinemaScope were launched in the USA. CinemaScope used a single camera and projector to produce a wide-screen effect with an anamorphic lens. The 3-D cameras were clumsy and the audiences disliked wearing the obligatory glasses. The new wide-screen cinema was accompanied by the introduction of Stereographic sound, which eventually became standard.
1959	The first film in Smell-O-Vision, *The Scent of Mystery*, was released. The process did not catch on.
1980	Most major films were released in Dolby stereo.
1981	Designated 'the Year of Color Film' by director Martin Scorsese in a campaign to draw attention to, and arrest, the deterioration of colour film shot since 1950.
1982	One of the first and most effective attempts at feature-length, computer-generated animation was *Tron*, Walt Disney's $20-million bid to break into the booming fantasy market. 3-D made a short-lived comeback.
1987	US House Judiciary Committee petitioned by leading Hollywood filmmakers to protect their work from electronic 'colorization', the new process by which black-and-white films were tinted for television transmission.
1988	Robert Zemeckis's (1952–) *Who Framed Roger Rabbit* set new technical standards in combining live action with cartoon animation.

include *Bringing Up Baby* 1938 and *Gentlemen Prefer Blondes* 1953. His final film was *Rio Lobo* 1970.

Hitchcock Alfred 1899–1980. British film director who became a US citizen in 1955. A master of the suspense thriller, he was noted for his meticulously drawn storyboards that determined his camera angles and for his cameo 'walk-ons' in his own films. His *Blackmail* 1929 was the first successful British talking film; *The Thirty-Nine Steps* 1935 and *The Lady Vanishes* 1939 are British suspense classics.

He went to Hollywood 1940, where his films included *Rebecca* 1940, *Notorious* 1946, *Strangers on a Train* 1951, *Rear Window* 1954, *Vertigo* 1958, *Psycho* 1960, and *The Birds* 1963. His last film was *Family Plot* 1976. He also hosted two US television mystery series, *Alfred Hitchcock Presents* 1955-62 and *The Alfred Hitchcock Hour* 1963-65.

Huston John 1906–1987. US film director, screenwriter, and actor. An impulsive and individualistic film maker, he often dealt with the themes of greed, treachery in human relationships, and the loner. His works as a director include *The Maltese Falcon* 1941 (his debut), *The Treasure of the Sierra Madre* 1948 (in which his father Walter Huston starred and for which both won Academy Awards), *Key Largo* 1948, *The African Queen* 1951, *Moby Dick* 1956, *The Misfits* 1961, *Fat City* 1972, *Prizzi's Honor* 1984, and his last, *The Dead* 1987. His daughter is the actress Anjelica Huston.

Jennings Humphrey 1907–1950. British documentary filmmaker who introduced a poetic tone and subjectivity to factually based material. He was active in the General Post Office Film Unit from 1934 and his wartime films vividly portrayed London in the Blitz: *London Can Take It* 1940, *This Is England* 1941, and *Fires Were Started* 1943.

Kubrick Stanley 1928– . US director and producer. His films include *Paths of Glory* 1957, *Dr Strangelove* 1964, *2001: A Space Odyssey* 1968, *A Clockwork Orange* 1971, and *The Shining* 1979.

A former photographer for *Life* magazine, he forged an early reputation with several low-budget features, notably *The Killing* 1956, and subsequently relocated to England. More than any of his American contemporaries, he achieved complete artistic control over his projects, which have been eclectic in subject matter and ambitious in scale and technique. His other films include *Lolita* 1962, and *Full Metal Jacket* 1987.

Kurosawa Akira 1929– . Japanese director whose film *Rashomon* 1950 introduced Western audiences to Japanese cinema. Epics such as *Shichinin no samurai/Seven Samurai* 1954 combine spectacle with intimate human drama. His other films include *Drunken Angel* 1948, *Yojimbo* 1961, *Kagemusha* 1981, and *Ran* 1985.

Lang Fritz 1890–1976. Austrian film director whose films are characterized by a strong sense of fatalism and moral inquiry. His German films include *Metropolis* 1927, *M* 1931, in which Peter Lorre starred as a child-killer, and the series of Dr Mabuse films, after which he fled from the Nazis to Hollywood in 1936. His US films include *Fury* 1936, *You Only Live Once* 1937, *Scarlet Street* 1945, *Rancho Notorious* 1952, and *The Big Heat* 1953. He returned to Germany and directed a third picture in the Dr Mabuse series in 1960.

Lean David 1908–1991. British film director. His films, noted for their storytelling flair and atmospheric quality, include early work codirected with playwright Noël Coward. *Brief Encounter* 1946 established Lean as a leading talent. Among his later films are such accomplished epics as *The Bridge on the River Kwai* 1957 (Academy Award), *Lawrence of Arabia* 1962 (Academy Award), and *Dr Zhivago* 1965. The critics' antipathy to *Ryan's Daughter* 1970 caused him to withdraw from filmmaking for over a decade, but *A Passage to India* 1984 represented a return to form.

Méliès Georges 1861–1938. French film pioneer. From 1896 to 1912 he made over 1,000 films, many of them imaginative fantasies (*Le Voyage dans la Lune/A Trip to the Moon* 1902). He developed trick effects, slow motion, double exposure, and dissolves, and in 1897 built Europe's first film studio at Montreuil.

Born in Paris, Méliès started out as a stage magician. His interest in cinema was sparked by the Lumière brothers' *cinématographe*, premiered 1895. He constructed a camera and founded a production company, Star Film. Méliès failed to develop as a filmmaker and he went bankrupt 1913.

Ophuls Max. Adopted name of Max Oppenheimer 1902–1957. German film director, initially in the theatre, whose style is characterized by a bitter-sweet tone and intricate camera movement. He worked in Europe and the USA, attracting much critical praise for such films as *Letter from an Unknown Woman* 1948, *La Ronde* 1950, and *Lola Montes* 1955. His son is the documentary filmmaker Marcel Ophuls (1927–).

Ozu Yasujiro 1903–1963. One of Japan's leading film director who became known in the West only in his last years. *Tokyo Monogatari/Tokyo Story* 1953 illustrates his typical low camera angles and his predominant theme of middle-class family life. Other major films include *Late Spring* 1949 and *Autumn Afternoon* 1962.

Pasolini Pier Paolo 1922–1975. Italian director, poet, and novelist. His early work is coloured by his experience of life in the poor districts of Rome, where he lived from 1950, and illustrates the decadence and inequality of society from a Marxist viewpoint. Among his films are *Accattone!* 1961, *Mamma Roma* 1962, *Il vangelo secondo Mateo/The Gospel According to St Matthew* 1964, *Decameron* 1970, *I racconti de Canterbury/The Canterbury Tales* 1972, and *Salò/The 120 Days of Sodom* 1975.

Porter Edwin Stanton 1869–1941. US director, a pioneer of film narrative. His 1903 film *The Great Train Robbery* lasted 12 minutes – then an unusually long time for a film – and contained an early use of the close-up. More concerned with the technical than the artistic side of his films, which include *The Teddy Bears* 1907 and *The Final Pardon* 1912, Porter abandoned filmmaking 1916.

Powell Michael 1905–1990. English film director and producer. Some of his most memorable films were made in collaboration with Hungarian screenwriter Emeric Pressburger (1902–1988), with whom he formed a company, the Archers, in 1942. They produced a succession of ambitious and richly imaginative films, including *The Life and Death of Colonel Blimp* 1943, *A Matter of Life and Death* 1946, *Black Narcissus* 1947, *The Red Shoes* 1948, and the opera movie *The Tales of Hoffman* 1951. On his own, Powell later made *Peeping Tom* 1960, a voyeuristic horror film.

Ray Satyajit 1921–1992. Indian film director, internationally known for his trilogy of life in his native Bengal: *Pather Panchali*, *Unvanquished*, and *The World of Apu* 1955–59. Later films include *The Music Room* 1958, *Charulata* 1964, *The Chess Players* 1977, and *The Home and the World* 1984.

Reed Carol 1906–1976. British film producer and director, an influential figure in the British film industry of the 1940s. His films include *Odd Man Out* 1947, *The Fallen Idol* and *The Third Man* both 1950 (both written by Graham Greene), and *Our Man in Havana* 1959. His later films included the Academy Award-winning *Oliver!* 1968.

Renoir Jean 1894–1979. French director whose films, characterized by their humanism and naturalistic technique, include *Boudu sauvé des eaux/Boudu Saved from Drowning* 1932, *La Grande Illusion* 1937, and *La Règle du Jeu/The Rules of the Game* 1939. In 1975 he received an honorary Academy Award for his life's work. He was the son of the painter Pierre-Auguste Renoir.

Rossellini Roberto 1906–1977. Italian film director. His World War II trilogy, *Roma città aperta/Rome, Open City* 1945, *Paisà/Paisan* 1946, and *Germania anno zero/Germany Year Zero* 1947, had a quality of direct realism which made it a landmark of European cinema.

In 1949 he made *Stromboli*, followed by other films in which his wife Ingrid Bergman appeared. After their divorce he made *General della Rovere* 1959 and embarked on television work including a feature-length film for French TV *La Prise de Pouvoir par Louis XIV/The Rise of Louis XIV* 1966. He and Ingrid Bergman were the parents of actress Isabella Rossellini (1952–   ).

Scorsese Martin 1942–   . US director whose films concentrate on complex characterization and the themes of alienation and guilt. His influential and forceful work includes *Mean Streets* 1973, *Taxi Driver* 1976, *Raging Bull* 1980, *The Color of Money* 1986, *After Hours* 1987, *The Last Temptation of Christ* 1988, and *Cape Fear* 1991.

Spielberg Steven 1947–   . US director, writer, and producer of such films as *Jaws* 1975, *Close Encounters of the Third Kind* 1977, *Raiders of the Lost Ark* 1981, and *ET* 1982. Immensely successful, his films usually combine cliff-hanging suspense with heartfelt sentimentality. He also directed *Indiana Jones and the Temple of Doom* 1984, *The Color Purple* 1985, *Empire of the Sun* 1987, *Indiana Jones and the Last Crusade* 1989, *Hook* 1992, *Jurassic Park* 1993, and *Schindler's list* 1993.

Sternberg Josef von 1894–1969. Austrian film director, in the USA from childhood. He is best remembered for his seven films with Marlene Dietrich, including *The Blue Angel/Der blaue Engel* 1930, *Blonde Venus* 1932, and *The Devil Is a Woman* 1935, all of which are marked by his expressive use of light and shadow. His subsequent career was sporadic, culminating in the Japanese-made *Saga of Anatahan* 1953.

Stroheim Erich von. Assumed name of Erich Oswald Stroheim 1885–1957. Austrian actor and director, in Hollywood from 1914. He was successful as an actor in villainous roles, then embarked on a career as a director. Such films as *Foolish Wives* 1922 won widespread praise, but his progress foundered on his extravagance (*Greed* 1923), and he returned to acting in such international films as *La Grande Illusion* 1937 and *Sunset Boulevard* 1950.

Sturges Preston. Adopted name of Edmond Biden 1898–1959. US film director and writer who enjoyed great success with a series of satirical comedies in the early 1940s, including *Sullivan's Travels* 1941, *The Palm Beach Story* 1942, and *The Miracle of Morgan's Creek* 1943. His last film *Diary of Major Thompson* 1955 was made in France.

Tarkovsky Andrei 1932–1986. Soviet film director whose work is characterized by an epic style combined with intense personal spirituality. His films include *Solaris* 1972, *Mirror* 1975, *Stalker* 1979, and *The Sacrifice* 1986. The last was made in Sweden, following his exile from the USSR in 1984.

Tati Jacques. Stage name of Jacques Tatischeff 1908–1982. French comic actor, director, and writer. He portrayed Monsieur Hulot, the embodiment of polite opposition to modern mechanization, in a series of films starting with *Les Vacances de M Hulot/Monsieur Hulot's Holiday* 1953, and including *Mon Oncle/My Uncle* 1959 and *Playtime* 1968.

Truffaut François 1932–1984. French New Wave film director and actor, formerly a critic. A popular, romantic, and intensely humane filmmaker, he wrote and directed a series of semi-autobiographical films starring Jean-Pierre Léaud, beginning with *Les Quatre Cent Coups/The 400 Blows* 1959. His other films include *Jules et Jim* 1961, *Fahrenheit 451* 1966, *L'Enfant sauvage/The Wild Child* 1970, and *La Nuit américaine/Day for Night* 1973 (Academy Award).

His love of cinema led to a job as film critic for *Cahiers du Cinema* during the 1950s before embarking on his career as director. His later work includes *The Story of Adèle H* 1975 and *The Last Metro* 1980. He was influenced by Alfred Hitchcock, and also by French comic traditions.

Vigo Jean. Adopted name of Jean Almereida 1905–1934. French director of intensely lyrical and semi-surrealist films. He made only two shorts, *A Propos de Nice* 1930 and *Taris Champion de Natation* 1934; and two feature films, *Zéro de conduite/Nothing for Conduct* 1933 and *L'Atalante* 1934. His promising career was tragically cut short by leukemia.

Visconti Luchino 1906–1976. Italian film, opera, and theatre director. The film *Ossessione* 1942 pioneered neorealist cinema despite being subject to censorship problems from the fascist government; later works include *Rocco and His Brothers* 1960, *The Leopard* 1963, *The Damned* 1969, and *Death in Venice* 1971. His powerful social commentary led to clashes with the Italian government and Roman Catholic Church.

Wajda Andrzej 1926– . Polish film and theatre director, one of the major figures in postwar European cinema. His films are often concerned with the predicament and disillusionment of individuals caught up in political events. His works include *Ashes and Diamonds* 1958, *Man of Marble* 1977, *Man of Iron* 1981, *Danton* 1982, and *Korczak* 1990. He has also worked in television and theatre. He made a television film version of Joseph Conrad's *The Shadow Line* 1976.

Welles (George) Orson 1915–1985. US actor and film and theatre director, whose first film was *Citizen Kane* 1941, which he produced, directed, and starred in. Using innovative lighting, camera angles and movements, he made it a landmark in the history of cinema, yet he directed very few films subsequently in Hollywood, and later worked mostly in Europe. His performances as an actor include the character of Harry Lime in *The Third Man* 1949.

In 1937 he founded the Mercury Theater, New York, with John Houseman, where their repertory productions included a modern-dress version of *Julius Caesar*. Welles's realistic radio broadcast of H G Wells's *The War of the Worlds* 1938 caused panic and fear of Martian invasion in the USA. He directed the films *The Magnificent Ambersons* 1942, *The Lady from Shanghai* 1948 with his wife Rita Hayworth, *Touch of Evil* 1958, and *Chimes at Midnight* 1967, a Shakespeare adaptation. As his career declined he became a familiar voice and face in US television commercials, and made guest appearances on TV shows.

Awards for Best Film from four top festivals

Cannes Film Festival

Palme d'Or for Best Film

1985	When Father Was Away on Business (Yug)
1986	The Mission (UK)
1987	Under the Sun of Satan (Fr)
1988	Pelle the Conqueror (Den)
1989	sex, lies and videotape (US)
1990	Wild at Heart (US)
1991	Barton Fink (US)
1992	The Best Intentions (Swe)
1993	The Piano (NZ/Australia); Farewell My Concubine (Hong Kong/China)

Venice Film Festival

Golden Lion for Best Film

1985	Sans toit ni loi (aka Vagabonde) (Fr)
1986	Le Rayon Vert (Fr)
1987	Au Revoir les Enfants (Fr)
1988	La Leggenda del Santo Bevitore (The Legend of the Holy Drinker) (It)
1989	Beiqing Chengshi (City of Sadness) (Taiwan)
1990	Rosencrantz and Guildenstern are Dead (UK)
1991	Urga (Russia)
1992	Story of Qiu Ju (China)
1993	Short Cuts (US); Three Colours Blue (Pol)

Berlin Film Festival

Golden Bear for Best Film

1985	Wetherby (UK); Die Frau und der Fremde (FRG)
1986	Stammheim (FRG)
1987	The Theme (USSR)
1988	Red Sorghum (China)
1989	Rain Man (US)
1990	Skylarks on a String (Czech); Music Box (US)
1991	La Casa del Sorriso (House of Smiles) (It)
1992	Grand Canyon (US)
1993	Woman from the Lake of Centred Souls (China); Wedding Banquet (Taiwan)
1994	In the Name of the Father (US/Ireland)

British Academy of Film and Television Arts (BAFTA)

Best Film Awards

1985	The Killing Fields (UK)
1986	The Purple Rose of Cairo (US)
1987	A Room with a View (UK)
1988	Jean de Florette (Fr)
1989	The Last Emperor (US)
1990	Dead Poets Society (US)
1991	GoodFellas (US)
1992	The Commitments (UK)
1993	Howards End (UK)

Motion picture Academy Awards (Oscars)

1928 Best Picture: *Wings*; Best Director: Frank Borzage *Seventh Heaven* and Lewis Milestone *Two Arabian Nights*; Best Actor: Emil Jannings *The Way of All Flesh*, *The Last Command*; Best Actress, Janet Gaynor *Seventh Heaven*, *Street Angel*, *Sunrise*

1929 Best Picture: *The Broadway Melody*; Best Director: Frank Lloyd *The Divine Lady*; Best Actor: Warner Baxter *In Old Arizona*; Best Actress: Mary Pickford *Coquette*

1930 Best Picture: *All Quiet on the Western Front*; Best Director: Lewis Milestone *All Quiet on the Western Front*; Best Actor: George Arliss *Disraeli*; Best Actress: Norma Shearer *The Divorcee*

1931 Best Picture: *Cimarron*; Best Director: Norman Taurog *Skippy*; Best Actor: Lionel Barrymore *A Free Soul*; Best Actress: Marie Dressler *Min and Bill*

1932 Best Picture: *Grand Hotel*; Best Director: Frank Borzage *Bad Girl*; Best Actor: Fredric March *Dr Jekyll and Mr Hyde* and Wallace Beery *The Champ*; Best Actress: Helen Hayes *The Sin of Madelon Claudet*

1933 Best Picture: *Cavalcade*; Best Director: Frank Lloyd *Cavalcade*; Best Actor: Charles Laughton *The Private Life of Henry VIII*; Best Actress: Katharine Hepburn *Morning Glory*

1934 Best Picture: *It Happened One Night*; Best Director: Frank Capra *It Happened One Night*; Best Actor: Clark Gable *It Happened One Night*; Best Actress: Claudette Colbert *It Happened One Night*

1935 Best Picture: *Mutiny on the Bounty*; Best Director: John Ford *The Informer*; Best Actor: Victor McLaglen *The Informer*; Best Actress: Bette Davis *Dangerous*

1936 Best Picture: *The Great Ziegfeld*; Best Director: Frank Capra *Mr Deeds Goes to Town*; Best Actor: Paul Muni *The Story of Louis Pasteur*; Best Actress: Luise Rainer *The Great Ziegfeld*

1937 Best Picture: *The Life of Emile Zola*; Best Director: Leo McCarey *The Awful Truth*; Best Actor: Spencer Tracy *Captains Courageous*; Best Actress: Luise Rainer *The Good Earth*

1938 Best Picture: *You Can't Take It With You*; Best Director: Frank Capra *You Can't Take It With You*; Best Actor: Spencer Tracy *Boys Town*; Best Actress: Bette Davis *Jezebel*

1939 Best Picture: *Gone With the Wind*; Best Director: Victor Flemming *Gone With the Wind*; Best Actor: Robert Donat *Goodbye Mr Chips*; Best Actress: Vivien Leigh *Gone With the Wind*

1940 Best Picture: *Rebecca*; Best Director: John Ford *The Grapes of Wrath*; Best Actor: James Stewart *The Philadelphia Story*; Best Actress: Ginger Rogers *Kitty Foyle*

1941 Best Picture: *How Green Was My Valley*; Best Director: John Ford *How Green Was My Valley*; Best Actor: Gary Cooper *Sergeant York*; Best Actress: Joan Fontaine *Suspicion*

1942 Best Picture: *Mrs Miniver*; Best Director: William Wyler *Mrs Miniver*; Best Actor: James Cagney *Yankee Doodle Dandy*; Best Actress: Greer Garson *Mrs Miniver*

1943 Best Picture: *Casablanca*; Best Director: Michael Curtiz *Casablanca*; Best Actor: Paul Lukas *Watch on the Rhine*; Best Actress: Jennifer Jones *The Song of Bernadette*

1944 Best Picture: *Going My Way*; Best Director: Leo McCarey *Going My Way*; Best Actor: Bing Crosby *Going My Way*; Best Actress: Ingrid Bergman *Gaslight*

1945 Best Picture: *The Lost Weekend*; Best Director: Billy Wilder *The Lost Weekend*; Best Actor: Ray Milland *The Lost Weekend*; Best Actress: Joan Crawford *Mildred Pierce*

1946 Best Picture: *The Best Years of Our Lives*; Best Director: William Wyler *The Best Years of Our Lives*; Best Actor: Fredric March *The Best Years of Our Lives*; Best Actress: Olivia de Havilland *To Each His Own*

1947 Best Picture: *Gentleman's Agreement*; Best Director: Elia Kazan *Gentleman's Agreement*; Best Actor: Ronald Coleman *A Double Life*; Best Actress: Loretta Young *The Farmer's Daughter*

1948 Best Picture: *Hamlet*; Best Director: John Huston *Treasure of Sierra Madre*; Best Actor: Laurence Olivier *Hamlet*; Best Actress: Jane Wyman *Johnny Belinda*

1949 Best Picture: *All the King's Men*; Best Director: Joseph L Mankiewicz *A Letter to Three Wives*; Best Actor: Broderick Crawford *All the King's Men*; Best Actress: Olivia de Havilland *The Heiress*

1950 Best Picture: *All About Eve*; Best Director: Joseph L Mankiewicz *All About Eve*; Best Actor: José Ferrer *Cyrano de Bergerac*; Best Actress: Judy Holliday *Born Yesterday*

1951 Best Picture: *An American in Paris*; Best Director: George Stevens *A Place in the Sun*; Best Actor: Humphrey Bogart *The African Queen*; Vivien Leigh *A Streetcar Named Desire*

1952 Best Picture: *The Greatest Show on Earth*; Best Director: John Ford *The Quiet Man*; Best Actor: Gary Cooper *High Noon*; Best Actress: Shirley Booth *Come Back Little Sheba*

1953 Best Picture: *From Here to Eternity*; Best Director: Fred Zinnemann *From Here to Eternity*; Best Actor: William Holden *Stalag 17*; Best Actress: Audrey Hepburn *Roman Holiday*

1954 Best Picture: *On the Waterfront*; Best Director: Elia Kazan *On the Waterfront*; Best Actor: Marlon Brando *On the Waterfront*; Best Actress: Grace Kelly *The Country Girl*

1955 Best Picture: *Marty*; Best Director: Delbert Mann *Marty*; Best Actor: Ernest Borgnine *Marty*; Best Actress: Anna Magnani *The Rose Tattoo*

1956 Best Picture: *Around the World in 80 Days*; Best Director: George Stevens *Giant*; Best Actor: Yul Brynner *The King and I*; Best Actress: Ingrid Bergman *Anastasia*

1957 Best Picture: *The Bridge on the River Kwai*; Best Director: David Lean *The Bridge on the River Kwai*; Best Actor: Alec Guinness *The Bridge on the River Kwai*; Best Actress: Joanne Woodward *The Three Faces of Eve*

1958 Best Picture: *Gigi*; Best Director: Vincente Minnelli *Gigi*; Best Actor: David Niven *Separate Tables*; Best Actress: Susan Hayward *I Want to Live!*

1959 Best Picture: *Ben Hur*; Best Director: William Wyler *Ben Hur*; Best Actor: Charlton Heston *Ben Hur*; Best Actress: Simone Signoret *Room at the Top*

Motion picture Academy Awards (Oscars) *(cont.)*

1960 Best Picture: *The Apartment*; Best Director: Billy Wilder *The Apartment*; Best Actor: Burt Lancaster *Elmer Gantry*; Best Actress: Elizabeth Taylor *Butterfield 8*

1961 Best Picture: *West Side Story*; Best Director: Robert Wise and Jerome Robbins *West Side Story*; Best Actor: Maximillian Schell *Judgment at Nuremberg*; Best Actress: Sophia Loren *Two Women*

1962 Best Picture: *Lawrence of Arabia*; Best Director: David Lean *Lawrence of Arabia*; Best Actor: Gregory Peck *To Kill a Mockingbird*; Best Actress: Anne Bancroft *The Miracle Worker*

1963 Best Picture: *Tom Jones*; Best Director: Tony Richardson *Tom Jones*; Best Actor: Sidney Poitier *Lilies of the Field*; Best Actress: Patricia Neal *Hud*

1964 Best Picture: *My Fair Lady*; Best Director: George Cukor *My Fair Lady*; Best Actor: Rex Harrison *My Fair Lady*; Best Actress: Julie Andrews *My Fair Lady*

1965 Best Picture: *The Sound of Music*; Best Director: Robert Wise *The Sound of Music*; Best Actor: Lee Marvin *Cat Ballou*; Best Actress: Julie Christie *Darling*

1966 Best Picture: *A Man for All Seasons*; Best Director: Fred Zinnemann *A Man for All Seasons*; Best Actor: Paul Scofield *A Man for All Seasons*; Best Actress: Elizabeth Taylor *Who's Afraid of Virginia Woolf?*

1967 Best Picture: *In the Heat of the Night*; Best Director: Mike Nichols *The Graduate*; Best Actor: Rod Steiger *In the Heat of the Night*; Best Actress: Katharine Hepburn *Guess Who's Coming to Dinner*

1968 Best Picture: *Oliver!*; Best Director: Sir Carol Reed *Oliver!*; Best Actor: Cliff Robertson *Charly*; Best Actress: Katharine Hepburn *The Lion in Winter* and Barbra Streisand *Funny Girl*

1969 Best Picture: *Midnight Cowboy*; Best Director: John Schlesinger *Midnight Cowboy*; Best Actor: John Wayne *True Grit*; Best Actress: Maggie Smith *The Prime of Miss Jean Brodie*

1970 Best Picture: *Patton*; Best Director: Franklin J Schaffner *Patton*; Best Actor: George C Scott *Patton*; Best Actress: Glenda Jackson *Women in Love*

1971 Best Picture: *The French Connection*; Best Director: William Friedkin *The French Connection*; Best Actor: Gene Hackman *The French Connection*; Best Actress: Jane Fonda *Klute*

1972 Best Picture: *The Godfather*; Best Director: Bob Fosse *Cabaret*; Best Actor: Marlon Brando *The Godfather*; Best Actress: Liza Minnelli *Cabaret*

1973 Best Picture: *The Sting*; Best Director: George Roy Hill *The Sting*; Best Actor: Jack Lemmon *Save the Tiger*; Best Actress: Glenda Jackson *A Touch of Class*

1974 Best Picture: *The Godfather Part II*; Best Director: Francis Ford Coppola *The Godfather Part II*; Best Actor: Art Carney *Harry and Tonto*; Best Actress: Ellen Burstyn *Alice Doesn't Live Here Anymore*

1975 Best Picture: *One Flew Over the Cuckoo's Nest*; Best Director: Milos Forman *One Flew Over the Cuckoo's Nest*; Best Actor: Jack Nicholson *One Flew Over the Cuckoo's Nest*; Best Actress: Louise Fletcher *One Flew Over the Cuckoo's Nest*

1976 Best Picture: *Rocky*; Best Director: John G Avildsen *Rocky*; Best Actor: Peter Finch *Network*; Best Actress: Faye Dunaway *Network*

1977 Best Picture: *Annie Hall*; Best Director: Woody Allen *Annie Hall*; Best Actor: Richard Dreyfuss *The Goodbye Girl*; Best Actress: Diane Keaton *Annie Hall*

1978 Best Picture: *The Deer Hunter*; Best Director: Michael Cimino *The Deer Hunter*; Best Actor: Jon Voight *Coming Home*; Best Actress: Jane Fonda *Coming Home*

1979 Best Picture: *Kramer vs Kramer*; Best Director: Robert Benton *Kramer vs Kramer*; Best Actor: Dustin Hoffman *Kramer vs Kramer*; Best Actress: Sally Field *Norma Rae*

1980 Best Picture: *Ordinary People*; Best Director: Robert Redford *Ordinary People*; Best Actor: Robert De Niro *Raging Bull*; Best Actress: Sissy Spacek *Coal Miner's Daughter*

1981 Best Picture: *Chariots of Fire*; Best Director: Warren Beatty *Reds*; Best Actor: Henry Fonda *On Golden Pond*; Best Actress: Katharine Hepburn *On Golden Pond*

1982 Best Picture: *Gandhi*; Best Director: Richard Attenborough *Gandhi*; Best Actor: Ben Kingsley *Gandhi*; Best Actress: Meryl Streep *Sophie's Choice*

1983 Best Picture: *Terms of Endearment*; Best Director: James L Brooks *Terms of Endearment*; Best Actor: Robert Duvall *Tender Mercies*; Best Actress: Shirley Maclaine *Terms of Endearment*

1984 Best Picture: *Amadeus*; Best Director: Milos Forman *Amadeus*; Best Actor: F Murray Abraham *Amadeus*; Best Actress: Sally Field *Places in the Heart*

1985 Best Picture: *Out of Africa*; Best Director: Sydney Pollack *Out of Africa*; Best Actor: William Hurt *Kiss of the Spider Woman*; Best Actress: Geraldine Page *The Trip to Bountiful*

1986 Best Picture: *Platoon*; Best Director: Oliver Stone *Platoon*; Best Actor: Paul Newman *The Color of Money*; Best Actress: Marlee Matlin *Children of a Lesser God*

1987 Best Picture: *The Last Emperor*; Best Director: Bernardo Bertolucci *The Last Emperor*; Best Actor: Michael Douglas *Wall Street*; Best Actress: Cher *Moonstruck*

1988 Best Picture: *Rain Man*; Best Director: Barry Levington *Rain Man*; Best Actor: Dustin Hoffman *Rain Man*; Best Actress: Jodie Foster *The Accused*

1989 Best Picture: *Driving Miss Daisy*; Best Director: Oliver Stone *Born on the Fourth of July*; Best Actor: Daniel Day-Lewis *My Left Foot*; Best Actress: Jessica Tandy *Driving Miss Daisy*

1990 Best Picture: *Dances With Wolves*; Best Director: Kevin Costner *Dances With Wolves*; Best Actor: Jeremy Irons *Reversal of Fortune*; Best Actress: Kathy Bates *Misery*

1991 Best Picture: *The Silence of the Lambs*; Best Director: Jonathan Demme *The Silence of the Lambs*; Best Actor: Anthony Hopkins *The Silence of the Lambs*; Best Actress: Jodie Foster *The Silence of the Lambs*

1992 Best Picture: *Unforgiven*; Best Director: Clint Eastwood *Unforgiven*; Best Actor: Al Pacino *Scent of a Woman* ; Best Actress: Emma Thompson *Howard's End*

DANCE

Genres

African traditional dance tribal and regional African dances with a primarily ritualistic function. These rhythmically complex dances are performed to celebrate the important events in people's lives and are part of their everyday experience. In most cases the dance focuses on the circle, with soloists splitting off and then returning to the main group. Movement is generally directed towards the ground rather than upwards.

avant-garde dance experimental dance form that rejects the conventions of modern dance. It is often performed in informal spaces – museums, rooftops, even scaling walls.

In the USA, avant-garde dance stemmed mainly from the collaboration between Merce Cunningham in New York and musician Robert Dunn, which resulted in the Judson Dance Theater. While retaining technique and rhythm, Cunningham deleted the role of choreographer, thus giving dancers a new freedom. The Judson collective went further, denying even the necessity for technique and concentrating on the use of everyday movements – walking, spinning, jumping. In the UK, leading exponents of avant- garde dance techniques include Michael Clark from the mid-1980s and Rosemary Butcher. In Germany, Pina Bausch with her Wuppertal Tanztheater (dance theatre), established 1974, has been considered the most compelling influence in European dance since Diaghilev. Her works, often several hours long, blend dance, music, dialogue, gesture, psychology, comedy, and stark fear, and may be performed on floors covered with churned earth, rose petals, or water..

Avant-garde dance repertory

Date	Title	Choreographer	Place
1969	Moving Earth	Kei Takei	New York
1970	Walking on the Wall	Trisha Brown	New York
1971	Education of the Girlchild	Meredith Monk	New York
1978	Café Müller	Pina Bausch	Essen
1986	The Watteau Duet	Karole Armitage	New York
1988	I Am Curious Orange	Michael Clark	Amsterdam

ballet theatrical representation in stylized dance form in which music also plays a major part in telling a story or conveying a mood. Some such form of entertainment existed in ancient Greece, but Western ballet as we know it today first appeared in Italy. From there it was brought by Catherine de' Medici to France in the form of a spectacle combining singing, dancing, and declamation. In the 20th century Russian ballet has had a vital influence on the Classical tradition in the West, and ballet developed further in the USA through the work of George Balanchine and American Ballet Theater, and in the UK through the influence of Marie Rambert. Modern dance is a separate development.

history The first important dramatic ballet, the *Ballet comique de la reine*, was produced 1581 by the Italian Balthasar de Beaujoyeux at the French court and was performed by male courtiers, with ladies of the court forming the *corps de ballet*. In 1661 Louis XIV founded *L'Académie royale de danse*, to which all subsequent ballet activities throughout the world can be traced. Long, flowing court dress was worn by the dancers until the 1720s when Marie-Anne Camargo, the first great ballerina, shortened her skirt to reveal her ankles, thus allowing greater movement *à terre* and the development of dancing *en l'air*. It was not until the early 19th century that a Paris costumier, Maillot, invented tights, thus allowing complete muscular freedom. The first of the great ballet masters was Jean-Georges Noverre, and great contemporary dancers were Teresa Vestris, Anna Friedrike Heinel, Jean Dauberval, and Maximilien Gardel. Carlo Blasis is regarded as the founder of Classical ballet since he defined the standard conventional steps and accompanying gestures.

Romantic ballet The great Romantic era of Taglioni, Elssler, Grisi, Grahn, and Cerrito began about 1830 but survives today only in the ballets *Giselle* 1841 and *La Sylphide* 1832. Characteristics of this era were the new calf-length Romantic white dress and the introduction of dancing on the toes, *sur les pointes*. The technique of the female dancer was developed, but the role of the male dancer was reduced to that of her partner.

Russian ballet was introduced to the West by Sergei Diaghilev, who set out for Paris 1909, at about the same time that Isadora Duncan, a fervent opponent of classical ballet, was touring Europe. Associated with Diaghilev were Mikhail Fokine, Vaslav Nijinsky, Anna Pavlova, Léonide Massine, George Balanchine, and Serge Lifar. Ballets presented by his company, before its break-up after his death 1929, included *Les Sylphides*, *Schéhérazade*, *Petrouchka*, and *Blue Train*. Diaghilev and Fokine pioneered a new and exciting combination of the perfect technique of imperial Russian dancers and the appealing naturalism favoured by Isadora Duncan. In Russia ballet continues to flourish, the two chief companies being the Kirov and the Bolshoi. Best-known ballerinas are Galina Ulanova and Maya Plisetskaya, and male dancers include the late Rudolf Nureyev, Mikhail Baryshnikov, and Alexander Godunov, now dancing in the West, as are the husband-and-wife team Vyacheslav Gordeyev and Nadezhda Pavlova.

American ballet was firmly established by the founding of Balanchine's School of American Ballet 1934, and by de Basil's Ballets Russes de Monte Carlo and Massine's Ballet Russe de Monte Carlo, which also carried on the Diaghilev tradition. In 1939 Lucia Chase and Richard Pleasant founded American Ballet Theater. From 1948 the New York City Ballet, under the guiding influence of Balanchine, developed a genuine American Neo-Classic style.

British ballet Marie Rambert initiated 1926 the company that developed into the Ballet Rambert, and launched the careers of choreographers such as Fred-

The ballet repertory

Date	Ballet	Composer	Choreographer	Place
1670	Le Bourgeois Gentilhomme	Lully	Beauchamp	Chambord
1735	Les Indes Galantes	Rameau	Blondy	Paris
1761	Don Juan	Gluck	Angiolini	Vienna
1778	Les Petits Riens	Mozart	Noverre	Paris
1801	The Creatures of Prometheus	Beethoven	Viganò	Vienna
1828	La Fille Mal Gardée	Hérold	Aumer	Paris
1832	La Sylphide	Schneitzhoeffer	F Taglioni	Paris
1841	Giselle	Coralli	Perrot	Paris
1842	Napoli	Gade/Helsted/Lumbye/Paulli	Bournonville	Copenhagen
1844	La Esmeralda	Pugni	Perrot	London
1869	Don Quixote	Minkus	M Petipa	Moscow
1870	Coppélia	Delibes	Saint-Léon	Paris
1876	Sylvia	Delibes	Mérante	Paris
1877	La Bayadère	Minkus	M Petipa	St Petersburg
1877	Swan Lake	Tchaikovsky	Reisinger	Moscow
1882	Namouna	Lalo	L Petipa	Paris
1890	The Sleeping Beauty	Tchaikovsky	M Petipa	St Petersburg
1892	Nutcracker	Tchaikovsky	M Petipa/Ivanov	St Petersburg
1898	Raymonda	Glazunov	M Petipa	St Petersburg
1905	The Dying Swan	Saint-Saëns	Fokine	St Petersburg
1907	Les Sylphides	Chopin	Fokine	St Petersburg
1910	Carnival	Schumann	Fokine	St Petersburg
1910	The Firebird	Stravinsky	Fokine	Paris
1911	Petrushka	Stravinsky	Fokine	Paris
1911	Le Spectre de la Rose	Weber	Fokine	Monte Carlo
1912	L'Après-midi d'un Faune	Debussy	Nijinsky	Paris
1912	Daphnis and Chloe	Ravel	Fokine	Paris
1913	Jeux	Debussy	Nijinsky	Paris
1913	The Rite of Spring	Stravinsky	Nijinsky	Paris
1915	El Amor Brujo	Falla	Imperio	Madrid
1917	Parade	Satie	Massine	Paris
1919	La Boutique Fantasque	Rossini/Respighi	Massine	London
1919	The Three-Cornered Hat	Falla	Massini	London
1923	The Creation of the World	Milhaud	Börlin	Paris
1923	Les Noces	Stravinsky	Nijinska	Paris
1924	Les Biches	Poulenc	Nijinska	Monte Carlo
1927	The Red Poppy	Glière	Lashchilin/Tikhomirov	Moscow
1928	Apollon Musagète	Stravinsky	Balanchine	Paris
1928	Le Baiser de la fée	Tchaikovsky	Nijinska	Paris
1928	Bolero	Ravel	Nijinska	Paris
1929	The Prodigal Son	Prokofiev	Balanchine	Paris
1929	La Valse	Ravel	Nijinska	Monte Carlo
1931	Bacchus and Ariadne	Roussel	Lifar	Paris
1931	Façade	Walton	Ashton	London
1931	Job	Vaughan Williams	de Valois	London
1937	Checkmate	Bliss	de Valois	Paris
1937	Les Patineurs	Meyerbeer/Lambert	Ashton	London
1938	Billy the Kid	Copland	Loring	Chicago
1938	Gaîté Parisienne	Offenbach/Rosenthal	Massine	Monte Carlo
1938	Romeo and Juliet	Prokofiev	Psota	Moravia
1942	Gayaneh	Khachaturian	Anisimova	Molotov-Perm
1942	The Miraculous Mandarin	Bartók	Milloss	Milan
1942	Rodeo	Copland	de Mille	New York
1944	Appalachian Spring	Copland	Graham	Washington
1944	Fancy Free	Bernstein	Robbins	New York
1945	Cinderella	Prokofiev	Zakharov	Moscow
1949	Carmen	Bizet	Petit	London
1951	Pineapple Poll	Sullivan/Mackerras	Cranko	London
1956	Spartacus	Khachaturian	Jacobson	Leningrad
1957	Agon	Stravinsky	Balanchine	New York
1959	Episodes	Webern	Balanchine	New York
1962	A Midsummer Night's Dream	Mendelssohn	Balanchine	New York

The ballet repertory *(cont.)*

Date	Ballet	Composer	Choreographer	Place
1962	*Pierrot Lunaire*	Schoenberg	Tetley	New York
1964	*The Dream*	Mendelssohn/Lanchbery	Ashton	London
1965	*The Song of the Earth*	Mahler	MacMillan	Stuttgart
1966	*Romeo and Juliet*	Prokofiev	MacMillan	London
1967	*Anastasia*	Martinu	MacMillan	New York
1968	*Enigma Variations*	Elgar	Ashton	London
1969	*The Taming of the Shrew*	Scarlatti/Stolze	Cranko	Stuttgart
1972	*Duo Concertant*	Stravinsky	Balanchine	New York
1974	*Elite Syncopations*	Joplin and others	MacMillan	London
1976	*A Month in the Country*	Chopin/Lanchbery	Ashton	London
1978	*Mayerling*	Liszt/Lanchbery	MacMillan	London
1978	*Symphony of Psalms*	Stravinsky	Kylián	Scheveningen
1980	*Gloria*	Poulenc	MacMillan	London
1980	*Rhapsody*	Rachmaninov	Ashton	London
1981	*St Matthew Passion*	Bach	Neumeier	Hamburg
1982	*The Golden Age*	Shostakovich	Grigorovich	Moscow
1984	*Different Drummer*	Webern/Schoenberg	MacMillan	London
1987	*In the Middle, Somewhat Elevated*	Willems	Forsythe	Paris
1988	*L'allegro, il penseroso ed il moderato*	Handel	Morris	Brussels
1989	*Falling Angels*	Reich	Kylián	Amsterdam
1991	*Winter Dreams*	Tchaikovsky	MacMillan	London

erick Ashton and Anthony Tudor. The national company, the Royal Ballet (so named 1956), grew from foundations laid by Ninette de Valois and Frederick Ashton 1928. British dancers include the late Margot Fonteyn, Alicia Markova, Anton Dolin, Antoinette Sibley, Anthony Dowell, David Wall, Merle Park, and Lesley Collier; Britain's leading choreographer was the late Kenneth MacMillan.

belly dancing Westernized form of *rakshaki*, a traditional Egyptian dance form that has spread through the Middle East. It is characterized by the primary use of the hips, spine, shoulders, and stomach muscles rather than the legs, although jumps, turning, and precise footwork are features of the original form. The dance is now usually performed by women and is accompanied by traditional instruments. Traditionally, *rakshaki* was performed by both women and men; different forms exist for the two sexes.

butoh dance Japanese *ankoku butō* 'dance of darkness'. Japanese avant-garde dance. Developed by Tatsumi Hijikata in the 1960s, the form draws on both Japanese traditions and the European avant-garde. It is characterized by stillness, which is contrasted with frantic movements and an emotional intensity represented in a highly stylized manner. The dancers' faces and bodies are often painted white.

contact improvisation improvised movement sequences often in avant-garde dance. The sequences are the result of intuitive communication leading to contact between two or more dancers, which is used to explore the changes in the flow of movement between them. Contact improvisation is used both as a choreographic tool and as a form of therapy through movement.

dervish dance religious dance of Islam. Part of the mystical Sufi tradition, its aim is to reach spiritual awareness with a trance-like state created by continual whirling. This spinning symbolizes the Earth's orbit of the Sun.

flamenco music and dance of the Andalusian gypsies of S Spain, evolved from Andalusian and Arabic folk music. The *cante* (song) is sometimes performed as a solo but more often accompanied by guitar music and passionate improvised dance. Hand clapping, finger clicking (castanets are a more recent addition), and enthusiastic shouts are all features. Male flamenco dancers excel in powerful, rhythmic footwork while the female dancers place emphasis on the graceful and erotic movements of their hands and bodies.

folk dance dance characteristic of a particular people, nation, or region. Many European folk dances are derived from the dances accompanying the customs and ceremonies of pre-Christian times. Some later became ballroom dances (for example, the minuet and waltz). Once an important part of many rituals, folk dance has tended to die out in industrialized countries. Examples of folk dance are Morris dance, farandole, and jota.

jazz dance dance based on African techniques and rhythms, developed by black Americans around 1917. It entered mainstream dance in the 1920s, mainly in show business, and from the 1960s the teachers and choreographers Matt Mattox and Luigi expanded its vocabulary. Contemporary choreographers as diverse as Jerome Robbins and the late Alvin Ailey have used it in their work.

modern dance 20th-century dance idiom developed in reaction against the rigidity of traditional ballet by those seeking a freer and more immediate means of dance expression. Leading exponents include Martha Graham and Merce Cunningham in the USA, Isadora Duncan, and Loie Fuller in Europe. The first generation of modern dance – Martha Graham, Doris Humphrey, and Charles Weidman – emerged from Ruth St Denis and Ted Shawn's Denishawn School in Los Angeles 1915. Doris Humphrey opened a school and performing group in New York 1928. The Humphrey-Weidman technique was based on the kinetic theory of *fall and recovery*. Humphrey's most famous protégé was José Limón. In the UK, the London Contemporary Dance Theatre and school was set up 1967 by Graham's pupil, Robert Cohan. It is the only European institute authorized to teach Graham Technique. In Germany, the originators of a modernist movement known as Central European dance were Jacques Dalcroze and Rudolph Laban. The leading exponents, Mary Wigman, Harald Kreutzberg, and Kurt Jooss, had some influence on modern dance.

Martha Graham's distinctive technique is based on *contraction and release*, using the stomach and pelvic area as a dynamic centre of movement. From her company and School of Contemporary Dance, opened 1927 in New York, a long line of dancers and choreographers continues to emerge. Among them, Erick Hawkins, Merce Cunningham, Glenn Tetley, Paul Taylor, and Dan Waggoner have each evolved his own style.

tap dancing rapid step dance, derived from clog dancing. Its main characteristic is the tapping of toes and heels accentuated by steel 'taps' affixed to the shoes. It was popularized in vaudeville and in 1930s films by such dancers as Fred Astaire and Bill 'Bojangles' Robinson.

Dance: chronology

1000 BC	King David danced 'with all his might' before the ark of the Covenant in Jerusalem – one of the earliest known instances of ritual dance.
405	*Bacchants* by Euripides was staged in Athens. The play demanded a considerable amount of dancing.
142	Consul Scipio Aemilianus Africanus closed the burgeoning dance schools of Rome in a drive against hedonism.
774 AD	Pope Zacharias forbade dancing.
1050	The *Ruodlieb*, a poem written by a monk at Tegernsee, Bavaria, contained the first European reference to dancing in couples.
1313	Rabbi Hacén ben Salomo of Zaragoza, in Aragon, like many other Jews in medieval times, was the local dancing master.
1489	A rudimentary allegorical ballet was performed in honour of the marriage of the Duke of Milan, at Tortona, Italy.
1581	In Paris, the first modern-style unified ballet, the *Ballet Comique de la Reine*, was staged at the court of Catherine de' Medici.
1588	Dance and ballet's first basic text, *L'Orchésographie*, by the priest Jehan Tabouret, was printed in Langres, near Dijon.
1651	In London, John Playford published *The English Dancing Master*. The 18th edition (1728) described 900 country dances.
1661	Louis XIV founded L'Académie Royale de Danse in Paris.
1670	The first classic ballet, *Le Bourgeois Gentilhomme*, was produced in Chambord, France.
1681	La Fontaine, the first professional female ballet dancer, made her debut in *Le Triomphe de L'amour* at the Paris Opéra.
1734	The dancer Marie Sallé adopted the gauze tunic, precursor to the Romantic tutu, and Marie Camargo shortened her skirts.
1738	The Kirov Ballet was established in St Petersburg, Russia.
1760	The great dancer and choreographer Jean-Georges Noverre published in Lyons *Lettres sur la Danse et sur les Ballets*, one of the most influential of all ballet books.
1776	The Bolshoi Ballet was established in Moscow.
1778	Noverre and Mozart collaborated on *Les Petits Riens* in Paris. The cast included the celebrated Auguste Vestris.
late 1700s	The waltz originated in Austria and Germany from a popular folk dance, the *Ländler*.
1820	Carlo Blasis, teacher and choreographer, published his *Traité élémentaire théoretique et pratique de l'arte de la danse* in Milan which, together with his later works of dance theory, codified techniques for future generations of dancers.
1821	The first known picture of a ballerina *sur les pointes*, the French Fanny Bias by F Waldeck, dates from this year.
1832	The first performance of *La Sylphide* at the Paris Opéra opened the Romantic era of ballet and established the central significance of the ballerina. Marie Taglioni, the producer's daughter, who created the title role, wore the new-style Romantic tutu.
1841	Ballet's Romantic masterpiece *Giselle*, with Carlotta Grisi in the leading role, was produced in Paris.
1845	Four great rival ballerinas of the Romantic era – Taglioni, Grisi, Fanny Cerrito, and Lucille Grahn – appeared together in Perrot's *Pas de Quatre* in London.
1866	*The Black Crook*, the ballet extravaganza from which US vaudeville and musical comedy developed, began its run of 474 performances in New York.
1870	*Coppélia*, 19th-century ballet's comic masterpiece, was presented in Paris.

Dance: chronology *(cont.)*

1877	*La Bayadère* and *Swan Lake* were premiered in Moscow, but the latter failed through poor production and choreography. The Petipa-Ivanov version, in which Pierina Legnani performed 32 *fouettés*, established the work 1895.
1897	Anna Pavlova made her debut in St Petersburg with the Imperial Russian Ballet.
1905	Isadora Duncan appeared in Russia, making an immense impression with her 'antiballet' innovations derived from Greek dance.
1906	Vaslav Nijinsky made his debut in St Petersburg.
1909	The first Paris season given by Diaghilev's troupe of Russian dancers, later to become known as the Ballets Russes, marked the beginning of one of the most exciting periods in Western ballet.
1913	The premiere of Stravinsky's *The Rite of Spring* provoked a scandal in Paris.
1914	The foxtrot developed from the two-step in the USA.
1915	The Denishawn School of Modern Dance was founded in Los Angeles.
1926	Martha Graham, one of the most innovative figures in Modern dance, gave her first recital in New York. In England, students from the Rambert School of Ballet, opened by Marie Rambert in 1920, gave their first public performance in *A Tragedy of Fashion*, the first ballet to be choreographed by Frederick Ashton.
1928	The first performance of George Balanchine's *Apollon Musagète* in Paris, by the Ballets Russes, marked the birth of Neo-Classicism in ballet.
1931	Ninette de Valois's Vic-Wells Ballet gave its first performance in London. In 1956 the company became the Royal Ballet.
1933	The Hollywood musical achieved artistic independence through Busby Berkeley's kaleidoscopic choreography in *Forty-Second Street* and Dave Gould's airborne finale in *Flying Down to Rio*, in which Fred Astaire and Ginger Rogers appeared together for the first time.
1939	The American Ballet Theater was founded in New York.
1940	The Dance Notation Bureau was established in New York for recording ballets and dances.
1948	The New York City Ballet was founded with George Balanchine as artistic director and principal choreographer. The film *The Red Shoes* appeared, choreographed by Massine and Robert Helpmann, starring Moira Shearer.
1950	The Festival Ballet, later to become the London Festival Ballet, was created by Alicia Markova and Anton Dolin, who had first danced together with the Ballets Russes de Monte Carlo 1929.
1952	Gene Kelly starred and danced in the film *Singin' in the Rain*.
1953	The US experimental choreographer Merce Cunningham, who often worked with the composer John Cage, formed his own troupe.
1956	The Bolshoi Ballet opened its first season in the West at Covent Garden in London, with Galina Ulanova dancing in *Romeo and Juliet*.
1957	Jerome Robbins conceived and choreographed the musical *West Side Story*, demonstrating his outstanding ability to work in both popular and Classical forms.
1960	The progressive French choreographer Maurice Béjart became director of the Brussels-based *Ballet du XXième Siècle* company.
1961	Rudolf Nureyev defected from the USSR while dancing with the Kirov Ballet in Paris. He was to have a profound influence on male dancing in the West. The South African choreographer John Cranko became director and chief choreographer of the Stuttgart Ballet, transforming it into a major company.
1962	Glen Tetley's ballet *Pierrot Lunaire*, in which he was one of the three dancers, was premiered in New York. In the same year he joined the Nederlands Dans Theater.
1965	US choreographer Twyla Tharp produced her first works.
1966	The School of Contemporary Dance was founded in London, from which Robin Howard and the choreographer Robert Cohan created the London Contemporary Dance Theatre, later to become an internationally renowned company. The choreographer Norman Morrice rejoined the Ballet Rambert as director and the company began to concentrate on contemporary works.
1968	Arthur Mitchell, the first black principal dancer to join the New York City Ballet, founded the Dance Theatre of Harlem.
1974	Mikhail Baryshnikov defected from the USSR while dancing with the Kirov Ballet in Toronto, and made his US debut with the American Ballet Theater.
1977	The release of Robert Stigwood's film *Saturday Night Fever* popularized disco dancing worldwide.
1980	Natalia Makarova, who had defected from the USSR 1979, staged the first full-length revival of Petipa's *La Bayadère* in the West with the American Ballet Theater in New York.
1981	Wayne Sleep, previously principal dancer with the Royal Ballet, starred as lead dancer in Andrew Lloyd-Webber's musical *Cats*, choreographed by Gillian Lynne.
1983	Peter Martins, principal dancer with the New York City Ballet, became choreographer and codirector with Jerome Robbins on the death of Balanchine. Break dancing became widely popular in Western inner cities.
1984	The avant-garde group Michael Clark and Company made its debut in London.
1990	*Maple Leaf Rag*, Martha Graham's final work, was premiered in New York City.

Great 20th-century Choreographers

Ailey Alvin 1931–1989. US dancer, choreographer, and director. His Alvin Ailey City Center Dance Theater, formed 1958, was the first truly multiracial modern dance company. Ailey's highly individual choreography blends modern, jazz, and classical dance, and celebrates rural and urban black America in pieces like *Blues Suite* 1958, and the company signature piece *Revelations* 1960, which has resonances of church revivalist meetings.

Alston Richard 1948– . English choreographer. His modernist style concentrates on light, speedy, lyrical movements. Among his pieces are *Bell High* 1980, *Sacre du printemps* 1981, and *Midsummer* 1983. He was artistic director of the Rambert Dance Company 1986- 92.

Ashton Frederick 1904–1988. English choreographer and dancer. He was director of the Royal Ballet, London, 1963–70. He studied with Marie Rambert before joining the Sadler's Wells (now Royal) Ballet 1935 as chief choreographer. His many works and long association with Margot Fonteyn, for whom he created her most famous roles, contributed to the worldwide reputation of British ballet and to the popularity of ballet in the mid-20th century.

Balanchine George 1904–1983. Russian-born US choreographer. After leaving the USSR 1924, he worked with Diaghilev in France. Moving to the USA 1933, he became a major influence on dance, starting the New York City Ballet 1948. He was the most influential 20th-century choreographer of ballet in the USA. He developed an *American Neo-Classic* dance style and made the New York City Ballet one of the world's great companies.

Bausch Pina 1940– . German avant-garde dance choreographer, director from 1974 of the Wuppertal Tanztheater. Her works incorporate dialogue, elements of psychoanalysis, comedy, and drama, and have been performed on floors covered with churned earth (*Le Sacre du printemps* 1975), water (*Arien* 1979), and rose petals (*Nelken* 1982).

Cranko John 1927–1973. South African-born British choreographer. He was a pivotal figure in the ballet boom of the 1960s. He joined Sadler's Wells, London, 1946 as a dancer, becoming their resident choreographer 1950. In 1961 he became director of the Stuttgart Ballet, where he achieved the *Stuttgart Ballet Miracle*, turning it into a world-class company with a vital and exhilarating repertory. His ballets include *Romeo and Juliet* 1958 and *Onegin* 1965; and one-act ballets such as *Pineapple Poll* 1951 and *Jeu de cartes* 1965.

Cunningham Merce 1919– . US choreographer and dancer. He is recognized as the father of postmodernist, or experimental, dance. He liberated dance from its relationship with music, allowing it to obey its own dynamics. Along with his friend and collaborator, composer John Cage, he introduced chance into the creative process, such as tossing coins to determine options. Influenced by Martha Graham, he formed his own avant-garde dance company and

school in New York 1953. His works include *The Seasons* 1947, *Antic Meet* 1958, *Squaregame* 1976, and *Arcade* 1985.

DeMille Agnes George 1905–1993. US choreographer. After becoming a member of the Ballet Theater, she choreographed a long string of Broadway hits, including *Oklahoma!* 1943, *Carousel* 1945, *Brigadoon* 1947, *Gentlemen Prefer Blondes* 1949, and *Paint Your Wagon* 1951. She founded the Agnes DeMille Dance Theater 1953.

Graham Martha 1893–1991. US dancer, choreographer, teacher, and director. The greatest exponent of modern dance in the USA, she developed a distinctive vocabulary of movement, the **Graham Technique**, now taught worldwide. Her pioneering technique, designed to express inner emotion and intention through dance forms, represented the first real alternative to classical ballet.

Lubovitch Lar 1943– . US modern-dance choreographer. He founded the Lar Lubovitch Dance Company 1976. He was the first to use Minimalist music, for which he created a new style of movement in works like *Marimba* 1977 and *North Star* 1978.

MacMillan Kenneth 1929–1992. Scottish choreographer. He was director of the Royal Ballet 1970–77 and then principal choreographer 1977–92. A daring stylist, he often took risks with his choreography, expanding the ballet's vocabulary with his frequent use of historical sources, religious music, and occasional use of dialogue. His works include *Romeo and Juliet* 1965 (filmed 1966) for Margot Fonteyn and Rudolf Nureyev.

Massine Léonide 1895–1979. Russian choreographer and dancer with the Ballets Russes. He was a creator of comedy in ballet and also symphonic ballet using concert music. His works include the first Cubist-inspired ballet, *Parade* 1917, *La Boutique fantasque* 1919, and *The Three-Cornered Hat* 1919.

Nijinsky Vaslav 1890–1950. Russian dancer and choreographer. Noted for his powerful but graceful technique, he was a legendary member of Diaghilev's Ballets Russes, for whom he choreographed Debussy's *Prélude à l'après-midi d'un faune* 1912 and *Jeux* 1913, and Stravinsky's *Le Sacre du printemps/The Rite of Spring* 1913.

Robbins Jerome 1918– . US dancer and choreographer. He was co-director of the New York City Ballet 1969–83 (with George Balanchine). His ballets are internationally renowned and he is considered the greatest US-born ballet choreographer. He also choreographed the musicals *The King and I* 1951, *West Side Story* 1957, and *Fiddler on the Roof* 1964.

Tharp Twyla 1941– . US modern-dance choreographer and dancer. A phenomenal success in the 1970s, Tharp's work both entertains and challenges audiences with her ability to create serious and beautifully constructed ballets with an often amusing or flippant veneer. She has fused many dance styles including ballet, jazz, modern, tap, and avant-garde dance. Her works include *Eight Jelly Rolls* 1971, *Deuce Coupe* 1973 (music by the Beach Boys), and *Push Comes to Shove* 1976 with Mikhail Baryshnikov, which was one of the most popular works of the decade.

LITERATURE AND LANGUAGE

Great Writers

Abú Nuwás Hasan ibn Háni 762–*c.* 815. Arab poet celebrated for the freedom, eroticism, and ironic lightness of touch he brought to traditional forms.

Andersen Hans Christian 1805–1875. Danish writer. His fairy tales such as 'The Ugly Duckling', 'The Emperor's New Clothes', and 'The Snow Queen', gained him international fame and have been translated into many languages.

Ariosto Ludovico 1474–1533. Italian poet, born in Reggio. He wrote Latin poems and comedies along Classical lines, including the poem *Orlando Furioso* 1516, 1532, an epic treatment of the *Roland* story, and considered to be the perfect poetic expression of the Italian Renaissance.

Machado de Assis Joaquim Maria 1839–1908. Brazilian writer and poet. He is regarded as the greatest Brazilian novelist. His sceptical, ironic wit is well displayed in his 30 volumes of novels and short stories, including *Epitaph for a Small Winner* 1880 and *Dom Casmurro* 1900.

Asturias Miguel Ángel 1899–1974. Guatemalan author and diplomat. He published poetry, Guatemalan legends, and novels, such as *El Señor Presidente/The President* 1946, *Men of Corn* 1949, and *Strong Wind* 1950, attacking Latin-American dictatorships and 'Yankee imperialism'. Nobel prize 1967.

Atwood Margaret (Eleanor) 1939– . Canadian novelist, short-story writer, and poet. Her novels, which often treat feminist themes with wit and irony, include *The Edible Woman* 1969, *Life Before Man* 1979, *Bodily Harm* 1981, *The Handmaid's Tale* 1986, and *Cat's Eye* 1989.

Austen Jane 1775–1817. English novelist whose books are set within the confines of middle-class provincial society, and show her skill at drawing characters and situations with delicate irony. Her principal works are *Sense and Sensibility* 1811 (like its successors, published anonymously), *Pride and Prejudice* 1813, *Mansfield Park* 1814, *Emma* 1816, *Persuasion* 1818, and *Northanger Abbey* 1818. She died at Winchester and is buried in the cathedral.

Baldwin James 1924–1987. US writer, born in New York City, who portrayed the condition of black Americans in contemporary society. His works include the novels *Go Tell It on the Mountain* 1953, *Another Country* 1962, and *Just Above My Head* 1979; the play *The Amen Corner* 1955; and the autobiographical essays *Notes of a Native Son* 1955 and *The Fire Next Time* 1963. He was active in the civil rights movement.

Balzac Honoré de 1799–1850. French novelist. His first success was *Les Chouans/The Chouans* and *La Physiologie du mariage/The Physiology of Marriage* 1829, inspired by Scott. This was the beginning of the long series of novels *La Comédie humaine/The Human Comedy* (planned as 143 volumes, of which 80 were completed), depicting vice and folly in contemporary French society. He also wrote the Rabelaisian *Contes drolatiques/Ribald Tales* 1833.

Bashō Pen name of Matsuo Munefusa 1644–1694. Japanese poet who was a master of the *haiku*, a 17-syllable poetic form with lines of 5, 7, and 5 syllables, which he infused with subtle allusiveness and made the accepted form of poetic expression in Japan. His most famous work is *Oku-no-hosomichi/The Narrow Road to the Deep North* 1694, an account of a visit to northern Japan, which consists of haikus interspersed with prose passages.

Baudelaire Charles Pierre 1821–1867. French poet, whose work combined rhythmical and musical perfection with a morbid romanticism and eroticism, finding beauty in decadence and evil. His first book of verse, *Les Fleurs du mal/Flowers of Evil* 1857, was condemned by the censor as endangering public morals, but was enormously influential, paving the way for Arthur Rimbaud, Paul Verlaine, and the symbolist school.

Bellow Saul 1915– . Canadian-born US novelist of Russian descent, whose finely styled works and skilled characterizations of life, especially contemporary Jewish-American life, won him the Nobel Prize for Literature 1976. His works usually portray an individual's frustrating relationship with the ongoing events of an indifferent society, and include the picaresque *The Adventures of Augie March* 1953, the philosophically speculative *Herzog* 1964, *Humboldt's Gift* 1975, *The Dean's December* 1982, and *The Bellarosa Connection* 1989.

Blake William 1757–1827. English poet, painter, and mystic, a leading figure in the Romantic period. His visionary, symbolic poems include *Songs of Innocence* 1789 and *Songs of Experience* 1794. He engraved the text and illustrations for his works and hand-coloured them, mostly in watercolour. He also illustrated works by John Milton and William Shakespeare.

Boccaccio Giovanni 1313–1375. Italian poet, chiefly known for the collection of tales called the *Decameron* 1348–53. The bawdiness and exuberance of this work, as well as its narrative skill and characterization, made the work enormously popular and influential, inspiring Chaucer, Shakespeare, Dryden, and Keats, among many others.

Böll Heinrich 1917–1985. West German novelist. A radical Catholic and anti-Nazi, he attacked Germany's political past and the materialism of its contemporary society. His many publications include poems, short stories, and novels which satirize German society, for example *Billard um Halbzehn/Billiards at Half-Past Nine* 1959 and *Gruppenbild mit Dame/Group Portrait with Lady* 1971. Nobel Prize for Literature 1972.

Borges Jorge Luis 1899–1986. Argentinian poet and short-story writer. In 1961 he became director of the National Library, Buenos Aires, and was professor of English literature at the university there. He is known for his fantastic and paradoxical work *Ficciones/Fictions* 1944.

Brontë family of English writers, including the three sisters *Charlotte* (1816–55), *Emily Jane* (1818–48) and *Anne* (1820–49), and their brother *Patrick Branwell* (1817–48). Their most enduring works are Charlotte Brontë's *Jane Eyre* 1847 and Emily Brontë's *Wuthering Heights* 1847. Later works include Anne's *The Tenant of Wildfell Hall* 1848 and Charlotte's *Shirley* 1849 and *Villette* 1853.

Burns Robert 1759–1796. Scottish poet who used the Scots dialect at a time when it was not considered suitably 'elevated' for literature. Burns's first volume, *Poems, Chiefly in the Scottish Dialect*, appeared in 1786. In addition to his poetry Burns wrote or adapted many songs, including 'Auld Lang Syne'.

Byron George Gordon, 6th Baron Byron 1788–1824. English poet who became the symbol of Romanticism and political liberalism throughout Europe in the 19th century. His reputation was established with the first two cantos of *Childe Harold* 1812. Later works include *The Prisoner of Chillon* 1816, *Beppo* 1818, *Mazeppa* 1819, and, most notably, *Don Juan* 1819–24. He left England in 1816, spending most of his later life in Italy. In 1823 he sailed for Greece to further the Greek struggle for independence, but died of fever at Missolonghi.

Camoëns or *Camões*, Luís Vaz de 1524–1580. Portuguese poet and soldier. He went on various military expeditions, and was shipwrecked in 1558. His poem, *Os Lusiades/The Lusiads*, published 1572, tells the story of the explorer Vasco da Gama and incorporates much Portuguese history; it has become the country's national epic. His posthumously published lyric poetry is also now valued.

Camus Albert 1913–1960. Algerian-born French writer. A journalist in France, he was active in the Resistance during World War II. His novels, which owe much to existentialism, include *L'Etranger/The Outsider* 1942, *La Peste/The Plague* 1948, and *L'Homme Révolté/The Rebel* 1952. He was awarded the Nobel Prize for Literature 1957.

Cao Chan or *Ts'ao Chan* 1719–1763. Chinese novelist. His tragic love story *Hung Lou Meng/The Dream of the Red Chamber* published 1792, involves the downfall of a Manchu family and is semi-autobiographical.

Carroll Lewis. Pen name of Charles Lutwidge Dodgson 1832–1898. English mathematician and writer of children's books, including the classics *Alice's Adventures in Wonderland* 1865 and its sequel *Through the Looking Glass* 1872. He also published mathematics books under his own name.

Cervantes Saavedra, Miguel de 1547–1616. Spanish novelist, playwright, and poet, whose masterpiece, *Don Quixote* (in full *El ingenioso hidalgo Don Quixote de la Mancha*) was published 1605. In 1613, his *Novelas Ejemplares/Exemplary Novels* appeared, followed by *Viaje del Parnaso/The Voyage to Parnassus* 1614. A spurious second part of *Don Quixote* prompted Cervantes to bring out his own second part in 1615, often considered superior to the first in construction and characterization.

Chaucer Geoffrey *c.* 1340–1400. English poet, the greatest and most influential English poet of the Middle Ages. In his masterpiece, *The Canterbury Tales* (*c.* 1387), a collection of tales told by pilgrims on their way to the shrine of Thomas à Becket, he showed his genius for metre and characterization. His other work includes the French-influenced *Romance of the Rose* and an adaptation of Boccaccio's *Troilus and Criseyde*. The great popularity of his work assured the dominance of the southern English dialect in literature.

Conrad Joseph 1857–1924. English novelist of Polish parentage, born Teodor Jozef Konrad Korzeniowski in the Ukraine. His novels include *Almayer's Folly* 1895, *Lord Jim* 1900, *Heart of Darkness* 1902, *Nostromo* 1904, *The Secret Agent* 1907, and *Under Western Eyes* 1911. His works vividly evoke the mysteries of sea life and exotic foreign settings and explore the psychological isolation of the 'outsider'.

Dante Alighieri 1265–1321. Italian poet. His masterpiece *La Divina Commedia/The Divine Comedy* 1307–21, the greatest poem of the Middle Ages, is an epic account in three parts of his journey through Hell, Purgatory, and Paradise, during which he is guided part of the way by the poet Virgil; on a metaphorical level the journey is also one of Dante's own spiritual development. Other works include the philosophical prose treatise *Convivio/The Banquet* 1306–08, the first major work of its kind to be written in Italian rather than Latin; *Monarchia/On World Government* 1310–13, expounding his political theories; *De vulgari eloquentia/Concerning the Vulgar Tongue* 1304–06, an original Latin work on Italian, its dialects, and kindred languages; and *Canzoniere/Lyrics*, containing his scattered lyrics.

Darío Rubén. Pen name of Félix Rubén García Sarmiento 1867–1916. Nicaraguan poet. His first major work *Azul/Azure* 1888, a collection of prose and verse influenced by French Symbolism, created a sensation. He went on to establish *modernismo*, the Spanish-American modernist literary movement, distinguished by an idiosyncratic and deliberately frivolous style that broke away from the prevailing Spanish provincialism and adapted French poetic models. His vitality and eclecticism influenced every poet writing in Spanish after him, both in the New World and in Spain.

Defoe Daniel 1660–1731. English novelist and journalist. His best-known work, *Robinson Crusoe* 1719, was greatly influential in the development of the novel. An active pamphleteer and political critic, he was imprisoned 1702–04 following publication of the ironic *The Shortest Way With Dissenters*. Fictional works include *Moll Flanders* 1722 and *A Journal of the Plague Year* 1724. Altogether he produced over 500 books, pamphlets, and journals.

Dickens Charles 1812–1870. English novelist, popular for his memorable characters and his portrayal of the social evils of Victorian England. In 1836 he published the first number of the *Pickwick Papers*, followed by *Oliver Twist* 1838, the first of his 'reforming' novels; *Nicholas Nickleby* 1839; *Barnaby Rudge* 1840; *The Old Curiosity Shop* 1841; and *David Copperfield* 1849. Among his later books are *Hard Times* 1854; *Little Dorritt* 1857; *A Tale of Two Cities* 1859; and *Great Expectations* 1861.

Donne John 1571–1631. English metaphysical poet whose work is characterized by subtle imagery and figurative language. In 1615 Donne took orders in the Church of England and as dean of St Paul's Cathedral, London, was noted for his sermons. His poetry includes the sonnets 'Batter my heart, three person'd God' and 'Death be not proud', elegies, and satires.

Dos Passos John 1896–1970. US author. He made his reputation with the war novels *One Man's Initiation* 1919 and *Three Soldiers* 1921. His major work is the trilogy *U.S.A.* 1930–36, which gives a panoramic view of US life through the device of placing fictitious characters against the setting of real newspaper headlines and contemporary events.

Dostoievsky Fyodor Mihailovich 1821–1881. Russian novelist. Remarkable for their profound psychological insight, Dostoievsky's novels have greatly influenced Russian writers, and since the beginning of the 20th century have been increasingly influential abroad. In 1849 he was sentenced to four years' hard labour in Siberia, followed by army service, for printing socialist propaganda. *The House of the Dead* 1861 recalls his prison experiences, followed by his major works *Crime and Punishment* 1866, *The Idiot* 1868–69, and *The Brothers Karamazov* 1880.

Duras Marguerite 1914– . French writer. Her works include short stories (*Des Journées entières dans les arbres*), plays (*La Musica*), film scripts (*Hiroshima mon amour* 1960), and novels such as *Le Vice-Consul* 1966, evoking an existentialist world from the setting of Calcutta, and *Emily L.* 1989. *La vie materielle* (published in France 1987) appeared in England as *Practicalities* 1990. Her autobiographical novel, *La Douleur*, is set in Paris in 1945.

Eliot George. Pen name of Mary Ann Evans 1819–1880. English novelist who portrayed Victorian society, including its intellectual hypocrisy, with realism and irony. In 1857 she published the story 'Amos Barton', the first of the *Scenes of Clerical Life*. This was followed by the novels *Adam Bede* 1859, *The Mill on the Floss* 1860, and *Silas Marner* 1861. *Middlemarch* 1872 is now considered one of the greatest novels of the 19th century. Her final book *Daniel Deronda* 1876 was concerned with anti-Semitism. She also wrote poetry.

Eliot T(homas) S(tearns) 1888–1965. US poet, playwright, and critic who lived in London from 1915. His first volume of poetry, *Prufrock and Other Observations* 1917, introduced new verse forms and rhythms, and expressed the disillusionment of the generation affected by World War I; further collections include *The Waste Land* 1922, which established his central position in modern poetry; *The Hollow Men* 1925, and *Old Possum's Book of Practical Cats* 1939. *Four Quartets* 1943 revealed his religious vision. His plays include *Murder in the Cathedral* 1935 and *The Cocktail Party* 1949. He was also an influential literary critic, and helped to reassess the importance of Donne. He was awarded the Nobel Prize for Literature in 1948.

Faulkner William 1897–1962. US novelist who wrote in an experimental stream-of-consciousness style. His works include *The Sound and the Fury* 1929, dealing with a Southern US family in decline; *As I Lay Dying* 1930; *Light in August* 1932, a study of

segregation; *The Unvanquished* 1938, stories of the Civil War; and *The Hamlet* 1940, *The Town* 1957, and *The Mansion* 1959, a trilogy covering the rise of the materialist Snopes family. He was awarded the Nobel Prize for Literature in 1949.

Fielding Henry 1707–1754. English novelist whose narrative power influenced the form and technique of the novel and helped to make it the most popular form of literature in England. In 1742 he parodied Richardson's novel *Pamela* in his *Joseph Andrews*, which was followed by *Jonathan Wild the Great* 1743; his masterpiece *Tom Jones* 1749, which he described as a 'comic epic in prose'; and *Amelia* 1751.

Firdawsi Mansûr Abu'l-Qâsim *c.* 935–*c.* 1020. Persian poet, the greatest epic poet of Persia. His *Shahnama/The Book of Kings* relates the history of Persia in 60,000 verses, and includes the legend of Sohrab and Rustum, in which the father unknowingly kills the son in battle.

Fitzgerald F(rancis) Scott (Key) 1896–1940. US novelist and short-story writer. His early autobiographical novel *This Side of Paradise* 1920 made him known in the postwar society of the East Coast, and *The Great Gatsby* 1925 epitomizes the Jazz Age.

Flaubert Gustave 1821–1880. French novelist, one of the greatest of the 19th century. His masterpiece, noted for its psychological realism, is *Madame Bovary* 1857. He entered Paris literary circles 1840, but in 1846 moved to Rouen, where he remained for the rest of his life. *Salammbô* 1862 earned him the Legion of Honour 1866, and was followed by *L'Education sentimentale/Sentimental Education* 1869, and *La Tentation de Saint Antoine/The Temptation of St Anthony* 1874. Flaubert also wrote the short stories *Trois contes/Three Tales* 1877.

García Márquez Gabriel 1928– . Colombian novelist. His sweeping novel *Cien años de soledad/One Hundred Years of Solitude* 1967 (which tells the story of a family over a period of six generations) is an example of magic realism, a technique used to heighten the intensity of realistic portrayal of social and political issues by introducing grotesque or fanciful material. His other books include *El amor en los tiempos del célera/Love in the Time of Cholera* 1985. Nobel Prize for Literature 1982.

Gide André 1869–1951. French novelist, born in Paris. His work is largely autobiographical and concerned with the dual themes of self-fulfilment and renunciation. It includes *L'Immoraliste/The Immoralist* 1902, *La Porte étroite/Strait Is the Gate* 1909, *Les Caves du Vatican/The Vatican Cellars* 1914, and *Les Faux-monnayeurs/The Counterfeiters* 1926; and an almost lifelong *Journal*. Nobel Prize for Literature 1947.

Goethe Johann Wolfgang von 1749–1832. German poet, novelist, and dramatist, generally considered the founder of modern German literature, and leader of the Romantic *Sturm und Drang* movement. His works include the autobiographical *Die Leiden des Jungen Werthers/The Sorrows of the Young Werther* 1774 and *Faust* 1808, his masterpiece. A visit to Italy 1786–88 inspired the classical dramas *Iphigenie auf Tauris/Iphigenia in Tauris* 1787 and *Tasso* 1790.

Gogol Nicolai Vasilyevich 1809–1852. Russian writer. His first success was a collection of stories, *Evenings on a Farm near Dikanka* 1831–32, followed by *Mirgorod* 1835. Later works include *Arabesques* 1835, the comedy play *The Inspector General* 1836, and the picaresque novel *Dead Souls* 1842, which satirizes Russian provincial society.

Grass Günter 1927– . German writer. Born in Danzig, he studied at the art academies of Düsseldorf and Berlin, worked as a writer and sculptor (first in Paris and later in Berlin), and in 1958 won the coveted 'Group 47' prize. The grotesque humour and socialist feeling of his novels *Die Blechtrommel/The Tin Drum* 1959 and *Der Butt/The Flounder* 1977 are also characteristic of many of his poems.

Greene (Henry) Graham 1904–1991. English writer, whose novels of guilt, despair, and penitence, include *The Man Within* 1929, *Brighton Rock* 1938, *The Power and the Glory* 1940, *The Heart of the Matter* 1948, *The Third Man* 1950, *The Honorary Consul* 1973, *Monsignor Quixote* 1982, and *The Captain and the Enemy* 1988.

Hâfiz Shams al-Din Muhammad *c.* 1326–1390. Persian lyric poet, who was born in Shiraz and taught in a Dervish college there. His *Diwan*, a collection of short odes, extols the pleasures of life and satirizes his fellow Dervishes.

Hardy Thomas 1840–1928. English novelist and poet. His novels, set in rural 'Wessex' (his native West Country), portray intense human relationships played out in a harshly indifferent natural world. They include *Far From the Madding Crowd* 1874, *The Return of the Native* 1878, *The Mayor of Casterbridge* 1886, *The Woodlanders* 1887, *Tess of the D'Urbervilles* 1891, and *Jude the Obscure* 1895. The latter, portraying social attitudes towards education, marriage, divorce, and suicide, aroused great antagonism, which reinforced his decision to confine himself to verse. His poetry includes the *Wessex Poems* 1898, and several volumes of lyrics.

Heine Heinrich 1797–1856. German romantic poet and journalist, who wrote *Reisebilder* 1826 and *Buch der Lieder/Book of Songs* 1827. From 1831 he lived mainly in Paris, working as a correspondent for German newspapers. Schubert and Schumann set many of his lyrics to music.

Hemingway Ernest 1898–1961. US writer. War, bullfighting, and fishing were used symbolically in his writings to represent honour, dignity, and primitivism – prominent themes in his short stories and novels – which included *A Farewell to Arms* 1929, *For Whom the Bell Tolls* 1940, and *The Old Man and the Sea* 1952. His deceptively simple writing styles attracted many imitators. He received the Nobel Prize for Literature in 1954.

Homer lived *c.* 8th century BC. Legendary Greek epic poet. According to tradition he was a blind minstrel and the author of the *Iliad* and the *Odyssey*, which are probably based on much older stories, passed on orally, concerning war with Troy in the 12th century BC.

Horace 65–8 BC. Roman lyric poet and satirist. He became a leading poet under the patronage of Emperor Augustus. His works include *Satires* 35–30 BC; the four books of *Odes* about 25–24 BC; *Epistles*, a series of verse letters; and a critical work, *Ars poetica*.

Hugo Victor (Marie) 1802–1885. French poet, novelist, and dramatist. The *Odes et poésies diverses* appeared 1822, and his verse play *Hernani* 1830 established him as the leader of French Romanticism. More volumes of verse followed between his series of dramatic novels, which included *The Hunchback of Notre Dame* 1831 and *Les Misérables* 1862.

Huxley Aldous (Leonard) 1894–1963. English writer. The satirical disillusionment of his first novel, *Crome Yellow* 1921, continued throughout *Antic Hay* 1923, *Those Barren Leaves* 1925, *Point Counter Point* 1928, and *Brave New World* 1932, in which human beings are mass-produced in laboratories and rendered incapable of freedom by indoctrination and drugs.

Iqbāl Muhammad 1875–1938. Islamic poet and thinker. His literary works, in Urdu and Persian, were mostly verse in the classical style, suitable for public recitation. He sought through his writings to arouse Muslims to take their place in the modern world.

Ishiguro Kazuo 1954– . Japanese-born British novelist. His novel *An Artist of the Floating World* won the 1986 Whitbread Prize, and *The Remains of the Day* won the 1989 Booker Prize.

James Henry 1843–1916. US novelist, who lived in Europe from 1875 and became a naturalized British subject 1915. His novels deal with the impact of sophisticated European culture on the innocent American. They include *The Portrait of a Lady* 1881, *Washington Square* 1881, *The Bostonians* 1886, *The Ambassadors* 1903, and *The Golden Bowl* 1904. He also wrote more than a hundred shorter works of fiction, notably the supernatural tale *The Turn of the Screw* 1898.

Johnson Samuel, known as 'Dr Johnson', 1709–1784. English lexicographer, author, and critic, also a brilliant conversationalist and the dominant figure in 18th-century London literary society. His *Dictionary*, published 1755, remained authoritative for over a century, and is still remarkable for the vigour of its definitions. In 1764 he founded the 'Literary Club', whose members included Reynolds, Burke, Goldsmith, Garrick, and Boswell, Johnson's biographer.

Joyce James (Augustine Aloysius) 1882–1941. Irish writer, born in Dublin, who revolutionized the form of the English novel with his 'stream of consciousness' technique. His works include *Dubliners* 1914 (short stories), *Portrait of the Artist as a Young Man* 1916, *Ulysses* 1922, and *Finnegans Wake* 1939.

Kafka Franz 1883–1924. Czech novelist, born in Prague, who wrote in German. His three unfinished allegorical novels *Der Prozess/The Trial* 1925, *Der Schloss/The Castle* 1926, and *Amerika/America* 1927 were posthumously published despite his instructions that they should be destroyed. His short stories include 'Die Verwandlung/The Metamorphosis' 1915, in which a man turns into a huge insect.

Kālidāsa lived 5th century AD. Indian epic poet and dramatist. His works, in Sanskrit, include the classic drama *Sakuntala*, the love story of King Dushyanta and the nymph Sakuntala.

Keats John 1795–1821. English poet, a leading figure of the Romantic movement. He published his first volume of poetry 1817; this was followed by *Endymion, Isabella*, and *Hyperion* 1818, 'The Eve of St Agnes', his odes 'To Autumn', 'On a Grecian Urn', and 'To a Nightingale', and 'Lamia' 1819. His final volume of poems appeared in 1820.

Kerouac Jack 1923–1969. US novelist who named and epitomized the Beat Generation of the 1950s. His books, all autobiographical, include *On the Road* 1957, *Big Sur* 1963, and *Desolation Angel* 1965.

Kipling (Joseph) Rudyard 1865–1936. English writer, born in India. His stories for children include the *Jungle Books* 1894–1895, *Stalky and Co* 1899, and the *Just So Stories* 1902. Other works include the novel *Kim* 1901, the short story 'His Gift', poetry, and the unfinished autobiography *Something of Myself* 1937. In his heyday he enjoyed enormous popularity, and although subsequently denigrated for alleged 'jingoist imperialism', his work is increasingly valued for its complex characterization and subtle moral viewpoints. Nobel prize 1907.

La Fontaine Jean de 1621–1695. French poet. He was born at Château-Thierry, and from 1656 lived largely in Paris, the friend of Molière, Racine, and Boileau. His works include *Fables* 1668–94 and *Contes* 1665–74, a series of witty and bawdy tales in verse.

Lafontaine Oskar 1943– . German socialist politician, federal deputy chair of the Social Democrat Party (SPD) from 1987. Leader of the Saar regional branch of the SPD from 1977 and former mayor of Saarbrucken, West Germany, he was dubbed 'Red Oskar' because of his radical views on military and environmental issues. His attitude became more conservative once he had become minister-president of Saarland in 1985.

Lawrence D(avid) H(erbert) 1885–1930. English writer whose work expresses his belief in emotion and the sexual impulse as creative and true to human nature. His novels include *Sons and Lovers* 1913, *The Rainbow* 1915, *Women in Love* 1921, and *Lady Chatterley's Lover* 1928 (the latter was banned as obscene in the UK until 1960). Lawrence also wrote short stories (for example 'The Woman Who Rode Away') and poetry.

Leopardi Giacomo, Count Leopardi 1798–1837. Italian romantic poet. The first collection of his uniquely pessimistic poems, *I Versi/Verses*, appeared in 1824, and was followed by his philosophical *Operette morali/Minor Moral Works* 1827, in prose, and *I Canti/Lyrics* 1831.

Levi Primo 1919–1987. Italian novelist. He joined the anti-Fascist resistance during World War II, was captured, and sent to the concentration camp at Auschwitz. He wrote of these experiences in *Se questo è un uomo/If This Is a Man* 1947.

Lewis (Harry) Sinclair 1885–1951. US novelist. He made a reputation with satirical novels: *Main Street* 1920, depicting American small-town life; *Babbitt* 1922, the story of a real-estate dealer of the Midwest

caught in the conventions of his milieu; *Arrowsmith* 1925, a study of the pettiness in medical science; and *Elmer Gantry* 1927, a satiric portrayal of evangelical religion. *Dodsworth*, a gentler novel of a US industrialist, was published 1929. He was the first American to be awarded the Nobel Prize for Literature 1930.

Li Po 705–762. Chinese poet. He used traditional literary forms, but his exuberance, the boldness of his imagination, and the intensity of his feeling have won him recognition as perhaps the greatest of all Chinese poets. Although he was mostly concerned with higher themes, he is also remembered for his celebratory verses on drinking.

London Jack (John Griffith) 1876–1916. US novelist, author of the adventure stories *The Call of the Wild* 1903, *The Sea Wolf* 1904, and *White Fang* 1906.

Lorca Federico García 1898–1936. Spanish poet and playwright, born in Granada. *Romancero gitano/Gipsy Ballad-book* 1928 shows the influence of the Andalusian songs of the area. In 1929–30 Lorca visited New York, and his experiences are reflected in *Poeta en Nuevo York* 1940. His poems include *Lament*, written for the bullfighter Mejías. He was shot by the Falangists during the Spanish Civil War.

Machado de Assis Joaquim Maria 1839–1908. Brazilian writer and poet. He is regarded as the greatest Brazilian novelist. His sceptical, ironic wit is well displayed in his 30 volumes of novels and short stories, including *Epitaph for a Small Winner* 1880 and *Dom Casmurro* 1900.

Mann Thomas 1875–1955. German novelist and critic, concerned with the theme of the artist's relation to society. His first novel was *Buddenbrooks* 1901, which, followed by *Der Zauberberg/The Magic Mountain* 1924, led to a Nobel prize 1929. Later works include *Dr Faustus* 1947 and *Die Bekenntnisse des Hochstaplers Felix Krull/Confessions of Felix Krull* 1954. Notable among his works of short fiction is *Der Tod in Venedig/Death in Venice* 1913.

Manzoni Alessandro, Count Manzoni 1785–1873. Italian poet and novelist, author of the historical romance, *I promessi sposi/The Betrothed* 1825–27, set in Spanish-occupied Milan during the 17th century. Verdi's *Requiem* commemorates him.

Maupassant Guy de 1850–1893. French author who established a reputation with the short story 'Boule de Suif/Ball of Fat' 1880 and wrote some 300 short stories in all. His novels include *Une Vie/A Woman's Life* 1883 and *Bel-Ami* 1885. He was encouraged as a writer by Flaubert.

Melville Herman 1819–1891. US writer, whose *Moby-Dick* 1851 was inspired by his whaling experiences in the South Seas. These experiences were also the basis for earlier fiction, such as *Typee* 1846 and *Omoo* 1847. He published several volumes of verse, as well as short stories (*The Piazza Tales* 1856). *Billy Budd* was completed just before his death and published 1924. Although most of his works were unappreciated during his lifetime, today he is one of the most highly regarded of US authors.

Milton John 1608–1674. English poet. His early poems include the pastoral *L'allegro* and *Il penseroso* 1632, the masque *Comus* 1633, and the elegy *Lycidas*

1637. His middle years were devoted to the Puritan cause and pamphleteering, including one advocating divorce, and another (*Areopagitica*) freedom of the press. From 1649 he was (Latin) secretary to the Council of State, his assistants (as his sight failed) including Marvell. The masterpieces of his old age are his epic poems on biblical themes, *Paradise Lost* 1667, *Paradise Regained* 1677, and the classic drama *Samson Agonistes* 1677.

Mishima Yukio 1925–1970. Japanese novelist whose work often deals with sexual desire and perversion, as in *Confessions of a Mask* 1949 and *The Temple of the Golden Pavilion* 1956. He committed hara-kiri (ritual suicide) as a protest against what he saw as the corruption of the nation and the loss of the samurai warrior tradition.

Montaigne Michel Eyquem de 1533–1592. French writer, regarded as the creator of the essay form. In 1580 he published the first two volumes of his *Essais*, the third volume appeared in 1588. Montaigne deals with all aspects of life from an urbanely sceptical viewpoint. Through the translation by John Florio in 1603 he influenced Shakespeare and other English writers.

Musil Robert 1880–1942. Austrian novelist, author of the unfinished *Der Mann ohne Eigenschaften/The Man without Qualities* (three volumes, 1930–43). Its hero shares the author's background of philosophical study and scientific and military training, and is preoccupied with the problems of the self viewed from a mystic but agnostic viewpoint.

Nabokov Vladimir 1899–1977. US writer who left his native Russia 1917 and began writing in English in the 1940s. His most widely known book is *Lolita* 1955, the story of the middle-aged Humbert Humbert's infatuation with a precocious child of 12. His other books include *Laughter in the Dark* 1938, *The Real Life of Sebastian Knight* 1945, *Pnin* 1957, and his memoirs *Speak, Memory* 1947.

Naipaul V(idiadhar) S(urajprasad) 1932– . British writer, born in Trinidad of Hindu parents. His novels include *A House for Mr Biswas* 1961, *The Mimic Men* 1967, *A Bend in the River* 1979, and *Finding the Centre* 1984. His brother *Shiva(dhar) Naipaul* (1940–85) was also a novelist (*Fireflies* 1970) and journalist.

Neruda Pablo. Pen name of Neftalí Ricardo Reyes y Basualto 1904–1973. Chilean poet and diplomat. His work includes lyrics and the epic poem of the American continent *Canto General* 1950. Nobel Prize for Literature 1971. He served as consul and ambassador to many countries.

Orwell George. Pen name of Eric Arthur Blair 1903–1950. English author. His books include the satire *Animal Farm* 1945, which included such sayings as 'All animals are equal, but some are more equal than others', and the prophetic *Nineteen Eighty-Four* 1949, portraying the dangers of excessive state control over the individual. Other works include *Down and Out in Paris and London* 1933 and *Homage to Catalonia* 1938.

Ovid (Publius Ovidius Naso) 43 BC–AD 17. Roman poet. His poetry deals mainly with the themes of love (*Amores* 20 BC), (*Ars amatoria* 1 BC), mythology (*Metamorphoses* AD 2), and exile (*Tristia* AD 9–12).

Pasternak Boris Leonidovich 1890–1960. Russian poet and novelist. His novel *Dr Zhivago* 1957 was banned in the USSR as a 'hostile act', and followed by a Nobel prize (which he declined). *Dr Zhivago* has since been unbanned and Pasternak posthumously rehabilitated.

Paz Octavio 1914– . Mexican poet and essayist. His works reflect many influences, including Marxism, surrealism, and Aztec mythology. His celebrated poem *Piedra del sol/Sun Stone* 1957 uses contrasting images, centring upon the Aztec Calendar Stone (representing the Aztec universe), to symbolize the loneliness of individuals and their search for union with others. Nobel Prize for Literature 1990.

Perrault Charles 1628–1703. French author of the fairy tales *Contes de ma mère l'oye/Mother Goose's Fairy Tales* 1697, which include 'Sleeping Beauty', 'Little Red Riding Hood', 'Blue Beard', 'Puss in Boots', and 'Cinderella'.

Pessoa Fernando 1888–1935. Portuguese poet. Born in Lisbon, he was brought up in South Africa and was bilingual in English and Portuguese. His verse is considered to be the finest written in Portuguese this century. He wrote under three assumed names, which he called 'heteronyms' – Alvaro de Campos, Ricardo Reis, and Alberto Caeiro – for each of which he invented a biography.

Petrarch (Italian *Petrarca*) Francesco 1304–1374. Italian poet, born in Arezzo, a devotee of the Classical tradition. His *Il Canzoniere* is composed of sonnets in praise of his idealized love 'Laura', whom he first saw 1327 (she was a married woman and refused to become his mistress). His 14-line sonnets, in a form which was given the name Petrarchan, were influential for centuries.

Poe Edgar Allan 1809–1849. US writer and poet. His short stories are renowned for their horrific atmosphere (as in *The Fall of the House of Usher* 1839) and acute reasoning (for example, *The Gold Bug* 1843 and *The Murders in the Rue Morgue* 1841, in which the investigators Legrand and Dupin anticipate Conan Doyle's Sherlock Holmes). His most famous poem is 'The Raven' 1844.

Pope Alexander 1688–1744. English poet and satirist. He established his reputation with the precocious *Pastorals* 1709 and *Essay on Criticism* 1711, which were followed by a parody of the heroic epic *The Rape of the Lock* 1712–14 and 'Eloisa to Abelard' 1717. Other works include a highly Neo-Classical translation of Homer's *Iliad* and *Odyssey* 1715–26.

Pound Ezra 1885–1972. US poet who lived in London from 1908. His *Personae* and *Exultations* 1909 established the principles of the Imagist movement. His largest work was the series of *Cantos* 1925–1969 (intended to number 100), which attempted a massive reappraisal of history.

Proust Marcel 1871–1922. French novelist and critic. His immense autobiographical work *À la recherche du temps perdu/Remembrance of Things Past* 1913–27, consisting of a series of novels, is the expression of his childhood memories coaxed from his subconscious; it is also a precise reflection of life in provincial France at the end of the 19th century.

Pushkin Aleksandr 1799–1837. Russian poet and writer. He was exiled 1820 for his political verse and in 1824 was in trouble for his atheistic opinions. He wrote ballads such as *The Gypsies* 1827, and the novel in verse *Eugene Onegin* 1823–31. Other works include the tragic drama *Boris Godunov* 1825, and the prose pieces *The Captain's Daughter* 1836 and *The Queen of Spades* 1834. Pushkin's range was wide, and his willingness to experiment freed later Russian writers from many of the archaic conventions of the literature of his time.

Pynchon Thomas 1937– . US novelist who created a bizarre, labyrinthine world in his books, the first of which was *V* 1963. *Gravity's Rainbow* 1973 represents a major achievement in 20th-century literature, with its fantastic imagery and esoteric language, drawn from mathematics and science.

Rabelais François 1495–1553. French satirist, monk, and physician, whose name has become synonymous with bawdy humour. He was educated in the Renaissance humanist tradition and was the author of satirical allegories, including *La Vie inestimable de Gargantua/The Inestimable Life of Gargantua* 1535 and *Faits et dits héroïques du grand Pantagruel/Deeds and Sayings of the Great Pantagruel* 1533, about two giants (father and son), Gargantua and Pantagruel.

Richardson Samuel 1689–1761. English novelist, one of the founders of the modern novel. *Pamela* 1740–41, written in the form of a series of letters and containing much dramatic conversation, was sensationally popular all across Europe, and was followed by *Clarissa* 1747–48 and *Sir Charles Grandison* 1753–54.

Rilke Rainer Maria 1875–1926. Austrian writer, born in Prague. His prose works include the semi-autobiographical *Die Aufzeichnungen des Malte Laurids Brigge/Notebook of Malte Laurids Brigge* 1910, and his poetical works include *Die Sonnette an Orpheus/Sonnets to Orpheus* 1923 and *Duisener Elegien/Duino Elegies* 1923. His verse is characterized by a form of mystic pantheism that seeks to achieve a state of ecstasy in which existence can be apprehended as a whole.

Rimbaud (Jean Nicolas) Arthur 1854–1891. French Symbolist poet. His verse was chiefly written before the age of 20, notably *Les Illuminations* published 1886. From 1871 he lived with Verlaine.

Rousseau Jean-Jacques 1712–1778. French social philosopher and writer, born in Geneva, Switzerland. *Discourses on the Origins of Inequality* 1754 made his name: he denounced civilized society and postulated the paradox of the superiority of the 'noble savage'. *Social Contract* 1762 emphasized the rights of the people over those of the government, and stated that a government could be legitimately overthrown if it failed to express the general will of the people. It was a significant influence on the French Revolution. In the novel *Emile* 1762 he outlined a new theory of education, based on natural development and the power of example, to elicit the unspoiled nature and abilities of children. *Confessions*, published posthumously 1782, was a frank account of his occasionally immoral life and was a founding work of autobiography.

Salinger J(erome) D(avid) 1919– . US writer, author of the classic novel of mid-20th-century adolescence *The Catcher in the Rye* 1951. He also wrote short stories about a Jewish family named Glass, including *Franny and Zooey* 1961.

Sartre Jean-Paul 1905–1980. French author and philosopher, a leading proponent of existentialism in postwar philosophy. He published his first novel, *La Nausée/Nausea*, 1937, followed by the trilogy *Les Chemins de la Liberté/Roads to Freedom* 1944–45 and many plays, including *Huis Clos/In Camera* 1944.

Scott Walter 1771–1832. Scottish novelist and poet. His first works were translations of German ballads, followed by poems such as 'The Lady of the Lake' 1810 and 'Lord of the Isles' 1815. He gained a European reputation for his historical novels such as *Heart of Midlothian* 1818, *Ivanhoe* 1819, and *The Fair Maid of Perth* 1828. His last years were marked by frantic writing to pay off his debts, after the bankruptcy of his publishing company in 1826.

Shakespeare William 1564–1616. English dramatist and poet, the greatest English playwright; he also wrote numerous sonnets. (See entry in *Theatre* section for more.)

Shelley Percy Bysshe 1792–1822. English lyric poet, a leading figure in the Romantic movement. Expelled from Oxford university for atheism, he fought all his life against religion and for political freedom. This is reflected in his early poems such as *Queen Mab* 1813. He later wrote tragedies including *The Cenci* 1818, lyric dramas such as *Prometheus Unbound* 1820, and lyrical poems such as 'Ode to the West Wind'. He drowned while sailing in Italy.

Singer Isaac Bashevis 1904– . Polish-born US novelist and short-story writer. His works, written in Yiddish, then translated into English, often portray traditional Jewish life in Poland and the USA, and the loneliness of old age. They include *Gimpel the Fool* 1957, *The Slave* 1960, *Shosha* 1978, *Old Love* 1979, *Lost in America* 1981, *The Image and Other Stories* 1985, and *The Death of Methuselah* 1988. He has also written plays and books for children. In 1978 he was awarded the Nobel Prize for Literature.

Solzhenitsyn Alexander (Isayevich) 1918– . Soviet novelist, a US citizen from 1974. After military service, he was in prison and exile 1945–57 for anti-Stalinist comments. Much of his writing is semi-autobiographical and highly critical of the system, including *One Day in the Life of Ivan Denisovich* 1962 which deals with the labour camps under Stalin, and *The Gulag Archipelago* 1973, an exposé of the whole Soviet labour camp network. This led to his expulsion from the USSR 1974.

Soyinka Wole 1934– . Nigerian author who was a political prisoner in Nigeria 1967–69. His works include the play *The Lion and the Jewel* 1963; his prison memoirs *The Man Died* 1972; *Aké, The Years of Childhood* 1982, an autobiography, and *Isara*, a fictionalized memoir 1989. He was the first African to receive the Nobel Prize for Literature, in 1986.

Spenser Edmund *c.* 1552–1599. English poet, who has been called the 'poet's poet' because of his rich imagery and command of versification. He is known for his moral allegory *The Faerie Queene*, of which six books survive (three published 1590 and three 1596). Other books include *The Shepheard's Calendar* 1579, *Astrophel* 1586, the love sonnets *Amoretti* and the *Epithalamion* 1595.

Steinbeck John (Ernst) 1902–1968. US novelist. His realist novels, such as *In Dubious Battle* 1936, *Of Mice and Men* 1937, and *The Grapes of Wrath* 1939 (Pulitzer prize 1940), portray agricultural life in his native California, where migrant farm laborers from the Oklahoma dust bowl struggled to survive. He received the Nobel Prize for Literature in 1962.

Stendhal pen name of Marie Henri Beyle 1783–1842. French novelist. His novels *Le Rouge et le noir/The Red and the Black* 1830 and *La Chartreuse de Parme/The Charterhouse of Parme* 1839 were pioneering works in their treatment of disguise and hypocrisy; a review of the latter by Balzac in 1840 furthered Stendhal's reputation.

Sterne Laurence 1713–1768. Irish writer, creator of the comic anti-hero Tristram Shandy. *The Life and Opinions of Tristram Shandy, Gent* 1760–67, an eccentrically whimsical and bawdy novel, foreshadowed many of the techniques and devices of 20th-century novelists, including James Joyce. His other works include *A Sentimental Journey through France and Italy* 1768.

Stevenson Robert Louis 1850–1894. Scottish novelist and poet, author of the adventure novel *Treasure Island* 1883. Later works included the novels *Kidnapped* 1886, *The Master of Ballantrae* 1889, *Dr Jekyll and Mr Hyde* 1886, and the anthology *A Child's Garden of Verses* 1885.

Swift Jonathan 1667–1745. Irish satirist and Anglican cleric, author of *Gulliver's Travels* 1726, an allegory describing travel to lands inhabited by giants, miniature people, and intelligent horses. Other works include *The Tale of a Tub* 1704, attacking corruption in religion and learning; contributions to the Tory paper *The Examiner*, of which he was editor 1710–11; the satirical *A Modest Proposal* 1729, which suggested that children of the poor should be eaten; and many essays and pamphlets.

Tagore Rabindranath 1861–1941. Bengali Indian writer, born in Calcutta, who translated into English his own verse *Gitanjali* ('song offerings') 1912 and his verse play *Chitra* 1896. Nobel prize 1913.

Tennyson Alfred, 1st Baron Tennyson 1809–1892. English poet, poet laureate 1850–96, whose verse has a majestic, musical quality. His works include 'The Lady of Shalott', 'The Lotus Eaters', 'Ulysses', 'Break, Break, Break', 'The Charge of the Light Brigade'; the longer narratives *Locksley Hall* 1832 and *Maud* 1855; the elegy *In Memoriam* 1850; and a long series of poems on the Arthurian legends *The Idylls of the King* 1857–85.

Thackeray William Makepeace 1811–1863. English novelist and essayist, born in Calcutta, India. He was a regular contributor to *Fraser's Magazine* and *Punch*. *Vanity Fair* 1847–48 was his first novel, followed by *Pendennis* 1848, *Henry Esmond* 1852 (and its sequel *The Virginians* 1857–59), and *The Newcomes* 1853–55, in which Thackeray's tendency to sentimentality is most marked.

Tolstoy Leo Nikolaievich 1828–1910. Russian novelist who wrote *Tales from Sebastopol* 1856, *War and Peace* 1863–69, and *Anna Karenina* 1873–77. From 1880 Tolstoy underwent a profound spiritual crisis and took up various moral positions, including passive resistance to evil, rejection of authority (religious or civil) and private ownership, and a return to basic mystical Christianity. He was excommunicated by the Orthodox Church, and his later works were banned.

Turgenev Ivan Sergeievich 1818–1883. Russian writer, notable for poetic realism, pessimism, and skill in characterization. His works include the play *A Month in the Country* 1849, and the novels *A Nest of Gentlefolk* 1858, *Fathers and Sons* 1862, and *Virgin Soil* 1877. His series *A Sportsman's Sketches* 1852 criticized serfdom.

Twain Mark. Pen name of Samuel Langhorne Clemens 1835–1910. US writer. He established his reputation with the comic masterpiece *The Innocents Abroad* 1869 and two classic American novels, in dialect, *The Adventures of Tom Sawyer* 1876 and *The Adventures of Huckleberry Finn* 1885. He also wrote satire, as in *A Connecticut Yankee at King Arthur's Court* 1889.

Verlaine Paul 1844–1896. French lyric poet who was influenced by the poets Baudelaire and Rimbaud. His volumes of verse include *Poèmes saturniens/Saturnine Poems* 1866, *Fêtes galantes/Amorous Entertainments* 1869 and *Romances sans paroles/Songs without Words* 1874. In 1873 he was imprisoned for attempting to shoot Rimbaud. His later works reflect his attempts to lead a reformed life. He was acknowledged as leader of the Symbolist poets.

Villon François 1431–c. 1465. French poet who used satiric humour, pathos, and lyric power in works written in *argot* (slang) of the time. Very little of his work survives, but it includes the *Ballade des dames du temps jadis/Ballad of the Ladies of Former Times*, *Petit Testament* 1456, and *Grand Testament* 1461.

Virgil (Publius Vergilius Maro) 70–19 BC. Roman poet who wrote the *Eclogues* 37 BC, a series of pastoral poems; the *Georgics* 30 BC, four books on the art of farming; and his epic masterpiece, the *Aeneid* 29–19 BC.

Voltaire Pen name of François-Marie Arouet 1694–1778. French writer who believed in deism, and devoted himself to tolerance, justice, and humanity. He was threatened with arrest for *Lettres philosophiques sur les anglais/Philosophical Letters on the English* 1733 (essays in favour of English ways, thought, and political practice) and had to take refuge. Other writings include *Le Siècle de Louis XIV/The Age of Louis XIV* 1751; *Candide* 1759, a parody on Leibniz's 'best of all possible worlds'; and *Dictionnaire philosophique* 1764.

Walker Alice 1944– . US poet, novelist, critic, and essay writer. She was active in the US civil-rights movement in the 1960s and, as a black woman, wrote about the double burden of racist and sexist oppression that such women bear. Her novel *The Color Purple* 1983 (film, 1985) won the Pulitzer Prize.

Wharton Edith (born Jones) 1862–1937. US novelist. Her work, known for its subtlety and form and influenced by her friend Henry James, was mostly set

Nobel Prize for Literature (International)

1901	René F A Sully-Prodhomme (French)	1950	Bertrand Russell (British)
1902	Theodor Mommsen (German)	1951	Pär Lagerkvist (Swedish)
1903	Bjornsterne Bjornsen (Norwegian)	1952	François Mauriac (French)
1904	Frédéric Mistral (French)	1953	Sir Winston Churchill (British)
1905	Henryk Sienkiwicz (Polish)	1954	Ernest Hemingway (American)
1906	Giosue Carducci (Italian)	1955	Halldór Laxness (Icelandic)
1907	Rudyard Kipling (British)	1956	Juan Ramón Jiménez (Spanish)
1908	Rudolk Eucken (German)	1957	Albert Camus (French)
1909	Selma Lagerlöf (Swedish)	1958	Boris Pasternak, declined award (Russian)
1910	Paul von Heyse (German)	1959	Salvatore Quasimodo (Italian)
1911	Maurice Maeterlinck (Belgian)	1960	Saint-John Perse (French)
1912	Gerhart Hauptmann (German)	1961	Ivo Andrić (Yugoslav)
1913	Rabindranath Tagore (Indian)	1962	John Steinbeck (American)
1914	No award	1963	George Seferis (Greek)
1915	Romain Rolland (French)	1964	Jean-Paul Sartre, declined award (French)
1916	Verver von Heidenstan (Swedish)	1965	Mikhail Sholokhov (Russian)
1917	Karl Gjellerup (Danish)	1966	Shmuel Yosef Agnon (Israeli),
1918	No award		Nelly Sachs (German-born Swedish)
1919	Carl Spitteler (Swiss)	1967	Miguel Angel Asturias (Guatemalan)
1920	Knut Hamsun (Norwegian)	1968	Kawabata Yasunari (Japanese)
1921	Anatole France (French)	1969	Samuel Beckett (Irish)
1922	Jacinto Benavente y Martinez (Spanish)	1970	Aleksandr Solzhenitsyn (Russian)
1923	William Butler Yeats (Irish)	1971	Pablo Neruda (Chilean)
1924	Wladyslaw Stanislaw Reymont (Polish)	1972	Heinrich Böll (German)
1925	George Bernard Shaw (Irish)	1973	Patrick White (Australian)
1926	Grazia Deledda (Italian)	1974	Eyvind Johnson (Swedish),
1927	Henri Bergson (French)		Harry Martinson (Swedish)
1928	Sigrid Undsey (Norwegian)	1975	Eugenio Montale (Italian)
1929	Thomas Mann (German)	1976	Saul Bellow (American)
1930	Sinclair Lewis (American)	1977	Vicente Aleixandre (Spanish)
1931	Erik Axel Karlfeldt (Swedish)	1978	Isaac Bashevis Singer (American)
1932	John Galsworthy (British)	1979	Odysseus Lytis (Greek)
1933	Ivan Bunin (Russian)	1980	Czeslaw Milosz (Polish-American)
1934	Luigi Pirandello (Italian)	1981	Elias Canetti (Bulgarian-born German)
1935	No award	1982	Gabriel García Márquez (Colombian)
1936	Eugene O'Neill (American)	1983	William Golding (British)
1937	Roger Martin du Gard (French)	1984	Jaroslav Seifert (Czech)
1938	Pearl Buck (American)	1985	Claude Simon (French)
1939	Frans Enil Sillanpää (Finnish)	1986	Wole Soyinka (Nigerian)
1940–43	No award	1987	Joseph Brodsky (Russian-American)
1944	Johannes V Jensen (Danish)	1988	Naguib Mahfouz (Egyptian)
1945	Gabriela Mistral (Chilean)	1989	Camilo José Cela (Spanish)
1946	Hermann Hesse (German-born Swiss)	1990	Octavio Paz (Mexican)
1947	André Gide (French)	1991	Nadine Gordimer (South African)
1948	T S Eliot (American-born English)	1992	Derek Walcott (Santa Lucian)
1949	William Faulkner (American)	1993	Toni Morrison (American)

in New York society. It includes *The House of Mirth* 1905, which made her reputation; the grim, uncharacteristic novel of New England *Ethan Frome* 1911; *The Custom of the Country* 1913, and *The Age of Innocence* 1920.

Whitman Walt(er) 1819–1892. US poet who published *Leaves of Grass* 1855, which contains the symbolic 'Song of Myself'. It used unconventional free verse (with no rhyme or regular rhythm) and scandalized the public by its frank celebration of sexuality.

Woolf Virginia (née Virginia Stephen) 1882–1941. English novelist and critic. Her first novel, *The Voyage Out* 1915, explored the tensions experienced by women who want marriage and a career. In *Mrs Dalloway* 1925 she perfected her 'stream of consciousness' technique. Among her later books are *To the Lighthouse* 1927, *Orlando* 1928, and *The Years* 1937, which considers the importance of economic independence for women.

Wordsworth William 1770–1850. English Romantic poet. In 1797 he moved with his sister Dorothy to Somerset to be near Coleridge, collaborating with him on *Lyrical Ballads* 1798 (which included 'Tintern Abbey'). From 1799 he lived in the Lake District, and later works include *Poems* 1807 (including 'Intimations of Immortality') and *The Prelude* (written by 1805, published 1850). He was appointed poet laureate in 1843.

Yeats W(illiam) (B)utler 1865–1939. Irish poet. He was a leader of the Celtic revival and a founder of the Abbey Theatre in Dublin. His early work was romantic and lyrical, as in the poem 'The Lake Isle of Innisfree' and plays *The Countess Cathleen* 1892 and *The Land of Heart's Desire* 1894. His later books of poetry include *The Wild Swans at Coole* 1917 and *The Winding Stair* 1929. He was a senator of the Irish Free State 1922–28. Nobel prize 1923.

Zola Émile Edouard Charles Antoine 1840–1902. French novelist and social reformer. With *La Fortune des Rougon/The Fortune of the Rougons* 1867 he began a series of some 20 naturalistic novels, portraying the fortunes of a French family under the Second Empire. They include *Le Ventre de Paris/The Underbelly of Paris* 1873, *Nana* 1880, and *La Débâcle/The Debacle* 1892. In 1898 he published *J'accuse/I Accuse*, a pamphlet indicting the persecutors of Dreyfus, for which he was prosecuted for libel but later pardoned.

Booker Prize for Fiction (British)

1969	P H Newby *Something to Answer For*
1970	Bernice Rubens *The Elected Member*
1971	V S Naipaul *In a Free State*
1972	John Berger *G*
1973	J G Farrell *The Siege of Krishnapur*
1974	Nadine Gordimer *The Conservationist*; Stanley Middleton *Holiday (joint winners)*
1975	Ruth Prawer Jhabvala *Heat and Dust*
1976	David Storey *Saville*
1977	Paul Scott *Staying On*
1978	Iris Murdoch *The Sea, The Sea*
1979	Penelope Fitzgerald *Offshore*
1980	William Golding *Rites of Passage*
1981	Salman Rushdie *Midnight's Children*
1982	Thomas Keneally *Schindler's Ark*
1983	J M Coetzee *Life and Times of Michael K*
1984	Anita Brookner *Hotel du Lac*
1985	Keri Hulme *The Bone People*
1986	Kingsley Amis *The Old Devils*
1987	Penelope Lively *Moon Tiger*
1988	Peter Carey *Oscar and Lucinda*
1989	Kazuo Ishiguro *Remains of the Day*
1990	A S Byatt *Possession*
1991	Ben Okri *The Famished Road*
1992	Barry Unsworth *Sacred Hunger*; Michael Ondaatje *The English Patient*
1993	Roddy Doyle *Paddy Clarke Ha Ha Ha*

Pulitzer Prize for Fiction (American)

1917	No award	1950	A B Guthrie Jr *The Way West*
1918	Ernest Poole *His Family*	1951	Conrad Richter *The Town*
1919	Booth Tarkington *The Magnificent Ambersons*	1952	Herman Wouk *The Caine Mutiny*
1920	No award	1953	Ernest Hemingway *The Old Man and the Sea*
1921	Edith Wharton *The Age of Innocence*	1954	No award
1922	Booth Tarkington *Alice Adams*	1955	William Faulkner *A Fable*
1923	Willa Cather *One of Ours*	1956	Mackinley Kantor *Andersonville*
1924	Margaret Wilson *The Able McLaughlins*	1957	No award
1925	Edna Ferber *So Big*	1958	James Agee *A Death in the Family*
1926	Sinclair Lewis *Arrowsmith*	1959	Robert Lewis Taylor *The Travels of Jamie McPheeters*
1927	Louis Bromfield *Early Autumn*		
1928	Thornton Wilder *The Bridge at San Luis Rey*	1960	Allen Drury *Advise and Consent*
1929	Julia Peterkin *Scarlet Sister Mary*	1961	Harper Lee *To Kill a Mockingbird*
1930	Oliver LaFarge *Laughing Boy*	1962	Edwin O'Connor *The Edge of Sadness*
1931	Margaret Ayer Barnes *Years of Grace*	1963	William Faulkner *The Reivers*
1932	Pearl S Buck *The Good Earth*	1964	No award
1933	T S Stribling *The Store*	1965	Shirley Ann Grau *The Keepers of the House*
1934	Caroline Miller *Lamb in His Bosom*	1966	Katherine Anne Porter *The Collected Stories of Katherine Anne Porter*
1935	Josephine Winslow Johnson *Now in November*		
1936	Harold L Davis *Honey in the Horn*	1967	Bernard Malamud *The Fixer*
1937	Margaret Mitchell *Gone With the Wind*	1968	William Styron *The Confessions of Nat Turner*
1938	John Phillips Marquand *The Late George Apley*	1969	N Scott Momaday *House Made of Dawn*
1939	Marjorie Kinnan Rawlings *The Yearling*	1970	Jean Stafford *Collected Stories*
1940	John Steinbeck *The Grapes of Wrath*	1971	No award
1941	No award	1972	Wallace Stegner *Angle of Repose*
1942	Ellen Glasgow *In This Our Life*	1973	Eudora Welty *The Optimist's Daughter*
1943	Upton Sinclair *Dragon's Teeth*	1974	No award
1944	Martin Flavin *Journey in the Dark*	1975	Michael Shaara *The Killer Angels*
1945	John Hersey *A Bell for Adano*	1976	Saul Bellow *Humboldt's Gift*
1946	No award	1977	No award
1947	Robert Penn Warren *All the King's Men*	1978	James Alan McPherson *Elbow Room*
1948	James A Michener *Tales of the South Pacific*	1979	John Cheever *The Stories of John Cheever*
1949	James Gould Cozzens *Guard of Honor*	1980	Norman Mailer *The Executioner's Song*

Pulitzer Prize for Fiction (American) *(cont.)*

1981	John Kennedy Toole *A Confederacy of Dunces*
1982	John Updike *Rabbit is Rich*
1983	Alice Walker *The Color Purple*
1984	William Kennedy *Ironweed*
1985	Alison Lurie *Foreign Affairs*
1986	Larry McMurtry *Lonesome Dove*
1987	Peter Taylor *A Summons to Memphis*
1988	Toni Morrison *Beloved*
1989	Anne Tyler *Breathing Lessons*
1990	Oscar Hijuelos *The Mambo Kings Play Songs of Love*
1991	John Updike *Rabbit at Rest*
1992	Jane Simley *A Thousand Acres*
1993	Robert Olen Butler *A Good Scent from a Strange Mountain*

Prix Goncourt for fiction (French)

1980	Yves Navarre *Le Jardin d'acclimation*
1981	Lucien Bodard *Anne Marie*
1982	Dominique Fernandez *Dans la Main de l'ange*
1983	Frederick Tristan *Les Égares*
1984	Marguerite Duras *L'Amant*
1985	Yann Queffelec *Les Noces barbares*
1986	Michel Host *Valet de Nuit*
1987	Tahir Ben Jelloun *La Nuit Sacrée*
1988	Erik Orsenna *L'Exposition Coloniale*
1989	Jean Vautrin *Un Grand Pas Vers le Bon Dieu*
1990	Jean Rouault *Les Champs d'Honneur*
1991	Pierre Combescot *Les Filles du Calvaire*
1992	Patrick Chamoisean *Texaco*

Poets Laureate

1668	John Dryden	(1631–1700)
1689	Thomas Shadwell	(1642?–1692)
1692	Nahum Tate	(1652–1715)
1715	Nicholas Rowe	(1674–1718)
1718	Laurence Eusden	(1688–1730)
1730	Colley Cibber	(1671–1757)
1757	William Whitehead	(1715–1785)
1785	Thomas Warton	(1728–1790)
1790	Henry James Pye	(1745–1813)
1813	Robert Southey	(1774–1843)
1843	William Wordsworth	(1770–1850)
1850	Alfred, Lord Tennyson	(1809–1892)
1896	Alfred Austin	(1835–1913)
1913	Robert Bridges	(1844–1930)
1930	John Masefield	(1878–1967)
1968	Cecil Day Lewis	(1904–1972)
1972	Sir John Betjeman	(1906–1984)
1984	Ted Hughes	(1930–)

Grammar and Usage

adjective grammatical part of speech for words that describe nouns (for example, *new* and *beautiful*, as in 'a new hat' and 'a beautiful day'). Adjectives generally have three degrees (grades or levels for the description of relationships): the positive degree (*new, beautiful*) the comparative degree (*newer, more beautiful*), and the superlative degree (*newest, most beautiful*).

Some adjectives do not normally need comparative and superlative forms; one person cannot be 'more asleep' than someone else, a lone action is unlikely to be 'the most single-handed action ever seen', and many people dislike the expression 'most unique' or 'almost unique', because something unique is supposed to be the only one that exists. For purposes of emphasis or style these conventions may be set aside ('I don't know who is more unique; they are both remarkable people'). Double comparatives such as 'more bigger' are not grammatical in Standard English, but Shakespeare used a double superlative ('the most unkindest cut of all'). Some adjectives may have both the comparative and superlative forms (*commoner* and *more common*; *commonest* and *most common*), usually shorter words take on the suffixes -*er*/-*est* but occasionally they may be given the *more*/*most* forms for emphasis or other reasons ('Which of them is the *most clear*?').

adverb grammatical part of speech for words that modify or describe verbs ('She ran *quickly*'), adjectives ('a *beautifully* clear day'), and adverbs ('They did it *really* well'). Most adverbs are formed from adjectives or past participles by adding -*ly* (*quick: quickly*) or -*ally* (*automatic: automatically*).

Sometimes adverbs are formed by adding -*wise* (*likewise* and *clockwise*, as in 'moving *clockwise*'; in 'a *clockwise* direction', *clockwise* is an adjective). Some adverbs have a distinct form from their partnering adjective; for example, *good/well* ('It was *good* work; they did it *well*'). Others do not derive from adjectives (*very*, in '*very* nice'; *tomorrow*, in 'I'll do it *tomorrow*'); and some are unadapted adjectives (*pretty*, as in 'It's *pretty* good'). Sentence adverbs modify whole sentences or phrases: '*Generally*, it rains a lot here'; '*Usually*, the town is busy at this time of year.' Sometimes there is controversy in such matters. *Hopefully* is universally accepted in sentences like 'He looked at them *hopefully*' (= in a hopeful way), but some people dislike it in '*Hopefully*, we'll see you again next year' (= We hope that we'll see you again next year).

apostrophe mark (') used in written English and some other languages. In English it serves primarily to indicate either a missing letter (*mustn't* for *must not*) or number ('*47* for *1947*), or grammatical possession ('*John's* camera', '*women's* dresses'). It is often omitted in proper names (Publishers Association, Actors

Studio, *Collins Dictionary*). Many people otherwise competent in writing have great difficulty with the apostrophe, which has never been stable at any point in its history.

An apostrophe may precede the plural *s* used with numbers and abbreviations (*the 1970's, a group of P.O.W.'s*) but is equally often omitted (*the 1970s, a group of POWs*). For possessives of certain words ending with *s*, usage is split, as between *James's book* and *James' book*. Names and dates used adjectivally are not usually followed by an apostrophe ('a *1950s* car', 'a *Beatles* record'). The use of an apostrophe to help indicate a plural (as in a shopkeeper's *Apple's* and *Tomato's*, followed by their prices) is regarded by many as semiliterate.

article grammatical part of speech. There are two articles in English: the *definite article the*, which serves to specify or identify a noun (as in 'This is *the* book I need'), and the *indefinite article a* or (before vowels) *an*, which indicates a single unidentified noun ('They gave me *a* piece of paper and *an* envelope').

Some people use the form 'an' before *h* ('an historic building'); this practice dates from the 17th century, when an initial *h* was often not pronounced (as in '*h*onour'), and is nowadays widely considered rather grandiose.

asterisk starlike punctuation mark (*) used to link the asterisked word with a note at the bottom of a page, and to indicate that certain letters are missing from a word (especially a taboo word such as 'f**k').

An asterisk is also used to indicate that a word or usage is nonexistent; for example, 'In English we say three boys and not three *boy'.

colon punctuation mark (:) intended to direct the reader's attention forward, usually because what follows explains or develops what has just been written (for example, *The farmer owned the following varieties of dogs: a spaniel, a pointer, a terrier, a border collie, and three mongrels*).

comma punctuation mark (,) intended to provide breaks or pauses within a sentence; commas may come at the end of a clause, to set off a phrase, or in lists (for example, *apples, pears, plums, and pineapples*).

Some writers, uncertain where sentences properly end, use a comma instead of a period (or full stop), writing *We saw John last night, it was good to see him again*, rather than *We saw John last night. It was good to see him again*. The meaning is entirely clear in both cases. One solution in such situations is to use a *semicolon* (;), which bridges the gap between the close association of the comma and the sharp separation of the period. For parenthetical commas, see parenthesis.

conjunction grammatical part of speech that serves to connect words, phrases, and clauses; for example *and* in 'apples and pears' and *but* in 'we're going but they aren't'.

exclamation mark or *exclamation point* punctuation mark (!) used to indicate emphasis or strong emotion ('That's terrible!'). It is appropriate after interjections ('Rats!'), emphatic greetings ('Yo!'), and orders ('Shut up!'), as well as those sentences beginning *How* or *What* that are not questions ('How embarrassing!', 'What a surprise!').

The exclamation mark is most often seen in dialogue. Its use is kept to a minimum in narrative prose and technical writing.

Within a quotation an exclamation mark may be placed in square brackets to indicate that the writer or editor is surprised by something. The convention that all sentences in comic books end with an exclamation mark is on the wane.

grammar the rules of combining words into phrases, clauses, sentences, and paragraphs. Emphasis on the standardizing impact of print has meant that spoken or colloquial language is often perceived as less grammatical than written language, but all forms of a language, standard or otherwise, have their own grammatical systems of differing complexity. People often acquire several overlapping grammatical systems within one language; for example, one formal system for writing and standard communication and one less formal system for everyday and peer-group communication.

Originally 'grammar' was an analytical approach to writing, intended to improve the understanding and the skills of scribes, philosophers, and writers. When compared with Latin, English has been widely regarded as having less grammar or at least a simpler grammar; it would be truer, however, to say that English and Latin have different grammars, each complex in its own way. In linguistics (the contemporary study of language) grammar, or syntax, refers to the arrangement of the elements in a language for the purposes of acceptable communication in speech, writing, and print.

All forms of a language, standard or otherwise, have their grammars or grammatical systems, which children acquire through use; a child may acquire several overlapping systems within one language (especially a nonstandard form for everyday life and a standard form linked with writing, school, and national life). Not even the most comprehensive grammar book (or grammar) of a language like English, French, Arabic, or Japanese completely covers or fixes the implicit grammatical system that people use in their daily lives. The rules and tendencies of natural grammar operate largely in nonconscious ways but can, for many social and professional purposes, be studied and developed for conscious as well as inherent skills. See also parts of speech.

Recent theories of the way language functions include *phrase structure grammar*, *transformational grammar*, and *case grammar*.

hyphen punctuation mark (-) with two functions: to join words, parts of words, syllables, and so on, for particular purposes; and to mark a word break at the end of a line. Adjectival compounds (see adjective) are hyphenated because they modify the noun jointly rather than separately ('a small-town boy' is a boy from a small town; 'a small town boy' is a small boy from a town). The use of hyphens with adverbs is redundant unless an identical adjective exists (*well, late, long*): 'late-blooming plant' but 'brightly blooming plant'.

Phrasal verbs are not hyphenated ('things *turned out* well', 'it *washed up* on the beach') unless used adjectivally ('a well-*turned-out* crowd', 'a *washed-up* athlete'). Nouns formed from phrasal verbs are hyphenated or joined together ('a good *turnout* tonight', 'please do the *washing-up*'). In the use of certain prefixes, modern style is moving towards omitting the hyphen (*noncooperation*).

The hyphenation of compound nouns in English is by no means clear cut; the same person may inadvertently in one article write, for example *world view*, *worldview* and *world-view*.

inflection or *inflexion* in grammatical analysis, an ending or other element in a word that indicates its grammatical function (whether plural or singular, masculine or feminine, subject or object, and so on).

In a highly inflected language like Latin, nouns, verbs, and adjectives have many inflectional endings (for example, in the word *amabunt* the base *am* means 'love' and the complex *abunt* indicates the kind of verb, the future tense, indicative mood, active voice, third person, and plurality). English has few inflections: for example, the *s* for plural forms (as in *the books*) and for the third person singular of verbs (as in *He runs*).

noun grammatical part of speech that names a person, animal, object, quality, idea, or time. Nouns can refer to objects such as *house*, *tree* (**concrete nouns**); specific persons and places such as *John Alden*, the *White House* (**proper nouns**); ideas such as *love*, *anger* (**abstract nouns**). In English many simple words are both noun and verb (*jump*, *reign*, *rain*). Adjectives are sometimes used as nouns ('a *local* man', 'one of the *locals*').

A common noun does not begin with a capital letter (*child*, *cat*), whereas a proper noun does, because it is the name of a particular person, animal, or place (*Jane*, *Rover*, *Norfolk*). A concrete noun refers to things that can be sensed (*dog*, *box*), whereas an abstract noun relates to generalizations abstracted from life as we observe it (*fear*, *condition*, *truth*). A **countable noun** can have a plural form (*book*: *books*), while an **uncountable noun** or mass noun cannot (*dough*). Many English nouns can be used both countably and uncountably (*wine*: 'Have some *wine*; it's one of our best *wines*'). A **collective noun** is singular in form but refers to a group (*flock*, *group*, *committee*), and a **compound noun** is made up of two or more nouns (*teapot*, *baseball team*, *car-factory strike committee*). A **verbal noun** is formed from a verb as a gerund or otherwise (*build*: *building*; *regulate*: *regulation*).

participle in grammar, a form of the verb; in English either a **present participle** ending in *-ing* (for example, 'work*ing*' in 'They were *working*', '*working* men', and 'a hard-*working* team') or a **past participle** ending in *-ed* in regular verbs (for example, 'train*ed*' in 'They have been *trained* well', '*trained* soldiers', and 'a well- *trained* team').

In irregular verbs the past participle has a special form (for example, drive/driven; light/lit, burn/burned, burnt). The participle is used to open such constructions as '*Coming* down the stairs, she paused and ...' and '*Angered* by the news, he ...'. Such constructions, when not logically formed, may have irritating or ambiguous results. '*Driving* along a country road, a stone broke my windscreen' suggests that the stone was driving along the road. This illogical usage is a *misplaced participle*. A *dangling* or *hanging participle* has nothing at all to relate to: 'While *driving* along a country road there was a loud noise under the car.' Such sentences need to be completely re-expressed, except in some well-established usages where the participle can stand alone (for example, '*Taking* all things into consideration, your actions were justified').

part of speech the grammatical function of a word, described in the grammatical tradition of the Western world, based on Greek and Latin. The four major parts of speech are the noun, verb, adjective, and adverb; the minor parts of speech vary according to schools of grammatical theory, but include the article, conjunction, preposition, and pronoun.

In languages like Greek and Latin, the part of speech of a word tends to be invariable (usually marked by an ending, or inflection); in English, it is much harder to recognize the function of a word simply by its form. Some English words may have only one function (for example, *and* as a conjunction). Others may have several functions (for example, *fancy*, which is a noun in the phrase 'flights of *fancy*', a verb in '*Fancy* that!', and an adjective in 'a *fancy* hat').

period punctuation mark (.). The term 'period' is universally understood in English and is the preferred usage in North America; *full stop* is the preferred term in the UK. The period has two functions: to mark the end of a sentence and to indicate that a word has been abbreviated. It is also used in mathematics to indicate decimals and is then called a *point*.

Such abbreviations as acronyms are unlikely to have periods (NATO rather than N.A.T.O.), and contractions (incorporating the last letter of the word, for example Dr for 'doctor') may or may not have periods. In such contexts as fictional dialogue and advertising, periods sometimes follow incomplete sentences in an effort to represent speech more faithfully or for purposes of emphasis.

preposition in grammar, a part of speech coming before a noun or a pronoun to show a location (*in*, *on*), time (*during*), or some other relationship (for example, figurative relationships in phrases like '*by* heart' or '*on* time').

In the sentence 'Put the book *on* the table', *on* is a preposition governing the noun 'table' and relates the verb 'put' to the phrase 'the table', indicating where the book should go. Some words of English that are often prepositional in function may, however, be used adverbially, as in the sentences, 'He picked the book *up*' and 'He picked *up* the book', in which the ordering is different but the meaning the same. In such cases *up* is called an **adverbial particle** and the form *pick up* is a *phrasal verb*.

pronoun in grammar, a part of speech that is used in place of a noun, usually to save repetition of the noun (for example 'The people arrived around nine o'clock. *They* behaved as though we were expecting *them*').

They, *them*, *he*, and *she* are **personal pronouns** (representing people); *this*/*these*, and *that*/*those* are **demonstrative pronouns** (demonstrating or pointing to something: '*this* book and not *that* book'. Words like *that* and *who* can be **relative pronouns** in sentences like 'She said *that* she was coming' and 'Tell me *who* did it' relating one clause to another), and *myself* and *himself* are **reflexive pronouns** (reflecting back to a person, as in 'He did it *himself*').

Common spelling errors

These are the 50 most commonly misspelled words in English:

accommodation	handkerchief
appearance	humorous
address	height
amount	
achieve	immediately
beautiful	library
bicycle	literature
biscuit	league
business	
beginning	minute
committee	necessary
competition	neither
definitely	occasion
disappoint	
disappear	parallel
describe	prejudice
	possess
embarrass	profession
exaggerate	parliament
excellent	
excitement	receive
finally	sincerely
foreign	solemn
fulfil	sergeant
friend	soldier
grammar	unusual
government	until
	vicious

punctuation the system of conventional signs (punctuation marks) and spaces by means of which written and printed language is organized in order to be as readable, clear, and logical as possible.

It contributes to the effective layout of visual language; if a work is not adequately punctuated, there may be problems of ambiguity and unclear association among words. Conventions of punctuation differ from language to language, and there are preferred styles in the punctuation of a language like English. Some people prefer a fuller use of punctuation, while others punctuate lightly; comparably, the use of punctuation will vary according to the kind of passage being produced: a personal letter, a newspaper article, and a technical report are all laid out and punctuated in distinctive ways.

Standard punctuation marks and conventions include the period (full stop or point), comma, colon, semicolon, exclamation mark (or point), question mark, apostrophe, asterisk, hyphen, and parenthesis (including dashes, brackets, and the use of parenthetical commas).

question mark punctuation mark (?) used to indicate enquiry or doubt. When indicating enquiry, it is placed at the end of a *direct question* ('Who is coming?') but never at the end of an *indirect question* ('He asked us who was coming'). When indicating doubt, it usually appears between brackets, to show that a writer or editor is puzzled or uncertain about quoted text.

semicolon punctuation mark (;) with a function halfway between the separation of sentence from sentence by means of a period, or full stop, and the gentler separation provided by a comma. It also helps separate items in a complex list: 'pens, pencils, and paper; staples, such as rice and beans; tools, various; and rope'.

Rather than the abrupt 'We saw Mark last night. It was good to see him again', and the casual (and often condemned) 'We saw Mark last night, it was good to see him again', the semicolon reflects a link in a two-part statement and is considered good style: *We saw Mark last night; it was good to see him again*. In such cases an alternative is to use a comma followed by *and* or *but*.

verb the grammatical part of speech for what someone or something does (*to go*), experiences (*to live*), or is (*to be*). Verbs involve the grammatical categories known as number (singular or plural: 'He *runs*; they *run*'), voice (active or passive: 'She *writes* books; it *is written*'), mood (statements, questions, orders, emphasis, necessity, condition), aspect (completed or continuing action: 'She *danced*; she *was dancing*'), and tense (variation according to time: simple present tense, present progressive tense, simple past tense, and so on).

Many verbs are formed from nouns and adjectives by adding affixes (prison: *imprison*; light: *enlighten*; fresh: *freshen up*; pure: *purify*). Some words function as both nouns and verbs (*crack, run*), both adjectives and verbs (*clean; ready*), and as nouns, adjectives, and verbs (*fancy*). In the sentences 'They *saw* the accident', 'She *is working* today', and 'He *should have been trying to meet* them', the words in italics are verbs (and, in the last case) two verb groups together; these sentences show just how complex the verbs of English can be.

types of verb

A *transitive* verb takes a direct object ('He *saw* the house'). An *intransitive* verb has no object ('She *laughed*'). An *auxiliary or helping* verb is used to express tense and/or mood ('He *was* seen'; 'They *may* come'). A *modal* verb or *modal auxiliary* generally shows only mood; common modals are *may/might, will/would, can/could, shall/should, must*. The *infinitive* of the verb usually includes *to* (*to go, to run* and so on), but may be a bare infinitive (for example, after modals, as in 'She may *go*'). A *regular* verb forms tenses in the normal way (*I walk: I walked: I have walked*); irregular verbs do not (*swim: swam: swum; put: put: put*; and so on). Because of their conventional nature, regular verbs are also known as weak verbs, while some irregular verbs are strong verbs with special vowel changes across tenses, as in *swim: swam: swum* and *ride: rode: ridden*. A *phrasal verb* is a construction in which a particle attaches to a usually single-syllable verb (for example, *put* becoming *put up*, as in 'He put up some money for the project', and *put up with*, as in 'I can't put up with this nonsense any longer').

Common roots

The similarities of six words in Indo-European languages contrast with their differences in other language groups

English	month	mother	new	night	nose	three
Welsh	mis	mam	newydd	nos	trwyn	tri
Gaelic	mí	máthair	nua	oíche	srón	trí
French	mois	mère	nouveau	nuit	nez	trois
Spanish	mes	madre	nuevo	noche	nariz	tres
Portuguese	mês	mãe	novo	noite	nariz	três
Italian	mese	madre	nuovo	notte	naso	tre
Latin	mensis	mater	novus	nox	nasus	tres
German	Monat	Mutter	neu	Nacht	Nase	drei
Dutch	maand	moeder	nieuw	nacht	neus	drie
Icelandic	mánudur	módir	nýr	nótt	nef	brír
Swedish	månad	moder	ny	natt	näsa	tre
Polish	miesiąc	matka	nowy	noc	nos	trzy
Czech	měsć	matka	nový	noc	nos	tři
Rumanian	lună	mamă	nou	noapte	nas	trei
Albanian	muaj	nënë	iri	natë	hundë	tre,tri
Greek	men	meter	neos	nux	rhïs	treis
Russian	mesyats	mat'	novy	noch'	nos	tri
Lithuanian	menuo	motina	naujas	naktis	nosis	trys
Armenian	amis	mayr	nor	kisher	kit	yerek
Persian	māh	mādar	nau	shab	bini	se
Sanskrit	mās	matar	nava	nakt	nãs	trayas

NON-INDO-EUROPEAN LANGUAGES

	month	mother	new	night	nose	three
Basque	hilabethe	ama	berri	gai	sädär	hirur
Finnish	kuukausi	äiti	uusi	yö	nenä	kolme
Hungarian	hónap	anya	új	éjszaka	orr	három
Turkish	ay	anne	yeni	gece	burun	úç

Source: Katzner, Kenneth/The Languages of the World/Routledge & Kegan Paul, London 1986

Some word-borrowings from foreign languages

Afrikaans

Most borrowings into South African English and eventually into international English come from Afrikaans and Dutch.

kran(t)z	18c	('chaplet') a sheer rock face encircling the summit of a mountain or enclosing a valley; a precipice
sjambok	18c	(from Urdu: 'horse-whip') a heavy whip made of rhinoceros or hippopotamus hide, used for driving cattle or administering punishment
veld(t)	18c	('field') unenclosed country or open grassland
Afrikaner	19c	('an African') an Afrikaans-speaking white South African
biltong	19c	('buttock-tongue') strips of lean meat dried in the sun
Boer	19c	('farmer') a descendant of Dutch or Huguenot colonists, especially a farmer in the Transvaal, Cape Colony and the Orange Free State
laager		('camp') an encampment defended by a circle of wagons
trek	19c	('march') (one stage of) a long journey across country (originally by ox- wagon); to make such a journey
apartheid	20c	('separateness') in South Africa, the government system of rigorous separation between people of European descent and others; often applied to similar movements elsewhere
stompie	20c	('stump') a cigarette butt or partially smoked cigarette

Some word-borrowings from foreign languages *(cont.)*

Arabic

Arabic words borrowed into English usually relate to Islamic and Arab society and culture. Contact between the two languages dates from the Crusades (11th–13th centuries). At that time, for example, the founder of the *assassin* sect would tempt potential members with pleasures heightened by the use of *hashish*, experiences (seen as a foretaste of heaven) that took away their fear of death (see below).

admiral	13c	('of the commander') the commander-in-chief of a fleet or navy; a naval officer of the highest rank
zenith	14c	('way or path over the head') the highest point of the celestial sphere and the point of the sky directly overhead; *fig.* the highest point of anything
nadir	14c	('opposite to') the point in the celestial sphere diametrically opposite the zenith and directly under the observer; *fig.* the lowest point of anything
alcohol	16c	('kohl') a colourless, flammable liquid obtained by distillation, commonly an ingredient of intoxicating drinks
algebra	16c	('reunion of broken parts') the branch of mathematics that generalizes the arithmetical relations and properties of numbers by means of symbols
arsenal	16c	('factory') an establishment for the manufacture and/or storage of weapons
assassin	16c	('hashish-takers') a person who seeks to kill someone else, usually for political reasons
hashish	16c	('dry herb') a purified preparation of hemp, the leaves and seeds of which are hallucinogenic
alcove	17c	('vaulted chamber') an arched recess in a wall
hare(e)m	17c	('prohibited') a group of wives and concubines; the part of a Muslim dwelling where the women live in seclusion
imam	17c	('leader') the officiating priest of a mosque; a title given to certain Muslim leaders
sofa	17c	a long padded seat with back and ends for two or more people
Islam	19c	('submission, resignation') the religion founded by the prophet Mohammad

Farsi/Persian

Many Persian words have entered English through other languages. For example, *paradise* comes originally from the Old Persian word *pairidaeza* for park or pleasure ground, but passed through Greek *paradeisos*, Latin *paradisus* and French *paradis* before reaching English.

magus	14c	(through Greek and Latin) a Zoroastrian priest; an astrologer or magician
bazaar	16c	a market area; a charity sale
dervish	16c	('religious mendicant') a member of one of several Muslim orders of ascetics, some of whom engage in whirling dances
cummerbund	17c	('loin-cloth') a wide sash worn around the waist (especially with a dinner jacket)
kiosk	17c	(through Turkish; 'palace') an open-sided pavilion; a small booth selling cigarettes, newspapers, and snacks
narg(h)ile/ nargileh	19c	('coconut') an Oriental pipe in which the smoke bubbles through scented water before being inhaled through a tube
ayatollah	20c	(from Arabic: 'miraculous son of God') the title for an Iranian Shiite religious leader

Hebrew

Words and names from Hebrew have entered the English language since Anglo-Saxon times, mostly through the Bible. More recently, colloquialisms from Yiddish, such as *kosher* and *goy*, have entered the language, particularly in the USA.

amen	13c	('may it be so') a concluding formula in a prayer or wish
shibboleth	14c	('ear of corn') a peculiarity of custom or especially language which distinguishes one group of people from another
cinnamon	15c	the inner bark of a tropical Asian tree, used as a spice
hallelujah	16c	('praise the lord') an exclamation, used in moments of religious enthusiasm or of relief, joy, etc.
philistine	17c	('uncultured') originally a member of the non-Semitic people who lived along the southern sea coast of Palestine; a person hostile to art and culture
bar mitzvah	19c	('man of duty') (sometimes caps) the ceremony in a synagogue for a Jewish boy who has reached 13, the age of religious responsibility; the boy himself at the time of the ceremony
kosher	19c	('right') (food) prepared in accordance with Jewish law; legitimate, authentic
goy	20c	('nation') (through Yiddish) a colloquial Jewish name for a non-Jew (plural *goyim*)

Some word-borrowings from foreign languages *(cont.)*

kibbutz	20c	('gathering') an Israeli collective farming community (plural *kibbutzim*)
Yom Kippur	20c	('Day of Purgations') the annual Jewish fast observed on the tenth day of the seventh month

Hindi-Urdu

Many words taken from Hindi-Urdu have already been borrowed from other languages: in Hindi from Sanskrit; in Urdu from Persian and Arabic. In addition to contributing vocabulary to English, they have both borrowed extensively from it.

raja(h)	16c	(from Sanskrit: 'king') formerly, an Indian ruler; a Malay prince
bungalow	18c	('belonging to Bengal') a one-storey house
dungaree	17c	(after Dungri, a district of Bombay) coarse cotton fabric used mostly for work clothes; (in the plural) overalls made of this fabric
guru	17c	(from Sanskrit: 'teacher') a Hindu or Sikh spiritual leader; an influential teacher or mentor (often dismissive, as in *leftwing political guru*)
maharaja(h)	17c	(from Sanskrit: 'great king') the title of certain Indian princes
babu	18c	('father') a title of respect for a learned person or a clerk, applied to a stilted, unidiomatic. and florid English ('Babu English') regarded as characteristic of Indian clerks
sari/saree	18c	(from Sanskrit) a long strip of cloth worn as a garment by Indian women
swami	18c	(from Sanskrit: 'lord') a Hindu saint or religious leader (used especially as a title)
khaki	19c	(from Persian: 'dusty') a dull yellow-brown colour; cloth of this colour used for military uniforms
raj	19c	(from Sanskrit: 'rule') government or rule; *The Raj* British dominion in the Indian sub-continent before 1947
yoga	19c	(from Sanskrit: 'yoke, union') a Hindu system of philosophy using physical and mental exercises

Irish Gaelic

English has often been accused of 'killing' Irish Gaelic for political and social reasons. As a consequence of the large numbers of English and Scottish settlements from the 16th century onwards, and famine and large-scale emigration in the 19th century, the prestige and use of English in the previously predominantly Gaelic-speaking community increased dramatically. Most loan-words in English relate to Irish culture.

currach	15c	('boat') a coracle
leprechaun	17c	('small body') a small and often mischievous supernatural creature
banshee	18c	('fairy woman') a supernatural female being who wails under the windows of a house where death is imminent
blarney	18c	flattering or cajoling talk; to talk in such a way, named after a village near Cork
céilidh	19c	('companion'; also in Scotland) an informal social gathering, with conversation, music, dancing, and story-telling
poteen	19c	('little pot') an alcoholic spirit, illegally brewed (usually from potatoes)
smithereens	19c	(unknown origin) small fragments
Taoiseach	20c	('chieftain') the title of the prime minister of the Republic of Ireland

Japanese

Japanese words have entered English for over five centuries, reflecting life and culture. More recently, English words have travelled to Japan (e.g. *salary* and *man*), and taken on new meanings (as in *sarariman*, a low-level manager), then returned to English (as *salaryman*).

shōgun	17c	('army leader') from AD 794, hereditary commander of the army; from 1192 to 1867, virtual ruler of Japan
saké/saki	17c	rice wine
mikado	18c	('exalted door') formerly the title of the emperor
samurai	18c	from 11th to 19th centuries a warrior retainer of a prince or nobleman; a member of the military caste
futon	19c	padded quilt, laid on the floor for use as a bed
geisha	19c	('person of pleasing accomplishments') a woman skilled in the arts of entertaining men with music, dance, and conversation
hara-kiri	19c	('belly-cut') ceremonial suicide by disembowelling, formerly practised by samurai faced with disgrace (and more elegantly known as *seppuku*, also now a term in English)

Some word-borrowings from foreign languages (cont.)

kamikaze	19c	a mythical 'divine wind' which destroyed a fleet of invading Mongols; used of Japanese airmen who made suicidal crashed on to enemy targets 1939–45; now used to imply recklessness
kimono	19c	('silk thing') a long sashed robe with loose sleeves; a similar garment worn in the West
sushi	19c	a dish of shaped balls of cold rice with sliced of raw fish
tycoon	19c	('great prince') formerly the title of the shogun; anyone of great power, especially in industry
karate	20c	('open hand') a martial art, which injures by striking vital nerve centres in the body with the edge of the open hand or foot, or the elbows and legs
origami	20c	the art of 'folding paper' into decorative shapes

Russian

Russian words have not entered the English language on a large scale, but those that have tend to relate to traditional culture and Soviet and Communist usage after 1917.

tsar/czar	16c	(ultimately from Latin *Caesar*) the emperor of Russia until 1917; a tyrant, boss, or tycoon
shaman	17c	(from Sanskrit: 'religious exercise') a priest or medicine-man among the peoples of northern India
steppe	17c	('lowland') a grassy but treeless plain
balalaika	18c	a musical instrument like a guitar but with a triangular body and three strings
kulak	19c	('fist') a class of peasant farmers who owned their own land; often used pejoratively to refer to tight-fisted people
vodka	19c	('water') a spirit usually distilled from rye or potatoes
Bolshevik	20c	('bigger one') a member of the extreme wing of the Russian Social-Democratic Party (later the Communist Party) which followed Lenin and seized power in 1917; pejoratively, a revolutionary
cosmonaut	20c	(from Greek: 'universe sailor') a Soviet astronaut
glasnost	20c	('publicness') a declared Communist party policy after 1985 of greater official openness; greater freedom of speech and information
intelligentsia	20c	(from Latin: 'intelligence') people who claim to engage in superior intellectual activity, originally in pre-Revolution Russia (and often pejorative)
perestroika	20c	the 'restructuring' of the Soviet economic and political system proposed in 1979 and promoted by Mikhail Gorbachev from 1985 onwards
soviet	20c	('council') in the USSR, an elected government council at local, regional and national level; (cap) a citizen of the USSR; (cap) pertaining to the USSR
sputnik	20c	('fellow-traveller') an uncrewed Soviet artificial satellite set in orbit around the earth, especially between 1957 and 1961

Sanskrit

Sanskrit words have come into English either directly or through other languages such as Hindi, and usually relate to religion, philosophy, and culture.

Prana	17c	('Ancient') one of a group of sacred verse stories about Hindu gods and heroes
avatar	18c	('descent') the manifestation or incarnation of a principle or deity in human or animal form
Tantra	18c	('loom') any one of many Hindu and Buddhist works between the 7th and 17th centuries of a magical or mystical nature
ahimsa	19c	('non-injury') the Hindu, Buddhist, and Jain doctrine of harming no living being; non-violence
chakra	19c	('wheel') a mystical circle placed in the hands of images of Hindu gods; in yoga, one of the centres of spiritual power in the human body; the emblem on the flag of the Indian Union
karma	19c	('action') in Hinduism and Buddhism, the total of a person's actions in one incarnation, which determines their fate in the next; fate, destiny
mantra	19c	('device') a sacred text, usually from the Vedas, used as a prayer or incantation; a sacred word or syllable used for meditation
nirvana	19c	('blowing out') the extinction of individual existence with its desires and passions (a religious goal in Hinduism and Buddhism)
swastika	19c	('mark of well-being') an equal-armed cross with right-angled ends, a symbol of good fortune; adopted as an Aryan symbol by the Nazi Party in 1935
swaraj	20c	('self-rule') in British India, (the agitation in favour of) self-government

Turkish

Turkish has absorbed many Arabic and Persian words, particularly in the late 11th century. Borrowings into English generally relate to culture.

dolman	16c	('winding round') a long open-fronted robe or the jacket worn like a cape by a hussar; a woman's garment with loose sleeves

Some word-borrowings from foreign languages *(cont.)*

kaftan/caftan	16c	a partly open-fronted garment consisting of a long tunic with or without a belt
effendi	17c	('lord') a title of respect originally applied to learned people and government officials, now equivalent to *Mr*
pasha	17c	('chief') an Ottoman title for high-ranking officers
yog(h)urt	17c	sour milk curdled by bacteria
kilim	19c	a woven carpet without a pile made throughout Turkey macramé
	19c	(from Arabic: 'striped cloth') (the art of making) knotted and woven cord used as patterned ornaments
mezé	20c	('snack') an hors d'oeuvre, served especially with an aperitif

Welsh

Borrowings from Welsh into English mainly relate to Welsh culture.

cromlech	17c	('arched stone') a megalithic chamber tomb or dolmen; standing stone(s)
englyn	17c	a four-line stanza of prescribed form written in *cynghanedd* metre
flummery	17c	(unknown origin) a pudding made with coagulated wheatflour or oatmeal; mere flattery or nonsense
gorsedd	18c	('throne') a meeting of bards and druids, preliminary to an *eisteddfod*
cynghanedd	19c	a complex form of alliterative metre
cwm	19c	a valley; a deep rounded hollow with a steep side formed by a glacier; a cirque
eisteddfod	19c	('session') a festival of poetry, singing and music; a congress of Welsh bards and minstrels
hwyl	19c	emotional fervour, characteristic of poetry recitation
corgi	20c	('dwarf-dog') either of two breeds of short-legged dogs, originally from Wales

Main language groups

Language	Number of speakers (millions)	Language	Number of speakers (millions)
Mandarin	907	Hausa (N Nigeria, Niger, Cameroon)	36
English	456	Malayalam (Kerala, India)	35
Hindi	383	Persian (Iran, Afghanistan)	34
Spanish	362	Hakka (SE China)	33
Russian	293	Burmese (Myanmar)	31
Arabic	208	Oriya (C and E India)	31
Bengali	189	Romanian	26
Portuguese	177	Sundanese (Sunda Strait, Indonesia)	25
Malay-Indonesian	148	Assamese (India, Bangladesh)	23
Japanese	126	Dutch-Flemish (Netherlands, Belgium)	21
French	123	Pashtu (Pakistan, Afghanistan, Iran)	21
German	119	Serbo-Croatian	20
Urdu	96	Yoruba (SW Nigeria, Zou, Benin)	19
Punjabi (Punjab, Pakistan, India)	89	Amharic (Ethiopia)	18
Korean (Korea, China, Japan)	73	Igbo (Lower Niger, Nigeria)	17
Telugu (Andhra Pradesh, SE India)	71	Sindhi (SE Pakistan, W India)	17
Marathi (Maharashtra, India)	67	Azerbaijani	15
Tamil (Tamil Nadu, India, Sri Lanka)	67	Zhuang (S China)	15
Cantonese (China, Hong Kong)	65	Hungarian	14
Wu (Shanghai region, China)	64	Nepali (Nepal, NE India, Bhutan)	14
Italian	63	Cebuano (Bohol Sea, Philippines)	13
Javanese (Java, Indonesia)	61	Fula (Cameroon, Nigeria)	13
Vietnamese	61	Sinhalese (Sri Lanka)	13
Turkish	57	Uzbek	13
Min (SE China, Taiwan, Malaysia)	50	Czech	12
Thai	49	Malagasy (Madagascar)	12
Swahili	46	Greek	11
Ukrainian	46	Afrikaans (Southern Africa)	10
Polish	44	Byelorussian	10
Kannada (S India)	43	Kurdish (SW of Caspian Sea)	10
Tagalog (Philippines)	43	Madurese (Madura, Indonesia)	10
Gujarati (WC India, S Pakistan)	39	Oromo (W Ethiopia, N Kenya)	10

Proof correction symbols

Instruction	Textual mark	Marginal mark
Leave unchanged	----- under characters	(encircled mark)
Remove extraneous marks	Encircle marks to be removed	(mark)
Delete	/through character(s) or ⊢through words	(mark)
Delete and close up	⊢through character(s) or ⊢through character(s)	(mark)
Insert in text the matter indicated in the margin		New matter followed by ⅄
Substitute character or substitute part of one or more words	/through character or ⊢through words	New character or new word(s)
Substitute ligature e.g. æ for separate letters	⊢through characters affected	e.g. æ
Substitute or insert full stop or decimal point	/through character or ⅄	(dot in circle)
Substitute or insert comma, semicolon, colon, etc.	/through character or ⅄	, ; : ⊙ / ⟨ ⟩ /
Substitute or insert character in 'superior' position	/through character or ⅄	under character e.g.
Substitute or insert character in 'inferior' position	/through character or ⅄	over character e.g.
Substitute or insert single or double quotation marks or apostrophe	/through character or ⅄	and/or
Substitute or insert ellipsis	/through character or ⅄	...
Substitute or insert hyphen	/through character or ⅄	(mark)
Substitute or insert rule	/through character or ⅄	Give the size of the rule in the marginal mark 1 em 4 mm
Substitute or insert oblique	/through character or ⅄	(circle with slash)

Instruction	Textual mark	Marginal mark
Wrong fount. Replace by character(s) of correct fount	Encircle character(s)	(mark)
Change damaged character(s)	Encircle character(s)	(mark)
Set in or change to italic	‒‒‒ under character(s) Where space does not permit textual marks, encircle the affected area instead	(mark)
Change italic to upright type	Encircle character(s)	(mark)
Set in or change to capital letters	≡ under character(s)	(mark)
Set in or change to small capital letters	= under character(s)	(mark)
Set in or change to bold type	∿∿∿ under character(s)	(mark)
Set in or change to bold italic type	∿∿∿ under character(s)	(mark)
Change capital letters to lower-case letters	Encircle character(s)	(mark)
Change small capital letters to lower-case letters	Encircle character(s)	(mark)
Close up. Delete space between characters or words	⌒ linking characters e.g. a scribe	( )
Insert space between characters	│ between characters	Give the size of the space when necessary
Insert space between words	│ between words	Give the size of the space when necessary
Reduce space between characters	│ between characters	Give the amount by which the space is to be reduced, when necessary

Instruction	Textual mark	Marginal mark
Reduce space between words	between words	Give the amount by which the space is to be reduced, when necessary
Make space appear equal between characters or words	between characters or words	
Close up to normal interline spacing	each side of column linking lines	
Insert space between lines or paragraphs	or	Give the size of the space when necessary
Reduce space between lines or paragraphs	or	Give amount by which the space is to be reduced, when necessary
Start new paragraph		
Run on (no new paragraph)		
Transpose characters or words	between characters or words, numbered when necessary	
Transpose lines		
Transpose a number of lines	3 / 2 / 1	Rules extend from the margin into the text with each line to be transposed numbered in the correct sequence
Centre	[enclosing matter to be centred]	
Indent		Give the amount of the indent
Cancel indent		

Instruction	Textual mark	Marginal mark
Move matter specified distance to the right*	enclosing matter to be moved to the right	
Move matter specified distance to the left*	enclosing matter to be moved to the left	
Set line to specified measure*		
Set column to specified measure*		
Take over character(s), word(s) or line to next line, column or page		The textual mark surrounds the matter to be taken over and extends into the margin
Take back character(s), word(s) or line to previous line, column or page		The textual mark surrounds the matter to be taken back and extends into the margin
Raise matter*	over matter to be raised / under matter to be raised	
Lower matter*	over matter to be lowered / under matter to be lowered	
Move matter to position indicated*	Enclose matter to be moved and indicate new position	
Correct vertical alignment		
Correct horizontal alignment	Single line above and below misaligned matter	placed level with the head and foot of the relevant line

* Give the exact dimensions when necessary.

English and American sign language

Abbreviations, Symbols, and Acronyms

A in physics, symbol for *ampere*, a unit of electrical current.

A1 abbreviation for *first class* (of ships).

AA abbreviation for the British *Automobile Association*.

abb. abbreviation for *abbreviation*.

ab init. abbreviation for *ab initio* (Latin 'from the beginning').

ABM abbreviation for *anti-ballistic missile*.

a/c abbreviation for *account*.

AC in physics, abbreviation for *alternating current*.

ACAS abbreviation for *Advisory, Conciliation and Arbitration Service*.

ACT abbreviation for *Australian Capital Territory*.

AD in the Christian calender, abbreviation for *Anno Domini* (Latin 'in the year of the Lord'); used with dates.

ADB abbreviation for *Asian Development Bank*.

ADC in electronics, abbreviation for analogue-to-digital converter.

ADH abbreviation for *antidiuretic hormone*, part of the system maintaining a correct salt/water balance in vertebrates.

adj. in grammar, abbreviation for *adjective*.

ADP abbreviation for *adenosine diphosphate*, a raw material in the manufacture of ATP, the molecule used by all cells to drive their chemical reactions.

adv. abbreviation for *adverb*.

aet. abbreviation for *aetatis* (Latin 'of the age').

AEW abbreviation for *airborne early warning*, a military surveillance system.

AFD abbreviation for *accelerated freeze drying*, a common method of food preservation.

AFL-CIO abbreviation for *American Federation of Labor and Congress of Industrial Organizations*.

AG abbreviation for *Aktiengesellschaft* (German 'limited company').

AH with reference to the Muslim calendar, abbreviation for *anno hegirae* (Latin 'year of the flight' – of Muhammad, from Mecca to Medina).

AIDS abbreviation for *acquired immune deficiency syndrome*, the newest and gravest of sexually transmitted diseases or STDs.

AK abbreviation for *Alaska*.

AL abbreviation for *Alabama*.

ALADI abbreviation for *Asociacion Latino-Americana de Integration* or Latin American Integration Association, organization promoting trade in the region.

AM in physics, abbreviation for amplitude modulation, one way in which radio waves are altered for the transmission of broadcasting signals.

a.m. or **A.M.** abbreviation for *ante meridiem* (Latin 'before noon').

AMF abbreviation of *Arab Monetary Fund*.

amp in physics, abbreviation for *ampere*, a unit of electrical current.

ANC abbreviation for *African National Congress*; South African nationalist organization.

ANZUS acronym for *Australia, New Zealand, and the United States* (Pacific Security Treaty), a military alliance established 1951. It was replaced 1954 by the Southeast Asia Treaty Organization , (SEATO).

a.p. in physics, abbreviation for *atmospheric pressure*.

APC abbreviation for *armoured personnel carrier*, a battlefield vehicle.

approx. abbreviation for *approximately*.

AR abbreviation for *Arkansas*.

ASA abbreviation for *Association of South East Asia* (1961–67), replaced by ASEAN, *Association of Southeast Asian Nations*.

a.s.a.p. abbreviation for *as soon as possible*.

ASAT acronym for *antisatellite weapon*.

ASPAC abbreviation of *Asian and Pacific Council*.

ASSR abbreviation for *Autonomous Soviet Socialist Republic*.

AWACS acronym for *Airborne Warning and Control System*. The system incorporates a long-range surveillance and detection radar mounted on a Boeing E-3 sentry aircraft. It was used with great success in the 1991 Gulf War.

AZ abbreviation for *Arizona*.

BA in education, abbreviation for *Bachelor of Arts* degree.

BAFTA abbreviation for *British Academy of Film and Television Arts*.

BBC abbreviation for *British Broadcasting Corporation*.

BC in the Christian calendar, abbreviation for *before Christ*; used with dates.

BCE abbreviation for *before the Common Era*; used with dates (instead of BC) particularly by non-Christians, and some theologians in recognition of the multiplicity of belief worldwide.

BCG abbreviation for *bacillus of Calmette and Guérin*, used as a vaccine to confer active immunity to tuberculosis (TB).

Beds abbreviation for *Bedfordshire*.

Berks abbreviation for *Berkshire*.

BFI abbreviation for the *British Film Institute*.

BFPO abbreviation for *British Forces Post Office*.

bhp abbreviation for *brake horsepower*.

biog. abbreviation for *biography*.

BIS abbreviation for *Bank for International Settlements* based in Basel, Switzerland. Established 1930, it makes loans for national central banks, and helps to offset movements of funds between the major currencies.

BMA abbreviation for *British Medical Association*.

BNF abbreviation for *British Nuclear Fuels*.

BOT abbreviation for *Board of Trade*, former UK government organization, merged in the Department of Trade and Industry from 1970.

BP abbreviation for *British Pharmacopoeia*; also *British Petroleum*.

BR abbreviation for *British Rail*.

BSc abbreviation for *Bachelor of Science* degree. The US abbreviation is *BS*.

BST abbreviation for *British Summer Time*; *bovine somatotropin*.

BT abbreviation for *British Telecom*.

Btu symbol for *British thermal unit*.

Bucks abbreviation for *Buckinghamshire*.

c. abbreviation for *circa* (Latin 'about'); used with dates that are uncertain.

C abbreviation for *centum* (Latin 'hundred'); *century*; *centigrade*; *Celsius*.

C °C symbol for degrees Celsius (temperature scale).

CA abbreviation for *California*.

CACM abbreviation for *Central American Common Market*.

CAD abbreviation for *computer-aided design*.

cal symbol for *calorie*.

CAM abbreviation for *computer-aided manufacture*.

Cambs abbreviation for *Cambridgeshire*.

Cantab abbreviation for *Cantabrigiensis* (Latin 'of Cambridge').

cap. abbreviation for *capital*.

CAP abbreviation for *Common Agricultural Policy*.

CARICOM abbreviation for *Caribbean Community* and Common Market.

CB abbreviation for *citizens' band* (radio).

CBI abbreviation for *Confederation of British Industry*.

CC abbreviation for *county council*; *cricket club*.

cc symbol for *cubic centimetre*; abbreviation for *carbon copy/copies*.

CCASG abbreviation of *Cooperative Council for the Arab States of the Gulf*.

CD abbreviation for *compact disc*; certificate of deposit; *Corps Diplomatique* (French 'Diplomatic Corps').

CDU abbreviation for the centre-right *Christian Democratic Union* in the Federal Republic of Germany.

CE abbreviation for *Common Era*; *Church of England* (often *C of E*).

CEDA (*Confederación Español de Derechas Autónomas*) a federation of right-wing parties under the leadership of José Maria Gil Robles, founded during the Second Spanish Republic 1933 to provide a right-wing coalition in the Spanish Cortes.

CEGB abbreviation for the former (until 1990) *Central Electricity Generating Board*.

CentCom abbreviation for US *Central Command*, a military strikeforce.

CENTO abbreviation for *Central Treaty Organization*.

CET abbreviation for *Central European Time*.

cf. abbreviation for *confer* (Latin 'compare').

CFC abbreviation for *chlorofluorocarbon*.

CFE abbreviation for *conventional forces in Europe*. Talks between government representatives began in Vienna, Austria, in March 1989 designed to reduce the 'conventional' – that is, non-nuclear – forces (US, Soviet, French, British, and German) in Europe. A treaty was signed by NATO and Warsaw Pact representatives in Nov 1990, reducing the number of tanks, missiles, aircraft, and other forms of military hardware held by member states, but doubts remain about its verification.

Ches abbreviation for Cheshire.

CIA abbreviation for the US *Central Intelligence Agency*.

CID abbreviation for *Criminal Investigation Department*.

cif in economics, abbreviation for *cost, insurance, and freight* or *charged in full*. Many countries value their imports on this basis, whereas exports are usually valued *fob*. For balance of payments purposes, figures are usually adjusted to include the freight and insurance costs.

cm symbol for *centimetre*.

CND abbreviation for *Campaign for Nuclear Disarmament*.

c/o abbreviation for *care of*.

co. abbreviation for *company*.

CO abbreviation for *Commanding Officer*.

CO abbreviation for *Colorado*.

COD abbreviation for *cash on delivery*.

COI abbreviation for *Central Office of Information*.

COIN acronym for *co*ounter*in*surgency, the suppression by a state's armed forces of uprisings against the state.

Comintern abbreviation of *Com*munist *Intern*ational.

continuo abbreviation for *basso continuo*; in music, the bass line on which a keyboard player, often accompanied by a bass stringed instrument, built up a harmonic accompaniment in 17th-century Baroque music.

CPP abbreviation for *current purchasing power*.

CPVE *Certificate of Pre-Vocational Education* in the UK, educational qualification introduced 1986 for students over 16 in schools and colleges who want a one-year course of preparation for work or further vocational study.

CRT abbreviation for *cathode-ray tube*.

CSCE abbreviation for *Conference on Security and Cooperation in Europe*, popularly known as the Helsinki Conference.

CSE (Certificate of Secondary Education) in the UK, the examinations taken by the majority of secondary school pupils who were not regarded as academically capable of GCE O level, until the introduction of the common secondary examination system, GCSE, 1988.

CT abbreviation for *Connecticut*.

cu abbreviation for *cubic* (measure).

CV abbreviation for *curriculum vitae*.

cwo abbreviation for *cash with order*.

cwt symbol for *hundredweight*, a unit of weight equal to 112 pounds (50.802 kg).

cwt symbol for *hundredweight*, a unit of weight equal to 100 lb (45.36 kg) in the US and 112 lb (50.8 kg) in the UK and Canada.

d. abbreviation for *day*; *diameter*; *died*; in the UK, d was the sign for a *penny* (Latin *denarius*) until decimalization of the currency in 1971.

D abbreviation for *500* in the Roman numeral system.

DA abbreviation for *district attorney*.

DBE abbreviation for *Dame Commander of the Order of the British Empire*.

DC in music, the abbreviation for *da capo* (Italian 'from the beginning'); in physics, the abbreviation for *direct current* (electricity); the District of Columbia.

DD abbreviation for *Doctor of Divinity*.

DE abbreviation for *Delaware*.

DES abbreviation for *Department of Education and Science*.

DHSS abbreviation for *Department of Health and Social Security*, UK government department until divided 1988.

diag. abbreviation for *diagram*.

DM abbreviation for *Deutschmark*, the unit of currency in Germany.

DMus abbreviation for *Doctor of Music*.

DNA abbreviation for *deoxyribonucleic acid*.

do. abbreviation for *ditto*.

DPhil abbreviation for *Doctor of Philosophy*.

DPP abbreviation for *Director of Public Prosecutions*.

DSO abbreviation for *Distinguished Service Order*, British military medal.

DTI abbreviation for *Department of Trade and Industry*, UK government department.

E abbreviation for *east*.

EC abbreviation for *European Community*.

ECM abbreviation for *electronic countermeasures*, military jargon for disrupting telecommunications.

ECOWAS acronym for *Economic Community of West African States*.

ECSC abbreviation for *European Coal and Steel Community*.

ECT abbreviation for *electroconvulsive therapy*.

ECTU abbreviation for *European Confederation of Trade Unions*.

ECU abbreviation for *European Currency Unit*, official monetary unit of the EC. It is based on the value of the different currencies used in the European Monetary System.

EEC abbreviation for *European Economic Community*.

EFTA acronym for *European Free Trade Association*.

EFTPOS abbreviation of *electronic funds transfer at point of sale* the transfer of funds from one bank account to another by electronic means.

e.g. abbreviation for *exempli gratia* (Latin 'for the sake of example').

emf in physics, abbreviation for *electromotive force*.

EMS abbreviation for *European Monetary System*.

ENT in medicine, an abbreviation for *ear, nose, and throat*. It is usually applied to a specialist clinic or hospital department.

E & O E abbreviation for *errors and omissions excepted*.

EOKA acronym for *Ethnikí Organósis Kipriakóu Agónos* (National Organization of Cypriot Struggle) an underground organization formed by General George Grivas 1955 to fight for the independence of Cyprus from Britain and ultimately its union (*enosis*) with Greece.

EPLF abbreviation for *Eritrean People's Liberation Front*.

EPNS abbreviation for *electroplated nickel silver*.

ERM abbreviation for *Exchange Rate Mechanism*.

ERNIE (acronym from *e*lectronic *r*andom *n*umber *i*ndicator *e*quipment) machine designed and produced by the UK Post Office Research Station to select a series of random 9-figure numbers to indicate prizewinners in the government's national lottery.

ESA abbreviation for *European Space Agency*.

est. abbreviation for *estimate(d)*.

et al. abbreviation for *et alii* (Latin 'and others'); used in bibliography.

etc. abbreviation for *et cetera* (Latin 'and the rest').

Euratom acronym for *European Atomic Energy Commission*, forming part of the European Community organization.

Eutelsat acronym for *European Telecommunications Satellite Organization*.

ex lib. abbreviation for *ex libris* (Latin 'from the library of').

°F symbol for degrees *Fahrenheit*.

FA abbreviation for *Football Association*.

f.a.o. abbreviation for *for the attention of*.

FAO abbreviation for *Food and Agriculture Organization*.

FBI abbreviation for *Federal Bureau of Investigation*, agency of the US Department of Justice.

FDN abbreviation for *Nicaraguan Democratic Front*.

fem. in grammar, abbreviation for *feminine*.

ff abbreviation for *folios*; and *the following*; used in reference citation and bibliography.

fig. abbreviation for *figure*.

fl. abbreviation for *floruit* (Latin 'he/she flourished').

FL abbreviation for *Florida*.

FM in physics, abbreviation for *frequency modulation*. Used in radio, FM is constant in amplitude and varies the frequency of the carrier wave.

FNLA abbreviation for *Front National de Libération de l'Angola* (French 'National Front for the Liberation of Angola').

FO abbreviation for *Foreign Office*, British government department.

FRS abbreviation for *Fellow of the Royal Society*.

ft abbreviation for *foot*, a measure of distance.

FTC abbreviation for *Federal Trade Commission*, US anti-monopoly organization.

g symbol for *gram*.

GA abbreviation for *Georgia* (USA).

gal symbol for *gallon*.

GATT acronym for *General Agreement on Tariffs and Trade*.

GCC abbreviation for *Gulf Cooperation Council*.

GCE (*General Certificate of Education*) in the UK, the public examination formerly taken at the age of 16 at Ordinary level (O level) and at 18 at Advanced level (A level).

GCHQ abbreviation for *Government Communications Headquarters* (UK).

GCSE (*General Certificate of Secondary Education*) in the UK, from 1988, examination for 16-year old pupils, superseding both GCE O level and CSE, and offering qualifications for up to 60% of school leavers in any particular subject.

GDP abbreviation for *Gross Domestic Product*.

GDR abbreviation for *German Democratic Republic* (East Germany).

gen. in grammar, the abbreviation for *genitive*.

ger. in grammar, the abbreviation for *gerund*.

GHQ abbreviation for *general headquarters*.

GI abbreviation for *government issue*; hence (in the USA) a common soldier.

Glos abbreviation for *Gloucestershire*; county in SW England.

GNP abbreviation for *Gross National Product*.

GmbH abbreviation for *Gesellshaft mit beschrankter Haftung* (German 'limited liability company').

GP in medicine, the abbreviation for *general practitioner*.

GPU former name (1922–23) for KGB, the Soviet security service.

GRP abbreviation for *glass- reinforced plastic*, a plastic material strengthened by glass fibres, usually erroneously known as fibreglass.

GU abbreviation for *Guam*.

ha symbol for *hectare*.

Hants abbreviation for *Hampshire*.

Herts abbreviation for *Hertfordshire*.

HF in physics, the abbreviation for *high frequency*.

HGV abbreviation for *heavy goods vehicle*.

HI abbreviation for *Hawaii*.

HMSO abbreviation for *His/Her Majesty's Stationery Office*.

Hon. abbreviation for *Honourable*.

hp symbol for *horsepower*.

HQ abbreviation for *headquarters*.

HRH abbreviation for *His/Her Royal Highness*.

ht abbreviation for *height*.

HWM abbreviation for *high water mark*.

Hz in physics, the symbol for *hertz*.

IA abbreviation for *Iowa*.

IADB abbreviation of *Inter-American Development Bank*.

IAEA abbreviation for *International Atomic Energy Agency*.

IBA abbreviation for *Independent Broadcasting Authority*, former name of the Independent Television Commission, UK regulatory body for commercial television and radio.

ibid. abbreviation for *ibidem* (Latin 'in the same place'); used in reference citation.

ICBM abbreviation for *intercontinental ballistic missile*.

id. abbreviation for *idem* (Latin 'the same'); used in reference citation.

ID abbreviation for *Idaho*.

IDA abbreviation for *International Development Association*.

i.e. abbreviation for *id est* (Latin 'that is').

IEEE abbreviation for *Institute of Electrical and Electronic Engineers*, which sets technical standards for electrical equipment and computer data exchange.

IKBS (abbreviation of *intelligent knowledge-based system*) in computing, an alternative name for the more usual KBS, knowledge-based system.

ILEA abbreviation for *Inner London Education Authority*. Former UK educational body which administered education in London. It was abolished 1990 and replaced by smaller borough-based education authorities.

IL abbreviation for *Illinois*.

IMF abbreviation for *International Monetary Fund*.

in abbreviation for *inch*, a measure of distance.

IN abbreviation for *Indiana*.

Inc. abbreviation for *Incorporated*.

INF abbreviation for *intermediate nuclear forces*, as in the Intermediate Nuclear Forces Treaty.

IOM abbreviation for *Isle of Man*.

IOW abbreviation for *Isle of Wight*.

ir in physics, abbreviation for *infrared*.

IRCAM abbreviation of the French *Institut de Recherche et de Coordination Acoustique-Musique* organization in Paris for research into electronic music, using computers, and synthesizers, founded 1976.

ISBN abbreviation for *International Standard Book Number*, used for ordering or classifying book titles.

ITU abbreviation for *intensive therapy unit*, a high-technology facility for treating the critically ill or injured.

IUCN abbreviation for *International Union for the Conservation of Nature*.

IUPAC abbreviation for *International Union of Pure and Applied Chemistry*, organization that recommends the nomenclature to be used for naming substances, the units to be used, and which conventions are to be adopted when describing particular changes.

IWW abbreviation for *Industrial Workers of the World*.

J in physics, symbol for *joule*, SI unit of energy.

jnr., jr. abbreviation for *junior*.

JP abbreviation for *justice of the peace*.

KBE abbreviation for *Knight (Commander of the Order) of the British Empire*.

KC abbreviation for *King's Counsel*.

Kcal abbreviation for *kilocalorie*.

kg abbreviation for *kilogram*.

KG abbreviation for *Knight of the Order of the Garter*.

KGB abbreviation for *Komitet Gosudarstvennoye Bezhopaznosti* (Russian 'Committee of State Security').

km symbol for *kilometre*.

kph or *km/h* symbol for *kilometres per hour*.

KS abbreviation for *Kansas*.

kW abbreviation for *kilowatt*.

KY abbreviation for *Kentucky*.

L Roman numeral for 50.

l symbol for *litre*, a measure of liquid volume.

LA abbreviation for *Louisiana*; *Los Angeles*.

Lab. abbreviation for *Labour* or *Labrador*, Canada.

LAES abbreviation for *Latin American Economic System*, organization for cooperation in the region.

Lancs abbreviation for *Lancashire*.

lat. abbreviation for *latitude*.

lb symbol for *pound* (weight).

lbw abbreviation for *leg before wicket* (cricket).

lc in abbreviation for *lower case*, or 'small' letters, as opposed to capitals.

LEA in the UK, abbreviation for *local education authority*.

Leics abbreviation for *Leicestershire*.

LF in physics, abbreviation for *low frequency*.

Lib. abbreviation for *Liberal*.

LIFFE acronym for *London International Financial Futures Exchange*, one of the exchanges in London where futures contracts are traded. It opened Sept 1982.

light-dependent resistor (LDR) component of electronic circuits whose resistance varies with the level of illumination on its surface. LDRs are used in light-measuring or light-sensing instruments (for example, in the exposure-meter circuit of an automatic camera) and in switches (such as those that switch on street lights at dusk).

Lincs abbreviation for *Lincolnshire*.

loc. cit. abbreviation for *loco citato* (Latin 'at the place cited'); used in reference citation.

log in mathematics, abbreviation for *logarithm*.

long. abbreviation for *longitude*.

Ltd abbreviation for *Limited*.

LW abbreviation for *long wave*, a radio wave with a wavelength of over 1,000 m/3,300 ft; one of the main wavebands into which radio frequency transmissions are divided.

LWM abbreviation for *low water mark*.

m symbol for *metre*.

M Roman numeral for *1,000*.

MA abbreviation for *Master of Arts* degree of education; the state of *Massachusetts*.

MAD abbreviation for *mutual assured destruction*; the basis of the theory of deterrence by possession of nuclear weapons.

MAFF abbreviation for *Ministry of Agriculture, Fisheries and Food*.

Man. abbreviation for *Manitoba*, Canadian province.

masc. in grammar, the abbreviation for *masculine*.

max. abbreviation for *maximum*.

MBE abbreviation for *Member (of the Order) of the British Empire*.

MCC abbreviation for *Marylebone Cricket Club*.

MD abbreviation for *Doctor of Medicine*; *Maryland*.

ME abbreviation for *Maine*.

ME abbreviation for *Middle English*, the period of the English language from 1050 to 1550.

MEP abbreviation for *Member of the European Parliament*.

Messrs abbreviation for *messieurs* (French 'sirs' or 'gentlemen') used in formal writing to address an organization or group of people.

MFA abbreviation for *Multi-Fibre Arrangement*.

mg symbol for *milligram*.

Mgr in the Roman Catholic Church, the abbreviation for *Monsignor*.

mi symbol for *mile*.

MI abbreviation for *Michigan*.

MICV abbreviation for *mechanized infantry combat vehicle*.

Middx abbreviation for *Middlesex*, former county of England.

MIDI abbreviation for *Musical Instrument Digital Interface*, a manufacturer's standard allowing different pieces of digital music equipment used in composing and recording to be freely connected.

min. abbreviation for *minute* (time); *minimum*.

MIRV abbreviation for *multiple independently targeted re-entry vehicle*, used in nuclear warfare.

ml symbol for *millilitre*.

MLR abbreviation for *minimum lending rate*.

mm symbol for *millimetre*.

mmHg symbol for *millimetre of mercury*.

MN abbreviation for *Minnesota*.

MO abbreviation for *Missouri*.

MOD abbreviation for *Ministry of Defence*.

MOH abbreviation for *Medical Officer of Health*.

mp in chemistry, the abbreviation for *melting point*.

MP abbreviation for *member of Parliament*.

mpg abbreviation for *miles per gallon*.

mph abbreviation for *miles per hour*.

Mr abbreviation for *mister*; title used before a name to show that the person is male.

MRBM abbreviation for *medium-range ballistic missile*.

Mrs title used before a name to show that the person is married and female; partly superseded by Ms, which does not indicate marital status. Mrs was originally an abbreviation for *mistress*.

Ms title used before a woman's name; pronounced 'miz'. Unlike Miss or Mrs, it can be used by married or unmarried women, and was introduced by the women's movement in the 1970s to parallel Mr, which also does not distinguish marital status.

MS abbreviation for *Mississippi*.

MSc in education, abbreviation for *Master of Science* degree. The US abbreviation is *MS*.

MSC abbreviation for *Manpower Services Commission*.

MS(S) abbreviation for *manuscript(s)*.

MT abbreviation for *Montana*.

MU in economics, the abbreviation for *monetary unit*.

MVD Soviet Ministry of Internal Affairs, name of the secret police 1946–53; now the KGB.

n. abbreviation for *noun*.

N abbreviation for *north*; *newton*; in chemistry, symbol for *nitrogen*.

NASA National Aeronautics and Space Administration, the US government agency, founded 1958, for spaceflight and aeronautical research. Its headquarters are in Washington DC and its main installation is at the Kennedy Space Center.

NATO abbreviation for *North Atlantic Treaty Organization*.

NB abbreviation for *New Brunswick*; *nota bene* (Latin 'note well'), used in references and citations.

NBS abbreviation for *National Bureau of Standards*, the US federal standards organization, on whose technical standards all US weights and measures are based.

NC abbreviation for *North Carolina*.

ND abbreviation for *North Dakota*.

NE abbreviation for *Nebraska*.

NEDC abbreviation for *National Economic Development Council*.

nem. con. abbreviation for *nemine contradicente* (Latin 'with no one opposing').

nem. diss. abbreviation for *nemine dissentiente* (Latin 'with no one dissenting').

NERC abbreviation for *Natural Environment Research Council*.

NF abbreviation for *Newfoundland*.

NH abbreviation for *New Hampshire*.

NHS abbreviation for *National Health Service*, the UK state-financed health service.

NIEO abbreviation for *New International Economic Order*.

NJ abbreviation for *New Jersey*.

NKVD the Soviet secret police 1934–38, replaced by the KGB. The NKVD was reponsible for Stalin's infamous purges.

NM abbreviation for *New Mexico*.

n.o. abbreviation for *not out* (cricket).

no. or *No.* abbreviation for *number*.

nom. in grammar, abbreviation for *nominative*.

Northants abbreviation for *Northamptonshire*.

Northd abbreviation for *Northumberland*.

Notts abbreviation for *Nottinghamshire*.

NPA abbreviation for *New People's Army* (Philippines).

NS abbreviation for *Nova Scotia*.

NSW abbreviation for *New South Wales*.

NT abbreviation for *Northern Territory*, Australia.

NTP abbreviation for *normal temperature and pressure*, former name for STP (*standard temperature and pressure*).

NV abbreviation for *Nevada*.

NY abbreviation for *New York*.

NZ abbreviation for *New Zealand*.

o/a abbreviation for *on account*.

OAPEC abbreviation of *Organization of Arab Petroleum Exporting Countries*.

ob. abbreviation for *obiit* (Latin 'he/she died').

OBE abbreviation for *Officer of the Order of the British Empire*.

OCAM acronym from *Organisation Commune Africaine et Mauricienne*, body for economic cooperation in Africa.

ODA abbreviation for *Overseas Development Administration*.

OE abbreviation for *Old English*.

OGPU former name 1923–34 of the Soviet secret police, now the KGB.

OH abbreviation for *Ohio*.

OHMS abbreviation for *On Her (His) Majesty's Service*.

OIC abbreviation for *Organization of the Islamic Conference*, international Muslim solidarity association.

OK abbreviation for *Oklahoma*.

o.n.o. abbreviation for *or near(est) offer*.

Ont. abbreviation for *Ontario*.

op. cit. abbreviation for *opere citato* (Latin 'in the work cited'), used in reference citation.

OPEC abbreviation for *Organization of Petroleum-Exporting Countries*.

OR abbreviation for *Oregon*.

OT abbreviation for *Old Testament*.

OU abbreviation for *Open University*.

OXFAM abbreviation for *Oxford Committee for Famine Relief*.

Oxon. abbreviation for *Oxoniensis* (Latin 'of Oxford').

oz symbol for *ounce*.

p in music, the abbreviation for *piano* (Italian 'softly').

p(p). abbreviation for *page(s)*.

p.a. abbreviation for *per annum* (Latin 'yearly').

PA abbreviation for *Pennsylvania*.

part. in grammar, the abbreviation for *participle*.

PAYE abbreviation for *pay as you earn*.

PC abbreviation for *personal computer*; *politically correct; police constable*; *Privy Councillor*.

PCB abbreviation for *polychlorinated biphenyl*; *printed circuit board*.

PCM abbreviation for *pulse-code modulation*.

PEN abbreviation for *Poets, Playwrights, Editors, Essayists, Novelists*, literary association established 1921 by C A ('Sappho') Dawson Scott, to promote international understanding among writers.

per pro abbreviation for *per procurationem* (Latin 'by the agency of').

PhD abbreviation for *Doctor of Philosophy* degree.

Phil. abbreviation for *Philadelphia*.

plc abbreviation for *public limited company*.

PLO abbreviation for *Palestine Liberation Organization*.

plur. in grammar, the abbreviation for *plural*.

PM abbreviation for *prime minister*.

p.m. or *P.M.* abbreviation for *post meridiem* (Latin 'after noon').

PO abbreviation for *Post Office*.

pp abbreviation for *per procurationem* (Latin 'by proxy').

ppm abbreviation for *parts per million*. An alternative (but numerically equivalent) unit used in chemistry is milligrams per litre (mg l⁻¹).

PR abbreviation for *public relations*; *proportional representation*.

PR abbreviation for *Puerto Rico*.

pref. in grammar, the abbreviation for *prefix*.

pro tem abbreviation for *pro tempore* (Latin 'for the time being').

PS abbreviation for *post scriptum* (Latin 'after writing').

PSBR abbreviation for *public sector borrowing requirement*.

pt abbreviation for *pint*.

PTO abbreviation for *please turn over*.

PX abbreviation for *Post Exchange*, a US organization that provides shopping and canteen facilities for armed forces at home and abroad. The British equivalent is the NAAFI.

QB abbreviation for *Queen's Bench*.

QC abbreviation for *Queen's Counsel*.

QED abbreviation for *quod erat demonstrandum* (Latin 'which was to be proved').

Qld abbreviation for *Queensland*.

quant. suff. abbreviation for *quantum sufficit* (Latin 'as much as suffices').

Que. abbreviation for *Québec*.

qv abbreviation for *quod vide* (Latin 'which see').

RA abbreviation for *Royal Academy* of Art, London, founded 1768.

RAC abbreviation for the British *Royal Automobile Club*.

RAF abbreviation for *Royal Air Force*.

RC abbreviation for *Red Cross*; *Roman Catholic*.

re abbreviation for Latin *'with regard to'*.

RI abbreviation for *Rhode Island*.

RIBA abbreviation for *Royal Institute of British Architects*.

RIP abbreviation for *requiescat in pace* (Latin 'may he/she rest in peace').

RN abbreviation for *Royal Navy*.

RNLI abbreviation for *Royal National Lifeboat Institution*.

RPI abbreviation for *retail price index*.

rpm abbreviation for *revolutions per minute*.

RPV abbreviation for *remotely piloted vehicle*, a flying TV camera for military use.

RSFSR abbreviation for *Russian Soviet Federal Socialist Republic*, the largest constituent republic of the USSR.

RSPB abbreviation for *Royal Society for the Protection of Birds*.

RSPCA abbreviation for *Royal Society for the Prevention of Cruelty to Animals*.

RSV abbreviation for *Revised Standard Version* of the Bible.

RSVP abbreviation for *répondez s'il vous plaît* (French 'please reply').

Rt Hon. abbreviation for *Right Honourable*, the title of British members of Parliament.

S abbreviation for *south*.

SA abbreviation for *South Africa*; *South Australia*.

SAARC abbreviation for *South Asian Association for Regional Cooperation*.

SADCC abbreviation for *Southern African Development Coordination Conference*, economic organization of countries in the region.

SADCC abbreviation of *Southern African Development Coordination Conference*.

s.a.e. abbreviation for *stamped addressed envelope*.

SALT abbreviation for *Strategic Arms Limitation Talks*, a series of US-Soviet negotiations 1969–79.

SAS abbreviation for *Special Air Service*; also for *Scandinavian Airlines System*.

Sask. abbreviation for *Saskatchewan*.

SBS acronym for *Special Boat Service*, the British Royal Navy's equivalent of the Special Air Service.

sc. abbreviation for *scilicet* (Latin 'let it be understood').

SC abbreviation for *South Carolina*.

SD abbreviation for *South Dakota*.

SDI abbreviation for *Strategic Defense Initiative*.

SDLP abbreviation for *Social Democratic and Labour Party* (Northern Ireland).

SDP abbreviation for *Social Democratic Party*.

SDR abbreviation for *special drawing right*.

SEATO abbreviation for *Southeast Asia Treaty Organization*.

sec or *s* abbreviation for *second*, a unit of time.

SELA abbreviation for *Sistema Economico Latino-Americana* or Latin American Economic System.

seq. abbreviation for *sequentes* (Latin 'the following').

SERC abbreviation for *Science and Engineering Research Council*.

SERPS abbreviation for *State Earnings-Related Pension Schemes*, the UK state pension scheme.

SFSR abbreviation for *Soviet Federal Socialist Republic*.

SHAEF abbreviation for *Supreme Headquarters Allied Expeditionary Force*. World War II military centre established 15 Feb 1944 in London, where final plans were made for the Allied invasion of Europe (under US general Eisenhower).

SHAPE abbreviation for *Supreme Headquarters Allied Powers Europe*, situated near Mons, Belgium, and the headquarters of NATO's Supreme Allied Commander Europe (SACEUR).

SHF in physics, the abbreviation for *superhigh frequency*.

SI abbreviation for *Système International [d'Unités]* (French 'International System [of Metric Units]').

SIB abbreviation for *Securities and Investments Board*, UK regulating body.

sing. abbreviation for *singular*.

SIS abbreviation for *Special Intelligence Service*.

SJ abbreviation for *Society of Jesus*.

SLBM abbreviation for *submarine-launched ballistic missile*.

SLD abbreviation for *Social and Liberal Democrats*.

SLR abbreviation for *single-lens reflex*, a type of camera in which the image can be seen through the lens before a picture is taken.

SOS internationally recognized distress signal, using letters of the Morse code (...–––...).

SPC abbreviation for *South Pacific Commission*, economic organization of countries in the region.

SPF abbreviation for *South Pacific Forum*, organization of countries in the region.

SPQR abbreviation for *Senatus Populusque Romanus*, Latin 'the Senate and the Roman People'.

sq abbreviation for *square* (measure).

Sr abbreviation for *senior*; for *señor*.

SSR abbreviation for *Soviet Socialist Republic*.

Staffs abbreviation for *Staffordshire*.

START abbreviation for *Strategic Arms Reduction Talks*.

suff. in grammar, abbreviation for *suffix*.

t symbol for *ton* or *tonne*.

tal. qual. abbreviation for *talis qualis* (Latin 'just as they come').

Tas. abbreviation for *Tasmania*.

TASM abbreviation for *tactical air-to-surface missile*.

Tass acronym for the Soviet news agency *T*elegrafnoye *A*gentstvo *S*ovyetskovo *S*oyuza.

TB abbreviation for the infectious disease *tuberculosis*.

TD abbreviation for *Teachta Dála* (Irish 'a member of the Irish parliament').

temp. abbreviation for *temperature*; *temporary*.

TIR abbreviation for *Transports Internationaux Routiers* (French 'International Road Transport').

TM abbreviation for *transcendental meditation*.

TN abbreviation for *Tennessee*.

TT abbreviation for *Tourist Trophy*; *teetotal*; *tuberculin tested*.

TTL abbreviation for *transistor-transistor logic*, a family of integrated circuits with fast switching speeds commonly used in building electronic devices.

TUC abbreviation for *Trades Union Congress*.

TX abbreviation for *Texas*.

UDC abbreviation for *urban district council*.

UFO abbreviation for *unidentified flying object*.

UHT abbreviation for *ultra heat treated*.

UK abbreviation for the *United Kingdom*.

UKAEA abbreviation for *United Kingdom Atomic Energy Authority*.

UN abbreviation for the *United Nations*.

UNCTAD acronym for *United Nations Commission on Trade and Development*.

UNEP acronym for *United Nations Environmental Programme*.

UNHCR abbreviation for *United Nations High Commission for Refugees*.

UNICEF acronym for *United Nations International Children's Emergency Fund*.

UNITA *National Union for the Total Independence of Angola* Angolan nationalist movement backed by South Africa.

US abbreviation for the *United States of America* (popular and most frequent name used by speakers of American English for the nation).

USA abbreviation (official) for the *United States of America*; *US Army*.

USDA abbreviation for the *US Department of Agriculture*.

USGS abbreviation for the *US Geological Survey*, part of the department of the interior.

USIA abbreviation for *US Information Agency*.

USO abbreviation for *United Service Organizations*.

USS abbreviation for *US Ship*.

USSR abbreviation for the *Union of Soviet Socialist Republics*.

UV in physics, abbreviation for *ultraviolet*.

V Roman numeral for *five*; in physics, symbol for *volt*.

v in physics, symbol for *velocity*.

VAT abbreviation for *value-added tax*.

vb in grammar, abbreviation for *verb*.

VDU (abbreviation for *visual display terminal*) an electronic output device for displaying the data processed by a computer on a screen.

v.i. in grammar, abbreviation for *verb intransitive*.

VI abbreviation for *Virgin Islands*; *Vancouver Island*.

VIP abbreviation for *very important person*.

viz abbreviation for *videlicet* (Latin 'that is to say', 'namely').

VLF in physics, abbreviation for *very low frequency*.

voc. in grammar, abbreviation for *vocative*.

vol abbreviation for *volume*.

VR abbreviation for *velocity ratio*.

VSTOL abbreviation for *vertical/short takeoff and landing* aircraft capable of taking off and landing either vertically or using a very short length of runway.

v.t. in grammar, abbreviation for *verb transitive*.

VT abbreviation for *Vermont*.

W abbreviation for *west*; in physics, symbol for *watt*.

WA abbreviation for *Washington* (state); *Western Australia*.

w.c. abbreviation for *water closet*, another name for a toilet.

WCC abbreviation for *World Council of Churches*.

WCC abbreviation for *World Council of Churches*, international Christian body.

WHO acronym for *World Health Organization*.

WI abbreviation for *West Indies*; *Wisconsin*.

Wilts abbreviation for *Wiltshire*.

Worcs abbreviation for *Worcestershire*.

wpm abbreviation for *words per minute*.

wt abbreviation for *weight*.

WV abbreviation for *West Virginia*.

WWF abbreviation for *World Wide Fund for Nature* (formerly World Wildlife Fund).

WY abbreviation for *Wyoming*.

X Roman numeral *ten*; a person or thing unknown.

x in mathematics, an unknown quantity.

yd abbreviation for *yard*.

YHA abbreviation for *Youth Hostels Association*.

YMCA abbreviation for *Young Men's Christian Association*.

Yorks. abbreviation for *Yorkshire*.

YWCA abbreviation for *Young Women's Christian Association*.

Z in physics, the symbol for *impedance* (electricity and magnetism).

zB abbreviation for *zum Beispiel* (German 'for example').

ZST abbreviation for *zone standard time*.

Foreign Words and Phrases

Abbé (French 'abbot') a French title of respect used to address any clergyman.

addendum (Latin) something to be added, usually in writing, which qualifies a foregoing thesis or statement.

ad infinitum (Latin) to infinity, endlessly.

ad lib(itum) (Latin) 'freely' interpreted.

ad nauseam (Latin) to the point of disgust.

aide-de-camp (French) officer who acts as private secretary to a general and would normally accompany the general on any duty.

al fresco (Italian, 'in the cool') in the open air.

avant-garde (from French) in the arts, those artists or works that are in the forefront of new developments in their media. The term was introduced (as was 'reactionary') after the French Revolution, when it was used to describe any socialist political movement.

ballet blanc (French 'white ballet') a ballet, such as *Giselle*, in which the female dancers wear calf-length white dresses. The costume was introduced by Marie Taglioni in *La Sylphide* 1832.

belles lettres (French 'fine letters') literature that is appreciated more for its aesthetic qualities than for its content.

bête noire (French 'black beast') something particularly disliked.

Bildungsroman (German 'education novel') novel that deals with the psychological and emotional development of its protagonist, tracing his or her life from inexperienced youth to maturity. The first example of the type is generally considered to be Wieland's *Agathon* 1765–66.

billabong (Australian *billa bung* 'dead river') a stagnant pond.

billet doux (French 'sweet note') a letter to or from one's lover.

Blitzkrieg (German 'lightning war') swift military campaign, as used by Germany at the beginning of World War II 1939–41. The abbreviated form Blitz was applied to the German air raids on London 1940–41.

bloc (French) a group, generally used to describe politically allied countries, as in 'the Soviet bloc'.

bona vacantia (Latin 'empty goods') in law, the property of a person who dies without making a will and without relatives or dependants who would be entitled or might reasonably expect to inherit.

bon marché (French) cheap.

bon mot (French) a witty remark.

bonsai (Japanese) the art of producing miniature trees by selective pruning.

bon ton (French 'good tone') fashionable manners.

bon voyage (French) have a good journey.

bourgeois (French) a member of the middle class, implying that a person is unimaginative, conservative, and materialistic.

bric-à-brac (French) odds and ends, usually old, ornamental, less valuable than antiques.

cahier (French 'notebook') usually the working notes or drawings of a writer or artist.

caïque (French, from Turkish) long, narrow, light rowing boat.

canaille (French) the mob, rabble.

carpe diem (Latin 'seize the day') live for the present.

carte blanche (French 'white paper') no instructions, complete freedom to do as one wishes.

casus belli (Latin) a justification for war, grounds for a dispute.

caveat emptor (Latin) dictum that professes the buyer is responsible for checking the quality of non-warrantied goods purchased.

cave canem (Latin) beware of the dog.

céad míle fáilte (Irish 'a hundred thousand welcomes') a conventional form of greeting.

c'est la vie (French) that's life.

chacun à son goût (French) each to their own taste.

chambré (French) (of wine) at room temperature, as opposed to chilled.

chef d'oeuvre (French) a masterpiece.

cicisbeo (Italian) 18th-century term for an aristocratic married woman's lover, similar to *cavaliere servente*.

cogito, ergo sum (Latin) 'I think, therefore I am'; quotation from French philosopher René Descartes.

comme il faut (French 'as it should be') socially correct and acceptable.

compos mentis (Latin) of sound mind.

conquistador (Spanish for 'conqueror'), applied to such explorers and adventurers in the Americas as Cortés (Mexico) and Pizarro (Peru).

corrigendum (Latin) something to be corrected.

coup d'état or *coup* (French literally 'stroke of state') forcible takeover of the government of a country by elements from within that country, generally carried out by violent or illegal means.

coûte que coûte (French) whatever the cost.

crème de la crème (French 'the cream of the cream') the elite, the very best.

cri de coeur (French) a cry from the heart.

cuius regio, eius religio (Latin) those who live in a country should adopt the religon of its ruler.

cul-de-sac (French, literally 'bottom of the bag') a street closed off at one end; an inescapable situation.

curriculum vitae or *CV* (Latin, literally 'the course of one's life') an account of a person's education and previous employment, attached to a job application.

de bene esse (Latin 'of wellbeing') in law, doing what is the best possible in the circumstances; the term usually relates to evidence.

decree nisi (Latin) conditional order of divorce. A *decree absolute* is normally granted six weeks after the decree nisi, and from the date of the decree absolute the parties cease to be husband and wife.

de die in diem (Latin) day after day.

de facto (Latin) in fact.

de gustibus non est disputandum (Latin) there is no accounting for taste.

Dei gratia (Latin) by the grace of God.

déjà vu (French 'already seen') the feeling that something encountered for the first time has in fact been seen before.

de jure (Latin) according to law; legally.

de novo (Latin) from the beginning; anew.

Deo (ad)juvante (Latin) with God's help.

Deo gratias (Latin) thanks to God.

Deo volente (Latin) God willing.

de profundis (Latin 'from the depths') a cry from the depths of misery. From the Bible, Psalm 130: *De profundis clamavi ad te*; 'Out of the depths have I cried to thee'.

de rigueur (French 'of strictness') demanded by the rules of etiquette.

détente (French) a reduction of political tension and the easing of strained relations between nations; for example, the ending of the Cold War 1989–90.

de trop (French 'of too much') not wanted, in the way.

deus ex machina (Latin 'a god from a machine') a far-fetched or unlikely event that resolves an intractable difficulty.

Dieu et mon droit (French 'God and my right') motto of the royal arms of Great Britain.

doppelgänger (German 'double-goer') a ghostly apparition identical to a living person; a twin soul.

double entendre (French 'double meaning') an ambiguous word or phrase, usually one that is coarse or impolite.

dramatis personae (Latin) the characters in a play.

dulce et decorum est pro patria mori (Latin 'it is sweet and noble to die for one's country') quotation from Horace's *Odes*, also used by English poet Wilfred Owen as the title for his poem denouncing World War I.

Ecce Homo (Latin 'behold the man') the words of Pontius Pilate to the accusers of Jesus; the title of paintings showing Jesus crowned with thorns, presented to the people (John 19:5).

emeritus (Latin) someone who has retired from an official position but retains their title on an honorary basis, for example a *professor emeritus*.

éminence grise (French, literally 'grey eminence') a power behind a throne; that is, a manipulator of power without immediate responsibility. The nickname was originally applied (because of his grey cloak) to the French monk François Leclerc du Tremblay (1577–1638), also known as Père Joseph, who in 1612 became the close friend and behind-the-scenes adviser of Cardinal Richelieu.

enfant terrible (French 'terrible child') one whose rash and unconventional behaviour shocks and embarrasses others.

en masse (French) as a group, in a body, all together.

enosis (Greek) the movement, developed from 1930, for the union of Cyprus with Greece, which took place 1974.

en plein air (French) in the open air.

en route (French) on the way.

entente cordiale (French 'cordial understanding'), specifically, the agreement reached by Britain and France 1904 recognizing British interests in Egypt and French interests in Morocco. It formed the basis for Anglo-French cooperation before the outbreak of World War I 1914.

ergo (Latin) therefore; hence.

erratum (Latin) an error.

ersatz (German) artificial, substitute, inferior.

espadrille (French) a type of shoe made with a canvas upper and a rope sole.

et in arcadia ego (Latin 'I also in Arcadia') death exists even in Arcadia (a fabled land).

ex cathedra (Latin, literally 'from the chair') term describing a statement by the pope, taken to be indisputably true, and which must be accepted by Catholics.

exeunt (Latin 'they go out') a stage direction.

exit (Latin 'he/she goes out') a stage direction.

ex parte (Latin 'on the part of one side only') in law, term indicating that an order has been made after hearing only the party that made the application; for example, an ex parte injunction.

factotum (Latin 'do everything") someone employed to do all types of work.

fait accompli (French 'accomplished fact') something that has been done and cannot be undone.

faute de mieux (French) for want of better.

faux pas (French 'false step') a social blunder.

fellah (Arabic, plural *fellahin*) in Arab countries, a peasant farmer or farm labourer. In Egypt, approximately 60% of the fellah population live in rural areas, often in villages of 1,000–5,000 inhabitants.

fin de siècle (French 'end of century') the art and literature of the 1890s; decadent.

force majeure (French 'superior force') in politics, the use of force rather than the seeking of a political or diplomatic solution to a problem.

Gesellschaft (German 'society') a group whose concerns are of a formal and practical nature.

glasnost (Russian 'speaking aloud') Soviet leader Mikhail Gorbachev's policy of liberalizing various aspects of Soviet life, such as introducing greater freedom of expression and information and opening up relations with Western countries.

Götterdämmerung (German 'twilight of the gods') in Scandinavian mythology, the end of the world.

gulag (Russian) term for the system of prisons and labour camps used to silence dissidents and opponents of the Soviet regime.

hic jacet (Latin 'here lies') an epitaph.

honi soit qui mal y pense (French 'shamed be he who thinks evil of it') the motto of England's Order of the Garter.

hors de combat (French) out of action.

incunabula (Latin, originally from swaddling clothes) the birthplace, or early stages of anything; printed books produced before 1500, when printing was in its infancy.

in loco parentis (Latin) in a parental capacity.

in situ (Latin) in place, on the spot, without moving from position.

inter alia (Latin) among other things.

ipso facto (Latin) by that very fact.

j'adoube (French 'I adjust') used in chess to show that a player is touching a piece in order to correct its position rather than to move it.

je ne sais quoi (French 'I don't know what') a certain indescribable quality.

joie de vivre (French) finding pleasure in simply being alive.

kindergarten (German) another term for nursery school.

kohl (Arabic) powdered antimony sulphide, used in Asia and the Middle East to darken the area around the eyes. Commonly used eyeliners also contain carbon (bone black, lamp black, carbon black) or black iron oxide.

Kyrie eleison (Greek 'Lord have mercy') the words spoken or sung at the beginning of the mass in the Catholic, Orthodox, and Anglican churches.

laissez faire (French) theory that the state should not intervene in economic affairs, except to break up a monopoly. The phrase originated with the Physiocrats, 18th-century French economists whose maxim was *laissez faire et laissez passer*, (leave the individual alone and let commodities circulate freely).

lakh or *lac* or *lak* (from Hindi) in India or Pakistan, the sum of 100,000 (rupees).

Land federal state (German; plural *Länder*) of Germany or Austria.

Landtag legislature of each of the *Länder* (states) that form the federal republics of Germany and Austria.

Lebensphilosophie (German) philosophy of life.

Lebensraum (German 'living space') theory developed by Hitler for the expansion of Germany into E Europe, and in the 1930s used by the Nazis to justify their annexation of neighbouring states on the grounds that Germany was overpopulated.

lingua franca (Italian, literally 'Frankish tongue') any language that is used as a means of communication by groups who do not themselves normally speak that language; for example, English is a lingua franca used by Japanese doing business in Finland, or by Swedes in Saudi Arabia.

locus standi (Latin 'a place to stand') in law, the right to bring an action.

Lumpenproletariat (German 'ragged proletariat') the poorest of the poor: beggars, tramps, and criminals (according to Karl Marx).

Machtpolitik (German) power politics.

magnum opus (Latin) a great work of art or literature.

Mardi Gras (French 'fat Tuesday' from the custom of using up all the fat in the household before the beginning of Lent) Shrove Tuesday. A festival was traditionally held on this day in Paris, and there are carnivals in many parts of the world, including New Orleans, Louisiana, Italy, and Brazil.

mare nostrum (Latin 'our sea') Roman name for the Mediterranean.

matze (Yiddish) unleavened bread eaten during the Passover.

mea culpa (Latin 'my fault') an admission of guilt.

memento mori (Latin) a reminder of death.

menhir (Breton 'long stone') a prehistoric standing stone; see megalith.

mens sana in corpore sano (Latin) a healthy mind in a healthy body.

Messrs abbreviation for *messieurs* (French 'sirs' or 'gentlemen') used in formal writing to address an organization or group of people.

mise en scène (French 'stage setting') in cinema, the composition and content of the frame in terms of background scenery, actors, costumes, props, and lighting.

modus operandi (Latin) a method of operating.

modus vivendi (Latin 'way of living') a compromise between opposing points of view.

mores (Latin) the customs and manners of a society.

mot juste (French) the right word, just the word to suit the occasion.

muezzin (Arabic) a person whose job is to perform the call to prayer five times a day from the minaret of a Muslim mosque.

née (French 'born') followed by a surname, indicates the name of a woman before marriage.

nemo me impune lacessit (Latin 'no one injures me with impunity') the motto of Scotland.

neo- a new development of an older form, often in a different spirit. Examples include *neo-Marxism* and *Neo-Classicism*.

nil desperandum (Latin) never despair.

noblesse oblige (French) the aristocracy ought to behave honourably. The phrase is often used sarcastically to point out how removed this idea is from reality.

nom de plume (French 'pen name') a writer's pseudonym.

non sequitur (Latin 'it does not follow') a statement that has little or no relevance to the one that preceded it.

nuit blanche (French 'white night') a night without sleep.

nulli secundus (Latin) second to none.

obiit (Latin 'he/she died') found, for example, in inscriptions on tombstones, followed by a date.

ombudsman (from Swedish 'commissioner') official who acts on behalf of the private citizen in investigating complaints against the government. The post is of Scandinavian origin; it was introduced in Sweden 1809, Denmark 1954, and Norway 1962, and spread to other countries from the 1960s.

onus (Latin) a burden or responsibility.

outré (French) extreme, beyond the bounds of acceptability.

pace (Latin) with deference to, followed by a name, used to acknowledge contradiction of the person named.

padre (Italian 'father') a priest.

Pamyat nationalist Russian popular movement. Founded 1979 as a cultural and historical group attached to the Soviet Ministry of Aviation Industry, it grew from the mid-1980s, propounding a violently conservative and anti-Semitic Russian nationalist message.

parvenu (French 'arrived') a social upstart.

passé (French) out of date.

passim (Latin 'in many places') indicates that a reference occurs repeatedly throughout the work.

perestroika (Russian 'radical restructuring') in Soviet politics, the wide-ranging economic and political reforms initiated during Mikhail Gorbachev's leadership of the Soviet state.

per se (Latin) in itself.

pièce de résistance (French) the most outstanding item in a collection; the main dish of a meal.

pied-à-terre (French 'foot on the ground') a convenient second home, usually small and in a town or city.

pique (French) a feeling of slight irritation or resentment.

plus ça change, plus c'est la même chose (French) the more things change, the more they stay the same.

poste restante (French) a system whereby mail is sent to a certain post office and kept there until collected by the addressee.

post hoc, ergo propter hoc (Latin) after this, therefore on account of this.

postmortem (Latin) dissection of a dead body to determine the cause of death. It is also known as an *autopsy*.

post scriptum (abbreviation PS; Latin) something written below the signature on a letter.

prêt-à-porter (French) ready-to-wear clothes.

prima facie (Latin) at first sight.

pro rata (Latin) in proportion.

pro tem(pore) (Latin) for the time being.

putsch (Swiss German) term for a violent seizure of political power, such as Hitler and Ludendorff's abortive beer-hall putsch Nov 1923, which attempted to overthrow the Bavarian government.

quasi (Latin 'as if') apparently but not actually.

quid pro quo (Latin 'something for something') an exchange of one thing in return for another.

quod erat demonstrandum (abbreviation QED; Latin 'which was to be proved') added at the end of a geometry proof.

quod vide (abbreviation qv; Latin 'which see') indicates a cross-reference.

quo vadis? (Latin) where are you going?

qv abbreviation for *quod vide* (Latin 'which see').

raison d'être (French) a reason for existence.

réchauffé (French 're-heated') warmed up (as of leftover food); old, stale.

recherché (French 'sought after') rare.

revenons à nos moutons (French 'let us return to our sheep') let us get back to the subject.

ruat coelum (Latin 'though the heavens may fall') whatever happens.

rus in urbe (Latin) urban retreat where one could imagine oneself in the countryside.

Sachlichkeit (German) objectivity, matter-of-factness.

samovar (Russian) urn, heated by charcoal, used for making tea.

sang-froid (French 'cold blood') coolness, composure.

sans souci (French) without cares or worries.

savoir-faire (French) knowing what to do, how to behave.

Schadenfreude (German) malicious enjoyment at the misfortunes of others.

scilicet (Latin) namely, that is.

secrétaire (French) a small writing desk.

sic (Latin 'thus', 'so') sometimes found in brackets within a printed quotation to show that an apparent error is in the original.

si monumentum requiris, circumspice (Latin 'if you seek his monument, look about you') the epitaph of Christopher Wren in St Paul's Cathedral, London.

sine die (Latin 'without a day being appointed') indefinitely.

sine qua non (Latin 'without which not') absolutely essential.

soupçon (French 'suspicion') a very small amount, a dash.

sovkhoz (Russian) state-owned farm in the USSR where the workers are state employees. The sovkhoz differs from the *kolkhoz* where the farm is run by a collective.

status quo (Latin 'the state in which') the current situation, without change.

Sturm Abteilung (SA) (German, literally 'storm division') German terrorist militia, also known as *Brownshirts*, of the Nazi Party, established 1921 under the leadership of Röhm, in charge of physical training and political indoctrination.

Sturm und Drang (German, literally 'storm and stress') German early Romantic movement in literature and music, from about 1775, concerned with the depiction of extravagant passions. Writers associated with the movement include Herder, Goethe, and Schiller.

sub judice (Latin) not yet decided by a court of law.

Sûreté the criminal investigation department of the French police.

tabula rasa (Latin 'scraped tablet', from the Romans' use of wax-covered tablets which could be written on with a pointed stick and cleared by smoothing over the surface) a mind without any preconceived ideas.

tant mieux (French) so much the better.

tant pis (French) so much the worse.

tempus fugit (Latin) time flies.

terra firma (Latin) dry land; solid earth.

terra incognita (Latin) an unknown region.

terza rima (Italian 'third line') poetical metre used in Dante's *Divine Comedy*, consisting of three-line stanzas in which the second line rhymes with the first and third of the following stanza.

tête-à-tête (French 'head-to-head') private meeting between two people.

texte intégral (French 'the complete text') unabridged.

tour de force (French 'feat of strength') a remarkable accomplishment.

tout de suite (French) immediately.

tout ensemble (French 'all together') the overall effect.

trahison des clercs (French 'the treason of the intellectuals') the involvement of intellectuals in active politics.

tricoteuse (French 'knitter') in the French Revolution, one of the women who sat knitting in the National Convention and near the guillotine.

ultra (Latin) extreme.

uomo universale (Italian 'universal man'), someone who is at home in all spheres of knowledge; one of the ideals of the Renaissance.

urbi et orbi (Latin 'to the city and to the world') a papal proclamation.

ut pictura poesis (Latin) a poem is as a picture.

vade mecum (Latin 'go with me') a useful handbook carried about for reference.

veni, vidi, vici (Latin 'I came, I saw, I conquered') Julius Caesar's description of his victory over King Pharnaces II (63–47 BC) at Zela in 47 BC.

vérité (French 'realism'), as in *cinéma vérité*, used to describe a realistic or documentary style.

versus (abbreviation vs; Latin) against.

vice versa (Latin) the other way around.

vis-à-vis (French 'face-to-face') with regard to.

viva voce (Latin 'with living voice') an oral examination.

Völkerwanderung (German 'nations wandering') the migration of peoples, usually with reference to the Slavic and Germanic movement in Europe 2nd–11th centuries AD.

Weltanschauung (German 'worldview') a philosophy of life.

Weltpolitik (German 'world politics') term applied to German foreign policy after about 1890, which represented Emperor Wilhelm II's attempt to make Germany into a world power through an aggressive foreign policy on colonies and naval building combined with an increase in nationalism at home.

white elephant any useless and cumbersome gift. In Thailand the monarch would formerly present a white elephant to a person out of favour: being the country's sacred animal, it could not be used for work, and its upkeep was ruinously expensive.

yeti (Tibetan) another term for the abominable snowman.

Zeitgeist (German 'time spirit') spirit of the age.

zenana (Hindi) the part of a house used by the female members of the household.

Zugzwang (German) a position in chess from which it is impossible to move without worsening one's situation.

MUSIC

Musical Terms

a cappella choral music sung without instrumental accompaniment. It is characteristic of gospel music, doo-wop, and the evangelical Christian church movement.

acoustics in general, the experimental and theoretical science of sound and its transmission; in particular, that branch of the science that has to do with the phenomena of sound in a particular space such as a room or theatre.

alto voice or instrument between tenor and soprano. The sound of the traditional high male alto voice (also known as *countertenor*) is trumpetlike and penetrating; the low-register female *contralto* is rich and mellow in tone. The alto range is centred on the octave above middle C on the piano. Alto is also another name for the French viola.

anthem short, usually elaborate, religious choral composition, sometimes accompanied by the organ; also a song of loyalty and devotion.

aria solo vocal piece in an opera or oratorio, often in three sections, the third repeating the first after a contrasting central section.

atonality music in which there is an apparent absence of key; often associated with an expressionist style.

bagatelle short character piece, often for piano.

bar or *measure* modular unit of rhythm, shown in notation by vertical 'barring' of the musical continuum into sections of usually constant duration and rhythmic content.

barbershop a style of unaccompanied close-harmony singing of sentimental ballads, revived in the USA during the 19th century. Traditionally sung by four male voices, since the 1970s it has developed as a style of a cappella choral singing for both male and female voices.

baritone male voice pitched between bass and tenor, centred in the octave below middle C and rising to the F or G above. The range is well suited to lieder.

bass (1) lowest range of male voice; (2) lower regions of musical pitch; (3) in the violin family, a double bass.

bel canto Italian style of singing with emphasis on perfect technique and beautiful tone. The style began in the 18th century and reached its peak in the operas of Gioacchino Rossini, Gaetano Donizetti (1797–1848), and Vincenzo Bellini (1801–1835).

cadence termination of a musical line or phrase, expressed rhythmically and harmonically.

cadenza unaccompanied bravura passage (requiring elaborate, virtuoso execution) in the style of an improvisation for the soloist during a concerto.

canon echo form for two or more parts repeating and following a leading melody at regular time intervals to achieve a harmonious effect. It is often found in classical music; for example, Vivaldi and J S Bach employed it.

cantata extended work for voices, from the Italian, meaning 'sung', as opposed to sonata ('sounded') for instruments. A cantata can be sacred or secular, sometimes uses solo voices, and usually has orchestral accompaniment. The first printed collection of sacred cantata texts dates from 1670.

capriccio short instrumental piece, often humorous or whimsical in character.

chamber music music suitable for performance in a small room or chamber, rather than in the concert hall, and usually written for instrumental combinations, played with one instrument to a part, as in the string quartet.

clef symbol used to indicate the pitch of the lines of the staff in musical notation.

coda concluding section of a movement, added to indicate finality.

coloratura rapid ornamental vocal passage with runs and trills. A *coloratura soprano* is a light, high voice suited to such music.

concerto composition, usually in three movements, for solo instrument (or instruments) and orchestra. It developed during the 18th century from the *concerto grosso* form for string orchestra, in which a group of solo instruments is contrasted with a full orchestra.

contralto low-registered female voice; also called an *alto*.

counterpoint the art of combining different forms of an original melody with apparent freedom and yet to harmonious effect. Giovanni Palestrina and J S Bach were masters of counterpoint.

diatonic scale consisting of the seven notes of any major or minor key.

encore (French 'again') unprogrammed extra item, usually short and well known, played at the end of a concert to please an enthusiastic audience.

étude musical exercise designed to develop technique.

finale the last movement or section of a composition, by implication resolute in character.

fret inlaid ridge of ivory or metal, or of circlets of nylon, marking positions in the fingerboard of a plucked or bowed string instrument indicating changes of pitch.

fugue contrapuntal form (with two or more melodies) for a number of parts or 'voices', which enter successively in imitation of each other. It was raised to a high art by J S Bach.

gamelan Indonesian orchestra employing tuned gongs, xylophones, metallophones (with bars of metal), cymbals, drums, flutes, and fiddles, the music of which has inspired such Western composers as Debussy, Benjamin Britten, and Philip Glass (1937–).

Gregorian chant any of a body of plainsong choral chants associated with Pope Gregory the Great (540–604), which became standard in the Roman Catholic Church.

harmonics series of partial vibrations that combine to form a musical tone. The number and relative prominence of harmonics produced determines an instrument's tone colour (timbre). An oboe is rich in harmonics; a flute has few. Harmonics conform to successive divisions of the sounding air column or string: their pitches are harmonious.

impromptu short instrumental piece that suggests spontaneity. Composers of piano impromptus include Schubert and Chopin.

intermezzo short orchestral interlude often used between the acts of an opera to denote the passage of time; by extension, a short piece for an instrument to be played between other more substantial works.

key the diatonic scale around which a piece of music is written; for example, a passage in the key of C major will mainly use the notes of the C major scale. The term is also used for the lever activated by a keyboard player, such as a piano key.

libretto the text of an opera or other dramatic vocal work, or the scenario of a ballet.

lied musical setting of a poem, usually for solo voice and piano; referring to Romantic songs of Schubert, Schumann, Brahms, and Hugo Wolf.

madrigal form of secular song in four or five parts, usually sung without instrumental accompaniment. It originated in 14th-century Italy. Madrigal composers include Monteverdi and Thomas Morley (1557–1602).

melody distinctive sequence of notes. A melody may be a tune in its own right, or it may form a theme running through a longer piece of music.

metre accentuation pattern characteristic of a musical line; the regularity underlying musical rhythm.

mezzo-soprano female singing voice halfway between soprano and contralto.

middle C white note at the centre of the piano keyboard, indicating the division between left- and right-hand regions and between the treble and bass staves of printed music.

minuet European courtly dance of the 17th century, later used with the trio as the third movement in a classical symphony.

modulation movement from one key to another.

movement section of a large work, such as a symphony, which is often complete in itself.

nocturne lyrical, dreamy piece, often for piano, introduced by John Field (1782–1837) and adopted by Chopin.

opera dramatic musical work in which singing takes the place of speech. In opera, the music accompanying the action has paramount importance, although dancing and spectacular staging may also play their parts. Opera originated in late 16th-century Florence when the musical declamation, lyrical monologues, and choruses of Classical Greek drama were reproduced in current forms.

operetta light form of opera, with music, dance, and spoken dialogue. The story line is romantic and sentimental, often employing farce and parody. Its origins lie in the 19th-century *opéra comique* and is intended to amuse. Examples of operetta are Offen-

bach's (1819–1880) *Orphée aux enfers/Orpheus in the Underworld* 1858, Johann Strauss's *Die Fledermaus/The Bat* 1874, and *Pirates of Penzance* 1879 and *The Mikado* 1885 by W S Gilbert (1836–1911) and Arthur Sullivan (1842–1900).

opus term, used with a figure, to indicate the numbering of a composer's works, usually in chronological order.

oratorio dramatic, non-scenic musical setting of religious texts, scored for orchestra, chorus, and solo voices. Its origins lie in the *Laudi spirituali* performed by St Philip Neri's Oratory in Rome in the 16th century. The form reached perfection in such works as J S Bach's *Christmas Oratorio* and Handel's *Messiah*.

orchestration scoring of a composition for orchestra; the choice of instruments of a score expanded for orchestra (often by another hand). A work may be written for piano, and then transferred to an orchestral score.

overture piece of instrumental music, usually preceding an opera. There are also overtures to suites and plays, ballets, and 'concert' overtures, such as Elgar's *Cockaigne*.

prelude composition intended as the preface to further music, to set a mood for a stage work, as in Wagner's *Lohengrin*; as used by Chopin, a short piano work.

requiem in the Roman Catholic church, a mass for the dead. Musical settings include those by Palestrina, Mozart, Berlioz, and Verdi.

rhapsody instrumental fantasia, often based on folk melodies, such as Franz Lizst's *Hungarian Rhapsodies* 1853–54.

rhythm the patterning of music in movement; a recurring unit of long and short time values.

rondo form of instrumental music in which the principal section returns like a refrain. Rondo form is often used for the last movement of a sonata or concerto.

scale sequence of pitches that establishes a key, and in some respects the character of a composition. A scale is defined by its starting note and may be *major* or *minor* depending on the order of intervals. A *chromatic* scale is the full range of 12 notes: it has no key because there is no fixed starting point.

scherzo lively piece, usually in rapid triple (3/4) time; often used for the third movement of a symphony, sonata, or quartet.

serenade musical piece for chamber orchestra or wind instruments in several movements, originally intended for evening entertainment, such as Mozart's *Eine kleine Nachtmusik/A Little Night Music*.

sonata piece of instrumental music written for a soloist or a small ensemble and consisting of a series of related movements.

soprano the highest range of the female voice, about an octave higher than a contralto. Its range stretches from F above middle C to the C an octave and half above; however, some operatic roles require the extended upper range of a coloratura soprano.

suite set of instrumental pieces, sometimes assembled from a stage work, such as Tchaikovsky's *Nut-*

Major operas and their first performances

Date	Opera	Composer	Librettist	Place
1607	Orfeo	Monteverdi	Striggio	Mantua
1642	The Coronation of Poppea	Monteverdi	Busenello	Venice
1689	Dido and Aeneas	Purcell	Tate	London
1724	Julius Caesar in Egypt	Handel	Haym	London
1762	Orpheus and Eurydice	Gluck	Calzabigi	Vienna
1786	The Marriage of Figaro	Mozart	Da Ponte	Vienna
1787	Don Giovanni	Mozart	Da Ponte	Prague
1790	Così fan tutte	Mozart	Da Ponte	Vienna
1791	The Magic Flute	Mozart	Schikaneder	Vienna
1805	Fidelio	Beethoven	Sonnleithner	Vienna
1816	The Barber of Seville	Rossini	Sterbini	Rome
1821	Der Freischütz	Weber	Kind	Berlin
1831	Norma	Bellini	Romani	Milan
1835	Lucia di Lammermoor	Donizetti	Cammarano	Naples
1836	Les Huguenots	Meyerbeer	Scribe	Paris
1842	Russlan and Ludmilla	Glinka	Shirkov/Bakhturin	St Petersburg
1850	Lohengrin	Wagner	Wagner	Weimar
1851	Rigoletto	Verdi	Piave	Venice
1853	Il Trovatore	Verdi	Cammarano	Rome
1853	La Traviata	Verdi	Piave	Venice
1859	Faust	Gounod	Barbier/Carré	Paris
1865	Tristan und Isolde	Wagner	Wagner	Munich
1866	The Bartered Bride	Smetana	Sabina	Prague
1868	Die Meistersinger	Wagner	Wagner	Munich
1871	Aida	Verdi	Ghislanzoni	Cairo
1874	Boris Godunov	Mussorgsky	Mussorgsky	St Petersburg
1874	Die Fledermaus	Johann Strauss II	Haffner/Genée	Vienna
1875	Carmen	Bizet	Meilhac/Halévy	Paris
1876	The Ring of the Nibelung	Wagner	Wagner	Bayreuth
1879	Eugene Onegin	Tchaikovsky	Tchaikovsky/Shilovsky	Moscow
1881	The Tales of Hoffman	Offenbach	Barbier	Paris
1882	Parsifal	Wagner	Wagner	Bayreuth
1885	The Mikado	Sullivan	Gilbert	London
1887	Otello	Verdi	Boito	Milan
1890	Cavalleria Rusticana	Mascagni	Menasci/Targioni- Tozzetti	Rome
1890	Prince Igor	Borodin	Borodin	St Petersburg
1892	Pagliacci	Leoncavallo	Leocavallo	Milan
1892	Werther	Massenet	Blau/Milliet/Hartmann	Vienna
1896	La Bohème	Puccini	Giacosa/Illica	Turin
1900	Tosca	Puccini	Giacosa/Illica	Rome
1902	Pelléas et Mélisande	Debussy	Maeterlinck	Paris
1904	Jenůfa	Janáček	Janáček	Brno
1904	Madame Butterfly	Puccini	Giacosa/Illica	Milan
1905	Salome	Richard Strauss	Wilde/Lachmann	Dresden
1909	The Golden Cockerel	Rimsky-Korsakov	Byelsky	Moscow
1911	Der Rosenkavalier	Richard Strauss	Hofmannsthal	Dresden
1918	Duke Bluebeard's Castle	Bartók	Balázs	Budapest
1925	Wozzeck	Berg	Berg	Berlin
1935	Porgy and Bess	Gershwin	Ira Gershwin/Heyward	Boston
1937	Lulu	Berg	Berg	Zürich
1945	Peter Grimes	Britten	Slater	London
1946	War and Peace	Prokofiev	Prokofiev/Mendelson	Leningrad
1951	The Rake's Progress	Stravinsky	Auden/Kallman	Venice
1978	Paradise Lost	Penderecki	Fry	Chicago
1984	Akhnaten	Glass	Glass	Stuttgart
1986	The Mask of Orpheus	Birtwistle	Zinovieff	London
1989	New Year	Tippett	Tippett	Houston
1992	Dienstag aus LICHT	Stockhausen	Stockhausen	Portugal

cracker Suite 1891–92. Formerly, the term meant a grouping of old dance forms.

symphonic poem term originated by Liszt for his 13 one-movement orchestral works that interpret a story from literature or history, also used by many other composers. Richard Strauss preferred the term 'tone poem'.

symphony musical composition for orchestra, traditionally in four separate but closely related movements. It developed from the smaller sonata form, the Italian overture, and the dance suite of the 18th century.

syncopation the deliberate upsetting of rhythm by shifting the accent to a beat that is normally unaccented.

tempo the speed at which a piece is played.

tenor the highest range of adult male voice when not using falsetto. It covers a two-octave range centred on middle C and is the preferred voice for operatic heroic roles.

timbre the tone colour of an instrument.

tonality the observance of a key structure; that is, the recognition of the importance of a tonic or key note and of the diatonic scale built upon it.

vibrato slight but rapid fluctuation of intensity or pitch in voice or instrument.

Great Composers

Bach Johann Sebastian 1685–1750. German composer. He was a master of counterpoint, and his music epitomizes the Baroque polyphonic style. His orchestral music includes the six *Brandenburg Concertos*, other concertos for keyboard instrument and violin, and four orchestral suites. Bach's keyboard music, for clavier and organ, his fugues, and his choral music are of equal importance. He also wrote chamber music and songs.

Bartók Béla 1881–1945. Hungarian composer who developed a personal musical language, combining folk elements with mathematical concepts of tone and rhythmic proportion. His large output includes six string quartets, concertos, an opera, and graded teaching pieces for piano.

Beethoven Ludwig van 1770–1827. German composer and pianist whose mastery of musical expression in every genre made him the dominant influence on 19th-century music. Beethoven's repertoire includes concert overtures; the opera *Fidelio*; five piano concertos and two for violin (one unfinished); 32 piano sonatas, including the *Moonlight* and *Appassionata*; 17 string quartets; the *Mass in D (Missa solemnis)*; and nine symphonies, as well as many youthful works. He usually played his own piano pieces and conducted his orchestral works until he was hampered by deafness 1801; nevertheless he continued to compose.

Berg Alban 1885–1935. Austrian composer. He studied under Arnold Schoenberg and was associated with him as one of the leaders of the serial, or 12-tone, school of composition. His output includes orchestral, chamber, and vocal music as well as two operas, *Wozzeck* 1925, a grim story of working-class life, and the unfinished *Lulu* 1929–35.

Berlioz (Louis) Hector 1803–1869. French Romantic composer, the founder of modern orchestration. Much of his music was inspired by drama and literature and has a theatrical quality. He wrote symphonic works, such as *Symphonie fantastique* 1830-31 and *Roméo et Juliette* 1839; dramatic cantatas, including *La Damnation de Faust* 1846 and *L'Enfance du Christ* 1854; sacred music; and three operas.

Brahms Johannes 1833–1897. German composer, pianist, and conductor who is considered one of the greatest composers of symphonic music and songs. His works include four symphonies; lieder (songs); concertos for piano and for violin; chamber music; sonatas; and the choral *A German Requiem* 1868.

Britten (Edward) Benjamin 1913–1976. English composer. He often wrote for the individual voice; for example, the role in the opera *Peter Grimes* 1945, based on verses by George Crabbe, was created for English tenor Peter Pears (1910–1986). Among his many works are the *Young Person's Guide to the Orchestra* 1946; the chamber opera *The Rape of Lucretia* 1946; *Billy Budd* 1951; *A Midsummer Night's Dream* 1960; and *Death in Venice* 1973.

Bruckner (Joseph) Anton 1824–1896. Austrian Romantic composer. He was cathedral organist at Linz 1856–68, and from 1868 he was professor at the Vienna Conservatoire. His works include many choral pieces and 11 symphonies, the last unfinished. His compositions were influenced by Richard Wagner and Beethoven.

Chopin Frédéric (François) 1810–1849. Polish composer and pianist. He made his debut as a pianist at the age of eight. As a performer, Chopin revolutionized the technique of pianoforte-playing, turning the hands outwards and favouring a light, responsive touch. His compositions for piano, which include two concertos and other works with orchestra, are characterized by great volatility of mood, and rhythmic fluidity.

Debussy (Achille-) Claude 1862–1918. French composer. He broke with the dominant tradition of German Romanticism and introduced new qualities of melody and harmony based on the whole-tone scale, evoking oriental music. His work includes *Prélude à l'après-midi d'un faune* 1894 and the opera *Pelléas et Mélisande* 1902.

Dvořák Antonín (Leopold) 1841–1904. Czech composer. International recognition came with his series of *Slavonic Dances* 1877–86, and he was director of the National Conservatory, New York, 1892–95. Works such as his *New World Symphony* 1893 reflect his interest in American folk themes, including black and native American. He wrote nine symphonies; tone poems; operas, including *Rusalka* 1900; large-scale choral works; the *Carnival* 1891–92 and other overtures; violin and cello concertos; chamber music; piano pieces; and songs. His Romantic music extends the Classical tradition of Beethoven and Brahms and displays the influence of Czech folk music.

Elgar Edward (William) 1857–1934. English composer. His *Enigma Variations* appeared 1899, and although his choral work, the oratorio setting of John

Henry Newman's *The Dream of Gerontius*, was initially a failure, it was well received in Düsseldorf, Germany, in 1902. Many of his earlier works were then performed, including the *Pomp and Circumstance* marches.

Franck César Auguste 1822–1890. Belgian composer. His music, mainly religious and Romantic in style, includes the Symphony in D minor 1866–68, *Symphonic Variations* 1885 for piano and orchestra, the *Violin Sonata* 1886, the oratorio *Les Béatitudes/The Beatitudes* 1879, and many organ pieces.

Grieg Edvard Hagerup 1843–1907. Norwegian composer. Much of his music is small-scale, particularly his songs, dances, sonatas, and piano works. Among his orchestral works are the *Piano Concerto* 1869 and the incidental music for Henrik Ibsen's drama *Peer Gynt* 1876.

Handel Georg Friedrich 1685–1759. German composer who became a British subject 1726. His first opera, *Almira*, was performed in Hamburg 1705. In 1710 he was appointed Kapellmeister to the elector of Hanover (the future George I of England). In 1712 he settled in England, where he established his popularity with such works as the *Water Music* 1717 (written for George I). His great choral works include the *Messiah* 1742 and the later oratorios *Samson* 1743, *Belshazzar* 1745, *Judas Maccabaeus* 1747, and *Jephtha* 1752.

Haydn Franz Joseph 1732–1809. Austrian composer. A teacher of Mozart and Beethoven, he was a major exponent of the classical sonata form in his numerous chamber and orchestral works (he wrote more than 100 symphonies). He also composed choral music, including the oratorios *The Creation* 1798 and *The Seasons* 1801. He was the first great master of the string quartet.

Janáček Leoš 1854–1928. Czech composer. He became director of the Conservatoire at Brno in 1919 and professor at the Prague Conservatoire in 1920. His music, highly original and influenced by Moravian folk music, includes arrangements of folk songs, operas (*Jenůfa* 1904, *The Cunning Little Vixen* 1924), and the choral *Glagolitic Mass* 1926.

Liszt Franz 1811–1886. Hungarian pianist and composer. An outstanding virtuoso of the piano, he was an established concert artist by the age of 12. His expressive, romantic, and frequently chromatic works include piano music (*Transcendental Studies* 1851), symphonies, piano concertos, and organ music. Much of his music is programmatic; he also originated the symphonic poem.

Mahler Gustav 1860–1911. Austrian composer and conductor whose work displays a synthesis of Romanticism and new uses of chromatic harmonies and musical forms. He composed 14 symphonies, including three unnumbered (as a student), nine massive repertoire symphonies, the titled *Das Lied von der Erde/Song of the Earth* 1909, and the incomplete *Symphony No. 10*. He also wrote song cycles.

Mendelssohn (-Bartholdy) (Jakob Ludwig) Felix 1809–1847. German composer, also a pianist and conductor. As a child he composed and performed with his own orchestra and as an adult was helpful to Schumann's career. Among his best-known works

are *A Midsummer Night's Dream* 1827; the *Fingal's Cave* overture 1832; and five symphonies, which include the Reformation 1830, the Italian 1833, and the Scottish 1842. He was instrumental in promoting the revival of interest in J S Bach's music.

Messiaen Olivier 1908–1992. French composer and organist. His music is mystical in character, vividly coloured, and incorporates transcriptions of birdsong. Among his works are the *Quartet for the End of Time* 1941, the large-scale *Turangalîla Symphony* 1949, and solo organ and piano pieces.

Monteverdi Claudio (Giovanni Antonio) 1567–1643. Italian composer. He contributed to the development of the opera with *Orfeo* 1607 and *The Coronation of Poppea* 1642. He also wrote madrigals, motets, and sacred music, notably the *Vespers* 1610.

Mozart Wolfgang Amadeus 1756–1791. Austrian composer and performer who showed astonishing precocity as a child and was an adult virtuoso. He was trained by his father, **Leopold Mozart** (1719–1787). From an early age he composed prolifically, his works including 27 piano concertos, 23 string quartets, 35 violin sonatas, and more than 50 symphonies including the E flat K543, G minor K550, and C major K551 ('Jupiter') symphonies, all composed 1788. His operas include *Idomeneo* 1781, *Le Nozze di Figaro/The Marriage of Figaro* 1786, *Don Giovanni* 1787, *Così fan tutte/Thus Do All Women* 1790, and *Die Zauberflöte/The Magic Flute* 1791. Strongly influenced by Haydn, Mozart's music marks the height of the Classical age in its purity of melody and form.

Mussorgsky Modest Petrovich 1839–1881. Russian composer who was largely self-taught. His opera *Boris Godunov* was completed in 1869, although not produced in St Petersburg until 1874. Some of his works were 'revised' by Rimsky-Korsakov, and only recently has their harsh original beauty been recognized.

Nielsen Carl (August) 1865–1931. Danish composer. His works show a progressive tonality, as in his opera *Saul and David* 1902 and six symphonies.

Palestrina Giovanni Pierluigi da 1525–1594. Italian composer of secular and sacred choral music. Apart from motets and madrigals, he also wrote 105 masses, including *Missa Papae Marcelli*.

Prokofiev Sergey (Sergeyevich) 1891–1953. Russian composer. His music includes operas such as *The Love for Three Oranges* 1921; ballets, including *Romeo and Juliet* 1935; seven symphonies, including the *Classical Symphony* 1916–17; music for films; piano and violin concertos; songs and cantatas (for example, that composed for the 30th anniversary of the October Revolution); and *Peter and the Wolf* 1936.

Puccini Giacomo (Antonio Domenico Michele Secondo Maria) 1858–1924. Italian opera composer whose music shows a strong gift for melody and dramatic effect and whose operas combine exotic plots with elements of *verismo* (realism). They include *Manon Lescaut* 1893, *La Bohème* 1896, *Tosca* 1900, *Madame Butterfly* 1904, and the unfinished *Turandot* 1926.

Purcell Henry 1659–1695. English Baroque composer. His work can be highly expressive; for example, the opera *Dido and Aeneas* 1689 and music for Dryden's *King Arthur* 1691 and for *The Fairy Queen* 1692. He wrote more than 500 works, ranging from secular operas and incidental music for plays to cantatas and church music.

Rachmaninov Sergei (Vasilevich) 1873–1943. Russian composer, conductor, and pianist. After the 1917 Revolution he went to the USA. His dramatically emotional Romantic music has a strong melodic basis and includes operas, such as *Francesca da Rimini* 1906, three symphonies, four piano concertos, piano pieces, and songs. Among his other works are the *Prelude in C-Sharp Minor* 1882 and *Rhapsody on a Theme of Paganini* 1934 for piano and orchestra.

Ravel (Joseph) Maurice 1875–1937. French composer. His work is characterized by its sensuousness, unresolved dissonances, and tone colour. Examples are the piano pieces *Pavane pour une infante défunte* 1899 and *Jeux d'eau* 1901, and the ballets *Daphnis et Chloë* 1912 and *Boléro* 1928.

Rimsky-Korsakov Nikolay Andreyevich 1844– 1908. Russian composer. He used Russian folk idiom and rhythms in his Romantic compositions and published a text on orchestration. His operas include *The Maid of Pskov* 1873, *The Snow Maiden* 1882, *Mozart and Salieri* 1898, and *The Golden Cockerel* 1907, a satirical attack on despotism that was banned until 1909.

Rossini Gioacchino (Antonio) 1792–1868. Italian composer. His first success was the opera *Tancredi* 1813. In 1816 his 'opera buffa' *Il barbiere di Siviglia/The Barber of Seville* was produced in Rome. During 1815–23 he produced 20 operas, and took a leading part in creating the 19th-century Italian operatic style.

Saint-Saëns (Charles) Camille 1835–1921. French composer, pianist and organist. Among his many lyrical Romantic pieces are concertos, the symphonic poem *Danse macabre* 1875, the opera *Samson et Dalila* 1877, and the orchestral *Carnaval des animaux/Carnival of the Animals* 1886.

Schoenberg Arnold (Franz Walter) 1874–1951. Austro-Hungarian composer, a US citizen from 1941. After Romantic early works such as *Verklärte Nacht/Transfigured Night* 1899 and the *Gurre-lieder/Songs of Gurra* 1900–11, he experimented with atonality (absence of key), producing works such as *Pierrot Lunaire* 1912 for chamber ensemble and voice, before developing the 12-tone system of musical composition. This was further developed by his pupils Alban Berg and Anton Webern (1883–1945).

Schubert Franz (Peter) 1797–1828. Austrian composer. His ten symphonies include the incomplete eighth in B minor (the 'Unfinished') and the 'Great' in C major. He wrote chamber and piano music, including the 'Trout Quintet', and over 600 lieder (songs) combining the Romantic expression of emotion with pure melody. They include the cycles *Die schöne Müllerin/The Beautiful Maid of the Mill* 1823 and *Die Winterreise/The Winter Journey* 1827.

Schumann Robert Alexander 1810–1856. German Romantic composer. His songs and short piano pieces show simplicity combined with an ability to portray mood and emotion. Among his compositions are four symphonies, a violin concerto, a piano concerto, sonatas, and song cycles, such as *Dichterliebe/Poet's Love* 1840. Felix Mendelssohn championed many of his works.

Shostakovich Dmitry (Dmitriyevich) 1906–1975. Soviet composer. His music is tonal, expressive, and sometimes highly dramatic; it was not always to official Soviet taste. He wrote 15 symphonies, chamber music, ballets, and operas, the latter including *Lady Macbeth of Mtsensk* 1934, which was suppressed as 'too divorced from the proletariat', but revived as *Katerina Izmaylova* 1963.

Sibelius Jean (Christian) 1865–1957. Finnish composer. His works include nationalistic symphonic poems such as *En saga* 1893 and *Finlandia* 1900, a violin concerto 1904, and seven symphonies.

Smetana Bedřich 1824–1884. Czech composer whose music has a distinct national character, as in, for example, the operas *The Bartered Bride* 1866 and *Dalibor* 1868, and the symphonic suite *My Country* 1875–80.

Stockhausen Karlheinz 1928– . German composer of avant-garde music who has continued to explore new musical sounds and compositional techniques since the 1950s. His major works include *Gesang der Jünglinge* 1956, *Kontakte* 1960 (electronic music), and *Sirius* 1977. Since 1977 all his works have been part of *LICHT*, a cycle of seven musical ceremonies intended for performance on the evenings of a week. He completed the fourth, *Dienstag*, 1992.

Strauss Johann (Baptist) 1825–1899. Austrian conductor and composer, the son of composer *Johann Strauss* (1804–1849). In 1872 he gave up conducting and wrote operettas, such as *Die Fledermaus* 1874, and numerous waltzes, such as *The Blue Danube* and *Tales from the Vienna Woods*, which gained him the title 'the Waltz King'.

Strauss Richard (Georg) 1864–1949. German composer and conductor. He followed the German Romantic tradition but had a strongly personal style, characterized by his bold, colourful orchestration. He first wrote tone poems such as *Don Juan* 1889, *Till Eulenspiegel's Merry Pranks* 1895, and *Also sprach Zarathustra* 1896. He then moved on to opera with *Salome* 1905 and *Elektra* 1909, both of which have elements of polytonality. He reverted to a more traditional style with *Der Rosenkavalier* 1911.

Stravinsky Igor 1882–1971. Russian composer, later of French (1934) and US (1945) nationality. He studied under Rimsky-Korsakov and wrote the music for the ballets *The Firebird* 1910, *Petrushka* 1911, and *The Rite of Spring* 1913 (controversial at the time for their unorthodox rhythms and harmonies). His versatile work ranges from his Neo-Classical ballet *Pulcinella* 1920 to the choral- orchestral *Symphony of Psalms* 1930. He later made use of serial techniques in such works as the *Canticum Sacrum* 1955 and the ballet *Agon* 1953–57.

Tchaikovsky Pyotr Il'yich 1840–1893. Russian composer. His strong sense of melody, personal expression, and brilliant orchestration are clear

Some musical expressions

Expression	Meaning	Expression	Meaning
accelerando	gradually faster	*quasi*	sort of, rather
adagio, adagietto	easy-going	*ripieno*	the accompanying ensemble
agitato	agitated	*ritardando*	gradually coming to a stop
alla breve	four beat as two to the bar	*ritenuto*	pulling back
allargando	spreading out in tempo	*ritornello*	refrain
allegro, allegretto	with lightness of action	*rubato*	borrowed (time)
andante, andantino	with movement	*secco*	with a dry tone
brio, con	with spirit	*segno*	cue sign
calando	winding down, slower and softer	*segue*	follow on
		sempre	always
cantabile	singing	*sforzato, sforzando*	with a forced tone
capo (da)	from the top (beginning)	*smorzando*	smothering, stifling the tone
concerto	the solo (group)	*sotto voce*	in an undertone
crescendo	gradually louder	*spiccato*	bounced (of the bow off the string)
deciso	firmly		
diminuendo	gradually softer	*staccato, -issimo*	short, very short
divisi a 2, 3, etc.	divided in 2, 3, etc. parts	*subito*	sudden, suddenly
dolce, dolcissimo	soft and sweetly	*Takt*	(German) beat, metre, bar (measure)
doloroso	mournfully		
espressivo	with expression	*tema*	theme
flatterzunge	(German) fluttertongue	*tenuto*	holding back
fuoco, con	with fire	*tessitura*	range of instrument or voice
giocoso	with fun	*tranquillo*	calmly
grave	with gravity	*tanto*	so much
largo, larghetto	expansively	*troppo*	too much
legato	smoothly	*via*	remove (eg mute)
lento	slowly	*veloce*	at speed
l'istesso (tempo)	the same (tempo)	*vivo, vivace*	with life
loco	in (its usual) place	*voce, voci*	voice, voices
lungo, lunga	long	*volante*	as though flying
misterioso	mysteriously	*wieder*	(German) again
molto	much, very	*Zeitmass*	(German) tempo
pesante	weightily	*zingaresca*	gipsy
poco, pochissimo	a little, very little	*zu 2*	(German) 1. for 2 players; 2. in 2 parts
portamento	lifting (note to note)		
presto, prestissimo	at speed, at high speed		

throughout his many Romantic works, which include six symphonies, three piano concertos, a violin concerto, operas (for example, *Eugene Onegin* 1879), ballets (for example, *The Nutcracker* 1892), orchestral fantasies (for example, *Romeo and Juliet* 1870), and chamber and vocal music.

Varèse Edgard 1885–1965. French composer who settled in New York 1916 where he founded the New Symphony Orchestra 1919 to advance the cause of modern music. His work is experimental and often dissonant, combining electronic sounds with orchestral instruments, and includes *Hyperprism* 1923, *Intégrales* 1931, and *Poème Electronique* 1958.

Verdi Giuseppe (Fortunino Francesco) 1813–1901. Italian opera composer of the Romantic period, who took his native operatic style to new heights of dramatic expression. In 1842 he wrote the opera *Nabucco*, followed by *Ernani* 1844 and *Rigoletto* 1851. Other works include *Il Trovatore* and *La Traviata* both 1853, *Aida* 1871, and the masterpieces of his old age, *Otello* 1887 and *Falstaff* 1893. His *Requiem*

1874 commemorates novelist Alessandro Manzoni (1785–1873).

Vivaldi Antonio (Lucio) 1678–1741. Italian Baroque composer, violinist, and conductor. He wrote 23 symphonies, 75 sonatas, over 400 concertos, including the *Four Seasons* (*c.* 1725) for violin and orchestra, over 40 operas, and much sacred music. His work was largely neglected until the 1930s.

Wagner Richard 1813–1883. German opera composer. He revolutionized the 19th-century conception of opera, envisaging it as a wholly new art form in which musical, poetic, and scenic elements should be unified through such devices as the leitmotiv (recurring theme). His operas include *Tannhäuser* 1845, *Lohengrin* 1850, and *Tristan und Isolde* 1865. In 1872 he founded the Festival Theatre in Bayreuth; his masterpiece *Der Ring des Nibelungen/The Ring of the Nibelung*, a sequence of four operas, was first performed there in 1876. His last work, *Parsifal*, was produced in 1882.

Popular Music and Jazz

Armstrong Louis ('Satchmo') 1901–1971. US jazz cornet and trumpet player and singer. His Chicago recordings in the 1920s with the Hot Five and Hot Seven brought him recognition for his warm and pure trumpet tone, his skill at improvisation, and his quirky, gravelly voice. From the 1930s he also appeared in films.

Beach Boys, the US pop group formed 1961. They began as exponents of vocal-harmony surf music with Chuck Berry guitar riffs (their hits include 'Surfin' USA' 1963 and 'Help Me, Rhonda' 1965) but the compositions, arrangements, and production by Brian Wilson (1942–) became highly complex under the influence of psychedelic rock, peaking with 'Good Vibrations' 1966.

Beatles, the English pop group 1960–70. The members, all born in Liverpool, were John Lennon (1940–80, rhythm guitar, vocals), Paul McCartney (1942– , bass, vocals), George Harrison (1943– , lead guitar, vocals), and Ringo Starr (Richard Starkey, 1940– , drums). Using songs written largely by Lennon and McCartney, the Beatles dominated rock music and pop culture in the 1960s.

beat music pop music that evolved in the UK in the early 1960s, known in its purest form as Mersey beat, and as British Invasion in the USA. The beat groups included the Beatles (1960–70), the Hollies (1962–), and the Zombies (1962–67).

bebop or **bop** hot jazz style, rhythmically complex, virtuosic, and highly improvisational, developed in New York 1940–55 by Charlie Parker, Dizzy Gillespie, Thelonius Monk, and other black musicians disaffected with dance bands.

Berry Chuck (Charles Edward) 1926– . US rock-and-roll singer, prolific songwriter, and guitarist. His characteristic guitar riffs became staples of rock music, and his humorous storytelling lyrics were also emulated. He had a string of hits in the 1950s and 1960s beginning with 'Maybellene' 1955.

bhangra pop music evolved in the UK in the late 1970s from traditional Punjabi music, combining electronic instruments and ethnic drums. Bhangra bands include Holle Holle, Alaap, and Heera. A 1990s development is *bhangramuffin*, a ragga-bhangra fusion popularized by Apache Indian (Steve Kapur, 1967–).

big-band jazz swing music created in the late 1930s and 1940s by bands of 13 or more players, such as those of Duke Ellington and Benny Goodman. Big-band jazz relied on fixed arrangements, where there is more than one instrument to some of the parts, rather than improvisation. Big bands were mainly dance bands, and they ceased to be economically viable in the 1950s.

blues African-American music that originated in the rural American South in the late 19th century, characterized by a 12-bar construction and frequently melancholy lyrics. The guitar has been the dominant instrument; harmonica and piano are also common. Blues guitar and vocal styles have played a vital part in the development of jazz, rock, and pop music in general.

1920s–30s The **rural** or **delta blues** was usually performed solo with guitar or harmonica, by such artists as Robert Johnson (*c.* 1912–1938) and Bukka White (1906–1977), but the earliest recorded style, **classic blues**, by such musicians as W C Handy (1873–1958) and Bessie Smith (1894–1937), was sung with a small band.

1940s–50s **The urban blues**, using electric amplification, emerged in the northern cities, chiefly Chicago. As exemplified by Howlin' Wolf (1910–1976), Muddy Waters (1915–1983), and John Lee Hooker (1917–), urban blues became **rhythm and blues**.

1960s The jazz-influenced smooth guitar style of B B King (1925–) inspired many musicians of the **British blues boom**, including Eric Clapton.

1980s The 'blues *noir*' of Robert Cray (1953–) contrasted with the rock-driven blues playing of Stevie Ray Vaughan (1955–1990).

boogie-woogie jazz played on the piano, using a repeated motif for the left hand. It was common in the USA from around 1900 to the 1950s. Boogie-woogie players included Pinetop Smith (1904–1929), Meade 'Lux' Lewis (1905–1964), and Jimmy Yancey (1898–1951). Rock-and-roll pianist Jerry Lee Lewis adapted the style.

Bowie David. Stage name of David Jones 1947– . English pop singer, songwriter, and actor whose career has been a series of image changes. His hits include 'Jean Genie' 1973, 'Rebel, Rebel' 1974, 'Golden Years' 1975, and 'Underground' 1986. He has acted in plays and films, including Nicolas Roeg's *The Man Who Fell to Earth* 1976. His 1993 album was *Black Tie White Noise*.

Brown James 1928– . US rhythm-and-blues and soul singer, a pioneer of funk. Staccato horn arrangements and shouted vocals characterize his hits, which include 'Please, Please, Please' 1956, 'Papa's Got a Brand New Bag' 1965, and 'Say It Loud, I'm Black and I'm Proud' 1968. In that year his TV appearance appealing for calm succeeded in restraining race riots in US cities. In the 1980s and 1990s his records were subject to much electronic sampling by rap musicians.

Byrds, the US pioneering folk-rock group 1964–73. Emulated for their 12-string guitar sound, as on the hits 'Mr Tambourine Man' (a 1965 version of Bob Dylan's song) and 'Eight Miles High' 1966, they moved towards country rock in the late 1960s, setting another trend.

Cajun music originating in the French-speaking community of Louisiana, USA. It has a lively rhythm and features steel guitar, fiddle, and accordion. Since the 1930s Cajun has fed into and drawn from country-and-western music. Cajun musicians include accordionist Nathan Abshire (1913–1981) and the Balfa Brothers Band (1946–1978).

calypso West Indian satirical ballad with a syncopated beat. Calypso is a traditional song form of Trinidad, a feature of its annual carnival, with roots in W African praise singing. It was first popularized in the USA by Harry Belafonte (1927–) in 1956. Mighty Sparrow (1935–) is Trinidad's best-known calypso singer.

Charles Ray 1930– . US singer, songwriter, and pianist whose first hits were 'I've Got A Woman' 1955, 'What'd I Say' 1959, and 'Georgia On My Mind' 1960. He has recorded gospel, blues, rock, soul, country, and rhythm and blues.

Clapton Eric 1945– . English blues and rock guitarist, singer, and songwriter. Originally a blues purist, then one of the pioneers of heavy rock with Cream 1966-68, he returned to the blues after making the landmark album *Layla and Other Assorted Love Songs* 1970 by Derek and the Dominos. Solo albums include *Journeyman* 1989 and the acoustic *Unplugged* 1992.

Coleman Ornette 1930– . US alto saxophonist and jazz composer. In the late 1950s he rejected the established structural principles of jazz for free avant-garde improvisation. He has worked with small and large groups, ethnic musicians of different traditions, and symphony orchestras. His albums include *The Shape of Jazz to Come* 1959, *Chappaqua Suite* 1965, and *Skies of America* 1972.

Coltrane John (William) 1926–1967. US jazz saxophonist who first came to prominence 1955 with the Miles Davis quintet, later playing with Thelonious Monk 1957. He was a powerful and individual artist, whose performances featured much experimentation. His 1960s quartet was highly regarded for its innovations in melody and harmony.

Costello Elvis. Stage name of Declan McManus 1954– . English rock singer, songwriter, and guitarist whose intricate yet impassioned lyrics have made him one of Britain's foremost songwriters. The great stylistic range of his work was evident from his 1977 debut *My Aim Is True* and was further extended 1993 when he collaborated with the classical Brodsky Quartet on the song cycle *The Juliet Letters*.

country and western or *country music* the popular music of the white US South and West; it evolved from the folk music of the English, Irish, and Scottish settlers and has a strong blues influence. Characteristic instruments are slide guitar, mandolin, and fiddle. Lyrics typically extol family values and traditional sex roles, and often have a strong narrative element. Country music encompasses a variety of regional styles, and ranges from mournful ballads to fast and intricate dance music.

history
1920s Jimmie Rodgers (1897–1933) wrote a series of 'Blue Yodel' songs that made him the first country-music recording star.

1930s Nashville, Tennessee, became a centre for the country-music industry, with the Grand Ole Opry a showcase for performers. The Carter Family arranged and recorded hundreds of traditional songs. Hollywood invented the singing cowboy.

1940s Hank Williams (1923–1953) emerged as the most significant singer and songwriter; *western swing* spread from Texas.

1950s The *honky-tonk* sound; Kentucky *bluegrass*; ballad singers included Jim Reeves (1923–1964) and Patsy Cline (1932–1963).

1960s Songs of the Bakersfield, California, school, dominated by Buck Owens (1929–) and Merle Haggard (1937–), contrasted with lush Nashville

productions of singers such as George Jones (1931–) and Tammy Wynette (1942–).

1970s Dolly Parton (1946–) and Emmylou Harris (1947–); the Austin, Texas, *outlaws* Willie Nelson (1933–) and Waylon Jennings (1937–); *country rock* pioneered by Gram Parsons (1946–1973).

1980s Neotraditionalist *new country* represented by Randy Travis (1963–), Dwight Yoakam (1957–), and k d lang (1961–).

1990s US pop charts invaded by cowboy-hat-wearing singers like Garth Brooks (1961–).

Crosby Bing (Harry Lillis) 1904–1977. US film actor and singer who achieved world success with his distinctive style of crooning in such songs as 'Pennies from Heaven' 1936 (featured in a film of the same name) and 'White Christmas' 1942. He won an acting Oscar for *Going My Way* 1944, and made a series of 'road' film comedies with Dorothy Lamour and Bob Hope, the last being *Road to Hong Kong* 1962.

Davis Miles (Dewey, Jr) 1926–1991. US jazz trumpeter, composer, and bandleader, one of the most influential and innovative figures in jazz. He pioneered bebop with Charlie Parker 1945, cool jazz in the 1950s, and jazz-rock fusion from the late 1960s. His albums include *Birth of the Cool* 1957 (recorded 1949 and 1950), *Sketches of Spain* 1959, *Bitches Brew* 1970, and *Tutu* 1985.

Dire Straits UK rock group formed 1977 by guitarist, singer, and songwriter Mark Knopfler (1949–). Their tasteful musicianship was tailormade for the new compact-disc audience, and their 1985 LP *Brothers in Arms* went on to sell 20 million copies. Other albums include *On Every Street* 1991. Knopfler is also much in demand as a producer.

disco music international style of dance music of the 1970s with a heavily emphasized beat, derived from *funk*. It was designed to be played in discotheques rather than performed live; hence the production was often more important than the performer, and drum machines came to dominate. Disco music was celebrated in the 1977 film *Saturday Night Fever*.

Dixieland jazz jazz style that originated in New Orleans, USA, in the early 20th century, dominated by cornet, trombone, and clarinet. The trumpeter Louis Armstrong emerged from this style. The *trad jazz* movement in the UK in the 1940s–50s was a Dixieland revival. The Rebirth Brass Band of New Orleans plays a funky 1990s version.

Doors, the US psychedelic rock group formed 1965 in Los Angeles with Jim Morrison (1943–1971) on vocals. Their first hit was 'Light My Fire' from their debut album *The Doors* 1967. They were noted for Morrison's poetic lyrics and flamboyant performance.

Dylan Bob. Adopted name of Robert Allen Zimmerman 1941– . US singer and songwriter whose lyrics provided catchphrases for a generation and influenced innumerable songwriters. He began in the folk-music tradition. His early songs, as on his albums *Freewheelin'* 1963 and *The Times They Are A-Changin'* 1964, were associated with the US civil-rights movement and antiwar protest. From 1965 he worked in an individualistic rock style, as on the albums *Highway 61 Revisited* 1965 and *Blonde on Blonde* 1966. Later work includes *Blood on the Tracks* 1975 and *Good As I Been to You* 1992.

Ellington Duke (Edward Kennedy) 1899–1974. US pianist who had an outstanding career as a composer and arranger of jazz. He wrote numerous pieces for his own jazz orchestra, accentuating the strengths of individual virtuoso instrumentalists, and became one of the leading figures in jazz over a 55-year period. Some of his most popular compositions include 'Mood Indigo', 'Sophisticated Lady', 'Solitude', and 'Black and Tan Fantasy'. He was one of the founders of big-band jazz.

Fitzgerald Ella 1918–1996. US jazz singer, recognized as one of the finest, most lyrical voices in jazz, both in solo work and with big bands. She is celebrated for her smooth interpretations of George and Ira Gershwin and Cole Porter songs.

funk dance music of black US origin, relying on heavy percussion in polyrhythmic patterns. Leading exponents include James Brown and George Clinton (1940–   ).

Gershwin George 1898–1937. US composer who wrote both 'serious' music, such as the tone poem *Rhapsody in Blue* 1924 and *An American in Paris* 1928, and popular musicals and songs, many with lyrics by his brother *Ira Gershwin* (1896–1983), including 'I Got Rhythm', "S Wonderful', and 'Embraceable You'. His opera *Porgy and Bess* 1935 incorporated jazz rhythms and popular song styles in an operatic format.

Gillespie Dizzy (John Birks) 1917–1993. US jazz trumpeter who, with Charlie Parker, was the chief creator and exponent of the bebop style (*Groovin' High* is a CD reissue of their seminal 78-rpm recordings).

Goodman Benny (Benjamin David) 1909–1986. US clarinetist, nicknamed the 'King of Swing' for the new jazz idiom he introduced with arranger Fletcher Henderson (1897–1952). In 1934 he founded his own 12-piece band, which combined the expressive improvisatory style of black jazz with disciplined precision ensemble playing. He is associated with such numbers as 'Blue Skies' and 'Let's Dance'.

gospel music vocal music developed in the 1920s in the black Baptist churches of the US South from spirituals. Outstanding among the early gospel singers was Mahalia Jackson, but from the 1930s to the mid-1950s male harmony groups predominated, among them the Dixie Hummingbirds, the Swan Silvertones, and the Five Blind Boys of Mississippi. The style they developed was continued into the 1990s.

grunge rock-music style of the early 1990s, characterized by a thick, abrasive, distorted sound. Grunge evolved from punk in the Seattle, Washington, USA, area and came to prominence with the chart success of the band Nirvana 1991. The Melvins (formed in Seattle early 1980s) pioneered grunge with their turbid, slow-moving sound. Pearl Jam (formed in Seattle 1990), with their powerful singer, have been the most commercially successful grunge-inspired group in the wake of Nirvana.

Guthrie Woody (Woodrow Wilson) 1912–1967. US folk singer and songwriter whose left-wing protest songs, 'dustbowl ballads', and 'talking blues' influenced, among others, Bob Dylan; they include 'Deportees', 'Hard Travelin'', and 'This Land Is Your Land'.

hardcore of any music style, the more extreme and generally less commercial end of the spectrum: hardcore techno is a minimalist electronic dance music; hardcore rap is aggressive or offensive; hardcore punk jettisons form and melody for speed and noise.

Hawkins Coleman (Randolph) 1904–1969. US virtuoso tenor saxophonist. He was, until 1934, a soloist in the swing band led by Fletcher Henderson (1898–1952), and was an influential figure in bringing the jazz saxophone to prominence as a solo instrument.

heavy metal rock style characterized by histrionic guitar solos and a macho swagger. Heavy metal developed out of the hard rock of the late 1960s and early 1970s, was performed by such groups as Led Zeppelin and Deep Purple, and enjoyed a resurgence in the late 1980s. Bands include Van Halen (formed 1974), Def Leppard (formed 1977), and Guns n' Roses (formed 1987).

Hendrix Jimi (James Marshall) 1942–1970. US rock guitarist, songwriter, and singer, legendary for his virtuoso experimental technique. *Are You Experienced?* 1967 was his first album. He greatly expanded the vocabulary of the electric guitar and influenced both rock and jazz musicians.

hip-hop popular music originating in New York in the early 1980s, created with scratching (a percussive effect obtained by manually rotating a vinyl record) and heavily accented electronic drums behind a rap vocal. Within a decade, digital sampling had largely superseded scratching. The term 'hip-hop' also comprises break dancing and graffiti.

Holiday Billie ('Lady Day'). Stage name of Eleanora Gough McKay 1915–1959. US jazz singer, known for her emotionally charged delivery and idiosyncratic phrasing; she brought a blues feel to performances with swing bands. Songs she made her own include 'Stormy Weather', 'Strange Fruit' and 'I Cover the Waterfront'.

Holly Buddy. Stage name of Charles Hardin Holley 1936–1959. US rock-and-roll singer, guitarist, and songwriter, born in Lubbock, Texas. Holly had a distinctive, hiccuping vocal style and was an early experimenter with recording techniques. Many of his hits with his band, the Crickets, such as 'That'll Be the Day' 1957, 'Peggy Sue' 1957, and 'Maybe Baby' 1958, have become classics.

house music dance music of the 1980s originating in the inner-city clubs of Chicago, USA, combining funk with European high-tech pop (techno), and using dub, digital sampling, and cross-fading. *Acid house* has minimal vocals and melody, instead surrounding the mechanically emphasized 4/4 beat with stripped-down synthesizer riffs and a wandering bass line. Other variants include *hip house*, with rap elements, and *acid jazz*.

indie (short for *independent*) any record label that is neither owned nor distributed by one of the large conglomerates ('majors') that dominate the industry.

Without a corporate bureaucratic structure, the independent labels are often quicker to respond to new trends and more idealistic in their aims. What has become loosely known as *indie music* therefore tends to be experimental, amateurish, or at the cutting edge of street fashion.

Jackson Michael 1958– . US rock singer and songwriter whose videos and live performances are meticulously choreographed. His first solo hit was 'Got to Be There' 1971; his worldwide popularity peaked with the albums *Thriller* 1982 and *Bad* 1987. The follow-up was *Dangerous* 1991.

jazz polyphonic, syncopated music characterized by solo virtuosic improvisation, which developed in the USA at the turn of the 20th century. Initially music for dancing, often with a vocalist, it had its roots in black American and other popular music. As jazz grew increasingly complex and experimental, various distinct forms evolved. Seminal musicians include Louis Armstrong, Charlie Parker, and John Coltrane.

jazz chronology
1880–1900 Originated chiefly in New Orleans from ragtime.

1920s During Prohibition, the centre of jazz moved to Chicago (Louis Armstrong, Bix Beiderbecke) and St Louis. By the end of the decade the focus had shifted to New York City (Art Tatum, Fletcher Henderson), to radio and recordings.

1930s The *swing* bands used call-and-response arrangements with improvised solos of voice and instruments (Paul Whiteman, Benny Goodman).

1940s Swing grew into the *big-band* era with jazz composed as well as arranged (Glenn Miller, Duke Ellington); rise of *West Coast* jazz (Stan Kenton) and rhythmically complex, highly improvised *bebop* (Charlie Parker, Dizzy Gillespie, Thelonius Monk).

1950s Jazz had ceased to be dance music; *cool jazz* (Stan Getz, Miles Davis, Lionel Hampton, Modern Jazz Quartet) developed in reaction to the insistent, 'hot' bebop and *hard bop*.

1960s Free-form or *free jazz* (Ornette Coleman, John Coltrane).

1970s Jazz rock (US group Weather Report, formed 1970; British guitarist John McLaughlin, 1942–); jazz funk (US saxophonist Grover Washington Jr, 1943–); more eclectic free jazz (US pianist Keith Jarrett, 1945–).

1980s Resurgence of tradition (US trumpeter Wynton Marsalis, 1962– ; British saxophonist Courtney Pine, 1965–) and avant-garde (US chamber-music Kronos Quartet, formed 1978; anarchic British group Loose Tubes, 1983–89).

karaoke amateur singing in public to prerecorded backing tapes. Karaoke originated in Japan and spread to other parts of the world in the 1980s. Karaoke machines are jukeboxes of backing tracks to well-known popular songs, usually with a microphone attached and lyrics displayed on a video screen.

lang k d 1961– . Canadian singer. Her mellifluous voice and androgynous image gained her a wide following beyond the country-music field where she first established herself. Her albums include *Angel With a*

Lariat 1987, *Shadowland* 1988, *Absolute Torch and Twang* 1989, and the mainstream *Ingénue* 1992.

Lennon John (Ono) 1940–1980. UK rock singer, songwriter, and guitarist, in the USA from 1971; a founder member of the Beatles. Both before the band's break-up 1969 and in his solo career, he collaborated intermittently with his wife **Yoko Ono** (1933–). 'Give Peace a Chance', a hit 1969, became an anthem of the peace movement. His solo work alternated between the confessional and the political, as on the album *Imagine* 1971. He was shot dead by a fan.

Madonna Stage name of Madonna Louise Veronica Ciccone 1958– . US pop singer and actress who presents herself on stage and in videos with an exaggerated sexuality. Her first hit was 'Like a Virgin' 1984; others include 'Material Girl' 1985 and 'Like a Prayer' 1989. Her films include *Desperately Seeking Susan* 1985, *Dick Tracy* 1990, and the documentary *In Bed with Madonna* 1991. Her dance album *Erotica* 1992 coincided with the publication of her book *Sex*.

Marley Bob (Robert Nesta) 1945–1981. Jamaican reggae singer and songwriter, a Rastafarian whose songs, many of which were topical and political, popularized reggae worldwide in the 1970s. They include 'Get Up, Stand Up' 1973 and 'No Woman No Cry' 1974; his albums include *Natty Dread* 1975 and *Exodus* 1977.

Miller Glenn 1904–1944. US trombonist and, as bandleader, exponent of the big-band swing sound from 1938. He composed his signature tune 'Moonlight Serenade' (a hit 1939). Miller became leader of the US Army Air Force Band in Europe 1942, made broadcasts to troops throughout the world during World War II, and disappeared without a trace on a flight between England and France.

Mingus Charles 1922–1979. US jazz bassist and composer. He played with Louis Armstrong, Duke Ellington, and Charlie Parker. Based on the West Coast until 1951, he took part in the development of cool jazz, and his experimentation with atonality and dissonant effects opened the way for the new style of free collective jazz improvisation of the 1960s.

Monk Thelonious (Sphere) 1917–1982. US jazz pianist and composer who took part in the development of bebop. He had a highly idiosyncratic style, but numbers such as 'Round Midnight' and 'Blue Monk' have become standards. Monk worked in New York during the Depression, and became popular in the 1950s.

Morrison Van (George Ivan) 1945– . Northern Irish singer and songwriter whose jazz-inflected Celtic soul style was already in evidence on *Astral Weeks* 1968 and has been highly influential. Among other albums are *Tupelo Honey* 1971, *Veedon Fleece* 1974, and *Hymns to the Silence* 1991.

New Age instrumental or ambient music of the 1980s, often semi-acoustic or electronic; less insistent than rock.

New Wave style that evolved parallel to punk in the second half of the 1970s. It shared the urban aggressive spirit of punk but was musically and lyrically more sophisticated; examples are the early work of Elvis Costello and Talking Heads.

Parker Charlie (Charles Christopher 'Bird', 'Yardbird') 1920–1955. US alto saxophonist and jazz composer, associated with the trumpeter Dizzy Gillespie in developing the bebop style. His skilful improvisations inspired performers on all jazz instruments.

pop music or *popular music* any contemporary music not categorizable as jazz or classical. Pop became distinct from folk music with the advent of sound-recording techniques, and has incorporated blues, country and western, and music-hall elements; electronic amplification and other technological innovations have played a large part in the creation of new styles. The traditional format is a song of roughly three minutes with verse, chorus, and middle eight bars.

1910s The singer Al Jolson was one of the first recording stars. Ragtime was still popular.

1920s In the USA Paul Whiteman and his orchestra played jazz that could be danced to, country singer Jimmie Rodgers reached a new record-buying public, the blues was burgeoning; in the UK popular singers included Al Bowlly (1899–1941, born in Mozambique).

1930s Crooner Bing Crosby and vocal groups such as the Andrews Sisters were the alternatives to swing bands.

1940s Rhythm and blues evolved in the USA while Frank Sinatra was a teen idol and Glenn Miller played dance music; the UK preferred such singers as Vera Lynn.

1950s In the USA *doo-wop* group vocalizing preceded *rockabilly* and the rise of *rock and roll* (Elvis Presley, Chuck Berry). British pop records were often cover versions of US originals.

1960s The Beatles and the *Mersey beat* transcended UK borders, followed by the Rolling Stones, *hard rock* (the Who, Led Zeppelin), and *art rock* (Genesis, Yes). In the USA *surf music* (group harmony vocals or guitar-based instrumentals) preceded *Motown*, *folk rock* (the Byrds, Bob Dylan), and *blues rock* (Jimi Hendrix, Janis Joplin). *Psychedelic rock* evolved from 1966 on both sides of the Atlantic (the Doors, Pink Floyd, Jefferson Airplane).

1970s The first half of the decade produced *glitter rock* (David Bowie), *heavy metal*, and *disco*; in the UK also *pub rock* (a return to basics, focusing on live performance); *reggae* spread from Jamaica. From 1976 *punk* was ascendant; the US term *New Wave* encompassed bands not entirely within the punk idiom (Talking Heads, Elvis Costello).

1980s Punk continued as *hardcore* or mutated into *gothic*; dance music developed regional US variants: *hip-hop* (New York), *go-go* (Washington DC), and *house* (Chicago). Live audiences grew, leading to anthemic *stadium rock* (U2, Bruce Springsteen) and increasingly elaborate stage performances (Michael Jackson, Prince, Madonna). An interest in *world music* sparked new fusions.

1990s Rap, hard rock, and heavy metal predominated in the USA at the start of the decade; on the UK *indie* scene, dance music (Happy Mondays, Primal Scream) and a new wave of guitar groups (Ride, Lush) drew on the psychedelic era. Germany in particular produced minimalist *techno* dance music.

Reggae gave way to *ragga*. *Grunge* emerged from Seattle, Washington, USA.

Porter Cole (Albert) 1892–1964. US composer and lyricist, mainly of musical comedies. His witty, sophisticated songs like 'Let's Do It' 1928, 'I Get a Kick Out of You' 1934, and 'Don't Fence Me In' 1944 have been widely recorded and admired. His shows, many of which were made into films, include *The Gay Divorcee* 1932 and *Kiss Me Kate* 1948.

Presley Elvis (Aron) 1935–1977. US singer and acoustic guitarist, the most influential performer of the rock-and-roll era. With his recordings for Sun Records in Memphis, Tennessee, 1954–55 and early hits such as 'Heartbreak Hotel', 'Hound Dog', and 'Love Me Tender', all 1956, he created an individual vocal style, influenced by Southern blues, gospel music, country music, and rhythm and blues. His records continued to sell in their millions into the 1990s.

Prince Stage name of Prince Rogers Nelson 1960– . US pop musician who composes, arranges, and produces his own records and often plays all the instruments. His albums, including *1999* 1982, *Purple Rain* 1984, and the 1992 release with a symbol instead of a name, contain elements of rock, funk, and jazz. His stage shows are energetic and extravagant. He has also starred in several films, including *Graffiti Bridge* 1990. In 1993, Prince announced that he had changed his name to that of the symbol used on his 1992 album.

psychedelic rock or *acid rock* pop music that usually involves advanced electronic equipment for both light and sound. The free-form improvisations and light shows that appeared about 1966, attempting to suggest or improve on mind-altering drug experiences, had by the 1980s evolved into stadium performances with lasers and other special effects.

punk rock style of the late 1970s that stressed aggressive, amateurish performance within a three-chord, three-minute format, as exemplified by the Sex Pistols. The lyrics and associated fashions were designed to shock or intimidate. Punk rock began in the UK but drew heavily on earlier US garage bands. Hardcore punk and grunge are derivations.

ragga type of reggae music with a rhythmic, rapid-fire, semi-spoken vocal line. A macho swagger is a common element in the lyrics. Influenced by rap, ragga developed around 1990 from toasting, the earliest talkover style. Performers and fans of ragga call themselves *ragamuffins*. Ragga performers include the Jamaicans Shabba Ranks, Anthony Red Rose, and Ninja Man; the ragga-rapper Daddy Freddy entered the *Guinness Book of Records* for cramming 528 syllables into 60 seconds (May 1991).

ragtime syncopated music ('ragged time') in 2/4 rhythm, usually played on piano. It developed in the USA among black musicians in the late 19th century; it was influenced by folk tradition, minstrel shows, and marching bands, and was later incorporated into jazz. Scott Joplin was a leading writer of ragtime pieces, called 'rags'.

raï Algerian pop music developed in the 1970s from the Bedouin song form *melhoun*, using synthesizers and electronic drums. Singers often take the name Cheb or Cheba ('young'); for example, Cheb Khaled, Cheb Mami.

rap music rapid, rhythmic chant over a prerecorded repetitive backing track. Rap emerged in New York 1979 as part of the hip-hop culture, although the macho, swaggering lyrics that initially predominated have ancient roots in ritual boasts and insults. By the 1990s, the main schools were gangsta rap (violent) and conscious rap (extolling peaceful coexistence), divided more by content than style, and the more relaxed jazz rap.

Reed Lou 1942– . US rock singer, songwriter, and guitarist; member (1965–70 and 1993–) of the New York avant-garde group *the Velvet Underground*, one of the most influential bands of the 1960s. His solo work deals largely with urban alienation and angst, and includes the albums *Berlin* 1973, *Street Hassle* 1978, and *New York* 1989.

reggae predominant West Indian popular music of the 1970s and 1980s, characterized by a heavily accented offbeat and a thick bass line. The lyrics often refer to Rastafarianism. Musicians include Bob Marley, Lee 'Scratch' Perry (1940– , performer and producer), and the group Black Uhuru (1974–). Reggae is also played in the UK, South Africa, and elsewhere.

remix the studio practice of reassembling a recording from all or some of its individual components, often with the addition of new elements. As a commercial concept, remixes accompanied the rise of the 12-inch single in the 1980s.

rhythm and blues (R & B) US popular music of the 1940s–60s, which drew on swing and jump-jazz rhythms and blues vocals, and was a progenitor of rock and roll. It diversified into soul, funk, and other styles. R & B artists include Bo Diddley (1928–), Jackie Wilson (1934–84), and Etta James (*c.* 1938–).

Robinson Smokey (William) 1940– . US singer, songwriter, and record producer, associated with Motown records from its conception. He was lead singer of the Miracles 1957–72 (hits include 'Shop Around' 1961, 'The Tears of a Clown' 1970) and his solo hits include 'Cruisin'' 1979 and 'Being With You' 1981. His light tenor voice and wordplay characterize his work.

rock and roll pop music born of a fusion of rhythm and blues and country and western and based on electric guitar and drums. In the mid-1950s, with the advent of Elvis Presley, it became the heartbeat of teenage rebellion in the West and also had considerable impact on other parts of the world. It found perhaps its purest form in late-1950s rockabilly, the style of white Southerners in the USA; the blanket term 'rock' later came to comprise a multitude of styles.

Rolling Stones, the British band formed 1962, once notorious as the 'bad boys' of rock. Original members included Mick Jagger (1943–), Keith Richards (1943–), and Brian Jones (1942–1969). Classic early hits like 'Satisfaction' 1965 and the albums from *Beggars Banquet* 1968 to *Exile on Main Street* 1972 have been rated among their best work; other albums include *Some Girls* 1978 and *Steel Wheels* 1989. A rock-and-roll institution, the Rolling Stones were still performing and recording in the 1990s.

salsa Latin big-band dance music popularized by Puerto Ricans in New York City in the 1970s–80s

and by, among others, the Panamanian singer Rubén Blades (1948–).

Simon Paul 1942– . US pop singer and songwriter. In a folk-rock duo with Art Garfunkel (1942–), he had such hits as 'Mrs Robinson' 1968 and 'Bridge Over Troubled Water' 1970. Simon's solo work includes the critically acclaimed album *Graceland* 1986, for which he drew on Cajun and African music, and *The Rhythm of the Saints* 1990.

Sinatra Frank (Francis Albert) 1915– . US singer and film actor, celebrated for his phrasing and emotion, especially on love ballads. He is particularly associated with the song 'My Way'. His films from 1941 include *From Here to Eternity* 1953 (Academy Award) and *Guys and Dolls* 1955. He was still performing in the 1980s.

Smiths, the English four-piece rock group (1982–87) from Manchester. Their songs, with lyrics by singer Morrissey (1959–) and tunes by guitarist Johnny Marr (1964–), drew on diverse sources such as rockabilly and Mersey beat, with confessional humour and images of urban desolation. They had an intensely dedicated following in Britain and were one of the most popular indie bands. Morrissey went on to a solo career and Marr became a part-time member of The The and Electronic.

soca Latin Caribbean dance music, a mixture of *so*ul and *ca*lypso but closer to the latter. A soca band is likely to include conga drums, synthesizer, and a small horn section, as well as electric guitar, bass, and drums. Soca originated on Trinidad in the 1970s.

Sondheim Stephen (Joshua) 1930– . US composer and lyricist. He wrote the lyrics of Leonard Bernstein's *West Side Story* 1957 and composed witty and sophisticated musicals, including *A Little Night Music* 1973, *Pacific Overtures* 1976, *Sweeney Todd* 1979, *Into the Woods* 1987, and *Sunday in the Park with George* 1989.

soul music emotionally intense style of rhythm and blues sung by, among others, Sam Cooke (1935–1964), Aretha Franklin (1942–), and Al Green (1946–). With elements of blues, gospel music, and jazz, it emerged in the 1950s. Sometimes all popular music made by African-Americans is labelled soul music.

Spector Phil 1940– . US record producer, known for the 'wall of sound', created using a large orchestra, distinguishing his work in the early 1960s with vocal groups such as the Crystals and the Ronettes. He withdrew into semi-retirement in 1966 but his influence can still be heard.

Springsteen Bruce 1949– . US rock singer, songwriter, and guitarist, born in New Jersey. His work combines music in traditional rock idiom and reflective lyrics about working-class life and the pursuit of the American dream on such albums as *Born to Run* 1975, *Born in the USA* 1984, and *Human Touch* 1992.

stadium rock epic style of rock music developed in the 1980s. As live audiences grew, performers had to adapt their delivery and material to the size of the auditorium. Stadium rock is a music of broad gesture, windswept and brooding. The Irish U2 and Scottish Simple Minds (formed 1977) are formative stadium-rock bands.

steel band musical ensemble common in the West Indies, consisting mostly of percussion instruments made from oil drums that give a sweet, metallic ringing tone.

Supremes, the US vocal group, pioneers of the Motown sound, formed 1959 in Detroit. Beginning in 1962, the group was a trio comprising, initially, Diana Ross (1944–　), Mary Wilson (1944–　), and Florence Ballard (1943–1976). The most successful female group of the 1960s, they had a string of pop hits beginning with 'Where Did Our Love Go?' 1964 and 'Baby Love' 1964. Diana Ross left to pursue a solo career 1969.

swing music jazz style popular in the 1930s–40s, a big-band dance music with a simple harmonic base of varying tempo from the rhythm section (percussion, guitar, piano), harmonic brass and woodwind sections (sometimes strings), and superimposed solo melodic line from, for example, trumpet, clarinet, or saxophone. Exponents included Benny Goodman, Duke Ellington, and Glenn Miller, who introduced jazz to a mass white audience.

syncopation the deliberate upsetting of rhythm by shifting the accent to a beat that is normally unaccented.

Velvet Underground, the US avant-garde rock group formed 1965, dissolved 1969–72; reformed 1993. Their experiments with dissonance and abrasive noise proved highly influential in subsequent decades, as did the street-smart lyrics of guitarist and vocalist Lou Reed. Their albums include *The Velvet Underground and Nico* 1967, *White Light/White Heat* 1968, and *Loaded* 1970. Songs like 'Waiting for the Man' and 'Sweet Jane' have become classics, and the Velvet Underground's sound, image, and attitude have been endlessly imitated and invoked. A Velvet Underground reunion took place with the original line-up in Paris 1991 and led to a European tour 1993.

world music or *roots music* any music whose regional character has not been lost in the melting pot of the pop industry. Examples are W African *mbalax*, E African soukous, S African mbaqanga, French Antillean zouk, Javanese gamelan, Latin American salsa and lambada, Cajun music, European folk music, and rural blues, as well as combinations of these (flamenco guitar and kora; dub polka).

1920s Afro-Cuban dance music popularized in the USA by bandleader Xavier Cugat (1900–1990). Highlife music developed in W Africa.

1930s Latin American dances like samba and rumba became Western ballroom dances.

1940s Afro-Cuban rhythms fused with American jazz to become Cubop.

1950s The cool-jazz school imported bossa nova from Brazil. US bandleader Tito Puente (1923–　) popularized Latin dances mambo and cha-cha-cha. Calypso appeared in the pop charts.

1960s Miriam Makeba took South African folk and pop to the West. The Beatles introduced Indian sitar music. Folk-rock recycled traditional songs.

1970s Jamaican reggae became international and was an influence on punk. Cuban singer Celia Cruz established herself in the USA as the 'queen of salsa'. Malian guitarist Ali Farka Touré (1939–　) brought a blues feel to traditional African melodies.

1980s World music was embraced by several established pop stars and various African, Latin American, Bulgarian, Yemenite, and other styles became familiar in the West. Zairean Papa Wemba was one of many Third World singers recording in France.

UK best-selling singles, 1956–1993

Year	Title	Artist	Year	Title	Artist
1956	*I'll Be Home*	Pat Boone	1976	*Save Your Kisses For Me*	Brotherhood of Man
1957	*Love Letters in the Sand*	Pat Boone			
1958	*All I Have To Do Is Dream*	The Everly Brothers	1977	*Don't Give Up On Us*	David Soul
			1978	*Rivers Of Babylon/Brown Girl In The Ring*	Boney M
1959	*Livin' Doll*	Cliff Richard			
1960	*Cathy's Clown*	The Everly Brothers	1979	*Bright Eyes*	Art Garfunkel
			1980	*Don't Stand So Close To Me*	The Police
1961	*Runaway*	Del Shannon	1981	*Tainted Love*	Soft Cell
1962	*Stranger On The Shore*	Acker Bilk	1982	*Come On Eileen*	Dexys Midnight Runners
1963	*From Me To You*	The Beatles			
1964	*I Love You Because*	Jim Reeves	1983	*Karma Chameleon*	Culture Club
1965	*I'll Never Find Another You*	The Seekers	1984	*Do They Know It's Christmas*	Band Aid
1966	*Distant Drum*	Jim Reeves	1985	*The Power Of Love*	Jennifer Rush
1967	*Release Me*	Engelbert Humperdinck	1986	*Don't Leave Me This Way*	The Communards
			1987	*Never Gonna Give You Up*	Rick Astley
1968	*What A Wonderful World*	Louis Armstrong	1988	*Mistletoe And Wine*	Cliff Richard
1969	*My Way*	Frank Sinatra	1989	*Ride On Time*	Black Box
1970	*The Wonder Of You*	Elvis Presley	1990	*Unchained Melody*	The Righteous Brothers
1971	*My Sweet Lord*	George Harrison			
1972	*Amazing Grace*	Royal Scots Dragoon Guards	1991	*Everything I Do (I Do It For You)*	Bryan Adams
1973	*Tie A Yellow Ribbon*	Dawn	1992	*I Will Always Love You*	Whitney Houston
1974	*Tiger Feet*	Mud	1993	*I'll Do Anything for Love (But I Won't Do That)*	Meat Loaf
1975	*Bye Bye Baby*	Bay City Rollers			

Source: The Independent/CIN

1990s New fusions, such as Afro-Gaelic, punk Ukrainian, and bhangramuffin, appeared.

Young Neil 1945– . Canadian rock guitarist, singer, and songwriter, in the USA from 1966. His high, plaintive voice and loud, abrasive guitar make his work instantly recognizable, despite abrupt changes of style throughout his career. His albums include *Rust Never Sleeps* 1979 (with the group Crazy Horse), *Harvest Moon* 1992 (a nod to his bestselling *Harvest* 1972), and *Unplugged* 1993.

zydeco dance music originating in Louisiana, USA, similar to Cajun but more heavily influenced by blues and West Indian music. Zydeco is fast and bouncy, using instruments like accordion, saxophone, and washboard. It was widely popularized by singer and accordion player Clifton Chenier (1925–1987).

PHOTOGRAPHY

Terms

aperture in a camera, an opening that allows light to pass through the lens to strike the film. Controlled by shutter speed and the iris diaphragm, it can be set mechanically or electronically at various diameters.

ASA numbering system for rating the speed of films, devised by the American Standards Association. It has now been superseded by *ISO*, the International Standards Organization.

autochrome single-plate additive colour process devised by the Lumière brothers 1903. It was the first commercially available process, in use 1907–35.

calotype paper-based photograph using a wax paper negative, the first example of the negative/positive process invented by the English photographer Fox Talbot around 1834.

camera apparatus used in photography, consisting of a lens system set in a light-proof box inside of which a sensitized film or plate can be placed. The lens collects rays of light reflected from the subject and brings them together as a sharp image on the film; it has apertures marked with f-numbers, or f-stops, that reduce or increase the amount of light. Apertures also control depth of field. A shutter controls the amount of time light has to affect the film. There are small-, medium-, and large-format cameras; the format refers to the size of recorded image and the dimensions of the print obtained.

A simple camera has a fixed shutter speed and aperture, chosen so that on a sunny day the correct amount of light is admitted. More complex cameras allow the shutter speed and aperture to be adjusted; most have a built-in exposure meter to help choose the correct combination of shutter speed and aperture for the ambient conditions and subject matter. The most versatile camera is the single-lens reflex (SLR) which allows the lens to be removed and special lenses attached. A pin-hole camera has a small (pin-sized) hole instead of a lens. It must be left on a firm support during exposures, which are up to ten seconds with slow film, two seconds with fast film, and five minutes for paper negatives in daylight. The pin-hole camera gives sharp images from close-up to infinity.

camera obscura darkened box with a tiny hole for projecting the inverted image of the scene outside on to a screen inside.

Cibachrome process of printing photographs directly from transparencies. It can be home-processed and the rich, saturated colours are highly resistant to fading. It was introduced 1963.

cine camera camera that takes a rapid sequence of still photographs – 24 frames (pictures) each second. When the pictures are projected one after the other at the same speed on to a screen, they appear to show movement, because our eyes hold on to the image of one picture before the next one appears.

The cine camera differs from an ordinary still camera in having a motor that winds the film on. The film is held still by a claw mechanism while each frame is exposed. When the film is moved between frames, a semicircular disc slides between the lens and the film and prevents exposure.

daguerreotype single-image process using mercury vapour and an iodine-sensitized silvered plate; it was invented by Louis Daguerre 1838.

developing process that produces a visible image on exposed photographic film, involving the treatment of the exposed film with a chemical developer.

The developing liquid consists of a reducing agent that changes the light-altered silver salts in the film into darker metallic silver. The developed image is made permanent with a fixer, which dissolves away any silver salts which were not affected by light. The developed image is a negative, or reverse image: darkest where the strongest light hit the film, lightest where the least light fell. To produce a positive image the negative is itself photographed, and the development process reverses the shading, producing the final print. Colour and black-and-white film can be obtained as direct reversal, slide, or transparency material. Slides and transparencies are used for projection or printing with a positive-to-positive process such as Cibachrome.

dye-transfer print print made by a relatively permanent colour process that uses red, yellow, and blue separation negatives printed together.

exposure meter instrument used in photography for indicating the correct exposure – the length of time the camera shutter should be open under given light conditions. Meters use substances such as cadmium sulphide and selenium as light sensors. These materials change electrically when light strikes them, the change being proportional to the intensity of the incident light. Many cameras have a built-in exposure meter that sets the camera controls automatically as the light conditions change.

film, photographic strip of transparent material (usually cellulose acetate) coated with a light-sensitive emulsion, used in cameras to take pictures. The emulsion contains a mixture of light-sensitive silver halide salts (for example, bromide or iodide) in gelatin. When the emulsion is exposed to light, the silver salts are invisibly altered, giving a latent image, which is then made visible by the process of developing. Films differ in their sensitivities to light, this being indicated by their speeds. Colour film consists of several layers of emulsion, each of which records a different colour in the light falling on it.

In *colour film* the front emulsion records blue light, then comes a yellow filter, followed by layers that record green and red light respectively. In the developing process the various images in the layers are dyed yellow, magenta (red), and cyan (blue), respectively. When they are viewed, either as a transparency or as a colour print, the colours merge to produce the true colour of the original scene photographed.

f-number or *f-stop* measure of the relative aperture of a telescope or camera lens; it indicates the light-gathering power of the lens. In photography, each successive f-number represents a halving of exposure speed.

Photography: chronology

1515   Leonardo da Vinci described the camera obscura.
1750   The painter Canaletto used a camera obscura as an aid to his painting in Venice.
1790   Thomas Wedgwood in England made photograms – placing objects on leather, sensitized using silver nitrate.
1826   Nicephore Niépce (1765–1833), a French doctor, produced the world's first photograph from nature on pewter plates with a camera obscura and an eight-hour exposure.
1835   Niépce and L J M Daguerre produced the first Daguerreotype camera photograph.
1839   Daguerre was awarded an annuity by the French government and his process given to the world.
1840   Invention of the Petzval lens, which reduced exposure time by 90%. Herschel discovered sodium thiosulphate as a fixer for silver halides.
1841   Fox Talbot's calotype process was patented – the first multicopy method of photography using a negative/positive process, sensitized with silver iodide.
1844   Fox Talbot published the first photographic book, *The Pencil of Nature*.
1845   Hill and Adamson began to use calotypes for portraits in Edinburgh.
1851   Fox Talbot used a one-thousandth of a second exposure to demonstrate high-speed photography. Invention of the wet-collodion-on-glass process and the waxed-paper negative. Photographs were displayed at the Great Exhibition in London.
1852   The London Society of Arts exhibited 779 photographs.
1855   Roger Fenton made documentary photographs of the Crimean War from a specially constructed caravan with portable darkroom.
1859   Nadar in Paris made photographs underground using battery-powered arc lights.
1860   Queen Victoria was photographed by Mayall. Abraham Lincoln was photographed by Matthew Brady for political campaigning.
1861   The single-lens reflex plate camera was patented by Thomas Sutton. The principles of three-colour photography were demonstrated by Scottish physicist James Clerk Maxwell.
1862   Nadar took aerial photographs over Paris.
1870   Julia Margaret Cameron used long lenses for her distinctive portraits.
1871   Gelatin-silver bromide was developed.
1878   In the USA Eadweard Muybridge analysed the movements of animals through sequential photographs, using a series of cameras.
1879   The photogravure process was invented.
1880   A silver bromide emulsion was fixed with hypo. Photographs were first reproduced in newspapers in New York using the half-tone engraving process. The first twin-lens reflex camera was produced in London. Gelatin-silver chloride paper was introduced.
1884   George Eastman produced flexible negative film.
1889   The Eastman Company in the USA produced the Kodak No 1 camera and roll film, facilitating universal, hand-held snapshots.
1891   The first telephoto lens. The interference process of colour photography was developed by the French doctor Gabriel Lippmann.
1897   The first issue of Alfred Stieglitz's *Camera Notes* in the USA.
1902   In Germany, Deckel invented a prototype leaf shutter and Zeiss introduced the Tessar lens.
1904   The autochrome colour process was patented by the Lumière brothers.
1905   Alfred Stieglitz opened the gallery '291' in New York promoting photography. Lewis Hine used photography to expose the exploitation of children in US factories, causing protective laws to be passed.
1907   The autochrome process began to be factory-produced.
1914   Oskar Barnack designed a prototype Leica camera for Leitz in Germany.
1924   Leitz launched the first 35mm camera, the Leica, delayed because of World War I. It became very popular with photojournalists because it was quiet, small, dependable, and had a range of lenses and accessories.
1929   Rolleiflex produced a twin-lens reflex camera in Germany.
1935   In the USA, Mannes and Godowsky invented Kodachrome transparency film, which produced sharp images and rich colour quality. Electronic flash was invented in the USA.
1936   *Life* magazine, significant for its photojournalism, was first published in the USA.
1938   *Picture Post* magazine was introduced in the UK.
1940   Multigrade enlarging paper by Ilford was made available in the UK.
1942   Kodacolour negative film was introduced.
1945   The zone system of exposure estimation was published in the book *Exposure Record* by Ansel Adams.
1947   Polaroid black and white instant process film was invented by Dr Edwin Land, who set up the Polaroid corporation in Boston, Massachusetts. The principles of holography were demonstrated in England by Dennis Gabor.
1955   Kodak introduced Tri-X, a black and white 200 ASA film.
1959   The zoom lens was invented by the Austrian firm of Voigtlander.
1960   The laser was invented in the USA, making holography possible. Polacolor, a self-processing colour film, was introduced by Polaroid, using a 60-second colour film and dye diffusion technique.
1963   Cibachrome, paper and chemicals for printing directly from transparencies, was made available by Ciba-Geigy of Switzerland. One of the most permanent processes, it is marketed by Ilford in the UK.

Photography: chronology (cont.)

1966	The International Center of Photography was established in New York.
1969	Photographs were taken on the Moon by US astronauts.
1970	A charge-coupled device was invented at Bell Laboratories in New Jersey, USA, to record very faint images (for example in astronomy). *Rencontres Internationales de la Photographie*, the annual summer festival of photography with workshops, was founded in Arles, France.
1971	Opening of the Photographers' Gallery, London, and the Photo Archive of the Bibliothèque Nationale, Paris.
1972	The SX70 system, a single-lens reflex camera with instant prints, was produced by Polaroid.
1975	The Center for Creative Photography was established at the University of Arizona.
1980	Ansel Adams sold an original print, *Moonrise: Hernandez*, for $45,000, a record price, in the USA. *Voyager 1* sent photographs of Saturn back to Earth across space.
1983	The National Museum of Photography, Film and Television opened in Bradford, England.
1985	The Minolta Corporation in Japan introduced the Minolta 7000 – the world's first body-integral autofocus single-lens reflex camera.
1988	The electronic camera, which stores pictures on magnetic disc instead of on film, was introduced in Japan.
1990	Kodak introduced PhotoCD which converts 35mm camera pictures (on film) into digital form and stores them on compact disc (CD) for viewing on TV.
1992	Japanese company Canon introduced a camera with autofocus controlled by the user's eye. The camera focuses on whatever the user is looking at.
1993	Man Ray's *Glass Tears* became world's most expensive photograph when it fetched £122,500 at Sotheby's

focus the distance that a lens must be moved in order to focus a sharp image on the light-sensitive film at the back of the camera. The lens is moved away from the film to focus the image of closer objects. The focusing distance is often marked on a scale around the lens; however, some cameras now have an automatic focusing (autofocus) mechanism that uses an electric motor to move the lens.

f-stop another name for f-number.

hypo sodium thiosulphate, discovered 1819 by John Herschel, and used as a fixative for photographic images since 1837.

ISO numbering system for rating the speed of films, devised by the International Standards Organization.

negative/positive reverse image, which when printed is again reversed, restoring the original scene. It was invented by Fox Talbot about 1834.

orthochromatic photographic film or paper of decreased sensitivity, which can be processed with a red safelight. Using it, blue objects appear lighter and red ones darker because of increased blue sensitivity.

panchromatic film highly sensitive black-and-white film made to render all visible spectral colours in correct grey tones. Panchromatic film is always developed in total darkness.

photogram picture produced on photographic material by exposing it to light, but without using a camera.

photography process for reproducing images on sensitized materials by various forms of radiant energy, including visible light, ultraviolet, infrared, X-rays, atomic radiations, and electron beams. Photography was developed in the 19th century; among the pioneers were L J M Daguerre in France and Fox Talbot in the UK. Colour photography dates from the early 20th century.

The most familiar photographic process depends upon the fact that certain silver compounds (called halides) are sensitive to light. A photographic film is coated with these compounds and, in a camera, is exposed to light. An image, or picture, of the scene before the camera is formed on the film because the silver halides become activated (light-altered) where light falls but not where light does not fall. The image is made visible by the process of developing, made permanent by fixing, and, finally, is usually printed on paper. Motion-picture photography uses a camera that exposes a roll of film to a rapid succession of views that, when developed, are projected in equally rapid succession to provide a moving image.

Polaroid camera instant-picture camera, invented by Edwin Land in the USA 1947; colour Polaroid cameras were introduced 1963. A modern camera produces black-and-white prints in a few seconds, and colour prints in less than a minute. It ejects a piece of film on paper immediately after the picture has been taken. The film consists of layers of emulsion and colour dyes together with a pod of chemical developer. When the film is ejected the pod bursts and processing occurs in the light.

rangefinder instrument for determining the range or distance of an object from the observer; used to focus a camera or to sight a gun accurately. A *rangefinder camera* has a rotating mirror or prism that alters the image seen through the viewfinder, and a secondary window. When the two images are brought together into one, the lens is sharply focused.

reflex camera camera that uses a mirror and prisms to reflect light passing through the lens into the viewfinder, showing the photographer the exact scene that is being shot. When the shutter button is released the mirror springs out of the way, allowing light to reach the film. The most common type is the single-lens reflex (SLR) camera. The twin-lens reflex (TLR) camera has two lenses: one has a mirror for viewing, the other is used for exposing the film.

SLR abbreviation for *single-lens reflex*, a type of camera in which the image can be seen through the lens before a picture is taken. A small mirror directs light entering the lens to the viewfinder. When a picture is taken the mirror moves rapidly aside to allow the light to reach the film. The SLR allows different lenses, such as close-up or zoom lenses, to be used because the photographer can see exactly what is being focused on.

telephoto lens photographic lens of longer focal length than normal that takes a very narrow view and gives a large image through a combination of telescopic and ordinary photographic lenses.

thaumatrope disc with two different pictures at opposite ends of its surface. The images combine into one when rapidly rotated because of the persistence of visual impressions.

35 mm width of photographic film, the most popular format for the camera today. The 35-mm camera falls into two categories, the single-lens reflex (SLR) and the rangefinder.

TLR camera twin-lens reflex camera that has a viewing lens of the same angle of view and focal length mounted above and parallel to the taking lens.

transparency picture on slide film. This captures the original in a positive image (direct reversal) and can be used for projection or printing on positive-to-positive print material; for example, by the Cibachrome or Kodak R-type process. Slide film is usually colour but can be obtained in black and white.

wide-angle lens photographic lens of shorter focal length than normal, taking in a wider angle of view.

zoetrope optical toy with a series of pictures on the inner surface of a cylinder. When the pictures are rotated and viewed through a slit, it gives the impression of continuous motion.

zone system system of exposure estimation invented by Ansel Adams that groups infinite tonal gradations into ten zones, zone 0 being black and zone 10 white. An f-stop change in exposure is required from zone to zone.

zoom lens photographic lens that, by variation of focal length, allows speedy transition from long shots to close-ups.

Famous Photographers

Abbott Berenice 1898–1991. US photographer best known for her portrait studies of artists in the 1920s and for her comprehensive documentation of New York City in the 1930s, culminating in the publication of *Changing New York* 1939. Her straightforward style was partially influenced by French photograher Eugène Atget, whose work she rescued from obscurity.

Adams Ansel 1902–1984. US photographer known for his printed images of dramatic landscapes and organic forms of the American West. Light and texture were important elements in his photographs. He was associated with the zone system of exposure estimation and was a founder member (with Imogen Cunningham and Edward Weston) of the 'f/64' group, which advocated precise definition. The Yosemite National Park and the High Sierras in California featured prominently in his work throughout his life.

Adamson Robert. Scottish photographer who collaborated with David Octavius Hill.

Arbus Diane 1923–1971. US photographer. Although she practised as a fashion photographer for 20 years, Arbus is best known for her later work, which examined the fringes of American society, the misfits, the eccentrics, and the bizarre. Her work has been attacked as cruel and voyeuristic, but it is essentially sympathetic in its unflinching curiosity. *A Box of Ten Photographs*, a limited edition of her work, was published 1970.

Atget Eugène 1857–1927. French photographer. He took up photography at the age of 40, and for 30 years documented urban Paris, leaving some 10,000 images. His photographs were sometimes used by painters and he was admired by the Surrealists. After his death his work was rescued and promoted by the photographer Berenice Abbott.

Avedon Richard 1923– . US photographer. A fashion photographer with *Harper's Bazaar* magazine in New York from the mid-1940s, he moved to *Vogue* 1965. He later became the highest-paid fashion and advertising photographer in the world. His work consists of intensely realistic images, chiefly portraits, made with large-format cameras.

Bailey David 1938– . British fashion photographer. His work for *Vogue* magazine in the 1960s and his black-and-white portraits of celebrities did much to define the image of 'swinging London'. He has published several books, including *Box of Pin-Ups* 1965 and *Goodbye Baby and Amen* 1969.

Beaton Cecil 1904–1980. English photographer whose elegant and sophisticated fashion pictures and society portraits often employed exotic props and settings. He adopted a simpler style for his wartime photographs of bomb-damaged London. He also worked as a stage and film designer.

Bourke-White Margaret 1906–1971. US photographer. As an editor of *Fortune* magazine 1929–33, she travelled extensively in the USSR, publishing several collections of photographs. Later, with husband Erskine Caldwell, she also published photo collections of American and European subjects. She began working for *Life* magazine 1936, and covered combat in World War II and documented India's struggle for independence.

Brady Mathew B *c.* 1823–1896. US photographer. Famed for his skill in photographic portraiture, he published *The Gallery of Illustrious Americans* 1850. With the outbreak of the US Civil War 1861 Brady and his staff became the foremost photographers of battle scenes and military life. Although his war photos were widely reproduced Brady later suffered a series of financial reverses and died in poverty.

Brandt Bill 1905–1983. British photographer, born in Germany. During the 1930s he made a series of social records contrasting the lives of the rich and the poor, some of which were presented in his book *The English at Home* 1936. During World War II he documented conditions in London in the Blitz. The strong contrasts in his black-and-white prints often produced a gloomy and threatening atmosphere. His outstanding creative work was his treatment of the nude, published in *Perspective of Nudes* and *Shadows of Light*, both 1966.

Brassäi adopted name of Gyula Halesz 1899–1986. French photographer of Hungarian origin who chronicled, mainly by flash, the nightlife of Paris: prostitutes, street cleaners, and criminals. These pictures were published as *Paris by Night* 1933. Later he turned to more abstract work.

Cameron Julia Margaret 1815–1879. British photographer who made lively and dramatic portraits of the Victorian intelligentsia, often posed as historical or literary figures. Her sitters included her friends Sir John Herschel and the poet Alfred Lord Tennyson, whose *Idylls of the King* she illustrated 1872, and Charles Darwin. She used a large camera, five-minute exposures, and wet plates.

Capa Robert. Adopted name of André Friedmann 1913–1954. US photographer, born in Hungary, who specialized in war photography. He covered the Spanish Civil War as a freelance and World War II for *Life* and *Collier's* magazines. His pictures emphasize the human tragedy of war. He was a founder member of the Magnum photographic agency, a cooperative. He died while on an assignment in Vietnam.

Cartier-Bresson Henri 1908– . French photographer, considered one of the greatest photographic artists. His documentary work was shot in black and white, using a small-format Leica camera. His work is remarkable for its tightly structured composition and his ability to capture the decisive moment. He was a cofounder (with Robert Capa and others) of the cooperative photo agency Magnum.

Cunningham Imogen 1883–1976. US photographer. Her early photographs were romantic but she gradually rejected pictorialism, producing clear and detailed plant studies 1922–29. With Ansel Adams and Edward Weston, she was a founder member of the 'f/64' group which advocated precise definition. From the mid-1930s she concentrated on portraiture.

Daguerre Louis Jacques Mande 1789–1851. French pioneer of photography. Together with Joseph Niépce, he is credited with the invention of photography (though others were reaching the same point simultaneously). In 1838 he invented the daguerreotype, a single image process superseded ten years later by Fox Talbot's negative/positive process.

Doisneau Robert 1912– . French photographer known for his sensitive and often witty depictions of ordinary people and everyday situations within the environs of Paris. His most famous image, *Baiser de l'Hôtel de Ville/The Kiss at the Hôtel de Ville*, was produced for *Life* magazine 1950.

Eggleston William 1937– . US photographer whose banal scenes of life in the deep South are transformed by his use of the dye-transfer technique into intense, superreal images of richly saturated colour. In 1984 he documented Elvis Presley's home, Graceland.

Evans Walker 1903–1975. US photographer best known for his documentary photographs of people in the rural American South during the Great Depression. Many of his photographs appeared in James Agee's book *Let Us Now Praise Famous Men* 1941.

Fenton Roger 1819–1869. English photographer, best known for his comprehensive documentation of the Crimean War 1855. He was a founder member of the Photographic Society (later the Royal Photographic Society) in London 1853 but completely gave up photography 1860.

Hill David Octavius 1802–1870 and Robert R Adamson 1821–1848. Scottish photographers who worked together 1843–48, making extensive use of the calotype process in their portraits of leading members of the Free Church of Scotland and their views of Edinburgh and the Scottish fishing village of Newhaven. They produced around 2,500 calotypes. Their work was rediscovered around 1900.

Hine Lewis 1874–1940. US sociologist and photographer. His dramatic photographs of child-labour conditions in US factories at the beginning of the 20th century led to changes in state and local labour laws. His photographs of immigrants arriving at New York's Ellis Island, their tenement homes and the sweatshops in which they worked, published 1908, are considered the first photo story.

Hosking Eric (John) 1909–1990. English wildlife photographer known for his documentation of British birds, especially owls. Beginning at the age of eight and still photographing in Africa at 80, he covered all aspects of birdlife and illustrated a large number of books, published between 1940 and 1990.

Karsh Yousuf 1908– . Canadian portrait photographer, born in Armenia. He is known for his formal and dramatically lit studies of the famous, in which he attempts to capture their 'inward power'. His most notable picture is the defiant portrait of Winston Churchill which appeared on the cover of *Life* magazine 1941.

Kertész André 1894–1986. Hungarian-born US photographer whose spontaneity had a great impact on photojournalism. A master of the 35-mm-format camera, he recorded his immediate environment (Paris, New York) with wit and style.

Koudelka Josef 1939– . Czech photographer best known for his photographs of East European Romanies, whose vanishing way of life he has recorded. He also photographed the Soviet invasion of Czechoslovakia 1968 and the inauguration of Václav Havel as president of Czechoslovakia 1989.

Land Edwin Herbert 1909–1991. US inventor of the Polaroid Land camera 1947, which developed the film in one minute inside the camera and produced an 'instant' photograph.

Lange Dorothea 1895–1965. US photographer who was hired in 1935 by the federal Farm Security Administration to document the westward migration of farm families from the Dust Bowl of the S central USA. Her photographs, characterized by a gritty realism, were widely exhibited and subsequently published as *An American Exodus: A Record of Human Erosion* 1939.

Le Gray Gustave 1820–1882. French photographer who in 1850 invented the waxed-paper negative, a more efficient version of the calotype, where the paper is waxed before being coated with silver iodide. He also experimented with printing images using more than one negative, notably in his detailed seascapes which use a separate negative for sea and sky.

Leibovitz Annie 1950– . US photographer whose elaborately staged portraits of American celebrities appeared first in *Rolling Stone* magazine and later in *Vanity Fair*. The odd poses in which her sitters allow themselves to be placed suggest an element of self-mockery.

McCullin Don(ald) 1935– . British war photographer who started out as a freelance photojournalist for Sunday newspapers. His coverage of hostilities in the Congo 1967, Vietnam 1968, Biafra 1968 and 1970, and Cambodia 1970 is notable for his pessimistic vision. He has published several books of his work, among them *Destruction Business*.

Man Ray adopted name of Emmanuel Rudnitsky 1890–1977. US photographer, painter, and sculptor, active mainly in France; associated with the Dada movement. His pictures often showed Surrealist images, like the photograph *Le Violon d'Ingres* 1924.

In 1922 he invented the ***rayograph***, a black-and-white image obtained without a camera by placing objects on sensitized photographic paper and exposing them to light; he also used the technique of solarization (partly reversing the tones on a photograph). His photographs include portraits of many artists and writers.

Mapplethorpe Robert 1946–1989. US art photographer known for his use of racial and homoerotic imagery in chiefly fine platinum prints. He developed a style of polished elegance in his gallery art works, whose often culturally forbidden subject matter caused controversy.

Meiselas Susan 1948– . US freelance war photographer who has covered conflicts in Nicaragua and El Salvador. Her brilliant cibachrome prints seem anti-heroic in their intention.

Modotti Tina 1896–1942 Italian photographer who studied with Edward Weston and went to Mexico with him 1923. As well as her sensitive studies of Mexican women, she recorded the work of the Mexican muralists and made near-abstract prints of stairs and flowers.

Moholy-Nagy Laszlo 1895–1946. US photographer, born in Hungary. He lived in Germany 1923–29, where he was a member of the Bauhaus school, and fled from the Nazis 1935. Through the publication of his illuminating theories and practical experiments, he had great influence on 20th-century photography and design.

Munkácsi Martin 1896–1963. US photographer born in Hungary. After a successful career in Budapest and then Berlin, where he was influenced by the New Photography movement, he moved to the USA 1934. There he worked as a fashion photographer pioneering a more lively and natural style of photograph for such magazines as *Harper's Bazaar* and *Ladies' Home Journal*.

Muybridge Eadweard. Adopted name of Edward James Muggeridge 1830–1904. British photographer. He made a series of animal locomotion photographs in the USA in the 1870s and proved that, when a horse trots, there are times when all its feet are off the ground. He also explored motion in birds and humans.

Nadar adopted name of Gaspard-Félix Tournachon 1820–1910. French portrait photographer and caricaturist. He took the first aerial photographs (from a balloon 1858) and was the first to take flash photographs (using magnesium bulbs).

Namuth Hans 1915–1990. German-born US photographer who specialized in portraits and documentary work. He began as a photojournalist in Europe in the 1930s and opened a portrait studio in New York in 1950. His work includes documentation of the Guatemalan Mam Indians (published as *Los Todos Santeros* 1989) and of US artists from the 1950s (published as *Artists 1950–1981*). He also carried out assignments for magazines.

Parkinson Norman. Adopted name of Ronald William Parkinson Smith 1913–1990. English fashion and portrait photographer who caught the essential glamour of each decade from the 1930s to the 1980s. Long associated with the magazines *Vogue* and *Queen*, he was best known for his colour work, and from the late 1960s took many official portraits of the royal family.

Penn Irving 1917– . US fashion, advertising, portrait, editorial, and fine art photographer. In 1948 he took the first of many journeys to Africa and the Far East, resulting in a series of portrait photographs of local people, avoiding sophisticated technique. He was associated for many years with *Vogue* magazine in the USA.

Renger-Patzsch Albert 1897–1966. German photographer. He was a leading figure of the New Photography movement which emphasized objectivity of vision. His influential book *Die Welt ist schön/The World is Beautiful* 1928 was a disparate collection of objects, from plants to industrial machinery, all photographed in the same way.

Rodchenko Alexander 1891–1956. Russian avant-garde painter and designer who took up photography 1924. The aim of his work, in all media, was to create a visual language that would reflect the new revolutionary times. In his photographs everyday objects were presented in close-up, from strange angles, or from high viewpoints, an approach similar to that of the Hungarian Laszlo Moholy-Nagy.

Sander August 1876–1964. German portrait photographer whose long-term project was to create a vast composite portrait, *Man of the Twentieth Century*. Concentrating on German society, he turned his dispassionate gaze on every walk of life – from butchers to bankers – in a way that combined the individual with the archetypal. Much of his work was destroyed when his Cologne studio was bombed 1944.

Siskind Aaron 1903–1991. US art photographer who began as a documentary photographer and in 1940 made a radical change towards a poetic exploration of forms and planes, inspired by the Abstract Expressionist painters.

Steichen Edward 1897–1973. Luxembourg-born US photographer, who with Alfred Stieglitz helped to establish photography as an art form. His style evolved during his career from painterly impressionism to realism.

During World War I he helped to develop aerial photography, and in World War II he directed US naval-combat photography. He turned to fashion and advertising 1923–38, working mainly for *Vogue* and *Vanity Fair* magazines. He was in charge of the Museum of Modern Art's photography collection 1947–62, where in 1955 he organized the renowned 'Family of Man' exhibition.

Stieglitz Alfred 1864–1946. US photographer who was mainly responsible for the recognition of photography as an art form. After forming the multimedia Photo-Secession Group at 291 Fifth Avenue, New York, with Edward Steichen, he began the magazine *Camera Work* 1902–17. His cloud series, the portraits of the painter Georgia O'Keeffe (whom he married 1924), and his studies of New York City, are his most famous works. Through exhibitions, competitions, and publication at his galleries, he helped establish a photographic esthetic.

Strand Paul 1890–1976. US photographer and film maker who studied with Lewis Hine and was encouraged by Alfred Stieglitz. After his early, near-abstract studies of New York, he turned to predominantly rural subjects which celebrate human dignity in a clear and straightforward manner. His portfolios, which include *Photographs of Mexico* 1940 and *Time in New England*, were always meticulously printed.

Talbot William Henry Fox 1800–1877. English pioneer of photography. He invented the paper-based calotype process, the first negative/positive method. Talbot made photograms several years before Louis Daguerre's invention was announced. In 1851 he made instantaneous photographs and in 1852 photo engravings. *The Pencil of Nature* 1844–46 was the first book of photographs published.

Weston Edward 1886–1958. US photographer. A founding member of the 'f/64' group (after the smallest lens opening), a school of photography advocating sharp definition. He is noted for the technical mastery, composition, and clarity in his California landscapes, clouds, gourds, cactuses, and nude studies.

In his photography, Weston aimed for realism. He never used artificial light and seldom enlarged, cropped, or retouched his negatives. His aesthetic principle dominated American photography for many years.

Woolcott Marion Post 1910–1990. US documentary photographer best known for her work for the Farm Security Administration (with Walker Evans and Dorothea Lange), showing the conditions of poor farmers in the late 1930s in Kentucky and the deep South.

THEATRE

Genres

Absurd, Theatre of the avant-garde drama originating with a group of playwrights in the 1950s, including Beckett, Ionesco, Genet, and Pinter. Their work expressed the belief that in a godless universe human existence has no meaning or purpose and therefore all communication breaks down. Logical construction and argument gives way to irrational and illogical speech and to its ultimate conclusion, silence, as in Beckett's play *Breath* 1970.

autos sacramentales Spanish 'religious plays'. Spanish drama form, related to the mystery plays in England, and well established by the 13th century. These traditional performances were redeveloped in the 17th century by dramatists Lope de Vega and Calderón, whose masterpiece in this form is *El gran teatro del mundo/The Great Theatre of the World* 1641.

burlesque in the 17th and 18th centuries, a form of satirical comedy parodying a particular play or dramatic genre. For example, John Gay's *The Beggar's Opera* 1728 is a burlesque of 18th-century opera, and Richard Brinsley Sheridan's *The Critic* 1777 satirizes the sentimentality in contemporary drama. In the USA from the mid-19th century, burlesque referred to a sex and comedy show invented by Michael Bennett Leavitt 1866 with acts including acrobats, singers, and comedians. During the 1920s striptease was introduced in order to counteract the growing popularity of the movies; Gypsy Rose Lee was the most famous stripper. Burlesque was frequently banned in the USA.

cabaret theatrical revue traditionally combining satire and song in cafés or bars. Originating in Paris in the late 19th century in venues such as the Moulin Rouge, cabaret was embraced by avant-garde writers and artists. In Germany in the 1920s, Berlin became a centre for an increasingly political cabaret, later suppressed by the Nazis. In Britain, satirical revue was revived by the Cambridge Footlights theatre group in *Beyond the Fringe* 1961, before cabaret and alternative comedy combined to provide a new generation of stand-up entertainers during the 1980s, notably from the Comedy Store group in London.

circus entertainment, often held in a large tent ('big top'), involving performing animals, acrobats, and clowns. In 1871 Phineas T Barnum created the 'Greatest Show on Earth' in the USA. The popularity of animal acts decreased in the 1980s. Originally, in Roman times, a circus was an arena for chariot races and gladiatorial combats.

comedy drama that aims to make its audience laugh, usually with a happy or amusing ending, as opposed to tragedy. The comic tradition was established by the Greek dramatists Aristophanes and Menander, and the Roman writers Terence and Plautus. In medieval times, the Vices and Devil of the Morality plays developed into the stock comic characters of the Renaissance *comedy of humours* with such notable villains as Ben Jonson's Mosca, in *Volpone*. The timeless comedies of Shakespeare and Molière were followed in England during the 17th century by the witty *comedy of manners* of Restoration writers such as George Etherege, William Wycherley, and William Congreve. Their often coarse but always vital comedies were toned down in the later Restoration dramas of Richard Sheridan and Oliver Goldsmith. Sentimental comedy dominated most of the 19th century, though little is remembered in the late 20th century, which prefers the realistic tradition of Shaw and the elegant social comedies of Wilde. The polished comedies of Nöel Coward and Terence Rattigan from the 1920s to 1940s were eclipsed during the late 1950s and the 1960s by a trend towards satire and cynicism as seen in the works of Joe Orton and Peter Nichols, alongside absurdist comedies by Samuel Beckett and Jean Genet. From the 1970s the 'black comedies' of Alan Ayckbourn have dominated the English stage. Genres of comedy include pantomime, satire, farce, black comedy, and commedia dell'arte.

commedia dell'arte popular form of Italian improvised comic drama in the 16th and 17th centuries, performed by trained troupes of actors and using stock characters and situations. It exerted considerable influence on writers such as Molière and Carlo Goldoni, and on the genres of pantomime, harlequinade, and the Punch and Judy show. It laid the foundation for a tradition of mime, strong in France, that has continued with the contemporary mime of Jean-Louis Barrault and Marcel Marceau.

Cruelty, Theatre of theory advanced by Antonin Artaud in his book *Le Théâtre et son double* 1938 and adopted by a number of writers and directors. It aims to shock the audience into an awareness of basic, primitive human nature through the release of feelings usually repressed by conventional behaviour. In the UK Artaud's ideas particularly influenced the producer and director Peter Brook.

farce a broad form of comedy involving stereotyped characters in complex, often improbable situations frequently revolving around extramarital relationships (hence the term 'bedroom farce'). Originating in the physical knockabout comedy of Greek satyr plays and the broad humour of medieval religious drama, the farce was developed and perfected during the 19th century by Eugène Labiche (1815–1888) and Georges Feydeau (1862–1921) in France and Arthur Pinero in England.

fringe theatre plays that are anti-establishment or experimental, and performed in informal venues, in contrast to mainstream commercial theatre. In the UK, the term originated in the 1960s from the activities held on the 'fringe' of the Edinburgh Festival. Notable 'fringe' writers include Howard Brenton and David Hare. Fringe groups that tour the country include Belt and Braces, Hull Truck, and Joint Stock. The US equivalent is off-off-Broadway (off-Broadway is mainstream theatre that is not on Broadway).

kabuki drama originating in late 16th-century Japan, drawing on Nō, puppet plays, and folk dance. Kabuki

Theatre: chronology

c. 3200 BC	Beginnings of Egyptian religious drama, essentially ritualistic.
c. 600 BC	Choral performances (dithyrambs) in honour of Dionysus formed the beginnings of Greek tragedy, according to Aristotle.
500–300 BC	Great age of Greek drama which included tragedy, comedy, and satyr plays (grotesque farce).
468 BC	Sophocles' first victory at the Athens festival. His use of a third actor altered the course of the tragic form.
458 BC	Aeschylus' *Oresteia* were first performed.
c. 425–388 BC	Comedies of Aristophanes including *The Birds* 414, *Lysistrata* 411, and *The Frogs* 405. In tragedy the importance of the chorus diminished under Euripides, author of *The Bacchae* 405.
c. 350 BC	Menander's 'New Comedy' of social manners developed.
c. 240 BC–AD 500	Emergence of Roman drama, adapted from Greek originals. Plautus, Terence, and Seneca were the main playwrights.
c. AD 375	Kālidāsa's *Sakuntalā* marked the height of Sanskrit drama in India.
c. 1250–1500	European mystery (or miracle) plays flourished, first in the churches, later in marketplaces, and were performed in England by town guilds.
c. 1375	Nō (or Noh) drama developed in Japan.
c. 1495	*Everyman*, the best known of all the morality plays, was first performed.
1500–1600	Italian commedia dell'arte troupes performed popular, improvised comedies; they were to have a large influence on Molière and on English harlequinade and pantomime.
c. 1551	Nicholas Udall wrote *Ralph Roister Doister*, the first English comedy.
c. 1576	The first English playhouse, The Theatre, was built by James Burbage in London.
1587	Christopher Marlowe's play *Tamburlaine the Great* marked the beginning of the great age of Elizabethan and Jacobean drama in England.
c. 1589	Thomas Kyd's play *Spanish Tragedy* was the first of the 'revenge' tragedies.
c. 1590–1612	Shakespeare's greatest plays, including *Hamlet* and *King Lear*, were written.
1604	Inigo Jones designed *The Masque of Blackness* for James I, written by Ben Jonson.
1614	Lope de Vega's *Fuenteovejuna* marked the Spanish renaissance in drama. Other writers include Calderón de la Barca.
1637	Pierre Corneille's *Le Cid* established classical tragedy in France.
1642	An act of Parliament closed all English theatres.
1660	With the restoration of Charles II to the English throne, dramatic performances recommenced. The first professional actress appeared as Desdemona in Shakespeare's *Othello*.
1664	Molière's *Tartuffe* was banned for three years by religious factions.
1667	Jean Racine's first success, *Andromaque*, was staged.
1680	The Comédie Française was formed by Louis XIV.
1700	William Congreve, the greatest exponent of Restoration comedy, wrote *The Way of the World*.
1716	The first known American theatre was built in Williamsburg, Virginia.
1728	John Gay's *The Beggar's Opera* was first performed.
1737	The Stage Licensing Act in England required all plays to be approved by the Lord Chamberlain before performance.
1747	The actor David Garrick became manager of the Drury Lane Theatre, London.
1773	In England, Oliver Goldsmith's *She Stoops to Conquer* and Richard Sheridan's *The Rivals* 1775 established the 'comedy of manners'. Goethe's *Götz von Berlichingen* was the first *Sturm und Drang* (literally, storm and stress) play.
1781	Friedrich Schiller's *Die Räuber/The Robbers*.
1784	Beaumarchais's *Le Mariage de Figaro/The Marriage of Figaro* (written 1778) was first performed.
1830	Victor Hugo's *Hernani* caused riots in Paris. His work marked the beginning of a new Romantic drama, changing the course of French theatre.
1878	Henry Irving became actor-manager of the Lyceum with Ellen Terry as leading lady.
1879	Henrik Ibsen's *A Doll's House*, an early example of realism in European theatre.
1888	August Strindberg wrote *Miss Julie*.
1893	George Bernard Shaw wrote *Mrs Warren's Profession* (banned until 1902 because it deals with prostitution). Shaw's works brought the new realistic drama to Britain and introduced social and political issues as subjects for the theatre.
1895	Oscar Wilde's comedy *The Importance of Being Earnest*. Alfred Jarry's *Ubu Roi*, a forerunner of Surrealism.
1896	The first performance of Anton Chekhov's *The Seagull* failed.
1899	The Abbey Theatre, Dublin, founded by W B Yeats and Lady Gregory, marked the beginning of an Irish dramatic revival.
1904	Chekhov's *The Cherry Orchard*. The Academy of Dramatic Art (Royal Academy of Dramatic Art 1920) was founded in London to train young actors.
1919	The Theater Guild was founded in the USA to perform less commercial new plays.
1920	*Beyond the Horizon*, Eugene O'Neill's first play, marked the beginning of serious theatre in the USA.

Theatre: chronology (cont.)

1921	Luigi Pirandello's *Six Characters in Search of an Author* introduced themes of the individual and exploration of reality and appearance.
1928	Bertolt Brecht's *Die Dreigroschenoper/The Threepenny Opera* with score by Kurt Weill; other political satires by Karel Čapek and Elmer Rice. In the USA Jerome Kern's *Show Boat* with Paul Robeson, and other musical comedies by Cole Porter, Irving Berlin, and George Gershwin, became popular.
1930s	US social-protest plays of Clifford Odets, Lillian Hellman, Thornton Wilder, and William Saroyan.
1935	T S Eliot's *Murder in the Cathedral*.
1935–39	WPA Federal Theater Project in the USA.
1938	Publication of Antonin Artaud's *Theatre and Its Double*.
1943	The first of the musicals, *Oklahoma!*, opened.
1944–45	Jean-Paul Sartre's *Huis Clos/In Camera*; Jean Anouilh's *Antigone*; Arthur Miller's *Death of a Salesman*.
post–1945	Resurgence of German-language theatre, including Wolfgang Borchert, Max Frisch, Friedrich Dürrenmatt, and Peter Weiss.
1947	Tennessee Williams's *A Streetcar Named Desire*. First Edinburgh Festival, Scotland, with fringe theatre events.
1953	Arthur Miller's *The Crucible* opened in the USA; *En attendant Godot/Waiting for Godot* by Samuel Beckett exemplified the Theatre of the Absurd.
1956	The English Stage Company was formed at the Royal Court Theatre to provide a platform for new dramatists. John Osborne's *Look Back in Anger* was included in its first season.
1957	Leonard Bernstein's *West Side Story* opened in New York.
1960	Harold Pinter's *The Caretaker* was produced in London.
1960s	Off-off-Broadway theatre, a more daring and experimental type of drama, began to develop in New York.
1961	The Royal Shakespeare Company was formed in the UK under the directorship of Peter Hall.
1963–64	The UK National Theatre Company was formed at the Old Vic under the directorship of Laurence Olivier.
1967	Success in the USA of *Hair*, the first of the 'rock' musicals; Tom Stoppard's *Rosencrantz and Guildenstern are Dead* was produced at the Old Vic, London.
1968	Abolition of theatre censorship in the UK.
1975	*A Chorus Line*, to become the longest-running musical, opened in New York.
1980	Howard Brenton's *The Romans in Britain* led in the UK to a private prosecution of the director for obscenity.
1987	The Japanese Ninagawa Company performed Shakespeare's *Macbeth* in London.
1989	Discovery of the remains of the 16th-century Rose and Globe theatres, London.
1990	The Royal Shakespeare Company suspended its work at the Barbican Centre, London, for six months, pleading lack of funds.
1993	Agatha Christie's *The Mousetrap* entered its 41st year in the West End, London, the longest-running play in the world.

was first popularized 1603; its colourful, lively spectacle became popular through the 17th and 18th centuries, although from 1629 only men were allowed to act, in the interests of propriety. The art was modernized and its following revived in the 1980s by Ennosuke III (1940–   ). Unlike Nō actors, kabuki actors do not wear masks; and many specialize in particular types of character, female impersonators (*onnagata*) being the biggest stars.

masque spectacular and essentially aristocratic entertainment with a fantastic or mythological theme in which music, dance, and extravagant costumes and scenic design figured larger than plot. Originating in Italy, it reached its height of popularity at the English court between 1600 and 1640, with the collaboration of Ben Jonson as writer and Inigo Jones as stage designer. The masque powerfully influenced the development of ballet and opera, and the elaborate frame in which it was performed developed into the proscenium arch.

melodrama play or film with romantic and sensational plot elements, often unsubtly acted. Originally it meant a play accompanied by music. The early melodramas used extravagant theatrical effects to heighten violent emotions and actions artificially. By the end of the 19th century, melodrama had become a popular genre of stage play.

mime type of acting in which gestures, movements, and facial expressions replace speech. It has developed as a form of theatre, particularly in France, where Marcel Marceau and Jean Louis Barrault have continued the traditions established in the 19th century by Deburau and the practices of the commedia dell'arte in Italy. In ancient Greece, mime was a crude, realistic comedy with dialogue and exaggerated gesture.

morality play didactic medieval European verse drama, in part a development of the mystery play (or miracle play), in which human characters are replaced by personified virtues and vices, the limited humorous elements being provided by the Devil. Morality plays, such as *Everyman*, flourished in the 15th century. They exerted an influence on the development of Elizabethan drama.

musical 20th-century form of dramatic musical performance, combining elements of song, dance, and the spoken word, often characterized by lavish staging and large casts. It developed from the operettas and musical comedies of the 19th century.

The *operetta* is a light-hearted entertainment with extensive musical content: Jaques Offenbach, Johann Strauss, Franz Lehár, and Gilbert and Sullivan all composed operettas. The *musical comedy* is an anglicization of the French *opéra bouffe*, of which the first was *A Gaiety Girl* 1893, mounted by George Edwardes (1852–1915) at the Gaiety Theatre, London. Typical musical comedies of the 1920s were *The Student Prince* 1924 and *The Desert Song* 1926, by Sigmund Romberg. The 1930s and 1940s were an era of sophisticated musical comedies with many filmed examples and a strong US presence (Irving Berlin, Jerome Kern, Cole Porter, and George Gershwin). In 1943 the word 'comedy' was dropped and the era of the 'musical' arrived with Rodgers and Hammerstein's *Oklahoma!*; this show introduced an integration of plot and music, which was developed in Lerner and Loewe's *My Fair Lady* 1956 and Leonard Bernstein's *West Side Story* 1957. In England in the 1930s and 1940s Noël Coward and Ivor Novello also wrote stylish musicals. Sandy Wilson's *The Boy Friend* 1953 revived the British musical and was followed by hits such as Lionel Bart's *Oliver!* 1960. Musicals began to branch into religious and political themes with *Oh What a Lovely War!* 1963, produced by Joan Littlewood and Charles Chiltern, and the Andrew Lloyd Webber musicals *Jesus Christ Superstar* 1970 and *Evita* 1978. Another category of musical, substituting a theme for conventional plotting, includes Stephen Sondheim's *Company* 1970, Hamlisch and Kleban's *A Chorus Line* 1975, and Lloyd Webber's *Cats* 1981, using verses by T S Eliot. In the 1980s 19th-century melodrama was popular, for example *Phantom of the Opera* 1986 and *Les Misérables* 1987 (both Lloyd Webber.)

music hall British light theatrical entertainment, in which singers, dancers, comedians, and acrobats perform in 'turns'. Music hall originated in the 17th century, when tavern-keepers acquired the organs that the Puritans had banished from churches. On certain nights organ music was played, and this resulted in a weekly entertainment known as the 'free and easy'. The music hall's heyday was at the beginning of the 20th century, with such artistes as Marie Lloyd, Harry Lauder, and George Formby. The US equivalent is vaudeville.

mystery play or *miracle play* medieval religious drama based on stories from the Bible. Mystery plays were performed around the time of church festivals, reaching their height in Europe during the 15th and 16th centuries. A whole cycle running from the Creation to the Last Judgement was performed in separate scenes on mobile wagons by various town guilds. Four English cycles survive: Coventry, Wakefield (or Townley), Chester, and York. Versions are still performed, such as the York cycle in York.

Nō or *Noh* the classical, aristocratic Japanese drama, which developed from the 14th to the 16th centuries and is still performed. There is a repertory of some 250 pieces, of which five, one from each of the several classes devoted to different subjects, may be put on in a performance lasting a whole day. Dance, mime, music, and chanting develop the mythical or historical themes. All the actors are men, some of whom wear masks and elaborate costumes; scenery is limited. Nō developed from popular rural entertainments and religious performances staged at shrines and temples by travelling companies. The leader of one of these troupes, Kan'ami (1333–1384), and his son and successor Zeami (1363–1443/4) wrote a number of Nō plays and are regarded as the founders of the form. Symbolism and suggestion dominate action, and the slow, stylized dance is the strongest element. Flute, drums, and chorus supply the music. Nō influenced kabuki drama.

pageant originally the wagon on which medieval mystery plays were performed. The term was later applied to the street procession of songs, dances, and historical tableaux that became fashionable during the 1920s and exist today in forms such as the Lord Mayor's Show in London, England. The open-air entertainment *Son et Lumière* is related to the pageant.

pantomime in the British theatre, a traditional Christmas entertainment with its origins in the harlequin spectacle of the 18th century and burlesque of the 19th century, which gave rise to the tradition of the principal boy being played by an actress and the dame by an actor. The harlequin's role diminished altogether as themes developed on folktales such as *The Sleeping Beauty* and *Cinderella*, and with the introduction of additional material such as popular songs, topical comedy, and audience participation. The term 'pantomime' was also applied to Roman dumbshows performed by a masked actor, to 18th-century ballets with mythical themes, and, in 19th-century France, to the wordless Pierrot plays from which modern mime developed.

puppet theatre drama performed with puppets manipulated by usually unseen operators. By the 16th and 17th centuries refined versions of the travelling puppet shows became popular with the aristocracy, and puppets were extensively used in caricature and satire until the 19th century. There has been a revival of interest in the 20th century, partly stimulated by the influence of the *joruri* tradition in Japan, and by leading exponents of rod puppets such as Obraztsov and his Moscow Puppet Theatre, and by Fluck and Law, whose satirical *Spitting Image* puppets, caricaturing public figures, have appeared on British television.

Wayang Kulit is Indonesian shadow puppet theatre, with characters drawn from the Sanskrit epic tradition contrasted with grotesque demons and clowns. Performances, with jointed puppets cut from leather, are accompanied by the brass gong orchestra known as the gamelan, and may last all through the night, on private or public celebrations. Similar forms of shadow puppet theatre are found in India and Malaya.

revue stage presentation involving short satirical and topical items in the form of songs, sketches, and monologues; it originated in the late 19th century. In Britain the first revue seems to have been *Under the Clock* 1893 by Seymour Hicks (1871–1949) and Charles Brookfield. The 1920s revues were spectacular entertainments, but the 'intimate revue' became increasingly popular, employing writers such as Noël

Recent theatre award winners

American Theater Wing Antoinette Perry (Tony) Awards, 1986–1993 (Best Play, Best Musical, and Best Revival production)

1986	*I'm Not Rappaport, The Mystery of Edwin Drood, Sweet Charity*
1987	*Fences, Les Miserables, All My Sons*
1988	*M. Butterfly, The Phantom of the Opera, Anything Goes*
1989	*The Heidi Chronicles, Jerome Robbins' Broadway, Our Town*
1990	*The Grapes of Wrath, City of Angels, Gypsy*
1991	*Lost in Yonkers, The Will Rogers Follies, Fiddler on the Roof*
1992	*Dancing at Lughnasa, Crazy for You, Guys and Dolls*
1993	*Angels in America, Kiss of the Spider Women, Anna Christie*

The Laurence Olivier Awards, presented by The Society of West End Theatre (Best Play, Best Musical, and Best Comedy)

1986	*Les Liaisons Dangereuses, The Phantom of the Opera, When We Are Married*
1987	*Serious Money, Follies, Three Men on a Horse*
1988	*Our Country's Good, Candide, Shirley Valentine*
1989/90	*Racing Demon, Return to the Forbidden Planet, Single Spies*
1991	*Dancing at Lughnasa, Sunday in the Park with George, Out of Order*
1992	*Death and the Maiden, Carmen Jones, La Bête*
1993	*Six Degrees of Separation, Crazy for You, The Rise and Fall of Little Voice*

Evening Standard Drama Awards (Best Play, Best Musical, and Best Comedy)

1986	*Les Liaisons Dangereuses, The Phantom of the Opera, A Month of Sundays*
1987	*A Small Family Business, Follies, Serious Money*
1988	*Aristocrats,* (award for Best Musical was not presented), *Lettice and Lovage*
1989	*Ghetto, Miss Saigon, Henceforward*
1990	*Shadowlands, Into the Woods, Man of the Moment* and *Jeffrey Bernard is Unwell* (joint award)
1991	*Dancing at Lughnasa, Carmen Jones, Kvetch*
1992	*Angels in America, Kiss of the Spider Woman, The Rise and Fall of Little Voice*
1993	*Arcadia, City of Angels, Jamais Vu*

Coward. During the 1960s the satirical revue took off with the Cambridge Footlights' production *Beyond the Fringe*, establishing the revue tradition among the young and at fringe theatrical events.

theatre-in-the-round theatrical performance that has the audience watching from all sides. In a reaction against the picture-frame stage of the 19th century, a movement began in the mid-20th century to design theatres with the performing area placed centrally in the auditorium. Notable examples are The Arena Stage in Washington DC, USA 1961 and the Royal Exchange in Manchester, England 1976. The concept was promoted in productions by Margo Jones (1913–1955) in Dallas, USA, who wrote a book on her work, *Theater-in-the-Round* 1951.

tragedy a play dealing with a serious theme, traditionally one in which a character meets disaster as a result either of personal failings or circumstances beyond his or her control. Historically the Greek view of tragedy, as defined by Aristotle and expressed by the great tragedians Aeschylus, Euripides, and Sophocles, has been predominant in the western tradition. In the 20th century, tragedies in the narrow Greek sense – that is, concerned with exalted personages and written in an elevated manner – have virtually died out. Tragedy has been replaced by dramas with 'tragic' implications or overtones, as in the work of Ibsen, O'Neill, Tennessee Williams, Pinter, and Osborne, for example, or by the hybrid tragicomedy. *Revenge tragedy* was a form of Elizabeth and Jacobean drama in which revenge formed the mainspring of the action. Characterized by bloody deeds, intrigue, and high melodrama, it was pioneered by Thomas Kyd with *The Spanish Tragedy* c. 1589, Shakespeare's *Titus Andronicus c.* 1592, and Cyril Tourneur's *The Revenger's Tragedy c.* 1606. Its influence is apparent in tragedies such as Shakespeare's *Hamlet* and *Macbeth*.

Biographies

Aeschylus *c.* 525–*c.* 456 BC. Athenian dramatist, who developed Greek tragedy by introducing the second actor, thus enabling true dialogue and dramatic action to occur independently of the chorus. Ranked with Euripides and Sophocles as one of the three great tragedians, Aeschylus composed some 90 plays between 500–456 BC, of which seven survive in his name: *Persians* 472 BC, *Seven Against Thebes* 467, *Suppliants* 463, the *Oresteia* trilogy, and *Prometheus Bound* (the last, although attributed to him, is of uncertain authorship).

Albee Edward 1928– . US playwright. His internationally performed plays are associated with the Theatre of the Absurd and include *The Zoo Story* 1960, *The American Dream* 1961, *Who's Afraid of Virginia Woolf?* 1962 (his most successful play; also filmed with Elizabeth Taylor and Richard Burton as the quarrelling, alcoholic, academic couple 1966), and *Tiny Alice* 1965. *A Delicate Balance* 1966 and *Seascape* 1975 both won Pulitzer prizes.

Anouilh Jean 1910–1987. French dramatist. His plays, influenced by the Neo-Classical tradition, include *Antigone* 1942, *L'Invitation au château/Ring Round the Moon* 1947, *Colombe* 1950, and *Becket* 1959, about St Thomas à Becket and Henry II.

Aristophanes *c.* 448–380 BC. Greek comedic dramatist. Of his 11 extant plays (of a total of over 40), the early comedies are remarkable for the violent satire with which he ridiculed the democratic war leaders. He also satirized contemporary issues such as the new learning of Socrates in *The Clouds* 423 BC and the power of women in *Lysistrata* 411 BC. The chorus plays a prominent role, frequently giving the play its title, as in *The Wasps* 422 BC, *The Birds* 414 BC, and *The Frogs* 405 BC.

Artaud Antonin 1896–1948. French theatre director. Although his play, *Les Cenci/The Cenci* 1935, was a failure, his concept of the *Theatre of Cruelty*, intended to release feelings usually repressed in the unconscious, has been an important influence on modern dramatists such as Albert Camus and Jean Genet and on directors and producers. Declared insane 1936, Artaud was confined in an asylum.

Ayckbourn Alan 1939– . English playwright. His prolific output, characterized by comic dialogue and experiments in dramatic structure, includes the trilogy *The Norman Conquests* 1974, *A Woman in Mind* 1986, *Henceforward* 1987, and *Man of the Moment* 1988.

Barker Howard 1946– . English playwright whose plays, renowned for their uncompromising and poetically dense language, confront the issues of private ambition and the exploitation of power. Among his works are *Victory* 1982; *The Castle* 1985; *The Last Supper*, *The Possibilities*, and *The Bite of the Night*, all 1988; and *Seven Lears* 1989. Essentially, his plays examine the human spirit when it is subjected to dictatorship, whether mental or physical.

Baylis Lilian 1874–1937. English theatre manager, who was responsible for re-opening Sadler's Wells Theatre, London 1931. From 1934 Sadler's Wells specialized in productions of opera and ballet: the resultant companies eventually became the Royal Ballet and the English National Opera.

Beckett Samuel 1906–1989. Irish novelist and dramatist who wrote in French and English. His *En attendant Godot/Waiting for Godot* 1952 is possibly the most universally known example of Theatre of the Absurd, in which life is taken to be meaningless. This genre is taken to further extremes in *Fin de Partie/Endgame* 1957 and *Happy Days* 1961. Nobel Prize for Literature 1969.

Berkoff Steven 1937– . English dramatist and actor whose abrasive and satirical plays, often informed by classical literature, include *East* 1975, *Greek* 1979, and *West* 1983. Berkoff's production of Oscar Wilde's *Salome* was staged 1991. In 1968 he set up the London Theatre Group, whose highly physical productions have included Berkoff's adaptations of Kafka's *Metamorphosis* 1969 and *The Trial* 1970, and Poe's *The Fall of the House of Usher* 1974.

Bond Edward 1935– . English dramatist. His early work aroused controversy because of the savagery of some of his imagery, for example, the brutal stoning of a baby by bored youths in *Saved* 1965. Other works include *Early Morning* 1968, the last play to be banned in the UK by the Lord Chamberlain; *Lear* 1972, a

reworking of Shakespeare's play; *Bingo* 1973, an account of Shakespeare's last days; and *The War Plays* 1985.

Boucicault Dion(ysus) Larner 1822–1890. Irish dramatist and actor. His first success was with the social comedy *London Assurance* 1841, and during his long career he wrote or adapted about 200 plays, many of them melodramas, including *The Corsican Brothers* 1852 and *Louis XI* 1855. He moved to the USA 1872 where *The Poor of New York* 1857, *The Octoroon* 1859, and *The Colleen Bawn* 1860 had been produced.

Branagh Kenneth 1960– . British actor and director. He cofounded, with David Parfitt, the Renaissance Theatre Company 1987, was a notable Hamlet and Touchstone in 1988, and in 1989 directed and starred in a film of Shakespeare's *Henry V*.

Brecht Bertolt 1898–1956. German dramatist and poet who aimed to destroy the 'suspension of disbelief' usual in the theatre – to this end he developed a number of 'alienation techniques' – and to express Marxist ideas. He adapted John Gay's *Beggar's Opera* as *Die Dreigroschenoper/The Threepenny Opera* 1928, set to music by Kurt Weill. Later plays include *Galileo* 1938, *Mutter Courage/Mother Courage* 1941, set during the Thirty Years' War, and *Der kaukasische Kreidekreis/The Caucasian Chalk Circle* 1949. In 1949 he established the Berliner Ensemble theatre group in East Germany.

Brook Peter 1925– . English director renowned for his experimental productions. His work with the Royal Shakespeare Company included a production of Shakespeare's *A Midsummer Night's Dream* 1970, set in a white gymnasium and combining elements of circus and commedia dell'arte. In the same year he established Le Centre International de Créations Théâtrales/The International Centre for Theatre Research in Paris. Brook's later productions transcend Western theatre conventions and include *The Conference of the Birds* 1973, based on a Persian story, and *The Mahabharata* 1985–88, a cycle of three plays based on the Hindu epic. His films include *Lord of the Flies* 1962 and *Meetings with Remarkable Men* 1979.

Büchner Georg 1813–1837. German dramatist. His characters were often individuals pitted against the forces of society. Büchner's plays include *Danton's Death* 1835, which chronicles the power struggle between Danton and Robespierre during the French Revolution; and *Woyzeck* 1836, unfinished at his death, which depicts the despair of a common soldier, crushed by his social superiors. Büchner's third play is the comedy *Leonce and Lena* 1836. Unperformed until well after his death, his plays have been repeatedly produced in the 20th century.

Chekhov Anton (Pavlovich) 1860–1904. Russian dramatist and writer of short stories. His plays concentrate on the creation of atmosphere and delineation of internal development, rather than external action. His first play, *Ivanov* 1887, was a failure, as was *The Seagull* 1896 until revived by Stanislavsky 1898 at the Moscow Art Theatre, for which Chekhov went on to write his finest plays: *Uncle Vanya* 1899, *The Three Sisters* 1901, and *The Cherry Orchard* 1904.

Churchill Caryl 1938– . English playwright. Her predominantly radical and feminist works include

Top Girls 1982, a study of the hazards encountered by 'career' women throughout history; *Serious Money* 1987, which satirized the world of London's brash young financial brokers; and *Mad Forest* 1990, set in Romania during the overthrow of the Ceauşescu regime.

Congreve William 1670–1729. English dramatist and poet. His first success was the comedy *The Old Bachelor* 1693, followed by *The Double Dealer* 1694, *Love for Love* 1695, the tragedy *The Mourning Bride* 1697, and *The Way of the World* 1700. His plays, which satirize the social affectations of the time, are characterized by elegant wit and wordplay.

Corneille Pierre 1606–1684. French dramatist. His many tragedies, such as *Oedipe* 1659, glorify the strength of will governed by reason, and established the French classical dramatic tradition for the next two centuries. His first play, *Mélite*, was performed 1629, followed by others that gained him a brief period of favour with Cardinal Richelieu. *Le Cid* 1636 was attacked by the Academicians, although it received public acclaim. Later plays were based on Aristotle's unities; Louis XIV approved, and he was elected to the Académie 1647 .

Coward Noël 1899–1973. English playwright, actor, producer, director, and composer, who epitomized the witty and sophisticated man of the theatre. From his first success with *The Young Idea* 1923, he wrote and appeared in plays and comedies on both sides of the Atlantic such as *Hay Fever* 1925, *Private Lives* 1930 with Gertrude Lawrence, *Design for Living* 1933, and *Blithe Spirit* 1941. Coward also wrote for and acted in films, including the patriotic *In Which We Serve* 1942 and the sentimental *Brief Encounter* 1945.

de Filippo Eduardo 1900–1984. Italian actor and dramatist. He founded his own company in Naples 1932, which was strongly influenced by the commedia dell'arte, and for which he wrote many plays. These include his finest comedies, *Filumena Marturano* 1946, *Napoli milionaria!* 1945, *Questi fantasmi!/These Ghosts!* 1946, *Grande magia/Grand Magic* 1951, and *Saturday, Sunday, Monday* 1959.

Donellan Declan 1953– . British theatre director, cofounder of the **Cheek by Jowl** theatre company 1981, and associate director of the National Theatre from 1989. His irreverent and audacious productions include many classics, such as Racine's *Andromaque* 1985, Corneille's *Le Cid* 1987, and Ibsen's *Peer Gynt* 1990; and Stephen Sondheim's musical *Sweeney Todd* 1993.

Euripides *c.* 485–*c.* 406 BC. Athenian tragic dramatist, ranked with Aeschylus and Sophocles as one of the three great tragedians, though he had more influence on the development of later drama than either Aeschylus or Sophocles. Drawing on the sophists, he transformed tragedy with unheroic themes. He wrote about 90 plays, of which 18 and some long fragments survive. These include *Alcestis* 438 BC, *Medea* 431, *Hippolytus* 428, the satyr-drama *Cyclops* about 424–423, *Electra, Trojan Women* 415, *Iphigenia in Tauris* 413, *Iphigenia in Aulis* about 414–412, and *The Bacchae* about 405 (the last two were produced shortly after his death).

Eyre Richard (Charles Hastings) 1943– . English stage and film director who succeeded Peter Hall as artistic director of the National Theatre, London, 1988. His stage productions include *Guys and Dolls* 1982, *Bartholomew Fair* 1988, and *Richard III* 1990, which he set in 1930s Britain. His films include *The Ploughman's Lunch* 1983 and *Laughterhouse* (US *Singleton's Pluck*) 1984.

Feydeau Georges 1862–1921. French comic dramatist. He is the author of over 60 farces and light comedies, which have been repeatedly revived in France at the Comédie Française and abroad. These include *La dame de chez Maxim/The Girl from Maxim's* 1899, *Une puce à l'oreille/A Flea in her Ear* 1907, *Feu la mère de Madame/My Late Mother-in-Law*, and *Occupe-toi d'Amélie/Look after Lulu*, both 1908.

Fo Dario 1926– . Italian playwright and actor. His plays are predominantly political satires, combining black humour with slapstick. They include *Morte accidentale di un anarchico/Accidental Death of an Anarchist* 1970, and *Non si paga non si paga/Can't Pay? Won't Pay!* 1975/1981.

Ford John 1586–*c.* 1640. English poet and dramatist. His play *'Tis Pity She's a Whore* (performed about 1626, printed 1633) is a study of incest between brother and sister.

Friel Brian 1929– . Northern Irish dramatist whose work often deals with the social and historical pressures that contribute to the Irish political situation. His first success was with *Philadelphia, Here I Come!* 1964, which dealt with the theme of exile. In 1980 he founded the Field Day Theatre Company, which produced *Translations* 1981, a study of British cultural colonialism in 19th-century Ireland. Other plays include *The Freedom of the City* 1973, about victims of the Ulster conflict, *Faith Healer* 1980, and the critically acclaimed *Dancing at Lughnasa* 1990.

Genet Jean 1910–1986. French dramatist, novelist, and poet, an exponent of the Theatre of Cruelty. His turbulent life and early years spent in prison are reflected in his drama, characterized by ritual, roleplay, and illusion, in which his characters come to act out their bizarre and violent fantasies. His plays include *Les Bonnes/The Maids* 1947, *Le Balcon/The Balcony* 1957, and two plays dealing with the Algerian situation: *Les Nègres/The Blacks* 1959 and *Les Paravents/The Screens* 1961.

Goethe Johann Wolfgang von 1749–1832. German poet, novelist, and dramatist, generally considered the founder of modern German literature, and leader of the Romantic *Sturm und Drang* ('storm and stress') movement. His works include the autobiographical *Die Leiden des Jungen Werthers/The Sorrows of Young Werther* 1774 and *Faust* 1808, his masterpiece. A visit to Italy 1786–88 inspired the classical dramas *Iphigenie auf Tauris/Iphigenia in Tauris* 1787 and *Torquato Tasso* 1790.

Goldoni Carlo 1707–1793. Italian dramatist, born in Venice. He wrote popular comedies for the Sant'Angelo theatre, including *La putta onorata/The Respectable Girl* 1749, *I pettegolezzi delle donne/Women's Gossip* 1750, and *La locandiera/Mine Hostess* 1753. In 1761 he moved to Paris, where he directed the Italian theatre and wrote more plays, including *L'Eventail/The Fan* 1763.

Grotowski Jerzy 1933– . Polish theatre director. His ascetic theory of performance in *Towards a Poor Theatre* 1968 has had a great influence on experimental theatre in the USA and Europe. His most famous productions were *Akropolis* 1962, *The Constant Prince* 1965, and *Apocalypsis cum Figuris* 1969, which he toured widely.

Guthrie Tyrone 1900–1971. British theatre director, notable for his experimental approach. Administrator of the Old Vic and Sadler's Wells theatres 1939–45, he helped found the Ontario (Stratford) Shakespeare Festival 1953 and the Minneapolis theatre now named after him.

Hall Peter (Reginald Frederick) 1930– . English theatre, opera, and film director. He was director of the Royal Shakespeare Theatre in Stratford-on-Avon 1960–68 and developed the Royal Shakespeare Company 1968–73 until appointed director of the National Theatre 1973–88, succeeding Laurence Olivier. He was appointed artistic director of opera at Glyndebourne 1984. He founded the Peter Hall Company 1988.

Hare David 1947– . British dramatist and director, whose plays include *Slag* 1970, *Teeth 'n' Smiles* 1975, *Pravda* 1985 (with Howard Brenton), and *Wrecked Eggs* 1986.

Ibsen Henrik (Johan) 1828–1906. Norwegian playwright and poet, whose realistic and often controversial plays revolutionized European theatre. Driven into exile 1864–91 by opposition to the satirical *Love's Comedy* 1862, he wrote the verse dramas *Brand* 1866 and *Peer Gynt* 1867, followed by realistic plays dealing with social issues, including *Pillars of Society* 1877, *A Doll's House* 1879, *Ghosts* 1881, *An Enemy of the People* 1882, and *Hedda Gabler* 1891. By the time he returned to Norway, he was recognized as the country's greatest living writer. His later plays, which are more symbolic, include *The Master Builder* 1892, *Little Eyolf* 1894, *John Gabriel Borkman* 1896, and *When We Dead Awaken* 1899.

Ionesco Eugène 1912–1994. Romanian-born French dramatist. He was a leading exponent of the Theatre of the Absurd. Most of his plays are in one act and concern the futility of language as a means of communication. These include *La Cantatrice chauve/The Bald Prima Donna* 1950 and *La Leçon/The Lesson* 1951. Later full-length plays include *Rhinocéros* 1958 and *Le Roi se meurt/Exit the King* 1961.

Jonson Ben(jamin) 1572–1637. English dramatist, poet, and critic. *Every Man in his Humour* 1598 established the English 'comedy of humours', in which each character embodies a 'humour', or vice, such as greed, lust, or avarice. This was followed by *Every Man out of his Humour* 1599, *Cynthia's Revels* 1600 and *Poetaster* 1601. His first extant tragedy is *Sejanus* 1603, with Burbage and Shakespeare as members of the original cast. The plays of his middle years include *Volpone, or The Fox* 1606, *The Alchemist* 1610, and *Bartholomew Fair* 1614.

Kantor Tadeusz 1915–1990. Polish theatre director and scene designer. He founded his experimental theatre Cricot 2 in 1955, and produced such plays as the *Dead Class* 1975, with which he became internationally known. Later productions include *Wielopole, Wielopole* 1980, *Let the Artists Die* 1985, and *I Shall Never Return* 1988.

Kazan Elia´ 1909– . US stage and film director, a founder of the Actors Studio 1947. Plays he directed include *The Skin of Our Teeth* 1942, *A Streetcar Named Desire* 1947, and *Cat on a Hot Tin Roof* 1955; films include *Gentlemen's Agreement* 1948, *East of Eden* 1954, and *The Visitors* 1972.

Littlewood Joan 1914– . English theatre director. She was responsible for many vigorous productions at the Theatre Royal, Stratford (London) 1953–75, such as *A Taste of Honey* 1959, *The Hostage* 1959–60, and *Oh, What a Lovely War* 1963. She established the Theatre Workshop 1945.

Lorca Federico García 1898–1936. Spanish poet and playwright, born in Granada. His plays include *Bodas de sangre/Blood Wedding* 1933 and *La casa de Bernarda Alba/The House of Bernarda Alba* 1936. His poems include *Lament*, written for the bullfighter Mejías. Lorca was shot by the Falangists during the Spanish Civil War.

Mamet David 1947– . US playwright. His plays, with their vivid, freewheeling language and sense of ordinary US life, include *American Buffalo* 1977, *Sexual Perversity in Chicago* 1978, *Glengarry Glen Ross* 1984 (filmed 1992), *Speed-the-Plow* 1988, and *Oleanna* 1992, about a sexual harrassment case.

Marlowe Christopher 1564–1593. English poet and dramatist. His work includes the blank-verse plays *Tamburlaine the Great* c. 1587, *The Jew of Malta* c. 1589, *Edward II* and *Dr Faustus*, both c. 1592, the poem *Hero and Leander* 1598, and a translation of Ovid's *Amores*.

McGrath John 1935– . Scottish dramatist and director. He founded the socialist 7:84 Theatre Companies in England 1971 and Scotland 1973, and is the author of such plays as *Events Guarding the Bofors Gun* 1966; *The Cheviot, the Stag, and the Black, Black Oil* 1973, a musical account of the economic exploitation of the Scottish highlands; and *The Garden of England* 1985.

Matura Mustapha 1939– . Trinidad-born British dramatist. Cofounder of the Black Theatre Cooperative 1978, his plays deal with problems of ethnic diversity and integration. These include *As Time Goes By* 1971, *Play Mas* 1974, and *Meetings* 1981. Other works include *Playboy of the West Indies* 1984 and *Trinidad Sisters* 1988, his adaptations of plays by Synge and Chekhov, and *The Coup* 1991.

Meyerhold Vsevolod 1874–1940. Russian actor and director. Before the revolution of 1917 he developed a strong interest in commedia dell'arte and stylized acting. He developed a system of actor-training known as bio-mechanics, which combined insights drawn from sport, the circus, and modern studies of time and motion. A member of the Moscow Art Theatre, he was briefly director of its Studio theatre under Stanislavsky 1905. He produced the Russian poet Mayakovsky's futurist *Mystery-Bouffe* 1918 and 1921, and later his *The Bed Bug* 1929.

Miller Arthur 1915– . US playwright. His plays deal with family relationships and contemporary American values, and include *Death of a Salesman* 1949 and *The Crucible* 1953, based on the Salem witch trials and reflecting the communist witch-hunts of Senator Joe McCarthy. He was married 1956–61 to the film star Marilyn Monroe, for whom he wrote the film *The Misfits* 1960. Among other plays are *All My Sons* 1947, *A View from the Bridge* 1955, and *After the Fall* 1964, based on his relationship with Monroe.

Mnouchkine Ariane 1939– . French theatre director. She founded the Theatre du Soleil 1964, which established a reputation with a vigorous production of Arnold Wesker's *The Kitchen* 1967. After 1968, the company began to devise its own material, firstly with *The Clowns* 1969, which was followed by *1789* 1970, an exploration of the French Revolution, and *L'Age d'Or* 1975, concerning the exploitation of immigrant workers. She has also collaborated with the writer Helene Cixous on *Sihanouk* 1985, a production about Cambodia, and directed *Les Atrides* 1992, a version of Aeschylus' *Oresteia*.

Molière Pen name of Jean Baptiste Poquelin 1622–1673. French satirical playwright from whose work modern French comedy developed. One of the founders of the Illustre Théâtre 1643, he was later its leading actor. In 1655 he wrote his first play, *L'Etourdi*, followed by *Les Précieuses Ridicules* 1659. His satires include *L'Ecole des femmes* 1662, *Le Misanthrope* 1666, *Le Bourgeois Gentilhomme* 1670, and *Le Malade imaginaire* 1673. Other satiric plays include *Tartuffe* 1664 (banned until 1697 for attacking the hypocrisy of the clergy), *Le Médecin malgré lui* 1666, and *Les Femmes savantes* 1672.

Müller Heiner 1929– . German dramatist whose scripts have played a leading role in contemporary avant-garde theatre in Germany and abroad. Early political works, showing the influence of Brecht, (*The Scab* 1950, and *The Correction* 1958) were followed by *Mauser* 1970, *Cement* 1972 (on the Russian revolution), *Hamletmachine* 1977, and *Medea-material* 1982.

O'Casey Sean. Adopted name of John Casey 1884–1964. Irish dramatist. His early plays are tragicomedies, blending realism with symbolism and poetic with vernacular speech: *The Shadow of a Gunman* 1922, *Juno and the Paycock* 1925, *The Plough and the Stars* 1926, and *The Silver Tassie* 1929. Later plays include *Red Roses for Me* 1946 and *The Drums of Father Ned* 1960.

Odets Clifford 1906–1963. US playwright, associated with the Group Theater and the most renowned of the social-protest playwrights of the Depression era. His plays include *Waiting for Lefty* 1935, about a taxi drivers' strike, *Awake and Sing* 1935, *Golden Boy* 1937, and *The Country Girl* 1950. In the late 1930s he became a successful Hollywood film writer and director, but he continued to write plays.

Olivier Laurence (Kerr), Baron Olivier 1907–1989. English actor and director. For many years associated with the Old Vic theatre, he was director of the National Theatre company 1962–73. His stage roles include Henry V, Hamlet, Richard III, and Archie

Rice in John Osborne's *The Entertainer*. His acting and direction of filmed versions of Shakespeare's plays received critical acclaim – for example, *Henry V* 1944 and *Hamlet* 1948. Olivier, appeared on screen in many films, including *Wuthering Heights* 1939, *Sleuth* 1972, and *The Boys from Brazil* 1978.

O'Neill Eugene (Gladstone) 1888–1953. US playwright, the leading dramatist between World Wars I and II. His plays include *Anna Christie* 1922, *Desire under the Elms* 1924, *The Iceman Cometh* 1946, and the posthumously produced autobiographical drama *Long Day's Journey into Night* 1956 (written 1940). Other plays include *Strange Interlude* 1928 (which lasts five hours) and *Mourning Becomes Electra* 1931 (a trilogy on the theme of Orestes from Greek mythology). He was awarded the Nobel prize for Literature 1936.

Orton Joe 1933–1967. English dramatist in whose black comedies surreal and violent action takes place in genteel and unlikely settings. Plays include *Entertaining Mr Sloane* 1964, *Loot* 1966, and *What the Butler Saw* 1968. His diaries deal frankly with his personal life. He was murdered by his lover Kenneth Halliwell.

Osborne John (James) 1929–1994. English dramatist. He became one of the first Angry Young Men (anti-establishment writers of the 1950s) of British theatre with his debut play, *Look Back in Anger* 1956. Other plays include *The Entertainer* 1957, *Luther* 1960, and *Watch It Come Down* 1976.

Ostrovsky Alexander Nikolaevich 1823–1886. Russian playwright, founder of the modern Russian theatre. He dealt satirically with the manners of the middle class in numerous plays – for example, *A Family Affair* 1850. His fairy-tale play *The Snow Maiden* 1873 inspired the composers Tchaikovsky and Rimsky-Korsakov.

Pinter Harold 1930– . English dramatist, originally an actor. He specializes in the tragicomedy of the breakdown of communication, broadly in the tradition of the Theatre of the Absurd – for example, *The Birthday Party* 1958 and *The Caretaker* 1960. Later plays include *The Homecoming* 1965, *Old Times* 1971, *Betrayal* 1978, and *Mountain Language* 1988. Pinter's work is known for its pauses, allowing the audience to read between the lines. He writes for radio and television, and his screenplays include *The Go-Between* 1969 and *The French Lieutenant's Woman* 1982.

Pirandello Luigi 1867–1936. Italian writer. His plays include *La morsa/The Vice* 1912, *Sei personaggi in cerca d'autore/Six Characters in Search of an Author* 1921, and *Enrico IV/Henry IV* 1922. The themes and treatment of his plays anticipated the work of Brecht, O'Neill, Anouilh, and Genet. Nobel Prize 1934.

Piscator Erwin 1893–1966. German theatre director. He introduced the idea of epic theatre, using slide-projection, music, dance, and film to create a revolutionary social drama in the *Red Revue* 1921 and in *Hoppla, That's Life!* 1927. While in the USA 1939–51 he produced an adaptation of Tolstoy's *War and Peace* 1942, but returned to directing in Germany 1951, and produced plays by Ralf Hochhuth.

Planchon Roger 1931– . French theatre director, actor, and dramatist. After early productions of the plays of Adamov and Brecht he established a theatre company in Villeurbanne, outside Lyon, France 1957; it inherited the name Théâtre National Populaire in 1973. Major productions of Shakespeare (*Henry V* 1957) and Molière (*Tartuffe* 1962 and 1973) were followed by Pinter's *No Man's Land* 1979 and Racine's *Athalie* 1980.

Racine Jean 1639–1699. French dramatist and exponent of the classical tragedy in French drama. His subjects came from Greek mythology and he observed the rules of classical Greek drama. Most of his tragedies have women in the title role, for example *Andromaque* 1667, *Iphigénie* 1674, and *Phèdre* 1677. After the failure of *Phèdre* in the theatre he no longer wrote for the secular stage, but wrote two religious dramas, *Esther* 1689 and *Athalie* 1691, which achieved posthumous success.

Reinhardt Max 1873–1943. Austrian producer and director, whose Expressionist style was predominant in German theatre and film during the 1920s and 1930s. Directors such as Murnau and Lubitsch, and actors such as Dietrich worked with him. He co-directed the US film *A Midsummer Night's Dream* 1935.

Saint-Denis Michel 1897–1971. French director and actor. He founded both the Compagnie des Quinze 1930, and the London Theatre Studio 1936-39. From 1946–52 he was director of the Old Vic Theatre school, and became an artistic adviser for the Lincoln Centre in New York 1957, and later for the Royal Shakespeare Company in Britain 1962.

Schiller Johann Christoph Friedrich von 1759–1805. German dramatist, poet, and historian. He wrote *Sturm und Drang* verse and became the foremost German dramatist with his classic dramas *Wallenstein*, *Maria Stuart* 1800, *Die Jungfrau von Orleans/The Maid of Orleans* 1801, and *Wilhelm Tell/William Tell* 1804. He also wrote essays on aesthetics. Much of his work concerns the aspirations for political freedom and the avoidance of mediocrity.

Shakespeare William 1564–1616. English dramatist and poet. Established in London by 1589 as an actor and a playwright, he was England's unrivalled dramatist until his death, and is considered the greatest English playwright. His plays, written in blank verse, can be broadly divided into lyric plays, including *Romeo and Juliet* and *A Midsummer Night's Dream*; comedies, including *The Comedy of Errors*, *As You Like It*, *Much Ado About Nothing*, and *Measure For Measure*; historical plays, such as *Henry VI* (in three parts), *Richard III*, and *Henry IV* (in two parts), which often showed cynical political wisdom; and tragedies, such as *Hamlet*, *Macbeth*, and *King Lear*. He also wrote numerous sonnets.

Shaw George Bernard 1856–1950. Irish dramatist. He was also a critic and novelist, and an early member of the socialist Fabian Society. His plays combine comedy with political, philosophical, and polemic aspects, aiming to make an impact on his audience's social conscience as well as their emotions. They include *Arms and the Man* 1894, *Devil's Disciple* 1897, *Man and Superman* 1905, *Pygmalion*

Shakespeare: the plays

Title	Performed
Early plays	
Henry VI Part I	1589–92
Henry VI Part II	1589–92
Henry VI Part III	1589–92
The Comedy of Errors	1592–93
The Taming of the Shrew	1593–94
Titus Andronicus	1593–94
The Two Gentlemen of Verona	1594–95
Love's Labours Lost	1594–95
Romeo and Juliet	1594–95
Histories	
Richard III	1592–93
Richard II	1593–96
King John	1596–97
Henry IV Part I	1597–98
Henry IV Part II	1597–98
Henry V	1599
Roman plays	
Julius Caesar	1599–1600
Antony and Cleopatra	1607–08
Coriolanus	1607–08
The 'great' or 'middle' comedies	
A Midsummer Night's Dream	1595–96
The Merchant of Venice	1596–97
Much Ado About Nothing	1598–99
As You Like It	1599–1600
The Merry Wives of Windsor	1600–01
Twelfth Night	1601–02
The great tragedies	
Hamlet	1600–01
Othello	1604–05
King Lear	1605–06
Macbeth	1605–06
Timon of Athens	1607–08
The 'dark' comedies	
Troilus and Cressida	1601–02
All's Well That Ends Well	1602–03
Measure for Measure	1604–05
Late plays	
Pericles	1608–09
Cymbeline	1609–10
The Winter's Tale	1610–11
The Tempest	1611–12
Henry VIII	1612–13

1913, and *St Joan* 1924. Nobel prize 1925. Altogether Shaw wrote more than 50 plays and became a byword for wit. His theories were further explained in the voluminous prefaces to the plays, and in books.

Shepard Sam 1943– . US dramatist and actor. His work combines colloquial American dialogue with striking visual imagery, and includes *The Tooth of Crime* 1972 and *Buried Child* 1978, for which he won a Pulitzer Prize. *Seduced* 1979 is based on the life of the recluse Howard Hughes. He has acted in a number of films, including *The Right Stuff* 1983, *Fool for Love* 1986, based on his play of the same name, and *Steel Magnolias* 1989.

Sheridan Richard Brinsley 1751–1816. Irish dramatist and politician, born in Dublin. His social comedies include *The Rivals* 1775, celebrated for the character of Mrs Malaprop, *The School for Scandal* 1777, and *The Critic* 1779. In 1776 he became lessee of the Drury Lane Theatre. He became a member of Parliament in 1780.

Simon (Marvin) Neil 1927– . US playwright. His stage plays (which were made into films) include the wryly comic *Barefoot in the Park* 1963, *The Odd Couple* 1965, and *The Sunshine Boys* 1972, and the more serious, autobiographical trilogy *Brighton Beach Memoirs* 1983, *Biloxi Blues* 1985, and *Broadway Bound* 1986. He has also written screenplays and co-written musicals, including *Sweet Charity* 1966, *Promises, Promises* 1968, and *They're Playing Our Song* 1978.

Sophocles *c*. 496–406 BC. Athenian dramatist, attributed with having developed tragedy by introducing a third actor and scene-painting, and ranked with Aeschylus and Euripides as one of the three great tragedians. He wrote some 120 plays, of which seven tragedies survive. These are *Antigone* 441 BC, *Oedipus the King*, *Electra*, *Ajax*, *Trachiniae*, *Philoctetes* 409 BC, and *Oedipus at Colonus* 401 (produced after his death). In his tragedies heroic determination leads directly to violence unless, as in *Philoctetes* and *Oedipus at Colonus*, it contains an element of resignation.

Stanislavsky Konstantin Sergeivich 1863–1938. Russian actor, director, and teacher of acting. He rejected the declamatory style of acting in favour of a more realistic approach, concentrating on the psychological basis for the development of character. His ideas, which he described in *My Life in Art* 1924 and other works, had considerable influence on acting techniques in Europe and the USA. The Actors Studio is based on this approach.

Stein Peter 1937– . German theatre director. Artistic director of the politically radical Berlin Schaubühne 1970–85, Stein's early productions included Edward Bond's *Saved* 1967 and Goethe's *Torquato Tasso* 1969. These foreshadowed the spectacular staging of Ibsen's *Peer Gynt* 1971, and his exploratory show *Shakespeare's Memory* 1976. His final productions for the Schaubühne included Genet's *The Blacks* 1983 and Chekhov's *Three Sisters* 1984.

Stoppard Tom 1937– . Czechoslovak-born British playwright whose works use wit and wordplay to explore logical and philosophical ideas. His play *Rosencrantz and Guildenstern are Dead* 1966 was followed by comedies including *The Real Inspector Hound* 1968, *Jumpers* 1972, *Travesties* 1974, *Dirty Linen* 1976, *The Real Thing* 1982, *Hapgood* 1988, and *Arcadia* 1993. He has also written for radio, television, and the cinema.

Strasberg Lee 1902–1982. US actor and artistic director of the Actors Studio from 1948, who developed Method acting from Stanislavsky's system; pupils have included Marlon Brando, Paul Newman, Julie Harris, Kim Hunter, Geraldine Page, Al Pacino, and Robert de Niro.

Strindberg August 1849–1912. Swedish playwright and novelist. His plays, influential in the development of dramatic technique, are in a variety of styles including historical plays, symbolic dramas (the two-part *Dödsdansen/The Dance of Death* 1901), and 'chamber plays', such as *Spöksonaten/The Ghost [Spook] Sonata* 1907. *Fadren/The Father* 1887 and *Fröken Julie/Miss Julie* 1888 are among his works.

Synge J(ohn) M(illington) 1871–1909. Irish playwright, a leading figure in the Irish dramatic revival of the early 20th century. His six plays reflect the speech patterns of the Aran Islands and W Ireland. They include *In the Shadow of the Glen* 1903, *Riders to the Sea* 1904, and *The Playboy of the Western World* 1907, which caused riots at the Abbey Theatre, Dublin, when first performed.

Vega Lope Felix de (Carpio) 1562–1635. Spanish poet and dramatist, one of the founders of modern Spanish drama. He wrote epics, pastorals, odes, sonnets, novels, and, reputedly, over 1,500 plays (of which 426 are still in existence), mostly tragicomedies. He set out his views on drama in *Arte nuevo de hacer comedias/The New Art of Writing Plays* 1609, while reaffirming the classical form. *Fuenteovejuna* 1614 has been acclaimed as the first proletarian drama.

Webster John *c*. 1580–1634. English dramatist who ranks after Shakespeare as the greatest tragedian of his time and is the Jacobean whose plays are most frequently performed today. His two great plays *The White Devil* 1608 and *The Duchess of Malfi* 1614 are dark, violent tragedies obsessed with death and decay and infused with poetic brilliance.

Wedekind Frank 1864–1918. German dramatist. He was a forerunner of Expressionism with *Frühlings Erwachen/The Awakening of Spring* 1891, and *Der Erdgeist/The Earth Spirit* 1895 and its sequel *Der Marquis von Keith*. *Die Büchse der Pandora/Pandora's Box* 1904 was the source for Berg's opera *Lulu*.

Wilde Oscar (Fingal O'Flahertie Wills) 1854–1900. Irish writer. With his flamboyant style and quotable conversation, he dazzled London society and, on his lecture tour 1882, the USA. He published his only novel, *The Picture of Dorian Gray*, 1891, followed by the elegant, witty social comedies including *Lady Windermere's Fan* 1892, *A Woman of No Importance* 1893, *The Importance of Being Earnest* and *An Ideal Husband*, both 1895. The drama *Salome* 1893, based on the biblical character, was written in French; considered scandalous by the British censor, it was first performed in Paris 1896 with the actress Sarah Bernhardt in the title role. In 1895 he was imprisoned for two years for homosexual offences; he died in exile.

Wilder Thornton (Niven) 1897–1975. US playwright and novelist. He won Pulitzer prizes for the novel *The Bridge of San Luis Rey* 1927, and for the plays *Our Town* 1938 and *The Skin of Our Teeth* 1942. His farce *The Matchmaker* 1954 was filmed 1958. In 1964 it was adapted into the hit stage musical *Hello, Dolly!*, also made into a film.

Williams Tennessee (Thomas Lanier) 1911–1983. US playwright, born in Mississippi. His work is characterized by fluent dialogue and searching analysis of the psychological deficiencies of his characters. His plays, usually set in the Deep South against a background of decadence and degradation, include *The Glass Menagerie* 1945, *A Streetcar Named Desire* 1947, and *Cat on a Hot Tin Roof* 1955, the last two of which earned Pulitzer Prizes.

Wilson Robert 1944– . US avant-garde theatre director who specializes in non-narrative, elaborately visual theatre productions such as *Deafman Glance* 1971, *Ka Mountain* at the Shiraz Festival, Iran 1972, and *The Life and Times of Joseph Stalin* 1973. Later productions include *Einstein on the Beach* 1976 and 1992, operatic productions of Euripides' tragedies *Medea* 1984 and *Alcestis* 1986, *The Black Rider* 1990, and *Alice* 1992.

SOCIETY

CLOTHES AND FASHION

Designers of Today

Armani Giorgio 1935– . Italian fashion designer. He launched his first menswear collection 1974 and the following year started designing women's clothing. His work is known for understated styles, precise tailoring, and fine fabrics. He designs for young men and women under the Emporio label.

Cardin Pierre 1922– . French pioneering fashion designer whose clothes are bold and fantastic. He was the first to launch menswear (1960) and designer ready-to-wear collections (1963). His name has become well known as a label since he gave it to a perfume and luxury goods such as scarves and luggage.

Comme des Garçons trade name of Rei Kawakubo 1942– . Japanese fashion designer whose asymmetrical, seemingly shapeless designs, which are often sombre in colour and sometimes torn and crumpled, combine Eastern and Western ideas of clothing. She became a freelance designer 1966, after working in a Japanese textile company, and formed Comme des Garçons in 1969. In the early 1980s her avant-garde designs received acclaim in Paris and were widely influential. She continued to question conventions in 1993 when she produced outfits turned inside out, with unpicked seams and slashed hems, as well as jackets and coats with three sleeves.

Conran Jasper 1959– . English fashion designer known for using quality fabrics to create comfortable garments. He launched his first collection 1978 and has rarely altered the simple, successful style he then adopted. He has also designed costumes for the stage.

Courrèges André 1923– . French fashion designer who is credited with inventing the miniskirt 1964. His 'space-age' designs – square-shaped short skirts and trousers – were copied worldwide in the 1960s. He has become familiar since the 1960s for tailored designs often in pastel shades.

Dolce e Gabbana Domenico Dolce 1958– and Stefano Gabbana 1963– . Italian fashion designers, established 1982, who showed their first women's collection in 1985 and became well known for designs centring around bra-tops, corset-style dresses, and stretch leggings, inspired by Sicilian culture. They launched a menswear collection 1990 and in 1991 began designing the mainstream label Complice for the Milanese manufacturing company Girombelli.

Farhi Nicole. French fashion designer who works in the UK producing understated easy-to-wear styles in natural earth-toned coloured fabrics and knitwear. She began designing for the mainstream fashion label French Connection and for Stephen Marks in 1973 (the Stephen Marks label was changed to Nicole Farhi in 1983). In 1989 she launched a menswear line, with soft unstructured jackets and casual separates.

Galliano John 1960– . British fashion designer whose elegant and innovative designs are often inspired by historical motifs (for example, 'Dickensian-style' clothing), the elements of which he redesigns to create progressive collections. He became known before graduating from St Martin's School of Art in 1984 for his technical expertise and imaginative flair. In 1990 he designed the costumes for a production of Ashley Page's ballet *Corrulao*, performed by the Ballet Rambert. In the same year he began showing his collections in Paris.

Gaultier Jean-Paul 1952– . French fashion designer who, after working for Pierre Cardin, launched his first collection in 1978, designing clothes that went against fashion trends, inspired by London's street style. He designed the costumes for Peter Greenaway's film *The Cook, the Thief, His Wife and Her Lover* 1989 and the singer Madonna's outfits for her world tour 1990, and launched a new denim line in 1993.

Hamnett Katharine 1948– . British fashion designer with her own business from 1979. Her oversized T-shirts promoting peace and environmental campaigns attracted attention 1984. She produces well-cut, inexpensive designs for men and women, predominantly in natural fabrics.

Jackson Betty 1940– . British fashion designer who produced her first collection 1981 and achieved an international reputation as a designer of young, up-to-the-minute clothes. She rescales separates into larger proportions and makes them in boldly coloured fabrics. In 1991 she launched her own accessory range.

Karan Donna 1948– . US fashion designer. For many years she worked for the Anne Klein company, producing Anne Klein sportswear until 1984 when she founded her own label. As well as trendy, wearable sportswear in bright colours, and tight, clingy clothes such as the bodysuit, she produced executive workwear. In 1989 she launched a second, less expensive, ready-to-wear line, DKNY. In 1992–93 she moved away from the structured look of the 1980s to produce lighter, casual, and more fluid outfits.

Kenzo trade name of Kenzo Takada 1940– . Japanese fashion designer, active in France from 1964. He opened his shop Jungle JAP 1970, and by 1972 was well established. He is known for unconventional designs based on traditional Japanese clothing. He also produces innovative designs in knitted fabrics.

Klein Calvin (Richard) 1942– . US fashion designer whose collections are characterized by the smooth and understated, often in natural fabrics – mohair, cashmere, wool, and suede in subtle colours. He set up his own business 1968 specializing in designing coats and suits, and expanded into sportswear in the mid-1970s. His designer jeans became a status symbol during the same period.

Klein Roland 1938– . French fashion designer, active in the UK from 1965. He opened his own-label shop 1979 and from 1991 designed menswear for the Japanese market.

Lacroix Christian 1951– . French fashion designer who opened his couture and ready-to-wear business in 1987, after working with Jean Patou 1981–87. He made headlines with his fantasy creations, including the short puffball skirt, rose prints, and low décolleté necklines.

Lagerfeld Karl (Otto) 1939– . German fashion designer, and a leading figure on the fashion scene from the early 1970s. As design director at Chanel for both the couture and ready-to-wear collections from 1983, he updated the Chanel look. He showed his first collection under his own label 1984.

Lauren Ralph 1939– . US fashion designer, producing menswear under the Polo label from 1968, womenswear from 1971, childrenswear, and home furnishings from 1983. He also designed costumes for the films *The Great Gatsby* 1973 and *Annie Hall* 1977.

Margiela Martin. Belgian fashion designer whose innovative 'deconstruction' designs have questioned conventions of dress since he launched his first collection in 1988. Taking used fabrics and second-hand clothes, he reworks the pieces, often making familiar garments into new outfits.

Missoni knitwear fashion label established in the UK 1953 by Italian designers Rosita and Ottavio Missoni. Producing individual pieces of knitwear, characterized by bold colours and geometric patterns, Missoni has become an international business and has raised the profile of knitwear on the fashion scene.

Miyake Issey 1938– . Japanese fashion designer, active in Paris from 1965. He showed his first collection in New York and Tokyo 1971, and has been showing in Paris since 1973. His 'anti-fashion' looks combined Eastern and Western influences: a variety of textured and patterned fabrics were layered and wrapped round the body to create linear and geometric shapes. His inspired designs have had a considerable influence on the fashion scene.

Montana Claude 1949– . French fashion designer who promoted the broad-shouldered look. He established his own business and launched his first collection 1977, becoming well known for black leather oufits with wide-shouldered jackets narrowed sharply at the waist, slim-fitting skirts, and trousers worn with chains. His designs were the antithesis of contemporary fashion and were widely influential. After 1984 he moved away from the structured look to softer, rounded shapes.

Mugler Thierry 1946– . French fashion designer who launched his first collection 1971 under the label Café de Paris. By 1973 he was designing under his own label. Strongly influenced by 1940s and 1950s fashion, his designs had broad shoulders and well-defined waists. His catwalk shows are often spectacular.

Muir Jean 1933– . British fashion designer who worked for Jaeger 1956–61 and set up her own fashion house 1961. In 1991 she launched a knitwear collection. Her clothes are characterized by soft, classic, tailored shapes in leather and soft fabrics.

Oldfield Bruce 1950– . English fashion designer who set up his own business 1975. His evening wear is worn by the British royal family, film stars, and socialites.

Ozbek Rifat 1953– . Turkish fashion designer whose opulent and influential clothing is often inspired by diverse cultures. He showed his first collection in London 1984, changed direction in 1990 when he produced a collection that was entirely white, and began showing designs in Milan in 1991, with a collection inspired by native American dress.

Quant Mary 1934– . British fashion designer who popularized the miniskirt in the UK, and is well known for being one of the first designers to make clothes specifically for the teenage and early twenties market, producing bold, simple outfits that were in tune with the 1960s. In the 1970s she extended into cosmetics and textile design.

Red or Dead UK fashion design label established 1982 by Wayne Hemingway. Initially he sold clothing designed by his wife Geraldine, and customized heavy industrial footwear to make an anti-fashion statement, which was partly responsible for the trend for Doc Martens workwear boots. In 1987 he designed his own-label footwear range, and in 1988 launched clothing collections for men and women, which became popular in London's clubland.

Richmond John 1960– . British fashion designer who produces unconventional street and clubland designs. He worked in the partnership Richmond/Cornejo 1984–87, creating upmarket leather jackets and separates, before setting up his own fashion label 1987. He continued to experiment with leather, producing jackets with tattoo-printed sleeves in 1989 and jackets covered with graffiti in 1990. In 1989 he expanded his range with the 'Destroy' line which combines the basic elements of his signature with lower prices. He staged his first solo show in 1991.

Saint-Laurent Yves (Henri Donat Mathieu) 1936– . French fashion designer who has had an exceptional influence on fashion in the second half of the 20th century. He began working for Christian Dior 1955 and succeeded him as designer on Dior's death 1957. He established his own label 1962 and went on to create the first 'power-dressing' looks for men and women: classical, stylish city clothes.

Smith Paul 1946– . British menswear designer whose clothes are stylistically simple and practical. He opened his first shop 1970 and showed his first collection in Paris 1976. He launched a toiletry range in 1986 and a childrenswear collection 1991.

Storey Helen 1959– . British fashion designer who launched her own label 1984. She opened Boyd and Storey with fellow fashion designer Karen Boyd 1987, and in 1989 designed a range of shoes for Dr Martens UK. She staged her first solo catwalk show 1990 and launched a menswear collection 1991, followed by a '2nd Life' collection in 1992, made of second-hand clothes recycled to make new outfits.

Valentino Mario 1927–1991. Italian shoe designer. Born in Naples, he began his career designing specialist shoes, which brought him fame in the 1950s. His commercial flair steered him towards many different areas. By 1956 he had a shoe-manufacturing company in Naples and a number of shops around the world.

Versace Gianni 1946–1997. Italian fashion designer. He opened his own business and presented a menswear collection in 1978. He diversified into women's wear, accessories, perfumes, furs, and costumes for opera, theatre, and ballet, using simple shapes and strong colours to create provocative clothing. He was shot dead in 1997.

Westwood Vivienne 1941– . British fashion designer who first attracted attention in the mid-1970s as co-owner of a shop with the rock-music entrepreneur Malcolm McLaren (1946–), which became a focus for the punk movement in London. Early in the 1980s her Pirate and New Romantics looks gained her international recognition. Westwood's dramatic clothes continue to have a wide influence on the public and other designers.

Yamamoto Yohji 1943– . Japanese fashion designer who formed his own company 1972 and showed his first collection 1976. He is an uncompromising, nontraditionalist designer who swathes and wraps the body in unstructured, loose, voluminous garments.

EDUCATION

Terms

adult education in the UK, voluntary classes and courses for adults provided mainly in further-education colleges, adult-education institutes, and school premises. Adult education covers a range of subjects from flower arranging to electronics and can lead to examinations and qualifications. The Open College, Open University, and Workers' Educational Association are adult-education bodies.

Most adult education is provided by Local Education Authorities (LEAs) and fees for classes are subsidized. In 1992 the government restricted subsidy to work-related courses, a proposal which met with strong opposition from bodies as diverse as the LEAs and the Women's Institute.

Assisted Places Scheme in UK education, a scheme established 1980 by which the government assists parents with the cost of fees at independent schools on a means-tested basis.

Baccalauréat French examination (or 'Bac') providing the school-leaving certificate and qualification, including vocational options, for university entrance.

The examination is also available on an international basis as an alternative to English A levels. The curriculum for the International Baccalauriat (IB) is much broader than the UK system, with a minimum of six compulsory subjects including a foreign language. The IB is offered in 52 countries. In the UK the IB can be taken in a growing number of colleges and sixth forms.

boarding school school offering board and lodging as well as tuition to its students. In the UK, most boarding education in the UK is provided in the private, fee-paying sector, but there are a number of state schools with boarding facilities. The number of boarding pupils in the UK is now in decline.

city technology college in the UK, one of a proposed network of some 20 schools, financed jointly by government and industry, designed to teach technological subjects in inner-city areas to students aged 11 to 18. By 1993 only 15 of the schools had opened, industry having proved reluctant to fund the scheme, which was abandoned in its original form.

CTCs have caused controversy (a) because of government plans to operate the schools independently of local education authorities; (b) because of selection procedures; and (c) because of the generous funds they receive in comparison with other schools. The government has been encouraging local authority and grant-maintained schools to opt for CTC status at reduced expense.

coeducation education of both boys and girls in one institution. In most countries coeducation has become favoured over single-sex education, although there is some evidence to suggest that girls perform better in a single-sex institution, particularly in maths and science. However, the new national curriculum in the UK will make it impossible for girls to drop science and technology at an early stage.

There has been a marked switch away from single-sex education in favour of coeducation over the last 20 years in the UK. In the USA, 90% of schools and colleges are coeducational. In 1954, the former USSR returned to its earlier coeducational system, which was partly abolished in 1944. In Islamic countries, coeducation is discouraged beyond the infant stage on religious principles.

college of higher education in the UK, a college in which a large proportion of the work undertaken is at degree level or above. Colleges of higher education are centrally funded by the Universities and Colleges Funding Council.

comprehensive school in the UK, a secondary school which admits pupils of all abilities, and therefore without any academic selection procedure. Most secondary education in the USA and the former USSR has always been comprehensive, but in W Europe most countries (including France and the UK) have switched from a selective to a comprehensive system within the last 20 years.

In England, the 1960s and 1970s saw slow but major reform of secondary education, in which most state-funded local authorities replaced selective grammar schools (those taking only the most academic 20% of children) and secondary modern schools (for the remainder), with comprehensive schools capable of providing suitable courses for children of all abilities. By 1987, only 3% of secondary pupils were still in grammar schools. Scotland and Wales have switched completely to comprehensive education, while Northern Ireland retains a largely selective system.

conductive education specialized method of training physically disabled children suffering from conditions such as cerebral palsy. The method was pioneered at the Peto Institute in Budapest, Hungary, and has been taken up elsewhere.

curriculum the range of subjects offered within an institution or course. Until 1988, the only part of the school curriculum prescribed by law in the UK was religious education. Growing concern about the low proportion of 14- and 16-year-olds opting to study maths, science, and technology, with a markedly low take-up rate among girls, led to the central government in the Education Reform Act 1988 introducing a compulsory national curriculum, which applies to all children of school age (5–16) in state schools. There are three core subjects in the curriculum – English, maths, and science – and seven foundation subjects: technology, history, geography, music, art, physical education, and a foreign language. A review of the national curriculum was made in 1993 after complaints that it was seriously loaded.

daycare all-day care for babies and young children, usually of working mothers. Daycare in the UK is not regarded as part of the education system but some daycare centres are now working in cooperation with schools to ensure that four- and five-year-olds are not excluded from nursery education. There is controversy among psychologists about the effects on children of spending so much time with their peers when very young. Some early research indicated that daycare for very young children could make them insecure and aggressive, but research in the USA in 1990 indicated beneficial effects.

distance learning home-based study by correspondence course or by radio, television, or audio or video tape. The establishment of the Open University 1969 put the UK in the forefront of distance learning. The Open College and individual institutions in the UK also offer distance-learning packages.

Eleven Plus examination test designed to select children for grammar school education in the UK, at the time when local authorities provided separate grammar, secondary modern, and occasionally technical schools for children over the age of 11. The examination became defunct on the introduction of comprehensive schools in Scotland, Wales, and most of England during the 1960s and 1970s, although certain education authorities retain the selective system and the Eleven Plus.

further education college college in the UK for students over school-leaving age that provides courses for skills towards an occupation or trade, and general education at a level below that of a degree course. FE colleges were removed from local authority control in 1993.

GCSE (*General Certificate of Secondary Education*) in the UK, from 1988, examination for 16-year-old pupils, superseding both GCE O level and CSE, and offering qualifications for up to 60% of school-leavers in any particular subject. The GCSE includes more practical and course work than O level, although course work was reduced in syllabuses from 1993. GCSE subjects are organized as part of the national curriculum.

grammar school in the UK, a secondary school catering for children of high academic ability, about 20% of the total, usually measured by the Eleven Plus examination. Most grammar schools have now been replaced by comprehensive schools. By 1991 the proportion of English children in grammar schools was less than 3%.

In the USA, the term is sometimes used for a primary school (also called elementary school).

grant-maintained school in the UK, a state school that has voluntarily withdrawn itself from local authority support (an action called *opting out*), and instead is maintained directly by central government. The first was Skegness Grammar School in 1989. The schools are managed by their own boards of governors.

health education teaching and counselling on healthy living, including hygiene, nutrition, and sex education, and advice on alcohol and drug abuse, smoking, and other threats to health. Health education in most secondary schools is also included within a course of personal and social education, or integrated into subjects such as biology, home economics, or physical education.

higher education in most countries, education beyond the age of 18 leading to a university or college degree or similar qualification.

independent school school run privately without direct assistance from the state. In the UK, just over 7% of children attended private fee-paying schools in 1991. The proportion rose during the 1980s and fell back for the first time in a decade in 1993. The sector includes most boarding education in the UK. Although most independent secondary schools operate a highly selective admissions policy for entrants at the age of 11 or 13, some specialize in the teaching of slow learners or difficult children and a few follow particular philosophies of progressive education. A group of old-established and prestigious independent schools are known as public schools.

Ivy League eight long-established colleges and universities in the US with prestigious academic and social reputations: Brown, Columbia, Cornell, Dartmouth, Harvard, Pennsylvania, Princeton, and Yale. The members of the Ivy League compete in intercollegiate athletics.

literacy ability to read and write. The level at which functional literacy is set rises as society becomes more complex, and it becomes increasingly difficult for an illiterate person to find work and cope with the other demands of everyday life.

Nearly 1 billion adults in the world, most of them women, are unable to read or write. Africa has the world's highest illiteracy rate: 54% of the adult population. Asia has 666 million illiterates, 75% of the world total. Surveys in the USA, the UK, and France in the 1980s found far greater levels of functional illiteracy than official figures suggest, and revealed a lack of basic general knowledge, but no standard of measurement has been agreed.

magnet school school that specializes in a particular area of the curriculum; for example, science, sport, or the arts. Magnet schools were established in the USA from 1954 in some inner cities, with the aim of becoming centres of excellence in their particular field.

Critics maintain that magnet schools attract talented pupils and staff away from equally deserving schools in the surrounding neighbourhood. In the UK, the idea of introducing magnet schools has been discussed since 1987 but no action has been taken.

mixed-ability teaching practice of teaching children of all abilities in a single class. Although this is normal practice in British primary schools, most secondary schools begin to divide children according to ability, either in sets or, more rarely, streams, as they approach public examinations at age 16.

modular course a course, usually leading to a recognized qualification, that is divided into short and often optional units, which are assessed as they are completed. In the UK system, an accumulation of modular credits may lead to the award of a GCSE pass, a BTEC diploma, or a degree. Modular schemes are becoming increasingly popular as a means of allowing students to take a wider range of subjects.

multicultural education education aimed at preparing children to live in a multiracial society by giving them an understanding of the culture and history of different ethnic groups.

national curriculum in the UK from 1988, a course of study in ten subjects common to all primary and secondary state schools. The national curriculum is divided into three core subjects – English, maths, and science – and seven foundation subjects: geography, history, technology, a foreign language (for secondary school pupils), art, music, and physical education. There are four stages, on completion of which the pupil's work is assessed. The stages are for ages 5–7, 7–11, 11–14, and 14–16. The scheme were set up through the Education Reform Act 1988.

national vocational qualification (NVQ) in the UK, a certificate of attainment of a standardized level of skill and competence. A national council for NVQs was set up 1986 in an effort by the government in cooperation with employers to rationalize the many unrelated vocational qualifications then on offer. The objective is to fit all qualifications to four levels of attainment, roughly equivalent to the GCSE, A level, and degree system of academic qualifications.

nursery school or *kindergarten* educational establishment for children aged three to five, initiated in the mid-19th century. In the UK, the Education Act 1944 did not make nursery school compulsory but increasing parental pressure from the 1960s led to a slow expansion. At the end of the 1980s the UK lagged behind most European countries in the provision of nursery-school places. Although 45% of three- and four-year-olds were in education in 1992, only half of these were in genuine nursery classes or schools; the rest were in primary classes.

Open College in the UK, a network launched by the former Manpower Services Commission 1987 to enable people to gain and update technical and vocational skills by means of distance teaching, such as correspondence courses, radio, and television.

Open University institution established in the UK 1969 to enable mature students without qualifications to study to degree level without regular attendance. Open University teaching is based on a mixture of correspondence courses, TV and radio lectures and demonstrations, personal tuition organized on a regional basis, and summer schools. It has been widely copied; by the National University Consortium in the USA, for example, set up in 1980.

opting out in UK education, schools that choose to be funded directly from the Department of Education and Science are said to be 'opting out' of local-authority control. The Education Act 1988 gave this option to all secondary schools and the larger primary schools, and in 1990 it was extended to all primary schools. However, by 1993 only 500 of 27,000 schools had opted out.

parent–teacher association (PTA) group attached to a school consisting of parents and teachers who support the school by fund-raising and other activities. In the UK, PTAs are organized into a national federation, the National Confederation of PTAs, which increasingly acts a pressure group for state schools.

Throughout the USA, PTAs are active as political pressure groups and as a way to involve parents in the public education process.

polytechnic formerly part of the UK educational system, an institution for higher education offering courses mainly at degree level and concentrating on full-time vocational courses, although many polytechnics provided a wide range of part-time courses at advanced levels.

In April 1989 the polytechnics in England and Wales became independent corporations. In 1992 all polytechnics and some colleges of higher education became universities. The new UK university sector consisted of 104 institutions.

preparatory school fee-paying independent school. In the UK, it is a junior school that prepares children for entry to a senior school at about age 13. In the USA, it is a school that prepares students for university entrance at about age 18.

primary education the education of children between the ages of 5 and 11 in the state school system in England and Wales, and up to 12 in Scotland.

private school alternative name in the UK for a fee-paying independent school.

progressive education teaching methods that take as their starting point children's own aptitudes and interests, encouraging children to follow their own investigations and lines of inquiry.

public school in England and Wales, a prestigious fee-paying independent school. In Scotland, the USA, and many other English-speaking countries, a 'public' school is a state-maintained school, and independent schools are generally known as 'private' schools.

remedial education special classes or teaching strategies that aim to help children with learning difficulties catch up with children within the normal range of achievement.

secondary education in the UK, education from the age of 11 (12 in Scotland) until school-leaving at 16 or later.

special education often in separate 'special schools', for children with specific physical or mental problems or disabilities.

statement in UK education, the results of an assessment of the special educational needs of a child with physical or mental disabilities. Under the Education Act 1981, less able children are entitled to such an assessment by various professionals to establish what their needs are and how they might be met. Approximately 2.5% children were in receipt of statements in 1992.

streaming the practice of dividing pupils for all classes according to an estimate of their overall ability, with arrangements for 'promotion' and 'demotion' at the end of each academic year.

student finance payment for higher education, whether by grants, loans, parents, or the student working part time. In the UK, students in higher education have their fees paid by their local education authority and are eligible for a maintenance grant, means-tested on their parents' income. In 1990 the government introduced a system of top-up loans intended gradually to replace 50% of the grant entitlement. At the same time students were debarred from previously available welfare benefits, and the National Union of Students argued that this left many worse off. In 1991–92 37% of higher education students applied for loans.

teacher training in the UK, teachers are trained by means of either a four-year Bachelor of Education (BEd) degree, which integrates professional training and the study of academic subjects, or a postgraduate Certificate of Education (PGCE), which provides one year of professional training to graduate students. The majority of BEd students train to teach in primary schools and two-thirds of PGCE students to teach specialist subjects in secondary schools.

In the 1970s the numbers of teacher training places fell sharply in line with school pupil numbers. By the late 1980s there were considerable difficulties in filling all training places, especially in such subjects as science, maths, and technology. By 1993, however, demand for training places had increased and the teacher shortage had largely disappeared as result of rising graduate unemployment.

tertiary college in the UK, a college for students over 16 that combines the work of a sixth form and a further education college.

Third Age late middle age and over. A Université du Troisième Age was established in France 1972 to offer people over 50 the opportunity to continue their education. In the UK, the University of the Third Age established 1982 has no teachers and no qualifications for entry, but aims to help its 120 local groups to pursue any topics that interest them.

university institution of higher learning for those who have completed primary and secondary education.

The number of university students in the UK almost doubled after the major expansion of the 1960s to stand at 303,000 in 1991. There was an even greater increase in degree-level students in the public-sector colleges, which educated more graduates than the universities. In 1992, polytechnics and some colleges of higher education already awarding degrees became universities. The more generous funding of traditional universities was phased out and a joint funding council established. Research is funded separately from teaching, and the new universities have gained access to research funds for the first time.

The USA has both state universities (funded by the individual states) and private universities. The oldest and many of the most prestigious universities are private.

Recent innovations in secondary education include universities serving international areas – for example, the Middle East Technical University 1961 in Ankara, Turkey, supported by the United Nations; the United Nations University 1974 in Tokyo; and the British Open University 1969.

vocational education education relevant to a specific job or career. The term refers to medical and legal education in the universities as well as higher and further education courses in professional and craft skills. In the UK, the TVEI (Technical and Vocational Education Initiative) was intended to expand pre-vocational education in schools but was being run down in the early 1990s.

work experience the opportunity for pupils or students to gain practical experience of working within industry for a short period of time. Typically, 15–16 year olds spend 1–2 weeks in a work experience placement. It helps them gain some understanding of the world of work and of the opportunities that might be available to them when they leave full-time education.

Youth Training Scheme (YTS) in the UK, a one- or two-year course of job-training and work experience for unemployed school-leavers aged 16 and 17, from 1989 provided by employer-led Training and Enterprise Councils at local levels and renamed Youth Training. On the basis of a government promise of training places for all school-leavers without jobs, social security cover was withdrawn. However, places have not always matched demand, leaving some school leavers in financial difficulties.

Opponents of youth training argue that it is a form of cheap forced labour, that it does not provide young people with the high-technology skills that will be needed in the future, and that it is underpaid.

HEALTH AND MEDICINE

Medical Terms

abortion ending of a pregnancy before the fetus is developed sufficiently to survive outside the uterus. Loss of a fetus at a later gestational age is termed premature stillbirth. Abortion may be accidental (miscarriage) or deliberate (termination of pregnancy).

Methods of deliberate abortion vary according to the gestational age of the fetus. Up to 12 weeks, the cervix is dilated and a suction curette passed into the uterus to remove its contents, a procedure called dilation and curretage (D and C). An alternative is the abortion pill mifepristone, licensed in the UK from 1991. Within 24 hours of ingestion, it leads to the expulsion of the foetus from the uterus, and can be used at an earlier stage in pregnancy than other methods. Over 12 weeks, a prostaglandin pessary is introduced into the vagina, which induces labour, producing a miscarriage.

Worldwide, an estimated 150,000 unwanted pregnancies are terminated each day by induced abortion. One-third of these abortions are performed outside the law in unsafe conditions, resulting in about 500 deaths a day.

allergy special sensitivity of the body that makes it react, with an exaggerated response of the natural immune defence mechanism, especially with histamines, to the introduction of an otherwise harmless foreign substance (allergen).

amniocentesis sampling the amniotic fluid surrounding a fetus in the womb for diagnostic purposes. It is used to detect Down's syndrome and other genetic abnormalities.

blood pressure pressure, or tension, of the blood against the inner walls of blood vessels, especially the arteries, due to the muscular pumping activity of the heart. Abnormally high blood pressure (see hypertension) may be associated with various conditions or arise with no obvious cause; abnormally low blood pressure (hypotension) occurs in shock and after excessive fluid or blood loss from any cause.

Caesarean section surgical operation to deliver a baby by cutting through the mother's abdominal and uterine walls. It may be recommended for almost any obstetric complication implying a threat to mother or baby. Britain's Caesarean rate of around 14% of births is one of the highest in Europe.

cervical smear removal of a small sample of tissue from the cervix (neck of the womb) to screen for changes implying a likelihood of cancer. The procedure is also known as the *Pap test* after its originator, George Papanicolau.

chemotherapy any medical treatment with chemicals. It usually refers to treatment of cancer with cytotoxic and other drugs. The term was coined by German bacteriologist Paul Ehrlich (1854–1915) for the use of synthetic chemicals against infectious diseases.

contraceptive any drug, device, or technique that prevents pregnancy. The contraceptive pill contains female hormones that interfere with egg production or the first stage of pregnancy. The 'morning-after' pill can be taken up to 72 hours after unprotected intercourse. Barrier contraceptives include condoms (sheaths) and diaphragms, also called caps or Dutch caps; they prevent the sperm entering the cervix (neck of the womb). Intrauterine devices, also known as IUDs or coils, cause a slight inflammation of the lining of the womb; this prevents the fertilized egg from becoming implanted. A sponge impregnated with spermicide inserted into the vagina kills the sperm.

Other contraceptive methods include sterilization (women) and vasectomy (men); these are usually nonreversible. 'Natural' methods include withdrawal of the penis before ejaculation (coitus interruptus), and avoidance of intercourse at the time of ovulation (rhythm method). These methods are unreliable and normally only used on religious grounds.

The effectiveness of a contraceptive method is often given as a percentage. To say that a method has 95% effectiveness means that, on average, out of 100 healthy couples using that method for a year, 95 will not conceive.

convulsion series of violent contractions of the muscles over which the patient has no control. It may be associated with loss of consciousness. Convulsions may arise from any one of a number of causes, including brain disease (such as epilepsy), injury, high fever, poisoning, and electrocution.

dermatology medical specialty concerned with the diagnosis and treatment of skin disorders. It is a rapidly expanding field owing to the proliferation of industrial chemicals affecting workers, and the universal use of household cleaners, cosmetics, and sun screens.

dialysis tecnhique for removing waste products from the blood in chronic or acute kidney failure. There are two main methods: haemodialysis and peritoneal dialysis.

endoscopy examination of internal organs or tissues by an instrument allowing direct vision. An endoscope is equipped with an eyepiece, lenses, and its own light source to illuminate the field of vision. The endoscope used to examine the digestive tract is a flexible fibreoptic instrument swallowed by the patient.

gallstone pebblelike, insoluble accretion formed in the human gall bladder or bile ducts from cholesterol or calcium salts present in bile. Gallstones may be symptomless or they may cause pain, indigestion, or jaundice. They can be dissolved with medication or removed, either by means of an endoscope or, along with the gall bladder, in an operation known as cholecystectomy.

geriatrics branch of medicine concerned with diseases and problems of the elderly.

gynaecology branch of medicine concerned with disorders of the female reproductive system.

haematology branch of medicine concerned with disorders of the blood.

hormone-replacement therapy (HRT) use of oral oestrogen and progestogen to help limit the effects of the menopause in women. The treatment was first used in the 1970s.

hospice residential facility specializing in palliative care for terminally ill patients and their relatives.

hysterectomy surgical removal of all or part of the uterus (womb). The operation is performed to treat fibroids (benign tumours growing in the uterus) or cancer; also to relieve heavy menstrual bleeding. A woman who has had a hysterectomy will no longer menstruate and cannot bear children.

Instead of a full hysterectomy it is sometimes possible to remove the lining of the womb, the endometrium, using either diathermy or a laser.

immunization conferring immunity to infectious disease by artificial methods. The most widely used technique is vaccination. Four out of five children around the world were by 1991 immunized against six diseases: measles, tetanus, polio, diphtheria, whooping cough, and tuberculosis.

inflammation defensive reaction of the body tissues to disease or damage, including redness, swelling, and heat. Denoted by the suffix *-itis* (as in appendicitis), it may be acute or chronic, and may be accompanied by the formation of pus. It is an essential part of the healing process.

intrauterine device (IUD) or *coil*, a contraceptive device that is inserted into the womb (uterus). It is a tiny plastic object, sometimes containing copper. By causing a mild inflammation of the lining of the uterus it prevents fertilized eggs from becoming implanted. The success rate is about 98%, but there is a very small risk of a pelvic infection leading to infertility.

in vitro fertilization (IVF) ('fertilization in glass') allowing eggs and sperm to unite in a laboratory to form embryos. The embryos produced may then either be implanted into the womb of the otherwise infertile mother (an extension of artificial insemination), or used for research. The first baby to be produced by this method was born 1978 in the UK. In cases where the fallopian tubes are blocked, fertilization may be carried out by intra-vaginal culture, in which egg and sperm are incubated (in a plastic tube) in the mother's vagina, then transferred surgically into the uterus.

mammography X-ray procedure used to detect breast cancer at an early stage, before the tumours can be seen or felt.

nursing care of the sick, the very young, the very old, and the disabled. Organized training originated 1836 in Germany, and was developed in Britain by the work of Florence Nightingale (1820–1920), who, during the Crimean War, established standards of scientific, humanitarian care in military hospitals. Nurses give day-to-day care and carry out routine medical and surgical procedures under the supervision of a physician.

In the UK there are four National Boards (England, Scotland, Wales, and Northern Ireland) for Nursing, Midwifery and Health Visiting, and the Royal College of Nursing (1916) is the professional body.

nutrition the science of food, and its effect on health and disease. Nutrition is the study of the basic nutrients required to sustain life, their bioavailability in foods and overall diet, and the effects upon them of cooking and storage. *Malnutrition* can be caused by underfeeding, an imbalanced diet, and overfeeding.

obstetrics medical speciality concerned with the management of pregnancy, childbirth, and the immediate postnatal period.

oncology branch of medicine concerned with the diagnosis and treatment of neoplasms, especially cancer.

ophthalmology medical speciality concerned with diseases of the eye and its surrounding tissues.

orthopaedics branch of medicine concerned with the surgery of bones and joints.

pacemaker medical device implanted under the skin of a patient whose heart beats irregularly. It delivers minute electric shocks to stimulate the heart muscles at regular intervals and restores normal heartbeat. The latest pacemakers are powered by radioactive isotopes for long life and weigh no more than 15 g/0.5 oz.

paediatrics or *pediatrics* medical speciality concerned with the care of children.

pain sense that gives an awareness of harmful effects on or in the body. It may be triggered by stimuli such as trauma, inflammation, and heat. Pain is transmitted by specialized nerves and also has psychological components controlled by higher centres in the brain. Drugs that control pain are also known as analgesics.

paraplegia paralysis of the lower limbs, involving loss of both movement and sensation; it is usually due to spinal injury.

physiotherapy treatment of injury and disease by physical means such as exercise, heat, manipulation, massage, and electrical stimulation.

poison or *toxin* any chemical substance that, when introduced into or applied to the body, is capable of injuring health or destroying life. The liver removes some poisons from the blood.

In the UK, the National Poisons Information Service, founded 1963, provides eight regional centres in the major city hospitals, where data on cases of poisoning is collected.

prematurity the condition of an infant born before the full term. In obstetrics, an infant born after less than 37 weeks' gestation is described as premature. In hospitals with advanced technology, specialized neonatal units can save babies born as early as 24 weeks.

prophylaxis any measure taken to prevent disease, including exercise and vaccination. Prophylactic (preventive) medicine is an aspect of public-health provision that is receiving increasing attention.

psychosomatic physical symptom or disease, thought to arise from emotional or mental factors. The term 'psychosomatic' has been applied to many conditions, including asthma, migraine, hypertension, and peptic ulcers. Whereas it is unlikely that these and other conditions are wholly due to psychological factors, emotional states such as anxiety or depression do have a distinct influence on the frequency and severity of illness.

radiotherapy treatment of disease by radiation from X-ray machines or radioactive sources. Radiation, which reduces the activity of dividing cells, is of special value for its effect on malignant tissues, certain nonmalignant tumours, and some diseases of the skin.

remission temporary disappearance of symptoms during the course of a disease.

resuscitation steps taken to revive anyone on the brink of death. The most successful technique for life-threatening emergencies, such as electrocution, near-drowning, or heart attack, is mouth-to-mouth resuscitation. Medical and paramedical staff are trained in cardiopulmonary resuscitation: the use of specialized equipment and techniques to attempt to restart the breathing and/or heartbeat and stabilize the patient long enough for more definitive treatment.

retrovirus any of a family (*Retroviridae*) of viruses containing the genetic material RNA rather than the more usual DNA. Retroviruses include those causing AIDS and some forms of leukaemia.

screening or *health screening* the systematic search for evidence of a disease, or of conditions that may precede it, in people who are not suffering from any symptoms. The aim of screening is to try to limit ill health from diseases that are difficult to prevent and might otherwise go undetected. Examples are hypothyroidism and phenylketonuria, for which all newborn babies in Western countries are screened; breast cancer and cervical cancer; and stroke, for which high blood pressure is a known risk factor.

spastic person with cerebral palsy. The term is also applied generally to limbs with impaired movement, stiffness, and resistance to passive movement, and to any body part (such as the colon) affected with spasm.

spermicide any cream, jelly, pessary, or other preparation that kills the sperm cells in semen. Spermicides are used for contraceptive purposes, usually in combination with a condom or diaphragm. Sponges impregnated with spermicide have been developed but are not yet in widespread use. Spermicide used alone is only 75% effective in preventing pregnancy.

sterilization any surgical operation to terminate the possibility of reproduction. In women, this is normally achieved by sealing or tying the Fallopian tubes (tubal ligation) so that fertilization can no longer take place. In men, the transmission of sperm is blocked by vasectomy.

tomography the obtaining of plane-section X-ray photographs, which show a 'slice' through any object. Crystal detectors and amplifiers can be used that have a sensitivity 100 times greater than X-ray film, and, in conjunction with a computer system, can detect, for example, the difference between a brain tumour and healthy brain tissue. In modern medical imaging there are several types, such as the CAT scan (computerized axial tomography).

transfusion intravenous delivery of blood or blood products (plasma, red cells) into a patient's circulation to make up for deficiencies due to disease, injury, or surgical intervention. Cross-matching is carried out to ensure the patient receives the right type of blood, unless a store of the patient's own blood is used.

transplant transfer of a tissue or organ from one human being to another or from one part of the body to another (skin grafting). In most organ transplants, the operation is for life-saving purposes, though the immune system tends to reject foreign tissue. Careful matching and immunosuppressive drugs must be used, but these are not always successful.

trauma painful emotional experience or shock with lasting psychic consequences; any physical damage or injury.

tumour overproduction of cells in a specific area of the body, often leading to a swelling or lump. Tumours are classified as *benign* or *malignant* (cancerous). Benign tumours grow more slowly, do not invade surrounding tissues, do not spread to other parts of the body, and do not usually recur after removal.

ultrasound scanning or *ultrasonography* the use of ultrasonic pressure waves to create a diagnostic image. It is a safe, noninvasive technique that often eliminates the need for exploratory surgery. An ultrasound beam can also be used to alleviate pain in joints and muscles.

vaccine any preparation of modified viruses or bacteria that is introduced into the body, usually either orally or by a hypodermic syringe, to induce the specific antibody reaction that produces immunity against a particular disease.

  In the UK, children are routinely vaccinated against diphtheria, tetanus, whooping cough, polio, measles, mumps, German measles, and tuberculosis.

X-ray electromagnetic radiation with a short wavelength. X-rays pass through most body tissues, although dense areas such as bone prevent their passage, showing up as white areas on X-ray photographs. The X-rays used in radiotherapy have very short wavelengths that penetrate tissues deeply and destroy them. X-rays are dangerous and can cause cancer.

The Human Body

Achilles tendon tendon pinning the calf muscle to the heel bone. It is one of the largest in the human body.

adenoids masses of lymphoid tissue, similar to tonsils, located in the upper part of the throat, behind the nose. They are part of a child's natural defences against the entry of germs but usually shrink and disappear by the age of ten.

adrenal gland or *suprarenal gland* gland situated on top of the kidney. The adrenals are soft and yellow, and consist of two parts: the cortex and medulla. The *cortex* (outer part) secretes various steroid hormones, controls salt and water metabolism, and regulates the use of carbohydrates, proteins, and fats. The *medulla* (inner part) secretes the hormones adrenaline and noradrenaline which, during times of stress, cause the heart to beat faster and harder, increase blood flow to the heart and muscle cells, and dilate airways in the lungs, thereby delivering more oxygen to cells throughout the body and in general preparing the body for 'fight or flight'.

alimentary canal the tube through which food passes; it extends from the mouth to the anus. It is a complex organ, adapted for digestion. In adults, it is about 9 m/30 ft long, consisting of the mouth cavity, pharynx, oesophagus, stomach, and the small and large intestines.

antibody protein molecule produced in the blood by lymphocytes in response to the presence of foreign or invading substances (antigens); such substances include the proteins carried on the surface of infecting microorganisms. Antibody production is one aspect of immunity.

aorta the chief artery, the dorsal blood vessel carrying oxygenated blood from the left ventricle of the heart. It branches to form smaller arteries, which in turn supply all body organs except the lungs. Loss of elasticity in the aorta provides evidence of atherosclerosis, which may lead to heart disease.

artery vessel that carries blood from the heart to the rest of the body. It is built to withstand considerable pressure, having thick walls that are impregnated with muscle and elastic fibres. During contraction of the heart muscles, arteries expand in diameter to allow for the sudden increase in pressure that occurs; the resulting pulse or pressure wave can be felt at the wrist. Not all arteries carry oxygenated (oxygen-rich) blood; the pulmonary arteries convey deoxygenated (oxygen-poor) blood from the heart to the lungs.

blood liquid circulating in the arteries, veins, and capillaries. Blood carries nutrients and oxygen to individual cells and removes waste products, such as carbon dioxide. It is also important in the immune response and in the distribution of heat throughout the body.

bone hard connective tissue comprising the skeleton of most vertebrate animals. It consists of a network of collagen fibres impregnated with mineral salts (largely calcium phosphate and calcium carbonate) that give the bone great strength; within this solid matrix are bone cells, blood vessels, and nerves. (See table on following page.)

bone marrow substance found inside the cavity of bones. In early life it produces red blood cells but

The composition of blood

There are approximately 5 litres/10½ pt of blood in the circulation. It accounts for 7–8% of body weight. Blood consists of:

erythrocytes (red blood cells), of which 54% is haemoglobin. Normal count: 4–6 million per cu mm.

leukocytes (white blood cells). Normal count: 4,500–11,000 per cu mm.

thrombocytes (platelets). Normal count: 150,000–300,000 per cu mm.

plasma: 90% water, 7% proteins, plus nutrients, salts, nitrogen waste, carbon dioxide and hormones.

Plasma accounts for 60% of blood volume, and the erythrocytes account for most of the remaining 40%.

later on lipids (fat) accumulate and its colour changes from red to yellow.

brain mass of interconnected nerve cells, forming the anterior part of the central nervous system, whose activities it coordinates and controls. In 1990 scientists at Johns Hopkins University, Baltimore, USA, succeeded in culturing human brain cells. (See *Life Sciences* for more.)

bronchus one of a pair of large tubes (bronchii) branching off from the windpipe and passing into the vertebrate lung. Cartilaginous rings give rigidity and prevent collapse during breathing movements. Numerous glands secrete a slimy mucus, which traps dust and other particles; the mucus is constantly being propelled upwards to the mouth by thousands of tiny hairs or cilia. The bronchus is adversely effected by several respiratory diseases and by smoking, which damages the cilia.

cranium the dome-shaped area of the skull, consisting of several fused plates, that protects the brain.

ear organ of hearing. It responds to the vibrations that constitute sound, and these are translated into nerve signals and passed to the brain. The ear consists of three parts: outer ear, middle ear, and inner ear. Three fluid-filled canals of the inner ear detect changes of position; this mechanism, with other sensory inputs, is responsible for the sense of balance.

eye organ of vision, a roughly spherical structure contained in a bony socket. Light enters it through the cornea, and passes through the circular opening (pupil) in the iris (the coloured part of the eye). The ciliary muscles act on the lens (the rounded transparent structure behind the iris) to change its shape, so that images of objects at different distances can be focused on the retina. This is at the back of the eye, and is packed with light-sensitive cells (rods and cones), connected to the brain by the optic nerve.

Fallopian tube or *oviduct* one of two tubes that carry eggs from the ovary to the uterus. An egg is fertilized by sperm in the Fallopian tubes, which are lined with cells whose cilia move the egg towards the uterus.

gall bladder small muscular sac, situated on the underside of the liver and connected to the small intestine by the bile duct. It stores bile from the liver.

hair threadlike structure growing from the skin. Each hair grows from a pit-shaped follicle embedded in the second layer of the skin, the dermis. It consists of dead cells impregnated with the protein keratin. There are about a million hairs on the average person's head. Each grows at the rate of 5–10 mm/ 0.2–0.4 in per month, lengthening for about three years before being replaced by a new one. In 1990 scientists succeeded for the first time in growing human hair in vitro.

heart muscular organ that rhythmically contracts to force blood around the body. The beating of the heart is controlled by the autonomic nervous system and an internal control centre or pacemaker, the sinoatrial node.

hormone product of the endocrine glands, concerned with control of body functions. The main glands are the thyroid, parathyroid, pituitary, adrenal, pancreas, uterus, ovary, and testis. Hormones bring about

Bones of the human body

Skull	No. of bones		No. of bones
occipital	1	lunate	1
parietal: one pair	2	triquetral	1
sphenoid	1	pisiform	1
ethmoid	1	trapezium	1
inferior nasal conchae: two	2	trapezoid	1
frontal: one pair, fused	1	capitate	1
nasal: one pair	2	hamate	1
lacrimal: one pair	2	metacarpals	5
temporal: one pair	2	phalanges (fingers):	
maxilla: one pair	2	first digit	2
zygomatic: one pair	2	second digit	3
vomer	1	third digit	3
palatine: one pair	2	fourth digit	3
mandible: one pair, fused (jawbone)	1	fifth digit	3
Total	22	Total	30

The ears		Pelvic girdle	
malleus (hammer)	2	ilium, ischium and pubis (combined):	
incus (anvil)	2	one pair of hip bones, innominate	2
stapes (stirrups)	2		
Total	6	Lower extremity (each leg)	

Vertebrae		femur (thighbone)	1
cervical	7	tibia	1
thoracic	12	fibula	1
lumbar	5	patella (kneebone)	1
sacral: five, fused to form the sacrum	1	tarsus (ankle):	
coccyx: between three and five, fused	1	talus	1
Total	26	calcaneus	1
		navicular	1

Vertebral ribs		cuneiform, medial	1
ribs, 'true': seven pairs	14	cuneiform, intermediate	1
ribs, 'false': five pairs of which		cuneiform, lateral	1
two pairs are floating	10	cuboid	1
Total	24	metatarsals	5
		phalanges (toes):	

Sternum (breastbone)		first digit	2
manubrium	1	second digit	3
sternebrae	1	third digit	3
xiphisternum	1	fourth digit	3
Total	3	fifth digit	3
		Total	30

Throat		Total	
hyoid	1	skull	22

Pectoral girdle		the ears	6
clavicle: one pair (collar bone)	2	vertebrae	26
scapula (including coracoid):		vertebral ribs	24
one pair (shoulder blade)	2	sternum	3
Total	4	throat	1
		pectoral girdle	4

Upper extremity (each arm)		upper extremity (arms): 2 x 30	60
forearm:		hip bones	2
humerus	1	lower extremity (legs): 2 x 30	60
radius	1	**Total**	**208**
ulna	1		
carpus (wrist):			
scaphoid	1		

changes in the functions of various organs according to the body's requirements. The pituitary gland, at the base of the brain, is a centre for overall coordination of hormone secretion; the thyroid hormones determine the rate of general body chemistry; the adrenal hormones prepare the organism during stress for 'fight or flight'; and the sexual hormones such as oestrogen govern reproductive functions.

joint the point where two bones meet. Some joints allow no motion (the sutures of the skull), others allow a very small motion (the sacroiliac joints in the lower back), but most allow a relatively free motion. Of these, some allow a gliding motion (one vertebra of the spine on another), some have a hinge action (elbow and knee), and others allow motion in all directions (hip and shoulder joints) by means of a

the human body

Key
1. brain
2. eye
3. carotid artery
4. jugular vein
5. subclavian artery
6. superior vena cava
7. aorta
8. subclavian vein
9. heart
10. lungs
11. diaphragm
12. liver
13. stomach
14. gall bladder
15. kidney
16. pancreas
17. small intestine
18. large intestine
19. appendix
20. bladder
21. femoral artery
22. femoral vein

Key
1. cranium (skull)
2. mandible
3. clavicle
4. scapula
5. sternum
6. rib cage
7. humerus
8. vertebra
9. ulna
10. radius
11. pelvis
12. coccyx
13. metacarpals
14. phalanges
15. femur
16. patella
17. fibula
18. tibia
19. metatarsals
20. phalanges
21. superficial (upper) layer of muscles

ball-and-socket arrangement. The ends of the bones at a moving joint are covered with cartilage for greater elasticity and smoothness, and enclosed in an envelope (capsule) of tough white fibrous tissue lined with a membrane which secretes a lubricating and cushioning synovial fluid. The joint is further strengthened by ligaments.

kidney one of a pair of organs responsible for water regulation, excretion of waste products, and maintaining the ionic composition of the blood. The kidneys are situated on the rear wall of the abdomen. Each one consists of a number of long tubules; the outer parts filter the aqueous components of blood, and the inner parts selectively reabsorb vital salts, leaving waste products in the remaining fluid (urine), which is passed through the ureter to the bladder.

liver large organ with many regulatory and storage functions. It is situated in the upper abdomen, and weighs about 2 kg/4.5 lb. It receives the products of digestion, converts glucose to glycogen (a long-chain carbohydrate used for storage), and breaks down fats. It removes excess amino acids from the blood, converting them to urea, which is excreted by the kidneys. The liver also synthesizes vitamins, produces bile and blood-clotting factors, and removes damaged red cells and toxins such as alcohol from the blood.

lung large cavity of the body, used for gas exchange. It is essentially a sheet of thin, moist membrane that is folded so as to occupy less space. The lung tissue, consisting of multitudes of air sacs and blood vessels, is very light and spongy, and functions by bringing inhaled air into close contact with the blood so that oxygen can pass into the organism and waste carbon dioxide can be passed out. The efficiency of lungs is enhanced by breathing movements, by the thinness and moistness of their surfaces, and by a constant supply of circulating blood.

lymph nodes small masses of lymphatic tissue in the body that occur at various points along the major lymphatic vessels. Tonsils and adenoids are large lymph nodes. As the lymph passes through them it is filtered, and bacteria and other microorganisms are engulfed by cells known as macrophages.

muscle contractile tissue that produces locomotion and maintains the movement of body substances. Muscle is made of long cells that can contract to between one-half and one-third of their relaxed length. (See *Life Sciences* for more.)

nerve strand of nerve cells enclosed in a sheath of connective tissue joining the central and the autonomic nervous systems with receptor and effector organs. A single nerve may contain both motor and sensory nerve cells, but they act independently.

oesophagus passage by which food travels from mouth to stomach. It is about 23 cm/9 in long, with its upper end at the bottom of the pharynx, immediately behind the windpipe.

ovary the organ that generates the ovum. The ovaries are two whitish rounded bodies about 25 mm/1 in by 35 mm/1.5 in, located in the abdomen near the ends of the Fallopian tubes. Every month, from puberty to the onset of the menopause, an ovum is released from the ovary. This is called ovulation, and forms part of the menstrual cycle.

pancreas accessory gland of the digestive system located close to the duodenum. When stimulated by the hormone secretin, it secretes enzymes into the duodenum that digest starches, proteins, and fats. In adults, it is about 18 cm/7 in long, and lies behind and below the stomach. It contains groups of cells called the islets of Langerhans, which secrete the hormones insulin and glucagon that regulate the blood sugar level.

parathyroid one of a pair of small endocrine glands. Two such pairs are located behind the thyroid gland. They secrete parathyroid hormone, which regulates the amount of calcium in the blood.

pelvis the lower area of the abdomen featuring the bones and muscles used to move the legs. The *pelvic girdle* is a set of bones that allows movement of the legs in relation to the rest of the body and provides sites for the attachment of relevant muscles.

penis male reproductive organ, used for internal fertilization; it transfers sperm to the female reproductive tract. The penis is made erect by vessels that fill with blood, and contains the urethra, through which urine is passed.

pharynx interior of the throat, the cavity at the back of the mouth. Its walls are made of muscle strengthened with a fibrous layer and lined with mucous membrane. The internal nostrils lead backwards into the pharynx, which continues downwards into the oesophagus and (through the epiglottis) into the windpipe. On each side, a Eustachian tube enters the pharynx from the middle ear cavity. The upper part (nasopharynx) is an airway, but the remainder is a passage for food.

prostate gland gland surrounding and opening into the urethra at the base of the bladder in males. The prostate gland produces an alkaline fluid that is released during ejaculation; this fluid activates sperm, and prevents their clumping together.

red blood cell or *erythrocyte* the most common type of blood cell, responsible for transporting oxygen around the body. It contains haemoglobin, which combines with oxygen from the lungs to form oxyhaemoglobin. When transported to the tissues these cells are able to release the oxygen because the oxyhaemoglobin splits into its original constituents.

rib long, usually curved bone that extends laterally from the spine in 12 pairs in the chest area. The ribs protect the lungs and heart, and allow the chest to expand and contract easily.

skull collection of flat and irregularly shaped bones (or cartilage) that enclose the brain and the organs of sight, hearing, and smell, and provide support for the jaws. The skull consists of 22 bones joined by sutures. The floor of the skull is pierced by a large hole for the spinal cord and a number of smaller apertures through which other nerves and blood vessels pass.

spinal cord major component of the central nervous system. It is enclosed by the bones of the spine, and links the peripheral nervous system to the brain.

stomach the first cavity in the digestive system, a bag of muscle situated just below the diaphragm. Food enters it from the oesophagus, is digested by the acid and enzymes secreted by the stomach lining, and then passes into the duodenum.

testis (plural *testes*) the organ that produces sperm in males. It is one of a pair of oval structures (testicles) that descend from the body cavity during development, to hang outside the abdomen in a scrotal sac.

throat passage that leads from the back of the nose and mouth to the trachea and oesophagus. It includes the pharynx and the larynx, the latter being at the top of the trachea.

thyroid endocrine gland situated in the neck in front of the trachea. It secretes several hormones, principally thyroxine, an iodine-containing hormone that stimulates growth, metabolism, and other functions of the body. The thyroid gland may be thought of as the regulator gland of the body's metabolic rate.

tongue muscular organ usually attached to the floor of the mouth. It has a thick root attached to a U-shaped bone (hyoid), and is covered with a mucous membrane containing nerves and taste buds. It directs food to the teeth and into the throat for chewing and swallowing. It is crucial for speech.

trachea or *windpipe* tube that forms an airway from the larynx to the upper part of the chest. Its diameter

Western medicine: chronology

c. 400 BC	Hippocrates recognized that disease had natural causes.
c. AD 200	Galen consolidated the work of the Alexandrian doctors.
1543	Andreas Vesalius gave the first accurate account of the human body.
1628	William Harvey discovered the circulation of the blood.
1768	John Hunter began the foundation of experimental and surgical pathology.
1785	Digitalis was used to treat heart disease; the active ingredient was isolated 1904.
1798	Edward Jenner published his work on vaccination.
1877	Patrick Manson studied animal carriers of infectious diseases.
1882	Robert Koch isolated the bacillus responsible for tuberculosis.
1884	Edwin Klebs isolated the diphtheria bacillus.
1885	Louis Pasteur produced a vaccine against rabies.
1890	Joseph Lister demonstrated antiseptic surgery.
1895	Wilhelm Röntgen discovered X-rays.
1897	Martinus Beijerinck discovered viruses.
1899	Felix Hoffman developed aspirin; Sigmund Freud founded psychiatry.
1900	Karl Landsteiner identified the first three bloodgroups, later designated A, B, and O.
1910	Paul Ehrlich developed the first specific antibacterial agent, Salvarsan, a cure for syphilis.
1922	Insulin was first used to treat diabetes.
1928	Alexander Fleming discovered penicillin.
1932	Gerhard Domagk discovered the first antibacterial sulphonamide drug, Prontosil.
1937	Electro-convulsive therapy (ECT) was developed.
1940s	Lithium treatment for manic-depressive illness was developed.
1950s	Antidepressant drugs and beta-blockers for heart disease were developed. Manipulation of the molecules of synthetic chemicals became the main source of new drugs. Peter Medawar studied the body's tolerance of transplanted organs and skin grafts.
1950	Proof of a link between cigarette smoking and lung cancer was established.
1953	Francis Crick and James Watson announced the structure of DNA. Jonas Salk developed a vaccine against polio.
1958	Ian Donald pioneered diagnostic ultrasound.
1960s	A new generation of minor tranquillizers called benzodiazepines was developed.
1967	Christiaan Barnard performed the first human heart-transplant operation.
1971	Viroids, disease-causing organisms even smaller than viruses, were isolated outside the living body.
1972	The CAT scan, pioneered by Godfrey Hounsfield, was first used to image the human brain.
1975	César Milstein developed monoclonal antibodies.
1978	World's first *test-tube baby* was born in the UK.
1980s	AIDS (acquired immune-deficiency syndrome) was first recognized in the USA. Barbara McClintock's discovery of the transposable gene was recognized.
1980	The World Health Organization reported the eradication of smallpox.
1983	The virus responsible for AIDS, now known as human immunodeficiency virus (HIV), was identified by Luc Montagnier at the Institut Pasteur, Paris; Robert Gallo at the National Cancer Institute, Maryland, USA discovered the virus independently 1984.
1984	The first vaccine against leprosy was developed.
1987	The world's longest-surviving heart-transplant patient died in France, 18 years after his operation.
1989	Grafts of fetal brain tissue were first used to treat Parkinson's disease.
1990	Gene for maleness discovered by UK researchers.
1991	First successful use of gene therapy (to treat severe combined immune deficiency) was reported in the USA.

is about 1.5 cm/0.6 in and its length 10 cm/4 in. It is strong and flexible, and reinforced by rings of cartilage. In the upper chest, the trachea branches into two tubes: the left and right bronchi, which enter the lungs.

uterus hollow muscular organ of females, located between the bladder and rectum, and connected to the Fallopian tubes above and the vagina below. The embryo develops within the uterus, and is attached to it after implantation via the placenta and umbilical cord. The lining of the uterus changes during the menstrual cycle. The outer wall of the uterus is composed of smooth muscle, capable of powerful contractions (induced by hormones) during childbirth.

vagina the front passage in females, linking the uterus to the exterior. It admits the penis during sexual intercourse, and is the birth canal down which the fetus passes during delivery.

Psychological Disorders

agoraphobia phobia involving fear of open spaces and crowded places. The anxiety produced can be so severe that some sufferers are confined to their homes for many years.

anorexia lack of desire to eat, especially the pathological condition of *anorexia nervosa*, usually found in adolescent girls and young women, who may be obsessed with the desire to lose weight. Compulsive eating, or bulimia, often accompanies anorexia. In anorexia nervosa, the patient refuses to eat and finally becomes unable to do so. The result is severe emaciation and, in rare cases, death.

anxiety emotional state of fear or apprehension. Anxiety is a normal response to potentially dangerous situations. Abnormal anxiety can either be free-floating, experienced in a wide range of situations, or it may be phobic, when the sufferer is excessively afraid of an object or situation.

behaviour therapy application of behavioural principles, derived from learning theories, to the treatment of clinical conditions such as phobias, obsessions, sexual and interpersonal problems. For example, in treating a phobia the person is taken into the feared situation in gradual steps. Over time, the fear typically reduces, and the problem becomes less acute.

claustrophobia phobia involving fear of enclosed spaces.

clinical psychology discipline dealing with the understanding and treatment of health problems, particularly mental disorders. The main problems dealt with include anxiety, phobias, depression, obsessions, sexual and marital problems, drug and alcohol dependence, childhood behavioural problems, psychoses (such as schizophrenia), mental handicap, and brain damage (such as dementia).

cognitive therapy treatment for emotional disorders, such as depression and anxiety, that encourages the patient to challenge the distorted and unhelpful thinking that is characteristic of these problems. The treatment includes behaviour therapy and has been most helpful for people suffering from depression.

delusion false belief that is unshakeably held. Delusions are a prominent feature of schizophrenia and paranoia, but may also occur in severe depression and manic depression.

depression emotional state characterized by sadness, unhappy thoughts, apathy, and dejection. Sadness is a normal response to major losses such as bereavement or unemployment. After childbirth, postnatal depression is common. However, clinical depression, which is prolonged or unduly severe, often requires treatment, such as antidepressant medication, cognitive therapy, or, in very rare cases, electroconvulsive therapy (ECT), in which an electrical current is passed through the brain.

drug and alcohol dependence physical or psychological craving for addictive drugs such as alcohol, nicotine (in cigarettes), tranquillizers, heroin, or stimulants (for example, amphetamines). Such substances can alter mood or behaviour. When dependence is established, sudden withdrawal from the drug can cause unpleasant physical and/or psychological reactions, which may be dangerous.

dyslexia malfunction in the brain's synthesis and interpretation of sensory information, popularly known as 'word blindness'. It results in difficulty with reading and writing. A similar disability with figures is called dyscalculia.

electroconvulsive therapy (ECT) or *electroshock therapy* treatment for schizophrenia and depression, given under anaesthesia and with a muscle relaxant. An electric current is passed through the brain to induce alterations in the brain's electrical activity. The treatment can cause distress and loss of concentration and memory, and so there is much controversy about its use and effectiveness.

hyperactivity condition of excessive activity in young children, combined with inability to concentrate and difficulty in learning. The cause is not known, although some food additives have come under suspicion. Modification of the diet may help, and in the majority of cases there is improvement at puberty.

hypnosis artificially induced state of relaxation in which suggestibility is heightened. Hypnosis is sometimes used to treat addictions to tobacco or overeating, or to assist amnesia victims.

hysteria according to the work of Austrian psychoanalyst Sigmund Freud (1856–1939), the conversion of a psychological conflict or anxiety feeling into a physical symptom, such as paralysis, blindness, recurrent cough, vomiting, and general malaise. The term is little used today in diagnosis.

manic depression mental disorder characterized by recurring periods of depression which may or may not alternate with periods of inappropriate elation (mania) or overactivity. Sufferers may be genetically predisposed to the condition. Some cases have been improved by taking prescribed doses of lithium.

mental handicap impairment of intelligence. It can be very mild, but in more severe cases, it is associated with social problems and difficulties in living independently. A person may be born with a mental handicap (for example, Down's syndrome) or may acquire it through brain damage. There are between 90 and 130 million people in the world suffering such disabilities.

nervous breakdown popular term for a reaction to overwhelming psychological stress. It has no equivalent in medicine: a patient said to be suffering from a nervous breakdown may in fact be going through an episode of depression, manic depression, anxiety, or even schizophrenia.

neurosis general term referring to emotional disorders, such as anxiety, depression, and obsessions. The main disturbance tends to be one of mood; contact with reality is relatively unaffected, in contrast to the effects of psychosis.

obsession repetitive unwanted thought or compulsive action that is often recognized by the sufferer as being irrational, but which nevertheless causes distress. It can be associated with the irresistible urge of an individual to carry out a repetitive series of actions.

paranoia mental disorder marked by delusions of grandeur or persecution. In popular usage, paranoia means baseless or exaggerated fear and suspicion.

phobia excessive irrational fear of an object or situation – for example, agoraphobia (fear of open spaces and crowded places), acrophobia (fear of heights), and claustrophobia (fear of enclosed places). Behaviour therapy is one form of treatment.

postnatal depression mood change occurring in many mothers a few days after the birth of a baby. It is usually a short-lived condition but can sometimes

Phobias

air	aerophobia	hair	chaetophobia
animals	zoophobia	heart conditions	cardiophobia
bacteria	bacteriophobia, microphobia	heat	thermophobia
		heaven	ouranophobia
beards	pogonophobia	heights	acrophobia, altophobia
bees	apiphobia, melissophobia	hell	hadephobia, stygiophobia
being alone	monophobia, autophobia	home	domatophobia, oikophobia
being buried alive	taphophobia	horses	hippophobia
being cold	frigophobia	human beings	anthrophobia
being touched	haphephobia	ice, frost	cryophobia
birds	ornithophobia	ideas	ideophobia
blood	haematophobia	illness	nosemaphobia
blushing	ereuthophobia, eyrythrophobia	imperfection	atelophobia
		infection	mysophobia
books	bibliophobia	infinity	apeirophobia
cancer	cancerophobia, carcinophobia	injustice	dikephobia
		inoculations, injections	trypanophobia
cats	ailurophobia, gatophobia	insanity	lyssophobia, maniaphobia
chickens	alektorophobia	insects	entomophobia
childbirth	tocophobia	itching	acarophobia, scabiophobia
children	paediphobia	jealousy	zelophobia
cold	cheimatophobia	lakes	limnophobia
colour	chromatophobia, chromophobia, psychrophobia	leaves	phyllophobia
		leprosy	leprophobia
		lice	pediculophobia
comets	cometophobia	lightning	astraphobia
contamination	misophobia	machinery	mechanophobia
crossing a bridge	gephyrophobia	many things	polyphobia
crossing streets	dromophobia	marriage	gamophobia
crowds	demophobia, ochlophobia	meat	carnophobia
darkness	achulophobia, nyctophobia	men	androphobia
dawn	eosophobia	metals	metallophobia
daylight	phengophobia	meteors	meteorophobia
death, corpses	necrophobia, thanatophobia	mice	musophobia
deformity	dysmorphophobia	mind	psychophobia
demons	demonophobia	mirrors	eisoptrophobia
dirt	mysophobia	money	chrometophobia
disease	nosophobia, pathophobia	monsters, monstrosities	teratophobia
disorder	ataxiophobia	motion	kinesophobia, kinetophobia
dogs	cynophobia	music	musicophobia
draughts	anemophobia	narrowness	anginaphobia
dreams	oneirophobia	needles	belonophobia
drinking	dipsophobia	night, darkness	achluophobia
drugs	pharmacophobia	noise	phonophobia
duration	chronophobia	novelty	cainophobia
dust	amathophobia, koniphobia	nudity	gymnotophobia
eating	phagophobia	number 13	triskaidekaphobia, terdekaphobia
enclosed spaces	claustrophobia		
everything	pantophobia	odours	osmophobia
faeces	coprophobia	one thing	monophobia
failure	kakorrphiaphobia	open spaces	agoraphobia
fatigue	kopophobia, ponophobia	pain	algophobia, odynophobia
fears	phobophobia	parasites	parasitophobia
fire	pyrophobia	physical love	erotophobia
fish	ichthyophobia	pins	enetophobia
flying, the air	aerophobia	places	topophobia
fog	homichlophobia	pleasure	hedonophobia
food	sitophobia	poison	toxiphobia
freedom	eleutherophobia	poverty	peniaphobia
germs	spermophobia	precipices	cremnophobia
ghosts	phasmophobia	pregnancy	maieusiophobia
God	theophobia	punishment	poinephobia
going to bed	clinophobia	rain	ombrophobia
graves	taphophobia	reptiles	batrachophobia

Phobias (cont.)

responsibility	hypegiaphobia	stealing	kleptophobia
ridicule	katagalophobia	stillness	eremophobia
rivers	potamophobia	stings	cnidophobia
robbery	harpaxophobia	strangers	xenophobia
ruin	atephobia	strong light	photophobia
rust	iophobia	stuttering	laliophobia
sacred things	hierophobia	sun	heliophobia
Satan	Satanophobia	surgical operations	ergasiophobia
school	scholionophobia	teeth	odontophobia
sea	thalassophobia	thinking	phronemophobia
semen	spermatophobia	thunder	brontophobia,
sex	genophobia		keraunophobia
sexual intercourse	coitophobia	touch	haptophobia
shadows	sciophobia	travel	hodophobia
shock	hormephobia	travelling by train	siderodromophobia
sin	hamartiophobia	trees	dendrophobia
sinning	peccatophobia	trembling	tremophobia
skin	dermatophobia	vehicles	amaxophobia, ochophobia
sleep	hypnophobia	venereal disease	cypridophobia
smell	olfactophobia	void	kenophobia
smothering, choking	pnigerophobia	vomiting	emetophobia
snakes	ophidiophobia, ophiophobia	walking	basiphobia
snow	chionophobia	wasps	spheksophobia
soiling	rypophobia	water	hydrophobia
solitude	eremitophobia,	weakness	asthenophobia
	eremophobia	wind	ancraophobia
sound	akousticophobia	women	gynophobia
sourness	acerophobia	words	logophobia
speaking aloud	phonophobia	work	ergophobia
speed	tachophobia	worms	helminthophobia
spiders	arachnophobia	wounds, injury	traumatophobia
stars	siderophobia	writing	graphophobia

persist; the most severe form of postnatal depressive illness, *puerperal psychosis*, requires hospital treatment. In mild cases, antidepressant drugs and hormone treatment may help.

psychiatry branch of medicine dealing with the diagnosis and treatment of mental disorder, normally divided into the areas of *neurotic conditions*, including anxiety, depression, and hysteria, and *psychotic disorders*, such as schizophrenia. Psychiatric treatment consists of analysis, drugs, or electroconvulsive therapy.

In practice there is considerable overlap between psychiatry and clinical psychology, the fundamental difference being that psychiatrists are trained medical doctors (holding an MD degree) and may therefore prescribe drugs, whereas psychologists may hold a PhD but do not need a medical qualification to practise.

psychoanalysis theory and treatment method for neuroses, developed by Austrian physician Sigmund Freud (1856–1939). The main treatment method involves the free association of ideas, and their interpretation by patient and analyst. It is typically prolonged and expensive and its effectiveness has been disputed.

psychology systematic study of human and animal behaviour. The first psychology laboratory was founded 1879 by Wilhelm Wundt (1832–1920) in Leipzig, Germany. The subject includes diverse areas of study and application, among them the roles of instinct, heredity, environment, and culture; the processes of sensation, perception, learning, and memory; the bases of motivation and emotion; and the functioning of thought, intelligence, and language.

psychosis or *psychotic disorder* general term for a serious mental disorder where the individual commonly loses contact with reality and may experience hallucinations (seeing or hearing things that do not exist) or delusions (fixed false beliefs). For example, in a paranoid psychosis an individual may believe that others are plotting against him or her. A major type of psychosis is schizophrenia (which may be biochemically induced).

psychotherapy treatment approaches for psychological problems involving talking rather than surgery or drugs. Examples include cognitive therapy and psychoanalysis.

schizophrenia psychosis of unknown origin that can lead to profound changes in personality and behaviour, including paranoia and hallucinations. Contrary to popular belief, it does not involve a split personality. Modern treatment approaches include drugs, family therapy, stress reduction, and rehabilitation.

senile dementia dementia associated with old age, often caused by Alzheimer's disease.

stress any event or situation that makes demands on a person's mental or emotional resources. Stress can be caused by overwork, anxiety about exams, money,

Psychology: chronology

1846 E H Weber reported on his pioneering quantitative investigations on touch in *On Touch and Common Sensibility*.

1860 G T Fechner published his *Elements of Psychophysics*, in which he presented the first statistical treatment of psychological data.

1879 Wilhelm Wundt founded the first psychological laboratory in Leipzig.

1885 H Ebbinghaus published his experimental researches on memory.

1890 William James published the first comprehensive psychology text, *Principles of Psychology*.

1895 Joseph Breuer and Sigmund Freud published *Studies on Hysteria*, containing the first writings on psychoanalysis.

1896 The first clinical psychology clinic founded, by Lightner Witmer at the University of Pennsylvania, and first use of the term 'clinical psychology'.

1900 Freud's *The Interpretation of Dreams* published.

1905 Alfred Binet and Théodore Simon developed the first effective intelligence test.

1908 The first textbooks of social psychology, by William McDougall and E A Ross, appear.

1910 Max Wertheimer, Wolfgang Köhler, and Kurt Koffka founded the Gestalt School in Frankfurt.

1913 J B Watson's article *Psychology as a Behaviorist Views it* published and the behaviourist movement thus launched.

1923 Jean Piaget's *The Language and the Thought of the Child* published, the first of his many books on the development of thinking.

1927 C Spearman proposed in *The Abilities of Man*, that two kinds of factor comprise intelligence, a general factor ('g') and specific factors.

1929 H Berger published his findings on the electroencephalogram (EEG).

1938 B F Skinner published *The Behavior of Organisms*, detailing his studies of operant conditioning and his radical behaviourism.

1943 C L Hull published his influential book *Principles of Behavior: An Introduction to Behavior Theory*, the most rigorous account of conditioning and learning from the perspective of behaviourism.

1947 Hans Eysenck published *Dimensions of Personality*, a large-scale study of neuroticism and introversion–extroversion.

1948 Nobert Wiener coined the term 'cybernetics' and published *Cybernetics: Control and Communication in the Animal and Machine*.

1949 D O Hebb's classic *Organization of Behaviour* re-emphasized the role of central (brain) processes in the explanation of behaviour.

1950 Alan Turing's famous article *Computing Machinery and Intelligence* published, in which he proposes a test of whether a machine can be said to think. *The Authoritarian Personality* by Theodor W Adorno and others published.

1953 E Aserinksy and N Kleitman publish the first account of rapid-eye-movement (REM) sleep.

1957 L Festinger's *A Theory of Cognitive Dissonance* published. Noam Chomsky published *Syntactic Structures*, a seminal work in psycholinguistics, that revolutionized the study of language.

1958 A Newell and H A Simon, with J C Shaw, published their article on human problem-solving, the first account of the information-processing approach to human psychology. Donald E Broadbent published his influential book *Perception and Communication*, a detailed account of information-processing psychology.

1960 G A Miller, E Galanter, and K Pribam applied the idea of a hierarchically structured computer program to the whole of psychology in their *Plans and the Structure of Behaviour*.

1961 A Newell and H A Simon published their pioneering computational model of human problem solving, the General Problem Solver.

1962 M S Gazzaniga, J E Bogen, and R W Sperry first reported on the 'split-brain' phenomenon in epileptic patients.

1963 Stanley Milgram published his first studies of obedience and the conditions under which individuals will inflict harm when instructed to.

1967 Konovski published *Integrative Activity of the Brain*, an influential melding of conditioning principles with sensation and motivation. Ulric Neisser's *Cognitive Psychology* marked renewed interest in the study of cognition after years in which behaviourism had dominated.

1968 R C Atkinson and R M Shiffin developed their theory of interacting memory systems in cognitive processing.

1970 T Shallice and E K Warrington provided the first of much evidence from brain-damaged patients that short-term memory is in parallel with long-term memory and is best viewed as a collection of separate processing modules.

1972 E Tulving distinguished episodic memory (for personal experience) and semantic memory (for general knowledge and facts about the world).

1983 J A Fodor published *The Modularity of Mind* arguing that the mind is a set of independent, computational input systems and central systems, or more general cognitive processes, corresponding to what the individual 'believes'.

1985 A new view of intelligence proposed by Robert J Sternberg in his *Beyond IQ: A Triarchic Theory of Intelligence*.

1986 J L McClelland and D E Rumelhart developed complex computational networks using parallel processing to simulate human learning and categorization.

1988 An important collection of articles by psychologists, neuropsychologists, and others published in *Consciousness in Contemporary Science*, edited by A J Marcel and E Bisiach.

1989 The mathematician, Roger Penrose, in his *The Emperor's New Mind*, argued that the computational account of the mind is incomplete, particularly concerning consciousness.

1992 The philosopher, John Searle, in *The Rediscovery of the Mind*, argued for the return of consciousness to its position as the central topic in psychology and cognitive science.

or job security, unemployment, bereavement, poor relationships, marriage breakdown, sexual difficulties, poor living or working conditions, and constant exposure to loud noise.

Many changes that are apparently for the better, such as being promoted at work, going to a new school, moving house, and getting married, are also sources of stress. Stress can cause, or aggravate, physical illnesses, among them psoriasis, eczema, asthma, and stomach and mouth ulcers. Apart from removing the source of stress, acquiring some control over it and learning to relax when possible are the best treatments.

Diseases and Disorders

acne skin eruption, mainly occurring among adolescents and young adults, caused by inflammation of the sebaceous glands which secrete an oily substance (sebum), the natural lubricant of the skin. Sometimes the openings of the glands become blocked and they swell; the contents decompose and pimples form on the face, back, and chest.

AIDS (acronym for *acquired immune deficiency syndrome*) the gravest of the sexually transmitted diseases, or STDs. It is caused by the human immunodeficiency virus (HIV), now known to be a retrovirus, an organism first identified 1983. HIV is transmitted in body fluids, mainly blood and sexual secretions.

The estimated incubation period between infection with HIV and outbreak of AIDS is 9.8 years. The effect of the virus in those who become ill is the devastation of the immune system, leaving the victim susceptible to (opportunistic) diseases that would not otherwise develop. Some AIDS victims die within a few months of the outbreak of symptoms, some survive for several years; roughly 50% are dead within three years. There is no cure for the disease.

By Feb 1991, 323,378 AIDS cases in 159 countries had been reported to the World Health Organization (WHO), which estimated that over 1.3 million cases might have occurred worldwide, of which about 400,000 were a result of transmission before, during, or shortly after birth.

By mid-1993, WHO reported an estimated 14 million people infected with the HIV virus worldwide. In the UK, 7,341 AIDS cases had been reported by April 1993, with 4,572 deaths.

alcoholism dependence on alcoholic liquor. It is characterized as an illness when consumption of alcohol interferes with normal physical or emotional health. Excessive alcohol consumption may produce physical and psychological addiction and lead to nutritional and emotional disorders. The direct effect is cirrhosis of the liver, nerve damage, and heart disease, and the condition is now showing genetic predisposition.

Alzheimer's disease common manifestation of dementia, thought to afflict one in 20 people over 65. Attacking the brain's 'grey matter', it is a disease of mental processes rather than physical function, characterized by memory loss and progressive intellectual impairment. The disease may result from a defective protein circulating in the blood; some forms of early-onset Alzheimer's disease, it was discovered 1991, are caused by a gene defect on chromosome 21.

anaemia condition caused by a shortage of haemoglobin, the oxygen-carrying component of red blood cells. The main symptoms are fatigue, pallor, breathlessness, palpitations, and poor resistance to infection. Treatment depends on the cause; untreated anaemia taxes the heart and may prove fatal.

angina or *angina pectoris* severe pain in the chest due to impaired blood supply to the heart muscle because a coronary artery is narrowed. Faintness and difficulty in breathing accompany the pain. Treatment is by drugs, such as nitroglycerin and amyl nitrite; rest is important.

appendicitis inflammation of the appendix, a small, blind extension of the bowel in the lower right abdomen. In an acute attack, the pus-filled appendix may burst, causing a potentially lethal spread of infection. Treatment is by removal (appendicectomy).

arthritis inflammation of the joints, with pain, swelling, and restricted motion. Many conditions may cause arthritis, including gout and trauma to the joint.

More common in women, *rheumatoid arthritis* usually begins in middle age in the small joints of the hands and feet, causing a greater or lesser degree of deformity and painfully restricted movement. It is alleviated by drugs, and surgery may be performed to correct deformity.

Osteoarthritis, a degenerative condition, tends to affect larger, load-bearing joints, such as the knee and hip. It appears in later life, especially in those whose joints may have been subject to earlier stress or damage; one or more joints stiffen and may give considerable pain. Joint replacement surgery is nearly always successful.

asthma difficulty in breathing due to spasm of the bronchi (air passages) in the lungs. Attacks may be provoked by allergy, infection, stress, or emotional upset. It may also be increasing as a result of air pollution and occupational hazards. Treatment is with bronchodilators to relax the bronchial muscles and thereby ease the breathing, and in severe cases by inhaled steroids that reduce inflammation of the bronchi.

Although the symptoms are similar to those of bronchial asthma, *cardiac asthma* is an unrelated condition and is a symptom of heart deterioration.

atherosclerosis thickening and hardening of the walls of the arteries, associated with atheroma.

autoimmunity condition where the body's immune responses are mobilized not against 'foreign' matter, such as invading germs, but against the body itself. Diseases considered to be of autoimmune origin include myasthenia gravis, rheumatoid arthritis, and lupus erythematosus. In 1990 in Israel a T-cell vaccine was produced that arrests the excessive reproduction of T-lymphocytes attacking healthy target tissues.

back pain aches in the region of the spine. Low back pain can be caused by a very wide range of medical conditions. About half of all episodes of back pain will resolve within a week, but severe back pain can be chronic and disabling. The causes include muscle sprain, a prolapsed intervertebral disc, and vertebral collapse due to osteoporosis or cancer. Treatment methods include rest, analgesics, physiotherapy, and exercises.

blindness complete absence or impairment of sight. It may be caused by heredity, accident, disease, or deterioration with age. Aids to the blind include the use of the Braille and Moon alphabets in reading and writing; electronic devices that convert print to recognizable mechanical speech; guide dogs; and sonic torches.

blood poisoning condition in which poisons are spread throughout the body by pathogens in the bloodstream.

bronchitis inflammation of the bronchi (air passages) of the lungs, usually caused initially by a viral infection, such as a cold or flu. It is aggravated by environmental pollutants, especially smoking, and results in a persistent cough, irritated mucus-secreting glands, and large amounts of sputum.

cancer group of diseases characterized by abnormal proliferation of cells. Cancer (malignant) cells are usually degenerate, capable only of reproducing themselves (tumour formation). Malignant cells tend to spread from their site of origin by travelling through the bloodstream or lymphatic system.

There are more than 100 types of cancer. Some, like lung or bowel cancer, are common; others are rare. The likely cause remains unexplained. Triggering agents (carcinogens) include chemicals such as those found in cigarette smoke, other forms of smoke, asbestos dust, exhaust fumes, and many industrial chemicals. Some viruses can also trigger the cancerous growth of cells, as can X-rays and radioactivity. Dietary factors are important in some cancers; for example, lack of fibre in the diet may predispose people to bowel cancer and a diet high in animal fats and low in fresh vegetables and fruit increases the risk of breast cancer. Psychological stress may increase the risk of cancer, more so if the person concerned is not able to control the source of the stress. In some families there is a genetic tendency towards a particular type of cancer.

Cancer is one of the leading causes of death in the industrialized world, yet it is by no means incurable, particularly in the case of certain tumours, including Hodgkin's disease, acute leukaemia, and testicular cancer. Cures are sometimes achieved with specialized treatments, such as surgery, chemotherapy with cytotoxic drugs, and irradiation, or a combination of all three. Monoclonal antibodies have been used therapeutically against some cancers, with limited success. There is also hope of combining a monoclonal antibody with a drug that will kill the cancer cell to produce a highly specific magic bullet drug. In 1990 it was discovered that the presence in some patients of a particular protein, p-glycoprotein, actively protects the cancer cells from drugs intended to destroy them. If this action can be blocked, the cancer should become far easier to treat. However, at present public health programmes are more concerned with prevention and early detection.

cataract eye disease in which the crystalline lens or its capsule becomes opaque, causing blindness. Fluid accumulates between the fibres of the lens and gives place to deposits of albumin. These coalesce into rounded bodies, the lens fibres break down, and areas of the lens or the lens capsule become filled with opaque products of degeneration. It is estimated (1991) that more than 25 million people around the world are blind because of cataracts. The treatment is surgical replacement of the opaque lens with an artificial implant.

chickenpox or *varicella* common acute disease, caused by a virus of the herpes group and transmitted by airborne droplets. Chickenpox chiefly attacks children under the age of ten. The incubation period is two to three weeks. One attack normally gives immunity for life.

cirrhosis any degenerative disease in an organ of the body, especially the liver, characterized by excessive development of connective tissue, causing scarring and painful swelling. Cirrhosis of the liver may be caused by an infection such as viral hepatitis, by chronic alcoholism or drug use, blood disorder, or malnutrition. If cirrhosis is diagnosed early, it can be arrested by treating the cause; otherwise it will progress to jaundice, oedema, vomiting of blood, coma, and death.

cot death or *sudden infant death syndrome* (SIDS) death of an apparently healthy baby during sleep. It is most common in the winter months, and strikes more boys than girls. The cause is not known.

cystic fibrosis hereditary disease characterized by the production of abnormally thick mucus and excessively salty sweat. In cystic fibrosis sufferers the airways become clogged, resulting in frequent, often severe infections; nutrition is impaired because mucus blockage of the pancreatic ducts inhibits the passage of digestive enzymes.

Unknown in Africans, cystic fibrosis is the commonest inherited disease among Caucasians. In the UK one person in 20 carries the defective gene. If both parents are carriers, there is a one-in-four chance of cystic fibrosis occurring in their child. Since the discovery of the cystic fibrosis gene in 1989, screening tests have been developed for carriers; the disease can be detected in the unborn child.

In the past, most cystic fibrosis sufferers died in infancy; today most survive into adulthood. Modern management is by diet and drugs, daily physiotherapy to keep the airways clear, and the use of antibiotics to combat infection; enzyme preparations are given to aid digestion. Some patients benefit from heart-lung transplants. Cystic fibrosis is seen as a promising test case for gene-replacement therapy. In 1992 the prospect of a cure improved greatly when a healthy version of the cystic-fibrosis gene was successfully introduced into the lung tissue of rats.

cystitis inflammation of the bladder, usually caused by bacterial infection, and resulting in frequent and painful urination. Treatment is by antibiotics and copious fluids with vitamin C.

deafness lack or deficiency in the sense of hearing, either inborn or caused by injury or disease of the middle or inner ear. Of assistance are hearing aids, lip-reading, a cochlear implant in the ear in combination with a special electronic processor, sign language (signs for concepts), and 'cued speech' (manual clarification of ambiguous lip movement during speech).

dementia mental deterioration as a result of physical changes in the brain. It may be due to degenerative change, circulatory disease, infection, injury, or chronic poisoning. *Senile dementia*, a progressive loss of mental abilities such as memory and orientation, is typically a problem of old age, and can be accompanied by depression.

dermatitis inflammation of the skin, usually related to allergy. *Dermatosis* refers to any skin disorder and may be caused by contact or systemic problems.

diabetes disease *diabetes mellitus* in which a disorder of the islets of Langerhans in the pancreas prevents the body producing the hormone insulin, so that sugars cannot be used properly. Treatment is by strict dietary control and oral or injected insulin, depending on the type of diabetes. Experimental work is under way to transplant islets of Langerhans cells into diabetics. Without treatment the patient may go blind, ulcerate, lapse into diabetic coma, and die. Early-onset diabetes tends to be more severe than that developing in later years. In 1989 it was estimated that 4% of the world's population had diabetes.

diarrhoea excessive action of the bowels so that the faeces are fluid or semifluid. It is caused by intestinal irritants (including some drugs and poisons), infection with harmful organisms (as in dysentery, salmonella, or cholera), or allergies; most diarrhoea is viral in origin.

Diarrhoea is the biggest killer of children in the world. The World Health Organization estimates that 4.5 million children die each year from dehydration as a result of diarrhoeal disease in Third World countries. It can be treated by giving an accurately measured aqueous solution of salt and glucose by mouth in large quantities (to restore the electrolyte balance in the blood).

Down's syndrome condition caused by a chromosomal abnormality (the presence of an extra copy of chromosome 21) which in humans produces mental retardation, a flattened face, coarse and straight hair, and a fold of skin at the inner edge of the eye (hence the former name 'mongolism').

All people with Down's syndrome who live long enough eventually develop early-onset Alzheimer's disease, which led to the discovery in 1991 that some forms of early-onset Alzheimer's disease are caused by a gene defect on chromosome 21.

drug misuse illegal use of drugs for nonmedicinal purposes. Under the UK Misuse of Drugs Acts drugs used illegally comprise: (1) *most harmful* heroin, morphine, opium, and other narcotics; hallucinogens, such as mescaline and LSD, and injectable amphetamines, such as methedrine; (2) *less harmful* narcotics such as codeine and cannabis; stimulants of the amphetamine type, such as Benzedrine and barbiturates; (3) *least harmful* milder drugs of the amphetamine type. *Designer drugs*, for example ecstasy, are usually modifications of the amphetamine molecule, altered in order to evade the law as well as for different effects. Crack, a smokable form of cocaine, became available to drug users in the 1980s.

eczema inflammatory skin condition, a form of dermatitis, marked by dryness, rashes, itching, the formation of blisters, and the exudation of fluid. It may

be allergic in origin and is sometimes complicated by infection.

endometriosis common gynaecological complaint in which patches of endometrium (the lining of the womb) are found outside the uterus. Endometriosis may be treated with analgesics, hormone preparations, or surgery.

epilepsy disorder characterized by a tendency to develop fits, which are convulsions or abnormal feelings caused by abnormal electrical discharges in the cerebral hemispheres of the brain. Epilepsy can be controlled with a number of anticonvulsant drugs. Most epileptics have infrequent fits that have little impact on their daily lives. Epilepsy is common in the Third World, with up to 30 sufferers per 1,000 people in some areas; in industrialized countries the figure is 3–5 per 1,000.

food poisoning any acute illness characterized by vomiting and diarrhoea and caused by eating food contaminated with harmful bacteria (for example, listeriosis), poisonous food (for example, certain mushrooms, puffer fish), or poisoned food (such as lead or arsenic introduced accidentally during processing). A frequent cause of food poisoning is salmonella bacteria. These come in many forms, and strains are found in cattle, pigs, poultry, and eggs. The most dangerous food poison is the bacillus that causes botulism. This is rare but leads to muscle paralysis and, often, death.

gastroenteritis inflammation of the stomach and intestines, giving rise to abdominal pain, vomiting, and diarrhoea. It may be caused by food or other poisoning, allergy, or infection, and is dangerous in babies.

German measles or *rubella* mild, communicable virus disease, usually caught by children. It is marked by a sore throat, pinkish rash, and slight fever, and has an incubation period of two to three weeks. If a woman contracts it in the first three months of pregnancy, it may cause serious damage to the unborn child.

glandular fever or *infectious mononucleosis* viral disease characterized at onset by fever and painfully swollen lymph nodes (in the neck); there may also be digestive upset, sore throat, and skin rashes. Lassitude persists for months and even years, and recovery can be slow.

glaucoma condition in which pressure inside the eye (intraocular pressure) is raised abnormally as excess fluid accumulates. It occurs when the normal flow of intraocular fluid out of the eye is interrupted. As pressure rises, the optic nerve suffers irreversible damage, leading to a reduction in the field of vision and, ultimately, loss of eyesight.

gout hereditary form of arthritis, marked by an excess of uric acid crystals in the tissues, causing pain and inflammation in one or more joints (usually of the feet or hands), and posing a long-term threat to the blood vessels and kidneys. It is worsened by drinking alcohol. Acute attacks are treated with anti-inflammatories. The disease is ten times more common in men than women.

haemophilia any of several inherited diseases in which normal blood clotting is impaired. The sufferer experiences prolonged bleeding from the slightest wound, as well as painful internal bleeding without apparent cause. Haemophilias are nearly always sex-linked, transmitted through the female line only to male infants. Treatment is with a protein involved in the clotting of blood.

haemorrhoids or *piles* distended blood vessels (varicose veins) in the area of the anus.

hay fever allergic reaction to pollen, causing sneezing, inflammation of the eyes, and asthmatic symptoms. Sufferers experience irritation caused by powerful body chemicals related to histamine produced at the site of entry. Treatment is by antihistamine drugs.

heart attack sudden onset of gripping central chest pain, often accompanied by sweating and vomiting, caused by death of a portion of the heart muscle following obstruction of a coronary artery by thrombosis (formation of a blood clot). Half of all heart attacks result in death within the first two hours, but in the remainder survival has improved following the widespread use of streptokinase and aspirin to treat heart-attack victims.

heartburn burning sensation below the breastbone (sternum). It results from irritation of the lower oesophagus (gullet) by excessively acid stomach contents, as sometimes happens during pregnancy and in cases of duodenal ulcer or obesity. It is often due to a weak valve at the entrance to the stomach that allows its contents to well up into the oesophagus.

hepatitis any inflammatory disease of the liver, usually caused by a virus. Other causes include alcohol, drugs, gallstones, lupus erythematosus, and amoebic dysentery. Symptoms include weakness, nausea, and jaundice.

The viral disease *hepatitis A* (infectious or viral hepatitis) is spread by contaminated food, often seafood, and via the oro-faecal route. Incubation is about four weeks. The virus causing *hepatitis B* (serum hepatitis) is contained in all body fluids, and very easily transmitted. Some people become carriers. Those with the disease may be sick for weeks or months. The illness may be mild, or it may result in death from liver failure. A successful vaccine was developed in the late 1970s.

hernia or *rupture* protrusion of part of an internal organ through a weakness in the surrounding muscular wall, usually in the groin or navel. The appearance is that of a rounded soft lump or swelling.

herpes any of several infectious diseases caused by viruses of the herpes group. *Herpes simplex I* is the causative agent of a common inflammation, the cold sore. *Herpes simplex II* is responsible for genital herpes, a highly contagious, sexually transmitted disease characterized by painful blisters in the genital area. It can be transmitted in the birth canal from mother to newborn. *Herpes zoster* causes shingles; another herpes virus causes chickenpox. A number of antivirals treat these infections.

hypertension abnormally high blood pressure due to a variety of causes, leading to excessive contraction of the smooth muscle cells of the walls of the arteries. It increases the risk of kidney disease, stroke, and heart attack.

hypothermia condition in which the deep (core) temperature of the body spontaneously drops. If it is not discovered, coma and death ensue. Most at risk are the aged and babies (particularly if premature).

impotence physical inability to perform sexual intercourse (the term is not usually applied to women). Impotent men fail to achieve an erection, and this may be due to illness, the effects of certain drugs, or psychological factors.

incontinence failure or inability to control evacuation of the bladder or bowel (or both in the case of double incontinence). It may arise as a result of injury, childbirth, disease, or senility.

infection invasion of the body by disease-causing organisms (pathogens, or germs) that become established, multiply, and produce symptoms. Bacteria and viruses cause most diseases, but there are other microorganisms, protozoans, and other parasites.

Most pathogens enter and leave the body through the digestive or respiratory tracts. Polio, dysentery, and typhoid are examples of diseases contracted by ingestion of contaminated foods or fluids. Organisms present in the saliva or nasal mucus are spread by airborne or droplet infection; fine droplets or dried particles are inhaled by others when the affected individual talks, coughs, or sneezes. Diseases such as measles, mumps, and tuberculosis are passed on in this way. The common cold is passed from hand to hand, which then touches the eye or nose. A less common route of entry is through the skin, either by contamination of an open wound (as in tetanus) or by penetration of the intact skin surface, as in a bite from a malaria-carrying mosquito. Relatively few diseases are transmissible by skin-to-skin contact. Glandular fever and herpes simplex (cold sore) may be passed on by kissing, and the group now officially bracketed as sexually transmitted diseases (STDs) are mostly spread by intimate contact.

influenza any of various virus infections primarily affecting the air passages, accompanied by systemic effects such as fever, chills, headache, joint and muscle pains, and lassitude. Treatment is with bed rest and analgesic drugs such as aspirin and paracetamol. Vaccines are effective against known strains but will not give protection against newly evolving viruses.

jaundice yellow discolouration of the skin and whites of the eyes caused by an excess of bile pigment in the bloodstream. Mild jaundice is common in newborns, but a serious form occurs in rhesus disease. Bile pigment is normally produced by the liver from the breakdown of red blood cells, then excreted into the intestines. A build-up in the blood is due to abnormal destruction of red cells (as in some cases of anaemia), impaired liver function (as in hepatitis), or blockage in the excretory channels (as in gallstones or cirrhosis). The jaundice gradually recedes following treatment of the underlying cause.

laryngitis inflammation of the larynx, causing soreness of the throat, a dry cough, and hoarseness. The acute form is due to a virus or other infection, excessive use of the voice, or inhalation of irritating smoke, and may cause the voice to be completely lost. With rest, the inflammation usually subsides in a few days.

leukaemia any one of a group of cancers of the blood cells, with widespread involvement of the bone marrow and other blood-forming tissue. The central feature of leukaemia is runaway production of white blood cells that are immature or in some way abnormal. These rogue cells, which lack the defensive capacity of healthy white cells, overwhelm the normal ones, leaving the victim vulnerable to infection. Treatment is with radiotherapy and cytotoxic drugs to suppress replication of abnormal cells, or by bone-marrow transplantation.

malaria infectious parasitic disease of the tropics transmitted by mosquitoes, marked by periodic fever and an enlarged spleen. When a female mosquito of the *Anopheles* genus bites a human who has malaria, it takes in with the human blood one of four malaria protozoa of the genus *Plasmodium*. This matures within the insect and is then transferred when the mosquito bites a new victim. Malaria affects an estimated 267 million people (1993) in 103 countries, claiming up to 2 million lives a year. Quinine, the first drug used against malaria, has now been replaced by synthetics, such as chloroquine, used to prevent or treat the disease. However, chloroquine-resistant strains of the main malaria parasite, *Plasmodium fulciparum*, are spreading rapidly in many parts of the world.

Tests on a vaccine were begun 1986 in the USA. One experimental vaccine, devised in Colombia in the mid-1980s and widely tested in Latin America, is undergoing trials in Thailand, Tanzania, and the USA.

ME (abbreviation for *myalgic encephalitis*) or *postviral fatigue syndrome* or *chronic fatigue syndrome* a debilitating condition still not universally accepted as a genuine disease. The condition occurs after a flulike attack and has a diffuse range of symptoms. These strike and recur for years and include extreme fatigue, muscular pain, weakness, and depression.

measles or *rubeola* acute virus disease spread by airborne infection. Symptoms are fever, severe catarrh, small spots inside the mouth, and a raised, blotchy red rash appearing for about a week after two weeks' incubation. Prevention is by vaccination.

melanoma mole or growth containing the dark pigment melanin. Malignant melanoma is a type of skin cancer developing in association with a pre-existing mole. Unlike other skin cancers, it is associated with brief but excessive exposure to sunlight. Once rare, this disease is now frequent, owing to the increasing popularity of holidays in the sun. Most at risk are those with fair hair and light skin, and those who have had a severe sunburn in childhood.

meningitis inflammation of the meninges (membranes) surrounding the brain, caused by bacterial or viral infection. The severity of the disease varies from mild to rapidly lethal, and symptoms include fever, headache, nausea, neck stiffness, delirium, and (rarely) convulsions. Bacterial meningitis, though treatable by antibiotics, is the more serious threat. Diagnosis is by lumbar puncture. The treatment for viral meningitis is rest.

migraine acute, sometimes incapacitating headache (generally only on one side), accompanied by nausea, that recurs, often with advance symptoms such as flashing lights. No cure has been discovered, but ergotamine normally relieves the symptoms. Some sufferers learn to avoid certain foods, such as chocolate, which suggests an allergic factor.

motor neuron disease or *amyotrophic lateral sclerosis* chronic disease in which there is progressive degeneration of the nerve cells (neurons) that instigate movement. It leads to weakness, wasting, and loss of muscle function, and usually proves fatal within two or three years of onset. Motor neuron disease occurs in both hereditary and sporadic forms, but its causes remain unclear. In the UK some 1,200 new cases are diagnosed each year.

multiple sclerosis (MS) incurable chronic disease of the central nervous system, occurring in young or middle adulthood. It is characterized by degeneration of the myelin sheath that surrounds nerves in the brain and spinal cord. It is also known as disseminated sclerosis. Its cause is unknown.

Depending on where the demyelination occurs – which nerves are affected – the symptoms of MS can mimic almost any neurological disorder. Typically seen are unsteadiness, ataxia (loss of muscular coordination), weakness, speech difficulties, and rapid involuntary movements of the eyes. The course of the disease is episodic, with frequent intervals of remission.

mumps virus infection marked by fever and swelling of the parotid salivary glands (such as those under the ears). It is usually minor in children, although meningitis is a possible complication. In adults the symptoms are severe and it may cause sterility in adult men. An effective vaccine against mumps, measles, and rubella (MMR vaccine) is now offered to children aged 18 months.

muscular dystrophy any of a group of inherited chronic muscle disorders marked by weakening and wasting of muscle. Muscle fibres degenerate, to be replaced by fatty tissue, although the nerve supply remains unimpaired. Death occurs in early adult life.

The commonest form, Duchenne muscular dystrophy, strikes boys, usually before the age of four. The child develops a waddling gait and an inward curvature (lordosis) of the lumbar spine. The muscles affected by dystrophy and the rate of progress vary. There is no cure, but physical treatments can minimize disability.

myalgic encephalomyelitis the full name of ME, or chronic fatigue syndrome.

osteoarthritis degenerative disease of the joints in later life, sometimes resulting in disabling stiffness and wasting of muscles. Formerly thought to be due to wear and tear, it has been shown to be less common in the physically active. It appears to be linked with crystal deposits (in the form of calcium phosphate) in cartilage.

osteoporosis disease in which the bone substance becomes porous and brittle. It is common in older people, affecting more women than men. It may be treated with calcium supplements and etidronate.

Osteoporosis may occur in women whose ovaries have been removed, unless hormone-replacement therapy (HRT) is instituted; it may also occur as a side effect of long-term treatment with corticosteroids. Early menopause in women, childlessness, small body build, lack of exercise, heavy drinking, smoking, and hereditary factors may be contributory factors.

otitis inflammation of the ear. *Otitis externa*, occurring in the outer ear canal, is easily treated with antibiotics. Inflamed conditions of the middle ear (*otitis media*) or inner ear (*otitis interna*) are more serious, carrying the risk of deafness and infection of the brain.

Parkinson's disease or *parkinsonism* or *paralysis agitans* degenerative disease of the brain characterized by a progressive loss of mobility, muscular rigidity, tremor, and speech difficulties. The condition is mainly seen in people over the age of 50.

Parkinson's disease destroys a group of cells called the *substantia nigra* ('black substance') in the upper part of the brainstem. These cells are concerned with the production of a neurotransmitter known as dopamine, which is essential to the control of voluntary movement. The almost total loss of these cells, and of their chemical product, produces the disabling effects.

The drug L-dopa, introduced in the 1960s, postpones the terminal phase of the disease. Brain grafts with dopamine-producing cells were pioneered in the early 1980s, and attempts to graft Parkinson's patients with fetal brain tissue have been made. In 1989 a large US study showed that the drug deprenyl may slow the rate at which disability progresses in patients with early Parkinson's disease.

pneumonia inflammation of the lungs, generally due to bacterial or viral infection but also to particulate matter or gases. It is characterized by a build-up of fluid in the alveoli, the clustered air sacs (at the end of the air passages) where oxygen exchange takes place.

Symptoms include fever and pain in the chest. With widespread availability of antibiotics, infectious pneumonia is much less common than it was. However, it remains a dire threat to patients whose immune systems are suppressed (including transplant recipients and AIDS and cancer victims) and to those who are critically ill or injured.

polio (*poliomyelitis*) viral infection of the central nervous system affecting nerves that activate muscles. The disease used to be known as infantile paralysis. Two kinds of vaccine are available, one injected and one given by mouth. The World Health Organization expects that polio will be eradicated by 2000.

premenstrual tension (PMT) or *premenstrual syndrome* medical condition caused by hormone changes and comprising a number of physical and emotional features that occur cyclically before menstruation and disappear with its onset. Symptoms include mood changes, breast tenderness, a feeling of bloatedness, and headache.

psoriasis chronic, recurring skin disease characterized by raised, red, scaly patches, usually on the scalp, back, arms, and/or legs. Tar preparations, steroid creams, and ultraviolet light are used to treat it, and sometimes it disappears spontaneously. Psori-

asis may be accompanied by a form of arthritis (inflammation of the joints). It is a common disease, affecting 2% of the UK population.

puerperal fever infection of the genital tract of the mother after childbirth, due to lack of aseptic conditions. Formerly often fatal, it is now rare and treated with antibiotics.

rabies or *hydrophobia* disease of the central nervous system that can afflict all warm-blooded creatures. It is almost invariably fatal once symptoms have developed. Its transmission to humans is generally by a bite from an infected dog. Injections of rabies vaccine and antiserum may save those bitten by a rabid animal from developing the disease.

rheumatic fever or *acute rheumatism* acute or chronic illness characterized by fever and painful swelling of joints. Some victims also experience involuntary movements of the limbs and head, a form of chorea.

Rheumatic fever, which strikes mainly children and young adults, is always preceded by a streptococcal infection such as scarlet fever or a severe sore throat, usually occurring a couple of weeks beforehand. It is treated with bed rest, antibiotics, and painkillers. The most important complication of rheumatic fever is damage to the heart valve, producing rheumatic heart disease, which may lead to disability and death.

rubella technical term for German measles.

scabies contagious infection of the skin caused by the parasitic itch mite *Sarcoptes scaboi*, which burrows under the skin to deposit eggs. Treatment is by antiparasitic creams and lotions.

sciatica persistent pain in the leg, along the sciatic nerve and its branches. Causes of sciatica include inflammation of the nerve or pressure on, or inflammation of, a nerve root leading out of the lower spine.

septicaemia technical term for blood poisoning.

shingles common name for herpes zoster, a disease characterized by infection of sensory nerves, with pain and eruption of blisters along the course of the affected nerves.

shock circulatory failure marked by a sudden fall of blood pressure and resulting in pallor, sweating, fast (but weak) pulse, and sometimes complete collapse. Causes include disease, injury, and psychological trauma. Treatment depends on the cause. Rest is needed, and, in the case of severe blood loss, restoration of the normal circulating volume.

sickle-cell disease hereditary chronic blood disorder common among people of black African descent; also found in the E Mediterranean, parts of the Persian Gulf, and in NE India. It is characterized by distortion and fragility of the red blood cells, which are lost too rapidly from the circulation. This often results in anaemia.

sinusitis painful inflammation of one of the sinuses, or air spaces, that surround the nasal passages. Most cases clear with antibiotics and nasal decongestants, but some require surgical drainage.

spina bifida congenital defect in which part of the spinal cord and its membranes are exposed, due to incomplete development of the spine.

Spina bifida, usually present in the lower back, varies in severity. The most seriously affected babies may be paralysed below the waist. There is also a risk of mental retardation and death from hydrocephalus, which is often associated. Surgery is performed to close the spinal lesion shortly after birth, but this does not usually cure the disabilities caused by the condition.

stroke or *cerebrovascular accident* or *apoplexy* interruption of the blood supply to part of the brain due to a sudden bleed in the brain (cerebral haemhorrhage) or embolism or thrombosis. Strokes vary in severity from producing almost no symptoms to proving rapidly fatal. In between are those (often recurring) that leave a wide range of impaired function, depending on the size and location of the event. The disease of the arteries that predisposes to stroke is atherosclerosis. High blood pressure (hypertension) is also a precipitating factor. Strokes can sometimes be prevented by surgery (as in the case of some aneurysms), or by use of anticoagulant drugs or vitamin E or daily aspirin to minimize the risk of stroke due to blood clots.

syphilis venereal disease caused by the spiral-shaped bacterium (spirochete) *Treponema pallidum*. Untreated, it runs its course in three stages over many years, often starting with a painless hard sore, or chancre, developing within a month on the area of infection (usually the genitals). The second stage, months later, is a rash with arthritis, hepatitis, and/or meningitis. The third stage, years later, leads eventually to paralysis, blindness, insanity, and death. The Wassermann test is a diagnostic blood test for syphilis.

With widespread availability of antibiotics, syphilis is now increasingly cured in the industrialized world, at least to the extent that the final stage of the disease is rare. The risk remains that the disease may go undiagnosed or that it may be transmitted by a pregnant woman to her fetus.

tetanus or *lockjaw* acute disease caused by the toxin of the bacillus *Clostridium tetani*, which usually enters the body through a wound. The bacterium is chiefly found in richly manured soil. Untreated, in seven to ten days tetanus produces muscular spasm and rigidity of the jaw spreading to the other muscles, convulsions, and death. There is a vaccine, and the disease may be treatable with tetanus antitoxin and antibiotics.

thrombosis condition in which a blood clot forms in a vein or artery, causing loss of circulation to the area served by the vessel. If it breaks away, it often travels to the lungs, causing pulmonary embolism. Thrombosis in veins of the legs is often seen in association with phlebitis, and in arteries with atheroma. Thrombosis increases the risk of heart attack (myocardial infarct) and stroke. It is treated by surgery and/or anticoagulant drugs.

thrush or *candidiasis* infection usually of the mouth (particularly in infants), but also sometimes of the vagina, caused by a yeastlike fungus (genus *Candida*). It is seen as white patches on the mucous membranes. Thrush may be caused by antibiotics removing natural antifungal agents from the body. It is treated with a further antibiotic.

toxic shock syndrome rare condition marked by rapid onset of fever, vomiting, and low blood pressure, sometimes leading to death. It is caused by a toxin of the bacterium *Staphylococcus aureus*, normally harmlessly present in the body, which may accumulate, for example, if a tampon used during a period remains unchanged beyond four to six hours.

travel sickness nausea and vomiting caused by the motion of cars, boats, or other forms of transport. Constant vibration and movement may stimulate changes in the fluids of the semicircular canals (responsible for balance) of the inner ear, to which the individual fails to adapt, and to which are added visual and psychological factors. Some proprietary remedies contain antihistamine drugs.

tropical disease any illness found mainly in hot climates. The most important tropical diseases worldwide are malaria, schistosomiasis, leprosy, and river blindness. Malaria kills about 1.5 million people each year, and produces chronic anaemia and tiredness in 100 times as many, while schistosomiasis is responsible for 1 million deaths a year. All the main tropical diseases are potentially curable, but the facilities for diagnosis and treatment are rarely adequate in the countries where they occur.

tuberculosis (TB) formerly known as *consumption* or *phthisis* infectious disease caused by the bacillus *Mycobacterium tuberculosis*. It takes several forms, of which pulmonary tuberculosis is by far the most common. A vaccine, BCG, was developed around 1920 and the first antituberculosis drug, streptomycin, in 1944.

In pulmonary TB, a patch of inflammation develops in the lung, with formation of an abscess. Often, this heals spontaneously, leaving only scar tissue. The dangers are of rapid spread through both lungs (what used to be called 'galloping consumption') or the development of miliary tuberculosis (spreading in the bloodstream to other sites) or tuberculous meningitis. In addition to streptomycin there are two other drugs used to treat TB: rifampicin and isoniazid.

Active tuberculosis is rare in the affluent parts of the world, although in the USA from 1985 there was an 18% rise each year (to 1992) in the number of TB cases, with a high proportion of drug-resistant strains of the disease. In the UK in 1992 there were 5,861 new cases reported.

varicose veins or *varicosis* condition where the veins become swollen and twisted. The veins of the legs are most often affected; other vulnerable sites include the rectum (haemorrhoids) and testes. The affected veins can be injected with a substance that makes them shrink, or surgery may be needed.

vomiting expulsion of the contents of the stomach through the mouth. It may have numerous causes, including direct irritation of the stomach, severe pain, dizziness, and emotion. Sustained or repeated vomiting may indicate serious disease, and dangerous loss of water, salt, and acid may result (as in bulimia).

whooping cough or *pertussis* acute infectious disease, seen mainly in children, caused by colonization of the air passages by the bacterium *Bordetella pertussis*. There may be catarrh, mild fever, and loss of appetite, but the main symptom is violent coughing, associated with the sharp intake of breath that is the characteristic 'whoop', and often followed by vomiting and severe nose bleeds. The cough may persist for weeks.

Types of Drugs

anabolic steroid any hormone of the steroid group that stimulates tissue growth. It is used to treat some anaemias and breast cancers, and may help to break up blood clots. Its use in sports to increase muscle bulk is widely condemned. Side effects include aggressive behaviour, masculinization in women, and, in children, reduced height.

anaesthetic drug that produces loss of sensation or consciousness; the resulting state is *anaesthesia*, in which the patient is insensitive to stimuli. Anaesthesia may also happen as a result of nerve disorder.

Pain is felt when electrical stimuli travel along a nerve pathway, from peripheral nerve fibres to the brain via the spinal cord. An anaesthetic agent acts either by preventing stimuli from being sent (local), or by removing awareness of them (general). In cases where general anaesthesia is not called for, a substance may be applied to the skin or tissue surface; a local agent may be injected into the tissues under the skin in the area to be treated; or a regional block of sensation may be achieved by injection into a nerve. Spinal anaesthetic, such as epidural, is injected into the tissues surrounding the spinal cord, producing loss of feeling in the lower part of the body.

analgesic agent for relieving pain. Opiates alter the perception or appreciation of pain and are effective in controlling 'deep' visceral (internal) pain. Non-opiates, such as aspirin, paracetamol, and NSAIDs (nonsteroidal anti-inflammatory drugs), relieve musculoskeletal pain and reduce inflammation in soft tissues.

antibiotic drug that kills or inhibits the growth of bacteria and fungi. It is derived from living organisms such as fungi or bacteria, which distinguishes it from synthetic antimicrobials.

The earliest antibiotics, the penicillins, came into use from 1941. Each class and individual antibiotic acts in a different way and may be effective against either a broad spectrum or a specific type of disease-causing agent. Use of antibiotics has become more selective as side effects, such as toxicity, allergy, and resistance, have become better understood. Bacteria have the ability to develop immunity following repeated or subclinical (insufficient) doses, so more advanced and synthetic antimicrobials are continually required to overcome them.

antidepressant any drug used to relieve symptoms in depressive illness. The two main groups are the tricyclic antidepressants (TCADs) and the monoamine oxidase inhibitors (MAOIs), which act by altering chemicals available to the central nervous system. Both may produce serious side effects and are restricted.

anti-inflammatory any substance that reduces swelling in soft tissues. Antihistamines relieve allergic reactions; aspirin and NSAIDs are effective in joint and musculoskeletal conditions; rubefacients

(counterirritant liniments) ease painful joints, tendons, and muscles. Steroids, because of their severe side effects, are only prescribed if other therapy is ineffective, or if a condition is life-threatening. A corticosteroid injection into the affected joint usually gives long-term relief from inflammation.

antiseptic any substance that kills or inhibits the growth of microorganisms. The use of antiseptics was pioneered by English surgeon Joseph Lister (1827–1912). He used carbolic acid (phenol), which is a weak antiseptic; substances such as TCP are derived from this.

antiviral any drug that acts against viruses, usually preventing them from multiplying. Most viral infections are not susceptible to antibiotics. Antivirals have been difficult drugs to develop, and do not necessarily cure viral diseases.

aspirin acetylsalicylic acid, a popular pain-relieving drug (analgesic) developed in the early 20th century for headaches and arthritis. It inhibits prostaglandins, and is derived from the white willow tree *Salix alba*.

beta-blocker any of a class of drugs that block impulses that stimulate certain nerve endings (beta receptors) serving the heart muscles. This reduces the heart rate and the force of contraction, which in turn reduces the amount of oxygen (and therefore the blood supply) required by the heart. Beta-blockers are banned from use in competitive sports. They may be useful in the treatment of angina, arrhythmia, and raised blood pressure, and following myocardial infarctions. They must be withdrawn from use gradually.

codeine opium derivative that provides analgesia in mild to moderate pain. It also suppresses the cough centre of the brain. It is an alkaloid, derived from morphine but less toxic and addictive.

corticosteroid any of several steroid hormones secreted by the cortex of the adrenal glands; also synthetic forms with similar properties. Corticosteroids have anti-inflammatory and immunosuppressive effects and may be used to treat a number of conditions including rheumatoid arthritis, severe allergies, asthma, some skin diseases, and some cancers. Side effects can be serious, and therapy must be withdrawn very gradually.

insulin protein hormone, produced by specialized cells in the islets of Langerhans in the pancreas, that regulates the metabolism (rate of activity) of glucose, fats, and proteins. Insulin was discovered by Canadian physician Frederick Banting (1891–1941), who pioneered its use in treating diabetes.

Human insulin has now been produced from bacteria by genetic engineering techniques, but may increase the chance of sudden, unpredictable hypoglycaemia, or low blood sugar. In 1990 the Medical College of Ohio developed gelatine capsules and an aspirinlike drug which helps the insulin pass into the bloodstream.

L-dopa chemical, normally produced by the body, which is converted by an enzyme to dopamine in the brain. It is essential for integrated movement of individual muscle groups. As a treatment, it relieves the rigidity of Parkinson's disease but may have significant side effects, such as extreme mood changes, hal-

Common plant-derived drugs

Major drugs derived from plants

Plant	Drug	Use
Amazonian liana	Curare	Muscle relaxant
Annual mugwort	Artemisinin	Antimalarial
Autumn crocus	Colchicine	Antitumor agent
Belladonna	Atropine	Anticholinergic
Coca	Cocaine	Local anesthetic
Common thyme	Thymol	Antifungal
Ergot fungus	Ergotamine	Analgesic
Foxglove	Digitoxin, digitalis	Cardiotonic
Indian snakeroot	Reserpine	Antihypertensive
Meadowsweet	Salicylic acid*	Analgesic
Mexican yam	Diosgenin	Birth-control pill
Nux vomica	Strychnine	CNS stimulant
Opium poppy	Codeine, morphine	Analgesic (& antitussive)
Pacific yew	Taxol	Antitumor agent
Recured thornapple	Scopolamine	Sedative
Rosy periwinkle	Vincristine, vinblastine	Antileukemia
Velvet bean	L-Dopa	Antiparkinsonian
White willow	Salicin*	Analgesic
Yellow cinchona	Quinine	Antimalarial, Antipyretic

* Compound formed from salicylic acid and acetic acid is called acetylsalicylic acid: better known as aspirin.

Source: Atlas of the Environment/WWF

lucinations, and uncontrolled writhing movements. It is often given in combination with other drugs to improve its effectiveness at lower doses.

mifepristone (formerly *RU-486*) abortion pill first introduced in France 1989, and effective in 94% of patients up to 10 weeks pregnant when administered in conjunction with a prostaglandin. It was licensed in the UK in 1991.

oxytocin hormone that stimulates the uterus in late pregnancy to initiate and sustain labour. After birth, it stimulates the uterine muscles to contract, reducing bleeding at the site where the placenta was attached.

paracetamol analgesic, particularly effective for musculoskeletal pain. It is as effective as aspirin in reducing fever, and less irritating to the stomach, but has little anti-inflammatory action (as for joint pain). An overdose can cause severe, often irreversible or even fatal, liver and kidney damage.

penicillin any of a group of antibiotic (bacteria-killing) compounds obtained from filtrates of moulds of the genus *Penicillium* (especially *P. notatum*) or produced synthetically. Penicillin was the first antibiotic to be discovered (by Scottish bacteriologist Alexander Fleming, 1881–1955); it kills a broad spectrum of bacteria, many of which cause disease in humans.

pill, the commonly used term for any oral contraceptive pill, based on female hormones. The *combined pill*, which contains synthetic hormones similar to oestrogen and progesterone, stops the production of eggs and makes the mucus produced by the cervix hostile to sperm. It is the most effective

form of contraception apart from sterilization, being more than 99% effective. The *minipill*, or progesterone-only pill, prevents implantation of a fertilized egg into the wall of the uterus. The minipill has a slightly higher failure rate, especially if not taken at the same time each day, but has fewer side effects and is considered safer for long-term use.

placebo any harmless substance, often called a 'sugar pill', that has no chemotherapeutic value. The use of placebos in medicine is limited to drug trials, where a placebo is given alongside the substance being tested, to compare effects. Placebos have been known to cause changes in blood pressure, perceived pain, and rates of healing.

premedication combination of drugs given before surgery to prepare a patient for general anaesthesia.

steroid short for anabolic steroid.

warfarin poison that induces fatal internal bleeding in rats; neutralized with sodium hydroxide, it is used in medicine as an anticoagulant: it prevents blood clotting by inhibiting the action of vitamin K. It is often given as a preventive measure, to reduce the risk of thrombosis or embolism after major surgery. It can be taken orally and begins to act several days after the initial dose.

zidovudine (formerly *AZT*) antiviral drug used in the treatment of AIDS. It is not a cure for AIDS but is effective in prolonging life; it does not, however, delay the onset of AIDS in people carrying the virus. Zidovudine was developed in the mid-1980s and approved for use by 1987. Taken every four hours, it reduces the risk of opportunistic infection and relieves many neurological complications. However, frequent blood monitoring is required to control anaemia, a potentially life-threatening side effect of zidovudine. Blood transfusions are often necessary, and the drug must be withdrawn if bone-marrow function is severely affected.

Alternative Therapies

acupuncture ancient Chinese medical art based on a theory of physiology that posits a network of life-energy pathways or 'meridians' in the human body and some 800 'acupuncture points' where metal needles may be inserted to affect the energy flow for purposes of preventive or remedial therapy or to produce a local anaesthetic effect. Numerous studies and surveys have attested the efficacy of the method, which is widely conceded by orthodox practitioners despite the lack of an acceptable scientific explanation.

Alexander technique method of correcting established bad habits of posture, breathing, and muscular tension which Australian therapist F M Alexander maintained cause many ailments. Back troubles, migraine, asthma, hypertension, and some gastric and gynaecological disorders are among the conditions said to be alleviated by the technique, which is also effective in the prevention of disorders, particularly those of later life. The technique also acts as a general health promoter, promoting relaxation and enhancing vitality.

applied kinesiology extension of chiropractic developed in the USA in the 1960s and 1970s, principally by US practitioner Dr George Goodheart. Relating to the science of kinesiology, or muscle testing, the Chinese principle that there exist energy pathways in the body and that disease results from local energy blockages or imbalances, Goodheart developed both diagnostic and therapeutic techniques, working on the body's musculature, which have proved particularly effective with stress-related ailments.

aromatherapy medicinal use of oils and essences derived from plants, flowers, and wood resins. Bactericidal properties and beneficial effects upon physiological functions are attributed to the oils, which are sometimes ingested but generally massaged into the skin. Aromatherapy was practised in the ancient world and revived in the 1960s in France, where today it is an optional component of some courses available to postgraduate medical students.

astrological diagnosis casting of a horoscope to ascertain a person's susceptibility to specific kinds of disease. From statistical evidence that offspring tend to have the same planetary positions in their charts as a parent, astrologers infer that there is a significant correlation between genetic and planetary influences, and that medical horoscopes, by pinpointing pathological tendencies, can be a useful tool of preventive medicine.

aura diagnosis ascertaining a person's state of health from the colour and luminosity of the aura, the 'energy envelope' of the physical body commonly claimed to be seen by psychics. A study carried out by the Charing Cross Hospital Medical School (London) confirmed that the aura can be viewed by high-frequency electrophotography techniques and is broadly indicative of states of health, but concluded that aura diagnosis cannot identify specific abnormalities.

autogenics system designed to facilitate mental control of biological and physiological functions generally considered to be involuntary. Effective in inducing relaxation, assisting healing processes, and relieving psychosomatic disorders, autogenics is regarded as a precursor of biofeedback. It was developed in the 1900s by German physician Johannes Schultz.

Bach flower healing homoeopathic system of therapy using extracts of wild flowers. It seeks to alleviate mental and emotional causes of disease rather than their physical symptoms. The system was developed in the 1920s by English physician Edward Bach.

Bates eyesight training method developed by US opthalmologist William Bates (1860–1931) to enable people to correct problems of vision without wearing glasses. The method is of proven effectiveness in relieving all refractive conditions, correcting squints, lazy eyes, and similar problems, but does not claim to treat eye disease.

biochemic tissue salts therapy the correction of imbalances or deficiencies in the body's resources of essential mineral salts. There are 12 tissue salts in the body and the healthy functioning of cells depends on their correct balance, but there is scant evidence that disease is due to their imbalance and can be cured by supplements, as claimed by German physician W H Schuessler in the 1870s, though many people profess to benefit from the 'Schuessler remedies'.

bioenergetics extension of Reichian therapy principles designed to promote, by breathing, physical exercise, and the elimination of muscular blockages, the free flow of energy in the body and thus restore optimum health and vitality. Bioenergetics was developed in the 1960s by US physician Alexander Lowen.

biofeedback the use of electrophysiological monitoring devices to 'feed back' information about internal processes and thus facilitate conscious control. Developed in the USA in the 1960s, independently by neurophysiologist Barbara Brown and neuropsychiatrist Joseph Kamiya, the technique is effective in alleviating hypertension and preventing associated organic and physiological dysfunctions.

chiropractic technique of manipulation of the spine and other parts of the body, based on the principle that disorders are attributable to aberrations in the functioning of the nervous system, which manipulation can correct.

clinical ecology ascertaining environmental factors involved in illnesses, particularly those manifesting nonspecific symptoms such as fatigue, depression, allergic reactions, and immune system malfunctions, and prescribing means of avoiding or minimizing these effects.

colour therapy application of light of appropriate wavelength to alleviate ailments or facilitate healing. Coloured light affects not only psychological but also physiological states — for instance, long exposure to red light raises blood pressure and speeds up heartbeat and respiration rates, whereas exposure to blue has the reverse effect.

crystal therapy the application of crystals to diseased or disordered physical structures or processes to effect healing or stabilizing.

cupping ancient folk-medicine method of drawing blood to the surface of the body by applying cups or glasses in which a vacuum has been created, found to be effective in alleviating (though not curing) rheumatism, lumbago, arthritis, asthma, and bronchitis.

diatetics the prescription of dietary regimens to promote health or healing. Although no one quarrels with the general principle that diet affects health, the preventative or curative effects of specific diets, such as the raw vegetable diets sometimes prescribed for cancer patients, are disputed by orthodox medicine.

electrocrystal diagnosis technique recently developed by British biologist Harry Oldfield, based on the finding that stimulated electromagnetic fields of the human body resonate at a particular frequency which varies with individuals, and that actual or incipient disease can be pinpointed by a scanning device responsive to local deviations from the person's norm.

endogenous endocrinotherapy the fostering of hormonal balance in the body by regulating the activities of the endocrine glands by external manipulation, without recourse to introduced stimulants, suppressants, or supplements.

fasting total abstinence from food for a limited period. This is prescribed by some naturopaths to eliminate body toxins or make available for recuperative purposes the energy normally used by the digestive system. Prolonged fasting can be dangerous.

Gerson therapy radical nutritional therapy for degenerative diseases, particularly cancer, developed by German-born US physician Max Gerson (1881–1959).

hair analysis diagnostic technique for ascertaining deficiencies or excesses of mineral resources in the body, using a sophisticated analytic procedure called atomic-emission spectroscopy.

herbalism prescription and use of plants and their derivatives for medication. Herbal products are favoured by alternative practitioners as 'natural medicine', as opposed to modern synthesized medicines and drugs, which are regarded with suspicion because of the dangers of side-effects and dependence.

holistic medicine umbrella term for an approach that virtually all alternative therapies profess, which considers the overall health and lifestyle profile of a patient, and treats specific ailments not primarily as conditions to be alleviated but rather as symptoms of more fundamental disease.

homoeopathy or **homeopathy** system of medicine based on the principle that symptoms of disease are part of the body's self-healing processes, and on the practice of administering extremely diluted doses of natural substances found to produce in a healthy person the symptoms manifest in the illness being treated. Developed by German physician Samuel Hahnemann (1755-1843), the system is widely practised today as an alternative to allopathic medicine, and many controlled tests and achieved cures testify its efficacy.

hydrotherapy use of water, externally or internally, for health or healing. Programmed hot and/or cold applications or immersions, sometimes accompanied by local low-voltage stimulation, are used to alleviate tension and stress. Some hydrotherapists specialize in colonic or high colonic irrigation, the thorough washing-out and detoxification of the digestive system.

hypnotherapy use of hypnotic trance and post-hypnotic suggestions to relieve stress-related conditions such as insomnia and hypertension, or to break health-inimical habits or addictions.

ionization therapy enhancement of the atmosphere of an environment by instrumentally boosting the negative ion content of the air.

iridology diagnostic technique based on correspondences between specific areas of the iris and bodily functions and organs.

magnet therapy use of applied magnetic fields to regulate potentially pathogenic disorders in the electrical charges of body cells and structures.

megavitamin therapy administration of large doses of vitamins to combat conditions considered wholly or in part due to their deficiency.

music therapy use of music as an adjunct to relaxation therapy, or in psychotherapy to elicit expressions of suppressed emotions by prompting patients to dance, shout, laugh, cry, or whatever, in response.

naturopathy the facilitating of the natural self-healing processes of the body. Naturopaths are the GPs of alternative medicine and often refer clients to other specialists, particularly in manipulative therapies, to complement their own work of seeking — through diet, the prescription of natural medicines and supplements, and lifestyle counselling — to restore or augment the vitality of the body and thereby its optimum health.

osteopathy system of physical manipulation to treat mechanical stress. Osteopaths are generally consulted to treat problems of the musculo-skeletal structure such as back pain.

psionic medicine system of medical diagnosis and therapy developed by British physician George Lawrence in the 1930s and subsequently. Diagnosis is effected by dowsing a small blood sample with the aid of a pendulum to ascertain deficiencies or imbalances affecting the body's vitality, and treatment is by the administration of homoeopathic remedies.

pulsed high frequency (PHF) instrumental application of high-frequency radio waves in short bursts to damaged tissue to relieve pain, reduce bruising and swelling, and speed healing.

radionics healing method said to work on the 'subtle energy' level of the organism. Critics regard the radionic 'black box' — invented early in the century by US physician Albert Adams and later modified by his follower Ruth Drown — as a fraudulent quasi-scientific instrument, though practitioners maintain that it is an enabling device to effect psychic healing at a distance, and claim numerous successes, both diagnostic and curative

reflexology manipulation and massage of the feet to ascertain and treat disease or dysfunction elsewhere in the body.

Reichian therapy general term for a group of body-therapies based on the theory propounded in the 1930s by Wilhelm Reich, that many functional and organic illnesses are attributable to constriction of the flow of vital energies in the body by tensions that become locked into the musculature. Bioenergetics and Rolfing are related approaches.

relaxation therapy development of regular and conscious control of physiological processes and their related emotional and mental states, and of muscular tensions in the body, as a way of relieving stress and its results. Meditation, hypnotherapy, autogenics, and biofeedback are techniques commonly employed.

Rolfing technique of deep muscular manipulation developed in the 1960s and 1970s by US physiologist Ira Rolf. Also known as 'structural integration', the treatment is designed to correct gravitational imbalance in body postures and movements, and to relieve muscular rigidities and inflexibilities, thus enhancing general health and vitality.

shiatsu or **acupressure** Japanese method of massage derived from acupuncture which treats organic

Nobel Prize for Physiology or Medicine

1901	Emil von Behring (Germany): discovery that the body produces antitoxins, and development of serum therapy for diseases such as diphtheria
1902	Ronald Ross (UK): role of the Anopheles mosquito in transmitting malaria
1903	Niels Finsen (Denmark): use of ultraviolet light to treat skin diseases
1904	Ivan Pavlov (Russia): physiology of digestion
1905	Robert Koch (Germany): investigations and discoveries in relation to tuberculosis
1906	Camillo Golgi (Italy) and Santiago Ramón y Cajal (Spain): fine structure of nervous system
1907	Charles Laveran (France): discovery that certain protozoa can cause disease
1908	Ilya Mechnikov (Russia) and Paul Ehrlich (Germany): work on immunity
1909	Emil Kocher (Switzerland): physiology, pathology, and surgery of the thyroid gland
1910	Albrecht Kossel (Germany): study of cell proteins and nucleic acids
1911	Allvar Gullstrand (Sweden): refraction of light through the different components of the eye
1912	Alexis Carrel (USA): techniques for connecting severed blood vessels and transplanting organs
1913	Charles Richet (France): allergic responses
1914	Robert Bárány (Austria): physiology and pathology of the equilibrium organs of the inner ear
1915–1918	no prizes awarded
1919	Jules Bordet (Belgium): work on immunity
1920	August Krogh (Denmark): discovery of mechanism regulating the dilation and constriction of blood capillaries
1921	no prizes awarded
1922	Archibald Hill (UK): production of heat in contracting muscle; Otto Meyerhof (Germany): relationship between oxygen consumption and metabolism of lactic acid in muscle
1923	Frederick Banting (Canada) and John Macleod (UK): discovery and isolation of the hormone insulin
1924	Willem Einthoven (Netherlands): invention of the electrocardiograph
1925	no prizes awarded
1926	Johannes Fibiger (Denmark): discovery of a parasite Spiroptera carcinoma that causes cancer
1927	Julius Wagner-Jauregg (Austria): use of induced malarial fever to treat paralysis caused by mental deterioration
1928	Charles Nicolle (France): role of the body louse in transmitting typhus
1929	Christiaan Eijkman (Netherlands): discovery of a cure for beriberi, a vitamin-deficiency disease; Frederick Hopkins (UK): discovery of trace substances, now known as vitamins, that stimulate growth
1930	Karl Landsteiner (USA): discovery of human blood groups
1931	Otto Warburg (Germany): discovery of respiratory enzymes that enable cells to process oxygen
1932	Charles Sherrington (UK) and Edgar Adrian (UK): function of neurons (nerve cells)
1933	Thomas Morgan (USA): role of chromosomes in heredity
1934	George Whipple (USA), George Minot (USA), and William Murphy (USA): treatment of pernicious anaemia by increasing the amount of liver in the diet
1935	Hans Spemann (Germany): organizer effect in embryonic development
1936	Henry Dale (UK) and Otto Loewi (Germany): chemical transmission of nerve impulses
1937	Albert Szent-Györgi (Hungary): investigation of biological oxidation processes and of the action of vitamin C (ascorbic acid)
1938	Corneille Heymans (Belgium): mechanisms regulating respiration
1939	Gerhard Domagk (Germany): discovery of the first antibacterial sulphonamide drug
1940–42	no prizes awarded
1943	Carl Dam (Denmark): discovery of vitamin K; Edward Doisy (USA): chemical nature of vitamin K
1944	Joseph Erlanger (USA) and Herbert Gasser (USA): transmission of impulses by nerve fibres
1945	Alexander Fleming (UK): discovery of the bactericidal effect of penicillin; Ernst Chain (UK) and Howard Florey (Australia): isolation of penicillin and its development as an antibiotic drug
1946	Hermann Muller (USA): discovery that X-ray irradiation can cause mutation
1947	Carl Cori (USA) and Gerty Cori (USA): production and breakdown of glycogen (animal starch); Bernardo Houssay (Argentina): function of the pituitary gland in sugar metabolism
1948	Paul Müller (Switzerland): discovery of the first synthetic contact insecticide DDT
1949	Walter Hess (Switzerland): mapping areas of the midbrain that control the activities of certain body organs; Antonio Egas Moniz (Portugal): therapeutic value of prefrontal lobotomy in certain psychoses
1950	Edward Kendall (USA), Tadeus Reichstein (Poland), and Philip Hench (USA): structure and biological effects of hormones of the adrenal cortex
1951	Max Theiler (South Africa): discovery of a vaccine against yellow fever
1952	Selman Waksman (USA): discovery of streptomycin, the first antibiotic effective against tuberculosis
1953	Hans Krebs (UK): discovery of the citric acid cycle; Fritz Lipmann (USA): discovery of coenzyme A, a nonprotein compound that acts in conjunction with enzymes to catalyse metabolic reactions leading up to the citric acid cycle
1954	John Enders (USA), Thomas Weller (USA), and Frederick Robbins (USA): cultivation of the polio virus in the laboratory
1955	Hugo Theorell (Sweden): nature and action of oxidation enzymes
1956	André Cournand (USA), Werner Forssmann (Germany), and Dickinson Richards Jr (USA): technique for passing a catheter into the heart for diagnostic purposes
1957	Daniel Bovet (Switzerland): discovery of synthetic drugs used as muscle relaxants in anaesthesia

Nobel Prize for Physiology or Medicine *(cont.)*

1958	George Beadle (USA) and Edward Tatum (USA): discovery that genes regulate precise chemical effects; Joshua Lederberg (USA): genetic recombination and the organization of bacterial genetic material
1959	Severo Ochoa (USA) and Arthur Kornberg (USA): discovery of enzymes that catalyse the formation of RNA (ribonucleic acid) and DNA (deoxyribonucleic acid)
1960	Macfarlane Burnet (Australia) and Peter Medawar (UK): acquired immunological tolerance of transplanted tissues
1961	Georg von Békésy (USA): investigations into the mechanism of hearing within the cochlea of the inner ear
1962	Francis Crick (UK), James Watson (USA), and Maurice Wilkins (UK): discovery of the double-helical structure of DNA and of the significance of this structure in the replication and transfer of genetic information
1963	John Eccles (Australia), Alan Hodgkin (UK), and Andrew Huxley (UK): ionic mechanisms involved in the communication or inhibition of impulses across neuron (nerve cell) membranes
1964	Konrad Bloch (USA) and Feodor Lynen (West Germany): cholesterol and fatty-acid metabolism
1965	François Jacob (France), André Lwoff (France), and Jacques Monod (France): genetic control of enzyme and virus synthesis
1966	Peyton Rous (USA): discovery of tumour- inducing viruses; Charles Huggins (USA): hormonal treatment of prostatic cancer
1967	Ragnar Granit (Sweden), Haldan Hartline (USA), and George Wald (USA): physiology and chemistry of vision
1968	Robert Holley (USA), Har Gobind Khorana (USA), and Marshall Nirenberg (USA): interpretation of genetic code and its function in protein synthesis
1969	Max Delbruck (USA), Alfred Hershey (USA), and Salvador Luria (USA): replication mechanism and genetic structure of viruses
1970	Bernard Katz (UK), Ulf von Euler (Austria), and Julius Axelrod (USA): storage, release, and inactivation of neurotransmitters
1971	Earl Sutherland(USA): discovery of cyclic AMP, a chemical messenger that plays a role in the action of many hormones
1972	Gerald Edelman (USA) and Rodney Porter (UK): chemical structure of antibodies
1973	Karl von Frisch (Austria), Konrad Lorenz (Austria), and Nikolaas Tinbergen (Netherlands): animal behaviour patterns
1974	Albert Claude (USA), Christian de Duve (Belgium), and George Palade (USA): structural and functional organization of the cell
1975	David Baltimore (USA), Renato Dulbecco (USA), and Howard Temin (USA): interactions between tumour-inducing viruses and the genetic material of the cell
1976	Baruch Blumberg (USA) and Carleton Gajdusek (USA): new mechanisms for the origin and transmission of infectious diseases
1977	Roger Guillemin (USA) and Andrew Schally (USA): discovery of hormones produced by the hypothalamus region of the brain; Rosalyn Yalow (USA): radioimmunoassay techniques by which minute quantities of hormone may be detected
1978	Werner Arber (Switzerland), Daniel Nathans (USA), and Hamilton Smith (USA): discovery of restriction enzymes and their application to molecular genetics
1979	Allan Cormack (USA) and Godfrey Hounsfield (UK): development of the CAT scan
1980	Baruj Benacerraf (USA), Jean Dausset (France), and George Snell (USA): genetically determined structures on the cell surface that regulate immunological reactions
1981	Roger Sperry (USA): functional specialization of the brain's cerebral hemispheres; David Hubel (USA) and Torsten Wiesel (Sweden): visual perception
1982	Sune Bergström (Sweden), Bengt Samuelson (Sweden), and John Vane (UK): discovery of prostaglandins and related biologically reactive substances
1983	Barbara McClintock (USA): discovery of mobile genetic elements
1984	Niels Jerne (Denmark), Georges Köhler (West Germany), and César Milstein (UK): work on immunity and discovery of a technique for producing highly specific, monoclonal antibodies
1985	Michael Brown (USA) and Joseph L Goldstein (USA): regulation of cholesterol metabolism
1986	Stanley Cohen (USA) and Rita Levi-Montalcini (Italy): discovery of factors that promote the growth of nerve and epidermal cells
1987	Susumu Tonegawa (Japan): process by which genes alter to produce a range of different antibodies
1988	James Black (UK), Gertrude Elion (USA), and George Hitchings (USA): principles governing the design of new drug treatment
1989	Michael Bishop (USA) and Harold Varmus (USA): discovery of oncogenes, genes carried by viruses that can trigger cancerous growth in normal cells
1990	Joseph Murray (USA) and Donnall Thomas (USA): pioneering work in organ and cell transplants
1991	Erwin Neher (Germany) and Bert Sakmann (Germany): discovery of how gatelike structures (ion channels) regulate the flow of ions into and out of cells
1992	Edmond Fisher (USA) and Edwin Krebs (USA): isolating and describing the action of the enzyme responsible for reversible protein phosphorylation, a major biological control mechanism
1993	Phillip Sharp (USA) and Richard Roberts (UK): discovery of split genes (genes interrupted by nonsense segments of DNA)

or physiological dysfunctions by applying finger or palm-of-the-hand pressure to parts of the body remote from the affected part.

sound therapy treatment based on the finding that human blood cells respond to sound frequencies by changing colour and shape, and the hypothesis that therefore sick or rogue cells can be healed or harmonized by sound. The therapy was in 1991 being developed and researched by French musician and acupuncturist Fabien Maman and US physicist Joel Sternheimer. It is claimed that sound frequencies applied to acupuncture points are as effective as needles.

spiritual healing or *psychic healing* the alleged transmission of energy from or through a healer, who may practise hand healing or absent healing through prayer or meditation.

thanatology study of the psychological aspects of the experiences of death and dying and its application in counselling and assisting the terminally ill. It was pioneered by US psychiatrist Elizabeth Kübler-Ross in the 1970s.

visualization use of guided mental imagery to activate and focus the body's natural self-healing processes. When used in the treatment of cancer patients, together with complementary techniques, some remarkable remissions have been attributed to visualization.

vitalistic medicine generic term for a range of therapies that base their practice on the theory that disease is engendered by energy deficiency in the organism as a whole or a dynamic dysfunction in the affected part. Such deficiencies or dysfunctions are regarded as antecedent to the biochemical effects in which disease becomes manifest and upon which orthodox medicine focuses. Acupuncture, crystal therapy, homoeopathy, magnet therapy, naturopathy, radionics, and Reichian therapy are all basically vitalistic.

zone therapy alternative name for reflexology.

INTERNATIONAL ORGANIZATIONS

International Organizations

Amazon Pact treaty signed 1978 by Bolivia, Brazil, Colombia, Ecuador, Guyana, Peru, Surinam, and Venezuela to protect and control the industrial or commercial development of the Amazon River.

Andean Group (Spanish *Grupo Andino*) South American organization aimed at economic and social cooperation between member states. It was established under the Treaty of Cartagena 1969, by Bolivia, Chile, Colombia, Ecuador, and Peru; Venezuela joined 1973, but Chile withdrew 1976. The organization is based in Lima, Peru.

Antarctic Treaty international agreement aiming to promote scientific research and keep Antarctica free from conflict. It dates from 1961, and in 1991 a 50-year ban on mining activity was secured.

The treaty was signed 1959 between 12 nations with an interest in Antarctica, and came into force 1961, initially for a 30-year period. By 1993 a total of 38 countries were party to it. Its provisions (covering the area south of latitude 60°S) neither accepted nor rejected any nation's territorial claims, but barred any new ones; imposed a ban on military operations and large-scale mineral extraction; and allowed for free exchange of scientific data from bases. In 1980 the treaty was extended to conserve marine resources within the larger area bordered by the Antarctic Convergence.

Arab League organization of Arab states established in Cairo 1945 to promote Arab unity, primarily in opposition to Israel. The original members were Egypt, Syria, Iraq, Lebanon, Transjordan (Jordan 1949), Saudi Arabia, and Yemen. They were later joined by Algeria, Bahrain, Djibouti, Kuwait, Libya, Mauritania, Morocco, Oman, Palestine, Qatar, Somalia, Sudan, Tunisia, and the United Arab Emirates. In 1979 Egypt's membership was suspended and the league's headquarters transferred to Tunis in protest against the Egypt-Israeli peace, but Egypt was readmitted as a full member May 1989, and in March 1990 its headquarters returned to Cairo.

Arab Maghreb Union (AMU) association formed 1989 by Algeria, Libya, Mauritania, Morocco, and Tunisia to formulate common policies on military, economic, international, and cultural issues.

Asian and Pacific Council (ASPAC) organization established 1966 to encourage cultural and economic cooperation in Oceania and Asia. Its members include Australia, Japan, South Korea, Malaysia, New Zealand, the Philippines, Taiwan, and Thailand.

Asia-Pacific Economic Cooperation Conference (APEC) trade group comprising Pacific Asian countries, formed 1989 to promote multilateral trade and economic cooperation between member states. Its members are Australia, Brunei, Canada, China, Hong Kong, Indonesia, Japan, Malaysia, New Zealand, the Philippines, Singapore, South Korea, Thailand, and the USA.

Association of South East Asian Nations (ASEAN) regional alliance formed 1967; it took over the nonmilitary role of the Southeast Asia Treaty Organization 1975. Its members are Indonesia, Malaysia, the Philippines, Singapore, Thailand, and (from 1984) Brunei; its headquarters are in Jakarta, Indonesia. The six member states signed an agreement 1992 to establish an ASEAN free trade area (AFTA) by the beginning of 2008.

Benelux (acronym from *Belgium, the Netherlands, and Luxembourg*) customs union agreed by Belgium, the Netherlands, and Luxembourg 1948, fully effective 1960. It was the precursor of the European Community.

Caribbean Community and Common Market (CARICOM) organization for economic and foreign policy coordination in the Caribbean region, established by the Treaty of Chaguaramas 1973 to replace the former Caribbean Free Trade Association. Its members are Antigua and Barbuda, Bahamas, Barbados, Belize, Dominica, Grenada, Guyana, Jamaica, Montserrat, St Christopher–Nevis, St Lucia, St Vincent and the Grenadines, and Trinidad and Tobago. The British Virgin Islands and the Turks and Caicos Islands are associate members, and the Dominican Republic, Haiti, Mexico, Puerto Rico, Surinam, and Venezuela are observers. CARICOM headquarters are in Kingston, Jamaica.

CERN nuclear research organization founded 1954 as a cooperative enterprise among European governments. It has laboratories at Meyrin, near Geneva, Switzerland. It was originally known as the *Conseil Européen pour la Recherche Nucléaire* but subsequently renamed *Organisation Européenne pour la Recherche Nucléaire*, although still familiarly known as CERN. It houses the world's largest particle accelerator, the Large Electron–Positron Collider (LEP), with which notable advances have been made in particle physics.

Commonwealth of Independent States (CIS) successor body to the Union of Soviet Socialist Republics, established Jan 1992 by Armenia, Azerbaijan, Belarus, Kazakhstan, Kyrgyzstan, Moldova, the Russian Federation, Tajikistan, Turkmenistan, Ukraine, and Uzbekistan. It has no real, formal political institutions and its role is uncertain. Its headquarters are in Minsk (Mensk), Belarus.

Conference on Security and Cooperation in Europe (CSCE) international forum attempting to reach agreement in security, economics, science, technology, and human rights. The CSCE first met at the Helsinki Conference in Finland 1975. By the end of 1992, having admitted the former republics of the USSR, as well as Croatia, Slovenia, the Czech Republic, and Slovakia, its membership had risen to 52 states; Yugoslavia's membership was suspended 1992.

The second conference, in Paris Nov 1990, was hailed as marking the formal end of the Cold War. Reversing a long-standing policy of noninterference in members' internal affairs, the CSCE agreed in 1991 that fact-finding teams could be sent to investigate alleged human-rights abuses in any member country. A ministerial bureaucracy, an Office for Democratic Institutions, and a Conflict Prevention Centre were established 1992. A third conference, in Helsinki July 1992, debated the Yugoslav problem and gave the CSCE the power to authorize military responses of the North Atlantic Treaty Organization (NATO), the Western European Union (WEU), and the European Community (EC) within Europe.

Council of Europe body constituted 1949 in Strasbourg, France (still its headquarters), to secure 'a greater measure of unity between the European countries'. The widest association of European states, it has a *Committee* of foreign ministers, a *Parliamentary Assembly* (with members from national parliaments), and a *European Commission* investigating violations of human rights.

The first session of the *Consultative Assembly* opened Aug 1949, the members then being the UK, France, Italy, Belgium, the Netherlands, Sweden, Denmark, Norway, the Republic of Ireland, Luxembourg, Greece, and Turkey; Iceland, Germany, Austria, Cyprus, Switzerland, Malta, Portugal, Spain, Liechtenstein, Finland, and San Marino joined subsequently. With the collapse of communism in E Europe, the Council acquired a new role in assisting the establishment of Western- style democratic and accountable political systems in the region, and several countries applied for membership. Hungary joined 1990, Czechoslovakia and Poland 1991; Romania and Yugoslavia applied for membership 1991 and Albania for observer status.

Council of the Entente (CE, *Conseil de l'Entente*) organization of W African states for strengthening economic links and promoting industrial development. It was set up 1959 by Benin, Burkina Faso, Ivory Coast, and Niger; Togo joined 1966 when a Mutual Aid and Loan Guarantee Fund was established. The headquarters of the CE are in Abidja'n, Ivory Coast.

Danube Commission organization that ensures the freedom of navigation on the river Danube, from Ulm in Germany to the Black Sea, to people, shipping, and merchandise of all states, in conformity with the Danube Convention 1948. The commission comprises representatives of all the states through which the Danube flows: Germany, Austria, Slovakia, Hungary, Bulgaria, and Romania. Its headquarters are in Budapest, Hungary.

Economic Community of Central African States (*Communauté Économique des États de l'Afrique Centrale* CEEAC) organization formed 1983 to foster economic cooperation between member states, which include Burundi, Cameroon, Central African Republic, Chad, Congo, Equatorial Guinea, Gabon, Rwanda, São Tomé and Principe, and Zaire. Angola has observer status.

Economic Community of West African States (ECOWAS, *Communauté Economique des Etats de l'Afrique de l'Ouest*) organization for the promotion of economic cooperation and development, established 1975 by the Treaty of Lagos. Its members include Benin, Burkina Faso, Cape Verde, Gambia, Ghana, Guinea, Guinea-Bissau, Ivory Coast, Liberia, Mali, Mauritania, Niger, Nigeria, Senegal, Sierra Leone, and Togo. Its headquarters are in Lagos, Nigeria.

Economic Cooperation Organization (ECO) Islamic regional grouping formed 1985 by Iran, Pakistan, and Turkey to reduce customs tariffs and promote commerce, with the aim of eventual customs union. In 1992 the newly independent republics of Azerbaijan, Kyrgyzstan, Tajikistan, Turkmenistan, and Uzbekistan were admitted into ECO.

European Free Trade Association (EFTA) organization established 1960 consisting of Austria, Finland, Iceland, Norway, Sweden, Switzerland, and (from 1991) Liechtenstein, previously a nonvoting associate member. There are no import duties between members.

Of the original members, Britain and Denmark left 1972 to join the European Community, as did Portugal 1985. In 1973 the EC signed agreements with EFTA members, setting up a free-trade area of over 300 million consumers. Trade between the two groups amounted to over half of total EFTA trade. A further pact signed 1991 between the EC and EFTA provided for a European Economic Area (EEA) to be set up, allowing EFTA greater access to the EC market by ending many of the restrictions. The area would span 19 nations and 380 million people.

European Space Agency (ESA) organization of European countries (Austria, Belgium, Denmark, France, Germany, Ireland, Italy, the Netherlands, Norway, Spain, Sweden, Switzerland, and the UK) that engages in space research and technology. It was founded 1975, with headquarters in Paris.

General Agreement on Tariffs and Trade (GATT) see entry in *International Economics* section.

G7 or *Group of Seven* the seven wealthiest nations in the world: the USA, Japan, Germany, France, the UK, Italy, and Canada. Since 1975 their heads of government have met once a year to discuss economic and, increasingly, political matters.

Group of Eight organization founded 1987 to develop a unified policy by Latin American debtor nations towards international creditors. Its members include Argentina, Brazil, Colombia, Mexico, Peru, and Uruguay. Panama was suspended from membership 1990.

Group of Rio international alliance formed 1987 from the Contadora Group to establish a general peace treaty for South America as 'a permanent mechanism for joint political action'. The original Contadora members – Colombia, Mexico, Panama, and Venezuela – were joined by Argentina, Bolivia, Brazil, Chile, Ecuador, Paraguay, Peru, and Uruguay.

Gulf Cooperation Council (GCC) Arab organization for promoting peace in the Persian Gulf area, established 1981. Its declared purpose is 'to bring about integration, coordination, and cooperation in economic, social, defence, and political affairs among Arab Gulf states'. Its members include Bahrain, Kuwait, Oman, Qatar, Saudi Arabia, and the United Arab Emirates; its headquarters are in Riyadh, Saudi Arabia.

Islamic Conference Organization (ICO) association of 44 states in the Middle East, Africa, and

Asia, established 1971 to promote Islamic solidarity between member countries, and to consolidate economic, social, cultural, and scientific cooperation. Headquarters in Niger.

Latin American Economic System (LAES/SELA *Sistema Económico Latino-Americana*) international organization for economic, technological, and scientific cooperation in Latin America, aiming to create and promote multinational enterprises in the region and provide markets. It was founded 1975 as the successor to the Latin American Economic Coordination Commission; its members are Argentina, Barbados, Bahamas, Bolivia, Brazil, Chile, Colombia, Costa Rica, Cuba, Dominican Republic, Ecuador, El Salvador, Grenada, Guatemala, Guyana, Haiti, Honduras, Jamaica, Mexico, Nicaragua, Panama, Paraguay, Peru, Spain, Surinam, Trinidad and Togabo, Uruguay, and Venezuela. Its headquarters are in Caracas, Venezuela.

Latin American Integration Association (*Asociación Latino-Americana de Integración* ALADI) organization aiming to create a common market in Latin America; to promote trade it applies tariff reductions preferentially on the basis of the different stages of economic development that individual member countries have reached. It was formed in 1990 to replace the Latin American Free Trade Association, and its members are Argentina, Bolivia, Brazil, Chile, Colombia, Ecuador, Mexico, Paraguay, Peru, Uruguay, and Venezuela. Its headquarters are in Montevideo, Uruguay.

Lomé Convention convention in 1975 that established economic cooperation between the European Community and African, Caribbean, and Pacific countries. It was renewed 1979 and 1985.

Mercosur international organization formed 1991 to establish a South American common market by the end of 1994. Its members include Argentina, Brazil, Paraguay, and Uruguay.

North American Free Trade Agreement (NAFTA) agreement between the United States, Canada, and Mexico, agreed August 1992 and ratified by the US Congress November 1993. The first trade pact of its kind to link two highly-industrialized countries to a developing one, it will create a free market of 360 million people, with a total GDP of US$6.45 trillion. From January 1994 tariffs began to be progressively eliminated over a 10 to 15 year period, and investment by Canada and the USA into low-wage Mexico progressively increased. Although the agreement was initially viewed with caution by the Canadian government and opposed by US labor unions, it was welcomed by the European Union, provided it operated within agreed GATT rules.

North Atlantic Treaty Organization (NATO) association set up 1949 to provide for the collective defence of the major W European and North American states against the perceived threat from the USSR. (For more, see entry in *Warfare* section.)

Organisation Commune Africaine et Mauricienne (OCAM; English 'Joint African and Mauritian Organization') organization founded 1965 to strengthen the solidarity and close ties between member states, raise living standards, and coordinate economic policies. The membership includes Benin,

Burkina Faso, Central African Republic, Ivory Coast, Niger, Rwanda, Senegal, and Togo. Through the organization, members share an airline, a merchant fleet, and a common postal and communications system. The headquarters of OCAM are in Bangui in the Central African Republic.

Organization for Economic Cooperation and Development (OECD) international organization of 24 industrialized countries that provides a forum for discussion and coordination of member states' economic and social policies. Founded 1961, with its headquarters in Paris, the OECD superseded the Organization for European Economic Cooperation, which had been established 1948 to implement the Marshall Plan.

Organization of African Unity (OAU) association established 1963 to eradicate colonialism and improve economic, cultural, and political cooperation in Africa. Its membership expanded to 51 countries when Namibia joined after independence 1990. The secretary general is Salim Ahmed Salim of Tanzania. Its headquarters are in Addis Ababa, Ethiopia.

Organization of American States (OAS) association founded 1948 by a charter signed by representatives of 30 North, Central, and South American states. It aims to maintain peace and solidarity within the hemisphere, and is also concerned with the social and economic development of Latin America. By 1991, membership had expanded to 35. OAS headquarters are in Washington DC.

Organization of Arab Petroleum Exporting Countries (OAPEC) body established 1968 to safeguard the interests of its members and encourage cooperation in economic activity within the petroleum industry. Its members are Algeria, Bahrain, Egypt, Iraq, Kuwait, Libya, Qatar, Saudi Arabia, Syria, and the United Arab Emirates; headquarters in Kuwait.

Organization of Central American States (*Organización de Estados Centroamericanos* ODECA) international association, first established 1951 and superseded 1962, promoting common economic, political, educational, and military aims in Central America. The association was responsible for establishing the Central American Common Market 1960. Its members are Costa Rica, El Salvador, Guatemala, Honduras, and Nicaragua, provision being made for Panama to join at a later date. The permanent headquarters are in Guatemala City.

Organization of Petroleum-Exporting Countries (OPEC) body established 1960 to coordinate price and supply policies of oil-producing states. Its concerted action in raising prices in the 1970s triggered worldwide recession but also lessened demand so that its influence was reduced by the mid-1980s. OPEC members in 1991 were: Algeria, Ecuador, Gabon, Indonesia, Iran, Iraq, Kuwait, Libya, Nigeria, Qatar, Saudi Arabia, the United Arab Emirates, and Venezuela.

Preferential Trade Area for Eastern and Southern African States (PTA) organization established 1981 with the object of increasing economic and commercial cooperation between member states, harmonizing tariffs, and reducing trade barriers, with the eventual aim of creating a common market. Members include (1992) Angola, Burundi, Comoros, Djibouti, Ethiopia, Kenya, Lesotho, Malawi, Mauritius, Mozambique, Rwanda, Somalia, Sudan, Swaziland, Tanzania, Uganda, Zaire, Zambia, and Zimbabwe. The headquarters of the PTA are in Lusaka, Zambia.

Rarotonga Treaty agreement that formally declares the South Pacific a nuclear-free zone. The treaty was signed 1987 by Australia, Fiji, Indonesia, New Zealand, and the USSR.

South Asian Association for Regional Cooperation (SAARC) international organization formed 1985 to foster economic cooperation between its member states, which include Bangladesh, Bhutan, India, the Maldives, Nepal, Pakistan, and Sri Lanka. Its headquarters are in Delhi, India.

Southeast Asia Treaty Organization (SEATO) collective military system 1954–77 established by Australia, France, New Zealand, Pakistan, the Philippines, Thailand, the UK, and the USA, with Vietnam, Cambodia, and Laos as protocol states. After the Vietnam War SEATO was phased out.

Southern African Development Coordination Conference (SADCC) organization of countries in the region working together to reduce their economic dependence on South Africa. It was established 1980 and focuses on transport and communications, energy, mining, and industrial production. The member states are Angola, Botswana, Lesotho, Malawi, Mozambique, Namibia, Swaziland, Tanzania, Zambia, and Zimbabwe; headquarters in Gaborone, Botswana.

South Pacific Bureau for Economic Cooperation (SPEC) organization founded 1973 for the purpose of stimulating economic cooperation and the development of trade in the region. The headquarters of SPEC are in Suva, Fiji.

South Pacific Commission (SPC) organization to promote economic and social cooperation in the region, established 1948. Its members include (1993) American Samoa, Australia, Belau, Cook Islands, the Federated States of Micronesia, Fiji, France, French Polynesia, Guam, Kiribati, the Marshall Islands, Nauru, New Caledonia, New Zealand, Niue, Northern Marinas, Papua New Guinea, Pitcairn Islands, Solomon Islands, Tokelau, Tonga, Tuvalu, the UK, the USA, Vanuatu, Wallis and Fortuna, and Western Samoa. Its headquarters are in Nouméa, New Caledonia.

South Pacific Forum (SPF) association of states in the region to discuss common interests and develop common policies, created 1971 as an offshoot of the South Pacific Commission. Member countries include (1992) Australia, Cook Islands, Fiji, Kiribati, Marshall Islands, the Federated States of Micronesia, Nauru, New Zealand, Niue, Papua New Guinea, Solomon Islands, Tonga, Tuvalu, Vanuatu, and Western Samoa. In 1985 the forum adopted a treaty for creating a nuclear-free zone in the Pacific.

Unrepresented Nations' and Peoples' Organization (UNPO) international association founded 1991 to represent ethnic and minority groups unrecognized by the United Nations and to defend the right to self-determination of oppressed peoples around the world. The founding charter was signed by representatives of Tibet, the Kurds, Turkestan, Armenia, Estonia, Georgia, the Volga region, the Crimea, the Greek minority in Albania, North American Indians, Australian Aborigines, West Irians, West Papuans, the minorities of the Cordillera in the Philippines, and the non-Chinese in Taiwan.

Warsaw Pact or *Eastern European Mutual Assistance Pact* military alliance 1955–91 between the USSR and East European communist states, originally established as a response to the admission of West Germany into NATO. Its military structures and agreements were dismantled early in 1991; a political organization remained until the alliance was officially dissolved July 1991.

Western European Union (WEU) organization established 1955 as a consultative forum for military issues among the W European governments: Belgium, France, the Netherlands, Italy, Luxembourg, the UK, Germany, and (from 1988) Spain and Portugal.

World Council of Churches (WCC) international organization aiming to bring together diverse movements within the Christian church. Established 1945, it has a membership of more than 100 countries and more than 300 churches; headquarters in Geneva, Switzerland.

The European Community (EC)

The EC is a political and economic alliance consisting of the European Coal and Steel Community (1952), European Economic Community (EEC, popularly called the Common Market, 1957), and the European Atomic Energy Community (Euratom, 1957). In 1995 there were more than 360 million people in the EC countries. A single market with free movement of goods and capital was established Jan 1993. A European Charter of Social Rights was approved at the Maastricht summit Dec 1991 by all members except the UK. In September 1995 the EU's member nations stated their commitment to the attainment of monetary union by 1999, and in December of the same year they agreed to call the new currency the euro.

Founding members
Belgium, France, West Germany, Italy, Luxembourg, Netherlands

Current members
Austria, Belgium, Denmark, Finland, France, Germany, Greece, Republic of Ireland, Italy, Luxembourg, Netherlands, Portugal, Spain, Sweden, UK

Aims
The aims of the EC include the expansion of trade, reduction of competition, the abolition of restrictive trading practices, the encouragement of free movement of capital and labour within the community, and the establishment of a closer union among European people. The Maastricht Treaty 1991 provides the framework for closer economic and political union. The EU reached agreement on closer economic and political cooperation with 12 Middle Eastern and North African countries in the Barcelona Declaration in Nov 1995, and an agreement between the USA and the EU to move towards closer economic and political cooperation was signed in Dec 1995.

Maastricht Treaty
The meeting in Maastricht Dec 1991 secured agree-

Who's who at the EC Commission, 1993–94

President	Jacques Santer (Luxembourg)
Vice-President	Manuel Marin (Spain)
Vice-President	Sir Leon Brittan (UK)
Competition	Karel Van Miert (Belgium)
External relations with Europe	Hans van den Broek (the Netherlands)
External relations with Africa, the Caribbean, and the Pacific,	João de Deus Pinheiro (Portugal)
Employment and social affairs	Padraig Flynn (Republic of Ireland)
Relations with the European Parliament	Marcelio Oreja (Spain)
Science, research, and development	Edith Cresson (France)
Environment and nuclear safety	Ritt Bjerregaard (Denmark)
Regional policies	Monika Wulf-Mathies (Germany)
Transport	Neil Kinnock (UK)
Internal market	Mario Monti (Italy)
Fisheries	Emma Bonino (Italy)
Economic and financial affairs	Yves-Thibault de Silguy (France)
Energy and Euratom Supply Agency	Christos Papoutsis (Greece)
Immigration, home affairs, and justice	Anita Gradin (Sweden)
Agriculture and rural development	Franz Fischler (Austria)
Budget	Erkki Liikanen (Finland)

ment on a treaty framework for European union, including political and monetary union, with a timetable for implementation, and for a new system of police and military EC cooperation. Compromises were agreed between all 12 nations at an Edinburgh summit Dec 1992, and the treaty was ratified by all member states 1993.

Budget
In 1993 51.2% of the EU's budget was spent on its Common Agricultural Policy (CAP), down from 58.2% in 1992 and 60% in 1990. A package of reforms to cut spending under the CAP was agreed in 1992 and implemented in 1994. Prior to the reforms, more than 80% of EU spending on agricultural support went to less than 20% of its farmers. Agricultural subsidies in 1992 totalled £88 billion, an increase of 6% on the previous year.

Constituent institutions
Common Agricultural Policy (CAP)
established 1962
purpose to ensure reasonable standards of living for farmers in member states by controlling outputs, giving financial grants, and supporting prices to even-out fluctuations

European Atomic Energy Community (EURATOM)
established 1957
purpose the cooperation of member states in nuclear research and the development of large-scale nonmilitary nuclear energy

European Coal and Steel Community (ECSC)
established 1952
purpose the creation of a single European market for coal, iron ore, and steel by the abolition of customs duties and quantitative restrictions

European Court of Justice
established 1957
purpose to ensure the treaties that established the Community are observed and to adjudicate on disputes between members on the interpretation and application of the laws of the Community
base Luxembourg

European Economic Community (EEC)
(popularly called the Common Market)
established 1957
purpose the creation of a single European market for the products of member states by the abolition of tariffs and other restrictions on trade

European Investment Bank (EIB)
established 1958
purpose to finance capital investment that will assist the steady development of the Community

European Monetary System (EMS)
established 1979
purpose to bring financial cooperation and monetary stability to the Community. Central to the EMS is the Exchange Rate Mechanism (ERM), a voluntary system of semi-fixed exchange rates based on the European Currency Unit (ECU), planned as a stepping stone towards the introduction of a common currency, the euro.

Central organs and methods of working of the Community
European Commission
membership 20: two each from France, Germany, Italy, Spain, and the UK, and one each from Austria, Belgium, Denmark, Finland, Greece, Ireland, Luxembourg, the Netherlands, Portugal, and Spain. The members are nominated by each state for a four-year, renewable term of office. One member is chosen as president for a two-year, renewable term. The post of president is a mixture of head of government and head of the European civil service
operational methods the commissioners are drawn proportionately from member states, and each takes an oath on appointment not to promote national interests. They head a staff of 13,000, with 20 directorates-general, each responsible for a particular department
base Brussels

EC Commission presidents from 1966

term	name	nationality
1966–70	Jean Rey	Belgian
1970–72	Franco Malfatti	Italian
1972–73	Sicco Mansholt	Dutch
1973–77	François-Xavier Ortoll	French
1977–81	Roy Jenkins	British
1981–85	Gaston Thom	Luxembourgian
1985–94	Jaques Delors	French
1995–	Jacques Santer	Luxembourgian

Council of Ministers
membership one minister from each of the 15 member countries

Presidency of the EC's Council of Ministers

The order until the end of 1998 is:

Denmark	1 January 1993–30 June 1993
Belgium	1 July 1993–31 December 1993
Greece	1 January 1994–30 June 1994
Germany	1 July 1994–31 December 1994
France	1 January 1995–30 June 1995
Spain	1 July 1995–31 December 1995
Italy	1 January 1996–30 June 1996
Ireland	1 July 1996–31 December 1996
Netherlands	1 January 1997–30 June 1997
Luxembourg	1 July 1997–31 December 1997
United Kingdom	1 January 1998–30 June 1998
Portugal	1 July 1998–31 December 1998

Source: The European Companion 1993

operational methods it is the supreme decision-taking body of the Community. The representatives vary according to the subject matter under discussion. If it is economic policy it will be the finance ministers, if it is agricultural policy, the agriculture ministers. It is the foreign ministers, however, who tend to be the most active. The presidency of the Council changes hands at six-monthly intervals, each member state taking its turn
base Brussels

Committee of Permanent Representatives (COREPER)
membership a subsidiary body of officials, often called 'ambassadors', who act on behalf of the Council. The members of COREPER are senior civil servants who have been temporarily released by member states to work for the Community
operational methods COREPER receives proposals from the Council of Ministers for consideration in detail before the Council decides on action
base Brussels.

Economic and Social Committee
membership representatives from member countries covering a wide range of interests, including employers, trade unionists, professional people, and farmers
operational methods a consultative body advising the Council of Ministers and the Commission
base Brussels

European Parliament
membership determined by the populations of member states. The total number of seats is 518, of which France, Germany, Italy, and the UK have 81 each, Spain has 60, the Netherlands 25, Belgium, Greece, and Portugal 24 each, Denmark 16, Ireland 15, and Luxembourg 6. Members are elected for five-year terms in large Euro-constituencies. Voting is by a system of proportional representation in all countries except the UK
role and powers mainly consultative, but it does have power to reject the Community budget and to dismiss the Commission if it has good grounds for doing so. It debates Community present and future policies and its powers will undoubtedly grow as the political nature of the Community becomes clearer
base Luxembourg and Strasbourg

United Nations

The UN is an association of states for international peace, security, and cooperation, with its headquarters in New York. The UN was established 1945 as a successor to the League of Nations, and has played a role in many areas, such as refugees, development assistance, disaster relief, and cultural cooperation. Its membership stands at 183 states (1993), and the total proposed budget for 1992/93 was $2,006 million. Boutros Boutros-Ghali became secretary general 1992.

Members contribute financially according to their resources, an apportionment being made by the General Assembly, with the addition of voluntary contributions from some governments to the funds of the UN. These finance the programme of assistance carried out by the UN intergovernmental agencies, the *United Nations Children's Fund* (UNICEF), the UN refugee organizations, and the *United Nations Special Fund* for developing countries. Total unpaid contributions of about $988 million had by the end of 1991 brought the UN to the brink of insolvency; fewer than half the members had paid their full contributions. By the deadline of 31 Jan 1993, only 18 member states had paid their annual dues in full; the UN was owed $500 million in arrears, approximately half of it from the USA.

The six official working languages are English, French, Russian, Spanish, Chinese, and Arabic.

Background
The UN charter was drawn up at the San Francisco Conference 1945, based on proposals drafted at the Dumbarton Oaks conference. The original intention was that the UN's Security Council would preserve the wartime alliance of the USA, USSR, and Britain (with France and China also permanent members) in order to maintain the peace. This never happened because of the outbreak of the Cold War.

The influence in the UN, originally with the Allied states of World War II, is now more widely spread. Although part of the value of the UN lies in recognition of member states as sovereign and equal, the rapid increase in membership of minor (in some cases minute) states was causing concern by 1980 (154 members) as lessening the weight of voting decisions. Taiwan, formerly a permanent member of the Security Council, was expelled 1971 on the admission of China. The breakup of the USSR and the increasing recognition of independent states throughout the world resulted in a further increase in UN membership between 1990 and 1992. The Russian Federation took over the Soviet permanent seat on the Security Council.

The principal UN institutions
All are based in New York except the International Court of Justice in The Hague.

General Assembly one member from each of 178 member states who meet annually for a session generally lasting from late Sept to the end of the year; it can be summoned at any time for an emergency session. Decisions are made by simple majority voting, but on certain important issues, such as the condemnation of an act by one of its members, a two-thirds majority is needed.

Security Council five permanent members (China, France, the UK, the USA, Russia) with the power of veto, so their support is requisite for all decisions, plus ten other members, elected for two-year terms by a two-thirds vote of the General Assembly; retiring members are not eligible for re-election. Any UN member may be invited to participate in the Security Council's discussions (though not to vote) if they bear on its interests. The council may undertake investigations into disputes and make recommendations to the parties concerned, and may call on all members to take economic or military measures to enforce its decisions; it has at its disposal a Military Staff Committee, composed of the chiefs of staff of the permanent member countries. The presidency of the Security Council is held for a month at a time by a representative of a member state, in English-language alphabetical order.

Economic and Social Council 54 members elected for three years, one-third retiring in rotation; presidency rotating on same system as Security Council. It initiates studies of international economic, social, cultural, educational, health, and related matters, and may make recommendations to the General Assembly. It operates largely through specialized commissions of international experts on economics, transport and communications, human rights, status of women, and so on, as well as regional commissions and hundreds of nongovernmental agencies that have been granted consultative status. It coordinates the activities of the *Food and Agriculture Organization* (FAO).

Trusteeship Council responsible for overseeing the administration of the UN trust territories. Its members are China, France, the Russian Federation, the UK, and the USA. It holds one regular session a year and can meet in special sessions if required.

International Court of Justice 15 independent judges, elected by the Security Council and the General Assembly on the basis of their competence in international law and irrespective of their nationalities, except that no two judges can be nationals of the same state. They serve for nine years and may be immediately re-elected. The president and vice president are elected by the court for three-year terms. Decisions are by majority vote of the judges present, and the president has a casting vote. Only states, not individuals, can be parties to cases before the court. There is no appeal.

United Nations Secretary Generals

Term	Name	Nationality
1946–53	Trygve Lie	Norwegian
1953–61	Dag Hammarskjöld	Swedish
1961–71	U Thant	Burmese
1972–81	Kurt Waldheim	Austrian
1982–92	Javier Pérez de Cuéllar	Peruvian
1992–	Boutros Boutros-Ghali	Egyptian

Secretariat the chief administrator of the UN is the secretary general, who has under- and assistant secretaries general and a large international staff. The secretary general is appointed by the General Assembly for a renewable five-year term.

UN specialized agencies

Food and Agriculture Organization (FAO)
established 1945
responsibilities to raise levels of nutrition and standards of living, to improve the production and distribution of food and agricultural products particularly for the less developed parts of the world, and to sponsor relief in emergency situations
headquarters Rome

General Agreement on Tariffs and Trade (GATT)
established 1948
responsibilities a multilateral treaty which lays down a common code of conduct in international trade, providing a forum for discussion of trade problems, with the object of reducing trade barriers.
headquarters Geneva

International Atomic Energy Agency (IAEA)
established 1957
responsibilities to accelerate and enlarge the contribution of atomic energy to peace, health and prosperity throughout the world and to prevent its diversion from peaceful purposes to military ends
headquarters Vienna

International Bank for Reconstruction and Development (IBRD) — (*World Bank*)
established 1945
responsibilities to provide funds and technical assistance to help the economies of the poorer nations of the world
headquarters Washington DC

International Civil Aviation Organization (ICAO)
established 1947
responsibilities to establish technical standards for safety and efficiency in air navigation, to develop regional plans for ground facilities and services for civil aviation, and generally provide advice to airline operators
headquarters Montréal

International Development Association (IDA)
established 1960
responsibilities as an agency of the World Bank, to provide financial and technical help to the poorest nations
headquarters Washington DC

International Finance Corporation (IFC)
established 1956
responsibilities as an affiliate of the World Bank, to make investments in companies, to assist their development, or provides loans
headquarters Washington DC

International Fund for Agricultural Development (IFAD)
established 1977
responsibilities to mobilize funds for agricultural and rural development
headquarters Rome

International Labour Organization (ILO)
established 1919, becoming part of the UN in 1946
responsibilities to improve labour conditions, raise living standards and promote productive employment through international cooperation

headquarters International Labour Conference, its supreme deliberative body, meets annually in Geneva; International Labour Office and International Institute for Labour Studies, both based permanently in Geneva; a training institution, particularly concerned with the needs of developing countries, based in Turin

International Maritime Organization (IMO)
established 1948
responsibilities to promote cooperation between governments on technical matters affecting merchant shipping, with the object of improving safety at sea
headquarters London

International Monetary Fund (IMF)
established 1945
responsibilities to promote international monetary cooperation and to help remedy any serious disequilibrium in a country's balance of payments by allowing it to draw on the resources of the Fund while it takes measures to correct the imbalance.
headquarters Washington DC

International Telecommunication Union (ITU)
established 1932
responsibilities to maintain and extend international cooperation in improving telecommunications of all kinds by promoting the development of technical skills and services and harmonizing national activities
headquarters Geneva

United Nations Centre for Human Settlements (UNCHS; Habitat)
established 1978
responsibilities to service the intergovernmental Commission on Human Settlements by providing planning, construction, land development, and finance
headquarters Nairobi

United Nations Children's Emergency Fund (UNICEF)
established 1953
responsibilities to meet the emergency needs of children in developing countries
headquarters New York

United Nations Conference on Trade and Development (UNCTAD)
established 1964
responsibilities to promote international trade, particularly in developing countries
headquarters Geneva

United Nations Development Programme (UNDP)
established 1961
responsibilities to promote higher standards of living in the poorer nations and to try to remedy the economic imbalance between industrialized and developing countries, to be achieved mainly by the economically advanced countries providing financial and technical help, and by adopting economic and commercial policies favouring the less advanced nations
headquarters New York.

United Nations Disaster Relief Coordinator (UNDRO)
established 1972.
responsibilities to provide a 24-hour service for monitoring natural disasters and emergencies; to promote disaster prevention; and to coordinate preparedness and relief
headquarters Geneva

United Nations Educational, Scientific and Cultural Organization (UNESCO)
established 1946
responsibilities to promote peace by encouraging international collaboration in education, science, and culture
headquarters Paris

United Nations Environment Programme (UNEP)
established 1972
responsibilities to monitor the state of the environment and to promote environmentally sound developments throughout the world
headquarters Nairobi

United Nations Fund for Population Activities (UNFPA)
established 1972
responsibilities to provide finance for projects in the areas of family planning, education, and research into population trends and the needs of particular age groups
headquarters New York

United Nations High Commissioner for Refugees (UNHCR)
established 1951
responsibilities to provide international protection for refugees and to find solutions to their problems
headquarters Geneva

United Nations Institute for Training and Research (UNITAR)
established 1965
responsibilities to improve the effectiveness of the UN through training and research
headquarters New York

United Nations Research Institute for Social Development (UNRISD)
established 1964
responsibilities to conduct research into problems and policies of social and economic development
headquarters Geneva

Universal Postal Union (UPU)
established 1875
responsibilities to improve the standards of postal services and promote international cooperation
headquarters Berne

World Food Council (WFC)
established 1974
responsibilities to stimulate national and international policies and programmes for alleviating world hunger, and to improve the global food system
headquarters Rome

World Food Programme (WFP)
established 1963
responsibilities to improve social and economic development through food aid, and to provide emergency relief
headquarters Rome

World Health Organization (WHO)
established 1948
responsibilities to assist all peoples in attaining the highest possible levels of health
headquarters Geneva

UN membership

Country	Year of admission	Contribution to UN budget (%)	Country	Year of admission	Contribution to UN budget (%)
Afghanistan	1946	0.01	Ghana†	1957	0.01
Albania	1955	0.01	Greece†	1945	0.35
Algeria	1962	0.16	Grenada	1974	0.01
Angola	1976	0.01	Guatemala†	1945	0.02
Antigua & Barbuda	1981	0.01	Guinea	1958	0.01
Argentina†	1945	0.57	Guinea-Bissau	1974	0.01
Armenia	1992	0.13	Guyana	1966	0.01
Australia†	1945	1.51	Haiti†	1945	0.01
Austria	1955	0.75	Honduras†	1945	0.01
Azerbaijan	1992	0.22	Hungary	1955	0.18
Bahamas	1973	0.02	Iceland	1946	0.03
Bahrain	1971	0.03	India†	1945	0.36
Bangladesh	1974	0.01	Indonesia	1950	0.16
Barbados	1966	0.01	Iran†	1945	0.77
Belarus†	1945	0.48	Iraq†	1945	0.13
Belgium†	1945	1.06	Ireland	1955	0.18
Belize	1981	0.01	Israel	1949	0.23
Benin	1960	0.01	Italy	1955	4.29
Bhutan	1971	0.01	Jamaica	1962	0.01
Bolivia†	1945	0.01	Japan	1956	12.45
Bosnia-Herzegovina	1992	0.04	Jordan	1955	0.01
Botswana	1966	0.01	Kazakhstan	1992	0.35
Brazil†	1945	1.59	Kenya	1963	0.01
Brunei	1984	0.03	Kuwait	1963	0.25
Bulgaria	1955	0.13	Kyrgyzstan	1992	0.06
Burkina Faso	1960	0.01	Laos	1955	0.01
Burundi	1962	0.01	Latvia	1991	0.13
Cambodia	1955	0.01	Lebanon†	1945	0.01
Cameroon	1960	0.01	Lesotho	1966	0.01
Canada†	1945	3.11	Liberia†	1945	0.01
Cape Verde	1975	0.01	Libya	1955	0.24
Central African Republic	1960	0.01	Liechtenstein	1990	0.01
Chad	1960	0.01	Lithuania	1991	0.15
Chile†	1945	0.08	Luxembourg†	1945	0.06
China†	1945	0.77	Macedonia	1993	***
Colombia†	1945	0.13	Madagascar	1960	0.01
Comoros	1975	0.01	Malawi	1964	0.01
Congo	1960	0.01	Malaysia	1957	0.12
Costa Rica†	1945	0.01	Maldives	1965	0.01
Côte d'Ivoire	1960	0.02	Mali	1960	0.01
Croatia	1992	0.13	Malta	1964	0.01
Cuba†	1945	0.09	Marshall Islands	1991	0.01
Cyprus	1960	0.02	Mauritania	1961	0.01
Czech Republic	1993	***	Mauritius	1968	0.01
Denmark†	1945	0.65	Mexico†	1945	0.88
Djibouti	1977	0.01	Micronesia	1991	0.01
Dominica	1978	0.01	Moldova	1992	0.15
Dominican Republic†	1945	0.02	Monaco	1993	***
Ecuador†	1945	0.03	Mongolia	1961	0.01
Egypt†	1945	0.07	Morocco	1956	0.03
El Salvador†	1945	0.01	Mozambique	1975	0.01
Equatorial Guinea	1968	0.01	Myanmar (Burma)	1948	0.01
Eritrea	1993	***	Namibia	1990	0.01
Estonia	1991	0.07	Nepal	1955	0.01
Ethiopia†	1945	0.01	Netherlands†	1945	1.50
Fiji	1970	0.01	New Zealand†	1945	0.24
Finland	1955	0.57	Nicaragua†	1945	0.01
France†	1945	6.00	Niger	1960	0.01
Gabon	1960	0.02	Nigeria	1960	0.20
Gambia	1965	0.01	North Korea	1991	0.05
Georgia	1992	0.21	Norway†	1945	0.55
Germany **	1973/1990	8.93	Oman	1971	0.03

UN membership *(cont.)*

Country	Year of admission	Contribution to UN budget (%)
Pakistan	1947	0.06
Panama†	1945	0.02
Papua New Guinea	1975	0.01
Paraguay†	1945	0.02
Peru†	1945	0.06
Philippines†	1945	0.07
Poland†	1945	0.47
Portugal	1955	0.20
Qatar	1971	0.05
Romania	1955	0.17
Russian Federation *	1945	6.71
Rwanda	1962	0.01
St Christopher–Nevis	1983	0.1
St Lucia	1979	0.01
St Vincent & Grenadines	1980	0.01
San Marino	1992	0.01
São Tomé e Principe	1975	0.01
Saudi Arabia†	1945	0.96
Senegal	1960	0.01
Seychelles	1976	0.01
Sierra Leone	1961	0.01
Singapore	1965	0.12
Slovak Republic	1993	***
Slovenia	1992	0.09
Solomon Isles	1978	0.01
Somalia	1960	0.01
South Africa†	1945	0.41
South Korea	1991	0.69
Spain	1955	1.98
Sri Lanka	1955	0.01
Sudan	1956	0.01
Surinam	1975	0.01
Swaziland	1968	0.01
Sweden	1946	1.11

Country	Year of admission	Contribution to UN budget (%)
Syria†	1945	0.04
Tajikistan	1992	0.05
Tanzania	1961	0.01
Thailand	1946	0.11
Togo	1960	0.01
Trinidad & Tobago	1962	0.05
Tunisia	1956	0.03
Turkey†	1945	0.27
Turkmenistan	1992	0.06
Uganda	1962	0.01
Ukraine†	1945	1.87
United Arab Emirates	1971	0.21
United Kingdom†	1945	5.02
United States of America†	1945	25.00
Uruguay†	1945	0.04
Uzbekistan	1992	0.26
Vanuatu	1981	0.01
Venezuela†	1945	0.49
Vietnam	1977	0.01
Western Samoa	1976	0.01
Yemen **	1947	0.01
Yugoslavia†	1945	0.16
Zaire	1960	0.01
Zambia	1964	0.01
Zimbabwe	1980	0.01

†   *founder members*
*   *became a separate member upon the demise of the USSR which was a founder member 1945*
**   *represented by two countries until unification 1990*
*** *contributions to be determined*

The sovereign countries that are not UN members are Andorra, Kiribati, Nauru, Switzerland, Taiwan, Tonga, Tuvalu, and Vatican City.

World Intellectual Property Organization (WIPO)
established 1974
responsibilities to protect intellectual property, which, in general, means patents and trademarks, throughout the world
headquarters Geneva

World Meteorological Organization (WMO)
established 1947
responsibilities to facilitate worldwide cooperation in the creation and maintenance of a network of stations for making meteorological observations and to ensure the rapid exchange of information
headquarters Geneva

United Nations Development Programme (UNDP)
Regional Commissions Established to promote cooperation between under- or less-developed countries, and to assist their economic and social development, through research and the coordination of national policies:

Economic Commission for Africa (ECA)
established 1958
membership 50 states, representing virtually the whole of north, central, and southern Africa.
headquarters Addis Ababa

Economic and Social Commission for Asia and the Pacific (ESCAP)
established 1947
membership 35 full and 10 associate members. Most of the full members are states in Asia or Oceania but other countries with interests in the regions, such as the USA, the UK, France, and the Netherlands also enjoy full membership. The associate members are the smaller countries of the region
headquarters Bangkok

Economic Commission for Europe (ECE).
established 1947
membership all European countries except Switzerland, which participates in a consultative capacity. The USA is also a consultant
headquarters Geneva

Economic Commission for Latin America (ECLA)
established 1948
membership 33 members, including, in addition to the countries of the region, Canada, France, the Netherlands, the UK, and the USA
headquarters Santiago

Economic Commission for Western Asia
(ECWA)
established 1973
membership 14 members, which comprise 13 countries plus the Palestine Liberation Organization (PLO), all situated in the Middle East or north or central Africa
headquarters Amman

UN peacekeeping operations 1993

Location	Year of establishment	Number of personnel	Annual cost $m
Angola	1991	298	67
Bosnia	1991	23,000	222
Cambodia	1992	19,000	637
Cyprus	1964	1,500	31
El Salvador	1991	530	35
Iraq-Kuwait	1991	353	67
Lebanon	1978	5,643	144
Mozambique	1992	7,500	200
Palestine/Israel/ Golan Heights	1948/1974	74	64
Somalia	1992	30,800	1,500
Totals		*88,698*	*2,967*

The British Commonwealth

The British Commonwealth is a voluntary association of 50 countries and their dependencies that once formed part of the British Empire and are now independent sovereign states. They are all regarded as 'full members of the Commonwealth'. Additionally, there are some 20 territories that are not completely sovereign and remain dependencies of the UK or another of the fully sovereign members, and are regarded as 'Commonwealth countries'. Heads of government meet every two years, apart from those of Nauru and Tuvalu; however, Nauru and Tuvalu have the right to participate in all functional activities. The Commonwealth has no charter or constitution, and is founded more on tradition and sentiment than on political or economic factors.

Queen Elizabeth II was the formal head but not the ruler of 16 member states in 1992; 5 member states had their own monarchs; and 29 were republics. The Commonwealth secretariat, headed from Oct 1989 by Nigerian Emeka Anyaoko (1933–   ) as secretary general, is based in London. The secretariat's staff come from a number of member countries, which also pay its operating costs.

On 15 May 1917 Jan Smuts, representing South Africa in the imperial war cabinet of World War I, suggested that 'British Commonwealth of Nations' was

The British Commonwealth

Country	Capital	Date joined	Area in sq km	Constitutional status
in Africa				
Botswana	Gaborone	1966	582,000	sovereign republic
British Indian Ocean Territory	Victoria	1965	60	British dependent territory
Gambia	Banjul	1965	10,700	sovereign republic
Ghana	Accra	1957	238,300	sovereign republic
Kenya	Nairobi	1963	582,600	sovereign republic
Lesotho	Maseru	1966	30,400	sovereign constitutional monarchy
Malawi	Zomba	1964	118,000	sovereign republic
Mauritius	Port Louis	1968	2,000	sovereign republic
Namibia	Windhoek	1990	824,000	sovereign republic
Nigeria	Lagos	1960	924,000	sovereign republic
St Helena	Jamestown	1931	100	British dependent territory
Seychelles	Victoria	1976	450	sovereign republic
Sierra Leone	Freetown	1961	73,000	sovereign republic
Swaziland	Mbabane	1968	17,400	sovereign republic
Tanzania	Dodoma	1961	945,000	sovereign republic
Uganda	Kampala	1962	236,900	sovereign republic
Zambia	Lusaka	1964	752,600	sovereign republic
Zimbabwe	Harare	1980	390,300	sovereign republic
in the Americas				
Anguilla	The Valley	1931	155	British dependent territory
Antigua and Barbuda	St John's	1981	400	sovereign constitutional monarchy*
Bahamas	Nassau	1973	13,900	sovereign constitutional monarchy*
Barbados	Bridgetown	1966	400	sovereign constitutional monarchy*
Belize	Belmopan	1982	23,000	sovereign constitutional monarchy*
Bermuda	Hamilton	1931	54	British dependent territory
British Virgin Islands	Road Town	1931	153	British dependent territory
Canada	Ottawa	1931	9,958,400	sovereign constitutional monarchy*
Cayman Islands	Georgetown	1931	300	British dependent territory
Dominica	Roseau	1978	700	sovereign republic

The British Commonwealth *(cont.)*

Country	Capital	Date joined	Aea in sq km	Constitutional status
Falkland Islands	Port Stanley	1931	12,100	British dependent territory
Grenada	St George's	1974	300	sovereign constitutional monarchy*
Guyana	Georgetown	1966	215,000	sovereign republicJamaica Kingston
		1962	11,400	sovereign constitutional monarchy*
Montserrat	Plymouth	1931	100	British dependent territory
St Christopher–Nevis	Basseterre	1983	300	sovereign constitutional monarchy*
St Lucia	Castries	1979	600	sovereign constitutional monarchy*
St Vincent and the Grenadines	Kingstown	1979	400	sovereign constitutional monarchy*
Trinidad and Tobago	Port of Spain	1962	5,100	sovereign republic
Turks and Caicos Islands	Grand Turk	1931	400	British dependent territory

in the Antarctic

Country	Capital	Date joined	Aea in sq km	Constitutional status
Australian Antarctic Territory	uninhabited	1936	5,403,000	Australian external territory
British Antarctic Territory	uninhabited	1931	390,000	British dependent territory
Falkland Islands Dependencies	uninhabited	1931	1,600	British dependent territories
Ross Dependency	uninhabited	1931	453,000	New Zealand associated territory

in Asia

Country	Capital	Date joined	Aea in sq km	Constitutional status
Bangladesh	Dhaka	1972	144,000	sovereign republic
Brunei	Bandar Seri Begawan	1984	5,800	sovereign monarchy
Hong Kong	Victoria	1931	1,100	British crown colony
India	Delhi	1947	3,166,800	sovereign republic
Malaysia	Kuala Lumpur	1957	329,800	sovereign constitutional monarchy
Maldives	Malé	1982	300	sovereign republic
Pakistan	Islamabad	1947†	803,900	sovereign republic
Singapore	Singapore	1965	600	sovereign republic
Sri Lanka	Colombo	1948	66,000	sovereign republic

in Australasia and the Pacific

Country	Capital	Date joined	Aea in sq km	Constitutional status
Australia	Canberra	1931	7,682,300	sovereign constitutional monarchy*
Cook Islands	Avarua	1931	300	New Zealand associated territory
Norfolk Island	Kingston	1931	34	Australian external territory
Kiribati	Tawawa	1979	700	sovereign republic
Nauru	Yaren	1968	21	sovereign republic
New Zealand	Wellington	1931	268,000	sovereign constitutional monarchy*
Niue	Alofi	1931	300	New Zealand associated territory
Papua New Guinea	Port Moresby	1975	462,800	sovereign constitutional monarchy*
Pitcairn Islands	Adamstown	1931	5	British dependent territory
Solomon Islands	Honiara	1978	27,600	sovereign constitutional monarchy*
Tokelau	Nukunonu	1931	10	New Zealand associated territory
Tonga	Nuku'alofa	1970	700	sovereign monarchy
Tuvalu	Funafuti	1978	24	sovereign constitutional monarchy*
Vanuatu	Villa	1980	15,000	sovereign republic
Western Samoa	Apia	1970	2,800	sovereign republic

in Europe

Country	Capital	Date joined	Aea in sq km	Constitutional status
Channel Islands		1931	200	UK crown dependencies
Cyprus	Nicosia	1961	9,000	sovereign republic
Gibraltar	Gibraltar	1931	6	British dependent territory
Malta	Valletta	1964	300	sovereign republic
Isle of Man	Douglas	1931	600	UK crown dependency
United Kingdom	London	1931	244,100	sovereign constitutional monarchy*
England	London			
Northern Ireland	Belfast			
Scotland	Edinburgh			
Wales	Cardiff			
Total			**33,089,900**	

* Queen Elizabeth II constitutional monarch and head of state
† left 1972 and rejoined 1989

the right title for the British Empire. The name was recognized in the Statute of Westminster 1931, but after World War II a growing sense of independent nationhood led to the simplification of the title to the Commonwealth.

Human-Rights and Relief Organizations

Action Aid
established 1972
objectives to help children, families, and communities in the world's poorest countries to overcome poverty, and to secure lasting improvements in the quality of their lives
areas of operation 18 countries in Africa, Asia, and Latin America
membership over 110,000 sponsors and supporters
annual budget (1990) £20,216,000
headquarters London

Amnesty International
established 1961
objectives to free all prisoners of conscience; to ensure fair and prompt trials for political prisoners; to abolish the death penalty, torture, and other cruel treatment of prisoners; to end extrajudicial executions and 'disappearances'. Amnesty International also opposes similar abuses by opposition groups. Politically unaligned
areas of operation organized sections in 47 countries (24 in Latin America, Asia, Africa, Middle East)
membership more than 6,000 volunteer groups active in more than 70 countries and 1,100,000 individual members, subscribers, and regular donors in more than 150 countries and territories
annual budget (1991) £12.9 million
headquarters international secretariat, London

Campaign for Nuclear Disarmament (CND)
established 1958
objectives to campaign for the dismantling of nuclear weapons, bases, and alliances; also campaigns against nuclear power. Politically unaligned
areas of operation mainly the UK
membership 60,000 plus affiliated organizations
annual budget (1990) £842,000 and £477,000 (publications wing)
headquarters London

Human Rights Watch *established* 1978
objectives to monitor and publicize human-rights abuses by governments, especially attacks on those who defend human rights in their own countries
areas of operation separate committees focus on one area each:
Africa Watch, *Americas Watch*, *Asia Watch*, *Middle East Watch*; *Helsinki Watch* monitors compliance with the 1975 Helsinki accords by the 35 signatory countries
annual budget does not accept financial support from governments or government-funded agencies
headquarters New York

Minority Rights Group
established 1965
objectives to promote human rights and increase awareness of minority issues

areas of operation Europe, Australia, North America, India
membership non-membership organization
headquarters London

Oxfam (Oxford Committee for Famine Relief)
established 1942
objectives to relieve poverty, distress, and suffering in any part of the world
areas of operation worldwide, particularly in developing countries
membership not a membership organization
annual budget (1990) £62m
headquarters Oxford

The Red Cross
established 1864 by the Geneva Convention; the Muslim equivalent is the Red Crescent
objectives to assist the wounded and prisoners in war, and war-related victims such as refugees and the disabled; to aid victims of natural disasters — floods, earthquakes, epidemics, famine, and accidents — and to organize emergency relief operations worldwide
membership non-membership organization
annual budget (1991) £64 million
areas of operation worldwide
headquarters Geneva, Switzerland

Save the Children Fund
established 1919
objectives to promote the rights of children to care, good health, material welfare, and moral, spiritual, and educational development, throughout the world
areas of operation more than 50 Third World countries and the UK
membership over 850 branches in the UK
annual budget (1990) £52m
headquarters London

Survival International
established 1969
objectives to support tribal peoples and their right to decide their own future, and to help them protect their lands, environment, and way of life
areas of operation more than 60 countries worldwide
membership 12,000
annual budget (1990) £530,000
headquarters London

Voluntary Service Overseas (VSO)
established 1958
objectives to help Third World development by providing opportunities for people with skills to make a practical contribution as volunteers
areas of operation 40 developing countries worldwide
membership 45 local groups
annual budget (1990) £15.7m
headquarters London

War on Want
established 1952
objectives to support development work in developing countries and to campaign in Europe on world poverty
areas of operation Bangladesh, Cambodia, Vietnam, Sri Lanka, India, Philippines, South Africa, Namibia, Ethiopia, Eritrea, West Bank and Gaza Strip, Brazil, Chile, Nicaragua, El Salvador, Guatemala, Jamaica
membership (1992) 1,400 individual members and trade-union affiliations
annual budget (1992) £990,000
headquarters London

LAW

Terms

accessory a criminal accomplice who aids in commission of a crime that is actually committed by someone else. An accomplice may be either 'before the fact' (assisting, ordering, or procuring another to commit a crime) or 'after the fact' (giving assistance after the crime). An accomplice present when the crime is committed is an 'abettor'.

accomplice person who acts with another in the commission or attempted commission of a crime, either as a principal or as an accessory.

acquittal the setting free of someone charged with a crime after a trial. In English courts it follows a verdict of 'not guilty', but in Scotland the verdict may be either 'not guilty' or 'not proven'. Acquittal by the jury must be confirmed by the judge.

action any proceeding in a civil court of law, including an ecclesiastical court. Actions in the High Court are commenced by the plaintiff issuing a writ, which will usually include a concise statement about the nature of the claim and the damages being sought from the defendant.

act of God some sudden and irresistible act of nature that could not reasonably have been foreseen or prevented, such as floods, storms, earthquakes, or sudden death.

act of Parliament in Britain, a change in the law originating in Parliament and called a statute. Before an act receives the royal assent and becomes law it is a *bill*. The US equivalent is an act of Congress.

An act of Parliament may be either public (of general effect), local, or private. The body of English statute law comprises all the acts passed by Parliament: the existing list opens with the Statute of Merton, passed in 1235. An act (unless it is stated to be for a definite period and then to come to an end) remains on the statute book until it is repealed.

How an act of Parliament becomes law: *1 first reading of the bill* The title is read out in the House of Commons (H of C) and a minister names a day for the second reading. *2* The bill is officially printed. *3 second reading* A debate on the whole bill in the H of C followed by a vote on whether or not the bill should go on to the next stage. *4 committee stage* A committee of MPs considers the bill in detail and makes amendments. *5 report stage* The bill is referred back to the H of C which may make further amendments. *6 third reading* The H of C votes whether the bill should be sent on to the House of Lords. *7 House of Lords* The bill passes through much the same stages in the Lords as in the H of C. (Bills may be introduced in the Lords, in which case the H of C considers them at this stage.) *8 last amendments* The H of C considers any Lords' amendments, and may make further amendments which must usually be agreed by the Lords. *9 royal assent* The Queen gives her formal assent. *10* The bill becomes an act of Parliament at royal assent, although it may not come into force until a day appointed in the act.

adjournment the postponement of the hearing of a case for later consideration. If a hearing is adjourned *sine die* ('without day') it is postponed for an indefinite period. If a party requests an adjournment, the court may find the costs of the adjournment have been unnecessarily incurred and make an order for costs against that party.

adoption permanent legal transfer of parental rights and duties in respect of a child from one person to another.

adultery voluntary sexual intercourse between a married person and someone other than his or her legal partner. It is one factor that may prove 'irretrievable breakdown' of marriage in actions for judicial separation or divorce in Britain.

advocate (Latin *advocatus*, one summoned to one's aid, especially in a lawcourt) professional pleader in a court of justice. A more common term for a professional advocate is barrister or counsel. In many tribunals lay persons may appear as advocates.

affidavit legal document, used in court applications and proceedings, in which a person swears that certain facts are true.

alibi a provable assertion that the accused was at some other place when a crime was committed.

alien a person who is not a citizen of a particular nation. In the UK, under the British Nationality Act 1981, an alien is anyone who is neither a British Overseas citizen (for example Commonwealth) nor a member of certain other categories; citizens of the Republic of Ireland are not regarded as aliens. Aliens may not vote or hold public office in the UK.

alimony in the USA, money allowance given by court order to a former spouse after separation or divorce. The right has been extended to relationships outside marriage and is colloquially termed palimony. Alimony is separate and distinct from court orders for child support.

amnesty release of political prisoners under a general pardon, or a person or group of people from criminal liability for a particular action; for example, the occasional amnesties in the UK for those who surrender firearms that they hold illegally.

appeal application for a re-hearing of all or part of an issue that has already been dealt with by a lower court or tribunal. The outcome can be a new decision on all or part of the points raised, or the previous decision may be upheld. In criminal cases, an appeal may be against conviction and either the prosecution or the defence may appeal against sentence. In the UK, summary trials (involving minor offences) are heard in the magistrates' court and appeals against conviction or sentence are heard in the crown court. The appeal in the crown court takes the form of a full retrial but no jury is present. Appeal against conviction or sentence in the crown court is heard by the criminal division of the Court of Appeal. The House of Lords is the highest appellate court within the UK. Further appeal may lie to either the European Court of Justice or the European Court of Human Rights.

arbitration submission of a dispute to a third, unbiased party for settlement. It may be personal litigation, a trade-union issue, or an international dispute.

arrest apprehension and detention of a person suspected of a crime classified as sufficiently serious (an 'arrestable' offence). In Britain, an arrest may be made on a magistrate's warrant, but a police constable is empowered to arrest without warrant in all cases where he or she has reasonable ground for thinking a serious offence has been committed.

arson malicious and wilful setting fire to property. A capital offence until 1921, it still carries a maximum sentence of life imprisonment.

assault intentional act or threat of physical violence against a person. In English law it is both a crime and a tort (a civil wrong). The kinds of criminal assault are common (ordinary); aggravated (more serious, such as causing actual bodily harm); or indecent (of a sexual nature).

Attorney General in England, principal law officer of the crown and head of the English Bar; the post is one of great political importance. In England, Wales, and Northern Ireland, the consent of the Attorney General is required for bringing certain criminal proceedings where offences against the state or public order are at issue (for example incitement to racial hatred). Under the Criminal Justice Act 1988, cases can be referred to the Court of Appeal by the Attorney General if it appears to him or her that the sentencing of a person convicted of a serious offence has been unduly lenient.

bail the setting at liberty of a person in legal custody on an undertaking (usually backed by some security, given either by that person or by someone else) to attend at a court at a stated time and place. If the person does not attend, the bail may be forfeited.

barrister in the UK, a lawyer qualified by study at the Inns of Court to plead for a client in court. In Scotland such lawyers are called advocates. Barristers also undertake the writing of opinions on the prospects of a case before trial. They act for clients through the intermediary of solicitors. In the highest courts, only barristers can represent litigants but this distinction between barristers and solicitors seems likely to change in the 1990s. When pupil barristers complete their training they are 'called to the Bar': this being the name of the ceremony in which they are admitted as members of the profession. A Queen's Counsel (silk) is a senior barrister appointed on the recommendation of the Lord Chancellor.

bigamy the offence of marrying a person while already lawfully married to another. In some countries marriage to more than one wife or husband is lawful; see also polygamy.

blackmail criminal offence of extorting money with menaces or threats of detrimental action, such as exposure of some misconduct on the part of the victim.

blasphemy written or spoken insult directed against religious belief or sacred things with deliberate intent to outrage believers.

Breathalyzer trademark for an instrument for on-the-spot checking by police of the amount of alcohol consumed by a suspect driver. The driver breathes into a plastic bag connected to a tube containing a chemical that changes colour in the presence of alcohol. Another method is to use a gas chromatograph, again from a breath sample.

brief the written instructions sent by a solicitor to a barrister before a court hearing.

burden of proof in court proceedings, the duty of a party to produce sufficient evidence to prove that his or her case is true. In English and US law a higher standard of proof is required in criminal cases (beyond all reasonable doubt), than in civil cases (on the balance of probabilities).

burglary offence committed when a trespasser enters a building intending to steal, do damage to property, grievously harm any person, or rape a woman. Entry need only be effective so, for example, a person who puts their hand through a broken shop window to steal something may be guilty of burglary. In English and Welsh courts, burglary is considered a serious offence especially if committed during the hours of darkness. Where the burglary is aggravated by the use of weapons or explosives, the offender may be imprisoned for life.

capital punishment punishment by death. Methods of execution include electrocution, lethal gas, hanging, shooting, lethal injection, garrotting, and decapitation. 44 countries have abolished the death penalty for all offences, and 17 (including the UK) have done so for all but exceptional crimes such as wartime crimes. 25 countries can be considered abolitionist *de facto*, that is they retain the death penalty in law but have not carried out any executions for the past ten years or more. Capital punishment is retained

Countries that have abolished the death penalty since 1976

1976	Portugal*; Canada**
1978	Denmark*; Spain**
1979	Luxembourg, Nicaragua, Norway*; Brazil (1), Fiji, Peru**
1981	France*
1982	The Netherlands*
1983	Cyprus, El Salvador**
1984	Argentina (2), Australia**
1985	Australia*
1987	The Philippines, Haiti, Liechtenstein, German Democratic Republic*
1989	Cambodia, New Zealand, Romania*
1990	Andorra, Czech and Slovak Federative Republic, Hungary, Ireland, Mozambique, Namibia, São Tomé e Príncipe*; Nepal** (3)
1992	Switzerland
1993	Guinea-Bissau*

* for all offences   ** for ordinary offences

1. Brazil had abolished the death penalty in 1882 but reintroduced it in 1969 while under military rule.

2. Argentina had abolished the death penalty for all offences in 1921 and again in 1972 but reintroduced it 1976 following a military coup.

3. Nepal had abolished the death penalty for murder in 1946 but reintroduced it in 1985 after bomb explosions killed several people.

and used in 92 countries, including the USA (37 states), China, Islamic countries, and the ex-Soviet republics.

The International Covenant on Civil and Political Rights 1977 ruled out imposition of the death penalty on those under the age of 18. The covenant was signed by President Carter on behalf of the USA, but in 1989 the US Supreme Court decided that it could be imposed from the age of 16 for murder, and that the mentally retarded could also face the death penalty. In 1990, in the USA there were over 2,000 prisoners on death row (awaiting execution).

care order in Britain, a court order that places a child in the care of a local authority; this may be with foster parents or in a community home.

child abuse the molesting of children by parents and other adults. It can give rise to various criminal charges and has become a growing concern since the early 1980s. In the UK, a local authority can take abused children away from their parents by obtaining a care order from a juvenile court under the Children's and Young Persons Act 1969 (replaced by the Children's Act 1989).

civil disobedience deliberate breaking of laws considered unjust, a form of nonviolent direct action; the term was coined by the US writer Henry Thoreau in an essay of that name 1849. It was advocated by Mahatma Gandhi to prompt peaceful withdrawal of British power from India. Civil disobedience has since been employed by, for instance, the US civil-rights movement in the 1960s and the peace movement in the 1980s.

civil law legal system based on Roman law. It is one of the two main European legal systems, English (common) law being the other. Civil law may also mean the law relating to matters other than criminal law, such as contract and tort. Inside the Commonwealth, Roman law forms the basis of the legal systems of Scotland and Québec and is also the basis of that of South Africa.

commissioner for oaths in English law, a person appointed by the Lord Chancellor with power to administer oaths or take affidavits. All practising solicitors have these powers but must not use them in proceedings in which they are acting for any of the parties or in which they have an interest.

committal proceedings in the UK, a preliminary hearing in a magistrate's court to decide whether there is a case to answer before a higher court. The media may only report limited facts about committal proceedings, such as the name of the accused and the charges, unless the defendant asks for reporting restrictions to be lifted.

common law that part of the English law not embodied in legislation. It consists of rules of law based on common custom and usage and on judicial decisions. English common law became the basis of law in the USA and many other English-speaking countries.

compulsory purchase in the UK, the right of the state and authorized bodies to buy land required for public purposes even against the wishes of the owner. Under the Land Compensation Act 1973, fair recompense is payable.

consent, age of age at which consent may legally be given to sexual intercourse by a girl or boy. In the UK it is 16 (18 for male homosexual intercourse).

consumer protection laws and measures designed to ensure fair trading for buyers. Responsibility for checking goods and services for quality, safety, and suitability has in the past few years moved increasingly away from the consumer to the producer.

contempt of court behaviour that shows lack of respect for the authority of a court of law, such as disobeying a court order, breach of an injunction, or improper use of legal documents. Behaviour that disrupts, prejudices, or interferes with court proceedings either inside or outside the courtroom may also be contempt. The court may punish contempt with a fine or imprisonment.

contract of employment the legal basis of an agreement between an employer and an employee.

copyright law applying to literary, musical, and artistic works (including plays, recordings, films, photographs, radio and television broadcasts, and, in the USA and the UK, computer programs), which prevents the reproduction of the work, in whole or in part, without the author's consent.

coroner official who investigates the deaths of persons who have died suddenly by acts of violence or under suspicious circumstances, by holding an inquest or ordering a postmortem examination (autopsy). The coroner's court aims not to establish liability but to find out how, where, and why the death occurred. A coroner must be a barrister, solicitor, or medical practitioner with at least five years' professional service. In Scotland similar duties are performed by the procurator-fiscal. The coroner alone decides which witnesses should be called, and legal aid is not available for representation in a coroner's court. Nor may any of the parties make a closing speech to the jury.

corporal punishment physical punishment of wrongdoers – for example, by whipping. It is still used as a punishment for criminals in many countries, especially under Islamic law. It was abolished as a punishment for criminals in Britain 1967 but only became illegal for punishing schoolchildren in state schools 1986. Corporal punishment of children by parents is illegal in some countries, including Sweden, Finland, Denmark, and Norway.

court martial court convened for the trial of persons subject to military discipline who are accused of violations of military laws.

criminal law body of law that defines the public wrongs (crimes) that are punishable by the state and establishes methods of prosecution and punishment. It is distinct from civil law, which deals with legal relationships between individuals (including organizations), for example contract law.

In England and Wales crimes are either: *indictable offences* (serious offences triable by judge and jury in a crown court); *summary offences* dealt with in magistrates' courts; or *hybrid offences* tried in either kind of court according to the seriousness of the case and the wishes of the defendant. Crown courts have power to punish more severely those found guilty than a magistrates' court. Punishments include imprisonment, fines, suspended terms of imprisonment (which only come into operation if the offender is guilty of further offences during a specified period), probation, and community service. Overcrowding in prisons and the cost of imprisonment have led to recent experiments with noncustodial sentences such as electronic tags fixed to the body to reinforce curfew orders on convicted criminals in the community.

custody the state of being held in confinement by the police or prison authorities. Following an arrest, a person may either be kept in custody or released on bail. Custody is also the legal guardianship of a child; a parent, guardian, or authority who has custody of a child usually exercises all parental rights.

damages compensation for a tort (such as personal injuries caused by negligence) or breach of contract. In the case of breach of contract the complainant can claim all the financial loss he or she has suffered. Damages for personal injuries include compensation for loss of earnings, as well as for the injury itself. The court might reduce the damages if the claimant was partly to blame. In the majority of cases, the parties involved reach an out-of-court settlement (a compromise without going to court).

decree nisi conditional order of divorce. A *decree absolute* is normally granted six weeks after the decree nisi, and from the date of the decree absolute the parties cease to be husband and wife.

deed legal document that passes an interest in property or binds a person to perform or abstain from some action. Deeds are of two kinds: indenture and deed poll. *Indentures* bind two or more parties in mutual obligations. A *deed poll* is made by one party only, such as when a person changes his or her name.

defamation an attack on a person's reputation by libel or slander.

defence collective term for the defendant and his or her legal advisors and representatives. It is also the case made in answer to the action or claim being made against the defendant.

defendant a person against whom court proceedings are brought.

Director of Public Prosecutions (DPP) in the UK, the head of the Crown Prosecution Service (established 1985), responsible for the conduct of all criminal prosecutions in England and Wales. The DPP was formerly responsible only for the prosecution of certain serious crimes, such as murder.

divorce legal dissolution of a lawful marriage. It is distinct from an annulment, which is a legal declaration that the marriage was invalid. The ease with which a divorce can be obtained in different countries varies considerably and is also affected by different religious practices.

easement rights that a person may have over the land of another. A common example is a right of way; others are the right to bring water over another's land and the right to a sufficient quantity of light.

ecclesiastical law church law. In England, the Church of England has special ecclesiastical courts to administer church law. Each diocese has a consistory court with a right of appeal to the Court of Arches (in the archbishop of Canterbury's jurisdiction) or the Chancery Court of York (in the archbishop of York's jurisdiction). They deal with the constitution of the Church of England, church property, the clergy, services, doctrine, and practice. These courts have no influence on churches of other denominations, which are governed by the usual laws of contract and trust.

employment law law covering the rights and duties of employers and employees. During the 20th century, statute law rather than common law has increasingly been used to give new rights to employees. Industrial tribunals are statutory bodies that adjudicate in disputes between employers and employees or trade unions and deal with complaints concerning unfair dismissal, sex or race discrimination, and equal pay. Discrimination against employees on the ground of their sex or race is illegal under the Sex Discrimination Act 1975 and the Race Relations Act 1976.

English law one of the major European legal systems, Roman law being the other. English law has spread to many other countries, including former English colonies such as the USA, Canada, Australia, and New Zealand.

equal opportunities the right to be employed or considered for employment without discrimination on the grounds of race, gender, physical or mental handicap.

equity system of law supplementing the ordinary rules of law where the application of these would operate harshly in a particular case; sometimes it is regarded as an attempt to achieve 'natural justice'. So understood, equity appears as an element in most legal systems, and in a number of legal codes judges are instructed to apply both the rules of strict law and the principles of equity in reaching their decisions.

escrow document sealed and delivered to a third party and not released or coming into effect until some condition has been fulfilled or performed, whereupon the document takes full effect.

executor a person appointed in a will to carry out the instructions of the deceased. A person so named has the right to refuse to act. The executor also has a duty to bury the deceased, prove the will, and obtain a grant of probate (that is, establish that the will is genuine and obtain official approval of his or her actions).

extradition surrender, by one state or country to another, of a person accused of a criminal offence in the state or country to which that person is extradited. When two nations are involved, extradition is usually governed by a treaty between the two countries concerned. A country usually will not allow extradition for political offences or an offence that it does not treat as a crime, even though it is a crime in the requesting country.

foreclosure the transfer of title of a mortgaged property from the mortgagor (borrower, usually a home owner) to the mortgagee (loaner, for example a bank) if the mortgagor is in breach of the mortgage agreement, usually by failing to make a number of payments on the mortgage (loan).

forgery the making of a false document, painting, or object with deliberate intention to deceive or defraud. The most common forgeries involve financial instruments such as cheques or credit-card transactions or money (counterfeiting). There are also literary forgeries, forged coins, and forged antiques.

fraud an act of deception resulting in injury to another. To establish fraud it has to be demonstrated that (1) a false representation (for example, a factually untrue statement) has been made, with the intention that it should be acted upon; (2) the person making the representation knows it is false or does not attempt to find out whether it is true or not; and (3) the person to whom the representation is made acts upon it to his or her detriment. A contract based on fraud can be declared void, and the injured party can sue for damages.

freehold in England and Wales, ownership of land for an indefinite period. It is contrasted with a leasehold, which is always for a fixed period. In practical effect, a freehold is absolute ownership.

grievous bodily harm (GBH) in English law, very serious physical damage suffered by the victim of a crime. The courts have said that judges should not try to define grievous bodily harm but leave it to the jury to decide.

hearsay evidence evidence given by a witness based on information passed to that person by others rather than evidence experienced at first hand by the witness. It is usually not admissible as evidence in criminal proceedings.

homicide the killing of a human being. This may be unlawful, lawful, or excusable, depending on the circumstances. Unlawful homicides include murder, manslaughter, infanticide, and causing death by dangerous driving. Lawful homicide occurs where, for example, a police officer is justified in killing a criminal in the course of apprehension or when a person is killed in self-defence or defence of others.

illegitimacy the status of a child born to a mother who is not legally married; a child may be legitimized by subsequent marriage of the parents. The nationality of the child is usually that of the mother.

indemnity an undertaking to compensate another for damage, loss, trouble, or expenses, or the money paid by way of such compensation – for example, under insurance agreements.

injunction court order that forbids a person to do something, or orders him or her to take certain action. Breach of an injunction is contempt of court.

inquest inquiry held by a coroner into an unexplained death. At an inquest, a coroner is assisted by a jury of between 7 and 11 people. Evidence is on oath, and medical and other witnesses may be summoned.

international law body of rules generally accepted as governing the relations between countries, pioneered by Hugo Grotius, especially in matters of human rights, territory, and war. The scope of the law is now extended to space – for example, the 1967 treaty that (among other things) banned nuclear weapons from space. *The Genocide Convention* 1948 declares that acts of killing, causing serious bodily harm, prevention of births, forcible transfer of children, the deliberate infliction of conditions of life calculated to bring about the physical destruction of a group, if those acts are 'committed with intent to destroy, in whole or in part, a national, ethnical, racial or religious group', are international crimes. *The Geneva Convention* is a series of international conventions on the laws of war. The Geneva Protocol of 1925 prohibits the use of gas and bacteriological warfare. The 1949 conventions include provision for the protection of sick and wounded soldiers, prisoners of war and certain groups of civilians; a Protocol of 1977 extends such protection and further regulates the law of bombing. Some of the Geneva conventions have been extended to cover civil wars and wars of national liberation.

intestacy absence of a will at a person's death. In law, special legal rules apply on intestacy for appointing administrators to deal with the deceased person's affairs, and for disposing of the deceased person's property in accordance with statutory provisions.

judge person invested with power to hear and determine legal disputes.

judicial review in English law, action in the High Court to review the decisions of lower courts, tribunals, and administrative bodies. Various court orders can be made: *certiorari* (which quashes the decision); *mandamus* (which commands a duty to be performed); *prohibition* (which commands that an action should not be performed because it is unauthorized); a *declaration* (which sets out the legal rights or obligations); or an *injunction*.

jurisprudence the science of law in the abstract – that is, not the study of any particular laws or legal system, but of the principles upon which legal systems are founded.

jury body of lay people (usually 12) sworn to decide the facts of a case and reach a verdict in a court of law. Juries, used mainly in English-speaking countries, are implemented primarily in criminal cases, but also sometimes in civil cases; for example, inquests and libel trials.

juvenile offender young person who commits a criminal offence. In UK law, young people under the age of 17 are commonly referred to as juveniles, although for some purposes a distinction is made between 'children' (under the age of 14) and 'young persons' (14–16). A juvenile under the age of ten may not be found guilty of an offence. Most legal proceedings in respect of juveniles are brought in specially constituted magistrates' courts known as juvenile courts, where the procedure is simpler and less formal than in an adult magistrates' court. Members of the public are not admitted and the name of the juvenile may not be disclosed in any report of the proceedings.

King's Counsel in England, a barrister of senior rank; the term is used when a king is on the throne and *Queen's Counsel* when the monarch is a queen.

larceny in the USA, and formerly in the UK, theft, the taking of personal property without consent and with the intention of permanently depriving the owner of it. In the UK until 1827 larceny was divided into 'grand larceny', punishable by death or transportation for life, and 'petty larceny', when the stolen articles were valued at less than a shilling (one-twentieth of a pound; approximately two weeks' wages for a labourer at the time).

law lords in England, the ten Lords of Appeal in Ordinary who, together with the Lord Chancellor and other peers, make up the House of Lords in its judicial capacity. The House of Lords is the final court of appeal in both criminal and civil cases. Law lords rank as life peers.

leasehold land or property held by a tenant (lessee) for a specified period, (unlike freehold, outright ownership) usually at a rent from the landlord (lessor).

legacy gift of personal property made by a testator in a will and transferred on the testator's death to the legatee. *Specific legacies* are definite named objects; a *general legacy* is a sum of money or item not specially identified; a *residuary legacy* is all the remainder of the deceased's personal estate after debts have been paid and the other legacies have been distributed.

legal aid public assistance with legal costs. In Britain it is given only to those below certain thresholds of income and unable to meet the costs. There are separate provisions for civil and criminal cases. Since 1989 legal aid is administered by the Legal Aid Board.

libel defamation published in a permanent form, such as in a newspaper, book, or broadcast.

licensing laws laws governing the sale of alcoholic drinks. Most countries have some restrictions on the sale of alcoholic drinks, if not an outright ban, as in the case of Islamic countries.

lien the right to retain goods owned by another until the owner has satisfied a claim against him by the person in possession of the goods. For example, the goods may have been provided as security for a debt.

Lord Advocate chief law officer of the crown in Scotland who has ultimate responsibility for criminal prosecutions in Scotland. The Lord Advocate does not usually act in inferior courts, where prosecution is carried out by procurators-fiscal acting under the Lord Advocate's instructions.

Lord Chancellor UK state official, originally the royal secretary, today a member of the cabinet, whose office ends with a change of government. The Lord Chancellor acts as speaker of the House of Lords, may preside over the Court of Appeal, and is head of the judiciary.

magistrate in English law, a person who presides in a magistrates' court: either a justice of the peace (with no legal qualifications, and unpaid) or a stipendiary magistrate. Stipendiary magistrates are paid, qualified lawyers working mainly in London and major cities.

maintenance payments to support children or a spouse, under the terms of an agreement, or by a court order. In Britain, financial provision orders are made on divorce, but a court action can also be brought for maintenance without divorce proceedings. Applications for maintenance of illegitimate children are now treated in the same way as for legitimate children.

malpractice in US law, negligence by a professional person, usually a doctor, that may lead to an action for damages by the client. Such legal actions result in doctors having high insurance costs that are reflected in higher fees charged to their patients.

manslaughter in English law, the unlawful killing of a human being in circumstances less culpable than murder – for example, when the killer suffers extreme provocation, is in some way mentally ill (diminished responsibility), did not intend to kill but did so accidentally in the course of another crime or by behaving with criminal recklessness, or is the survivor of a genuine suicide pact that involved killing the other person.

maritime law that part of the law dealing with the sea: in particular, fishing areas, ships, and navigation. Seas are divided into *internal waters* governed by a state's internal laws (such as harbours, inlets); *territorial waters* (the area of sea adjoining the coast over which a state claims rights); the *continental shelf* (the seabed and subsoil that the coastal state is entitled to exploit beyond the territorial waters); and the *high seas*, where international law applies.

martial law replacement of civilian by military authorities in the maintenance of order.

minor legal term for those under the age of majority, which varies from country to country but is usually between 18 and 21. In the USA (from 1971 for voting, and in some states for nearly all other purposes) and certain European countries (in Britain since 1970) the age of majority is 18. Most civic and legal rights and duties only accrue at the age of majority: for example, the rights to vote, to make a will, and (usually) to make a fully binding contract, and the duty to act as a juror.

motoring law law affecting the use of vehicles on public roads. It covers the licensing of vehicles and drivers, and the criminal offences that can be committed by the owners and drivers of vehicles.

murder unlawful killing of one person by another. In the USA, first-degree murder requires proof of premeditation; second-degree murder falls between first-degree murder and manslaughter.

negligence negligence consists in doing some act that a 'prudent and reasonable' person would not do, or omitting to do some act that such a person would do. Negligence may arise in respect of a person's duty towards an individual or towards other people in general. Breach of the duty of care that results in reasonably foreseeable damage is a tort. *Contributory negligence* is a defence sometimes raised where the defendant to an action for negligence claims that the plaintiff by his or her own action contributed to the cause of the action.

neighbourhood watch local crime-prevention scheme. Under the supervision of police, groups of residents agree to increase watchfulness in order to prevent crimes such as burglary and vandalism in their area.

oath solemn promise to tell the truth or perform some duty, combined with a declaration naming a deity or something held sacred.

obscenity law law established by the Obscene Publications Act 1959 prohibiting the publishing of any material that tends to deprave or corrupt.

parole conditional release of a prisoner from jail. The prisoner remains on licence until the date release would have been granted, and may be recalled if the authorities deem it necessary. Under the Criminal Justice Act 1991 parole is automatic for sentences under four years.

party a person who takes part in legal proceedings. Parties to a civil action may include one or more plaintiffs or defendants. In the UK, the parties in a criminal trial include the Crown (as prosecutor) and one or more defendants.

patent or *letters patent* documents conferring the exclusive right to make, use, and sell an invention for a limited period. Ideas are not eligible; neither is anything not new. In 1987 the USA began issuing patents for new animal forms (new types of livestock and assorted organisms) being created by gene splitting. The payment of $909.5 million by Eastman Kodak to Polaroid 1990 was a record sum for infringement of patent.

perjury the offence of deliberately making a false statement on oath (or affirmation) when appearing as a witness in legal proceedings, on a point material to the question at issue. In Britain and the USA it is punishable by a fine, imprisonment, or both.

perverting the course of justice the criminal offence of acting in such a way as to prevent justice being done. Examples are tampering with evidence, misleading the police or a court, and threatening witnesses or jurors.

picketing gathering of workers and their trade-union representatives to try to persuade others to support them in an industrial dispute. In the UK, the Employment Act 1980 restricted the right to picket to a striker's own place of work and outlawed secondary picketing (that is, at other workplaces). This allows employers or other persons picketed to sue pickets who are not at their own workplace and who are attempting to persuade other workers to break their contracts.

plaintiff person who brings a civil action in a court of law seeking relief (for example, damages).

poaching illegal hunting of game and fish on someone else's property.

police civil law-and-order force. In the UK it is responsible to the Home Office, with 56 autonomous police forces, generally organized on a county basis; mutual aid is given in circumstances such as mass picketing in the 1984–85 miners' strike, but there is no national police force or police riot unit (such as the French CRS riot squad). Unlike most other police forces, the British are armed only on special occasions, but arms issues grow more frequent.

power of attorney legal authority to act on behalf of another, for a specific transaction, or for a particular period.

precedent common law principle that, in deciding a particular case, judges are bound to follow any applicable principles of law laid down by superior courts in earlier reported cases.

probate formal proof of a will. In the UK, if a will's validity is unquestioned, it is proven in 'common form'; the executor, in the absence of other interested parties, obtains at a probate registry a grant upon his or her own oath. Otherwise, it must be proved in 'solemn form': its validity established at a probate court (in the Chancery Division of the High   Court), those concerned being made parties to the action.

probation the placing of offenders under supervision of probation officers in the community, as an alternative to prison.

procurator fiscal officer of a Scottish sheriff's court who (combining the role of public prosecutor and coroner) inquires into suspicious deaths and carries out the preliminary questioning of witnesses to crime.

prosecution the party instituting legal proceedings. In the UK, the prosecution of a criminal case is begun by bringing the accused (defendant) before a magistrate, either by warrant or summons, or by arrest without warrant. Most criminal prosecutions are conducted by the Crown Prosecution Service, although other government departments may also prosecute some cases; for example, the Department of Inland Revenue. An individual may bring a private prosecution, usually for assault.

provost chief magistrate of a Scottish burgh, approximate equivalent of an English mayor.

proxy person authorized to stand in another's place; also the document conferring this right. The term usually refers to voting at meetings, but marriages by proxy are possible.

public inquiry in English law, a legal investigation where witnesses are called and evidence is produced in a similar fashion to a court of law. Inquiries may be held as part of legal procedure, or into a matter of public concern.

quarter session former local criminal court in England, replaced 1972 by crown courts.

Queen's Counsel (QC) in England, a barrister appointed to senior rank by the Lord Chancellor. When the monarch is a king the term is *King's Counsel (KC)*.

rape sexual intercourse without the consent of the subject. Most cases of rape are of women by men. A new ruling in 1991 made rape within marriage an offence; in the first prosecution of such a case a London man was found guilty of raping his wife and jailed for five years.

receiver person appointed by a court to collect and manage the assets of an individual, company, or partnership in serious financial difficulties. In the case of bankruptcy, the assets may be sold and distributed by a receiver to creditors.

redundancy rights in British law, the rights of employees to a payment (linked to the length of their employment) if they lose their jobs because they are no longer needed. The statutory right was introduced 1965, but payments are often made in excess of the statutory scheme.

remand the committing of an accused but not convicted person into custody or to release on bail pending a court hearing.

reply, right of right of a member of the public to respond to a media statement. A statutory right of reply, enforceable by a Press Commission, as exists in many Western European countries, failed to reach the statute book in the UK in 1989. There is no legal provision in the UK that any correction should receive the same prominence as the original statement and legal aid is not available in defamation cases, so that only the wealthy are able to sue. However, the major newspapers signed a Code of Practice in 1989 that promised some public protection.

reprieve legal temporary suspension of the execution of a sentence of a criminal court. It is usually associated with the death penalty. It is distinct from a pardon (extinguishing the sentence) and commutation (alteration) of a sentence (for example, from death to life imprisonment).

rule of law doctrine that no individual, however powerful, is above the law. The principle had a significant influence on attempts to restrain the arbitrary use of power by rulers and on the growth of legally enforceable human rights in many Western countries. It is often used as a justification for separating legislative from judicial power.

Scots law the legal system of Scotland. Owing to its separate development, Scotland has a system differing from the rest of the UK, being based on civil law. Its continued separate existence was guaranteed by the Act of Union with England in 1707.

settlement out of court a compromise reached between the parties to a legal dispute. Most civil legal actions are settled out of court, reducing legal costs and avoiding the uncertainty of the outcome of a trial.

sheriff in England and Wales, the crown's chief executive officer in a county for ceremonial purposes; in Scotland, the equivalent of the English county-court judge, but also dealing with criminal cases; and in the USA the popularly elected head law-enforcement officer of a county, combining judicial authority with administrative duties.

show trial public and well-reported trial of people accused of crimes against the state. In the USSR in the 1930s and 1940s, Stalin carried out show trials against economic saboteurs, Communist Party members, army officers, and even members of the Bolshevik leadership.

slander spoken defamatory statement; if written, or broadcast on radio or television, it constitutes libel.

solicitor in the UK, a member of one of the two branches of the English legal profession, the other being a barrister. A solicitor is a lawyer who provides all-round legal services (making wills, winding up estates, conveyancing, divorce, and litigation). A solicitor cannot appear at High Court level, but must brief a barrister on behalf of his or her client. Solicitors may become circuit judges and recorders. In the USA the general term is lawyer or attorney.

subpoena order requiring someone who might not otherwise come forward of his or her own volition to give evidence before a court or judicial official at a specific time and place. A witness who fails to comply with a subpoena is in contempt of court.

summons court order officially delivered, requiring someone to appear in court on a certain date.

tagging, electronic long-distance monitoring of the movements of people charged with or convicted of a crime, thus enabling them to be detained in their homes rather than in prison. In the UK, legislation passed 1991 allowed for its use as an aid to bail and as a means of enforcing punishment, for example a curfew. The system is in use in the USA.

telephone tapping listening in on a telephone conversation, without the knowledge of the participants; in the UK and the USA a criminal offence if done without a warrant or the consent of the person concerned. In the UK, the Interception of Communications Act 1985 allows a tribunal to investigate a complaint from any person believing they have been subject to an interception. Court of Human Rights for widespread telephone tapping by police.

theft dishonest appropriation of another's property with the intention of depriving him or her of it permanently. In Britain, under the Theft Act 1968, the maximum penalty is ten years' imprisonment. The act placed under a single heading forms of theft that had formerly been dealt with individually; for example, burglary and larceny.

tort wrongful act for which someone can be sued for damages in a civil court. It includes such acts as libel, trespass, injury done to someone (whether intentionally or by negligence), and inducement to break a contract (although breach of contract itself is not a tort). In general a tort is distinguished from a crime in that it affects the interests of an individual rather than of society at large, but some crimes can also be torts (for example, assault).

treason act of betrayal, in particular against the sovereign or the state to which the offender owes allegiance. Treason is punishable in Britain by death.

treasure trove in England, any gold or silver, plate or bullion, found concealed in a house or the ground, the owner being unknown. Normally, treasure originally hidden, and not abandoned, belongs to the crown, but if the treasure was casually lost or intentionally abandoned, the first finder is entitled to it against all but the true owner. Objects buried with no intention of recovering them, for example in a burial mound, do not rank as treasure trove, and belong to the owner of the ground.

trespass going on to the land of another without authority. In law, a landowner has the right to eject a trespasser by the use of reasonable force and can sue for any damage caused. A trespasser who refuses to leave when requested may, in certain circumstances, be committing a criminal offence under the Public Order Act 1986 (designed to combat convoys of caravans trespassing on farm land).

trial the determination of an accused person's innocence or guilt by means of the judicial examination of the issues of the case in accordance with the law of the land. The two parties in a trial, the defendant and plaintiff, or their counsels, put forward their cases and question the witnesses; on the basis of this evidence the jury or other tribunal body will decide on the innocence or guilt of the defendant.

tribunal strictly, a court of justice, but used in English law for a body appointed by the government to arbitrate in disputes, or investigate certain matters. Tribunals usually consist of a lawyer as chair, sitting with two lay assessors.

trust arrangement whereby a person or group of people (the trustee or trustees) hold property for others (the beneficiaries) entitled to the beneficial interest.

verdict a jury's decision, usually a finding of 'guilty' or 'not guilty'. In Scotland a third option is 'not proven' where the jury is not convinced either way. In Britain majority verdicts are acceptable if a unanimous verdict cannot be reached.

ward of court in the UK, a child whose guardian is the High Court. Any person may, by issuing proceedings, make the High Court guardian of any child within its jurisdiction. No important step in the child's life can then be taken without the court's leave.

will declaration of how a person wishes his or her property to be disposed of after death. It also appoints administrators of the estate (executors) and may contain wishes on other matters, such as place of burial or use of organs for transplant. Wills must comply with formal legal requirements of the local jurisdiction.

witness person who was present at some event (such as an accident, a crime, or the signing of a document) or has relevant special knowledge (such as a medical expert) and can be called on to give evidence in a court of law.

writ document issued by a court requiring performance of certain actions.

Legal and Penal Institutions

Bar, the the profession of barristers collectively. To be *called to the Bar* is to become a barrister. Prospective barristers in the UK must complete a course of study in law and be admitted to one of the four Inns of Court before they can be 'called'. The General Council of the Bar and of the Inns of Court (known as the Bar Council) is the professional governing body of the Bar.

borstal in the UK, formerly a place of detention for offenders aged 15–21. The name was taken from Borstal prison near Rochester, Kent, where the system was first introduced 1908. From 1983 borstal institutions were officially known as youth custody centres, and have been replaced by *young offender institutions*.

Citizens' Advice Bureau (CAB) UK organization established 1939 to provide information and advice to the public on any subject, such as personal or financial problems, house purchase, or consumer rights. If required, the bureau will act on behalf of citizens, drawing on its own sources of legal and other experts. There are more than 900 bureaux located all over the UK.

county court English court of law created by the County Courts Act 1846 and now governed by the Act of 1984. It exists to try civil cases, such as actions on contract and tort where the claim does not exceed £5,000, and disputes about land, such as between landlord and tenant. County courts are presided over by one or more circuit judges. An appeal on a point of law lies to the Court of Appeal.

Court of Appeal UK court comprising two divisions: a Civil Division and a Criminal Division set up under the Criminal Appeals Act 1968. The Court of Appeal consists of 16 Lord Justices of Appeal and a number of ex-officio judges, for example, the Lord Chancellor, the Master of the Rolls, and the President of the Family Division. Usually, three judges sit, but where a case raises new or important issues, up to seven judges may form the court. The Criminal Division of the Court of Appeal has the power to revise sentences or quash a conviction on the grounds that in all the circumstances of the case the verdict is unsafe or unsatisfactory, or that the judgement of the original trial judge was wrong in law, or that there was a material irregularity during the course of the trial. The Court of Appeal in 1991 had a backlog of appeals by people charged and prosecuted by the West Midlands Serious Crime Squad, which was disbanded due to corruption.

Court of Protection in English law, a department of the High Court that deals with the estates of people who are incapable, by reason of mental disorder, of managing their own property and affairs.

Criminal Injuries Compensation Board UK board established 1964 to administer financial compensation by the state for victims of crimes of violence. Victims can claim compensation for their injuries, but not for damage to property. The compensation awarded is similar to the amount that would be obtained for a court in damages from personal injury.

Criminal Investigation Department (CID) detective branch of the London Metropolitan Police, established 1878, comprising a force of about 4,000 men and women recruited entirely from the uniformed police and controlled by an assistant commissioner. Such branches are also found in the regional police forces.

crown court in England and Wales, any of several courts that hear serious criminal cases referred from magistrates' courts after committal proceedings. They replaced quarter sessions and assizes, which were abolished 1971. Appeals against conviction or sentence at magistrates' courts may be heard in crown courts. Appeal from a crown court is to the Court of Appeal.

Crown Prosecution Service body established by the Prosecution of Offences Act 1985, responsible for prosecuting all criminal offences in England and Wales. It is headed by the Director of Public Prosecutions (DPP), and brings England and Wales in line with Scotland (which has a procurator fiscal) in having a prosecution service independent of the police.

European Court of Human Rights court that hears cases referred from the European Commission of Human Rights, if the commission has failed to negotiate a friendly settlement in a case where individuals' rights have been violated by a member state. The court sits in Strasbourg and comprises one judge for every state that is a party to the 1950 convention. Court rulings have forced the Republic of Ireland to drop its constitutional ban on homosexuality, and Germany to cease to exclude political left- and right-wingers from the civil service.

European Court of Justice the court of the European Community (EC), which is responsible for interpreting Community law and ruling on breaches by member states and others of such law. It sits in Luxembourg with judges from the member states.

Inns of Court four private legal societies in London, England: Lincoln's Inn, Gray's Inn, Inner Temple, and Middle Temple. All barristers (advocates in the English legal system) must belong to one of the Inns of Court. The main function of each Inn is the education, government, and protection of its members. Each is under the administration of a body of Benchers (judges and senior barristers).

International Court of Justice main judicial organ of the United Nations, in The Hague, the Netherlands. It hears international law disputes as well as playing an advisory role to UN organs. It was set up by the UN charter 1945 and superseded the World Court. There are 15 judges, each from a different member state.

Interpol (acronym for *Inter*national Criminal *Pol*ice Organization) agency founded following the Second International Judicial Police Conference 1923 with its headquarters in Vienna, and reconstituted after World War II with its headquarters in Paris. It has an international criminal register, fingerprint file, and methods index.

Land Registry, HM official body set up in 1925 to register legal rights to land in England and Wales. There has been a gradual introduction, since 1925, of compulsory registration of land in different areas of the country. This requires the purchaser of land to register details of his or her title and all other rights (such as mortgages and easements) relating to the land. Once registered, the title to the land is guaranteed by the Land Registry, subject to those interests that cannot be registered; this makes the buying and selling of land easier and cheaper. The records are open to public inspection (since Dec 1990).

Law Commission in the UK, either of two statutory bodies established in 1965 (one for England and Wales and one for Scotland) which consider proposals for law reform and publish their findings. They also keep British law under constant review, systematically developing and reforming it by, for example, the repeal of obsolete and unnecessary enactments.

law courts bodies that adjudicate in legal disputes. Civil and criminal cases are usually dealt with by separate courts. In many countries there is a hierarchy of courts that provide an appeal system.

In England and Wales the court system was reorganized under the Courts Act 1971. The higher courts are: the *House of Lords* (the highest court for the whole of Britain), which deals with both civil and criminal appeals; the *Court of Appeal*, which is divided between criminal and civil appeal courts; the *High Court of Justice* dealing with important civil cases; *crown courts*, which handle criminal cases; and *county courts*, which deal with civil matters. *Magistrates' courts* deal with minor criminal cases and are served by justices of the peace or stipendiary (paid) magistrates; and *juvenile courts* are presided over by specially qualified justices. There are also special courts, such as the Restrictive Practices Court and the Employment Appeal Tribunal. The courts are organized in six circuits. The towns of each circuit are first-tier (High Court and circuit judges dealing with both criminal and civil cases), second-tier (High Court and circuit judges dealing with criminal cases only), or third-tier (circuit judges dealing with criminal cases only). Cases are allotted according to gravity among High Court and circuit judges and recorders (part-time judges with the same jurisdiction as circuit judges). In 1971 solicitors were allowed for the first time to appear in and conduct cases at the level of the crown courts, and solicitors as well as barristers of ten years' standing became eligible for appointment as recorders, who after five years become eligible as circuit judges. In 1989 a Green Paper proposed (1) omitting the Bar's monopoly of higher courts, removing demarcation between barristers and solicitors; (2) cases to be taken on a 'no win, no fee' basis (as already happens in Scotland). In the UK in 1989 there were 5,500 barristers and 47,000 solicitors. In Scotland, the supreme civil court is the Court of Session, with appeal to the House of Lords; the highest criminal court is the *High Court of Justiciary*, with no appeal to the House of Lords.

magistrates' court in England and Wales, a local law court that mainly deals with minor criminal cases, but also decides, in committal proceedings, whether more serious criminal cases should be referred to the crown court. It deals with some civil matters, too, such as licensing certain domestic and matrimonial proceedings, and may include a juvenile court. A magistrates' court consists of between two and seven lay justices of the peace (who are advised on the law by a clerk to the justices), or a single paid lawyer called a stipendiary magistrate.

Old Bailey popular name for the Central Criminal Court in London, situated in a street of that name in the City of London, off Ludgate Hill.

Police Complaints Authority in the UK, an independent group of a dozen people set up under the Police and Criminal Evidence Act 1984 to supervise the investigation of complaints against the police by members of the public. When the investigation of a complaint is completed the authority must make a public declaration of its decision. It can order disciplinary action to be taken against police officers. Alternatively, a complainant may take a case to court. The number of successful civil actions against the police rises every year.

prison place of confinement for those convicted of contravening the laws of the state; most countries claim to aim also at rehabilitation. The approximate number of people in prison in the UK (1993) was 53,000. It costs 30 times more per year to keep a prisoner in custody than it would for 100 hours' community service.

Experiments have been made in Britain and elsewhere in 'open prisons' without bars, which included releasing prisoners in the final stages of their sentence to work in ordinary jobs outside the prison, and the provision of aftercare on release. Attempts to deal with the increasing number of young offenders include, from 1982, accommodation in community homes in the case of minor offences, with (in more serious cases) 'short, sharp shock' treatment in detention centres (although the latter was subsequently found to have little effect on reconviction rates).

In April 1992, The Wolds, Britain's first privatized prison, opened. Situated near Hull, it accommodates 320 remand prisoners.

Writers to the Signet society of Scottish solicitors. Their predecessors were originally clerks in the secretary of state's office entrusted with the preparation of documents requiring the signet, or seal. Scottish solicitors may be members of other societies, such as the Royal Faculty of Procurators in Glasgow.

young offender institution in the UK, establishment of detention for lawbreakers under 17 (juveniles) and 17–21 (young adults). The period of detention depends on the seriousness of the offence and on the age and sex of the offender. A number of statutory requirements support the principle that a custodial sentence in a young offender institution should be used only as a last resort. The institution was introduced by the Criminal Justice Act 1988.

MEDIA

Television and Radio Networks

British Broadcasting Corporation (BBC) UK state-owned broadcasting network, established as a private company 1922 and converted to a public body 1927. It operates television and national and local radio stations, and is financed solely by the sale of television viewing licences; it is not allowed to carry advertisements. Overseas radio broadcasts (World Service) have a government subsidy.

BSkyB (British Sky Broadcasting) British group of satellite TV channels, formed 1990 by a merger between Sky Television and British Satellite Broadcasting.

Cable News Network (CNN) international television news channel; the 24-hour service was founded 1980 by US entrepreneur Ted Turner and has its headquarters in Atlanta, Georgia. CNN is owned by Turner Broadcasting – which also owns the satellite channels TBS, TNT, and Headline News.

Capital Cities/ABC US television and radio network, one of the three biggest in the country. The company owns eight TV and 21 radio stations, three cable TV channels, nine daily newspapers, as well as weekly papers, shopping guides, and magazines. ABC was founded 1943 when NBC was forced to sell off one of its two networks. It was taken over by Capital Cities in 1986.

CBC (Canadian Broadcasting Corporation or Société Radio-Canada) the national radio and television service of Canada. CBC was set up in 1936. It is primarily government-funded; the rest (about 30%) comes from advertising. It was the first system to use a geostationary satellite.

CBS (Columbia Broadcasting System) US television and radio network. Founded in 1927 as a rival radio network to NBC, CBS set up its first TV station in New York in 1931. It owns seven TV stations, 21 radio stations and, in 1991, acquired Midwest Communications, which included TV, radio stations, and a sports cable channel.

European Broadcasting Union (EBU) organization of W European public and national broadcasters, set up in 1950. The EBU manages Eurovision, founded 1954, a network for the exchange of programmes and news, and Euroradio, founded 1989.

Independent Television Commission (ITC) (formerly the Independent Broadcasting Authority) UK corporate body established by legislation to provide commercially funded television (ITV from 1955) and local radio (ILR from 1973) services. In the 1980s, services expanded to include the launching of Channel 4 (1982) and the provision of satellite television: services broadcast directly by satellite into homes (DBS).

NBC (National Broadcasting Company) US television and radio network. NBC, founded 1926, is a wholly owned subsidiary of RCA (Radio Corporation of America), which was bought in 1985 by General Electric, which also owns the Financial News Network. Besides its broadcast network, NBC also has a 24-hour news channel, CNBC.

PBS (Public Broadcasting System) US public TV network of more than 300 stations. PBS and NPR (National Public Radio) were created by the Corporation for Public Broadcasting, which was set up by President Lyndon Johnson in 1967, to distribute programmes to educational TV and radio. Both are financed by a mix of government funding and public donations.

RTE (Radio Telefis Eireann) the national radio and television service of the Republic of Ireland. Radio broadcasting began in Dublin 1926 and in Cork 1927. Television broadcasting started 1961. Both are financed by a mix of licence fees and advertising revenues.

Visnews TV news agency. Visnews, founded 1957 and based in London, has 35 bureaus worldwide, and provides international news to CBS, Fox, and NBC, which has a 37.5% stake in the company. Its other shareholders are Reuters, which is the majority shareholder, and the BBC. In late 1991, Visnews became the first international news agency from a noncommunist country to be approved to set up a bureau in Havana, Cuba.

Worldwide Television News TV news agency that supplies international news to CNN, PBS, ABC, and CBS, among others. It was founded in 1956, and is jointly owned by Capital Cities/ABC (80%), Nine Network Australia (10%), and Britain's Independent Television News (10%).

Europe's Top Media Conglomerates

Reed/Elsevier UK-Dutch media conglomerate, created 1992 by a merger of Reed International and Elsevier. Subsidiaries include IPC, Britain's largest magazine publisher, whose titles include *New Scientist* and *TV Times*.

Fininvest Italian media conglomerate. Owned by Sivio Berlusconi, Fininvest owns Italy's three largest commercial television channels, a group of Italian magazines, and has interests in television in Germany, France, and Spain; it also owns a substantial chunk of the Mondadori publishing company.

Bertelsmann German-based international media conglomerate. Bertelsmann has a 38.9% stake in the German satellite TV station RTL-Plus and 24.9% of the channel Vox, new in 1993; it also owns German magazine publisher Grüner & Jahr and, in the USA, Doubleday, Bantam, Dell, and RCA Records. In the UK it owns Transworld Publishing.

Axel Springer German media conglomerate. It is Germany's largest newspaper publisher – it owns *Die Welt* and *Bild Zeitung* – and has stakes in the TV channels Sat 1, RTL-Plus, and Tele 5. It is also a major book publisher, and owns a variety of magazines and newspapers in E Europe.

Hachette French media conglomerate. Hachette is a major French book publisher, and owns *Elle* and French TV magazines, and the US publishers Grolier and Diamandis (*Women's Day*). Hachette merged at the beginning of 1993 with the missile, transport, and electronics company Matra.

Heinrich Bauer German media conglomerate, the country's largest publisher of consumer magazines. Bauer also publishes newspapers and the UK's *Take a Break* and *Bella*.

Hersant French media conglomerate, privately held. The Hersant family owns a number of French newspapers, including *Le Figaro* and *France Soir*, and has interests in TV and local radio.

CLT Luxembourg-based broadcasting group. It owns Radio Luxembourg, 48.1% of Germany's RTL-Plus television channel, and a variety of other TV and radio stations in France, Belgium, Germany, the Netherlands, the Czech Republic, and Ireland, as well as several magazines.

United Newspapers British newspaper group. It owns the *Daily Express* and the *Daily Star* in Britain, and a variety of other newspapers in the USA and the UK, plus Yorkshire Post Newspapers, Link House (*Exchange & Mart*), Morgan Grampian, and Extel Financial.

RCS Editori Italian media group. RCS Editori controls about 30% of the Italian press; it also has interests in book publishing and women's magazines, and a 5% stake in the UK's Carlton Television. Its US arm is RCS Rizzoli, which owns the Rizzoli bookstores and is expanding into magazines.

Other Groups

News International/News Corporation one of the largest international media conglomerates, owned by Rupert Murdoch. Based in Australia, News Corporation owns 67% of the Australian press; *The Times* and the *Sun* in the UK; and *TV Guide* in the USA. It also owns the US Fox network and 50% of Britain's BSkyB satellite-channel group, plus the publisher Harper Collins. Rupert Murdoch controls 35%.

Pearson UK-based media group. Pearson owns publishers Pearson Longman, Pitman, Penguin, and Addison Wesley; it also owns the UK's *Financial Times*, 50% of *The Economist*, the Profile electronic newspaper database service, 20% of Yorkshire Television, and has a stake in BSkyB.

Time-Warner the world's biggest media conglomerate, formed by the 1989 merger between Time-Life and Warner Brothers. Time-Warner owns the US magazines *Time*, *People*, *Sports Illustrated*, and *Fortune*, and the USA's second biggest cable-TV operator and the satellite subscription service and film studio Home Box Office. It also has a 10% stake in Turner Broadcasting System, owner of CNN.

Dow Jones US media and financial services group. Based in New York, Dow Jones owns the *Wall Street Journal* and *Barron's* (weekly financial newspaper), and supplies financial news around the world in affiliation with Associated Press.

Gannett US media group. Gannett owns the USA's largest newspaper chain plus *USA Today*, Harris polls, and a host of local TV and radio stations.

UK Media Watchdogs

Advertising Standards Authority (ASA) organization founded by the UK advertising industry 1962 to promote higher standards of advertising in the media (excluding television and radio, which have their own authority). It is financed by the advertisers, who pay 0.1% supplement on the cost of advertisements. It advises the media not to publish advertisements that might breach the British Code of Advertising Practice, but has no statutory power.

Broadcasting Complaints Commission UK body responsible for dealing with complaints of invasion of privacy or unjust treatment on television or radio. It is a statutory body, formed 1981.

Broadcasting Standards Council UK body concerned with handling complaints on treatment of sex and violence. It was established 1988 and is responsible for drawing up a code on standards of taste and decency in TV and radio.

Press Complaints Commission (PCC) UK organization that replaced the Press Council (founded 1953) in 1991. It serves to preserve the freedom of the press, maintain standards, consider complaints, and report on monopoly developments. In July 1992 it made a landmark ruling in favour of the right of the press to disclose information on public figures' personal lives, deeming such information to be in the public interest.

International news agencies

Country	Agency		Headquarters
Albania	Albanian Telegraphic Agency	ATA	Tirana
Algeria	Algeria Presse Service	APS	Algiers
Angola	Angola Agêcia Naticiosa N'gola Press	ANGOP	Luanda
Argentina	Agence Los Diarios	ALD	Buenos Aires
	Noticias Argentinas	NA	Buenos Aires
Australia	Australian Associated Press	AAP	Sydney
	Australian United Press	AUP	Melbourne
Austria	Austria Presse Agentur	APA	Vienna
Bangladesh	Bangladesh Sangbad Sangstha	BSS	Dhaka
	Eastern News Agency	ENA	Dhaka
Barbados	Caribbean News Agency	CANA	Bridgetown
Belgium	Agence Belga	BELGA	Brussels
	Agence Europe	AE	Brussels
	Centre d'Information de Presse	CIP	Brussels
Botswana	Botswana Press Agency	BOPA	Gaborone
Brazil	Agencia Meridional	AM	Rio de Janeiro
	Agencia Nacional	AN	Brasília
Bulgaria	Bulgarska Telegrafitscheka Agentzia	BTA	Sofia
	Sofia Press Agency	SOFIAPRES	Sofia
Cambodia	Saporamean Kampuchea	SPK	Phnom Penh
Canada	Canadian Press	CP	Toronto
Chile	Agencia Informativa Orbe de Chile	AIO	Santiago
China	China News Service	CNS	Beijing
	Xinhua		Beijing
Colombia	Colprensa		Bogotá
Croatia	Hrvatska Izvjestajna Novinska Agencija	HINA	Zagreb
Cuba	Prensa Latina	PRELA	Havana
Cyprus	Cyprus News Agency	CNA	Nicosia
Czech Republic	Ceskoslovenska Tiskova Kancelar	CSTK	Prague
	Orbis Press Agency	OPA	Prague
Denmark	Ritzaus Bureau	RB	Copenhagen
Egypt	Middle East News Agency	MENA	Cairo
Estonia	Eesti Teadate Agentuur	ETA	Tallinn
Finland	Oy Suomen Tietoimisto Notisbyran Ab	OTTFNB	Helsinki
France	Agence France Presse	AFP	Paris
	Agence Parisienne de Presse	APP	Paris
	Presse Services	PS	Paris
Germany	Allgemeiner Deutscher Nachrichtendienst	ADN	Berlin
	Deutsche Presse Agentur	DPA	Hamburg
Ghana	Ghana News Agency	GNA	Accra
Greece	Athenagence	ANA	Athens
Guatemala	Inforpress Centroamericana	IC	Guatemala City
Guinea	Agence Guinéenne de Presse	GNA	Conakry
Guyana	Guyana News Agency	GNA	Georgetown
Hungary	Magyar Tavariti Iroda	MTI	Budapest
India	Press Trust of India	PTI	Bombay
	United News of India	UNI	New Delhi
Indonesia	Indonesian National News Agency	ANTARA	Jakarta
Iran	Islamic Republic News Agency	IRNA	Tehran
Iraq	Iraqi News Agency	INA	Baghdad
Israel	Associated Israel Press	ITIM	Tel Aviv
	Jewish Telegraphic Agency	JTA	Jerusalem
Italy	Agenzia Nazionale Stampa Associate	ANSA	Rome
	Inter Press Service	IPS	Rome
Ivory Coast	Agence Ivoirienne de Presse	AIP	Abidja'n
Jamaica	Jampress		Kingston
Japan	Jiji Tsushin-Sha	JIJI	Tokyo
	Kyodo Tsushin		Tokyo
Jordan	Jordan News Agency	BATRA	Amman
Kenya	Kenya News Agency	KNA	Nairobi
Korea	Korean Central News Agency	KCNA	Pyongyang
Kuwait	Kuwait News Agency	KUNA	Kuwait City

International news agencies *(cont.)*

Laos	Khao San Pathet Lao	KPL	Vientiane
Latvia	Latvijas Telegrafa Agentura	LETA	Riga
Libya	Jamahiriya News Agency	JANA	Tripoli
Malaysia	Malaysian National News Agency	BERNAMA	Kuala Lumpur
Mexico	Noticias Mexicanas	NOTIMEX	Mexico City
Netherlands	Algemeen Nederlands Persbureau	ANP	The Hague
New Zealand	New Zealand Press Agency	NZPA	Wellington
	South Pacific News Service	SOPAC-NEWS	Wellington
Nigeria	News Agency of Nigeria	NAN	Lagos
Norway	Norsk Presse Service	NPS	Oslo
	Norsk Telegrambyra	NTB	Oslo
Pakistan	Associated Press of Pakistan	APP	Islamabad
	Pakistan Press International	PPI	Karachi
	United Press of Pakistan	UPP	Karachi
Philippines	Philippines News Agency	PNA	Manila
Poland	Polska Agencija Prasowa	PAP	Warsaw
Portugal	Agencia Lusa de Informacao	ALI	Lisbon
Romania	Romanian News Agency	ROMPRESS	Bucharest
Russia	Agentstvo Pechati Novosti	NOVOSTI	Moscow
	Information Telegraph Agency of Russia	ITAR-TASS	Moscow
Saudi Arabia	Saudi Press Agency	SPA	Riyadh
Senegal	Agence de Presse Senegalaise	APS	Dakar
	Pan-African News Agency	PANA	Dakar
Sierra Leone	Sierra Leone News Agency	SLENA	Freetown
Slovenia	Slovenska Tiskovna Agencija	STA	Ljubljana
South Africa	South African Press Association	SAPA	Johannesburg
South Korea	Naewoe Press		Seoul
	Yonhap (United) Press Agency	YONHAP	Seoul
Spain	Agencia EFE		Madrid
	Logos Agencia de Informacion	LAI	Madrid
Sweden	Svensk Internationella Pressbyran	SIP	Stockholm
	Tidningarnes Telegrambyra	TT	Stockholm
Switzerland	Schweizerische Depeschenagentur	SDA	Berne
Syria	Agence Arabe Syrienne d'Information	AASA	Damascus
Taiwan	Central News Agency	CNA	Taipei
Tunisia	Tunis Afrique Presse	TAP	Tunis
Turkey	Anadol Ajansi	AA	Ankara
	Hurriyet Haber Ajasi	HHA	Istanbul
UK	Exchange and Telegraph Company	EXTEL	London
	Press Association	PA	London
	Reuters		London
USA	Associated Press	AP	New York
	United Press International	UPI	New York
Vatican City State	Agenzia Internazionale Fides		Vatican City
Vietnam	Vietnam News Agency	VNA	Hanoi
Zimbabwe	Zimbabwe Inter-Africa News Agency		Harare

Newspapers and their circulations

Title	Frequency	Circulation	Location
Australia			
Herald-Sun	daily	680,000	Melbourne
Sunday Herald-Sun	weekly	600,000	Melbourne
Sunday Telegraph	weekly	562,000	Sydney
Daily Telegraph Mirror	daily	480,000	Sydney
Sun	daily	362,000	Brisbane
Sunday Mail	weekly	268,000	Adelaide
Mercury	daily	54,000	Hobart
Adelaide Advertiser	daily	213,000	Adelaide
Canberra Times	daily	44,000	Canberra
Austria			
Neue Kronenzeitung	daily	1,000,000	Vienna
Die Ganze Woche	2 weekly	850,000	Vienna
Kurier	daily & Sun	620,000	Vienna
Kleine Zeitung	weekly	275,000	Graz
Belgium			
Groupe AZ (Dutch)	weekly	2,800,000	Brussels
Groupe AZ (French)	weekly	1,625,000	Brussels
Deze Week in	weekly	840,000	Roeselare
Belgique No 1	weekly	530,000	Brussels
Vlan	weekly	425,000	Brussels
Het Nieuwsblad	daily	382,000	Groot-Bijgaarden
De Standaard	daily	382,000	Groot-Bijgaarden
Publi-Hebdo	weekly	382,000	Liege
L'Echo	weekly	380,000	Brussels
Hier Groep	weekly	350,000	Hasselt
De Gentenaar	daily	326,000	Ghent
Antwerpse Post	weekly	313,000	Antwerp
Die Nieuwe Gazet Antwerp	daily	299,000	Antwerp
Bulgaria			
Duma	daily	300,000	Sofia
Otechestven Front	daily	280,000	Sofia
Canada			
Toronto Sun	daily	500,000	Toronto, Ontario
La Presse	daily	311,000	Montreal, Québec
Vancouver Sun	daily	267,000	Vancouver, British
Columbia			
Winnipeg Free Press	daily	227,000	Winnipeg, Manitoba
Calgary Herald	daily	163,000	Calgary, Alberta
Chronicle-Herald	daily	87,000	Halifax, Novia Scotia
Leader-Post	daily	69,000	Regina, Saskatchewan
Telegraph-Journal	daily	62,000	Moncton, New Brunswick
Evening Telegram	daily	58,000	St John's, Newfoundland
Guardian	daily	19,700	Charlottetown, Prince Edward Island
Czech Republic			
Práce	daily	350,000	Prague
Rudé Právo	daily	280,000	Prague
France			
Le Dauphiné Libéré	daily	813,000	Veurey-Voroize
Ouest-France	daily	739,000	Rennes
France-Dimanche	weekly	706,000	Paris
Le Figaro	daily	429,000	Paris
Ici Paris	weekly	423,000	Paris
Le Monde	daily	381,000	Paris
Sud-Ouest	daily	368,000	Bordeaux
Le Parisien	daily	366,000	Paris
le Journal Dimanche	weekly	360,000	Paris

Newspapers and their circulations *(cont.)*

Title	Frequency	Circulation	Location
Le Progrès	daily	354,000	Lyons
France Soir	daily	334,000	Paris
La Nouvelle République du Centre-Ouest	daily	271,000	Tours
VSD	weekly	262,000	Paris
Nice Matin	daily	258,000	Nice
L'Est Républicain	daily	251,000	Heillecourt
La Montagne	daily	250,000	Clermont Ferrand
Germany			
Bild	daily	4,416,000	Hamburg
Westdeutsche Allgemeine Zeitung	daily	1,236,000	Essen
Sonntag Aktuell	weekly	877,000	Stuttgart
Super Zeitung	daily	600,000	Munich
Sächsische Zeitung	daily	513,000	Dresden
Hannoversche Allgemeine Zeitung	daily	511,000	Hannover
Stuttgarter Zeitung	daily	510,000	Stuttgart
Die Zeit	weekly	488,000	Hamburg
Leipziger Volkszeitung	daily	484,000	Leipzig
Express Köln	daily	437,000	Cologne
Berliner Zeitung	daily	425,000	Berlin
Das Volk	daily	401,000	Erfurt
Rheinische Post	daily	391,000	Düsseldorf
Süddeutsche Zeitung	daily	386,000	Magdeburg
Volksstimme	daily	379,000	Magdeburg
Frankfurter Allgemeine Zeitung	daily	367,000	Frankfurt/Main
Südwest Presse	daily	367,000	Ulm
Augsberger Allgemeine	daily	362,000	Augsburg
Junge Welt	daily	330,000	Berlin
Nürnberger Nachrichten	daily	325,000	Nuremburg
Nordwest Zeitung	daily	317,000	Oldenburg
Neue Osnabrücker Zeitung	daily	299,000	Osnabruck
Ostee Zeitung	daily	293,000	Rostock
Lausitzer Rundschau	daily	291,000	Cottbus
BZ-Berlin	daily	279,000	Berlin
Hessische Niedersäch Allgemeine	daily	272,000	Kassel
Bild Berlin	daily	250,000	Berlin
Ireland			
Sunday World	weekly	263,000	Dublin
Italy			
La Repubblica	daily	826,000	Rome
La Gazzetta Dello Sport	daily	815,000	Milan
Corriere Della Sera	daily	645,000	Milan
Corriere Dello Sport-Stadio	daily	542,000	Rome
La Stampa	daily	407,000	Turin
Il Messaggero	daily	400,000	Rome
Il Sole 24 Ore	daily	259,000	Milan
The Netherlands			
De Telegraaf	daily	726,000	Amsterdam
De Volkskrant	daily	340,000	Amsterdam
Algemeen Dagblad	daily	417,000	Rotterdam
Norway			
Aftenposten	daily	263,000	Oslo
Poland			
Gazeta Wyborcza	daily	550,000	Warsaw
Zycie Warsawy	daily	250,000	Warsaw
Romania			
România Liberia	daily	400,000	Bucharest
Ardevarul	daily	250,000	Bucharest

Newspapers and their circulations *(cont.)*

Title	Frequency	Circulation	Location
Russia			
Trud	daily	21,429,000	Moscow
Komsomolskaya Pravda	daily	20,354,000	Moscow
Izvestiya	daily	10,130,000	Moscow
Pravda	daily	7,700,000	Moscow
Selskaya Zhizn	daily	5,772,000	Moscow
Sovetski Sport	daily	4,863,000	Moscow
Sotsialisticheskaya Industriya	daily	1,500,000	Moscow
Rabochaya Tribuna	daily	1,405,000	Moscow
Moskovskaya Pravda	daily	725,000	Moscow
Vechernaya Moskva	daily	650,000	Moscow
Slovakia			
Práca	daily	260,000	Bratislava
Pravda	daily	260,000	Bratislava
Spain			
El Pais	daily	378,000	Madrid
ABC	daily	280,000	Madrid
Sweden			
Expressen	daily	575,000	Stockholm
Dagens Nyheter	daily	519,000	Stockholm
Aftonbladet	daily	480,000	Stockholm
Göteborg-Posten	daily	281,000	Gothenburg
Turkey			
Sabah	daily	507,000	Istanbul
Milliyet	daily	250,000	Istanbul
United Kingdom			
News of the World	weekly	4,845,000	London
The Sun	daily	3,690,000	London
Daily Mirror	daily	2,911,000	London
Sunday Mirror	weekly	2,810,000	London
The People	weekly	2,279,000	London
The Mail on Sunday	weekly	1,907,000	London
Daily Mail	daily	1,702,000	London
Daily Express	daily	1,563,000	London
Sunday Post	weekly	1,198,000	Dundee
Sunday Times	weekly	1,148,000	London
Daily Telegraph	daily	1,059,000	London
Daily Star	daily	859,000	London
Sunday Telegraph	weekly	569,000	London
The Observer	weekly	555,000	London
Today	daily	471,000	London
The Guardian	daily	413,000	London
The Times	daily	390,000	London
The Independent	daily	377,000	London
The Independent on Sunday	weekly	372,000	London
Sunday Sport	weekly	370,000	London
Financial Times	daily	286,000	London
Daily Sport	daily	210,000	Manchester
The European	weekly	167,000	London
Glasgow Herald	daily	122,000	Glasgow
The Scotsman	daily	86,000	Edinburgh
United States			
Wall Street Journal	Mon–Fri	1,857,000	New York, NY
USA Today	Mon–Fri	1,748,000	Arlington, VA
The New York Times	daily & Sun	1,687,000	New York, NY
Daily News	daily & Sun	1,401,000	New York, NY
LA Times	daily & Sun	1,196,000	Los Angeles, CA
Washington Post	daily & Sun	1,137,000	Washington, DC
Chicago Tribune	daily & Sun	1,102,000	Chicago, IL

Newspapers and their circulations *(cont.)*

Title	Frequency	Circulation	Location
Philadelphia Enquirer	daily & Sun	978,000	Philadelphia, PA
The Boston Globe	daily & Sun	792,000	Boston, MA
Star-Ledger	daily & Sun	693,000	Newark, NJ
Star Tribune	daily & Sun	667,000	Minneapolis, MN
Free Press	daily & Sun	636,000	Detroit, MI
Houston Chronicle	daily & Sun	621,000	Houston, TX
Post Dispatch	daily & Sun	562,000	St Louis, MO
Plain Dealer	daily	561,000	Cleveland, OH
Miami Herald	daily & Sun	520,000	Miami, FL
Republic	daily	517,000	Phoenix, AZ
Journal	daily & Sun	505,000	Milwaukee, WI
Sun	daily	494,000	Baltimore, MD
Oregonian	daily & Sun	432,000	Portland, OR
Star	daily & Sun	411,000	Indianapolis, IN
Rocky Mountain News	daily & Sun	408,000	Denver, CO
Register	daily & Sun	346,000	Des Moines, IA
Oklahoman	daily & Sun	326,000	Oklahoma City, OK
Courier Journal	daily & Sun	325,000	Louisville, KY
Atlanta Constitution	Mon–Fri	317,000	Atlanta, GA
Hartford Courant	daily & Sun	315,000	Hartford, CT
Observer	daily & Sun	299,000	Charlotte, NC
Commercial Appeal	daily & Sun	289,000	Memphis, TN
World Herald	daily & Sun	284,000	Omaha, NE
Times Picayune	daily & Sun	279,000	New Orleans, LA
Bulletin	Mon–Fri	265,000	Providence, RI
Times	daily	234,000	Seattle, WA
Arkansas Democrat	daily	224,000	Little Rock, AR
News	daily	207,000	Birmingham, AL
Wichita Eagle	daily & Sun	199,000	Wichita, KS
State	daily & Sun	173,000	Columbia, SC
Las Vegas Review Journal	daily & Sun	165,000	Las Vegas, NV
Journal	daily & Sun	158,000	Albuquerque, NM
Tribune	daily & Sun	141,000	Salt Lake City, UT
News Journal	daily	140,000	Wilmington, DE
Clarion Ledger	daily	123,000	Jackson, MS

daily = Monday–Saturday. Circulations are approximate.

Advertising restrictions on European television

Products	Benelux	Denmark	France	Germany	Greece	Ireland	Italy	Netherlands	Portugal	Spain	UK
Cigarettes	×	×	×	×	×	×	×	×	×	×	×
Cigars	×	×	×	×	×	×	×	×	×	×	×
Beer/wine	✓	×	×			✓	✓	✓	✓	✓	
Spirits	✓	×	×	✓	×	✓	✓	✓	✓	✓	×
Medical services		×		✓		✓	✓	✓	✓		✓
Pharmaceuticals	×	✓	✓	✓	×	✓	✓	✓		✓	
Family planning			×		×				✓		✓
Personal hygiene	✓		✓	✓		✓	✓				✓
Gambling			✓	×			×		×		×
Loans			✓				×				
Political parties	✓	×		×	✓	×		×		×	✓
Religion	×	×		×	×	×		×		×	✓
Travel agents			×				✓				
Dieting		×	✓					✓			
Aimed at children	✓	✓	✓	✓	✓	✓		✓		✓	

× *TV advertising prohibited by law*
✓ *TV advertising subject to restriction of copy/time of transmission*

Source: Media Map 1992/CIT

POLITICS

Political Ideologies

absolutism or *absolute monarchy* system of government in which the ruler or rulers have unlimited power. The principle of an absolute monarch, given a right to rule by God (the divine right of kings), was extensively used in Europe during the 17th and 18th centuries. Absolute monarchy is contrasted with limited or constitutional monarchy, in which the sovereign's powers are defined or limited.

anarchism political belief that society should have no government, laws, police, or other authority, but should be a free association of all its members. It does not mean 'without order'; most theories of anarchism imply an order of a very strict and symmetrical kind, but they maintain that such order can be achieved by cooperation. Anarchism must not be confused with nihilism (a purely negative and destructive activity directed against society); anarchism is essentially a pacifist movement.

authoritarianism rule of a country by a dominant elite who repress opponents and the press to maintain their own wealth and power. They are frequently indifferent to activities not affecting their security, and rival power centres, such as trade unions and political parties, are often allowed to exist, although under tight control. An extreme form is totalitarianism.

collectivism position in which the collective (such as the state) has priority over its individual members. It is the opposite of individualism, which is itself a variant of anarchy.

communism revolutionary socialism based on the theories of the political philosophers Karl Marx (1818–1883) and Friedrich Engels (1820–1895), emphasizing common ownership of the means of production and a planned economy. The principle held is that each should work according to their capacity and receive according to their needs. Politically, it seeks the overthrow of capitalism through a proletarian revolution.

The first communist state was the USSR after the revolution of 1917. Revolutionary socialist parties and groups united to form communist parties in other countries (in the UK 1920). After World War II, communism was enforced in those countries that came under Soviet occupation. China emerged after 1961 as a rival to the USSR in world communist leadership, and other countries attempted to adapt communism to their own needs. The late 1980s saw a movement for more individual freedoms in many communist countries, culminating in the abolition or overthrow of communist rule in Eastern European countries and Mongolia, and further state repression in China. The failed hard-line coup in the USSR against President Gorbachev 1991 resulted in the effective abandonment of communism there.

conservatism approach to government favouring the maintenance of existing institutions and identified with a number of Western political parties, such as the British Conservative, US Republican, German Christian Democratic, and Australian Liberal parties. It tends to be explicitly nondoctrinaire and pragmatic but generally emphasizes free-enterprise capitalism, minimal government intervention in the economy, rigid law and order, and the importance of national traditions.

democracy government by the people, usually through elected representatives. In the modern world democracy has developed from the American and French revolutions.

In *direct democracy* the whole people meets for the making of laws or the direction of executive officers, for example in Athens in the 5th century BC (and allegedly in modern Libya). Direct democracy today is represented mainly by the use of the referendum, as in the UK, France, Switzerland, and certain states of the USA.

The two concepts underlying *liberal democracy* are the right to representative government and the right to enjoy individual freedom. In practice the principal features of a liberal democratic system include representative institutions based on majority rule, through free elections and a choice of political parties; accountability of the government to the electorate; freedom of expression, assembly, and the individual, guaranteed by an independent judiciary; and limitations on the power of government.

It is estimated that almost one-third (1.6 billion) of the world's population live within political systems founded on liberal democracy. While it is an ideology that has been successfully implemented in all parts of the world, this type of political system tends to flourish best in high-income, First World states.

Social democracy is founded on the belief in the gradual evolution of a democratic socialism within existing political structures. The earliest was the German *Sozialdemokratische Partei* (SPD), today one of the two main German parties, created in 1875 from August Bebel's earlier German Social Democratic Workers' Party, founded 1869. Parties along the lines of the German model were founded in the last two decades of the 19th century in a number of countries, including Austria, Belgium, the Netherlands, Hungary, Poland, and Russia. The British Labour Party is in the social democratic tradition.

egalitarianism belief that all citizens in a state should have equal rights and privileges. Interpretations of this can vary, from the notion of equality of opportunity to equality in material welfare and political decision-making. Some states clearly reject any thought of egalitarianism; most accept the concept of equal opportunities but recognize that people's abilities vary widely. Even those states that claim to be socialist find it necessary to have hierarchical structures in the political, social, and economic spheres. Egalitarianism was one of the principles of the French Revolution.

fascism political ideology that denies all rights to individuals in their relations with the state; specifically, the totalitarian nationalist movement founded in Italy 1919 by Benito Mussolini and followed by Adolf Hitler's Germany 1933. The fascist party, the *Partitio Nazionale Fascista*, controlled Italy 1922–43.

Fascism was essentially a product of the economic and political crisis of the years after World War I. Fascism protected the existing social order by forcible suppression of the working-class movement and by providing scapegoats for popular anger such as outsiders who lived within the state: Jews, foreigners, or blacks; it also prepared the citizenry for the economic and psychological mobilization of war.

imperialism policy of extending the power and rule of a government beyond its own boundaries. A country may attempt to dominate others by direct rule or by less obvious means such as control of markets for goods or raw materials. The latter is often called neo-colonialism.

individualism view in which the individual takes precedence over the collective: the opposite of collectivism. The term *possessive individualism* has been applied to the writings of John Locke (1632–1704) and Jeremy Bentham (1748–1832), describing society as comprising individuals interacting through market relations.

liberalism political and social theory that favours representative government, freedom of the press, speech, and worship, the abolition of class privileges, the use of state resources to protect the welfare of the individual, and international free trade. It is historically associated with the Liberal Party in the UK and the Democratic Party in the USA.

Liberalism developed during the 17th–19th centuries as the distinctive theory of the industrial and commercial classes in their struggle against the power of the monarchy, the church, and the feudal landowners. The classical statement of liberal principles is found in *On Liberty* 1859 and other works of the British philosopher J S Mill (1806–1873).

Maoism form of communism based on the ideas and teachings of Chinese communist leader Mao Zedong (1893–1976). It involves an adaptation of Marxism to suit conditions in China and apportions a much greater role to agriculture and the peasantry in the building of socialism, thus effectively bypassing the capitalist (industrial) stage envisaged by Marx.

Marxism or *dialectical materialism* philosophical system, developed by the 19th-century German social theorists Karl Marx (1818–1883) and Friedrich Engels (1820–1895). As applied to history it supposes that human society, having passed through successive stages of slavery, feudalism, and capitalism, must advance to communism. The stubborn resistance of any existing system to change necessitates its complete overthrow in the *class struggle* – in the case of capitalism, by the proletariat (working class) – rather than gradual modification. Marxism is the basis of communism.

nationalism movement that consciously aims to unify a nation, create a state, or liberate it from foreign or imperialistic rule. Nationalist movements became a potent factor in European politics during the 19th century; since 1900 nationalism has become a strong force in Asia and Africa and in the late 1980s revived strongly in E Europe.

neo-nazism or *neo-fascism* term applied to the upsurge in radical and political intolerance occuring in Western Europe from the 1980s. In Austria, Belgium, France, Germany, and Italy the growth of extreme right-wing political groupings, coupled with racial violence – particularly in Germany – has revived memories of the Nazi period, which post-war politicians have vowed must never be allowed to happen again. Sparked in part by a rapid influx of immigrants at a time of world recession, xenophobia took on new and violent extremes, particularly in the hands of previously marginalized political parties. Another factor that influenced the recent rise in neo-nazism has been the liberalization of politics in the post-cold war world, unleashing anti-liberal forces that were previously kept in check by authoritarian regimes.

The German neo-Nazi movement, consisting of dozens of competing groups, claimed approximately 80,000 members in 1993.

pluralism the view that decision-making in contemporary liberal democracies is the outcome of competition among several interest groups in a political system characterized by free elections, representative institutions, and open access to the organs of power. This concept is opposed by corporatism and other approaches that perceive power to be centralized in the state and its principal elites (the Establishment).

socialism movement aiming to establish a classless society by substituting public for private ownership of the means of production, distribution, and exchange. The term has been used to describe positions as widely apart as anarchism and social democracy. Socialist ideas appeared in classical times; in early Christianity; among later Christian sects such as the Anabaptists and Diggers; and, in the 18th and early 19th centuries, were put forward as systematic political aims by Jean-Jacques Rousseau (1712–1778), Claude Saint-Simon (1760–1825), François Fourier (1772–1837), and Robert Owen (1771–1858), among others. Most countries in W Europe have a strong socialist party; for example, in Germany the Social Democratic Party and in Britain the Labour Party.

Thatcherism political outlook comprising a belief in the efficacy of market forces, the need for strong central government, and a conviction that self-help is preferable to reliance on the state, combined with a strong element of nationalism. The ideology is associated with Margaret Thatcher but stems from an individualist view found in Britain's 19th-century Liberal and 20th-century Conservative parties, and is no longer confined to Britain.

theocracy political system run by priests, as was once found in Tibet. In practical terms it means a system where religious values determine political decisions. The closest modern example was Iran during the period when Ayatollah Khomeini was its religious leader, 1979–89.

totalitarianism government control of all activities within a country, overtly political or otherwise, as in fascist or communist dictatorships. Examples of totalitarian regimes are Italy under Benito Mussolini 1922–45; Germany under Adolph Hitler 1933–45; the USSR under Joseph Stalin from the 1930s until his death in 1953; more recently Romania under Nicolae Ceauşescu 1974–89.

Trotskyism form of Marxism advocated by the Russian Leon Trotsky (1879–1940). Its central concept is that of **permanent revolution**. In his view a proletarian revolution, leading to a socialist society, could not be achieved in isolation, so it would be necessary to spark off further revolutions throughout Europe and ultimately worldwide. This was in direct opposition to the Stalinist view that socialism should be built and consolidated within individual countries.

Political Terms

affirmative action government policy of positive discrimination that favours members of minority ethnic groups and women in such areas as employment and education, designed to counter the effects of long-term discrimination against them. In Europe, Sweden, Belgium, the Netherlands, and Italy actively promote affirmative action through legal and financial incentives.

alliance agreement between two or more states to come to each other's assistance in the event of war. Alliances were criticized after World War I as having contributed to the outbreak of war, but NATO has been a major part of the post-1945 structure of international relations (as was the Warsaw Pact until its dissolution 1991).

ambassador officer of the highest rank in the diplomatic service, who represents the head of one sovereign state at the court or capital of another.

apartheid racial-segregation policy of the government of South Africa, which was legislated 1948, when the Afrikaner National Party gained power, and partly repealed 1991. Nonwhites (classified as Bantu, coloured or mixed, or Indian) do not share full rights of citizenship with the 4.5 million whites (for example, the 23 million black people cannot vote in parliamentary elections), and many public facilities and institutions were until 1990 (and in some cases remain) restricted to the use of one race only; the establishment of Black National States ('homelands') was another manifestation of apartheid. In 1991 President de Klerk repealed the key elements of apartheid, and democratic elections were set for 1994.

The term has also been applied to similar movements and other forms of racial separation, for example social or educational, in other parts of the world.

arms control attempts to limit the arms race between the superpowers by reaching agreements to restrict the production of certain weapons. (See *disarmament* in **Warfare** for more.)

autonomy political self-government of a state or, more commonly, a subdivision of a state. Autonomy may be based upon cultural or ethnic differences and often leads eventually to independence.

ballot the process of voting in an election. In political elections in democracies ballots are usually secret: voters indicate their choice of candidate on a voting slip that is placed in a sealed ballot box. *Ballot rigging* is a term used to describe elections that are fraudulent because of interference with the voting process or the counting of votes.

blockade cutting-off of a place by hostile forces by land, sea, or air so as to prevent any movement to or fro, in order to compel a surrender without attack or to achieve some other political aim (for example, the Berlin blockade 1948 by the USSR).

cabinet the group of ministers holding a country's highest executive offices who decide government policy. In Britain the cabinet system originated under the Stuarts. Under William III it became customary for the king to select his ministers from the party with a parliamentary majority. The US cabinet, unlike the British, does not initiate legislation, and its members, appointed by the president, must not be members of Congress.

citizenship status as a member of a state. In most countries citizenship may be acquired either by birth or by naturalization. The status confers rights, such as voting and the protection of the law, and also imposes responsibilities, such as military service, in some countries.

coalition association of political groups, usually for some limited or short-term purpose, such as fighting an election or forming a government when one party has failed to secure a majority in a legislature.

constitution body of fundamental laws of a state, laying down the system of government and defining the relations of the legislature, executive, and judiciary to each other and to the citizens. Since the French Revolution almost all countries (the UK is an exception) have adopted written constitutions; that of the USA (1787) is the oldest.

council in local government in England and Wales, a popularly elected local assembly charged with the government of the area within its boundaries. Under the Local Government Act 1972, they comprise three types: county councils, district councils, and parish councils.

coup d'état or *coup* forcible takeover of the government of a country by elements from within that country, generally carried out by violent or illegal means. It differs from a revolution in typically being carried out by a small group (for example, of army officers or opposition politicians) to install its leader as head of government, rather than being a mass uprising by the people.

détente (French) reduction of political tension and the easing of strained relations between nations – for example, the ending of the Cold War 1989–90, although it was first used in the 1970s to describe the easing East–West relations, trade agreements, and cultural exchanges.

dictatorship term or office of an absolute ruler, overriding the constitution. Although dictatorships were common in Latin America during the 19th century, the only European example during this period was the rule of Napoleon III. The crises following World War I produced many dictatorships, including the regimes of Kemal Atatürk in Turkey and Józef Piłsudski in Poland (nationalist); Benito Mussolini in Italy, Adolf Hitler in Germany, Miguel Primo de Rivera and Francisco Franco in Spain, and Antonio Salazar in Portugal (all right-wing); and Joseph Stalin in the USSR (communist).

diplomacy process by which states attempt to settle their differences through peaceful means such as negotiation or arbitration.

dissident in one-party states, a person intellectually dissenting from the official line. Dissidents have been sent into exile, prison, labour camps, and mental institutions, or deprived of their jobs. In China the number of prisoners of conscience increased after the 1989 Tiananmen Square massacre, and in South Africa, despite the release of Nelson Mandela in 1990, numerous political dissidents have remained in jail.

ethnic cleansing the forced expulsion of one ethnic group by another. The term has been frequently used in relation to the Serbian policy toward Moslems in Bosnia-Herzegovina during 1992 and thereafter. The practice of ethnic cleansing has been formally condemned by the United Nations.

federalism system of government in which two or more separate states unite under a common central government while retaining a considerable degree of local autonomy. A federation should be distinguished from a *confederation*, a looser union of states for mutual assistance. Switzerland, the USA, Canada, Australia, and Malaysia are all examples of federal government, and many supporters of the European Community see it as the forerunner of a federal Europe.

glasnost former Soviet leader Mikhail Gorbachev's policy of liberalizing various aspects of Soviet life, such as introducing greater freedom of expression and information and opening up relations with Western countries. Glasnost was introduced and adopted by the Soviet government 1986.

high commissioner representative of one independent Commonwealth country in the capital of another, ranking with ambassador.

judiciary in constitutional terms, the system of courts and body of judges in a country. The independence of the judiciary from other branches of the central authority is generally considered to be an essential feature of a democratic political system. This independence is often written into a nation's constitution and protected from abuse by politicians.

left wing the socialist parties of the political spectrum. The term originated in the French National Assembly of 1789, where the nobles sat in the place of honour to the right of the president, and the commons sat to the left. This arrangement has become customary in European parliaments, where the progressives sit on the left and the conservatives on the right. It is also usual to speak of the right, left, and centre, when referring to the different elements composing a single party.

lobby individual or pressure group that sets out to influence government action. The lobby is prevalent in the USA, where the term originated in the 1830s from the practice of those wishing to influence state policy waiting for elected representatives in the lobby of the Capitol.

local government that part of government dealing mainly with matters concerning the inhabitants of a particular area or town, usually financed at least in part by local taxes. In the USA and UK, local government has comparatively large powers and responsibilities.

mandate in politics, the right (given by the electors) of an elected government to carry out its programme of policies.

In history, mandate referred to a territory whose administration was entrusted to Allied states by the League of Nations under the Treaty of Versailles after World War I. Mandated territories were former German and Turkish possessions (including Iraq, Syria, Lebanon, and Palestine). When the United Nations replaced the League of Nations 1945, mandates that had not achieved independence became known as trust territories.

manifesto published prospectus of a political party, setting out the policies that the party will pursue if elected to govern. When elected to power a party will often claim that the contents of its manifesto constitute a mandate to introduce legislation to bring these policies into effect.

militia body of civilian soldiers, usually with some military training, who are on call in emergencies, distinct from professional soldiers. In Switzerland, the militia is the national defence force, and every able-bodied man is liable for service in it. In the UK the *Territorial Army* and in the USA the *National Guard* have supplanted earlier voluntary militias.

nationalization policy of bringing a country's essential services and industries under public ownership. It was pursued, for example, by the UK Labour government 1945–51. In recent years the trend has in many countries (the UK, France, and Japan, for example) reversed (privatization). Assets in the hands of foreign governments or companies may also be nationalized; for example, Iran's oil industry, the Suez Canal, and US-owned fruit plantations in Guatemala, all in the 1950s.

parliament legislative body of a country. The world's oldest parliament is the Icelandic Althing, which dates from about 930. The UK Parliament is usually dated from 1265.

In the UK, Parliament is the supreme legislature, comprising the *House of Commons* and the *House of Lords*. The origins of Parliament are in the 13th century, but its powers were not established until the late 17th century. The powers of the Lords were curtailed 1911, and the duration of parliaments was fixed at five years, but any parliament may extend its own life, as happened during both world wars. The UK Parliament meets in the Palace of Westminster, London.

perestroika in Soviet politics, the wide-ranging economic and political reforms initiated from 1985 by Mikhail Gorbachev, finally leading to the demise of the USSR. Originally, in the economic sphere, *perestroika* was conceived as involving 'intensive development' concentrating on automation and improved labour efficiency. It evolved to attend increasingly to market indicators and incentives ('market socialism') and the gradual dismantling of the Stalinist central-planning system, with decision-taking being devolved to self-financing enterprises.

president the usual title of the head of state in a republic; the power of the office may range from the equivalent of a constitutional monarch to the actual head of the government.

prime minister or *premier* head of a parliamentary government, usually the leader of the largest party. In countries with an executive president, the prime minister is of lesser standing, whereas in those with dual executives, such as France, power is shared with the president.

privatization policy or process of selling or transferring state-owned or public assets and services (notably nationalized industries) to private investors. Privatization of services involves the government contracting private firms to supply services previously supplied by public authorities. The term 'privatization' is used even when the state retains a majority share of an enterprise.

The policy has been pursued by the post-1979 Conservative administration in the UK, and by recent governments in France, Japan, Italy, New Zealand, and elsewhere. By 1988 the practice had spread worldwide with communist countries such as China and Cuba selling off housing to private tenants.

propaganda systematic spreading (propagation) of information or disinformation, usually to promote a religious or political doctrine with the intention of instilling particular attitudes or responses. Examples of the use of propaganda are the racial doctrines put forth by Nazism in World War II, and some of the ideas and strategies propagated by the USA and the USSR during the Cold War (1945–90).

purge removal (for example, from a political party) of suspected opponents or persons regarded as undesirable (often by violent means). During the 1930s purges were conducted in the USSR under Joseph Stalin, carried out by the secret police against political opponents, Communist Party members, minorities, civil servants, and large sections of the armed forces' officer corps. Some 10 million people were executed or deported to labour camps from 1934 to 1938.

rainbow coalition or *rainbow alliance* loose, left-of-centre alliance of people from several different sections of society that are traditionally politically underrepresented, such as nonwhite ethnic groups. Its aims include promoting minority rights and equal opportunities.

referendum procedure whereby a decision on proposed legislation is referred to the electorate for settlement by direct vote of all the people. A referendum was held in the UK for the first time 1975 on the issue of membership of the European Community. In 1992 several European countries (Ireland, Denmark, France) held referenda on whether or not to ratify the Maastricht Treaty on closer European economic and political union.

A similar device is the *recall*, whereby voters are given the opportunity of demanding the dismissal from office of officials.

refugee person fleeing from oppressive or dangerous conditions (such as political, religious, or military persecution) and seeking refuge in a foreign country. Their numbers grow every year: in 1970 they numbered 2.5 million; in 1985, 10 million; in 1987, 12 million; in 1990, 15 million; in 1991, 17 million. In 1993 there were an estimated 19 million refugees worldwide, whose resettlement and welfare were the responsibility of the United Nations High Commission for Refugees (UNHCR). An estimated average of 3,000 people a day become refugees.

Major refugee movements in 20th-century Europe include: Jews from the pogroms of Russia 1881–1914 and again after the Revolution; White Russians from the USSR after 1917; Jews from Germany and other Nazi-dominated countries 1933–45; the displaced people of World War II; and from 1991 victims of the the civil wars in Croatia and Bosnia-Herzegovina.

right wing the more conservative or reactionary section of a political party or spectrum. It originated in the French national assembly 1789, where the nobles sat in the place of honour on the president's right, whereas the commons were on his left (hence left wing).

sanction economic or military measure taken by a state or number of states to enforce international law. The first use of sanctions was the attempted economic boycott of Italy (1935–36) during the Abyssinian War by the League of Nations; a current example is the sanctions against South Africa on human-rights grounds by the UN and other organizations from 1985.

shuttle diplomacy in international relations, the efforts of an independent mediator to achieve a compromise solution between belligerent parties, travelling back and forth from one to the other.

sovereignty absolute authority within a given territory. The possession of sovereignty is taken to be the distinguishing feature of the state, as against other forms of community. The term has an internal aspect, in that it refers to the ultimate source of authority within a state, such as a parliament or monarch, and an external aspect, where it denotes the independence of the state from any outside authority.

state territory that forms its own domestic and foreign policy, acting through laws that are typically decided by a government and carried out, by force if necessary, by agents of that government. It can be argued that growth of regional international bodies such as the European Community means that states no longer enjoy absolute sovereignty.

summit or *summit conference* meeting of heads of government to discuss common interests, especially the US–Soviet summits 1959–90, of which there were 15. The term was first used during World War II; and the Yalta Conference and Potsdam Conference 1945 were summits that did much to determine the political structure of the postwar world. Later summits have been of varying importance, being partly used as public-relations exercises.

terrorism systematic violence in the furtherance of political aims, often perpetrated by small guerrilla groups.

trade union organization of employed workers formed to undertake collective bargaining with employers and to try to achieve improved working conditions for its members. Attitudes of government to unions and of unions to management vary greatly from country to country. Probably the most effective trade-union system is that of Sweden, and the internationally best known is Poland's Solidarity.

unilateralism support for *unilateral nuclear disarmament*: scrapping a country's nuclear weapons without waiting for other countries to agree to do so at the same time.

veto (Latin 'I forbid') exercise by a sovereign, branch of legislature, or other political power, of the right to prevent the enactment or operation of a law, or the taking of some course of action. At the United Nations, members of the Security Council can exercise a veto on resolutions.

vote expression of opinion by ballot, show of hands, or other means. In systems that employ direct vote, the plebiscite and referendum are fundamental mechanisms. In parliamentary elections the results can be calculated in a number of ways. The main electoral systems are: *simple plurality* or *first past the post*, with single-member constituencies (USA, UK, India, Canada); *absolute majority*, achieved for example by the *alternative vote*, where the voter, in single-member constituencies, chooses a candidate by marking preferences (Australia), or by the *second ballot*, where, if a clear decision is not reached immediately, a second ballot is held (France, Egypt); *proportional representation*, achieved for example by the *party list* system (Israel, most countries of Western Europe, and several in South America), the *additional member* system (Germany), the *single transferable vote* (Ireland and Malta), and the *limited vote* (Japan).

All British subjects over 18, except peers, the insane, and felons, are entitled to vote in UK local government and parliamentary elections. A register is prepared annually, and since 1872 voting has been by secret ballot. Under the Corrupt and Illegal Practices Act 1883, any candidate attempting to influence voters by gifts, loans or promises, or by intimidation, is liable to a fine or imprisonment. The voting system is by a simple majority in single-member constituencies.

welfare state political system under which the state (rather than the individual or the private sector) has responsibility for the welfare of its citizens. Services such as unemployment and sickness benefits, family allowances and income supplements, pensions, medical care, and education may be provided and financed through state insurance schemes and taxation.

Internationally, the aim of creating a welfare state has been adopted in several countries, particularly in Scandinavia. The welfare-state concept was built into the political structures of communist states, led by the USSR, but even here economic realities tempered its practical implementation.

UK Central Government

Central government in the UK is currently based on 16 major departments of state, each headed by a minister who is a member of the cabinet, and 16 minor departments or subdepartments.

MAJOR DEPARTMENTS

Ministry of Agriculture, Fisheries and Food
Ministry of Defence
Department for Education
Department of Employment
Department of the Environment Foreign and Commonwealth Office
Department of Health Department for National Heritage
Home Office
Northern Ireland Office
Scottish Office
Department of Social Security
Department of Trade and Industry
Department of Transport
Treasury *
Welsh Office

* The Treasury is the one department with two cabinet representatives, the chancellor of the Exchequer and the chief secretary to the Treasury, and, since the prime minister is formally also First Lord of the Treasury, it can be argued that the cabinet representation is threefold.

MINOR DEPARTMENTS

Board of Inland Revenue
Central Office of Information
Department of National Savings
Export Credits Guarantee Department
H M Customs and Excise Department
Her Majesty's Household
Her Majesty's Stationery Office
Law Officers' Department
Lord Advocate's Department
Lord Chancellor's Department
Office of Arts and Libraries
Office of the Minister for the Civil Service
Overseas Development Administration
Parliamentary Counsel's Office
Paymaster General's Office
Privy Council Office*

* Direct representation in the cabinet.

NONDEPARTMENTAL CABINET MEMBERS

Apart from the prime minister, there are three members of the cabinet without specific departmental responsibilities : Lord President of the Council, who is Leader of the House of Commons; Lord Privy Seal, who is Leader of the House of Lords; and Chancellor of the Duchy of Lancaster, who is responsible for the implementation of the Citizens' Charter, for science, and for civil-service reform.

MINISTERIAL GRADINGS

The top-ranking ministers are members of the cabinet. Most cabinet ministers heading departments are now styled secretary of state. The exceptions are: the minister of Agriculture, Fisheries, and Food; the Lord Chancellor; the chancellor of the Exchequer; and the President of the Board of Trade.

The other ministers, in descending order of rank, are:

minister of state who may be of cabinet rank (may sometimes be styled minister of state and sometimes minister)

undersecretary of state (may sometimes be styled minister) *parliamentary undersecretary* (in the cases of Agriculture, Fisheries, and Food; and the Treasury; styled parliamentary secretary)

When the minister heading a major department is styled secretary of state, junior ministers in that department are styled parliamentary undersecretaries. In other cases they are styled parliamentary secretaries.

CIVIL-SERVICE GRADINGS

The three most senior grades in the home civil service, found in all major departments, are: permanent secretary, deputy secretary, undersecretary.

TYPICAL STRUCTURE OF A DEPARTMENT

All departments have specific, distinctive features but most conform to the following pattern:

political head: secretary of state, supported by one or more ministers of state and junior ministers

nonpolitical head: permanent secretary, supported by administrative, executive, and clerical staff.

MAJOR DEPARTMENTS

Ministry of Agriculture, Fisheries, and Food
established 1955, through combination of existing agriculture, fisheries, and food ministries
responsibilities agriculture, horticulture, fisheries, and food policies
ministerial team minister, one minister of state, two parliamentary secretaries
head Gillian Shephard
permanent staff 10,400
administrative headquarters Whitehall Place, London SW1

Ministry of Defence
established 1964, when Admiralty, War Office, and Air Defence were brought together in one ministry
responsibilities national defence, including overall control of the Royal Navy, Army, and Royal Air Force, and arms procurement
ministerial team secretary of state, two ministers of state, one parliamentary undersecretary
head Malcolm Rifkind
permanent staff 98,000, including Royal Ordnance factories
administrative headquarters Whitehall, London SW1

Department for Education
established 1944, as the Ministry of Education
responsibilities education and scientific research policies
ministerial team secretary of state, one minister of state, one parliamentary undersecretary
head John Patten
permanent staff 2,600
administrative headquarters York Road, London SE1

Department of Employment
established 1970 in its present form. The original Ministry of Labour was formed in 1917
responsibilities employment and training policies
ministerial team secretary of state, one minister of state, two parliamentary undersecretaries

head David Hunt
permanent staff 53,700
administrative headquarters Tothill Street, London SW1

Department of the Environment
established 1970, bringing together ministries of Housing and Local Government, Transport, and Building and Works. Transport returned to an independent status in 1975
responsibilities housing, construction, local government, sport and recreation policies, and preservation of the environment
ministerial team secretary of state, three ministers of state, one parliamentary undersecretary
head John Selwyn Gummer
permanent staff 19,400
administrative headquarters Marsham Street, London SW1

Foreign and Commonwealth Office
established 1782, as the Foreign Office
responsibilities conduct of foreign policy, representation of British interests abroad, relations with other members of the Commonwealth, overseas aid policy and administration
ministerial team secretary of state, four ministers of state, one parliamentary undersecretary
head Douglas Hurd
permanent staff 8,300
administrative headquarters Downing Street, London SW1

Department of Health
established 1988, following the division of the Department of Health and Social Security into two separate departments. Ministry of Health formed in 1919
responsibilities operation of the national health service and overall policies on health
ministerial team secretary of state, one minister of state, three parliamentary undersecretaries
head Virginia Bottomley
permanent staff 11,400, excluding NHS staff
administrative headquarters Whitehall, London SW1

Department for National Heritage
established 1992
responsibilities broadcasting and the media, the arts, sport and recreation, the national lottery
ministerial team secretary of state, one minister of state
head Peter Brooke
permanent staff not yet known
administrative headquarters Whitehall, London SW1

Home Office
established 1782
responsibilities administration of justice, penal system (including the prison and probation services), police, fire, civil defence, licensing (including marriage, liquor, theatres, and cinemas), radio and television broadcasting, immigration and nationality policies
ministerial team secretary of state, two ministers of state, two parliamentary undersecretaries
head Michael Howard
permanent staff 45,000

administrative headquarters Queen Anne's Gate, London SW1

Northern Ireland Office
established 1972
responsibilities direct government of Northern Ireland, including administration of security, law and order, and economic, industrial, and social policies
ministerial team secretary of state, one minister of state, one parliamentary undersecretary
head Patrick Mayhew
permanent staff 29,500
administrative headquarters Whitehall, London SW1, and Belfast

Scottish Office
established 1707 in England, 1938 in Scotland
responsibilities administration for Scotland of policies on agriculture and fisheries, education, industrial development, law and order, and health
ministerial team secretary of state, two ministers of state, two parliamentary undersecretaries
head Ian Lang
permanent staff 13,000
administrative headquarters Whitehall, London SW1, and Edinburgh

Department of Social Security
established 1988, after being part of the Department of Health and Social Security
responsibilities administration of social-service policies, including pensions, unemployment, income support, and disability benefits
ministerial team secretary of state, one minister of state, three parliamentary undersecretaries
head Peter Lilley
permanent staff 78,000
administrative headquarters Whitehall, London SW1

Department of Trade and Industry
established 1970, bringing together the Board of Trade, founded in 1786, and the Ministry of Technology, formed in 1964; took over the responsibilities of the Department of Energy in 1992
responsibilities administration of policies on international trade, industry, competition, industrial research and assistance to exporters
ministerial team President of the Board of Trade (secretary of state), three ministers of state, three parliamentary undersecretaries
head Michael Heseltine
permanent staff 12,500
administrative headquarters Victoria Street, London SW1

Department of Transport
established 1975, in its present form
responsibilities land, sea, and air transport policies, including sponsorship of British Rail, and construction and maintenance of motorways and trunk roads
ministerial team secretary of state, two ministers of state, two parliamentary undersecretaries
head John MacGregor
permanent staff 16,000
administrative headquarters Marsham Street, London SW1

Treasury
established 1612
responsibilities control of public expenditure, national economic policy, including monetary and fiscal measures, efficiency in the public sector, international finance, and oversight of the financial system
ministerial team chancellor of the Exchequer, chief secretary (of cabinet rank), three ministers of state rank (paymaster general, financial secretary, and economic secretary), one parliamentary secretary
chancellor Kenneth Clarke
chief secretary Michael Portillo
permanent staff 3,200
administrative headquarters Parliament Street, London SW1

Welsh Office
established 1951
responsibilities administration for Wales of policies on agriculture, education, health and social services, local government, planning, sport, and tourism. It is also responsible for promoting the Welsh language and culture
ministerial team secretary of state, one minister of state, one parliamentary undersecretary
head John Redwood
permanent staff 2,300
administrative headquarters Whitehall, London SW1, and Cardiff

MINOR DEPARTMENTS

Board of Inland Revenue
parent department Treasury
responsibilities collection of central government taxes, other than VAT and customs and excise duties, throughout the UK

Cabinet Office
parent department Cabinet
responsibilities services the cabinet and all its committees and subcommittees; it organizes meetings; prepares and distributes agendas and cabinet papers, including minutes; and decides, with the prime minister, which issues should go to the full cabinet and which to one of its committees or subcommttees

Central Office of Information (COI)
parent department Treasury
resposibilities operation of government information services

Customs and Excise Department
parent department Treasury
responsibilities collection of customs and excise duties, including VAT

Department of National Savings
parent department Treasury
responsibilities management of government savings schemes

Exports Credits Guarantee Department
parent department Department of Trade and Industry
responsibilities management of government scheme to underwrite finance for exporters

Her Majesty's Household
parent department Lord Chamberlain
responsibilities management of the affairs of the royal household

Her Majesty's Stationery Office (HMSO)
parent department Treasury
responsibilities production and sale of government publications

Law Officers' Department
parent department freestanding, under Attorney General
responsibilities legal advice to the government and representation of the Crown in court

Lord Advocate's Department
parent department freestanding
responsibilities administration of law in Scotland

Lord Chancellor's Department
parent department freestanding, under Lord Chancellor
responsibilities administration of civil law in England and Wales, including the appointment of the judiciary in lower courts and advice on appointments in the higher courts

The Lord Chancellor also presides over sittings in the House of Lords

Office of Arts and Libraries
parent department Privy Council Office, under Lord President of the Council
responsibilities promotion of the arts

Office of the Minister for the Civil Service
parent department prime minister
responsibilities management of the home civil service

Overseas Development Administration (ODA)
parent department Foreign and Commonwealth Office
responsibilities administration of development assistance to overseas countries

Parliamentary Counsel's Office
parent department freestanding
responsibilities drafting of parliamentary legislation

Paymaster General's Office
parent department Treasury
responsibilities administration of payment of government financial liabilities

Privy Council Office
parent department freestanding, under Lord President of the Council
responsibilities a miscellany of duties, including management of the civil service and promotion of the arts

Significant political thinkers

Lived	Name	Chief work	Published
551–479 BC	Confucius	The Analects	
c. 428–347	Plato	The Republic, The Laws	
384–22	Aristotle	Constitution of the Athenians, Politics	
1225–1274	St Thomas Aquinas	Summa contra Gentiles/ Against the Errors of the Infidels	1259–64
1469–1527	Niccolò Machiavelli	Il principe/The Prince	1583
		Discorsi/Discourses	1531
1588–1679	Thomas Hobbes	The Leviathan	1651
1632–1704	John Locke	Treatise on Civil Government	1690
1712–1778	Jean-Jacques Rousseau	Du Contrat social/Social Contract	1762
1729–1797	Edmund Burke	Thoughts on the Present Discontents	1770
		Reflections on the Revolution in France	1790
1737–1809	Thomas Paine	The Rights of Man	1791
1748–1832	Jeremy Bentham	Fragments on Government	1776
1770–1831	Georg Wilhelm Friedrich Hegel	Philosophie des Rechts/ Philosophy of Right	1821
1772–1837	Charles Fourier	Le nouveau Monde industriel/ The New Industrial World	1829
1806–1873	John Stuart Mill	On Liberty	1859
1809–1865	Pierre Joseph Proudhon	Qu'est-ce que la propriété?/ What is Property?	1840
1818–1883	Karl Marx	The Communist Manifesto (with F Engels)	1848
		Das Kapital/Capital	1867–95
1820–1895	Friedrich Engels	The Communist Manifesto (with K Marx) 1848 Origins of the Family, Private Property, and the State	1884
1869–1948	Mohandas K Gandhi	Collected Works	1958
1876–1924	Vladimir Ilyich Lenin	What Is to be Done?	1902
		Imperialism	1917
1889–1945	Adolf Hitler	Mein Kampf/My Struggle	1925–27
1891–1937	Antonio Gramsci	Quaderni di carcere/Prison Notebooks	1947
1893–1976	Mao Zedong	Little Red Book	
1899–1992	Friedrich August von Hayek	The Road to Serfdom	1944

Nobel Peace Prize

1901	Jean Henri Dunant (Switzerland): founder of the Red Cross. Frédéric Passy (France): advocate of international arbitration and peace
1902	Elie Ducommun (Switzerland) and Charles Albert Gobat (Switzerland): work for peace within the International Peace Bureau
1903	Sir William Cremer (UK): advocate of international arbitration
1904	Institute of International Law
1905	Bertha von Suttner (Austria): influential peace novels
1906	Theodore Roosevelt (USA): mediation at end of Russo-Japanese war 1904
1907	Ernesto Teodoro Moneta (Italy): founder of International League for peace and president of International Peace Conference 1906. Louis Renault (France): international arbitration
1908	Klas Pontus Arnoldson (Sweden): mediating dissolution of Norwegian–Swedish Union. Fredrik Bajer (Denmark): work for female emancipation and the peace movement
1909	Baron d'Estournelles de Constant (France): diplomat. Auguste Beernaert (Belgium): work at the Hague Peace Conferences
1910	International Peace Bureau
1911	Tobias Asser (Netherlands): forming the Permanent Court of Justice (1899 Hague Peace Conference). Alfred Fried (Austria): co-founder of German peace movement
1912	Elihu Root (USA): international arbitration
1913	Henri Lafontaine (Belgium): president of International Peace Bureau
1914–16	No award
1917	International Red Cross Committee
1918	No award
1919	Woodrow Wilson (USA)
1920	Léon Bourgeois (France): advocate of the League of Nations and international cooperation
1921	Karl Branting (Sweden): conciliatory international diplomacy. Christian Lous Lance (Norway): work as secretary-general of Inter-Parliamentary Union
1922	Fridtjof Nansen (Norway): relief work after World War I
1923–24	No award
1925	Sir Austen Chamberlain (UK): work on the Locarno Pact 1925. Charles G Dawes (USA): reorganization of German reparation payments
1926	Aristide Briand (France) and Gustav Stresemann (Germany): work for European reconciliation
1927	Ferdinand Buisson (France): co-founder of League of Human Rights 1898. Ludwig Quidde (Germany): work for peace in Germany
1928	No award
1929	Frank B Kellogg (USA): Kellogg–Briand Pact 1928
1930	Nathan Söderblom (Sweden): efforts for peace through church unity
1931	Jane Addams (USA): support of women's suffrage. Nicholas Murray Butler (USA): work in forming Carnegie Endowment for International Peace
1932	No award
1933	Sir Norman Angell (UK): work on the economic futility of war
1934	Arthur Henderson (UK): work for disarmament
1935	Carl von Ossietzky (Germany): opposition to Nazi rearmament
1936	Carlos Saavedra Lamas (Argentina): efforts to end the Chaco War 1932–35
1937	Viscount Cecil of Chetwood (UK): drafting the League of Nations Covenant 1919
1938	Nansen International Office for Refugees
1939–43	No award
1944	International Red Cross Committee
1945	Cordell Hull (USA): for his part in organizing the United Nations
1946	Emily Greene Balch (USA): leader of the women's movement for peace. John R Mott (USA): for work in international missionary movements
1947	American Friends Service Committee (USA) and Friends Service Council (UK): promotion of peace through programmes of social service
1948	No award
1949	Lord Boyd-Orr (UK): work on nutritional requirements
1950	Ralph Bunche (USA): negotiating the Arab–Israeli truce 1949
1951	Léon Juhaut (France): co-founder of International Confederation of Free Trade Unions
1952	Albert Schweitzer (Germany): medical and other work in Africa
1953	George C Marshall (USA): Marshall (European recovery) plan
1954	Office of the United Nations High Commissioner for Refugees
1955–56	No award
1957	Lester B Pearson (Canada): efforts to solve the Suez Crisis 1956
1958	Dominique Georges Pire (Belgium): aid to displaced Europeans after World War II
1959	Philip Noel-Baker (UK): advocate of world disarmament
1960	Albert Lutuli (South Africa): non-violent struggle against apartheid

Nobel Peace Prize *(cont.)*

1961	Dag Hammarskjöld (Sweden): Secretary-General of the United Nations (posthumously awarded)
1962	Linus Pauling (USA): campaigns for the control of nuclear weapons and nuclear testing
1963	International Red Cross Committee: for relief work after natural disasters
1964	Martin Luther King Jr (USA): black civil rights leader
1965	United Nations Children's Fund
1966–67	No award
1968	René Cassin (France): principal author of the UN Declaration of Human Rights
1969	International Labour Organization
1970	Norman E Borlaug (USA): agricultural technology
1971	Willy Brandt (Germany): reconciliation between West and East Germany
1972	No award
1973	Henry Kissinger (USA) and Le Duc Tho (North Vietnam) (declined): peace settlement of the Vietnam War
1974	Eisaku Satō anti-nuclear policies. Sean MacBride (Ireland): campaign for human rights
1975	Andrei D Sakharov (Russia): advocacy of human rights and disarmament
1976	Mairead Corrigan and Betty Williams (Northern Ireland): campaigning to end sectarian strife in Northern Ireland
1977	Amnesty International: work to secure the release of political prisoners
1978	Menachem Begin (Israel) and Anwar el-Sadat (Egypt): Israel–Egypt peace treaty 1979
1979	Mother Teresa of Calcutta (Macedonia): help with the destitute in India
1980	Adolfo Pérez Esquivel (Argentina): work for human rights in Latin America
1981	United Nations High Commissioner for Refugees
1982	Alva Myrdal (Sweden) and Alfonso Garciá Robles (Mexico): advocacy of nuclear disarmament
1983	Lech Walesa (Poland): the Solidarity movement
1984	Desmond Tutu (South Africa): peaceful anti-apartheid work
1985	International Physicians for the Prevention of Nuclear War
1986	Elie Wiesel (France): writer and human rights activist
1987	Oscar Arias Sánchez (Costa Rica): promoting peace in Central America
1988	United Nations peacekeeping forces
1989	The Dalai Lama (Tibet): spiritual and exiled temporal leader of Tibet
1990	Mikhail Gorbachev (Russia): promoting greater openness in the USSR and helping to end the Cold War
1991	Aung San Suu Kyi (Burma): non-violent campaign for democracy
1992	Rigoberta Menchu (Guatemala): campaign for indigenous people
1993	Nelson Mandela and Frederik Willem de Klerk (South Africa): work towards dismantling apartheid and negotiating transition to non-racial democracy

RELIGION

Religious Traditions

bce/ce before the common era (BCE) and common era (CE) are abbreviations used in this section to replace, respectively, before Christ (BC) and anno Domini (AD).

African religions there is a wide variety of belief and practice in African religion. Most indigenous African religions are basically polytheistic (believing in a number of gods), but there is often a concept of one High God, generally a creator who has withdrawn from interaction with the world. There are also many spirits, which are present in all natural objects: water is seen as a particularly powerful force. Dead ancestors are very important in African religions, and are consulted before major undertakings. If offended, they can cause natural disasters and sterility, so they must be placated with offerings. In society, healers are highly regarded, as they deal with supernatural powers, as do diviners, but the most powerful human figure is the chief-king, who is surrounded by prohibitions because he is so dangerous: he is the life of the tribe incarnate, though because of this he may be required to sacrifice himself to preserve the health of his people.

Australian Aboriginal religion the creation story of the Australian Aborigines is recorded in the **Dreamtime** stories. These reveal how giant human and other animals sprang from the earth, sea, and sky and criss-crossed the empty continent of Australia on a journey known as Dreamtime. At the end of their journey they returned into the earth where it is believed their spirits still exist. The places where they travelled or sank back into the land became mountain ranges, rocks, and sites full of sacred meaning.

Every sacred site has its own Dreamtime story that is part of the sacred law and must be re-enacted at certain times of the year in order to maintain the life of the land and the Dreamtime. Each Australian Aborigine has their own particular Dreamtime Ancestor although they are related to many other ancestors through kinship. When hunting, Aborigines are careful never to trap, maim, or kill the animals who are associated with their kinship ancestors.

Buddhism one of the great world religions, which originated in India about 500 BCE. It derives from the teaching of Buddha, who is regarded as one of a series of such enlightened beings; there are no gods. The chief doctrine is that of **karma**, good or evil deeds meeting an appropriate reward or punishment either in this life or (through reincarnation) a long succession of lives. The main divisions in Buddhism are **Theravāda** (or **Hīnayāna**) in SE Asia and **Mahāyāna** in N Asia; **Lamaism** in Tibet and **Zen** in Japan are among the many Mahāyāna sects. Its symbol is the lotus. There are approximately 315 million (1992) Buddhists worldwide.

scriptures The only complete canon of the Buddhist scriptures is that of the Sinhalese (Sri Lanka) Buddhists, in Pāli, but other schools have essentially the same canon in Sanskrit. The scriptures, known as *pitakas* (baskets), date from the 2nd to 6th centuries CE. There are three divisions: *vinaya* (discipline), listing offences and rules of life; the sūtras (discourse), or *dharma* (doctrine), the exposition of Buddhism by Buddha and his disciples; and *abhidharma* (further doctrine), later discussions on doctrine.

beliefs The self is not regarded as permanent, as it is subject to change and decay. It is attachment to the things that are essentially impermanent that cause delusion, suffering, greed, and aversion, the origin of karma, and they in turn create further karma and the sense of self is reinforced. Actions which incline towards selflessness are called 'skilful karma' and they are on the path leading to enlightenment. In the **Four Noble Truths** the Buddha acknowledged the existence and source of suffering, and showed the way of deliverance from it through the **Eightfold Path**. The aim of following the Eightfold Path is to break the chain of karma and achieve dissociation from the body by attaining *nirvana* ('blowing out') – the eradication of all desires, either in annihilation or by absorption of the self in the infinite. Supreme reverence is accorded to the historical Buddha (Śākyamuni, or, when referred to by his clan name, Gautama), who is seen as one in a long and ongoing line of Buddhas, the next one (Maitreya) being due *c.* CE 3000.

divisions: Theravāda Buddhism, the School of the Elders, also known as *Hīnayāna* or Lesser Vehicle, prevails in SE Asia (Sri Lanka, Thailand, and Burma), and emphasizes the mendicant, meditative life as the way to break the cycle of *samsāra*, or death and rebirth. Its three alternative goals are *arahat*: one who has gained insight into the true nature of things; *Paccekabuddha*, an enlightened one who lives alone and does not teach; and fully awakened *Buddha*. Its scriptures are written in *Pāli*, an Indo-Aryan language with its roots in N India. In India itself Buddhism had virtually died out by the 13th century, and was replaced by Hinduism. However, it has 5 million devotees in the 20th century and is still growing.

Mahāyāna, or Greater Vehicle arose at the beginning of the Christian era. This tradition emphasized the eternal, formless principle of the Buddha as the essence of all things. It exhorts the individual not merely to attain personal nirvana, but to become a trainee Buddha, or *bodhisattva*, and so save others; this meant the faithful could be brought to enlightenment by a bodhisattva without following the austeri-

Followers of major faiths

Christianity	1,833,022,000
Islam	1,025,585,000
Hinduism	732,812,000
Buddhism	314,939,000
Sikhism	18,000,000
Judaism	17,822,000
Confucianism	8,028,000
Jainism	3,794,000
Baha'ism	3,517,000
Shintoism	3,222,800

Source: David B. Barrett (1992)

ties of Theravāda, and the cults of various Buddhas and bodhisattvas arose. Mahāyāna Buddhism also emphasizes *shunyata*, or the experiential understanding of the emptiness of all things, even Buddhist doctrine.

Mahāyāna Buddhism prevails in N Asia (China, Korea, Japan, and Tibet). In the 6th century CE Mahāyāna spread to China with the teachings of Bodhidharma and formed Ch'an, which became established in Japan from the 12th century as *Zen Buddhism*. Zen emphasizes silent meditation with sudden interruptions from a master to encourage awakening of the mind. Japan also has the lay organization *Sōka Gakkai* (Value Creation Society), founded 1930, which equates absolute faith with immediate material benefit; by the 1980s it was followed by more than 7 million households.

Esoteric, Tantric, or Diamond Buddhism became popular in Tibet and Japan, and holds that enlightenment is already within the disciple and with the proper guidance, (that is privately passed on by a master) can be realized.

Christianity world religion derived from the teaching of Jesus in the first third of the 1st century, with a present-day membership of about 1 billion. It is divided into different groups or denominations which differ in some areas of belief and practice. Its main divisions are the Roman Catholic, Eastern Orthodox, and Protestant churches. There are approximately 1,833 million (1992) Christian believers worldwide.

beliefs Christianity is based on the belief that the man Jesus, born about 2000 years ago, is 'the Christ', the Son of God, and that his death and resurrection broke down the barrier that human sinfulness put between humanity and God. Christians believe in one God with three aspects or persons: God the Father, God the Son (Jesus), and God the Holy Spirit, who is the power of God working in the world. Christians believe in God the Creator, who came to Earth as Jesus, was crucified, resurrected three days after his death, appeared to his disciples, and then ascended into heaven.

Christians believe that Jesus is alive and present in the world as the Holy Spirit. The main commandments are to love God and to love one's neighbour as oneself, which, if followed successfully, lead to an afterlife in heaven.

divisions: Orthodox Church or *Eastern Orthodox Church* or *Greek Orthodox Church* a federation of self-governing Christian churches mainly found in E and SE Europe, Russia, and parts of Asia. The centre of worship is the Eucharist. There is a married clergy, except for bishops; the Immaculate Conception is not accepted. The highest rank in the church is that of Ecumenical Patriarch, or Bishop of Istanbul. There are approximately 135 million (1990) adherents.

The church's teaching is based on the Bible, and the Nicene Creed (as modified by the Council of Constantinople 381) is the only confession of faith used. The celebration of the Eucharist has changed little since the 6th century. The ritual is elaborate, and accompanied by singing in which both men and women take part, but no instrumental music is used. Besides the seven sacraments, the prayer book contains many other services for daily life. During the marriage service, the bride and groom are crowned.

Its adherents include Greeks, Russians, Romanians, Serbians, Bulgarians, Georgians, and Albanians. In the last 200 years the Orthodox Church has spread into China, Korea, Japan, and the USA, as well as among the people of Siberia and central Asia. Some of the churches were founded by the apostles and their disciples; all conduct services in their own languages and follow their own customs and traditions, but are in full communion with one another. There are many monasteries, for example Mount Athos in Greece, which has flourished since the 10th century. The senior church of Eastern Christendom is that of Constantinople (Istanbul).

Protestantism one of the main divisions of Christianity, which emerged from Roman Catholicism at the Reformation. The chief denominations are the Anglican Communion (Episcopalian in the USA), Baptists, Lutherans, Methodists, Pentecostals, and Presbyterians, with a total membership of about 327 million (1990).

Protestantism takes its name from the protest of Luther and his supporters at the Diet of Spires 1529 against the decision to reaffirm the edict of the Diet of Worms against the Reformation. The first conscious statement of Protestantism as a distinct movement was the Confession of Augsburg 1530. The chief characteristics of original Protestantism are the acceptance of the Bible as the only source of truth, the universal priesthood of all believers, and forgiveness of sins solely through faith in Jesus Christ. The Protestant church minimalises the liturgical aspects of Christianity and emphasizes the preaching and hearing of the word of God before sacramental faith and practice. The many interpretations of doctrine and practice are reflected in the various denominations. The ecumenical movement of the 20th century has unsuccessfully attempted to reunite various Protestant denominations and, to some extent, the Protestant churches and the Catholic church. During the last 20 years there has been a worldwide upsurge in Christianity taking place largely outside the established church.

Roman Catholicism one of the main divisions of the Christian religion, separate from the Eastern Orthodox Church from 1054, and headed by the pope. For history and beliefs, see Christianity. Membership is about 920 million (1990), concentrated in S Europe, Latin America, and the Philippines.

The Protestant churches separated from the Catholic with the Reformation in the 16th century, to which the Counter-Reformation was a response. An attempt to update Catholic doctrines in the late 19th century was condemned by Pope Pius X in 1907, and more recent moves have been rejected by John Paul II.

doctrine The focus of liturgical life is the Mass or Eucharist, and attendance is obligatory on Sundays and Feasts of Obligation such as Christmas or Easter. The Roman Catholic differs from the other Christian churches in that it acknowledges the supreme jurisdiction of the pope, infallible when he speaks *ex cathedra* ('from the throne'); in the doctrine of the Immaculate Conception (which states that the Virgin Mary, the mother of Jesus, was conceived without the original sin with which all other human beings are born); and in according a special place to the Virgin Mary.

organization Since the Second Vatican Council 1962–66, major changes have taken place. They include the use of vernacular or everyday language instead of Latin in the liturgy, and increased freedom amongst the religious and lay orders. The pope has an episcopal synod of 200 bishops elected by local hierarchies to collaborate in the government of the church. The priesthood is celibate and there is a strong emphasis on the monastic orders.

Confucianism the body of beliefs and practices that are based on the Chinese classics and supported by the authority of the philosopher Confucius (Kong Zi). The origin of things is seen in the union of **yin** and **yang**, the passive and active principles. Human relationships follow the patriarchal pattern. For more than 2,000 years Chinese political government, social organization, and individual conduct was shaped by Confucian principles. In 1912, Confucian philosophy, as a basis for government, was dropped by the state. There are approximately 8 million Confucian believers (1992) worldwide.

The writings on which Confucianism is based include the ideas of a group of traditional books edited by Confucius, as well as his own works, such as the *Analects*, and those of some of his pupils. The *I Ching* is included among the Confucianist texts.

doctrine Until 1912 the emperor of China was regarded as the father of his people, appointed by heaven to rule. The Superior Man was the ideal human and filial piety was the chief virtue. Accompanying a high morality was a kind of ancestor worship.

practices Under the emperor, sacrifices were offered to heaven and earth, the heavenly bodies, the imperial ancestors, various nature gods, and Confucius himself. These were abolished at the Revolution in 1912, but ancestor worship (better expressed as reverence and remembrance) remained a regular practice in the home.

Under communism Confucianism continued. The defence minister Lin Biao was associated with the religion, and although the communist leader Mao Zedong undertook an anti-Confucius campaign 1974–76, this was not pursued by the succeeding regime.

Hinduism religion originating in N India about 4,000 years ago, which is superficially and in some of its forms polytheistic, but has a concept of the supreme spirit, Brahman, above the many divine manifestations. These include the triad of chief gods (the Trimurti): Brahma, Vishnu, and Siva (creator, preserver, and destroyer). Central to Hinduism are the beliefs in reincarnation and karma; the oldest scriptures are the *Vedas*. Temple worship is almost universally observed and there are many festivals. There are approximately 732 million (1992) Hindus worldwide. Women are not regarded as the equals of men but should be treated with kindness and respect. Muslim influence in N India led to the veiling of women and the restriction of their movements from about the end of the 12th century.

roots Hindu beliefs originated in the Indus Valley civilization dating from about 4500 years ago. Much of the tradition that is now associated with Hinduism stems from the ritual and religion of the Aryans who invaded N India about 3000 years ago.

scriptures The *Veda* collection of hymns, compiled by the Aryans, was followed by the philosophical *Upanishads*, centring on the doctrine of Brahman, and the epics *Rāmāyana* and *Mahābhārata* (which includes the *Bhagavad-Gītā*), all from before the Christian era.

beliefs Hindu belief and ritual can vary greatly even between villages. Some deities achieve widespread popularity such as Krishna, Hanuman, Lakshmi, and Durga; others, more localised and specialised, are referred to particularly in times of sickness or need. Some deities manifest themselves in different incarnations or avatars such as Rama or Krishna: both avatars of the god Vishnu. Underlying this multi-faceted worship is the creative strength of Brahman, the Supreme Being. Hindus believe that all living things are part of Brahman: they are sparks of atman or divine life that transmute from one body to another, sometimes descending into the form of a plant or an insect, sometimes the body of a human. This is all according to its karma or past actions which are the cause of its sufferings or joy as it rises and falls in *samsara* (the endless cycle of birth and death). Humans have the opportunity, through knowledge and devotion, to break the karmic chain and achieve final liberation or moksha. The atman is then free to return to Brahman.

The creative force of the universe is recognised in the god Brahma, once he has brought the cosmos into being it is sustained by Vishnu and then annihilated by the god Shiva, only to be created once more by Brahma. Vishnu and Shiva are, respectively, the forces of light and darkness, preservation and destruction, with Brahma as the balancing force that enables the existence and interaction of life. The cosmos is seen as both real and an illusion (*maya*), since its reality is not lasting; the cosmos is itself personified as the goddess Maya.

practice Hinduism has a complex of rites and ceremonies performed within the framework of the *jati* or caste system under the supervision of the Brahman priests and teachers. In India, caste is traditionally derived from the four classes of early Hindu society: brahmans (priests), kshatriyas (nobles and warriors), vaisyas (traders and cultivators), and sudras (servants). A fifth class, the untouchables, regarded as polluting in its origins, remained (and still largely remains) on the edge of Hindu society. The Indian Constituent Assembly 1947 made discrimination against the Schedules Castes or Depressed Classes illegal, but strong prejudice continues.

Western influence The International Society for Krishna Consciousness (ISKON), the western organization of the Hare Krishna movement, was introduced to the west by Swami Prabhupada (1896–1977). Members are expected to lead ascetic lives. It is based on devotion to Krishna which includes study of the *Bhagavad-Gītā*, temple and home ritual, and the chanting of the name Hare (saviour) Krishna. Members are expected to avoid meat, eggs, alcohol, tea, coffee, drugs, and gambling. Sexual relationships should be for procreation within the bonds of marriage.

Islam religion founded in the Arabian peninsula in the early 7th century CE. It emphasizes the oneness of

God, his omnipotence, benificence, and inscrutability. The sacred book is the **Koran** of the prophet Muhammad, the Prophet or Messenger of Allah. There are two main Muslim sects: **Sunni** and **Shi'ite**. Other schools include **Sufism**, a mystical movement originating in the 8th century. There are over 1,025 million Muslims (1992) worldwide.

beliefs The fundamental beliefs of Islam are contained in the Adhan: 'I bear witness that there is no God but Allah and Muhammad is the Prophet of Allah.' Creation, Fall of Adam, angels and jinns, heaven and hell, Day of Judgment, God's predestination of good and evil, and the succession of scriptures revealed to the prophets, including Moses and Jesus, but of which the perfect, final form is the **Koran** or **Quran**, divided into 114 **suras** or chapters, said to have been divinely revealed to Muhammad; the original is said to be preserved beside the throne of Allah in heaven.

Islamic law Islam embodies a secular law (the **Shari'a** or 'Highway'), which is clarified for Shi'ites by reference to their own version of the **sunna**, 'practice' of the Prophet as transmitted by his companions and embodied in the Hadith; the Sunni sect also take into account *ijma'*, the endorsement by universal consent of practices and beliefs among the faithful. For the Sufi, the **Shari'a**, is the starting point on the 'Sufi Path' to self-enlightenment. A **mufti** is a legal expert who guides the courts in their interpretation. (In Turkey until the establishment of the republic 1924 the mufti had supreme spiritual authority.)

organization There is no organized church or priesthood, although Muhammad's descendants (the Hashim family) and popularly recognized holy men, mullahs, and ayatollahs are accorded respect.

observances The Shari'a includes the observances known as 'The Five Pillars of the Faith', which are binding on all adult believers. The observances include: *shahada* or profession of the faith; *salat* or worship five times a day facing the holy city of Mecca (the call to prayer is given by a muezzin, usually from the minaret or tower of a mosque); *zakat* or obligatory almsgiving; *saum* or fasting dawn to sunset through Ramadan (ninth month of the year, which varies with the calendar); and the *hajj* or pilgrimage to Mecca at least once in a lifetime.

history Islam began as a militant and missionary religion, and between 711 and 1492 spread east into India, west over N Africa, then north across Gibraltar into the Iberian peninsula. During the Middle Ages, Islamic scholars preserved ancient Greco-Roman learning, while the Dark Ages prevailed in Christian Europe. Islam was seen as an enemy of Christianity by European countries during the Crusades, and Christian states united against a Muslim nation as late as the Battle of Lepanto 1571. Driven from Europe, Islam remained established in N Africa and the Middle East.

Islam is a major force in the Arab world and is a focus for nationalism among the peoples of Soviet Central Asia. It is also a significant factor in Pakistan, Indonesia, Malaysia, and parts of Africa. It is the second largest religion in the UK. Since World War II there has been a resurgence of fundamentalist Islam Iran, Libya, Afghanistan, and elsewhere. In the UK 1987 the manifesto *The Muslim Voice* demanded

rights for Muslim views on education (such as single-sex teaching) and on the avoidance of dancing, mixed bathing, and sex education.

divisions: Shi'ite or **Shiah** member of a sect of Islam who believe that Ali was Muhammad's first true successor. The term Shi'ite originally referred to shi'a ('the partisans') of Ali. They are doctrinally opposed to the Sunni Muslims. They developed their own law differing only in minor directions, such as inheritance and the status of women. Holy men have greater authority in the Shi'ite sect than in the Sunni sect. They are prominent in Iran, the Lebanon, and Indo-Pakistan, and are also found in Iraq, Bahrain, and the eastern province of Saudi Arabia. In the aftermath of the Gulf War 1991, many thousands of Shi'ites in Iraq were forced to take refuge in the marshes of S Iraq, after unsuccessfully rebelling against Saddam Hussein. Shi'ite sacred shrines were desecrated and atrocities committed by the armed forces on civilians. There are approximately 129 million Shi'ites (1990) worldwide.

Breakaway sub-sects include the **Alawite** sect, to which the ruling party in Syria belongs; the **Ismaili** sect, with the Aga Khan IV (1936–) as its spiritual head; and the Baha'i religion founded from a Muslim splinter group.

Sufism a mystical movement of Islam which originated in the 8th century. Sufis believe that deep intuition is the only real guide to knowledge. The movement has a strong strain of asceticism. The name derives from the *suf*, a rough woollen robe worn as an indication of disregard for material things. There are a number of groups or brotherhoods within Sufism, each with its own method of meditative practice, one of which is the whirling dance of the dervishes.

Sunni a member of the larger of the two main sects of Islam. Sunni Muslims believe that the first three caliphs were all legitimate successors of the prophet Muhammad, and that guidance on belief and life should come from the Koran and the Hadith, and from the Shari'a, not from a human authority or spiritual leader. Imams in Sunni Islam are educated lay teachers of the faith and prayer leaders. The name derives from the *Sunna*, Arabic 'code of behaviour', the body of traditional law evolved from the teaching and acts of Muhammad. There are approximately 690 million (1990) Sunni Muslims worldwide.

Jainism ancient Indian religion, sometimes regarded as an offshoot of Hinduism. Jains believe that non-injury to living beings is the highest religion, and their code of ethics is based on sympathy and compassion for all forms of life. They also believe in karma. In Jainism there is no deity and, like Buddhism, it is a monastic, ascetic religion. There are two main sects: the Digambaras and the Swetambaras. Jainism practises the most extreme form of non-violence (*ahimsā*) of all Indian sects, and influenced the philosophy of Mahātmā Gāndhī. Jains number approximately 4 million (1992); there are Jain communities throughout the world but the majority live in India.

Jainism's sacred books record the teachings of Mahavira (*c.* 540–468 BCE), the last in a line of 24 great masters called Tirthankaras (or *jinas*, 'those who overcome'). Mahavira was born in Vessali (now Bihar), E India. He became an ascetic at the age of 30, achieved enlightenment at 42, and preached for 30 years.

During the 3rd century BCE two divisions arose regarding the extent of austerities. The Digambaras ('sky-clad') believe that enlightenment can only occur when all possessions have been given up, including clothes, and that it can only be achieved when a soul is born into a human male body. Monks of this sect go naked on the final stages of their spiritual path. The Swetambaras ('white-clad') believe that both human sexes can achieve enlightenment and that nakedness is not a prerequisite. Jain derives its name from ancient prophets known as jinas ('those who overcome').

Judaism the religion of the ancient Hebrews and their descendents the Jews, based, according to the Old Testament, on a covenant between God and Abraham about 2000 BCE, and the renewal of the covenant with Moses about 1200 BCE. It rests on the concept of one eternal, invisible God, whose will is revealed in the *Torah* and who has a special relationship with the Jewish people. The Torah comprises the first five books of the Bible (the Pentateuch), which contains the history, laws, and guide to life for correct behaviour. Besides those living in Israel, there are large Jewish populations today in the USA, the ex-USSR, the UK and Commonwealth nations, and in Jewish communities throughout the world. There are approximately 18 million Jews (1992), with about 9 million in the Americas, 5 million in Europe, and 4 million in Asia, Africa, and the Pacific.

scriptures The *Talmud* combines the *Mishna*, rabbinical commentary on the law handed down orally from CE 70 and put in writing about 200, and the *Gemara*, legal discussions in the schools of Palestine and Babylon from the 3rd and 4th centuries. The *Haggadah* is a part of the Talmud dealing with stories of heroes. The *Midrash* is a collection of commentaries on the scriptures written 400–1200, mainly in Palestine. Along with the *Torah* they are regarded as authoritative sources of Jewish ritual, worship, and practice.

observances The *synagogue* (in US non-Orthodox usage *temple*) is the local building for congregational worship (originally simply the place where the Torah was read and expounded); its characteristic feature is the Ark, the enclosure where the Torah scrolls are kept. *Rabbis* are ordained teachers schooled in the Jewish law and ritual who act as spiritual leaders and pastors of their communities; some devote themselves to study. Religious practices include: circumcision, daily services in Hebrew, observance of the *Sabbath* (sunset on Friday to sunset Saturday) as a day of rest, and, among Orthodox Jews, strict dietary laws. High Holy days include *Rosh Hashanah* marking the Jewish New Year (first new moon after the autumn equinox) and, a week later, the religious fast *Yom Kippur* (Day of Atonement). Other holidays are celebrated throughout the year to commemorate various events of Biblical history.

history In the late Middle Ages when Europe and Western Asia were divided into Christian and Islamic countries, the Jewish people also found itself divided into two main groups. Jews in central and eastern Europe, namely in Germany and Poland, were called *Ashkenazi*. *Sefardic* Jews can trace their tradition back to the Mediterranean countries, particularly Spain and Portugal under Muslim rule. When they were expelled in 1492 they settled in north Africa, the Levant, the Far East, and northern Europe. The two traditions differ in a number of ritual and cultural ways but their theology and basic Jewish practice is the same. The Hassidic sects of eastern Europe and some north African and Oriental countries also differ from other groups in their rites but they, too, maintain the concept of divine authority.

divisions In the 19th and early 20th centuries there was a move by some Jewish groups away from traditional or orthodox observances. This trend gave rise to a number of groups within Judaism. *Orthodox Jews*, who form the majority, assert the supreme authority of the Torah, adhere to all the traditions of Judaism, including the strict dietary laws and the segregation of women in the synagogue. *Reform Judaism* rejects the idea that Jews are the chosen people, has a liberal interpretation of the dietary laws, and takes a critical attitude toward the Torah. *Conservative Judaism* is a compromise between Orthodox and Reform in its acceptance of the traditional law, making some allowances for modern conditions, although its services and ceremonies are closer to Orthodox than to Reform. *Liberal Judaism*, or *Reconstructionism*, goes further than Reform in attempting to adapt Judaism to the needs of the modern world and to interpret Torah in the light of current scholarship. In all the groups except Orthodox, women are not segregated in the synagogue, and there are female rabbis in both Reform and Liberal Judaism. In the 20th century many people who call themselves Jews prefer to identify Judaism with a historical and cultural tradition rather than with strict religious observance, and a contemporary debate (complicated by the history of non-Jewish attitudes towards Jews) centres on the question of how to define a Jew. As in other religions, fundamentalist movements have emerged, for example, Gush Emunim.

North American indigenous religions these form a wide variety, but have some features in common, especially a belief that everything in nature is alive and contains powerful forces which can be helpful or harmful to humans. If the forces are to be helpful, they must be treated with respect, and so hunting and other activities require ritual and preparation. Certain people are believed to be in contact with or possessed by the spirit world and so to have special powers; but each individual can also seek power and vision through ordeals and fasting.

Shinto the indigenous religion of Japan. It combines an empathetic oneness with natural forces and loyalty to the reigning dynasty as descendants of the Sun goddess, Amaterasu-Omikami. Traditional Shinto followers stressed obedience and devotion to the emperor, and an aggressive nationalistic aspect was developed by the Meiji rulers. Today Shinto has discarded these aspects. There are about 3.2 million (1992) adherents worldwide.

Shinto is the Chinese transliteration of the Japanese *Kami-no-Michi*. Shinto ceremonies appeal to the Kami, the mysterious forces of nature manifest in topographical features such as mountains, trees, stones, springs, and caves. Shinto focuses on purity, devotion, and sincerity; aberrations can be cleansed through purification rituals. In addition, purification procedures make the worshipper presentable and acceptable when making requests before the Kami.

Shinto's holiest shrine is at Ise, near Kyoto, where in the temple of the Sun Goddess is preserved the mirror that she is supposed to have given to Jimmu, the first emperor, in the 7th century BCE. Sectarian Shinto consists of 130 sects; the sects are officially recognized but not state-supported (as was state Shinto until its disestablishment after World War II and Emperor Hirohito's disavowal of his divinity 1946).

There is no Shinto philosophical literature although there are texts on mythologies, ceremonial and administrative procedures, religious laws, and chronicles or ruling families and temple construction.

Sikhism religion professed by 14 million Indians, living mainly in the Punjab. Sikhism was founded by Nanak (1469–c. 1539). Sikhs believe in a single God who is the immortal creator of the universe and who has never been incarnate in any form, and in the equality of all human beings; Sikhism is strongly opposed to caste divisions. There are approximately 18 million (1992) adherents worldwide.

Their holy book is the *Guru Granth Sahib*. Guru Gobind Singh (1666–1708) instituted the *Khanda-di-Pahul*, (the Baptism of the Sword), and established the *Khalsa* ('pure'), the company of the faithful. The Khalsa wear the five Ks: *kes*, long hair; *kangha*, a comb; *kirpan*, a sword; *kachh*, short trousers; and *kara*, a steel bracelet. Sikh men take the last name 'Singh' ('lion') and women 'Kaur' ('princess').

beliefs Human beings can make themselves ready to find God by prayer and meditation but can achieve closeness to God only as a result of God's *nadar* (grace). Sikhs believe in reincarnation and that the ten human gurus were teachers through whom the spirit of Guru Nanak was passed on to live today in the *Guru Granth Sahib* and the Khalsa.

practice Sikhs do not have a specific holy day, but hold their main services on the day of rest of the country in which they are living. Daily prayer is important in Sikhism, and the gurdwara functions as a social as well as religious centre; it contains a kitchen, the *langar*, where all, male and female, Sikh and non-Sikh, may eat together as equals. Sikh women take the same role as men in religious observances, for example, in reading from the *Guru Granth Sahib* at the gurdwara. Festivals in honour of the ten human gurus include a complete reading of the *Guru Granth Sahib*; Sikhs also celebrate at the time of some of the major Hindu festivals, but their emphasis is on aspects of Sikh belief and the example of the gurus. Sikhs avoid the use of all nonmedicinal drugs and, in particular, tobacco.

history On Nanak's death he was followed as guru by a succession of leaders who converted the Sikhs (the word means 'disciple') into a military confraternity which established itself as a political power. The last of the gurus, Guru Gobind Singh, instituted the *Khanda-di-Pahul* ('baptism of the sword') and established the Khalsa. Gobind Singh was assassinated by a Muslim 1708, and since then the *Guru Granth Sahib* has taken the place of a leader.

Upon the partition of India many Sikhs migrated from W to E Punjab, and in 1966 the efforts of Sant Fateh Singh (c. 1911–1972) led to the creation of a Sikh state within India by partition of the Punjab. However, the Akali separatist movement agitates for a completely independent Sikh state, Khalistan, and a revival of fundamentalist belief and was headed from 1978 by Sant Jarnail Singh Bhindranwale (1947–1984), killed in the siege of the Golden Temple, Amritsar. In retaliation for this, the Indian prime minister Indira Gandhi was assassinated in Oct of the same year by her Sikh bodyguards. Heavy rioting followed, in which 1,000 Sikhs were killed. Mrs Gandhi's successor, Rajiv Gandhi, reached an agreement for the election of a popular government in the Punjab and for state representatives to the Indian parliament with the moderate Sikh leader Sant Harchand Singh Longowal, who was himself killed 1985 by Sikh extremists.

South American indigenous religions religious beliefs and practice are diverse and since early Indian contact with whites there has been some reconciliation between Christian and local belief, and also the emergence of new religious movements. Many of the local religions have the concept of a supreme religious force or god, but this force is often so remote or great that it is not worshipped directly. There are many powerful spirits, including souls of the ancestors, that inhabit and influence the natural environment and the lives of humans. To maintain harmony with the forest, rivers, or animals, these spirits are respected and frequently associated with creation myths or as the harbingers of fortune or suffering, and as such are not hunted – for example, the anaconda snake amongst the Sarema people of the Amazonian rainforest.

Taoism Chinese philosophical system, traditionally founded by the Chinese philosopher Lao Zi 6th century BCE. He is also attributed authorship of the scriptures, *Tao Te Ching*, which were apparently compiled 3rd century BCE. The 'tao' or 'way' denotes the hidden principle of the universe, and less stress is laid on good deeds than on harmonious interaction with the environment, which automatically ensures right behaviour. The second major work is that of Zhuangzi (c. 389–286 BCE), *The Way of Zhuangzi*. The magical side of Taoism is illustrated by the *I Ching* or *Book of Changes*, a book of divination. There are approximately 190 million (1990) Taoists worldwide.

beliefs The universe is believed to be kept in balance by the opposing forces of yin and yang that operate in dynamic tension between themselves. Yin is female and watery: the force in the moon and rain which reached its peak in the winter; yang is masculine and solid: the force in the sun and earth which reaches its peak in the summer. The interaction of yin and yang is believed to shape all life.

This magical, ritualistic aspect of Taoism developed from the 2nd century CE and was largely responsible for its popular growth; it stresses physical immortality, which was attempted by means ranging from dietary regulation and fasting to alchemy. By the 3rd century, worship of gods had begun to appear, including that of the stove god Tsao Chun. From the 4th century, rivalry between Taoists and Mahāyāna Buddhists was strong in China, leading to persecution of one religion by the other; this was resolved by mutual assimilation, and Taoism developed monastic communities similar to those of the Buddhists.

Taoist texts record the tradition of mental and physical discipline, and methods to use in healing, exorcism, and the quest for immortality.

Zoroastrianism pre-Islamic Persian religion founded by the Persian prophet Zarathustra or Zoroaster (Greek), and still practised by the Parsees in India. The *Zendavesta* are the sacred scriptures of the faith. The theology is dualistic, *Ahura Mazda* or *Ormuzd* (the good God) being perpetually in conflict with *Ahriman* (the evil God), but the former is assured of eventual victory. There are approximately 150,000 (1990) adherents worldwide.

beliefs Humanity has been given free will to choose between the two powers, thus rendering believers responsible for their fate after death in heaven or hell. Moral and physical purity is central to all aspects of Zoroastrianism *yasna* or worship: since life and work are part of worship, there should be purity of action. Fire is considered sacred, and Ahura Mazda believed to be present when the ritual flame is worshipped at home or in the temple. It is believed that there will be a second universal judgement at *Frashokereti*, a time when the dead will be raised and the world cleansed of unnatural impurity.

The Parsee community in Bombay is now the main centre of Zoroastrianism, but since conversion is generally considered impossible, the numbers in India have been steadily decreasing at the rate of 10% per decade since 1947. Parsee groups, mainly in Delhi and outside India have been pushing for the acceptance of converts, but the concern of the majority in Bombay is that their religious and cultural heritage will be lost.

Religious Movements

Baha'i movement founded in 19th century Persia by a Muslim splinter group, Babis. It evolved into the Baha'i religion under the leadership of Baha'ullah. His message in essence was that all great religious leaders are manifestations of the unknowable God and all scriptures are sacred. There is no priesthood: all Baha'is are expected to teach, and to work towards world unification. There are about 4.5 million (1990) Baha'is worldwide.

Jehovah's Witness member of a religious organization originating in the USA 1872 under Charles Taze Russell (1852–1916). Jehovah's Witnesses attach great importance to Christ's second coming, which Russell predicted would occur 1914, and which Witnesses still believe is imminent. All Witnesses are expected to take part in house-to-house preaching; there are no clergy. There are approximately 6.75 million (1990) adherents worldwide.

Mormon or *Latter-day Saint* member of a Christian sect, the *Church of Jesus Christ of Latter-day Saints*, founded at Fayette, New York, in 1830 by Joseph Smith. According to Smith, Mormon was an ancient prophet in North America whose *Book of Mormon*, of which Smith claimed divine revelation, is accepted by Mormons as part of the Christian scriptures. In the 19th century the faction led by Brigham Young was polygamous. It is a missionary church with headquarters in Utah and a worldwide membership of about 5 million.

Rajneesh meditation meditation based on the teachings of the Indian Shree Rajneesh (born Chaadra Mohan Jain), established in the early 1970s. Until 1989 he called himself *Bhagwan* (Hindi 'God'). His followers, who number about half a million worldwide, regard themselves as Sannyas, or Hindu ascetics; they wear orange robes and carry a string of prayer beads. They are not expected to observe any specific prohibitions but to be guided by their instincts.

Rastafarianism religion originating in the West Indies, based on the ideas of Marcus Garvey, who called on black people to return to Africa and set up a black-governed country there. When Haile Selassie (*Ras Tafari*, 'Lion of Judah') was crowned emperor of Ethiopia 1930, this was seen as a fulfilment of prophecy and Rastafarians acknowledged him as the Messiah, the incarnation of God (*Jah*). The use of ganja (marijuana) is a sacrament. There are no churches. There were about one million Rastafarians by 1990.

Scientology (Latin *scire* 'to know' and Greek *logos* 'branch of learning') an 'applied religious philosophy' based on dianetics, founded in California in 1954 by L Ron Hubbard as the *Church of Scientology*. Through a form of psychotherapy it claims to 'increase man's spiritual awareness', but its methods of recruiting and retaining converts have met criticism. Its headquarters from 1959 have been in Sussex, England.

Seventh Day Adventist, often called an *Adventist*. A member of the Protestant religious sect of the same name. It originated in the US in the fervent expectation of Christ's Second Coming, or advent, that swept across New York State following William Miller's prophecy that Christ would return on Oct 22, 1844. When this failed to come to pass, a number of Millerites, as his followers were called, reinterpreted his prophetic speculations and continued to maintain that the millennium was imminent. Adventists observe Saturday as the Sabbath and emphasize healing, temperance, and diet; many are vegetarians. The sect has about 500,000 members in the US.

transcendental meditation (TM) technique of focusing the mind, based in part on Hindu meditation. Meditators are given a *mantra* (a special word or phrase) to repeat over and over to themselves; such meditation is believed to benefit the practitioner by relieving stress and inducing a feeling of well-being and relaxation. It was introduced to the West by Maharishi Mahesh Yogi and popularized by the Beatles in the late 1960s.

Unification Church or *Moonies* church founded in Korea 1954 by the Reverend Sun Myung Moon. The theology unites Christian and Taoist ideas and is based on Moon's book *Divine Principle*, which teaches that the original purpose of creation was to set up a perfect family, in a perfect relationship with God. The church has met with criticism over its recruiting methods and use of finances. The number of members (often called 'moonies') is about 200,000 worldwide.

Unitarianism a Christian denomination that rejects the orthodox doctrine of the Trinity and gives a pre-eminent position to Jesus as a religious teacher, while denying his deity. Unitarians believe in individual conscience and reason as a guide to right action, rejecting the doctrines of original sin, the atonement, and eternal punishment. There are approximately 750,000 adherents (1990) worldwide.

Rites of Passage

Most religions mark certain important stages in a person's life, such as birth, initiation, marriage, and death, by special ceremonies or rites of passage. These rituals provide a way of publicly recognizing a change of status; they are also a time for the whole community to reaffirm its faith.

Birth rites Birth is often a time of rejoicing, but it is also a time of new responsibility. The rituals associated with birth mark the child's entrance into a new community and the adult's commitment to that child.

Hindu birth rites begin with the choice of a suitable day for conception, and continue through pregnancy; the mother-to-be must avoid certain foods and recite verses from the Hindu holy books. When the baby is born, there are a number of further ceremonies including naming the child, the calculation of a horoscope, and the inscription of the word 'aum' (the elemental sound of the universe) in honey on the child's tongue. The last of these ceremonies, the shaving of the child's hair, may take place up to two years after the birth. Hindus believe that these ceremonies will help the child towards a better rebirth.

Sikh birth rites Sikhs believe that the first words a child should hear are those of the Mool Mantra, the beginning of the Sikh holy book, and so, as soon as the baby is born, it is washed and the words of the Mool Mantra whispered into its ear. A few weeks later the child is taken to the gurdwara, the Sikh place of worship, to be named. The initial of the name is chosen by opening the *Guru Granth Sahib* at random and choosing the first letter of the hymn on the left hand page.

Muslim birth rites the first words which a Muslim baby will hear are those of the call to prayer, which is used to call Muslims to the mosque or place of worship each day; these words, which contain the basic beliefs of Islam, are whispered into its ears. Seven days later, the child is named. This ceremony involves the shaving of the baby's head. If the child is a boy, he will also be circumcised at this time, to recall Abraham and his son Ismail.

Jewish birth rites the surgical operation of *circumcision* consists of the removal of a small part of the foreskin. All Jewish boys must be circumcised on the eighth day after birth, as long as health permits. During circumcision a prayer is said which recalls the covenant or agreement God made with Abraham and the ceremony marks the boy's entry into this covenant. If the child is a girl, her name is announced in the synagogue (the Jewish place of worship) by the father on the first Sabbath after her birth.

Christian birth rites universal in the Christian church from its beginning has been the religious initiation rite of *baptism* (Greek 'to dip'), involving immersion in or sprinkling with water. In the baptismal ceremony, sponsors or godparents make vows on behalf of the child which are renewed by the child at confirmation. Baptism was originally administered to adults by immersion, and infant baptism has been common only since the 6th century. In some of the Protestant churches, adults are still baptized by immersion in a pool of water. The immersion symbolizes death and new life.

Chinese birth rites Chinese babies are not named for the first month after birth; then the Full Month ceremony is held, with special foods, including red eggs which are symbols of luck and new life. The name given to the baby is a nickname designed to convince any malevolent spirits that the child is not worth stealing.

Initiation rites Initiation is a passage into full membership of a group, whether religious or social. It gives the individual both rights and responsibilities.

Sikh initiation rites the tenth guru of Sikhism, Guru Gobind Singh, set up a brotherhood of dedicated Sikhs, the Khalsa; any sufficiently mature and dedicated Sikh may apply to join the Khalsa. The ceremony is conducted by five members of the Khalsa in the presence of the *Guru Granth Sahib*, the Sikh holy book; it involves special prayers, the sharing of karah parshad (a sweet mixture) to symbolize the equality of Sikhs, and the drinking and sprinkling of amrit (sugar and water). Those initiated in the Khalsa should always wear five things known as the Five K's: uncut hair; a steel bracelet; a short sword; a comb; and kaccha, a type of shorts.

Jewish initiation is marked by the *bar mitzvah* (Hebrew 'son of the commandment'), initiation of a boy at the age of 13 into the adult Jewish community; less common is the bat mitzvah for girls. In the synagogue, the boy says a special bar mitzvah prayer promising to keep God's commandments, and accept responsibility for his actions before God. He then reads a passage from the Torah in the synagogue on the Sabbath. After this, he is regarded as a full member of the congregation.

Christian initiation is marked by *confirmation*, a rite by which a previously baptized person is admitted to full membership of the Christian church.

It consists of the laying on of hands by a bishop in order that the confirmed person may receive the gift of the Holy Spirit, the third aspect of the Trinity. Among Anglicans, the rite is deferred until the child is able to comprehend the fundamental beliefs of Christian doctrine.

Marriage rites Marriage involves not only a change in status for the two people concerned, but also a new set of relationships for their families and the probability of children. In many cultures the choice of marriage partner is made by the parents, though the participants usually have some say in the matter.

Hindu marriage rites Hindu weddings may take place at the bride's home or in a temple. The bride usually wears a red sari and her hands and feet are painted with patterns in henna, an orange dye. Offerings are made before a sacred fire and prayers said; the bride and groom take seven steps around the fire, which symbolize food, strength, wealth, good fortune, children, the seasons, and everlasting friendship.

Sikh wedding rites a Sikh wedding may be held anywhere, as long as the *Guru Granth Sahib* is present. During the ceremony, the couple show their assent to the marriage by bowing to the holy book. The couple walk together round the *Guru Granth Sahib* four times as a hymn written by the fourth Guru is sung: this hymn contains all the basic teachings of Sikhism.

Jewish wedding rites the ceremony usually takes place in the synagogue, the place of worship. The bride and groom, with their parents, stand under a canopy or chupah. Blessings are recited by the rabbi, the religious leader, and the groom gives the bride a ring. The couple are now legally married and the *ketubah* or marriage contract, is read out. At the end of the ceremony the groom steps on and shatters a glass as a reminder, amidst the happiness, of the destruction of the Temple at Jerusalem.

Christian marriage rites Christian marriages are usually celebrated at the place of worship (church or chapel). The groom is accompanied by a helper, or best man, while the bride is escorted by her father, who officially 'gives' her to her new husband, and by attendants (bridesmaids). The couple make promises to love, honour and care for each other, and exchange rings.

Muslim marriage rites Muslim weddings may take place in the bride's home or in the place of worship, the mosque. The bride and groom are normally in separate rooms throughout the short ceremony. There is often a reading from the Koran, and a talk on the duties of marriage. The couple must both consent to the marriage, and rings are exchanged.

Chinese wedding rites in Chinese weddings, the concept of yin and yang, the two complementary forces which make up the universe, plays a prominent part; among their other attributes yin is seen as female and yang as male. There is a series of rituals leading up to the wedding, including the giving of gifts, an exchange of horoscopes (a prediction of a person's fortune), and a payment to the bride's family. The ceremony itself involves offerings and prayers to the bridegroom's ancestors and the household gods.

Death rites Death rites fulfil three main purposes: to comfort and strengthen the dying person, to comfort those left behind, and to ensure the best possible outcome for the deceased person in the next world or next birth. In several religions, such as Sikhism, Judaism, and Islam, people are encouraged to speak a declaration of faith before death, and Sikhs and Muslims read from their holy books to the dying person. Some religions discourage mourning, because they feel that death should not be regarded as a tragedy for the individual, especially after a long life, while others, such as Judaism, set time aside for the family to grieve. There are many ways in which religions try to help the deceased in the afterlife. The Chinese offer practical help: since the afterlife may have resemblances to this life, replicas of useful goods, cars, washing machines, and money, are burnt at the funeral for the use of the deceased who will, with the other ancestors, now watch over the family.

Holy Books

Many religions have a book or books which are regarded as holy or as providing special wisdom. These books are treated with great reverence and copies may be kept in a place particularly set aside or have specific ceremonies associated with them. Such books are sometimes referred to as scriptures.

Buddhist Buddhist literature is divided into two groups, the teachings and discourses of the Buddha himself, and the teachings of saints, sages, and scholars. Since Buddhism was transmitted by word of mouth for about five hundred years after the death of the Buddha, it is difficult to say which of these writings contain the original word of the Buddha and which are later additions. One of the fundamental differences between the Hīnayāna and Mahāyāna schools is the attribution of the Buddha's word to the various texts. The Buddha's words are assembled in the *Tipitaka* or *Tripitaka* (three baskets) containing sutra (discourses), vinaya (rules of discipline), abhidharma (further knowledge). Important texts in this group include the commentaries on the Buddha's word by Buddhagosa in the Theravāda tradition and Nagarjuna and Asanga in the early Indian Mahāyāna tradition.

Chinese Since Chinese religion is a mixture of Buddhism, Confucianism and Taoism, the Chinese generally respect the writings of all three. The main text of Taoism is the *Tao Te Ching*, attributed to the traditional founder of Taoism, Lao Zi, although its date and authorship are obscure. Confucianism's main writings are those of Confucius himself, especially the *Analects* or 'selected sayings'. Confucius is traditionally the author of the Five Classics: *Su Ching*, *Shi Ching*, *Li Chi*, *I Ching*, and the annals of *Lu*.

Christian The Christian *Bible* (Greek *ta biblia* 'the books') consists of the *Old Testament*, the first five books of the Hebrew Bible, and the *New Testament*, originally written in Greek, containing the Gospels, Acts of the Apostles, Letters, and Revelation. It is believed that the books of the New Testament were written within a hundred years of the death of Christ, and from the 4th century were recognized by the Christian church as canonical. Early church history is recorded in the *Acts of the Apostles*, the life of Jesus Christ in the four *Gospels*, the epistles are the letters of St Paul and other Christian leaders to fellow Christians, and the New Testament closes with the *Book of Revelation* which records St John's vision of the end of time and Christ's second coming.

Hindu *Veda* (Sanskrit, divine knowledge). The most sacred of the Hindu scriptures, hymns written in an old form of Sanskrit; the oldest may date from 1500 or 2000 BCE. The four main collections are: the Rigveda (hymns and praises); Yajurveda (prayers and sacrificial formulae); Sāmaveda (hymns); and Atharvaveda, (spells, charms, and chants).

Rāmāyana Hindu epic of 24,000 stanzas written in Sanskrit. It was assembled in its received form between the 1st century BCE and 1st century CE. The story reveals how Rama, an incarnation of the god Vishnu, and his friend Hanuman (the monkey chieftain) strive to recover Rama's wife, Sita, abducted by

The Bible

The Books of the Old Testament

Name of book	Chapters	Date written
The Pentateuch or the Five Books of Moses		
Genesis	50	mid 8th–century BC
Exodus	40	950–586 BC
Leviticus	27	mid 7th–century BC
Numbers	36	850–650 BC
Deuteronomy	34	mid–7th century BC
Joshua	24	c. 550 BC
Judges	21	c. 550 BC
Ruth	4	end 3rd century BC
1 Samuel	31	c. 900 BC
2 Samuel	24	c. 900 BC
1 Kings	22	550–600 BC
2 Kings	25	550–600 BC
1 Chronicles	29	c. 300 BC
2 Chronicles	36	c. 300 BC
Ezra	10	c. 450 BC
Nehemiah	13	c. 450 BC
Esther	10	c. 200 BC
Job	42	600–400 BC
Psalms	150	6th–2nd century BC
Proverbs	31	350–150 BC
Ecclesiastes	12	c. 200 BC
Song of Solomon	8	3rd century BC
Isaiah	66	end 3rd century BC
Jeremiah	52	604 BC
Lamentations	5	586–536 BC
Ezekiel	48	6th century BC
Daniel	12	c. 166 BC
Hosea	14	c. 732 BC
Joel	3	c. 500 BC
Amos	9	775–750 BC
Obadiah	1	6th–3rd century BC
Jonah	4	600–200 BC
Micah	7	end 3rd century BC
Nahum	3	c. 626 BC
Habakkuk	3	c. 600 BC
Zephaniah	3	3rd century BC
Haggai	2	c. 520 BC
Zechariah	14	c. 520 BC
Malachi	4	c. 430 BC

The Books of the New Testament

Name of book	Chapters	Date written
The Gospels		
Matthew	28	before AD 70
Mark	16	before AD 70
Luke	24	AD 70–80
John	21	AD 90–100
The Acts	28	AD 70–80
Romans	16	AD 120
1 Corinthians	16	AD 57
2 Corinthians	13	AD 57
Galatians	6	AD 53
Ephesians	6	AD 140
Philippians	4	AD 63
Colossians	4	AD 140
1 Thessalonians	5	AD 50–54
2 Thessalonians	3	AD 50–54
1 Timothy	6	before AD 64
2 Timothy	4	before AD 64
Titus	3	before AD 64
Philemon	1	AD 60–62
Hebrews	13	AD 80–90
James	5	before AD 52
1 Peter	5	before AD 64
2 Peter	3	before AD 64
1 John	5	AD 90–100
2 John	1	AD 90–100
3 John	1	AD 90–100
Jude	1	AD 75–80
Revelation	22	AD 81–96

the demon king Ravana. It upholds the Hindu ideal of a relationship between a man and woman.

Mahābhārata Sanskrit ('great poem of the Bharatas') Hindu epic of 90,000 stanzas probably written between the 2nd century BCE and the end of the 1st century CE. With the Rāmāyana, it forms the two great epics of Hindu literature. The story is set on the Upper Ganges plain and deals with the fortunes of two rival families, the Kauravas and the Pandavas. It reveals the ethical values of ancient Hindu society and individual responsibility in particular. The central and most popular part is the *Bhagavad-Gītā* or *Song of the Blessed One*, a religious and philosophical poem delivered by Krishna to the hero Arjuna. The *Bhagavad-Gītā* is regarded as one of the essential Hindu religious texts.

Jain The Swetabaras' canon is the *Siddhanta* assembled in the 5th century CE which includes accounts of the monastic discipline and teachings of Mahavira. The Digambaras' canon is made of two early Pakrit texts (Indian vernacular language) supplemented by commentaries from later scholars. There is also a large body of literature, dating from the 8th century CE, including narratives, commentaries, and cosmologies on existing texts. This later material is generally accepted by both Jain groups.

Jewish The *Torah* contains the first five books of the Hebrew Bible and it is given absolute religious authority by orthodox Jews. As well as referring to the first five books of Moses, the *Torah* is sometimes used as a term for the whole Hebrew Bible. The First Five Books of Moses contain 613 laws covering social and religious customs and histories of the early patriarchs of the Jewish nation. The Hebrew Bible contains two further sections, the Prophets and the Writings.

The Oral Law, traditionally revealed to Moses on Mount Sinai alongside the Written Law, is codified in the Mishna which was compiled after the destruction of the Temple CE 70. Further debates and interpretations by rabbis on the Torah's law and guidance are recorded in the Gemara and Midrash. The combined texts of the Mishna, Gemara, and Midrash, together with later rabbinical commentaries, are recorded in the *Talmud*, the main compilation of traditional Jewish thought.

Muslim *Koran* more properly, Quran, though both are transliterations; the sacred book of Islam. Written in the purest Arabic, it contains 114 suras or chapters, and is stated to have been divinely revealed to the prophet Muhammad from Allah through the angel Jibra'el; the original is supposed to be preserved beside the throne of Allah in heaven.

Sikh The Sikh holy book is the *Guru Granth Sahib*, also known as the *Adi Granth* ('first book'). It is a collection of hymns by the Sikh gurus or teachers, as well as by Muslim and Hindu writers, which was compiled largely by the fifth guru, Guru Arjan, and completed by the tenth guru, Guru Gobind Singh. On the death of the tenth guru, the *Guru Granth Sahib* took over the role of teacher and leader of the Sikhs. Guidance is sought by opening the holy book at random and reading verses. Any copy of the *Guru Granth Sahib* must have a special room to itself; people entering the room must cover their heads and remove their shoes. All copies of the holy book are identical, having 1,430 pages, and written in Gurmukhi, the written form of Punjabi.

Religious Figures

Abraham *c.* 2300 BCE. in the Old Testament, founder of the Jewish nation. Jehovah promised him heirs and land for his people in Canaan (Israel), renamed him Abraham ('father of many nations'), and tested his faith by a command (later retracted) to sacrifice his son Isaac. Jehovah's promise to Abraham was fulfilled when the descendants of Abraham's grandson, Jacob, were led out of Egypt by Moses.

Abu Bakr or *Abu-Bekr* 573–634. 'Father of the virgin', name used by Abd-el-Ka'aba from about 618 when the prophet Muhammad married his daughter Ayesha. He was a close adviser to Muhammad in the period 622–32. On the prophet's death, he became the first caliph, adding Mesopotamia to the Muslim world and instigating expansion into Iraq and Syria.

Ali *c.* 598–660. 4th caliph of Islam. He was born in Mecca, the son of Abu Talib, uncle to the prophet Muhammad, who gave him his daughter Fatima in marriage. On Muhammad's death 632, Ali had a claim to succeed him, but this was not conceded until 656. After a stormy reign, he was assassinated. Around Ali's name the controversy has raged between the Sunni and the Shi'ites, the former denying his right to the caliphate and the latter supporting it.

Asoka lived *c.* 273–238 BCE. Indian emperor, and Buddhist convert from Hinduism. He issued edicts, carved on pillars and rock faces throughout his dominions, promoting wise government and the cultivation of moral virtues according to Buddhist teachings. Many still survive,and are amongst the oldest deciphered texts in India. In Patna there are the remains of a hall built by him.

Augustine, St ?–605. First archbishop of Canterbury, England. He was sent from Rome to convert England to Christianity by Pope Gregory I. He landed at Ebbsfleet in Kent 597, and soon after baptized Ethelbert, king of Kent, along with many of his subjects. He was consecrated bishop of the English at Arles in the same year, and appointed archbishop

601, establishing his see at Canterbury. Feast day 26 May.

Bodhidharma 6th century CE. Indian Buddhist and teacher. He entered China from S India about 520, and was the founder of the Ch'an school (Zen is the Japanese derivation). Ch'an focuses on contemplation leading to intuitive meditation, a direct pointing to and stilling of the human mind. In the 20th century, Zen has attracted many followers in the west.

Buddha 'enlightened one', title of Prince *Gautama Siddhārtha* *c.*563–483 BCE. Religious leader, founder of Buddhism, born at Lumbini in Nepal. At the age of 29, he left his wife and son and a life of luxury, to escape from the material burdens of existence. After six years of austerity he realized that asceticism, like overindulgence, was futile, and chose the middle way of meditation. He became enlightened under a bo or bodhi tree in Bihar, India. He began teaching at Varanasi, and founded the Sangha, or order of monks. He spent the rest of his life travelling around N India, and died at Kusinagara in Uttar Pradesh.

Confucius Latinized form of *K'ung Tzu*, 'Kong the master' 551–479 BCE. Chinese sage whose name is given to Confucianism. He devoted his life to relieving suffering among the poor through governmental and administrative reform. His emphasis on tradition and ethics attracted a growing number of pupils during his lifetime. *The Analects of Confucius*, a compilation of his teachings, was published after his death. Within three hundred years of the death of Confucius his teaching was adopted by the Chinese state, and remained so until 1912.

Ghazzali, al- 1058–1111. Muslim philosopher and one of the most celebrated Sufis (Muslim mystics). He was responsible for easing the conflict between the Sufi and the Ulama, a body of Muslim religious and legal scholars.

Gobind Singh 1666–1708. Indian religious leader, the tenth and last guru (teacher) of Sikhism, 1675–1708, and founder of the Sikh brotherhood known as the Khalsa. On his death, the Sikh holy book, the *Guru Granth Sahib*, replaced the line of human gurus as the teacher and guide of the Sikh community.

Jesus *c.* 4 BCE–CE 29 or 30. Hebrew preacher on whose teachings Christianity was founded. According to the accounts of his life in the four Gospels, he was born in Bethlehem, Palestine, son of God and the Virgin Mary, and brought up by Mary and her husband Joseph as a carpenter in Nazareth. After adult baptism, he gathered 12 disciples, but his preaching antagonized the Roman authorities and he was executed by crucifixion. Three days later there came reports of his resurrection and, later, his ascension to heaven.

Lao Zi or *Lao Tzu* *c.* 604–531 BCE. Chinese philosopher, commonly regarded as the founder of Taoism, with its emphasis on the Tao, the inevitable and harmonious way of the universe. Nothing certain is known of his life, and he is variously said to have lived in the 6th or the 4th century BCE. The *Tao Te Ching*, the Taoist scripture, is attributed to him but apparently dates from the 3rd century BCE.

Popes of the last 500 years

1492–1503	Alexander VI	1676–89	Innocent XI
1503	Pius III	1689–91	Alexander VIII
1503–13	Julius II	1691–1700	Innocent XII
1513–21	Leo X	1700–21	Clement XI
1522–3	Hadrian VI	1721–4	Innocent XIII
1523–34	Clement VII	1724–30	Benedict XIII
1534–49	Paul III	1730–40	Clement XII
1550–5	Julius III	1740–58	Benedict XIV
1555	Marcellus II	1758–69	Clement XIII
1555–9	Paul IV	1769–74	Clement XIV
1559–65	Pius IV	1775–99	Pius VI
1566–72	Pius V	1800–23	Pius VII
1572–85	Gregory XIII	1823–9	Leo XII
1585–90	Sixtus V	1829–30	Pius VIII
1590	Urban VII	1831–46	Gregory XVI
1590–1	Gregory XIV	1846–78	Pius IX
1591	Innocent IX	1878–1903	Leo XIII
1592–1605	Clement VIII	1903–14	Pius X
1605	Leo XI	1914–22	Benedict XV
1605–21	Paul V	1922–39	Pius XI
1621–3	Gregory XV	1939–58	Pius XII
1623–44	Urban VIII	1958–63	John XXIII
1644-55	Innocent X	1963–78	Paul VI
1655–67	Alexander VII	1978	John Paul I
1667–9	Clement IX	1978–	John Paul II
1670–6	Clement X		

Luther Martin 1483–1546. German Christian church reformer, a founder of Protestantism. While he was a priest at the University of Wittenberg, he wrote an attack on the sale of indulgences (remissions of punishment for sin) in 95 theses which he nailed to a church door 1517, in defiance of papal condemnation. The Holy Roman Emperor Charles V summoned him to the Diet of Worms 1521, where he refused to retract his objections. Originally intending reform, his protest led to schism, with the emergence, following the Augsburg Confession 1530, of a new Protestant church. Luther is regarded as the instigator of the Protestant revolution, and Lutherism is now the major religion of many north European countries including Germany, Sweden, and Denmark.

Mahavira c. 540–468 BCE. Indian teacher and scholar. He was born into the warrior-king caste in Vessili (now Bihar). He became an ascetic at 30, achieved enlightenment at 42, and preached for 30 years. He was last in a line of 24 Jain masters called *Tirthankaras* or jinas ('those who overcome').

Maimonides Moses (Moses Ben Maimon) 1135–1204. Jewish rabbi and philosopher, born in Córdoba, Spain. Known as one of the greatest Hebrew scholars, he attempted to reconcile faith and reason. He was author of the *Thirteen Principles of Faith*.

Moses c. 13th century BCE. Hebrew lawgiver and judge who led the Israelites out of Egypt to the promised land of Canaan. On Mount Sinai he claimed to have received from Jehovah the oral and written Law, including the *Ten Commandments* engraved on tablets of stone. The first five books of the Old Testament – in Judaism, the *Torah* – are ascribed to him.

Muhammad or *Mohammed*, *Mahomet* c. 570–632. Prophet of Islam, born in Mecca on the Arabian peninsula. He began his prophetic mission c. 610 CE

when it is believed he began to receive the revelations of the *Koran,* revealed to him by God (it was later written down by his followers), through the angel Jibra'el (Gabriel). He fled from persecution to the town now known as Medina in 622: the flight, *Hegira*, marks the beginning of the Islamic era.

Nanak 1469–c. 1539. Indian guru and founder of Sikhism, a religion based on the unity of God and the equality of all human beings. He was strongly opposed to caste divisions. He was the first of ten human gurus in the Sikh faith.

Paul, St c. 3–c. CE 68. Christian missionary and martyr; in the New Testament, one of the apostles and author of 13 epistles. He is said to have been converted by a vision on the road to Damascus. His emblems are a sword and a book; feast day 29 June.

Shankara 799–833. Hindu philosopher who wrote commentaries on some of the major Hindu scriptures, as well as hymns and essays on religious ideas. Shankara was responsible for the final form of the Advaita Vedanta school of Hindu philosophy, which teaches that Brahman, the supreme being, is all that exists in the universe, everything else is illusion. Shankara was fiercely opposed to Buddhism and may have influenced its decline in India.

Zoroaster or *Zarathustra* 6th century BCE. Persian prophet and religious teacher, founder of Zoroastrianism. Zoroaster believed that he had seen God, Ahura Mazda, in a vision. His first vision came at the age of 30 and, after initial rejection and violent attack, he converted King Vishtaspa. Subsequently, his teachings spread rapidly, becoming the official religion of the kingdom. Zoroastrianism was a dualistic theology: the god of absolute purity and goodness, Ahura Mazda, being opposed by the twin spirit of violence and death: Angra Mainyu. According to tradition, Zoroaster was murdered at the age of 70 while praying at the altar.

Holy Places

The concept of *pilgrimage*, a journey to sacred places inspired by religious devotion, is common to many religions. For Hindus the holy places include Benares and the purifying Ganges; for Buddhists, Bodhgaya, the site of the Buddha's enlightenment; the Tooth of the Buddha in Sri Lanka; and numerous temples and sacred mountains throughout China and south-east Asia; for the ancient Greeks, the shrines at Delphi, Ephesus, among others; for the Jews, the Western Wall at Jerusalem; and for Muslims, Mecca. Among Christians, pilgrimages were common by the second century, and as a direct result of the established necessity of making pilgrimages there arose the numerous hospices catering for pilgrims, the religious orders of knighthood, and the Crusades. The great centres of Christian pilgrimages have been, or are, Jerusalem, Rome, the tomb of St James of Compostella in Spain, the shrine of Becket at Canterbury, and the holy places at La Salette and Lourdes in France.

Amritsar city in the Punjab, India, founded 1577. It is the religious centre of the Sikhs and contains the Golden Temple and Guru Nanak University 1969, named after the first Sikh Guru.

Jerusalem ancient city of Palestine, which is a holy place for Jews, Christians, and Muslims. It was divided in 1948 between the new republic of Israel and Jordan. In 1950, the western New City was proclaimed as the Israeli capital, and following the Israeli capture of the eastern Old City in 1967 from the Jordanians, it was affirmed in 1980 that the united city was the country's capital, but the United Nations does not recognize the claim.

history by 1400 BCE Jerusalem was ruled by a king subject to Egypt, but *c.* 1000 BCE David, the second king of Israel, made it the capital of a united Jewish kingdom. It was captured by Nebuchadnezzar 586 BCE, who deported its population. Later conquerors include Alexander the Great and Pompey (63 BCE), and it was under Roman rule that Jesus Christ was executed. In 70 CE a Jewish revolt led to its complete destruction by Titus. It was first conquered by Islam in 637; was captured by Crusaders, Christians who were fighting the Muslims in Israel, 1099, and recaptured by Saladin 1187, to remain under almost unbroken Islamic rule until the British occupation of Palestine in 1917.

Notable buildings include the Church of the Holy Sepulchre (built 335), and the mosque of the Dome of the Rock. The latter was built on the site of Solomon's Temple, and the Western ('wailing') Wall, held sacred by Jews, is part of the walled platform on which the Temple once stood.

Temple the centre of Jewish national worship at Jerusalem. Three temples occupied the site: Solomon's Temple, which was destroyed by Nebuchadnezzar; Zerubbabel's Temple, built after the return from Babylon; and Herod's Temple, which was destroyed by the Romans in 70 CE. The Mosque of Omar occupies the site. The Wailing Wall is the surviving part of the western wall of the platform of the enclosure of the Temple of Herod, so-called by tourists because of the chanting style of the Jews in their prayers there. Under Jordanian rule Jews had no access to the place, but took this part of the city in the 1967 campaign.

Mecca city of Saudi Arabia, the holiest city of the Muslim world, where the Prophet was born. It stands in the desert, in a valley about 72 km/45 mi east of Jidda, its port on the Red Sea, with which it is linked by a motorway, and long before the time of Muhammad was a commercial centre, caravan junction, and place of pilgrimage. In the centre of Mecca is the Great Mosque, in whose courtyard is the Kaaba; it also contains the well Zam-Zam, associated by tradition with Ishmael, the son of Abraham, and his mother Hagar, and the Maqām Ibrāhīm, a holy stone believed to bear the imprint of Abraham's foot.

kaaba the oblong building in the quadrangle of the Great Mosque at Mecca into the south-east corner of which is built the black stone declared by Muhammad to have been given to Abraham by Gabriel, and devoutly revered by Muslim pilgrims. The name means chamber.

Medina city in Saudi Arabia, about 355 km/220 mi north of Mecca. To Muslims it is a holy city second only to Mecca, since Muhammad lived here for many years after he fled from Mecca, and died here. The Mosque of the Prophet is believed to contain Muhammad's tomb, and those of the caliphs or Muslim leaders Abu Bakr, Omar, and Fatima, Muhammad's daughter.

Varanasi or Benares Indian city on the sacred Ganges river in Uttar Pradesh. It is holy to Hindus with a 5 km/3 mi frontage of stairways (ghats), leading up from the river to innumerable streets, temples, and the 1,500 golden shrines. The ritual of purification is practised daily by thousands of devout Hindus, who bathe from the ghats in the sacred river. At the burning ghats, the ashes, following cremation, are scattered on the river, a ritual followed to ensure a favourable reincarnation.

Festivals

Buddhist festivals

Wesak the day of the Buddha's birth, enlightenment, and death. A large act of worship is held and gifts given to monks; captive animals may be freed.

Dhammacakka celebrates the preaching of the Buddha's first sermon. Visits are made to monasteries and gifts are given to the monks.

Bodhi Day Mahāyāna Buddhist celebration of the Buddha's enlightenment.

Chinese festivals

New Year time when the Kitchen God, whose picture is in every home, returns to heaven to report on the family's behaviour during the year. There are elaborate lion dances and fireworks, and vegetarian feasts are eaten.

Ching Ming a time for visiting ancestral tombs, making offerings and remembering the dead.

Dragon Boat Festival celebrates the story of a brave official who persuaded a harsh emperor to relent over his crippling taxation of the people by drowning himself. Races are held between boats carved to resemble dragons, in memory of the boat chase to save the official's body from being eaten by dragons and demons.

Moon Festival commemorates the story of a brave woman who defied her husband, a wicked king, to stop him obtaining immortality, and was carried off by the gods to live on the moon. The festival is held at the harvest full moon and the moon is greeted with incense, lanterns and feasting.

Winter Festival time of feasting to build up strength for the winter ahead.

Christian festivals

Epiphany annual festival (6 Jan) of the Christian church, celebrating the coming of the Magi or wise men to Bethlehem with gifts for the infant Christ, and symbolizing the manifestation of Christ to the world. It is the twelfth day after Christmas, and marks the end of the Christmas festivities. In many countries the night before, called *Twelfth Night*, is marked by the giving of gifts.

Shrove Tuesday the day before Ash Wednesday. The name comes from the Anglo-Saxon *scrifan*, to shrive, and in former times it was the time for confession before Lent. Another name for it is Pancake Tuesday; the pancakes are a survival of merry-making in anticipation of Lenten abstinence.

Ash Wednesday first day of Lent, the period in the Christian calendar leading up to Easter; in the Catholic church the foreheads of the congregation are marked with a cross in ash, as a sign of penitence.

Lent in the Christian church, the forty days' period of fasting which precedes Easter, beginning on Ash Wednesday, but omitting Sundays.

Palm Sunday the Sunday before Easter, and first day of Holy Week; so-called to commemorate Christ's entry into Jerusalem, when the crowd strewed palm leaves in his path.

Good Friday (probably a corruption of God's Friday). In the Christian church, the Friday before Easter, which is kept in memory of the Crucifixion (the death of Jesus).

Easter feast of the Christian church, commemorating the Resurrection of Christ. It usually falls around the time of the Jewish Passover since Christ's crucifixion coincided with the time of this festival. The English name derives from Eostre, Anglo-Saxon goddess of spring, who was honoured in April. Eggs are given at this time as a symbol of new life.

Whitsun celebrates the filling of the followers of Jesus with the Holy Spirit, which Christians believe to be the third aspect of God, after Jesus had returned to heaven. As the disciples went out and told everyone about Jesus, so at Whitsun many Christians go on processions around the parish boundaries.

Advent the time leading up to Christmas; a time of preparation for Christians.

Christmas day on which the birth of Christ is celebrated by Christians. Although the actual birth date is unknown, the choice of a date near the winter solstice owned much to missionary desire to facilitate conversion of pagans, for example in Britain 25 Dec had been kept as a festival long before the introduction of Christianity. Many of its customs also have a non-Christian origin.

Hindu festivals

Mahashivaratri Festival of Siva, who is celebrated as lord of the dance, dancing on the demon of ignorance.

Holi a harvest time festival in honour of Krishna, when bonfires are lit; people throw coloured water at each other and play games and tricks as a reminder of Krishna's mischievous behaviour.

Rama Naumi celebration of the Birth of Rama. An eight-day fast during which the Rāmāyana is recited; the fast is broken on the ninth day with fruit and nuts, and offerings are made to Rama.

Raksha Bandhan a family festival in which sisters present their brothers with a bracelet of thread to protect them from harm, in return for which the brothers promise to look after their sisters.

Janmashtami celebration of the birthday of Krishna. Children act out stories of Krishna, and a statue of the young Krishna is used in the celebrations.

Dusshera a festival (also known as Durga Puja) which lasts ten days; the great goddess Devi is worshipped in her many forms.

Divali a new year festival which honours Lakshmi, goddess of fortune. Lights are lit in every window.

Jewish festivals

Purim celebrates the story of Esther, a Jewish woman who risked her life to save her people from treacherous slaughter. The story is read from a scroll in the synagogue, and the congregation boo and hiss when the villain's name is read out. It is a time for noisy parties and merriment.

Passover (Pesach) festival which commemorates the escape from slavery in Egypt. A special meal, the seder meal, is eaten and the story of how the Jews were saved by God from this bondage is told.

Shavuot or Pentecost commemorates the giving of the ten commandments to Moses.

Rosh Hashanah the two-day festival at the start of the Jewish New Year (first new moon after the autumn equinox), a time for repentence and forgiveness. This reflective period is brought to a close nine days later at Yom Kippur. Rosh Hashanah begins on the first day of the month of Tishri (Sept–Oct), the seventh month of the Jewish year.

Yom Kippur (Day of Atonement) day of Jewish religious fast held on the tenth day of Tishri. Final forgiveness is sought for past deeds and the Kol Nidrei is sung in the synagogue to end the old vows of the past year and to prepare for the demands of the coming year. The festival ends with the blowing of the shofar, the ram's horn.

Succot the feast of Tabernacles (tents), a reminder of the time the Israelites spent wandering in the wilderness. Temporary homes of branches are built at the synagogue and sometimes at home.

Hanukkah celebrates the recapture and rededication of the Temple of Jerusalem by Judah Maccabee in 165 BCE. The festival lasts eight days; each day, a new candle is lit on a special candlestick or menorah.

Muslim festivals

The Muslim calendar is lunar, and correspondences with the Western calendar cannot be given; festivals fall 11–12 days earlier each year.

Lailat ul-Isra Wal Mi'raj celebrates Muhammad's night journey by horse to Jerusalem and up to heaven.

Lailat ul-Barah the night of forgiveness; a time to prepare for Ramadan.

Ramadan the ninth month of the Muslim year, throughout which a strict fast is observed during the hours of daylight.

Lailat ul-Qadr commemorates the night the Koran was first revealed to Muhammad.

Eid ul-Fitr the end of the fast of Ramadan. Gifts are given to charity, new clothes are worn and sweets are given.

Eid ul-Adha celebrates the faith of the prophet Abraham, who was prepared to sacrifice his son Ismail when Allah asked him to. Lamb is eaten and shared with the poor, as a reminder of the sheep which Allah provided as a sacrifice instead of Ismail.

Day of Hijra commemorates the journey of Muhammad from Mecca to Medina.

Sikh festivals

Hola Mohalla a three-day festival held at the time of the Hindu festival Holi. Sporting competitions and other tests of skill take place.

Religious festivals

Date	Festival	Religion	Event commemorated
6 Jan	Epiphany	Western Christian	coming of the Magi
6–7 Jan	Christmas	Orthodox Christian	birth of Jesus
18–19 Jan	Epiphany	Orthodox Christian	coming of the Magi
Jan–Feb	New Year	Chinese	return of Kitchen god to heaven
Feb–Mar	Shrove Tuesday	Christian	day before Lent
	Ash Wednesday	Christian	first day of Lent
	Purim	Jewish	story of Esther
	Mahashivaratri	Hindu	Siva
Mar–Apr	Palm Sunday	Western Christian	Jesus's entry into Jerusalem
	Good Friday	Western Christian	crucifixion of Jesus
	Easter Sunday	Western Christian	resurrection of Jesus
	Passover	Jewish	escape from slavery in Egypt
	Holi	Hindu	Krishna
	Holi Mohalla	Sikh	(coincides with Holi)
	Rama Naumi	Hindu	birth of Rama
	Ching Ming	Chinese	remembrance of the dead
13 Apr	Baisakhi	Sikh	founding of the Kalsa
Apr–May	Easter	Orthodox Christian	death and resurrection of Jesus
	Lailut ul-Isra wal Mi'raj	Muslim	Prophet Muhammad's journey to Jerusalem and then up to Heaven
	Lailat ul-Bara'h	Muslim	forgiveness before Ramadan
May–Jun	Shavuot	Jewish	giving of Ten Commandments to Moses
	Lailat ul-Qadr	Muslim	revelation of the Qur'an to Muhammad
	Eid ul-Fitr	Muslim	end of Ramadan
	Pentecost (Whitsun)	Christian	Jesus's followers receiving the Holy Spirit
	Wesak	Buddhist	day of Buddha's birth, enlightenment, and death
	Martyrdom of Guru Arjan	Sikh	death of fifth guru of Sikhism
June	Dragon Boat Festival	Chinese	Chinese martyr
Jul	Dhammacakka	Buddhist	preaching of Buddha's first sermon
	Eid ul-Adha	Muslim	Abraham's willingness to sacrifice his son
Aug	Raksha Bandhan	Hindu	family
Aug–Sept	Janmashtami	Hindu	birthday of Khrishna
Sept	Moon Festival	Chinese	Chinese hero
Sept–Oct	Rosh Hashanah	Jewish	start of Jewish New Year
	Yom Kippur	Jewish	day of Atonement
	Succot	Jewish	Israelites' time in the wilderness
Oct	Dusshera	Hindu	goddess Devi
Oct–Nov	Divali	Hindu	goddess Lakshmi
	Divali	Sikh	release of Guru Hargobind from prison
Nov	Guru Nanak's Birthday	Sikh	founder of Sikhism
1 Nov	All Saint's Day	Christian	deceased Christian saints and holy people
2 Nov	All Soul's Day	Christian	Christian deceased
	Bodhi Day	Buddhist (Mahāyāna)	Buddha's enlightenment
Dec	Hanukkah	Jewish	recapture of Temple of Jerusalem
	Winter Festival	Chinese	time of feasting
25 Dec	Christmas	Western Christian	birth of Christ
Dec–Jan	Birthday of Guru Gobind Sind	Sikh	last (tenth) human guru of Sikhism
	Martyrdom of Guru Tegh Bahadur	Sikh	ninth guru of Sikhism

Baisakhi originally a harvest festival, it now celebrates the founding of the Khalsa, the Sikh brotherhood, and commemorates those Sikhs killed by British troops in Amritsar on Baisakhi, 1919.

Martyrdom of Guru Arjan commemorates the death of the fifth guru, Guru Arjan, who built the Golden Temple at Amritsar and compiled the main part of the Sikh holy book.

Divali celebrates the release from prison of the sixth guru, Guru Hargobind, who also managed to secure the release of 51 Hindu princes who were imprisoned with him.

Guru Nanak's birthday celebrates the birth of the founder of the first guru of Sikhism.

Martyrdom of Guru Tegh Bahadur the ninth guru, martyred for the faith.

Birthday of Guru Gobind Singh The tenth and last human guru of Sikhism, and the founder of the Khalsa.

Christian festivals and holy days

1 January	The naming of Jesus	25 July	St James the Apostle
	The Circumcision of Christ	6 August	The Transfiguration of our Lord
	The Solemnity of Mary Mother of God	24 August	St Bartholomew the Apostle
6 January	Epiphany	1 September	New Year (Eastern Orthodox Church)
25 January	The Conversion of St Paul	8 September	The Nativity of the Blessed Virgin Mary
2 February	The Presentation of Christ in the Temple	14 September	The Exaltation of the Holy Cross
19 March	St Joseph of Nazareth, husband of the	21 September	St Matthew the Apostle
	Blessed Virgin Mary	29 September	St Michael and All Angels (Michaelmas)
25 March	The Annunciation of Our Lord to the	18 October	St Luke the Evangelist
	Blessed Virgin Mary	28 October	St Simon and St Jude, Apostles
25 April	St Mark the Evangelist	1 November	All Saints
1 May	St Philip and St James, Apostles	21 November	Presentation of the Blessed Virgin Mary
14 May	St Matthias the Apostle		in the Temple
31 May	The Visitation of the Blessed Virgin	30 November	St Andrew the Apostle
	Mary	8 December	The Immaculate Conception of the
11 June	St Barnabas the Apostle		Blessed Virgin Mary
24 June	The Birth of St John the Baptist	25 December	Christmas
29 June	St Peter and St Paul, Apostles	26 December	St Stephen the first Martyr
3 July	St Thomas the Apostle	27 December	St John the Evangelist
22 July	St Mary Magdalen	28 December	The Holy Innocents

Movable Christian feasts 1994–2025

	Ash Wednesday	Easter Day	Ascension Day	Pentecost (Whit Sunday)	Advent Sunday
1994	16 Feb	3 April	12 May	22 May	27 Nov
1995	1 March	16 April	25 May	4 June	3 Dec
1996	21 Feb	7 April	16 May	26 May	1 Dec
1997	12 Feb	30 March	8 May	18 May	30 Nov
1998	25 Feb	12 April	21 May	31 May	29 Nov
1999	17 Feb	4 April	13 May	23 May	28 Nov
2000	8 March	23 April	1 June	11 June	3 Dec
2001	28 Feb	15 April	24 May	3 June	2 Dec
2002	13 Feb	31 March	9 May	19 May	1 Dec
2003	5 March	20 April	29 May	8 June	30 Nov
2004	25 Feb	11 April	20 May	30 May	28 Nov
2005	9 Feb	27 March	5 May	15 May	27 Nov
2006	1 March	16 April	25 May	4 June	3 Dec
2007	21 Feb	8 April	17 May	27 May	2 Dec
2008	6 Feb	23 March	1 May	11 May	30 Nov
2009	25 Feb	12 April	21 May	31 May	29 Nov
2010	17 Feb	4 April	13 May	23 May	28 Nov
2011	9 March	24 April	2 June	12 June	27 Nov
2012	22 Feb	8 April	17 May	27 May	2 Dec
2013	13 Feb	31 March	9 May	19 May	1 Dec
2014	5 March	20 April	29 May	8 June	30 Nov
2015	18 Feb	5 April	14 May	24 May	29 Nov
2016	10 March	27 March	5 May	15 May	27 Nov
2017	1 March	16 April	25 May	4 June	3 Dec
2018	14 Feb	1 April	10 May	20 May	2 Dec
2019	6 March	21 April	30 May	9 June	1 Dec
2020	26 Feb	12 April	21 May	31 May	29 Nov
2021	17 Feb	4 April	13 May	23 May	28 Nov
2022	2 March	17 April	26 May	5 June	27 Nov
2023	22 Feb	9 April	18 May	28 May	3 Dec
2024	14 Feb	31 March	9 May	19 May	1 Dec
2025	5 March	20 April	29 May	8 June	30 Nov

Advent Sunday is the fourth Sunday before Christmas Day
Ash Wednesday is the first day of Lent, and falls in the seventh week before Easter
Holy Week is the week before Easter Day, and includes Palm Sunday, Maundy Thursday, Good Friday, and Easter Eve.
Ascension Day is 40 days after Easter Day.
Pentecost (Whit Sunday) is seven weeks after Easter Day.
Trinity Sunday is eight weeks after Easter Day.

Hindu festivals

January	Makar Sankranti/Til Sankranti/Lohri, Pongal, Kumbha Mela at Prayag (every 12 years)
January–February	Vasanta Panchami/Shri Panchami/Saraswati Puja, Bhogali Bihu, Mahashivratri
20 February	Ramakrishna Utsav
February–March	Holi
March–April	Ugadi, Basora, Rama Navami, Hanuman Jayanti
April	Vaisakhi
April–May	Akshaya Tritiya, Chittrai
May–June	Ganga Dasa-hara, Nirjala Ekadashi, Snan-yatra
June–July	Ratha-yatra/Jagannatha, Ashadhi Ekadashi/Toli Ekadashi
July–August	Teej, Naga Panchami, Raksha Bandhan/Shravana Purnima/Salono/Rakhi Purnima
August–September	Onam, Ganesha Chaturthi, Janamashtami/Krishna Jayanti
September–October	Mahalaya/Shraddha/Pitri Paksha/Kanagat, Navaratri/Durga Puja/Dassehra, Lakshmi Puja
2 October	Gandhi Jayanti
October–November	Divali/Deepavali Chhath, Karttika Ekadashi/Devuthna Ekadashi/Tulsi Ekadashi Karttika Purnima/Tripuri Purnima, Hoi, Skanda Shasti
November–December	Vaikuntha Ekadashi, Lakshmi Puja (Orissa)

Buddhist festivals

Myanmar

16–17 April	New Year
May–June	The Buddha's Birth, Enlightenment and Death
July	The Buddha's First Sermon Beginning of the Rains Retreat
October	End of the Rains Retreat
November	Kathina Ceremony

China

June–August	Summer Retreat
August	Festival of Hungry Ghosts; Gautama Buddha's Birth; Kuan-Yin

Sri Lanka

13 April	New Year
May–June	The Buddha's Birth, Enlightenment and Death
June–July	Establishment of Buddhism in Sri Lanka
July	The Buddha's First Sermon
July–August	Procession of the Month of Asala
September	The Buddha's First Visit to Sri Lanka
December–January	Arrival of Sanghamitta

Thailand

13–16 April	New Year
May	The Buddha's Enlightenment
May–June	The Buddha's Cremation
July–October	Rains Retreat
October	End of the Rains Retreat
November	Kathina Ceremony; Festival of Lights
February	All Saints' Day

Tibet

February	New Year
May	The Buddha's Birth, Enlightenment and Death
June	Dzamling Chisang
June–July	The Buddha's First Sermon
October	The Buddha's Descent from Tushita
November	Death of Tsongkhapa
January	The Conjunction of Nine Evils and the Conjunction of Ten Virtues

Patron saints

Saint	Occupation
Adam	gardeners
Albert the Great	scientists
Alphonsus Liguori	theologians
Amand	brewers, hotelkeepers
Andrew	fishermen
Angelico	artists
Anne	miners
Apollonia	dentists
Augustine	theologians
Barbara	builders, miners
Bernadino (Feltre)	bankers
Bernadino of Siena	advertisers
Camillus de Lellis	nurses
Catherine of Alexandria	librarians, philosophers
Cecilia	musicians, poets, singers
Christopher	motorists, sailors
Cosmas and Damian	barbers, chemists, doctors, surgeons
Crispin	shoemakers
Crispinian	shoemakers
David	poets
Dismas	undertakers
Dominic	astronomers
Dorothy	florists
Eligius	blacksmiths, jewellers, metalworkers
Erasmus	sailors
Fiacre	gardeners, taxi drivers
Florian	firemen
Francis de Sales	authors, editors, journalists
Francis of Assisi	merchants
Francis of Paola	sailors
Gabriel	messengers, postal workers, radio workers, television workers
Genesius	actors, secretaries
George	soldiers
Gregory	singers
Gregory the Great	musicians, teachers
Homobonus	tailors
Honoratus	bakers
Isidore	farmers
Ivo	lawyers
James	labourers
Jean-Baptiste Vianney	priests
Jerome	librarians
Joan of Arc	soldiers
John Baptist de la Salle	teachers
John Bosco	labourers
John of God	book trade, nurses, printers
Joseph	carpenters
Joseph (Arimathea)	gravediggers, undertakers
Joseph (Cupertino)	astronauts
Julian the Hospitaler	hotelkeepers
Lawrence	cooks
Leonard	prisoners
Louis	sculptors
Lucy	glassworkers, writers
Luke	artists, butchers, doctors, glassworkers, sculptors, surgeons
Martha	cooks, housewives, servants, waiters
Martin of Tours	soldiers
Matthew	accountants, bookkeepers, tax collectors
Michael	grocers, policemen
Our Lady of Loreto	aviators
Peter	fishermen
Raymond Nonnatus	midwives
Sebastian	athletes, soldiers
Thérèse of Lisieux	florists
Thomas (Apostle)	architects, builders
Thomas Aquinas	philosophers, scholars, students, theologians
Thomas More	lawyers
Vitus	actors, comedians, dancers
Wenceslaus	brewers
Zita	servants

Saints' days

January
1 Basil (E), Fulgentius, Telemachus
2 Basil and Gregory of Nazianzus (W), Macarius of Alexandria, Seraphim of Sarov
3 Geneviève
4 Angela of Foligno
5 Simeon Stylites (W)
7 Cedda, Lucian of Antioch (W), Raymond of Penyafort
8 Atticus (E), Gudule, Severinus
9 Hadrian the African
10 Agatho, Marcian
12 Ailred, Benedict Biscop
13 Hilary of Poitiers
14 Kentigern
15 Macarius of Egypt, Maurus, Paul of Thebes
16 Honoratus
17 Antony of Egypt
19 Wulfstan
20 Euthymius, Fabian, Sebastian
21 Agnes, Fructuosus, Maximus (E), Meinrad
22 Timothy (G), Vincent
23 Ildefonsus
24 Babylas (W), Francis de Sales
25 Gregory of Nazianzus (E)
26 Paula, Timothy and Titus, Xenophon (E)
27 Angela Merici
28 Ephraem Syrus (E), Paulinus of Nola, Thomas Aquinas
29 Gildas
31 John Bosco, Marcella

February
1 Bride, Pionius
3 Anskar, Blaise (W),Werburga, Simeon (E)
4 Gilbert of Sempringham, Isidore of Pelusium, Phileas
5 Agatha, Avitus
6 Dorothy, Paul Miki and companions, Vedast
8 Theodore (G), Jerome Emiliani
9 Teilo
10 Scholastica
11 Benedict of Aniane, Blaise (E), Caedmon, Gregory II
12 Meletius
13 Agabus (W), Catherine dei Ricci, Priscilla (E)
14 Cyril and Methodius (W), Valentine (W)
16 Flavian (E), Pamphilus (E), Valentine (E)
18 Bernadette (France), Colman, Flavian (W), Leo I (E)
20 Wulfric
21 Peter Damian
23 Polycarp
25 Ethelbert, Tarasius, Walburga
26 Alexander (W), Porphyrius
27 Leander
28 Oswald of York

March
1 David
2 Chad, Simplicius
3 Ailred
4 Casimir
6 Chrodegang
7 Perpetua and Felicity
8 Felix, John of God, Pontius

9 Frances of Rome, Gregory of Nyssa, Pacian
10 John Ogilvie, Macarius of Jerusalem, Simplicius
11 Constantine, Oengus, Sophronius
12 Gregory (the Great)
13 Nicephorus
14 Benedict (E)
15 Clement Hofbauer
17 Gertrude, Joseph of Arimathea (W), Patrick
18 Anselm of Lucca, Cyril of Jerusalem, Edward
19 Joseph
20 Cuthbert, John of Parma, Martin of Braga
21 Serapion of Thmuis
22 Catherine of Sweden, Nicholas of Flüe
23 Turibius de Mongrovejo
30 John Climacus

April
1 Hugh of Grenoble, Mary of Egypt (E), Melito
2 Francis of Paola, Mary of Egypt (W)
3 Richard of Chichester
4 Isidore of Seville
5 Juliana of Liège, Vincent Ferrer
7 Hegesippus, John Baptist de la Salle
8 Agabus (E)
10 Fulbert
11 Gemma Galgani, Guthlac, Stanislaus
12 Julius I, Zeno
13 Martin I
15 Aristarchus, Pudus (E), Trophimus of Ephesus
17 Agapetus (E), Stephen Harding
18 Mme Acarie
19 Alphege, Leo IX
21 Anastasius (E), Anselm, Beuno, Januarius (E)
22 Alexander (C)
23 George
24 Egbert, Fidelis of Sigmaringen, Mellitus
25 Mark, Phaebadius
27 Zita
28 Peter Chanel, Vitalis and Valeria
29 Catherine of Siena, Hugh of Cluny, Peter Martyr, Robert
30 James (the Great) (E), Pius V

May
1 Asaph, Joseph the Worker, Walburga
2 Athanasius
3 Phillip and James (the Less)(W)
4 Gotthard
5 Hilary of Arles
7 John of Beverley
8 John (E), Peter of Tarantaise
10 Antoninus, Comgall, John of Avila, Simon (E)
11 Cyril and Methodius (E), Mamertus
12 Epiphanius, Nereus and Achilleus, Pancras
14 Matthias (W)
16 Brendan, John of Nepomuk, Simon Stock
17 Robert Bellarmine, Paschal Baylon
18 John I
19 Dunstan, Ivo, Pudens (W), Pudentiana (W)
20 Bernadino of Siena
21 Helena (E)
22 Rita of Cascia
23 Ivo of Chartres
24 Vincent of Lérins

Saints' days *(cont.)*

25 Aldhelm, Bede, Gregory VII, Mary Magdalene de Pazzi
26 Philip Neri, Quadratus
27 Augustine of Canterbury
30 Joan of Arc

June
1 Justin Martyr, Pamphilus
2 Erasmus, Marcellinus and Peter, Nicephorus (G), Pothinus
3 Charles Lwanga and companions, Clotilde, Kevin
4 Optatus, Petrock
5 Boniface
6 Martha (E), Norbert
7 Paul of Constantinople (W), Willibald
8 William of York
9 Columba, Cyril of Alexandria (E), Ephraem (W)
11 Barnabas, Bartholomew (E)
12 Leo III
13 Anthony of Padua
15 Orsisius, Vitus
17 Alban, Botulph
19 Gervasius and Protasius, Jude (E), Romuald
20 Alban
21 Alban of Mainz, Aloysius Gonzaga
22 John Fisher and Thomas More, Nicetas, Pantaenus (C), Paulinus of Nola
23 Etheldreda
24 Birth of John the Baptist
25 Prosper of Aquitaine
27 Cyril of Alexandria (W), Ladislaus
28 Irenaeus
29 Peter and Paul
30 First Martyrs of the Church of Rome

July
1 Cosmas and Damian (E), Oliver Plunket
3 Anatolius, Thomas
4 Andrew of Crete (E), Elizabeth of Portugal, Ulrich
5 Anthony Zaccaria
6 Maria Goretti
7 Palladius, Pantaenus
8 Kilian, Aquila and Prisca (W)
11 Benedict (W), Pius I
12 John Gualbert, Veronica
13 Henry II, Mildred, Silas
14 Camillus of Lellis, Deusdedit, Nicholas of the Holy Mountain(E)
15 Bonaventure, Jacob of Nisibis, Swithin, Vladimir
16 Eustathius, Our Lady of Mt Carmel
17 Ennodius, Leo IV, Marcellina, Margaret (E), Scillitan Martyrs
18 Arnulf, Philastrius
19 Marcrina, Symmachus
20 Aurelius, Margaret (W)
21 Lawrence of Brindisi, Praxedes
22 Mary Magdalene
23 Apollinaris, Bridget of Sweden
25 Anne and Joachim (E), Christopher, James (the Great) (W)
26 Anne and Joachim (W)
27 Pantaleon
28 Innocent I, Samson, Victor I
30 Peter Chrysologus, Silas (G)

31 Giovanni Colombini, Germanus, Joseph of Arimathea (E), Ignatius of Loyola

August
1 Alphonsus Liguori, Ethelwold
2 Eusebius of Vercelli, Stephen I
4 Jean-Baptiste Vianney
6 Hormisdas
7 Cajetan, Sixtus II and companions
8 Dominic
9 Matthias (G)
10 Laurence, Oswald of Northumbria
11 Clare, Susanna
13 Maximus (W), Pontian and Hippolytus, Radegunde
14 Maximilian Kolbe
15 Arnulf, Tarsicius
16 Roch, Simplicianus, Stephen of Hungary
17 Hyacinth
19 John Eudes, Sebaldus
20 Bernard, Oswin, Philibert
21 Jane Frances de Chantal, Pius X
23 Rose of Lima, Sidonius Apollinaris
24 Bartholomew (W), Ouen
25 Joseph Calasanctius, Louis IX, Menas of Constantinople
26 Blessed Dominic of the Mother of God, Zephyrinus
27 Caesarius, Monica
28 Augustine of Hippo
29 Beheading of John the Baptist, Sabina
30 Pammachius
31 Aidan, Paulinus of Trier

September
1 Giles, Simeon Stylites (E)
2 John the Faster (E)
3 Gregory (the Great)
4 Babylas (E), Boniface I
5 Zacharias (E)
9 Peter Claver, Nicholas of Tolentino, Pulcheria
11 Deiniol, Ethelburga, Paphnutius
13 John Chrysostom (W)
15 Catherine of Genoa, Our Lady of Sorrows
16 Cornelius, Cyprian of Carthage, Euphemia, ninian
17 Robert Bellarmine, Hildegard, Lambert, Satyrus
19 Januarius (W), Theodore of Tarsus
20 Agapetus or Eustace (W)
21 Matthew (W)
23 Adamnan, Linus
25 Sergius of Rostov
26 Cosmas and Damian (W), Cyprian of Carthage, John (E)
27 Frumentius (W), Vincent de Paul
28 Exuperius, Wenceslaus
29 Michael (Michaelmas Day), Gabriel and Raphael
30 Jerome, Otto

October
1 Remigius, Romanos, Teresa of the Child Jesus
2 Leodegar (Leger)
3 Teresa of Lisieux, Thomas de Cantilupe
4 Ammon, Francis of Assisi, Petronius
6 Bruno, Thomas (G)
9 Demetrius (W), Denis and companions, Dionysius of Paris, James (the Less) (E), John Leonardi

Saints' days *(cont.)*

10   Francis Borgia, Paulinus of York
11   Atticus (E), Bruno, Nectarius
12   Wilfrid
13   Edward the Confessor
14   Callistus I, Cosmas Melodus (E)
15   Lucian of Antioch (E), Teresa of Avila
16   Gall, Hedwig, Lullus, Margaret Mary Alacoque
17   Ignatius of Antioch, Victor
18   Luke
19   John de Bréboeuf and Isaac Jogues and
     companions, Paul of the Cross, Peter of Alcántara
21   Hilarion, Ursula
22   Abercius
23   John of Capistrano, James
24   Anthony Claret
25   Crispin and Crispinian, Forty Martyrs of England and
     Wales, Gaudentius
26   Demetrius (E)
28   Fermilian (E), Simon and Jude
30   Serapion of Antioch
31   Wolfgang

November
1   All Saints, Cosmas and Damian (E)
2   Eustace (E), Victorinus
3   Hubert, malachy, Martin de Porres, Pirminius,
     Winifred
4   Charles Borromeo, Vitalis and Agricola
5   Elizabeth (W)
6   Illtyd, Leonard, Paul of Constantinople (E)
7   Willibrord
8   Elizabeth (E), Willehad
9   Simeon Metaphrastes (E)
10   Justus, Leo I (W)
11   Martin of Tours (W), Menas of Egypt, Theodore of
     Studios
12   Josaphat, Martin of Tours (E), Nilus the Ascetic
13   Abbo, John Chrysostom (E), Nicholas I
14   Dubricius, Gregory Palamas (E)
15   Albert the Great, Machutus
16   Edmund of Abingdon, Eucherius, Gertrude (the
     Great), Margaret of Scotland, Matthew (E)

17   Elizabeth of Hungary, Gregory Thaumaturgus,
     Gregory of Tours, Hugh of Lincoln
18   Odo, Romanus
19   Mechthild, Nerses
20   Edmund the Martyr
21   Gelasius
22   Cecilia
23   Amphilocius, Clement I (W), Columban, Felicity,
     Gregory of Agrigentum
25   Clement I (E), Mercurius, Mesrob
26   Siricius
27   Barlam and Josaphat
28   Simeon Metaphrastes
29   Cuthbert Mayne
30   Andrew, Frumentius (G)

December
1   Eligius
2   Chromatius
3   Francis Xavier
4   Barbara, John Damascene, Osmund
5   Clement of Alexandria, Sabas
6   Nicholas
7   Ambrose
10   Miltiades
11   Damasus, Daniel
12   Jane Frances de Chantal, Spyridon (E), Vicelin
13   Lucy, Odilia
14   John of the Cross, Spyridon (W)
16   Eusebius
18   Frumentius (C)
20   Ignatius of Antioch (G)
21   Peter Canisius, Thomas
22   Anastasia (E), Chrysogonus (E)
23   John of Kanty
26   Stephen (W)
27   John (W), Fabiola, Stephen (E)
29   Thomas à Becket, Trophimus of Arles
31   Sylvester

C = Coptic; G = Greek; E = Eastern; W = Western

Sport

Events and Records

angling fishing with rod and line. *Freshwater fishing* embraces game fishing, in which members of the salmon family, such as salmon and trout, are taken by spinners (revolving lures) and flies (imitations of adult or larval insects); and coarse fishing, in which members of the carp family, pike, perch, and eels are taken by baits or lures, and (in the UK) are returned to the water virtually unharmed. In *sea fishing* the catch includes flatfish, bass, and mackerel; big-game fishes include shark, tuna or tunny, marlin, and swordfish. World championships take place for most branches of the sport.

WORLD FRESHWATER CHAMPIONSHIPS

first held 1957

individual
1982 Kevin Ashurst *(England)*
1983 Wolf-Rüdiger Kremkus *(West Germany)*
1984 Bobby Smithers *(England)*
1985 Dave Roper *(England)*
1986 Lud Wever *(Holland)*
1987 Clive Branson *(Wales)*
1988 Jean-Pierre Fouquet *(France)*
1989 Tom Pickering *(England)*
1990 Bob Nudd *(England)*
1991 Bob Nudd *(England)*
1992 David Wesson *(Australia)*
1993 Russell Owen *(Wales)*

team
1982 Holland
1983 Belgium
1984 Luxembourg
1985 England
1986 Italy
1987 England
1988 England
1989 Wales
1990 France
1991 England
1992 Italy
1993 England

archery shooting with a bow and arrow at a circular target made up of ten concentric scoring zones. The highest score (10 points) is obtained by hitting the central, gold-coloured zone. Competitions usually take the form of Double FITA (Fédération Internationale de Tir à l'Arc) rounds – that is, 72 arrows are fired at each of four targets from distances of 90, 70, 50, and 30 m (70, 60, 50, and 30 m for women). The highest possible score is 2,880.

WORLD CHAMPIONSHIP

first held 1931; now contested every two years

men: individual
1983 Richard McKinney *(USA)*
1985 Richard McKinney *(USA)*
1987 Vladimir Ashéyer *(USSR)*
1989 Stanislav Zabrodsky *(USSR)*
1991 Simon Fairweather *(Australia)*
1993 Richard McKinney *(USA)*

men: team
1983 USA
1985 South Korea
1987 South Korea
1989 USSR
1991 South Korea
1993 South Korea

women: individual
1983 Jin-Ho Kim *(South Korea)*
1985 Irina Soldatova *(USSR)*
1987 Ma Xiagjuan *(China)*
1989 Soo Nyung-Kim *(South Korea)*
1991 Soo Nyung-Kim *(South Korea)*
1993 Kim Hyo-Jung *(South Korea)*

women: team
1983 South Korea
1985 USSR
1987 China
1989 South Korea
1991 South Korea
1993 South Korea

athletics competitive track and field events consisting of running, throwing, and jumping disciplines. *Running events* range from sprint races (100 metres) and hurdles to the marathon (26 miles 385 yards). *Jumping events* are the high jump and long jump, and, for men only, the triple jump and pole vault. *Throwing events* are javelin, discus, shot put, and hammer throw (men only).

OLYMPIC GAMES

events staged since 1896

Barcelona Olympics 1992 (25th Olympic Games)

track and field
men/women
100 metres: Linford Christie *(UK)*/Gail Devers *(USA)*
200 metres: Michael Marsh *(USA)*/Gwen Torrence *(USA)*
400 metres: Quincy Watts *(USA)*/Marie-Jose Perec *(France)*
800 metres: William Tanui *(Kenya)*/Ellen van Langen *(Netherlands)*
1,500 metres: Fermin Cacho *(Spain)*/Hassiba Boulmerka *(Algeria)*
3,000 metres: — /Yelina Romanova *(Unified Team*)*
5,000 metres: Dieter Baumann *(Germany)*/ —
10,000 metres: Khalid Skah *(Morocco)*/Derartu Tulu *(Ethiopia)*
marathon: Hwang Young Cho *(South Korea)*/Valentina Yegorova *(Unified Team)*
110-metre hurdles: Mark McCoy *(Canada)*/Paraskevi Patoulidou *(Greece)*
400-metre hurdles: Kevin Young *(USA)*/Sally Gunnell *(UK)*
3,000-metre steeplechase: Matthew Birir *(Kenya)*/ —
10,000-metre walk: — /Chen Yueling *(China)*
20,000-metre walk: Daniel Plaza Montero *(Spain)*/ —
50,000-metre walk: Andrei Perlov *(Unified Team)*/ —
400-metre relay: USA/USA
1,600-metre relay: USA/Unified Team
high jump: Javier Sotomayor *(Cuba)*/ Heike Henkel *(Germany)*

long jump: Carl Lewis *(USA)*/Heike Drechsler *(Germany)*
triple jump: Mike Conley *(USA)*/ —
pole vault: Maksim Tarassov *(Unified Team)*/ —
javelin: Jan Zelezny *(Czechoslovakia)*/Silke Renke *(Germany)*
hammer: Andrei Abduvaliyev *(Unified Team)*/ —
discus: Romas Ubartas *(Lithuania)*/Maritza Marten Garcia *(Cuba)*
shot put: Mike Stulce *(USA)*/Svetlana Kriveleva *(Unified Team)*
decathlon: Robert Zmelik *(Czechoslovakia)*/ —
heptathlon: — /Jackie Joyner-Kersee *(USA)*
* *Commonwealth of Independent States plus Georgia*

WORLD RECORDS
at 1 November 1993

men
100 metres: 9.86 sec Carl Lewis *(USA)*
200 metres: 19.72 sec Pietro Mennea *(Italy)*
400 metres: 43.29 sec Butch Reynolds *(USA)*
800 metres: 1 min 41.73 sec Sebastian Coe *(UK)*
1,000 metres: 2 min 12.18 sec Sebastian Coe *(UK)*
1,500 metres: 2 min 28.82 sec Noureddine Morceli *(Morocco)*
mile: 3 min 44.39 sec Noureddine Morceli *(Morocco)*
2,000 metres: 4 min 50.81 sec Said Aouita *(Morocco)*
3,000 metres: 7 min 28.96 sec Moses Kiptanui *(Kenya)*
5,000 metres: 12 min 58.39 sec Said Aouita *(Morocco)*
10,000 metres: 26 min 58.38 sec Yobes Ondieki (Kenya)
20,000 metres: 56 min 55.6 sec Arturo Barrios *(Mexico)*
20,994 metres: 1 hr Jos Hermans *(Holland)*
25,000 metres: 1 hr 13 min 55.8 sec Toshihiko Seko *(Japan)*
30,000 metres: 1 hr 29 min 18.8 sec Toshihiko Seko *(Japan)*
110-metre hurdles: 12.91 sec Colin Jackson *(UK)*
400-metre hurdles: 46.78 sec Kevin Young *(USA)*
3,000-metre steeplechase: 8 min 2.08 sec Moses Kiptanui *(Kenya)*
400-metre relay: 37.40 sec USA
1,600-metre relay: 2 min 54.29 sec USA
3,200-metre relay: 7 min 03.89 sec UK
6,000-metre relay: 14 min 38.8 sec West Germany
high jump: 2.45 metres Javier Sotomayor *(Cuba)*
pole vault: 6.13 metres Sergey Bubka *(USSR)*
long jump: 8.95 metres Mike Powell *(USA)*
triple jump: 17.97 metres Willie Banks *(USA)*
shot: 23.12 metres Randy Barnes *(USA)*
discus: 74.08 metres Jurgen Schult *(East Germany)*
hammer: 86.74 metres Yuriy Sedykh *(USSR)*
javelin: 95.66 metres Jan Zelezny *(RCS)*
decathlon: 8,891 points Dan O'Brien *(USA)*
marathon: 2 hr 6 min 50 sec Belayneh Dinsamo *(Ethiopia)*

women
100 metres: 10.49 sec Florence Griffith-Joyner *(USA)*
200 metres: 21.34 sec Florence Griffith-Joyner *(USA)*
400 metres: 47.60 sec Marita Koch *(East Germany)*
800 metres: 1 min 53.28 sec Jarmila Kratochvilova *(Czechoslovakia)*
1,500 metres: 3 min 50.46 sec Qu Yunxia *(China)*
mile: 4 min 15.61 sec Paula Ivan *(Romania)*
2,000 metres: 5 min 28.69 sec Maricica Puica *(Romania)*
3,000 metres: 8 min 06.11 sec Wang Junxia *(China)*
5,000 metres: 14 min 37.33 sec Ingrid Kristiansen *(Norway)*
10,000 metres: 29 min 31.78 sec Wang Junxia *(China)*

20,000 metres: 1 hr 29 min 29.2 sec Karolina Szabo *(Hungary)*
30,000 metres: 1 hr 49 min 5.6 sec Karolina Szabo *(Hungary)*
100-metre hurdles: 12.21 sec Yordanka Donkova *(Bulgaria)*
400-metre hurdles: 52.74 sec Sally Gunnell *(UK)*
400-metre relay: 41.37 sec *(East Germany)*
800-metre relay: 1 min 28.15 sec *(East Germany)*
1,600-metre relay: 3 min 15.17 sec *(USSR)*
high jump: 2.09 metres Stefka Kostadinova *(Bulgaria)*
long jump: 7.52 metres Galina Chistiakova *(Russia)*
shot: 22.63 metres Natalya Lisovskaya *(Russia)*
discus: 76.80 metres Gaby Reinsch *(Germany)*
javelin: 80.00 metres Petra Felke *(Germany)*
heptathlon: 7,291 points Jackie Joyner-Kersee *(USA)*

WORLD CROSS-COUNTRY CHAMPIONSHIP

men: individual
1988 John Ngugi *(Kenya)*
1989 John Ngugi *(Kenya)*
1990 Khaled Skah *(Morocco)*
1991 Khaled Skah *(Morocco)*
1992 John Ngugi *(Kenya)*
1993 William Sigei *(Kenya)*

women: individual
1988 Ingrid Kristiansen *(Norway)*
1989 Annette Sergant *(France)*
1990 Lynn Jennings *(USA)*
1991 Lynn Jennings *(USA)*
1992 Lynn Jennings *(USA)*
1993 Albertina Dias *(Portugal)*

men: team
1988 Kenya
1989 Kenya
1990 Kenya
1991 Kenya
1992 Kenya
1993 Kenya

women: team
1988 USSR
1989 USSR
1990 USSR
1991 Kenya/Ethiopia
1992 Kenya
1993 Kenya

badminton indoor racket game, similar to lawn tennis but played with a shuttlecock (a half sphere of cork or plastic with a feather or nylon skirt) instead of a ball. It may be played by two or four players. The game takes place on a court 13.4 m/44 ft long and 5.2 m/17 ft wide (6.1 m/20 ft wide for doubles), with a raised net across the middle. The object of the game is to prevent the opponent from being able to return the shuttlecock.

WORLD CHAMPIONSHIP
first held 1977; now contested every two years

men
1983 Icuk Sugiarto *(Indonesia)*
1985 Han Jian *(China)*
1987 Yang Yang *(China)*
1989 Yang Yang *(China)*
1991 Zao Zinhua *(China)*
1993 Joko Suprianto *(Indonesia)*

women
1983 Li Lingwei *(China)*
1985 Han Aiping *(China)*
1987 Han Aiping *(China)*
1989 Li Lingwei *(China)*
1991 Tang Jiu Hong *(China)*
1993 Susi Susanti *(Indonesia)*

THOMAS CUP

men's team championship, first held 1949
1970 Indonesia
1973 Indonesia
1976 Indonesia
1979 Indonesia
1982 China
1984 Indonesia
1986 China
1988 China
1990 China
1992 Malaysia

UBER CUP

women's team championship, first held 1957
1969 Japan
1972 Japan
1975 Indonesia
1978 Japan
1981 Japan
1984 China
1986 China
1988 China
1990 China
1992 China

baseball national summer game of the USA, derived in the 19th century from the English game of rounders. Baseball is a bat-and-ball game played between two teams, each of nine players. The field is marked out in the form of a diamond, with a base at each corner. The ball is struck with a cylindrical bat, and the players try to score ('make a run') by circuiting the bases. A 'home run' is a circuit on one hit.

WORLD SERIES

first held 1903 as an end-of-season game between the winners of the two professional leagues, the National League and the American League, and established as a series of seven games 1905
1982 St Louis Cardinals
1983 Baltimore Orioles
1984 Detroit Tigers
1985 Kansas City Royals
1986 New York Mets
1987 Minnesota Twins
1988 Los Angeles Dodgers
1989 Oakland Athletics
1990 Cincinatti Reds
1991 Minnesota Twins
1992 Toronto Blue Jays
1993 Toronto Blue Jays

basketball ball game between two teams of five players on a rectangular enclosed court. The object is to throw the large inflated ball through a circular hoop and net positioned at the end of each courts, 3.05 m/10 ft above the ground. Players move the ball by passing it or by dribbling it (bouncing it on the floor) while running.

WORLD CHAMPIONSHIPS

first held 1950 for men, 1953 for women; contested every four years

men
1954 USA
1959 Brazil
1963 Brazil
1967 USSR
1970 Yugoslavia
1974 USSR
1978 Yugoslavia
1982 USSR
1986 USA
1990 Yugoslavia

women
1957 USA
1959 USSR
1964 USSR
1967 USSR
1971 USSR
1975 USSR
1979 USA
1983 USSR
1986 USA
1990 USA

NBA (NATIONAL BASKETBALL ASSOCIATION)
CHAMPIONSHIP

US end-of-season contest, first held 1947, between the top teams of the two professional leagues, the Western Conference and the Eastern Conference
1982 Los Angeles Lakers
1983 Philadelphia 76ers
1984 Boston Celtics
1985 Los Angeles Lakers
1986 Boston Celtics
1987 Los Angeles Lakers
1988 Los Angeles Lakers
1989 Detroit Pistons
1990 Detroit Pistons
1991 Chicago Bulls
1992 Chicago Bulls
1993 Chicago Bulls

billiards indoor game played, normally by two players, with tapered poles (cues) and composition balls (one red, two white) on a rectangular table covered with a green feltlike cloth (baize). The table has six pockets, one at each corner and in each of the long sides at the middle. Scoring strokes are made by potting the red ball, potting the opponent's ball, or potting another ball off one of these two. The cannon (when the cue ball hits the two other balls on the table) is another scoring stroke.

WORLD PROFESSIONAL CHAMPIONSHIP

instituted 1870, on a challenge basis, and restored as an annual tournament 1980
1982 Rex Williams *(England)*
1983 Rex Williams *(England)*
1984 Mark Wildman *(England)*
1985 Ray Edmonds *(England)*
1986 Robert Foldvari *(Australia)*

1987 Norman Dagley *(England)*
1988 Norman Dagley *(England)*
1989 Mike Russell *(England)*
1990 Mike Russell *(England)*
1991 Mike Russell *(England)*
1992 Geet Sethi *(India)*

bobsleighing or **bobsledding** racing steel-bodied, steerable toboggans, crewed by two or four people, down mountain ice-chutes at speeds of up to 130 kph/80 mph.

WORLD CHAMPIONSHIP
four-crew championship introduced 1924, two-crew 1931; Olympic winners automatically become world champions
two-person/four-person
1983 Switzerland/Switzerland
1984 East Germany/East Germany
1985 East Germany/East Germany
1986 East Germany/Switzerland
1987 Switzerland/Switzerland
1988 USSR/Switzerland
1989 East Germany/Switzerland
1990 Switzerland/Switzerland
1991 Germany/Germany
1992 Switzerland/Switzerland
1993 Germany/Switzerland

bowls outdoor and indoor game popular in Commonwealth countries. The outdoor game is played on a finely cut grassed area called a rink, with biased bowls 13 cm/5 in in diameter. It is played as either singles, pairs, triples, or fours. The object is to position one's bowl (or bowls) as near as possible to the jack (target). *Lawn bowls* is played on a flat surface; *crown green bowls* is played on a rink with undulations and a crown at the centre of the green.

WORLD OUTDOOR CHAMPIONSHIP
first held 1966 for men, and 1969 for women
men: singles
1972 Maldwyn Evans *(Wales)*
1976 Doug Watson *(South Africa)*
1980 David Bryant *(England)*
1984 Peter Bellis *(New Zealand)*
1988 David Bryant *(England)*
1992 Tony Allcock *(England)*
women: singles
1973 Elsie Wilke *(New Zealand)*
1977 Elsie Wilke *(New Zealand)*
1981 Norma Shaw *(England)*
1985 Merle Richardson *(Australia)*
1988 Janet Ackland *(Wales)*
1992 Margaret Johnston *(Ireland)*

WORLD INDOOR CHAMPIONSHIP
first held 1979 for men, 1988 for women
men: singles
1988 Hugh Duff *(Scotland)*
1989 Richard Corsie *(Scotland)*
1990 John Price *(Wales)*
1991 Richard Corsie *(Scotland)*
1992 Ian Schuback *(Australia)*
1993 Richard Corsie *(Scotland)*
women: singles
1988 Margaret Johnston *(Ireland)*

1989 Margaret Johnston *(Ireland)*
1990 Fleur Bougourd *(England)*
1991 Mary Price *(England)*
1992 Sarah Gourlay *(Scotland)*

WATERLOO HANDICAP
crown green tournament first held 1907
1982 Dennis Mercer
1983 Stan Frith
1984 Steve Ellis
1985 Tommy Johnstone
1986 Brian Duncan
1987 Brian Duncan
1988 Ingham Gregory
1989 Brian Duncan
1990 John Bancroft
1991 John Eccles
1992 Brian Duncan

boxing fighting with gloved fists, almost entirely a male sport. Contests take place in a square, roped ring 4.3–6.1 m/14–20 ft square. All rounds last 3 minutes. Amateur bouts last three rounds and professional championship bouts for as many as 12 or 15 rounds. Boxers are classified according to weight and may not fight in a division lighter than their own. The weight divisions in professional boxing range from straw-weight (also known as paperweight and mini-flyweight), under 49 kg/108 lb, to heavyweight, over 88 kg/195 lb.

WORLD CHAMPIONSHIP
(WBC = World Boxing Council; WBA = World Boxing Association; IBF = International Boxing Federation; WBO = World Boxing Organization)
heavyweight
1986 Tim Witherspoon (*USA*, WBA)
1986 Trevor Berbick (*Canada*, WBC)
1986 Mike Tyson (*USA*, WBC)
1986 James Smith (*USA*, WBA)
1987 Mike Tyson (*USA*, WBA)
1987 Tony Tucker (*USA*, IBF)
1987 Mike Tyson (*USA*, undisputed)
1989 Francesco Damiani (*Italy*, WBO)
1990 James Douglas (*USA*, undisputed)
1990 Evander Holyfield (*USA*, undisputed)
1992 Riddick Bowe (*(USA)*, WBA, IBF)
1992 Lennox Lewis (*(UK)*, WBC)
1992 Michael Moorer (*(USA)*, WBO)
1993 Tommy Morrison (*(USA)*, WBO)
1993 Michael Bentt (*(USA)*, WBO)
1993 Evander Holyfield (*(USA)*, WBA, IBF)
great heavyweight champions include:
John L Sullivan (bare-knuckle champion) 1882–92
Jim Corbett (first Marquess of Queensberry champion) 1892–97
Jack Dempsey 1919–26
Joe Louis 1937–49
Rocky Marciano 1952–56
Muhammad Ali 1964–67, 1974–78, 1978–79
Larry Holmes 1978–85
Mike Tyson 1986–1990

canoeing propelling a lightweight, shallow boat, pointed at both ends, by paddles or sails. Currently, canoes are made from fibreglass, but original boats were of wooden construction covered in bark or skin. Two types of canoe are used: the *kayak*, and the *Canadian-style* canoe. The kayak, derived from the Eskimo model, has a keel and the canoeist sits. The Canadian style canoe has no keel and the canoeist kneels.

OLYMPIC GAMES

event introduced 1936
men: kayak singles
500 metres
1980 Vladimir Parfenovich *(USSR)*
1984 Ian Ferguson *(New Zealand)*
1988 Zsolt Gyulay *(Hungary)*
1992 Mikko Kolehmainen *(Finland)*

1,000 metres
1980 Rudiger Helm *(East Germany)*
1984 Alan Thompson *(New Zealand)*
1988 Greg Barton *(USA)*
1992 Clint Robinson *(Australia)*

kayak pairs
500 metres
1980 USSR
1984 New Zealand
1988 New Zealand
1992 Germany

1,000 metres
1980 USSR
1984 Canada
1988 USA
1992 Germany

kayak fours
1,000 metres
1980 East Germany
1984 New Zealand
1988 Hungary
1992 Germany

Canadian singles
500 metres
1980 Sergey Postrekhin *(USSR)*
1984 Larry Cain *(Canada)*
1988 Olaf Heukrodt *(East Germany)*
1992 Nikolai Bukhalov *(Germany)*

1,000 metres
1980 Lubomir Lubenov *(Bulgaria)*
1984 Ulrich Eicke *(West Germany)*
1988 Ivan Klementiev *(USSR)*
1992 Nikolai Bukhalov *(Germany)*

Canadian pairs
500 metres
1980 Hungary
1984 Yugoslavia
1988 USSR
1992 Unified Team*

1,000 metres
1980 Romania
1984 Romania
1988 USSR
1992 Germany

women: kayak singles
500 metres
1980 Birgit Fischer *(East Germany)*
1984 Agneta Anderson *(Sweden)*
1988 Vania Guecheva *(Bulgaria)*
1992 Birgit Schmidt *(Germany)*

kayak pairs
500 metres
1980 East Germany
1984 Sweden
1988 East Germany
1992 Germany
* *Commonwealth of Independent States plus Georgia*

---

cricket bat-and-ball game between two teams of 11 players each. It is played with a small solid ball and long flat-sided wooden bats, on a round or oval field, at the centre of which is a finely mown pitch, 20 m/22 yd long. At each end of the pitch is a wicket made up of three upright wooden sticks (stumps), surmounted by two smaller sticks (bails). The object of the game is to score more runs than the opposing team. A run is normally scored by the batsman striking the ball and exchanging ends with his or her partner until the ball is returned by a fielder, or by hitting the ball to the boundary line for an automatic four or six runs.

COUNTY CHAMPIONSHIP

first held officially 1890
1983 Essex
1984 Essex
1985 Middlesex
1986 Essex
1987 Nottinghamshire
1988 Worcestershire
1989 Worcestershire
1990 Middlesex
1991 Essex
1992 Essex
1993 Middlesex

AXA EQUITY AND LAW LEAGUE

(formerly Refuge Assurance League), first held 1969
1982 Sussex
1983 Yorkshire
1984 Essex
1985 Essex
1986 Hampshire
1987 Worcestershire
1988 Worcestershire
1989 Lancashire
1990 Derbyshire
1991 Nottinghamshire
1992 Middlesex
1993 Glamorgan

NATWEST TROPHY

(formerly the Gillette Cup), first held 1963
1983 Somerset
1984 Middlesex
1985 Essex
1986 Sussex
1987 Nottinghamshire
1988 Middlesex
1989 Warwickshire
1990 Lancashire
1991 Hampshire
1992 Northamptonshire
1993 Warwickshire

BENSON AND HEDGES CUP

first held 1972
1983 Middlesex
1984 Lancashire

1985 Leicestershire
1986 Middlesex
1987 Yorkshire
1988 Hampshire
1989 Nottinghamshire
1990 Lancashire
1991 Worcestershire
1992 Hampshire
1993 Derbyshire

WORLD CUP
first held 1975, contested every four years
1975 West Indies
1979 West Indies
1983 India
1987 Australia
1992 Pakistan

curling game resembling bowls that is played on ice, between two teams of four players each. Each player has two disclike stones, of equal size, fitted with a handle. The object of the game is to slide the stones across the ice so that they are positioned as near as possible to a target object (the tee), those nearest scoring. The stone may be curled in one direction or another according to the twist given as it leaves the hand. The match is played for an agreed number of heads or shots, or by time.

WORLD CHAMPIONSHIP
first held 1959 for men, 1979 for women

men
1988 Norway
1989 Canada
1990 Canada
1991 Scotland
1992 Switzerland
1993 Canada

women
1988 West Germany
1989 Canada
1990 Norway
1991 Norway
1992 Sweden
1993 Canada

cycling cycle racing can take place on oval artificial tracks, on the road, or across country (cyclo-cross). *Stage races* are run over gruelling terrain and can last anything from three to five days up to three and a half weeks, as in the Tour de France, Tour of Italy, and Tour of Spain. *Criteriums* are fast, action-packed races around the closed streets of town or city centres. *Road races* are run over a prescribed circuit, which the riders will lap several times. Such a race will normally cover a distance of approximately 100 mi/160 km. *Track racing* takes place on a concrete or wooden banked circuit, either indoors or outdoors. In *time trialing* each rider races against the clock, with all the competitors starting at different intervals.

TOUR DE FRANCE
first held 1903
1983 Laurent Fignon *(France)*
1984 Laurent Fignon *(France)*
1985 Bernard Hinault *(France)*

1986 Greg LeMond *(USA)*
1987 Stephen Roche *(Ireland)*
1988 Pedro Delgado *(Spain)*
1989 Greg LeMond *(USA)*
1990 Greg LeMond *(USA)*
1991 Miguel Indurain *(Spain)*
1992 Miguel Indurain *(Spain)*
1993 Miguel Indurain *(Spain)*

TOUR OF BRITAIN
(formerly the Milk Race), first held 1951
1982 Yuri Kashirin *(USSR)*
1983 Matt Eaton *(USA)*
1984 Oleg Czougeda *(USSR)*
1985 Erik van Lancker *(Belgium)*
1986 Joey McLoughlin *(UK)*
1987 Malcolm Elliott *(UK)*
1988 Vasily Zhdanov *(USSR)*
1989 Brian Walton *(Canada)*
1990 Shane Sutton *(Australia)*
1991 Chris Walker *(UK)*
1992 Conor Henry *(Ireland)*
1993 Chris Lillywhite *(UK)*

WORLD PROFESSIONAL ROAD RACE CHAMPIONS
first held 1927
1982 Giuseppe Saroni *(Italy)*
1983 Greg LeMond *(USA)*
1984 Claude Criquielon *(Belgium)*
1985 Joop Zoetemelk *(Holland)*
1986 Moreno Argentin *(Italy)*
1987 Stephen Roche *(Ireland)*
1988 Maurizio Fondriest *(Italy)*
1989 Greg LeMond *(USA)*
1990 Rudy Dhaenens *(Belgium)*
1991 Gianni Bugno *(Italy)*
1992 Gianni Bugno *(Italy)*
1993 Lance Armstrong *(USA)*

darts indoor game played on a circular board. Darts about 13 cm/5 in long are thrown at segmented targets, and score points according to their landing place.

WORLD CHAMPIONSHIP
first held 1978
1983 Keith Deller *(England)*
1984 Eric Bristow *(England)*
1985 Eric Bristow *(England)*
1986 Eric Bristow *(England)*
1987 John Lowe *(England)*
1988 Bob Anderson *(England)*
1989 Jocky Wilson *(Scotland)*
1990 Phil Taylor *(England)*
1991 Dennis Priestley *(England)*
1992 Phil Taylor *(England)*
1993 John Lowe *(England)*

diving sport of entering water either from a springboard (3 m/10 ft) above the water, or from a platform, or highboard, (10 m/33 ft) above the water. Various starts are adopted, and twists and somersaults may be performed in midair. Points are awarded and the level of difficulty of each dive is used as a multiplying factor.

OLYMPIC GAMES
springboard diving
men
1980 Aleksandr Portnov *(USSR)*

1984 Greg Louganis *(USA)*
1988 Greg Louganis *(USA)*
1992 Mark Lenzi *(USA)*

women
1980 Irina Kalinina *(USSR)*
1984 Sylvie Bernier *(Canada)*
1988 Gao Min *(China)*
1992 Gao Min *(China)*

platform diving
men
1980 Falk Hoffmann *(East Germany)*
1984 Greg Louganis *(USA)*
1988 Greg Louganis *(USA)*
1992 Sun Shuwei *(China)*

women
1980 Martina Jäschke *(East Germany)*
1984 Zhou Jihong *(China)*
1988 Xu Yanmei *(China)*
1992 Fu Mingxia *(China)*

equestrianism skill in horse riding, as practised under International Equestrian Federation rules. *Showjumping* is horse-jumping over a course of fences. The winner is usually the competitor with fewest 'faults' (penalty marks given for knocking down or refusing fences), but in timed competitions it is the competitor completing the course most quickly, additional seconds being added for mistakes. *Dressage* tests the horse's obedience skills, and the rider's control. Tests consist of a series of movements at walk, trot, canter, with each movement marked by judges who look for suppleness, balance, and the special harmony between rider and horse. *Three-Day Eventing* tests the all-round abilities of a horse and rider in dressage, cross-country, and showjumping.

WORLD CHAMPIONSHIP

show jumping; first held 1953 for men, 1965 for women; since 1978 men and women have competed together

men
1953 Francisco Goyoago *(Spain)*
1954 Hans-Günter Winkler *(West Germany)*
1955 Hans-Günter Winkler *(West Germany)*
1956 Raimondo D'Inzeo *(Italy)*
1960 Raimondo D'Inzeo *(Italy)*
1966 Pierre d'Oriola *(France)*
1970 David Broome *(UK)*
1974 Hartwig Steenken *(West Germany)*

women
1965 Marion Coakes *(UK)*
1970 Janou Lefebvre *(France)*
1974 Janou Tissot (born Lefebvre) *(France)*

mixed
1978 Gerd Wiltfang *(West Germany)*
1982 Norbert Koof *(West Germany)*
1986 Gail Greenough *(Canada)*
1990 Eric Navet *(France)*

EUPOPEAN CHAMPIONSHIP

show jumping; first held 1957 with men and women competing separately; since 1975 they have competed together
1977 Johan Heins *(Holland)*
1979 Gerd Wiltfang *(West Germany)*
1981 Paul Schockemohle *(West Germany)*

1983 Paul Schockemohle *(West Germany)*
1985 Paul Schockemohle *(West Germany)*
1987 Pierre Durand *(France)*
1989 John Whitaker *(UK)*
1991 Eric Navet *(France)*
1993 Jean-Lou Bigot *(France)*

BRITISH SHOWJUMPING CHAMPIONSHIP

first held 1961
1982 Paul Schockemohle *(West Germany)*
1983 John Whitaker *(UK)*
1984 John Ledingham *(Ireland)*
1985 Paul Schockemohle *(West Germany)*
1986 Paul Schockemohle *(West Germany)*
1987 Nick Skelton *(UK)*
1988 Nick Skelton *(UK)*
1989 Nick Skelton *(UK)*
1990 Joe Turi *(UK)*
1991 Michael Whitaker *(UK)*
1992 Michael Whitaker *(UK)*
1993 Michael Whitaker *(UK)*

THREE-DAY EVENTING WORLD CHAMPIONSHIP

1974 Bruce Davidson *(USA)*
1978 Bruce Davidson *(USA)*
1982 Lucinda Green (born Prior-Palmer) *(UK)*
1986 Virginia Leng (born Holgate) *(UK)*
1990 Blyth Tait *(New Zealand)*

BADMINTON HORSE TRIALS

three-day eventing; first held 1949
1983 Lucinda Green *(UK)*
1984 Lucinda Green *(UK)*
1985 Virginia Holgate *(UK)*
1986 Ian Stark *(UK)*
1987 cancelled
1988 Ian Stark *(UK)*
1989 Virginia Leng *(UK)*
1990 Nicola McIrvine *(UK)*
1991 Rodney Powell *(UK)*
1992 Mary Thompson *(UK)*
1993 Virginia Leng *(UK)*

fencing sport of fighting with swords including the *foil*, derived from the light weapon used in practice duels; the *épée*, a heavier weapon derived from the duelling sword proper; and the *sabre*, with a curved handle and narrow V-shaped blade. In sabre fighting, cuts count as well as thrusts. Masks and protective jackets are worn, and hits are registered electronically in competitions.

WORLD CHAMPIONSHIP

first held 1921; Olympic winners automatically become world champions

foil: men
1988 Stefano Cerioni *(Italy)*
1989 Alexandr Koch *(West Germany)*
1990 Philippe Omnes *(France)*
1991 Ingo Weissenborn *(Germany)*
1992 Philippe Omnes *(France)*
1993 Alexandr Koch *(Germany)*

foil: women
1988 Anja Fichtel *(West Germany)*
1989 Olga Velichko *(USSR)*
1990 Anja Fichtel *(Germany)*

1991 Giovanna Trillini *(Italy)*
1992 Giovanna Trillini *(Italy)*
1993 Francessa Botolozzi *(Italy)*

épée: men
1988 Arnd Schmitt *(West Germany)*
1989 Manuel Pereira *(Spain)*
1990 Thomas Gerull *(Germany)*
1991 Andrei Chouvalov *(USSR)*
1992 Eric Srecki *(France)*
1993 Pavel Kolobkov *(Russia)*

épée: women
1989 Anja Straub *(Switzerland)*
1990 Taimi Chappe *(Cuba)*
1991 Mariann Horvath *(Hungary)*
1992 not an Olympic event
1993 Olga Jermakova *(Russia)*

sabre: men
1988 Jean-François Lamour *(France)*
1989 Grigoriy Kirienko *(USSR)*
1990 Gyorgy Nebald *(Hungary)*
1991 Grigoriy Kirienko *(USSR)*
1992 Bence Szabo *(Hungary)*
1993 Grigoriy Kirienko *(Russia)*

football, American contact sport played between two teams of 11 players, with an inflated oval ball. Players are well padded for protection and wear protective helmets. The game is played on a field 91.4 m/100 yd long and 48.8 m/53.3 yd wide, marked out with a series of parallel lines giving a gridiron effect. There is a goalpost at each end of the field, and beyond this an endzone 9 m/10 yd long. Points are scored by running or passing the ball across the goal line (touchdown); by kicking it over the goal's crossbar after a touchdown (conversion or point after touchdown), or from the field during regular play (field goal); or by tackling an offensive player who has the ball in the end zone, or blocking an offensive team's kick so it goes out of bounds from the end zone (safety). A touchdown counts 6 points, a field goal 3, a safety 2, and a conversion 1. Games are divided into four quarters of 15 minutes each.

SUPER BOWL

first held 1967
1983 Washington Redskins
1984 Los Angeles Raiders
1985 San Francisco 49ers
1986 Chicago Bears
1987 New York Giants
1988 Washington Redskins
1989 San Francisco 49ers
1990 San Francisco 49ers
1991 New York Giants
1992 Washington Redskins
1993 Dallas Cowboys
1994 Dallas Cowboys

football, association or *soccer* form of football originating in the UK, popular in Europe and Latin America. It is played between two teams each of 11 players, on a field 90–120 m/100–130 yd long and 45–90 m/ 50–100 yd wide, with an inflated spherical ball. The object of the game is to kick or head the ball into the opponents' goal, an area 7.31 m/8 yd wide and

2.44 m/8 ft high. Games are divided into two halves of 45 minutes each, the teams changing ends at half-time.

In the UK the game is played according to the rules laid down by the Football Association, founded 1863. Slight amendments to the rules take effect in certain competitions and overseas matches as laid down by the sport's world governing body, Fédération Internationale de Football Association (FIFA, 1904).

WORLD CUP

first held 1930; contested every four years
1954 West Germany
1958 Brazil
1962 Brazil
1966 England
1970 Brazil
1974 West Germany
1978 Argentina
1982 Italy
1986 Argentina
1990 West Germany

EUROPEAN CHAMPIONSHIP

instituted 1958, first final 1960; contested every four years
1960 USSR
1964 Spain
1968 Italy
1972 West Germany
1976 Czechoslovakia
1980 West Germany
1984 France
1988 Holland
1992 Denmark

EUROPEAN CHAMPIONS CUP

first held 1955
1983 SV Hamburg *(West Germany)*
1984 Liverpool *(England)*
1985 Juventus *(Italy)*
1986 Steaua Bucharest *(Romania)*
1987 FC Porto *(Portugal)*
1988 PSV Eindhoven *(Holland)*
1989 AC Milan *(Italy)*
1990 AC Milan *(Italy)*
1991 Red Star Belgrade *(Yugoslavia)*
1992 Barcelona *(Spain)*

EUROPEAN CUP WINNERS' CUP

first held 1960
1983 Aberdeen *(Scotland)*
1984 Juventus *(Italy)*
1985 Everton *(England)*
1986 Dinamo Kiev *(USSR)*
1987 Ajax *(Holland)*
1988 Mechelen *(Belgium)*
1989 Barcelona *(Spain)*
1990 Sampdoria *(Italy)*
1991 Manchester United *(England)*
1992 Werder Bremen *(Germany)*
1993 Parma *(Italy)*

UEFA CUP

(formerly Inter Cities Fairs Cup) first held 1955
1983 Anderlecht *(Belgium)*
1984 Tottenham Hotspur *(England)*
1985 Real Madrid *(Spain)*
1986 Real Madrid *(Spain)*

1987 IFK Gothenburg *(Sweden)*
1988 Bayer Leverkusen *(West Germany)*
1989 Napoli *(Italy)*
1990 Juventus *(Italy)*
1991 Internazionale Milan *(Italy)*
1992 Ajax *(Holland)*
1993 Juventus *(Italy)*

UK CHAMPIONSHIPS

FA CUP

a knockout club competition, first held 1872
1983 Manchester United
1984 Everton
1985 Manchester United
1986 Liverpool
1987 Coventry City
1988 Wimbledon
1989 Liverpool
1990 Manchester United
1991 Tottenham Hotspur
1992 Liverpool
1993 Arsenal

FOOTBALL LEAGUE CUP

(currently known as the Coca-Cola Cup, formerly the Rumbelows Cup, the Milk Cup and the Littlewoods Cup) first final 1961 in two stages, now a single game
1983 Liverpool
1984 Liverpool
1985 Norwich City
1986 Oxford United
1987 Arsenal
1988 Luton Town
1989 Nottingham Forest
1990 Nottingham Forest
1991 Sheffield Wednesday
1992 Manchester United
1993 Arsenal

PREMIER LEAGUE CHAMPIONS

(Formerly Division One Champions), Football League founded 1888—89
1982—83 Liverpool
1983—84 Liverpool
1984—85 Everton
1985—86 Liverpool
1986—87 Everton
1987—88 Liverpool
1988—89 Arsenal
1989—90 Liverpool
1990—91 Arsenal
1991—92 Leeds United
1992—93 Manchester United

SCOTTISH PREMIER DIVISION

Scottish League formed 1899—91, reformed into three divisions 1975—76
1982—83 Dundee United
1983—84 Aberdeen
1984—85 Aberdeen
1985—86 Celtic
1986—87 Rangers
1987—88 Celtic
1988—89 Rangers
1989—90 Rangers
1990—91 Rangers
1991—92 Rangers
1992—93 Rangers

SCOTTISH FA CUP

first final held 1874
1983 Aberdeen
1984 Aberdeen
1985 Celtic
1986 Aberdeen
1987 St Mirren
1988 Celtic
1989 Celtic
1990 Aberdeen
1991 Motherwell
1992 Rangers
1993 Rangers

football, Australian Rules game that combines aspects of Gaelic football, rugby, and association football; it is played between two teams of 18 players, with an inflated oval ball. It is unique to Australia. The game is played on an oval pitch, 164.4 m/180 yd long and 137 m/150 yd wide, with a pair of goalposts, 6 m/19 ft high, at each end. On either side of each pair of goalposts is a smaller post. Each team is placed in five lines of three persons each, and three players follow the ball all the time. Points are scored by kicking the ball between the goalposts, without its being touched on the way (goal, 6 points), or by passing the ball between a goalpost and one of the smaller posts, or causing it to hit a post (behind, 1 point).

VICTORIA FOOTBALL LEAGUE PREMIERSHIP TROPHY

first contested 1897
1982 Carlton
1983 Hawthorn
1984 Essendon
1985 Essendon
1986 Hawthorn
1987 Carlton
1988 Hawthorn
1989 Hawthorn
1990 Collingwood
1991 Hawthorn
1992 West Coast
1993 Essendon

football, Gaelic kicking and catching game played mainly in Ireland, between two teams of 15 players each. It is played with an inflated spherical ball, on a field 76–91 m/84–100 yd long and 128–146 m/140–160 yd wide. At each end is a set of goalposts 4.88 m/16 ft high, with a crossbar 2.44 m/8 ft above the ground, and a net across its lower half. Goals are scored by kicking the ball into the net (3 points) or over the crossbar (1 point).

ALL-IRELAND CHAMPIONSHIP

first played 1887
1982 Offaly
1983 Dublin
1984 Kerry
1985 Kerry
1986 Kerry
1987 Meath
1988 Meath
1989 Cork

1990 Cork
1991 Down
1992 Donegal

golf outdoor game in which a small rubber-cored ball is hit with a wooden- or iron-faced club. Its object is to sink the ball in a hole that can be anywhere between 90 m/100 yd and 457 m/500 yd away, using the least number of strokes. The faces of the clubs have varying angles and are styled for different types of shot.

Most golf courses consist of 18 holes and are approximately 5,500 m/6,000 yd in length. Each hole is made up of distinct areas: the *tee*, from where plays start at each hole; the *green*, a finely manicured area where the hole is located; the *fairway*, the grassed area between the tee and the green, not cut as finely as the green; and the *rough*, the perimeter of the fairway, which is left to grow naturally. Natural hazards such as trees, bushes, and streams make play more difficult, and there are additional artificial hazards in the form of sand-filled bunkers.

BRITISH OPEN

first held 1860
1983 Tom Watson *(USA)*
1984 Severiano Ballesteros *(Spain)*
1985 Sandy Lyle *(UK)*
1986 Greg Norman *(Australia)*
1987 Nick Faldo *(UK)*
1988 Severiano Ballesteros *(Spain)*
1989 Mark Calcavecchia *(USA)*
1990 Nick Faldo *(UK)*
1991 Ian Baker-Finch *(Australia)*
1992 Nick Faldo *(UK)*
1993 Greg Norman *(Australia)*

UNITED STATES OPEN

first held 1895
1983 Larry Nelson *(USA)*
1984 Fuzzy Zoeller *(USA)*
1985 Andy North *(USA)*
1986 Ray Floyd *USA)*
1987 Scott Simpson *(USA)*
1988 Curtis Strange *(USA)*
1989 Curtis Strange *(USA)*
1990 Hale Irwin *(USA)*
1991 Payne Stewart *(USA)*
1992 Tom Kite *(USA)*
1993 Lee Janzen *(USA)*

MASTERS

first held 1934
1983 Severiano Ballesteros *(Spain)*
1984 Ben Crenshaw *(USA)*
1985 Bernhard Langer *(West Germany)*
1986 Jack Nicklaus *(USA)*
1987 Larry Mize *(USA)*
1988 Sandy Lyle *(UK)*
1989 Nick Faldo *(UK)*
1990 Nick Faldo *(UK)*
1991 Ian Woosnam *(UK)*
1992 Fred Couples *(USA)*
1993 Bernard Langer *(Germany)*

UNITED STATES PGA

first held 1916
1982 Ray Floyd *(USA)*
1983 Hal Sutton *(USA)*
1984 Lee Trevino *(USA)*
1985 Hubert Green *(USA)*
1986 Bob Tway *(USA)*
1987 Larry Nelson *(USA)*
1988 Jeff Sluman *(USA)*
1989 Payne Stewart *(USA)*
1990 Wayne Grady *(Australia)*
1991 John Daly *(USA)*
1992 Nick Price *(Zimbabwe)*
1993 Paul Azinger *(USA)*

greyhound racing spectator sport, invented in 1919 in the USA, that has a number of greyhounds pursuing a mechanical hare around a circular or oval track. It is popular in the UK and Australia, attracting much on- and offcourse betting.

GREYHOUND DERBY

UK, first held 1927
1983 I'm Slippy
1984 Whisper Wishes
1985 Pagan Swallow
1986 Tico
1987 Signal Park
1988 Hit the Lid
1989 Lartigue Note
1990 Slippy Blue
1991 Ballinderry Ash
1992 Farloe Melody
1993 Ringa Hustle

gymnastics competitive physical exercises. *Men's gymnastics* includes exercises on apparatus such as the horizontal bar, parallel bars, horse vault, pommel horse, and rings, and on an area of floor 12 m/13 yd square. *Women's gymnastics* includes work on the asymmetric bars, side horse vault, and beam, and floor exercises. Each exercise is marked out of ten by a set of judges, who look for suppleness, balance, control, and innovation. *Rhythmic gymnastics*, is choreographed to music and performed by individuals or six-woman teams, with small hand apparatus such as a ribbon, ball, or hoop.

WORLD CHAMPIONSHIP

first held 1903 for men, 1934 for women; contested every two years; Olympic champions automatically become world champions

men: individual/team
1974 Shigeru Kasamatsu *(Japan)*/Japan
1978 Nikolai Adrianov *(USSR)*/Japan
1979 Aleksandr Ditiatin *(USSR)*/USSR
1981 Yuri Korolev *(USSR)*/USSR
1983 Dimitri Belozertchev *(USSR)*/China
1985 Yuri Korolev *(USSR)*/USSR
1987 Dimitri Belozertchev *(USSR)*/USSR
1989 Igor Korobichensky *(USSR)*/USSR
1991 Gregori Misutin *(USSR)*/USSR
1992 Vitaly Scherbo (*Unified Team* *)/Unified Team
1993 Vitaly Scherbo (*Belarus*)/Belarus

women: individual/team
1974 Ludmila Tourischeva *(USSR)*/USSR
1978 Elena Mukhina *(USSR)*/USSR
1979 Nelli Kim *(USSR)*/Romania
1981 Olga Bitcherova *(USSR)*/USSR

1983 Natalia Yurchenko *(USSR)*/USSR
1985 Elena Shoushounova *(USSR)* and Oksana Omeliantchik *(USSR)*/USSR
1987 Aurelia Dobre *(Romania)*/Romania
1989 Svetlana Boginskaya *(USSR)*/USSR
1991 Kim Zmeskal *(USA)*/USSR
1992 Tatyana Gutsu *(Unified Team)*/Unified Team
1993 Shannon Miller *(USA)*/USA
Commonwealth of Independent States plus Georgia

handball game resembling football, but played with the hands instead of the feet. The indoor game has seven players in a team; the outdoor version (field handball) has 11. The indoor court is 40 m/43.8 yd long and 20 m/21.9 yd wide, with goals 2 m/6.6 ft high and 3 m/9.8 ft wide.

OLYMPIC GAMES
indoor event introduced 1972 for men, 1976 for women

men
1972 Yugoslavia
1976 USSR
1980 East Germany
1984 Yugoslavia
1988 USSR
1992 Unified Team*

women
1976 USSR
1980 USSR
1984 Yugoslavia
1988 South Korea
1992 South Korea
* *Commonwealth of Independent States plus Georgia*

hockey or *field hockey* stick-and-ball game played by two teams of 11 players each. Its object is to strike the solid white ball, by means of a hooked stick, into the opposing team's goal. The game is played on a pitch 91.5 m/100 yd long and 54.9 m/60 yd wide, with a goal, 2.13 m/7 ft high and 3.65 m/4 yd wide, at each end. All shots at goal must be made from within a striking 'circle', a semicircle of 14.64 m/16 yd radius in front of each goal. The game is divided into two 35-minute periods.

OLYMPIC GAMES
event introduced 1908 for men, 1980 for women

men
1980 India
1984 Pakistan
1988 Great Britain
1992 Germany

women
1980 Zimbabwe
1984 Netherlands
1988 Australia
1992 Spain

WORLD CUP
men's tournament first held 1971 and contested every four years; women's tournament first held 1974 and contested every four years

men
1971 Pakistan
1973 Holland

1975 India
1978 Pakistan
1982 Pakistan
1986 Australia
1990 Holland

women
1974 Holland
1976 West Germany
1978 Holland
1981 West Germany
1983 Holland
1986 Holland
1990 Holland

horse racing the sport of racing mounted or driven horses. Two popular forms in Britain are *flat racing*, for thoroughbred horses over a flat course, and *National Hunt racing*, in which the horses have to clear obstacles. Forms of National Hunt racing include *steeplechasing*, a development of foxhunting, in which horses jump over fixed fences 0.9–1.2 m/3–4 ft high (the amateur version is point-to-point), and *hurdling*, in which the horses negotiate less taxing, and movable, fences. *Harness racing* is popular in North America. It is for standard-bred horses pulling a two-wheeled 'sulky' on which the driver sits. Leading races include The Hambletonian and Little Brown Jug.

DERBY
first held 1780; 1 mi 4 furlongs long
horse/jockey
1983 Teenoso/Lester Piggott
1984 Secreto/Christy Roche
1985 Slip Anchor/Steve Cauthen
1986 Shahrastani/Walter Swinburn
1987 Reference Point/Steve Cauthen
1988 Kahyasi/Ray Cochrane
1989 Nashwan/Willie Carson
1990 Quest for Fame/Pat Eddery
1991 Generous/Alan Munro
1992 Dr Devious/John Reid
1993 Commander In Chief/Michael Kinane

OAKS
first held 1779; 1 mi 4 furlongs long
horse/jockey
1982 Time Charter/Billy Newnes
1983 Sun Princess/Willie Carson
1984 Circus Plume/Lester Piggott
1985 Oh So Sharp/Steve Cauthen
1986 Midway Lady/Ray Cochrane
1987 Unite/Walter Swinburn
1988 Diminuendo/Steve Cauthen
1989 Snow Bride/Steve Cauthen
1990 Salsabil/Willie Carson
1991 Jet Ski Lady/Christy Roche
1992 User Friendly/George Duffield
1993 Intrepidity/Michael Roberts

1,000 GUINEAS
first held 1814; 1 mi long
horse/jockey
1983 Ma Biche/Freddy Head
1984 Pebbles/Philip Robinson
1985 Oh So Sharp/Steve Cauthen

1986 Midway Lady/Ray Cochrane
1987 Miesque/Freddy Head
1988 Ravinella/Gary Moore
1989 Musical Bliss/Walter Swinburn
1990 Salsabil/Willie Carson
1991 Shadayid/Willie Carson
1992 Hatoof/Walter Swinburn
1993 Sayyedati/Walter Swinburn

2,000 GUINEAS

first held 1809; 1 mi long

horse/jockey
1983 Lomond/Pat Eddery
1984 El Gran Senor/Pat Eddery
1985 Shadeed/Lester Piggott
1986 Dancing Brave/Greville Starkey
1987 Don't Forget Me/Willie Carson
1988 Doyoun/Walter Swinburn
1989 Nashwan/Walter Swinburn
1990 Tirol/Michael Kinane
1991 Mystiko/Michael Roberts
1992 Rodrigo de Triano/Lester Piggott
1993 Zafonic/Pat Eddery

ST LEGER

the oldest English classic, first held 1776; 1 mi 6 furlongs 127 yd long

horse/jockey
1982 Touching Wood/Paul Cook
1983 Sun Princess/Willie Carson
1984 Commanche Run/Lester Piggott
1985 Oh So Sharp/Steve Cauthen
1986 Moon Madness/Pat Eddery
1987 Reference Point/Steve Cauthen
1988 Minster Son/Willie Carson
1989 Michelozza/Steve Cauthen
1990 Snurge/Richard Quinn
1991 Toulon/Pat Eddery
1992 User Friendly/George Duffield
1993 Bob's Return/Philip Robinson

GRAND NATIONAL

steeplechase; first held 1847; 4 mi 4 furlongs long
horse/jockey (amateurs are shown as Mr)
1983 Corbiere/Ben De Haan
1984 Hallo Dandy/Neale Doughty
1985 Last Suspect/Hywel Davies
1986 West Tip/Richard Dunwoody
1987 Maori Venture/Steve Knight
1988 Rhyme N'Reason/Brendan Powell
1989 Little Polveir/Jimmy Frost
1990 Mr Frisk/Marcus Armytage
1991 Seagram/Nigel Hawke
1992 Party Politics/Carl Llewellyn
1993 void

PRIX DE L'ARC DE TRIOMPHE

first held 1920; 2,400 m long
horse/jockey
1983 All Along/Walter Swinburn
1984 Sagace/Yves Saint-Martin
1985 Rainbow Quest/Pat Eddery
1986 Dancing Brave/Pat Eddery
1986 Lieutenant's Lark/Robbie Davis
1987 Trempolino/Pat Eddery
1988 Tony Bin/John Reid
1989 Caroll House/Michael Kinane

1990 Saumarez/Gerald Mosse
1991 Suave Dancer/Cash Asmussen
1992 Subotica/Thierry Jarnet
1993 Urban Sea/Eric St Martin

hurling or *hurley* stick-and-ball game played between two teams of 15 players each, popular in Ireland. Its object is to hit the ball, by means of a curved stick, into the opposing team's goal. If the ball passes under the goal's crossbar 3 points are scored; if it passes above the crossbar 1 point is scored.

ALL-IRELAND CHAMPIONSHIP

first held 1887
1982 Kilkenny
1983 Kilkenny
1984 Cork
1985 Offaly
1986 Cork
1987 Galway
1988 Galway
1989 Tipperary
1990 Cork
1991 Tipperary
1992 Limerick

ice hockey game played on ice between two teams of six, developed in Canada from hockey. A rubber disc (puck) is used in place of a ball. Players wear skates and protective clothing.

OLYMPIC GAMES

event introduced 1920
1976 USSR
1980 United States
1984 USSR
1988 USSR
1992 Unified Team*

* *Commonwealth of Independent States plus Georgia*

STANLEY CUP

end-of-season playoff tournament conducted between the top teams of the Canadian and US National Hockey League conferences

1988 Edmonton Oilers
1989 Calgary Flames
1990 Edmonton Oilers
1991 Pittsburgh Penguins
1992 Pittsburgh Penguins
1993 Montreal Canadiens

judo form of wrestling of Japanese origin. The two combatants wear loose-fitting, belted jackets and trousers to facilitate holds, and falls are broken by a square mat; when one has established a painful hold that the other cannot break, the latter signifies surrender by slapping the ground with a free hand. Degrees of proficiency are indicated by the colour of the belt: for novices, white; after examination, brown (three degrees); and finally, black (nine degrees).

WORLD CHAMPIONSHIP

first held 1956 for men, 1980 for women; contested every two years
men: open class
1983 Angelo Parisi *(France)*

1985 Yoshimi Masaki *(Japan)*
1987 Noayo Ogawa *(Japan)*
1989 Noayo Ogawa *(Japan)*
1991 Noayo Ogawa *(Japan)*
1993 Roman Kubacki *(Poland)*

women: open class
1984 Ingrid Berghmans *(Belgium)*
1986 Ingrid Berghmans *(Belgium)*
1987 Fengliang Gao *(China)*
1989 Estela Rodriguez *(Cuba)*
1991 Zhuang Xiaoyan *(China)*
1993 Barbara Maksymov *(Russia)*

---

lacrosse Canadian ball game, adopted from the North American Indians, and named from a fancied resemblance of the lacrosse stick (crosse) to a bishop's crosier. Thongs across the curved end of the crosse form a pocket to carry the small rubber ball. The field is approximately 100 m/110 yd long and a minimum 55 m/60 yd wide in the men's game, which is played with ten players per side; the women's field is larger, and there are twelve players per side. The goals are just under 2 m/6 ft square, with loose nets.

WORLD CHAMPIONSHIP
first held 1967 for men, 1969 for women

men
1967 USA
1974 USA
1978 Canada
1982 USA
1986 USA
1990 USA

women
1969 UK
1974 USA
1978 Canada
1982 USA
1986 Australia
1989 USA

---

motorcycle racing speed contests on motorcycles. It has many different forms: *road racing* over open roads; *circuit racing* over purpose-built tracks; *speedway* over oval-shaped dirt tracks; *motocross* (or *scrambling*) over natural terrain, incorporating hill climbs; and *trials*, also over natural terrain, but with the addition of artificial hazards. For finely tuned production machines, there exists a season-long world championship Grand Prix series with various categories for machines with engine sizes 125–500 cc.

WORLD CHAMPIONSHIP
Grand Prix racing; first held 1949
500cc class

rider/manufacturer
1982 Franco Uncini/Suzuki *(Italy)*
1983 Freddie Spencer/Honda *(USA)*
1984 Eddie Lawson/Yamaha *(USA)*
1985 Freddie Spencer/Honda *(USA)*
1986 Eddie Lawson/Yamaha *(USA)*
1987 Wayne Gardner/Honda *(Australia)*
1988 Eddie Lawson/Yamaha *(USA)*
1989 Eddie Lawson/Honda *(USA)*
1990 Wayne Rainey/Yamaha *(USA)*

1991 Wayne Rainey/Yamaha *(USA)*
1992 Wayne Rainey/Yamaha *(USA)*
1993 Kevin Scwantz/Suzuki *(USA)*

ISLE OF MAN TOURIST TROPHY
road race; first held 1907
Senior TT
rider/manufacturer
1983 Rob McElnea/Suzuki *(UK)*
1984 Rob McElnea/Suzuki *(UK)*
1985 Joey Dunlop/Honda *(Ireland)*
1986 Roger Burnett/Honda *(UK)*
1987 Joey Dunlop/Honda *(Ireland)*
1988 Joey Dunlop/Honda *(Ireland)*
1989 Steve Hislop/Honda *(UK)*
1990 Carl Fogarty/Honda *(UK)*
1991 Steve Hislop/Honda *(UK)*
1992 Steve Hislop/Norton *(UK)*
1993 Joey Dunlop/Honda *(Ireland)*

WORLD CHAMPIONSHIP
speedway; first held 1936
individual
1982 Bruce Penhall *(USA)*
1983 Egon Müller *(West Germany)*
1984 Erik Gundersen *(Denmark)*
1985 Erik Gundersen *(Denmark)*
1986 Hans Nielsen *(Denmark)*
1987 Hans Nielsen *(Denmark)*
1988 Erik Gundersen *(Denmark)*
1989 Hans Nielsen *(Denmark)*
1990 Per Jonsson *(Sweden)*
1991 Jan Pedersen *(Denmark)*
1992 Gary Havelock *(England)*
1993 Sam Ermolenko *(USA)*

pairs
event introduced 1970
1982 Dennis Sigalos and Bobby Schwartz *USA)*
1983 Kenny Carter and Peter Collins *(England)*
1984 Peter Collins and Chris Morton *(England)*
1985 Erik Gundersen and Tommy Knudsen *Denmark)*
1986 Erik Gundersen and Hans Nielsen *(Denmark)*
1987 Erik Gundersen and Hans Nielsen *(Denmark)*
1988 Erik Gundersen and Hans Nielsen *(Denmark)*
1989 Erik Gundersen and Hans Nielsen *(Denmark)*
1990 Hans Nielsen and Jan Pedersen *(Denmark)*
1991 Hans Nielsen, Jan Pedersen, and Tommy Knudsen *(Denmark)*
1992 Grey Hancock, Sam Ermolenko, and Ronnie Correy *(USA)*
1993 Tony Rickardsson, Per Jonsson, and Henrik Gustafsson *(Sweden)*

team
event introduced 1960
1982 USA
1983 Denmark
1984 Denmark
1985 Denmark
1986 Denmark
1987 Denmark
1988 Denmark
1989 England
1990 USA
1991 Denmark
1992 USA
1993 USA

WORLD CHAMPIONSHIP

motocross; first held 1957

500cc class
rider/manufacturer
1982 Brad Lackey/Suzuki *(USA)*
1983 Håkan Carlqvist/Yamaha *(Sweden)*
1984 André Malherbe/Honda *(Belgium)*
1985 Dave Thorpe/Honda *(UK)*
1986 Dave Thorpe/Honda *(UK)*
1987 Georges Jobé/Honda *(Belgium)*
1988 Eric Geboers/Honda *(Belgium)*
1989 Dave Thorpe/Honda *(UK)*
1990 Eric Geboers/Honda *(Belgium)*
1991 Georges Jobé/Honda *(Belgium)*
1992 Georges Jobé/Honda *(Belgium)*
1993 Jacky Martens/Husqvarna *(Belgium)*

motor racing competitive racing of motor vehicles. It has forms as diverse as hill-climbing, stock-car racing, rallying, sports-car racing, and Formula One Grand Prix racing. The first organized race was from Paris to Rouen 1894.

WORLD DRIVERS' CHAMPIONSHIP

Formula One Grand Prix racing; instituted 1950

driver/manufacturer
1983 Nelson Piquet/Ferrari *(Brazil)*
1984 Niki Lauda/McLaren *(Austria)*
1985 Alain Prost/McLaren *(France)*
1986 Alain Prost/Williams *(France)*
1987 Nelson Piquet/Williams *(Brazil)*
1988 Ayrton Senna/McLaren *(Brazil)*
1989 Alain Prost/McLaren *(France)*
1990 Ayrton Senna/McLaren *(Brazil)*
1991 Ayrton Senna/McLaren *(Brazil)*
1992 Nigel Mansell/Williams *(UK)*
1993 Alain Prost/Williams *(France)*

LE MANS GRAND PRIX D'ENDURANCE

(Le Mans 24-Hour Race) first held 1923
1983 Vern Schuppan *(Austria)*, Al Holbert *(USA)*, and Hurley Haywood *(USA)*
1984 Klaus Ludwig *(West Germany)* and Henri Pescarolo *(France)*
1985 Klaus Ludwig *(West Germany)*, 'John Winter' *(West Germany)*, and Paolo Barilla *(Italy)*
1986 Hans Stuck *(West Germany)*, Derek Bell *(UK)*, and Al Holbert *(USA)*
1987 Hans Stuck *(West Germany)*, Derek Bell *(UK)*, and Al Holbert *(USA)*
1988 Jan Lammers *(Holland)*, Johnny Dumfries *(UK)*, and Andy Wallace *(UK)*
1989 Jochen Mass *(West Germany)*, Manuel Reuter *(West Germany)*, and Stanley Dickens *(Sweden)*
1990 John Nielsen *(Denmark)*, Price Cobb *(USA)*, and Martin Brundle *(UK)*
1991 Volker Weidler *(Germany)*, John Herbert *(UK)*, and Bertrand Gachot *(Belgium)*
1992 Derek Warwick *(UK)*, Yannick Dalmas *(France)*, and Mark Blundell *(UK)*
1993 Geoff Brabham *(Australia)*, Christophe Bouchut *(France)*, Eric Helary *(France)*

INDIANAPOLIS 500

first held 1911

driver/manufacturer
1983 Tom Sneva/March—Cosworth *(USA)*

1984 Rick Mears/March—Cosworth *(USA)*
1985 Danny Sullivan/March—Cosworth *(USA)*
1986 Bobby Rahal/March—Cosworth *(USA)*
1987 Al Unser, Jr/March—Cosworth *(USA)*
1988 Rick Mears/Penske—Chevrolet *(USA)*
1989 Emerson Fittipaldi/Penske—Chevrolet *(Brazil)*.
1990 Arie Luyendyk/Lola—Chevrolet *(Holland)*
1991 Rick Mears/Penske—Chevrolet *(USA)*
1992 Al Unser, Jr/Galmer—Chevy A *(USA)*
1993 Emerson Fittipaldi/Penske—Chevrolet *(Brazil)*

MONTE CARLO RALLY

1983 Walter Röhrl *(West Germany)*
1984 Walter Röhrl *(West Germany)*
1985 Ari Vatanen *(Finland)*
1986 Henri Toivonen *(Finland)*
1987 Mikki Biasion *(Italy)*
1988 Bruno Saby *(France)*
1989 Mikki Biasion *(Italy)*
1990 Didier Auriol *(France)*
1991 Carlos Sainz *(Spain)*
1992 Didier Auriol *(France)*
1993 Didier Auriol *(France)*

LOMBARD— RAC RALLY

(formerly RAC International Rally of Great Britain) first held 1927
1982 Hannu Mikkola *(Finland)*
1983 Stig Blomqvist *(Sweden)*
1984 Ari Vatanen *(Finland)*
1985 Henri Toivonen *(Finland)*
1986 Timo Salonen *(Finland)*
1987 Juha Kankkunen *(Finland)*
1988 Markku Alén *(Finland)*
1989 Pentti Arikkala *(Finland)*
1990 Carlos Sainz *(Spain)*
1991 Juha Kankkunen *(Finland)*
1992 Carlos Sainz *(Spain)*

netball a women's game, developed from basketball, played by two teams of seven players each. It is played on a hard court 30.5 m/100 ft long and 15.25 m/50 ft wide. At each end is a goal, consisting of a post 3.05 m/10 ft high, at the top of which is attached a circular hoop and net. The object of the game is to pass an inflated spherical ball through the opposing team's net. The ball is thrown from player to player; no contact is allowed between players, and none may run with the ball.

WORLD CHAMPIONSHIP

first held 1963; contested every four years
1963 Australia
1967 New Zealand
1971 Australia
1975 Australia
1979 Australia, New Zealand, and Trinidad and Tobago
1983 Australia
1987 New Zealand
1991 Australia

orienteering sport of cross-country running and route-finding. Competitors set off at one-minute intervals and have to find their way, using map and compass, to various checkpoints (approximately 0.8 km/ 0.5 mi apart), where their control cards are marked.

WORLD CHAMPIONSHIP

first held 1966

individual (men/women)
1983 Morten Berglia *(Norway)*/Annichen Kringstad *(Norway)*
1985 Kari Sallinen *(Finland)*/Annichen Kringstad *(Norway)*
1987 Kent Olsson *(Sweden)*/Arja Hannus *(Sweden)*
1989 Peter Thoresen *(Norway)*/Marita Skogum *(Sweden)*
1991 Jorgen Martensson *(Sweden)*/Katarina Olch *(Hungary)*

relay (men/women)
1983 Norway/Sweden
1985 Norway/Sweden
1987 Norway/Norway
1989 Norway/Sweden
1991 Switzerland/Sweden

polo stick-and-ball game played between two teams of four on horseback. It is played on the largest pitch of any game, measuring up to 274 m/300 yd by 182 m/200 yd. A small solid ball is struck with the side of a long-handled mallet through goals at each end of the pitch. A typical match lasts about an hour, and is divided into 'chukkas' of $7^1/_2$ minutes each. No pony is expected to play more than two chukkas in the course of a day.

COWDRAY PARK GOLD CUP

British Open Championship; first held 1956
1982 Southfield
1983 Falcons
1984 Southfield
1985 Maple Leafs
1986 Tramontana
1987 Tramontana
1988 Tramontana
1989 Tramontana
1990 Hildon
1991 Tramontana
1992 Black Bears
1993 Alcatel

rowing propulsion of a boat by oars, either by one rower with two oars (sculling) or by crews (two, four, or eight persons) with one oar each, often with a coxswain.

WORLD CHAMPIONSHIP

first held 1962 for men, 1974 for women; Olympic winners automatically become world champions

men—-single sculls
1983 Peter-Michael Kolbe *(West Germany)*
1984 Pertti Karppinen *(Finland)*
1985 Pertti Karppinen *(Finland)*
1986 Peter-Michael Kolbe *(West Germany)*
1987 Thomas Lange *(East Germany)*
1988 Thomas Lange *(East Germany)*
1989 Thomas Lange *(East Germany)*
1990 Uri Janson *(USSR)*
1991 Thomas Lange *(Germany)*
1992 Thomas Lange *(Germany)*
1993 Derek Porter *(Canada)*

women—-single sculls
1983 Jutta Hampe *(East Germany)*

1984 Valeria Racila *(Romania)*
1985 Cornelia Linse *(East Germany)*
1986 Jutta Hampe *(East Germany)*
1987 Magdalena Georgeyeva *(Bulgaria)*
1988 Jutta Hampe *(East Germany)*
1989 Elisabeta Lipa *(Romania)*
1990 Birgit Peter *(Germany)*
1991 Silke Laumann *(Canada)*
1992 Elisabeta Lipa *(Romania)*
1993 Jane Thieme *(Germany)*

THE BOAT RACE

first held 1829; rowed annually by crews from Oxford and Cambridge Universities, between Putney and Mortlake on the river Thames
1986 Cambridge
1987 Oxford
1988 Oxford
1989 Oxford
1990 Oxford
1991 Oxford
1992 Oxford
1993 Cambridge

wins
Cambridge 70
Oxford 68

rugby league the professional form of rugby football founded in England 1895 as the Northern Union when a dispute about pay caused northern clubs to break away from the Rugby Football Union. The game is similar to rugby union, but the number of players is reduced from 15 to 13, and other rule changes have made the game more open and fast-moving.

CHALLENGE CUP

first held 1897
1983 Featherstone Rovers
1984 Widnes
1985 Wigan
1986 Castleford
1987 Halifax
1988 Wigan
1989 Wigan
1990 Wigan
1991 Wigan
1992 Wigan
1993 Wigan

PREMIERSHIP TROPHY

introduced at the end of the 1974—75 season; a knockout competition involving the top eight clubs in the first division
1983 Widnes
1984 Hull Kingston Rovers
1985 St Helens
1986 Warrington
1987 Wigan
1988 Widnes
1989 Widnes
1990 Widnes
1991 Hull
1992 Wigan
1993 St Helens

rugby union the amateur form of rugby football in which there are 15 players on each side. It is played with an inflated oval ball, on a field 69 m/75 yd long and 100 m/110 yd wide. At each end of the field is an H-shaped set of goalposts 5.6 m/18.5 ft wide, with a crossbar 3 m/10 ft above the ground. Points are scored by 'touching down', or grounding, the ball beyond the goal line (try, 4 points), or by kicking it over the goal's crossbar after a touchdown (conversion, 2 points), from the field during regular play (dropped goal, 3 points), or in response to a penalty against the opposing team (3 points).

WORLD CUP

William Webb Ellis Trophy; first held 1987
1987 New Zealand
1991 Australia

INTERNATIONAL CHAMPIONSHIP

instituted 1884, now a tournament between England, France, Ireland, Scotland, and Wales
1983 France and Ireland
1984 Scotland
1985 Ireland
1986 France
1987 France
1988 France and Wales
1989 France
1990 Scotland
1991 England
1992 England
1993 France

COUNTY CHAMPIONSHIP

first held 1889
1983 Gloucestershire
1984 Gloucestershire
1985 Middlesex
1986 Warwickshire
1987 Yorkshire
1988 Lancashire
1989 Durham
1990 Lancashire
1991 Cornwall
1992 Lancashire
1993 Lancashire

PILKINGTON CUP

formerly the John Player Special Cup, the English club knockout tournament, first held 1971—72
1983 Bristol
1984 Bath
1985 Bath
1986 Bath
1987 Bath
1988 Harlequins
1989 Bath
1990 Bath
1991 Harlequins
1992 Bath
1993 Leicester

SCOTTISH CLUB CHAMPIONSHIP

first held 1974

Division One
1983 Gala
1984 Hawick
1985 Hawick
1986 Hawick
1987 Hawick
1988 Kelso
1989 Kelso
1990 Melrose
1991 Boroughmuir
1992 Melrose
1993 Melrose

SWALEC WELSH CUP

(formerly the Schweppes Welsh Cup), the Welsh club knockout tournament, first held 1971—72
1983 Pontypool
1984 Cardiff
1985 Llanelli
1986 Cardiff
1987 Cardiff
1988 Llanelli
1989 Neath
1990 Neath
1991 Llanelli
1992 Llanelli
1993 Llanelli

shinty (Gaelic *camanachd*) stick-and-ball game, resembling hurling, popular in the Scottish Highlands. It is played between two teams of 12 players each, on a field 132–183 m/144–200 yd long and 64–91 m/70–99 yd wide. A curved stick (caman) is used to propel a leather-covered cork-and-worsted ball into the opposing team's goal (hail).

CAMANACHD CUP

instituted 1896
1983 Kyles Athletic
1984 Kingussie
1985 Newtonmore
1986 Newtonmore
1987 Kingussie
1988 Kingussie
1989 Kingussie
1990 Skye
1991 Kingussie
1992 Fort William
1993 Kingussie

skating self-propulsion on ice by means of bladed skates, or on other surfaces by skates with small rollers. The chief competitive ice-skating events are figure skating, for singles or pairs, ice-dancing, and simple speed skating.

WORLD CHAMPIONSHIP

ice-skating; first held 1896

men
1988 Brian Boitano *(USA)*
1989 Kurt Browning *(Canada)*
1990 Kurt Browning *(Canada)*
1991 Kurt Browning *(Canada)*
1992 Viktor Petrenko *(USSR)*
1993 Kurt Browning *(Canada)*

women
1988 Katarina Witt *(East Germany)*
1989 Midoria Ito *(Japan)*
1990 Jill Trenary *(USA)*
1991 Kristi Yamaguchi *(USA)*
1992 Kristi Yamaguchi *(USA)*
1993 Oksana Baiul *(Ukraine)*

pairs
1988 Oleg Vasilyev and Yelena Valova *(USSR)*

1989 Sergey Grinkov and Ekaterina Gordeeva *(USSR)*
1990 Sergey Grinkov and Ekaterina Gordeeva *(USSR)*
1991 Artur Dmitriev and Natalya Mishkuteniok*(USSR)*
1992 Artur Dmitriev and Natalya Mishkuteniok*(USSR)*
1993 Lloyd Eisler and Isabelle Brasseur *(Canada)*

ice dance
1988 Andrei Bukin and Natalia Bestemianova *(USSR)*
1989 Sergey Ponomarenko and Marina Klimova *(USSR)*
1990 Sergey Ponomarenko and Marina Klimova *(USSR)*
1991 Paul Duchesnay and Isabelle Duchesnay *(France)*
1992 Sergey Ponomarenko and Marina Klimova *(USSR)*
1993 Alexandr Zhulin and Maia Usova *(Russia)*

skiing self-propulsion on snow by means of elongated runners (skis) for the feet, slightly bent upward at the tip. Events include downhill; slalom, in which a series of turns between flags have to be negotiated; cross-country racing; and ski jumping, when jumps of over 150 m/490 ft are achieved from ramps up to 90 m/295 ft high. Speed-skiing uses skis approximately $1/3$ longer and wider than normal, with which speeds of up to 200 kmph have been recorded.

OLYMPIC GAMES
events introduced 1936

men : downhill
1976 Franz Klammer *(Austria)*
1980 Leonhard Stock *(Austria)*
1984 William Johnson *(USA)*
1988 Pirmin Zurbriggen *(Switzerland)*
1992 Patrick Ortlieb *(Austria)*

men : slalom
1976 Piero Gros *(Italy)*
1980 Ingemar Stenmark *(Sweden)*
1984 Phil Mahre *(USA)*
1988 Alberto Tomba *(Italy)*
1992 Christian Jagge *(Norway)*

women : downhill
1976 Rosi Mittermaier *(West Germany)*
1980 Annemarie Moser-Proll *(Austria)*
1984 Michela Figini *(Switzerland)*
1988 Marina Kiehl *(Germany)*
1992 Kerrin Lee-Gartner *(Canada)*

women : slalom
1976 Rosi Mittermaier *(West Germany)*
1980 Hanni Wenzel *(Liechtenstein)*
1984 Paoletta Magoni *(Italy)*
1988 Vreni Schneider *(Switzerland)*
1992 Petra Krönberger *(Austria)*

ALPINE WORLD CUP
first held 1967

men - overall
1983 Phil Mahre *(USA)*
1984 Pirmin Zurbriggen *(Switzerland)*
1985 Marc Girardelli *(Luxembourg)*
1986 Marc Girardelli *(Luxembourg)*
1987 Pirmin Zurbriggen *(Switzerland)*
1988 Pirmin Zurbriggen *(Switzerland)*
1989 Marc Girardelli *(Luxembourg)*
1990 Pirmin Zurbriggen *(Switzerland)*
1991 Marc Girardelli *(Luxembourg)*
1992 Paul Accola *(Switzerland)*
1993 Marc Girardelli *(Luxembourg)*

women - overall
1983 Tamara McKinney *(USA)*
1984 Erika Hess *(Switzerland)*
1985 Michela Figini *(Switzerland)*
1986 Maria Walliser *(Switzerland)*
1987 Maria Walliser *(Switzerland)*
1988 Michela Figini *(Switzerland)*
1989 Vreni Schneider *(Switzerland)*
1990 Petra Krönberger *(Austria)*
1991 Petra Krönberger *(Austria)*
1992 Petra Krönberger *(Austria)*
1993 Anita Wachter *(Austria)*

snooker indoor game derived from billiards. It is played with 22 balls: 15 red, one each of yellow, green, brown, blue, pink, and black, and one white cueball. Red balls are worth one point when sunk, while the coloured balls have ascending values from two points for the yellow to seven points for the black.

WORLD PROFESSIONAL CHAMPIONSHIP
first held 1927
1983 Steve Davis *(England)*
1984 Steve Davis *(England)*
1985 Dennis Taylor *(Northern Ireland)*
1986 Joe Johnson *(England)*
1987 Steve Davis *(England)*
1988 Steve Davis *(England)*
1989 Steve Davis *(England)*
1990 Stephen Hendry *(Scotland)*
1991 John Parrott *(England)*
1992 Stephen Hendry *(Scotland)*
1993 Stephen Hendry *(Scotland)*

WORLD AMATEUR CHAMPIONSHIP
first held 1963
1980 Jimmy White *(England)*
1982 Terry Parsons *(Wales)*
1984 O B Agrawal *(India)*
1985 Paul Mifsud *(Malta)*
1986 Paul Mifsud *(Malta)*
1987 Darren Morgan *(Wales)*
1988 James Wattana *(Thailand)*
1989 Ken Doherty *(Ireland)*
1990 Stephen O'Connor *(Ireland)*
1991 Noppadon Noppachom *(Thailand)*
1992 Neil Mosley *(England)*
1993 Neil Mosley *(England)*

softball a form of baseball played with similar equipment. The two main differences are the distances between the bases (18.29 m/60 ft) and that the ball is pitched underhand in softball. There are two forms of the game, *fast pitch* and **slow pitch**; in the latter the ball must be delivered to home plate in an arc that must be not less than 2.4 m/8 ft at its height.

WORLD CHAMPIONSHIP
fast pitch; introduced 1965 for women, 1966 for men; now contested every four years

men
1966 USA
1968 USA
1972 Canada
1976 Canada, New Zealand, and USA

1980 USA
1984 New Zealand
1988 USA
1992 Canada

women
1965 Australia
1970 Japan
1974 USA
1978 USA
1982 New Zealand
1986 USA
1990 USA

squash or **squash rackets** racket-and-ball game usually played by two people on an enclosed court. Each player hits the small rubber ball against the front wall of the court alternately. The object is to win points by playing shots the opponent cannot return to the wall. There are two forms of the game: the American form, which is played in North and some South American countries and the English, which is played mainly in Europe, Pakistan, and Commonwealth countries such as Australia and New Zealand. In English singles, the court is 6.4 m/21 ft wide and 10 m/32 ft long. Doubles squash is played on a larger court.

WORLD OPEN CHAMPIONSHIP
first held 1975

men
1982 Jahangir Khan *(Pakistan)*
1983 Jahangir Khan *(Pakistan)*
1984 Jahangir Khan *(Pakistan)*
1985 Jahangir Khan *(Pakistan)*
1986 Ross Norman *(New Zealand)*
1987 Jansher Khan *(Pakistan)*
1988 Jahangir Khan *(Pakistan)*
1989 Jansher Khan *(Pakistan)*
1990 Jansher Khan *(Pakistan)*
1991 Rodney Martin *(Australia)*
1992 Jansher Khan *(Pakistan)*

women
1981 Rhonda Thorne *(Australia)*
1983 Vicky Cardwell *(Australia)*
1985 Sue Devoy *(New Zealand)*
1987 Sue Devoy *(New Zealand)*
1989 Martine Le Moignan *(UK)*
1990 Sue Devoy *(New Zealand)*
1991 Sue Devoy *(New Zealand)*
1992 Sue Devoy *(New Zealand)*
1993 Michelle Martin *(Australia)*

surfing riding on the crest of large waves while standing on a narrow, keeled surfboard, usually of a light synthetic material such as fibreglass, about 1.8 m/6 ft long (or 2.4–7 m/8–9 ft known as the Malibu), as first developed in Hawaii and Australia.

WORLD PROFESSIONAL CHAMPIONSHIP
first held 1970

men
1987 Damien Hardman *(Australia)*
1988 Barton Lynch *(Australia)*
1989 Martin Potter *(UK)*
1990 Tommy Curren *(USA)*

1991 Damien Hardman *(Australia)*
1992 Kelly Slater *(USA)*

women
1987 Wendy Botha *(South Africa)*
1988 Frieda Zamba *(USA)*
1989 Wendy Botha *(South Africa)*
1990 Pam Burridge *(Australia)*
1991 Wendy Botha *(South Africa)*
1992 Wendy Botha *(Australia ex-South Africa)*

WORLD AMATEUR CHAMPIONSHIP
first held 1964

men
1982 Tommy Curren *(USA)*
1984 Scott Farnsworth *(USA)*
1986 Mark Sainsbury *(Australia)*
1988 Fabio Gouveia *(Brazil)*
1990 Heifara Tahutini *(Tahiti)*

women
1982 Jenny Gill *(Australia)*
1984 Janice Aragon *(USA)*
1986 Connie Nixon *(Australia)*
1988 Pauline Menczer *(Australia)*
1990 Kathy Newman *(Australia)*

swimming self-propulsion of the body through water. There are four strokes in competitive swimming: *freestyle* (or *front crawl*), the fastest stroke; *breaststroke*, the slowest stroke; *backstroke*; and *butterfly*, the newest stroke, developed in the USA from breaststroke. Swimmers enter the water with a 'racing plunge' (a form of dive) with the exception of the backstroke, when competitors start in the water. Distances of races vary between 50 m/54.7 yd and 1,500 m/1,641 yd. Olympic-size pools are 50 m/55 yd long and have eight lanes. *Synchronized swimming* is a form of 'ballet' performed in and under water.

OLYMPIC GAMES

event introduced 1896 for men, 1912 for women
Barcelona Olympics 1992 (25th Olympic Games)

men/women
100 metres backstroke: Mark Tewkesbury *(Canada)*/Kristina Egerszegi *(Hungary)*
200 metres backstroke: Martin Lopez-Zubero *(Spain)*/Kristina Egerszegi *(Hungary)*
100 metres breaststroke: Nelson Diebel *(USA)*/Yelena Roudkovskaya *(Unified Team*)*
200 metres breaststroke: Mike Barrowman *(USA)*/Kyoko Iwasaki *(Japan)*
100 metres butterfly: Pablo Morales *(USA)*/Qian Hong *(China)*
200 metres butterfly: Melvin Stewart *(USA)*/Summer Sanders *(USA)*
50 metres freestyle: Aleksandr Popov *(Unified Team)*/Yang Wenyi *(China)*
100 metres freestyle: Aleksandr Popov *(Unified Team)*/Zhuang Yong *(China)*
200 metres freestyle: Yevgeny Sadovyi *(Unified Team)*/Nicole Haislett *(USA)*
400 metres freestyle: Yevgeny Sadovyi *(Unified Team)*/Dagmar Hase *(Germany)*
800 metres freestyle: — /Janet Evans *(USA)*
1,500 metres freestyle: Kieren Perkins *(Australia)*/ —

200 metres individual medley: Tamás Darnyi *(Hungary)*/Lin Li *(China)*
400 metres individual medley: Tamás Darnyi *(USA)*/Kristina Egerszegi *(Hungary)*
400 metres freestyle relay: USA/USA
800 metres freestyle relay: Unified Team/ —
400 metres medley relay: USA/USA
synchronized swimming (individual): — /Kristen Babb-Sprague *(USA)*
synchronized swimming (duet): — /Karen Josephson and Sarah Josephson *(USA)*

* *Commonwealth of Independent States plus Georgia*

most gold medals:
9 Mark Spitz *(USA)* 1968, 1972
8 Matt Biondi *(USA)* 1984, 1988, 1992
6 Kristin Otto *(East Germany)* 1988
5 Charles Daniels *(USA)* 1904, 1908
5 Johnny Weissmuller *(USA)* 1924, 1928
5 Don Schollander *(USA)* 1964, 1968
4 Henry Taylor *(UK)* 1906, 1908
4 Murray Rose *(Australia)* 1956, 1960
4 Dawn Fraser *(Australia)* 1956, 1960, 1964
4 Roland Matthes *(East Germany)* 1968, 1972
4 John Naber *(USA)* 1976
4 Kornelia Ender *(East Germany)* 1976
4 Vladimir Salnikov *(USSR)* 1980, 1988
4 Tamás Darnyi *(Hungary)* 1988, 1992
4 Janet Evans *(USA)* 1988, 1992

most medals:
11 Mark Spitz *(USA)* 1968, 1972
11 Matt Biondi *(USA)* 1984, 1988, 1992
8 Charles Daniels *(USA)* 1904, 1908
8 Roland Matthes *(East Germany)* 1968, 1972
8 Henry Taylor *(UK)* 1906, 1908, 1912, 1920
8 Dawn Fraser *(Australia)* 1956, 1960, 1964
8 Kornelia Ender *(East Germany)* 1972, 1976
8 Shirley Babashoff *(USA)* 1972, 1976

---

table tennis or ***ping pong*** indoor game played on a rectangular table by two or four players. Play takes place on a table measuring 2.74 m/9 ft long by 1.52 m/5 ft wide. Across the middle is a 15.25 cm/6 in high net over which the ball must be hit. The players use small, wooden paddles covered in sponge or rubber. Points are scored by forcing the opponent(s) into an error. The first to score 21 wins the game. A match may consist of three or five games. Volleying is not allowed. In doubles play, the players must hit the ball in strict rotation.

WORLD CHAMPIONSHIP
first held 1926, now contested every two years

men's team
1983 China
1985 China
1987 China
1989 Sweden
1991 Sweden
1993 Sweden

women's team
1983 China
1985 China
1987 China
1989 China

1991 Korea
1993 China

men's singles
1983 Guo Yue-Hua *(China)*
1985 Jiang Jialiang *(China)*
1987 Jiang Jialiang *(China)*
1989 Jan-Ove Waldner *(Sweden)*
1991 Jorgen Persson *(Sweden)*
1993 Jean-Philippe Gatien *(France)*

women's singles
1983 Cao Yan-Hua *(China)*
1985 Cao Yan-Hua *(China)*
1987 He Zhili *(China)*
1989 Qiuo Hong *(China)*
1991 Deng Yalping *(China)*
1993 Hyun Jung-hwa *(South Korea)*

---

tennis, lawn racket-and-ball game for two or four players, invented towards the end of the 19th century. It may be played on a grass, wood, shale, clay, or concrete surface. The object of the game is to strike the ball into the prescribed area of the court, with oval-headed rackets (strung with gut or nylon), in such a way that it cannot be returned. The game is won by those first winning four points (called 15, 30, 40, game), unless both sides reach 40 (deuce), when two consecutive points are needed to win. A set is won by winning six games with a margin of two over opponents, though a tie-break system operates, that is at six games to each side (or in some cases eight) except in the final set.

The Grand Slam events are the Wimbledon Championship, the United States Open, French Open, and Australian Open.

WIMBLEDOM CHAMPIONSHIPS

All-England Lawn Tennis Club championships; first held 1877; grass surface

men's singles
1983 John McEnroe *(USA)*
1984 John McEnroe *(USA)*
1985 Boris Becker *(West Germany)*
1986 Boris Becker *(West Germany)*
1987 Pat Cash *(Australia)*
1988 Stefan Edberg *(Sweden)*
1989 Boris Becker *(West Germany)*
1990 Stefan Edberg *(Sweden)*
1991 Michael Stich *(Germany)*
1992 Andre Agassi *(USA)*
1993 Pete Sampras *(USA)*

women's singles
1983 Martina Navratilova *(USA)*
1984 Martina Navratilova *(USA)*
1985 Martina Navratilova *(USA)*
1986 Martina Navratilova *(USA)*
1987 Martina Navratilova *(USA)*
1988 Steffi Graf *(West Germany)*
1989 Steffi Graf *(West Germany)*
1990 Martina Navratilova *(USA)*
1991 Steffi Graf *(Germany)*
1992 Steffi Graf *(Germany)*
1993 Steffi Graf *(Germany)*

UNITED STATES OPEN

first held 1881 as the United States Championship; became the United States Open 1968; concrete surface

men's singles
1983 Jimmy Connors *(USA)*
1984 John McEnroe *(USA)*
1985 Ivan Lendl *(Czechoslovakia)*
1986 Ivan Lendl *(Czechoslovakia)*
1987 Ivan Lendl *(Czechoslovakia)*
1988 Mats Wilander *(Sweden)*
1989 Boris Becker *(West Germany)*
1990 Pete Sampras *(USA)*
1991 Stefan Edberg *(Sweden)*
1992 Stefan Edberg *(Sweden)*
1993 Pete Sampras (USA)

women's singles
1983 Martina Navratilova *(USA)*
1984 Martina Navratilova *(USA)*
1985 Hana Mandlikova *(Czechoslovakia)*
1986 Martina Navratilova *(USA)*
1987 Martina Navratilova *(USA)*
1988 Steffi Graf *(West Germany)*
1989 Steffi Graf *(West Germany)*
1990 Gabriela Sabatini *(Argentina)*
1991 Monica Seles *(Yugoslavia)*
1992 Monica Seles *(Yugoslavia)*
1993 Steffi Graf (Germany)

FRENCH OPEN

first held 1891 (a national championship until 1924); clay
surface
men's singles
1983 Yannick Noah *(France)*
1984 Ivan Lendl *(Czechoslovakia)*
1985 Mats Wilander *(Sweden)*
1986 Ivan Lendl *(Czechoslovakia)*
1987 Ivan Lendl *(Czechoslovakia)*
1988 Mats Wilander *(Sweden)*
1989 Michael Craig *(USA)*
1990 Andres Gomez *(Ecuador)*
1991 Jim Courier *(USA)*
1992 Jim Courier *(USA)*
1993 Sergi Bruguera *(Spain)*
women's singles
1983 Chris Evert-Lloyd *(USA)*
1984 Martina Navratilova *(USA)*
1985 Chris Evert-Lloyd *(USA)*
1986 Chris Evert-Lloyd *(USA)*
1987 Steffi Graf *(West Germany)*
1988 Steffi Graf *(West Germany)*
1989 Arantxa Sanchez Vicario *(Spain)*
1990 Monica Seles *(Yugoslavia)*
1991 Monica Seles *(Yugoslavia)*
1992 Monica Seles *(Yugoslavia)*
1993 Steffi Graf *(West Germany)*

AUSTRALIAN OPEN

first held 1905 (a national championship until 1925); clay
surface
men's singles
1983 Mats Wilander *(Sweden)*
1984 Mats Wilander *(Sweden)*
1985 Stefan Edberg *(Sweden)*
1987 Stefan Edberg *(Sweden)*
1988 Mats Wilander *(Sweden)*
1989 Ivan Lendl *(Czechoslovakia)*
1990 Ivan Lendl *(Czechoslovakia)*
1991 Boris Becker *(Germany)*
1992 Jim Courier *(USA)*
1993 Jim Courier *(USA)*

women's singles
1983 Martina Navratilova *(USA)*
1984 Chris Evert-Lloyd *(USA)*
1985 Martina Navratilova *(USA)*
1987 Hana Mandlikova *(Czechoslovakia)*
1988 Steffi Graf *(West Germany)*
1989 Steffi Graf *(West Germany)*
1990 Steffi Graf *(West Germany)*
1991 Monica Seles *(Yugoslavia)*
1992 Monica Seles *(Yugoslavia)*
1993 Monica Seles *(Yugoslavia)*

DAVIS CUP

first contested 1900
1982 USA
1983 Australia
1984 Sweden
1985 Sweden
1986 Australia
1987 Sweden
1988 West Germany
1989 West Germany
1990 USA
1991 France
1992 USA

trampolining gymnastics performed on a sprung
canvas sheet that allows the performer to reach great
heights before landing again. Marks are gained for
carrying out difficult manoeuvres. Synchronized
trampolining and tumbling are also popular forms of
the sport.

WORLD CHAMPIONSHIP

first held 1964

men
1974 Richard Tisson *(France)*
1976 Richard Tisson *(France)* and Evgeni Janes *(USSR)*
1978 Evgeni Janes *(USSR)*
1980 Stewart Matthews *(UK)*
1982 Carl Furrer *(UK)*
1984 Lionel Pioline *(France)*
1986 Lionel Pioline *(France)*
1988 Vadim Krasonchapka *(USSR)*
1990 Alexandr Moskalenko *(USSR)*
1992 Alexandr Moskalenko *(USSR)*
women
1974 Alexandra Nicholson *(USA)*
1976 Svetlana Levina *(USSR)*
1978 Tatyana Anisimova *(USSR)*
1980 Ruth Keller *(Switzerland)*
1982 Ruth Keller *(Switzerland)*
1984 Sue Shotton *(UK)*
1986 Tatyana Lushina *(USSR)*
1988 Khoperla Rusudum *(USSR)*
1990 Elena Merkulova *(USSR)*
1992 Elena Merkulova *(USSR)*

volleyball an indoor and outdoor game played
between two teams of six players each. The court
measures 18 m/59 ft by 9 m/29 ft 6 in, and has a
raised net drawn across its centre. Players hit an
inflated spherical ball over the net with their hands or
arms, the aim being to ground the ball in the opponents' court. The ball may not be hit more than three
times on one team's side of the net.

WORLD CHAMPIONSHIP

first held 1949 for men, 1952 for women; Olympic winners automatically become world champions

men
1974 Poland
1976 Poland
1978 USSR
1980 USSR
1982 USSR
1984 USA
1986 USA
1988 USA
1990 Italy
1992 Brazil

women
1974 Japan
1976 Japan
1978 Cuba
1980 USSR
1982 China
1984 China
1986 USA
1988 USSR
1990 USSR
1992 Cuba

---

water polo (formerly *soccer-in-water*) sport played in a swimming pool, between two teams of seven players each. An inflated ball is passed among the players, who must swim around the pool without touching the bottom. Goals are scored when the ball is thrown past the opposing team's goalkeeper and into a net.

WORLD CHAMPIONSHIP

first held 1973; contested every four years since 1978
1973 Hungary
1975 USSR
1978 Italy
1982 USSR
1986 Yugoslavia
1990/91 Yugoslavia

---

water skiing sport in which a person is towed across water on a ski or skis, by means of a rope (23 m/75 ft long) attached to a speedboat. Competitions are held for overall performances, slalom, tricks, and jumping.

WORLD CHAMPIONSHIP

first held 1949; contested every two years

men—overall
1973 George Athans *(Canada)*
1975 Carlos Suarez *(Venezuela)*
1977 Mike Hazelwood *(UK)*
1979 Joel McClintock *(Canada)*
1981 Sammy Duvall *(USA)*
1983 Sammy Duvall *(USA)*
1985 Sammy Duvall *(USA)*
1987 Sammy Duvall *(USA)*
1989 Patrice Martin *(France)*
1991 Patrice Martin *(France)*
1993 Patrice Martin *(France)*

women—overall
1973 Lisa St John *(USA)*
1975 Liz Allan-Shetter *(USA)*

1977 Cindy Todd *(USA)*
1979 Cindy Todd *(USA)*
1981 Karin Roberge *(USA)*
1983 Ana-Maria Carrasco *(Venezuela)*
1985 Karen Neville *(Australia)*
1987 Deena Brush *(USA)*
1989 Deena Mapple (née Brush) *(USA)*
1991 Karen Neville *(Australia)*
1993 Natalya Rumiantseva *(Russia)*

---

weightlifting the sport of lifting the heaviest possible weight above one's head to the satisfaction of judges. In international competitions there are two standard lifts: snatch and jerk. In the **snatch**, the bar and weights are lifted from the floor to a position with the arms outstretched and above the head in one continuous movement. The arms must be locked for two seconds for the lift to be good. The **jerk** is a two-movement lift: from the floor to the chest, and from the chest to the outstretched position. The aggregate weight of the two lifts counts.

OLYMPIC GAMES

Barcelona Olympics (25th Olympics) 1992
52 kg: Ivan Ivanov *(Bulgaria)*
56 kg: Chun Byung-Kwan *(South Korea)*
60 kg: Naim Suleymanoglu *(Turkey)*
67.5 kg: Israel Militossyan *(Unified Team*)*
75 kg: Fyodor Kassapu *(Unified Team)*
82.5 kg: Pyrros Dimas *(Greece)*
90 kg: Kakhi Kakhiashvili *(Unified Team)*
100 kg: Viktor Tregubov *(Unified Team)*
110 kg: Ronny Weller *(Germany)*
110+ kg: Aleksandr Kurlovich *(Unified Team)*
* Commonwealth of Independent States plus Georgia

---

wrestling fighting without the use of fists. The two main modern international styles are **Greco-Roman**, concentrating on above-waist holds, and **freestyle**, which allows the legs to be used to hold or trip; in both, the aim is to throw the opponent to the ground. Competitors are categorized according to weight: there are ten weight divisions in each style of wrestling, ranging from light-flyweight (under 48 kg) to super-heavyweight (over 100 kg). The professional form of the sport has become popular, partly due to television coverage, but is regarded by purists as an extension of show-business. Many countries have their own forms of wrestling. **Glima** is unique to Iceland; **kushti** is the national style practised in Iran; **schwingen** has been practised in Switzerland for hundreds of years; and **sumo** is the national sport of Japan.

OLYMPIC GAMES

Barcelona Olympics (25th Olympics) 1992
Greco-Roman
light-flyweight (48 kg): Oleg Koutherenko *(Unified Team*)*
flyweight (52 kg): Jon Ronningen *(Norway)*
bantamweight (57 kg): An Han Bong *(South Korea)*
featherweight (62 kg): M Akif Pirim *(Turkey)*
lightweight (68 kg): Attila Repka *(Hungary)*
welterweight (74 kg): Mnatsakan Iskandaryan *(Unified Team)*
middleweight (82 kg): Peter Farkas *(Hungary)*

light-heavyweight (90 kg): Maik Bullmann *(Germany)*
heavyweight (100 kg): Hector Milian Perez *(Cuba)*
super-heavyweight (over 100 kg): Aleksandr Karelin *(Unified Team)*

freestyle
light-flyweight: Kim II*(North Korea)*
flyweight: Li Hak Son *(North Korea)*
bantamweight: Alejandro Puerto Diaz *(Cuba)*
featherweight: John Smith *(USA)*
lightweight: Arsen Fadzyev *(Unified Team)*
welterweight: Park Jang Sun *(South Korea)*
middleweight: Kevin Jackson *(USA)*
light-heavyweight: Makharbek Khadartsev *(Unified Team)*
heavyweight: Lery Khabelov *(Unified Team)*
super-heavyweight: Bruce Baumgartner *(USA)*

* *Commonwealth of Independent States plus Georgia*

yachting racing a small, light sailing vessel. At the Olympic Games, seven categories exist: Soling, Flying Dutchman, Star, Finn, Tornado, 470, and Windglider (or windsurfing/boardsailing), which was introduced at the 1984 Los Angeles games. The Finn and Windglider are solo events; the Soling class is for three-person crews; all other classes are for crews of two.

AMERICA'S CUP

first held 1870; now contested approximately every four years; all winners have been US boats, except for *Australia II* 1983
1962 *Weatherly*
1964 *Constellation*
1967 *Intrepid*
1970 *Intrepid*
1974 *Courageous*
1977 *Courageous*
1980 *Freedom*
1983 *Australia II*
1987 *Stars and Stripes*
1988 *Stars and Stripes*
1992 *America 3*

ADMIRAL'S CUP

first held 1957; national teams consisting of three boats compete over three inshore courses and two offshore courses; contested every two years
1973 West Germany
1975 UK
1977 UK
1979 Australia
1981 UK
1983 West Germany
1985 West Germany
1987 New Zealand
1989 UK
1991 France
1993 Germany

Biographies

Agostini Giacomo 1943– . Italian motorcyclist who won a record 122 grand prix and 15 world titles. His world titles were at 350cc and 500cc and he was five times a dual champion. In addition he was ten times winner of the Isle of Man Tourist Trophy (TT) races; a figure only bettered by Mike Hailwood and Joey Dunlop.

CAREER HIGHLIGHTS

world titles
350cc: 1968–73 (MV Agusta), 1974 (Yamaha)
500cc: 1966–72 (MV Agusta), 1975 (Yamaha)

Isle of Man TT wins
Junior TT: 1966, 1968–70, 1972 (all MV Agusta)
Senior TT: 1968–72 (all MV Agusta)

Alexeev Vasiliy 1942– . Soviet weightlifter who broke 80 world records 1970–77, a record for any sport. He was Olympic super-heavyweight champion twice, world champion seven times, and European champion on eight occasions. At one time the most decorated man in the USSR, he was regarded as the strongest man in the world. He carried the Soviet flag at the 1980 Moscow Olympics opening ceremony, but retired shortly afterwards.

CAREER HIGHLIGHTS

Olympic champion: 1972, 1976
world champion: 1970–71, 1973–75, 1977
European champion: 1970–78

Ali Muhammad. Adopted name of Cassius Marcellus Clay, Jr 1942– . US boxer. Olympic light-heavyweight champion 1960, he went on to become world professional heavyweight champion 1964, and was the only man to regain the title twice. Ali had his title stripped from him 1967 for refusing to be drafted into the US Army. He was known for his fast footwork and extrovert nature.

CAREER HIGHLIGHTS

fights: 61
wins: 56 (37 knockouts)
draws: 0
defeats: 5
first professional fight: 29 Oct 1960 v. Tunny Hunsaker *(USA)*
last professional fight: 11 Dec 1981 v. Trevor Berbick *(Canada)*

Aouita Said 1960– . Moroccan runner. Outstanding at middle and long distances, he won the 1984 Olympic and 1987 World Championship 5,000-metres title. In 1985 he held world records at both 1,500 and 5,000 metres, the first person for 30 years to hold both. He has since broken the 2 miles, 3,000 metres, and 2,000 metres world records.

CAREER HIGHLIGHTS

Olympic Games
1984: gold 5,000 metres

world records
1985: 1,500 metres, 5,000 metres
1987: 2,000 metres, 3,000 metres, 5,000 metres
1989: 3,000 metres

world championships
1987: gold 5,000 metres

world best
2 miles: 1987

Ashe Arthur Robert, Jr 1943–1993. US tennis player and coach, renowned for his exceptionally strong serve. He won the US national men's singles title at Forest Hills and the first US Open 1968. He won the Australian men's title 1970 and Wimbledon 1975. Cardiac problems ended his playing career 1979, but he continued his involvement with the sport as captain of the US Davis Cup team.

Ballesteros Seve(riano) 1957– . Spanish golfer who came to prominence 1976 and has won several leading tournaments in the USA, including the Masters Tournament 1980 and 1983. He has also won the British Open three times: in 1979, 1984, and 1988.

CAREER HIGHLIGHTS

British Open: 1979, 1984, 1988
Ryder Cup (individual): 1979, 1983, 1985, 1987, 1989, 1991
Ryder Cup (team): 1985,1987, tie 1989
PGA Championship: 1983, 1991
US Masters: 1980, 1983
World Match-Play Championship: 1981–82, 1984–85, 1991

Bannister Roger Gilbert 1929– . English track and field athlete, the first person to run a mile in under four minutes. He achieved this feat at Oxford, England, on 6 May 1954 in a time of 3 min 59.4 sec. Bannister also broke the four-minute barrier at the 1954 Commonwealth Games in Vancouver, Canada.

Beckenbauer Franz 1945– . German football player who made over 100 appearances for his country. He captained West Germany to the 1972 European Championship and the 1974 World Cup, and was twice European Footballer of the Year. After retiring as a player, he became West Germany's team manager, taking them to the runners-up spot in the 1986 World Cup and victory in the 1990 World Cup. He is the only person both to captain and manage a winning World Cup team.

CAREER HIGHLIGHTS

as player
World Cup: 1974
European Championship: 1972
European Cup: 1974–76
European Footballer of the Year: 1972, 1976
as manager
World Cup: 1990

Becker Boris 1967– . German tennis player. In 1985 he became the youngest winner of a singles title at Wimbledon at the age of 17. He has won the title three times and helped West Germany to win the Davis Cup 1988 and 1989. He also won the US Open 1989 and the Grand Prix Masters/ATP Tour World Championship 1992.

CAREER HIGHLIGHTS

Wimbledon
singles: 1985, 1986, 1989
US Open
singles: 1989

Australian Open
singles: 1991
Grand Prix Masters
1988

Best George 1946– . Irish footballer. He won two League championship medals and was a member of the Manchester United side that won the European Cup in 1968. Best joined Manchester United as a youth and made his debut at 17; seven months later he made his international debut for Northern Ireland. Trouble with managers, fellow players, and the media led to his early retirement.

CAREER HIGHLIGHTS

Football League
appearances: 411
goals: 147
League championship: 1965, 1967
Footballer of the Year: 1968
internationals
appearances: 37
goals: 9
European Cup: 1968
European Footballer of the Year: 1968

Blanco Serge 1958– . French rugby union player, renowned for his pace, skill, and ingenuity on the field. Blanco played a world-record 93 internationals before his retirement in 1991, scoring 38 tries of which 34 were from full back – another world record. He was instrumental in France's Grand Slam wins of 1981 and 1987.

Border Allan 1955– . Left-handed batsman and captain of the Australian cricket team since 1985. At the start of the 1993 Ashes series, he held world records for most runs in test cricket (10,262), most appearances in test matches (141) and most appearances in one day internationals (256). Plays in Australia for Queensland after starting career with NSW, and has also played for Gloucestershire and Essex in England.

CAREER HIGHLIGHTS

Test cricket runs: 10,695 average: 51.17 best: 205 not out v. New Zealand 1987–88 wickets: 38 average: 38.53 best: 7 for 46 v. West Indies 1988–89

Borg Bjorn 1956– . Swedish tennis player who won the men's singles title at Wimbledon five times 1976–80, a record since the abolition of the challenge system 1922. He also won six French Open singles titles. In 1990 Borg announced plans to return to professional tennis, but he enjoyed little competitive success.

CAREER HIGHLIGHTS

Wimbledon
singles: 1976–80
French Open
singles: 1974–75, 1978–81
Davis Cup
1975 (member of winning Sweden team)

Grand Prix Masters
1980–81
WCT Champion
1976
ITF World Champion
1978–80

Botham Ian (Terrence) 1955– . English cricketer whose test record places him among the world's greatest all-rounders. He has played county cricket for Somerset, Worcestershire, and Durham as well as playing in Australia. He played for England 1977-89 and returned to the England side 1991. He retired from cricket in 1993. Botham has raised money for leukaemia research with walks from John o'Groats to Land's End in the UK, and across the Alps.

CAREER HIGHLIGHTS

all first-class matches
runs: 19,399
average: 33.97
best: 228 (Somerset v. Gloucestershire 1980)
wickets: 1,172
average: 27.21
best: 8 for 34 (England v. Pakistan 1978)
test cricket
appearances: 102
runs: 5,200
average: 33.54
best: 208 (England v. India 1982)
wickets: 383
average: 28.40
best: 8 for 34 (England v. Pakistan 1978)
catches: 120

Boycott Geoffrey 1940– . English cricketer born in Yorkshire, England's most prolific run-maker with 8,114 runs in test cricket until overtaken by David Gower in 1992. He played in 108 test matches and in 1981 overtook Gary Sobers' world record total of test runs. Twice, in 1971 and 1979, his average was over 100 runs in an English season. Boycott was banned as a test player in 1982 for taking part in matches against South Africa. He was released by Yorkshire after a dispute in 1986 and has not played first-class cricket since.

CAREER HIGHLIGHTS

all first-class matches
runs: 48,426
average: 56.83
best: 261 not out (MCC v. WIBC President's X I 1973–74)
test cricket
runs: 8,114
average: 47.72
best: 246 not out (England v. India 1967)

Bradman Don (Donald George) 1908– . Australian test cricketer with the highest average in test history. From 52 test matches he averaged 99.94 runs per innings. He only needed four runs from his final test innings to average 100 but was dismissed at second ball. Bradman played for Australia for 20 years and was captain 1936–48. He twice scored triple centuries against England and in 1930 scored 452 not out for New South Wales against Queensland, the highest first-class innings until 1959.

CAREER HIGHLIGHTS

all first-class matches
runs: 28,067
average: 95.14
best: 452 not out (New South Wales v. Queensland 1930)
test cricket
runs: 6,996
average: 99.94
best: 334 (Australia v. England 1930)

Bristow Eric 1957– . English darts player nicknamed 'the Crafty Cockney'. He has won all the game's major titles, including the world professional title a record five times between 1980 and 1986.

CAREER HIGHLIGHTS

world professional champion: 1980–81, 1984–86
World Masters: 1977, 1979, 1981, 1983–84
World Cup (individual): 1983, 1985, 1987, 1989
World Cup (team): 1979, 1981, 1983, 1985, 1987, 1989
British Open: 1978, 1981, 1983, 1985–86
News of the World: 1983–84
World Pairs: 1987 (with Peter Locke)

Bryant David 1931– . English flat-green (lawn) bowls player. He has won every honour the game has offered, including four outdoor world titles (three singles and one triples) 1966–88 and three indoor titles 1979–81. He retired 1993.

CAREER HIGHLIGHTS

world outdoor champion: 1966, 1980, 1988
world indoor champion: 1979–81
Commonwealth Games
singles: 1962, 1970, 1974, 1978
fours: 1962
English Bowling Association titles
singles: 1960, 1966, 1971–73, 1975
pairs: 1965, 1969, 1974
triples: 1966, 1977
fours: 1957, 1968–69, 1971

Budge Donald 1915– . US tennis player. He was the first to perform the Grand Slam when he won the Wimbledon, French, US, and Australian championships all in 1938. He won 14 Grand Slam events in all, including Wimbledon singles twice.

CAREER HIGHLIGHTS

Wimbledon
singles: 1937–38
doubles: 1937–38
mixed: 1937–38
US Open
singles: 1937–38
doubles: 1936, 1938
mixed: 1937–38
French Open
singles: 1938

Australian Open
singles: 1938

Campese David– . 1962 Australian rugby union player, one of the outstanding entertainers of the game. He holds the world record for the most tries scored in international rugby (57 international tries by 1 Nov 1993). Australia's most capped player, he was a key element in their 1991 World Cup victory.

Carson Willie (William Hunter) 1942– . Scottish jockey who has ridden three Epsom Derby winners as well as the winners of most major races worldwide. The top flat-race jockey on five occasions, Carson has had over 3,000 wins in Britain. For many years he rode for the royal trainer, Major Dick Hern. To the start of the 1993 season, he has ridden 16 Classic winners and a total of 3,434 winners since 1962.

CAREER HIGHLIGHTS
Champion Jockey
1972–73, 1978, 1980, 1983
Derby
1979 (Troy)
1980 (Henbit)
1989 (Nashwan)

Caslavska Vera 1943– . Czechoslovak gymnast, the first of the great present-day stylists. She won a record 21 world, Olympic, and European gold medals 1959–68; she also won eight silver and three bronze medals.

CAREER HIGHLIGHTS
Olympic champion
overall individual: 1964, 1968
beam: 1964, 1968
vault: 1964, 1968
floor exercise: 1968
world champion
overall individual: 1966
vault: 1962, 1966

Charlton Bobby (Robert) 1937– . English footballer, younger brother of Jack Charlton, who scored a record 49 goals in 106 appearances. An elegant midfield player who specialized in fierce long-range shots, Charlton spent most of his playing career with Manchester United. On retiring he had an unsuccessful spell as manager of Preston North End. He later became a director of Manchester United.

CAREER HIGHLIGHTS
Football League appearances: 644; goals: 206
international appearances: 106; goals: 49
World Cup: 1966
Football League championship: 1965, 1967
FA Cup: 1963
European Cup: 1968
Footballer of the Year: 1966
European Footballer of the Year: 1966

Christie Linford 1960– . Jamaican-born English sprinter who, with his win in the 1993 World Cham-
pionships, became the first track athlete ever to hold World Olympic, European, and Commonwealth titles simultaneously. He has won more medals in major events than any other athlete in British athletics history. His time of 9.87 seconds was, in 1993, the second-fastest time ever recorded.

CAREER HIGHLIGHTS
Olympic games
1988: silver 100 metres; silver 400-metre relay
1992: gold 100 metres
Commonwealth games
1990: gold 100 metres; gold 400-metre relay
European championships
1986: gold 100 metres
1990: gold 100 metres
World Cup
1989: gold 100 metres
1992: gold 100 metres
World Athletic Championships
1993: gold 100 metres

Clark Jim (James) 1936–1968. Scottish-born motor-racing driver who was twice world champion 1963 and 1965. He spent all his Formula One career with Lotus. Clark won 25 Formula One Grand Prix races, a record at the time, before losing his life at Hockenheim, West Germany, in April 1968 during a Formula Two race.

CAREER HIGHLIGHTS
world champion
1963 (Lotus)
1965 (Lotus)
Formula One Grand Prix
races: 72
wins: 25

Cobb Ty(rus Raymond), nicknamed 'the Georgia Peach' 1886–1961. US baseball player, one of the greatest batters and base runners of all time. He played for Detroit and Philadelphia 1905–28, and won the American League batting average championship 12 times. He holds the record for runs scored (2,254) and batting average (0.367). He had 4,191 hits in his career – a record that stood for almost 60 years.

Coe Sebastian 1956– . English middle-distance runner, Olympic 1,500-metre champion 1980 and 1984. Coe became Britain's most prolific world-record breaker with eight outdoor world records and three indoor world records 1979–81. After his retirement in 1990 he pursued a political career with the Conservative party, and in 1992 was elected member of Parliament for Falmouth and Camborne in Cornwall.

CAREER HIGHLIGHTS
Olympic Games
1980: gold 1,500 metres, silver 800 metres
1984: gold 1,500 metres, silver 800 metres
world records
1979: 800 metres, one mile, 1,500 metres
1980: 1,000 metres

1981: 800 metres, 1,000 metres, one mile (twice)
1982: 3,200-metre relay

Comaneci Nadia 1961– . Romanian gymnast. She won three gold medals at the 1976 Olympics at the age of 14, and was the first gymnast to record a perfect score of 10 in international competition. Upon retirement she became a coach of the Romanian team, but defected to Canada 1989.

CAREER HIGHLIGHTS
Olympic Games
1976: gold beam, vault, floor exercise
1980: gold beam, parallel bars

Connolly Maureen 1934–1969. US tennis player, nicknamed 'Little Mo' because she was just 157 cm/5 ft 2 in tall. In 1953 she became the first woman to complete the Grand Slam by winning all four major tournaments. All her singles titles (at nine major championships) and her Grand Slam titles were won between 1951 and 1954. Her career ended 1954 after a riding accident.

CAREER HIGHLIGHTS
Wimbledon
singles: 1952–54
US Open
singles: 1951–53
French Open
singles: 1953–54
doubles: 1954
mixed: 1954
Australian Open
singles: 1953
doubles: 1953

Connors Jimmy 1952– . US tennis player who won the Wimbledon title 1974, and subsequently won ten Grand Slam events. He was one of the first players to popularize the two-handed backhand.

CAREER HIGHLIGHTS
Wimbledon
singles: 1974, 1982
doubles: 1973
US Open
singles: 1974, 1976, 1978, 1982–83
doubles: 1975
Australian Open
singles: 1974
Grand Prix Masters
1978

Court Margaret (born Smith) 1942– . Australian tennis player. The most prolific winner in the women's game, she won a record 64 Grand Slam titles, including 25 at singles. Court was the first from her country to win the ladies title at Wimbledon 1963, and the second woman after Maureen Connolly to complete the Grand Slam 1970.

CAREER HIGHLIGHTS
Wimbledon
singles: 1963, 1965, 1970

doubles: 1964, 1969
mixed: 1963, 1965–66, 1968, 1975
US Open
singles: 1962, 1965, 1968–70, 1973
doubles: 1963, 1968–70, 1973, 1975
mixed: 1961–65, 1969–70, 1972
French Open
singles: 1962, 1964, 1969–70, 1973
doubles: 1964–66, 1973
mixed: 1963–65, 1969
Australian Open
singles: 1960–66, 1969–71, 1973
doubles: 1961–63, 1965, 1969–71, 1973
mixed: 1963–64

Cruyff Johan 1947– . Dutch football player, an outstanding European player in the 1970s. He was capped 48 times by his country, scoring 33 goals. He spent most of his career playing with Ajax and Barcelona and was named European Footballer of the Year on three occasions. As a coach he took both clubs to domestic and European honours.

CAREER HIGHLIGHTS
as player:
European Cup
1971–73 (with Ajax)
as coach:
European Cup Winners Cup
1987 (with Ajax)
1989 (with Barcelona)
European Cup
1992 (with Barcelona)
European Footballer of the Year
1971, 1973, 1974
World Club Champions
1972 (with Ajax)

Davis Steve 1957– . English snooker player, who has won every major honour in the game since turning professional 1978. Davis won his first major title 1980 when he won the Coral UK Championship. He has been world champion six times, and has also won world titles at pairs and with the England team.

CAREER HIGHLIGHTS
UK Open
1980–81, 1984–87, 1993
World Professional Champion
1981, 1983–84, 1987–89
World Pairs Championship (with Tony Meo)
1982–83, 1985–86
Benson & Hedges Masters
1982, 1988
World Team Championship
1981, 1983, 1988–89
Rothmans Grand Prix
1985, 1988–89

Dempsey Jack 1895–1983. US heavyweight boxing champion, nicknamed 'the Manassa Mauler'. He beat Jess Willard 1919 to win the title and held it until 1926, when he lost it to Gene Tunney. In a re-match the following year (the 'Battle of the Long Count') Dempsey narrowly lost his chance to regain the title, when after knocking out Tunney in the seventh round he failed to return to a neutral corner, and thereby obliged the referee to delay the start of the count.

CAREER HIGHLIGHTS
fights: 79
wins: 64
draws: 9
defeats: 6

DiMaggio Joe 1914– . US baseball player with the New York Yankees 1936–51. In 1941 he set a record by getting hits in 56 consecutive games. He was an outstanding fielder, played centre field, hit 361 home runs, and had a career average of 0.325. He was once married to the actress Marilyn Monroe.

Edberg Stefan 1966– . Swedish lawn-tennis player, twice winner of Wimbledon 1988 and 1990. He won the junior Grand Slam 1983 and his first Grand Slam title – the Australian Open – 1985, repeated 1987. Other Grand Slam singles titles include the US Open 1991 and 1992. At Wimbledon in 1987 he became the first male player in 40 years to win a match without conceding a game.

CAREER HIGHLIGHTS
Wimbledon
singles: 1988, 1990
Australian Open
singles: 1985, 1987
doubles: 1987
US Open
singles: 1991, 1992
doubles: 1987
Grand Prix Masters
1989

Edwards Gareth 1947– . Welsh rugby union player. He was appointed captain of his country when only 20 years old. Edwards appeared in seven championship winning teams, five Triple Crown winning teams, and two Grand Slam winning teams. In 53 international matches he scored a record 20 tries.

CAREER HIGHLIGHTS
international championship: 1969, 1970*, 1971, 1975–76, 1978
Triple Crown: 1969, 1971, 1976–78
Grand Slam: 1971, 1976, 1978
British Lions tours: 1968 to South Africa, 1971 to New Zealand, 1974 to South Africa
* denotes title shared

Evert Chris(tine) 1954– . US tennis player renowned for her outstanding two-handed backhand and baseline technique. She won her first Wimbledon title 1974, and has since won 21 Grand Slam titles. From 1974–89 she never failed to reach the quarter-finals at Wimbledon. She became the first woman tennis player to win $1 million in prize money.

CAREER HIGHLIGHTS
Wimbledon
singles: 1974, 1976, 1981
doubles: 1976
US Open
singles: 1975–78, 1980, 1982
French Open
singles: 1974–75, 1979–80, 1983, 1985–86
doubles: 1974–75
Australian Open
singles: 1982, 1984

Faldo Nick 1957– . English golfer who was the first Briton in 54 years to win three British Open titles, and the only person after Jack Nicklaus to win two successive US Masters titles (1989 and 1990). He is one of only six golfers to win the Masters and British Open in the same year.

CAREER HIGHLIGHTS
British Open: 1987, 1989, 1992
US Masters: 1989, 1990
PGA Championship: 1978, 1980–81, 1989
Ryder Cup winning team: 1985, 1987, tie 1989
World Match-Play Championship: 1989, 1992
European Open: 1992

Ferrari Enzo 1898–1988. Italian founder of the Ferrari car manufacturing company, which specializes in Grand Prix racing cars and high-quality sports cars. He was a racing driver for Alfa Romeo in the 1920s, went on to become one of their designers and in 1929 took over their racing division. In 1947 the first 'true' Ferrari was seen. The Ferrari car has won more world championship Grands Prix than any other car.

Finney Tom (Thomas) 1922– . English footballer, known as the 'Preston Plumber'. His only Football League club was his home-town team, Preston North End. He played for England 76 times, in every forward position. He was celebrated for his ball control and goal-scoring skills, and was the first person to win the Footballer of the Year award twice.

CAREER HIGHLIGHTS
Football League appearances: 433; goals: 187
international appearances: 76; goals: 30
FA Cup (runners-up medal): 1954
Footballer of the Year: 1954, 1957

Francome John 1952– . English jockey who holds the record for the most National Hunt winners (over hurdles or fences). Between 1970 and 1985 he rode 1,138 winners from 5,061 mounts – the second person (after Stan Mellor) to ride 1,000 winners. He took up training after retiring from riding.

CAREER HIGHLIGHTS
Champion Jockey: 1979, 1981–85 (shared title 1982)
Cheltenham Gold Cup: 1978
Champion Hurdle: 1981
Hennessy Cognac Gold Cup: 1983–84
King George VI Chase: 1982

Gascoigne Paul ('Gazza') 1967– . English footballer who has played for Tottenham Hotspur 1988–91 and for Lazio, Italy, from 1992. At the 1990 World Cup semifinal against West Germany, he committed a foul for which he was booked (cautioned by the referee), meaning that he would be unable to play in the final, should England win. His tearful response drew public sympathy, and he was subsequently lionized by the British press.

Gavaskar Sunil Manohar 1949– . Indian cricketer. Between 1971 and 1987 he scored a record 10,122 test runs in a record 125 matches (including 106 consecutive tests) until overtaken by Allan Border in 1993.

CAREER HIGHLIGHTS

all first-class matches
runs: 25,834
average: 51.46
best: 340 (Bombay v. Bengal, 1981–82)
test cricket
runs: 10,122
average: 51.12
best: 236 not out (India v. West Indies, 1983–84)

Gooch Graham Alan 1953– . English cricketer who plays for Essex county and England. He made his first-class cricket debut in 1973, and was first capped for England two years later. Banned for three years for captaining a team for a tour of South Africa in 1982, he was later re-instated as England captain in 1989. He scored a world record 456 runs in a test match against India in 1990. In 1993 he joined the select band of cricketers to reach the milestone of 100 centuries.

CAREER HIGHLIGHTS

all first-class matches (to end of 1993 season)
runs: 38,149
average: 48.65
best: 333 (England v. India 1990)
wickets: 231
average: 35.18
best: 7-14 (Essex v. Worcestershire 1982)
test cricket (to end of 1993 season)
appearances: 107
runs: 8,293
average: 43.87
best: 333 (England v. India 1990)
wickets: 22
average: 43.63
best: 3-39 (England v. Pakistan 1992)

Gower David 1957– . English left-handed cricketer who played for Leicestershire 1975–89 and for Hampshire from 1990. In 1992, during the third test against Pakistan, he became England's highest-scoring batsman in test cricket, surpassing Geoffrey Boycott's record of 8,114 runs.

CAREER HIGHLIGHTS

all first-class matches (to end of 1993 season)
runs: 26,339
average: 40.08
best: 228 (Leicestershire v. Glamorgan 1989)
test cricket (to end of 1993 season)
appearances (to April 1991): 117

runs: 8,231
average: 44.25
best: 215 (England v. Australia 1985)

Grace W(illiam) G(ilbert) 1848–1915. English cricketer. By profession a doctor, he became the best batsman in England. He began playing first-class cricket at the age of 16, scored 152 runs in his first test match, and scored the first triple century 1876. Throughout his career, which lasted nearly 45 years, he scored more than 54,000 runs.

CAREER HIGHLIGHTS

all first-class matches
runs: 54,896
average: 39.55
best: 344 MCC v. Kent, 1876
wickets: 2,876
average: 17.92
best: 10-49 MCC v. Oxford University, 1886
test cricket
runs: 1,098
average: 32.29
best: 170 v. Australia, 1886
wickets: 9
average: 26.22
best: 2-12 v Australia, 1890

Graf Steffi 1969– . German tennis player who brought Martina Navratilova's long reign as the world's number-one female player to an end. Graf reached the semifinal of the US Open 1985 at the age of 16, and won five consecutive Grand Slam singles titles 1988–89.

CAREER HIGHLIGHTS

Wimbledon
singles: 1988–89, 1991, 1992, 1993
doubles: 1988
US Open
singles: 1988–89, 1993
French Open
singles: 1987–88, 1993
Australian Open
singles: 1988–90
Olympics
gold: 1988

Green Lucinda (born Prior-Palmer) 1953– . English three-day eventer. She has won the Badminton Horse Trials a record six times 1973–84 and was world individual champion 1982.

Gretzky Wayne 1961– . Canadian ice-hockey player, probably the best in the history of the National Hockey League (NHL). Gretsky played with the Edmonton Oilers 1979–88 and with the Los Angeles Kings from 1988. He took just 11 years to break the NHL scoring record of 1,850 goals (accumulated by Gordie Howe over 26 years) and won the Hart Memorial Trophy as the NHL's most valuable player of the season a record nine times (1980–87, 1990–91).

CAREER HIGHLIGHTS

Stanley Cup: 1984, 1985, 1987, 1988

Hart Memorial Trophy (NHL's most valuable player): 1980–87, 1989
Ross Trophy (most points in regular season): 1981–87

Griffith-Joyner (born Griffith) Delorez Florence 1959– . US track athlete, nicknamed 'Flo-Jo', who won three gold medals at the 1988 Seoul Olympics, the 100 and 200 metres and the sprint relay. Her time in the 200 metres was a world record 21.34 seconds.

Hadlee Richard John 1951– . New Zealand cricketer. In 1987 he surpassed Ian Botham's world record of 373 wickets in test cricket and went on to set the record at 431 wickets. He played for Canterbury and Nottinghamshire in England, and retired from international cricket 1990.

CAREER HIGHLIGHTS
all first-class matches
runs: 12,052
average: 31.78
best: 210 not out (Nottinghamshire v. Middlesex 1984)
wickets: 1,490
average: 18.11
best: 9 for 52 (New Zealand v. Australia 1985–86)
test cricket
appearances: 86
runs: 3,124
average: 27.16
best: 151 not out (New Zealand v. Sri Lanka 1986–87)
wickets: 431
average: 22.29
best: 9 for 52 (New Zealand v. Australia 1985–86)

Hanley Ellery 1965– . English rugby league player, a regular member of the Great Britain team since 1984 and the inspiration behind Wigan's domination of the sport in the 1980s. Hanley started his career in 1981 with Bradford Northern before his transfer to Wigan 1985 for a then world record £85,000. He has since won all the top honours of the game in Britain as well as earning a reputation in Australia, the world's top rugby league nation. He joined Leeds in 1991.

CAREER HIGHLIGHTS
Challenge Cup: 1985, 1988–91
Division One Championship: 1987, 1990–91
Regal Trophy: 1986–87, 1989–90
Lancashire County Cup: 1986–89
Premiership Trophy: 1987

Hendry Stephen 1970– . Scottish snooker player. Hendry was the youngest winner ever of a professional tournament when he claimed the 1986 Scottish professional title, and won his first ranking event in the 1987 Rothmans Grand Prix. During the 1989–90 season he replaced Steve Davis as the top-ranking player, and became the youngest world champion ever.

CAREER HIGHLIGHTS
Embassy World Professional Championship: 1990, 1992, 1993
Rothmans Grand Prix: 1987, 1990, 1991
MIM/Pearl Assurance British Open: 1988, 1991

Benson and Hedges Masters: 1989–91, 1992, 1993
UK Open: 1989–90

Hick Graeme 1966– . Rhodesian-born cricketer who became Zimbabwe's youngest professional cricketer at the age of 17. A prolific batsman, he joined Worcestershire, England, in 1984. He achieved the highest score in England in the 20th century in 1988 against Somerset with 405 not out. He made his test debut for England in 1991 after a seven-year qualification period.

CAREER HIGHLIGHTS
all first-class cricket (to end of 1993 season)
runs: 20,605
average: 59.37
best: 405 (Worcestershire v. Somerset 1988)
test cricket (to end of 1993 season)
appearances: 18
runs: 972
average: 31.35
best: 178 (England v. India 1993)

Hill Graham 1929–1975. English motor-racing driver. He won the Dutch Grand Prix in 1962, progressing to the world driver's title in 1962 and 1968. In 1972 he became the first world driver's champion to win the Le Mans Grand Prix d' Endurance (Le Mans 24-Hour Race). Hill started his Formula One career with Lotus 1958, went to BRM 1960–66, returned to Lotus 1967–69, moved to Brabham 1970–72, and formed his own team, Embassy Shadow, 1973–75. He was killed in an air crash. His son Damon won his first Grand Prix in 1993, making them the first father and son to both win a Grand Prix.

CAREER HIGHLIGHTS
world champion
1962 BRM
1968 Lotus
Formula One Grand Prix
races: 176
wins: 14
Le Mans Grand Prix d'Endurance
1972 Matra-Simca
Indianapolis 500
1966 Lola Ford

Hobbs Jack (John Berry) 1882–1963. English cricketer who represented his country 61 times. In first-class cricket he scored a world record 61,237 runs, including a record 197 centuries, in a career that lasted nearly 30 years.
CAREER HIGHLIGHTS
all first-class matches
runs: 61,237
average: 50.65
test cricket
runs: 5,410
average: 56.94
best: 211 v. South Africa, 1924

Howe Gordie 1926– . Canadian ice-hockey player who played for the Detroit Red Wings (National

Hockey League) 1946–71 and then the New England Whalers (World Hockey Association). In the NHL, he scored more goals (801), assists (1,049), and points (1,850) than any other player in ice-hockey history until beaten by Wayne Gretsky. Howe played professional hockey until he was over 50.

Hutton Len (Leonard) 1916–1990. English cricketer. He captained England in 23 test matches 1952–56 and was England's first professional captain. In 1938 at the Oval he scored 364 against Australia, a world record test score until beaten by Gary Sobers 1958.

CAREER HIGHLIGHTS
all first-class matches
runs: 40,140
average: 55.51
best: 364 England v. Australia, 1938
test cricket
runs: 6,971
average: 55.51
best: 364 (England v. Australia, 1938)

Johnson Jack 1878–1968. US heavyweight boxer. He overcame severe racial prejudice to become the first black heavyweight champion of the world 1908 when he travelled to Australia to challenge Tommy Burns. The US authorities wanted Johnson 'dethroned' because of his colour but could not find suitable challengers until 1915, when he lost the title in a dubious fight decision to the giant Jess Willard.

CAREER HIGHLIGHTS
fights: 107
wins: 86
draws: 11
defeats: 10

Jones Bobby (Robert Tyre) 1902–1971. US golfer who was the game's greatest amateur player. He never turned professional but won 13 major amateur and professional tournaments, including the Grand Slam of the amateur and professional opens of both the USA and Britain 1930. Jones finished playing competitive golf 1930, but maintained his contacts with the sport and was largely responsible for inaugurating the US Masters.

CAREER HIGHLIGHTS
British Open: 1926–27, 1930
US Open: 1923, 1926, 1929–30
British Amateur: 1930
US Amateur: 1924–25, 1927–28, 1930
US Walker Cup (team): 1922, 1924, 1926, 1928*, 1930*
* *indicates playing captain*

Khan Imran 1952– . Pakistani cricketer. He played county cricket for Worcestershire and Sussex in the UK, and made his test debut for Pakistan 1971, subsequently playing for his country 85 times. In first-class cricket he has scored over 16,000 runs and taken over 1,200 wickets. He captained Pakistan to victory in the 1992 World Cup.

CAREER HIGHLIGHTS
test cricket
appearances: 88
runs: 3,807
average: 37.69
best: 136 (Pakistan v. Australia 1989–90)
wickets: 362
average: 22.81
best: 8–58 (Pakistan v. Sri Lanka 1981–82)

Khan Jahangir 1963– . Pakistani squash player who won the world open championship a record six times 1981–85 and 1988. He was ten times British Open champion 1982–91, and World Amateur champion 1979, 1983, and 1985. After losing to Geoff Hunt of Australia in the final of the 1981 British Open he did not lose again until Nov 1986 when he lost to Ross Norman of New Zealand in the World Open final. He announced his retirement 1993.

King Billie Jean (born Moffitt) 1943– . US tennis player. She won a record 20 Wimbledon titles between 1961 and 1979 (including six singles titles), and her 39 Grand Slam events at singles and doubles are third only to Navratilova and Margaret Court.

CAREER HIGHLIGHTS
Wimbledon
singles: 1966–68, 1972–73, 1975
doubles: 1961–62, 1965, 1967–68, 1970–73, 1979
mixed: 1967, 1971, 1973–74
US Open
singles: 1967, 1971–72, 1974
doubles: 1964, 1967, 1974, 1978, 1980
mixed: 1967, 1971, 1973, 1976
French Open
singles: 1972
doubles: 1972
mixed: 1967, 1970
Australian Open
singles: 1968
mixed: 1968

Klammer Franz 1953– . Austrian skier who won a record 35 World Cup downhill races between 1974 and 1985. He was the combined world champion 1974, Olympic gold medallist 1976, and the World Cup downhill champion 1975–78 and 1983.

Korbut Olga 1955– . Soviet gymnast who attracted world attention at the 1972 Olympic Games with her lively floor routine. She won gold medals for the beam and floor exercises, a silver for the parallel bars, and another gold as member of the winning Soviet team.

CAREER HIGHLIGHTS
Olympic Games
1972: gold beam, floor exercise, team
1976: team

Kristiansen Ingrid 1956– . Norwegian athlete, an outstanding long-distance runner of 5,000 metres,

10,000 metres, marathon, and cross-country races. She has won all the world's leading marathons. In 1986 she knocked 45.68 seconds off the world 10,000 metres record. She was the world cross-country champion 1988 and won the London marathon 1984–85 and 1987–88.

Latynina Larissa Semyonovna 1935– . Soviet gymnast, winner of more Olympic medals than any person in any sport. She won 18 between 1956 and 1964, including nine gold medals. During her career she won a total of 12 individual Olympic and world championship gold medals.

CAREER HIGHLIGHTS

Olympic champion
team: 1956, 1960, 1964
overall individual: 1956, 1960
floor exercise: 1956*, 1960, 1964
vault: 1956
world championship
team: 1958, 1962
overall individual: 1958, 1962
vault: 1958
beam: 1958
floor exercise: 1962
asymmetric bars: 1958
* denotes shared title

Lauda Niki 1949– . Austrian motor racing driver who won the world championship in 1975, 1977 and 1984. He was also runner-up in 1976 just six weeks after a serious accident at Nurburgring, Germany, which left him badly burned. Lauda was Formula Two champion in 1972, and drove for March, BRM, Ferrari, and Brabham before his retirement in 1978. He returned to the sport in 1984 and won his third world title in a McLaren before eventually retiring in 1985 to concentrate on his airline business, Lauda-Air.

CAREER HIGHLIGHTS

world champion
1975 Ferrari
1977 Ferrari
1984 McLaren

Formula One Grand Prix
races: 171
wins: 25

Laver Rod(ney George) 1938– . Australian tennis player. He was one of the greatest left-handed players, and the only player to perform the Grand Slam twice (1962 and 1969). He won four Wimbledon singles titles, the Australian title three times, the US Open twice, and the French Open twice. He turned professional after winning Wimbledon in 1962 but returned when the championships were opened to professionals in 1968.

CAREER HIGHLIGHTS

Wimbledon
singles: 1961–62, 1968–69
doubles: 1971
mixed: 1959–60

US Open
singles: 1962, 1969
French Open
singles: 1962, 1969
doubles: 1961
mixed: 1961
Australian Open
singles: 1960, 1962, 1969
doubles: 1959–61, 1969

Leonard Sugar Ray 1956– . US boxer. In 1988 he became the first man to have won world titles at five officially recognized weights. He was Olympic light-welterweight champion 1976, and won his first professional title in 1979 when he beat Wilfred Benitez for the WBC welterweight title. He later won titles at junior middleweight (WBA version) 1981, middleweight (WBC) 1987, light-heavyweight (WBC) 1988, and super-middleweight (WBC) 1988. He retired 1992.

Lewis Carl (Frederick Carlton) 1961– . US track and field athlete who won eight gold medals and one silver in three successive Olympic Games 1984, 1988, and 1992. At the 1984 Olympic Games he equalled the performance of Jesse Owens, winning gold medals in the 100 and 200 metres, 400-metre relay, and long jump.

CAREER HIGHLIGHTS

Olympic Games
1984: gold 100 metres, 200 metres, 400-metre relay, long jump
1988: gold 100 metres, long jump; silver 200 metres
1992: gold long jump, 400-metre relay

Lewis Lennox 1966– . British-born heavyweight boxer who represented Canada in the super-heavyweight division. Turning professional in 1989, he won the European heavyweight title in 1990 and British title in 1991. In 1992 he became the first British-born boxer this century to win the world heavyweight title, when reigning champion Riddick Bowe refused to fight him. He then successfully defended his WBC crown against Tony Tucker and Frank Bruno in 1993.

Lillee Dennis 1949– . Australian cricketer regarded as the best fast bowler of his generation. He made his test debut in the 1970–71 season and subsequently played for his country 70 times. Lillee was the first to take 300 wickets in test cricket. He played Sheffield Shield cricket for Western Australia and at the end of his career made a comeback with Tasmania.

CAREER HIGHLIGHTS

test cricket (to the beginning of the 1992 season)
appearances: 70
wickets: 355
average: 23.92

Lineker Gary 1960– . English footballer who scored over 250 goals in 550 games for Leicester, Everton, Barcelona, and Tottenham. With 48 goals in 80 internationals he failed by one goal to equal

Bobby Charlton's record of 49 goals for England. Lineker was elected Footballer of the Year in 1986 and 1992 and was leading scorer at the 1986 World Cup finals. In 1993 he moved to Japan to play for Nagoya Grampus Eight.

CAREER HIGHLIGHTS

FA Cup: 1991 (with Tottenham)
European Cup Winners Cup: 1989 (with Barcelona)
Footballer of the Year: 1986, 1992

Lopez Nancy 1957– . US golfer who turned professional in 1977 and in 1979 became the first woman to win $200,000 in a season. She has won the US LPGA title three times 1978, 1985, and 1989, and has won over 35 tour events, and $3 million in prize money.

Louis Joe. Assumed name of Joseph Louis Barrow 1914–1981. US boxer, nicknamed 'the Brown Bomber'. He was world heavyweight champion between 1937 and 1949 and made a record 25 successful defences (a record for any weight). Louis was the longest-reigning world heavyweight champion at 11 years and 252 days before announcing his retirement in 1949. He made a comeback and lost to Ezzard Charles in a world title fight in 1950.

CAREER HIGHLIGHTS

professional fights: 66
wins: 63
knockouts: 49
defeats: 3
1st professional fight: 4 July 1934 v. Jack Kracken
last professional fight: 26 Oct 1951 v. Rocky Marciano

McBride Willie John 1940– . Irish rugby union player. He was capped 63 times by Ireland, and won a record 17 British Lions caps. He played on five Lions tours 1962, 1966, 1968, 1971, and in 1974 as captain when they returned from South Africa undefeated.

CAREER HIGHLIGHTS

British Lions tours
1962 South Africa
1966 Australia and New Zealand
1968 South Africa
1971 Australia and New Zealand
1974 South Africa (captain)
1983 New Zealand (manager)

McEnroe John Patrick 1959– . US tennis player whose brash behaviour and fiery temper on court dominated the men's game in the early 1980s. He was three times winner of the Wimbledon men's title 1981, 1983, and 1984. He also won three successive US Open titles 1979–81 and again in 1984. A fine doubles player, McEnroe also won ten Grand Slam doubles titles, seven in partnership with Peter Fleming.

CAREER HIGHLIGHTS

Wimbledon
singles: 1981, 1983, 1984
doubles: 1979, 1981, 1983, 1984, 1992

US Open
singles: 1979–81, 1984
doubles: 1979, 1981, 1983, 1989
French Open
mixed doubles: 1977
Grand Prix Masters
singles: 1979, 1984, 1985
doubles: 1979–85

Mansell Nigel 1954– . English motor-racing driver. Runner-up in the world championship on two occasions, he became world champion in 1992 and in the same year announced his retirement from Formula One racing. He won 30 Grand Prix races – more than any other British driver. Mansell started his Formula One career with Lotus 1980 and won the European Grand Prix 1985. He drove for the Williams team 1985–88, then for Ferrari 1989–90, before returning to Williams 1991–92. He joined the Newman-Haas team in 1993 and became the first to win the IndyCar championship in his debut season.

Mantle Mickey (Charles) 1931– . US baseball player. Signed by the New York Yankees, he broke into the major leagues 1951. A powerful switch-hitter (able to bat with either hand), he also excelled as a centre-fielder. In 1956 he won baseball's Triple Crown, leading the American League in batting average, home runs, and runs batted in. He retired 1969 after 18 years with the Yankees and seven World Series championships.

Maradona Diego 1960– . Argentine footballer who was voted the best player of the 1980s by the world's press. He has won over 80 international caps, and helped his country to two successive World Cup finals. Maradona played for Argentinos Juniors and Boca Juniors before leaving South America for Barcelona, Spain, 1982, for a transfer fee of approximately £5 million. In 1993 he moved from the Spanish club Seville back to Argentina to play for Newell's Old Boys.

CAREER HIGHLIGHTS

World Cup: 1986
UEFA Cup: 1989
Italian League: 1987, 1990
Italian Cup: 1987
Spanish Cup: 1983
South American footballer of the year: 1979, 1980

Marciano Rocky (Rocco Francis Marchegiano) 1923–1969. US boxer, world heavyweight champion 1952–56. He retired after 49 professional fights, the only heavyweight champion to retire undefeated. He was killed in a plane crash.

CAREER HIGHLIGHTS

professional fights: 49
wins: 49
knockouts: 43
defeats: 0
1st professional fight: 17 March 1947 v. Lee Epperson
(USA)
last professional fight: 21 Sept 1955 v. Archie Moore
(USA)

Matthews Stanley 1915– . English footballer who played for Stoke City, Blackpool, and England. An outstanding right-winger, he won the nickname 'the Wizard of the Dribble' because of his ball control. Matthews played nearly 700 Football League games, and won 54 international caps. He continued to play first-division football after the age of 50. He was the first European Footballer of the Year 1956.

CAREER HIGHLIGHTS

Football League appearances: 698, goals: 71
international appearances: 54, goals: 11
FA Cup: 1953
Footballer of the Year: 1948, 1963
European Footballer of the Year: 1956

Merckx Eddie 1945– . Belgian cyclist, known as 'the Cannibal', who won the Tour de France a joint record five times 1969–74. Merckx turned professional 1966 and won his first classic race, the Milan–San Remo, the same year. He went on to win 24 classics as well as the three major tours (of Italy, Spain, and France) a total of 11 times.

He was world professional road-race champion three times and in 1971 won a record 54 races in the season. He rode 50 winners in a season four times. He retired in 1977.

CAREER HIGHLIGHTS

Tour de France: 1969–72, 1974
Tour of Italy: 1968, 1970, 1972–74
Tour of Spain: 1973
world professional champion: 1967, 1971, 1974
world amateur champion: 1964

Miandad Javed 1957– . Pakistani test cricketer, his country's leading run-maker. He scored a century on his test debut in 1976 and has since become one of a handful of players to make 100 test appearances. He has captained his country and helped Pakistan to win the 1992 World Cup. His highest score of 311 was made when he was aged 17.

CAREER HIGHLIGHTS

test cricket (to end of 1993 season)
appearances: 117
runs: 8,465
average: 54.26
best: 280 not out v. India 1982–83

Montana Joe 1956– . US football player who has appeared in four winning Super Bowls as quarterback for the San Francisco 49ers 1982, 1985, 1989, and 1990, winning the Most Valuable Player award in 1982, 1985, and 1990. He had a record five touchdown passes in the 1990 Super Bowl.

Moore Bobby (Robert Frederick) 1941–1993. English footballer who led the England team to victory against West Germany in the 1966 World Cup final at Wembley Stadium. A superb defender, he played 108 games for England 1962–70 (until 1978, a world-record number of international appearances) and was captain 90 times. His Football League career, spent at West Ham 1968–74 and Fulham 1974–77, spanned 19 years and 668 matches.

CAREER HIGHLIGHTS

Football League appearances: 668; goals: 25
international appearances: 108; goals: 2
World Cup: 1966
European Cup Winners Cup: 1965
FA Cup: 1964
Footballer of the Year: 1964
World Cup Player of Players: 1966

Namath Joe (Joseph William) 1943– . US football player. In 1965 Namath signed with the New York Jets of the newly established American Football League. In 1969 Namath led the Jets to a historic upset victory over the Baltimore Colts in the Super Bowl. After leaving the Jets 1977, Namath joined the Los Angeles Rams; however, knee injuries forced his retirement as a player the following year. He later became a sports broadcaster and actor.

Navratilova Martina 1956– . Czech tennis player who became a naturalized US citizen 1981. The most outstanding woman player of the 1980s, she had 55 Grand Slam victories by 1991, including 18 singles titles. She has won the Wimbledon singles title a record nine times, including six in succession 1982–87.

CAREER HIGHLIGHTS

Wimbledon
singles: 1978–79, 1982–87, 1990
doubles: 1976, 1979, 1981–84, 1986
mixed: 1985, 1993
US Open
singles: 1983–84, 1986–87
doubles: 1977–78, 1980, 1983–84, 1986–90
mixed: 1985, 1987
French Open
singles: 1982, 1984
doubles: 1975, 1982, 1984–88
mixed: 1974, 1985
Australian Open
singles: 1981, 1983, 1985
doubles: 1980, 1982–85, 1987–89

Nicklaus Jack (William) 1940– . US golfer, nicknamed 'the Golden Bear'. He won a record 20 major titles, including 18 professional majors between 1962 and 1986. He played for the US Ryder Cup team six times 1969–81 and was nonplaying captain 1983 and 1987 when the event was played over the course he designed at Muirfield Village, Ohio. In 1988 he was voted Golfer of the Century.

CAREER HIGHLIGHTS

US Amateur: 1959, 1961
US Open: 1962, 1967, 1972, 1980
British Open: 1966, 1970, 1978
US Masters: 1963, 1965–66, 1972, 1975, 1986
US PGA Championship: 1963, 1971, 1973, 1975, 1980
US Ryder Cup (team): 1969, 1971, 1973, 1975, 1977

Owens Jesse (James Cleveland) 1913–1980. US track and field athlete who excelled in the sprints, hurdles, and the long jump. At the 1936 Berlin Olympics he won four gold medals, and the Nazi leader Hitler is said to have stormed out of the stadium in disgust at the black man's triumph. Owens held the world long-jump record for 25 years 1935–60. At Ann Arbor, Michigan, on 25 May 1935, he broke six world records in less than an hour.

CAREER HIGHLIGHTS

Olympic Games
1936: gold 100 metres, 200 metres, 400-metre relay, long jump

world records:
1935: 100 yards, 200 metres, 220 yards, 200-metre hurdles, 220-yd hurdles, long jump
1936: 100 metres, 100 yards, 400-metre relay (US National team)

Palmer Arnold (Daniel) 1929– . US golfer who helped to popularize the professional sport in the USA in the 1950s and 1960s. He won the US amateur title 1954, and went on to win all the world major professional trophies except the US PGA Championship. In the 1980s he enjoyed a successful career on the US Seniors Tour.

CAREER HIGHLIGHTS

US Open: 1960
British Open: 1961–62
Masters: 1958, 1960, 1962, 1964
World Match-Play: 1964, 1967
US Ryder Cup: 1961, 1963*, 1965, 1967, 1971, 1973, 1975**

* playing captain; ** nonplaying captain

Pelé Adopted name of Edson Arantes do Nascimento 1940– . Brazilian soccer player who was celebrated as one of the finest inside-forwards in the history of the game. A prolific goal scorer, he appeared in four World Cup competitions 1958–70 and led Brazil to three championships 1958, 1962, and 1970. He spent most of his playing career with the Brazilian team Santos, before ending it with the New York Cosmos in the USA.

Piggott Lester 1935– . English jockey. He has adopted a unique high riding style and is renowned as a brilliant tactician. A champion jockey 11 times between 1960 and 1982, he has ridden a record nine Derby winners. He retired from riding 1985 and took up training. In 1987 he was imprisoned for tax evasion. He returned to racing in 1990 and has ridden 4,435 winners, including a record 30 Classics, in Britain to the start of the 1993 season.

CAREER HIGHLIGHTS

Champion Jockey: 1960, 1964–71, 1981–82
Derby: 1954, 1957, 1960, 1968, 1970, 1972, 1976–77, 1983
Oaks: 1957, 1959, 1966, 1975, 1981, 1984
St Leger: 1960–61, 1967–68, 1970–72, 1984
1,000 Guineas: 1970, 1981
2,000 Guineas: 1957, 1968, 1970, 1985, 1992
Irish 2,000 Guineas: 1992

Platini Michel 1955– . French football player who was the inspiration of the French team that won the 1984 European Championship. He represented his country on 72 occasions, scoring a record 41 goals and playing in three World Cups, and was the first to be elected European Footballer of the Year on three successive years 1983–85. He became manager of the French national team in 1988.

CAREER HIGHLIGHTS

European Championship: 1984
French Cup: 1978 (with Nancy)
French Championship: 1981 (with St Etienne)
Italian Championship: 1984, 1986 (with Juventus)
European Cup: 1985 (with Juventus)
European Cup Winners Cup: 1984 (with Juventus)
European Footballer of the Year: 1983–85

Prost Alain 1955– . French motor-racing driver who was world champion 1985, 1986, and 1989, the first French world drivers' champion. He raced in Formula One events from 1980 and had his first Grand Prix win 1981, driving a Renault. In 1984 he began driving for the McLaren team. To the end of the 1993 season he had won 51 Grands Prix from 199 starts. He announced his retirement in 1993.

CAREER HIGHLIGHTS

world champion
1985 Marlboro McLaren–TAG
1986 Marlboro McLaren–TAG
1989 Marlboro McLaren–Honda
1993 Williams–Renault

Formula One Grand Prix (to end of 1993 season)
races: 199
wins: 51 (record)

Rhodes Wilfred 1877–1973. English cricketer who took more wickets than anyone else in the game – 4,187 wickets from 1898 to 1930 – and also scored 39,802 first-class runs. Playing for Yorkshire, Rhodes made a record 763 appearances in the county championship. He took 100 wickets in a season 23 times and completed the 'double' of 1,000 runs and 100 wickets in a season 16 times (both records). He played his 58th and final game for England, against the West Indies 1930, when he was 52 years old, the oldest ever test cricketer.

CAREER HIGHLIGHTS

all first-class matches
runs: 39,802
average: 30.83
best: 267 not out Yorkshire v. Leicestershire, 1921
wickets: 4,187
average: 16.71
best: 9-24 C I Thornton's XI v. Australians, 1899

test cricket
runs: 2,325
average: 30.19
best: 179 v. Australia, 1911-12
wickets: 127
average: 26.96
best: 8-68 v. Australia, 1903-04

Richards Gordon 1905–1986. English jockey and trainer who was champion on the flat a record 26 times between 1925 and 1953. He started riding 1920 and rode 4,870 winners from 21,834 mounts before retiring 1954 and taking up training. He rode the winners of all the classic races but only once won the Derby (on Pinza 1953). In 1947 he rode a record 269 winners in a season.

CAREER HIGHLIGHTS

Champion Jockey: 1925, 1927-29, 1931-40, 1942-53
Derby: 1953
Oaks: 1930, 1942
St Leger: 1930, 1937, 1940, 1942, 1944
1,000 Guineas: 1942, 1948, 1951
2,000 Guineas: 1938, 1942, 1947

Richards Viv (Isaac Vivian Alexander) 1952– . West Indian cricketer, captain of the West Indies team 1986–91. He has played for the Leeward Islands and, in the UK, for Somerset and Glamorgan. A prolific run-scorer, he holds the record for the greatest number of runs made in test cricket in one calendar year (1,710 runs in 1976). He retired from international cricket after the West Indies tour of England in 1991. He retired from first-class cricket at the end of the 1993 season

CAREER HIGHLIGHTS

all first-class cricket
runs: 36,212
average: 49.33
best: 322 (Somerset v. Warwickshire 1985)
wickets: 223
average: 45.15
best: 5 for 88 (West Indies v. Queensland 1981-82)
test cricket
appearances: 121
runs: 8,540
average: 50.23
best: 291 (v. England 1976)
wickets: 32
average: 61.37
best: 2 for 17 (v. Pakistan 1988)

Rodnina Irina 1949– . Soviet ice skater. Between 1969 and 1980 she won 23 world, Olympic, and European gold medals in pairs competitions. Her partners were Alexei Ulanov and then Alexsandr Zaitsev.

CAREER HIGHLIGHTS

Olympic champion: 1972, 1976, 1980
world champion: 1969-78
European champion: 1969-78

Ruth Babe (George Herman) 1895–1948. US baseball player, regarded by many as the greatest of all time. He played in ten World Series and hit 714 home runs, a record that stood from 1935 to 1974 and led to the nickname 'Sultan of Swat'. He is still the holder of the record for most bases in a season: 457 in 1921. Yankee Stadium is known as 'the house that Ruth built' because of the money he brought into the club.

CAREER HIGHLIGHTS

games: 2,503
runs: 2,174
home runs: 714
average: .342
World Series wins: 1915–16, 1918, 1923, 1927–28, 1932

Sawchuk Terry (Terrance Gordon) 1929–1970. Canadian ice-hockey player, often considered the greatest goaltender of all time. He played for Detroit, Boston, Toronto, Los Angeles, and New York Rangers 1950–67, and holds the National Hockey League record of 103 shut-outs (games in which he did not concede a goal).

Scudamore Peter 1958– . English National Hunt jockey who was champion jockey 1982 (shared with John Francome) and from 1986 to 1992. In 1988–89 he rode a record 221 winners. In April 1993 he announced his retirement from the sport with a world record of 1,677 winners.

Seles Monica 1973– . Yugoslavian tennis player who won her first Grand Slam title, the French Open, at the age of 16. She dominated the major events in 1991 but withdrew from Wimbledon and consequently missed the chance to achieve the Grand Slam. In the same year she became the youngest woman player ever to achieve number-one ranking. In 1993 she was stabbed by a spectator during the Hamburg Open. The enforced break from the game meant her missing most major tournaments in 1993.

CAREER HIGHLIGHTS

US Open
singles: 1991, 1992
French Open
singles: 1990–92
Australian Open
singles: 1991, 1992, 1993

Senna Ayrton 1960– . Brazilian motor-racing driver. He had his first Grand Prix win in the 1985 Portuguese Grand Prix, and progressed to the world driver's title in 1988, 1990, and 1991. By the end of the 1993 season he had 41 wins in 158 starts.

Shilton Peter 1949– . English international footballer, an outstanding goalkeeper, who has set records for the highest number of Football League appearances (991 to start of 1993–94 season) and England caps (125). First capped by England 1970 he announced his retirement from international football in 1990, after the England–West Germany World Cup semifinal. In 1992 he became manager of Plymouth Argyle.

Shoemaker Willie (William Lee) 1931– . US jockey whose career, from 1949 to 1990, was outstandingly successful. He rode 8,833 winners from 40,351 mounts and his earnings exceeded $123 million. He retired Feb 1990 after finishing fourth on Patchy Groundfog at Santa Anita, California.

CAREER HIGHLIGHTS

Kentucky Derby: 1955, 1959, 1965, 1986
Preakness Stakes: 1963, 1967
Belmont Stakes: 1957, 1959, 1962, 1967, 1975
leading US money winner: 1951, 1953–54, 1958–64

Sobers Gary (Garfield St Aubrun) 1936–   . West Indian test cricketer. One of the game's great all-rounders, he holds the record for the highest test innings (365 not out). Sobers played English county cricket with Nottinghamshire and while playing for them against Glamorgan at Swansea in 1968, he established a world record by scoring six 6s in one over. He played for the West Indies 93 times.

CAREER HIGHLIGHTS

all first-class cricket
runs: 28,315
average: 54.87
best: 365 not out West Indies v. Pakistan 1957–58
wickets: 1,043
average: 27.74
best: 9-49 West Indies v. Kent 1966
test cricket
runs: 8,032
average: 57.78
best: 365 not out v. Pakistan 1957–58
wickets: 235
average: 34.03
best: 6-73 v. Australia 1968–69

Spitz Mark Andrew 1950–   . US swimmer. He won a record seven gold medals at the 1972 Olympic Games, all in world record times. He won 11 Olympic medals in total (four in 1968) and set 26 world records between 1967 and 1972. After retiring in 1972 he became a movie actor, two of his films being elected candidates for 'The Worst of Holly-wood'.

CAREER HIGHLIGHTS

Olympic medals
1968: gold – 400 metres freestyle relay, 800 metres freestyle relay; silver – 100 metres butterfly; bronze – 100 metres freestyle
1972: gold – 100 metres freestyle, 200 metres freestyle, 100 metres butterfly, 200 metres butterfly, 400 metres freestyle relay, 800 metres freestyle relay, 400 metres medley relay

Stewart Jackie (John Young) 1939–   . Scottish motor-racing driver. Until surpassed by Alain Prost in 1987, Stewart held the record for the most Formula One Grand Prix wins (27). With manufacturer Ken Tyrrell, Stewart built up one of the sport's great partnerships. His last race was the 1973 Canadian Grand Prix. He pulled out of the next race (which would have been his 100th) because of the death of his team-mate François Cevert. He is now a motor-racing commentator.

CAREER HIGHLIGHTS

world champion
1969 Matra
1971 Tyrrell
1973 Tyrrell

Formula One Grand Prix
races: 99
wins: 27
first: 1965 (South African Grand Prix; BRM)
last: 1973 (Canadian Grand Prix; Tyrrell)

Thompson Daley (Francis Morgan) 1958–   . English decathlete who has broken the world record four times since winning the Commonwealth Games decathlon title 1978. He has won two more Commonwealth titles (1982, 1986), two Olympic gold medals (1980, 1984), three European medals (silver 1978; gold 1982, 1986), and a world title (1983).

Torvill and Dean English ice-dance champions Jayne Torvill (1957–) and Christopher Dean (1959–). They won the world title four times 1981–84 and were the 1984 Olympic champions. They turned professional shortly thereafter but returned to international competition in 1994.

Tyson Mike (Michael Gerald) 1966–   . US heavyweight boxer, undisputed world champion from Aug 1987 to Feb 1990 (when he was defeated by James 'Buster' Douglas). He won the World Boxing Council heavyweight title 1986 when he beat Trevor Berbick to become the youngest world heavyweight champion ever. He beat James 'Bonecrusher' Smith for the World Boxing Association title 1987 and later that year became the first undisputed champion since 1978 when he beat Tony Tucker for the International Boxing Federation title. Of Tyson's first 25 opponents, 15 were knocked out in the first round. In 1992 he was imprisoned for rape.

Witt Katarina 1965–   . German ice-skater. She was 1984 Olympic champion (representing East Germany) and by 1990 had won four world titles (1984–85, 1987–88) and six consecutive European titles (1983–88). After four years as a professional she returned to competitive skating in 1993.

Woosnam Ian 1958–   . Welsh golfer who, in 1987, became the first UK player to win the World Match-Play Championship. He has since won many tournaments, including the World Cup 1987, World Match-Play 1990, and US Masters 1991. Woosnam was Europe's leading money-winner in 1987 (as a result of winning the $1 million Sun City Open in South Africa) and again in 1990. He was ranked Number One in the world for 50 weeks in 1991–92.

CAREER HIGHLIGHTS

Ryder Cup (individual): 1983, 1985, 1987, 1989, 1991
Ryder Cup (team): 1985,1987, tie 1989
US Masters: 1991
World Match-Play Championship: 1987, 1990
World Cup (individual): 1987, 1991
World Cup (team): 1987 (Wales)

Sites of summer Olympic Games*

1896	Athens, Greece
1900	Paris, France
1904	St Louis, USA
1908	London, England
1912	Stockholm, Sweden
1920	Antwerp, Belgium
1924	Paris, France
1928	Amsterdam, Netherlands
1932	Los Angeles, USA
1936	Berlin, Germany
1948	London, England
1952	Helsinki, Finland
1956	Melbourne, Australia
1960	Rome, Italy
1964	Tokyo, Japan
1968	Mexico City, Mexico
1972	Munich, W Germany
1976	Montreal, Canada
1980	Moscow, USSR
1984	Los Angeles, USA
1988	Seoul, S Korea
1992	Barcelona, Spain
1996	Atlanta, USA
2000	Sydney, Australia

Winter Olympic Games were started in 1924.

The 1906 Games were not recognized by the International Olympic Committee. In 1916, 1940, and 1944 the Games were not held because of the two World Wars. Sixty-two nations, including the USA, boycotted the 1980 Games; the 1984 Games were boycotted by the USSR and most of Eastern Europe. In 1992, athletes from the 12 former Soviet republics formed the Unified Team, while the Independent Olympic Participants (I.O.P.) consisted of athletes from Serbia, Montenegro, and Macedonia.

Sites of the Commonwealth Games

British Empire Games

1930 Hamilton, Canada
1934 London, England
1938 Sydney, Australia
1950 Auckland, New Zealand

British Empire and Commonwealth Games

1954 Vancouver, Canada
1958 Cardiff, Wales
1962 Perth, Australia
1966 Kingston, Jamaica

British* Commonwealth Games

1970 Edinburgh, Scotland
1974 Christchurch, New Zealand
1978 Edmonton, Canada
1982 Brisbane, Australia
1986 Edinburgh, Scotland
1990 Auckland, New Zealand
1994 Victoria, Canada

* the word 'British' has been dropped from the title.

TRANSPORT

Air Transport

People first took to the air in balloons and began powered flight in airships, but the history of flying is dominated by the aeroplane. The aeroplane is a development of the model glider, first flown by Sir George Cayley (1773–1857) in 1804. It was not until the invention of the petrol engine that powered flight become feasible. The Wright brothers in the USA first achieved success, when they flew their biplane *Flyer* on 17 Dec 1903. In Europe, France led the way in aviation – the Voisin brothers pioneered aeroplane design and much publicity was attracted by Louis Blériot who crossed the Channel in 1909 and by the Reims air races of that year. The first powered flight in the UK was made by S F Cody in 1908. In 1912 Sopwith and Bristol both built small biplanes.

The stimulus of World War I (1914–18) and the rapid development of the petrol engine led to increased power, and speeds rose to 320 kph/200 mph. Streamlining the body of planes became imperative: the body, wings, and exposed parts were reshaped to reduce drag. Eventually the biplane was superseded by the internally braced monoplane structure – for example, the Hawker Hurricane and Supermarine Spitfire fighters and the Avro Lancaster and Boeing Flying Fortress bombers of World War II (1939–45).

The German Heinkel 178, built 1939, ushered in a new era in aviation. It was the first jet plane, driven, not as all planes before it, with a propeller, but by a jet of hot gases. The first British jet aircraft, the Gloster E.28/39 flew from Cranwell, Lincolnshire, on 15 May 1941, powered by a jet engine invented by Frank Whittle. Twin-jet Meteor fighters were in use by the end of the war. The rapid development of the jet plane led to enormous increases in power and speed until air-compressibility effects were felt near the speed of sound, which at first seemed to be the limit for flight speed (the sound barrier). To exceed supersonic speed, streamlining only the aircraft body became insufficient: wings were swept back, engines buried in wings and tail units, and bodies were even eliminated in all-wing delta designs.

In the 1950s the first jet airliners, such as the Comet, were introduced into service. Today jet planes dominate both military and civilian aviation, although many light planes still use piston engines and propellers. The late 1960s saw the introduction of the jumbo jet, and in 1976 the Anglo-French Concorde, which makes a transatlantic crossing in under three hours, came into commercial service.

During the 1950s and 1960s research was done on V/STOL (vertical and/or short take-off and landing) aircraft. The British Harrier jet fighter has been the only VTOL aircraft to achieve commercial success, but STOL technology has fed into subsequent generations of aircraft. The 1960s and 1970s also saw the development of variable geometry ('swing-wing') aircraft, whose wings can be swept back in flight to achieve higher speeds. In the 1980s much progress has been made in 'fly-by-wire' aircraft with computer-aided controls.

International partnerships have developed both civilian and military aircraft. The Panavia Tornado is a joint project of British, German, and Italian aircraft companies. It is an advanced swing-wing craft with multiple military functions – interception, strike, ground support, and reconnaissance. The Airbus is a wide-bodied airliner built jointly by companies from France, Germany, the UK, the Netherlands, and Spain.

aeroplane heavier-than-air craft supported in flight by fixed wings: it may be unpowered (a glider) or powered, when it is propelled by the thrust of a jet engine or propeller. It must be designed aerodynamically, since streamlining ensures maximum flight efficiency. The shape of a plane depends on its use and operating speed – aircraft operating at well below the speed of sound need not be as streamlined as supersonic aircraft.

Efficient streamlining prevents the formation of shock waves over the body surface and wings, which would cause instability and power loss. The wing of an aeroplane has the cross-sectional shape of an aerofoil, being broad and curved at the front, flat underneath, curved on top, and tapered to a sharp point at the rear. The wings' shape is such that air passing above them is speeded up, reducing pressure below atmospheric pressure, while that above is slowed. This results in a force acting vertically upwards, called lift, which counters the aircraft's weight. In level flight, lift equals weight. The wings develop sufficient lift to support the plane when they move quickly through the air. The thrust that causes propulsion comes from the reaction to the air stream accelerated backwards by the propeller or the gases shooting backwards from the jet exhaust. In flight the engine thrust must overcome the air resistance, or drag. Drag depends on frontal area (large in the case of an airliner; small in the case of a fighter plane) and shape (drag coefficient); in level flight, drag equals thrust. The drag is reduced by streamlining the plane, resulting in higher speed and reduced fuel consumption for a given power. Carrying less fuel for a given distance means a larger payload (cargo or passengers) can be carried.

Planes are constructed using light but strong aluminium alloys such as duralumin (with copper, magnesium, and so on). For supersonic planes special stainless steel and titanium may be used in areas subjected to high heat loads. The structure of the plane, or the airframe (wings, fuselage, and so on) consists of a surface skin of alloy sheets supported at intervals by struts known as ribs and stringers. The structure is bonded together by riveting or by powerful adhesives such as epoxy resins. In certain critical areas, which have to withstand very high stresses (such as the wing roots), body panels are machined from solid metal for extra strength.

Fastest aeroplane – the Lockheed SR-71, holder of the world air-speed record of 3,529 kph/2,193 mph (over Mach 3.3).

Fastest airliner – Concorde, which can cruise at up to 2,333 kph/1,450 mph (Mach 2.2).

Largest airliner – Boeing 747, with a wingspan of 59.6 m/195.7 ft and a length of 70.7 m/231.8 ft.

Flight: chronology

1783	First human flight, by Jean F Pilâtre de Rozier and the Marquis d'Arlandes, in Paris, using a hot-air balloon made by Joseph and Etienne Montgolfier; first ascent in a hydrogen-filled balloon by Jacques Charles and M N Robert in Paris.
1785	Jean-Pierre Blanchard and John J Jeffries made the first balloon crossing of the English Channel.
1852	Henri Giffard flew the first steam-powered airship over Paris.
1853	George Cayley flew the first true aeroplane, a model glider 1.5 m/5 ft long.
1891-96	Otto Lilienthal piloted a glider in flight.
1903	First powered and controlled flight of a heavier-than-air craft (aeroplane) by Orville Wright, at Kitty Hawk, North Carolina, USA.
1908	First powered flight in the UK by Samuel Cody.
1909	Louis Blériot flew across the English Channel in 36 minutes.
1914-18	World War I stimulated improvements in speed and power.
1919	First E–W flight across the Atlantic by Albert C Read, using a flying boat; first nonstop flight across the Atlantic E–W by John William Alcock and Arthur Whitten Brown in 16 hours, 27 minutes; first complete flight from Britain to Australia by Ross Smith and Keith Smith.
1923	Juan de la Cieva flew the first autogiro with a rotating wing.
1927	Charles Lindbergh made the first W–E solo nonstop flight across the Atlantic.
1928	First transpacific flight, from San Francisco to Brisbane, by Charles Kinsford Smith and C T P Ulm.
1930	Frank Whittle patented the jet engine; Amy Johnson became the first woman to fly solo from England to Australia.
1937	The first fully pressurized aircraft, the Lockheed XC-35, came into service.
1939	Erich Warsitz flew the first Heinkel jet plane, in Germany; Igor Sikorsky designed the first helicopter, with a large main rotor and a smaller tail rotor.
1939-45	World War II – developments included the Hawker Hurricane and Supermarine Spitfire Fighters, and Avro Lancaster and Boeing Flying Fortress bombers.
1947	A rocket-powered plane, the Bell X-1, was the first aircraft to fly faster than the speed of sound.
1949	The de Havilland Comet, the first jet airliner, entered service; James Gallagher made the first nonstop round-the-world flight, in a Boeing Superfortress.
1953	The first vertical takeoff aircraft, the Rolls-Royce 'Flying Bedstead', was tested.
1968	The world's first supersonic airliner, the Russian TU-144, flew for the first time.
1970	The Boeing 747 jumbo jet entered service, carrying 500 passengers.
1976	Anglo-French Concorde, making a transatlantic crossing in under three hours, came into commercial service. A Lockheed SR-17A, piloted by Eldon W Joersz and George T Morgan, set the world air-speed record of 3,529.56 kmh/2,193.167 mph over Beale Air Force Base, California, USA.
1978	A US team made the first transatlantic crossing by balloon, in the helium-filled *Double Eagle II*.
1979	First crossing of the English Channel by a human-powered aircraft, *Gossamer Albatross*, piloted by Bryan Allen.
1981	The solar-powered *Solar Challenger* flew across the English Channel, from Paris to Kent, taking 5 hours for the 262 km/162.8 mi journey.
1986	Dick Rutan and Jeana Yeager made the first nonstop flight around the world without refuelling, piloting *Voyager*, which completed the flight in 9 days, 3 minutes, 44 seconds.
1987	Richard Branson and Per Lindstrand made the first transatlantic crossing by hot-air balloon.
1988	*Daedelus*, a human-powered craft piloted by Kanellos Kanellopoulos, flew 118 km/74 mi across the Aegean Sea.
1991	Richard Branson and Per Lindstrand crossed the Pacific Ocean in the hot-air balloon *Virgin Otsouka Pacific Flyer* from the southern tip of Japan to NW Canada in 46 hours, 15 minutes.
1992	US engineers demonstrated a model radio-controlled ornithopter, the first aircraft to be successfully propelled and manoeuvred by flapping wings.
1993	The US Federal Aviation Authority made the use of an automatic on-board collision avoidance system (TCAS-2) mandatory in US airspace.

Largest volume aeroplane – the Guppy-201, with a usable volume of 1,104 cu m/39,000 cu ft.

airship a power-driven balloon. All airships have streamlined envelopes or hulls, which contain the inflation gas, and are either non-rigid, semi-rigid, or rigid. In 1900, Count Ferdinand von Zeppelin pioneered the rigid type, named after him, which were later used for bombing raids on the UK in World War I. The destruction by fire of the British R101 in 1930 halted airship building in Britain, but the Germans continued and built the 248-m/812-ft-long *Hindenburg*. However, this airship exploded at Lakehurst, New Jersey 1937, marking the effective end of airship travel. The early airships were vulnerable because they used hydrogen for inflation. It is the lightest gas, but highly flammable. After World War II, interest grew in airships using the nonflammable gas helium. They cause minimum noise, can lift enormous loads, and are economical on fuel. In 1987, the US Navy commissioned the British airship industry to build large numbers of airships for use in coastguard patrol. In recent years, airships have also been used commercially for the promotion of products and services.

balloon bag or envelope of impermeable fabric that rises from the ground when filled with a gas that is lighter than the surrounding air. In 1783, the first successful human ascent was piloted by Pilâtre de Rozier in Paris, in a hot-air balloon designed by the Montgolfier brothers. During the French Revolution balloons were used for observation; in World War II they were used to defend London against low-flying aircraft. Balloons continue in use for sport, and as an economical means of meteorological, infrared, gamma-ray, and ultraviolet observation. The first transatlantic crossing by gas balloon (from Presque Isle, Maine to Miserey, France) was made 11–17 Aug 1978 by a US team.

helicopter an aircraft that achieves both lift and propulsion by means of a rotary wing, or rotor, on top of the fuselage. It can take off and land vertically, move in any direction, or remain stationary in the air. Igor Sikorsky built the first practical single rotor craft, in the USA 1939. The rotor of a helicopter has two or more blades, which are of aerofoil cross-section, like an aeroplane's wings. Lift and propulsion are achieved by angling the blades as they rotate. A single-rotor helicopter must also have a small tail rotor to counter the tendency of the body to spin in the opposite direction to the main rotor. Twin-rotor helicopters, like the Boeing Chinook, have their rotors turning in opposite directions, and this prevents the body from spinning.

Helicopters are now widely used in passenger service, rescue missions on land and sea, police pursuits and traffic control, firefighting, and agriculture. In war they carry troops and equipment into difficult terrain, make aerial reconnaissance and attacks, and carry wounded to aid stations. Helicopters are increasingly being associated with naval aircraft carriers, as many as 30 helicopters being used on larger carriers, in combination with V/STOL aircraft, such as Harriers. The helicopter may possess depth charges and homing torpedoes guided to submarine or surface targets beyond the carrier's attack range. It may also use dunking sonar to find targets beyond the carrier's own radar horizon.

jet propulsion a method of propulsion in which an object is propelled in one direction by a jet, or stream of gases, moving in the other. This follows from Newton's celebrated third law of motion 'to every action, there is an equal and opposite reaction'. The most widespread application of the jet principle is in the jet engine, the commonest kind of aero-engine.

The jet engine is a type of gas turbine. Air, after passing through a forward-facing intake, is compressed by a compressor, or fan, and fed into a combustion chamber. Fuel (usually kerosene) is sprayed in and ignited. The hot gas produced expands rapidly rearwards, spinning a turbine that drives the compressor before being finally ejected from a rearward-facing tail pipe, or nozzle, at very high speed. Reaction to the jet of gases streaming backwards produces a propulsive thrust forwards, which acts on the aircraft through its engine-mountings, not from any pushing of the hot gas stream against the static air.

rocket a projectile driven by the reaction of gases produced by a fast-burning fuel. Unlike the jet engine, which is also a reaction engine, the rocket engine carries its own oxygen supply to burn its fuel and is totally independent of any surrounding atmosphere. As rockets are the only form of propulsion available that can function in a vacuum, they are essential to the exploration of outer space. Multistage rockets have to be used for this, consisting of a number of rockets joined together. In the 1990s, the most powerful rocket system is the Russian Energiya, capable of placing 100 tonnes/110 tons into low Earth orbit.

Rail Transport

Tracks to carry goods waggons were in use at collieries in the 18th century, but the first practical public passenger service was that between Stockton and Darlington in 1825, under the power of Stephenson's engine 'Locomotion'. A railway boom ensued, and railways were the major form of land transport for passengers and goods until after World War II when the private car, coach services, internal air services, and road haulage door-to-door destroyed their monopoly. In the UK the railways (known as British Rail from 1965) were nationalized in 1948, and the network shrank steadily. In the USA and Canada railways made the 19th-century exploitation of the central and western territories possible, and in the USA underpinned the victory of the north in the Civil War, the 'Railway War'.

In countries with less developed road systems and large areas of difficult terrain, the railway is still important, as in India, China, South America, and Russia. Electrification, or the use of diesel electric engines, has superseded the steam engine in most countries, and there has been some revival in the popularity of the train for longer distance 'inter-city' services.

The 1970s saw diesel high-speed trains (HSTs) introduced in the UK, followed by super-fast networks in Japan and France.

monorail a railway that runs on a single (mono) rail. It was invented in 1882 to carry light loads, and when run by electricity was called a *telpher*. The most successful monorail, the Wuppertal Schwebebahn, has been running in Germany since 1901. It is a suspension monorail, where the passenger cars hang from an arm fixed to a trolley that runs along the rail. Today most monorails are of the straddle type, where the passenger cars run on top of the rail. They are used to transport passengers between terminals at some airports – as at Birmingham, where the monorail works on the maglev (magnetic levitation) principle.

tramway a transport system for use in cities, by which wheeled vehicles run along parallel rails. It originated in collieries in the 18th century. The earliest passenger system was established in 1832, in New York, and by the 1860s horse-drawn trams plied in London and Liverpool. Trams are now powered either by electric conductor rails below ground, or conductor arms connected to overhead wires, but their use on public roads is very limited because of their lack of manoeuvrability. Greater flexibility is achieved with the *trolleybus*, similarly powered by conductor arms overhead but without tracks. In the 1990s both trams and trolley buses were being revived in some areas. Both vehicles have the advantage of being nonpolluting to the local environment.

Rail transport: chronology

1500s	Tramways – wooden tracks along which trolleys ran – were in use in mines.
1804	Richard Trevithick built the first steam locomotive and ran it on a track at the Pen-y-darren ironworks in South Wales.
1825	British engineer George Stephenson built the first public railway to carry steam trains – the Stockton and Darlington line.
1829	Stephenson designed his locomotive *Rocket*, which trounced its rivals at the Rainhill trials.
1830	Stephenson completed the Liverpool and Manchester Railway, the first steam passenger line; the first US-built locomotive, *Best Friend of Charleston*, went into service on the South Carolina Railroad.
1835	Germany pioneered steam railways in Europe, using *Der Adler*, a locomotive built by Stephenson.
1863	Robert Fairlie, a Scot, patented a locomotive with pivoting driving bogies, allowing tight curves in the track . London opened the world's first underground railway, powered by steam.
1869	The first US transcontinental railway was completed at Promontory, Utah, when the Union Pacific and the Central Pacific railroads met; George Westinghouse of the USA invented the compressed-air brake.
1879	Werner von Siemens demonstrated an electric train in Germany; Volk's Electric Railway along the Brighton seafront was the world's first public electric railway.
1883	Charles Lartique built the first monorail, in Ireland.
1885	The trans-Canada continental railway was completed, from Montreal in the east to Port Moody, British Columbia, in the west.
1890	The first electric underground railway opened in London.
1901	The world's most successful monorail, the Wuppertal Schwebebahn, went into service.
1912	The first diesel locomotive took to the rails in Germany.
1938	The British steam locomotive *Mallard* set a steam-rail speed record of 201 kph/125 mph.
1941	Swiss Federal Railways introduced a gas-turbine locomotive.
1964	Japan National Railways inaugurated the 512- km/320-mi New Tokaido line between Osaka and Tokyo, on which run the 210-kph/130-mph 'bullet' trains.
1973	British Rail's High Speed Train (HST) set a diesel rail speed record of 229 kph/143 mph.
1979	Japan National Railways' maglev test vehicle ML-500 attained a speed of 517 kph/321 mph.
1981	France's TGV superfast trains began operation between Paris and Lyons, regularly attaining a peak speed of 270 kph/168 mph.
1987	British Rail set a new diesel-traction speed record of 238.9 kph/148.5 mph, on a test run between Darlington and York; France and the UK began work on the Channel Tunnel, a railway link connecting the two countries, running beneath the English Channel. Japanese maglev MUV- 001 test train reaches speed with passengers of 400 kph/249 mph.
1988	The West German Intercity Experimental train reached 405 kph/252 mph on test run between Würzburg amd Fulda.
1990	A new rail-speed record of 515 kph/320 mph was established by a French TGV train, on a stretch of line between Tours and Paris.
1991	British and French twin tunnels met 23 km/14 mi out to sea to form the Channel tunnel.
1992	Trams returned to the streets of Manchester, England, after an absence of 40 years; towns in France and the US followed suit.
1994	Channel tunnel opened, linking England and France.

Road Transport

Specially constructed, reinforced tracks became necessary with the invention of wheeled vehicles in about 3000 BC and most ancient civilizations had some form of road network. The Romans developed engineering techniques that were not equalled for another 1,400 years. Until the late 18th century most European roads were haphazardly maintained, making winter travel difficult. In the UK the turnpike system of collecting tolls created some improvement. The Scottish engineers Thomas Telford and John McAdam introduced sophisticated construction methods in the early 19th century. Recent developments have included durable surface compounds and machinery for rapid ground preparation.

bicycle a pedal-driven two-wheeled vehicle. It consists of a metal frame mounted on two large wire-spoked wheels, with handlebars in front and a seat between the front and back wheels. The first pedal-bicycle was invented by Kirkpatrick Macmillan, a Scot, in about 1840, pneumatic tyres being added from 1846, and by 1888 these had been improved by J B Dunlop to boost the cycling craze of the turn of the century. Design changes were then minor until the small-wheeled Moulton bicycle appeared after World War II. The bicycle is an energy-efficient, nonpolluting form of transport and it is estimated that 800 million bicycles are in use throughout the world – outnumbering cars three to one. China, India, Denmark, and the Netherlands are countries with a high use of bicycles.

car a small self-propelled vehicle able to be run and be steered on normal roads. Most are four-wheeled and have water-cooled, piston-type internal-combustion engines fuelled by petrol or diesel.

Although it is recorded that in 1479 one Gilles de Dom was paid 25 livres by the treasurer of Antwerp for supplying a self-propelled vehicle, the forerunner of the automobile is generally agreed to be Nicolas-Joseph Cugnot's cumbrous steam carriage 1769, still preserved in Paris. Another Parisian, Étienne Lenoir, made the first gas engine in 1860, and in 1885 Benz built and ran the first petrol-driven motor car. Panhard 1890 (front radiator, engine under the bonnet, sliding-pinion gearbox, wooden ladder-chassis) and Mercedes 1901 (honeycomb radiator, in-line four-cylinder engine, gate-change gearbox, pressed-steel chassis) set the pattern for the modern car.

A typical modern medium-sized saloon car has a semi-monocoque construction in which the body panels, suitably reinforced, support the road loads through independent front and rear sprung suspension, with seats located within the wheelbase for comfort. It is usually powered by a petrol engine using a carburettor to mix petrol and air for feeding to the engine cylinders (typically four or six). The engine is usually water cooled. From the engine, power is transmitted through a clutch to a four- or five-speed gearbox and thence, in a front-engine rear-drive car, through a drive (propeller) shaft to a differential gear, which drives the rear wheels. In a front-engine front-wheel drive car, clutch, gearbox, and final drive are incorporated with the engine unit. An increasing number of high-performance cars are being offered with four-wheel drive. This gives vastly superior roadholding in wet and icy conditions.

internal-combustion engine a heat engine in which fuel is burned inside the engine, contrasting with an external-combustion engine (such as the steam engine) in which fuel is burned in a separate unit. The petrol and diesel engine are both internal-combustion engines. They are reciprocating piston engines in

Car: chronology

1769 Nicholas-Joseph Cugnot in France built a steam tractor.

1860 Jean Etienne Lenoir built a gas-fuelled internal-combustion engine.

1831 The UK government passed the 'Red Flag' Act, requiring a man to precede a 'horseless carriage' with a red flag.

1876 Nikolaus August Otto improved the gas engine, making it a practical power source.

1885 Gottlieb Daimler developed a successful lightweight petrol engine and fitted it to a bicycle to create the prototype of the modern motorbike; Karl Benz fitted his lightweight petrol engine to a three-wheeled carriage to pioneer the motor car.

1886 Gottlieb Daimler fitted his engine to a four-wheeled carriage to produce a four-wheeled motor car.

1891 René Panhard and Emile Levassor established the modern design of cars by putting the engine in front.

1896 Frederick Lanchester introduced epicyclic gearing, which foreshadowed automatic transmission.

1901 The first Mercedes took to the roads. It was the direct ancestor of the modern car; Ransome Olds in the USA introduced mass production on an assembly line.

1906 Rolls-Royce introduced the legendary Silver Ghost, which established their reputation for superlatively engineered cars.

1908 Henry Ford used assembly-line production to manufacture his famous Model T, nicknamed the Tin Lizzie because lightweight steel sheets were used for the body, which looked 'tinny'.

1911 Cadillac introduced the electric starter and dynamo lighting.

1913 Ford introduced the moving conveyor belt to the assembly line, further accelerating production of the Model T.

1922 The Lancia Lambda featured unitary (all-in-one) construction and independent front suspension.

1928 Cadillac introduced the synchromesh gearbox, greatly facilitating gear changing.

1934 Citroën pioneered front-wheel drive in their 2CV model.

1936 Fiat introduced their baby car, the Topolino, 500 cc.

1938 Germany produced their 'people's car', the Volkswagen 'beetle'.

1948 Jaguar launched the XK120 sports car; Michelin introduced the radial-ply tyre and Goodrich the tubeless tyre.

1950 Dunlop announced the disc brake.

1951 Buick and Chrysler in the USA introduced power steering.

1952 Rover's gas-turbine car set a speed record of 243 kph/152 mph.

1954 Bosch introduced fuel-injection for cars.

1957 Felix Wankel built his first rotary petrol engine.

1959 BMC (now Rover) introduced the Issigonis-designed Mini, with front-wheel drive, transverse engine, and independent rubber suspension.

1966 California introduced legislation regarding air pollution by cars.

1972 Dunlop introduced safety tyres, which sealed themselves after a burst.

1979 American Sam Barrett exceeded the speed of sound in the rocket-engined *Budweiser Rocket*, reaching 1,190.377 kph/739.666 mph, a speed not officially recognized as a record because of timing difficulties.

1980 The first mass-produced car with four-wheel drive, the Audi Quattro, was introduced; Japanese car production overtook that of the USA.

1981 BMW introduced the on-board computer, which monitored engine performance and indicated to the driver when a service was required.

1983 British driver Richard Noble set an official speed record in the jet-engined *Thrust 2* of 1,019.4 kph/ 633.468 mph; Austin Rover introduced the Maestro, the first car with a 'talking dashboard' that alerted the driver to problems.

1987 The solar-powered *SunRaycer* travelled 3,000 km/1,864 mi from Darwin to Adelaide, Australia, in six days.

1990 Fiat of Italy, and Peugeot of France launched electric passenger cars on the market.

1991 European Parliament voted to adopt stringent controls of car emissions.

1993 A Japanese electric car, the *IZA*, built by the Tokyo Electric Power Company, reached a speed of 176 kph/ 109 mph (10 kph/6 mph faster than the previous record for an electric car). The *Honda Dream* won the Darwin-to-Adelaide race for solar-powered cars in record time, achieving an average speed of 85 kph/53 mph and a top speed of 125 kph/77 mph which pistons move up and down in cylinders to effect the engine operating cycle. This may be a four-stroke cycle or a two-stroke cycle. Gas turbines and jet and rocket engines are sometimes also considered to be internal-combustion engines because they burn their fuel inside their combustion chambers.

motorcycle or **motorbike** a two-wheeled vehicle propelled by a petrol engine. Gottlieb Daimler, who went on to produce the motorcar, created the first motorcycle when he installed his lightweight petrol engine in a bicycle frame in 1885. The first really successful two-wheel design was devised by Michael and Eugene Werner in France 1901. They adopted the classic motorcycle layout with the engine low down between the wheels. Harley Davidson in the USA and Triumph in the UK began manufacture 1903. Road races like the Isle of Man TT (Tourist Trophy), established in 1907, helped improve motorcycle design and it soon evolved into more or less its present form. Today Japanese motorcycles, such as Honda, Suzuki, Yamaha, and Kawasaki, dominate the world market. The Japanese make a wide variety of machines, from mopeds (lightweights with pedal assistance) to streamlined superbikes capable of speeds up to 250 kph/160 mph.

Countries that drive on the left

Anguilla	Grenada	Montserrat	South Africa
Antigua	Guyana	Mozambique	Sri Lanka
Australia	Hong Kong	Namibia	Surinam
Bahamas	India	Nepal	Swaziland
Bangladesh	Indonesia	New Zealand	Tanzania
Barbados	Ireland (Republic of)	Norfolk Island	Thailand
Bermuda	Jamaica	Pakistan	Tonga
Bhutan	Japan	Papua New Guinea	Trinidad and Tobago
Botswana	Kenya	St Christopher-Nevis	Tuvalu
Brunei	Kiribati	St Lucia	Uganda
Cook Islands	Lesotho	St Vincent	UK (including Guernsey,
Cyprus	Malaysia	Seychelles	Jersey and the Isle of Man)
Dominica	Malawi	Singapore	Virgin Islands (British)
Falkland Islands	Malta	Solomon Islands	Zambia
Fiji	Mauritius	Somalia	Zimbabwe

Sea Transport

People have travelled on and across the seas, for various purposes, throughout history. The Greeks and Phoenicians built wooden ships, propelled by oar or sail, to transport themselves and their goods across the sea. The Romans and Carthaginians built war galleys equipped with rams and several tiers of oars. The oak ships of the Vikings were designed for rough seas, and propelled by oar and sail. The Crusader fleet of Richard the Lionheart was largely of sail. By 1840 iron had largely replaced wood, although fast-sailing clippers, introduced in the mid-1800s, made effective use of wooden planks on iron frames. The USA and the UK experimented with steam propulsion as the 19th century opened. The paddle-wheel-propelled *Comet* appeared 1812, the Canadian *Royal William* crossed the Atlantic 1833, and the English *Great Western* steamed from Bristol to New York 1838. Pettit Smith first used the screw propeller in the *Archimedes* 1839, and after 1850 the paddle-wheel became largely obsolete, its use being confined to the inland waterways, particularly the great American rivers. The introduction of the internal-combustion engine and turbine completed the revolution in propulsion until the advent after World War II of nuclear-powered vessels, chiefly submarines.

More recently hovercraft and wave-piercing catamarans (vessels with a long pointed main hull and two outriggers) have been developed for specialized purposes, particularly as short-distance ferries – for example, the catamarans introduced 1991 by Hover-speed cross the English Channel from Dover to Calais in 35 min, cruising at a speed of 35 knots (84.5 kph/52.5 mph). Sailing ships in automated form for cargo purposes, and maglev (magnetic-levitation) ships, are in development.

Largest ship – the oil tanker *Happy Giant*, which is 458 m/1,505 ft long, with a beam of 69 m/226 ft. Of 564,739 tonnes deadweight, she was launched 1979.

Longest and largest passenger liner – the *Norway*, launched 1961 as the *France*. Of 70,202 gross tonnage, she measures 316 m/1,035 ft long.

hovercraft a vehicle that rides on a cushion of high-pressure air, free from all contact with the surface beneath, invented by British engineer Christopher Cockerell 1959. Hovercraft need a smooth terrain when operating overland, and are best adapted to use on lakes, sheltered coastal waters, river estuaries and swamps. They are useful in places where harbours have not been established. Large hovercraft (SR-N4) operate a swift car-ferry service across the English Channel, taking only about 35 minutes between Dover and Calais.

hydrofoil boat a boat whose hull rises out of the water when it travels at speed. The boat gets its lift from a set of hydrofoils, wings which are partially submerged underwater. The hydrofoils develop lift in the water in much the same way that aeroplane wings develop lift in the air, enabling the boat to skim the water's surface.

jetfoil an advanced type of hydrofoil boat built by Boeing, propelled by water jets. It features horizon-

Sea transport: chronology

8000–7000 BC	Reed boats developed in Mesopotamia and Egypt; dug-out canoes used in NW Europe.
4000–3000 BC	Egyptians used single-masted square-rigged ships on Nile.
1200 BC	Phoenicians built keeled boats with hulls of wooden planks.
1st century BC	Chinese invented the rudder.
AD 200	Chinese built ships with several masts.
200–300	Arabs and Romans developed fore-and-aft rigging that allowed boats to sail across the direction of wind.
800–900	Square-rigged Viking longboats crossed the North Sea to Britain, the Faroe Islands, and Iceland.
1090	Chinese invented the magnetic compass.
1400–1500	Three-masted ships devleoped in western Europe, stimulating voyages of exploration.
1620	Dutch engineer Cornelius Drebbel invented the submarine.
1776	US engineer David Bushnell built a handpowered submarine, *Turtle*, with buoyancy tanks.
1777	The first boat with an iron hull built in Yorkshire, England.
1783	French engineer Jouffroy d'Abbans built the first paddle-driven steam boat.
1802	Scottish engineer William Symington launched the first stern paddle-wheel steamer *Charlotte Dundas*.
1836	The screw propeller was patented, by Francis Pettit Smith in the UK.
1838	British engineer Isambard Kingdom Brunel's *Great Western*, the first steamship built for crossing the Atlantic, sailed from Bristol to New York in 15 days.
1845	*Great Britain*, also built by Isambard Kingdom Brunel, became the first propeller-driven iron ship to cross the Atlantic.
1845	The first clipper ship, *Rainbow*, was launched in the USA.
1863	*Plongeur*, the first submarine powered by an air-driven engine was launched in France.
1866	The British clippers *Taeping* and *Ariel* sailed, laden with tea, from China to London in 99 days.
1886	German engineer Gottlieb Daimler built the first boat powered by an internal-combustion engine.
1897	English engineer Charles Parson fitted a steam turbine to *Turbinia*, making it the fastest boat of the time.
1900	Irish-American John Philip Holland designed the first modern submarine *Holland VI*, fitted with an electric motor for underwater sailing and an internal-combustion engine for surface travel; E Forlanini of Italy built the first hydrofoil.
1902	The French ship *Petit-Pierre* became the first boat to be powered by a diesel engine.
1955	The first nuclear-powered submarine, *Nautilus*, was built; the hovercraft was patented by British inventor Christopher Cockerell.
1959	The first nuclear-powered ship, the Soviet ice-breaker *Lenin*, was commissioned; the US *Savannah* became the first nuclear-powered merchant (passenger and cargo) ship.
1980	Launch of the first wind-assisted commercial ship for half a century, the Japanese tanker *Shin-Aitoku-Maru*.
1983	German engineer Ortwin Fries invented a hinged ship designed to bend into a V-shape in order to scoop up oil spillages in its jaws.
1989	*Gentry Eagle* set a record for the fastest crossing of the Atlantic by a power vessel, taking 2 days, 14 hours, 7 minutes.
1990	*Hoverspeed Great Britain*, a wave-piercing catamaran, crossed the Atlantic in 3 days, 7 hours, 52 minutes, setting a record for the fastest crossing by a passenger vessel. The world's largest car and passenger ferry the *Silja Serenade* entered service between Stockholm and Helsinki, carrying 2500 passengers and 450 cars.

tal, fully submerged hydrofoils fore and aft, and has a sophisticated computerized control system to maintain its stability in all waters. Jetfoils have been in service worldwide since 1975. A jetfoil service currently operates between Dover and Ostend, with a passage time of 1 hr 40 min.

submarine an underwater ship, especially a warship. The first underwater boat was constructed for King James I of England by the Dutch scientist Cornelius van Drebbel 1620. A century and a half later, David Bushnell in the USA designed a submarine called *Turtle* for attacking British ships. In both world wars submarines, from the oceangoing to the midget type, played a vital role. The conventional submarine of this period was driven by diesel engine on the sur-

face and by battery-powered electric motors underwater. The diesel engine also drove a generator that produced electricity to charge the batteries.

In 1955 the USA launched the first nuclear-powered submarine, *Nautilus*. The US nuclear submarine *Ohio*, USA, in service from 1981, is 170 m/560 ft long and carries 24 Trident missiles, each with 12 independently targetable nuclear warheads. The nuclear warheads on US submarines have a range that is being extended to 11,000 km/6.750 mi. Operating depth is usually up to 300 m/1,000 ft, and nuclear power speeds of 30 knots (i.e. 55 kph/34 mph) are reached. As in all nuclear submarines, propulsion is by steam turbine driving a propellor. The steam is raised using the heat given off by the nuclear reactor. European road distances.

Road distances between some UK towns, in miles *(To convert statute miles to kilometres, multiply by 1.6093)*

	Aberdeen	Birmingham	Bristol	Cambridge	Cardiff	Dover	Edinburgh	Exeter	Glasgow	Holyhead	Hull
Birmingham	430										
Bristol	511	85									
Cambridge	468	101	156								
Cardiff	532	107	45	191							
Dover	591	202	198	121	234						
Edinburgh	130	293	373	337	395	457					
Exeter	584	157	81	233	119	248	446				
Glasgow	149	291	372	349	393	490	45	444			
Holyhead	457	151	232	246	209	347	325	305	319		
Hull	361	136	227	157	246	278	229	297	245	215	
Leeds	336	115	216	143	236	265	205	288	215	163	59
Liverpool	361	98	178	195	200	295	222	250	220	104	126
London	543	118	119	60	155	77	405	170	402	263	215
Manchester	354	88	167	153	188	283	218	239	214	123	97
Newcastle	239	198	291	224	311	348	107	361	150	260	121
Norwich	501	161	217	62	252	167	365	295	379	309	153
Nottingham	402	59	151	82	170	202	268	222	281	174	92
Oxford	497	63	74	82	109	148	361	152	354	218	188
Penzance	696	272	195	346	232	362	561	112	559	419	411
Plymouth	624	199	125	275	164	290	488	45	486	347	341
Shrewsbury	412	48	128	142	110	243	276	201	272	104	164
Southampton	571	128	75	133	123	155	437	114	436	296	253
Stranraer	241	307	386	361	406	503	130	457	88	332	259
York	325	128	221	153	241	274	191	291	208	190	38

Road distances between some European cities, in kilometres *(To convert to statute miles, multiply by 0.6214.)*

	Athens	Barcelona	Brussels	Calais	Cherbourg	Cologne	Copenhagen	Geneva	Gibraltar	Hamburg
Barcelona	3,313									
Brussels	2,963	1,318								
Calais	3,175	1,326	204							
Cherbourg	3,339	1,294	583	460						
Cologne	2,762	1,498	206	409	785					
Copenhagen	3,276	2,218	966	1,136	1,545	760				
Geneva	2,610	803	677	747	853	1,662	1,418			
Gibraltar	4,485	1,172	2,256	2,224	2,047	2,436	3,196	1,975		
Hamburg	2,977	2,018	597	714	1,115	460	460	1,118	2,897	
Hook of Holland	3,030	1,490	172	330	731	269	269	895	2,428	550
Lisbon	4,532	1,304	2,084	2,052	1,827	2,290	2,971	1,936	676	2,671
Lyons	2,753	645	690	739	789	714	1,458	158	1,817	1,159
Madrid	3,949	636	1,558	1,550	1,347	1,764	2,498	1,439	698	2,198
Marseilles	2,865	521	1,011	1,059	1,101	1,035	1,778	425	1,693	1,479
Milan	2,282	1,014	925	1,077	1,209	911	1,537	328	2,185	1,238
Munich	2,179	1,365	747	977	1,160	583	1,104	591	2,565	3,805
Paris	3,000	1,033	285	280	340	465	1,176	513	1,971	877
Rome	817	1,460	1,511	1,662	1,794	1,497	2,050	995	2,631	1,751
Stockholm	3,927	2,868	1,616	1,786	2,196	1,403	650	2,068	3,886	949
Vienna	1,991	1,802	1,175	1,381	1,588	937	1,455	1,019	2,974	1,155

Leeds													
72	Liverpool												
196	210	London											
43	34	199	Manchester										
91	170	280	141	Newcastle									
173	232	115	183	258	Norwich								
73	107	128	71	156	123	Nottingham							
171	164	56	153	253	144	104	Oxford						
401	366	283	355	477	407	336	265	Penzance					
328	294	215	281	410	336	265	193	78	Plymouth				
116	64	162	69	216	205	81	113	315	242	Shrewsbury			
235	241	76	227	319	192	171	67	227	155	190	Southampton		
232	234	419	226	164	393	295	371	572	502	287	447	Stranraer	
24	100	209	71	83	185	86	185	406	340	144	252	228	

Hook of Holland									
2,280	Lisbon								
863	1,778	Lyons							
1,730	668	1,281	Madrid						
1,183	1,762	320	1,157	Marseilles					
1,098	2,250	328	1,724	618	Milan				
851	2,507	724	2,010	1,109	331	Munich			
457	1,799	471	1,273	792	856	821	Paris		
1,683	2,700	1,048	2,097	1,011	586	946	1,476	Rome	
1,500	3,231	2,108	3,188	2,428	2,187	1,754	1,827	2,707	Stockholm
1,205	2,935	1,157	2,409	1,363	898	428	1,249	1,209	2,105

Air distances between major cities in statute miles

	Bangkok	Beijing	Berlin	Cairo	Cape Town	Caracas	Chicago
Bangkok		2,046	5,352	4,523	6,300	10,555	8,570
Beijing	2,046		4,584	4,698	8,044	8,950	6,604
Berlin	5,352	4,584		1,797	5,961	5,238	4,414
Cairo	4,523	4,698	1,797		4,480	6,342	6,141
Cape Town	6,300	8,044	5,961	4,480		6,366	8,491
Caracas	10,555	8,950	5,238	6,342	6,366		2,495
Chicago	8,570	6,604	4,414	6,141	8,491	2,495	
Hong Kong	1,077	1,217	5,443	5,066	7,376	10,165	7,797
Honolulu	6,609	5,077	7,320	8,848	11,535	6,021	4,256
London	5,944	5,074	583	2,185	5,989	4,655	3,958
Los Angeles	7,637	6,250	5,782	7,520	9,969	3,632	1,745
Madrid	6,337	5,745	1,165	2,087	5,308	4,346	4,189
Melbourne	4,568	5,643	9,918	8,675	6,425	9,717	9,673
Mexico City	9,793	7,753	6,056	7,700	8,519	2,234	1,690
Montreal	8,338	6,519	3,740	5,427	7,922	2,438	745
Moscow	4,389	3,607	1,006	1,803	6,279	6,177	4,987
New York	8,669	6,844	3,979	5,619	7,803	2,120	714
Paris	5,877	5,120	548	1,998	5,786	4,732	4,143
Rio de Janeiro	9,994	10,768	6,209	6,143	3,781	2,804	5,282
Rome	5,494	5,063	737	1,326	5,231	5,195	4,824
San Francisco	7,931	5,918	5,672	7,466	10,248	3,902	1,859
Singapore	883	2,771	6,164	5,137	6,008	11,402	9,372
Stockholm	5,089	4,133	528	2,096	6,423	5,471	4,331
Tokyo	2,865	1,307	5,557	5,958	9,154	8,808	6,314
Warsaw	5,033	4,325	322	1,619	5,935	5,559	4,679
Washington DC	8,807	6,942	4,181	5,822	7,895	2,047	596

	Montreal	Moscow	New Delhi	New York	Paris	Rio de Janeiro	Rome
Bangkok	8,338	4,389	1,813	8,669	5,877	9,994	5,494
Beijing	6,519	3,607	2,353	6,844	5,120	10,768	5,063
Berlin	3,740	1,006	3,598	3,979	548	6,209	737
Cairo	5,427	1,803	2,758	5,619	1,998	6,143	1,326
Cape Town	7,922	6,279	5,769	7,803	5,786	3,781	5,231
Caracas	2,438	6,177	8,833	2,120	4,732	2,804	5,195
Chicago	745	4,987	7,486	714	4,143	5,282	4,824
Hong Kong	7,736	4,437	2,339	8,060	5,990	11,009	5,774
Honolulu	4,918	7,047	7,412	4,969	7,449	8,288	8,040
London	3,254	1,564	4,181	3,469	214	5,750	895
Los Angeles	2,427	6,068	7,011	2,451	5,601	6,330	6,326
Madrid	3,448	2,147	4,530	3,593	655	5,045	851
Melbourne	10,395	8,950	6,329	10,359	10,430	8,226	9,929
Mexico City	2,317	6,676	9,120	2,090	5,725	4,764	6,377
Montreal		4,401	7,012	331	3,432	5,078	4,104
Moscow	4,401		2,698	4,683	1,554	7,170	1,483
New York	331	4,683	7,318		3,636	4,801	4,293
Paris	3,432	1,554	4,102	3,636		5,684	690
Rio de Janeiro	5,078	7,170	8,753	4,801	5,684		5,707
Rome	4,104	1,483	3,684	4,293	690	5,707	
San Francisco	2,543	5,885	7,691	2,572	5,577	6,613	6,259
Singapore	9,203	5,228	2,571	9,534	6,673	9,785	6,229
Stockholm	3,714	716	3,414	3,986	1,003	6,683	1,245
Tokyo	6,471	4,660	3,638	6,757	6,053	11,532	6,142
Warsaw	4,022	721	3,277	4,270	852	6,455	820
Washington DC	489	4,876	7,500	205	3,840	4,779	4,497

Hong Kong	Honolulu	Lima	London	Los Angeles	Madrid	Melbourne	Mexico City
1,077	6,609	12,244	5,944	7,637	6,337	4,568	9,793
1,217	5,077	10,349	5,074	6,250	5,745	5,643	7,753
5,443	7,320	6,896	583	5,782	1,165	9,918	6,056
5,066	8,848	7,726	2,185	7,520	2,087	8,675	7,700
7,376	11,535	6,072	5,989	9,969	5,308	6,425	8,519
10,165	6,021	1,707	4,655	3,632	4,346	9,717	2,234
7,797	4,256	3,775	3,958	1,745	4,189	9,673	1,690
	5,556	11,418	5,990	7,240	6,558	4,595	8,788
5,556		5,947	7,240	2,557	7,872	5,505	3,789
5,990	7,240	6,316		5,439	785	10,500	5,558
7,240	2,557	4,171	5,439		5,848	7,931	1,542
6,558	7,872	5,907	785	5,848		10,758	5,643
4,595	5,505	8,059	10,500	7,931	10,758		8,426
8,788	3,789	2,639	5,558	1,542	5,643	8,426	
7,736	4,918	3,970	3,254	2,427	3,448	10,395	2,317
4,437	7,047	7,862	1,564	6,068	2,147	8,950	6,676
8,060	4,969	3,639	3,469	2,451	3,593	10,359	2,090
5,990	7,449	6,370	214	5,601	655	10,430	5,725
11,009	8,288	2,342	5,750	6,330	5,045	8,226	4,764
5,774	8,040	6,750	895	6,326	851	9,929	6,377
6,905	2,398	4,518	5,367	347	5,803	7,856	1,887
1,605	6,726	11,689	6,747	8,767	7,080	3,759	10,327
5,063	6,875	7,166	942	5,454	1,653	9,630	6,012
1,791	3,859	9,631	5,959	5,470	6,706	5,062	7,035
5,147	7,366	7,215	905	5,922	1,427	9,598	6,337
8,155	4,838	3,509	3,674	2,300	3,792	10,180	1,885

San Francisco	Singapore	Stockholm	Teheran	Tokyo	Vienna	Warsaw	Washington
7,931	883	5,089	3,391	2,865	5,252	5,033	8,807
5,918	2,771	4,133	3,490	1,307	4,648	4,325	6,942
5,672	6,164	528	2,185	5,557	326	322	4,181
7,466	5,137	2,096	1,234	5,958	1,481	1,619	5,822
10,248	6,008	6,423	5,241	9,154	5,656	5,935	7,895
3,902	11,402	5,471	7,320	8,808	5,372	5,559	2,047
1,859	9,372	4,331	6,502	6,314	4,698	4,679	596
6,905	1,605	5,063	3,843	1,791	5,431	5,147	8,155
2,398	6,726	6,875	8,070	3,859	7,632	7,366	4,838
5,367	6,747	942	2,743	5,959	771	905	3,674
347	8,767	5,454	7,682	5,470	6,108	5,922	2,300
5,803	7,080	1,653	2,978	6,706	1,128	1,427	3,792
7,856	3,759	9,630	7,826	5,062	9,790	9,598	10,180
1,887	10,327	6,012	8,184	7,035	6,320	6,337	1,885
2,543	9,203	3,714	5,880	6,471	4,009	4,022	489
5,885	5,228	716	1,532	4,660	1,043	721	4,876
2,572	9,534	3,986	6,141	6,757	4,234	4,270	205
5,577	6,673	1,003	2,625	6,053	645	852	3,840
6,613	9,785	6,683	7,374	11,532	6,127	6,455	4,779
6,259	6,229	1,245	2,127	6,142	477	820	4,497
	8,448	5,399	7,362	5,150	5,994	5,854	2,441
8,448		5,936	4,103	3,300	6,035	5,843	9,662
5,399	5,936		2,173	5,053	780	494	4,183
5,150	3,300	5,053	4,775		5,689	5,347	6,791
5,854	5,843	494	1,879	5,689		347	4,472
2,441	9,662	4,183	6,341	6,791	4,438	4,472	

Worst railway disasters in various countries

Place/country	Date	No. killed	Cause
Modane, France	1917	543	Runaway and derailment
Balvano, nr Salerno, Italy	1944	526	Stalled in Armi Tunnel
Near Torre, Leon Province, Spain	1944	500-800	Double collision and fire inside tunnel
Montgomery, Pakistan	1957	250	Collision
Near Buenos Aires, Argentina	1970	236	Collision
Near Gretna Green, Scotland	1915	227	Double collision
Nowy Dwor, Poland	1949	c. 200	Derailment
Osaka, Japan	1940	200	Collision
Near Aracaju, Brazil	1946	185	Wreck
Kendal, Jamaica	1957	178	Derailed into ravine
Near Waiouru, New Zealand	1953	155	Bridge collapse
Near Tchery, Russia	1882	c. 150	Derailment
Northern Nigeria, Nigeria	1970	c. 150*	–
Marudaiyar River, India	1956	143	Derailment
Near Magdeburg, Germany	1939	132	Collision
Harrow & Wealdstone, England	1952	112	Double collision
Pardubice, Czechoslovakia	1960	110	Collision
Nashville, Tennessee, USA	1918	c. 101	Head-on collision
Near Kishiney, Roumania	1938	c. 100	Collision
Beloeil, nr St Hilaire, Canada	1864	99	Train ran through open drawbridge
Custoias, nr Oporto, Portugal	1964	94	Wreck
Java, Indonesia	1959	92	Derailed into ravine
Woerden, Netherlands	1962	91	Collision
Near Durban, South Africa	1965	81	Derailment
Armagh, Northern Ireland	1889	80	Runaway collision
Granville, nr Sydney, Australia	1977	80	Collision with bridge
Near Toungoo, Burma	1965	76	Collision
Münchenstein, Switzerland	1891	71	Birs Bridge collapse
Near Seoul, South Korea	1954	56	–
Negros Island, Philippines	1954	56	–
Budapest, Hungary	1968	c. 43	Collision
Belgrade, Yugoslavia	1971	34	Fire
Abergele, Wales	1868	33	Runaway collision

* A further 52 survivors were killed in a lorry on their way to hospital.

WARFARE

Military Terms

admiral highest-ranking naval officer. In the UK Royal Navy and the US Navy, in descending order, the ranks of admiral are: admiral of the fleet (fleet admiral in the USA), admiral, vice admiral, and rear admiral.

air force a nation's fighting aircraft and the organization that maintains them.

history The emergence of the aeroplane at first brought only limited recognition of its potential value as a means of waging war. Like the balloon, used since the American Civil War, it was considered a way of extending the vision of ground forces. A unified air force was established in the UK 1918, Italy 1923, France 1928, Germany 1935 (after repudiating the arms limitations of the Versailles treaty), and the USA 1947 (it began as the Aeronautical Division of the Army Signal Corps in 1907, and evolved into the Army's Air Service Division by 1918; by 1926 it was the Air Corps and in World War II the Army Air Force). The main specialized groupings formed during World War I – such as *combat*, *bombing*, *reconnaissance*, and *transport* – were adapted and modified in World War II; activity was extended, with self-contained tactical air forces to meet the needs of ground commanders in the main theatres of land operations and for the attack on and defence of shipping over narrow seas.

During the period 1945–60 piston-engine aircraft were superseded by jet aircraft. Computerized guidance systems lessened the difference between missile and aircraft, and flights of unlimited duration became possible with air-to-air refuelling. For example, the US Strategic Air Command's bombers were capable of patrolling 24 hours a day armed with thermonuclear weapons. It was briefly anticipated that the pilot might become obsolete, but the continuation of conventional warfare and the evolution of tactical nuclear weapons led in the 1970s and 1980s to the development of advanced combat aircraft able to fly supersonically beneath an enemy's radar on strike and reconnaissance missions, as well as so-called stealth aircraft that cannot be detected by radar.

Allied Mobile Force (AMF) permanent multinational military force established 1960 to move immediately to any NATO country under threat of attack. Its headquarters are in Heidelberg, Germany.

Allies, the in World War I, the 23 countries allied against the Central Powers (Germany, Austria-Hungary, Turkey, and Bulgaria), including France, Italy, Russia, the UK, Australia and other Commonwealth nations, and, in the latter part of the war, the USA; and in World War II, the 49 countries allied against the Axis powers (Germany, Italy, and Japan), including France, the UK, Australia and other Commonwealth nations, the USA, and the USSR. In the 1991 Gulf War, there were 28 countries in the Allied coalition.

Armistice Day anniversary of the armistice signed 11 Nov 1918, ending World War I.

armour body protection worn in battle. Chain mail was developed in the Middle Ages but the craft of the armourer in Europe reached its height in design in the 15th century, when knights were completely encased in plate armour that still allowed freedom of movement. Medieval Japanese armour was articulated, made of iron, gilded metal, leather, and silk. Contemporary bulletproof vests and riot gear are forms of armour. The term is used in a modern context to refer to a mechanized armoured vehicle, such as a tank. Since World War II armour for tanks and ships has been developed beyond an increasing thickness of steel plate, becoming an increasingly light, layered composite, including materials such as ceramics.

arms trade sale of arms from a manufacturing country to another nation. It is estimated that 56% of the world's arms exports end up in Third World countries. The proportion of global military expenditure accounted for by Third World countries was about 18% in 1993 (up from 6% in 1965, but down from 24% in 1989). Arms exports are known in the trade as 'arms transfers'. In the UK, the Defence Export Services, a department of the Ministry of Defence, is responsible for British arms exports. Its annual budget is about £10 million.

army organized military force for fighting on the ground. A national army is used to further a political policy by force either within the state or on the territory of another state. Most countries have a national army, maintained at the expense of the state, and raised either by conscription (compulsory military service) or voluntarily (paid professionals). Private armies may be employed by individuals and groups. Following the ending of the Cold War, the US, and the former Soviet and European armies are to be substantially cut by the mid-1990s. The UK army will be cut from 155,000 to 119,000.

artillery collective term for military firearms too heavy to be carried. Artillery can be mounted on tracks, wheels, ships, or aeroplanes and includes cannons and rocket launchers.

AWACS (acronym for *Airborne Warning And Control System*) surveillance system that incorporates a long-range surveillance and detection radar mounted on a Boeing E-3 sentry aircraft. It was used with great success in the 1991 Gulf War.

battalion or *unit* basic personnel unit in the military system, usually consisting of four or five companies and about 600–700 soldiers. A battalion is commanded by a lieutenant colonel. Several battalions form a brigade.

battleship class of large warships with the biggest guns and heaviest armour. In 1991, four US battleships were in active service. They are now all decommissioned.

biological warfare the use of living organisms, or of infectious material derived from them, to bring about death or disease in humans, animals, or plants. It was condemned by the Geneva Convention 1925, to which the United Nations has urged all states to adhere. Nevertheless research in this area continues; the Biological

Weapons Convention 1972 permits research for defence purposes but does not define how this differs from offensive-weapons development. In 1990 the US Department of Defense allocated $60 million to research, develop, and test defence systems. Advances in genetic engineering make the development of new varieties of potentially offensive biological weapons more likely. At least ten countries have this capability.

Russian president Boris Yeltsin signed a decree to comply with the treaty in 1992. Although the treaty was originally ratified by the Kremlin three months after its original signing, national laws ensuring compliance were never passed.

bomb container filled with explosive or chemical material and generally used in warfare. There are also incendiary bombs and nuclear bombs and missiles. Any object designed to cause damage by explosion can be called a bomb (car bombs, letter bombs). Initially dropped from aeroplanes (from World War I), bombs were in World War II also launched by rocket (V1, V2). The 1960s saw the development of missiles that could be launched from aircraft, land sites, or submarines. Although high explosive is increasingly delivered by means of missiles, free fall and so-called 'smart' or laser-guided munitions are still widely used.

The rapid development of *laser guidance systems* in the 1970s meant that precise destruction of small but vital targets could be more effectively achieved with standard 450 kg/1,000 lb high-explosive bombs. The laser beam may be directed at the target by the army from the ground, or alternatively from high-performance aircraft accompanying the bombers, for example, the Laser Ranging Marker Target System (LRMTS). The effectiveness of these systems was demonstrated during the Gulf War of 1991.

brigade military formation consisting of a minimum of two battalions, but more usually three or more, as well as supporting arms. There are typically about 5,000 soldiers in a brigade, which is commanded by a brigadier. Two or more brigades form a division.

carrier warfare naval warfare involving aircraft carriers. Carrier warfare was conducted during World War II in the battle of the Coral Sea May 1942, which stopped the Japanese advance in the South Pacific, and in the battle of Midway Islands June 1942, which weakened the Japanese navy through the loss of four aircraft carriers. The US Navy deployed six aircraft carriers during the Gulf War 1991.

Central Command military strike force consisting of units from the US army, navy, and air force, which operates in the Middle East and North Africa. Its headquarters are in Fort McDill, Florida. It was established 1979, following the Iranian hostage crisis and the Soviet invasion of Afghanistan, and was known as the Rapid Deployment Force until 1983. It commanded coalition forces in the Gulf War 1991.

chemical warfare use in war of gaseous, liquid, or solid substances intended to have a toxic effect on humans, animals, or plants. Together with biological warfare, it was banned by the Geneva Convention 1925, although this has not always been observed. In 1989, when the 149-nation Conference on Chemical Weapons unanimously voted to outlaw chemical weapons, the total US stockpile was estimated at 30,000 tonnes and the Soviet stockpile variously at 30,000 and 300,000 tonnes.

In a deal with the USA, the USSR offered to eliminate its stocks; the USA began replacing its stocks with new binary nerve-gas weapons. In 1990 President Bush offered to destroy all US chemical weapons if the convention to outlaw them, signed in Paris on 13 Jan 1993, were ratified. The Conventional Weapons Convention (CWC) will enter into force 180 days after the 65th signatory has ratified the convention, but in no case earlier than 13 Jan 1995. By mid-Feb 1993, 136 countries had signed the convention. Some 20 nations currently hold chemical weapons, including Iraq, Iran, Israel, Syria, Libya, South Africa, China, Ethiopia, North Korea, Myanmar, Taiwan, and Vietnam.

civil defence or *civil protection* organized activities by the civilian population of a state to mitigate the effects of enemy attack on them. The threat of nuclear weapons in the post-World War II period led to the building of fallout shelters in the USA, the USSR, and elsewhere. China has networks of tunnels in cities that are meant to enable the population to escape nuclear fallout and reach the countryside, but which do not protect against the actual blast. Sweden and Switzerland have highly developed civil-defence systems.

A new structure of 'Home Defence' is now being created in Britain, in which the voluntary services, local authorities, the Home Service Force, and the Territorial Army would cooperate. Regulations came into force 1983 compelling local authorities to take part in civil-defence exercises. Councils have to provide blast-proof bunkers and communication links, train staff, and take part in the exercises. In July 1991 it was announced that much of the Home Defence infrastructure would be severely cut back since the Cold War had ended.

COIN acronym for *co*unter *in*surgency, the suppression by a state's armed forces of uprisings against the state. Also called internal security (IS) operations of counter-revolutionary warfare (CRW). The British army has been engaged in COIN operations in Northern Ireland since 1969.

commando member of a specially trained, highly mobile military unit. The term originated in South Africa in the 19th century, where it referred to Boer military reprisal raids against Africans and, in the South African Wars, against the British. Commando units have often carried out operations behind enemy lines.

company a subunit of a battalion. It consists of about 120 soldiers, and is commanded by a major in the British army, a captain or major in the US army. Four or five companies make a battalion.

conscription legislation for all able-bodied male citizens (and female in some countries, such as Israel) to serve with the armed forces. It originated in France 1792, and in the 19th and 20th centuries became the established practice in almost all European states. Modern conscription systems often permit alternative national service for conscientious objectors.

In Britain conscription was introduced in March 1916 but was abolished after World War I. It was introduced for the first time in peace April 1939, when all men aged 20 became liable to six months' military training. The National Service Act, passed Sept 1939, made all men between 18 and 41 liable to military service, and in 1941 women also became liable to be called up for the women's services as an alternative to industrial service. Men reaching the age of 18 continued to be called up until 1960. Conscription remains the norm for most NATO and Warsaw Pact countries as well as neutral states. In the USSR 21% of those called up in 1990 failed to respond. It is also practised by governments in the Third World. In South Africa, the penalty for evading conscription is up to six years' imprisonment.

corps a military formation consisting of 2-5 divisions. Its strength is between 50,000 and 120,000 men. All branches of the army are represented. A corps is commanded by a lieutenant general or, in the USA, a three-star general. Two or more corps form an army group.

deception the use of dummies, decoys, and electronics to trick the enemy into believing in and preparing to defend against armies that do not exist. The Allied ground offensive in the 1991 Gulf War was launched 160 km/100 mi W of where the Iraqi army was led to believe it would take place. The deception techniques used completely wrong-footed the Iraqi forces.

Delta Force US antiguerrilla force, based at Fort Bragg, North Carolina, and modelled on the British Special Air Service.

destroyer small, fast warship designed for antisubmarine work. Destroyers played a critical role in the convoy system in World War II. Modern destroyers often carry guided missiles and displace 3,700–5,650 tonnes.

disarmament reduction of a country's weapons of war. Most disarmament talks since World War II have been concerned with nuclear-arms verification and reduction, but biological, chemical, and conventional weapons have also come under discussion at the United Nations and in other forums.

division military formation consisting of two or more brigades. A major general at divisional headquarters commands the brigades and also additional artillery, engineers, attack helicopters, and other logistic support. There are 10,000 or more soldiers in a division. Two or more divisions form a corps.

early warning advance notice of incoming attack, often associated with nuclear attack. There are early-warning radar systems in the UK (Fylingdales), Alaska, and Greenland. *Airborne early warning* (AEW) is provided by sentry planes; NATO has such a system.

explosive any material capable of a sudden release of energy and the rapid formation of a large volume of gas, leading when compressed to the development of a high-pressure wave (blast). Examples include gelignite, dynamite, nitroglycerin, nitrobenzine, TNT (trinitoluene), and RDX (Research Department Explosive).

fallout harmful radioactive material released into the atmosphere in the debris of a nuclear explosion and descending to the surface of the Earth. Such material

can enter the food chain, cause radiation sickness, and last for hundreds of thousands of years.

field marshal the highest rank in many European armies. A British field marshal is equivalent to a 5-star US general (of the army).

firearm weapon from which projectiles are discharged by the combustion of an explosive. Firearms are generally divided into two main sections: *artillery* (ordnance or cannon), with a bore greater than 2.54 cm/1 in, and *small arms*, with a bore of less than 2.54 cm/1 in. Although gunpowder was known in Europe 60 years previously, the invention of guns dates from 1300–25, and is attributed to Berthold Schwartz, a German monk.

frigate escort warship smaller than a destroyer. Before 1975 the term referred to a warship larger than a destroyer but smaller than a light cruiser. In the 18th and 19th centuries a frigate was a small, fast sailing warship.

general senior military rank, the ascending grades being major general, lieutenant general, and general. The US rank of general of the army, or 5-star general, is equivalent to the British field marshal.

guerrilla irregular soldier fighting in a small unofficial unit, typically against an established or occupying power, and engaging in sabotage, ambush, and the like, rather than pitched battles against an opposing army. Guerrilla tactics have been used both by resistance armies in wartime (for example, the Vietnam War) and in peacetime by national liberation groups and militant political extremists (for example the PLO; Tamil Tigers).

Political activists who resort to violence, particularly *urban guerrillas*, tend to be called 'freedom fighters' by those who support their cause, 'terrorists' by those who oppose it. Efforts by governments to put a stop to their activities have had only sporadic success. The Council of Europe has set up the European Convention on the Suppression of Terrorism, to which many governments are signatories. In the UK the Prevention of Terrorism Act 1984 is aimed particularly at the Irish Republican Army (IRA). The Institute for the Study of Terrorism was founded in London 1986.

Gurkha member of a people living in the mountains of Nepal, whose young men have been recruited since 1815 for the British and Indian armies. There are currently five battalions of Gurkhas in the British Army (though the cuts of July 1991 will reduce these to two by 1996). There are many more Gurkhas in the Indian Army.

Home Service Force (HSF) military unit established in the UK 1982, linked to the Territorial Army (TA) and recruited from volunteers aged 18-60 with previous army (TA or regular) experience. It was introduced to guard key points and installations likely to be the target of enemy 'special forces' and saboteurs, so releasing other units for mobile defence roles. It was stood down in 1992.

ICBM abbreviation for *intercontinental ballistic missile*.

Luftwaffe German air force. In World War I and, as reorganized by the Nazi leader Hermann Goering in

1933, in World War II. The Luftwaffe also covered anti-aircraft defence and the launching of the flying bombs V1 and V2.

manoeuvre to move around the battlefield so as to gain an advantage over the enemy. It implies rapid movement, shock action, and surprise. Bold manoeuvre warfare can be synonymous with Blitzkrieg or a swift military campaign. An example of manoeuvre warfare was the wide-ranging encirclement of the Iraqi army by coalition forces in the 1991 Gulf War.

marines fighting force that operates both on land and at sea. The *US Marine Corps* (1775) is constituted as an arm of the US Navy. It is made up of infantry and air support units trained and equipped for amphibious landings under fire. The *Corps of Royal Marines* founded by Charles I in 1664 is the British equivalent, numbering approximately 7,000 (1993). It is part of the Royal Navy.

mercenary soldier hired by the army of another country or by a private army. Mercenary military service originated in the 14th century, when cash payment on a regular basis was the only means of guaranteeing soldiers' loyalty. In the 20th century mercenaries have been common in wars and guerrilla activity in Asia, Africa, and Latin America.

Article 47 of the 1977 Additional Protocols to the Geneva Convention stipulates that 'a mercenary shall not have the right to be a combatant or a prisoner of war' but leaves a party to the Protocols the freedom to grant such status if so wished.

minesweeper small naval vessel for locating and destroying mines at sea. A typical minesweeper weighs about 725 tonnes, and is built of reinforced plastic (immune to magnetic and acoustic mines). Remote-controlled miniature submarines may be used to lay charges next to the mines and destroy them.

mobilization preparation of armed forces (land, sea, air) for active service.

MRBM abbreviation for *medium-range ballistic missile*, such as the French M-5 ballistic missile.

navy fleet of ships, usually a nation's warships and the organization to maintain them. In the early 1990s, the UK had a force of small carriers, destroyers, frigates, and submarines. In the light of 1991 Armed Forces reductions, the Royal Navy is to be reduced from around 50 to 40 destroyers and frigates, and the submarine fleet to be cut by 50%.

NBC abbreviation for *nuclear, biological, and chemical warfare* term used to describe the form of warfare fought with weapons of mass destruction. The only case of nuclear warfare to date was the dropping of two nuclear weapons on Hiroshima and Nagasaki by the US Air Force in 1945, with the purpose of forcing Japan to surrender in World War II. Biological warfare is a weapon that is difficult to use in the field of battle but which could be used as a strategic weapon to poison water supplies or cause epidemics. Chemical weapons were first used during World War I in the form of mustard gas, and they have been used since in Vietnam, Afghanistan, and during the Iran–Iraq war by the Iraqis.

North Atlantic Treaty Organization (NATO) association set up 1949 to provide for the collective defence of the major W European and North American states against the perceived threat from the USSR. Its chief body is the Council of Foreign Ministers (who have representatives in permanent session), and there is an international secretariat in Brussels, Belgium, and also the Military Committee consisting of the Chiefs of Staff. The military headquarters SHAPE (Supreme Headquarters Allied Powers, Europe) is in Chièvres, near Mons, Belgium. In Oct 1991, it was agreed that NATO's nuclear arsenal in Europe would be reduced by 80%. There were also plans for NATO forces to be reduced by up to 30% by the mid-1990s. It was agreed July 1992 that the Conference on Security and Cooperation in Europe (CSCE) would in future authorize all NATO's military responses within Europe. After the E European Warsaw Pact was disbanded 1991, the *North Atlantic Cooperation Council*, was established, including all the former Soviet republics, with the aim of building greater security in Europe. In May 1991 a meeting of NATO defence ministers endorsed the creation of a UK-commanded, 100,000-strong 'rapid-reaction corps' (RRC) adaptable to post-Cold War contingencies. The new force is to be operational from late 1994 and to be used solely inside NATO territory, unless otherwise agreed by all members of the alliance.

nuclear warfare war involving the use of nuclear weapons. Nuclear-weapons research began in Britain 1940, but was transferred to the USA after it entered World War II. The research programme, known as the Manhattan Project, was directed by J Robert Oppenheimer. The first test explosion was at Alamogordo, New Mexico, 16 July 1945; the first use in war was by the USA against Japan 6 Aug 1945 over Hiroshima and three days later at Nagasaki. *atom bomb* The original weapon relied on use of a chemical explosion to trigger a chain reaction. *hydrogen bomb* A much more powerful weapon than the atom bomb, it relies on the release of thermonuclear energy by the condensation of hydrogen nuclei to helium nuclei (as happens in the Sun). The first detonation was at Eniwetok Atoll, Pacific Ocean, 1952 by the USA. *neutron bomb* or *enhanced radiation weapon* (ERW) a very small hydrogen bomb that has relatively high radiation but relatively low blast, designed to kill (in up to six days) by a brief neutron radiation that leaves buildings and weaponry intact. *nuclear methods of attack* now include aircraft bombs, missiles (long- or short-range, surface to surface, air to surface, and surface to air), depth charges, and high-powered landmines ('atomic demolition munitions') to destroy bridges and roads.

The major subjects of disarmament negotiations are *intercontinental ballistic missiles* (ICBMs), which have from 1968 been equipped with clusters of warheads (which can be directed to individual targets) and are known as multiple independently targetable re-entry vehicles (MIRVs). The 1980s US-designed MX (Peacekeeper) carries up to ten warheads in each missile. In 1989, the UK agreed to purchase submarine-launched Trident missiles from the USA. Each warhead has eight independently targetable re-entry vehicles (each nuclear-armed) with a range of about 6,400 km/4,000 mi to eight separate targets within about 240 km/150 mi of the central aiming point. The

Trident system was scheduled to enter service within the Royal Navy in the mid-1990s.

nuclear methods of defence include: *antiballistic missile* (ABM) Earth-based systems with two types of missile, one short-range with high acceleration, and one comparatively long-range for interception above the atmosphere; *Strategic Defense Initiative* (announced by the USA 1983 to be operative from 2000; popularly known as the 'Star Wars' programme) 'directed energy weapons' firing laser beams would be mounted on space stations, and by burning holes in incoming missiles would either collapse them or detonate their fuel tanks.

The worldwide total of nuclear weapons in 1990 was about 50,000, and the number of countries possessing nuclear weapons stood officially at five – USA, USSR, UK, France, and China – although some other nations were thought either to have a usable stockpile of these weapons (Israel) or the a bility to produce them quickly (Brazil, India, Pakistan, South Africa). Successive arms-reduction treaties between 1990 and 1993 have, however, resulted in agreements to reduce the worldwide figure to approximately 10,000 by 2003. In the 1991 Minsk Agreement – 'The Creation of the Commonwealth of Independent States' – Belarus, Ukraine, and Kazakhstan declared they would become non-nuclear.

The UK nuclear warhead programme costs £607 million a year.

platoon in the army, the smallest infantry subunit. It contains 30–40 soldiers and is commanded by a lieutenant or second lieutenant. There are three or four platoons in a company.

prisoner of war (POW) person captured in war, who has fallen into the hands of, or surrendered to, an opponent. Such captives may be held in prisoner-of-war camps. The treatment of POWs is governed by the Geneva Convention.

Rapid Reaction Force (or *RRF*) any military unit that is maintained at a high state of readiness to react to an emergency. Specifically, it refers to the corps-sized unit, the formation of which was announced by NATO in May 1991 to meet threats anywhere in its area of responsibility.

reconnaissance the gathering of information about a military objective. This can be carried out by a reconnaissance ('recce') patrol or from a small, fast-moving vehicle or an aircraft configured for reconnaissance, or a remotely piloted vehicle (RPV). The SAS (Special Air Service) carried out invaluable reconnaissance work in the 1991 Gulf War. Less precise information was provided by satellites.

Red Army name of the army of the USSR until 1946; later known as the *Soviet Army*. It developed from the Red Guards, volunteers who carried out the Bolshevik revolution, and took its name from the red flag under which it fought. The Chinese revolutionary army was also called the Red Army.

regiment military formation equivalent to a battalion in parts of the British army, and to a brigade in the armies of many other countries. In the British infantry, a regiment may include more than one battalion, and soldiers belong to the same regiment throughout their career.

Royal Air Force (RAF) the air force of Britain. The RAF was formed 1918 by the merger of the Royal Naval Air Service and the Royal Flying Corps. The RAF numbers approximately 85,000 (1991), with some 48 front-line squadrons of aircraft out of approximately 600 aircraft. The 1991 defence cuts will reduce this by 15 squadrons and by 75,000 personnel.

Royal British Legion full name of the British Legion, a nonpolitical body promoting the welfare of war veterans and their dependants.

Royal Marines British military force trained for amphibious warfare.

services, armed the air, sea, and land forces of a country; also called the armed forces.

SHAPE acronym for *Supreme Headquarters Allied Powers Europe*, situated near Mons, Belgium, and the headquarters of NATO's Supreme Allied Command Europe (SACEUR).

SLBM abbreviation for *submarine-launched ballistic missile*.

Special Air Service (SAS) specialist British regiment recruited from regiments throughout the army. It has served in Malaysia, Oman, Yemen, the Falklands, Northern Ireland, and during the 1991 Gulf War, as well as against international urban guerrillas, as in the siege of the Iranian embassy in London 1980.

Strategic Defense Initiative (SDI) also called *Star Wars* attempt by the USA to develop a defence system against incoming nuclear missiles, based in part outside the Earth's atmosphere. The essence of the SDI is to attack enemy missiles at several different stages of their trajectory, using advanced laser and particle-beam technology, thus increasing the chances of disabling them. It was announced by President Reagan in March 1983, and the research had by 1990 cost over $16.5 billion. In 1988, the joint Chiefs of Staff announced that they expected to be able to intercept no more than 30% of incoming missiles. Israel, Japan, and the UK are among the nations assisting in SDI research and development. In 1987 President Gorbachev acknowledged that the USSR was developing a similar defence system.

The SDI programme was subsequently scaled down dramatically, and it is now certain that the original concept will not be deployed. The scaled-down version is known as Global Protection Against Limited Strikes (GPALS). The overall programme was renamed the Ballistic Missile Defence Organization (BMDO) in May 1993.

tank armoured fighting vehicle that runs on tracks and is fitted with weapons systems capable of defeating other tanks and destroying life and property. The term was originally a code name for the first effective tracked and armoured fighting vehicle, invented by the British soldier and scholar Ernest Swinton, and used in the battle of the Somme 1916. A tank consists of a body or hull of thick steel, on which are mounted machine guns and a larger gun. The hull contains the crew (usually consisting of a commander, driver, and one or two soldiers), engine, radio, fuel tanks, and ammunition. The tank travels on caterpillar tracks that enable it to cross rough ground and debris. It is known today as an MBT (main battle tank).

Territorial Army British force of volunteer soldiers, created from volunteer regiments (incorporated 1872) as the *Territorial Force* 1908. It was raised and administered by county associations, and intended primarily for home defence. It was renamed Territorial Army 1922. Merged with the Regular Army in World War II, it was revived 1947, and replaced by a smaller, more highly trained Territorial and Army Volunteer Reserve, again renamed Territorial Army 1979.

war act of force, usually on behalf of the state, intended to compel a declared enemy to obey the will of the other. The aim is to render the opponent incapable of further resistance by destroying its capability and will to bear arms in pursuit of its own aims. War is therefore a continuation of politics carried on with violent and destructive means, as an instrument of policy. The estimated figure for loss of life in Third World wars since 1945 is 17 million.

War is generally divided into **strategy**, the planning and conduct of a war, and **tactics**, the deployment of forces in battle. Types of war include: *guerrilla war* the waging of low-level conflict by irregular forces against an occupying army or against the rear of an enemy force. Examples include Mao Zedong's campaign against the Nationalist Chinese and T E Lawrence's Arab revolt against the Turks. *low-intensity conflict* US term for its interventions in the Third World, ranging from drug-running to funding and training guerrillas, and fought with political, economic, and cultural weapons as well as by military means. *civil war* the waging of war by opposing parties, or members of different regions, within a state. The American Civil War 1861–65, the English Civil War of the 17th century, and the Spanish Civil War 1936–39 are notable examples. *limited war* the concept that a war may be limited in both geographical extent and levels of force exerted and have aims that stop short of achieving the destruction of the enemy. The Korean War 1950–53 falls within this category. *total war* the waging of war against both combatants and noncombatants, taking the view that no distinction should be made between them. The Spanish Civil War marked the beginning of this type of warfare, in which bombing from the air included both civilian and military targets. *absolute war* the view that there should be no limitations, such as law, compassion, or prudence, in the application of force, the sole aim being to achieve the complete annihilation of one's opponent. Such a concept contradicts the notion, formulated by Clausewitz, of war as an instrument of political dialogue since it implies that no dialogue is actually intended. It has been claimed that nuclear warfare would assume such proportions and would be in accordance with the doctrine of mutually assured destruction (MAD).

warship fighting ship armed and crewed for war. The supremacy of the battleship at the beginning of the 20th century was rivalled during World War I by the development of submarine attack, and was rendered obsolescent in World War II with the advent of long-range air attack. Today the largest and most important surface warships are the aircraft carriers.

aircraft carriers The large-scale aircraft carrier was temporarily out of favour, as too vulnerable, until the resumption of building, especially by the USSR, in the late 1970s and 1980s. The USS *Carl Vinson* (1982)

weighs 81,600 tonnes. Some countries, such as the UK, have opted for *mini-carriers* with vertical takeoff aircraft and long-range helicopters. Minicarriers evolved in the early 1970s and have been advocated by US military reformers. *submarines* The first nuclear-powered submarine was the US *Nautilus* 1955; the first Polaris was the *George Washington* 1960. Submarines fall into two classes: the specially designed, almost silent *attack submarine*, intended to release its fast torpedoes and missiles at comparatively close range, and the *ballistic-missile submarine* with guided missiles of such long range that the submarine itself is virtually undetectable to the enemy. For the USA these submarines form one leg of the strategic 'triad' of land-based missiles, crewed bombers, and submarine-launched missiles. *battleships* The US Navy has recommissioned and modernized several World War II battleships for shore bombardment and force projection purposes. These were used with great effect during the 1991 Gulf War. They have since been decommissioned.

withdrawal an orderly movement of forces in a rearward direction in order to occupy more favourable ground. It is voluntary and controlled, unlike a retreat.

women's services the organized military use of women on a large scale, a 20th-century development. First, women replaced men in factories, on farms, and in noncombat tasks during wartime; they are now found in combat units in many countries, including the USA, Cuba, the UK, Russia, and Israel.

Treaties and Conferences

Georgetown, Declaration of call, at a conference in Guyana of nonaligned countries 1972, for a multipolar system to replace the two world power blocs, and for the Mediterranean Sea and Indian Ocean to be neutral.

Helsinki Conference international meeting 1975 at which 35 countries, including the USSR and the USA, attempted to reach agreement on cooperation in security, economics, science, technology, and human rights.

INF abbreviation for *intermediate nuclear forces*, as in the Intermediate Nuclear Forces Treaty.

Intermediate Nuclear Forces Treaty agreement signed 8 Dec 1987 between the USA and the USSR to eliminate all ground-based nuclear missiles in Europe that were capable of hitting only European targets (including European Russia). It reduced the countries' nuclear arsenals by some 2,000 (4% of the total). The treaty included provisions for each country to inspect the other's bases.

Paris, Treaty of any of various peace treaties signed in Paris. In the 20th century these have included: *1919–20* the conference preparing the Treaty of Versailles at the end of World War I was held in Paris; *1946* after World War II, the peace treaties between the Allies and Italy, Romania, Hungary, Bulgaria, and Finland; *1951* treaty signed by France, West Germany, Italy, Belgium, Netherlands, and Luxembourg, embodying the Schuman Plan to set up a single coal and steel authority; *1973* ending US participation in the Vietnam War.

SALT abbreviation for *Strategic Arms Limitation Talks*, a series of US–Soviet negotiations 1969–79.

START acronym for *Strategic Arms Reduction Talks*.

Strategic Arms Limitation Talks (SALT) series of US–Soviet discussions 1969–79 aimed at reducing the rate of nuclear-arms build-up. The talks, delayed by the Soviet invasion of Czechoslovakia 1968, began in 1969 between the US president Lyndon Johnson and the Soviet leader Leonid Brezhnev. Neither the SALT I accord (effective 1972–77) nor SALT II called for reductions in nuclear weaponry, merely a limit on the expansion of these forces. SALT II was mainly negotiated by US president Ford before 1976 and signed by Brezhnev and US president Carter in Vienna in 1979. It was never fully ratified because of the Soviet occupation of Afghanistan, although the terms of the accord were respected by both sides until US president Reagan exceeded its limitations during his second term 1985–89. SALT talks were superseded by START negotiations under Reagan, and the first significant reductions began under Soviet president Gorbachev.

Strategic Arms Reduction Talks (START) phase in peace discussions dealing with disarmament, initially involving the USA and the Soviet Union and from 1992 the USA and Russia. It began with talks in Geneva 1983, leading to the signing of the Intermediate Nuclear Forces (INF) Treaty 1987. Reductions of about 30% in strategic nuclear weapons systems were agreed 1991 (START I). More significant cuts were agreed 3 Jan 1993 (START II), when Presidents Bush and Yeltsin brought the START process to a dramatic conclusion by signing the START II Treaty, agreeing to reduce their strategic nuclear warheads to 3,000–3,500 weapons each by 2003. The treaty will be put into effect in two stages, with interim ceilings to be reached in the first seven years after the treaty enters into force. The treaty has yet to be ratified.

Versailles, Treaty of peace treaty after World War I between the Allies and Germany, signed 28 June 1919. It established the League of Nations. Germany surrendered Alsace-Lorraine to France, and large areas in the east to Poland, and made smaller cessions to Czechoslovakia, Lithuania, Belgium, and Denmark. The Rhineland was demilitarized, German rearmament was restricted, and Germany agreed to pay reparations for war damage. The treaty was never ratified by the USA, which made a separate peace with Germany and Austria 1921.

Yalta Conference in 1945, a meeting at which the Allied leaders Churchill (UK), Roosevelt (USA), and Stalin (USSR) completed plans for the defeat of Germany in World War II and the foundation of the United Nations. It took place in Yalta, a Soviet holiday resort in the Crimea.

Wars and Leaders

Alamein, El, Battles of in World War II, two decisive battles in the western desert, N Egypt. In the *First Battle of El Alamein* 1–27 July 1942 the British 8th Army under Auchinleck held the German and Italian forces under Rommel. In the *Second Battle of El Alamein* 23 Oct–4 Nov 1942 Montgomery defeated Rommel.

Arab-Israeli Wars series of wars between Israel and various Arab states in the Middle East since the founding of the state of Israel 1948. *First Arab-Israeli War* 15 May 1948–13 Jan/24 March 1949. As soon as the independent state of Israel had been proclaimed by the Jews, it was invaded by combined Arab forces. The Israelis defeated them and went on to annex territory until they controlled 75% of what had been Palestine under British mandate. *Second Arab-Israeli War* 29 Oct–4 Nov 1956. After Egypt had taken control of the Suez Canal and blockaded the Straits of Tiran, Israel, with British and French support, invaded and captured Sinai and the Gaza Strip, from which it withdrew under heavy US pressure after the entry of a United Nations force. *Third Arab-Israeli War* 5–10 June 1967, the *Six Day War*. It resulted in the Israeli capture of the Golan Heights from Syria; the eastern half of Jerusalem and the West Bank from Jordan; and, in the south, the Gaza Strip and Sinai peninsula as far as the Suez Canal. *Fourth Arab-Israeli War* 6-24 Oct 1973, the 'October War' or *Yom Kippur War*, so called because the Israeli forces were attacked by Egypt and Syria on the Day of Atonement, the holiest day of the Jewish year. After nearly three weeks of heavy fighting, with heavy losses, a cease-fire was agreed. *Fifth Arab-Israeli War* From 1978 the presence of Palestinian guerrillas in Lebanon led to Arab raids on Israel and Israeli retaliatory incursions, but on 6 June 1982 Israel launched a full-scale invasion. By 14 June Beirut was encircled, and Palestine Liberation Organization (PLO) and Syrian forces were evacuated (mainly to Syria) 21–31 Aug, but in Feb 1985 there was a unilateral Israeli withdrawal from the country without any gain or losses incurred. Israel maintains a 'security zone' in S Lebanon and supports the South Lebanese Army militia as a buffer against Palestinian guerrilla incursions.

Arnhem, Battle of in World War II, airborne operation by the Allies, 17–26 Sept 1944, to secure a bridgehead over the Rhine, thereby opening the way for a thrust towards the Ruhr and a possible early end to the war. It was only partially successful, with 7,600 casualties. Arnhem is a city in the Netherlands, on the Rhine SE of Utrecht.

Arras, Battle of battle of World War I, April–May 1917. It was an effective but costly British attack on German forces in support of a French offensive, which was only partially successful, on the Siegfried Line. British casualties totalled 84,000 as compared to 75,000 German casualties.

Atlantic, Battle of the continuous battle fought in the Atlantic Ocean during World War II by the sea and air forces of the Allies and Germany, to control the supply routes to the UK. The number of U-boats destroyed by the Allies during the war was nearly 800. At least 2,200 convoys of 75,000 merchant ships crossed the Atlantic, protected by US naval forces. Before the US entry into the war 1941, destroyers were supplied to the British under the Lend-Lease Act 1941. Fiftieth anniversary celebrations took place in Liverpool, England, in late May 1993.

Bataan peninsula in Luzon, the Philippines, which was defended against the Japanese in World War II by US and Filipino troops under General MacArthur 1 Jan–9 April 1942. MacArthur was evacuated, but some 67,000 Allied prisoners died on the *Bataan Death March* to camps in the interior.

Bradley Omar Nelson 1893–1981. US general in World War II. In 1943 he commanded the 2nd US Corps in their victories in Tunisia and Sicily, leading to the surrender of 250,000 Axis troops, and in 1944 led the US troops in the invasion of France. His command, as the 12th Army Group, grew to 1.3 million troops, the largest US force ever assembled.

Britain, Battle of World War II air battle between German and British air forces over Britain lasting 10 July–31 Oct 1940. At the outset the Germans had the advantage because they had seized airfields in the Netherlands, Belgium, and France, which were basically safe from attack and from which SE England was within easy range. On 1 Aug 1940 the Luftwaffe had about 4,500 aircraft of all kinds, compared to about 3,000 for the RAF. The Battle of Britain had been intended as a preliminary to the German invasion plan *Seelöwe* (Sea Lion), which Hitler indefinitely postponed 17 Sept and abandoned 10 Oct, choosing instead to invade the USSR.

Bulge, Battle of the or *Ardennes offensive* in World War II, Hitler's plan, code-named 'Watch on the Rhine', for a breakthrough by his field marshal Rundstedt aimed at the US line in the Ardennes 16 Dec 1944–28 Jan 1945. There were 77,000 Allied casualties and 130,000 German, including Hitler's last powerful reserve, his Panzer elite. Although US troops were encircled for some weeks at Bastogne, the German counteroffensive failed.

Caporetto former name of Kobarid (see entry), a village in Slovenia.

Cassino town in S Italy, 80 km/50 mi NW of Naples, at the foot of Monte Cassino; population (1981) 31,139. It was the scene of heavy fighting during World War II 1944, when most of the town was destroyed. It was rebuilt 1.5 km/1 mi to the N. The abbey on the summit of Monte Cassino, founded by St Benedict 529, was rebuilt 1956.

Clausewitz Karl von 1780–1831. Prussian officer and writer on war, born near Magdeburg. His book *Vom Kriege/On War* 1833, translated into English 1873, gave a new philosophical foundation to the art of war and put forward a concept of strategy that was influential until World War I.

D-day 6 June 1944, the day of the Allied invasion of Normandy under the command of General Eisenhower, with the aim of liberating Western Europe from German occupation. The Anglo-American invasion fleet landed on the Normandy beaches on the stretch of coast between the Orne River and St Marcouf. Artificial harbours known as 'Mulberries' were constructed and towed across the Channel so that equipment and armaments could be unloaded onto the beaches. After overcoming fierce resistance the allies broke through the German defences; Paris was liberated on 25 Aug, and Brussels on 2 Sept.

de Gaulle Charles André Joseph Marie 1890–1970. French general and first president of the Fifth Repub-

lic 1958-69. He organized the Free French troops fighting the Nazis 1940-44, was head of the provisional French government 1944-46, and leader of his own Gaullist party. In 1958 the national assembly asked him to form a government during France's economic recovery and to solve the crisis in Algeria. He became president at the end of 1958, having changed the constitution to provide for a presidential system, and served until 1969.

Desert Storm, Operation codename of the military action to eject the Iraqi army from Kuwait 1991. The build-up phase was codenamed *Operation Desert Shield* and lasted from Aug 1990, when Kuwait was first invaded by Iraq, to Jan 1991 when Operation Desert Storm was unleashed, starting the Gulf War. Desert Storm ended with the defeat of the Iraqi army in the Kuwaiti theatre of operations late Feb 1991. The cost of the operation was $53 billion.

Dönitz Karl 1891–1980. German admiral, originator of the wolf-pack submarine technique, which sank 15 million tonnes of Allied shipping in World War II. He succeeded Hitler in 1945, capitulated, and was imprisoned 1946–56.

Dunkirk (French *Dunkerque*) seaport on the north coast of France, in Nord *département*, on the Strait of Dover. Dunkirk was close to the front line during much of World War I, and in World War II, 337,131 Allied troops (including about 110,000 French) were evacuated from the beaches as German forces approached.

Falklands War war between Argentina and Britain over disputed sovereignty of the Falkland Islands. It was initiated when Argentina invaded and occupied the islands 2 April 1982, declaring the Falkland Islands and other British-held South Atlantic islands part of the new Argentine province of Tierra del Fuego. On the following day, the United Nations Security Council passed a resolution calling for Argentina to withdraw. A British task force was immediately dispatched and, after a fierce conflict in which over 1,000 Argentine and British lives were lost, 12,000 Argentine troops surrendered and the islands were returned to British rule 14-15 June 1982. The cost of the Falklands War was £1.6 billion.

Fuchs Klaus (Emil Julius) 1911–1988. German spy who worked on atom-bomb research in the USA in World War II, and subsequently in the UK. He was imprisoned 1950–59 for passing information to the USSR, and resettled in eastern Germany.

Fuller John Frederick Charles 1878–1966. British major general and military theorist who propounded the concept of armoured warfare which, when interpreted by the Germans, became *blitzkrieg* in 1940.

Gallipoli port in European Turkey. In World War I, at the instigation of Winston Churchill, an unsuccessful attempt was made Feb 1915–Jan 1916 by Allied troops to force their way through the Dardanelles and link up with Russia. The campaign was fought mainly by Australian and New Zealand (ANZAC) forces, who suffered heavy losses. An estimated 36,000 Commonwealth troops died during the nine-month campaign.

Galtieri Leopoldo 1926– . Argentine general, president 1981–82. A leading member from 1979 of the ruling right-wing military junta and commander of the army, Galtieri became president in 1981. Under his leadership the junta ordered the seizure 1982 of the Falkland Islands (Malvinas), a British colony in the SW Atlantic claimed by Argentina. After the surrender of his forces he resigned as army commander and was replaced as president. He and his fellow junta members were tried for abuse of human rights and court-martialled for their conduct of the war; he was sentenced to 12 years in prison in 1986.

Gulf War war 16 Jan–28 Feb 1991 between Iraq and a coalition of 28 nations led by the USA. The invasion and annexation of Kuwait by Iraq on 2 Aug 1990 provoked a build-up of US troops in Saudi Arabia, eventually totalling over 500,000. The UK subsequently deployed 42,000 troops, Egypt 20,000, France 15,000, and other nations smaller contingents. An air offensive lasting six weeks, in which 'smart' weapons came of age, destroyed about one-third of Iraqi equipment and inflicted massive casualties. A 100-hour ground war followed, which effectively destroyed the remnants of the 500,000-strong Iraqi army in or near Kuwait. The cost of the war is estimated to be $60–70 billion. A sum approximating $54.5 billion was donated by the Japanese, Germans, and Saudi Arabians towards the cost of conducting the war.

Hiroshima industrial city and port on the south coast of Honshu Island, Japan, destroyed by the first wartime use of an atomic bomb 6 Aug 1945. The city has largely been rebuilt since the war. Towards the end of World War II the city was utterly devastated by the US atomic bomb. More than 10 sq km/4 sq mi were obliterated, with very heavy damage outside that area. Casualties totalled at least 137,000 out of a population of 343,000: 78,150 were found dead, others died later.

Iwo Jima largest of the Japanese Volcano Islands in the W Pacific Ocean, 1,222 km/760 mi S of Tokyo; area 21 sq km/8 sq mi. Annexed by Japan 1891, it was captured by the USA 1945 after fierce fighting. It was returned to Japan 1968.

Jutland, Battle of naval battle of World War I, fought between England and Germany on 31 May 1916, off the W coast of Jutland. Its outcome was indecisive, but the German fleet remained in port for the rest of the war.

Khe Sanh in the Vietnam War, US Marine outpost near the Laotian border and just south of the demilitarized zone between North and South Vietnam. Garrisoned by 4,000 Marines, it was attacked unsuccessfully by 20,000 North Vietnamese troops 21 Jan–7 April 1968.

Kobarid formerly *Caporetto* village on the river Isonzo in NW Slovenia. Originally in Hungary, it was in Italy from 1918, and in 1947 became Kobarid. During World War I, German-Austrian troops defeated Italian forces there 1917.

Liddell Hart Basil 1895–1970. British military strategist. He was an exponent of mechanized warfare, and his ideas were adopted in Germany in 1935 in creating the 1st Panzer Division, combining motorized infantry and tanks. From 1937 he advised the UK War Office on army reorganization.

Marne, Battles of the in World War I, two unsuccessful German offensives. In the *First Battle* 6–9 Sept 1914, von Moltke's advance was halted by the British Expeditionary Force and the French under Foch; in the *Second Battle* 15 July–4 Aug 1918, Ludendorff's advance was defeated by British, French, and US troops under the French general Pétain, and German morale crumbled.

Montgomery Bernard Law, 1st Viscount Montgomery of Alamein 1887–1976. British field marshal. In World War II he commanded the 8th Army in N Africa in the Second Battle of El Alamein 1942. As commander of British troops in N Europe from 1944, he received the German surrender 1945.

Okinawa largest of the Japanese Ryuku Islands in the W Pacific; area 2,250 sq km/869 sq mi. It was captured by the USA in the *Battle of Okinawa* 1 Apr–21 June 1945, with 47,000 US casualties (12,000 dead) and 60,000 Japanese (only a few hundred survived as prisoners); the island was returned to Japan 1972.

Passchendaele village in W Flanders, Belgium, near Ypres. The Passchendaele ridge before Ypres was the object of a costly and unsuccessful British offensive in World War I, between July and Nov 1917; British casualties numbered nearly 400,000.

Patton George (Smith) 1885–1945. US general in World War II, known as 'Blood and Guts'. He was appointed to command the 2nd Armored Division 1940 and became commanding general of the First Armored Corps 1941. In 1942 he led the Western Task Force that landed at Casablanca, Morocco. After commanding the 7th Army, he led the 3rd Army across France and into Germany, and in 1945 took over the 15th Army.

Pearl Harbor US Pacific naval base in Oahu, Hawaii, USA, the scene of a Japanese aerial attack 7 Dec 1941, which brought the USA into World War II. The attack took place while Japanese envoys were holding so-called peace talks in Washington. More than 2,000 members of US armed forces were killed, and a large part of the US Pacific fleet was destroyed or damaged. The local commanders Admiral Kummel and Lt-Gen Short were relieved of their posts and held responsible for the fact that the base was totally unprepared at the time of the attack, but recent information indicates that warnings of the attack given to the USA (by British intelligence) were withheld from Kummel and Short by President Roosevelt. US public opinion was very much against entering the war, and Roosevelt wanted an excuse to change popular sentiments and take the USA into the war.

Rommel Erwin 1891–1944. German field marshal. He served in World War I, and in World War II he played an important part in the invasions of central Europe and France. He was commander of the N African offensive from 1941 (when he was nicknamed 'Desert Fox') until defeated in the Battles of El Alamein. Rommel was commander in chief for a short time against the Allies in Europe 1944 but (as a sympathizer with the Stauffenberg plot against Hitler) was forced to commit suicide.

Russo-Japanese War war between Russia and Japan 1904–05, which arose from conflicting ambi-

World War I: chronology

1914 outbreak	On 28 June the heir to the Austrian throne was assassinated in Sarajevo, Serbia; on 28 July Austria declared war on Serbia; as Russia mobilized, Germany declared war on Russia and France, taking a short cut in the west by invading Belgium; on 4 Aug Britain declared war on Germany; dominions within the Empire, including Australia, were automatically involved.
Western Front	The German advance reached within a few miles of Paris, but an Allied counterattack at the Marne drove them back to the Aisne River; the opposing lines then settled into trench warfare.
Eastern Front	The German commander Hindenburg halted the Russian advance through the Ukraine and across Austria-Hungary at the Battle of Tannenberg in E Prussia.
Africa	By Sept most of Germany's African colonies were in Allied hands; guerrilla warfare centred in Cameroon until 1916 and military operations in German East Africa until November 1918.
Middle East	On 1 Nov Turkey entered the war on the side of the Central Powers and soon attacked Russia in the Caucasus Mountains.
1915 Western Front	Several offensives on both sides resulted in insignificant gains. At Ypres, Belgium, the Germans used poison gas for the first time.
Eastern Front	The German field marshals Mackensen and Hindenburg drove back the Russians and took Poland.
Middle East	British attacks against Turkey in Mesopotamia (Iraq), the Dardanelles, and at Gallipoli (where 7,600 Anzacs were killed) were all unsuccessful.
Italy	Italy declared war on Austria; Bulgaria joined the Central Powers.
War at sea	Germany declared all-out U-boat war, but the sinking of the British ocean liner *Lusitania* (with Americans among the 1,198 lost) led to demands that the USA enter the war.
1916 Western Front	The German attack at Verdun was countered by the Allies on the river Somme, where tanks were used for the first time.
Eastern Front	Romania joined the Allies but was soon overrun by Germany.
Middle East	Kut-al-Imara, Iraq, was taken from the British by the Turks.
War at sea	The Battle of Jutland between England and Germany, although indecisive, put a stop to further German naval participation in the war.
1917	The USA entered the war in April. British and Empire troops launched the third battle at Ypres and by Nov had taken Passchendaele.
1918 Eastern Front	On 3 March Soviet Russia signed the Treaty of Brest-Litovsk with Germany, ending Russian participation in the war (the Russian Revolution 1917 led into their civil war 1918–21).
Western Front	Germany began a final offensive. In April the Allies appointed the French marshal Foch supreme commander, but by June (when the first US troops went into battle) the Allies had lost all gains since 1915, and the Germans were on the river Marne. The battle at Amiens marked the launch of the victorious Allied offensive.
Italy	At Vittorio Veneto the British and Italians finally defeated the Austrians.
German capitulation	This began with naval mutinies at Kiel, followed by uprisings in the major cities. Kaiser Wilhelm II abdicated, and on 11 Nov the armistice was signed.
1919	18 June, peace treaty of Versailles. (The USA signed a separate peace accord with Germany and Austria 1921.)

tions in Korea and Manchuria, specifically, the Russian occupation of Port Arthur (modern Lüda) 1896 and of the Amur province 1900. Japan successfully besieged Port Arthur May 1904–Jan 1905, took Mukden (modern Shenyang) on 29 Feb–10 March, and on 27 May defeated the Russian Baltic fleet, which had sailed halfway around the world to Tsushima Strait. A peace was signed 23 Aug 1905. Russia surrendered its lease on Port Arthur, ceded S Sakhalin to Japan, evacuated Manchuria, and recognized Japan's interests in Korea.

Schwarzkopf (H) Norman (nicknamed 'Stormin' Norman') 1934– . US general who was supreme commander of the Allied forces in the Gulf War 1991. He planned and executed a blitzkrieg campaign, 'Desert Storm', sustaining remarkably few casualties in the liberation of Kuwait. He was a battalion commander in the Vietnam War and deputy commander of the 1983 US invasion of Grenada. A graduate of the military academy at West Point, Schwarzkopf obtained a master's degree in guided-missile engineering. He became an infantryman and later a paratrooper, and did two tours of service in Vietnam. Maintaining the 28-member Arab–Western military coalition against Iraq 1991 extended his diplomatic skills, and his success in the Gulf War made him a popular hero in the USA. He retired from the army Aug 1991.

Sevastopol or *Sevastopol*, a port, resort, and fortress in the Crimea, Ukraine. It is the base of the (former) Black Sea fleet. It was besieged by the English and French during the Crimean War (Oct 1854–Sept 1855) and in World War II by the Germans (Nov 1941–July 1942, but was retaken by the USSR in 1944.

Sinai Egyptian peninsula, at the head of the Red Sea; area 65,000 sq km/25,000 sq mi. Resources include oil, natural gas, manganese, and coal; irrigation water from the river Nile is carried under the Suez Canal. Sinai was occupied by Israel 1967–82. After the Battle of Sinai 1973, Israel began a gradual withdrawal from the area, under the disengagement agreement 1975 and the Camp David peace treaty 1979, and restored the whole of Sinai to Egyptian control by April 1982.

Sino-Japanese Wars two wars waged by Japan against China 1894–95 and 1931–45 to expand to the mainland. Territory gained in the First Sino-Japanese War (Korea) and in the 1930s (Manchuria, Shanghai) was returned at the end of World War II. *First Sino-Japanese War* 1894–95. Under the treaty of Shimonoseki, Japan secured the 'independence' of Korea, cession of Taiwan and the nearby Pescadores Islands, and the Liaodong peninsula (for a naval base). France, Germany, and Russia pressured Japan into returning the last-named, which Russia occupied 1896 to establish Port Arthur (now Lüda); this led to the Russo-Japanese War 1904–05. *Second Sino-Japanese War* 1931–45. 1931– 37 The Japanese occupied Manchuria, which they formed into the puppet state of Manchukuo. They also attacked Shanghai, and moved into NE China. 1937 Chinese leaders Chiang Kai-shek and Mao Zedong allied to fight the Japanese; war was renewed as the Japanese overran NE China and seized Shanghai and Nanjing. 1938 Japanese capture of Wuhan and Guangzhou was followed by the transfer of the Chinese capital to Chongqing; a period of stalemate followed. 1941 Japanese attack on the USA (see Pearl Harbor) led to the extension of lend-lease aid to China and US entry into war against Japan and its allies. 1944 A Japanese offensive threatened Chongqing. 1945 The Chinese received the Japanese surrender at Nanjing in Sept, after the Allies had concluded World War II.

Stalingrad former name (1925–61) of the Russian city of Volgograd (see entry).

Tirpitz Alfred von 1849–1930. German admiral. As secretary for the navy 1897–1916, he created the German navy and planned the World War I U-boat campaign.

Tonkin Gulf Incident clash that triggered US entry into the Vietnam War in Aug 1964. Two US destroyers (USS *C Turner Joy* and USS *Maddox*) reported that they were fired on by North Vietnamese torpedo boats. It is unclear whether hostile shots were actually fired, but the reported attack was taken as a pretext for making air raids against North Vietnam. On 7 Aug the US Congress passed the *Tonkin Gulf Resolution*, which allowed President Johnson to 'take all necessary steps, including the use of armed forces' to help SEATO (South-East Asia Treaty Organization) members 'defend their freedom'. This resolution formed the basis for the considerable increase in US military involvement in the Vietnam War; it was repealed 1970 in the light of evidence that the Johnson administration contrived to deceive Congress about the incident.

Verdun fortress town in NE France on the Meuse. During World War I it became the symbol of French resistance, withstanding a German onslaught 1916.

Vietnam War 1954–75. War between communist North Vietnam and US-backed South Vietnam. 200,000 South Vietnamese soldiers, 1 million North Vietnamese soldiers, and 500,000 civilians were killed. 56,555 US soldiers were killed 1961–75, a fifth of them by their own troops. The war destroyed 50% of the country's forest cover and 20% of agricultural land. Cambodia, a neutral neighbour, was bombed by the US 1969–75, with 1 million killed or wounded.

Volgograd formerly (until 1925) *Tsaritsyn* and (1925–61) *Stalingrad*, an industrial city (metal goods, machinery, sawmills, oil refining) in SW Russia, on the river Volga; population (1987) 988,000. Its successful defence 1942–43 against Germany was a turning point in World War II. The German 6th army under field marshal Friedrich Paulus captured Stalingrad 1943, but was forced to surrender to the USSR under marshal Georgi Zhukov. After intense fighting, the Germans lost 70,000 men.

World War I 1914–1918. War between the Central European Powers (Germany, Austria-Hungary, and allies) on one side and the Triple Entente (Britain and the British Empire, France, and Russia) and their

Notable naval battles

Year	Site	Conflict
480 BC	Salamis	Greek victory over Persian fleet.
405 BC	Aegospotami	Athenian fleet defeated by Spartans.
31 BC	Actium	Fleets of Antony and Cleopatra of Egypt defeated by Roman fleet of Octavian.
AD 1340	Sluis	British victory over French navy.
1457	Matelino	Victory of papal fleet over Ottoman navy.
1571	Lepanto	Defeat of Ottoman Empire by the Holy League (Italian states and Spain).
1588	Gravelines	British defeat of Spanish Armada.
1591	Azores	British victory over Spanish fleet.
1592	Yellow Sea	Japanese victory over Korean navy.
1666	Four Days' War	Dutch victory over British navy.
1759	Quiberon Bay	British victory during Seven Years' War.
1782	Les Saintes	British victory over French navy off Dominica in the Caribbean.
1797	Cape St Vincent	British victory over French and Spanish fleets off SW Portugal.
1798	Nile (Aboukir Bay)	French defeat by British navy.
1801	Copenhagen/Baltic	British victory over Danish fleet.
1805	Trafalgar	British victory over French navy.
1813	Lake Erie	American victory over British fleet.
1905	Tsushima	Japanese victory over Russian fleet.
1914	Falkland Islands	British victory over German navy.
1916	Jutland	British against German navy (indecisive result).
1942	Midway	Defeat of Japanese navy in Pacific by USA.

World War II: chronology

1939 Sept	German invasion of Poland; Britain and France declared war on Germany; the USSR invaded Poland; fall of Warsaw (Poland divided between Germany and USSR).
Nov	The USSR invaded Finland.
1940 March	Soviet peace treaty with Finland.
April	Germany occupied Denmark, Norway, the Netherlands, Belgium, and Luxembourg. In Britain, a coalition government was formed under Churchill.
May	Germany outflanked the defensive French Maginot Line.
May–June	Evacuation of 337,131 Allied troops from Dunkirk, France, across the Channel to England.
June	Italy declared war on Britain and France; the Germans entered Paris; the French prime minister Pétain signed an armistice with Germany and moved the seat of government to Vichy.
July–Oct	Battle of Britain between British and German air forces.
Sept	Japanese invasion of French Indochina.
Oct	Abortive Italian invasion of Greece.
1941 April	Germany occupied Greece and Yugoslavia.
June	Germany invaded the USSR; Finland declared war on the USSR.
July	The Germans entered Smolensk, USSR.
Dec	The Germans came within 40 km/25 mi of Moscow, with Leningrad (now St Petersburg) under siege. First Soviet counteroffensive. Japan bombed Pearl Harbor, Hawaii, and declared war on the USA and Britain. Germany and Italy declared war on the USA.
1942 Jan	Japanese conquest of the Philippines.
June	Naval battle of Midway, the turning point of the Pacific War.
Aug	German attack on Stalingrad (now Volgograd), USSR.
Oct–Nov	Battle of El Alamein in N Africa, turn of the tide for the Western Allies.
Nov	Soviet counteroffensive on Stalingrad.
1943 Jan	The Casablanca Conference issued the Allied demand of unconditional surrender; the Germans retreated from Stalingrad.
March	The USSR drove the Germans back to the river Donetz.
May	End of Axis resistance in N Africa.
July	A coup by King Victor Emmanuel and Marshal Badoglio forced Mussolini to resign.
Aug	Beginning of the campaign against the Japanese in Burma (now Myanmar); US Marines landed on Guadalcanal, Solomon Islands.
Sept	Italy surrendered to the Allies; Mussolini was rescued by the Germans who set up a Republican Fascist government in N Italy; Allied landings at Salerno; the USSR retook Smolensk.
Oct	Italy declared war on Germany.
Nov	The US Navy defeated the Japanese in the Battle of Guadalcanal.
Nov–Dec	The Allied leaders met at the Tehran Conference.
1944 Jan	Allied landing in Nazi-occupied Italy: Battle of Anzio.
March	End of the German U-boat campaign in the Atlantic.
May	Fall of Monte Cassino, S Italy.
6 June	D-day: Allied landings in Nazi-occupied and heavily defended Normandy.
July	The bomb plot by German generals against Hitler failed.
Aug	Romania joined the Allies.
Sept	Battle of Arnhem on the Rhine; Soviet armistice with Finland.
Oct	The Yugoslav guerrilla leader Tito and Soviets entered Belgrade.
Dec	German counteroffensive, Battle of the Bulge.
1945 Feb	The Soviets reached the German border; Yalta conference; Allied bombing campaign over Germany (Dresden destroyed); the US reconquest of the Philippines was completed; the Americans landed on Iwo Jima, south of Japan.
April	Hitler committed suicide; Mussolini was captured by Italian partisans and shot.
May	German surrender to the Allies.
June	US troops completed the conquest of Okinawa (one of the Japanese Ryukyu Islands).
July	The Potsdam Conference issued an Allied ultimatum to Japan.
Aug	Atom bombs were dropped by the USA on Hiroshima and Nagasaki; Japan surrendered.

allies, including the USA (which entered 1917), on the other side. An estimated 10 million lives were lost and twice that number were wounded.

World War II 1939–1945. War between Germany, Italy, and Japan (the Axis powers) on one side, and Britain, the Commonwealth, France, the USA, the USSR, and China (the Allied powers) on the other. An estimated 55 million lives were lost, 20 million of them citizens of the USSR. The war was fought in the

Atlantic and Pacific theatres. In May 1945 Germany surrendered, but Japan fought on until the USA dropped atomic bombs on Hiroshima and Nagasaki in August.

Ypres (Flemish *Ieper*) Belgian town in W Flanders, 40 km/25 mi S of Ostend, a site of three major battles 1914–17 fought in World War I. The Menin Gate 1927 is a memorial to British soldiers lost in these battles.

Civil wars and related battles

Period	Civil war/battle	Conflict
c. 800 BC	Mahābhārata	Kaurava and Pandava families' rivalry on Upper Ganges plain.
88–*c.* 28 BC	Roman Civil Wars	Military factions in power struggle.
AD 220–65	Three Kingdoms War	In China, civil war between the Wei, Shu, and Wu kingdoms.
1180–85	Gempei War	In Japan, Minamoto clan rose against rival Taira.
1185	Dannoura	Naval defeat of Taira by Minamoto forces.
1265	Evesham	English royal forces led by Prince Edward defeated the army of Simon de Montfort in second Barons' War.
1298	Falkirk	English forces of Edward I put down Scottish revolt of William Wallace.
1314	Bannockburn	English defeated by Scots forces under Robert the Bruce.
1331–36	Genkō War	Japanese imperial forces put an end to the Kamakura shogunate.
1333	Halidon Hill	Nationalist Scots defeated by Edward Baliol.
1336–92	Nambokuchō	Japanese succession dispute between Northern Court in Kyoto and Southern Court in Yoshino.
1355–67	Chu Yuan-chang Rebellion	In China, uprising against Mongol Yuan dynasty.
1455–85	Wars of the Roses	English wars between the houses of Lancaster and York.
1460	Wakefield	Victory of Lancaster over York.
1464	Hexham	Yorkist victory over forces of Henry Beaufort.
1467–77	Ōnin War	Kyoto area of Japan devastated by feudal factions.
1471	Barnet	Defeat of Lancaster by York.
1485	Bosworth Field	Defeat of Yorkist king Richard III by Henry (VII).
1513	Flodden Field	Defeat of the Scots by the English army.
1556	Panipat	Mogul forces of Akbar defeated a Hindu army near Delhi.
1562–98	French Wars of Religion	Catholics versus Protestants (Huguenots) and fight for control of the expiring Valois dynasty.
1600	Sekigahara	Victory of Tokugawa Ieyasu over rivals ensured him control of Japan.
1642–49	English Civil War	Parliamentarians under Oliver Cromwell against Royalists.
1642	Edgehill	Indecisive result.
1644	Marston Moor	Royalist defeat by Parliamentarians and Scots.
1645	Naseby	Defeat of Royalists by Cromwell's troops.
1648–52	The Fronde	Revolts against French absolutism during the minority of Louis XIV.
1685	Sedgemoor	Duke of Monmouth's rebellion crushed by forces of James II.
1690	Boyne	Deposed James II defeated by William III of Great Britain and Ireland.
1698	Killiecrankie	Victory for supporters of James II.
1715	The Fifteen	Unsuccessful Jacobite rebellion by Scots against Hanoverian king George I.
1745–46	The Forty-Five	Unsuccessful Jacobite rebellion by Scots against English crown.
1745	Prestonpans	English forces defeated by Jacobites in Scotland.
1746	Culloden	Defeat of the Jacobite rebels.
1850–64	Taiping Rebellion	Opposition to Manchu dynasty in China.
1857–58	Indian Mutiny	Revolt of Indian soldiers against British colonizers.
1861–65	American Civil War	Secession of Southern states (Confederacy) from North (Union).
1861–62	Bull Run	Confederate army victories.
1863	Gettysburg	Union victory over the Confederacy.
1865	Appomattox	Confederate army surrender.
1927–37 and 1946–49	Chinese Civil War	Communist overthrow of Guomindang nationalist government.
1948–49	Huai-Hai	Communist victory over nationalist forces.
1936–39	Spanish Civil War	Right-wing Nationalist revolt against left-wing Republican government.
1937	Guernica	Defeat of Basques by Nationalists supported by Nazi Germany.
1944–49	Greek Civil War	US-sponsored royalist suppression of socialist movement.
1948–55	Burmese (Myanmar) Civil War.	Ethnic separatists and communists against socialist government.
1948–	Karen insurgence in Burma	Separatist movement of ethnic group.
1950–62	Indonesian Civil War	Revolts in Sumatra and the South Moluccas against the dominance of Java.
1955–72	Sudanese Civil War	Muslim north against non-Muslim south.
1959–75	Laotian and Vietnamese Civil Wars	Communists against right-wing governments.
1960–67	Congolese Civil War	Secession attempt by Katanga from the Republic of the Congo (now Zaire).
1961–75	Angolan War of Independence	Three nationalist movements against Portuguese colonial rulers.
1961–	Kurdish revolts	Separatist uprisings by Kurds especially in Iraq and Iran.
1962–70	North Yemen Civil War	Royalists against republicans.
1962–	Irian Jaya conflict	Popular resistance in W New Guinea to Indonesian rule.

Civil wars and related battles *(cont.)*

1963–68	Cypriot Civil War	Turkish community in Cyprus withdrew recognition of Greek Cypriot government.
1963–	Eritrean revolt	Secessionist movement in N Ethiopia.
1964–74	Mozambique War of Independence	Nationalist opposition to Portuguese colonial rule.
1965–79	Zimbabwe Civil War	Popular resistance to white-only rule in what was then Rhodesia.
1965–	Chad Civil War	Resistance by Muslim north to government.
1966–89	Namibian War of Independence	Popular resistance to South African rule.
1967–70	Nigerian (Biafran) Civil War	Attempted secession of state of Biafra.
1969–	Northern Ireland Troubles	Civil insurgence against British rule in Northern Ireland.
1970–	Cambodian Civil Wars	Communist Khmer Rouge against US-backed right wing and other groups.
1975–89	Angolan Civil Wars	Cuban-backed left and South African-backed right-wing forces.
1975–	Lebanese Civil War	Christian Phalangists, Muslim militias, Druse socialists, Syrian and Israeli interventions.
1975–	Western Sahara dispute	Partition of territory between Morocco and Mauritania rejected by Polisario separatist guerrillas.
1975–	East Timor guerrilla war	Popular resistance to Indonesian rule.
1976–92	Mozambique Civil War	Right-wing insurgence backed by South Africa.
1977–91	Ogaden secession	Somalian-backed breakaway from Ethiopia.
1977–	Sri Lanka guerrilla war	Ethnic Tamil separatist rebellion.
1978–90	Nicaraguan Civil War	US-sponsored right-wing guerrilla war to overthrow socialist government.
1979–	Afghan War	Muslim guerrillas (mujaheddin) against communist government and one another.
1984–	Indian separatist unrest	Sikhs in Punjab; Muslims in Kashmir, disputed with Pakistan.
1987–	Palestinian Intifada	Arab resistance movement in Israel-occupied West Bank and Gaza.
1990–	Liberian Civil War	Government overthrown by rival armed groups.
1991–	Somalian Civil War	Government overthrown by rival armed groups.
1992–	Yugoslavian Civil War	Disintegration of republic amid interethnic violence.

Zhukov Georgi Konstantinovich 1896–1974. Marshal of the USSR in World War II and minister of defence 1955–57. As chief of staff from 1941, he defended Moscow 1941, counterattacked at Stalingrad (now Volgograd) 1942, organized the relief of Leningrad (now St Petersburg) 1943, and led the offensive from the Ukraine March 1944 which ended in the fall of Berlin. He subsequently commanded the Soviet occupation forces in Germany.

Weapons and Equipment

aircraft carrier sea-going base for military aircraft. After World War II the cost and vulnerability of such large vessels were thought to have outweighed their advantages. However, by 1980 the desire to have a means of destroying enemy aircraft beyond the range of a ship's own weapons, especially on convoy duty, led to a widespread revival of aircraft carriers of 20,000–30,000 tonnes. Aircraft carriers are equipped with combinations of fixed-wing aircraft, helicopters, missile launchers, and anti-aircraft guns.

armoured personnel carrier (APC) wheeled or tracked military vehicle designed to transport up to ten people. Armoured to withstand small-arms fire and shell splinters, it is used on battlefields.

assault ship naval vessel designed to land and support troops and vehicles under hostile conditions.

bayonet short sword attached to the muzzle of a firearm. The new British Army rifle, the SA-80, is fitted with a bayonet; its predecessor, the SLR, was similarly equipped and used, with its bayonet, during the 1982 Falklands conflict.

binary weapon weapon consisting of two substances that in isolation are harmless but when mixed together form a poisonous nerve gas. They are loaded into the delivery system separately and combine after launch.

enhanced radiation weapon another name for the neutron bomb.

fuel-air explosive warhead containing a highly flammable petroleum and oxygen mixture; when released over a target, this mixes with the oxygen in the atmosphere and produces a vapour which, when ignited, causes a blast approximately five times more powerful than conventional high explosives. Fuel-air explosives were used by the US Air Force in the 1991 Gulf War to flatten Iraqi defensive positions.

Harrier the only truly successful vertical takeoff and landing fixed-wing aircraft, often called the *jump jet*. Built in Britain, it made its first flight 1966. It has a single jet engine and a set of swivelling nozzles. These deflect the jet exhaust vertically downwards for takeoff and landing, and to the rear for normal flight. Designed to fly from confined spaces with minimal ground support, it can refuel in midair.

incendiary bomb a bomb containing inflammable matter. Usually dropped by aircraft, incendiary bombs were used in World War I, and were a major weapon in attacks on cities in World War II. To hinder firefighters, delayed-action high-explosive bombs were usually dropped with them. In the Vietnam War, US forces used napalm in incendiary bombs.

machine gun rapid-firing automatic gun. The fore-runner of the modern machine gun was the Gatling (named after its US inventor R J Gatling 1818–1903), perfected in the USA in 1860 and used in the American Civil War. The Maxim of 1884 was recoil-operated, but some later types have been gas-operated (Bren) or recoil assisted by gas (some versions of the Browning). The *sub-machine gun*, exploited by Chicago gangsters in the 1920s, was widely used in World War II; for instance the Thompson, often called the Tommy gun.

mechanized infantry combat vehicle (MICV) tracked military vehicle designed to fight as part of an armoured battle group; that is, with tanks. It is armed with a quick-firing cannon and one or more machine guns. MICVs have replaced armoured personnel carriers.

mine explosive charge on land or sea, or in the atmosphere, designed to be detonated by contact, vibration (for example, from an enemy engine), magnetic influence, or a timing device. Countermeasures include metal detectors (useless for plastic types), specially equipped helicopters, and (at sea) minesweepers.

missile rocket-propelled weapon, which may be nuclear-armed. Modern missiles are often classified according to range into *intercontinental ballistic missiles* (ICBMs, capable of reaching targets over 5,500 km/3,400 mi), *intermediate-range missiles* (1,100 km/680 mi–2,750 km/1,700 mi), and *short-range missiles* (under 1,100 km/680 mi). They are also categorized as *surface-to-surface missiles* (SSM), *air-to-air missiles* (AAM), *surface-to-air missiles* (SAM), or *air-to-surface missiles* (ASM).

A *ballistic missile* is one whose trajectory is governed by gravity once the power is shut off. The first long-range ballistic missile used was the V2 launched by Germany against Britain in World War II. Outside the industrialized countries, 22 states had active ballistic-missile programmes by 1989, and 17 had deployed these weapons: Afghanistan, Argentina, Brazil, Cuba, Egypt, India, Iran, Iraq, Israel, North Korea, South Korea, Libya, Pakistan, Saudi Arabia, South Africa, Syria, and Taiwan.

A *cruise missile* is in effect a pilotless, computer-guided aircraft; it can be sea-launched from submarines or surface ships, or launched from the air or the ground. Tomahawk cruise missiles launched from both US submarines and battleships lying offshore were devastatingly effective and accurate against targets deep within Iraq during the 1991 Gulf War.

Battlefield missiles used in the 1991 Gulf War include anti-tank missiles and short-range attack missiles. NATO announced in 1990 that it was phasing out ground-launched nuclear battlefield missiles, and these are being replaced by types of tactical air-to-surface missile (TASM), also with nuclear warheads.

mortar method of projecting a bomb via a high trajectory at a target up to 6–7 km/3–4 mi away. A mortar bomb is stabilized in flight by means of tail fins. The high trajectory results in a high angle of attack and makes mortars more suitable than artillery for use in built-up areas or mountains; mortars are less accurate, however. Artillery also differs in firing a projectile through a rifled barrel, thus creating greater muzzle velocity.

napalm fuel used in flamethrowers and incendiary bombs. Produced from jellied petrol, it is a mixture of *na*phthenic and *palm*itic acids. Napalm causes extensive burns because it sticks to the skin even when aflame. It was widely used by the US Army during the Vietnam War.

Patriot missile ground-to-air medium-range missile system used in air defence. It has high-altitude coverage, electronic jamming capability, and excellent mobility. US Patriot missiles were tested in battle against Scud missiles fired by the Iraqis in the 1991 Gulf War, successfully intercepting 24 missiles out of about 85 attempts.

periscope optical instrument designed for observation from a concealed position such as a submerged submarine. In its basic form it consists of a tube with parallel mirrors at each end, inclined at 45° to its axis. The periscope attained prominence in naval and military operations of World War I.

remotely piloted vehicle (RPV) crewless mini-aircraft used for military surveillance and to select targets in battle. RPVs barely show up on radar, so they can fly over a battlefield without being shot down, and they are equipped to transmit TV images to an operator on the ground. RPVs were used by Israeli forces in 1982 in Lebanon and by the Allies in the 1991 Gulf War. The US system is called Aquila and the British system Phoenix.

rifle firearm that has spiral grooves (rifling) in its barrel. When a bullet is fired, the rifling makes it spin, thereby improving accuracy. Rifles were first introduced in the late 18th century.

Scud surface-to-surface missile designed and produced in the USSR, that can be armed with a nuclear, chemical, or conventional warhead. The *Scud-B*, deployed on a mobile launcher, was the version most commonly used by the Iraqi army in the Gulf War 1991. It is a relatively inaccurate weapon. The Scud-B has a range of 300 km/180 mi; modified by the Iraqi army into the *al-Hussayn*, it was capable of projecting a smaller payload (about 500 kg/ 1,100 lb) for a distance of up to 650 km/400 mi, and was used during the Gulf War to hit Israel and Saudi Arabia.

Semtex plastic explosive, manufactured in the Czech Republic. It is safe to handle (it can only be ignited by a detonator) and difficult to trace, since it has no smell. It has been used by extremist groups in the Middle East and by the IRA in Northern Ireland. 0.5kg of Semtex is thought to have been the cause of an explosion that destroyed a Pan-American Boeing 747 in flight over Lockerbie, Scotland, in Dec 1988, killing 270 people.

small arms one of the two main divisions of firearms: guns that can be carried by hand. The first small arms were portable handguns in use in the late 14th century, supported on the ground and ignited by hand. Today's small arms range from breech-loading single-shot rifles and shotguns to sophisticated automatic and semiautomatic weapons. In 1980, there were 11,522 deaths in the USA caused by hand-held guns; in the UK, there were 8. From 1988 guns accounted for more deaths among teenage US males than all other causes put together.

The arms trade

The leading exporters and importers of major conventional weapons, 1987-91

Exporters	1987	1988	1989	1990	1991	1987-91
USSR	17,745	15,115	14,887	9,663	3,930	61,339
USA	13,691	11,867	11,969	11,234	11,195	59,957
France	3,232	2,374	2,861	1,950	804	11,220
UK	2,171	1,690	2,661	1,575	999	9,097
China	2,917	1,930	929	954	1,127	7,857
Germany, FR	784	1,309	780	1,226	2,015	6,115
Czechoslovakia	954	927	715	669	0	3,264
Italy	599	732	225	149	172	1,878
Netherlands	317	631	459	142	208	1,758
Brazil	666	507	288	165	2	1,629
Sweden	474	585	302	103	59	1,524
Israel	408	155	382	108	119	1,172
Spain	169	231	602	80	47	1,128
Yugoslavia	3	4	0	60	661	728
Egypt	234	277	78	42	5	636
Others	1,506	983	1,089	883	771	5,233
Total	*45,870*	*39,317*	*38,228*	*29,004*	*22,114*	*174,532*

To the developing world

Total	*32,162*	*24,054*	*21,735*	*16,720*	*12,336*	*107,007*

To the industralized world

Total	*13,708*	*15,263*	*16,492*	*12,284*	*9,778*	*67,525*

Importers						
India	5,475	4,009	4,461	1,607	2,009	17,561
Saudi Arabia	2,617	2,441	1,914	2,487	1,138	10,597
Iraq	5,438	2,759	1,526	596	0	10,319
Japan	1,644	2,177	2,795	2,094	1,040	9,750
Afghanistan	901	1,275	2,615	2,419	1,220	8,430
Turkey	1,203	1,419	1,138	1,067	1,559	6,384
Egypt	2,850	493	248	1,203	667	5,461
Spain	1,457	1,681	912	674	231	4,955
Czechoslovakia	1,167	1,197	1,557	716	47	4,684
Korea, North	751	1,734	1,518	612	15	4,631
Israel	1,940	604	120	228	1,676	4,567
Greece	92	819	1,471	929	1,081	4,393
Poland	1,012	1,247	1,225	334	137	3,954
Angola	1,599	1,171	88	748	0	3,606
Korea, South	720	1,184	1,101	370	177	3,551
Others	17,005	15,106	15,539	12,919	11,119	71,687
Total	*45,870*	*39,317*	*38,228*	*29,004*	*22,114*	*174,532*

Source: SIPRI Yearbook

smart weapon programmable bomb or missile that can be guided to its target by laser technology, TV homing technology, or terrain-contour matching (TERCOM). A smart weapon relies on its pinpoint accuracy to destroy a target rather than on the size of its warhead. Examples are the cruise missile (Tomahawk), laser-guided artillery shells (Copperhead), laser-guided bombs, and short-range TV-guided missiles (SLAM). Smart weapons were first used on the battlefield in the Gulf War 1991, but only 3% of all the bombs dropped or missiles fired were smart. Of that 3%, it was estimated that 50–70% hit their targets, which is a high accuracy rate.

stealth technology methods used to make an aircraft as invisible as possible, primarily to radar detection but also to detection by visual means and heat sensors. This is achieved by a combination of aircraft-design elements: smoothing off all radar-reflecting sharp edges; covering the aircraft with radar-absorbent materials; fitting engine coverings that hide the exhaust and heat signatures of the aircraft; and other, secret technologies.

The US F-117A stealth fighter-bomber was used during the 1991 Gulf War to attack targets in Baghdad completely undetected. The B-2 bomber, a larger stealth aircraft, is being put into limited production.

TASM (abbreviation for *tactical air-to-surface missile*) missile with a range of under 500 km/300 mi and a nuclear warhead. TASMs are being developed independently by the USA and France to replace the surface-to-surface missiles being phased out by NATO from 1990.

torpedo self-propelled underwater missile, invented 1866 by British engineer Robert Whitehead. Modern torpedoes are homing missiles; some resemble mines in that they lie on the seabed until activated by the acoustic signal of a passing ship. A television camera enables them to be remotely controlled, and in the final stage of attack they lock on to the radar or sonar signals of the target ship.

U-2 US military reconnaissance aeroplane, used in secret flights over the USSR from 1956 to photograph military installations. In 1960 a U-2 was shot down over the USSR and the pilot, Gary Powers, was captured and imprisoned. He was exchanged for a US-held Soviet agent two years later.

U-boat German submarine. The title was used in both world wars.

vertical takeoff and landing craft (VTOL) aircraft that can take off and land vertically. Helicopters, airships, and balloons can do this, as can a few fixed-wing aeroplanes, like the convertiplane.

Armed forces ranks

The following tables lists equivalent ranks in the three armed forces in the UK:

Army	Royal Air Force	Navy
Field Marshal	Marshal of the RAF	Admiral of the Fleet
General	Air Chief Marshal	Admiral
Lieutenant-General	Air Marshal	Vice-Admiral
Major-General	Air Vice-Marshal	Rear-Admiral
Brigadier	Air Commodore	Commodore (1st and 2nd Class)
Colonel	Group Captain	Captain
Lieutenant-Colonel	Wing Commander	Commander
Major	Squadron Leader	Lieutenant Commander
Captain	Flight Lieutenant	Lieutenant
Lieutenant	Flying Officer	Sub-Lieutenant
Second Lieutenant	Pilot Officer	Acting Sub-Lieutenant

THE WORLD

HISTORY

The Seven Wonders of the World

The Seven Wonders of the World are ancient works of art and architecture, considered by the Greek and Roman worlds to be awe-inspiring in size or splendour. Usually considered to include the following:

The Pyramids of Egypt

These monumental masonry structures are located on the west bank of the Nile, over a 60 mile distance southwards from Gizeh, near Cairo. They were built from 3000 to 1800 BC as royal tombs. The oldest pyramid is that of Zoser at Saqqara, built c. 2650 BC. The Great Pyramid of Cheops is a solid mass of limestone covering more than 13 acres/5 ha.

The Hanging Gardens of Babylon

These gardens are said to have been built by King Nebuchadnezzar II around 600 BC, supposedly to please one of his Persian concubines, who was pining for the mountains of her homeland. The gardens were laid out on a brick terrace about 400 ft/120 m square, and rising nearly 82 ft/25 m above the ground, watered from storage tanks on the highest terrace.

The Statue of Zeus at Olympia

This statue was made of marble, inlaid with ivory and gold. Constructed by the sculptor Phidias about 430 BC, it is said to have been 400 ft/12 m high.

The Colossus of Rhodes

This bronze statue of Apollo was erected about 280 BC by the sculptor Chares, who worked on it for 12 years. It stood at the harbour entrance of the seaport of Rhodes.

The Temple of Artemis

This temple, one of the greatest of ancient times, was erected at Ephesus about 350 BC. It was burned by the Goths in AD 262.

The Tomb of Mausolus

This marble tomb was built by Queen Artemisia for her husband Mausolus who died in 353 BC. It stood at Halicarnassus in Asia Minor (now part of SE Turkey). Adorned with the work of four sculptors, it stood about 135 ft/40 m high. It is the source of the term mausoleum.

The Pharos of Alexandria

This marble watchtower and lighthouse stood on the island of Pharos in the harbour of Alexandria. It was built about 270 BC, during the reign of King Ptolemy II, by the Greek architect Sostratos. Estimates of its height range from 200 to 600 ft/60 to 180 m.

Ancient Egypt

5000 BC	Egyptian culture already well established in the Nile Valley, with Neolithic farming villages.
3200	Menes united Lower Egypt (the delta) with his own kingdom of Upper Egypt.
2800	The architect Imhotep built the step pyramid at Sakkara.
c. 2600	Old Kingdom reached the height of its power and the kings of the 4th dynasty built the pyramids at Gîza.
c. 2200–1800	Middle Kingdom, under which the unity lost towards the end of the Old Kingdom was restored.
1730	Invading Asian Hyksos people established their kingdom in the Nile Delta.
c. 1580	New Kingdom established by the 18th dynasty following the eviction of the Hyksos, with its capital at Thebes. The high point of ancient Egyptian civilization under the pharaohs Thothmes, Hatshepsut, Amenhotep, Ikhnaton (who moved the capital to Akhetaton), and Tutankhamen.
c. 1321	19th dynasty Ramses I built a temple at Karnak, Ramses II the temple at Abu Simbel.
1191	Ramses III defeated the Indo-European Sea Peoples, but after him there was decline, and power within the country passed from the pharaohs to the priests of Ammon.
1090–663	Late New Kingdom: during this period Egypt was often divided between two or more dynasties; the nobles became virtually independent.
8th–7th centuries	Brief interlude of rule by kings from Nubia.
666	The Assyrians under Ashurbanipal occupied Thebes.
663–609	Psammetichus I restored Egypt's independence and unity.
525	Egypt was conquered by Cambyses and became a Persian province.
c. 405–340	Period of independence.
332	Conquest by Alexander the Great. On the division of his empire, Egypt went to one of his generals, Ptolemy I, and his descendants, the Macedonian dynasty.
30	Death of Cleopatra, last of the Macedonians, and conquest by the Roman emperor Augustus; Egypt became a province of the Roman and Byzantine empires.
AD 641	Conquest by the Arabs; the Christianity of later Roman rule was for the most part replaced by Islam.

Ancient Greece from the Mycenaean age to the death of Alexander the Great: chronology

1600–1200 BC	Bronze Age Mycenaean civilization flourished, using early written form of Greek language.
1200–1100	Mycenean centres fell. Use of writing apparently ended.
c. 1100	Dorian Greeks settled in Peloponnese (S Greece).
c. 1000	Ionian Greeks left the mainland for E Aegean area.
c. 800	City wall built at Smyrna (Ionia).
c. 750–700	Greeks colonized areas in Sicily, S Italy, and Black Sea, encouraged by the oracle at Delphi. Writing re-appeared. Sparta pursued war against Messenia. Chalcis and Eretria were rivals in Euboea. Homer's epic poems compiled.
c. 680	Gyges of Lydia began attacks on Ionian Greek cities.
c. 670	Sparta conquered Messenia. Pheidon consolidated power of Argos in NE Peloponnese.
c. 665	Corinthians colonized Corcyra (Corfu), winning the first Greek naval battle.
c. 650–585	Cypselus and his son Periander ruled as tyrants in Corinth.
c. 630	Greek colony established at Cyrene, N Africa.
c. 620	Severe law code of Draco introduced in Athens.
c. 600	Greek colony set up at Massilia (now Marseille). Greek traders established at Naucratis in the Nile Delta. Coinage introduced in Lydia.
594–93	Solon was elected archon (magistrate) at Athens, and achieved economic and political reforms.
560–510	Pisistratus and his sons ruled as tyrants at Athens. Athenian influence established in N Greece and the Dardanelles (Turkey).
556–555	Chilon increased the power of the ephors (senior magistrates) at Sparta.
546	Croesus of Lydia defeated by Cyrus the Great of Persia, who had already subdued the Ionian Greeks.
527	Death of Pisistratus.
514	Hipparchus, son of Pisistratus, assassinated in Athens.
510	Hippias, last of the Pisistratids, was expelled from Athens. The city saw the gradual introduction of democracy by Cleisthenes.
c. 510–500	Formation of the Peloponnesian League, led by Sparta.
499–94	Revolt against Persia by Ionian Greeks, supported by Athens. Miletus was destroyed, and the revolt defeated.
c. 494	Defeat of Argos by Sparta.
493	Themistocles elected archon at Athens, and fortified Piraeus harbour.
492	Persian expedition to N Greece led by Mardonius.
490	Persian campaign against Athens defeated at the Battle of Marathon.
from 483	Athenians started to build warships on the advice of Themistocles.
480–79	Persian invasion of Greece under Xerxes defeated at Battles of Salamis 480 (at sea), and Plataea 479 (on land). Carthaginians defeated by Gelon of Syracuse at Battle of Himera, Sicily 480.
477	Formation of the Delian League by Athens and Ionian Greeks against Persia.
c. 465	Revolt of the Messenians against Sparta.
461	Confirmation of democracy (legal and political) at Athens.
c. 450	Attacks of Delian League on Persian possessions ended.
443–29	Pericles pre-eminent as statesman and general in Athens until his death.
440	Attempted secession of Samos from the Delian League crushed by Athens.
431	Peloponnesian War between Athens and Sparta began.
421	Peace of Nicias signed by Athens and Sparta.
415–13	Athenian expedition against Syracuse defeated. Nicias died.
411	Right-wing coup in Athens failed.
405	Athenian fleet defeated at Battle of Aegospotami by Spartan admiral Lysander.
404	Surrender of Athens. Lysander installed the rule of the Thirty in Athens. Alcibiades died.
403	Democracy re-established at Athens.
395–86	Spartan supremacy challenged in Corinthian War.
382	Thebes garrisoned by Sparta.
371	Sparta defeated by the Thebans under Epaminondas at Battle of Leuctra.
369	City of Messene founded. Messenia became independent of Sparta.
362	Epaminondas died.
358–36	Reign of Philip II of Macedon.
351–38	Expansionist policies of Philip of Macedon opposed by the Athenian orator Demosthenes.
338	Philip of Macedon secured control of mainland Greece at Battle of Chaeronea.
336–323	Reign of Alexander the Great of Macedon.
334	Alexander invaded the Persian empire, winning Battle of Granicus near the Dardanelles.
333	Darius III of Persia defeated at Battle of Ipsus.
332	Persian dockyards destroyed. Siege of Tyre and capture of Egypt by Alexander.
331	Final defeat of Darius at Battle of Gaugamela.
330	Darius III died.
330–27	Campaigns by Alexander in the E Persian provinces.
327–24	Indian expedition by Alexander.
323	Alexander died. Athens and Thessaly revolted against Macedonian supremacy, but were defeated and the Macedonians garrisoned Athens. Demosthenes committed suicide.

Ancient Rome: chronology

753 BC	According to tradition, Rome was founded.
510	The Etruscan dynasty of the Tarquins was expelled and a republic established, with power concentrated in patrician hands.
450	Publication of the law code contained in the Twelve Tables.
396	Capture of Etruscan Veii, 15 km/9 mi N of Rome.
387	Rome sacked by Gauls.
367	Plebeians gained the right to be consuls (the two chief magistrates, elected annually).
338	Cities of Latium formed into a league under Roman control.
343–290	Sabines to the N, and the Samnites to the SE, were conquered.
280–272	Greek cities in S Italy subdued.
264–241	First Punic War against Carthage, ending in a Roman victory and the annexation of Sicily.
238	Sardinia seized from Carthage.
226–222	Roman conquest of Cisalpine Gaul (Lombardy, Italy). More conflict with Carthage, which was attempting to conquer Spain.
218	Second Punic War. Hannibal crossed the Alps and invaded Italy, winning a series of brilliant victories.
202	Victory of General Scipio Africanus Major over Hannibal at Zama was followed by the surrender of Carthage and relinquishing of its Spanish colonies.
188	Peace of Apamea confined the rule of the Seleucid king Antiochus the Great to Asia.
168	Final defeat of Macedon by Rome.
146	After a revolt, Greece became in effect a Roman province. Carthage was destroyed and its territory annexed.
133	Tiberius Gracchus suggested agrarian reforms and was murdered by the senatorial party. Roman province of Asia formed from the kingdom of Pergamum, bequeathed to Rome by the Attalid dynasty.
123	Tiberius' policy adopted by his brother Gaius Gracchus, who was likewise murdered.
91–88	Social War: revolt by the Italian cities forced Rome to grant citizenship to all Italians.
87	While Sulla was repelling an invasion of Greece by King Mithridates of Pontus (in Asia Minor), Marius seized power.
82–79	Sulla returned and established a dictatorship ruled by terror.
70	Sulla's constitutional changes were reversed by Pompey and Crassus.
66–63	Pompey defeated Mithridates and annexed Syria.
60	The First Triumvirate was formed, an alliance between Pompey and the democratic leaders Crassus and Caesar.
51	Caesar conquered Gaul as far as the Rhine.
49	Caesar crossed the Rubicon, returned to Italy and a civil war between him and Pompey's senatorial party began.
48	Pompey defeated at Pharsalus.
44	Caesar's dictatorship ended by his assassination.
43	Second Triumvirate formed by Octavian, Mark Antony, and Lepidus.
32	War between Octavian and Mark Antony.
31	Mark Antony defeated at Actium.
30	Egypt was annexed after the deaths of Mark Antony and Cleopatra.
27	Octavian took the name Augustus. He was by now absolute ruler, though in title he was only *princeps* (first citizen).
AD 14	Augustus died. Tiberius proclaimed as his successor.
43	Claudius added Britain to the empire.
70	Jerusalem sacked by Titus.
96–180	The empire enjoyed a golden age under the Flavian and Antonine emperors Nerva, Trajan, Hadrian, Antoninus Pius, and Marcus Aurelius Antoninus.
115	Trajan conquered Parthia, achieving the peak of Roman territorial expansion.
180	Marcus Aurelius died, and a century of war and disorder followed, with a succession of generals being put on the throne by their armies.
212	Caracalla granted citizenship to the communities of the empire.
284–305	Diocletian reorganized the empire, dividing power between himself and three others (the Tetrarchy).
313	Constantine I recognized the Christians' right to freedom of worship by the Edict of Milan.
330	Constantine made Constantinople his new imperial capital.
395	The empire divided into eastern and western parts.
410	Visigoths sacked Rome. Roman legions withdrew from Britain.
451–52	Huns raided Gaul and Italy.
455	Vandals sacked Rome.
476	Last Western emperor, Romulus Augustulus, deposed.

Roman emperors 27 BC–AD 285

Reign	Name
Julio-Claudian emperors	
27 BC–14 AD	Augustus
14–37	Tiberius I
37–41	Caligula (Gaius Caesar)
41–54	Claudius I
54–68	Nero
Civil wars	
68–69	Galba
69	Otho
69	Vitellius
Flavian emperors	
69–79	Vespasian
79–81	Titus
81–96	Domitian
96–98	Nerva
98–117	Trajan
117–38	Hadrian
Antonine emperors	
138–61*	Antoninus Pius
161–69*	Lucius Verus

*divided voluntarily between two brothers

Reign	Name
despotic emperors	
161–80	Marcus Aurelius
180–92	Commodus
193	Pertinax
193	Didius Julianus
the Severi	
193–211	Septimius Severus
211–17	Caracalla
217–18	Macrinus
218–22	Elagabalus
222–35	Severus Alexander
the soldier emperors	
235–38	Maximus I
238–44	Gordian III
244–49	Philip I, the Arab
249–51	Trajan Decius
251–53	Trebonianus Gallus
253–68	Gallienus
268–70	Claudius II
270–75	Aurelian
275–76	Tacitus
276	Florian
276–82	Probus
282–83	Carus
283–85	Carinus

Ottoman emperors 1280–1924

Reign	Osmanli dynasty
1280–1324	Osman I
1324–62	Orhan
1362–89	Murad I
1389–1402	Bayezid I, the Thunderbolt (deposed)
1402–03	Isa (claimed Anatolia)
1402–11	Suleiman (claimed Rumelia)
1409–13	Mesa (claimed Rumelia)
1413–21	Mehmed I (claimed Anatolia, 1402-13)
1421–51	Murad II (abdicated in favour of Mehmed II 1444-46)
1451–81	Mehmed II, the Conqueror
1481–1512	Bayezid II (deposed)
1512–20	Selim I, the Grim
1520–66	Suleiman I, the Magnificent
1566–74	Selim II, the Sot
1574–95	Murad III
1595–1603	Mehmed III
1603–17	Ahmed I
1617–18	Mustafa I (deposed)
1618–22	Osman II
1622–23	Mustafa I (restored; deposed)
1623–40	Murad IV
1640–48	Ibrahim (deposed)
1648–87	Mehmed IV (deposed)
1687–91	Suleiman II
1691–95	Ahmed II
1695–1703	Mustafa II (deposed)
1703–30	Ahmed III (deposed)
1730–54	Mahmud I
1754–57	Osman III
1757–74	Mustafa III
1774–89	Abdulhamid I
1789–1807	Selim III (deposed)
1807–08	Mustafa IV (deposed)
1808–39	Mahmud II
1839–61	Abdulmecid I
1861–76	Abdulaziz (deposed)
1876–76	Murad V (deposed)
1876–1909	Abdulhamid II (deposed)
1909–18	Mehmed V Resad
1918–22	Mehmed VI Vahiduddin (deposed)
1922–24	Abdulmecid II (deposed)

Holy Roman emperors

Reign	Name
Carolingian kings and emperors	
800–14	Charlemagne (Charles the Great)
814–40	Louis the Pious
840–55	Lothair I
855–75	Louis II
875–77	Charles II, the Bald
881–87	Charles III, the Fat
891–94	Guido of Spoleto
892–98	Lambert of Spoleto (co-emperor)
896–901	Arnulf (rival)
901–05	Louis III of Provence
905–24	Berengar
911–18	Conrad I of Franconia (rival)
Saxon kings and emperors	
918–36	Henry I, the Fowler
936–73	Otto I, the Great
973–83	Otto II
983–1002	Otto III
1002–24	Henry II, the Saint
Franconian (Salian) emperors	
1024–39	Conrad II
1039–56	Henry III, the Black
1056–1106	Henry IV
1077–80	Rudolf of Swabia (rival)
1081–93	Hermann of Luxembourg (rival)
1093–1101	Conrad of Franconia (rival)
1106–25	Henry V
1126–37	Lothair II
Hohenstaufen kings and emperors	
1138–52	Conrad III
1152–90	Frederick Barbarossa
1190–97	Henry VI
1198–1215	Otto IV
1198–1208	Philip of Swabia (rival)
1215–50	Frederick II
1246–47	Henry Raspe of Thuringia (rival)
1247–56	William of Holland

Reign	Name
1250–54	Conrad IV
1254–73	no ruler (the Great Interregnum)
Rulers from various noble families	
1257–72	Richard of Cornwall (rival)
1257–73	Alfonso X of Castile (rival)
1273–91	Rudolf I, Habsburg
1292–98	Adolf I of Nassau
1298–1308	Albert I, Habsburg
1308–13	Henry VII, Luxembourg
1314–47	Louis IV of Bavaria
1314–25	Frederick of Habsburg (co-regent)
1347–78	Charles IV, Luxembourg
1378–1400	Wenceslas of Bohemia
1400	Frederick III of Brunswick
1400–10	Rupert of the Palatinate
1411–37	Sigismund, Luxembourg
Habsburg emperors	
1438–39	Albert II
1440–93	Frederick III
1493–1519	Maximilian I
1519–56	Charles V
1556–64	Ferdinand I
1564–76	Maximilian II
1576–1612	Rudolf II
1612–19	Matthias
1619–37	Ferdinand II
1637–57	Ferdinand III
1658–1705	Leopold I
1705–11	Joseph I
1711–40	Charles VI
1742–45	Charles VII of Bavaria
Habsburg-Lorraine emperors	
745–65	Francis I of Lorraine
1765–90	Joseph II
1790–92	Leopold II
1792–1806	Francis II

Ming dynasty emperors of China

Reign	Name	Born
1368–98	Hongwu	1328
1398–1402	Jianwen	1377
1402–24	Yongle	1360
1424–25	Hongxi	1378
1425–35	Xuande	1399
1435–49	Zhengtong	1427*
1449–57	Jingtai	1428
1457–64	Tianshun	1427
1464–87	Chenghua	1447
1487–1505	Hongzhi	1470
1505–21	Zhengde	1491
1521–67	Jiajing	1507
1567–72	Longqing	1537
1572–1620	Wanli	1563
1620	Taichang	1582
1620–27	Tianqi	1605
1627–44	Chongzhen	1611

* Zhengtong was deposed in 1449 and held captive. He was restored, as Tianshun, in 1457.

Qing dynasty emperors of China

Reign	Name	Born
1644–61	Shunzhi	1638
1661–1722	Kangxi	1645
1722–35	Yongzheng	1678
1735–96	Qianlong	1711
1796–1820	Jiaqing	1760
1820–50	Daoguang	1782
1850–61	Xianfeng	1831
1861–75	Tongzhi	1856
1875–1908	Guangxu	1871
1908–12	Xuantong*	1906

* Personal name: P'u-i

Emperors of India

Reign	Name
Mauryan emperors	
325–297 BC	Chandragupta Maurya
297–272 BC	Bindusara
272–268 BC	interregnum
268–232 BC	Asoka
232–224 BC	Dasaratha
224–215 BC	Samprati
215–202 BC	Salisuka
202–195 BC	Devavarman
195–187 BC	Satadhanvan
187–185 BC	Brihadratha

Reign	Name
Gupta emperors	
AD 320–50	Chandragupta I
350–76	Samudragupta
376–415	Chandragupta II
415–55	Kumaragupta I
455–70	Skandagupta
470–75	Kumaragupta II
475–500	Budhagupta
500–15	Vainyagupta
515–30	Narasimhagupta
530–40	Kumaragupta III
540–50	Vishnugupta

Reign	Name
Mogul emperors	
Great Moguls	
1526–30	Babur (Zahiruddin Muhammad)
1530–56	Humayun (Nasiruddin Muhammad)*
1556–1605	Akbar (Jalaluddin Muhammad)
1605–27	Jahangir (Nuruddin)
1627–28	Dewar Baksh
1628–58	Shah Jahan (Shihabuddin; dethroned)
1658–1707	Aurangzeb (Muhiyuddin)
lesser Moguls	
1707–07	Azam Shah
1707–12	Shah Alam I (Muhammad Mu'azzam)
1712–12	Azim-ush Shan
1712–13	Jahandar Shah (Muhammad Muizzuddin)
1713–19	Farrukh Siyar (Jalaluddin Muhammad)
1719–19	Rafi ud-Darajat (Shamsuddin)
1719–19	Rafi ud-Daula Shah Jahan II
1719–19	Nikusiyar
1719–48	Muhammad Shah (Nasiruddin)
1748–54	Ahmad Shah Bahadur (Abu al-Nasir Muhammad)
1754–60	Alamgir II (Muhammad Azizuddin)
1760–60	Shah Jahan III
1760–1806	Shah Alam II (Jalaluddin Ali Jauhar; deposed briefly in 1788)
1806–37	Akbar Shah II (Muhiyuddin)
1837–58	Bahadur Shah II (Abul al-Zafar Muhammad Sirajuddin; banished)

Humayun was defeated 1540 and expelled from India until 1555, leaving N India under the control of Sher Shah Suri (died 1545), Islam Shah, and Sikandar Shah.

Inca emperors

Reign	Name	Relationship
the kingdom of Cuzco		
c. 1200	Manco Capac	traditional founder of Cuzco and the Inca royal house
	Sinchi Roca	son
	Lloque Yupanqui	son
	Mayta Capac	son
	Capac Yupanqui	son
	Inca Roca	son
	Yahuar Huaca	son
	Viracocha Inca	son
the empire		
1438–71	Pachacuti	son; abdicated, died 1471
1471–93	Topa Inca	son
1493–24	Huayna Capac	son
1524–32	Huascar	son; deposed, died 1532
1532	Atahualpa	brother; deposed, died 1533 in the Spanish conquest of the Inca Empire
the Vilcabamba state		
1533	Topa Hualpa	brother
1533–45	Manco Inca	brother
1545–60	Sayri Tupac	son
1560–71	Titu Cusi Yupanqui	brother
1571–72	Tupac Amaru	brother; deposed, died 1572 in the Spanish conquest of the Vilcabamba state

Aztec emperors

Reign*	Name
1372–91	Acamapichtli (chieftain at Tenochtitlán; traditional founder of Aztec royal house)
1391–1416	Huitzilihuitl (son)
1416–27	Chimalpopoca (son)
1427–40	Itzcoatl (son of Acamapichtli)
1468–81	Axayacatl (grandson of Itzcoatl)
1481–86	Tizoc (brother)
1486–1502	Ahuitzotl (brother)
1502–20	Montezuma II, Xocoyotzin (son of Axayacatl)
1520	Cuitlahuac (brother)
1520–21	Cuauhtemoc (son of Ahuitzotl)

* Dates before 1468 are approximate.

Emperors of Japan

Reign	Era name*	Relationship
Legendary and Yamato periods (to AD 710)		
40–10 BC	Jimmu	semi-mythical founder of the dynasty
10 BC–AD 20	Suizei	son
20–50	Annei	son
50–80	Itoku	son
80–110	Kōshō	son
110–40	Kōan	son
140–70	Kōrei	son
170–200	Kōgen	son
200–230	Kaika	son
230–258	Sujin	son
258–90	Suinin	son
290–322	Keikō	son
322–55	Seimu	son
355–62	Chūai	nephew
362–94	Ōjin	son
394–427	Nintoku	son
427–32	Richū	son
432–37	Hanzei	brother
437–54	Ingyō	brother
454–57	Ankō	son
457–89	Yūraku	brother
489–94	Seinei	son
494–97	Kenzō	grandson of Richū
497–504	Ninken	brother
504–10	Buretsu	son
510–27	Keitai	fifth in descent from Ōjin
527–35	Ankan	son
535–39	Senka	brother
539–71	Kimmei	brother
572–85	Bidatsu	son
585–87	Yōmei	brother
587–92	Sushun	brother
593–628	Suiko	sister
629–41	Jomei	grandson of Bidatsu
642–45	Kōgyoku	niece; abdicated
645–54	Kōtoku	brother
655–61	Saimei	ex-empress Kōgyoku
661–72	Tenji	son of Jomei
672	Kōbun	son
672–86	Temmu	son of Jomei
686–97	Jitō	daughter of Tenji; abdicated, died 703
697–707	Mommu	grandson of Temmu
Nara period (710–84)		
707–15	Gemmei	daughter of Tenji; abdicated, died 721
715–24	Genshō	sister of Mommu; abdicated, died 748
724–49	Shōmu	son of Mommu; abdicated, died 756
749–58	Kōken	daughter; abdicated
758–64	Junnin	grandson of Temmu; deposed, died 765
764–70	Shōtoku	ex-empress Kōken
770–81	Kōnin	grandson of Tenji; abdicated, died 782
Heian period (794–1185)		
781–806	Kammu	son
806–09	Heizei	son; abdicated, died 824
809–23	Saga	brother; abdicated, died 842
823–33	Junna	brother; abdicated, died 840
833–50	Nimmyō	son of Saga
850–58	Montoku	son
858–76	Seiwa	son; abdicated, died 881
876–84	Yōzei	son; deposed, died 949
884–87	Kōkō	son of Nimmyō
887–97	Uda	son; abdicated, died 931
897–930	Daigo	son; abdicated, died 930
930–46	Suzaku	son; abdicated, died 952
946–67	Murakami	brother
967–69	Reizei	son; abdicated, died 1011
969–84	En'yū	brother; abdicated, died 991
984–86	Kazan	son of Reizei; abdicated, died 1008
986–1011	Ichijō	son of En'yū; abdicated, died 1011
1011–16	Sanjō	son of Reizei; abdicated, died 1017
1016–36	Go-Ichijō	son of Ichijō
1036–45	Go-Suzaku	brother; abdicated, died 1045
1045–68	Go-Reizei	son
1068–73	Go-Sanjō	brother; abdicated, died 1073
1073–87	Shirakawa	son; abdicated, died 1129
1087–1107	Horikawa	son
1107–23	Toba	son; abdicated, died 1156
1123–42	Sutoku	son; abdicated, died 1164
1142–55	Konoe	brother
1155–58	Go-Shirakawa	brother; abdicated, died 1192
1158–65	Nijō	son; abdicated, died 1165
1165–68	Rokujō	son; abdicated, died 1176
1168–80	Takakura	son of Go-Shirakawa; abdicated, died 1181
1180–85	Antoku	son
Kamakura period (1192–1333)		
1183–98	Go-Toba	brother; abdicated, died 1239
1198–1210	Tsuchimikado	son; abdicated, died 1231
1210–21	Juntoku	brother; abdicated, died 1242
1221	Chūkyō	son; deposed, died 1234
1221–32	Go-Horikawa	grandson of Takakura; abdicated, died 1234
1232–42	Shijō	son

Emperors of Japan (cont.)

Reign	Era name*	Relationship
1242–46	Go-Saga	son of Tsuchimikado; abdicated,died 1272
1246–60	Go-Fukakusa	son; abdicated, died 1304
1260–74	Kameyama	brother; abdicated, died 1305
1274–87	Go-Uda	son; abdicated, died 1324
1287–98	Fushimi	son of Go-Fukakusa; abdicated, died 1317
1298–1301	Go-Fushimi	son; abdicated, died 1336
1301–08	Go-Nijō	son of Go-Uda
1308–1318	Hanazono	son of Fushimi; abdicated, died 1348

Nambokuchō period (1336–92)
The Southern Court

1318–39	Go-Daigo	son of Go-Uda
1339–68	Go-Murakami	son
1368–83	Chōkei	son; abdicated, died 1394
1383–92	Go-Kameyama	brother; abdicated, died 1424

The Northern Court

1331–33	Kōgon	son of Go-Fushimi; deposed, died 1364
1336–48	Kōmyō	brother; abdicated, died 1380
1348–51	Sukō	son of Kōgon; abdicated, died 1398
1352–71	Go-Kōgon	brother; abdicated, died 1374
1371–82	Go-En'yū	son; abdicated, died 1393

Muromachi period (1392–1568)

1382–1412	Go-Komatsu	son; abdicated, died 1433
1412–28	Shōkō	son
1428–64	Go-Hanazono	great-grandson of Sukō; abdicated, died 1471

Reign	Era name	Relationship
1464–1500	Go-Tsuchimikado	son
1500–26	Go-Kashiwabara	son
1526–57	Go-Nara	son
1557–86	Ōgimachi	son; abdicated, died 1593

Edo period (1603–1868)

1586–1611	Go-Yōzei	grandson; abdicated, died 1617
1611–1629	Go-Mizunoo	son; abdicated, died 1680
1629–43	Meishō	daughter; abdicated, died 1696
1643–54	Go-Kōmyō	brother
1655–63	Go-Sai	brother; abdicated, died 1685
1663–87	Reigen	brother; abdicated, died 1732
1687–1709	Higashiyama	son; abdicated, died 1710
1709–35	Nakamikado	son; abdicated, died 1737
1735–47	Sakuramachi	son; abdicated, died 1750
1747–62	Momozono	son
1762–71	Go-Sakuramachi	sister; abdicated, died 1813
1771–79	Go-Momozono	son of Momozono
1780–1817	Kōkaku	great-grandson of Higashiyama; abdicated, died 1840
1817–46	Ninkō	son
1846–67	Kōmei	son

modern period (from 1867)

1867–1912	Meiji Mutsuhito	son
1912–26	Taishō Yoshihito	son
1926–89	Shōwa Hirohito	son; regent 1921–26
1989–	Heisei Akihito	son

* Many emperors changed their era names for parts of their reign; for example, Higashiyama was known as Genroku 1688–1704 and as Hōei 1704–09.

Kings of France 751–1848

Reign	Name
Carolingian House (*Robertian House)	
751–68	Pepin the Short
768–814	Charlemagne
814–40	Louis I, the Pious
840–77	Charles I, the Bald
877–79	Louis II, the Stammerer
879–82	Louis III
879–84	Carloman
884–88	Charles II, the Fat
888–93	Eudes
893–922	Charles III, the Simple
922–23	Robert I
923–36	Rudolf*
936–54	Louis IV of Outremer
954–86	Lothair
986–87	Louis V, the Sluggard
Capetian House	
987–96	Hugh Capet
996–1031	Robert II, the Pious
1031–60	Henry I
1060–1108	Philip I
1108–37	Louis VI, the Fat
1137–80	Louis VII, the Younger
1180–1223	Philip II (Philip Augustus)
1223–26	Louis VIII, the Lion
1226–70	St Louis IX
1270–85	Philip III, the Bold
1285–1314	Philip IV, the Fair
1314–16	Louis X, the Stubborn
1316	John I
1316–22	Philip V, the Tall
1322–28	Charles IV, the Fair
House of Valois	
1328–50	Philip VI
1350–64	John II, the Good
1364–80	Charles V, the Wise
1380–1422	Charles VI, the Mad
1422–61	Charles VII, the Victorious
1461–83	Louis XI
1483–98	Charles VIII
1498–1515	Louis XII
1515–47	Francis I
1547–59	Henry II
1559–60	Francis II
1560–74	Charles IX
1574–89	Henry III
House of Bourbon	
1589–1610	Henry IV
1610–43	Louis XIII
1643–1715	Louis XIV
1715–74	Louis XV
1774–92	Louis XVI (deposed)
1792–1803	First Republic
1804–14	House of Bonaparte (First Empire)
1814–24	Louis XVIII
1824–30	Charles X (deposed)
1830–48	Louis Philippe I (deposed)

Rulers of Spain from 1516

Reign	Name
House of Habsburg	
1516–56	Charles I
1556–98	Philip II
1598–1621	Philip III
1621–65	Philip IV
1665–1700	Charles II
House of Bourbon	
1700–46	Philip V
1746–59	Ferdinand VI
1759–88	Charles III
1788–1808	Charles IV
1808	Ferdinand VII (deposed)
1808–13	Joseph Napoleon*
1813–33	Ferdinand VII (restored)
1833–68	Isabel II
1868–70	provisional government
1870–73	Amadeus I † (abdicated)
1873–74	first republic
1874–86	Alfonso XII
1886–1931	Alfonso XIII (deposed)
1931–39	second republic
1939–75	fascist state, General Francisco Franco head of state
1975–	Juan Carlos I

* House of Bonaparte
† House of Savoy

Kings of Italy 1861–1946

Reign	Name
1861–78	Victor Emmanuel II
1878–1900	Umberto I
1900–46	Victor Emmanuel III
1946–46	Umberto II (abdicated)

House of Habsburg

Reign	Name
emperors of Austria	
1804–35	Francis (Franz) I (of Austria) and II (as Holy Roman emperor until 1806)
1835–48	Ferdinand
emperors of Austria-Hungary	
1848–1916	Franz Josef
1916–18	Charles (Karl; abdicated)

Tsars of Russia 1547–1917

Reign	Name
House of Rurik	
1547–84	Ivan the Terrible
1584–98	Theodore I
1598	Irina
House of Gudonov	
1598–1605	Boris Gudonov
1605	Theodore II
usurpers	
1605–06	Dimitri III
1606–10	Basil IV
1610–13	interregnum
House of Romanov	
1613–45	Michael Romanov
1645–76	Alexis
1676–82	Theodore III
1682–96	Peter I and Ivan V (brothers)
1689–1725	Peter I, the Great*
1725–27	Catherine I
1727–30	Peter II
1730–40	Anna Ivanovna
1740–41	Ivan VI
1741–62	Elizabeth
1762	Peter III
1762–96	Catherine II, the Great
1796–1801	Paul I
1801–25	Alexander I
1825–55	Nicholas I
1855–81	Alexander II
1881–94	Alexander III
1894–1917	Nicholas II

The title of 'tsar' was replaced by 'emperor' from 1721.

Kings and Queens of Scotland 1005–1603

(from the unification of Scotland to the union of the crowns of Scotland and England)

Reign	Name
Celtic kings	
1005	Malcolm II
1034	Duncan I
1040	Macbeth
1057	Malcolm III Canmore
1095	Donald Ban (restored)
1097	Edgar
1107	Alexander I
1124	David
1153	Malcolm IV
1165	William the Lion
1214	Alexander II
1249	Alexander III
1286–90	Margaret of Norway
English domination	
1292–96	John Baliol
1296–1306	annexed to England
House of Bruce	
1306	Robert I, the Bruce
1329	David II
House of Stuart	
1371	Robert II
1390	Robert III
1406	James I
1437	James II
1460	James III
1488	James IV
1513	James V
1542	Mary
1567	James VI
1603	union of crowns

English sovereigns from 900

Reign	Name	Relationship
West Saxon kings		
901–25	Edward the Elder	son of Alfred the Great
925–40	Athelstan	son of Edward I
940–46	Edmund	half-brother of Athelstan
946–55	Edred	brother of Edmund
955–59	Edwy	son of Edmund
959–75	Edgar	brother of Edwy
975–78	Edward the Martyr	son of Edgar
978–1016	Ethelred II	son of Edgar
1016	Edmund Ironside	son of Ethelred
Danish kings		
1016–35	Canute	son of Sweyn I of Denmark, who conquered England in 1013
1035–40	Harold I	son of Canute
1040–42	Hardicanute	son of Canute
West Saxon kings (restored)		
1042–66	Edward the Confessor	son of Ethelred II
1066	Harold II	son of Godwin
Norman kings		
1066–87	William I	illegitimate son of Robert I the Magnificent, Duke of Normandy
1087–1100	William II	son of William I
1100–35	Henry I	son of William I
1135–54	Stephen	grandson of William II
House of Plantagenet		
1154–89	Henry II	son of Matilda (daughter of Henry I)
1189–99	Richard I	son of Henry II
1199–1216	John	son of Henry II
1216–72	Henry III	son of John
1272–1307	Edward I	son of Henry III
1307–27	Edward II	son of Edward I
1327–77	Edward III	son of Edward II
1377–99	Richard II	son of the Black Prince
House of Lancaster		
1399–1413	Henry IV	son of John of Gaunt
1413–22	Henry V	son of Henry IV
1422–61, 1470–71	Henry VI	son of Henry V

Reign	Name	Relationship
House of York		
1461–70, 1471–83	Edward IV	son of Richard, Duke of York
1483	Edward V	son of Edward IV
1483–85	Richard III	brother of Edward IV
House of Tudor		
1485–1509	Henry VII	son of Edmund Tudor, Earl of Richmond
1509–47	Henry VIII	son of Henry VII
1547–53	Edward VI	son of Henry VIII
1553–58	Mary I	daughter of Henry VIII
1558–1603	Elizabeth I	daughter of Henry VIII
House of Stuart		
1603–25	James I	great-grandson of Margaret (daughter of Henry VIII)
1625–49	Charles I	son of James I
1649–60	*the Commonwealth*	
House of Stuart (restored)		
1660–85	Charles II	son of Charles I
1685–88	James II	son of Charles I
1689–1702	William III and Mary	son of Mary (daughter of Charles I); daughter of James II
1702–14	Anne	daughter of James II
House of Hanover		
1714–27	George I	son of Sophia (granddaughter of James I)
1727–60	George II	son of George I
1760–1820	George III	son of Frederick (son of George II)
1820–30	George IV (regent 1811–20)	son of George III
1830–37	William IV	son of George III
1837–1901	Victoria	daughter of Edward (son of George III)
House of Saxe-Coburg		
1901–10	Edward VII	son of Victoria
House of Windsor		
1910–36	George V	son of Edward VII
1936	Edward VIII	son of George V
1936–52	George VI	son of George V
1952–	Elizabeth II	daughter of George VI

From colonialism to independence: the break-up of the empires

Colonial power/ current name of country colonized	Colonial names and history	Colonized	Independent
Belgium			
Zaïre	Belgian Congo	1885	1960
France			
Cambodia	Kampuchea 1970–89	1863	1953
Laos	French Indochina (protectorate)	1893	1954
Vietnam	Tonkin, Annam, Conchin-China to 1954 North and South Vietnam 1954–76	1858	1954
Burkina Faso	Upper Volta to 1984	1896	1960
Central African Republic	Ubangi-Shari	19th century	1960
Chad	French Equatorial Africa	19th century	1960
Côte d'Ivoire	Ivory Coast to 1986	1883	1960
Madagascar		1896	1960
Mali	French Sudan	19th century	1960
Niger		1912	1960
Algeria	colonized in 19th century; incorporated into France 1881	c. 1840	1962
The Netherlands			
Indonesia	Netherlands Indies	17th century	1949
Suriname	British colony 1650–67	1667	1975
Portugal			
Brazil		1532	1822
Uruguay	province of Brazil	1533	1828
Mozambique		1505	1975
Angola		1491	1975
Spain			
Paraguay	viceroyalty of Buenos Aires	1537	1811
Argentina	viceroyalty of Buenos Aires	16th century	1816
Chile		1541	1818
Costa Rica		1563	1821
Mexico	viceroyalty of New Spain	16th century	1821
Peru		1541	1824
Bolivia		16th century	1825
Ecuador	Greater Colombia 1822–30	16th century	1830
Venezuela	captaincy-general of Caracas to 1822 Greater Colombia 1822–30	16th century	1830
Honduras	federation of Central America 1821–38	1523	1838
El Salvador	federation of Central America 1821–39	16th century	1839
Guatemala	federation of Central America 1821–39	16th century	1839
Dominican Republic	Hispaniola to 1821 ruled by Haiti to 1844	16th century	1844
Cuba		1512	1902
Colombia	viceroyalty of New Granada to 1819 Greater Colombia to 1830	16th century	1903
Panama	part of Colombia to 1903	16th century	1903
Philippines	Spain 1565–1898, US 1898–1946	1565	1946
United Kingdom			
India	British E India Co. 18th century–1858	18th century	1947
Pakistan	British E India Co. 18th century–1858	18th century	1947
Myanmar	Burma until 1989	19th century	1948
Sri Lanka	Portuguese, Dutch 1602–1796; Ceylon 1802–1972	16th century	1948
Ghana	Gold Coast	1618	1957
Nigeria		1861	1960
Cyprus	Turkish to 1878, then British rule	1878	1960
Sierra Leone	British protectorate	1788	1961
Tanzania	German E Africa to 1921; British mandate from League of Nations/UN as Tanganyika	19th century	1961

From colonialism to independence: the break-up of the empires *(cont.)*

Colonial power/ current name of country colonized	Colonial names and history	Colonized	Independent
Jamaica	Spanish to 1655	17th century	1962
Trinidad & Tobago	Spanish 1532–1797; British 1797–1962	1532	1962
Uganda	British protectorate	1894	1962
Kenya	British colony from 1920	1895	1963
Malaysia	British interests from 1786; Federation of Malaya 1957–63	1874	1963
Malawi	British protectorate of Nyasaland 1907–53; Federation of Rhodesia & Nyasaland 1953–64	1891	1964
Malta	French 1798–1814	1798	1964
Zambia	N Rhodesia – British protectorate; Federation of Rhodesia & Nyasaland 1953–64	1924	1964
The Gambia		1888	1965
Singapore	Federation of Malaya 1963–65	1858	1965
Guyana	Dutch to 1796; British Guiana 1796–1966	1620	1966
Botswana	Bechuanaland – British protectorate	1885	1966
Lesotho	Basutoland	1868	1966
Mauritius		1814	1968
Bangladesh	British E India Co. 18th cent.–1858; British India 1858–1947; E Pakistan 1947–71	18th century	1971
Zimbabwe	S Rhodesia from 1923; UDI under Ian Smith 1965–79	1895	1980

Revolutions

Revolution any rapid, far-reaching, or violent change in the political, social, or economic structure of society. It has usually been applied to different forms of political change; the American Revolution (War of Independence) where colonists broke free from their colonial ties and established a sovereign, independent state; the French Revolution, where an absolute monarchy was overthrown by opposition from inside the country and a popular rising; and the Russian Revolution, where a repressive monarchy was overthrown by those seeking to institute widespread social and economic changes in line with a socialist model. While political revolutions are often associated with violence, there are other types of change, which often have just as much impact on society. Most notable is the Industrial Revolution, a process that has imposed massive changes on economies and societies since the mid-18th century. From the 1980s, a new 'silicon' revolution can be identified, involving the increasing use of computers to undertake tasks formerly done 'by hand'.

Industrial Revolution the sudden acceleration of technical development that occurred in Europe from the late 18th century, and which transferred the balance of political power from the landowner to the industrial capitalist, and created an organized industrial working class. The great achievement of the first phase (to 1830) was the invention of the steam engine in Britain, originally developed for draining mines, but rapidly put to use in factories and in the railways. In the second phase, from 1830 to the early 20th century, the Industrial Revolution enlarged its scope from Europe to the world, with some initial exploitation of 'colonial' possessions by European powers as a preliminary to their independent development. During this period, the internal combustion engine and electricity were developed. In 1911, Rutherford split the atom and opened up the prospect of nuclear power. Electronic devices were developed, which made possible automation at such a sophisticated level that even managerial decision-making came within the capabilities of machines.

French Revolution the forcible abolition of the *Ancien Régime* 'old order of things' (feudalism and absolute monarchy) 1789–99.
1789 5 May the States General (an assembly of the three 'estates', nobles, clergy, and commons) met at Versailles, bent on establishing a new constitution; *17 June* National Assembly formed by the Third Estate (commons); *14 July* Bastille was taken by the mob when Louis XVI attempted repressive moves.
1791 20 June flight of the royal family to Varennes; 14 Sept Louis, brought back as a prisoner, accepted the new constitution.
1792 20 April war declared on Austria, which threatened to suppress the revolution; *10 Aug* royal palace stormed by the French mob; *21 Sept* First Republic proclaimed.
1793 21 Jan Louis XVI executed; *2 June* overthrow of the moderate Girondists by the Jacobins; rule of the dictatorial Committee of Public Safety; *5 Sept* the mass executions of the Terror began.
1794 27 July (9 Thermidor under the Revolutionary calendar) fall of Robespierre and end of the Terror; the Directory (a body of five directors) established to hold a middle course between Royalism and Jacobinism. It ruled until Napoleon seized power in 1799.

Bastille a fortress prison in Paris, stormed by the mob at the beginning of the revolution on 14 July 1789, when it was found to contain only seven prisoners.

The governor and most of the garrison were killed and the building razed.

Commune of Paris first body that took this name between 1789–94 and acted as the municipal government of Paris from the storming of the Bastille to the fall of Robespierre.

Jacobins extremist republican club founded at Versailles in 1789, which later used a former Jacobin (Dominican) friary as its headquarters in Paris. It was led by Robespierre and closed after his execution in 1794.

Girondins right wing republicans of the French Revolution whose leaders came from the Gironde *departement* of France.

Robespierre Maximilien. French politician, 'the Sea Green Incorruptible'. As Jacobin leader in the National Convention, he supported the execution of Louis XVI and the overthrow of the Girondins, and as dominant member of the Committee of Public Safety, instituted the Reign of Terror in 1793. His extremist zeal made him enemies on both left and right, resulting in his overthrow and death by guillotine in July 1794.

Danton Georges Jacques. French lawyer and leading revolutionary. Influential in the early years of the revolution in Paris, he was instrumental in organizing the rising of 10 Aug 1792, which overthrew the monarchy. He also helped to instigate the revolutionary tribunal and the Committee of Public Safety in 1793. He led the Committee until July 1793 but was then superseded by Robespierre. An attempt to reassert his power failed and he was guillotined in 1794.

Marat Jean Paul 1743–1793. French revolutionary leader and journalist. He was the idol of the Paris revolutionary crowds, and was elected in 1792 to the National Convention, where he carried on a long struggle with the Girondins, ending in their overthrow in May 1793. In July he was murdered by Charlotte Corday.

revolutions of 1848 a series of revolts in various parts of Europe against monarchial rule. While some of the revolutionaries had republican ideas, many more were motivated by economic grievances. The revolution began in France and then spread to Italy, the Austrian Empire, and to Germany where the short-lived Frankfurt Parliament put forward ideas about German political unity. None of the revolutions enjoyed any lasting success, and most were violently suppressed within a few months.

Indian Mutiny (1857–58) the revolt of the Bengal Army against the British in India. The movement was confined to the north, from Bengal to the Punjab, and central India. Most support came from the army and recently dethroned princes, but in some areas it developed into a peasant rising or general revolt. Outstanding episodes were the seizure of Delhi by the rebels, and its seige and recapture by the British, and the defence of Lucknow by a British garrison. The mutiny led to the end of rule by the British East Indian Co. and its replacement by direct Crown administration.

Paris Commune the second body to bear this name. A provisional government of socialist and left-wing republicans, elected in March 1871 after an attempt by the right-wing National Assembly at Versailles to disarm the Paris National Guard, it held power until May, when the Versailles troops captured Paris and massacred at least 20,000 people. It is famous as the first socialist government in history.

Chinese Revolution a series of major political upheavals which began in 1911 with a nationalist revolt, which overthrew the Manchu imperial dynasty in 1912. Led by Sun Yat-sen (1923–25) and then by Chiang Kai-shek (1925–49), the nationalists came under increasing pressure form the growing communist movement. The 6,000 mile 'Long March' of the Chinese communists (1934–35) to escape from the nationalist forces saw Mao Zedong emerge as leader. After World War II, the conflict expanded into open civil war (1946–49) with the nationalists finally being defeated at Nanking. This effectively established communist rule in China under the leadership of Mao.

Sun Yat-sen or **Sun Zhong Shan** 1867–1925. Chinese revolutionary, founder of the Guomindang, and moving spirit behind the revolution of 1911 that overthrew the Manchu dynasty. He was briefly president 1912, but the reactionaries gained the ascendant, and he broke away to try to establish an independent republic in S China based in Canton. He lacked organizational ability, but his three 'people's principles' of nationalism, democracy, and social reform were influential.

Chiang Kai-shek or **Jiang Jie Shi** Chinese statesman. He took part in the revolution of 1911, and after the death of Sun Yat-sen was made commander-in-chief of the Guomindang armies in S China in 1925. The initial collaboration with the communists, broken in 1927, was resumed following the Xi An incident, and he nominally headed the struggle against the Japanese invaders, receiving the Japanese surrender in 1945. Civil war then resumed between communists and nationalists, and ended in the defeat of Chiang in 1949 and the limitation of his rule to Taiwan.

Mao Zedong or **Mao Tse-Tung** 1893–1976. Chinese statesman, the 'Great Helmsman'. Born in Hunan, he became the leader of the communists in 1927. After the rupture with the nationalists, led by Chiang Kai-shek, Mao Zedong and his troops undertook the 'Long March' of 10,000 km/6000 mi 1934–35 from SE to NW China, the prelude to his ascent to power. Again in nominal alliance with Chiang against the Japanese 1937–45, he subsequently defeated him, and proclaimed the People's Republic of China in 1949. As chairman of the Communist Party, he provided the pattern for the development of the country through the Great Leap Forward of 1959, and the Cultural Revolution of 1966 based on his thoughts contained in the 'Little Red Book'. His reputation plunged after his death, but was later somewhat restored.

Russian Revolution two revolutions of March and Nov 1917, which began with the overthrow of the Romanov Imperial dynasty and ended with the the establishment of a state run by Lenin and the Bolsheviks. The revolution of March 1917 arose in part from the repressive nature of tsarist government but primarily as a result of the mismanagement of World

War I after 1914. Riots in St Petersburg led to the abdication of Tsar Nicholas II and the formation of a provisional government under Kerensky. The provisional government ruled until Oct 1917 but found its power increasingly undermined by the soldiers' and workers' soviets in Petrograd (St Petersburg) and Moscow. During this period, the Bolsheviks under Lenin's guidance, had concentrated on gaining control of the soviets and advocating an end to the war and land reform. Under the slogan 'All power to the Soviets', they staged a coup on the night of 6–7 Nov that overthrew the government. The second All-Russian Congress of Soviets, which met the following day, proclaimed itself the new government of Russia. The Bolshevik seizure of power led to peace with Germany through the Treaty of Brest-Litovsk, but also to civil war as anti-Bolshevik elements within the army attempted to seize power. The war lasted until 1920, when the Red Army, organized by Trotsky, finally overcame 'white' opposition.

Lenin Vladimir Ilich Ulyanov 1870–1924. Born 22 April 1870 at Simbinsk (Ulyanovsk), Vladimir Ilich Ulyanov was converted to Marxism in 1889 and exiled to Siberia in 1895 as a result of subversive activity. After 1900, he spent most of his time in Western Europe, emerging as the leader of the more radical Bolshevik section of Russian Social Democracy. Returning to Russia in April 1917 with German help, Lenin assumed control of the Bolshevik movement and was instrumental in organizing the coup of 6–7 Nov. From then until his death in 1924, he effectively controlled Russia, establishing Bolshevik rule and the beginnings of communism. In addition, he consolidated his position as a great Marxist theoretician, modifying traditional Marxist doctrine to fit the objective conditions prevailing in Russia, a doctrine known as Marxism–Leninism which became the basis of communist ideology.

Trotsky Leon 1879–1940. Born 7 Nov 1879 at Yanovka. Communist theorist, agitator, and collaborator with Lenin after the two met in exile in London in 1902. Trotsky was a leading member of the Bolshevik movement in 1917 and helped organize the overthrow of the provisional government. He was instrumental in building up the Red Army to the point where it could win the civil war and acted as commissioner for foreign affairs until 1924. He was ousted during the power struggle which followed Lenin's death, but he remained active in opposing Stalin's rule until he was assassinated in Aug 1940.

Cuban Revolution the overthrow of the Batista regime in Jan 1959 by Fidel Castro and the 26 July Movement. Having led abortive coups in 1953 and 1956, Castro succeeded in overthrowing Batista with a force of only 5,000 men. Politically non-aligned, Castro was increasingly forced to seek Eastern Bloc help for government as a result of US opposition, which culminated in the abortive 'Bay of Pigs' invasion of 1961, sponsored by the CIA. The missile crisis of 1962 highlighted Russian involvement in Cuba. Between 1959 and 1974, Cuba, led by Castro, his brother Raúl, and initially, Che Guevara, adopted economic and social policies based on the principles of Marxism–Leninism and relied almost exclusively on communist help. After 1974, in an attempt to stabilise the economy, Castro reintroduced incentives

into society with the maxim that each 'should receive according to his work' rather than according to his need.

Castro Ruz Fidel 1927– . Cuban prime minister. Of wealthy parentage, Castro was educated at Jesuit schools and, after studying law at the University of Havana, gained a reputation through his work for poor clients. He strongly opposed the Batista dictatorship, and with his brother Raúl, took part in an unsuccessful attack on the army barracks at Santiago de Cuba in 1953. After spending some time in exile in the US and Mexico, Castro attempted a secret landing in Cuba in 1956 in which all but 11 of his supporters were killed. He eventually gathered an army of over 5,000 which overthrew Batista in 1959 and he became prime minister a few months later. He became president in 1976, and in 1979 also president of the Non-Aligned Movement. His brother Raúl was appointed minister of armed forces in 1959.

Guevara Ernesto 'Che' 1928–67. Revolutionary. Born in Argentina, he was trained as a doctor, but in 1953 left the country because of his opposition to Peron. In effecting the Cuban revolution of 1959, he was second only to Castro and his brother, but in 1965 moved on to fight against white mercenaries in the Congo, and then to Bolivia, where he was killed in an unsuccessful attempt to lead a peasant rising. His revolutionary technique using minimum resources has been influential, but his orthodox Marxism has been obscured by romanticizing disciples.

Chilean Revolution the period between 1970 and 1973 and the presidency of Salvador Allende, the world's first democratically elected Marxist head of state. Allende was brought to power in 1970 as the head of the Popular Unity alliance of socialists, communists, and radicals, a victory which owed more to the disunity of the Christian Democrat opposition than a major shift in voter preferences. Allende was committed to extensive social and economic reforms to be carried out within the existing political structure – the so-called 'peaceful road to socialism'. Nationalization of key industries and increased contacts with Eastern Bloc countries strained Chile's traditional economic relations with the USA and the West. His failure to stabilize the economy created widespread opposition; Allende was unable to fulfil the expectations of his supporters or quell the fears of his opponents about the pace of change. This led to increasing political polarization which culminated in a military coup in Sept 1973. The Allende regime was overthrown and replaced by a four-man junta led by General Pinochet.

Allende Gossens Salvador 1908– . Born in Valparaiso, Chile, Allende became a Marxist activist in the 1930s and rose to prominence as a left-wing presidential candidate in 1952, 1958, and 1964. In each election he had the support of the socialist and communist movements but was defeated by the Christian Democrats and Nationalists. Elected in 1970 as the candidate of the Popular Front alliance, Allende never succeeded in keeping the electoral alliance together in government. His failure to solve the country's economic problems or to deal with political subversion allowed the army to stage the 1973 coup which brought about Allende's death, and those of many of his supporters.

Nicaraguan Revolution the revolt led by the FSLN (Sandinist National Liberation Front named after Augusto Cesar Sandino, killed by the National Guard in 1934) against the dictatorship established by the father of the president Anastasio 'Tacho' Somoza. The dictatorship of the Somoza family had been underwritten by US support but this was of little help in 1978–79 when the Sandinistas mounted a full scale challenge to the regime and the hated National Guard. Somoza was forced into exile and assassinated in Paraguay in 1980. Since the revolution, the Sandinistas have taken political control of the country, introducing socialist policies and receiving help from Eastern Bloc countries, while US aid has dried up. The Sandinista government has had to contend with severe economic problems and also the activities of a counter-revolutionary movement, the Contras, operating in the north of the country with US monetary and technical support.

Iranian Revolution the revolution in Iran 1979 that deposed the shah 15 Jan and led to the popular return of Ayatollah Khomeini 1 Feb. Opposition to the shah's one-party regime (introduced 1975) became so great that he was forced to quit the country, leaving the way open for Khomeini's return. Khomeini, exiled for 25 years, had led an effective campaign from France. He appointed Mehdi Bazargan as prime minister 1979–80; real power, however, remained with Khomeini's Islamic Revolutionary Council. Revolutionary forces took control of the country, and Khomeini announced the establishment of the Islamic Republic, in which a return was made to the strict observance of Muslim principles and tradition. The harshness of the Islamic codes caused increasing opposition to Khomeini's regime, which led to a power struggle after his death 1989. The more moderate Hoshemi Rafsanjani became president.

revolutions of 1989 a series of revolutions in various countries of Eastern Europe against communist rule. By 1990, most had moved from monist to pluralist political systems.

Mikhail Gorbachev's official encouragement of *perestroika* (radical restructuring), and *glasnost* (greater political openness), largely for economic reasons, unleashed a wave of simmering discontent, both within the USSR (notably in the Baltic states of Estonia, Latvia, and Lithuania, and in Belarus, the Ukraine, and Moldova) and in several East European countries. Until the late 1980s, any potentially damaging discontent, however widespread, had been kept in check by the use of, or threat of military force controlled from Moscow – as in the termination of the Prague Spring experiment 1968 in Czechoslovakia.

Bulgaria, Czechoslovakia, East Germany, Hungary, Poland, Romania, Albania, and Yugoslavia were not as 'reluctantly content' with their lot as had been supposed, though they still subscribed to a form of one-party communism. Though many of the countries achieved bloodless coups (Bulgaria, Czechoslovakia, and Hungary), some were more dramatic: Romania's 'Christmas Revolution' 1989, in which Nicolae Ceauşescu was shot, was short and bloody. East Germany's revolution witnessed the symbolic dismantling of the Berlin Wall Nov 1989, with formal unification of East and West Germany Oct 1990. In Yugoslavia, the multiparty systems established in Slovenia and Croatia led to several republics calling for secession, and fighting between Serbs and Croats in Croatia 1991.

ASIA and AUSTRALASIA

AFRICA and the MIDDLE EAST

2.5 million BC

2.5 million *Homo habilis* used stone tools in Africa.
1.7 million *Homo habilis* built first structured habitats.
1 million *Homo erectus* able to control fire.
c. 130,000 *Homo sapiens* in Africa.

800,000 *Homo erectus* began colonizing Asia.
c. 50,000 Modern humans in Asia.

30,000 Tools in use in Japan.
30,000–10,000 Aboriginal migration to Australia from S India, Sri Lanka and SE Asia.
c. 10,000 Harvesting of wild seeds in SW Asia.

10,000

c. 7500 First agriculture in SW Asia.

c. 8500 Wheat and barley cultivated in Jordan.
c. 7500 Goats and sheep domesticated in Near East.
c. 7000 Walled settlement at Jericho.
c. 5000 Sumerians settled in Mesopotamia.

c. 4000 Rice grown in China. Indus valley became a population centre.

5000

3000

c. 3500 Height of Sumerian civilization.
c. 3000 Menes united Egypt. Semitic tribes occupied Assyria.
2600 Egyptians retaliated at Palestinian attacks on trade caravans. Semitic tribes in Syria and N Africa.
c. 2500 Great Pyramids at Giza built.
c. 2350 Sargon founded Akkadian Empire.
c. 2200 Tribesmen from Iran destroyed Akkadian Empire.
1925 Hittites conquered Babylon.

2850 Start of legendary 'golden age' in China.
2800–2200 Sage Kings period in China.

c. 2500 Indus civilization began in India.
2500–250 Jomon culture in Japan.
2200–1700 Xia dynasty in China.

2000

c. 1760–c. 1122 Shang dynasty in China.

c. 1650 Hittite Old Kingdom established.
c. 1580 Hyksos driven out of Egypt. Egypt reunited under Ahmose.
1400–1200 Hittite New Empire.

c. 1500 Aryan invasion of India. Collapse of Indus civilization.
c. 1400 Iron Age under way in India and W Asia.
1285 Egyptians and Hittites fought over, then divided, Syria.
c. 1122–256 Zhou dynasty in China.

c. 1250 Israelites under Moses left Egypt.
1200–332 Phoenicians built up empire.
1175 Egypt split into two kingdoms.
1100–612 Assyrian Empire in Mesopotamia.
1025 Hebrew monarchy founded.
970 Death of King David.
970–c. 937 Reign of King Solomon.
850 Phoenicians founded Carthage.

1000

750 Foundation of Kushan kingdom.

660 Jimmu became first emperor of Japan.

721 Assyrians conquered Israel.
689 Assyrians destroyed Babylon.
c. 625 End of Assyrian Empire.
550 Cyrus seized Median throne and began to build empire.
529 Persians conquered Egypt.
c. 522 Massacre of Magi priests in Persia.

570 Taoism founded.
560 Sakya Muni (later Buddha) born.
551 Confucius born.

500

500 Vedda conquered by Sinhalese in Sri Lanka.

403–221 'Warring states' period in China.

332 Macedonians under Alexander the Great conquered Asia Minor, Phoenicia, Persia, and Egypt.

321–185 Mauryan dynasty in India.
313 Tibet founded.
300 Agriculture began in Japan.

221–206 Qin dynasty in China.

EUROPE

AMERICAS

2.5 million BC

2.5 million BC

800,000 Europe colonized by *Homo erectus*.
c. 130,000 *Homo erectus* in Europe, able to control fire.

60,000–35,000 Ice Age landbridge between Asia and Alaska allowed migration from Siberia towards America.

c. 35,000 Modern humans in Europe.

40,000 Probable arrival of modern humans in Australia.

c. 15,000 Date of cave wall paintings at Lascaux, France.

c. 23,000 Modern humans in Americas.
9000 South America settled by peoples from Central America.

10,000

8400 Domesticated dogs in America.
8000 Ciboney people of S America reached Hispaniola.

c. 6000 First farming communities appeared in SE Europe. S Sweden inhabited.

c. 5000 Domestication of llamas in South America. Agriculture developed in Mexico.

5000

5000–4000 Inuit people arrived in N America.

c. 3000 Minoan civilization in Crete. Athens first inhabited.

3000

2600 Maya civilization began in the Yucatán peninsula.

2500 Agriculture developed in S America.

c. 2500 Stonehenge built in England.

c. 2200–1450 Middle Minoan age flourished because of control of sea.

2000

c. 1700 Bronze Age began in Europe.
1674 Hyksos invaded Europe.
c. 1580 Start of Mycenean civilization.

1500 Olmec civilization in Central America. Farming settlements developed in Peru.

c. 1300 First Celts appeared, in Upper Danube region.

1200 Sack of Troy.
1120 End of Mycenean civilization.

1200–800 Chavin culture blossomed in Peru (to 200).
1000–500 Zapotecs built ceremonial centre Monte Albán.

1000

c. 900 Etruscans settled in Italy.
c. 800 Building of Carthage.
776 First Olympic Games, in Greece.
753 Traditional date for founding of Rome.
736–716 First Messenian War.
650–630 Second Messenian War.

510 Roman republic founded.
499–404 Greek-Persian wars.
431–404 Peloponnesian wars.
4th century Gauls entered N Italy.
399 Death of Socrates.
359 Philip became king of Macedonia.

c. 500 Beginning of Maya civilization.

500

300 Olmec disappeared, replaced by regional cultures.

264–41 First Punic War (Rome and Carthage).
225 Romans defeated Gauls at Talamone.
218–201 Second Punic War.

ASIA and AUSTRALASIA	AFRICA and the MIDDLE EAST
206 Han dynasty began in China. **185–30** Shunga dynasty in India. **155–50** Indio-Greek kingdom in Indus valley, founded by Menander. **108** China annexed Korea.	**133** Asia Minor became a province of Rome. **64** Romans conquered Syria.

AD

1st century Kushans invaded India. **58** Buddhism introduced to China. **91** Han invaded Mongolia.	**4** Birth of Jesus Christ. **30** Jesus Christ crucified. **50** Rise of kingdom of Axum in NE Africa. **70** Revolt of Jews against Rome. Jerusalem sacked. **106** Jordan became part of Roman province of Arabia.

200

200 Huns invaded Afghanistan, ruling to 540. **201–250** Andgra dynasty in S India. **220** End of Han dynasty in China. Three Kingdoms period to 581. **225** End of Andgra dynasty in S India. **270–550** Gupta Empire in India.	**220** Goths invaded Asia Minor and Balkan Peninsula. **224** Foundation of Sassanian Empire in Persia.

300

4th century Ainu people driven into N Japan.	**330** Constantine the Great shifted seat of power to Byzantium, renamed Constantinople, and briefly united Roman Empire.

400

400–500 Mon kingdom in Burma.	

500

c. 500 Huns secured control over NW India. **550** End of Gupta Empire.	**525** Abyssinians conquered Yemen. **534** Byzantines reconquered N Africa. **539–562** War between Byzantines and Persia. **570** Muhammad, founder of Islam, born in Mecca. **572–591** War between Byzantines and Persia. **575** Persians overthrew Abyssinians in Yemen.

600

581–618 Sui dynasty united China. **600–650** Harsha dynasty in India. **607** First Japanese ambassadors to China. **618–907** Tang dynasty in China. **636** Rise of feudal nobility in Japan. **638** Burma founded. **644** China invaded Korea. **645** Reform in Japan at start of Nara period (645– 784).	**618** Persians conquered Egypt. **622** Flight of Muhammad to Medina. **633–41** Arabs conquered Persia. **632** Death of Muhammad. **637** Sassanian Empire destroyed by Muslims. **639–42** Arabs conquered Egypt. **650** Byzantine Empire partly overrun by Muslims. **661** Ommayad dynasty of the Islamic empire founded. **697** Arabs destroyed Carthage.

700

c. 700–800 Hinduism drove Buddhism from India. **712** Moslems conquered Sindh. **740** Gurjara dynasty united N India and defeated the Arabs. **753–63** Rebellion by Anlu-shan increased China's vulnerability to invaders.	**750–1258** Abbasid caliphate founded in Baghdad. **760** Turkish Empire founded.

800

800 Rajputs began to set up kingdom in India.	**809** Death of Haroun-al-Raschid began 200 years of chaos in Arab Empire.

EUROPE	AMERICAS	
216 Hannibal crossed the Alps. **c. 200** Romans began to conquer Spain. **149–46** Third Punic War. Carthage destroyed.		
	100 Teotihuacán established.	
60 First triumvirate formed. **50** Romans conquered Gaul. **43** Second triumvirate formed. **31** Battle of Actium. Roman Empire founded.		
		AD
43 Romans invaded Britain. **98** Trajan became Roman emperor, with Empire at its largest. **122–26** Hadrian's Wall built.		
	200–1000 Arawak Indians migrated from NE South America to Caribbean.	**200**
268 Goths sacked Athens, Sparta, and Corinth.		
	300 Rise of Maya civilization in Central America.	**300**
360 Huns invaded Europe. **395** Roman Empire split into Western and Eastern (Byzantine) Empires. **c. 400–500** Picts, Saxons, Jutes, and Angles invaded Britain.		**400**
410 Goths sacked Rome. Romans withdrew from Britain. **470** Huns withdrew from Europe. **476** Fall of the (Western) Roman Empire. **481** Clovis founded Frankish kingdom. **496** Franks conquered Alemanni (Germany).		
	500–1600 American Indians in Mississippi basin became farmers with small settlements. **550** Toltec kingdom continued Teotihuacán civilization.	**500**
	600–1000 Rise of Ayamará in Bolivia.	**600**
664 Synod of Whitby decided to adopt Roman, not Celtic, form of Christianity for Britain. **685** Picts stopped Northumbrians invading Scotland. **711** Moors invaded Spain. **720** Moors invaded France. **732** Moors driven out of France.		**700**
771 Charlemagne conquered Saxony and continued campaign for Carolingians. **793** Viking raids on Britain began. **800** Charlemagne crowned Holy Roman Emperor. **811** Bulars defeated Byzantines.		**800**

ASIA and AUSTRALASIA

AFRICA and the MIDDLE EAST

845 Buddhism proscribed in China.

867 Basil I began Macedonian dynasty of Byzantine empire (to 1056).

900

c. 907 Chola power established in S India.
907–960 Civil war in China.

909 Fatimid dynasty founded in N Africa.

960–1279 Song dynasty in China.

969 Fatimids conquered Egypt.

1000

1050–1200 Start of main Muslim invasions into India from Afghanistan. Collapse of Hindu kingdoms.

c. 1000 Rise of Kanem empire (N Nigeria).
1045 Byzantines conquered Armenia.
c. 1050 Almoravid empire in Morocco began. Egyptian anarchy ended by Badr al Jamali.
1054 Abdallah ben Yasim began Muslim conquest of W Africa. End of kingdom of Ghana.
1055 Seljuk Turks took over caliphate.
1061 Almoravids conquered N Africa.
1071 Turks conquered Anatolia.

1096–99 First Crusade.

1100

1100–1192 Civil war in Japan.

1127–1279 Southern Song dynasty in China.

1147–49 Second Crusade.
1160 Normans expelled from N Africa.
1171 Saladin conquered Egypt.
1174 Saladin launched Holy War against Christians.
1176 Turks defeated Byzantium over Asia Minor in Battle of Myriokephalon.
1189–92 Third Crusade.

1190 Mongol leader Genghis Khan began to build Mongol Empire in E Asia.
1192 Kamakura shogunate began in Japan.

1200

1205 Hōjō family set up feudal government in Japan.
1206 Delhi sultanate founded. Mogul state founded.
1221 Mongols attacked Delhi sultanate.
1234 Mongols destroyed Jin Empire.

c. 1200 Christian Sudan kingdoms invaded by Muslims.
1202 Fourth Crusade.
1204 Crusaders sacked Constantinople.
1212 Children's Crusade.
1240 Mali Empire founded in W Africa.
1244 Egyptian Khwarazmi took Jerusalem.
1250–1517 Mameluke dynasty in Egypt.

1258 Mongols took Baghdad.
1260–1368 Yuan dynasty in China.
1274 Kublai Khan failed in attempt to invade Japan.
1275–95 Marco Polo's travels.
1279 Moguls in control over whole of China.
1281 Great Mongol attack on Japan, defeated.

1270 Ethiopia revitalized over next two centuries.

1300

1291 End of the Crusades.
1300 Ottoman Empire founded.

1325–51 Sultanate of Delhi at its height under Muhammad ibn Tughluq.

EUROPE

826 Arabs conquered Crete.
843 Treaty of Verdun broke up Frankish Empire.
844 Scotland unified under Kenneth MacAlpin.
855 Former Carolingian empire broken up.
874 Vikings settled in Iceland.
878 Treaty of Wedmore between Alfred and the Danes.
885–86 Viking siege of Paris.
900 Start of Christian reconquest of Spain.
907 Commercial treaties between Kiev and Constantinople.
959 Edgar crowned king of all England.
962 Otto I crowned Holy Roman emperor.
985 Viking settlements in Greenland.
987 Capet became king of France.
991 Renewed Viking raids on England.

1018 Byzantines conquered Bulgarians.
1023–91 Abbadid Muslim dynasty in Seville.

1054 Schism between Roman and Greek churches.
1061 Normans conquered Messina.

1066 Normans conquered England.
1077–1122 War between papacy and Holy Roman Empire.
1084 Normans sacked Rome.
1086 Domesday Book of England completed.

1122 Concordat of Worms.
1127 Normans completed conquest of Sicily.
1143 Benjamin of Tudela travelled to India via Constantinople, returning via Egypt and Sicily.
1144 Republican rule established in Rome.
1147 Portugal became independent monarchy.
1169 English invaded Ireland.
1170 Thomas à Becket murdered.

1177 Peace of Venice between Pope and Holy Roman Emperor.
1183 Peace of Constance between Pope, Holy Roman Emperor and the Lombards.

1204 King John of England lost Normandy to France.
1215 Magna Carta.
1223 Mongols overan S steppes of Russia.
1236 Arabs lost Córdoba to Castile.
1240 Mongols took Moscow and Kiev.
1241 Mongols defeated Germans and invaded Poland and Hungary, but later withdrew from Europe.
1259 Treaty of Paris (France and England).
1265 Birth of English Parliament.
1282 Sicilians rose against Normans.
1294 Start of Franco-Scottish alliance.

1306 Robert Bruce became King Robert I of Scotland.
1314 Battle of Bannockburn, Robert defeated English.

AMERICAS

850 Nahuas began invading from N Mexico. First Maya civilization in Yucatán and Guatemala collapsed.

900

985 Toltecs now controlled Mexico.
987–1185 League of Mayapán in South America.

1000 Chimú state formed in Peru. Peak of Mayan civilization in Yucatán. Caribs from South America destroyed Arawak culture in Caribbean. Viking Leif Ericsson said to have reached Nova Scotia.

1000

1100 Nahuas in control of central Mexican plateau.

1100

1168 Toltec capital Tula fell to the Aztecs.

1180 Toltec state fell to nomadic tribes.
1194 Chichen Itzá fell.

1200–50 Foundation of Aztec Empire in N Mexico.

1200

1250 Inca settled at Cuzco, S Peru. Chimú established in N Peru.

1300

1327 Tenochtitlán founded by Aztecs.

ASIA and AUSTRALASIA	AFRICA and the MIDDLE EAST

1350

1336 Kingdom of Vijayanagar founded in S India.
1339 Ashikaga shogunate in Japan. Political chaos.
1350 Siam founded.
1355 Illayas Shad established independent Bengal.
1363 Tamerlane began conquest of Asia.
1368 Mongol Yuan dynasty in China.
1368–1644 Ming dynasty in China.

1354 Turks took Gallipoli.

1375 Mamelukes captured Sis and overthrew Armenians.
1380 Tamerlane began series of conquests, including Persia, Georgia, Russia, and Egypt.
1390 Byzantines lost some territory to Turks.

1400

1396 Battle of Micopolis won by Bajazet.
1398–99 Tamerlane invaded India, annexing Punjab.
1401 Tamerlane conquered Damascus and Baghdad.
1403–24 Emperor Yongle extended territories in China.
1405–33 Zheng He's expeditions from China.
1428 First great peasant revolt in Japan.

1416 Venetians defeated Turks off Gallipoli.

1442 First black slaves sent to Portugal.
1445 Diniz Diaz reached Cape Verde.
1448 Portuguese built first European fort on African coast, at Arguin (Mauritania).

1450

1447 Break up of Tamerlane's empire.

1453 Turks with Mohammad II took Constantinople.
1455 Cadamosto explored Senegal.
1462 Castile captured Gibralta from Arabs.
1468 Songhai Empire began to grow in NW Africa.
1470 Portuguese reached Gold Coast of W Africa.

1479 Peace of Constantinople: Venice ceded territory to Turks.

1483 Russians began to explore Siberia.

1482 Portuguese set up trading base on Gold Coast (Ghana).
1484 Portuguese reached mouth of the Congo.
1488 Bartolomeu Diaz rounded Cape of Good Hope.

1489 Yasuf Adilshah became last independent ruler of Bijapur.

1498 Vasco da Gama reached India.

1500

1505 Trading contracts between India and Portugal.
1511 Portuguese reached Siam. Portuguese took Malacca.
1517 European traders gained access to China.

1501–1736 Safavid dynasty in Persia.
1505 Portuguese reached Mozambique.
1507 Cadamosto explored Gambia.

1516–17 Turks conquered Egypt.

1521 Tartars from Crimea invaded S Russia as far as Moscow.

1526 Babur founded Mogul dynasty (to 1761), and conquered most of India.
1529 Treaty of Saragossa: Spain and Portugal divided up Far East.

1531 Portuguese trading posts in Mozambique established.

EUROPE	AMERICAS	

1337 Hundred Years' War began between England and France.
1348–49 Black Death in Europe.
1356 Ottoman Turks entered Europe.
1360 Treaty of Brétigny ended first stage of Hundred Years' War.
1378–1417 Great Schism of Rome and Avignon.

1381 Peasants' Revolt in England.
1385 Portugal ensured independence from Spain.
1397 Union of Kalmar united Sweden, Norway, and Denmark (to 1520).

1401 Union of Poland and Lithuania.

1410 Battle of Tannenberg.
1415 Battle of Agincourt.

1453 End of Hundred Years' War.
1454 Peace of Lodi between Venice and Milan.
1455–85 Wars of the Roses.
1456 Turks conquered Athens.
1459 Turks overran Serbia.
1463 Turks conquered Bosnia. Turks at war with Venice (to 1479).

1475 Turkey took over Crimea.

1480 Ivan III of Moscow overthrew Mongols.
1481 Spanish Inquisition established.
1482 Peace of Arras.

1483 Burgundy and Brittany annexed by France.

1492 Spain conquered Granada from Muslims.

1504 Treaty of Lyons: France ceded Naples to Spain.
1511 Holy League formed.
1512–22 War between Russia and Poland.
1517 Protestant Reformation began.
1520 Field of the Cloth of Gold.
1521 Diet of Worms.
1526 League of Cognac: France, Florence, Venice, Milan, and papacy against Charles V.
1529 Peace of Cambrai.

1358 Tlatelolco founded.

1400–1500 Aztec empire grew to cover most of Mexico.

1428 Aztecs in control of central basin of Mexico.
1438 Inca rebuilt Cuzco and began expansion.
1440 Aztecs crowned Montezuma I. Battle of Cuzco: Inca defeated Chanca.
1441 Mayapán fell to Xius. Maya broken up into smaller states.

1476 Inca conquered Chimú (Ecuador).
1479 Treaty of Alvaovas between Spain and Portugal about Atlantic islands.
1480 Inca took over Bolivia.

1484 Inca conquered N and central Chile, and NW Argentina.

1492 Columbus reached West Indies.
1494 Treaty of Tordesillas.
1496 Aztecs captured Tehuantepec.
1497 Cabot landed at Newfoundland. Spanish settled Hispaniola.
1500 Aztecs took Soconuscuo, threatening Mayan territory.
1505 Spanish conquered Puerto Rico.
1511–26 Inca pacified N territories.

1519–21 Aztec empire fell to Cortés.

1532 Portuguese began to settle in Brazil.
1532–33 Inca fell to Pizarro.

1350

1400

1450

1500

ASIA and AUSTRALASIA

AFRICA and the MIDDLE EAST

1551 Turks took Tripoli.

1555 Accession of Akbar in India.

1569 Turks captured the Yemen.

1574 Portuguese began colonizing Angola.

1575

1575 Akbar conquered Bengal.

1582 Japan united under Hideyoshi.

1592–93 Hideyoshi's invasion of Korea repelled.

1591 Morocco conquered Songhay.

1600

1600 English East India Company formed.
1602 Dutch East India Company formed.
1603 Tokugawa shogunate began in Japan, based in Tokyo.
1606 First European sighting of Australia, from a Dutch ship.
1609 Portugal took Ceylon from Dutch.
1615 Tribes in N China started forming military groupings, later called Manchus.
1619 Dutch empire founded in East Indies.

1602–18 Turkey and Persia at war.

1621 Iraq reoccupied by Persia.

1624 Japan expelled Spanish.

1625

1627 Korea became a tributary state of China.

1632 Portuguese withdrew from Bengal.

1637 Russian explorers reached Pacific coast.
1639 Dutch took Trincomalee (in Ceylon) from Portuguese. Japan expelled Portuguese traders.
1641 Japan isolated itself from the rest of the world (to 1853). Dutch ousted Portuguese from Malacca.
1642 Tasman landed at Tasmania.
1644–1912 Qing (Manchu) dynasty in China.

1633 Portuguese expelled from Abyssinian territory.
1637 French settlements set up in Senegal.
1638 Dutch took Mauritius.

1650

1650 Rise of Ashanti in W Africa.
1652 Dutch founded Cape colony.

1658 Dutch took over rule of Ceylon from Portuguese.
1658–1707 Aurangzeb Empire in India.

1664 French East India Company formed.

EUROPE	AMERICAS
1534 Henry VIII broke with Rome. Jesuits founded. **1536** Union of England and Wales.	**1534** French reached Canada. **1536–1609** French and British began to penetrate Spanish Caribbean. **1538** Spain conquered Bolivia. **1539** Spain annexed Cuba.
1541 Turks conquered Hungary. **1547** Ivan the Terrible became tsar of Russia. **1552** Russia conquered Tatar state.	**c. 1545** Silver found in Peru and Mexico.
1562–98 French Wars of Religion. **1563–70** Sweden and Denmark at war. **1568** Dutch Revolt began. **1571** Battle of Lepanto.	**1565** Spanish settled Florida. **1567** Portuguese founded Rio de Janeiro.
1579 United Provinces (Dutch) proclaimed independence from Spain in Union of Utrecht. **1580** Spain conquered Portugal.	**1575** Frobisher reached Frobisher Bay, Canada. **1575** **1584** Raleigh annexed Virginia.
1588 English defeated Spanish Armada. **1589** Bourbon dynasty began in France. **1595–98** Franco-Spanish War. **1598** Edict of Nantes.	
1603 James I king of England and Scotland.	**1600** **1605** French settled in Nova Scotia. England claimed Barbados. **1607** English founded Jamestown, Virginia. **1608** Quebec founded.
1613–1917 Romanov dynasty in Russia. **1618** Outbreak of Thirty Years' War.	
	1619 First American legislature at Virginia. **1620** *Mayflower* arrived in New England. **1621** Dutch West India Company founded. Dutch took over Guyana. **1624–54** Dutch-Portuguese wars over Brazil. **1625** Dutch founded New Amsterdam. **1625** **1627** England secured Barbados. **1630** Great migration to the New World began. **1630–40** English and French made claims on West Indies possessions. **1634** English Catholics founded Maryland.
1635 French entered Thirty Years' War against Spain.	
1640 Portugal and Catalonia rebelled against Spain.	
1642–48 English Civil War. **1645–69** Turkey won war with Venice over Crete. **1648** Treaty of Westphalia ended Thirty Years' War. **1649** Charles I executed. Britain a republic to 1660.	**1642** Montreal founded. **1650** French began colonizing Canada. **1650**
1652–54 First Anglo-Dutch war. **1654–67** Russo-Polish war. **1656–59** Anglo-Spanish war. **1657–59** Dutch Republic and Portuguese at war. **1659** Treaty of Pyrenees ended Franco-Spanish war. **1660** Charles II restored in England. **1661–64** Turkey and Holy Roman Empire at war.	**1654** Portuguese drove Dutch from Brazil. **1655** English took Jamaica from Spanish. **1664** English seized New Amsterdam from Dutch.

ASIA and AUSTRALASIA	AFRICA and the MIDDLE EAST
	1665 Battle of Ambuila: Portuguese killed king of the Kongo kingdom.
1668 England acquired Bombay.	
1669 Hindus persecuted in India by Aurangzeb.	
1674 Sivaji defeated Mongols. Maratha kingdom invaded. **1676–78** Sikh uprisings in India. **1683** Taiwan (Formosa) incorporated into China. **1685** All Chinese ports opened to foreign trade.	
1689 Treaty of Nerchinsk between China and Russia over boundaries.	
1690 Mogul conquests of S India almost complete. **1693** China invaded Mongolia.	
c. 1700 British East India Company took control of key Indian ports.	**1699** Sultanate of Oman established on E coast of Africa.
1707 Death of Mogul emperor Aurangzeb: power struggle in India to 1761.	
	1711 Russo-Turkish war.
	1714 Tripoli gained independence from Turkey.
1720 Chinese invaded Tibet.	
1735–95 Chinese expanded into Turkestan, Annam (Vietnam), Burma, and Nepal.	**1729** Arabs took Mombasa from Portugal. **1734–35** Turko-Persian war. **1736–39** Russo-Turkish war.
1739 Persians pillaged Delhi.	
1747 Afghanistan united.	
1751 Britain captured Arcot, India, from French. China invaded Tibet. **1752** Fall of Toungoo dynasty in Burma. **1756** Black hole of Calcutta. **1757** Battle of Plassey: Britain defeated nawab of Bengal. **1759** China occupied E Turkestan. **1760** French defeated in India leaving British supreme. **1761** Battle of Panipat ended Maratha attempt to dominate India.	**1750** Ngwane III conquered Swaziland.

Left margin dates: 1670, 1700, 1725, 1750

EUROPE	AMERICAS	
1665–67 Second Anglo-Dutch war. **1667–68** War of Devolution by France against Spain. **1668** Triple Alliance of England, Netherlands, and Sweden against France. Spain recognized Portugal's independence. **1670** Secret Treaty of Dover between England and France. **1672–74** Third Anglo-Dutch war. **1678** Treaty of Nijmegen marked peak of Louis XIV's ambitions. **1683** Turkey's defeat at Vienna ended advance of Islam into Europe. **1685** Edict of Nantes revoked. Huguenot exodus. **1688** Revolution in England. **1688–97** War of the League of Augsburg (France against Grand Alliance). **1690** Battle of the Boyne in Ireland. **1695–96** Russo-Turkish war. **1697** Peace of Ryswick marked defeat of France by Grand Alliance. **1699** Turks lost Hungary to Austria. **1700–21** Great Northern War. **1701** Act of Settlement. **1701–13** War of the Spanish Succession. **1704** Britain captured Gibraltar. **1707** Union of England and Scotland. **1709** Battle of Poltava. **1713** Treaty of Utrecht. **1715** Jacobite rising. Death of Louis XIV. **1718** England declared war on Spain. **1721** Proclamation of the Russian Empire. **1725** Treaty of Vienna (Pragmatic Sanction). **1727–28** Spanish siege on Gibraltar. **1727–29** War between Britain and Spain. **1731** Treaty of Vienna (England, Holland, Spain, and Holy Roman emperor). **1740** Accessions of Frederick the Great and Maria Theresa. **1740–48** War of the Austrian Succession. **1745** Peace of Dresden. **1745–46** Last Jacobite uprising in Britain. **1762** Accession of Catherine the Great. **1763** Peace of Paris ended Seven Years' War.	**1670** Hudson's Bay Company founded. **1681** Pennsylvania colony founded by Quakers. **1683** Peace treaty between William Penn and North American Indians. **1697** French gained Haiti. **1699** French began to colonize Louisiana. **1710** British captured Nova Scotia from French. **1711** French captured Rio de Janeiro. **1713** British gained Newfoundland, Hudson Bay. **1733** Dawes gained control of Santa Cruz. Georgia became the 13th British crown colony. **1739** New Granada parted from Peru. **1750** Spanish-Portuguese treaty over South America. **1754** Seven Years' (French and Indian) War between Europeans in North America. **1758–60** British conquered French Canada. **1761** Britain gained control of West Indies. **1763** Peace of Paris: France lost American possessions to Britain. Ottawa Indians fought British.	**1670** **1700** **1725** **1750**

	ASIA and AUSTRALASIA	AFRICA and the MIDDLE EAST
1770	**1767–69** First Mysore War. **1768** Cook landed in New Zealand and E coast of Australia. **1769** Burmese recognized Chinese sovereignty. **1770** Cook claimed New South Wales as a colony. **1775–82** First Maratha War. **1780–84** Second Mysore War. **1784** India Act. Burma conquered Arakan. **1786** British took Malacca. **1788** Colonization of Australia began at Botany Bay. **1790–92** Third Mysore War.	 **1776** Dutch Afrikaners met Bantu. **1787** First European settlement of Freetown. **1792** British took Cape of Good Hope.
	1796 British took Ceylon. **1799** Kingdom of Mysore divided between Britain and Hyderabad.	**1794** Slave trade in French colonies ended. **1798** French invaded Egypt.
1800	**1800–50** Laos broken up into several states. **1803–05** First Maratha War in India. **1804** Castle Hill rising in New South Wales. **1804–08** Japan rejected Russian and British trading attempts. **1806** Sepoy mutiny at Vellore, India.	**1801** French defeated Turks at Heliopolis, but later left Egypt. **1801–24** Osei Bonsu reduced powers of Ashanti chiefs. **1804–08** Uthman dan Fodio led jihad against the Hausa. **1805** Mehemet Ali proclaimed pasha of Egypt. **1806** Britain seized Cape Colony from Dutch.
	1812 Chinese edict against Christianity. **1817** Ceylon revolt suppressed by British. **1817–18** Second Maratha War.	**1810** Fulani Empire of Sokoto (Nigeria) established. **1811** Massacre of Mamelukes. **1814** Cape Province sold to British.
	1819 Singapore founded as British colony. Kashmir conquered by Ranjit Singh. **1824** Assam ceded to Britain. **1824–26** First Anglo-Burmese War. **1824–51** General Chakri of Siam founded new dynasty.	**1818** Zulu kingdom formed by Shaka. Sheik Ahmuda's jihad. **1820** Ali Pasha's revolt crushed by Turks. **1820–22** Egypt conquered Sudan. **1822** Liberia founded for freed slaves. Mzilika rebelled against Shaka. **1824** Mzilika led Ndebele to western Transvaal. First Ashanti War.
1825	**1825–50** Java War.	

EUROPE	AMERICAS	
	1765 Britain imposed Stamp Act on American colonies.	
	1768–71 Cook explored Pacific.	
		1770
1772 First partition of Poland.		
	1773 Boston Tea Party.	
1774 Turkey left Crimea.	**1774** Declaration of Rights and Grievances.	
	1775–83 American War of Independence.	
	1776 Declaration of Independence issued. Viceroyalty of River Plate founded.	
	1780–81 Peruvian Indians revolted against Spanish.	
	1781 Battle of Yorktown.	
	1784 US began trade with China.	
	1787–89 US constitution formed.	
1789 French Revolution began.	**1789** Washington first US president.	
	1791 Canada divided in Upper and Lower Canada, and allowed representative government.	
1792 Russian Empire extended to Black Sea.		
1793 Execution of Louis XVI. Start of Revolutionary War. Second partition of Poland.		
1793–94 Reign of Terror in France.		
1795 Poland ceased to exist.	**1795** Treaty of San Lorenzo between US and Spain over border rights.	
	1796 Britain captured Guyana.	
1799 Napoleon seized power as first consul.		
	1800 Jefferson became US president.	**1800**
1801 Act of Union (Britain and Ireland).	**1800–15** Tripolitan War.	
1802 Peace of Amiens (Britain and France).		
1803 Britain and France at war again.	**1803** Louisiana Purchase of large tract of land from France.	
1804 Napoleon became emperor of the French.	**1804** Haiti independent.	
	1804–06 Lewis and Clark expedition in US to find land route to Pacific.	
1805 Battles of Trafalgar and Austerlitz.		
1806 Battle of Jena. End of Holy Roman Empire.		
1807 Treaty of Tilsit. Treaty of Fontainebleau. Slave trade abolished by Britain.	**1807** Colombian Independent Movement started in Venezuela.	
1808 Peninsular War started. Treaty of Bucharest ended Russo-Turkish war. Russia seized Finland.	**1809** Ecuador became part of Colombia.	
1811 Luddite riots began in England.	**1811** Paraguay and Venezuela gained independence. Battle of Tippecanoe.	
1812 Napoleon's retreat from Russia.	**1812–14** Anglo-American war.	
1813 Quadruple Alliance. Battle of Leipzig.		
1814 Congress of Vienna. Restoration of Bourbons in France.	**1814** Treaty of Ghent.	
1815 Napoleon's Hundred Days. Battle of Waterloo. German Confederation formed.	**1815** Battle of New Orleans.	
	1816 United Provinces of South America. Argentine independent.	
1818 Congress of Aix-la-Chapelle.	**1818** Chile independent.	
1819 Peterloo massacre in England.	**1819** Colombia independent.	
	1820 Missouri compromise.	
1821–32 Greek War of Independence.	**1821** Mexico, Central America, and Peru proclaimed independence.	
	1822 Brazil independent.	
	1823 Monroe Doctrine.	
1825 Decembrist uprising.	**1825** Bolivia independent.	**1825**

ASIA and AUSTRALASIA

1826 Straits Settlements formed by East India Company.
1828 Western Australia founded.

1830 Britain gained Mysore.
1830–54 Russia conquered Kazakhstan.

1834 South Australia founded.
1836 Uprising in Japan.

1837 Colonization of New Zealand began.
1838 Myall Creek massacre.
1838–42 First Afghan War.

1839–42 First Opium War.
1840 Treaty of Waitangi. Britain annexed New Zealand.
1841 Britain occupied Hong Kong.
1841–43 Reforms in Japan.
1842 Treaty of Nanking opened up Chinese trade with West, creating treaty ports. Massacre at Khyber Pass during British retreat from Afghanistan.
1843 French occupied Tahiti. Britain conquered Sind.
1845–49 Britain annexed Punjab. Sikh Wars.

1850 Victoria separated from New South Wales.
1850–64 Taiping Rebellion in China.

1852–54 Second Burmese War (with Britain).
1853 Britain annexed Nagpur.

1855 Treaty of Peshawar (Afghanistan and Britain).
1855–60 Second Opium War (China and Britain).
1856 Britain annexed Oudh. Tasmania became self-governing. US Admiral Perry entered Japanese ports.
1857–58 Indian Mutiny suppressed.
1858 Treaty of Aigun: Russia gained Amur from China.
1860 End of Opium War: Britain and France occupied Beijing. Peking Pact signed.
1860–70 Second Maori War.

1863 Cambodia became a French protectorate.

1867 Convict transportation to Australia ended.

AFRICA and the MIDDLE EAST

1826–7 Sheikh Ahmadu conquered Timbuktu.
1827 Battle of Navarino: Turkish and Egyptian fleets destroyed.

1830 Algeria became a French colony.

1836 Great Trek by Boers.

1838 Massacre of Zulus at Battle of Blood River.

1839 Mehemet Ali defeated Ottomans. Tanzimat Reforms began.
1840 Said ibn Sayyid took over Zanzibar. Matabeleland founded. Natal proclaimed.
1841 Mehemet Ali recognized as hereditary ruler of Egypt, virtually independent of Ottomans.
1842 French occupied Tahiti.

1843 Orange Free State founded. Natal became a British colony.

1846–53 Xhosa War.

1847 Liberia independent.

1850 Britain bought Danish settlements in W Africa.
1850–53 Anglo-Kaffir War.
1851 British occupied Lagos.

1853 Russo-Turkish war over Palestine.
1854 Orange Free State founded.

1856 Natal became a crown colony.
1856–57 Persia at war with Britain after taking Herat (Afghanistan).

1859 Morocco and Spain at war.

1861 Lagos ceded to Britain.

1862 Messina conquered by Tukolor al-Hajj Umar.

1830
1840
1850
1860

EUROPE

1827–29 Russo-Turkish war.

1830 Revolutions in France, Poland, Belgium, Italy.
1831 Young Italy movement formed.
1832 First Reform Act (Britain).
1833 Prussian Zollverein formed.
1834 Slavery ended in British colonies.

1837 Accession of Queen Victoria.

1839 First Chartist petition.

1845–51 Irish potato famine.
1846 Corn Laws repealed.

1847 Il Risorgimento founded.
1848 Revolutions throughout Europe. Communist Manifesto published.

1852 Fall of 2nd Republic in France. Napoleon III took power.
1854–56 Crimean War.

1856 Congress of Paris.

1859 France and Sardinia at war with Austria.
1860 Carlist uprising in Spain.

1861 Emancipation of Russian serfs. Unification of Italy.
1862 Bismarck prime minister of Prussia.
1863 Greek revolution.

1864 Denmark and France at war with Prussian alliance.
1866 Austro-Prussian War. Crete revolted against Turks.
1867 Second Great Reform Act in Britain. Garibaldi's march on Rome.

AMERICAS

1826 First Pan-American Congress in Panama.

1828 Uruguay independent. Treaty of Rio de Janeiro. Andrew Jackson elected US president.
1830 Partition of Gran Columbia. Removal of American Indians to reservations began.
1832 Black Hawk War. Britain occupied Falkland Islands.

1836 Battles of the Alamo and San Jacinto. Texas gained independence from Spain.
1837 Papineau and Mackenzie rebellions. Montreal rebellion.
1838 Durham Report. First crossing of Atlantic by steamship.
1839 Central America split into numerous states.

1840 Act of Union for Canada.

1842 Oregon Trail opened up. Webster-Ashburton Treaty

1845 Texas annexed by US.
1846 Oregon Treaty.
1846–48 Mexican-American War.
1848 Californian Gold Rush. Hawaii granted independence. Maya Indian revolt in Mexico suppressed.
1850 New US states compromised over slavery. California joined US.
1851 Cuba unsuccessfully declared independence.

1853–54 Gadsden Purchase.
1854 Elgin Treaty re Canadian trade by US and Britain.

1858–61 Mexican War of Reform.

1860 Confederacy formed by Southern states.

1861–65 American Civil War.

1863 Dutch abolished slavery in colonies. Slavery abolished in US. France occupied Mexico.
1864–70 Triple Alliance (Paraguayan) War.
1865 Rebellion in Jamaica.

1867 Alaska purchased by US from Russia. Dominion of Canada established. French left Mexico.
1867–70 Reconstruction Acts in US.

1830

1840

1850

1860

ASIA and AUSTRALASIA

1868 Meiji dynasty restored in Japan.

1874 Britain annexed Fiji.
1876 Korea independent.
1877 Queen Victoria became empress of India.
Satsuma rebellion in Japan.
1878–80 Second Anglo-Afghan War.

1880 French annexed Tahiti.

1882 French captured Hanoi.

1883–85 Sino-French War.

1885 Anglo-Russian crisis over Afghan boundary.
Indian National Congress met.
1885–86 Anglo-Burmese War: Britain annexed
Upper Burma, and rest joined India.
1887 French Indochina established.

1893 Durrand Agreement (India and Afghanistan
frontier defined).
1894–95 Sino-Japanese War over Korea.
1896 Manchuria Convention (Russia and China).

1898 Hundred Days' reform in China.

1900 Boxer Rebellion in China.
1901 Australian Commonwealth established. US
took over Philippines. Russia occupied Manchuria.
1902 Anglo-Japanese treaty.

1904–05 Russo-Japanese War.

1905 Partition of Bengal. Battle of Mukden.

1907 New Zealand an independent dominion. Dutch
conquered Sumatra.
1908 Dutch took over Bali. Muslim League formed.
1909 Indian Councils Act.
1910 Japan annexed Korea. China ended slavery.
1911–12 Revolution in China: republic established.

AFRICA and the MIDDLE EAST

1868 Basutoland became a British protectorate.
1869 Suez Canal opened.

1871 Britain annexed Kimberley diamond fields.

1873–74 Second Ashanti War.
1874 Gold Coast (Ghana) colony founded by
Britain.
1877 Britain annexed Transvaal.
1877–79 Last Xhosa War.

1879 Zulu Wars. Britain and France took control of
Egypt.

1881 First South African War. Revolt in Egypt.
French invaded Tunis.
1882 French left Egypt to British, who occupied
Cairo.
1883 Britain left Sudan.
1884 Berlin Conference accelerated European
'scramble for Africa'. Germany acquired SW Africa,
Togoland, Cameroons.
1885 Germany annexed Tanganyika and Zanzibar.

1886 Royal Niger Company formed.

1887 Ethiopia and Italy at war.

1889 Italy gained protectorate over Ethiopia.
1890 Rhodesia formed. Britain annexed Uganda.
Zanzibar Settlement (Britain and Germany).
1891 Anglo-Portuguese Convention on E Africa.
Anglo-Italian agreement on NE Africa.
1892 Anglo-German agreement over Cameroons.
1893 Matabele War: French gained Ivory Coast.

1895–96 Ethiopia won war with Italy.
1896 French annexed Madagascar. Britain won last
Ashanti War.
1898 Fashoda Incident. Britain agreed 99-year lease
on New Territories (Hong Kong).
1899–1902 Second South African War.
1900 North and South Nigeria became British
protectorates. Britain annexed Orange Free State
and Transvaal. First Pan-African Conference.
1902 End of South African War.
1903 Britain occupied North Nigeria (Sokoto).
1904 Germans massacred Herero rebels, SW
Africa.
1905 Moroccan crisis (France and Germany).
1906 Revolution in Iran. Algeciras Conference.

1908 Young Turk Revolution. Belgium took over
Congo Free State.
1910 South Africa became independent dominion.
1911 Agadir Crisis (Germany and France over
Morocco). Italy conquered Libya. Italy and Turkey
at war to 1912.
1914 Egypt and Cyprus declared British
protectorates.

1870

1880

1890

1900

1910

EUROPE	AMERICAS
1868 Military rising in Spain.	**1868** Ku Klux Klan formed.
	1868–78 Cuba and Spain at war.
1870 Third Republic in France. Italy annexed Rome.	**1869–70** Red River Rebellion.
1870–71 Franco-Prussian War.	**1871** British Columbia and Vancouver joined Dominion of Canada.
1872–76 2nd Carlist uprising in Spain.	**1871–86** Military conflict with Apaches.
	1873 Spain ended slavery in Puerto Rico.
1876 Turks massacred Bulgarians.	**1876** Battle of Little Big Horn.
1877–78 Russo-Turkish War.	
1878 Congress of Berlin.	
1879 Treaty of San Stefano (Russia and Turkey). Dual Alliance (Austria and Germany).	**1879** War of the Pacific: Chile beat Peru and Bolivia, which lost its coastline.
	c. 1880 End of Indian wars in Argentina and Chile.
1882 Triple Alliance (Italy, Germany, and Austria) formed.	
1886 Treaty of Bucharest ended Serbo-Bulgarian War.	**1886** Spain ended slavery in Cuba.
1887 Reinsurance Treaty of neutrality between Germany and Russia.	**1888** Slavery ended in Brazil.
1889 Great London Dock Strike.	**1889** Brazil became a republic.
1893 Franco-Russian alliance.	**1893** US overthrew Hawaiian government.
1894–1906 Dreyfus Affair in France.	**1895** Cuba rebelled against Spain.
1897 Greece and Turkey at war over Crete.	**1898** Spanish-American War over Cuba. US annexed Hawaii.
	1902 Cuba fully independent. Anglo-German force seized Venezuelan fleet.
1904 Entente Cordiale (Britain and France).	**1904** Treaty between Bolivia and Chile.
1905 Revolution in Russia. Sweden and Norway split.	**1906–09** US occupied Cuba.
1907 Triple Entente (France, Britain, and Russia).	
	1909–11 Civil war in Honduras.
1910 Revolution in Portugal.	**1910** Revolution in Mexico.
1912 Treaty of Lausanne.	**1912** Arizona and New Mexico joined US.
1914 Start of World War I between Central Powers and Allies (France and Germany). Battle of Tannenburg.	**1914** Panama Canal opened.

1870

1880

1890

1900

1910

ASIA and AUSTRALASIA	AFRICA and the MIDDLE EAST
1915 **1915** Twenty-one demands by Japan on China.	
	1916–18 Mesopotamia campaign. **1918** Britain captured Syria.
1919 Punjab riots. Amritsar Massacre. **1920**	**1919** Ottoman Empire dismantled. Arab Revolt in Egypt. **1920** Kenya a British colony. Turkish Revolution.
1921 Breakaway Chinese government set up under Sun Yat-sen.	**1921–58** Hashemite kingdom in Iraq. **1922** End of British protectorate in Egypt.
	1923 Turkish republic founded. Palestine, Transjordan, and Iraq mandated to Britain: Syria to France. **1924** N Rhodesia became a British protectorate.
1926 Chiang Kai-shek firmly in control in China. **1927** Chiang Kai-shek began purge of communists.	**1926** Independent Lebanon established.
	1929 Major Arab-Jewish conflict in Palestine.
1930 **1931** Mukden Incident. Japan occupied Manchuria to 1932. **1932** Indian Congress declared illegal.	**1932** Saudi Arabia established.
1933 Japan left League of Nations. **1934–35** Long March by Chinese communists. **1935** Burma separated from India. Philippines became self-governing. **1936** Japan signed Anti-Comintern Pact with Germany.	**1935–36** Ethiopia occupied by Italy. **1936** Arab-Jewish conflict in Palestine.
1937–45 Japan invaded China.	
1940	**1940** Italy expelled from Somalia, Eritrea, and Ethiopia.
1941 Japan attacked Pearl Harbor and began to overrun SE Asia. China joined Allies in World War II. **1942** Japan conquered Singapore.	**1941** World War II reached N Africa. **1942** Battle of El Alamein. **1943** End of Axis resistance in N Africa.
1944 Battle of Leyte Gulf. **1945** Atomic bombs dropped on Japan, which surrendered. US and USSR troops entered Korea. **1946–49** Civil war in China. **1947** Indonesia established. India, Pakistan, and Laos independent. **1948** Korea divided. Burma independent.	**1946** Jordan independent. **1948** Israel established. **1948** Apartheid began in South Africa. **1948–49** First Arab-Israeli War.
1949	

EUROPE

AMERICAS

EUROPE	AMERICAS	
1915 Italy joined Allies. Bulgaria joined Central Powers.		**1915**
1915–16 Gallipoli campaign.		
1916 Battles of Verdun, Jutland, and the Somme. Portugal and Romania joined war against Germany. Easter Rising in Ireland.	**1916** US bought Danish West Indies (Virgin Islands).	
1917 Revolutions in Russia.	**1917** US declared war on Germany. US bought Dutch West Indies.	
1918 Central Powers surrendered. Civil wars began in Ireland (to 1921), and Russia (to 1922).		
1919 Treaty of Versailles.	**1919** Woodrow Wilson advocated League of Nations.	
1920 League of Nations formed.	**1920** US Senate rejected Versailles settlement. Civil war in Mexico.	**1920**
1921 Irish Free State created in S Ireland.	**1920–33** Prohibition in US.	
1922 USSR formed. Mussolini prime minister in Italy.		
1923 French occupied Ruhr.		
	1924 US limited immigration and barred Japanese.	
1925 Locarno Conference.		
	1927 Kellogg-Briand pact.	
	1927–30 Cristeros Revolt in Mexico.	
1927 Kellogg-Briand pact.	**1928** Chaco War (Paraguay and Bolivia).	
1929 Yugoslavia created.	**1929** Wall Street Crash.	
1929–33 Great Depression.		
1930 Statute of Westminster in Britain.	**1930** Revolutions in Argentina and Brazil.	**1930**
	1932 Ottawa Conference.	
	1932–35 Bolivia and Paraguay at war.	
1933 Hitler became chancellor of Germany.	**1933** Roosevelt's New Deal.	
1934 Balkan Pact.		
1936 Rome-Berlin Axis formed. Germany and Japan signed Anti-Comintern Pact.		
1936–39 Spanish Civil War.		
1937 Italy joined Anti-Comintern Pact.		
1938 Munich Crisis.		
1939 Italy conquered Albania. Germany signed non-aggression pact with USSR. USSR invaded Finland. Germany invaded Czechoslovakia and Poland. Start of World War II.		
1940 Germany invaded France. Italy joined war against Allies. Germany began exterminating Jews.		**1940**
1941 Germany invaded USSR.	**1941** Japan bombed Pearl Harbor. US entered World War II.	
	1942 Brazil entered World War II.	
1943 Italy surrendered. USSR drove Germans back.		
1944 Normandy landings.		
1945 End of World War II.	**1945** United Nations formed.	
1945–48 Communist takeover in E Europe.		
1946–49 Greek Civil War.		
1948–49 Berlin blockade.	**1948** Organization of American States formed. Marshall Plan of aid for Europe.	
1949 North Atlantic Treaty Alliance formed. Germany divided into E and W. Comecon formed.		**1949**

ASIA and AUSTRALASIA	AFRICA and the MIDDLE EAST
1950	
1950–53 Korean War.	**1950** Anglo-Egyptian dispute over Suez Canal and Sudan.
1951 China occupied Tibet. French defeated by Vietminh. Colombo plan for economic development in S and SE Asia. Japan signed treaties of peace with 49 nations.	**1951** British troops entered canal zone.
	1952 Moroccan uprising against French.
	1952–55 Mau Mau campaign in Kenya.
	1953 Egypt became a republic.
1954 Vietnam independent and divided into North and South, which began a war. Laos and Cambodia independent. SEATO (SE Asian Treaty Organization) formed (to 1977).	**1954–62** Algerian War of Independence.
	1955 Baghdad Pact (Iran, Iraq, and Turkey).
1956 French recognized Moroccan and Tunisian independence.	**1956** Suez Crisis, and Canal nationalized. Morocco, Sudan, and Tunisia independent.
1957 Malaya independent.	**1957** Suez Canal reopened. Ghana independent.
1958 Singapore independent.	**1958** Revolution in Iraq. Egypt and Sudan formed United Arab Republic, which Yemen joined.
1960	
1959 China crushed uprising in Tibet, and had border clashes with India.	**1960** South Africa became a republic. Sharpeville massacre. Nigeria and Belgian Congo independent.
1962 Sino-Indian border clashes.	
1963 Military coup in S Vietnam.	**1963** Organization of African Unity formed. Kenya independent.
1964–66 War between Indonesia and Malaysia.	**1964** Tanzania founded. Malawi and Zambia independent. Palestine Liberation Organization formed.
1965 US marines entered Vietnam. India and Pakistan at war over Kashmir.	**1965** White Rhodesian government formed.
1966–76 Cultural Revolution in China.	
	1967 Six-day Arab-Israeli War. Suez Canal shut.
	1967–70 Biafra War in Nigeria.
1968 Tet Offensive in Vietnam.	**1969** Libyan revolution.
1970	**1970** Civil war in Jordan.
1971 Fighting in Indochina spread into Laos and Cambodia. Tension between India and Pakistan. Bangladesh proclaimed. China joined United Nations.	
1972 Sri Lanka independent.	**1972** Lebanese Civil War. Uganda expelled Asians.
1973 US troops left Vietnam.	**1973** Arab-Israeli (Yom Kippur) War. Oil prices raised.
	1974 Oil crisis.
1975 End of Vietnam War.	**1975** Suez Canal re-opened. Portuguese colonies gained independence.
1976 North and South Vietnam reunited.	**1976** Civil war in Angola. Soweto riots in South Africa.
1977 Military coup in Pakistan.	**1977** Israeli and Egyptian leaders visited each other's countries. Israel settled on West Bank.
1978 Military junta seized power in Afghanistan.	**1978** Camp David agreement. Border troubles between Israel and Lebanon.
1979 Civil war in Afghanistan. Russia entered Afghanistan. Chinese invaded Vietnam.	**1979** Islamic Revolution in Iran. Egypt and Israel signed peace treaty.
1979–88 Vietnam invaded Cambodia.	
1980	**1980** Rhodesia independent (Zimbabwe).
	1980–88 Iran-Iraq War.
	1981 President Sadat of Egypt assassinated.
	1982 Israel invaded Lebanon. Numerous atrocities in Beirut.
1984 UK affirmed agreement to return Hong Kong to China in 1997.	**1984** Ethiopian famine. Foreign nationals left Beirut.

EUROPE	**AMERICAS**	
1950 East Germany and Poland agreed frontier.	**1950–54** McCarthy anti-communist campaign.	**1950**
1951 Schuman Plan (France and Germany). **1952** End of Allied occupation of West Germany. Greece and Turkey joined NATO. **1953** Death of Stalin in USSR. **1954** Warsaw Pact formed. West Germany joined NATO.	**1953** Coup in Colombia. **1954** Revolution in Guatemala.	
1956 Soviet troops crushed uprising in Hungary. Polish revolt. **1957** European Economic Community established by six countries through Treaty of Rome.	**1956–57** Cuban Civil War. **1957** US Civil Rights Act. **1958** Alaska joined US. West Indies Federation formed. **1959** Cuban Revolution. Hawaii joined US. **1960** US invasion of Cuba failed.	
1961 Berlin Wall built.	**1961** Cuban Missile Crisis. Latin American Free Trade Association formed. **1962** Jamaica and Trinidad independent.	**1960**
1963 French vetoed British application to join EEC. Nuclear Test Ban Treaty signed in Moscow. **1964** Greek-Turkish tension over Cyprus.	**1963** Nuclear Test Ban Treaty. US President Kennedy assassinated. Race riots in Birmingham, Alabama. **1964** US Civil Rights Act.	
1966 France left NATO. **1967** Military coup in Greece. **1969** Violence in Northern Ireland.	**1968** Martin Luther King assassinated. **1969** US put men on the Moon.	
		1970
1972 British direct rule introduced in Northern Ireland. USSR signed SALT I accord. **1973** Britain, Ireland, and Denmark entered EEC. **1973–75** Helsinki Conference. **1974** Portuguese dictatorship overthrown. Partition of Cyprus. Northern Irish terrorism spread to British mainland. **1975** Democracy restored in Spain. Helsinki Agreement.	**1972** US signed SALT I accord. **1973** Military coup in Chile. **1974** Watergate scandal in US.	
1979 USSR signed SALT II accord.	**1979** US signed SALT II accord. Sandinistas overthrew Somoza in Nicaragua.	
1980 Solidarity formed in Poland.		**1980**
1981 Greece joined EC. **1982** Spain joined NATO. Falklands War (Britain and Argentina).	**1982** Falklands War (Argentina and Britain). **1983** US invaded Grenada.	

	ASIA and AUSTRALASIA	**AFRICA and the MIDDLE EAST**
1985		
	1986 Overthrow of President Marcos in Philippines.	**1986** US bombed Libya.
	1989 Soviet troops left Afghanistan. Democracy demonstrations in China crushed.	
1990		**1990** Dismantling of apartheid in South Africa began. Iraq invaded Kuwait. **1991** Gulf War. Middle East peace talks began.
1992	**1992** Muslims replaced communists to rule Afghanistan.	**1992** South Africa voted for majority rule: continued unrest. Civil war and famine in Somalia: US intervened.
	1993 Zemin became president of China.	**1993** Declaration of Principles signed between Israel and PLO.
1994		**1994** Mandela became president of South Africa. South Africa rejoined the Commonwealth. Israel withdrew from West Bank and Gaza Strip.
		1995 Cameroon and Mozambique admitted to the Commonwealth. Israeli prime minister, Yitzhak Rabin assassinated.
1996	**1996** First legislation in the world permitting euthanasia took effect in Northern Territory, Australia.	
1997	**1997** Hong Kong reverted to Chinese control. Fuji rejoined the Commonwealth.	**1997** Zaire renamed the Democratic Republic of Congo by Tutsi rebels. Laurent Kabila became president.

EUROPE

1985 Gorbachev came to power in USSR.
1986 Spain and Portugal joined EC.
1987 USSR signed Intermediate Nuclear Forces treaty.
1989 Berlin Wall opened. Revolutions in E Europe against communist rule.
1990 Germany reunified. Free elections in Hungary, Romania, Bulgaria, and Czechoslovakia.
1991 Civil war in Yugoslavia. USSR broke up into republics. Warsaw Pact disbanded. Gorbachev resigned.
1992 Yugoslavia broke up amid civil war. EC crisis over Maastricht Treaty. Czechoslovakia split into two.

1993 EC single market came into force. Czech and Slovak republics became separate countries. Maastrict Treaty came into force. Downing Street declaration set out principles for peace talks on Northern Ireland.

1994 Establishment of European Economic Area. IRA ceasefire.

1995 Austria, Finland and Sweden joined the EU. Chirac became president of France. Peace plan for Bosnia-Herzegovina signed.

1996 UN war tribunal investigated crimes against humanity committed during Yugoslavian civil war. IRA ceasefire broken.

1997 In Britain, Labour party, under Tony Blair, won general election. IRA restored ceasefire. Jospin became president of France.

AMERICAS

1986 Irangate scandal broke.
1987 US signed Intermediate Nuclear Forces treaty.

1991 US signed START treaty. New constitution in Colombia. Military coup in Haiti.

1992 Rio de Janeiro hosted Earth Summit.

1993 Jean Chrétien became prime minister of Canada.

1994 North American Free Trade Agreement (NAFTA)came into effect between Mexico, the USA, and Canada. Argentina, Brazil, Paraguay, and Uruguay signed pact creating the Souther Common Market (Mercosur).

1995 World Trade Organization inaugurated, succeeding GATT. Oklahoma City bombing.

1996 Bill Clinton re-elected president of USA.

1985

1990

1992

1994

1996

1997

WORLD LEADERS

Leaders of the Modern World (1945 to the present)

Adenauer Konrad 1876–1967. German Christian Democrat politician, chancellor of West Germany 1949–63. With the French president de Gaulle, he achieved the postwar reconciliation of France and Germany and strongly supported all measures designed to strengthen the Western bloc in Europe.

Alfonsín Foulkes Raúl Ricardo 1927– . Argentine politician, president 1983–89, leader of the moderate Radical Union Party (UCR). As president from the country's return to civilian government, he set up an investigation of the army's human-rights violations. Economic problems caused him to seek help from the International Monetary Fund and introduce austerity measures.

Allende Gossens Salvador 1908–1973. Chilean Marxist politician, president from 1970 until his death during a military coup in 1973. As president, Allende nationalized the banking and copper industries and instituted land reform, provoking the conservative elements in the country. As Chile's economy declined and strikes and disturbances supported by the US Central Intelligence Agency spread, the military staged a coup, during which Allende either was killed or committed suicide.

Amin (Dada) Idi 1926– . Ugandan politician, president 1971–79. He led the coup that deposed Milton Obote 1971, expelled the Asian community 1972, and exercised a reign of terror over his people. He fled to Libya when insurgent Ugandan and Tanzanian troops invaded the country 1979.

Andreotti Giulio 1919– . Italian Christian Democrat politician. He headed seven postwar governments: 1972–73, 1976–79 (four successive terms), and 1989–92 (two terms). In addition, he was defence minister eight times, and foreign minister five times. He was a fervent European. In 1993, Andreotti was among several high-ranking politicians under investigation for possible involvement in Italy's corruption network.

Antall Jozsef 1932– . Hungarian politician, prime minister 1990–1993. A former teacher and museum director, he led the centre-right Hungarian Democratic Forum (MDF) to electoral victory in April 1990, becoming Hungary's first post-communist prime minister. He promoted gradual, and successful, privatization and encouraged inward foreign investment. He was succeeded by Peter Boross.

Aquino (Maria) Corazon (born Cojuangco) 1933– . President of the Philippines 1986–92. She was instrumental in the nonviolent overthrow of President Ferdinand Marcos 1986. As president, she sought to rule in a conciliatory manner, but encountered opposition from left (communist guerrillas) and right (army coup attempts), and her land reforms were seen as inadequate.

Arafat Yassir 1929– . Palestinian nationalist politician, cofounder of al-Fatah 1956 and president of the Palestine Liberation Organization (PLO) from 1969. His support for Saddam Hussein after Iraq's invasion of Kuwait 1990 weakened his international standing, but he has since been influential in Middle East peace talks.

Assad Hafez al 1930– . Syrian Ba'athist politician, president from 1971. He became prime minister after a bloodless military coup 1970, and the following year was the first president to be elected by popular vote. Having suppressed dissent, he was re-elected 1978 and 1985. He is a Shia (Alawite) Muslim.

Attlee Clement (Richard), 1st Earl 1883–1967. British Labour politician. In the coalition government during World War II he was Lord Privy Seal 1940–42, dominions secretary 1942–43, and Lord President of the Council 1943–45, as well as deputy prime minister from 1942. As prime minister 1945–51, he introduced a sweeping programme of nationalization and a whole new system of social services.

Babangida Ibrahim 1941– . Nigerian politician and soldier, president 1985–1993. He became head of the Nigerian army in 1983 and in 1985 led a coup against President Buhari, assuming the presidency himself. In Jan 1992, responding to calls for a return to civilian rule, he announced dates for assembly and presidential elections later in the year. Alleging fraudulent electoral practices in the first primaries Sept 1992, Babangida subsequently delayed the date for a transition to civilian rule. In Nov 1993 General Sani Abacha took over as prime minister.

Balladur Edouard 1929– . French conservative politician, prime minister from 1993. He was the protégé of France's former premier and president, Georges Pompidou, during the 1960s and 1970s. Balladur later became a top adviser to former prime minister Jacques Chirac and was finance minister 1986–88. Following strong gains by the conservatives in the 1993 French election, Balladur was strongly placed for an eventual challenge for the presidency. Balladur is a strong supporter of the European Community and of maintaining close relations between France and Germany.

Banda Hastings Kamuzu 1902– . Malawi politician, president from 1966. He led his country's independence movement and was prime minister of Nyasaland (the former name of Malawi) from 1963. He became Malawi's first president 1966 and 1971 was named president for life; his rule has been authoritarian. Despite civil unrest during 1992, he has resisted calls for free, multiparty elections.

Bandaranaike Sirimavo (born Ratwatte) 1916– . Sri Lankan politician who succeeded her husband Solomon Bandaranaike to become the world's first female prime minister, 1960–65 and 1970–77, but was expelled from parliament 1980 for abuse of her powers while in office.

Begin Menachem 1913–1992. Israeli politician. He was leader of the extremist Irgun Zvai Leumi organization in Palestine from 1942, and prime minister of Israel 1977–83, as head of the right-wing Likud party. In 1978, Begin shared a Nobel Peace Prize with President Sadat of Egypt for work on the Camp David Agreements for a Middle East peace settlement.

Ben Bella Ahmed 1916– . Algerian politician. He was leader of the National Liberation Front (FLN) from 1952, the first prime minister of independent Algeria 1962–63, and its first president 1963–65. In 1965, Ben Bella was overthrown by Col Houari Boumédienne and detained until 1979. In 1985, he founded a new party, Mouvement pour la Démocratie en Algérie, and returned to Algeria 1990 after nine years in exile.

Ben-Gurion David. Adopted name of David Gruen 1886–1973. Israeli statesman and socialist politician, one of the founders of the state of Israel, the country's first prime minister 1948–53, and again 1955–63.

Bhutto Benazir 1953– . Pakistani politician, prime minister from 1993. She was leader of the Pakistan People's Party (PPP) from 1984 (in exile until 1986), and prime minister of Pakistan 1988–90, when the opposition manoeuvred her from office and charged her with corruption. She was the first female leader of a Muslim state.

Bhutto Zulfikar Ali 1928–1979. Pakistani politician, president 1971–73; prime minister from 1973 until the 1977 military coup led by General Zia ul-Haq. In 1978, Bhutto was sentenced to death for conspiring to murder a political opponent and was hanged the following year.

Blair, Tony (Anthony Charles Lynton) 1953– . British politician, leader of the Labour Party from 1994, prime minister from 1997. A centrist in the manner of his predecessor Smith, he became Labour's youngest leader by a large majority in the first fully democratic elections to the post July 1994. In 1995 he won approval of a new Labour Party charter, intended to distance the party from its traditional socialist base and promote 'social market' values. He and his party secured a landslide victory in the 1997 general election with a 179-seat majority.

Bokassa Jean-Bédel 1921– . President of the Central African Republic 1966–79 and later self-proclaimed emperor 1977–79. Commander in chief from 1963, in Dec 1965, he led the military coup that gave him the presidency. On 4 Dec 1976, he proclaimed the Central African Empire and one year later crowned himself as emperor for life. He was overthrown in 1979 and was in exile until 1986. Upon his return he was sentenced to death, but this was commuted to life imprisonment in 1988.

Bolger Jim (James) Brendan 1935– . New Zealand politician and prime minister from 1990. He held a variety of cabinet posts under Robert Muldoon's leadership 1977–84, and was an effective, if uncharismatic, leader of the opposition from March 1986, taking the National Party to electoral victory Oct 1990. In 1997 he lost the leadership of the NP to Jenny Shipley and subsequently resigned as prime minister.

Botha P(ieter) W(illem) 1916– . South African politician, prime minister 1978–84 and president 1984–89. Botha initiated a modification of apartheid, which later slowed in the face of Afrikaner (Boer) opposition. In 1984, he became the first executive state president. In 1989, he unwillingly resigned both party leadership and presidency after suffering a stroke, and was succeeded by F W de Klerk. dent in 1965 by a further coup.

Boutros-Ghali Boutros 1922– . Egyptian diplomat and politician, deputy prime minister 1991–92. He worked towards peace in the Middle East in the foreign ministry posts he held 1977–91. He became secretary general of the United Nations Jan 1992, and during his first year of office had to deal with the war in Bosnia-Herzegovina and famine in Somalia.

Bourguiba Habib ben Ali 1903– . Tunisian politician, first president of Tunisia 1957–87. In 1934, he founded the Destour Socialist Party (PSD), and led Tunisia's campaign for independence from France. He became prime minister 1956, president (for life from 1974) and prime minister of the Tunisian republic 1957; he was overthrown in a bloodless coup 1987.

Brandt Willy. Adopted name of Karl Herbert Frahm 1913–1992. German socialist politician, federal chancellor (premier) of West Germany 1969–74. He played a key role in the remoulding of the Social Democratic Party (SPD) as a moderate socialist force (leader 1964–87). As mayor of West Berlin 1957–66, Brandt became internationally known during the Berlin Wall crisis 1961. Nobel Peace Prize 1971.

Brezhnev Leonid Ilyich 1906–1982. Soviet leader. A protégé of Stalin and Khrushchev, he came to power (after he and Kosygin forced Khrushchev to resign) as general secretary of the Soviet Communist Party (CPSU) 1964–82 and was president 1977–82.

Brundtland Gro Harlem 1939– . Norwegian Labour politician. Environment minister 1974–76, she briefly took over as prime minister 1981, and was elected prime minister 1986 and again 1990. She chaired the World Commission on Environment and Development which produced the Brundtland Report, published as *Our Common Future* 1987. In 1992, she resigned as leader of the Norwegian Labour Party, a post she had held since 1981.

Bush George 1924– . 41st president of the USA 1989–93, a Republican. He was director of the Central Intelligence Agency (CIA) 1976-81 and US vice president 1981–89. As president, his response to the Soviet leader Gorbachev's diplomatic initiatives were initially criticized as inadequate, but his sending of US troops to depose his former ally, General Noriega of Panama, proved a popular move at home. Success in the 1991 Gulf War against Iraq further raised his standing. Domestic economic problems 1991–92 were followed by his defeat in the 1992 presidential elections by Democrat Bill Clinton.

Buthelezi Chief Gatsha 1928– . Zulu leader and politician, chief minister of KwaZulu, a black 'homeland' in the Republic of South Africa from 1970. He is the founder (1975) and president of Inkatha, a paramilitary organization for attaining a nonracial democratic political system. He has been accused of complicity in the factional violence between Inkatha and African National Congress supporters that has continued to rack the townships despite his signing of a peace accord with ANC leader, Nelson Mandela, Sept 1991.

Callaghan (Leonard) James, Baron Callaghan 1912– . British Labour politician. As chancellor of the Exchequer 1964–67, he introduced corporation and capital-gains taxes, and resigned following devaluation. He was home secretary 1967–70 and prime minister 1976–79 in a period of increasing economic stress.

Campbell Kim 1947– . Canadian Progressive Conservative politician and lawyer. She succeeded Brian Mulroney as prime minister 1993, becoming the first woman to hold this office. She held the posts of minister for state affairs and nothern development 1989–90, attorney general 1990–92, and defence minister 1992. Soon after taking over as prime minister, she lost the Oct 1993 election to the Liberal Party's candidate, Jean Chretien (1934–).

Carter Jimmy (James Earl) 1924– . 39th president of the USA 1977–81, a Democrat. In 1976, he narrowly wrested the presidency from Gerald Ford. Features of his presidency were the return of the Panama Canal Zone to Panama, the Camp David Agreements for peace in the Middle East, and the Iranian seizure of US embassy hostages. He was defeated by Ronald Reagan 1980.

Castro (Ruz) Fidel 1927– . Cuban communist politician, prime minister 1959–76 and president from 1976. He led two unsuccessful coups against the right-wing Batista regime and led the revolution that overthrew the dictator 1959. He raised the standard of living for most Cubans but dealt harshly with dissenters.

Cavaco Silva Anibal 1939– . Portuguese politician, finance minister 1980–81, and prime minister and Social Democratic Party (PSD) leader from 1985. Under his leadership Portugal joined the European Community 1985 and the Western European Union 1988.

Ceauşescu Nicolae 1918–1989. Romanian politician, leader of the Romanian Communist Party (RCP), in power 1965–89. He pursued a policy line independent of and critical of the USSR. He appointed family members, including his wife *Elena Ceauşescu*, to senior state and party posts, and governed in an increasingly repressive manner, zealously implementing schemes that impoverished the nation. The Ceauşescu were overthrown in a bloody revolutionary coup Dec 1989 and executed.

Chadli Benjedid 1929– . Algerian socialist politician, president 1979–92. An army colonel, he supported Boumédienne in the overthrow of Ben Bella 1965, and succeeded Boumédienne 1979, pursuing more moderate policies. Chadli resigned Jan 1992 following a victory for Islamic fundamentalists in the first round of assembly elections.

Chirac Jacques 1932– . French conservative politician, prime minister 1974–76 and 1986–88. He established the neo-Gaullist Rassemblement pour la République (RPR) 1976, and became mayor of Paris 1977.

Chissano Joaquim 1939– . Mozambique nationalist politician, president from 1986; foreign minister 1975–86. In Oct 1992, Chissano signed a peace accord with the leader of the rebel Mozambique National Resistance (MNR) party, bringing to an end 16 years of civil war.

Clinton Bill (William Jefferson) 1946– . 42nd president of the USA from 1993, a Democrat. He served as governor of Arkansas 1979–81, and 1983–93, establishing a liberal and progressive reputation. He became the first Democrat in the White House for 13 years. In Jan 1993, he delayed for six months an executive order to suspend the ban on homosexuals in the armed forces. In spring 1993, Congress passed his medium-term economic plan, combining spending cuts with tax increases targeted against the rich, to cut the huge federal budget deficit.

Collor de Mello Fernando 1949– . Brazilian politician, president 1990–92. As candidate of the centre-right National Reconstruction Party (PRN), he conducted the 1989 presidential campaign on a platform of rooting out government corruption and entrenched privileges. Rumours of his own past wrongdoings were rife by 1992, leading to his constitutional removal from office by a vote of impeachment in congress in Sept 1992. He resigned in Dec at the start of his trial, and was subsequently banned from public office for eight years. He was succeeded by Itamar Franco.

Craxi Bettino 1934– . Italian socialist politician, leader of the Italian Socialist Party (PSI) 1976–93, prime minister 1983–87. He has been accused of involvement in Italy's corruption network.

Dalai Lama 14th incarnation 1935– . Spiritual and temporal head of the Tibetan state until 1959, when he went into exile in protest against Chinese annexation and oppression. His people have continued to demand his return. The Dalai Lama was awarded the Nobel Peace Prize 1989 in recognition of his commitment to the nonviolent liberation of his homeland.

de Gaulle Charles André Joseph Marie 1890–1970. French general and first president of the Fifth Republic 1958–69. He organized the Free French troops fighting the Nazis 1940–44, was head of the provisional French government 1944–46, and leader of his own Gaullist party. In 1958, the national assembly asked him to form a government during France's economic recovery and to solve the crisis in Algeria. He became president at the end of 1958, having changed the constitution to provide for a presidential system, and served until 1969.

de Klerk F(rederik) W(illem) 1936– . South African National Party politician, president from 1989. He served in the cabinets of B J Vorster and P W Botha 1978–89, and replaced Botha as National Party leader Feb 1989 and as state president Aug 1989. In Feb 1990, he ended the ban on the African National Congress opposition movement and released its effective leader, Nelson Mandela. In Feb 1991, de Klerk promised the end of all apartheid legislation and a new multiracial constitution, and by June of the same year, had repealed all racially discriminating laws. In March 1992, a nationwide, whites-only referendum gave de Klerk a clear mandate to proceed with plans for major constitutional reform to end white minority rule. In Feb 1993, he and Nelson Mandela agreed to the formation of a government of national unity after free, nonracial elections in late 1993 or early 1994. De Klerk and Mandela shared the 1993 Nobel Prize for Peace.

Delors Jacques 1925– . French socialist politician, finance minister 1981–84. As president of the European Commission from 1984 he has overseen significant budgetary reform and the move towards a free European Community market in 1992, with increased powers residing in Brussels.

Demirel Suleyman 1924– . Turkish politician. Leader from 1964 of the Justice Party, he was prime minister 1965–71, 1975–77, and 1979–80. He favoured links with the West, full membership in the European Community, and foreign investment in Turkish industry.

Deng Xiaoping or *Teng Hsiao-ping* 1904–1997. Chinese political leader. A member of the Chinese Communist Party (CCP) from the 1920s, he took part in the Long March 1934–36. He was in the Politburo from 1955 until ousted in the Cultural Revolution 1966–69. Reinstated in the 1970s, he gradually took power and introduced a radical economic modernization programme. He retired from the Politburo 1987 and from his last official position (as chair of State Military Commission) March 1990. He appointed President Jiang Zemin to succeed him on his death in 1997.

Diouf Abdou 1935– . Senegalese left-wing politician, president from 1980. He became prime minister 1970 under President Leopold Senghor and, on his retirement, succeeded him, being re-elected in 1983, 1988, and 1993. His presidency has been characterized by authoritarianism.

Dubček Alexander 1921–1992. Czechoslovak politician, chair of the federal assembly 1989–92. He was a member of the Slovak resistance movement during World War II, and became first secretary of the Communist Party 1967–69. He launched a liberalization campaign (called the Prague Spring) that was opposed by the USSR and led to the Soviet invasion of Czechoslovakia 1968. He was arrested by Soviet troops and expelled from the party 1970. In 1989, he gave speeches at prodemocracy rallies, and after the fall of the hardline regime, he was elected speaker of the National Assembly in Prague, a position to which he was re-elected 1990. He was fatally injured in a car crash Sept 1992.

Duvalier François 1907–1971. Right-wing president of Haiti 1957–71. Known as *Papa Doc*, he ruled as a dictator, organizing the Tontons Macoutes ('bogeymen') as a private security force to intimidate and assassinate opponents of his regime. He rigged the 1961 elections in order to have his term of office extended until 1967, and in 1964, declared himself president for life. He was excommunicated by the Vatican for harassing the church, and was succeeded on his death by his son Jean-Claude Duvalier.

Duvalier Jean-Claude 1951– . Right-wing president of Haiti 1971–86. Known as *Baby Doc*, he succeeded his father François Duvalier, becoming, at the age of 19, the youngest president in the world. He continued to receive support from the USA but was pressured into moderating some elements of his father's regime, yet still tolerated no opposition. In 1986, with Haiti's economy stagnating and with increasing civil disorder, Duvalier fled to France, taking much of the Haitian treasury with him.

Eisenhower Dwight David ('Ike') 1890–1969. 34th president of the USA 1953–60, a Republican. A general in World War II, he commanded the Allied forces in Italy 1943, then the Allied invasion of Europe, and from Oct 1944 all the Allied armies in the West. As president he promoted business interests at home and conducted the Cold War abroad. His vice president was Richard Nixon.

Ershad Hussain Mohammad 1930– . Military ruler of Bangladesh 1982–90. He became chief of staff of the Bangladeshi army 1979 and assumed power in a military coup 1982. As president from 1983, Ershad introduced a successful rural-oriented economic programme. He was re-elected 1986 and lifted martial law, but faced continuing political opposition, which forced him to resign Dec 1990. In 1991, he was formally charged with the illegal possession of arms, convicted, and sentenced to ten years' imprisonment. He received a further sentence of three years' imprisonment Feb 1992 after being convicted of corruption.

Fahd 1921– . King of Saudi Arabia from 1982, when he succeeded his half-brother Khalid. As head of government, he has been active in trying to bring about a solution to the Middle East conflicts.

Franco Francisco (Paulino Hermenegildo Teódulo Bahamonde) 1892–1975. Spanish dictator from 1939. As a general, he led the insurgent Nationalists to victory in the Spanish Civil War 1936–39, supported by Fascist Italy and Nazi Germany, and established a dictatorship. In 1942, Franco reinstated a Cortes (Spanish parliament), which in 1947, passed an act by which he became head of state for life.

Franco Itamar 1931– . Brazilian politician and president since 1992. A member of the Liberal Front Party (PFL), he had had a long, but largely low-profile, career in Brazilian politics until his elevation to head of state. Although holding fundamentally different views on economic policy, he served as vice-president to President Fernando Collor until the latter's removal from office on charges of corruption Dec 1992. Franco, whose record was clean, became interim, then full, president. Criticizing his predecessor's economic modernization policies as 'unrealistic', he promised reform with stability but his first months in office attracted widespread criticism from both supporters and opponents.

Fujimori Alberto 1939– . President of Peru from July 1990. As leader of the newly formed Cambio 90 (Change 90) he campaigned on a reformist ticket and defeated his more experienced Democratic Front opponent. With no assembly majority, and faced with increasing opposition to his policies, he imposed military rule early 1992.

Gandhi Indira (born Nehru) 1917–1984. Indian politician, prime minister of India 1966–77 and 1980–84, and leader of the Congress Party 1966–77 and subsequently of the Congress (I) party. She was assassinated 1984 by members of her Sikh bodyguard, resentful of her use of troops to clear malcontents from the Sikh temple at Amritsar.

Gandhi Mohandas Karamchand, called *Mahatma* ('Great Soul') 1869–1948. Indian nationalist leader. A pacifist, he led the struggle for Indian independence from the UK by advocating nonviolent noncooperation (*satyagraha*, defence of and by truth) from 1915. He was imprisoned several times by the British authorities and was influential in the nationalist Congress Party and in the independence negotiations 1947. He was assassinated by a Hindu nationalist in the violence that followed the partition of British India into India and Pakistan.

Gandhi Rajiv 1944–1991. Indian politician, prime minister from 1984 (following his mother Indira Gandhi's assassination) to Nov 1989. As prime minister, he faced growing discontent with his party's elitism and lack of concern for social issues. He was assassinated by a bomb at an election rally.

Geingob Hage Gottfried 1941– . Namibian politician and prime minister. Geingob was appointed founding director of the United Nations Institute for Namibia in Lusaka, 1975. He became the first prime minister of an independent Namibia March 1990.

Giscard d'Estaing Valéry 1926– . French conservative politician, president 1974–81. He was finance minister to de Gaulle 1962–66 and Pompidou 1969–74. As leader of the Union pour la Démocratie Française, which he formed in 1978, Giscard sought to project himself as leader of a 'new centre'.

Goh Chok Tong 1941– . Singapore politician, prime minister from 1990. A trained economist, Goh became a member of parliament for the ruling People's Action Party 1976. Rising steadily through the party ranks, he was appointed deputy prime minister 1985, and subsequently chosen by the cabinet as Lee Kuan Yew's successor, first as prime minister and from 1992 also as party leader.

González Márquez Felipe 1942– . Spanish socialist politician, leader of the Socialist Workers' Party (PSOE), prime minister from 1982. Although PSOE was re-elected in 1989 and 1993, his popularity suffered from economic upheaval and allegations of corruption.

Gorbachev Mikhail Sergeyevich 1931– . Soviet president, in power 1985–91. As general secretary of the Communist Party (CPSU) 1985–91, and president of the Supreme Soviet 1988–91, he introduced liberal reforms at home (*perestroika* and *glasnost*), proposed the introduction of multiparty democracy, and attempted to halt the arms race abroad. He became head of state 1989. He was awarded the Nobel Peace Prize 1990 but his international reputation suffered in the light of harsh state repression of nationalist demonstrations in the Baltic states. Following an abortive coup attempt by hardliners Aug 1991, international acceptance of independence for the Baltic states, and accelerated moves towards independence in other republics, Gorbachev's power base as Soviet president was greatly weakened and in Dec 1991 he resigned.

Haughey Charles 1925– . Irish Fianna Fáil politician of Ulster descent. Dismissed 1970 from Jack Lynch's cabinet for alleged complicity in IRA gunrunning, he was afterwards acquitted. He was prime minister 1979–81, March–Nov 1982, and 1986–92, when he was replaced by Albert Reynolds.

Havel Václav 1936– . Czech dramatist and politician, president of Czechoslovakia 1989–92 and president of the Czech Republic from 1993. Havel became widely known as a human-rights activist. He was imprisoned 1979–83 and again 1989 for support of Charter 77, a human-rights manifesto. As president of Czechoslovakia he sought to preserve a united republic, but resigned in recognition of the breakup of the federation 1992. In 1993 he became president of the newly independent Czech Republic.

Hawke Bob (Robert) 1929– . Australian Labor politician, prime minister 1983–91, on the right wing of the party. He was president of the Australian Council of Trade Unions 1970–80. He announced his retirement from politics 1992.

Heath Edward (Richard George) 1916– . British Conservative politician, party leader 1965–75. As prime minister 1970–74, he took the UK into the European Community but was brought down by economic and industrial relations crises at home. He was replaced as party leader by Margaret Thatcher 1975, and became increasingly critical of her policies and her opposition to the UK's full participation in the EC. In 1990, he undertook a mission to Iraq in an attempt to secure the release of British hostages.

Hekmatyar Gulbuddin 1949– . Afghani Islamic fundamentalist guerrilla leader, prime minister from 1993. Strongly anticommunist, he resisted the takeover of Kabul by moderate mujaheddin forces April 1992 and refused to join the interim administration, continuing to bombard the city until being driven out. A year later he became prime minister by a peace agreement.

Ho Chi Minh adopted name of Nguyen Tat Thanh 1890–1969. North Vietnamese communist politician, premier and president 1954–69. Having trained in Moscow shortly after the Russian Revolution, he headed the communist Vietminh from 1941 and fought against the French during the Indochina War 1946–54, becoming president and prime minister of the republic at the armistice. Aided by the communist bloc, he did much to develop industrial potential. He relinquished the premiership 1955, but continued as president. In the years before his death, Ho successfully led his country's fight against US-aided South Vietnam in the Vietnam War 1954–75.

Honecker Erich 1912–1994. German communist politician, in power 1973–89, elected chair of the council of state (head of state) 1976. He governed in an outwardly austere and efficient manner and, while favouring East–West détente, was a loyal ally of the USSR. In Oct 1989, following a wave of prodemocracy demonstrations, he was replaced as leader of the Socialist Unity Party (SED) and head of state by Egon Krenz, and in Dec expelled from the Communist Party. Honecker was placed under house arrest in 1990, awaiting trial on charges of treason, corruption, and abuse of power. In 1993, he was allowed to go into exile in Chile, where he died in 1994.

Houphouët-Boigny Félix 1905–1993. Côte d'Ivoire right-wing politician. He held posts in French ministries, and became president of the

Republic of the Ivory Coast on independence 1960, maintaining close links with France, which helped to boost an already thriving economy and encourage political stability. Pro-Western and opposed to communist intervention in Africa, Houphouët-Boigny was strongly criticized for maintaining diplomatic relations with South Africa. He was re-elected for a seventh term 1990 in multiparty elections, amid allegations of ballot rigging and political pressure.

Hoxha Enver 1908–1985. Albanian Communist politician, the country's leader from 1954. He founded the Albanian Communist Party 1941, and headed the liberation movement 1939–44. He was prime minister 1944–54, combining with foreign affairs 1946–53, and from 1954 was first secretary of the Albanian Party of Labour. In policy he was a Stalinist and independent of both Chinese and Soviet communism.

Hun Sen 1950– . Cambodian political leader, prime minister from 1985. Originally a member of the Khmer Rouge army, he defected in 1977 to join Vietnam-based anti-Khmer Cambodian forces. His leadership has been characterized by the promotion of economic liberalization and a thawing in relations with exiled non-Khmer opposition forces as a prelude to a compromise political settlement. In Oct 1991, following a peace accord ending 13 years of civil war in Cambodia, Hun Sen agreed to rule the country in conjunction with the United Nations Transitional Authority in Cambodia (UNTAC) and representatives of the warring factions until UN-administered elections 1993.

Hussein ibn Talal 1935– . King of Jordan from 1952. By 1967, he had lost all his kingdom west of the river Jordan in the Arab-Israeli Wars, and in 1970, suppressed the Palestine Liberation Organization acting as a guerrilla force against his rule on the remaining East Bank territories. He has become a moderating force in Middle Eastern politics.

Hussein Saddam 1937– . Iraqi politician, in power from 1968, president from 1979, progressively eliminating real or imagined opposition factions as he gained increasing dictatorial control. He fought a bitter war against Iran 1980–88, with US economic aid, and dealt harshly with Kurdish rebels seeking independence, using chemical weapons against civilian populations. In 1990, he annexed Kuwait, to universal condemnation, before being driven out by a US-dominated coalition army Feb 1991. He subsequently sent the remainder of his army to crush the Kurds, bringing international charges of genocide against him and causing hundreds of thousands of Kurds to flee their homes in northern Iraq. His continued indiscriminate bombardment of Shi'ites in southern Iraq caused the UN to impose a 'no-fly zone' in the area Aug 1992. Alleging infringements of the zone, US-led warplanes bombed strategic targets in Iraq Jan 1993, forcing Hussein to back down and comply with repeated UN requests for access to inspect his arms facilities.

Iliescu Ion 1930– . Romanian president from 1990. A former member of the Romanian Communist Party (PCR) and of Nicolae Ceaușescu's government, Iliescu swept into power on Ceaușescu's fall as head of the National Salvation Front.

Jaruzelski Wojciech 1923– . Polish general, communist leader from 1981, president 1985–90. He imposed martial law for the first year of his rule, suppressed the opposition, and banned trade-union activity, but later released many political prisoners. In 1989, elections in favour of the free trade union Solidarity forced Jaruzelski to speed up democratic reforms, overseeing a transition to a new form of 'socialist pluralist' democracy and stepping down as president 1990.

Jayawardene Junius Richard 1906– . Sri Lankan politician. Leader of the United Nationalist Party from 1973, he became prime minister 1977 and the country's first president 1978–88.

Jiang Zemin 1926– . Chinese political leader, state president from 1993. He succeeded Zhao Ziyang as Communist Party leader after the Tiananmen Square massacre of 1989. Jiang is a cautious proponent of economic reform who held with unswerving adherence to the party's 'political line'.

Johnson Lyndon Baines 1908–1973. 36th president of the USA 1963–69, a Democrat. He was elected to Congress 1937–49 and the Senate 1949–60. Born in Texas, he brought critical Southern support as J F Kennedy's vice-presidential running mate 1960, and became president on Kennedy's assassination. After the Tonkin Gulf Incident, which escalated US involvement in the Vietnam War, support won by Johnson's Great Society legislation (civil rights, education, alleviation of poverty) dissipated, and he declined to run for re-election 1968.

Kádár János 1912–1989. Hungarian Communist leader, in power 1956–88, after suppressing the national uprising. As Hungarian Socialist Workers' Party (HSWP) leader and prime minister 1956–58 and 1961–65, Kádár introduced a series of market-socialist economic reforms, while retaining cordial political relations with the USSR.

Karadzic Radovan 1945– . Bosnian Serb political leader, president of the community's unofficial government 1992– . As leader, he launched the siege of Sarajevo in 1992, which escalated swiftly into a brutal civil war. Distrusted in the West and viewed as an intransigent figure, for many Bosnian Serbs he is considered a moderate.

Kaunda Kenneth (David) 1924– . Zambian politician, president 1964–91. Imprisoned in 1958–60 as founder of the Zambia African National Congress, he became in 1964 the first prime minister of Northern Rhodesia, then the first president of independent Zambia. In 1973, he introduced one-party rule. He supported the nationalist movement in Southern Rhodesia, now Zimbabwe, and survived a coup attempt 1980 thought to have been promoted by South Africa. He was elected chair of the Organization of African Unity 1987. In 1990, he was faced with wide anti-government demonstrations, leading to the acceptance of a multiparty political system. He lost the first multiparty election, in Nov 1991, to Frederick Chiluba.

Keating Paul 1954– . Australian politician, Labor Party (ALP) leader and prime minister from 1991. He was treasurer and deputy leader of the ALP 1983–91.

Kennedy John F(itzgerald) 'Jack' 1917–1963. 35th president of the USA 1961–63, a Democrat; the first Roman Catholic and the youngest person to be elected president. In foreign policy, he carried through the unsuccessful Bay of Pigs invasion of Cuba, and in 1963 secured the withdrawal of Soviet missiles from the island. His programme for reforms at home, called the *New Frontier*, was posthumously executed by Lyndon Johnson. Kennedy was assassinated while on a visit to Dallas, Texas, on 22 Nov 1963 by Lee Harvey Oswald (1939–1963), who was within a few days shot dead by Jack Ruby (1911–1967).

Kenyatta Jomo. Assumed name of Kamau Ngengi c. 1894–1978. Kenyan nationalist politician, prime minister from 1963, as well as the first president of Kenya from 1964 until his death. He led the Kenya African Union from 1947 (*KANU* from 1963) and was active in liberating Kenya from British rule.

Khaddhafi or *Gaddafi* or *Qaddafi*, Moamer al 1942– . Libyan revolutionary leader. Overthrowing King Idris 1969, he became virtual president of a republic, although he nominally gave up all except an ideological role 1974. He favours territorial expansion in N Africa reaching as far as Zaire, has supported rebels in Chad, and has proposed mergers with a number of countries. His theories, based on those of the Chinese communist leader Mao Zedong, are contained in a *Green Book*.

Khasbulatov Rusian 1943– . Russian politician and chairman of the Supreme Soviet since 1991. As the Russian first vice-president, he was initially a strong supporter of Boris Yeltsin, and, after the collapse of the 1991 anti-Gorbachev coup, became chairman of the Russian Supreme Soviet. Thereafter, however, relations between Yeltsin and Khasbulatov deteriorated rapidly, the latter repeatedly trying to block the Russian leader's economic and political reforms. Khasbulatov's critics accused him of shifting his ideological ground to pursue his personal ambitions.

Khomeini Ayatollah Ruhollah 1900–1989. Iranian Shi'ite Muslim leader, born in Khomein, central Iran. Exiled for opposition to the Shah from 1964, he returned when the Shah left the country 1979, and established a fundamentalist Islamic republic. His rule was marked by a protracted war with Iraq, and suppression of opposition within Iran, executing thousands of opponents.

Khrushchev Nikita Sergeyevich 1894–1971. Soviet politician, secretary general of the Communist Party 1953–64, premier 1958–64. He emerged as leader from the power struggle following Stalin's death and was the first official to denounce Stalin, in 1956. His de-Stalinization programme gave rise to revolts in Poland and Hungary 1956. Because of problems with the economy and foreign affairs (a breach with China 1960; conflict with the USA in the Cuban missile crisis 1962), he was ousted by Leonid Brezhnev and Alexei Kosygin.

Kim Il Sung 1912–1994. North Korean communist politician and marshal. He became prime minister 1948 and president 1972, retaining the presidency of the Communist Workers' party. He liked to be known as the 'Great Leader' and campaigned constantly for the reunification of Korea. His son *Kim Jong Il* (1942–), known as the 'Dear Leader', succeeded him.

Kim Young Sam 1927– . South Korean democratic politician, president from 1993. A member of the National Assembly from 1954 and president of the New Democratic Party (NDP) from 1974, he lost his seat and was later placed under house arrest because of his opposition to President Park Chung Hee. In 1983, he led a pro-democracy hunger strike but in 1987, failed to defeat Roh Tae-Woo in the presidential election. In 1990, he merged the NDP with the ruling party to form the new Democratic Liberal Party (DLP). In the Dec 1992 presidential election, he captured 42% of the national vote, and assumed office Feb 1993.

King Martin Luther Jr 1929–1968. US civil-rights campaigner, black leader, and Baptist minister. He first came to national attention as leader of the Montgomery, Alabama, bus boycott 1955, and was one of the organizers of the massive (200,000 people) march on Washington DC 1963 to demand racial equality. An advocate of nonviolence, he was awarded the Nobel Peace Prize 1964. He was assassinated in Memphis, Tennessee, by James Earl Ray (1928–).

Kohl Helmut 1930– . German conservative politician, leader of the Christian Democratic Union (CDU) from 1976, West German chancellor (prime minister) 1982–90. He oversaw the reunification of East and West Germany 1989–90 and in 1990, won a resounding victory to become the first chancellor of reunited Germany. His miscalculation of the true costs of reunification and their subsequent effects on the German economy led to a dramatic fall in his popularity.

Koivisto Mauno Henrik 1923– . Finnish politician, prime minister 1968–70 and 1979–82, and president since 1982. He gradually moved from the fringe of politics into active participation, becoming finance minister 1966–67 and prime minister 1968–72, leading a Social Democratic Party (SDP) coalition. He returned as head of government 1979–82 and then became president 1982, sharing power with Centre Party (KESK) prime minister, Esko Aho, in Finland's unusual 'dual executive'.

Kravchuk Leonid 1934– . Ukrainian politician, president from July 1990. Formerly a member of the Ukrainian Communist Party (UCP), he became its ideology chief in the 1980s. After the suspension of the UCP Aug 1991, Kravchuk became an advocate of independence and market-centred economic reform.

Landsbergis Vytautas 1932– . President of Lithuania 1990–1993. He became active in nationalist politics in the 1980s, founding and eventually chairing the anticommunist Sajudis independence movement 1988. When Sajudis swept to victory in the republic's elections March 1990, Landsbergis chaired the Supreme Council of Lithuania, becoming president. He immediately drafted the republic's declaration of independence from the USSR, which was recognized Sept 1991. He was succeeded by Algirdas Brazauskas 1993.

Lange David (Russell) 1942– . New Zealand Labour prime minister 1983–89. Lange, a barrister, was elected to the House of Representatives 1977. Labour had a decisive win in the 1984 general election on a non-nuclear military policy, which Lange immediately put into effect, despite criticism from the USA. He introduced a free-market economic policy and was re-elected 1987. He resigned Aug 1989 over a disagreement with his finance minister.

Lee Kuan Yew 1923– . Singapore politician, prime minister 1959–90. Lee founded the anticommunist Socialist People's Action Party 1954 and entered the Singapore legislative assembly 1955. He was elected the country's first prime minister 1959, and took Singapore out of the Malaysian federation 1965. He remained in power until his resignation 1990, and was succeeded by Goh Chok Tong. Until 1992, he held on to the party leadership.

Li Peng 1928– . Chinese communist politician, a member of the Politburo from 1985, and head of government from 1987. During the pro-democracy demonstrations of 1989 he supported the massacre of students by Chinese troops in Tiananmen Square and the subsequent execution of others. He sought improved relations with the USSR prior to its demise, and has favoured maintaining firm central and party control over the economy.

Lubbers Rudolph Franz Marie (Ruud) 1939– . Dutch politician, prime minister of the Netherlands from 1982. Leader of the Christian Democratic Appeal (CDA), he is politically right of centre. He became minister for economic affairs 1973.

Lumumba Patrice 1926–1961. Congolese politician, prime minister of Zaire 1960. Imprisoned by the Belgians, but released in time to attend the conference giving the Congo independence in 1960, he led the National Congolese Movement to victory in the subsequent general election. He was deposed in a coup d'état, and murdered some months later.

Machel Samora 1933–1986. Mozambique nationalist leader, president 1975–86. Machel was active in the liberation front Frelimo from its conception 1962, fighting for independence from Portugal. He became Frelimo leader 1966, and Mozambique's first president from independence 1975 until his death in a plane crash near the South African border.

Macmillan (Maurice) Harold, 1st Earl of Stockton 1894–1986. British Conservative politician, prime minister 1957–63; foreign secretary 1955 and chancellor of the Exchequer 1955–57. In 1963, he attempted to negotiate British entry into the European Economic Community, but was blocked by French president de Gaulle. Much of his career as prime minister was spent defending the retention of a UK nuclear weapon, and he was responsible for the purchase of US Polaris missiles 1962.

Major John 1943– . British Conservative politician, prime minister 1990-97. He was foreign secretary 1989 and chancellor of the Exchequer 1989–90. Despite divisions within the Conservative Party, Major was returned to power in the April 1992 general election; however, he subsequently faced mounting public dissatisfaction over a range of issues, including the sudden withdrawal of the pound from the European Monetary System (EMS), a drastic pit-closure programme, and past sales of arms to Iraq.

Criticized for weak leadership of his divided party, he resigned as leader of the Conservative Party after a crushing defeat in the 1997 general election.

Makarios III 1913–1977. Cypriot politician, Greek Orthodox archbishop 1950–77. A leader of the Resistance organization EOKA, he was exiled by the British to the Seychelles 1956–57 for supporting armed action to achieve union with Greece (*enosis*). He was president of the republic of Cyprus 1960–77 (briefly deposed by a Greek military coup July–Dec 1974).

Mandela Nelson (Rolihlahla) 1918 – . South African politician and lawyer, president from 1994. He was president of the African National Congress (ANC) 1991–97. Imprisoned from 1964, as organizer of the then banned ANC, he became a symbol of unity for the worldwide anti-apartheid movement. In Feb 1990 he was released, the ban on the ANC having been lifted, and entered into negotiations with the government about a multiracial future for South Africa. In May 1994 he was sworn in as South Africa's first post-apartheid president after the ANC won 62.65% of the vote in universal-suffrage elections. He shared the Nobel Prize for Peace 1993 with South African president F W de Klerk.

Manley Michael (Norman) 1924– 1997. Jamaican politician, leader of the socialist People's National Party from 1969, and prime minister 1972–80 and 1989–92. He resigned the premiership because of ill health March 1992 and was succeeded by P J Patterson. Manley left parliament April 1992. His father, *Norman Manley* (1893–1969), was the founder of the People's National Party and prime minister 1959–62.

Mao Zedong or *Mao Tse-tung* 1893–1976. Chinese political leader and Marxist theoretician. A founder of the Chinese Communist Party (CCP) 1921, Mao soon emerged as its leader. He organized the Long March 1934–35 and the war of liberation 1937–49, following which he established a People's Republic and communist rule in China; he headed the CCP and government until his death. His influence diminished with the failure of his 1958–60 Great Leap Forward, but he emerged dominant again during the 1966–69 Cultural Revolution. Mao adapted communism to Chinese conditions, as set out in the *Little Red Book*. Since 1978, the leadership of Deng Xiaoping has reinterpreted Maoism and criticized its policy excesses, but many of Mao's ideas remain valued.

Marcos Ferdinand 1917–1989. Filipino right-wing politician, president from 1965 to 1986, when he was forced into exile in Hawaii by a popular front led by Corazon Aquino. He was backed by the USA when in power, but in 1988, US authorities indicted him and his wife Imelda Marcos for racketeering, embezzlement.

Martens Wilfried 1936– . Prime minister of Belgium 1979–92, member of the Social Christian Party. He was president of the Dutch-speaking CVP 1972–79 and, as prime minister, headed several coalition governments in the period 1979–92 when he was replaced by Jean-Luc Dehaene heading a new coalition.

Masire Quett Ketumile Joni 1925– . President of Botswana from 1980. In 1962, with Seretse Khama, he founded the Botswana Democratic Party (BDP) and in 1965 was made deputy prime minister. After independence 1966, he became vice president and, on Khama's death 1980, president, continuing a policy of nonalignment. A centrist, he has helped Botswana become one of the most stable states in Africa.

Meciar Vladimir 1942– . Slovak politician, prime minister of the new state of Slovakia from January 1993. A dissident, he was expelled from the Communist Party 1970. As leader of the Movement for a Democratic Slovakia (HZDS), he sought an independent Slovak state. Meciar became prime minister of the Slovak republic 1990, within the federal system, and subsequently, the first prime minister of the new state, which formally came into being Jan 1993. With his Czech counterparts he played an important role in ensuring that the 'velvet revolution' of 1989 was translated into a similarly bloodless 'velvet divorce'.

Meir Golda 1898–1978. Israeli Labour (*Mapai*) politician. Born in Russia, she emigrated to the USA 1906, and in 1921 went to Palestine. She was foreign minister 1956–66 and prime minister 1969–74. Criticism of the Israelis' lack of preparation for the 1973 Arab-Israeli War led to election losses for Labour and, unable to form a government, she resigned.

Menem Carlos (Saul) 1935– . Argentine politician, president from 1989; leader of the Peronist (Justicialist Party) movement. As president, he introduced sweeping privatization and public spending cuts, released hundreds of political prisoners jailed under the Alfonsín regime, and sent two warships to the Gulf to assist the USA against Iraq in the 1992 Gulf War (the only Latin American country to offer support to the USA). He also improved relations with the UK.

Mengistu Haile Mariam 1937– . Ethiopian soldier and socialist politician, head of state 1977–91 (president 1987–91). He seized power in a coup and was confronted with severe problems of drought and secessionist uprisings, but survived with help from the USSR and the West until his violent overthrow.

Milosevic Slobodan 1941– . Serbian communist politician, party chief and president of Serbia from 1986; re-elected Dec 1990 in multiparty elections and again re-elected Dec 1992. Milosevic wielded considerable influence over the Serb-dominated Yugoslav federal army during the 1991–92 civil war and has continued to back Serbian militia in Bosnia-Herzegovina 1992–93, although publicly disclaiming any intention to 'carve up' the newly independent republic.

Mitterrand François 1916–1996. French socialist politician, president from 1981. He held ministerial posts in 11 governments 1947–58, and founded the French Socialist Party (PS) 1971. In 1985, he introduced proportional representation, allegedly to weaken the growing opposition from left and right. Since 1982, his administrations have combined economic orthodoxy with social reform.

Miyazawa Kiichi 1920– . Japanese right-wing politician. After holding a number of key government posts, he became leader of the ruling Liberal Democratic Party and prime minister Nov 1991. He was defeated June 1993 on a vote of confidence (triggered by demand for electoral reform), and resigned in July following a general election.

Mobutu Sese Seko Kuku Ngbeandu Wa Za Banga 1930–1997. President of Zaire (now the Democratic Republic of Congo) 1965–97. He assumed the presidency in a coup, and created a unitary state under a centralized government. The harshness of some of his policies and charges of corruption attracted widespread international criticism. In 1991 opposition leaders forced Mobutu to agree formally to give up some of his powers, but the president continued to oppose constitutional reform. The Alliance of Democratic Forces for the Liberation of Zaire–Congo (ADFL), led by Laurent Kabila, threatened Mobutu's regime. In May 1997, with Kabila's rebels poised to take the capital Kinshasa, government officials announced that President Mobutu was giving up his powers. Kabila claimed victory and the presidency, and renamed Zaire the Democratic Republic of Congo. Mobutu died in Rabat, Morocco, in Sept 1997.

Mohamad Mahathir bin 1925– . Prime minister of Malaysia from 1981 and leader of the United Malays National Organization (UMNO). His 'look east' economic policy emulates Japanese industrialization.

Moi Daniel arap 1924– . Kenyan politician, president from 1978. Leader of the Kenya African National Union (KANU), he became minister of home affairs 1964, vice president 1967, and succeeded Jomo Kenyatta as president. He enjoys the support of Western governments but has been widely criticized for Kenya's poor human-rights record. From 1988, his rule became increasingly authoritarian and in 1991, in the face of widespread criticism, he promised an eventual introduction of multiparty politics. In 1992, he was elected president in the first free elections amid widespread accusations of fraud.

Mubarak Hosni 1928– . Egyptian politician, president from 1981. Vice president to Anwar Sadat from 1975, Mubarak succeeded him on his assassination. He has continued to pursue Sadat's moderate policies, and has significantly increased the freedom of the press and of political association, while trying to repress the growing Islamic fundamentalist movement.

Mugabe Robert (Gabriel) 1925– . Zimbabwean politician, prime minister from 1980 and president from 1987. He was in detention in Rhodesia for nationalist activities 1964–74, then carried on guerrilla warfare from Mozambique. As leader of ZANU he was in an uneasy alliance with Joshua Nkomo of ZAPU (Zimbabwe African People's Union) from 1976. The two parties merged 1987. His failure to anticipate and respond to the 1991–92 drought in southern Africa adversely affected his popularity.

Muldoon Robert David 1921–1992. New Zealand National Party politician, prime minister 1975–84, during which time he pursued austere economic policies such as a wage-and-price policy to control inflation. Muldoon announced his retirement from politics 1992.

Mulroney Brian 1939– . Canadian politician, Progressive Conservative Party leader from 1983, prime minister 1984–93. He achieved a landslide in the 1984 election, and won the 1988 election on a platform of free trade with the USA. Opposition to the Meech Lake agreement, a prerequisite to signing the

1982 constitution, eventually forced him, in Feb 1993, to resign the leadership of the Conservative Party, though he remained prime minister until Kim Campbell was appointed his successor in June.

Museveni Yoweri Kaguta 1945– . Ugandan general and politician, president from 1986. He led the opposition to Idi Amin's regime 1971–78 and was minister of defence 1979–80 but, unhappy with Milton Obote's autocratic leadership, formed the National Resistance Army (NRA). When Obote was ousted in a coup in 1985, Museveni entered into a brief power-sharing agreement with his successor, Tito Okello, before taking over as president. Museveni leads a broad-based coalition government.

Najibullah Ahmadzai 1947– . Afghan communist politician, state president 1986-92. A member of the Politburo from 1981, he was leader of the People's Democratic Party of Afghanistan (PDPA) from 1986. Although his government initially survived the withdrawal of Soviet troops Feb 1989, continuing pressure from the mujaheddin forces resulted in his eventual overthrow. In the spring of 1992, he was captured while attempting to flee the country and placed under United Nations protection, pending trial by an Islamic court.

Nakasone Yasuhiro 1917– . Japanese conservative politician, leader of the Liberal Democratic Party (LDP) and prime minister 1982–87. He stepped up military spending and increased Japanese participation in international affairs, with closer ties to the USA. He was forced to resign his party post May 1989 as a result of having profited from insider trading in the Recruit scandal. After serving a two-year period of atonement, he rejoined the LDP April 1991.

Narasimha Rao P(amulaparti) V(enkata) 1921– . Indian politician, prime minister of India from 1991 and Congress (I) leader. He governed the state of Andhra Pradesh as chief minister 1971–73, and served in the Congress (I) cabinets of Indira and Rajiv Gandhi as minister of external affairs 1980–85 and 1988–90 and of human resources 1985–88. He took over the party leadership after the assassination of Rajiv Gandhi. Elected prime minister the following month, he instituted a reform of the economy.

Nasser Gamal Abdel 1918–1970. Egyptian politician, prime minister 1954–56 and from 1956 president of Egypt (the United Arab Republic 1958–71). In 1952, he was the driving power behind the Neguib coup, which ended the monarchy. His nationalization of the Suez Canal 1956 led to an Anglo-French invasion and the Suez Crisis, and his ambitions for an Egyptian-led union of Arab states led to disquiet in the Middle East (and in the West). Nasser was also an early and influential leader of the nonaligned movement.

Nazarbayev Nursultan 1940– . President of Kazakhstan from 1990. In the Soviet period he was prime minister of the republic 1984–89 and leader of the Kazakh Communist Party 1989–91, which established itself as the independent Socialist Party of Kazakhstan (SPK) Sept 1991. He advocates free-market policies, yet enjoys the support of the environmentalist lobby. He joined the Communist Party at 22 and left it after the failed Soviet coup 1991.

Nehru Jawaharlal 1889–1964. Indian nationalist politician, prime minister from 1947. Before the partition (the division of British India into India and Pakistan), he led the socialist wing of the nationalist Congress Party, and was second in influence only to Mohandas Gandhi. He was imprisoned nine times by the British 1921–45 for political activities. As prime minister from the creation of the dominion (later republic) of India in Aug 1947, he originated the idea of nonalignment (neutrality towards major powers). His daughter was Prime Minister Indira Gandhi.

Netanyahu ('Bibi') Binjamin 1949– . Israeli right-wing politician and diplomat, leader of the Likud (Consolidation Party) from 1993 and prime minister from 1996. As deputy foreign minister in the Likud-led government of Shamir, he was the chief Israeli spokesperson in the 1991–92 Middle East peace talks. A hard-line politician, he succeeded Yitzak Shamir to the Likud leadership in March 1993 following the party's 1992 electoral defeat. He is Israel's first directly-elected prime minister.

Nixon Richard (Milhous) 1913–1994. 37th president of the USA 1969–74, a Republican. He attracted attention as a member of the Un-American Activities Committee 1948, and was vice president to Eisenhower 1953–61. As president he was responsible for US withdrawal from Vietnam, and forged new links with China, but at home his culpability in the cover-up of the Watergate scandal and the existence of a 'slush fund' for political machinations during his re-election campaign 1972 led to his resignation 1974 when threatened with impeachment. He was granted a pardon 1974 by President Ford and turned to lecturing and writing.

Nkomo Joshua 1917– . Zimbabwean politician, vice-president from 1988. As president of ZAPU (Zimbabwe African People's Union) from 1961, he was a leader of the black nationalist movement against the white Rhodesian regime. He was a member of Robert Mugabe's cabinet 1980–82 and from 1987.

Nkrumah Kwame 1909–1972. Ghanaian nationalist politician, prime minister of the Gold Coast (Ghana's former name) 1952–57 and of newly independent Ghana 1957–60. He became Ghana's first president 1960 but was overthrown in a coup 1966. His policy of 'African socialism' led to links with the communist bloc.

Noriega Manuel (Antonio Morena) 1940– . Panamanian soldier and politician, effective ruler of Panama from 1982, as head of the National Guard, until deposed by the USA 1989. An informer for the US Central Intelligence Agency, he was known to be involved in drug trafficking as early as 1972. He enjoyed US support until 1987. In the 1989 US invasion of Panama, he was forcibly taken to the USA to stand trial. He was eventually convicted of drug trafficking and racketeering in 1992 and given a 40-year prison sentence.

Nujoma Sam 1929– . Namibian left-wing politician, president from 1990, founder and leader of SWAPO (the South-West Africa People's Organization) from 1959. He was exiled in 1960 and controlled guerrillas from Angolan bases until the first free elections were held 1989, taking office early the following year.

Nyerere Julius (Kambarage) 1922– . Tanzanian socialist politician, president 1964–85. He devoted himself from 1954 to the formation of the Tanganyika African National Union and subsequent campaigning for independence. He became chief minister 1960, was prime minister of Tanganyika 1961–62, president of the newly formed Tanganyika Republic 1962–64, and first president of Tanzania 1964–85.

Obote (Apollo) Milton 1924– . Ugandan politician who led the independence movement from 1961. He became prime minister 1962 and was president 1966–71 and 1980–85, being overthrown by first Idi Amin and then by Lt-Gen Tito Okello.

Ortega Saavedra Daniel 1945– . Nicaraguan socialist politician, head of state 1981–90. He was a member of the Sandinista Liberation Front (FSLN), which overthrew the regime of Anastasio Somoza 1979. US-sponsored Contra guerrillas opposed his government from 1982. In Feb 1990, Ortega lost the presidency to US-backed Violeta Chamorro.

Özal Turgut 1927–1993. Turkish Islamic right-wing politician, prime minister 1983–89, president 1989–93. He was responsible for improving his country's relations with Greece, but his prime objective was to strengthen Turkey's alliance with the USA. He died in office and was succeeded by Suleyman Demirel.

Palme (Sven) Olof 1927–1986. Swedish social-democratic politician, prime minister 1969–76 and 1982–86. As prime minister he carried out constitutional reforms, turning the Riksdag into a single-chamber parliament and stripping the monarch of power, and was widely respected for his support of Third World countries. He was assassinated Feb 1986.

Papandreou Andreas 1919–1996. Greek socialist politician, founder of the Pan-Hellenic Socialist Movement (PASOK); prime minister 1981–89, and again 1993–96. He lost the 1989 election after being implicated in an alleged embezzlement scandal, involving the diversion of funds to the Greek government from the Bank of Crete, headed by George Koskotas.

Paz (Estenssoro) Victor 1907– . President of Bolivia 1952–56, 1960–64, and 1985–89. He founded and led the Movimiento Nacionalista Revolucionario (MNR), which seized power 1952. His regime extended the vote to Indians, nationalized the country's largest tin mines, embarked on a programme of agrarian reform, and brought inflation under control.

Pérez de Cuéllar Javier 1920– . Peruvian diplomat, secretary general of the United Nations 1982–91. He raised the standing of the UN by his successful diplomacy in ending the Iran–Iraq War 1988 and securing the independence of Namibia 1989.

Perón Juan (Domingo) 1895–1974. Argentine politician, dictator 1946–55 and from 1973 until his death. His populist appeal to the poor was enhanced by the charisma and political work of his second wife

Eva (Evita) Perón. After her death in 1952 his popularity waned and he was deposed in a military coup 1955. He returned from exile to the presidency 1973, but died in office 1974, and was succeeded by his third wife Isabel Perón.

Pinochet (Ugarte) Augusto 1915– . Military ruler of Chile from 1973, when a coup backed by the US Central Intelligence Agency ousted and killed President Salvador Allende. Pinochet took over the presidency and governed ruthlessly, crushing all opposition. He was voted out of power when general elections were held in Dec 1989 but remained head of the armed forces until 1997.

Pol Pot (also known as *Saloth Sar*, *Tol Saut*, and *Pol Porth*) 1925– . Cambodian politician and leader of the Khmer Rouge communist movement that overthrew the government 1975. After widespread atrocities against the civilian population, his regime was deposed by a Vietnamese invasion 1979. Pol Pot continued to help lead the Khmer Rouge despite officially resigning from all positions in 1989.

Rabin Yitzhak 1922– 1995. Israeli Labour politician, prime minister 1974–77 and 1992-95. His policy of favouring Palestinian self-government in the occupied territories contributed to the success of the centre-left party in the 1992 elections. In Sept 1993 he signed a historic peace agreement with the Palestinian Liberation Organization (PLO), providing for a phased withdrawal of Israeli forces. He was awarded the 1994 Nobel Prize for Peace jointly with Israeli foreign minister, Shimon Peres, and PLO leader, Yassir Arafat. He was shot and killed by a young Israeli extremist while attending a peace rally in Tel Aviv Nov 1995.

Rafsanjani Hojatoleslam Ali Akbar Hashemi 1934– . Iranian politician and cleric, president from 1989. When his former teacher Ayatollah Khomeini returned after the revolution of 1979–80, Rafsanjani became the speaker of the Iranian parliament and, after Khomeini's death, state president and effective political leader. He was re-elected with a reduced majority 1993.

Ramos Fidel (Eddie) 1928– . Philippine politician and president from 1992. He was Corazon Aquino's staunchest ally as defence secretary, and was later nominated her successor.

Reagan Ronald (Wilson) 1911– . 40th president of the USA 1981–89, a Republican. He was governor of California 1966–74, and a former Hollywood actor. Reagan was a hawkish and popular president. He adopted an aggressive policy in Central America, attempting to overthrow the government of Nicaragua, and invading Grenada 1983. In 1987, Irangate was investigated by the Tower Commission; Reagan admitted that USA–Iran negotiations had become an 'arms for hostages deal', but denied knowledge of resultant funds being illegally sent to the Contras in Nicaragua. He increased military spending (sending the national budget deficit to record levels), cut social programmes, introduced deregulation of domestic markets, and cut taxes. His Strategic Defense Initiative, announced 1983, proved controversial owing to the cost and unfeasibility. He was succeeded by George Bush.

Reynolds Albert 1933– . Irish politician, prime minister from 1992. He joined Fianna Faíl 1977, and held various government posts including minister for industry and commerce 1987–88 and minister of finance 1989–92. He became prime minister when Charles Haughey was forced to resign Jan 1992, but his government was defeated on a vote of confidence Nov 1992. Subsequent elections gave no party an overall majority but, after prolonged negotiations, Reynolds succeeded in forming a Fianna Faíl–Labour coalition.

Robinson Mary 1944– . Irish Labour politician, president from 1990. She became a professor of law at 25. A strong supporter of women's rights, she has campaigned for the liberalization of Ireland's laws prohibiting divorce and abortion.

Rocard Michel 1930– . French socialist politician, prime minister 1988–91. A former radical, he joined the Socialist Party (PS) 1973, emerging as leader of its moderate social-democratic wing. He held ministerial office under President François Mitterrand 1981–85.

Sadat Anwar 1918–1981. Egyptian politician. Succeeding Nasser as president 1970, he restored morale by his handling of the Egyptian campaign in the 1973 war against Israel. In 1974, his plan for economic, social, and political reform to transform Egypt was unanimously adopted in a referendum. In 1977, he visited Israel to reconcile the two countries, and shared the Nobel Peace Prize with Israeli prime minister Menachem Begin 1978. He was assassinated by Islamic fundamentalists.

Salazar Antonio de Oliveira 1889–1970. Portuguese prime minister 1932–68 who exercised a virtual dictatorship. During World War II, he maintained Portuguese neutrality but fought long colonial wars in Africa (Angola and Mozambique) that impeded his country's economic development as well as that of the colonies.

Salinas de Gortiari Carlos 1948– . Mexican politician, president from 1988, a member of the dominant Institutional Revolutionary Party (RPI). Educated in Mexico and the USA, he taught at Harvard and in Mexico before joining the government in 1971 and thereafter held a number of posts, mostly in the economic sphere, including finance minister. He narrowly won the 1988 presidnetial election, despite allegations of fraud.

Sarney (Costa) José 1930– . Brazilian politician, member of the centre-left Democratic Movement (PMDB), president 1985–90. He was succeeded by Fernando Collor.

Schlüter Poul Holmskov 1929– . Danish right-wing politician, leader of the Conservative People's Party (KF) from 1974 and prime minister 1982–93. Having joined the KF in his youth, he trained as a lawyer and then entered the Danish parliament (Folketing) in 1964. His centre-right coalition survived the 1990 election and was reconstituted with Liberal support. In Jan 1993, Schlüter resigned, accused of dishonesty regarding his role in an incident involving Tamil refugees. He was succeeded by Poul Nyrup Rasmussen.

Schmidt Helmut 1918– . German socialist politician, member of the Social Democratic Party (SPD), chancellor of West Germany 1974–83. As chancellor, Schmidt introduced social reforms and continued Brandt's policy of Ostpolitik. With the French president Giscard d'Estaing, he instigated annual world and European economic summits. He was a firm supporter of NATO and of the deployment of US nuclear missiles in West Germany during the early 1980s.

Shamir Yitzhak 1915– . Polish-born Israeli right-wing politician; prime minister 1983–84 and 1986–92; leader of the Likud (Consolidation Party) until 1993. He was foreign minister under Menachem Begin 1980–83, and again foreign minister in the Peres unity government 1984–86.

Shevardnadze Edvard 1928– . Georgian politician, Soviet foreign minister 1985–91, head of state of Georgia from 1992. A supporter of Gorbachev, he was first secretary of the Georgian Communist Party from 1972 and an advocate of economic reform. In 1985, he became a member of the Politburo, working for détente and disarmament. In July 1991, he resigned from the Communist Party (CPSU) and, along with other reformers and leading democrats, established the Democratic Reform Movement. In March 1992, he was chosen as chair of Georgia's ruling military council, and in Oct elected speaker of parliament.

Shushkevich Stanislav 1934– . Belarus politician, president from 1991 after the attempted Soviet coup in Moscow. He was elected to parliament as a 'reform communist' 1990 and played a key role in the creation of the Commonwealth of Independent States as the successor to the Soviet Union.

Sihanouk Norodom 1922– . Cambodian politician, king 1941–55, prime minister 1955–70, when his government was overthrown by a military coup led by Lon Nol. With Pol Pot's resistance front, he overthrew Lon Nol 1975 and again became prime minister 1975–76, when he was forced to resign by the Khmer Rouge. He returned from exile Nov 1991 under the auspices of a United Nations-brokered peace settlement to head the Supreme National Council, a new coalition comprising all Cambodia's warring factions, including the Khmer Rouge. On his return, Sihanouk called for an international trial of the leaders of the Khmer Rouge on charges of genocide.

Smith Ian (Douglas) 1919– . Rhodesian politician. He was a founder of the Rhodesian Front 1962 and prime minister 1964–79. In 1965, he made a unilateral declaration of Rhodesia's independence, and, despite United Nations sanctions, maintained his regime with tenacity. In 1979, he was succeeded as prime minister by Bishop Abel Muzorewa, when the country was renamed Zimbabwe. He was suspended from the Zimbabwe parliament April 1987 and resigned in May as head of the white opposition party.

Soares Mario 1924– . Portuguese socialist politician, president from 1986. Exiled 1970, he returned to Portugal 1974, and, as leader of the Portuguese Socialist Party, was prime minister 1976–78. He resigned as party leader 1980, but in 1986 he was elected Portugal's first socialist president.

Stroessner Alfredo 1912– . Military leader and president of Paraguay 1954–89. As head of the armed forces from 1951, he seized power in a coup in 1954 sponsored by the right-wing ruling Colorado Party. Accused by his opponents of harsh repression, his regime spent heavily on the military to preserve his authority. He was ousted in an army-led coup and gained asylum in Brazil.

Suharto Raden 1921– . Indonesian politician and general. He ousted Sukarno to become president 1967. He ended confrontation with Malaysia, invaded East Timor 1975, and reached a cooperation agreement with Papua New Guinea 1979. His authoritarian rule has met with domestic opposition from the left.

Sukarno Achmed 1901–1970. Indonesian nationalist, president 1945–67. During World War II, he cooperated in the local administration set up by the Japanese, replacing Dutch rule. After the war, he became the first president of the new Indonesian republic, becoming president-for-life in 1966; he was ousted by Suharto.

Tambo Oliver 1917–1993. South African nationalist politician, in exile 1960–90, president of the African National Congress (ANC) 1977–91. Because of poor health, he was given the honorary post of national chair July 1991, and Nelson Mandela resumed the ANC presidency.

Thant, U 1909–1974. Burmese diplomat, secretary general of the United Nations 1962–71. He helped to resolve the US–Soviet crisis over the Soviet installation of missiles in Cuba, and made the controversial decision to withdraw the UN peacekeeping force from the Egypt–Israel border.

Thatcher Margaret Hilda (born Roberts), Baroness Thatcher of Kesteven 1925– . British Conservative politician, prime minister 1979–90. She was education minister 1970–74 and Conservative Party leader from 1975. In 1982, she sent British troops to recapture the Falkland Islands from Argentina. She confronted trade-union power during the miners' strike 1984–85, sold off majority stakes in many public utilities to the private sector, and reduced the influence of local government through such measures as the abolition of metropolitan councils, the control of expenditure through 'rate-capping', and the introduction of the community charge, or poll tax, from 1989. In 1990, splits in the cabinet over the issues of Europe and consensus government forced her resignation. An astute Parliamentary tactician, she tolerated little disagreement, either from the opposition or from within her own party. She was created a life peer 1992.

Tito adopted name of Josip Broz 1892–1980. Yugoslav communist politician, in power from 1945. In World War II, he organized the National Liberation Army to carry on guerrilla warfare against the German invasion 1941, and was created marshal 1943. As prime minister 1946–53 and president from 1953, he followed a foreign policy of 'positive neutralism'.

Trudeau Pierre (Elliott) 1919– . Canadian Liberal politician. He was prime minister 1968–79 and 1980–84. In 1980, having won again by a landslide on a platform opposing Québec separatism, he helped to defeat the Québec independence movement in a referendum. He repatriated the constitution from Britain 1982, but by 1984 had so lost support that he resigned.

Truman Harry S 1884–1972. 33rd president of the USA 1945–53, a Democrat. In Jan 1945, he became vice president to F D Roosevelt, and president when Roosevelt died in April that year. He used the atom bomb against Japan, launched the Marshall Plan to restore W Europe's economy, and nurtured the European Community and NATO (including the rearmament of West Germany).

Tutu Desmond (Mpilo) 1931– . South African priest, Anglican archbishop of Cape Town and general secretary of the South African Council of Churches 1979–84. One of the leading figures in the struggle against apartheid in the Republic of South Africa, he was awarded the Nobel Peace Prize 1984.

Ulbricht Walter 1893–1973. East German communist politician, in power 1960–71. He lived in exile in the USSR during Hitler's rule 1933–45. A Stalinist, he became first secretary of the Socialist Unity Party in East Germany 1950 and (as chair of the Council of State from 1960) was instrumental in the building of the Berlin Wall 1961. He established East Germany's economy and recognition outside the Eastern European bloc.

Vranitzky Franz 1937– . Austrian socialist politician, federal chancellor from 1986. A banker, he entered the political arena through the moderate, left-of-centre Socialist Party of Austria (SPÖ) and became minister of finance 1984. He succeeded Fred Sinowatz as federal chancellor 1986, heading an SPÖ–ÖVP (Austrian People's Party) coalition.

Waldheim Kurt 1918– . Austrian politician and diplomat, president 1986-92. He was secretary general of the United Nations 1972–81, having been Austria's representative there 1964–68 and 1970–71. He was elected president of Austria despite revelations that during World War II he had been an intelligence officer in an army unit responsible for transporting Jews to death camps. However, with mounting international pressure, in 1991 he announced that he would not run for re-election.

Wałesa Lech 1943– . Polish trade-union leader and president of Poland from 1990, founder of Solidarity (Solidarność) in 1980, an organization, independent of the Communist Party, which forced substantial political and economic concessions from the Polish government 1980–81 until being outlawed. During his presidency, his public standing diminished and economic problems increased. Nobel Peace Prize 1983.

Wilson (James) Harold, Baron Wilson of Rievaulx 1916–1995. British Labour politician, party leader from 1963, prime minister 1964–70 and 1974–76. His premiership was dominated by the issue of UK admission to membership of the European Community, the social contract (unofficial agreement with the trade unions), and economic difficulties. He was knighted 1976 and made a peer 1983.

Yeltsin Boris Nikolayevich 1931– . Russian politician, president of the Russian Soviet Federative Socialist Republic (RSFSR) 1990–91, and president of the newly independent Russian Federation from 1991. He directed the Federation's secession from the USSR and the formation of a new, decentralized confederation, the Commonwealth of Independent States (CIS), with himself as the most powerful leader. A referendum 1993 supported his policies of price deregulation and accelerated privatization, despite severe economic problems and civil unrest. He has consistently requested international aid to bring his country out of recession.

Zhao Ziyang 1918– . Chinese politician, prime minister 1980–87 and secretary of the Chinese Communist Party 1987–89. His reforms included self-management and incentives for workers and factories. He lost his secretaryship and other posts after the Tiananmen Square massacre in Beijing June 1989.

Zhelev Zhelyu 1935– . Bulgarian politician, president since 1990. He was expelled from the Bulgarian Communist Party because of his criticisms of Lenin; in 1989, he became head of the opposition movement, the Democratic Forces coalition. He was nominated, unopposed, for the presidency in 1990 after the demise of the 'reform communist' regime, and was directly elected to the post 1992. He is a proponent of market-centred economic reform and social peace.

Zhivkov Todor 1911– . Bulgarian Communist Party leader 1954–89, prime minister 1962–71, president 1971–89. His period in office was one of caution and conservatism. In 1991, he was tried for gross embezzlement.

Zia ul-Haq Mohammad 1924–1988. Pakistani general, in power from 1977 until his death, probably an assassination, in an aircraft explosion. He became army chief of staff 1976, led the military coup against Zulfikar Ali Bhutto 1977, and became president 1978. Zia introduced a fundamentalist Islamic regime and restricted political activity.

Prime ministers of the United Kingdom from 1721

Term	Name	Party	Term	Name	Party
1721–42	Sir Robert Walpole	Whig	1868–74	W E Gladstone	Liberal
1742–43	Earl of Wilmington	Whig	1874–80	Benjamin Disraeli	Conservative
1743–54	Henry Pelham	Whig	1880–85	W E Gladstone	Liberal
1754–56	Duke of Newcastle	Whig	1885–86	Marquess of Salisbury	Conservative
1756–57	Duke of Devonshire	Whig	1886	W E Gladstone	Liberal
1757–62	Duke of Newcastle	Whig	1886–92	Marquess of Salisbury	Conservative
1762–63	Earl of Bute	Tory	1892–94	W E Gladstone	Liberal
1763–65	George Grenville	Whig	1894–95	Earl of Rosebery	Liberal
1765–66	Marquess of Rockingham	Whig	1895–1902	Marquess of Salisbury	Conservative
1767–70	Duke of Grafton	Whig	1902–05	Arthur James Balfour	Conservative
1770–82	Lord North	Tory	1905–08	Sir H Campbell-Bannerman	Liberal
1782	Marquess of Rockingham	Whig	1908–15	H H Asquith	Liberal
1782–83	Earl of Shelburne	Whig	1915–16	H H Asquith	coalition
1783	Duke of Portland	coalition	1916–22	David Lloyd George	coalition
1783–1801	William Pitt the Younger	Tory	1922–23	Andrew Bonar Law	Conservative
1801–04	Henry Addington	Tory	1923–24	Stanley Baldwin	Conservative
1804–06	William Pitt the Younger	Tory	1924	Ramsay MacDonald	Labour
1806–07	Lord Grenville	coalition	1924–29	Stanley Baldwin	Conservative
1807–09	Duke of Portland	Tory	1929–31	Ramsay MacDonald	Labour
1809–12	Spencer Perceval	Tory	1931–35	Ramsay MacDonald	national coalition
1812–27	Earl of Liverpool	Tory			
1827	George Canning	coalition	1935–37	Stanley Baldwin	national coalition
1827–28	Viscount Goderich	Tory			
1828–30	Duke of Wellington	Tory	1937–40	Neville Chamberlain	national coalition
1830–34	Earl Grey	Tory			
1834	Viscount Melbourne	Whig	1940–45	Sir Winston Churchill	coalition
1834–35	Sir Robert Peel	Whig	1945–51	Clement Attlee	Labour
1835–41	Viscount Melbourne	Whig	1951–55	Sir Winston Churchill	Conservative
1841–46	Sir Robert Peel	Conservative	1955–57	Sir Anthony Eden	Conservative
1846–52	Lord Russell	Liberal	1957–63	Harold Macmillan	Conservative
1852	Earl of Derby	Conservative	1963–64	Sir Alec Douglas-Home	Conservative
1852–55	Lord Aberdeen	Peelite	1964–70	Harold Wilson	Labour
1855–58	Viscount Palmerston	Liberal	1970–74	Edward Heath	Conservative
1858–59	Earl of Derby	Conservative	1974–76	Harold Wilson	Labour
1859–65	Viscount Palmerston	Liberal	1976–79	James Callaghan	Labour
1865–66	Lord Russell	Liberal	1979–90	Margaret Thatcher	Conservative
1866–68	Earl of Derby	Conservative	1990–97	John Major	Conservative
1868	Benjamin Disraeli	Conservative	1997–	Tony Blair	Labour

Presidents of the USA

Term	Name	Party
1789–97	George Washington	Federalist
1797–1801	John Adams	Federalist
1801–09	Thomas Jefferson	Democratic-Republican
1809–17	James Madison	Democratic-Republican
1817–25	James Monroe	Democratic-Republican
1825–29	John Quincy Adams	Democratic-Republican
1829–37	Andrew Jackson	Democrat
1837–41	Martin Van Buren	Democrat
1841	William Henry Harrison	Whig
1841–45	John Tyler	Whig
1845–49	James Knox Polk	Democrat
1849-50	Zachary Taylor	Whig
1850–53	Millard Fillmore	Whig
1853–57	Franklin Pierce	Democrat
1857–61	James Buchanan	Democrat
1861–65	Abraham Lincoln	Republican
1865–69	Andrew Johnson	Democrat
1869–77	Ulysses S Grant	Republican
1877–81	Rutherford B Hayes	Republican
1881	James A Garfield	Republican
1881–85	Chester Alun Arthur	Republican
1885–89	Grover Cleveland	Democrat
1889–93	Benjamin Harrison	Republican
1893–97	Grover Cleveland	Republican
1897–1901	William McKinley	Republican
1901–09	Theodore Roosevelt	Republican
1909–13	William Howard Taft	Republican
1913–21	Woodrow Wilson	Democrat
1921–23	Warren Gamaliel Harding	Republican
1923–29	Calvin Coolidge	Republican
1929–33	Herbert C Hoover	Republican
1933–45	Franklin Delano Roosevelt	Democrat
1945–53	Harry S Truman	Democrat
1953–61	Dwight D Eisenhower	Republican
1961–63	John F Kennedy	Democrat
1963–69	Lyndon B Johnson	Democrat
1969–74	Richard M Nixon	Republican
1974–77	Gerald R Ford	Republican
1977–81	James Earl Carter	Democrat
1981–89	Ronald Reagan	Republican
1989–93	George Bush	Republican
1993–	Bill Clinton	Democrat

Prime ministers of Australia from 1901

Term	Name	Party
1901–03	Sir Edmund Barton	Protectionist
1903–04	Alfred Deacon	Protectionist
1904–04	John Watson	Labor
1904–05	Sir G Reid	Protectionist–Free Trade coalition
1905–08	Alfred Deakin	Protectionist
1908–09	Andrew Fisher	Labor
1909–10	Alfred Deakin	Protectionist–Free Trade coalition
1910–13	Andrew Fisher	Labor
1913–14	Sir J Cook	Liberal
1914–15	Andrew Fisher	Labor
1915–23	William Morris Hughes	Labor (National Labor from 1917)
1923–29	J H Scullin	
1932–39	Joseph Aloysius Lyons	United Australia–Country coalition
1939–41	R G Menzies	United Australia
1941–41	A W Fadden	Country–United Australia coalition
1941–45	John Curtin	Labor
1945	F M Forde	Labor
1945–49	J B Chifley	Labor
1949–66	R G Menzies	Liberal–Country coalition
1966–67	Harold Holt	Liberal–Country coalition
1967–68	John McEwen	Liberal–Country coalition
1968–71	J G Gorton	Liberal–Country coalition
1971–72	William McMahon	Liberal–Country coalition
1972–75	Gough Whitlam	Labor
1975–83	Malcolm Fraser	Liberal–National coalition
1983–91	Robert Hawke	Labor
1991–96	Paul Keating	Labor
1996-	John Howard	Liberal-National coalition

Prime ministers of Canada from 1867

Term	Name	Party
1867–73	John A Macdonald	Conservative
1873–78	Alexander Mackenzie	Liberal
1878–91	John A Macdonald	Conservative
1891–92	John J Abbott	Conservative
1892–94	John S D Thompson	Conservative
1894–96	Mackenzie Bowell	Conservative
1896	Charles Tupper	Conservative
1896–1911	Wilfred Laurier	Liberal
1911–20	Robert L Borden	Conservative
1920–21	Arthur Meighen	Conservative
1921–26	William L M King	Liberal
1926–26	Arthur Meighen	Conservative
1926–30	William L M King	Liberal
1930–35	Richard B Bennett	Conservative
1935–48	William L M King	Liberal
1948–57	Louis S St Laurent	Liberal
1957–63	John G Diefenbaker	Conservative
1963–68	Lester B Pearson	Liberal
1968–79	Pierre E Trudeau	Liberal
1979–80	Joseph Clark	Progressive Conservative
1980–84	Pierre E Trudeau	Liberal
1984	John Turner	Liberal
1984–93	Brian Mulroney	Progressive Conservative
1993	Kim Campbell	Progressive Conservative
1993–	Jean Chretien	Liberal

Prime Ministers of New Zealand from 1891

Term	Name	Party
1891–93	J Ballance	Liberal
1893–06	R J Seddon	Liberal
1906–06	W Hall-Jones	Liberal
1906–12	Joseph Ward	Liberal
1912–12	T Mackenzie	Liberal
1912–25	W F Massey	Reform
1925–28	J G Coates	Reform
1928–30	Joseph Ward	United
1930–35	G W Forbes	United
1935–40	M J Savage	Labour
1940–49	P Fraser	Labour
1949–57	S G Holland	National
1957–60	K J Holyoake	National
1957–60	Walter Nash	Labour
1960–72	K J Holyoake	National
1972–72	J Marshall	National
1972–74	N Kirk	Labour
1974–75	W Rowling	Labour
1975–84	R Muldoon	National
1984–89	D Lange	Labour
1989–90	G Palmer	Labour
1990	M Moore	Labour
1990–97	J Bolger	National
1997–	J Shipley	National

Prime ministers of India

Term	Name	Party
1949–64	Jawaharlal Nehru	Congress
1964–66	Lal Bahadur Shastri	Congress
1966–77	Indira Gandhi	Congress (I)
1977–79	Morarji Desai	Janata
1979–80	Charan Singh	Janata/Lok Dal
1980–84	Indira Gandhi	Congress (I)
1984–89	Rajiv Gandhi	Congress (I)
1989–90	Viswanath Pratap Singh	Janata Dal
1990–91	Chandra Shekhar	Janata Dal (Socialist)
1991–96	P V Narasimha Rao	Congress (I)
1996	Atal Behari Vaj Payee	Bharatiya Janata
1996-97	H D Deve Gowda	Janata Dal
1997-	Inder Kumar Gujral	Janata Dal

Prime ministers of Japan from 1945

Term	Name	Party
1945–46	Kijurō Shidehara	coalition
1946–47	Shigeru Yoshida	Liberal
1947–48	Tetsu Katayama	coalition
1948–48	Hitoshi Ashida	Democratic
1948–54	Shigeru Yoshida	Liberal
1954–56	Ichirō Hatoyama	Liberal*
1956–57	Tanzan Ishibashi	LDP
1957–60	Nobusuke Kishi	LDP
1960–64	Hayato Ikeda	LDP
1964–72	Eisaku Satō	LDP
1972–74	Kakuei Tanaka	LDP
1974–76	Takeo Miki	LDP
1976–78	Takeo Fukuda	LDP
1978–80	Masayoshi Ohira	LDP
1980–82	Zenkō Suzuki	LDP
1982–87	Yasuhiro Nakasone	LDP
1987–89	Noboru Takeshita	LDP
1989–89	Sōsuke Uno	LDP
1989–91	Toshiki Kaifu	LDP
1991–93	Kiichi Miyazawa	LDP
1993–94	Morohiro Hosokawa	JNP-led coalition
1994-94	Tsutoma Hata	Shinseito-led coalition
1994-	Tomiichi Murayama	SDPJ-led coalition

The conservative parties merged 1955 to form the Liberal Democratic Party (LDP, Jiyū-Minshūtō).

Presidents and Communist Party leaders of the USSR

Term	Name
Communist Party leaders	
1917–22	V I Lenin
1922–53	Joseph Stalin
1953–64	Nikita Khrushchev
1964–82	Leonid Brezhnev
1982–84	Yuri Andropov
1984–85	Konstantin Chernenko
1985–91	Mikhail Gorbachev
Presidents	
1917–22	V I Lenin
1922–46	Mikhail Kalinin
1946–53	N Shvernik
1953–60	Marshal K Voroshilov
1960–64	Leonid Brezhnev
1964–65	A Mikoyan
1965–77	N Podgorny
1977–82	Leonid Brezhnev
1982–83	V Kuznetsov (acting)
1983–84	Yuri Andropov
1984	V Kuznetsov (acting)
1984–85	Konstantin Chernenko
1985	V Kuznetsov (acting)
1985–89	Andrei Gromyko
1989–91	Mikhail Gorbachev

People's Republic of China: prime ministers and Communist Party leaders

Term	Name
Prime ministers	
1949–76	Zhou Enlai
1976–80	Hua Guofeng
1980–88	Zhao Ziyang
1988–	Li Peng
Communist Party leaders	
1935–76	Mao Zedong
1976–81	Hua Guofeng
1981–87	Hu Yaobang
1987–89	Zhao Ziyang
1989–	Jiang Zemin

Prime ministers and presidents of South Africa

Term	Name
Prime ministers	
1910–19	General L Botha
1919–24	General Jan Smuts
1924–39	General James Hertzog
1939–48	General Jan Smuts
1948–54	Daniel Malan
1954–58	J Strijdon
1958–66	Hendrik Verwoerd
1966–78	Balthazar Johannes Vorster
1978–84	Pieter Botha
Presidents*	
1984–89	Pieter Botha
1989–94	F W de Klerk
1994–	Nelson Mandela

* The post of prime minister was abolished 1984 and combined with that of president.

CONTINENTS

Continents

Africa second largest of the continents, three times the area of Europe

area 30,097,000 sq km/11,620,451 sq mi

largest cities (population over 1 million) Cairo, Algiers, Lagos, Kinshasa, Abidjan, Cape Town, Nairobi, Casablanca, El Gîza, Addis Ababa, Luanda, Dar-es Salaam, Ibadan, Douala, Mogadishu

physical dominated by a uniform central plateau comprising a southern tableland with a mean altitude of 1,070 m/3,000 ft that falls northwards to a lower elevated plain with a mean altitude of 400 m/1,300 ft. Although there are no great alpine regions or extensive coastal plains, Africa has a mean altitude of 610 m/2,000 ft, two times greater than Europe. The highest points are Mount Kilimanjaro 5,900 m/19,364 ft, and Mount Kenya 5,200 m/17,058 ft; the lowest point in Lac Assal in Djibouti −144 m/−471 ft. Compared with other continents, Africa has few broad estuaries or inlets and therefore has proportionately the shortest coastline (24,000 km/15,000 mi). The geographical extremities of the continental mainland are Cape Hafun in the E, Cape Almadies in the W, Ras Ben Sekka in the N, and Cape Agulhas in the S. The Sahel is a narrow belt of savanna and scrub forest which covers 700 million hectares of west and central Africa; 75% of the continents lies within the tropics

features Great Rift Valley, containing most of the great lakes of E Africa (except Lake Victoria); Atlas Mountains in NW; Drakensberg mountain range in SE; Sahara Desert (world's largest desert) in N;

Africa: history

14 million BC	Africa, which is considered the *cradle continent*, probably produced the first humanlike creatures.
3–5 million	Direct line of descent of modern humans was established in E Africa.
15,000	Agriculture first practised in Egypt.
10,000–2000	The originally fertile Sahara became a barrier desert between north and south.
5450–2500	Era of Saharan rock and cave paintings.
7th century BC– **6th century AD**	Assyria, Persia, Greece, Rome, and Byzantium in turn made conquests in N Africa. Meroe: the Egyptian and Negro tradition met in the Nubian kingdom of Kush.
320 BC–AD 50	The kingdom of Axum flourished in Ethiopia and gave rise to the later legend of Prester John.
AD 640	Islamic expansion began in N, E, and Central Africa.
300–1500	Period of the great medieval states: Ghana, Mali, Songhai, Benin, Ife, and the culture of Great Zimbabwe.
12th–15th centuries	Era of the Arab travellers: for example, Ibn Batuta; and of trade, for example, Kilwa.
1488	Diaz rounded the Cape of Good Hope.
15th–16th centuries	European sea trade in gold, ivory, timber, and pepper.
17th–19th centuries	Height of the Atlantic and Indian Ocean slave trade.
18th–19th centuries	European travellers in Africa: Park, Livingstone, Stanley, Speke, Mary Kingsley.
19th century	Colonial wars against well-organized native states: Ashanti, Dahomey, Zululand.
1880–90	Peak of European colonization in the *scramble for Africa*.
1899–1902	South African War, the first large-scale war between whites in Africa.
1920	League of Nations mandate system introduced the idea of European trusteeship.
1936	Italy's conquest of Ethiopia.
1942	World War II reached its turning point in the Battles of Alamein.
1951	Libya became the first independent state to be declared by the United Nations.
1952–60	Mau-Mau movement in Kenya began the ousting of white settlers south of the Sahara.
1954–62	The fight for independence in Algeria precipitated the end of the French Fourth Republic 1958.
1957	Ghana became independent, the first of the revived black nation states.
1963	Organization of African Unity (OAU) founded.
1967–70	Revolt of Biafra within the federation of Nigeria constituted the first civil war in a modern black state.
1975	Mozambique's independence led to the end of dictatorship in Portugal.
1979	Zimbabwe's achievement of independence left South Africa as the last white-ruled state in Africa.
1980	Future of the OAU doubtful due to division over Western Sahara and Libyan aggression towards Chad. Extensive food shortages in many parts of Central and East Africa.
1984	Increasing internal disaster in South Africa leading to violence between black population and minority white groups.
1988	Peace treaty between Angola, South Africa, and Cuba leading to Namibia's independence.
1990	Namibia declared independent. South Africa's African National Congress (ANC) party leader Nelson Mandela freed.
1991	North African states oppose Iraq on Kuwait invasion. Ethiopia's communist regime collapses.
1992	New constitution in South Africa leading to all-races majority rule approved by whites-only referendum. Southern Africa experienced the worst drought of the 20th century.

Namib, Kalahari, and Great Karoo deserts in S; Nile, Zaïre, Niger, Zambezi, Limpopo, Volta, and Orange rivers

products has 30% of the world's minerals including diamonds (51%) and gold (47%); produces 11% of world's crude petroleum, 58% of world's cocoa (Ivory Coast, Ghana, Cameroon, Nigeria) 23% of world's coffee (Uganda, Ivory Coast, Zaïre, Ethiopia, Cameroon, Kenya), 20% of the world's groundnuts (Senegal, Nigeria, Sudan, Zaïre), and 21% of the world's hardwood timber (Nigeria, Zaïre, Tanzania, Kenya)

population (1992) 656 million; more than double the 1960 population of 278 million, and estimated to rise above 1 billion by 2010; growth rate (1985–90) 3.05%; 27% of the world's undernourished people live in sub-Saharan Africa where an estimated 25 million are facing famine

language over 1,000 languages spoken in Africa; Niger-Kordofanian languages including Mandinke, Kwa, Lingala, Bemba, and Bantu (Zulu, Swahili, Kikuyu), spoken over half of Africa from Mauritania in the W to South Africa; Nilo-Saharan languages, including Dinka, Shilluk, Nuer, and Masai, spoken in Central Africa from the bend of the Niger river to the foothills of Ethiopia; Afro-Asiatic (Hamito-Semitic) languages, including Arabic, Berber, Ethiopian, and Amharic, N of Equator; Khoisan languages with 'click' consonants spoken in SW by Bushmen, Hottentots, and Nama people of Namibia

religion Islam in the N and on the E coast as far S as N Mozambique; animism below the Sahara, which survives alongside Christianity (both Catholic and Protestant) in many central and S areas.

Antarctica an ice-covered continent surrounding the South Pole

area 13,900,000 sq km/5,400,000 sq mi (the size of Europe and the USA combined)

physical formed of two blocs of rock with an area of about 8 million sq km/3 million sq mi, Antarctica is covered by a cap of ice that flows slowly towards its 22,400 km/14,000 mi coastline, reaching the sea in high ice cliffs. The most southerly shores are near the 78th parallel in the Ross and Weddell Seas. E Antarctica is a massive bloc of ancient rocks that surface in the Transantarctic Mountains of Victoria Land. Separated by a deep channel, W Antarctica is characterized by the mountainous regions of Graham Land, the Antarctic Peninsula, Palmer Land, and Ellsworth Land; the highest peak is Vinson Massif (5,139 m/16,866 ft). Little more than 1% of the land is ice-free. With an estimated volume of 24 million cu m/5.9 million cu mi, the ice-cap has a mean thickness of 1,880 m/6,170 ft and in places reaches depths of 5,000 m/16,000 ft or more. Each annual layer of snow preserves a record of global conditions, and where no melting at the surface of the bedrock has occurred the ice can be a million years old. Occupying 10% of the world's surface, the continent contains 90% of the world's ice and 70% of its fresh water. Winds are strong and temperatures are cold, particularly in the interior where temperatures can drop to −70°C/−100°F and below. Precipitation is largely in the form of snow or hoar-frost rather than rain which

Antarctic exploration

1773–7	English explorer James Cook first sailed in Antarctic seas, but exploration was difficult before the development of iron ships able to withstand ice pressure.
1819–21	Antarctica circumnavigated by Russian explorer Fabian Bellingshausen.
1823	British navigator James Weddell sailed into the sea named after him.
1841–42	Scottish explorer James Ross sighted the Great Ice Barrier named after him.
1895	Norwegian explorer Carsten Borchgrevink was one of the first landing party on the continent.
1898	Borchgrevink's British expedition first wintered in Antarctica.
1901–04	English explorer Robert Scott first penetrated the interior of the continent.
1907–08	English explorer Ernest Shackleton came within 182 km/113 mi of the Pole.
1911	Norwegian explorer Roald Amundsen reached the Pole, 14 Dec, overland with dogs.
1912	Scott reached the Pole, 18 Jan, initially aided by ponies.
1928–29	US naval officer Richard Byrd made the first flight to the Pole.
1935	US explorer Lincoln Ellsworth first flew across Antarctica.
1946–48	US explorer Finn Ronne's expedition proved the Antarctic to be one continent.
1957–58	English explorer Vivian Fuchs made the first overland crossing.
1959	Soviet expedition from the West Ice Shelf to the Pole.
1959	International Antarctic Treaty suspended all territorial claims, reserving an area south of 60°S latitude for peaceful purposes.
1961–62	Bentley Trench discovered, which suggested that there may be an Atlantic-Pacific link beneath the Continent.
1966–67	Specially protected areas established internationally for animals and plants.
1979	Fossils of ape-like humanoids resembling E Africa's Proconsul found 500 km/300 mi from the Pole.
1980	International Convention on the exploitation of resources – oil, gas, fish, and krill.
1982	First circumnavigation of Earth (2 Sept 1979–29 Aug 1982) via the Poles by English explorers Ranulph Fiennes and Charles Burton.
1990	Longest unmechanized crossing (6,100 km/3,182 mi) completed by a 6-person international team, using only skis and dogs.
1991	Antarctic Treaty imposing a 50-year ban on mining activity secured.
1992–93	Norwegian lawyer Erling Kagge skied unassisted to South Pole from Berkner Island in Weddell Sea; Ranulph Fiennes and Michael Strond crossed Antarctic continent on foot, unassisted, but had to be rescued before reaching ultimate destination of Scott's Base.

Arctic exploration

60,000–35,000 BC	Ancestors of the Inuit and American Indians began migration from Siberia to North America by the 'lost' landbridge of Beringia.
320 BC	Pytheas, Greek sailor contemporary with Alexander the Great, possibly reached Iceland.
9th–10th centuries AD	Vikings colonized Iceland and Greenland, which then had a much warmer climate.
***c.* 1000**	Norwegian sailor Leif Ericsson reached Baffin Island (NE of Canada) and Labrador.
1497	Genoese pilot Giovanni Caboto first sought the Northwest Passage as a trade route around North America for Henry VII of England.
1553	English navigator Richard Chancellor tried to find the Northeast Passage around Siberia and first established direct English trade with Russia.
1576	English sailor Martin Frobisher reached Frobisher Bay, but found only 'fools' gold' (iron pyrites) for Elizabeth I of England.
1594–97	Dutch navigator Willem Barents made three expeditions in search of the Northeast Passage.
1607	English navigator Henry Hudson failed to cross the Arctic Ocean, but his reports of whales started the northern whaling industry.
1670	Hudson's Bay Company started the fur trade in Canada.
1728	Danish navigator Vitus Bering passed Bering Strait.
1829–33	Scottish explorer John Ross discovered the North Magnetic Pole.
1845	Mysterious disappearance of English explorer John Franklin's expedition to the Northwest Passage stimulated further exploration.
1878–79	Swedish navigator Nils Nordensköld was the first European to discover the Northeast Passage.
1893–96	Norwegian explorer Fridtjof Nansen's ship *Fram* drifted across the Arctic, locked in the ice, proving that no Arctic continent existed.
1903–06	Norwegian explorer Roald Amundsen sailed through the Northwest Passage.
1909	US explorer Robert Peary, Matt Henson, and four Inuit reached the North Pole on 2 Apr.
1926	US explorer Richard Byrd and Floyd Bennett flew to the Pole on 9 May.
1926	Italian aviator Umberto Nobile and Amundsen crossed the Pole (Spitzbergen–Alaska) in the airship *Norge* on 12 May.
1954	First regular commercial flights over the short-cut polar route by Scandinavian Airlines.
1958	the US submarine *Nautilus* crossed the Pole beneath the ice.
1960	from this date a Soviet nuclear-powered icebreaker has kept open a 4,000 km/2,500 mi Asia-Europe passage along the north coast of Siberia 150 days a year.
1969	first surface crossing, by dog sled, of the Arctic Ocean (Alaska–Spitzbergen) by Wally Herbert, British Transarctic Expedition, Feb–May.
1977	The Soviet icebreaker *Arktika* made the first surface voyage to the Pole.
1982	first circumnavigation of Earth (2 Sept 1979–29 Aug 1982) via the Poles by Ranulph Fiennes and Charles Burton.
1988	Canadian and Soviet skiers attempted the first overland crossing from the USSR to Canada via the Pole.

rarely exceeds 50 mm/2 in in a year (less than the Sahara Desert). The Antarctic ecosystem is characterized by large numbers of relatively few species of higher plants and animals, and a short food chain from tiny marine plants to whales, seals, penguins, and other sea birds. Only two species of vascular plant are known, but there are about 60 species of moss, 100 species of lichen, and 400 species of algae. The crabeater seal is the most numerous wild large mammal in the world

features Mount Erebus on Ross Island is the world's southernmost active volcano; the Ross Ice Shelf is formed by several glaciers coalescing in the Ross Sea

products cod, Antarctic icefish and krill are fished in Antarctic waters. Whaling, which began in the early 20th century ceased during the 1960s as a result of overfishing. Petroleum, coal, and minerals such as palladium and platinum exist, but their exploitation is prevented by a 50-year ban on commercial mining agreed by 39 nations in 1991

population no permanent residents; settlement limited to scientific research stations with maximum population of 2,000 to 3,000 during the summer months. Sectors of Antarctica are claimed by Argentina, Australia, Chile, France, the UK, Norway, and New Zealand

history following multi-national scientific cooperation in Antarctica during the International Geophysical Year of 1957–58, 12 countries signed an Antarctic Treaty with a view to promoting scientific research and keeping Antarctica free from conflict. After it came into effect 1961, a further 27 countries acceded to the treaty. In response to overfishing in Antarctic waters, the Conservation of Antarctic Marine Living Resources was agreed 1980. In 1988 the Convention on the Regulation of Antarctic Mineral Resource Activities gave any signatory the right to veto mining activity on environmental grounds. While this provided a means of regulation, environmental pressure groups felt it would not prevent commercial exploitation. In 1991 an agreement was signed extending the Antarctic Treaty and imposing a 50-year ban on mining activity.

Arctic, the that part of the northern hemisphere surrounding the North Pole; arbitrarily defined as the region lying N of the Arctic Circle (66° 32'N) or N of the tree line. There is no Arctic continent – the greater part of the region comprises the Arctic Ocean which is the world's smallest ocean. Arctic climate, fauna, and flora extend over the islands and northern edges of continental land masses that surround the Arctic Ocean (Svalbard, Iceland, Greenland, Siberia, Scandinavia, Alaska, and Canada)

physical pack ice floating on the Arctic Ocean occupies almost the entire region between the North Pole and the coasts of North America and Eurasia, covering an area that ranges in diameter from 3,000 km/1,900 mi to 4,000 km/2,500 mi. The pack-ice reaches a maximum extent in Feb when its outer limit (influenced by the cold Labrador Current and the warm Gulf Stream) varies from 50°N along the coast of Labrador to 75°N in the Barents Sea N of Scandinavia. In spring the pack-ice begins to break up into ice floes which are carried by the S-flowing Greenland Current to the Atlantic Ocean. Arctic ice is at its minimum area in August. The greatest concentration of icebergs in Arctic regions is found in Baffin Bay. They are derived from the glaciers of W Greenland, then carried along Baffin Bay and down into the N Atlantic where they melt off Labrador and Newfoundland. The Bering Straits are icebound for more than six months each year, but the Barents Sea between Scandinavia and Svalbard is free of ice and is navigable throughout the year. Arctic coastlines, which have emerged from the sea since the last Ice Age, are characterized by deposits of gravel and disintegrated rock

climate permanent ice-sheets and year-round snow cover are found in regions where average monthly temperatures remain below 0°C/32°F, but on land areas where one or more summer months have average temperatues between freezing point and 10°C/50°F, a stunted, treeless tundra vegetation is found. Mean annual temperatures range from –23°C at the North Pole to –12°C on the coast of Alaska. In winter the Sun disappears below the horizon for a time, but the cold is less severe than in parts of E Siberia or Antarctica. During the short summer season there is a maximum of 24 hours of daylight at the summer solstice on the Artic Circle and six months constant light at the North Pole. Countries with Arctic coastlines established the International Arctic Sciences Committee in 1987 to study ozone depletion and climatic change

flora and fauna the plants of the relatively infertile Arctic tundra (lichens, mosses, grasses, cushion plants, and low shrubs) spring to life during the short summer season and remain dormant for the remaining ten months of the year. There are no annual plants, only perennials. Animal species include reindeer, caribou, musk ox, fox, hare, lemming, wolf, polar bear, seal, and walrus. There are few birds, except in summer, when insects, especially mosquitoes, are plentiful

natural resources the Arctic is rich in coal (Svalbard, Russia), oil and natural gas (Alaska, Canadian Arctic, Russia), and mineral resources, including gold, silver, copper, uranium, lead, zinc, nickel, and bauxite. Because of climatic conditions the Arctic is not suited to navigation and the exploitation of these resources. Murmansk naval base on the Kola Peninsula is the largest in the world

population there are about one million aboriginal people including the Aleuts of Alaska, North American Indians, the Lapps of Scandinavia and Russia, the Yakuts, Samoyeds, Komi, Chukchi, Tungus, and Dolgany of Russia, and the Inuit of Siberian Russia, the Canadian Arctic, and Greenland.

Asia largest of the continents, occupying one third of the total land surface of the world

area 44,000,000 sq km/17,000,000 sq mi

largest cities (population over 5 million) Tokyo, Shanghai, Osaka, Beijing, Seoul, Calcutta, Bombay, Jakarta, Bangkok, Tehran, Hong Kong, Delhi, Tianjin, Karachi

physical lying in the eastern hemisphere, Asia extends from the Arctic Circle to just over 10°S of the Equator. The Asia mainland, which forms the greater part of the Eurasian continent, lies entirely in the northern hemisphere and stretches from Cape Chelyubinsk at its N extremity to Cape Piai at the S tip of the Malay Peninsula. From Dezhneva Cape in the E, the mainland extends W over more than 165° longitude to Cape Baba in Turkey. Containing the world's highest mountains and largest inland seas, Asia can be divided into five physical units:

1) at the heart of the continent, a central triangle of plateaux at varying altitudes (Tibetan Plateau, Tarim Basin, Gobi Desert), surrounded by huge mountains chains which spread in all directions (Himalayas, Karakoram, Hindu Kush, Pamirs, Kunlun, Tien Shan, Altai);

2) the W plateaux and ranges (Elburz, Zagros, Taurus, Great Caucasus mountains) of Afghanistan, Iran, N Iraq, Armenia, and Turkey;

3) the lowlands of Turkestan and Siberia which stretch N of the central mountains to the Arctic Ocean and include large areas in which the subsoil is permanently frozen;

4) the fertile and densely populated E lowlands and river plains of Korea, China, and Indochina, and the islands of the East Indies and Japan;

5) the southern plateaux of Arabia, and the Deccan, with the fertile alluvial plains of the Euphrates, Tigris, Indus, Ganges, Brahmaputra, and Irrawaddy rivers.

In Asiatic Russia are the largest areas of coniferous forest (taiga) in the world. The climate shows great extremes and contrasts, the heart of the continent becoming bitterly cold in winter and extremely hot in summer. When the heated air over land rises, moisture-laden air from the surrounding seas flows in, bringing heavy monsoon rain to all SE Asia, China, and Japan between May and Oct

features Mount Everest at 8,872 m/29,118 ft, is the world's highest mountain; Dead Sea –394 m/–1,293 ft is the world's lowest point below sea level; rivers (over 3,200 km/2,000 mi) include Chiang Jiang (Yangtze), Huang He (Yellow River), Ob-Irtysh, Amur, Lena, Mekong, Yeni sei; lakes (over 18,000 sq km/7,000 sq mi) include Caspian Sea (the largest body of water in the world), Aral Sea, Baikal (largest freshwater lake in Eurasia), Balkhash; deserts include the Gobi, Takla Makan, Syrian Desert, Arabian Desert, Negev

products 62% of the population are employed in agriculture; Asia produces 46% of the world's cereal crops (91% of the world's rice); other crops include mangoes (India), groundnuts (India, China), 84% of the

Asia: history

2800–2200 BC	Sage kings, earliest Chinese legendary dynasty; civilization spread to all of China.
2500–1500	Indus Valley civilization.
563	Birth of the Buddha.
551	Birth of Confucius.
215	Great Wall of China begun.
320 BC–AD 550	Gupta dynasty in India.
1192	First Muslim kingdom of India established.
1279	Kublai Khan became emperor of China; Marco Polo visited.
1395	Tamerlane defeated the Golden Horde.
1526	Babur established Mogul empire in N India.
1600s	English East India Company chartered.
1757	Clive defeated the nawab of Bengal at Plassey.
1839–42	Opium War between Britain and China ended with ceding of Hong Kong to Britain and opening of treaty ports in China.
1854	US Commodore Perry forced Japanese shogun to grant commercial treaty.
1857–58	Sepoy Rebellion in India.
1894–95	Sino–Japanese War.
1912	Qin dynasty overthrown in republican revolution in China.
1931	Japan invaded China.
1941	Japan attacked US fleet at Pearl Harbor.
1947	India and Pakistan gained independence.
1949	Chiang Kai-shek forced by Chinese communists to flee to Taiwan, where he set up a US-backed Republic of China.
1950–53	Korean War.
1954	End of French colonialism in Indochina: Vietnam was divided into the communist north and the noncommunist south.
1955	US sent to advise South Vietnam against Vietcong communist insurgents, backed by North Vietnam and China.
1965	US troops sent to support South Vietnamese government in large numbers.
1971	East Pakistan declared independence as Bangladesh.
1975	Fall of South Vietnam to North Vietnam. Khmer Rouge seized power in Cambodia.
1976	Death of Mao Zedong.
1980	Trial of Gang of Four (including Mao's widow Jiang Qing).
1980s	Japan became world's richest nation.
1986	Agreement between British and Chinese governments on future 1997 administration of Hong Kong.
1989	Prodemocracy demonstrations in China bloodily repressed by government troops.

world's copra (Philippines, Indonesia), 93% of the world's rubber (Indonesia, Malaysia, Thailand), tobacco (China), flax (China, Russia), 95% of the world's jute (India, Bangladesh, China), cotton (China, India, Pakistan), silk (China, India), fish (Japan, China, Korea, Thailand); China pro-duces 55% of the world's tungsten; 45% of the world's tin is produced by Malaysia, China, and Indonesia; Saudi Arabia is the world's largest producer of oil

population (1992) 3.29 billion; the world's largest, though not the fastest-growing population, amounting to more than half the total number of people in the world; between 1950 and 1990 the death rate and infant mortality were reduced by more than 60%; growth rate (1985–90) 1.8%; projected to increase to 4.29 billion by 2010

language predominantly tonal languages (Chinese, Japanese) in the E, Indo-Iranian languages (Hindi, Urdu, Persian) in S Asia, Altaic languages (Mongolian, Turkish) in W and Central Asia, Semitic languages (Arabic, Hebrew) in the SW

religion the major religions of the world had their origins in Asia – Judaism and Christianity in the Middle East, Islam in Arabia, Buddhism, Hinduism, and Sikhism in India, Confucianism in China, and Shinto in Japan.

Europe second smallest continent, occupying 8% of the Earth's surface

area 10,400,000 sq km/4,000,000 sq mi

largest cities (population over 1.5 million) Athens, Barcelona, Berlin, Birmingham, Bucharest, Budapest, Hamburg, Istanbul, Kharkov, Kiev, Lisbon, London, Madrid, Manchester, Milan, Moscow, Paris, Rome, St Petersburg, Vienna, Warsaw

physical conventionally occupying that part of Eurasia to the west of the Ural Mountains, north of the Caucasus Mountains and north of the Sea of Marmara; Europe lies entirely in the northern hemisphere between 36°N and the Arctic Ocean. About two-thirds of the continent is a great plain which covers the whole of European Russia and spreads westward through Poland to the Low Countries and the Bay of Biscay. To the north lie the Scandinavian highlands rising to 2,470 m/8,110 ft at Glittertind, in the Jotenheim Range of Norway. To the south, a series of mountain ranges stretch from east to west (Caucasus, Balkans, Carpathians, Apennines, Alps, Pyrenees, and Sierra Nevada). The most westerly point of the mainland is Cape Roca in Portugal; the most southerly location is Tarifa Point in Spain; the most northerly point on the mainland is Nordkynn, in Norway. A line from the Baltic to the Black Sea

Europe: history

3000 BC	Bronze Age civilizations: Minoan, Mycenaean.
10–1000	Iron Age.
6th–4th centuries	Greek civilization at its height; Alexander the Great advances E to India.
3rd century	Rome in control of the Italian peninsula.
146	Greece a Roman province, and Carthage destroyed.
1st century	Augustus made the Rhine and Danube the Roman Empire's northern frontiers.
AD 1st century	Britain brought within the Roman Empire
2nd century	Roman Empire ceased to expand.
4th century	Christianity the established religion of the Roman Empire, which halved into E and W empires (see *Byzantine* empires).
4th–6th centuries	W Europe overrun by Anglo Saxons, Franks, Goths, Lombards. W Roman empire fell 476. Middle Ages begin; feudalism prevails.
7th–8th centuries	Christendom threatened by the Moors (Muslim Arabs) via the Mediterranean countries.
800	Charlemagne given title of emperor by the Pope; Holy Roman empire begins.
1073	Gregory VII began 200 years of conflict between the powers of the empire and papacy.
1096–1272	Crusades to take Jerusalem.
12th century	Setting up of German, Flemish, and Italian city states, which in the 14th–15th centuries fostered the Renaissance.
1453	Byzantine empire falls to the Turks.
16th–17th centuries	Dominated by rivalry of France and the Habsburgs, the Protestant Reformation, and the Catholic Counter Reformation.
17th century	Absolute monarchy came to prevail (Louis XIV) in Europe, although in Britain supremacy of Parliament established by Civil War.
18th century	War of the Austrian Succession and Seven Years' War ended in the loss of the French colonial empire to Britain and the establishment of Prussia as Europe's military power.
1789–95	French Revolution led to the Revolutionary and Napoleonic wars.
1821–29	Greek War of Independence marked the end of Turkish control of the Balkans.
1848	Year of revolutions against monarchial rule, beginning in France and spreading to Italy, the Austrian Empire, and Germany. Most were violently suppressed within a few months.
1914–1918	World War I arose from the Balkan question, Franco–German rivalry, and colonial differences; it destroyed the Austrian, Russian, and Turkish empires and paved the way for the Russian Revolution and the formation of the USSR.
1933	Hitler came to power in a defeated, impoverished Germany. His geopolitical aggression caused World War II.
1939–45	World War II resulted in decline of European colonial rule in Africa and Asia; emergence of Soviet power, and most of Western Europe under the military aegis of the USA (NATO); the Cold War begins.
1957	Establishment of the European Economic Community, the Common Market.
1973	Enlargement of the European Community to include Britain, Denmark, and the Irish Republic.
1979	First direct elections to the European Parliament.
1989–90	Beginning of democratization of Eastern bloc, including USSR, Poland, Romania, Czechoslovakia, East Germany, Lithuania. Unification of Germany.
1991	Baltic republics of Estonia, Latvia, and Lithuania regain independence; other Soviet republics follow.
1992	European Community becomes a single market.

divides Europe between an eastern continental region and a western region characterized by a series of peninsulas that include Scandinavia (Norway, Sweden, and Finland), Jutland (Denmark and Germany), Iberia (Spain and Portugal), and Italy and the Balkans (Greece, Albania, Croatia, Slovenia, Bosnia-Herzegovina, Yugoslavia, Bulgaria, and European Turkey). Because of the large number of bays, inlets, and peninsulas, the coastline is longer in proportion to its size than that of any other continent. The largest islands adjacent to continental Europe are the British Isles, Novaya Zemlya, Sicily, Sardinia, Crete, Corsica, Gotland (in the Baltic Sea), and the Balearic Islands; other more distant islands associated with Europe include Iceland, Svalbard, Franz Josef Land, Madeira, the Azores, and the Canary Islands. The greater part of Europe falls within the northern temperate zone which is modified by the Gulf Stream in the northwest; Central Europe has warm summers and cold winters; the Mediterranean coast has comparatively mild winters and hot summers

features Mount Elbruz 5,642 m/18,517 ft in the Caucasus mountains is the highest peak in Europe; Mont Blanc 4,807 m/15,772 ft is the highest peak in the Alps; lakes (over 5,100 sq km/2,000 sq mi) include Ladoga, Onega, Vänern; rivers (over 800 km/500 mi) include the Volga, Danube, Dnieper Ural, Don, Pechora, Dneister, Rhine, Loire, Tagus, Ebro, Oder, Prut, Rhône

products nearly 50% of the world's cars are produced in Europe (Germany, France, Italy, Spain, Russia, Georgia, Ukraine, Latvia, Belarus, UK); the rate of fertilizer consumption on agricultural land is four times greater than that in any other continent; Europe produces 43% of the world's barley (Germany, Spain, France, UK), 41% of its rye (Poland, Germany), 31% of its oats (Poland, Germany, Sweden, France), and

24% of its wheat (France, Germany, UK, Romania); Italy, Spain, and Greece produce more than 70% of the world's olive oil

population (1992) 727 million; growth rate (1985–90) 0.45%, projected population of 762 million by 2010

language mostly Indo-European, with a few exceptions, including Finno-Ugrian (Finnish and Hungarian), Basque and Altaic (Turkish); apart from a fringe of Celtic, the NW is Germanic; Letto-Lithuanian languages separate the Germanic from the Slavonic tongues of E Europe; Romance languages spread E-W from Romania through Italy and France to Spain and Portugal

religion Christianity (Protestant, Roman Catholic, Eastern Orthodox), Muslim (Turkey, Albania, Bosnia-Herzegovina, Yugoslavia, Bulgaria), Judaism.

North America third largest of the continents (including Greenland and Central America), and over twice the size of Europe

area 24,000,000 sq km/9,400,000 sq mi

largest cities (population over 1 million) Mexico City, New York, Chicago, Toronto, Los Angeles,

North America: history

c. 100,000–40,000 BC	Mongoloid Asian peoples migrated into North America. Settlement spread south and east.
c. 7000–1400 BC	Civilization developed.
1400–400 BC	Period of Olmec civilization.
C. AD 1000	First known European settlement, of Norsemen in *Vinland*, a part of Newfoundland.
1200 BC–AD 1521	Mayan civilization.
AD 1325–1521	Aztec civilization.
1492	Columbus sailed from Spain to the West Indies, so named because he mistook them for the East Indies; for the same reason, the native Americans he encountered were called *Indians*. The permanent settlement of North America by Europeans began.
1497	John Cabot sailed from England to Canada.
1502	Columbus discovered the Mayan civilization in Central America.
1521	The Spanish adventurer Hernan Cortes, greeted at first by the Aztecs as a god, destroyed their capital city and their empire and took Mexico; he subsequently colonized other parts of Central and North America.
1534	Jacques Cartier began to colonize Canada for France.
17th century	England and France began to colonize Canada.
1756–63	France defeated in wars with Britain for control of Canada. Continuing hostility resulted in the country's division into British and French sectors.
1775	Beginning of American Revolution (War of Independence).
1776	Declaration of Independence.
1783	Britain recognized the independence of the 13 colonies in the Treaty of Paris, and the USA now extended from the Atlantic seaboard to the Mississippi River.
1803	The Louisiana Purchase of land from France doubled the area of the USA.
early 1800s	Central American Federation (CAF) formed.
1812–14	French trade blockade of British shipping sparked the Anglo–American War of 1812.
1819	The USA bought Florida from Spain.
1821	Mexico and Central America won their independence from Spain.
1840	CAF disintegrated.
1841	Union of Upper (English) and Lower (French) Canada as Canada province; Dominion of Canada founded.
1848, 1851	The USA won the Southwestern states from Mexico in the Mexican War.
1861	The USA bought Alaska from Russia.
1861–65	The Civil War brought about the end of slavery.
1867	Canadian Confederation formed, with ties to Great Britain.
1898	Hawaii ceded itself to the USA.
1903	The USA leased the rights to the Panama Canal Zone.
1914	Panama Canal completed.
1948	Formation of OAS.
1949	Formation of NATO.
1961	The USA backed the abortive invasion of Cuba by anti-Castro Cuban exiles.
1969	US space launch was the first to put a person on the Moon.
1960s–70s	Opposition to the Vietnam War caused domestic discord in the USA.
1982	Canada gained its independence while remaining in the British Commonwealth.
1983	The USA invaded Grenada to preserve the existing government.
1989	The USA and Canada signed a free trade agreement. The USA invaded Panama and took its leader, General Noriega, into custody.
1900	Collapse of Meech Lake accords, designed to resolve Canadian constitutional issues.
1990–91	Gulf War: US-led coalition, joined by Canada and other nations, drove the invader Iraq from Kuwait.
1992	The USA, Canada, and Mexico reached accord on North American Free Trade Agreement, aimed at ending tariffs.

Montreal, Guadalajara, Monterrey, Philadelphia, Houston, Guatemala City, Vancouver, Detroit, San Diego, Dallas

physical occupying the N part of the landmass of the western hemisphere between the Arctic Ocean and the tropical SE tip of the isthmus that joins Central America to South America; the northernmost point on the mainland is the tip of Boothia Peninsula in the Canadian Arctic; the northernmost point on adjacent islands is Cape Morris Jesup on Greenland; the most westerly point on the mainland is Cape Prince of Wales, Alaska; the most westerly point on adjacent islands is Attu Island in the Aleutians; the most easterly point on the mainland lies on the SE coast of Labrador; the highest point is Mount McKinley, Alaska 6,194 m/20,320 ft; the lowest point is Badwater in Death Valley –86 m/–282 ft. In Canada and the USA, the Great Plains of the interior separate mountain belts to the E (Appalachians, Laurentian Highlands) and W (Rocky Mountains, Coast Mountains, Cascade Range, Sierra Nevada). The W range extends S into Mexico as the Sierra Madre. The Mississippi river system drains from the central Great Plains into the Gulf of Mexico; low coastal plains on the Atlantic coast are indented by the Gulf of St Lawrence, Bay of Fundy, Delaware Bay, Chesapeake Bay; the St Lawrence and Great Lakes form a rough crescent (with Lake Winnipeg, Lake Athabasca, the Great Bear, and the Great Slave lakes) around the exposed rock of the great Canadian/Laurentian shield, into which Hudson Bay break from the north; Greenland (the largest island in the world next to Australia) is a high, ice-covered plateau with a deeply indented coastline of fjords

features Lake Superior (the largest body of freshwater in the world); Grand Canyon on the Colorado river; Redwood National Park, California has some of the world's tallest trees; San Andreas Fault, California; deserts: Death Valley, Mojave, Sonoran; rivers (over 1,600 km/1,000 mi) include Mississippi, Missouri, Mackenzie, Rio Grande, Yukon, Arkansas, Colorado, Saskatchewan-Bow, Columbia, Red, Peace, Snake

products with abundant resources and an ever-expanding home market, the USA's fast-growing industrial and technological strength has made it less dependent on exports and a dominant economic power throughout the continent. Canada is the world's leading producer of nickel, zinc, uranium, potash, and linseed, and the world's second largest producer of asbestos, silver, titanium, gypsum, sulphur, and molybdenum; Mexico is the world's leading producer of silver and the fourth largest oil producer; the USA is the world's leading producer of salt and the second largest producer of oil and cotton; nearly 30% of the world's beef and veal is produced in North America

population (1988) 417 million, rising to an estimated 450 million by 2000; growth rate (1980–85): Canada 1.08%, USA 0.88%, Mexico 2.59%, Honduras 3.39%; the native American Indian, Inuit, and Aleut peoples are now a minority within a population predominantly of European immigrant origin. Many Africans were brought in as part of the slave trade

language English predominates in Canada, USA, and Belize; Spanish is the chief language of the countries of Latin America and a sizeable minority in the USA; French is spoken by about 25% of the population of Canada, and by people of the French département of St Pierre and Miquelon; indigenous non-European minorities, including the Inuit of Arctic Canada, the Aleuts of Alaska, North American Indians, and the Maya of Central America, have their own languages and dialects

religion Christian and Jewish religions predominate; 97% of Latin Americans, 47% of Canadians, and 21% of those living in the USA are Roman Catholic.

Oceania a general term for the islands of the central and S Pacific, including Australia, New Zealand, and the E half of New Guinea; although situated in the world's largest ocean, Oceania is the smallest continent in the world in terms of land surface

area 8,500,000 sq km/3,300,000 sq mi (land area)

largest cities (population over 500,000) Sydney, Melbourne, Brisbane, Perth, Adelaide, Auckland

physical stretching from the Tropic of Cancer in the N to the S tip of New Zealand, Oceania can be broadly divided into groups of volcanic and coral islands on the basis of the ethnic origins of their inhabitants: Micronesia (Guam, Kiribati, Mariana, Marshall, Caroline Islands), Melanesia (Papua New Guinea, Vanuatu, New Caledonia, Fiji, Solomon Islands) and Polynesia (Tonga, Samoa, Line Islands, Tuvalu, French Polynesia, Pitcairn); Australia (the largest island in the world) occupies more than 90% of the land surface; the highest point is Mount Wilhelm, Papua New Guinea 4,509 m/14,793 ft; the lowest point is Lake Eyre, South Australia –16 m/–52 ft; the longest river is the Murray in SE Australia 2,590 km/1,609 mi

features the Challenger Deep in the Mariana Trench –11,034 m/–36,201 ft is the greatest known depth of sea in the world; Ayers Rock in Northern Territory, Australia is the world's largest monolith; the Great Barrier Reef is the longest coral reef in the world; Mount Kosciusko 2,229 m/7,316 ft in New South Wales, is the highest peak in Australia; Mount Cook 3,764 m/21,353 ft is the highest peak in New Zealand

products with a small home market, Oceania has a manufacturing sector dedicated to servicing domestic requirements and a large export-oriented sector 70% of which is based on exports of primary agricultural or mineral products. Australia is a major producer of bauxite, nickel, silver, cobalt, gold, iron ore, diamonds, lead, and uranium; New Caledonia is a source of cobalt, chromite, and nickel; Papua and New Guinea produces gold and copper

Agricultural products include coconuts, copra, palm oil, coffee, cocoa, phosphates (Nauru), rubber (Papua New Guinea), 40% of the world's wool (Australia, New Zealand); New Zealand and Australia are, respectively, the world's second and third largest producers of mutton and lamb; fishing and tourism are also major industries

population 27 million, rising to 35 million by 2010; growth rate (1985–90) 1.37%; Australia accounts for 65% of the population; 1% of Australia's population are Aboriginal and 9% of the people of New Zealand are Maori

language English, French (French Polynesia, New Caledonia, Wallis and Fatuna, Vanuatu); a wide range of indigenous Aboriginal, Maori, Melanesian, Micronesian, and Polynesian languages and dialects (over 700 in Papua New Guinea) are spoken

religion predominantly Christian; 30% of the people of Tonga adhere to the Free Wesleyan Church; 70% of the people of Tokelau adhere to the Congregational Church; French overseas territories are largely Roman Catholic.

South America fourth largest of the continents, nearly twice as large as Europe, occupying 13% of the world's land surface

area 17,864,000 sq km/6,900,000 sq mi

largest cities (population over 2 million) Buenos Aires, São Paulo, Rio de Janeiro, Bogotá, Santiago, Lima, Caracas, Janeiro, Belo Horizonte

physical occupying the S part of the landmass of the western hemisphere, the South American continent stretches from Point Gallinas on the Caribbean coast of Colombia to Cape Horn at the southern tip of Horn Island which lies adjacent to Tierra del Fuego; the most southerly point on the mainland is Cape Froward on the Brunswick peninsula, S Chile; at its maximum width (5,120 km/3,200 mi) the continent stretches from Point Pariñas , Peru in the extreme W to Point Coqueiros, just N of Recife, Brazil, in the E; five-sixths of the continent lies in the southern hemisphere

and two-thirds within the tropics. South America can be divided into the following physical regions:

1) the Andes mountain system which begins as three separate ranges in the N and stretches the whole length of the W coast approximately 7,200 km/4,500 mi; the highest peak is Aconcagua 6,960 m/22,834 ft; the width of the Andes ranges from 40 km/25 mi in Chile to 640 km/400 mi in Bolivia; a narrow coastal belt lies between the Andes and the Pacific Ocean;

2) the uplifted remains of the old continental mass, with interior plains at an elevation of 610–1,520 m/2,000–5,000 ft, are found in the E and NE, in the Brazilian Highlands (half the area of Brazil) and Guiana Highlands;

3) the plain of the Orinoco river is an alluvial tropical lowland lying between the Venezuelan Andes and the Guiana Highlands. The tropical Amazon Plain stretches over 3,200 km/2,000 mi from the E foothills of the Andes to the Atlantic ocean, separating the Brazilian and Guiana highlands; once an inland sea, the Amazon basin was filled with sediment and then uplifted;

5) the Pampa-Chaco plain of Argentina, Paraguay, and Bolivia occupies a former bay of the Atlantic that has been filled with sediment brought down from the surrounding highlands;

6) the Patagonian Plateau in the S consists of a series of terraces that rise from the Atlantic Ocean to the foothills of the Andes; glaciation, wind, and rain have dissected these terraces and created rugged land forms

South America: history

20,000 BC	Humans began to populate the continent.
c.1000–500 BC	Chavín civilization flourished in Peru.
1494	Treaty of Tordesillas assigned what is now Brazil to Portugal, the rest of South America to Spain.
15th century	The Inca civilization developed in Peru.
16th century	Spain and Portugal invaded and conquered South America, killing and enslaving the people.
1513	The Spanish explorer Balboa discovered the Pacific Ocean.
1532–35	Francisco Pizarro conquered Peru and the Incas for Spain.
1780	Peruvian Túpac Amaru (José Condorcanqui), who claimed descent from Inca chieftains, led a revolt against Spanish rule and was executed.
19th century	Simon Bolívar and José de San Martín liberated South America's Spanish colonies. Brazil gained independence without struggle. Massive European immigration.
1818	Chile declared independence.
1822	Bolívar and San Martín met but failed to agree on plans for South American independence.
1865–70	President F S Lopez involved Paraguay in a war with Brazil, Argentina, and Uruguay. Paraguay was defeated and over half its population killed, including Lopez.
1879–83	Pacific War, between Chile and the forces of Bolivia and Peru, ended with Chile's acquisition of all of Bolivia's coastal territory and part of Peru's southern coast. Bolivia still seeks access to the coast.
1889	Brazilian monarchy overthrown and republic established.
1932–35	Chaco war, between Paraguay and Bolivia; the territorial dispute which caused it was settled by arbitration 1938.
1930s	US Marines intervened in Nicaragua.
1952	Bolivian revolution, with nationalization of the tin mines.
1970–73	CIA-backed military coup ended the rule of Salvador Allende's elected socialist government in Chile.
1977	Panama and the USA signed a treaty to give Panama control of the Panama Canal in 1999.
20th century	Rapid industrialization and population growth.
1980s	Widespread inability to meet interest payments on loans incurred from economically powerful countries to finance rapid industrialization and capture export markets.
1982	Argentina's invasion of the Falkland Islands triggered war with the UK; the UK regained the Islands.
1992	The first Earth Summit convened in Rio de Janeiro, Brazil, in an effort to cooperate in solving global environmental problems. Celebration in the USA of Columbus' first voyage to the New World; Native American representatives protested.

features Lake Titicaca (world's highest navigable lake); La Paz (highest capital city in the world); Atacama Desert; Inca ruins at Machu Picchu; rivers include the Amazon (world's largest and second longest), Parana, Madeira, São Francisco, Purus, Paraguay, Orinoco, Araguaia, Negro, Uruguay

products produces 44% of the world's coffee (Brazil, Colombia), 22% of its cocoa (Brazil), 35% of its citrus fruit, meat (Argentina, Brazil), soybeans (Argentina, Brazil), cotton (Brazil), linseed (Argentina); Argentina is the world's second largest producer of sunflower seed; Brazil is the world's largest producer of bananas, its second largest producer of tin and its third largest producer of manganese, tobacco, and mangoes; Peru is the world's second largest producer of silver; Chile is the world's largest producer of copper

population (1988) 285 million, rising to 550 million by 2000; growth rate (1980–85) 2.3%

language Spanish, Portuguese (chief language in Brazil), Dutch (Surinam), French (French Guiana), Amerindian languages; Hindi, Javanese, and Chinese spoken by descendants of Asian immigrants to Surinam and Guyana; a variety of Creole dialects spoken by those of African descent

religion 90–95% Roman Catholic; local animist beliefs among Amerindians; Hindu and Muslim religions predominate among the descendants of Asian immigrants in Surinam and Guyana.

COUNTRIES OF THE WORLD

Afghanistan

Republic of (*Jamhuria Afghanistan*)

area 652,090 sq km/251,707 sq mi
capital Kabul
towns Kandahar, Herat, Mazar-i-Sharif
physical mountainous in centre and NE, plains in N and SW
environment an estimated 95% of the urban population is without access to sanitation services
features Hindu Kush mountain range (Khyber and Salang passes, Wakhan salient and Panjshir Valley), Amu Darya (Oxus) River, Helmand River, Lake Saberi
head of state Burhanuddin Rabbani from 1992
head of government Gulbuddin Hekmatyar from 1993
political system emergent democracy
political parties Homeland Party (Hezb-i-Watan, formerly People's Democratic Party of Afghanistan, PDPA) Marxist-Leninist; Hezb-i-Islami and Jamiat-i-Islami, Islamic fundamentalist mujaheddin; National Liberation Front, moderate mujaheddin
exports dried fruit, natural gas, fresh fruits, carpets; small amounts of rare minerals, karakul lamb skins, and Afghan coats
currency afgháni
population (1992) 18,052,000 (more than 5 million became refugees after 1979); growth rate 0.6% p.a.
life expectancy (1986) men 43, women 41
languages Pushtu, Dari (Persian)
religion Muslim (80% Sunni, 20% Shi'ite)
literacy men 39%, women 8% (1985 est)
GNP $3.3 bn (1985); $275 per head
GDP $1,858 million; $111 per head

chronology
1747 Afghanistan became an independent emirate.
1839–42 and 1878–80 Afghan Wars instigated by Britain to counter the threat to British India from expanding Russian influence in Afghanistan.
1919 Afghanistan recovered full independence following Third Afghan War.
1953 Lt-Gen Daud Khan became prime minister and introduced reform programme.

1963 Daud Khan forced to resign and constitutional monarchy established.
1973 Monarchy overthrown in coup by Daud Khan.
1978 Daud Khan ousted by Taraki and the PDPA.
1979 Taraki replaced by Hafizullah Amin; USSR entered country to prop up government; they installed Babrak Karmal in power. Amin executed.
1986 Replacement of Karmal as leader by Dr Najibullah Ahmadzai. Partial Soviet troop withdrawal.
1988 New non-Marxist constitution adopted.
1989 Complete withdrawal of Soviet troops; state of emergency imposed in response to intensification of civil war.
1991 US and Soviet military aid withdrawn. Mujaheddin began talks with Russians and Kabul government.
1992 April: Najibullah government overthrown. June: after a succession of short-term presidents, Burhanuddin Rabbani named interim head of state; Islamic law introduced. Sept: Hezb-i-Islami barred from government participation after shell attacks on Kabul. Dec: Rabbani elected president for two-year term by constituent assembly.
1993 Jan: renewed bombardment of Kabul by Hezbi-Islami and other rebel forces. Interim parliament appointed by constituent assembly. March: peace agreement signed between Rabbani and dissident mujaheddin leader Gulbuddin Hekmatyar, under which Hekmatyar became prime minister.

Albania

Republic of (*Republika e Shqipërisë*)

area 28,748 sq km/11,097 sq mi
capital Tiranë
towns Shkodër, Elbasan, Vlorë, chief port Durrës
physical mainly mountainous, with rivers flowing E–W, and a narrow coastal plain
features Dinaric Alps, with wild boar and wolves
head of state Sali Berisha from 1992
head of government Alexander Meksi from 1992
political system emergent democracy
political parties Democratic Party of Albania (PSDS), moderate, market-oriented; Socialist Party

of Albania (PSS), ex-communist; Human Rights Union (HMU), Greek minority party
exports crude oil, bitumen, chrome, iron ore, nickel, coal, copper wire, electricity, tobacco, fruit, vegtables
currency lek
population (1992) 3,357,000; growth rate 1.9% p.a.
life expectancy men 69, women 73
languages Albanian, Greek
religion Muslim 70%, although all religion banned 1967–90
literacy 75% (1986)
GNP $2.8 bn (1986 est); $900 per head
GDP $1,313 million; $543 per head

chronology
c. 1468 Albania made part of the Ottoman Empire.
1912 Independence achieved from Turkey.
1925 Republic proclaimed.
1928–39 Monarchy of King Zog.
1939–44 Under Italian and then German rule.
1946 Communist republic proclaimed under the leadership of Enver Hoxha.
1949 Admitted into Comecon.
1961 Break with Khrushchev's USSR.
1967 Albania declared itself the 'first atheist state in the world'.
1978 Break with 'revisionist' China.
1985 Death of Hoxha.
1987 Normal diplomatic relations restored with Canada, Greece, and West Germany.
1988 Attendance of conference of Balkan states for the first time since the 1930s.
1990 One-party system abandoned; first opposition party formed.
1991 Party of Labour of Albania (PLA) won first multiparty elections; Ramiz Alia re-elected president; three successive governments formed. PLA renamed PSS.
1992 Presidential elections won by PSDS; Sali Berisha elected president. Alia and other former communist officials charged with corruption and abuse of power; totalitarian and communist parties banned.
1993 Jan: Nexhmije Hoxha, widow of Enver Hoxha, sentenced to nine years' imprisonment for misuse of government funds 1985–90.

Algeria

Democratic and Popular Republic of (*al-Jumhuriya al-Jazairiya ad-Dimuqratiya ash- Shabiya*)

area 2,381,741 sq km/919,352 sq mi
capital al-Jazair (Algiers)
towns Qacentina/Constantine; ports are Ouahran/Oran, Annaba/Bône
physical coastal plains backed by mountains in N; Sahara desert in S
features Atlas mountains, Barbary Coast, Chott Melrhir depression, Hoggar mountains
head of state Ali Kafi from 1992
head of government Redha Malek from 1993
political system semi-military rule
political parties National Liberation Front (FLN), nationalist socialist; Socialist Forces Front (FSS), Berber-based
exports oil, natural gas, iron, wine, olive oil
currency dinar
population (1992) 26,401,000 (83% Arab, 17% Berber); growth rate 3.0% p.a.
life expectancy men 59, women 62
languages Arabic (official); Berber, French
religion Sunni Muslim (state religion)
literacy men 63%, women 37% (1985 est)
GDP $64.6 bn; $2,796 per head

chronology
1954 War for independence from France led by the FLN.
1962 Independence achieved from France. Republic declared. Ahmed Ben Bella elected prime minister.
1963 Ben Bella elected Algeria's first president.
1965 Ben Bella deposed by military, led by Colonel Houari Boumédienne.
1976 New constitution approved.
1978 Death of Boumédienne.
1979 Benjedid Chadli elected president. Ben Bella released from house arrest. FLN adopted new party structure.
1981 Algeria helped secure release of US prisoners in Iran.
1983 Chadli re-elected.
1988 Riots in protest at government policies; 170 killed. Reform programme introduced. Diplomatic relations with Egypt restored.
1989 Constitutional changes proposed, leading to limited political pluralism.
1990 Fundamentalist Islamic Salvation Front (FIS) won Algerian municipal and provincial elections.
1991 Dec: FIS won first round of multiparty elections.
1992 Jan: Chadli resigned; military took control of government; Mohamed Boudiaf became president; FIS leaders detained. Feb: state of emergency declared. March: FIS ordered to disband. June: Boudiaf assassinated; Ali Kafi chosen as new head of state and Belnid Absessalem as prime minister.
1993 Belnid Absessalem replaced by Redha Malek.

Andorra

Principality of (*Principat d'Andorra*)
area 468 sq km/181 sq mi
capital Andorra-la-Vella
towns Les Escaldes
physical mountainous, with narrow valleys
features the E Pyrenees, Valira River
heads of state Joan Marti i Alanis (bishop of Urgel, Spain) and François Mitterrand (president of France)
head of government Oscar Riba Reig from 1989

political system semi-feudal co-principality
political party Democratic Party of Andorra
exports main industries are tourism and tobacco
currency French franc and Spanish peseta
population (1992) 57,100 (30% Andorrans, 61% Spanish, 6% French)
languages Catalan (official); Spanish, French
religion Roman Catholic
literacy 100% (1987)
GDP $300 million (1985)

chronology
1278 Treaty signed making Spanish bishop and French count joint rulers of Andorra (through marriage the king of France later inherited the count's right).
1970 Extension of franchise to third-generation female and second-generation male Andorrans.
1976 First political organization (Democratic Party of Andorra) formed.
1977 Franchise extended to first-generation Andorrans.
1981 First prime minister appointed by General Council.
1982 With the appointment of an Executive Council, executive and legislative powers were separated.
1991 Links with European Community (EC) formalized.
1993 First constitution approved in a referendum. Dec: first elections held.

Angola

People's Republic of (*República Popular de Angola*)

area 1,246,700 sq km/481,226 sq mi
capital and chief port Luanda
towns Lobito and Benguela, also ports; Huambo, Lubango
physical narrow coastal plain rises to vast interior plateau with rainforest in NW; desert in S
features Cuanza, Cuito, Cubango, and Cunene rivers; Cabinda enclave
head of state and government José Eduardo dos Santos from 1979
political system socialist republic
political parties People's Movement for the Liberation of Angola–Workers' Party (MPLA–PT),

Marxist-Leninist; National Union for the Total Independence of Angola (UNITA); National Front for the Liberation of Angola (FNLA)
exports oil, coffee, diamonds, palm oil, sisal, iron ore, fish
currency kwanza
population (1992) 10,609,000 (largest ethnic group Ovimbundu); growth rate 2.5% p.a.
life expectancy men 40, women 44
languages Portuguese (official); Bantu dialects
religions Roman Catholic 68%, Protestant 20%, animist 12%
literacy 20%
GDP $2.7 bn; $432 per head

chronology
1951 Angola became an overseas territory of Portugal.
1956 First independence movement formed, the MPLA.
1961 Unsuccessful independence rebellion.
1962 Second nationalist movement formed, the FNLA.
1966 Third nationalist movement formed, UNITA.
1975 Independence achieved from Portugal. Transitional government of independence formed from representatives of MPLA, FNLA, UNITA, and Portuguese government. MPLA proclaimed People's Republic of Angola under the presidency of Dr Agostinho Neto. FNLA and UNITA proclaimed People's Democratic Republic of Angola.
1976 MPLA gained control of most of the country. South African troops withdrawn, but Cuban units remained.
1977 MPLA restructured to become MPLA–PT.
1979 Death of Neto, succeeded by José Eduardo dos Santos.
1980 UNITA guerrillas, aided by South Africa, continued raids against the Luanda government and bases of the South West Africa People's Organization (SWAPO) in Angola.
1984 South Africa promised to withdraw its forces if the Luanda government guaranteed that areas vacated would not by filled by Cuban or SWAPO units (the Lusaka Agreement).
1985 South African forces officially withdrawn.
1986 Further South African raids into Angola. UNITA continued to receive South African support.

1988 Peace treaty, providing for the withdrawal of all foreign troops, signed with South Africa and Cuba.
1989 Cease-fire agreed with UNITA broke down and guerrilla activity restarted.
1990 Peace offer by rebels. Return to multiparty politics promised.
1991 Peace agreement signed, civil war between MPLA–PT and UNITA officially ended. Amnesty for all political prisoners.
1992 MPLA–PT's general-election victory fiercely disputed by UNITA, plunging the country into renewed civil war. UNITA offered, and eventually accepted, seats in the new government, but fighting continued.
1993 MPLA–PT made power-sharing agreement with UNITA. Dos Santos government recognized by US.

Antigua and Barbuda

State of

area Antigua 280 sq km/108 sq mi, Barbuda 161 sq km/62 sq mi, plus Redonda 1 sq km/0.4 sq mi
capital and chief port St John's
towns Codrington (on Barbuda)
physical low-lying tropical islands of limestone and coral with some higher volcanic outcrops; no rivers and low rainfall result in frequent droughts and deforestation
features Antigua is the largest of the Leeward Islands; Redonda is an uninhabited island of volcanic rock rising to 305 m/1,000 ft
head of state Elizabeth II from 1981, represented by governor general
head of government Vere C Bird from 1981
political system liberal democracy
political parties Antigua Labour Party (ALP), moderate, left of centre; Progressive Labour Movement (PLM), left of centre
exports sea-island cotton, rum, lobsters
currency Eastern Caribbean dollar
population (1992) 64,000; growth rate 1.3% p.a.
life expectancy 70 years
language English
media no daily newspaper; weekly papers all owned by political parties
religion Christian (mostly Anglican)

literacy 90% (1985)
GDP $173 million (1985); $2,200 per head

chronology
1493 Antigua visited by Christopher Columbus.
1632 Antigua colonized by English settlers.
1667 Treaty of Breda formally ceded Antigua to Britain.
1871–1956 Antigua and Barbuda administered as part of the Leeward Islands federation.
1967 Antigua and Barbuda became an associated state within the Commonwealth, with full internal independence.
1971 PLM won the general election by defeating the ALP.
1976 PLM called for early independence, but ALP urged caution. ALP won the general election.
1981 Independence from Britain achieved.
1983 Assisted US invasion of Grenada.
1984 ALP won a decisive victory in the general election.
1985 ALP re-elected.
1989 Another sweeping general election victory for the ALP under Vere Bird.
1991 Bird remained in power despite calls for his resignation.
1993 Lester Bird elected ALP leader.

Argentina

Republic of (*República Argentina*)

area 2,780,092 sq km/1,073,116 sq mi
capital Buenos Aires (to move to Viedma)
towns Rosario, Córdoba, Tucumán, Mendoza, Santa Fé; ports are La Plata and Bahía Blanca
physical mountains in W, forest and savanna in N, pampas (treeless plains) in E central area, Patagonian plateau in S; rivers Colorado, Salado, Paraná, Uruguay, Río de la Plata estuary
territories part of Tierra del Fuego; disputed claims to S Atlantic islands and part of Antarctica
environment an estimated 20,000 sq km/7,700 sq mi of land has been swamped with salt water
features Andes mountains, with Aconcagua the highest peak in the W hemisphere; Iguaçú Falls

head of state and government Carlos Menem from 1989
political system democratic federal republic
political parties Radical Civic Union Party (UCR), moderate centrist; Justicialist Party, right-wing Peronist
exports livestock products, cereals, wool, tannin, peanuts, linseed oil, minerals (coal, copper, molybdenum, gold, silver, lead, zinc, barium, uranium); the country has huge resources of oil, natural gas, hydroelectric power
currency peso
population (1992) 33,070,000 (mainly of Spanish or Italian origin, only about 30,000 American Indians surviving); growth rate 1.5% p.a.
life expectancy men 66, women 73
languages Spanish (official); English, Italian, German, French
religion Roman Catholic (state-supported)
literacy men 96%, women 95% (1985 est)
GDP $70.1 bn (1990); $2,162 per head

chronology
1816 Independence achieved from Spain, followed by civil wars.
1946 Juan Perón elected president, supported by his wife 'Evita'.
1952 'Evita' Perón died.
1955 Perón overthrown and civilian administration restored.
1966 Coup brought back military rule.
1973 A Peronist party won the presidential and congressional elections. Perón returned from exile in Spain as president, with his third wife, Isabel, as vice president.
1974 Perón died, succeeded by Isabel.
1976 Coup resulted in rule by a military junta led by Lt-Gen Jorge Videla. Congress dissolved, and hundreds of people, including Isabel Perón, detained.
1976–83 Ferocious campaign against left-wing elements, the 'dirty war'.
1978 Videla retired. Succeeded by General Roberto Viola, who promised a return to democracy.
1981 Viola died suddenly. Replaced by General Leopoldo Galtieri.
1982 With a deteriorating economy, Galtieri sought popular support by ordering an invasion of the British-held Falkland Islands. After losing the short war, Galtieri was removed and replaced by General Reynaldo Bignone.
1983 Amnesty law passed and democratic constitution of 1853 revived. General elections won by Raúl Alfonsín and the UCR. Armed forces under scrutiny.
1984 National Commission on the Disappearance of Persons (CONADEP) reported on over 8,000 people who had disappeared during the 'dirty war' of 1976–83.
1985 A deteriorating economy forced Alfonsín to seek help from the International Monetary Fund and introduce an austerity programme.
1986 Unsuccessful attempt on Alfonsín's life.
1988 Unsuccessful army coup.
1989 Carlos Menem, of the Justicialist Party, elected president.
1990 Full diplomatic relations with the UK restored. Menem elected Justicialist Party leader. Revolt by army officers thwarted.

1992 New currency introduced.
1993 Success for Justicialist Party in assembly elections.

Armenia
Republic of

area 29,800 sq km/11,500 sq mi
capital Yerevan
towns Kumayri (formerly Leninakan)
physical mainly mountainous (including Mount Ararat), wooded
features State Academia Theatre of Opera and Ballet; Yerevan Film Studio
head of state Levon Ter-Petrossian from 1990
head of government Gagik Arutyunyan from 1991
political system emergent democracy
products copper, molybdenum, cereals, cotton, silk
population (1992) 3,426,000 (90% Armenian, 5% Azeri, 2% Russian, 2% Kurd)
language Armenian
religion traditionally Armenian Christian

chronology
1918 Became an independent republic.
1920 Occupied by the Red Army.
1936 Became a constituent republic of the USSR.
1988 Feb: demonstrations in Yerevan called for transfer of Nagorno-Karabakh from Azerbaijan to Armenian control. Dec: earthquake claimed around 25,000 lives and caused extensive damage.
1989 Jan–Nov: strife-torn Nagorno-Karabakh placed under direct rule from Moscow. Pro-autonomy Armenian National Movement founded. Nov: civil war erupted with Azerbaijan over Nagorno-Karabakh.
1990 March: Armenia boycotted USSR constitutional referendum. Aug: nationalists secured control of Armenian supreme soviet; former dissident Levon Ter-Petrossian indirectly elected president; independence declared. Nakhichevan republic affected by Nagorno-Karabakh dispute.
1991 March: overwhelming support for independence in referendum. Dec: Armenia joined new Commonwealth of Independent States; Nagorno-Karabakh declared its independence; Armenia granted diplomatic recognition by USA.
1992 Admitted into United Nations and the Conference on Security and Cooperation in Europe. Conflict over Nagorno-Karabakh worsened.

Australia

Commonwealth of

area 7,682,300 sq km/2,966,136 sq mi
capital Canberra
towns Adelaide, Alice Springs, Brisbane, Darwin, Melbourne, Perth, Sydney, Hobart, Geelong, Newcastle, Townsville, Wollongong
physical the world's smallest, flattest, and driest continent (40% lies in the tropics, one-third is desert, and one- third is marginal grazing); Great Sandy Desert; Gibson Desert; Great Victoria Desert; Simpson Desert; the Great Barrier Reef (largest coral reef in the world, stretching 2,000 km/1,250 mi off E coast of Queensland); Great Dividing Range and Australian Alps in the E (Mount Kosciusko, 2,229 m/7,136 ft, Australia's highest peak). The fertile SE region is watered by the Darling, Lachlan, Murrumbridgee, and Murray rivers; rivers in the interior are seasonal. Lake Eyre basin and Nullarbor Plain in the S
territories Norfolk Island, Christmas Island, Cocos (Keeling) Islands, Ashmore and Cartier Islands, Coral Sea Islands, Heard Island and McDonald Islands, Australian Antarctic Territory
environment an estimated 75% of Australia's northern tropical rainforest has been cleared for agriculture or urban development since Europeans first settled there in the early 19th century
features Ayers Rock; Arnhem Land; Gulf of Carpentaria; Cape York Peninsula; Great Australian Bight; unique animal species include the kangaroo, koala, platypus, wombat, Tasmanian devil, and spiny anteater; of 800 species of bird, the budgerigar, cassowary, emu, kookaburra, lyre bird, and black swan are also unique as a result of Australia's long isolation from other continents
head of state Elizabeth II from 1952, represented by governor general
head of government Paul Keating from 1991
political system federal constitutional monarchy
political parties Australian Labor Party, moderate left of centre; Liberal Party of Australia, moderate, liberal, free enterprise; National Party of Australia (formerly Country Party), centrist non-metropolitan
exports world's largest exporter of sheep, wool, diamonds, alumina, coal, lead and refined zinc ores, and mineral sands; other exports include cereals, beef, veal, mutton, lamb, sugar, nickel (world's second

largest producer), iron ore; principal trade partners are Japan, the USA, and EC member states
currency Australian dollar
population (1992) 17,562,000; growth rate 1.5% p.a.
life expectancy men 75, women 80
languages English, Aboriginal languages
religions Anglican 26%, other Protestant 17%, Roman Catholic 26%
literacy 98.5.% (1988)
GDP $286.9 bn (1992)

chronology
1901 Creation of Commonwealth of Australia.
1911 Site acquired for capital at Canberra.
1927 Seat of government moved to Canberra.
1942 Statute of Westminster Adoption Act gave Australia autonomy from UK in internal and external affairs.
1944 Liberal Party founded by Robert Menzies.
1951 Australia joined New Zealand and the USA as a signatory to the ANZUS Pacific security treaty.
1966 Menzies resigned after being Liberal prime minister for 17 years, and was succeeded by Harold Holt.
1967 A referendum was passed giving Aborigines full citizenship rights.
1968 John Gorton became prime minister after Holt's death.
1971 Gorton succeeded by William McMahon, heading a Liberal–Country Party coalition.
1972 Gough Whitlam became prime minister, leading a Labor government.
1975 Senate blocked the government's financial legislation; Whitlam dismissed by the governor general, who invited Malcolm Fraser to form a Liberal–Country Party caretaker government. This action of the governor general, John Kerr, was widely criticized.
1977 Kerr resigned.
1978 Northern Territory attained self-government, with Darwin as its capital.
1983 Labor Party, returned to power under Bob Hawke, convened meeting of employers and unions to seek consensus on economic policy to deal with growing unemployment.
1986 Australia Act passed by UK government, eliminating last vestiges of British legal authority in Australia.
1988 Labor foreign minister Bill Hayden appointed governor general designate. Free-trade agreement with New Zealand signed.
1990 Hawke won record fourth election victory, defeating Liberal Party by small majority.
1991 Paul Keating became new Labor Party leader and prime minister.
1992 Keating's popularity declined as economic problems continued. Oath of allegiance to British crown abandoned.
1993 Labor Party won general election, entering fifth term of office.

Austria

Republic of (*Republik Österreich*)

area 83,500 sq km/32,374 sq mi
capital Vienna
towns Graz, Linz, Salzburg, Innsbruck
physical landlocked mountainous state, with Alps in

W and S and low relief in E where most of the population is concentrated

environment Hainburg, the largest primeval forest left in Europe, under threat from a dam project (suspended 1990)

features Austrian Alps (including Grossglockner and Brenner and Semmering passes); Lechtaler and Allgauer Alps N of river Inn; Carnic Alps on Italian border; river Danube

head of state Thomas Klestil from 1992

head of government Franz Vranitzky from 1986

political system democratic federal republic

political parties Socialist Party of Austria (SPÖ), democratic socialist; Austrian People's Party (ÖVP), progressive centrist; Freedom Party of Austria (FPÖ), moderate left of centre; United Green Party of Austria (VGÖ), conservative ecological; Green Alternative Party (ALV), radical ecological

exports lumber, textiles, clothing, iron and steel, paper, machinery and transport equipment, foodstuffs

currency schilling

population (1992) 7,857,000; growth rate 0.1% p.a.

life expectancy men 70, women 77

language German

religions Roman Catholic 85%, Protestant 6%

literacy 98% (1983)

GDP $184.7 bn (1992)

chronology

1867 Emperor Franz Josef established dual monarchy of Austria–Hungary.

1914 Archduke Franz Ferdinand assassinated by a Serbian nationalist; Austria–Hungary invaded Serbia, precipitating World War I.

1918 Habsburg empire ended; republic of Austria proclaimed.

1938 Austria incorporated into German Third Reich by Hitler (the *Anschluss*).

1945 Under Allied occupation, constitution of 1920 reinstated and coalition government formed by the SPÖ and the ÖVP.

1955 Allied occupation ended, and the independence of Austria formally recognized.

1966 ÖVP in power with Josef Klaus as chancellor.

1970 SPÖ formed a minority government, with Dr Bruno Kreisky as chancellor.

1983 Kreisky resigned and was replaced by Dr Fred Sinowatz, leading a coalition.

1986 Dr Kurt Waldheim elected president. Sinowatz resigned, succeeded by Franz Vranitzky. No party won an overall majority; Vranitzky formed a coalition of the SPÖ and the ÖVP, with ÖVP leader, Dr Alois Mock, as vice chancellor.

1989 Austria sought European Community membership.

1990 Vranitzky re-elected.

1991 Bid for EC membership endorsed by the Community.

1992 Thomas Klestil elected president, replacing Waldheim.

Azerbaijan

Republic of

area 86,600 sq km/33,400 sq mi

capital Baku

towns Gyandzha (formerly Kirovabad), Sumgait

physical Caspian Sea; the country ranges from semi-desert to the Caucasus Mountains

head of state Geidar Aliyev from 1993

head of government Suret Guseinov from 1993

political system emergent democracy

political parties Republican Democratic Party, ex-communist-dominated; Popular Front, democratic nationalist; Islamic Party, fundamentalist

products oil, iron, copper, fruit, vines, cotton, silk, carpets

population (1992) 7,237,000 (83% Azeri, 6% Russian, 6% Armenian)

language Turkic

religion traditionally Shi'ite Muslim

chronology

1917–18 A member of the anti-Bolshevik Transcaucasian Federation.

1918 Became an independent republic.

1920 Occupied by the Red Army.

1922–36 Formed part of the Transcaucasian Federal Republic with Georgia and Armenia.

1936 Became a constituent republic of the USSR.

1988 Riots followed Nagorno-Karabakh's request for transfer to Armenia.

1989 Jan–Nov: strife-torn Nagorno-Karabakh placed under direct rule from Moscow. Azerbaijan Popular Front established. Nov: civil war erupted with Armenia.

1990 Jan: Soviet troops dispatched to Baku to restore order. Aug: communists won parliamentary elections. Nakhichevan republic affected by Nagorno-Karabakh dispute.

1991 Aug: Azeri leadership supported attempted anti-Gorbachev coup in Moscow; independence declared. Sept: former communist Ayaz Mutalibov elected president. Dec: joined new Commonwealth of Independent States; Nagorno-Karabakh declared independence.

1992 Jan: admitted into Conference on Security and Cooperation in Europe; March: Mutalibov resigned; Azerbaijan became a member of the United Nations; accorded diplomatic recognition by the USA. June: Albulfaz Elchibey, leader of the Popular Front, elected president; renewed campaign against Armenia in the fight for Nagorno-Karabakh.

1993 Prime Minister Rakham Guseinov resigned. President Elchibey ousted, replaced by former Communist Party leader Geidar Aliyev. Suret Guseinov appointed prime minister.

Bahamas

Commonwealth of the

area 13,864 sq km/5,352 sq mi
capital Nassau on New Providence
towns Alice Town, Andros Town, Hope Town, Spanish Wells, Freeport, Moss Town, George Town
physical comprises 700 tropical coral islands and about 1,000 cays
features desert islands: only 30 are inhabited; Blue Holes of Andros, the world's longest and deepest submarine caves; the Exumas are a narrow spine of 365 islands
principal islands Andros, Grand Bahama, Great Abaco, Eleuthera, New Providence, Berry Islands, Biminis, Great Inagua, Acklins, Exumas, Mayaguana, Crooked Island, Long Island, Cat Island, Rum Cay, Watling (San Salvador) Island
head of state Elizabeth II from 1973, represented by governor general
head of government Hubert Ingraham from 1992
political system constitutional monarchy
political parties Progressive Liberal Party (PLP), centrist; Free National Movement (FNM), centre-left
exports cement, pharmaceuticals, petroleum products, crawfish, salt, aragonite, rum, pulpwood; over half the islands' employment comes from tourism

currency Bahamian dollar
population (1992) 264,000; growth rate 1.8% p.a.
languages English and some Creole
media three independent daily newspapers
religions 29% Baptist, 23% Anglican, 22% Roman Catholic
literacy 95% (1986)
GDP $2.7 bn (1987); $11,261 per head

chronology
1964 Independence achieved from Britain.
1967 First national assembly elections; Lynden Pindling became prime minister.
1972 Constitutional conference to discuss full independence.
1973 Full independence achieved.
1983 Allegations of drug trafficking by government ministers.
1984 Deputy prime minister and two cabinet ministers resigned. Pindling denied any personal involvement and was endorsed as party leader.
1987 Pindling re-elected despite claims of frauds.
1992 FNM led by Hubert Ingraham won absolute majority in assembly elections.

Bahrain

State of (*Dawlat al Bahrayn*)

area 688 sq km/266 sq mi
capital Manama on the largest island (also called Bahrain)
towns Muharraq, Jidd Hafs, Isa Town; oil port Mina Sulman
physical 35 islands, composed largely of sand-covered limestone; generally poor and infertile soil; flat and hot
environment a wildlife park on Bahrain preserves the endangered oryx; most of the south of the island is preserved for the ruling family's falconry
features causeway linking Bahrain to mainland Saudi Arabia; Sitra island is a communications centre for the lower Persian Gulf and has a satellite-tracking station
head of state and government Sheik Isa bin Sulman al-Khalifa from 1961
political system absolute emirate
political parties none
exports oil, natural gas, aluminium, fish
currency Bahrain dinar

population (1992) 531,000 (two-thirds are nationals); growth rate 4.4% p.a.
life expectancy men 67, women 71
languages Arabic (official); Farsi, English, Urdu
religion 85% Muslim (Shi'ite 60%, Sunni 40%)
literacy men 79%, women 64% (1985 est)
GDP $3.5 bn (1987); $7,772 per head

chronology
1861 Became British protectorate.
1968 Britain announced its intention to withdraw its forces. Bahrain formed, with Qatar and the Trucial States, the Federation of Arab Emirates.
1971 Qatar and the Trucial States withdrew from the federation and Bahrain became an independent state.
1973 New constitution adopted, with an elected national assembly.
1975 Prime minister resigned and national assembly dissolved. Emir and his family assumed virtually absolute power.
1986 Gulf University established in Bahrain. A causeway was opened linking the island with Saudi Arabia.
1988 Bahrain recognized Afghan rebel government.
1991 Bahrain joined United Nations coalition that ousted Iraq from its occupation of Kuwait.

Bangladesh

People's Republic of (*Gana Prajatantri Bangladesh*) (formerly *East Pakistan*)

area 144,000 sq km/55,585 sq mi
capital Dhaka (formerly Dacca)
towns ports Chittagong, Khulna
physical flat delta of rivers Ganges (Padma) and Brahmaputra (Jamuna), the largest estuarine delta in the world; annual rainfall of 2,540 mm/100 in; some 75% of the land is less than 3 m/10 ft above sea level; hilly in extreme SE and NE
environment deforestation on the slopes of the Himalayas increases the threat of flooding in the coastal lowlands of Bangladesh, which are also subject to devastating monsoon storms. The building of India's Farakka Barrage has reduced the flow of the Ganges in Bangladesh and permitted salt water to intrude further inland. Increased salinity has destroyed fisheries, contaminated drinking water, and damaged forests

head of state Abdur Rahman Biswas from 1991
head of government Begum Khaleda Zia from 1991
political system emergent democratic republic
political parties Bangladesh Nationalist Party (BNP), Islamic, right of centre; Awami League, secular, moderate socialist; Jatiya Dal (National Party), Islamic nationalist
exports jute, tea, garments, fish products
currency taka
population (1992) 110,602,000; growth rate 2.17% p.a.; just over 1 million people live in small ethnic groups in the tropical Chittagong Hill Tracts, Mymensingh, and Sylhet districts
life expectancy men 50, women 52
language Bangla (Bengali)
religions Sunni Muslim 85%, Hindu 14%
literacy men 43%, women 22% (1985 est)
GDP $17.6 bn (1987); $172 per head

chronology
1947 Formed into eastern province of Pakistan on partition of British India.
1970 Half a million killed in flood.
1971 Bangladesh emerged as independent nation, under leadership of Sheik Mujibur Rahman, after civil war.
1975 Mujibur Rahman assassinated. Martial law imposed.
1976–77 Maj-Gen Zia ur-Rahman assumed power.
1978–79 Elections held and civilian rule restored.
1981 Assassination of Maj-Gen Zia.
1982 Lt-Gen Ershad assumed power in army coup. Martial law reimposed.
1986 Elections held but disputed. Martial law ended.
1987 State of emergency declared in response to opposition demonstrations.
1988 Assembly elections boycotted by main opposition parties. State of emergency lifted. Islam made state religion. Monsoon floods left 30 million homeless and thousands dead.
1989 Power devolved to Chittagong Hill Tracts to end 14-year conflict between local people and army-protected settlers.
1990 Following mass antigovernment protests, President Ershad resigned; Shahabuddin Ahmad became interim president.
1991 Feb: elections resulted in coalition government with BNP dominant. April: cyclone killed around 139,000 and left up to 10 million homeless. Sept: parliamentary government restored; Abdur Rahman Biswas elected president.

Barbados

area 430 sq km/166 sq mi
capital Bridgetown
towns Speightstown, Holetown, Oistins
physical most easterly island of the West Indies; surrounded by coral reefs; subject to hurricanes June–Nov
features highest point Mount Hillaby 340 m/1,115 ft
head of state Elizabeth II from 1966, represented by governor general Hugh Springer from 1984
head of government prime minister Erskine Lloyd Sandiford from 1987
political system constitutional monarchy
political parties Barbados Labour Party (BLP), moderate, left of centre; Democratic Labour Party (DLP),

moderate, left of centre; National Democratic Party (NDP), centre

exports sugar, rum, electronic components, clothing, cement

currency Barbados dollar

population (1992) 259,000; growth rate 0.5% p.a.

life expectancy men 70, women 75

languages English and Bajan (Barbadian English dialect)

media two independent daily newspapers

religions 70% Anglican, 9% Methodist, 4% Roman Catholic

literacy 99% (1984)

GDP $1.4 bn (1987); $5,449 per head

chronology

1627 Became British colony; developed as a sugar-plantation economy, initially on basis of slavery.

1834 Slaves freed.

1951 Universal adult suffrage introduced. BLP won general election.

1954 Ministerial government established.

1961 Independence achieved from Britain. DLP, led by Errol Barrow, in power.

1966 Barbados achieved full independence within Commonwealth. Barrow became the new nation's first prime minister.

1972 Diplomatic relations with Cuba established.

1976 BLP, led by Tom Adams, returned to power.

1983 Barbados supported US invasion of Grenada.

1985 Adams died; Bernard St John became prime minister.

1986 DLP, led by Barrow, returned to power.

1987 Barrow died; Erskine Lloyd Sandiford became prime minister.

1989 New NDP opposition formed.

1991 DLP, under Erskine Sandiford, won general election.

Belarus

Republic of

area 207,600 sq km/80,100 sq mi

capital Minsk (Mensk)

towns Gomel, Vitebsk, Mogilev, Bobruisk, Grodno, Brest

physical more than 25% forested; rivers W Dvina, Dnieper and its tributaries, including the Pripet and Beresina; the Pripet Marshes in the E; mild and damp climate

environment large areas contaminated by fallout from Chernobyl

features Belovezhskaya Pushcha (scenic forest reserve)

head of state Stanislav Shushkevich from 1991

head of government Vyacheslav Kebich from 1990

political system emergent democracy

political parties Byelorussian Popular Front (Adradzhenne), moderate nationalist; Byelorussian Ecological Union (BEU); Byelorussian Social Democratic Party, moderate left of centre; Christian Democratic Union of Belarus, centrist; Communist Party, left-wing

products peat, agricultural machinery, fertilizers, glass, textiles, leather, salt, electrical goods, meat, dairy produce

currency rouble and dukat

population (1992) 10,321,000 (77% Byelorussian 'Eastern Slavs', 13% Russian, 4% Polish, 1% Jewish)

languages Byelorussian, Russian

religions Roman Catholic, Russian Orthodox, with Baptist and Muslim minorities

chronology

1918–19 Briefly independent from Russia.

1937–41 More than 100,000 people were shot in mass executions ordered by Stalin.

1941–44 Occupied by Nazi Germany.

1945 Became a founding member of the United Nations.

1986 April: fallout from the Chernobyl nuclear reactor in Ukraine contaminated a large area.

1989 Byelorussian Popular Front established as well as a more extreme nationalist organization, the Tolaka group.

1990 Sept: Byelorussian established as state language and republican sovereignty declared.

1991 April: Minsk hit by nationalist-backed general strike. Aug: declared independence from Soviet Union; CP suspended. Sept: reformist Shushkevich elected president. Dec: Commonwealth of Independent States formed in Minsk; Belarus accorded diplomatic recognition by USA.

1992 Jan: admitted into Conference on Security and Cooperation in Europe. May: protocols signed with USA agreeing to honour START disarmament treaty.

Belgium

Kingdom of (French *Royaume de Belgique*, Flemish *Koninkrijk België*)

area 30,510 sq km/11,784 sq mi
capital Brussels
towns Ghent, Liège, Charleroi, Bruges, Mons, Namur, Leuven; ports are Antwerp, Ostend, Zeebrugge
physical fertile coastal plain in NW, central rolling hills rise eastwards, hills and forest in SE
environment a 1989 government report judged the drinking water in Flanders to be 'seriously substandard' and more than half the rivers and canals in that region to be in a 'very bad' condition
features Ardennes Forest; rivers Scheldt and Meuse
head of state King Albert from 1993
head of government Jean-Luc Dehaene from 1992
political system liberal democracy
political parties Flemish Christian Social Party (CVP), centre-left; French Social Christian Party (PSC), centre-left; Flemish Socialist Party (SP), left of centre; French Socialist Party (PS), left of centre; Flemish Liberal Party (PVV), moderate centrist; French Liberal Reform Party (PRL), moderate centrist; Flemish People's Party (VU), federalist; Flemish Green Party (Agalev); French Green Party (Ecolo)
exports iron, steel, textiles, manufactured goods, petrochemicals, plastics, vehicles, diamonds
currency Belgian franc
population (1992) 10,021,000 (comprising Flemings and Walloons); growth rate 0.1% p.a.
life expectancy men 72, women 78
languages in the N (Flanders) Flemish (a Dutch dialect, known as *Vlaams*) 55%; in the S (Wallonia) Walloon (a French dialect) 32%; bilingual 11%; German (E border) 0.6%; all are official
religion Roman Catholic 75%
literacy 98% (1984)
GDP $218.7 bn (1992)

chronology
1830 Belgium became an independent kingdom.
1914 Invaded by Germany.
1940 Again invaded by Germany.
1948 Belgium became founding member of Benelux Customs Union.
1949 Belgium became founding member of Council

of Europe and NATO.
1951 Leopold III abdicated in favour of his son Baudouin.
1952 Belgium became founding member of European Coal and Steel Community.
1957 Belgium became founding member of the European Economic Community.
1971 Steps towards regional autonomy taken.
1972 German-speaking members included in the cabinet for the first time.
1973 Linguistic parity achieved in government appointments.
1974 Leo Tindemans became prime minister. Separate regional councils and ministerial committees established.
1978 Wilfried Martens succeeded Tindemans as prime minister.
1980 Open violence over language divisions. Regional assemblies for Flanders and Wallonia and a three-member executive for Brussels created.
1981 Short-lived coalition led by Mark Eyskens was followed by the return of Martens.
1987 Martens head of caretaker government after break-up of coalition.
1988 Following a general election, Martens formed a new CVP–PS–SP–PSC–VU coalition.
1992 Martens-led coalition collapsed; Jean-Luc Dehaene formed a new CVP-led coalition.
1993 Federal system adopted, based on Flanders, Wallonia, and Brussels. King Baudouin died; succeeded by his brother, Prince Albert of Liege.

Belize

(formerly *British Honduras*)

area 22,963 sq km/8,864 sq mi
capital Belmopan
towns ports Belize City, Dangriga and Punta Gorda; Orange Walk, Corozal
physical tropical swampy coastal plain, Maya Mountains in S; over 90% forested
environment since 1981 Belize has developed an extensive system of national parks and reserves to protect large areas of tropical forest, coastal mangrove, and offshore islands. Forestry has been replaced by agriculture and ecotourism, which are now the most important sectors of the economy; world's first jaguar reserve created 1986 in the Cockscomb Mountains

features world's second longest barrier reef; Maya ruins
head of state Elizabeth II from 1981, represented by governor general
head of government Manuel Esquivel from 1993
political system constitutional monarchy
political parties People's United Party (PUP), left of centre; United Democratic Party (UDP), moderate conservative
exports sugar, citrus fruits, rice, fish products, bananas
currency Belize dollar
population (1992) 196,000 (including Mayan minority in the interior); growth rate 2.5% p.a.
life expectancy (1988) 60 years
languages English (official); Spanish (widely spoken), native Creole dialects
media no daily newspaper; several independent weekly tabloids
religions Roman Catholic 60%, Protestant 35%
literacy 93% (1988)
GDP $247 million (1988); $1,220 per head

chronology
1862 Belize became a British colony.
1954 Constitution adopted, providing for limited internal self-government. General election won by George Price.
1964 Self-government achieved from the UK (universal adult suffrage introduced).
1965 Two-chamber national assembly introduced, with Price as prime minister.
1970 Capital moved from Belize City to Belmopan.
1973 British Honduras became Belize.
1975 British troops sent to defend the disputed frontier with Guatemala.
1980 United Nations called for full independence.
1981 Full independence achieved. Price became prime minister.
1984 Price defeated in general election. Manuel Esquivel formed the government. The UK reaffirmed its undertaking to defend the frontier.
1989 Price and the PUP won the general election.
1991 Diplomatic relations with Guatemala established.
1993 In general election UDP defeated PUP. Manuel Esquivel returned as prime minister. Dec: British government relinquished responsibility for external defence of the country.

Benin

People's Republic of (*République Populaire du Bénin*)

area 112,622 sq km/43,472 sq mi
capital Porto Novo (official), Cotonou (de facto)
towns Abomey, Natitingou, Parakou; chief port Cotonou
physical flat to undulating terrain; hot and humid in S; semiarid in N
features coastal lagoons with fishing villages on stilts; Niger River in NE
head of state and government Nicéphore Soglo from 1991
political system socialist pluralist republic
political parties Party of the People's Revolution of Benin (PRPB); other parties from 1990
exports cocoa, peanuts, cotton, palm oil, petroleum, cement, sea products

currency CFA franc
population (1992) 4,928,000; growth rate 3% p.a.
life expectancy men 42, women 46
languages French (official); Fon 47% and Yoruba 9% in south; six major tribal languages in north
religions animist 65%, Christian 17%, Muslim 13%
literacy men 37%, women 16% (1985 est)
GDP $1.6 bn (1987); $365 per head

chronology
1851 Under French control.
1958 Became self-governing dominion within the French Community.
1960 Independence achieved from France.
1960–72 Acute political instability, with switches from civilian to military rule.
1972 Military regime established by General Mathieu Kerekou.
1974 Kerekou announced that the country would follow a path of 'scientific socialism'.
1975 Name of country changed from Dahomey to Benin.
1977 Return to civilian rule under a new constitution.
1980 Kerekou formally elected president by the national revolutionary assembly.
1989 Marxist-Leninism dropped as official ideology. Strikes and protests against Kerekou's rule mounted; army deployed against protesters.
1991 Multiparty elections held. Kerekou defeated in presidential elections by Nicéphore Soglo.

Bhutan

Kingdom of (*Druk-yul*)

area 46,500 sq km/17,954 sq mi
capital Thimbu (Thimphu)
towns Paro, Punakha, Mongar
physical occupies southern slopes of the Himalayas; cut by valleys formed by tributaries of the Brahmaputra; thick forests in S
features Gangkar Punsum (7,529 m/24,700 ft) is one of the world's highest unclimbed peaks
head of state and government Jigme Singye Wangchuk from 1972
political system absolute monarchy
political parties none officially; illegal Bhutan People's Party (BPP)
exports timber, talc, fruit and vegetables, cement, distilled spirits, calcium carbide
currency ngultrum; also Indian currency
population (1992) 1,511,000; growth rate 2% p.a. (75% Ngalops and Sharchops, 25% Nepalese)

life expectancy men 44, women 43
languages Dzongkha (official, a Tibetan dialect), Sharchop, Bumthap, Nepali, and English
media one daily newspaper (*Kuensel*), published in Dzongkha, English, and Nepali editions; it gives the government's point of view
religions 75% Lamaistic Buddhist (state religion), 25% Hindu
literacy 5%
GDP $250 million (1987); $170 per head

chronology
1865 Trade treaty with Britain signed.
1907 First hereditary monarch installed.
1910 Anglo-Bhutanese Treaty signed.
1949 Indo-Bhutan Treaty of Friendship signed.
1952 King Jigme Dorji Wangchuk installed.
1953 National assembly established.
1959 4,000 Tibetan refugees given asylum.
1968 King established first cabinet.
1972 King died and was succeeded by his son Jigme Singye Wangchuk.
1979 Tibetan refugees told to take Bhutanese citizenship or leave; most stayed.
1983 Bhutan became a founding member of the South Asian Regional Association for Cooperation.
1988 King imposed 'code of conduct' suppressing Nepalese customs.
1990 Hundreds of people allegedly killed during prodemocracy demonstrations.

Bolivia

Republic of (*República de Bolivia*)

area 1,098,581 sq km/424,052 sq mi
capital La Paz (seat of government), Sucre (legal capital and seat of judiciary)
towns Santa Cruz, Cochabamba, Oruro, Potosí
physical high plateau (Altiplano) between mountain ridges (cordilleras); forest and lowlands (llano) in the E
features Andes, lakes Titicaca (the world's highest navigable lake, 3,800 m/12,500 ft) and Poopó; La Paz is world's highest capital city (3,600 m/11,800 ft)
head of state and government Gonzalo Sanchez de Lozado from 1993
political system emergent democratic republic
political parties National Revolutionary Movement

(MNR), centre right; Movement of the Revolutionary Left (MIR), left of centre; Solidarity Civil Union (UCS), radical free-market; Nationalist Democratic Action (ADN), right of centre
exports tin, antimony (second largest world producer), other nonferrous metals, oil, gas (piped to Argentina), agricultural products, coffee, sugar, cotton
currency boliviano
population (1992) 7,739,000; (Quechua 25%, Aymara 17%, mestizo (mixed) 30%, European 14%); growth rate 2.7% p.a.
life expectancy men 51, women 54
languages Spanish, Aymara, Quechua (all official)
religion Roman Catholic 95% (state-recognized)
literacy men 84%, women 65% (1985 est)
GDP $4.2 bn (1987); $617 per head

chronology
1825 Liberated from Spanish rule by Simón Bolívar; independence achieved (formerly known as Upper Peru).
1952 Dr Víctor Paz Estenssoro elected president.
1956 Dr Hernán Siles Zuazo became president.
1960 Estenssoro returned to power.
1964 Army coup led by the vice president, General René Barrientos.
1966 Barrientos became president.
1967 Uprising, led by 'Che' Guevara, put down with US help.
1969 Barrientos killed in plane crash, replaced by Vice President Siles Salinas. Army coup deposed him.
1970 Army coup put General Juan Torres González in power.
1971 Torres replaced by Col Hugo Banzer Suárez.
1973 Banzer promised a return to democratic government.
1974 Attempted coup prompted Banzer to postpone elections and ban political and trade-union activity.
1978 Elections declared invalid after allegations of fraud.
1980 More inconclusive elections followed by another coup, led by General Luis García. Allegations of corruption and drug trafficking led to cancellation of US and EC aid.

1981 García forced to resign. Replaced by General Celso Torrelio Villa.

1982 Torrelio resigned. Replaced by military junta led by General Guido Vildoso. Because of worsening economy, Vildoso asked congress to install a civilian administration. Dr Siles Zuazo chosen as president.

1983 Economic aid from USA and Europe resumed.

1984 New coalition government formed by Siles. Abduction of president by right-wing officers. The president undertook a five-day hunger strike as an example to the nation.

1985 President Siles resigned. Election result inconclusive; Dr Paz Estenssoro, at the age of 77, chosen by congress as president.

1989 Jaime Paz Zamora (MIR) elected president in power-sharing arrangement with Hugo Banzer Suárez, pledged to maintain fiscal and monetary discipline and preserve free- market policies.

1993 MNR won congressional and presidential elections.

Bosnia-Herzegovina

Republic of

area 51,129 sq km/19,745 sq mi
capital Sarajevo
towns Banja Luka, Mostar, Prijedor, Tuzla, Zenica
physical barren, mountainous country
features part of the Dinaric Alps, limestone gorges
population (1992) 4,397,000 including 44% Muslims, 33% Serbs, 17% Croats; a complex patchwork of ethnically mixed communities
head of state Alija Izetbegović from 1990
head of government Mile Akmadzic from 1992
political system emergent democracy
political parties Party of Democratic Action (SDA), Muslim-oriented; Serbian Democratic Party (SDS), Serbian nationalist; Christian Democratic Union (HDS), centrist; League of Communists, left-wing
products citrus fruits and vegetables; iron, steel, and leather goods; textiles
language Serbian variant of Serbo-Croatian
religions Sunni Muslim, Serbian Orthodox, Roman Catholic

chronology
1918 Incorporated in the future Yugoslavia.
1941 Occupied by Nazi Germany.

1945 Became republic within Yugoslav Socialist Federation.

1980 Upsurge in Islamic nationalism.

1990 Ethnic violence erupted between Muslims and Serbs. Communists defeated in multiparty elections; coalition formed by Serb, Muslim, and Croatian parties.

1991 May: Serbia–Croatia conflict spread disorder into Bosnia-Herzegovina. Aug: Serbia revealed plans to annex the SE part of the republic. Sept: Serbian enclaves established by force. Oct: 'sovereignty' declared. Nov: plebiscite by Serbs favoured remaining within Yugoslavia; Serbs and Croats established autonomous communities.

1992 Feb–March: Muslims and Croats voted overwhelmingly in favour of independence; referendum boycotted by Serbs. April: USA and EC recognized Bosnian independence. Ethnic hostilities escalated, with Serb forces occupying E and Croatian forces much of W; state of emergency declared; all- out civil war. May: admitted to United Nations. June: UN forces drafted into Sarajevo to break three-month siege of city by Serbs. Accusations of 'ethnic cleansing' being practised, particularly by Serbs. Oct: UN ban on military flights over Bosnia-Herzegovina. First British troops deployed, under UN control.

1993 UN-EC peace plan introduced, failed. USA began airdrops of food and medical supplies.

Botswana

Republic of

area 582,000 sq km/225,000 sq mi
capital Gaborone
towns Mahalpye, Serowe, Tutume, Francistown
physical desert in SW, plains in E, fertile lands and swamp in N
environment the Okavango Swamp is threatened by plans to develop the area for mining and agriculture
features Kalahari Desert in SW; Okavango Swamp in N, remarkable for its wildlife; Makgadikgadi salt pans in E; diamonds mined at Orapa and Jwaneng in partnership with De Beers of South Africa
head of state and government Quett Ketamile Joni Masire from 1980
political system democratic republic
political parties Botswana Democratic Party (BDP),

moderate centrist; Botswana National Front (BNF), moderate, left of centre
exports diamonds (third largest producer in world), copper, nickel, meat products, textiles
currency pula
population (1992) 1,359,000 (Bamangwato 80%, Bangwaketse 20%); growth rate 3.5% p.a.
life expectancy (1988) 59 years
languages English (official), Setswana (national)
religions Christian 50%, animist 50%
literacy (1988) 84%
GDP $2.0 bn (1988); $1,611 per head

chronology
1885 Became a British protectorate.
1960 New constitution created a legislative council.
1963 End of rule by High Commission.
1965 Capital transferred from Mafeking to Gaborone. Internal self-government achieved. Sir Seretse Khama elected head of government.
1966 Independence achieved from Britain. New constitution came into effect; name changed from Bechuanaland to Botswana; Seretse Khama elected president.
1980 Seretse Khama died; succeeded by Vice President Quett Masire.
1984 Masire re-elected.
1985 South African raid on Gaborone.
1987 Joint permanent commission with Mozambique established, to improve relations.
1989 The BDP and Masire re-elected.

Brazil

Federative Republic of (*República Federativa do Brasil*)

area 8,511,965 sq km/3,285,618 sq mi
capital Brasília
towns São Paulo, Belo Horizonte, Curitiba, Manaus, Fortaleza; ports are Rio de Janeiro, Belém, Recife, Pôrto Alegre, Salvador
physical the densely forested Amazon basin covers the northern half of the country with a network of rivers; the south is fertile; enormous energy resources, both hydroelectric (Itaipú dam on the Paraná, and Tucuruí on the Tocantins) and nuclear (uranium ores)

environment Brazil has one-third of the world's tropical rainforest. It contains 55,000 species of flowering plants (the greatest variety in the world) and 20% of all the world's bird species. During the 1980s at least 7% of the Amazon rainforest was destroyed by settlers who cleared the land for cultivation and grazing
features Mount Roraima, Xingu National Park; Amazon delta; Rio harbour
head of state and government Itamar Franco from 1992
political system emergent democratic federal republic
political parties Social Democratic Party (PDS), moderate, left of centre; Brazilian Democratic Movement Party (PMDB), centre-left; Liberal Front Party (PFL), moderate, left of centre; Workers' Party (PT), left of centre; National Reconstruction Party (PRN), centre-right
exports coffee, sugar, soya beans, cotton, textiles, timber, motor vehicles, iron, chrome, manganese, tungsten and other ores, as well as quartz crystals, industrial diamonds, gemstones; the world's sixth largest arms exporter
currency cruzado (introduced 1986; value = 100 cruzeiros, the former unit); inflation 1990 was 1,795%
population (1992) 151,381,000 (including 200,000 Indians, survivors of 5 million, especially in Rondônia and Mato Grosso, mostly living on reservations); growth rate 2.2% p.a.
life expectancy men 61, women 66
languages Portuguese (official); 120 Indian languages
religions Roman Catholic 89%; Indian faiths
literacy men 79%, women 76% (1985 est)
GDP $352 bn (1988); $2,434 per head

chronology
1822 Independence achieved from Portugal; ruled by Dom Pedro, son of the refugee King John VI of Portugal.
1889 Monarchy abolished and republic established.
1891 Constitution for a federal state adopted.
1930 Dr Getúlio Vargas became president.
1945 Vargas deposed by the military.
1946 New constitution adopted.
1951 Vargas returned to office.
1954 Vargas committed suicide.
1956 Juscelino Kubitschek became president.
1960 Capital moved to Brasília.
1961 João Goulart became president.
1964 Bloodless coup made General Castelo Branco president; he assumed dictatorial powers, abolishing free political parties.
1967 New constitution adopted. Branco succeeded by Marshal da Costa e Silva.
1969 Da Costa e Silva resigned and a military junta took over.
1974 General Ernesto Geisel became president.
1978 General Baptista de Figueiredo became president.
1979 Political parties legalized again.
1984 Mass calls for a return to fully democratic government.
1985 Tancredo Neves became first civilian president in 21 years. Neves died and was succeeded by the vice president, José Sarney.
1988 New constitution approved, transferring power from the president to the congress. Measures

announced to halt large-scale burning of Amazonian rainforest for cattle grazing.

1989 Forest Protection Service and Ministry for Land Reform abolished. International concern over how much of the Amazon has been burned. Fernando Collor (PRN) elected president Dec, pledging free-market economic policies.

1990 Government won the general election offset by mass abstentions.

1992 Collor charged with corruption and replaced by Vice President Itamar Franco.

1993 Collor indicted for 'passive corruption'. June: Collor appeared before supreme court.

Brunei

Islamic Sultanate of (*Negara Brunei Darussalam*)

area 5,765 sq km/2,225 sq mi
capital Bandar Seri Begawan
towns Tutong, Seria, Kuala Belait
physical flat coastal plain with hilly lowland in W and mountains in E; 75% of the area is forested; the Limbang valley splits Brunei in two, and its cession to Sarawak 1890 is disputed by Brunei
features Temburong, Tutong, and Belait rivers; Mount Pagon (1,850 m/6,070 ft)
head of state and of government HM Muda Hassanal Bolkiah Mu'izzaddin Waddaulah, Sultan of Brunei, from 1968
political system absolute monarchy
political party Brunei National United Party (BNUP)
exports liquefied natural gas (world's largest producer) and oil, both expected to be exhausted by the year 2000
currency Brunei dollar
population (1992) 268,000 (65% Malay, 20% Chinese – few Chinese granted citizenship); growth rate 12% p.a.
life expectancy 74 years
languages Malay (official), Chinese (Hokkien), English
religion 60% Muslim (official)
literacy 95%
GDP $3.4 bn (1985); $20,000 per head

chronology
1888 Brunei became a British protectorate.

1941–45 Occupied by Japan.
1959 Written constitution made Britain responsible for defence and external affairs.
1962 Sultan began rule by decree.
1967 Sultan abdicated in favour of his son, Hassanal Bolkiah.
1971 Brunei given internal self-government.
1975 United Nations resolution called for independence for Brunei.
1984 Independence achieved from Britain, with Britain maintaining a small force to protect the oil- and gasfields.
1985 A 'loyal and reliable' political party, the Brunei National Democratic Party (BNDP), legalized.
1986 Death of former sultan, Sir Omar. Formation of multiethnic BNUP.
1988 BNDP banned.

Bulgaria

Republic of (*Republika Bulgaria*)

area 110,912 sq km/42,812 sq mi
capital Sofia
towns Plovdiv, Ruse; Black Sea ports Burgas and Varna
physical lowland plains in N and SE separated by mountains that cover three-quarters of the country
environment pollution has virtually eliminated all species of fish once caught in the Black Sea. Vehicle-exhaust emissions in Sofia have led to dust concentrations more than twice the medically accepted level
features key position on land route from Europe to Asia; Black Sea coast; Balkan and Rhodope mountains; Danube River in N
head of state Zhelyu Zhelev from 1990
head of government Lyuben Berov from 1992
political system emergent democratic republic
political parties Union of Democratic Forces (UDF), right of centre; Bulgarian Socialist Party (BSP), left-wing, ex-communist; Movement for Rights and Freedoms (MRF), centrist; Civit Alliances for the Republic (CAR), left of centre
exports textiles, leather, chemicals, nonferrous metals, timber, machinery, tobacco, cigarettes (world's largest exporter)
currency lev
population (1992) 8,985,000 (including 900,000–1,500,000 ethnic Turks, concentrated in S and NE); growth rate 0.1% p.a.

life expectancy men 69, women 74
languages Bulgarian, Turkish
religions Eastern Orthodox Christian 90%, Sunni Muslim 10%
literacy 98%
GDP $25.4 bn (1987); $2,836 per head

chronology
1908 Bulgaria became a kingdom independent of Turkish rule.
1944 Soviet invasion of German-occupied Bulgaria.
1946 Monarchy abolished and communist-dominated people's republic proclaimed.
1947 Soviet-style constitution adopted.
1949 Death of Georgi Dimitrov, the communist government leader.
1954 Election of Todor Zhivkov as Communist Party general secretary; made nation a loyal satellite of USSR.
1971 Constitution modified; Zhivkov elected president.
1985–89 Large administrative and personnel changes to government made haphazardly under Soviet stimulus.
1987 New electoral law introduced multicandidate elections.
1989 Programme of 'Bulgarianization' resulted in mass exodus of Turks to Turkey. Nov: Zhivkov ousted by Petar Mladenov. Dec: opposition parties allowed to form.
1990 April: BCP renamed Bulgarian Socialist Party (BSP). Aug: Dr Zhelyu Zhelev elected president. Nov: government headed by Andrei Lukanov resigned, replaced Dec by coalition led by Dimitur Popov.
1991 July: new constitution adopted. Oct: UDF beat BSP in general election by narrow margin; formation of first noncommunist, UDF-minority government under Filip Dimitrov.
1992 Zhelev became Bulgaria's first directly elected president. Relations with West greatly improved. Dimitrov resigned after vote of no confidence; replaced by Lyuben Berov and non-party government.

Burkina Faso

The People's Democratic Republic of (formerly *Upper Volta*)

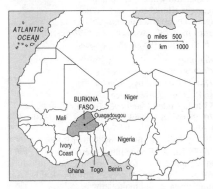

area 274,122 sq km/105,811 sq mi
capital Ouagadougou

towns Bobo-Dioulasso, Koudougou
physical landlocked plateau with hills in W and SE; headwaters of the river Volta; semiarid in N, forest and farmland in S
environment tropical savanna subject to overgrazing and deforestation
features linked by rail to Abidjan in Ivory Coast, Burkina Faso's only outlet to the sea
head of state and government Blaise Compaoré from 1987
political system transitional
political parties Organization for Popular Democracy–Workers' Movement (ODP–MT), nationalist left-wing; FP–Popular Front
exports cotton, groundnuts, livestock, hides, skins, sesame, cereals
currency CFA franc
population (1992) 9,515,000; growth rate 2.4% p.a.
life expectancy men 44, women 47
languages French (official); about 50 native Sudanic languages spoken by 90% of population
religions animist 53%, Sunni Muslim 36%, Roman Catholic 11%
literacy men 21%, women 6% (1985 est)
GDP $1.6 bn (1987); $188 per head

chronology
1958 Became a self-governing republic within the French Community.
1960 Independence from France, with Maurice Yaméogo as the first president.
1966 Military coup led by Col Lamizana. Constitution suspended, political activities banned, and a supreme council of the armed forces established.
1969 Ban on political activities lifted.
1970 Referendum approved a new constitution leading to a return to civilian rule.
1974 After experimenting with a mixture of military and civilian rule, Lamizana reassumed full power.
1977 Ban on political activities removed. Referendum approved a new constitution based on civilian rule.
1978 Lamizana elected president.
1980 Lamizana overthrown in bloodless coup led by Col Zerbo.
1982 Zerbo ousted in a coup by junior officers. Major Ouédraogo became president and Thomas Sankara prime minister.
1983 Sankara seized complete power.
1984 Upper Volta renamed Burkina Faso, 'land of upright men'.
1987 Sankara killed in coup led by Blaise Compaoré.
1989 New government party ODP–MT formed by merger of other pro-government parties. Coup against Compaoré foiled.
1991 New constitution approved. Compaoré re-elected president.
1992 Multiparty elections won by FP–Popular Front.

Burundi

Republic of (*Republika y'Uburundi*)

area 27,834 sq km/10,744 sq mi
capital Bujumbura
towns Gitega, Bururi, Ngozi, Muyinga
physical landlocked grassy highland straddling watershed of Nile and Congo
features Lake Tanganyika, Great Rift Valley

head of state transitional military group
head of government Sylvie Kinigi from 1993
political system one-party military republic
political party Union for National Progress (UPRONA), nationalist socialist
exports coffee, cotton, tea, nickel, hides, livestock, cigarettes, beer, soft drinks; there are 500 million tonnes of peat reserves in the basin of the Akanyaru River
currency Burundi franc
population (1992) 5,657,000 (of whom 15% are the Nilotic Tutsi, still holding most of the land and political power, 1% are Pygmy Twa, and the remainder Bantu Hutu); growth rate 2.8% p.a.
life expectancy men 45, women 48
languages Kirundi (a Bantu language) and French (both official), Kiswahili
religions Roman Catholic 62%, Protestant 5%, Muslim 1%, animist 32%
literacy men 43%, women 26% (1985)
GDP $1.1 bn (1987); $230 per head

chronology
1962 Separated from Ruanda-Urundi, as Burundi, and given independence as a monarchy under King Mwambutsa IV.
1966 King deposed by his son Charles, who became Ntare V; he was in turn deposed by his prime minister, Capt Michel Micombero, who declared Burundi a republic.
1972 Ntare V killed, allegedly by the Hutu ethnic group. Massacres of 150,000 Hutus by the rival Tutsi ethnic group, of which Micombero was a member.
1973 Micombero made president and prime minister.
1974 UPRONA declared the only legal political party, with the president as its secretary general.
1976 Army coup deposed Micombero. Col Jean-Baptiste Bagaza appointed president by the Supreme Revolutionary Council.
1981 New constitution adopted, providing for a national assembly.
1984 Bagaza elected president as sole candidate.
1987 Bagaza deposed in coup Sept. Maj Pierre Buyoya headed new Military Council for National Redemption.
1988 Some 24,000 majority Hutus killed by Tutsis.
1992 New constitution approved by referendum.
1993 Melchior Ndadaye, a Hutu, elected president. Oct: Ndadaye killed by military

Cambodia

State of (formerly *Khmer Republic* 1970–76, *Democratic Kampuchea* 1976–79, *People's Republic of Kampuchea* 1979–89)

area 181,035 sq km/69,880 sq mi
capital Phnom Penh
towns Battambang, the seaport Kompong Som
physical mostly flat forested plains with mountains in SW and N; Mekong River runs N–S
features ruins of ancient capital Angkor; Lake Tonle Sap
head of state Prince Norodom Sihanouk from 1991
head of government Prince Norodom Ranariddh from 1993
political system transitional
political parties Cambodian People's Party (CPP), reform socialist (formerly the communist Kampuchean People's Revolutionary Party (KPRP)); Party of Democratic Kampuchea (Khmer Rouge), ultranationalist communist; Khmer People's National Liberation Front (KPNLF), anticommunist; United Front for an Independent, Neutral, Peaceful, and Cooperative Cambodia (FUNCINPEC), moderate centrist
exports rubber, rice, pepper, wood, cattle
currency Cambodian riel
population (1992) 8,974,000; growth rate 2.2% p.a.
life expectancy men 42, women 45
languages Khmer (official), French
religion Theravāda Buddhist 95%
literacy men 78%, women 39% (1980 est)
GDP $592 mn (1987); $83 per head

chronology
1863–1941 French protectorate.
1941–45 Occupied by Japan.
1946 Recaptured by France.
1953 Independence achieved from France.
1970 Prince Sihanouk overthrown by US-backed Lon Nol.
1975 Lon Nol overthrown by Khmer Rouge.
1976–78 Khmer Rouge introduced an extreme communist programme, forcing urban groups into rural areas and bringing over 2.5 million deaths from famine, disease, and maltreatment.
1978–79 Vietnamese invasion and installation of Heng Samrin government.

1982 The three main anti-Vietnamese resistance groups formed an alliance under Prince Sihanouk.
1987 Vietnamese troop withdrawal began.
1989 Sept: completion of Vietnamese withdrawal. Nov: United Nations peace proposal rejected by Phnom Penh government.
1991 Oct: Peace agreement signed in Paris, providing for a UN Transitional Authority in Cambodia (UNTAC) to administer country in transition period in conjunction with all-party Supreme National Council; communism abandoned. Nov: Sihanouk returned as head of state.
1992 Political prisoners released; freedom of speech and party formation restored. Oct: Khmer Rouge refused to disarm in accordance with peace process. Dec: UN Security Council voted to impose limited trade embargo on area of country controlled by Khmer Rouge guerrillas.
1993 Free general elections resulted in win by FUNCINPEC over the CPP. Prince Norodom Ranariddh, FUNCINPEC leader, appointed prime minister.

Cameroon

Republic of (*République du Cameroun*)

area 475,440 sq km/183,638 sq mi
capital Yaoundé
towns chief port Douala; Nkongsamba, Garova
physical desert in far north in the Lake Chad basin, mountains in W, dry savanna plateau in the intermediate area, and dense tropical rainforest in S
environment the Korup National Park preserves 1,300 sq km/500 sq mi of Africa's fast-disappearing tropical rainforest. Scientists have identified nearly 100 potentially useful chemical substances produced naturally by the plants of this forest
features Mount Cameroon 4,070 m/13,358 ft, an active volcano on the coast, W of the Adamawa Mountains
head of state and of government Paul Biya from 1982
political system emergent democratic republic
political parties Democratic Assembly of the Cameroon People (RDPC), nationalist, left of centre; Social Democratic Front (SDF), centre-left; Social Movement for New Democracy (MSND), left of centre; Union of the Peoples of Cameroon (UPC), left of centre
exports cocoa, coffee, bananas, cotton, timber, rubber, groundnuts, gold, aluminium, crude oil
currency CFA franc

population (1992) 12,662,000; growth rate 2.7% p.a.
life expectancy men 49, women 53
languages French and English in pidgin variations (official); there has been some discontent with the emphasis on French – there are 163 indigenous peoples with their own African languages
media heavy government censorship
religions Roman Catholic 35%, animist 25%, Muslim 22%, Protestant 18%
literacy men 68%, women 45% (1985 est)
GDP $12.7 bn (1987); $1,170 per head

chronology
1884 Treaty signed establishing German rule.
1916 Captured by Allied forces in World War I.
1922 Divided between Britain and France.
1946 French Cameroon and British Cameroons made UN trust territories.
1960 French Cameroon became the independent Republic of Cameroon. Ahmadou Ahidjo elected president.
1961 Northern part of British Cameroon merged with Nigeria and southern part joined the Republic of Cameroon to become the Federal Republic of Cameroon.
1966 One-party regime introduced.
1972 New constitution made Cameroon a unitary state, the United Republic of Cameroon.
1973 New national assembly elected.
1982 Ahidjo resigned and was succeeded by Paul Biya.
1983 Biya began to remove his predecessor's supporters; accused by Ahidjo of trying to create a police state. Ahidjo went into exile in France.
1984 Biya re-elected; defeated a plot to overthrow him. Country's name changed to Republic of Cameroon.
1988 Biya re-elected.
1990 Widespread public disorder. Biya granted amnesty to political prisoners.
1991 Constitutional changes made.
1992 Ruling RDPC won in first multiparty elections in 28 years. Biya's presidential victory challenged by opposition.

Canada

area 9,970,610 sq km/3,849,674 sq mi
capital Ottawa
towns Toronto, Montréal, Vancouver, Edmonton, Calgary, Winnipeg, Quebec, Hamilton, Saskatoon, Halifax
physical mountains in W, with low-lying plains in interior and rolling hills in E. Climate varies from temperate in S to arctic in N
environment sugar maples are dying in E Canada as a result of increasing soil acidification; nine rivers in Nova Scotia are now too acid to support salmon or trout reproduction
features St Lawrence Seaway, Mackenzie River; Great Lakes; Arctic Archipelago; Rocky Mountains; Great Plains or Prairies; Canadian Shield; Niagara Falls; the world's second largest country
head of state Elizabeth II from 1952, represented by governor general
head of government Jean Chretien from 1993
political system federal constitutional monarchy

political parties Progressive Conservative Party, free-enterprise, right of centre; Liberal Party, nationalist, centrist; New Democratic Party (NDP), moderate left of centre

exports wheat, timber, pulp, newsprint, fish (salmon), furs (ranched fox and mink exceed the value of wild furs), oil, natural gas, aluminium, asbestos (world's second largest producer), coal, copper, iron, zinc, nickel (world's largest producer), uranium (world's largest producer), motor vehicles and parts, industrial and agricultural machinery, fertilizers, chemicals

currency Canadian dollar

population (1992) 27,737,000 – including 300,000 North American Indians, of whom 75% live on more than 2,000 reservations in Ontario and the four western provinces; some 300,000 Métis (people of mixed race) and 19,000 Inuit of whom 75% live in the Northwest Territories. Over half Canada's population lives in Ontario and Québec. Growth rate 1.1% p.a.

life expectancy men 72, women 79

languages English, French (both official; about 70% speak English, 20% French, and the rest are bilingual); there are also North American Indian languages and the Inuit Inuktitut

religion Roman Catholic 46%, Protestant 35%

literacy 99%

GDP $562 bn (1992)

chronology
1867 Dominion of Canada founded.
1949 Newfoundland joined Canada.
1957 Progressive Conservatives returned to power after 22 years in opposition.
1961 NDP formed.
1963 Liberals elected under Lester Pearson.
1968 Pearson succeeded by Pierre Trudeau.
1979 Joe Clark, leader of the Progressive Conservatives, formed a minority government; defeated on budget proposals.
1980 Liberals under Trudeau returned with a large majority. Québec referendum rejected demand for independence.
1982 Canada Act removed Britain's last legal control over Canadian affairs; 'patriation' of Canada's constitution.
1983 Clark replaced as leader of the Progressive Conservatives by Brian Mulroney.
1984 Trudeau retired and was succeeded as Liberal leader and prime minister by John Turner. Progressive Conservatives won the federal election with a large majority, and Mulroney became prime minister.
1988 Conservatives re-elected with reduced majority on platform of free trade with the USA.
1989 Free-trade agreement signed. Turner resigned as Liberal Party leader, and Ed Broadbent as NDP leader.
1990 Collapse of Meech Lake accord. Canada joined the coalition opposing Iraq's invasion of Kuwait.
1992 Gradual withdrawal of Canadian forces in Europe announced. Self-governing homeland for Inuit approved. Constitutional reform package, the Charlottetown agreement, rejected in national referendum.
1993 Mulroney resigned leadership of Conservative Party; Kim Campbell, the new party leader, became prime minister. Oct: Conservatives defeated in general election. Liberal leader Jean Chretien became prime minister. Dec: Kim Campbell resigned Conservative Party leadership.

Cape Verde
Republic of (*República de Cabo Verde*)

area 4,033 sq km/1,557 sq mi

capital Praia

towns Mindelo, Sal-Rei, Porto Novo

physical archipelago of ten volcanic islands 565 km/350 mi W of Senegal; the windward (Barlavento) group includes Santo Antão, São Vicente, Santa Luzia, São Nicolau, Sal, and Boa Vista; the leeward (Sotovento) group comprises Maio, São Tiago, Fogo, and Brava; all but Santa Luzia are inhabited

features strategic importance guaranteed by its domination of western shipping lanes; Sal, Boa Vista, and Maio lack water supplies but have fine beaches

head of state Mascarenhas Monteiro from 1991

head of government Carlos Viega from 1991

political system socialist pluralist state

political parties African Party for the Independence of Cape Verde (PAICV), African nationalist; Movement for Democracy (MPD)

exports bananas, salt, fish

currency Cape Verde escudo

population (1992) 346,000 (including 100,000 Angolan refugees); growth rate 1.9% p.a.

life expectancy men 57, women 61

language Creole dialect of Portuguese
religion Roman Catholic 80%
literacy men 61%, women 39% (1985)
GDP $158 million (1987); $454 per head

chronology
15th century First settled by Portuguese.
1951–74 Ruled as an overseas territory by Portugal.
1974 Moved towards independence through a transitional Portuguese–Cape Verde government.
1975 Independence achieved from Portugal. National people's assembly elected. Aristides Pereira became the first president.
1980 Constitution adopted providing for eventual union with Guinea-Bissau.
1981 Union with Guinea-Bissau abandoned and the constitution amended; became one-party state.
1991 First multiparty elections held. New party, MPD, won majority in assembly. Pereira replaced by Mascarenhas Monteiro.

Central African Republic
(*République Centrafricaine*)

area 622,436 sq km/240,260 sq mi
capital Bangui
towns Berbérati, Bouar, Bossangoa
physical landlocked flat plateau, with rivers flowing N and S, and hills in NE and SW; dry in N, rainforest in SW
environment an estimated 87% of the urban population is without access to safe drinking water
features Kotto and Mbali river falls; the Oubangui River rises 6 m/20 ft at Bangui during the wet season (June– Nov)
head of state André Kolingba from 1981
head of government Jean-Luc Mandaba from 1993
political system emergent democratic republic
political parties Central African Democratic Assembly (RDC), nationalist; all political activity has been banned since the 1981 coup, but the main opposition groups, although passive, still exist. They are the Patriotic Front Ubangi Workers' Party (FPO-PT), the Central African Movement for National Liberation (MCLN), and the Movement for the Liberation of the Central African People (MPLC)
exports diamonds, uranium, coffee, cotton, timber, tobacco
currency CFA franc
population (1992) 2,930,000 (more than 80 ethnic groups); growth rate 2.3% p.a.
life expectancy men 41, women 45

languages Sangho (national), French (official), Arabic, Hunsa, and Swahili
religions Protestant 25%, Roman Catholic 25%, Muslim 10%, animist 10%
literacy men 53%, women 29% (1985 est)
GDP $1 bn (1987); $374 per head

chronology
1960 Central African Republic achieved independence from France; David Dacko elected president.
1962 The republic made a one-party state.
1965 Dacko ousted in military coup led by Col Bokassa.
1966 Constitution rescinded and national assembly dissolved.
1972 Bokassa declared himself president for life.
1977 Bokassa made himself emperor of the Central African Empire.
1979 Bokassa deposed by Dacko following violent repressive measures by the self-styled emperor, who went into exile.
1981 Dacko deposed in a bloodless coup, led by General André Kolingba, and an all-military government established.
1983 Clandestine opposition movement formed.
1984 Amnesty for all political party leaders announced. President Mitterrand of France paid a state visit.
1985 New constitution promised, with some civilians in the government.
1986 Bokassa returned from France, expecting to return to power; he was imprisoned and his trial started. General Kolingba re-elected. New constitution approved by referendum.
1988 Bokassa found guilty and received death sentence, later commuted to life imprisonment.
1992 Abortive debate held on political reform; multiparty elections promised but then postponed.
1993 Feb: Enoch Derant Lakoue appointed prime minister. Oct: Jean-Luc Mandaba appointed prime minister after inconclusive general election.

Chad
Republic of (*République du Tchad*)

area 1,284,000 sq km/495,624 sq mi
capital Ndjamena (formerly Fort Lamy)
towns Sarh, Moundou, Abéché
physical landlocked state with mountains and part of Sahara Desert in N; moist savanna in S; rivers in S flow NW to Lake Chad
head of state Idriss Deby from 1990
head of government Fuidel Mounyar (interim) 1993

political system emergent democratic republic
political parties National Union for Independence and Revolution (UNIR), nationalist; Alliance for Democracy and Progress (RDP), centre-left; Union for Democracy and Progress (UPDT), centre-left
exports cotton, meat, livestock, hides, skins
currency CFA franc
population (1992) 5,961,000; growth rate 2.3% p.a. Nomadic tribes move N–S seasonally in search of water
life expectancy men 42, women 45
languages French, Arabic (both official), over 100 African languages spoken
religions Muslim 44% (N), Christian 33%, animist 23% (S)
literacy men 40%, women 11% (1985 est)
GDP $980 million (1986); $186 per head

chronology
1960 Independence achieved from France, with François Tombalbaye as president.
1963 Violent opposition in the Muslim north, led by the Chadian National Liberation Front (Frolinat), backed by Libya.
1968 Revolt quelled with France's help.
1975 Tombalbaye killed in military coup led by Félix Malloum. Frolinat continued its resistance.
1978 Malloum tried to find a political solution by bringing the former Frolinat leader Hissène Habré into his government but they were unable to work together.
1979 Malloum forced to leave the country; an interim government was set up under General Goukouni. Habré continued his opposition with his Army of the North (FAN).
1981 Habré now in control of half the country. Goukouni fled and set up a 'government in exile'.
1983 Habré's regime recognized by the Organization for African Unity (OAU), but in the north Goukouni's supporters, with Libya's help, fought on. Eventually a cease-fire was agreed, with latitude 16°N dividing the country.
1984 Libya and France agreed to a withdrawal of forces.
1985 Fighting between Libyan-backed and French-backed forces intensified.
1987 Chad, France, and Libya agreed on cease-fire proposed by OAU.
1988 Full diplomatic relations with Libya restored.
1989 Libyan troop movements reported on border; Habré re-elected, amended constitution.
1990 President Habré ousted in coup led by Idriss Deby. New constitution adopted.
1991 Several anti-government coups foiled.
1992 Anti-government coup foiled. Two new opposition parties approved.
1993 Fuidel Mounyar chosen as transitional prime minister pending multiparty elections.

Chile

Republic of (*República de Chile*)
area 756,950 sq km/292,257 sq mi
capital Santiago
towns Concepción, Viña del Mar, Temuco; ports Valparaíso, Antofagasta, Arica, Iquique, Punta Arenas
physical Andes mountains along E border, Atacama Desert in N, fertile central valley, grazing land and forest in S

territories Easter Island, Juan Fernández Islands, part of Tierra del Fuego, claim to part of Antarctica
features Atacama Desert is one of the driest regions in the world
head of state and government Patricio Aylwin from 1990
political system emergent democratic republic
political parties Christian Democratic Party (PDC), moderate centrist; National Renewal Party (RN), right-wing
exports copper (world's leading producer), iron, molybdenum (world's second largest producer), nitrate, pulp and paper, steel products, fishmeal, fruit
currency peso
population (1992) 13,599,000 (the majority are of European origin or are mestizos, of mixed American Indian and Spanish descent); growth rate 1.6% p.a.
life expectancy men 64, women 73
language Spanish
religion Roman Catholic 89%
literacy 94% (1988)
GDP $18.9 bn (1987); $6,512 per head

chronology
1818 Achieved independence from Spain.
1964 PDC formed government under Eduardo Frei.
1970 Dr Salvador Allende became the first democratically elected Marxist president; he embarked on an extensive programme of nationalization and social reform.
1973 Government overthrown by the CIA-backed military, led by General Augusto Pinochet. Allende killed. Policy of repression began during which all opposition was put down and political activity banned.
1983 Growing opposition to the regime from all sides, with outbreaks of violence.
1988 Referendum on whether Pinochet should serve a further term resulted in a clear 'No' vote.
1989 President Pinochet agreed to constitutional changes to allow pluralist politics. Patricio Aylwin (PDC) elected president (his term would begin 1990); Pinochet remained as army commander in chief.

1990 Aylwin reached accord on end to military junta government. Pinochet censured by president.
1992 Future US–Chilean free-trade agreement announced.
1993 Ruling coalition successful in general election.

China

People's Republic of (*Zhonghua Renmin Gonghe Guo*)

area 9,596,960 sq km/3,599,975 sq mi
capital Beijing (Peking)
towns Chongqing (Chungking), Shenyang (Mukden), Wuhan, Nanjing (Nanking), Harbin; ports Tianjin (Tientsin), Shanghai, Qingdao (Tsingtao), Lüda (Lü-ta), Guangzhou (Canton)
physical two-thirds of China is mountains or desert (N and W); the low-lying E is irrigated by rivers Huang He (Yellow River), Chang Jiang (Yangtze-Kiang), Xi Jiang (Si Kiang)
features Great Wall of China; Gezhouba Dam; Ming Tombs; Terracotta Warriors (Xi'ain); Gobi Desert; world's most populous country
head of state Jiang Zemin from 1993
head of government Li Peng from 1987
political system communist republic
political party Chinese Communist Party (CCP), Marxist-Leninist-Maoist
exports tea, livestock and animal products, silk, cotton, oil, minerals (China is the world's largest producer of tungsten and antimony), chemicals, light industrial goods
currency yuan
population (1992) 1,165,888,000 (the majority are Han or ethnic Chinese; the 67 million of other ethnic groups, including Tibetan, Uigur, and Zhuang, live in border areas). The number of people of Chinese origin outside China, Taiwan, and Hong Kong is estimated at 15–24 million. Growth rate 1.2% p.a.
life expectancy men 67, women 69
languages Chinese, including Mandarin (official), Cantonese, and other dialects
religions officially atheist, but traditionally Taoist, Confucianist, and Buddhist; Muslim 13 million; Catholic 3-6 million (divided between the 'patriotic' church established 1958 and the 'loyal' church subject to Rome); Protestant 3 million
literacy men 82%, women 66% (1985 est)

GDP $293.4 bn (1987); $274 per head

chronology
1949 People's Republic of China proclaimed by Mao Zedong.
1954 Soviet-style constitution adopted.
1956–57 Hundred Flowers Movement encouraged criticism of the government.
1958–60 Great Leap Forward commune experiment to achieve 'true communism'.
1960 Withdrawal of Soviet technical advisers.
1962 Sino-Indian border war.
1962–65 Economic recovery programme under Liu Shaoqi; Maoist 'socialist education movement' rectification campaign.
1966–69 Great Proletarian Cultural Revolution; Liu Shaoqi removed from power.
1969 Ussuri River border clashes with USSR.
1970–76 Reconstruction under Mao and Zhou Enlai.
1971 Entry into United Nations.
1972 US president Nixon visited Beijing.
1975 New state constitution. Unveiling of Zhou's 'Four Modernizations' programme.
1976 Deaths of Zhou Enlai and Mao Zedong; appointment of Hua Guofeng as prime minister and Communist Party chair. Vice Premier Deng Xiaoping in hiding. Gang of Four arrested.
1977 Rehabilitation of Deng Xiaoping.
1979 Economic reforms introduced. Diplomatic relations opened with USA. Punitive invasion of Vietnam.
1980 Zhao Ziyang appointed prime minister.
1981 Hu Yaobang succeeded Hua Guofeng as party chair. Imprisonment of Gang of Four.
1982 New state constitution adopted.
1984 'Enterprise management' reforms for industrial sector.
1986 Student prodemocracy demonstrations.
1987 Hu was replaced as party leader by Zhao, with Li Peng as prime minister. Deng left Politburo but remained influential.
1988 Yang Shangkun replaced Li Xiannian as state president. Economic reforms encountered increasing problems; inflation rocketed.
1989 Over 2,000 killed in prodemocracy student demonstrations in Tiananmen Square; international sanctions imposed.
1991 March: European Community and Japanese sanctions lifted. May: normal relations with USSR resumed. Sept: UK prime minister John Major visited Beijing. Nov: relations with Vietnam normalized.
1992 China promised to sign 1968 Nuclear Non-Proliferation Treaty. Historic visit by Japan's emperor.
1993 Jiang Zemin, Chinese Communist Party general secretary, set to replace Yang Shangkun as president.

Colombia

Republic of (*República de Colombia*)

area 1,141,748 sq km/440,715 sq mi
capital Bogotá
towns Medellín, Cali, Bucaramanga; ports Barranquilla, Cartagena, Buenaventura
physical the Andes mountains run N–S; flat coastland in W and plains (llanos) in E; Magdalena River runs N to Caribbean Sea; includes islands of Providencia, San Andrés, and Mapelo

features Zipaquira salt mine and underground cathedral; Lake Guatavita, source of the legend of 'El Dorado'
head of state and government Cesar Gaviria Trujillo from 1990
political system emergent democratic republic
political parties Liberal Party (PL), centrist; April 19 Movement (M-19); National Salvation Movement; Conservative Party, right of centre
exports emeralds (world's largest producer), coffee (world's second largest producer), cocaine (country's largest export), bananas, cotton, meat, sugar, oil, skins, hides, tobacco
currency peso
population (1992) 33,392,000 (mestizo 68%, white 20%, Amerindian 1%); growth rate 2.2% p.a.
life expectancy men 61, women 66; Indians 34
language Spanish
religion Roman Catholic 95%
literacy men 89%, women 87% (1987); Indians 40%
GDP $31.9 bn (1987); $1,074 per head

chronology
1886 Full independence achieved from Spain. Conservatives in power.
1930 Liberals in power.
1946 Conservatives in power.
1948 Left-wing mayor of Bogotá assassinated; widespread outcry.
1949 Start of civil war, 'La Violencia', during which over 250,000 people died.
1957 Hoping to halt the violence, Conservatives and Liberals agreed to form a National Front, sharing the presidency.
1970 National Popular Alliance (ANAPO) formed as a left-wing opposition to the National Front.
1974 National Front accord temporarily ended.
1975 Civil unrest because of disillusionment with the government.
1978 Liberals, under Julio Turbay, revived the accord and began an intensive fight against drug dealers.
1982 Liberals maintained their control of congress but lost the presidency. The Conservative president, Belisario Betancur, granted guerrillas an amnesty and freed political prisoners.
1984 Minister of justice assassinated by drug dealers; campaign against them stepped up.

1986 Virgilio Barco Vargas, Liberal, elected president by record margin.
1989 Drug cartel assassinated leading presidential candidate; Vargas declared antidrug war; bombing campaign by drug traffickers killed hundreds; police killed José Rodríguez Gacha, one of the most wanted cartel leaders.
1990 Cesar Gaviria Trujillo elected president. Liberals maintained control of congress.
1991 New constitution prohibited extradition of Colombians wanted for trial in other countries; several leading drug traffickers arrested. Oct: Liberal Party won general election.
1992 One of the drug cartel leaders, Pablo Escobar, escaped from prison.
1993 Dec: Escobar killed while attempting to avoid arrest.

Comoros

Federal Islamic Republic of (*Jumhurīyat al-Qumur al- Itthādīyah al-Islāmīyah*)

area 1,862 sq km/719 sq mi
capital Moroni
towns Mutsamudu, Domoni, Fomboni
physical comprises the volcanic islands of Njazídja, Nzwani, and Mwali (formerly Grande Comore, Anjouan, Moheli); at N end of Mozambique Channel

features active volcano on Njazídja; poor tropical soil
head of state Said Mohammad Djohar (interim administration) from 1989
head of government Halidi Abderamane Ibrahim from 1993
political system emergent democracy
political parties Comoran Union for Progress (Udzima), nationalist Islamic; National Union for Congolese Democracy (UNDC), left of centre; Popular Democratic Movement (MDP), centrist
exports copra, vanilla, cocoa, sisal, coffee, cloves, essential oils
currency CFA franc
population (1992) 497,000; growth rate 3.1% p.a.
life expectancy men 48, women 52
languages Arabic (official), Comorian (Swahili and Arabic dialect), Makua, French
religions Muslim (official) 86%, Roman Catholic 14%

literacy 15%
GDP $198 million (1987); $468 per head

chronology
1975 Independence achieved from France, but island of Mayotte remained part of France. Ahmed Abdallah elected president. The Comoros joined the United Nations.
1976 Abdallah overthrown by Ali Soilih.
1978 Soilih killed by mercenaries working for Abdallah. Islamic republic proclaimed and Abdallah elected president.
1979 The Comoros became a one-party state; powers of the federal government increased.
1985 Constitution amended to make Abdallah head of government as well as head of state.
1989 Abdallah killed by French mercenaries who took control of government; under French and South African pressure, mercenaries left Comoros, turning authority over to French administration and interim president Said Mohammad Djohar.
1990 Antigovernment coup foiled.
1992 Third transitional government appointed. Antigovernment coup foiled.
1993 General election failed to provide any one party with overall assembly majority. President Djohar appointed Halidi Abderamane Ibrahim prime minister.

Congo

Republic of (*République du Congo*)

area 342,000 sq km/132,012 sq mi
capital Brazzaville
towns chief port Pointe-Noire; N'Kayi, Loubomo
physical narrow coastal plain rises to central plateau, then falls into northern basin; Zaïre (Congo) River on the border with Zaire; half the country is rainforest
environment an estimated 93% of the rural population is without access to safe drinking water
features 70% of the population lives in Brazzaville, Pointe-Noire, or in towns along the railway linking these two places
head of state Pascal Lissouba from 1992
head of government Jacques-Joachim Yhombi-Opango from 1993
political system emergent democracy
political parties Pan-African Union for Social Democracy (UPADS), moderate left of centre; Congolese Labour Party (PCT), (Marxist-Leninist ideology abandoned 1990) left-wing; Union for Democratic Renewal (URD), moderate centrist; Ralley for Democracy and Development (RDD)

exports timber, petroleum, cocoa, sugar
currency CFA franc
population (1992) 2,692,000 (chiefly Bantu); growth rate 2.6% p.a.
life expectancy men 45, women 48
languages French (official); many African languages
religions animist 50%, Christian 48%, Muslim 2%
literacy men 79%, women 55% (1985 est)
GDP $2.1 bn (1983); $500 per head

chronology
1910 Became part of French Equatorial Africa.
1960 Achieved independence from France, with Abbé Youlou as the first president.
1963 Youlou forced to resign. New constitution approved, with Alphonse Massamba-Débat as president.
1964 The Congo became a one-party state.
1968 Military coup, led by Capt Marien Ngouabi, ousted Massamba-Débat.
1970 A Marxist state, the People's Republic of the Congo, was announced, with the PCT as the only legal party.
1977 Ngouabi assassinated. Col Yhombi-Opango became president.
1979 Yhombi-Opango handed over the presidency to the PCT, who chose Col Denis Sassou-Nguessou as his successor.
1984 Sassou-Nguessou elected for another five-year term.
1990 The PCT abandoned Marxist-Leninism and promised multiparty politics.
1991 1979 constitution suspended. Country renamed the Republic of Congo.
1992 New constitution approved and multiparty elections held, giving UPADS the most assembly seats. Pascal Lissouba elected president.
1993 Gen. Yhombi-Opango, RDD leader, appointed prime minister.

Costa Rica

Republic of (*República de Costa Rica*)

area 51,100 sq km/19,735 sq mi
capital San José
towns ports Limón, Puntarenas
physical high central plateau and tropical coasts; Costa Rica was once entirely forested, containing an estimated 5% of the Earth's flora and fauna. By 1983

only 17% of the forest remained; half of the arable land had been cleared for cattle ranching, which led to landlessness, unemployment (except for 2,000 politically powerful families), and soil erosion; the massive environmental destruction also caused incalculable loss to the gene pool

environment one of the leading centres of conservation in Latin America, with more than 10% of the country protected by national parks, and tree replanting proceeding at a rate of 150 sq km/60 sq mi per year

features Poas Volcano; Guayabo pre-Colombian ceremonial site

head of state and government Rafael Calderón from 1990

political system liberal democracy

political parties National Liberation Party (PLN), left of centre; Christian Socialist Unity Party (PUSC), centrist coalition; ten minor parties

exports coffee, bananas, cocoa, sugar, beef

currency colón

population (1992) 3,161,000 (including 1,200 Guaymi Indians); growth rate 2.6% p.a.

life expectancy men 71, women 76

language Spanish (official)

religion Roman Catholic 95%

literacy men 94%, women 93% (1985 est)

GDP $4.3 bn (1986); $1,550 per head

chronology

1821 Independence achieved from Spain.

1949 New constitution adopted. National army abolished. José Figueres, cofounder of the PLN, elected president; he embarked on ambitious socialist programme.

1958–73 Mainly conservative administrations.

1974 PLN regained the presidency and returned to socialist policies.

1978 Rodrigo Carazo, conservative, elected president. Sharp deterioration in the state of the economy.

1982 Luis Alberto Monge (PLN) elected president. Harsh austerity programme introduced to rebuild the economy. Pressure from the USA to abandon neutral stance and condemn Sandinista regime in Nicaragua.

1983 Policy of neutrality reaffirmed.

1985 Following border clashes with Sandinista forces, a US-trained antiguerrilla guard formed.

1986 Oscar Arias Sánchez won the presidency on a neutralist platform.

1987 Arias won Nobel Prize for Peace for devising a Central American peace plan.

1990 Rafael Calderón (PUSC) elected president.

Croatia

Republic of

area 56,538 sq km/21,824 sq mi

capital Zagreb

towns chief port: Rijeka (Fiume); other ports: Zadar, Sibenik, Split, Dubrovnik

physical Adriatic coastline with large islands; very mountainous, with part of the Karst region and the Julian and Styrian Alps; some marshland

features popular sea resorts along the extensive Adriatic coastline

head of state Franjo Tudjman from 1990

head of government Nikica Valentic from 1993

political system emergent democracy

political parties Christian Democratic Union (HDZ), right-wing, nationalist; Coalition of National Agreement, centrist; Communist Party, reform-communist

products cereals, potatoes, tobacco, fruit, livestock, metal goods, textiles

currency Croatian dinar

population (1992) 4,808,000 including 75% Croats, 12% Serbs, and 1% Slovenes

language Croatian variant of Serbo-Croatian

media no official censorship but no press or TV independent of government

religions Roman Catholic (Croats); Orthodox Christian (Serbs)

GNP $7.9 bn (1990); $1,660 per head

chronology

1918 Became part of the kingdom that united the Serbs, Croats, and Slovenes.

1929 The kingdom of Croatia, Serbia, and Slovenia became Yugoslavia. Croatia continued its campaign for autonomy.

1941 Became a Nazi puppet state following German invasion.

1945 Became constituent republic of Yugoslavia.

1970s Separatist demands resurfaced. Crackdown against anti-Serb separatist agitators.

1989 Formation of opposition parties permitted.

1990 April–May: Communists defeated by Tudjman-led Croatian Democratic Union (HDZ) in first free election since 1938. Sept: 'sovereignty' declared. Dec: new constitution adopted.

1991 Feb: assembly called for Croatia's secession. March: Serb-dominated Krajina announced secession from Croatia. June: Croatia declared independence; military conflict with Serbia; internal civil war ensued. July onwards: civil war intensified. Oct: Croatia formally seceded from Yugoslavia.

1992 Jan: United Nations peace accord reached in Sarajevo; Croatia's independence recognized by the European Community. March–April: UN peacekeeping forces drafted into Croatia. April: independence recognized by USA. May: became a member of the United Nations. Aug: Tudjman directly elected president; HDZ won assembly elections. Sept: Tudjman requested withdrawal of UN forces on expiry of mandate 1993.

1993 Jan: Croatian forces launched offensive to retake parts of Serb-held Krajina, violating the 1992 UN peace accord.

Cuba

Republic of (*República de Cuba*)

area 110,860 sq km/42,820 sq mi
capital Havana
towns Santiago de Cuba, Camagüey
physical comprises Cuba, the largest and westernmost of the West Indies, and smaller islands including Isle of Youth; low hills; Sierra Maestra mountains in SE
features 3,380 km/2,100 mi of coastline, with deep bays, sandy beaches, coral islands and reefs; more than 1,600 islands surround the Cuban mainland
head of state and government Fidel Castro Ruz from 1959
political system communist republic
political party Communist Party of Cuba (PCC), Marxist-Leninist
exports sugar, tobacco, coffee, nickel, fish
currency Cuban peso
population (1992) 10,848,000; 37% are white of Spanish descent, 51% mulatto, and 11% are of African origin; growth rate 0.6% p.a.
life expectancy men 72, women 75
language Spanish
religions Roman Catholic 85%; also Episcopalians and Methodists
literacy men 96%, women 95% (1988)
disposable national income $15.8 bn (1983); $1,590 per head

chronology
1492 Christopher Columbus landed in Cuba and claimed it for Spain.
1898 USA defeated Spain in Spanish-American War; Spain gave up all claims to Cuba.
1901 Cuba achieved independence; Tomás Estrada Palma became first president of the Republic of Cuba.
1933 Fulgencia Batista seized power.
1944 Batista retired.
1952 Batista seized power again to begin an oppressive regime.
1953 Fidel Castro led an unsuccessful coup against Batista.
1956 Second unsuccessful coup by Castro.

1959 Batista overthrown by Castro. Constitution of 1940 replaced by a 'Fundamental Law', making Castro prime minister, his brother Raúl Castro his deputy, and 'Che' Guevara his number three.
1960 All US businesses in Cuba appropriated without compensation; USA broke off diplomatic relations.
1961 USA sponsored an unsuccessful invasion at the Bay of Pigs. Castro announced that Cuba had become a communist state, with a Marxist-Leninist programme of economic development.
1962 Cuba expelled from the Organization of American States. Soviet nuclear missiles installed but subsequently removed from Cuba at US insistence.
1965 Cuba's sole political party renamed Communist Party of Cuba (PCC). With Soviet help, Cuba began to make considerable economic and social progress.
1972 Cuba became a full member of the Moscow-based Council for Mutual Economic Assistance.
1976 New socialist constitution approved; Castro elected president.
1976-81 Castro became involved in extensive international commitments, sending troops as Soviet surrogates, particularly to Africa.
1982 Cuba joined other Latin American countries in giving moral support to Argentina in its dispute with Britain over the Falklands.
1984 Castro tried to improve US–Cuban relations by discussing exchange of US prisoners in Cuba for Cuban 'undesirables' in the USA.
1988 Peace accord with South Africa signed, agreeing to withdrawal of Cuban troops from Angola.
1989 Reduction in Cuba's overseas military activities.
1991 Soviet troops withdrawn.
1992 Castro affirmed continuing support of communism.
1993 Mysterious epidemic swept the country, possibly linked to malnutrition.

Cyprus

Greek *Republic of Cyprus* (*Kypriakí Dimokratía*) in the south, and *Turkish Republic of Northern Cyprus* (*Kibris Cumhuriyeti*) in the north

area 9,251 sq km/3,571 sq mi, 37% in Turkish hands
capital Nicosia (divided between Greeks and Turks)
towns ports Limassol, Larnaca, Paphos (Greek); Morphou, and ports Kyrenia and Famagusta (Turkish)

physical central plain between two E–W mountain ranges

features archaeological and historic sites; Mount Olympus 1,953 m/6,406 ft (highest peak); beaches

heads of state and government Glafkos Clerides (Greek) from 1993, Rauf Denktaş (Turkish) from 1976

political system democratic divided republic

political parties Democratic Front (DIKO), centre-left; Progressive Party of the Working People (AKEL), socialist; Democratic Rally (DISY), centrist; Socialist Party (EDEK), socialist; *Turkish zone*: National Unity Party (NUP), Communal Liberation Party (CLP), Republican Turkish Party (RTP), New British Party (NBP)

exports citrus, grapes, raisins, Cyprus sherry, potatoes, clothing, footwear

currency Cyprus pound and Turkish lira

population (1992) 580,000 (Greek Cypriot 78%, Turkish Cypriot 18%); growth rate 1.2% p.a.

life expectancy men 72, women 76

languages Greek and Turkish (official), English

religions Greek Orthodox 78%, Sunni Muslim 18%

literacy 99% (1984)

GDP $3.7 bn (1987); $5,497 per head

chronology

1878 Came under British administration.

1955 Guerrilla campaign began against the British for enosis (union with Greece), led by Archbishop Makarios and General Grivas.

1956 Makarios and enosis leaders deported.

1959 Compromise agreed and Makarios returned to be elected president of an independent Greek-Turkish Cyprus.

1960 Independence achieved from Britain, with Britain retaining its military bases.

1963 Turks set up their own government in northern Cyprus. Fighting broke out between the two communities.

1964 United Nations peacekeeping force installed.

1971 Grivas returned to start a guerrilla war against the Makarios government.

1974 Grivas died. Military coup deposed Makarios, who fled to Britain. Nicos Sampson appointed president. Turkish army sent to northern Cyprus to confirm Turkish Cypriots' control; military regime in southern Cyprus collapsed; Makarios returned. Northern Cyprus declared itself the Turkish Federated State of Cyprus (TFSC), with Rauf Denktaş as president.

1977 Makarios died; succeeded by Spyros Kyprianou.

1983 An independent Turkish Republic of Northern Cyprus proclaimed but recognized only by Turkey.

1984 UN peace proposals rejected.

1985 Summit meeting between Kyprianou and Denktaş failed to reach agreement.

1988 Georgios Vassiliou elected president. Talks with Denktaş began, under UN auspices.

1989 Peace talks abandoned.

1992 UN-sponsored peace talks collapsed.

1993 Democratic Rally leader Glafkos Clerides narrowly won presidential election.

Czech Republic

(*Česká Republika*)

area 78,864 sq km/30,461 sq mi

capital Prague

towns Brno, Ostrava, Olomouc, Liberec, Plzeň, Ustí nad Labem, Hradec Králové

physical mountainous; rivers: Morava, Labe (Elbe), Vltava (Moldau)

environment considered in 1991 to be the most polluted country in E Europe. Pollution is worst in N Bohemia, which produced 70% of Czechoslovakia's coal and 45% of its coal-generated electricity. Up to 20 times the permissible level of sulphur dioxide is released over Prague, where 75% of the drinking water fails to meet the country's health standards

features summer and winter resort areas in Western Carpathian, Bohemian, and Sudetic mountain ranges

head of state Václav Havel from 1993

head of government Václav Klaus from 1993

political system emergent democracy

political parties Civic Democratic Party (CDP), right of centre; Civic Movement (CM), left of centre; Communist Party (CPCZ), left-wing; Czechoslovak People's Party, centrist nationalist

exports machinery, vehicles, coal, iron and steel, chemicals, glass, ceramics, clothing

currency new currency based on koruna

population (1991) 10,298,700 (with German and other minorities); growth rate 0.4% p.a.

life expectancy men 68, women 75

languages Czech (official)

religions Roman Catholic (75%), Protestant, Hussite, Orthodox

literacy 100%

GDP $26,600 million (1990); $2,562 per head

chronology

1526–1918 Under Habsburg domination.

1918 Independence achieved from Austro-Hungarian Empire; Czechs joined Slovaks in forming Czechoslovakia as independent nation.

1948 Communists assumed power in Czechoslovakia.

1968 Czech Socialist Republic created under new federal constitution.

1989 Nov: pro-democracy demonstrations in Prague; new political parties formed, including Czech-based Civic Forum under Václav Havel; Communist Party stripped of powers; political parties legalized. Dec: new 'grand coalition' government formed, including former dissidents; Havel appointed state president. Amnesty granted to 22,000 prisoners; calls for USSR to withdraw troops.

1990 July: Havel re-elected president in multiparty elections.

1991 Civic Forum split into CDP and CM; evidence of increasing Czech and Slovak separatism.

1992 June: Václav Klaus, leader of the Czech-based CDP, became prime minister; Havel resigned following Slovak gains in assembly elections. Aug: creation of separate Czech and Slovak states agreed.

1993 Jan: Czech Republic became sovereign state, with Klaus as prime minister. Havel elected president of the new republic. Admitted into United Nations, Conference on Security and Cooperation in Europe, and Council of Europe.

Denmark

Kingdom of (*Kongeriget Danmark*)

area 43,075 sq km/16,627 sq mi

capital Copenhagen

towns Aarhus, Odense, Aalborg, Esbjerg, all ports

physical comprises the Jutland peninsula and about 500 islands (100 inhabited) including Bornholm in the Baltic Sea; the land is flat and cultivated; sand dunes and lagoons on the W coast and long inlets (fjords) on the E; the main island is Sjælland (Zealand), where most of Copenhagen is located (the rest is on the island of Amager)

territories the dependencies of Faeroe Islands and Greenland

features Kronborg Castle in Helsingør (Elsinore); Tivoli Gardens (Copenhagen); Legoland Park in Sillund

head of state Queen Margrethe II from 1972

head of government Poul Nyrup Rasmussen from 1993

political system liberal democracy

political parties Social Democrats (SD), left of centre; Conservative People's Party (KF), moderate centre-right; Liberal Party (V), centre-left; Socialist People's Party (SF), moderate left-wing; Radical Liberals (RV), radical internationalist, left of centre; Centre Democrats (CD), moderate centrist; Progress Party (FP), radical antibureaucratic; Christian People's Party (KrF), interdenominational, family values

exports bacon, dairy produce, eggs, fish, mink pelts, car and aircraft parts, electrical equipment, textiles, chemicals

currency kroner

population (1992) 5,167,000; growth rate 0% p.a.

life expectancy men 72, women 78

languages Danish (official); there is a German-speaking minority

religion Lutheran 97%

literacy 99% (1983)

GDP $142.1 bn (1992)

chronology

1940–45 Occupied by Germany.

1945 Iceland's independence recognized.

1947 Frederik IX succeeded Christian X.

1948 Home rule granted for Faeroe Islands.

1949 Became a founding member of NATO.

1960 Joined European Free Trade Association (EFTA).

1972 Margrethe II became Denmark's first queen in nearly 600 years.

1973 Left EFTA and joined European Economic Community (EEC).

1979 Home rule granted for Greenland.

1985 Strong non-nuclear movement in evidence.

1990 General election; another coalition government formed.

1992 Rejection of Maastricht Treaty in national referendum.

1993 Poul Schlüter resigned; replaced by Poul Nyrup Rasmussen at head of Social Democrat-led coalition government. Second referendum approved the Maastricht Treaty after modifications.

Djibouti

Republic of (*Jumhouriyya Djibouti*)

area 23,200 sq km/8,955 sq mi

capital (and chief port) Djibouti

towns Tadjoura, Obock, Dikhil

physical mountains divide an inland plateau from a coastal plain; hot and arid

features terminus of railway link with Ethiopia; Lac Assal salt lake is the second lowest point on Earth (−144 m/−471 ft)

head of state and government Hassan Gouled Aptidon from 1977

political system authoritarian nationalism

political party People's Progress Assembly (RPP), nationalist

exports acts mainly as a transit port for Ethiopia

currency Djibouti franc

population (1992) 557,000 (Issa 47%, Afar 37%, European 8%, Arab 6%); growth rate 3.4% p.a.

life expectancy 50

languages French (official), Somali, Afar, Arabic
religion Sunni Muslim
literacy 20% (1988)
GDP $378 million (1987); $1,016 per head

chronology
1884 Annexed by France as part of French Somaliland.
1967 French Somaliland became the French Territory
of the Afars and the Issas.
1977 Independence achieved from France; Hassan
Gouled was elected president.
1979 All political parties combined to form the
People's Progress Assembly (RPP).
1981 New constitution made RPP the only legal
party. Gouled re-elected. Treaties of friendship
signed with Ethiopia, Somalia, Kenya, and Sudan.
1984 Policy of neutrality reaffirmed.
1987 Gouled re-elected for a third term.
1991 Amnesty International accused secret police of
brutality.
1992 Djibouti elected member of UN Security Council 1993–95.
1993 Gouled re-elected for a fourth term.

Dominica

Commonwealth of

area 751 sq km/290 sq mi
capital Roseau, with a deepwater port
towns Portsmouth, Marigot
physical second largest of the Windward Islands,
mountainous central ridge with tropical rainforest
features of great beauty, it has mountains of volcanic
origin rising to 1,620 m/5,317 ft; Boiling Lake (an
effect produced by escaping subterranean gas)
head of state Clarence Seignoret from 1983
head of government Eugenia Charles from 1980
political system liberal democracy
political parties Dominica Freedom Party (DFP),
centrist; Labour Party of Dominica (LPD), left-of-
centre coalition
exports bananas, coconuts, citrus, lime, bay oil
currency Eastern Caribbean dollar; pound sterling;
French franc
population (1992) 71,500 (mainly black African in
origin, but with a small Carib reserve of some 500);
growth rate 1.3% p.a.
life expectancy men 57, women 59

language English (official), but the Dominican
patois reflects earlier periods of French rule
media one independent weekly newspaper
religion Roman Catholic 80%
literacy 80%
GDP $91 million (1985); $1,090 per head

chronology
1763 Became British possession.
1978 Independence achieved from Britain. Patrick
John, leader of Dominica Labour Party (DLP),
elected prime minister.
1980 Dominica Freedom Party (DFP), led by Eugenia
Charles, won convincing victory in general election.
1981 Patrick John implicated in plot to overthrow
government.
1982 John tried and acquitted.
1985 John retried and found guilty. Regrouping of left-
of-centre parties resulted in new Labour Party of
Dominica (LPD). DFP, led by Eugenia Charles, re-
elected.
1990 Charles elected to a third term.
1991 Integration into Windward Islands confederation proposed.

Dominican Republic

(*República Dominicana*)

area 48,442 sq km/18,700 sq mi
capital Santo Domingo
towns Santiago de los Caballeros, San Pedro de
Macoris
physical comprises eastern two-thirds of island of
Hispaniola; central mountain range with fertile valleys
features Pico Duarte 3,174 m/10,417 ft, highest point
in Caribbean islands; Santo Domingo is the oldest
European city in the western hemisphere
head of state and government Joaquín Ricardo Balaguer from 1986
political system democratic republic
political parties Dominican Revolutionary Party
(PRD), moderate, left of centre; Christian Social
Reform Party (PRSC), independent socialist;
Dominican Liberation Party (PLD), nationalist
exports sugar, gold, silver, tobacco, coffee, nickel
currency peso
population (1992) 7,471,000; growth rate 2.3% p.a.
life expectancy men 61, women 65
language Spanish (official)

religion Roman Catholic 95%
literacy men 78%, women 77% (1985 est)
GDP $4.9 bn (1987); $731 per head

chronology
1492 Visited by Christopher Columbus.
1844 Dominican Republic established.
1930 Military coup established dictatorship of Rafael Trujillo.
1961 Trujillo assassinated.
1962 First democratic elections resulted in Juan Bosch, founder of the PRD, becoming president.
1963 Bosch overthrown in military coup.
1965 US Marines intervene to restore order and protect foreign nationals.
1966 New constitution adopted. Joaquín Balaguer, leader of PRSC, became president.
1978 PRD returned to power, with Silvestre Antonio Guzmán as president.
1982 PRD re-elected, with Jorge Blanco as president.
1985 Blanco forced by International Monetary Fund to adopt austerity measures to save the economy.
1986 PRSC returned to power, with Balaguer re-elected president.
1990 Balaguer re-elected by a small majority.

Ecuador

Republic of (*República del Ecuador*)

area 270,670 sq km/104,479 sq mi
capital Quito
towns Cuenca; chief port Guayaquil
physical coastal plain rises sharply to Andes Mountains, which are divided into a series of cultivated valleys; flat, low-lying rainforest in E
environment about 25,000 species became extinct 1965–90 as a result of environmental destruction
features Ecuador is crossed by the equator, from which it derives its name; Galápagos Islands; Cotopaxi is world's highest active volcano; rich wildlife in rainforest of Amazon basin
head of state and government Sixto Duran Ballen from 1992
political system emergent democracy republic
political parties Social Christian Party (PSC), right-wing; United Republican Party (PUR), right-of-

centre coalition; Ecuadorean Roldosist Party (PRE)
exports bananas, cocoa, coffee, sugar, rice, fruit, balsa wood, fish, petroleum
currency sucre
population (1992) 10,607,000; (mestizo 55%, Indian 25%, European 10%, black African 10%); growth rate 2.9% p.a.
life expectancy men 62, women 66
languages Spanish (official), Quechua, Jivaro, and other Indian languages
religion Roman Catholic 95%
literacy men 85%, women 80% (1985 est)
GDP $10.6 bn (1987); $1,069 per head

chronology
1830 Independence achieved from Spain.
1925–48 Great political instability; no president completed his term of office.
1948–55 Liberals in power.
1956 First conservative president in 60 years.
1960 Liberals returned, with José Velasco as president.
1961 Velasco deposed and replaced by the vice president.
1962 Military junta installed.
1968 Velasco returned as president.
1972 A coup put the military back in power.
1978 New democratic constitution adopted.
1979 Liberals in power but opposed by right- and left-wing parties.
1982 Deteriorating economy provoked strikes, demonstrations, and a state of emergency.
1983 Austerity measures introduced.
1984–85 No party with a clear majority in the national congress; Febres Cordero narrowly won the presidency for the Conservatives.
1988 Rodrigo Borja Cevallos elected president for moderate left-wing coalition.
1989 Guerrilla left-wing group *Alfaro Vive, Carajo* ('Alfaro lives, damn it'), numbering about 1,000, laid down arms after nine years.
1992 PUR leader Sixto Duran Ballen elected president; PSC became largest party in congress.

Egypt

Arab Republic of (*Jumhuriyat Misr al-Arabiya*)

area 1,001,450 sq km/386,990 sq mi
capital Cairo
towns Gîza; ports Alexandria, Port Said, Suez, Damietta

physical mostly desert; hills in E; fertile land along Nile valley and delta; cultivated and settled area is about 35,500 sq km/13,700 sq mi

environment the building of the Aswan Dam (opened 1970) on the Nile has caused widespread salinization and an increase in waterborne diseases in villages close to Lake Nasser. A dramatic fall in the annual load of silt deposited downstream has reduced the fertility of cropland and has led to coastal erosion and the consequent loss of sardine shoals

features Aswan High Dam and Lake Nasser; Sinai; remains of ancient Egypt (pyramids, Sphinx, Luxor, Karnak, Abu Simbel, El Faiyum)

head of state and government Hosni Mubarak from 1981

political system democratic republic

political parties National Democratic Party (NDP), moderate left of centre; Socialist Labour Party, right of centre; Socialist Liberal Party, free-enterprise; New Wafd Party, nationalist

exports cotton and textiles, petroleum, fruit and vegetables

currency Egyptian pound

population (1992) 55,979,000; growth rate 2.4% p.a.

life expectancy men 57, women 60

languages Arabic (official); ancient Egyptian survives to some extent in Coptic

media there is no legal censorship, but the largest publishing houses, newspapers, and magazines are owned and controlled by the state, as is all television. Questioning of prevalent values, ideas, and social practices is discouraged

religions Sunni Muslim 95%, Coptic Christian 5%

literacy men 59%, women 30% (1985 est)

GDP $34.5 bn (1987); $679 per head

chronology

1914 Egypt became a British protectorate.

1936 Independence achieved from Britain. King Fuad succeeded by his son Farouk.

1946 Withdrawal of British troops except from Suez Canal Zone.

1952 Farouk overthrown by army in bloodless coup.

1953 Egypt declared a republic, with General Neguib as president.

1956 Neguib replaced by Col Gamal Nasser. Nasser announced nationalization of Suez Canal; Egypt attacked by Britain, France, and Israel. Cease-fire agreed because of US intervention.

1958 Short-lived merger of Egypt and Syria as United Arab Republic (UAR). Subsequent attempts to federate Egypt, Syria, and Iraq failed.

1967 Six-Day War with Israel ended in Egypt's defeat and Israeli occupation of Sinai and Gaza Strip.

1970 Nasser died suddenly; succeeded by Anwar Sadat.

1973 Attempt to regain territory lost to Israel led to fighting; cease-fire arranged by US secretary of state Henry Kissinger.

1977 Sadat's visit to Israel to address the Israeli parliament was criticized by Egypt's Arab neighbours.

1978-79 Camp David talks in the USA resulted in a treaty between Egypt and Israel. Egypt expelled from the Arab League.

1981 Sadat assassinated, succeeded by Hosni Mubarak.

1983 Improved relations between Egypt and the Arab world; only Libya and Syria maintained a trade boycott.

1984 Mubarak's party victorious in the people's assembly elections.

1987 Mubarak re-elected. Egypt readmitted to Arab League.

1988 Full diplomatic relations with Algeria restored.

1989 Improved relations with Libya; diplomatic relations with Syria restored. Mubarak proposed a peace plan.

1990 Gains for independents in general election.

1991 Participation in Gulf War on US-led side. Major force in convening Middle East peace conference in Spain.

1992 Outbreaks of violence between Muslims and Christians. Earthquake devastated Cairo.

1993 President Mubarak sworn in for third term.

El Salvador

Republic of (*República de El Salvador*)

area 21,393 sq km/8,258 sq mi

capital San Salvador

towns Santa Ana, San Miguel

physical narrow coastal plain, rising to mountains in N with central plateau

features smallest and most densely populated Central American country; Maya archaeological remains

head of state and government Alfredo Cristiani from 1989

political system emergent democracy

political parties Christian Democrats (PDC), anti-imperialist; National Republican Alliance (ARENA), right-wing; National Conciliation Party (PCN), right-wing; Farabundo Marti Liberation Front (FMLN), left-wing

exports coffee, cotton, sugar

currency colón

population (1992) 5,460,000 (mainly of mixed Spanish and Indian ancestry; 10% Indian); growth rate 2.9% p.a.

life expectancy men 63, women 66

languages Spanish, Nahuatl

religion Roman Catholic 97%

literacy men 75%, women 69% (1985 est)

GDP $4.7 bn (1987); $790 per head

chronology

1821 Independence achieved from Spain.

1931 Peasant unrest followed by a military coup.
1961 Following a coup, PCN established and in power.
1969 'Soccer' war with Honduras.
1972 Allegations of human-rights violations; growth of left-wing guerrilla activities. General Carlos Romero elected president.
1979 A coup replaced Romero with a military-civilian junta.
1980 Archbishop Oscar Romero assassinated; country on verge of civil war. José Duarte became first civilian president since 1931.
1981 Mexico and France recognized the guerrillas as a legitimate political force, but the USA actively assisted the government in its battle against them.
1982 Assembly elections boycotted by left-wing parties and held amid considerable violence.
1986 Duarte sought a negotiated settlement with the guerrillas.
1988 Duarte resigned.
1989 Alfredo Cristiani (ARENA) became president in rigged elections; rebel attacks intensified.
1991 United Nations-sponsored peace accord signed by representatives of the government and the socialist guerrilla group, the FMLN.
1992 Peace accord validated; FMLN became political party.

Equatorial Guinea
Republic of (*República de Guinea Ecuatorial*)

area 28,051 sq km/10,828 sq mi
capital Malabo (Bioko)
towns Bata, Mbini (Río Muni)
physical comprises mainland Río Muni, plus the small islands of Corisco, Elobey Grande and Elobey Chico, and Bioko (formerly Fernando Po) together with Annobón (formerly Pagalu)
features volcanic mountains on Bioko
head of state and government Teodoro Obiang Nguema Mbasogo from 1979
political system emergent military republic
political party Democratic Party of Equatorial Guinea (PDGE), militarily controlled
exports cocoa, coffee, timber
currency ekuele; CFA franc
population (1992) 367,000 (plus 110,000 estimated to live in exile abroad); growth rate 2.2% p.a.
life expectancy men 44, women 48
languages Spanish (official); pidgin English is widely spoken, and on Annobón (whose people were formerly slaves of the Portuguese) a Portuguese

dialect; Fang and other African dialects spoken on Río Muni
religions nominally Christian, mainly Catholic, but in 1978 Roman Catholicism was banned
literacy 55% (1984)
GDP $90 million (1987); $220 per head

chronology
1778 Fernando Po (Bioko Island) ceded to Spain.
1885 Mainland territory came under Spanish rule; colony known as Spanish Guinea.
1968 Independence achieved from Spain. Francisco Macias Nguema became first president, soon assuming dictatorial powers.
1979 Macias overthrown and replaced by his nephew, Teodoro Obiang Nguema Mbasogo, who established a military regime. Macias tried and executed.
1982 Obiang elected president unopposed for another seven years. New constitution adopted.
1989 Obiang re-elected president.
1992 New constitution adopted; elections held, but president continued to nominate candidates for top government posts.

Eritrea
State of

area 125,000 sq km/48,250 sq mi
capital Asmara
towns Keren, Adigrat; ports: Asab, Massawa
physical coastline along the Red Sea 1,000 km/620 mi; narrow coastal plain that rises to an inland plateau
features Dahlak Islands
head of state and government Issaias Afewerki from 1993
political system emergent democracy
political parties Eritrean People's Liberation Front (EPLF), militant nationalist; Eritrean National Pact Alliance (ENPA), moderate, centrist
products coffee, salt, citrus fruits, grains, cotton
currency birr
population (1993) 4,000,000
life expectancy men 44, women 48
languages Amharic (official), Tigrinya (official), Arabic, Afar, Bilen, Hidareb, Kunama, Nara, Rashaida, Saho, and Tigre
religions Muslim, Coptic Christian

chronology
1962 Annexed by Ethiopia; secessionist movement began.
1974 Ethiopian emperor Haile Selassie deposed by military; Eritrean People's Liberation Front (EPLF) continued struggle for independence.
1990 Port of Massawa captured by Eritrean forces.
1991 Ethiopian president Mengistu Haile Mariam overthrown. EPLF secured the whole of Eritrea. Ethiopian government acknowledged Eritrea's right to secede. Issaias Afwerki became secretary general of provisional government.
1992 Transitional ruling council established
1993 National referendum supported independence; new state formally recognized by Ethiopia and UK. Transitional government established for four-year period. Issaias Afwerki elected chairman of state council and president.

Estonia

Republic of

area 45,000 sq km/17,000 sq mi
capital Tallinn
towns Tartu, Narva, Kohtla-Järve, Pärnu
physical lakes and marshes in a partly forested plain; 774 km/481 mi of coastline; mild climate
features Lake Peipus and Narva River forming boundary with Russian Federation; Baltic islands, the largest of which is Saaremaa Island
head of state Lennart Meri from 1992
head of government Mart Laar from 1992
political system emergent democracy
political parties Estonian Popular Front (Rahvarinne), nationalist; Association for a Free Estonia, nationalist; Fatherland Group, right-wing; International Movement, ethnic Russian; Estonian Green Party, environmentalist
products oil and gas (from shale), wood products, flax, dairy and pig products
currency kroon
population (1992) 1,592,000 (Estonian 62%, Russian 30%, Ukrainian 3%, Byelorussian 2%)
language Estonian, allied to Finnish
religion traditionally Lutheran

chronology
1918 Estonia declared its independence. March: Soviet forces, who had tried to regain control from occupying German forces during World War I, were

overthrown by German troops. Nov: Soviet troops took control after German withdrawal.
1919 Soviet rule overthrown with help of British navy; Estonia declared a democratic republic.
1934 Fascist coup replaced government.
1940 Estonia incorporated into USSR.
1941–44 German occupation during World War II.
1944 USSR regained control.
1980 Beginnings of nationalist dissent.
1988 Adopted own constitution, with power of veto on all centralized Soviet legislation. Popular Front (Rahvarinne) established to campaign for democracy. Estonia's supreme soviet (state assembly) voted to declare the republic 'sovereign' and autonomous in all matters except military and foreign affairs; rejected by USSR as unconstitutional.
1989 Estonian replaced Russian as main language.
1990 Feb: Communist Party monopoly of power abolished; multiparty system established. March: pro-independence candidates secured majority after republic elections; coalition government formed with Popular Front leader Edgar Savisaar as prime minister; Arnold Rüütel became president. May: prewar constitution partially restored.
1991 March: independence plebiscite overwhelmingly approved. Aug: full independence declared after abortive anti-Gorbachev coup; Communist Party outlawed. Sept: independence recognized by Soviet government and Western nations; admitted into United Nations and Conference on Security and Cooperation in Europe (CSCE).
1992 Jan: Savisaar resigned owing to his government's inability to alleviate food and energy shortages; new government formed by Tiit Vahl. June: New constitution approved. Sept: presidential election inconclusive; right-wing Fatherland Group did well in general election. Oct: Fatherland leader Lennart Meri chosen by parliament to replace Rüütel; Maart Laar became prime minister.

Ethiopia

People's Democratic Republic of (*Hebretesebawit Ityopia*, formerly also known as *Abyssinia*)

area 1,128,221 sq km/435,493 sq mi
capital Addis Ababa
towns Jimma , Dire Dawa
physical a high plateau with central mountain range divided by Rift Valley; plains in E; source of Blue Nile River
environment more than 90% of the forests of the Ethiopian highlands have been destroyed since 1900
features Danakil and Ogaden deserts; ancient remains (in Aksum, Gondar, Lalibela, among others); only African country to retain its independence during the colonial period
head of state and government Meles Zenawi from 1991
political system transition to democratic socialist republic
political parties Ethiopian People's Revolutionary Democratic Front (EPRDF), nationalist, left of centre; Tigré People's Liberation Front (TPLF); Ethiopian People's Democratic Movement (EPDM); Oromo People's Democratic Organization (OPDO)
exports coffee, pulses, oilseeds, hides, skins
currency birr

population (1992) 50,345,000 (Oromo 40%, Amhara 25%, Tigré 12%, Sidamo 9%); growth rate 2.5% p.a.
life expectancy 38
languages Amharic (official), Tigrinya, Orominga, Arabic
religions Sunni Muslim 45%, Christian (Ethiopian Orthodox Church, which has had its own patriarch since 1976) 40%
literacy 35% (1988)
GDP $4.8 bn (1987); $104 per head

chronology
1889 Abyssinia reunited by Menelik II.
1930 Haile Selassie became emperor.
1962 Eritrea annexed by Haile Selassie; resistance movement began.
1974 Haile Selassie deposed and replaced by a military government led by General Teferi Benti. Ethiopia declared a socialist state.
1977 Teferi Benti killed and replaced by Col Mengistu Haile Mariam.
1977–79 'Red Terror' period in which Mengistu's regime killed thousands of innocent people.
1981–85 Ethiopia spent at least $2 billion on arms.
1984 WPE declared the only legal political party.
1985 Worst famine in more than a decade; Western aid sent and forcible internal resettlement programmes undertaken.
1987 New constitution adopted, Mengistu Mariam elected president. New famine; food aid hindered by guerrillas.
1988 Mengistu agreed to adjust his economic policies in order to secure IMF assistance. Influx of refugees from Sudan.
1989 Coup attempt against Mengistu foiled. Peace talks with Eritrean rebels mediated by former US president Carter reported some progress.
1990 Rebels captured port of Massawa.
1991 Mengistu overthrown; transitional government set up by EPRDF. EPLF secured Eritrea; Eritrea's right to secede recognized. Meles Zenawi elected Ethiopia's new head of state and government.
1993 Eritrean independence recognized after referendum.

Fiji

Republic of

area 18,333 sq km/7,078 sq mi
capital Suva
towns ports Lautoka and Levuka
physical comprises 844 Melanesian and Polynesian islands and islets (about 110 inhabited), the largest being Viti Levu (10,429 sq km/4,028 sq mi) and Vanua Levu (5,550 sq km/2,146 sq mi); mountainous, volcanic, with tropical rainforest and grasslands
features almost all islands surrounded by coral reefs; high volcanic peaks; crossroads of air and sea services between N America and Australia
head of state Ratu Sir Penaia Ganilau from 1987
head of government Col Sitiveni Rabuka from 1992
political system democratic republic
political parties Alliance Party (AP), moderate centrist Fijian; National Federation Party (NFP), moderate left-of-centre Indian; Fijian Labour Party (FLP), left-of-centre Indian; United Front, Fijian
exports sugar, coconut oil, ginger, timber, canned fish, gold; tourism is important
currency Fiji dollar
population (1992) 748,000 (46% Fijian, holding 80% of the land communally, and 49% Indian, introduced in the 19th century to work the sugar crop); growth rate 2.1% p.a.
life expectancy men 67, women 71
languages English (official), Fijian, Hindi
religions Hindu 50%, Methodist 44%
literacy men 88%, women 77% (1980 est)
GDP $1.2 bn (1987); $1,604 per head

chronology
1874 Fiji became a British crown colony.
1970 Independence achieved from Britain; Ratu Sir Kamisese Mara elected as first prime minister.
1987 April: general election brought to power an Indian-dominated coalition led by Dr Timoci Bavadra. May: military coup by Col Sitiveni Rabuka removed new government at gunpoint; Governor General Ratu Sir Penaia Ganilau regained control within weeks. Sept: second military coup by Rabuka proclaimed Fiji a republic and suspended the constitution. Oct: Fiji ceased to be a member of the Commonwealth. Dec: civilian government restored with Rabuka retaining control of security as minister for home affairs.
1990 New constitution, favouring indigenous Fijians, introduced.
1992 General election produced coalition government; Col Rabuka named as president.

Finland

Republic of (*Suomen Tasavalta*)

area 338,145 sq km/130,608 sq mi
capital Helsinki

towns Tampere, Rovaniemi, Lahti; ports Turku, Oulu
physical most of the country is forest, with low   hills
and about 60,000 lakes; one-third is within the Arctic
Circle; archipelago in S; includes Åland Islands
features Helsinki is the most northerly national capital on the European continent; at the 70th parallel
there is constant daylight for 73 days in summer and
51 days of uninterrupted night in winter
head of state Mauno Koivisto from 1982
head of government Esko Aho from 1991
political system democratic republic
political parties Social Democratic Party (SDP),
moderate left of centre; National Coalition Party
(KOK), moderate right of centre; Centre Party (KP),
centrist, rural-oriented; Finnish People's Democratic
League (SKDL), left-wing; Swedish People's Party
(SFP), independent Swedish-oriented; Finnish Rural
Party (SMP), farmers and small businesses; Democratic Alternative, left-wing; Green Party
exports metal, chemical, and engineering products
(icebreakers and oil rigs), paper, sawn wood, clothing, fine ceramics, glass, furniture
currency markka
population (1992) 5,033,000; growth rate 0.5% p.a.
life expectancy men 70, women 78
languages Finnish 93%, Swedish 6% (both official),
small Saami- and Russian-speaking minorities
religions Lutheran 97%, Eastern Orthodox 1.2%
literacy 99%
GDP $109.6 bn (1992)

chronology
1809 Finland annexed by Russia.
1917 Independence declared from Russia.
1920 Soviet regime acknowledged independence.
1939 Defeated by USSR in Winter War.
1941 Allowed Germany to station troops in Finland
to attack USSR; USSR bombed Finland.
1944 Concluded separate armistice with USSR.
1948 Finno-Soviet Pact of Friendship, Cooperation,
and Mutual Assistance signed.
1955 Finland joined the United Nations and the
Nordic Council.
1956 Urho Kekkonen elected president; re-elected
1962, 1968, 1978.
1973 Trade treaty with European Economic Community signed.
1977 Trade agreement with USSR signed.
1982 Mauno Koivisto elected president; re-elected
1988.
1989 Finland joined Council of Europe.

1991 Big swing to the centre in general election. New
coalition government formed.
1992 Formal application for European Community
membership.

France

French Republic (République Française)

area (including Corsica) 543,965 sq km/209,970 sq
mi
capital Paris
towns Lyons, Lille, Bordeaux, Toulouse, Nantes,
Strasbourg; ports Marseille, Nice, Le Havre
physical rivers Seine, Loire, Garonne, Rhône, Rhine;
mountain ranges Alps, Massif Central, Pyrenees,
Jura, Vosges, Cévennes; the island of Corsica
territories Guadeloupe, French Guiana, Martinique,
Réunion, St Pierre and Miquelon, Southern and
Antarctic Territories, New Caledonia, French Polynesia, Wallis and Futuna
features Ardennes forest, Auvergne mountain
region, Riviera, Mont Blanc (4,810 m/15,781 ft),
caves of Dordogne with relics of early humans;
largest W European nation
head of state Jacques Chirac from 1995
head of government Lionel Jospin from 1997
political system liberal democracy
political parties Socialist Party (PS), left of centre;
Rally for the Republic (RPR), neo-Gaullist conservative; Union for French Democracy (UDF), centre-
right; Republican Party (RP), centre-right; French
Communist Party (PCF), Marxist-Leninist; National
Front, far right; Greens, environmentalist
exports fruit (especially apples), wine, cheese, wheat,
cars, aircraft, iron and steel, petroleum products,
chemicals, jewellery, silk, lace; tourism is very
important
currency franc
population (1992) 57,289,000 (including 4,500,000
immigrants, chiefly from Portugal, Algeria, Morocco,
and Tunisia); growth rate 0.3% p.a.
life expectancy men 71, women 79
language French (regional languages include
Basque, Breton, Catalan, and the Provençal dialect)
religions Roman Catholic 90%, Protestant 2%,
Muslim 1%
literacy 99% (1984)
GNP $1,324.9 bn (1992)

chronology
1944–46 Provisional government headed by General Charles de Gaulle; start of Fourth Republic.
1954 Indochina achieved independence.
1956 Morocco and Tunisia achieved independence.
1957 Entry into European Economic Community.
1958 Recall of de Gaulle after Algerian crisis; start of Fifth Republic.
1959 De Gaulle became president.
1962 Algeria achieved independence.
1966 France withdrew from military wing of NATO.
1968 'May events' uprising of students and workers.
1969 De Gaulle resigned after referendum defeat; Georges Pompidou became president.
1974 Giscard d'Estaing elected president.
1981 François Mitterrand elected Fifth Republic's first socialist president.
1986 'Cohabitation' experiment, with the conservative Jacques Chirac as prime minister.
1988 Mitterrand re-elected. Moderate socialist Michel Rocard became prime minister. Matignon Accord on future of New Caledonia approved by referendum.
1989 Greens gained 11% of vote in elections to European Parliament.
1991 French forces were part of the US-led coalition in the Gulf War. Edith Cresson became prime minister; Mitterrand's popularity rating fell rapidly.
1992 March: Socialist Party humiliated in regional and local elections; Greens and National Front polled strongly. April: Cresson replaced by Pierre Bérégovoy. Sept: referendum narrowly endorsed Maastricht Treaty.
1993 March: Socialist Party suffered heavy defeat in National Assembly elections. Edouard Balladur appointed prime minister; 'cohabitation' government re-established. May: suicide of Bérégovoy; Michel Rocard appointed PS leader.

Gabon

Gabonese Republic (*République Gabonaise*)

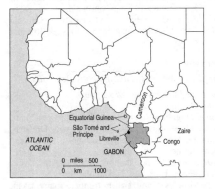

area 267,667 sq km/103,319 sq mi
capital Libreville
towns Port-Gentil and Owendo (ports); Masuku (Franceville)
physical virtually the whole country is tropical rainforest; narrow coastal plain rising to hilly int-erior with savanna in E and S; Ogooué River flows N–W
features Schweitzer hospital at Lambaréné; Trans-Gabonais railway

head of state and government Omar Bongo from 1967
political system emergent democracy
political parties Gabonese Democratic Party (PDG), nationalist; Morena Movement of National Recovery, left of centre
exports petroleum, manganese, uranium, timber
currency CFA franc
population (1992) 1,253,000 including 40 Bantu groups; growth rate 1.6% p.a.
life expectancy men 47, women 51
languages French (official), Bantu
religions Christian 96% (Roman Catholic 65%), small Muslim minority 1%, animist 3%
literacy men 70%, women 53% (1985 est)
GDP \$3.5 bn (1987); \$3,308 per head

chronology
1889 Gabon became part of the French Congo.
1960 Independence from France achieved; Léon M'ba became the first president.
1964 Attempted coup by rival party foiled with French help. M'ba died; he was succeeded by his protégé Albert-Bernard Bongo.
1968 One-party state established.
1973 Bongo re-elected; converted to Islam, he changed his first name to Omar.
1986 Bongo re-elected.
1989 Coup attempt against Bongo defeated.
1990 PDG won first multiparty elections since 1964 amidst allegations of ballot-rigging.
1993 Bongo re-elected

Gambia

Republic of The

area 10,402 sq km/4,018 sq mi
capital Banjul
towns Serekunda, Bakau, Georgetown
physical banks of the river Gambia flanked by low hills
features smallest state in black Africa; stone circles; Karantaba obelisk marking spot where Mungo Park began his journey to the Niger River 1796
head of state and government Dawda K Jawara from 1970
political system liberal democracy
political parties Progressive People's Party (PPP), moderate centrist; National Convention Party (NCP), left of centre
exports groundnuts, palm oil, fish
currency dalasi
population (1992) 921,000; growth rate 1.9% p.a.

life expectancy 42 (1988 est)
languages English (official), Mandinka, Fula and other native tongues
media no daily newspaper; two official weeklies sell about 2,000 copies combined and none of the other independents more than 700
religions Muslim 90%, with animist and Christian minorities
literacy men 36%, women 15% (1985 est)
GDP $189 million (1987); $236 per head

chronology
1843 The Gambia became a British crown colony.
1965 Independence achieved from Britain as a constitutional monarchy within the Commonwealth, with Dawda K Jawara as prime minister.
1970 Declared itself a republic, with Jawara as president.
1972 Jawara re-elected.
1981 Attempted coup foiled with the help of Senegal.
1982 Formed with Senegal the Confederation of Senegambia; Jawara re-elected.
1987 Jawara re-elected.
1989 Confederation of Senegambia dissolved.
1990 Gambian troops contributed to the stabilizing force in Liberia.

Georgia
Republic of

area 69,700 sq km/26,911 sq mi
capital Tbilisi
towns Kutaisi, Rustavi, Batumi, Sukhumi
physical largely mountainous with a variety of landscape from the subtropical Black Sea shores to the ice and snow of the crest line of the Caucasus; chief rivers are Kura and Rioni
features holiday resorts and spas on the Black Sea; good climate; two autonomous republics, Abkhazia and Adzharia; one autonomous region, South Ossetia
head of state Eduard Shevardnadze from 1992
head of government Tengiz Sigua from 1992
political system emergent democracy
political parties Georgian Popular Front, nationalist; Democratic National Party of Georgia, left of centre; National Independence Party, nationalist
products tea, citrus and orchard fruits, tung oil, tobacco, vines, silk, hydroelectricity
population (1992) 5,482,000 (Georgian 70%, Armenian 8%, Russian 8%, Azeri 6%, Ossetian 3%, Abkhazian 2%)

language Georgian
religion Georgian Church, independent of the Russian Orthodox Church since 1917
GNP $24,030,000 (1990); $4,410 per head

chronology
1918–21 Independent republic.
1921 Uprising quelled by Red Army and Soviet republic established.
1922–36 Linked with Armenia and Azerbaijan as the Transcaucasian Republic.
1936 Became separate republic within USSR.
1972 Drive against corruption by Georgian Communist Party (GCP) leader Eduard Shevardnadze.
1978 Outbreaks of violence by nationalists.
1981–88 Increasing demands for autonomy, spearheaded from 1988 by the Georgian Popular Front.
1989 March–April: Abkhazians demanded secession from Georgia, provoking inter-ethnic clashes. April: GCP leadership purged. July: state of emergency imposed in Abkhazia; interethnic clashes in South Ossetia. Nov: economic and political sovereignty declared.
1990 March: GCP monopoly ended. Oct: nationalist coalition triumphed in supreme-soviet elections. Nov: Zviad Gamsakhurdia became president. Dec: GCP seceded from Communist Party of USSR; calls for Georgian independence.
1991 April: declared independence. May: Gamsakhurdia popularly elected president. Aug: GCP outlawed and all relations with USSR severed. Sept: anti-Gamsakhurdia demonstrations; state of emergency declared. Dec: Georgia failed to join new Commonwealth of Independent States.
1992 Jan: Gamsakhurdia fled to Armenia; Tengiz Sigua appointed prime minister; Georgia admitted into Conference on Security and Cooperation in Europe. Eduard Shevardnadze appointed interim president. July: admitted into United Nations. Aug: fighting started between Georgian troops and Abkhazian separatists in Abkhazia in NW. Oct: Shevardnadze elected chair of new parliament. Clashes in South Ossetia and Abkhazia continued.
1993 Increased fighting with separatists. Georgia joined CIS. Shevardnadze forced to seek Russian military help.

Germany
Federal Republic of (*Bundesrepublik Deutschland*)

area 357,041 sq km/137,853 sq mi
capital Berlin
towns Cologne, Munich, Essen, Frankfurt-am-Main, Dortmund, Stuttgart, Düsseldorf, Leipzig, Dresden, Chemnitz, Magdeburg; ports Hamburg, Kiel, Cuxhaven, Bremerhaven, Rostock
physical flat in N, mountainous in S with Alps; rivers Rhine, Weser, Elbe flow N, Danube flows SE, Oder, Neisse flow N along Polish frontier; many lakes, including Müritz
environment acid rain causing *Waldsterben* (tree death) affects more than half the country's forests; industrial E Germany has the highest sulphur-dioxide emissions in the world per head of population
features Black Forest, Harz Mountains, Erzgebirge (Ore Mountains), Bavarian Alps, Fichtelgebirge, Thüringer Forest
head of state Richard von Weizsäcker from 1984

head of government Helmut Kohl from 1982

political system liberal democratic federal republic

political parties Christian Democratic Union (CDU), right of centre; Christian Social Union (CSU), right of centre; Social Democratic Party (SPD), left of centre; Free Democratic Party (FDP), liberal; Greens, environmentalist; Republicans, far right; Party of Democratic Socialism (PDS), reform-communist (formerly Socialist Unity Party: SED)

exports machine tools (world's leading exporter), cars, commercial vehicles, electronics, industrial goods, textiles, chemicals, iron, steel, wine, lignite (world's largest producer), uranium, coal, fertilizers, plastics

currency Deutschmark

population (1992) 80,293,000 (including nearly 5,000,000 'guest workers', *Gastarbeiter*, of whom 1,600,000 are Turks; the rest are Yugoslav, Italian, Greek, Spanish, and Portuguese); growth rate –0.7% p.a.

life expectancy men 68, women 74

languages German, Sorbian

religions Protestant 42%, Roman Catholic 35%

literacy 99% (1985)

GNP $1,775.1 bn (1992)

chronology

1945 Germany surrendered; country divided into four occupation zones (US, French, British, Soviet).

1948 Blockade of West Berlin.

1949 Establishment of Federal Republic under the 'Basic Law' Constitution with Konrad Adenauer as chancellor; establishment of the German Democratic Republic as an independent state.

1953 Uprising in East Berlin suppressed by Soviet troops.

1954 Grant of full sovereignty to both West Germany and East Germany.

1957 West Germany was a founder-member of the European Economic Community; recovery of Saarland from France.

1961 Construction of Berlin Wall.

1963 Retirement of Chancellor Adenauer.

1964 Treaty of Friendship and Mutual Assistance signed between East Germany and USSR.

1969 Willy Brandt became chancellor of West Germany.

1971 Erich Honecker elected SED leader in East Germany.

1972 Basic Treaty between West Germany and East Germany; treaty ratified 1973, normalizing relations between the two.

1974 Resignation of Brandt; Helmut Schmidt became chancellor.

1975 East German friendship treaty with USSR renewed for 25 years.

1982 Helmut Kohl became West German chancellor.

1987 Official visit of Honecker to the Federal Republic.

1988 Death of Franz-Josef Strauss, leader of the West German Bavarian CSU.

1989 West Germany: rising support for far right in local and European elections, declining support for Kohl. East Germany: mass exodus to West Germany began. Honecker replaced by Egon Krenz. National borders opened in Nov, including Berlin Wall. Reformist Hans Modrow appointed prime minister. Krenz replaced.

1990 March: East German multiparty elections won by a coalition led by the right-wing CDU. 3 Oct: official reunification of East and West Germany. 2 Dec: first all-German elections since 1932, resulting in a victory for Kohl.

1991 Kohl's popularity declined after tax increase. The CDU lost its Bundesrat majority to the SPD. Racist outbreaks continued with violent attacks on foreigners.

1992 Neo-Nazi riots against immigrants continued.

1993 Unemployment exceeded 7%; severe recession. Outbreaks of racist violence. Restrictions on refugee admission introduced.

Ghana

Republic of

area 238,305 sq km/91,986 sq mi

capital Accra

towns Kumasi, and ports Sekondi-Takoradi, Tema

physical mostly tropical lowland plains; bisected by river Volta

environment forested areas shrank from 8.2 million sq km/3.17 million sq mi at the beginning of the 20th century to 1.9 million sq km/730,000 sq mi by 1990

features world's largest artificial lake, Lake Volta; relics of traditional kingdom of Ashanti: 32,000 chiefs and kings

head of state and government Jerry Rawlings from 1981

political system emergent democracy

exports cocoa, coffee, timber, gold, diamonds, manganese, bauxite
currency cedi
population (1992) 15,237,000; growth rate 3.2% p.a.
life expectancy men 50, women 54
languages English (official) and African languages
media all media are government-controlled and the two daily newspapers are government-owned
religion animist 38%, Muslim 30%, Christian 24%
literacy men 64%, women 43% (1985 est)
GNP $3.9 bn (1983); $420 per head

chronology
1957 Independence achieved from Britain, within the Commonwealth, with Kwame Nkrumah as president.
1960 Ghana became a republic.
1964 Ghana became a one-party state.
1966 Nkrumah deposed and replaced by General Joseph Ankrah.
1969 Ankrah replaced by General Akwasi Afrifa, who initiated a return to civilian government.
1970 Edward Akufo-Addo elected president.
1972 Another coup placed Col Acheampong at the head of a military government.
1978 Acheampong deposed in a bloodless coup led by Frederick Akuffo; another coup put Flight-Lt Jerry Rawlings in power.
1979 Return to civilian rule under Hilla Limann.
1981 Rawlings seized power again, citing the incompetence of previous governments. All political parties banned.
1989 Coup attempt against Rawlings foiled.
1992 New multiparty constitution approved. Partial lifting of ban on political parties. Nov: Rawlings won presidency in national elections.
1993 Fourth republic of Ghana formally inaugurated in Rawlings' presence.

Greece

Hellenic Republic (*Elliniki Dimokratia*)

area 131,957 sq km/50,935 sq mi
capital Athens
towns Larisa; ports Piraeus, Thessaloníki, Patras, Iráklion
physical mountainous; a large number of islands, notably Crete, Corfu, and Rhodes
environment acid rain and other airborne pollutants are destroying the Classical buildings and ancient monuments of Athens

features Corinth canal; Mount Olympus; the Acropolis; many classical archaeological sites; the Aegean and Ionian Islands
head of state Constantine Karamanlis from 1990
head of government Andreas Papandreou from 1993
political system democratic republic
political parties Panhellenic Socialist Movement (PASOK), democratic socialist; New Democracy Party (ND), centre-right; Democratic Renewal (DR); Communist Party; Greek Left Party; Political Spring, moderate, left of centre
exports tobacco, fruit, vegetables, olives, olive oil, textiles, aluminium, iron, and steel
currency drachma
population (1992) 10,288,000; growth rate 0.3% p.a.
life expectancy men 72, women 76
language Greek
religion Greek Orthodox 97%
literacy men 96%, women 89% (1985)
GDP $79.2 bn (1992)

chronology
1829 Independence achieved from Turkish rule.
1912–13 Balkan Wars; Greece gained much land.
1941–44 German occupation of Greece.
1946 Civil war between royalists and communists; communists defeated.
1949 Monarchy re-established with Paul as king.
1964 King Paul succeeded by his son Constantine.
1967 Army coup removed the king; Col George Papadopoulos became prime minister. Martial law imposed, all political activity banned.
1973 Republic proclaimed, with Papadopoulos as president.
1974 Former premier Constantine Karamanlis recalled from exile to lead government. Martial law and ban on political parties lifted; restoration of the monarchy rejected by a referendum.
1975 New constitution adopted, making Greece a democratic republic.
1980 Karamanlis resigned as prime minister and was elected president.
1981 Greece became full member of European Economic Community. Andreas Papandreou elected Greece's first socialist prime minister.
1983 Five-year military and economic cooperation agreement signed with USA; ten-year economic cooperation agreement signed with USSR.
1985 Papandreou re-elected.
1988 Relations with Turkey improved. Major cabinet reshuffle after mounting criticism of Papandreou.
1989 Papandreou defeated. Tzannis Tzannetakis became prime minister; his all-party government collapsed. Xenophon Zolotas formed new unity government. Papandreou charged with corruption.
1990 New Democracy Party (ND) won half of parliamentary seats in general election but no outright majority; Constantine Mitsotakis became premier; formed new all-party government. Karamanlis re-elected president.
1992 Papandreou acquitted. Greece opposed recognition of independence of the Yugoslav breakaway republic of Macedonia.
1993 Parliament ratified the Maastricht Treaty. PASOK won general election and Papandreou returned as prime minister.

Grenada

area (including the Grenadines, notably Carriacou) 340 sq km/131 sq mi
capital St George's
towns Grenville, Hillsborough (Carriacou)
physical southernmost of the Windward Islands; mountainous
features Grand-Anse beach; Annandale Falls; Great Pool volcanic crater
head of state Elizabeth II from 1974, represented by governor general
head of government Nicholas Braithwaite from 1990
political system emergent democracy
political parties New National Party (NNP), centrist; Grenada United Labour Party (GULP), nationalist, left of centre; National Democratic Congress (NDC), centrist
exports cocoa, nutmeg, bananas, mace
currency Eastern Caribbean dollar
population (1992) 90,900, 84% of black African descent; growth rate –0.2% p.a.
life expectancy 69
language English (official); some French patois spoken
religion Roman Catholic 60%
literacy 85% (1985)
GDP $139 million (1987); $1,391 per head

chronology
1974 Independence achieved from Britain; Eric Gairy elected prime minister.
1979 Gairy removed in bloodless coup led by Maurice Bishop; constitution suspended and a People's Revolutionary Government established.
1982 Relations with the USA and Britain deteriorated as ties with Cuba and the USSR strengthened.
1983 After Bishop's attempt to improve relations with the USA, he was overthrown by left-wing opponents. A coup established the Revolutionary Military Council (RMC), and Bishop and three colleagues were executed. The USA invaded Grenada, accompanied by troops from other E Caribbean countries; RMC overthrown, 1974 constitution reinstated.
1984 The newly formed NNP won 14 of the 15 seats in the house of representatives and its leader, Herbert Blaize, became prime minister.
1989 Herbert Blaize lost leadership of NNP, remaining as head of government; he died and was succeeded by Ben Jones.

1990 Nicholas Braithwaite of the NDC became prime minister.
1991 Integration into Windward Islands confederation proposed.

Guatemala

Republic of (*República de Guatemala*)

area 108,889 sq km/42,031 sq mi
capital Guatemala City
towns Quezaltenango, Puerto Barrios (naval base)
physical mountainous; narrow coastal plains; limestone tropical plateau in N; frequent earthquakes
environment between 1960 and 1980 nearly 57% of the country's forest was cleared for farming
features Mayan archaeological remains, including site at Tikal
head of state and government Ramiro de Leon Carpio from 1993
political system democratic republic
political parties Guatemalan Christian Democratic Party (PDCG), Christian centre-left; Centre Party (UCN), centrist; National Democratic Cooperation Party (PDCN), centre-right; Revolutionary Party (PR), radical; Movement of National Liberation (MLN), extreme right-wing; Democratic Institutional Party (PID), moderate conservative; Solidarity Action Movement (MAS), right-wing
exports coffee, bananas, cotton, sugar, beef
currency quetzal
population (1992) 9,442,000 (Mayaquiche Indians 54%, mestizos (mixed race) 42%); growth rate 2.8% p.a. (87% of under-fives suffer from malnutrition)
life expectancy men 57, women 61
languages Spanish (official); 40% speak 18 Indian languages
religions Roman Catholic 80%, Protestant 20%
literacy men 63%, women 47% (1985 est)
GDP $7 bn (1987); $834 per head

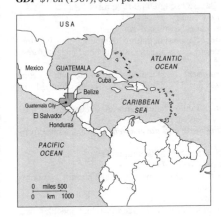

chronology
1839 Independence achieved from Spain.
1954 Col Carlos Castillo became president in US-backed coup, halting land reform.
1963 Military coup made Col Enrique Peralta president.
1966 Cesar Méndez elected president.
1970 Carlos Araña elected president.

1974 General Kjell Laugerud became president. Widespread political violence precipitated by the discovery of falsified election returns in March.
1978 General Fernando Romeo became president.
1981 Growth of antigovernment guerrilla movement.
1982 General Angel Anibal became president. Army coup installed General Ríos Montt as head of junta and then as president; political violence continued.
1983 Montt removed in coup led by General Mejía Victores, who declared amnesty for the guerrillas.
1985 New constitution adopted; PDCG won congressional elections; Vinicio Cerezo elected president.
1989 Coup attempt against Cerezo foiled. Over 100,000 people killed and 40,000 reported missing since 1980.
1991 Jorge Serrano Elías of the Solidarity Action Movement elected president. Diplomatic relations with Belize established.
1993 President Serrano deposed; Ramiro de Leon Carpio elected president by assembly.

Guinea

Republic of *(République de Guinée)*

area 245,857 sq km/94,901 sq mi
capital Conakry
towns Labé, Nzérékoré, Kankan
physical flat coastal plain with mountainous interior; sources of rivers Niger, Gambia, and Senegal; forest in SE
environment large amounts of toxic waste from industrialized countries have been dumped in Guinea
features Fouta Djallon, area of sandstone plateaus, cut by deep valleys
head of state and government Lansana Conté from 1984
political system military republic
political parties none since 1984
exports coffee, rice, palm kernels, alumina, bauxite, diamonds
currency syli or franc
population (1992) 7,232,000 (chief peoples are Fulani, Malinke, Susu); growth rate 2.3% p.a.
life expectancy men 39, women 42
languages French (official), African languages
media state-owned, but some criticism of the government tolerated; no daily newspaper
religions Muslim 85%, Christian 10%, local 5%
literacy men 40%, women 17% (1985 est)
GNP $1.9 bn (1987); $369 per head

chronology
1958 Full independence achieved from France; Sékou Touré elected president.
1977 Strong opposition to Touré's rigid Marxist policies forced him to accept return to mixed economy.
1980 Touré returned unopposed for fourth seven-year term.
1984 Touré died. Bloodless coup established a military committee for national recovery, led by Col Lansana Conté.
1985 Attempted coup against Conté while he was out of the country was foiled by loyal troops.
1990 Sent troops to join the multinational force that attempted to stabilize Liberia.
1991 Antigovernment general strike by National Confederation of Guinea Workers (CNTG).
1993 President Conté narrowly re-elected.

Guinea-Bissau

Republic of *(República da Guiné-Bissau)*

area 36,125 sq km/13,944 sq mi
capital Bissau
towns Mansâa, São Domingos
physical flat coastal plain rising to savanna in E
features the archipelago of Bijagós
head of state and government João Bernardo Vieira from 1980
political system emergent democracy
political party African Party for the Independence of Portuguese Guinea and Cape Verde (PAIGC), nationalist socialist
exports rice, coconuts, peanuts, fish, timber
currency peso
population (1992) 1,015,000; growth rate 2.4% p.a.
life expectancy 42; 1990 infant mortality rate was 14.8%
languages Portuguese (official), Crioulo (Cape Verdean dialect of Portuguese), African languages
religions animism 54%, Muslim 38%, Christian 8%
literacy men 46%, women 17% (1985 est)
GDP $135 million (1987); $146 per head

chronology
1956 PAIGC formed to secure independence from Portugal.
1973 Two-thirds of the country declared independent, with Luiz Cabral as president of a state council.
1974 Independence achieved from Portugal.
1980 Cape Verde decided not to join a unified state. Cabral deposed, and João Vieira became chair of a council of revolution.

1981 PAIGC confirmed as the only legal party, with Vieira as its secretary general.
1982 Normal relations with Cape Verde restored.
1984 New constitution adopted, making Vieira head of government as well as head of state.
1989 Vieira re-elected.
1991 Other parties legalized.
1992 Multiparty electoral commission established.

Guyana

Cooperative Republic of

area 214,969 sq km/82,978 sq mi
capital (and port) Georgetown
towns New Amsterdam, Mabaruma
physical coastal plain rises into rolling highlands with savanna in S; mostly tropical rainforest
features Mount Roraima; Kaietur National Park, including Kaietur Fall on the Potaro (tributary of Essequibo) 250 m/821 ft
head of state Janet Jagan from 1997
head of government Sam Hinds from 1992
political system democratic republic
political parties People's National Congress (PNC), Afro-Guyanan nationalist socialist; People's Progressive Party (PPP), Indian Marxist-Leninist
exports sugar, rice, rum, timber, diamonds, bauxite, shrimps, molasses
currency Guyanese dollar
population (1992) 748,000 (51% descendants of workers introduced from India to work the sugar plantations after the abolition of slavery, 30% black, 5% Amerindian); growth rate 2% p.a.
life expectancy men 66, women 71
languages English (official), Hindi, Amerindian
media one government-owned daily newspaper; one independent paper published three times a week, on which the government puts pressure by withholding foreign exchange for newsprint; one weekly independent in the same position. There is also legislation that restricts exchange of information between public officials, government, and the press
religions Christian 57%, Hindu 33%, Sunni Muslim 9%
literacy men 97%, women 95% (1985 est)
GNP $359 million (1987); $445 per head

chronology
1831 Became British colony under name of British Guiana.

1953 Assembly elections won by left-wing PPP; Britain suspended constitution and installed interim administration, fearing communist takeover.
1961 Internal self-government granted; Cheddi Jagan became prime minister.
1964 PNC leader Forbes Burnham led PPP–PNC coalition.
1966 Independence achieved from Britain.
1970 Guyana became a republic within the Commonwealth.
1981 Forbes Burnham became first executive president under new constitution.
1985 Burnham died; succeeded by Desmond Hoyte.
1992 PPP had decisive victory in assembly elections; Jagan became president.

Haiti

Republic of (*République d'Haïti*)

area 27,750 sq km/10,712 sq mi
capital Port-au-Prince
towns Cap-Haïtien, Gonaïves, Les Cayes
physical mainly mountainous and tropical; occupies W third of Hispaniola Island in Caribbean Sea; seriously deforested
features oldest black republic in the world; only French-speaking republic in the Americas; island of La Tortuga off N coast was formerly a pirate lair
head of state (interim) Joseph Nerette from 1991
head of government (interim) Robert Malval from 1993
political system transitional
political party National Progressive Party (PNP), right-wing military
exports coffee, sugar, sisal, cotton, cocoa, bauxite
currency gourde
population (1992) 6,764,000; growth rate 1.7% p.a.; one of highest population densities in the world; about 1.5 million Haitians live outside Haiti (in USA and Canada); about 400,000 live in virtual slavery in the Dominican Republic, where they went or were sent to cut sugar cane
life expectancy men 51, women 54
languages French (official, spoken by literate 10% minority), Creole (spoken by 90% black majority)
religion Christian 95% of which 80% Roman Catholic, voodoo 4%
literacy men 40%, women 35% (1985 est)
GDP $2.2 bn (1987); $414 per head

chronology
1804 Independence achieved from France.
1915 Haiti invaded by USA; remained under US control until 1934.
1957 Dr François Duvalier (Papa Doc) elected president.
1964 Duvalier pronounced himself president for life.
1971 Duvalier died, succeeded by his son, Jean-Claude (Baby Doc); thousands murdered during Duvalier era.
1986 Duvalier deposed; replaced by Lt-Gen Henri Namphy as head of a governing council.
1988 Feb: Leslie Manigat became president. Namphy staged a military coup in June, but another coup in Sept led by Brig-Gen Prosper Avril replaced him with a civilian government under military control.
1989 Coup attempt against Avril foiled; US aid resumed.
1990 Opposition elements expelled; Ertha Pascal-Trouillot acting president.
1991 Jean-Bertrand Aristide elected president but later overthrown in military coup led by Brig-Gen Raoul Cedras. Efforts to reinstate Aristide failed. Joseph Nerette became interim head of state.
1992 Economic sanctions imposed since 1991 were eased by the USA but increased by the Organization of American States. Marc Bazin appointed premier.
1993 Bazin resigned. Robert Malval nominated as prime minister. UN blockade introduced in an effort to force Aristide's return.

Honduras

Republic of (*República de Honduras*)

area 112,100 sq km/43,282 sq mi
capital Tegucigalpa
towns San Pedro Sula; ports La Ceiba, Puerto Cortés
physical narrow tropical coastal plain with mountainous interior, Bay Islands
features archaeological sites; Mayan ruins at Copán
head of state and government Rafael Leonardo Callejas from 1990
political system democratic republic
political parties Liberal Party of Honduras (PLH), centre-left; National Party (PN), right-wing
exports coffee, bananas, meat, sugar, timber (including mahogany, rosewood)
currency lempira

population (1992) 4,996,000 (mestizo, or mixed, 90%; Indians and Europeans 10%); growth rate 3.1% p.a.
life expectancy men 58, women 62
languages Spanish (official), English, Indian languages
religion Roman Catholic 97%
literacy men 61%, women 58% (1985 est)
GDP $3.5 bn (1987); $758 per head

chronology
1838 Independence achieved from Spain.
1980 After more than a century of mostly military rule, a civilian government was elected, with Dr Roberto Suazo as president; the commander in chief of the army, General Gustavo Alvarez, retained considerable power.
1983 Close involvement with the USA in providing naval and air bases and allowing Nicaraguan counter-revolutionaries ('Contras') to operate from Honduras.
1984 Alvarez ousted in coup led by junior officers, resulting in policy review towards USA and Nicaragua.
1985 José Azcona elected president after electoral law changed, making Suazo ineligible for presidency.
1989 Government and opposition declared support for Central American peace plan to demobilize Nicaraguan Contras based in Honduras; Contras and their dependents in Honduras in 1989 thought to number about 55,000.
1990 Rafael Callejas (PN) inaugurated as president.
1992 Border dispute with El Salvador dating from 1861 finally resolved.

Hungary

Republic of (*Magyar Köztársaság*)

area 93,032 sq km/35,910 sq mi
capital Budapest
towns Miskolc, Debrecen, Szeged, Pécs
physical Great Hungarian Plain covers E half of country; Bakony Forest, Lake Balaton, and Transdanubian Highlands in the W; rivers Danube, Tisza, and Raba
environment an estimated 35%–40% of the population live in areas with officially 'inadmissible' air and water pollution. In Budapest lead levels have reached 30 times the maximum international standards
features more than 500 thermal springs; Hortobágy National Park; Tokay wine area
head of state Arpád Göncz from 1990
head of government Peter Boross from 1993
political system emergent democratic republic
political parties over 50, including Hungarian Socialist Party (HSP), left of centre; Hungarian Democratic Forum (MDF), umbrella prodemocracy grouping; Alliance of Free Democrats (SzDSz), radical free-market opposition group heading coalition with Alliance of Young Democrats, Social Democrats, and Smallholders Party, right-wing; Hungarian Justice Party (MIP), populist-nationalist
exports machinery, vehicles, iron and steel, chemicals, fruit and vegetables
currency forint
population (1992) 10,303,000 (Magyar 92%, Romany 3%, German 2.5%; Hungarian minority in Romania has caused some friction between the two countries); growth rate 0.2% p.a.
life expectancy men 67, women 74

language Hungarian (or Magyar), one of the few languages of Europe with non-Indo-European origins; it is grouped with Finnish, Estonian, and others in the Finno-Ugric family
religions Roman Catholic 67%, other Christian denominations 25%
literacy men 99.3%, women 98.5% (1980)
GDP $26.1 bn (1987); $2,455 per head

chronology
1918 Independence achieved from Austro-Hungarian empire.
1919 A communist state formed for 133 days.
1920–44 Regency formed under Admiral Horthy, who joined Hitler's attack on the USSR.
1945 Liberated by USSR.
1946 Republic proclaimed; Stalinist regime imposed.
1949 Soviet-style constitution adopted.
1956 Hungarian national uprising; workers' demonstrations in Budapest; democratization reforms by Imre Nagy overturned by Soviet tanks, János Kádár installed as party leader.
1968 Economic decentralization reforms.
1983 Competition introduced into elections.
1987 VAT and income tax introduced.
1988 Kádár replaced by Károly Grosz. First free trade union recognized; rival political parties legalized.
1989 May: border with Austria opened. July: new four-person collective leadership of HSWP. Oct: new 'transitional constitution' adopted, founded on multiparty democracy and new presidentialist executive. HSWP changed name to Hungarian Socialist Party, with Nyers as new leader. Kádár 'retired'.
1990 HSP reputation damaged by 'Danubegate' bugging scandal. March–April: elections won by right-of-centre coalition, headed by Hungarian Democratic Forum (MDF). May: József Antall, leader of the MDF, appointed premier. Aug: Arpád Göncz elected president.
1991 Jan: devaluation of currency. June: legislation approved to compensate owners of land and property expropriated under communist government. Last Soviet troops departed. Dec: EC association pact signed.
1992 March: EC pact came into effect.
1993 József Antall died and was succeeded by Peter Boross.

Iceland

Republic of (*Lýdveldid ísland*)

area 103,000 sq km/39,758 sq mi
capital Reykjavík
towns Akureyri, Akranes
physical warmed by the Gulf Stream; glaciers and lava fields cover 75% of the country; active volcanoes (Hekla was once thought the gateway to Hell), geysers, hot springs, and new islands created offshore (Surtsey in 1963); subterranean hot water heats 85% of Iceland's homes
features Thingvellir, where the oldest parliament in the world first met AD 930; shallow lake Mývatn (38 sq km/15 sq mi) in N
head of state Vigdís Finnbogadóttir from 1980
head of government Davíd Oddsson from 1991
political system democratic republic
political parties Independence Party (IP), right of centre; Progressive Party (PP), radical socialist; People's Alliance (PA), socialist; Social Democratic Party (SDP), moderate, left of centre; Citizens' Party, centrist; Women's Alliance, women- and family-oriented
exports cod and other fish products, aluminium, diatomite
currency krona
population (1992) 261,000; growth rate 0.8% p.a.
life expectancy men 74, women 80
language Icelandic, the most archaic Scandinavian language
religion Evangelical Lutheran 95%
literacy 99.9% (1984)
GDP $6.6 bn (1992)

chronology
1944 Independence achieved from Denmark.
1949 Joined NATO and Council of Europe.
1953 Joined Nordic Council.
1976 'Cod War' with UK.
1979 Iceland announced 320-km/200-mi exclusive fishing zone.
1983 Steingrímur Hermannsson appointed to lead a coalition government.
1985 Iceland declared itself a nuclear-free zone.
1987 New coalition government formed by Thorsteinn Pálsson after general election.
1988 Vigdís Finnbogadóttir re-elected president for a third term; Hermannsson led new coalition.
1991 Davíd Oddsson led new IP–SDP (Independence Party and Social Democratic Party) centre-right coalition, becoming prime minister in the general election.

1992 Iceland defied world ban to resume whaling industry.

India

Republic of (Hindi *Bharat*)

area 3,166,829 sq km/1,222,396 sq mi
capital Delhi
towns Bangalore, Hyderabad, Ahmedabad, Kanpur, Pune, Nagpur; ports Calcutta, Bombay, Madras
physical Himalaya mountains on N border; plains around rivers Ganges, Indus, Brahmaputra; Deccan peninsula S of the Narmada River forms plateau between Western and Eastern Ghats mountain ranges; desert in W; Andaman and Nicobar Islands, Lakshadweep (Laccadive Islands)
environment the controversial Narmada Valley Project is the world's largest combined hydroelectric irrigation scheme. In addition to displacing a million people, the damming of the holy Narmada River will submerge large areas of forest and farmland and create problems of waterlogging and salinization
features Taj Mahal monument; Golden Temple, Amritsar; archaeological sites and cave paintings (Ajanta); world's second most populous country
head of state Shankar Dayal Sharma from 1992
head of government P V Narasimha Rao from 1991
political system liberal democratic federal republic
political parties All India Congress Committee (I), or Congress (I), cross-caste and cross-religion, left of centre; Janata Dal, left of centre; Bharatiya Janata Party (BJP), conservative Hindu-chauvinist; Communist Party of India (CPI), pro-Moscow Marxist-Leninist; Communist Party of India–Marxist (CPI–M), West Bengal-based moderate socialist
exports tea (world's largest producer), coffee, fish, iron and steel, leather, textiles, clothing, polished diamonds
currency rupee
population (1992) 889,700,000 (920 women to every 1,000 men); growth rate 2.0% p.a.
life expectancy men 56, women 55
languages Hindi (widely spoken in N India), English, and 14 other official languages: Assamese, Bengali, Gujarati, Kannada, Kashmiri, Malayalam, Marathi, Oriya, Punjabi, Sanskrit, Sindhi, Tamil, Telugu, Urdu
media free press; government-owned broadcasting
religions Hindu 80%, Sunni Muslim 10%, Christian 2.5%, Sikh 2%

literacy men 57%, women 29% (1985 est)
GDP $220.8 bn (1987); $283 per head

chronology
1947 Independence achieved from Britain.
1950 Federal republic proclaimed.
1962 Border skirmishes with China.
1964 Death of Prime Minister Nehru. Border war with Pakistan over Kashmir.
1966 Indira Gandhi became prime minister.
1971 War with Pakistan leading to creation of Bangladesh.
1975–77 State of emergency proclaimed.
1977–79 Janata Party government in power.
1980 Indira Gandhi returned in landslide victory.
1984 Indira Gandhi assassinated; Rajiv Gandhi elected with record majority.
1987 Signing of 'Tamil' Colombo peace accord with Sri Lanka; Indian Peacekeeping Force (IPKF) sent there. Public revelation of Bofors corruption scandal.
1988 New opposition party, Janata Dal, established by former finance minister V P Singh. Voting age lowered from 21 to 18.
1989 Congress (I) lost majority in general election, after Gandhi associates implicated in financial misconduct; Janata Dal minority government formed, with V P Singh prime minister.
1990 Central rule imposed in Jammu and Kashmir. V P Singh resigned; new minority Janata Dal government formed by Chandra Shekhar. Interethnic and religious violence in Punjab and elsewhere.
1991 Central rule imposed in Tamil Nadu. Shekhar resigned; elections called for May. May: Rajiv Gandhi assassinated. June: elections resumed, resulting in a Congress (I) minority government led by P V Narasimha Rao. Separatist violence continued.
1992 Congress (I) won control of state assembly and a majority in parliament in Punjab state elections. Split in Janata Dal opposition resulted in creation of National Front coalition party (including rump of Janata Dal party). Widespread communal violence killed over 1,200 people, mainly Muslims, following destruction of a mosque in Ayodhya, N India, by Hindu extremists.
1993 Sectarian violence in Bombay left 500 dead. Rao narrowly survived a confidence vote in parliament. Dec: the movement of former independents into the Congress party gave it a clear majority in parliament.

Indonesia

Republic of (*Republik Indonesia*)

area 1,919,443 sq km/740,905 sq mi
capital Jakarta
towns Bandung; ports Surabaya, Semarang, Tandjungpriok
physical comprises 13,677 tropical islands, of the Greater Sunda group (including Java and Madura, part of Borneo (Kalimantan), Sumatra, Sulawesi and Belitung), and the Lesser Sundas/Nusa Tenggara (including Bali, Lombok, Sumbawa, Sumba, Flores, and Timor), as well as Malaku/Moluccas and part of New Guinea (Irian Jaya)
environment comparison of primary forest and 30-year-old secondary forest has shown that logging in Kalimantan has led to a 20% decline in tree species
head of state and government T N J Suharto from 1967

political system authoritarian nationalist republic
political parties Golkar, ruling military-bureaucrat, farmers' party; United Development Party (PPP), moderate Islamic; Indonesian Democratic Party (PDI), nationalist Christian
exports coffee, rubber, timber, palm oil, coconuts, tin, tea, tobacco, oil, liquid natural gas
currency rupiah
population (1992) 184,796,000 (including 300 ethnic groups); growth rate 2% p.a.; Indonesia has the world's largest Muslim population; Java is one of the world's most densely populated areas
life expectancy men 52, women 55
languages Indonesian (official), closely allied to Malay; Javanese is the most widely spoken local dialect
religions Muslim 88%, Christian 10%, Buddhist and Hindu 2%
literacy men 83%, women 65% (1985 est)
GDP $69.7 bn (1987); $409 per head

chronology
17th century Dutch colonial rule established.
1942 Occupied by Japan; nationalist government established.
1945 Japanese surrender; nationalists declared independence under Achmed Sukarno.
1949 Formal transfer of Dutch sovereignty.
1950 Unitary constitution established.
1963 Western New Guinea (Irian Jaya) ceded by the Netherlands.
1965–66 Attempted communist coup; General T N J Suharto imposed emergency administration, carried out massacre of hundreds of thousands.
1967 Sukarno replaced as president by Suharto.
1975 Guerrillas seeking independence for S Moluccas seized train and Indonesian consulate in the Netherlands, held Western hostages.
1976 Forced annexation of former Portuguese colony of East Timor.
1986 Institution of 'transmigration programme' to settle large numbers of Javanese on sparsely populated outer islands, particularly Irian Jaya.
1988 Partial easing of travel restrictions to East Timor. Suharto re-elected for fifth term.
1989 Foreign debt reaches $50 billion; Western creditors offer aid on condition that concessions are made to foreign companies and that austerity measures are introduced.

1991 Democracy forums launched to promote political dialogue. Massacre in East Timor.
1992 The ruling Golkar party won the assembly elections.
1993 President Suharto re-elected for sixth consecutive five-year term.

Iran

Islamic Republic of (*Jomhori-e-Islami-e-Irân*; until 1935 *Persia*)

area 1,648,000 sq km/636,128 sq mi
capital Tehran
towns Isfahan, Mashhad, Tabriz, Shiraz, Ahvaz; chief port Abadan
physical plateau surrounded by mountains, including Elburz and Zagros; Lake Rezayeh; Dasht-Ekavir Desert; occupies islands of Abu Musa, Greater Tunb and Lesser Tunb in the Gulf
features ruins of Persepolis; Mount Demavend 5,670 m/18,603 ft
Leader of the Islamic Revolution Seyed Ali Khamenei from 1989
head of government Ali Akbar Hoshemi Rafsanjani from 1989
political system authoritarian Islamic republic
political party Islamic Republican Party (IRP), fundamentalist Islamic
exports carpets, cotton textiles, metalwork, leather goods, oil, petrochemicals, fruit
currency rial
population (1992) 59,570,000 (including minorities in Azerbaijan, Baluchistan, Khuzestan/Arabistan, and Kurdistan); growth rate 3.2% p.a
life expectancy men 57, women 57
languages Farsi (official), Kurdish, Turkish, Arabic, English, French
religions Shi'ite Muslim (official) 92%, Sunni Muslim 5%, Zoroastrian 2%, Jewish, Baha'i, and Christian 1%
literacy men 62%, women 39% (1985 est)
GDP $86.4 bn (1987); $1,756 per head

chronology
1946 British, US, and Soviet forces left Iran.
1951 Oilfields nationalized by Prime Minister Muhammad Mossadeq.
1953 Mossadeq deposed and the US-backed shah, Muhammad Reza Shah Pahlavi, took full control of the government.

1975 The shah introduced single-party system.
1978 Opposition to the shah organized from France by Ayatollah Khomeini.
1979 Shah left the country; Khomeini returned to create Islamic state. Revolutionaries seized US hostages at embassy in Tehran; US economic boycott.
1980 Start of Iran–Iraq War.
1981 US hostages released.
1984 Egyptian peace proposals rejected.
1985 Fighting intensified in Iran–Iraq War.
1988 Cease-fire; talks with Iraq began.
1989 Khomeini called for the death of British writer Salman Rushdie. June: Khomeini died; Ali Khamenei elected interim Leader of the Revolution; speaker of Iranian parliament Hoshemi Rafsanjani elected president. Secret oil deal with Israel revealed.
1990 Generous peace terms with Iraq accepted. Normal relations with UK restored.
1991 Imprisoned British business executive released. Nearly one million Kurds arrived in Iran from Iraq, fleeing persecution by Saddam Hussein after the Gulf War.
1992 Pro-Rafsanjani moderates won assembly elections.
1993 President Rafsanjani re-elected, but with a smaller vote.

Iraq

Republic of (*al Jumhouriya al 'Iraqia*)

area 434,924 sq km/167,881 sq mi
capital Baghdad
towns Mosul and port of Basra
physical mountains in N, desert in W; wide valley of rivers Tigris and Euphrates NW–SE
environment a chemical-weapons plant covering an area of 65 sq km/25 sq mi, situated 80 km/50 mi NW of Baghdad, has been described by the UN as the largest toxic waste dump in the world
features reed architecture of the marsh Arabs; ancient sites of Eridu, Babylon, Nineveh, Ur, Ctesiphon
head of state Saddam Hussein al- Tikriti from 1979
head of government Ahmed Hussain from 1993
political system one-party socialist republic
political party Arab Ba'ath Socialist Party, nationalist socialist
exports oil (prior to UN sanctions), wool, dates (80% of world supply)
currency Iraqi dinar

population (1992) 18,838,000 (Arabs 77%, Kurds 19%, Turks 2%); growth rate 3.6% p.a.
life expectancy men 62, women 63
languages Arabic (official); Kurdish, Assyrian, Armenian
religions Shi'ite Muslim 60%, Sunni Muslim 37%, Christian 3%
literacy men 68%, women 32% (1980 est)
GDP $42.3 bn (1987); $3,000 per head

chronology
1920 Iraq became a British League of Nations protectorate.
1921 Hashemite dynasty established, with Faisal I installed by Britain as king.
1932 Independence achieved from British protectorate status.
1958 Monarchy overthrown; Iraq became a republic.
1963 Joint Ba'athist-military coup headed by Col Salem Aref.
1968 Military coup put Maj-Gen al-Bakr in power.
1979 Al-Bakr replaced by Saddam Hussein.
1980 War between Iraq and Iran broke out.
1985 Fighting intensified.
1988 Cease-fire; talks began with Iran. Iraq used chemical weapons against Kurdish rebels seeking greater autonomy.
1989 Unsuccessful coup against President Hussein; Iraq launched ballistic missile in successful test.
1990 Peace treaty favouring Iran agreed. Aug: Iraq invaded and annexed Kuwait, precipitating another Gulf crisis. US forces massed in Saudi Arabia at request of King Fahd. United Nations resolutions ordered Iraqi withdrawal from Kuwait and imposed total trade ban on Iraq; UN resolution sanctioning force approved. All foreign hostages released.
1991 16 Jan: US-led forces began aerial assault on Iraq; Iraq's infrastructure destroyed by bombing. 23–28 Feb: land–sea–air offensive to free Kuwait successful. Uprisings of Kurds and Shi'ites brutally suppressed by surviving Iraqi troops. Talks between Kurdish leaders and Saddam Hussein about Kurdish autonomy. Allied troops withdrew after establishing 'safe havens' for Kurds in the north, leaving a rapid-reaction force near the Turkish border. Allies threatened to bomb strategic targets in Iraq if full information about nuclear facilities denied to UN.
1992 UN imposed a 'no-fly zone' over S Iraq to protect Shi'ites.
1993 Iraqi incursions into the 'no-fly zone' prompted US-led alliance aircraft to bomb 'strategic' targets in Iraq. USA also bombed a target in Baghdad in retaliation for an alleged plot against former president Bush, claiming that the action was taken in 'self-defence'.

Ireland

Republic of (*Eire*)

area 70,282 sq km/27,146 sq mi
capital Dublin
towns ports Cork, Dun Laoghaire, Limerick, Waterford
physical central plateau surrounded by hills; rivers Shannon, Liffey, Boyne
features Bog of Allen, source of domestic and national power; Macgillicuddy's Reeks, Wicklow

Mountains; Lough Corrib, lakes of Killarney; Galway Bay and Aran Islands

head of state Mary McAleese from 1997

head of government Bertie Ahern from 1997

political system democratic republic

political parties Fianna Fáil (Soldiers of Destiny), moderate centre-right; Fine Gael (Irish Tribe), moderate centre-left; Labour Party, moderate, left of centre; Progressive Democrats, radical free-enterprise

exports livestock, dairy products, Irish whiskey, microelectronic components and assemblies, mining and engineering products, chemicals, clothing; tourism is important

currency punt

population (1992) 3,519,000; growth rate 0.1% p.a.

life expectancy men 70, women 76

languages Irish Gaelic and English (both official)

religion Roman Catholic 94%

literacy 99% (1984)

GDP $48.8 (1992)

chronology

1916 Easter Rising: nationalists proclaimed a republic in Dublin; British crushed revolt and executed 15 leaders.

1919 Sinn Féin MPs formed Irish parliament in Dublin in defiance of British government.

1919–21 Irish Republican Army (IRA) waged guerrilla war against British forces.

1921 Anglo-Irish Treaty partitioned Ireland; N Ireland (Ulster) remained part of the United Kingdom; S Ireland won full internal self-government with dominion status.

1922 Irish Free State proclaimed; IRA split over Anglo-Irish Treaty led to civil war 1922–23.

1932 Anti-Treaty party, Fianna Fáil, came to power under Éamonn de Valéra.

1937 New constitution established Eire (Gaelic name for Ireland) as a sovereign state and refused to acknowledge partition.

1949 After remaining neutral in World War II, Eire left the Commonwealth and became the Republic of Ireland.

1973 Ireland joined European Economic Community.

1985 Anglo-Irish Agreement gave the Republic of Ireland a consultative role, but no powers, in the government of Northern Ireland.

1990 Mary Robinson became the first woman president of Ireland.

1993 Downing Street Declaration: joint Anglo-Irish peace proposal for Northern Ireland issued.

1994 Cease-fires announced by Catholic and Protestant paramilitaries in Northern Ireland.

1995 Ulster framework peace document issued.

1997 Fianna Fáil leader Bertie Ahern became prime minister; Mary MacAleese elected president.

Israel

State of (*Medinat Israel*)

area 20,800 sq km/8,029 sq mi (as at 1949 armistice)

capital Jerusalem (not recognized by the United Nations)

towns ports Tel Aviv/Jaffa, Haifa, Acre, Eilat; Bat-Yam, Holon, Ramat Gan, Petach Tikva, Beersheba

physical coastal plain of Sharon between Haifa and Tel Aviv noted since ancient times for fertility; central mountains of Galilee, Samariq, and Judea; Dead Sea, Lake Tiberias, and river Jordan Rift Valley along the E are below sea level; Negev Desert in the S; Israel occupies Golan Heights, West Bank, and Gaza

features historic sites: Jerusalem, Bethlehem, Nazareth, Masada, Megiddo, Jericho; caves of the Dead Sea scrolls

head of state Ezer Weizman from 1993

head of government Binyamin Netanyahu from 1996

political system democratic republic

political parties Israel Labour Party, moderate, left of centre; Consolidation Party (Likud), right of centre

exports citrus and other fruit, avocados, chinese leaves, fertilizers, diamonds, plastics, petrochemicals, textiles, electronics, electro-optics, precision instruments, aircraft, and missiles

currency shekel

population (1992) 5,239,000 (including 750,000 Arab Israeli citizens and over 1 million Arabs in the occupied territories); under the Law of Return 1950, 'every Jew shall be entitled to come to Israel as an immigrant'; those from the East and E Europe are Ashkenazim, and those from Mediterranean Europe (Spain, Portugal, Italy, France, Greece) and Arab N Africa are Sephardim (over 50% of the population is now of Sephardic descent). Between Jan 1990 and April 1991, 250,000 Soviet Jews emigrated to Israel. An Israeli-born Jew is a Sabra. About 500,000 Israeli Jews are resident in the USA. Growth rate 1.8% p.a.

life expectancy men 73, women 76

languages Hebrew and Arabic (official); Yiddish, European and W Asian languages

religions Israel is a secular state, but the predominant faith is Judaism 83%; also Sunni Muslim, Christian, and Druse

literacy Jewish 88%, Arab 70%

GDP $35 bn (1987); $8,011 per head

chronology

1948 Independent State of Israel proclaimed with David Ben-Gurion as prime minister; Israel repulsed invasion by Arab nations; many Palestinian Arabs settled in refugee camps in the Gaza Strip and West Bank.

1952 Col Gamal Nasser of Egypt stepped up blockade of Israeli ports and support of Arab guerrillas in Gaza.

1956 War between Israel and Egypt; Israeli invasion of Gaza and Sinai followed by withdrawal 1957.

1963 Levi Eshkol succeeded Ben-Gurion as prime minister.

1964 Palestine Liberation Organization (PLO) founded to unite Palestinian Arabs with the aim of overthrowing the state of Israel.

1967 Israel defeated Egypt, Syria, and Jordan in the Six-Day War; Gaza, West Bank, E Jerusalem, Sinai, and Golan Heights captured.

1969 Golda Meir (Labour) elected prime minister; Yassir Arafat became chair of the PLO; escalation of terrorism and border raids.

1973 Yom Kippur War: Israel repulsed surprise attack by Egypt and Syria.

1974 Golda Meir succeeded by Yitzhak Rabin.

1977 Right-wing Likud bloc took office under Menachem Begin; President Anwar Sadat of Egypt began peace initiative.

1979 Camp David talks ended with signing of peace treaty between Israel and Egypt; Israel withdrew from Sinai.

1980 United Jerusalem declared capital of Israel.

1982 Israeli forces invaded S Lebanon to drive out PLO guerrillas; occupation continued until 1985.

1985 Labour and Likud formed coalition government led by Shimon Peres 1985–86 and Yitzhak Shamir 1986–90.

1988 Israeli handling of Palestinian uprising (Intifada) in occupied territories provoked international criticism.

1990 Shamir headed Likud government following the breakup of the coalition; PLO formally recognized the state of Israel.

1991 Iraq launched missile attacks on Israel during Gulf War; Middle East peace talks began in Madrid.

1992 Labour government elected under Yitzhak Rabin.

1993 Rabin and Arafat signed peace accord; Israel granted limited autonomy to Gaza Strip and Jericho.

1994 Arafat became head of autonomous Palestinian authority in Gaza and Jericho; peace agreement between Israel and Jordan.

1995 Rabin assassinated by Jewish opponent of peace accord; Peres became prime minister.

1996 Likud government elected under Binyamin Netanyahu, critic of peace accord. Revival of communal violence; peace process threatened. The opening of a 2,000-year-old tunnel near the Al-Aqsa mosque in Jerusalem in Sept provoked renewed Palestinian–Israeli conflict.

1997 Israeli schoolgirls killed by Jordanian soldier. Jewish settlement in E Jerusalem widely condemned. Netanyahu's government investigated for corruption. Suicide bombs by Hamas in Jerusalem. Partial and limited West Bank withdrawal.

Italy

Republic of (*Repubblica Italiana*)

area 301,300 sq km/116,332 sq mi

capital Rome

towns Milan, Turin; ports Naples, Genoa, Palermo, Bari, Catania, Trieste

physical mountainous (Maritime Alps, Dolomites, Apennines) with narrow coastal lowlands; rivers Po, Adige, Arno, Tiber, Rubicon; islands of Sicily, Sardinia, Elba, Capri, Ischia, Lipari, Pantelleria; lakes Como, Maggiore, Garda

environment Milan has the highest recorded level of sulphur-dioxide pollution of any city in the world. The Po River, with pollution ten times higher than officially recommended levels, is estimated to discharge around 250 tonnes of arsenic into the sea each year

features continental Europe's only active volcanoes: Vesuvius, Etna, Stromboli; historic towns include Venice, Florence, Siena, Rome; Greek, Roman, Etruscan archaeological sites

head of state Oscar Luigi Scalfaro from 1992

head of government Carlo Azeglio Ciampi from 1993

political system democratic republic

political parties Christian Democratic Party (DC), Christian, centrist; Democratic Party of the Left (PDS), pro-European socialist; Italian Socialist Party (PSI), moderate socialist; Italian Social Movement–National Right (MSI–DN), neofascist; Italian Republican Party (PRI), social democratic, left of centre; Italian Social Democratic Party (PSDI), moderate left of centre; Liberals (PLI), right of centre

exports wine (world's largest producer), fruit, vegetables, textiles (Europe's largest silk producer), clothing, leather goods, motor vehicles, electrical goods, chemicals, marble (Carrara), sulphur, mercury, iron, steel
currency lira
population (1992) 57,103,000; growth rate 0.1% p.a.
life expectancy men 73, women 80 (1989)
languages Italian; German, French, Slovene, and Albanian minorities
religion Roman Catholic (state religion)
literacy 97% (1989)
GDP $1,223.6 bn (1992)

chronology
1946 Monarchy replaced by a republic.
1948 New constitution adopted.
1954 Trieste returned to Italy.
1976 Communists proposed establishment of broad-based, left–right government, the 'historic compromise'; rejected by Christian Democrats.
1978 Christian Democrat Aldo Moro, architect of the historic compromise, kidnapped and murdered by Red Brigade guerrillas infiltrated by Western intelligence agents.
1983 Bettino Craxi, a Socialist, became leader of broad coalition government.
1987 Craxi resigned; succeeding coalition fell within months.
1988 Christian Democrats' leader Ciriaco de Mita established a five-party coalition including the Socialists.
1989 De Mita resigned after disagreements within his coalition government; succeeded by Giulio Andreotti. De Mita lost his leadership of Christian Democrat Party; Communists formed a 'shadow government'.
1991 Referendum approved electoral reform.
1992 April: ruling coalition lost its majority in general election; President Cossiga resigned, replaced by Oscar Luigi Scalfaro in May. Giuliano Amato, deputy leader of PDS, accepted premiership. Sept: lira devalued and Italy withdrew from the Exchange Rate Mechanism.
1993 Investigation of corruption network exposed Mafia links with several notable politicians, including Craxi and Andreotti. Craxi resigned Socialist Party leadership; replaced by Giorgio Benvenuto and then Ottaviano del Turro. Referendum supported ending the proportional-representation electoral system. Amato resigned premiership; Carlo Ciampi, with no party allegiance, named as his successor.

Ivory Coast

Republic of (*République de la Côte d'Ivoire*)
area 322,463 sq km/124,471 sq mi
capital Yamoussoukro
towns Bouaké, Daloa, Man; ports Abidjan, San-Pédro
physical tropical rainforest (diminishing as exploited) in S; savanna and low mountains in N
environment an estimated 85% of the country's forest has been destroyed by humans
features Vridi canal, Kossou dam, Monts du Toura
head of state and government Henri Konan Bedie from 1993
political system emergent democratic republic
political party Democratic Party of the Ivory Coast (PDCI), nationalist, free-enterprise

exports coffee, cocoa, fish, timber, petroleum products
currency franc CFA
population (1992) 12,951,000; growth rate 3.3% p.a.
life expectancy men 52, women 55 (1989)
languages French (official), over 60 native dialects
media the government has full control of the media
religions animist 65%, Muslim 24%, Christian 11%
literacy 35% (1988)
GDP $7.6 bn (1987); $687 per head

chronology
1904 Became part of French West Africa.
1958 Achieved internal self-government.
1960 Independence achieved from France, with Félix Houphouët-Boigny as president of a one-party state.
1985 Houphouët-Boigny re-elected, unopposed.
1986 Name changed officially from Ivory Coast to Côte d'Ivoire.
1990 Houphouët-Boigny and PDCI re-elected.
1993 President Houphouët-Boigny died and was succeeded by parliamentary speaker, Henri Konan Bedie.

Jamaica

area 10,957 sq km/4,230 sq mi
capital Kingston
towns Montego Bay, Spanish Town, St Andrew
physical mountainous tropical island
features Blue Mountains (so called because of the haze over them) renowned for their coffee; partly undersea ruins of pirate city of Port Royal, destroyed by an earthquake 1692

head of state Elizabeth II from 1962, represented by governor general
head of government P J Patterson from 1992
political system constitutional monarchy
political parties Jamaica Labour Party (JLP), moderate, centrist; People's National Party (PNP), left of centre
exports sugar, bananas, bauxite, rum, cocoa, coconuts, liqueurs, cigars, citrus
currency Jamaican dollar
population (1992) 2,445,000 (African 76%, mixed 15%, Chinese, Caucasian, East Indian); growth rate 2.2% p.a.
life expectancy men 75, women 78 (1989)
languages English, Jamaican creole
media one daily newspaper 1834–1988 (except 1973–82), privately owned; sensational evening and weekly papers
religions Protestant 55.9%, Rastafarian 5%
literacy 82% (1988)
GDP $2.9 bn; $1,187 per head (1989)

chronology
1494 Columbus reached Jamaica.
1509–1655 Occupied by Spanish.
1655 Captured by British.
1944 Internal self-government introduced.
1962 Independence achieved from Britain, with Alexander Bustamante of the JLP as prime minister.
1967 JLP re-elected under Hugh Shearer.
1972 Michael Manley of the PNP became prime minister.
1980 JLP elected, with Edward Seaga as prime minister.
1983 JLP re-elected, winning all 60 seats.
1988 Island badly damaged by Hurricane Gilbert.
1989 PNP won a decisive victory with Michael Manley returning as prime minister.
1992 Manley resigned, succeeded by P J Patterson.
1993 Landslide victory for PNP in general election.

Japan

(*Nippon*)

area 377,535 sq km/145,822 sq mi
capital Tokyo
towns Fukuoka, Kitakyushu, Kyoto, Sapporo; ports Osaka, Nagoya, Yokohama, Kobe, Kawasaki
physical mountainous, volcanic; comprises over 1,000 islands, the largest of which are Hokkaido, Honshu, Kyushu, and Shikoku
features Mount Fuji, Mount Aso (volcanic), Japan Alps, Inland Sea archipelago
head of state (figurehead) Emperor Akihito (Heisei) from 1989
head of government Morihiro Hosokawa from 1993
political system liberal democracy
political parties Liberal Democratic Party (LDP), right of centre; Social Democratic Party of Japan (SDJP), former Socialist Party, left of centre but moving towards centre; Komeito (Clean Government Party), Buddhist, centrist; Democratic Socialist Party, centrist; Japanese Communist Party (JCP), socialist; Nihon Shinto, centrist reformist; Shinsei, right-wing reformist
exports televisions, cassette and video recorders, radios, cameras, computers, robots, other electronic and electrical equipment, motor vehicles, ships, iron, steel, chemicals, textiles

currency yen
population (1992) 124,310,000; growth rate 0.5% p.a.
life expectancy men 76, women 82 (1989)
language Japanese
religions Shinto, Buddhist (often combined), Christian; 30% claim a personal religious faith
literacy 99% (1989)
GDP $3,674.5 bn (1992)

chronology
1867 End of shogun rule; executive power passed to emperor. Start of modernization of Japan.
1894–95 War with China; Formosa (Taiwan) and S Manchuria gained.
1902 Formed alliance with Britain.
1904–05 War with Russia; Russia ceded southern half of Sakhalin.
1910 Japan annexed Korea.
1914 Joined Allies in World War I.
1918 Received German Pacific islands as mandates.
1931–32 War with China; renewed 1937.
1941 Japan attacked US fleet at Pearl Harbor 7 Dec.
1945 World War II ended with Japanese surrender. Allied control commission took power. Formosa and Manchuria returned to China.
1946 Framing of 'peace constitution'. Emperor Hirohito became figurehead ruler.
1952 Full sovereignty regained.
1958 Joined United Nations.
1968 Bonin and Volcano Islands regained.
1972 Ryukyu Islands regained.
1974 Prime Minister Tanaka resigned over Lockheed bribes scandal.
1982 Yasuhiro Nakasone elected prime minister.
1985 Yen revalued.
1987 Noboru Takeshita chosen to succeed Nakasone.
1988 Recruit scandal cast shadow over government and opposition parties.
1989 Emperor Hirohito (Shōwa) died; succeeded by his son Akihito. Many cabinet ministers implicated in Recruit scandal and Takeshita resigned; succeeded by Sosuke Uno. Aug: Uno resigned after sex scandal; succeeded by Toshiki Kaifu.
1990 Feb: new house of councillors' elections won by LDP. Public-works budget increased by 50% to encourage imports.
1991 Japan contributed billions of dollars to the Gulf War and its aftermath. Kaifu succeeded by Kiichi Miyazawa.
1992 Over 100 politicians implicated in new financial

scandal. Emperor Akihito made first Japanese imperial visit to China. Trade surpluses reached record levels.
1993 Worst recession of postwar era; trade surpluses, however, again reached record levels. LDP 'godfather' Shin Kanemaru charged with tax evasion. Government lost no-confidence vote over electoral reform. Miyazawa resigned. Morihiro Hosokawa chosen as prime minister. New party (Shinsei) formed from LDP faction.

Jordan

Hashemite Kingdom of (*Al Mamlaka al Urduniya al Hashemiyah*)

area 89,206 sq km/34,434 sq mi (West Bank 5,879 sq km/2,269 sq mi)
capital Amman
towns Zarqa, Irbid, Aqaba (the only port)
physical desert plateau in E; rift valley separates E and W banks of the river Jordan
features lowest point on Earth below sea level in the Dead Sea (–396 m/–1,299 ft); archaeological sites at Jerash and Petra
head of state King Hussein ibn Talai from 1952
head of government Abdul-Salam-al-Mujali from 1993
political system constitutional monarchy
political parties none
exports potash, phosphates, citrus, vegetables
currency Jordanian dinar
population (1992) 3,636,000; growth rate 3.6% p.a.
life expectancy men 67, women 71
languages Arabic (official), English
religions Sunni Muslim 92%, Christian 8%
literacy 71% (1988)
GDP $4.3 bn (1987); $1,127 per head (1988)

chronology
1946 Independence achieved from Britain as Transjordan.
1949 New state of Jordan declared.
1950 Jordan annexed West Bank.
1953 Hussein ibn Talai officially became king of Jordan.
1958 Jordan and Iraq formed Arab Federation that ended when the Iraqi monarchy was deposed.
1967 Israel captured and occupied West Bank. Martial law imposed.
1976 Lower house dissolved, political parties banned, elections postponed until further notice.

1982 Hussein tried to mediate in Arab-Israeli conflict.
1984 Women voted for the first time.
1985 Hussein and Yassir Arafat put forward framework for Middle East peace settlement. Secret meeting between Hussein and Israeli prime minister.
1988 Hussein announced decision to cease administering the West Bank as part of Jordan, passing responsibility to Palestine Liberation Organization, and the suspension of parliament.
1989 Prime Minister Zaid al-Rifai resigned; Hussein promised new parliamentary elections following criticism of economic policies. Riots over price increases up to 50% following fall in oil revenues. First parliamentary elections for 22 years; Muslim Brotherhood won 25 of 80 seats but exiled from government; martial law lifted.
1990 Hussein unsuccessfully tried to mediate after Iraq's invasion of Kuwait. Massive refugee problems as thousands fled to Jordan from Kuwait and Iraq.
1991 24 years of martial law ended; ban on political parties lifted.
1993 King Hussein publicly distanced himself from Iraqi leader Saddam Hussein. Abdul-Salam-al-Mujali appointed as new prime minister. Peace accord with Israel.

Kazakhstan

Republic of

area 2,717,300 sq km/1,049,150 sq mi
capital Alma-Ata
towns Karaganda, Semipalatinsk, Petropavlovsk
physical Caspian and Aral seas, Lake Balkhash; Steppe region
features Baikonur Cosmodrome (space launch site at Tyuratam, near Baikonur)
head of state Nursultan Nazarbayev from 1990
head of government Sergey Tereshchenko from 1991
political system emergent democracy
political parties Independent Socialist Party of Kazakhstan (SPK)
products grain, copper, lead, zinc, manganese, coal, oil
population (1992) 17,008,000 (Kazakh 40%, Russian 38%, German 6%, Ukrainian 5%)

languages Russian; Kazakh, related to Turkish
religion Sunni Muslim

chronology
1920 Autonomous republic in USSR.
1936 Joined the USSR and became a full union republic.
1950s Site of Nikita Khrushchev's ambitious 'Virgin Lands' agricultural extension programme.
1960s A large influx of Russian settlers turned the Kazakhs into a minority in their own republic.
1986 Riots in Alma-Alta after Gorbachev ousted local communist leader.
1989 Nursultan Nazarbayev became leader of the Kazakh Communist Party (KCP) and instituted economic and cultural reform programmes.
1990 Nazarbayev became head of state.
1991 March: support pledged for continued union with USSR; Aug: Nazarbayev condemned attempted anti-Gorbachev coup; KCP abolished and replaced by Independent Socialist Party of Kazakhstan. Dec: joined new Commonwealth of Independent States; independence recognized by USA.
1992 Admitted into United Nations and Conference on Security and Cooperation in Europe. Trade agreement with USA.
1993 New constitution adopted, increasing the authority of the president and making Kazakh the state language.

Kenya

Republic of (*Jamhuri ya Kenya*)

area 582,600 sq km/224,884 sq mi
capital Nairobi
towns Kisumu, port Mombasa
physical mountains and highlands in W and centre; coastal plain in S; arid interior and tropical coast
environment the elephant faces extinction as a result of poaching
features Great Rift Valley, Mount Kenya, Lake Nakuru (salt lake with world's largest colony of flamingos), Lake Turkana (Rudolf), national parks with wildlife, Malindini Marine Reserve, Olduvai Gorge
head of state and government Daniel arap Moi from 1978
political system authoritarian nationalism
political parties Kenya African National Union (KANU), nationalist, centrist; National Democratic Party (NDP), centrist (launched 1991, not accepted by government)

exports coffee, tea, fruits and vegetables, petroleum products
currency Kenya shilling
population (1992) 26,985,000 (Kikuyu 21%, Luo 13%, Luhya 14%, Kelenjin 11%; Asian, Arab, European); growth rate 4.2% p.a.
life expectancy men 59, women 63 (1989)
languages Kiswahili (official), English; there are many local dialects
religions Protestant 38%, Roman Catholic 28%, indigenous beliefs 26%, Muslim 6%
literacy 50% (1988)
GDP $6.9 bn (1987); $302 per head (1988)

chronology
1895 British East African protectorate established.
1920 Kenya became a British colony.
1944 African participation in politics began.
1950 Mau Mau campaign began.
1953 Nationalist leader Jomo Kenyatta imprisoned by British authorities.
1956 Mau Mau campaign defeated, Kenyatta released.
1963 Achieved internal self-government, with Kenyatta as prime minister.
1964 Independence achieved from Britain as a republic within the Commonwealth, with Kenyatta as president.
1967 East African Community (EAC) formed with Tanzania and Uganda.
1977 Collapse of EAC.
1978 Death of Kenyatta. Succeeded by Daniel arap Moi.
1982 Attempted coup against Moi foiled.
1983 Moi re-elected unopposed.
1984 Over 2,000 people massacred by government forces at Wajir.
1985-86 Thousands of forest villagers evicted and their homes destroyed to make way for cash crops.
1988 Moi re-elected. 150,000 evicted from state-owned forests.
1989 Moi announced release of all known political prisoners. Confiscated ivory burned in attempt to stop elephant poaching.
1990 Despite antigovernment riots, Moi refused multiparty politics.
1991 Increasing demands for political reform; Moi promised multiparty politics.
1992 Constitutional amendment passed. Dec: Moi re-elected in first direct elections despite allegations of fraud.

Kiribati

Republic of

area 717 sq km/277 sq mi
capital (and port) Bairiki (on Tarawa Atoll)
physical comprises 33 Pacific coral islands: the Kiribati (Gilbert), Rawaki (Phoenix), Banaba (Ocean Island), and three of the Line Islands including Kiritimati (Christmas Island)
environment the islands are threatened by the possibility of a rise in sea level caused by global warming. A rise of approximately 30 cm/1 ft by the year 2040 will make existing fresh water brackish and undrinkable
features island groups crossed by equator and International Date Line

head of state and government Teatao Teannaki from 1991
political system liberal democracy
political parties National Progressive Party, governing faction; opposition parties: Christian Democratic Party and the Kiribati United Party
exports copra, fish
currency Australian dollar
population (1992) 74,700; growth rate 1.7% p.a.
languages English (official), Gilbertese
religions Roman Catholic 48%, Protestant 45%
literacy 90% (1985)
GDP $26 million (1987); $430 per head (1988)

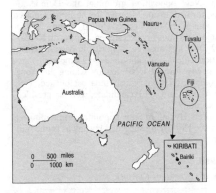

chronology
1892 Gilbert and Ellice Islands proclaimed a British protectorate.
1937 Phoenix Islands added to colony.
1950s UK tested nuclear weapons on Kiritimati (formerly Christmas Island).
1962 USA tested nuclear weapons on Kiritimati.
1975 Ellice Islands separated to become Tuvalu.
1977 Gilbert Islands granted internal self-goverment.
1979 Independence achieved from Britain, within the Commonwealth, as the Republic of Kiribati, with Ieremia Tabai as president.
1982 and 1983 Tabai re-elected.
1985 Fishing agreement with Soviet state-owned company negotiated, prompting formation of Kiribati's first political party, the opposition Christian Democrats.
1987 Tabai re-elected.
1991 Tabai re-elected but not allowed under constitution to serve further term; Teatao Teannaki elected president.

Korea, North

Democratic People's Republic of (*Chosun Minchuchui Inmin Konghwa-guk*)

area 120,538 sq km/46,528 sq mi
capital Pyongyang
towns Chongjin, Nampo, Wonsan
physical wide coastal plain in W rising to mountains cut by deep valleys in interior
environment the building of a hydroelectric dam at Kumgangsan on a tributary of the Han River has been opposed by South Korea as a potential flooding threat to central Korea
features separated from South Korea by a military demarcation line; the richer of the two Koreas in

mineral resources (copper, iron ore, graphite, tungsten, zinc, lead, magnesite, gold, phosphor, phosphates)
head of state Kim Jong Il from 1994
head of government Hong Song Nam from 1997
political system communism
political parties Korean Workers' Party (KWP), Marxist-Leninist-Kim Il Sungist (leads Democratic Front for the Reunification of the Fatherland, including North Korean Democratic Party and Religious Chungwoo Party)
exports coal, iron, copper, textiles, clothing, chemicals
currency won
population (1992) 22,227,000; growth rate 2.5% p.a.
life expectancy men 67, women 73 (1989)
language Korean
religions traditionally Buddhist, Confucian, but religious activity curtailed by the state
literacy 99% (1989)
GNP $20 bn; $3,450 per head (1988)

chronology
1910 Korea formally annexed by Japan.
1945 Russian and US troops entered Korea, forced surrender of Japanese, and divided the country in two. Soviet troops occupied North Korea.
1948 Democratic People's Republic of Korea declared.
1950 North Korea invaded South Korea to unite the nation, beginning the Korean War.
1953 Armistice agreed to end Korean War.
1961 Friendship and mutual assistance treaty signed with China.
1972 New constitution, with executive president, adopted. Talks took place with South Korea about possible reunification.
1980 Reunification talks broke down.
1983 Four South Korean cabinet ministers assassinated in Rangoon, Burma (Myanmar), by North Korean army officers.
1985 Increased relations with the USSR.
1989 Increasing evidence shown of nuclear-weapons development.
1990 Diplomatic contacts with South Korea and Japan suggested the beginning of a thaw in North Korea's relations with the rest of the world.
1991 Became a member of the United Nations. Signed nonaggression agreement with South Korea; agreed to ban nuclear weapons.
1992 Signed Nuclear Safeguards Agreement, allowing international inspection of its nuclear facilities.

Also signed a pact with South Korea for mutual inspection of nuclear facilities. Passed legislation making foreign investment in the country attractive. Yon Hyong Muk replaced by Kang Song San.
1993 Threatened to withdraw from Nuclear Non-Proliferation Treaty.

Korea, South

Republic of Korea (*Daehan Minguk*)

area 98,799 sq km/38,161 sq mi
capital Seoul
towns Taegu, ports Pusan, Inchon
physical southern end of a mountainous peninsula separating the Sea of Japan from the Yellow Sea
features Chomsongdae (world's earliest observatory); giant Popchusa Buddha; granite peaks of Soraksan National Park
head of state Kim Young Sam from 1992
head of government Lee Hoi Chang from 1993
political system emergent democracy
political parties Democratic Liberal Party (DLP), right of centre; Democratic Party, left of centre; Unification National Party (UNP), right of centre
exports steel, ships, chemicals, electronics, textiles and clothing, plywood, fish
currency won
population (1992) 43,663,000; growth rate 1.4% p.a.
life expectancy men 66, women 73 (1989)
language Korean
media freedom of the press achieved 1987; large numbers of newspapers with large circulations. It is prohibited to say anything favourable about North Korea
religions traditionally Buddhist, Confucian, and Chondokyo; Christian 28%
literacy 92% (1989)
GNP $171bn (1988); $2,180 per head (1986)
chronology
1910 Korea formally annexed by Japan.
1945 Russian and US troops entered Korea, forced surrender of Japanese, and divided the country in two. US military government took control of South Korea.
1948 Republic proclaimed.
1950-53 War with North Korea.
1960 President Syngman Rhee resigned amid unrest.
1961 Military coup by General Park Chung-Hee. Industrial growth programme.
1979 Assassination of President Park.
1980 Military takeover by General Chun Doo Hwan.

1987 Adoption of more democratic constitution after student unrest. Roh Tae Woo elected president.
1988 Former president Chun, accused of corruption, publicly apologized and agreed to hand over his financial assets to the state. Seoul hosted Summer Olympic Games.
1989 Roh reshuffled cabinet, threatened crackdown on protesters.
1990 Two minor opposition parties united with Democratic Justice Party to form ruling Democratic Liberal Party. Diplomatic relations established with the USSR.
1991 Violent mass demonstrations against the government. New opposition grouping, the Democratic Party, formed. Prime Minister Ro Jai Bong replaced by Chung Won Shik. Entered United Nations. Nonaggression and nuclear pacts signed with North Korea.
1992 DLP lost absolute majority in March general election; substantial gains made by Democratic Party and newly formed UNP, led by Chung Ju Wong. Diplomatic relations with China established. Dec: Kim Young Sam, DLP candidate, won the presidential election.
1993 Feb: Hwang In Sung appointed prime minister. Dec: Lee Hoi Chang succeeded Hwang as prime minister.

Kuwait

State of (*Dowlat al Kuwait*)

area 17,819 sq km/6,878 sq mi
capital Kuwait (also chief port)
towns Jahra, Ahmadi, Fahaheel
physical hot desert; islands of Failaka, Bubiyan, and Warba at NE corner of Arabian Peninsula
environment during the Gulf War 1990–91, 650 oil wells were set alight and about 300,000 tonnes of oil were released into the waters of the Gulf leading to pollution haze, photochemical smog, acid rain, soil contamination, and water pollution
features there are no rivers and rain is light; the world's largest desalination plants, built in the 1950s
head of state and government Jabir al-Ahmad al-Jabir al-Sabah from 1977
political system absolute monarchy
political parties none
exports oil
currency Kuwaiti dinar
population (1992) 1,190,000 (Kuwaitis 40%, Palestinians 30%); growth rate 5.5% p.a.

life expectancy men 72, women 76 (1989)
languages Arabic 78%, Kurdish 10%, Farsi 4%
religion Sunni Muslim 45%, Shi'ite minority 30%
literacy 71% (1988)
GNP $19.1 bn; $10,410 per head (1988)

chronology
1914 Britain recognized Kuwait as an independent sovereign state.
1961 Full independence achieved from Britain, with Sheik Abdullah al-Salem al-Sabah as emir.
1965 Sheik Abdullah died; succeeded by his brother, Sheik Sabah.
1977 Sheik Sabah died; succeeded by Crown Prince Jabir.
1983 Shi'ite guerrillas bombed targets in Kuwait; 17 arrested.
1986 National assembly suspended.
1987 Kuwaiti oil tankers reflagged, received US Navy protection; missile attacks by Iran.
1988 Aircraft hijacked by pro-Iranian Shi'ites demanding release of convicted guerrillas; Kuwait refused.
1989 Two of the convicted guerrillas released.
1990 Prodemocracy demonstrations suppressed. Aug: Kuwait annexed by Iraq. Emir set up government in exile in Saudi Arabia.
1991 Feb: Kuwait liberated by US-led coalition forces; extensive damage to property and environment. New government omitted any opposition representatives. Trials of alleged Iraqi collaborators criticized.
1992 Reconstituted national assembly elected on restricted franchise, with opposition party winning majority of seats.
1993 Jan: incursions by Iraq into Kuwait again created tension; US-led air strikes reassured Kuwaitis.

Kyrgyzstan
Republic of

area 198,500 sq km/76,641 sq mi
capital Bishkek (formerly Frunze)
towns Osh, Przhevalsk, Kyzyl-Kiya, Tormak
physical mountainous, an extension of the Tian Shan range
head of state Askar Akayev from 1990
head of government Tursunbek Chyngyshev from 1991

political system emergent democracy
political parties Democratic Kyrgyzstan, nationalist reformist; Asaba (Banner) Party and Free Kyrgyzstan Party, both opposition groupings; Social Democratic Party, nationalist
products cereals, sugar, cotton, coal, oil, sheep, yaks, horses
population (1992) 4,533,000 (Kyrgyz 52%, Russian 22%, Uzbek 13%, Ukrainian 3%, German 2%)
language Kyrgyz, a Turkic language
religion Sunni Muslim

chronology
1917–1924 Part of an independent Turkestan republic.
1924 Became autonomous republic within USSR.
1936 Became full union republic within USSR.
1990 June: ethnic clashes resulted in state of emergency being imposed in Bishkek. Nov: Askar Akayev, founder of Democratic movement, chosen as state president.
1991 March: Kyrgyz voters endorsed maintenance of Union in USSR referendum. Aug: President Akayev condemned anti-Gorbachev attempted coup in Moscow; Kyrgyz Communist Party, which supported the coup, suspended. Oct: Akayev directly elected president. Dec: joined new Commonwealth of Independent States and independence recognized by USA.
1992 Joined the United Nations and Conference on Security and Cooperation in Europe. Supreme Soviet (parliament) renamed the Uluk Kenesh.
1993 Formation of Social Democratic Party, supporting President Akayev.

Laos
Lao People's Democratic Republic (*Saathiaranagroat Prachhathippatay Prachhachhon Lao*)

area 236,790 sq km/91,400 sq mi
capital Vientiane
towns Luang Prabang (the former royal capital), Pakse, Savannakhet
physical landlocked state with high mountains in E; Mekong River in W; jungle covers nearly 60% of land
features Plain of Jars, where prehistoric people carved stone jars large enough to hold a person
head of state Nouhak Phoumsavan from 1992

head of government General Khamtay Siphandon from 1991
political system communism, one-party state
political party Lao People's Revolutionary Party (LPRP) (only legal party)
exports hydroelectric power from the Mekong is exported to Thailand; timber, teak, coffee, electricity
currency new kip
population (1992) 4,409,000 (Lao 48%, Thai 14%, Khmer 25%, Chinese 13%); growth rate 2.2% p.a.
life expectancy men 48, women 51 (1989)
languages Lao (official), French
religions Theravāda Buddhist 85%, animist beliefs among mountain dwellers
literacy 45% (1991)
GNP $500 million (1987); $180 per head (1988)

chronology
1893–1945 Laos was a French protectorate.
1945 Temporarily occupied by Japan.
1946 Retaken by France.
1950 Granted semi-autonomy in French Union.
1954 Independence achieved from France.
1960 Right-wing government seized power.
1962 Coalition government established; civil war continued.
1973 Vientiane cease-fire agreement. Withdrawal of US, Thai, and North Vietnamese forces.
1975 Communist-dominated republic proclaimed with Prince Souphanouvong as head of state.
1986 Phoumi Vongvichit became acting president.
1988 Plans announced to withdraw 40% of Vietnamese forces stationed in the country.
1989 First assembly elections since communist takeover.
1991 Constitution approved. Kaysone Phomvihane elected president. General Khamtay Siphandon named as new premier.
1992 Nov: Phomvihane died; replaced by Nouhak Phoumsavan. Dec: new national assembly created, replacing supreme people's assembly, and general election held (effectively one-party).

Latvia

Republic of

area 63,700 sq km/24,595 sq mi
capital Riga
towns Daugavpils, Liepāja, Jurmala, Jelgava, Ventspils
physical wooded lowland (highest point 312 m/1,024 ft), marshes, lakes; 472 km/293 mi of coastline; mild climate
features Western Dvina River; Riga is largest port on the Baltic after Leningrad
head of state Anatolijs Gorbunov from 1988
head of government Ivars Godmanis from 1990
political system emergent democratic republic
political parties Latvian Popular Front, nationalist; Latvian Social-Democratic Workers' Party; Latvian Way, moderate, nationalist
products electronic and communications equipment, electric railway carriages, motorcycles, consumer durables, timber, paper and woollen goods, meat and dairy products
currency Latvian rouble
population (1992) 2,685,000 (Latvian 52%, Russian 34%, Byelorussian 5%, Ukrainian 3%)

language Latvian
religions mostly Lutheran Protestant, with a Roman Catholic minority

chronology
1917 Soviets and Germans contested for control of Latvia.
1918 Feb: Soviet forces overthrown by Germany. Nov: Latvia declared independence. Dec: Soviet rule restored after German withdrawal.
1919 Soviet rule overthrown by British naval and German forces May–Dec; democracy established.
1934 Coup replaced established government.
1939 German-Soviet secret agreement placed Latvia under Russian influence.
1940 Incorporated into USSR as constituent republic.
1941–44 Occupied by Germany.
1944 USSR regained control.
1980 Nationalist dissent began to grow.
1988 Latvian Popular Front established to campaign for independence. Prewar flag readopted; official status given to Latvian language.
1989 Popular Front swept local elections.
1990 Jan: Communist Party's (CP) monopoly of power abolished. March–April: Popular Front secured majority in elections. April: Latvian CP split into pro-independence and pro-Moscow wings. May: unilateral declaration of independence from USSR, subject to transitional period for negotiation.
1991 Jan: Soviet troops briefly seized key installations in Riga. March: overwhelming vote for independence in referendum. Aug: full independence declared at time of anti-Gorbachev coup; CP outlawed. Sept: independence recognized by Soviet government and Western nations; joined United Nations (UN) and Conference on Security and Cooperation in Europe.
1992 Russia began pull-out of ex-Soviet troops, to be completed 1994. July: curbing of rights of noncitizens in Latvia prompted Russia to request minority protection by UN.
1993 Latvian Way, led by former CP ideological secretary Anatolijs Gorbunov, won most seats in general election.

Lebanon

Republic of (*al-Jumhouria al-Lubnaniya*)

area 10,452 sq km/4,034 sq mi
capital and port Beirut
towns ports Tripoli, Tyre, Sidon

physical narrow coastal plain; Bekka valley N–S between Lebanon and Anti-Lebanon mountain ranges
features Mount Hermon; Chouf Mountains; archaeological sites at Baalbeck, Byblos, Tyre; until the civil war, the financial centre of the Middle East
head of state Elias Hrawi from 1989
head of government Rafik al-Hariri from 1992
political system emergent democratic republic
political parties Phalangist Party, Christian, radical, right-wing; Progressive Socialist Party (PSP), Druse, moderate, socialist; National Liberal Party (NLP), Maronite, centre-left; Parliamentary Democratic Front, Sunni Muslim, centrist; Lebanese Communist Party (PCL), nationalist, communist
exports citrus and other fruit, vegetables; industrial products; jewellery; clothing; metal products
currency Lebanese pound
population (1992) 2,803,000 (Lebanese 82%, Palestinian 9%, Armenian 5%); growth rate –0.1% p.a.
life expectancy men 65, women 70 (1989)
languages Arabic, French (both official), Armenian, English
religions Muslim 57% (Shiite 33%, Sunni 24%), Christian (Maronite and Orthodox) 40%, Druse 3%
literacy 75% (1989)
GNP $1.8 bn; $690 per head (1986)

chronology
1920–41 Administered under French mandate.
1944 Independence achieved.
1948–49 Lebanon joined first Arab war against Israel. Palestinian refugees settled in the south.
1964 Palestine Liberation Organization (PLO) founded in Beirut.
1967 More Palestinian refugees settled in Lebanon.
1971 PLO expelled from Jordan; established headquarters in Lebanon.
1975 Outbreak of civil war between Christians and Muslims.
1976 Cease-fire agreed; Syrian-dominated Arab deterrent force formed to keep the peace but considered by Christians as a occupying force.
1978 Israel invaded S Lebanon in search of PLO fighters. International peacekeeping force established. Fighting broke out again.
1979 Part of S Lebanon declared an 'independent free Lebanon'.
1982 Bachir Gemayel became president but was assassinated before he could assume office; suc-

ceeded by his brother Amin Gemayel. Israel again invaded Lebanon. Palestinians withdrew from Beirut under supervision of international peacekeeping force. PLO moved its headquarters to Tunis.
1983 Agreement reached for the withdrawal of Syrian and Israeli troops but abrogated under Syrian pressure.
1984 Most of international peacekeeping force withdrawn. Muslim militia took control of W Beirut.
1985 Lebanon in chaos; many foreigners taken hostage.
1987 Syrian troops sent into Beirut.
1988 Agreement on a Christian successor to Gemayel failed; he established a military government; Selim al-Hoss set up rival government; threat of partition hung over the country.
1989 Christian leader General Michel Aoun declared 'war of liberation' against Syrian occupation; Saudi Arabia and Arab League sponsored talks that resulted in new constitution recognizing Muslim majority; René Muhawad named president, assassinated after 17 days in office; Elias Hrawi named successor; Aoun occupied presidential palace, rejected constitution.
1990 Release of Western hostages began. General Aoun surrendered and legitimate government restored, with Umar Karami as prime minister.
1991 Government extended control to the whole country. Treaty of cooperation with Syria signed. More Western hostages released. General Aoun pardoned.
1992 Karami resigned as prime minister; succeeded by Rashid al-Solh. Remaining Western hostages released. General election boycotted by many Christians; pro-Syrian administration re-elected; Rafik al-Hariri became prime minister.
1993 July: Israel launched attacks on S Lebanon against Hezbollah strongholds

Lesotho
Kingdom of

area 30,355 sq km/11,717 sq mi
capital Maseru
towns Teyateyaneng, Mafeteng, Roma, Quthing
physical mountainous with plateaus, forming part of South Africa's chief watershed
features Lesotho is an enclave within South Africa
political system constitutional monarchy
head of state King Letsie III from 1990

head of government Ntsu Mokhehle from 1993
political parties Basotho National Party (BNP), traditionalist, nationalist; Basutoland Congress Party (BCP); Basotho Democratic Alliance (BDA)
exports wool, mohair, diamonds, cattle, wheat, vegetables
currency maluti
population (1992) 1,854,000; growth rate 2.7% p.a.
life expectancy men 59, women 62 (1989)
languages Sesotho, English (official), Zulu, Xhosa
religions Protestant 42%, Roman Catholic 38%
literacy 59% (1988)
GNP $408 million; $410 per head (1988)

chronology
1868 Basutoland became a British protectorate.
1966 Independence achieved from Britain, within the Commonwealth, as the Kingdom of Lesotho, with Moshoeshoe II as king and Chief Leabua Jonathan as prime minister.
1970 State of emergency declared and constitution suspended.
1973 Progovernment interim assembly established; BNP won majority of seats.
1975 Members of the ruling party attacked by guerrillas backed by South Africa.
1985 Elections cancelled because no candidates opposed BNP.
1986 South Africa imposed border blockade, forcing deportation of 60 African National Congress members. General Lekhanya ousted Chief Jonathan in coup. National assembly abolished. Highlands Water Project agreement signed with South Africa.
1990 Moshoeshoe II dethroned by military council; replaced by his son Mohato as King Letsie III.
1991 Lekhanya ousted in military coup led by Col Elias Tutsoane Ramaema. Political parties permitted to operate.
1992 Ex-king Moshoeshoe returned from exile.
1993 Free elections ended military rule; Ntsu Mokhehle of BCP became prime minister.

Liberia

Republic of

area 111,370 sq km/42,989 sq mi
capital and port Monrovia
towns ports Buchanan, Greenville
physical forested highlands; swampy tropical coast where six rivers enter the sea
features nominally the world's largest merchant navy as minimal registration controls make Liberia's a flag of convenience; the world's largest rubber plantations
head of state and government Bismark Kuyon heading collective presidency from 1993
political system emergent democratic republic
political parties National Democratic Party of Liberia (NDLP), nationalist; Liberian Action Party (LAP); Liberian Unity Party (LUP); United People's Party (UPP); Unity Party (UP)
exports iron ore, rubber (Africa's largest producer), timber, diamonds, coffee, cocoa, palm oil
currency Liberian dollar
population (1992) 2,780,000; growth rate 3% p.a.
life expectancy men 53, women 56 (1989)
languages English (official), over 20 Niger-Congo languages

media two daily newspapers, one published under government auspices, the other independent and with the largest circulation (10,000 copies)
religions animist 65%, Muslim 20%, Christian 15%
literacy men 47%, women 23% (1985 est)
GNP $973 million; $450 per head (1988)

chronology
1847 Founded as an independent republic.
1944 William Tubman elected president.
1971 Tubman died; succeeded by William Tolbert.
1980 Tolbert assassinated in coup led by Samuel Doe, who suspended the constitution and ruled through a People's Redemption Council.
1984 New constitution approved. National Democratic Party of Liberia (NDPL) founded by Doe.
1985 NDPL won decisive victory in allegedly rigged general election. Unsuccessful coup against Doe.
1990 Rebels under former government minister Charles Taylor controlled nearly entire country by July. Doe killed during a bloody civil war between rival rebel factions. Amos Sawyer became interim head of government.
1991 Amos Sawyer re-elected president. Rebel leader Charles Taylor agreed to work with Sawyer. Peace agreement failed but later revived; UN peacekeeping force drafted into republic.
1992 Monrovia under siege by Taylor's rebel forces.
1993 Peace agreement between opposing groups signed in Benin, under OAU/UN auspices. Interim collective presidency established prior to elections in 1994.

Libya

Great Socialist People's Libyan Arab Jamahiriya (*al-Jamahiriya al-Arabiya al-Libya al-Shabiya al-Ishtirakiya al-Uzma*)

area 1,759,540 sq km/679,182 sq mi
capital Tripoli
towns ports Benghazi, Misurata, Tobruk
physical flat to undulating plains with plateaus and depressions stretch S from the Mediterranean coast to an extremely dry desert interior
environment plan to pump water from below the Sahara to the coast risks rapid exhaustion of nonrenewable supply (Great Manmade River Project)
features Gulf of Sirte; rock paintings of about 3000 BC in the Fezzan; Roman city sites include Leptis Magna, Sabratha
head of state and government Moamer al-Khaddhafi from 1969

political system one-party socialist state
political party Arab Socialist Union (ASU), radical, left-wing
exports oil, natural gas
currency Libyan dinar
population (1992) 4,447,000 (including 500,000 foreign workers); growth rate 3.1% p.a.
life expectancy men 64, women 69 (1989)
language Arabic
religion Sunni Muslim 97%
literacy 60% (1989)
GNP $20 bn; $5,410 per head (1988)

chronology
1911 Conquered by Italy.
1934 Colony named Libya.
1942 Divided into three provinces: Fezzan (under French control); Cyrenaica, Tripolitania (under British control).
1951 Achieved independence as the United Kingdom of Libya, under King Idris.
1969 King deposed in a coup led by Col Moamer al-Khaddhafi. Revolution Command Council set up and the Arab Socialist Union (ASU) proclaimed the only legal party.
1972 Proposed federation of Libya, Syria, and Egypt abandoned.
1980 Proposed merger with Syria abandoned. Libyan troops began fighting in Chad.
1981 Proposed merger with Chad abandoned.
1986 US bombing of Khaddhafi's headquarters, following allegations of his complicity in terrorist activities.
1988 Diplomatic relations with Chad restored.
1989 USA accused Libya of building a chemical-weapons factory and shot down two Libyan planes; reconciliation with Egypt.
1992 Khaddhafi under international pressure to extradite suspected Lockerbie and UTA (Union de Transports Aerians) bombers for trial outside Libya; sanctions imposed.

Liechtenstein

Principality of (*Fürstentum Liechtenstein*)

area 160 sq km/62 sq mi
capital Vaduz
towns Balzers, Schaan, Ruggell
physical landlocked Alpine; includes part of Rhine Valley in W

features no airport or railway station; easy tax laws make it an international haven for foreign companies and banks (some 50,000 companies are registered)
head of state Prince Hans Adam II from 1989
head of government Mario Frick from 1993
political system constitutional monarchy
political parties Fatherland Union (VU); Progressive Citizens' Party (FBP)
exports microchips, dental products, small machinery, processed foods, postage stamps
currency Swiss franc
population (1992) 29,600 (33% foreign); growth rate 1.4% p.a.
life expectancy men 78, women 83 (1989)
language German (official); an Alemannic dialect is also spoken
religions Roman Catholic 87%, Protestant 8%
literacy 100% (1989)
GNP $450 million (1986)
GDP $1 bn (1987); $32,000 per head

chronology
1342 Became a sovereign state.
1434 Present boundaries established.
1719 Former counties of Schellenberg and Vaduz constituted as the Principality of Liechtenstein.
1921 Adopted Swiss currency.
1923 United with Switzerland in a customs union.
1938 Prince Franz Josef II came to power.
1984 Prince Franz Joseph II handed over power to Crown Prince Hans Adam. Vote extended to women in national elections.
1989 Prince Franz Joseph II died; Hans Adam II succeeded him.
1990 Became a member of the United Nations (UN).
1991 Became seventh member of European Free Trade Association.
1993 Mario Frick became head of government at 28, the youngest in Europe.

Lithuania

Republic of

area 65,200 sq km/25,174 sq mi
capital Vilnius
towns Kaunas, Klaipeda, Siauliai, Panevezys
physical central lowlands with gentle hills in W and higher terrain in SE; 25% forested; some 3,000

small lakes, marshes, and complex sandy coastline
features river Nemen; white sand dunes on Kursiu Marios lagoon
head of state Algirdas Brazauskas from 1993
head of government Adolfas Slezevicius from 1993
political system emergent democracy
political parties Sajudis (Lithuanian Restructuring Movement), nationalist; Democratic Party, centrist; Humanism and Progress Party, reformist; Social Democratic Party, left of centre; Green Party, ecological; Christian Democratic Party, right of centre; Democratic Labour Party, 'reform communist'
products heavy engineering, electrical goods, shipbuilding, cement, food processing, bacon, dairy products, cereals, potatoes
currency Lithuanian rouble
population (1992) 3,802,000 (Lithuanian 80%, Russian 9%, Polish 7%, Byelorussian 2%)
language Lithuanian
religion predominantly Roman Catholic

chronology
1918 Independence declared following withdrawal of German occupying troops at end of World War I; USSR attempted to regain power.
1919 Soviet forces overthrown by Germans, Poles, and nationalist Lithuanians; democratic republic established.
1920–39 Province and city of Vilnius occupied by Poles.
1926 Coup overthrew established government; Antanas Smetona became president.
1939 Secret German-Soviet agreement brought most of Lithuania under Soviet influence.
1940 Incorporated into USSR as constituent republic.
1941 Lithuania revolted against USSR and established own government. During World War II Germany again occupied the country.
1944 USSR resumed rule.
1944–52 Lithuanian guerrillas fought USSR.
1972 Demonstrations against Soviet government.
1980 Growth in nationalist dissent, influenced by Polish example.
1988 Popular front formed, the Sajudis, to campaign for increased autonomy.
1989 Lithuanian declared the state language; flag of independent interwar republic readopted. Communist Party (CP) split into pro-Moscow and nationalist wings. Communist local monopoly of power abolished.

1990 Feb: nationalist Sajudis won elections. March: Vytautas Landsbergis became president; unilateral declaration of independence resulted in temporary Soviet blockade.
1991 Jan: Albertas Shiminas became prime minister. Soviet paratroopers briefly occupied key buildings in Vilnius. Sept: independence recognized by Soviet government and Western nations; Gediminas Vagnorius elected prime minister; CP outlawed; admitted into United Nations (UN) and Conference on Security and Cooperation in Europe (CSCE).
1992 July: Aleksandras Abisala became prime minister. Nov: DLP, led by Algirdas Brazauskas, won majority vote. Dec: Bronislovas Lubys appointed prime minister.
1993 Brazauskas elected president; Adolfas Slezevicius appointed prime minister.

Luxembourg

Grand Duchy of (*Grand-Duché de Luxembourg*)

area 2,586 sq km/998 sq mi
capital Luxembourg
towns Esch-sur-Alzette, Dudelange
physical on the river Moselle; part of the Ardennes (Oesling) forest in N
features seat of the European Court of Justice, Secretariat of the European Parliament, international banking centre; economically linked with Belgium
head of state Grand Duke Jean from 1964
head of government Jacques Santer from 1984
political system liberal democracy
political parties Christian Social Party (PCS), moderate, left of centre; Luxembourg Socialist Workers' Party (POSL), moderate, socialist; Democratic Party (PD), centre-left; Communist Party of Luxembourg, pro-European left-wing
exports pharmaceuticals, synthetic textiles, steel
currency Luxembourg franc
population (1992) 387,000; growth rate 0% p.a.
life expectancy men 71, women 78 (1989)
languages French (official), local Letzeburgesch, German
religion Roman Catholic 97%
literacy 100% (1989)
GNP $10.4 bn (1992)

chronology
1354 Became a duchy.

1482 Under Habsburg control.
1797 Ceded, with Belgium, to France.
1815 Treaty of Vienna created Luxembourg a grand duchy, ruled by the king of the Netherlands.
1830 With Belgium, revolted against Dutch rule.
1890 Link with Netherlands ended with accession of Grand Duke Adolphe of Nassau-Weilburg.
1948 With Belgium and the Netherlands, formed the Benelux customs union.
1960 Benelux became fully effective economic union.
1961 Prince Jean became acting head of state on behalf of his mother, Grand Duchess Charlotte.
1964 Grand Duchess Charlotte abdicated; Prince Jean became grand duke.
1974 Dominance of Christian Social Party challenged by Socialists.
1979 Christian Social Party regained pre-eminence.
1991 Pact agreeing European free-trade area signed in Luxembourg.
1992 Voted in favour of ratification of Maastricht Treaty on European union.

Macedonia

Former Yugoslav Republic of

area 25,700 sq km/9,920 sq mi
capital Skopje
physical mountainous; rivers: Struma, Vardar; Mediterranean climate with hot summers
head of state Kiro Gligorov from 1990
head of government Branko Crvenkovski from 1992
political system emergent democracy
political parties Internal Macedonian Revolutionary Organization–Democratic Party for Macedonian National Unity (VMRO–DMPNE), centrist; League of Communists, left-wing
population (1990) 1,920,000
language Macedonian, closely allied to Bulgarian and written in Cyrillic
religion Macedonian Orthodox Christian

chronology
1913 Ancient country of Macedonia divided between Serbia, Bulgaria, and Greece.
1918 Serbian part included in what was to become Yugoslavia.
1941–44 Occupied by Bulgaria.

1945 Created a republic within Yugoslav Socialist Federation.
1980 Rise of nationalism after death of Yugoslav leader Tito.
1990 Multiparty election produced inconclusive result.
1991 'Socialist' dropped from republic's name. Referendum supported independence.
1992 Independence declared, but international recognition withheld because of objections to name by Greece.
1993 Sovereignty recognized by UK and Albania; won United Nations membership, with Greece's approval, under provisional name of Former Yugoslav Republic of Macedonia.

Madagascar

Democratic Republic of (*Repoblika Demokratikañi Madagaskar*)

area 587,041 sq km/226,598 sq mi
capital Antananarivo
towns chief port Toamasina, Antseranana, Fianarantsoa, Toliary
physical temperate central highlands; humid valleys and tropical coastal plains; arid in S
environment according to 1990 UN figures, 93% of the forest area has been destroyed and about 100,000 species have been made extinct
features one of the last places to be inhabited, it evolved in isolation with unique animals (such as the lemur, now under threat from deforestation)
head of state Albert Zafy from 1993
head of government Francisque Raueny from 1993
political system emergent democratic republic
political parties National Front for the Defence of the Malagasy Socialist Revolution (FNDR); AKFM-Congress and AKFM-Renewal, both left of centre; Social Democratic Party (PSD), centre-left
exports coffee, cloves, vanilla, sugar, chromite, shrimps
currency Malagasy franc
population (1992) 12,804,000, mostly of Malayo-Indonesian origin; growth rate 3.2% p.a.
life expectancy men 50, women 53 (1989)
languages Malagasy (official), French, English
religions animist 50%, Christian 40%, Muslim 10%
literacy 53% (1988)
GNP $2.1 bn (1987); $280 per head (1988)

chronology
1885 Became a French protectorate.
1896 Became a French colony.
1960 Independence achieved from France, with Philibert Tsiranana as president.
1972 Army took control of the government.
1975 Martial law imposed under a national military directorate. New Marxist constitution proclaimed the Democratic Republic of Madagascar, with Didier Ratsiraka as president.
1976 Front-Line Revolutionary Organization (AREMA) formed.
1977 National Front for the Defence of the Malagasy Socialist Revolution (FNDR) became the sole legal political organization.
1980 Ratsiraka abandoned Marxist experiment.
1983 Ratsiraka re-elected, despite strong opposition from radical socialist National Movement for the Independence of Madagascar (MONIMA) under Monja Jaona.
1989 Ratsiraka re-elected for third term after restricting opposition parties.
1990 Political opposition legalized; 36 new parties created.
1991 Antigovernment demonstrations; opposition to Ratsiraka led to general strike. Ratsiraka formed new unity government.
1992 Constitutional reform approved by referendum. First multiparty elections won by Democrat coalition.
1993 Albert Zafy, leader of coalition, elected president. Francisque Raueny appointed prime minister.

Malawi

Republic of (*Malaŵi*)

area 118,000 sq km/45,560 sq mi
capital Lilongwe
towns Blantyre (largest city and commercial centre), Mzuzu, Zomba
physical landlocked narrow plateau with rolling plains; mountainous W of Lake Malawi
features one-third is water, including lakes Malawi, Chilara, and Malombe; Great Rift Valley; Nyika, Kasungu, and Lengare national parks; Mulanje Massif; Shire River
head of state and government Hastings Kamusu Banda from 1966 for life

political system one-party republic
political party Malawi Congress Party (MCP), multiracial, right-wing
exports tea, tobacco, cotton, peanuts, sugar
currency kwacha
population (1992) 9,484,000 (nearly 1 million refugees from Mozambique); growth rate 3.3% p.a.
life expectancy men 46, women 50 (1989)
languages English, Chichewa (both official)
religions Christian 75%, Muslim 20%
literacy 25% (1989)
GNP $1.2 bn (1987); $160 per head (1988)

chronology
1891 Became the British protectorate Nyasaland.
1964 Independence achieved from Britain, within the Commonwealth, as Malawi.
1966 Became a one-party republic, with Hastings Banda as president.
1971 Banda was made president for life.
1977 Banda released some political detainees and allowed greater freedom of the press.
1986–89 Influx of nearly a million refugees from Mozambique.
1992 Calls for multiparty politics. Countrywide industrial riots caused many fatalities. Western aid suspended over human-rights violations.
1993 Referendum overwhelmingly supported the ending of one-party rule. Dec: President Banda returned to office.

Malaysia

area 329,759 sq km/127,287 sq mi
capital Kuala Lumpur
towns Johor Baharu, Ipoh, Georgetown (Penang), Kuching in Sarawak, Kota Kinabalu in Sabah
physical comprises Peninsular Malaysia (the nine Malay states – Johore, Kedah, Kelantan, Negri Sembilan, Pahang, Perak, Perlis, Selangor, Trengganu – plus Malacca and Penang); and E Malaysia (Sabah and Sarawak); 75% tropical jungle; central mountain range; swamps in E
features Mount Kinabalu (highest peak in SE Asia); Niah caves (Sarawak)
head of state Rajah Azlan Muhibuddin Shah (sultan of Perak) from 1989
head of government Mahathir bin Mohamad from 1981
political system liberal democracy
political parties New United Malays' National Organization (UMNO Baru), Malay-oriented nationalist; Malaysian Chinese Association (MCA), Chinese-oriented conservative; Gerakan Party, Chinese-oriented, left of centre; Malaysian Indian Congress (MIC), Indian-oriented; Democratic Action Party (DAP), left of centre, multiracial but Chinese-dominated; Pan-Malayan Islamic Party (PAS), Islamic; Semangat '46 (Spirit of 1946), moderate, multiracial
exports pineapples, palm oil, rubber, timber, petroleum (Sarawak), bauxite
currency ringgit
population (1992) 18,630,000 (Malaysian 47%, Chinese 32%, Indian 8%, others 13%); growth rate 2% p.a.
life expectancy men 65, women 70 (1989)

languages Malay (official), English, Chinese, Indian, and local languages
religions Muslim (official), Buddhist, Hindu, local beliefs
literacy 80% (1989)
GNP $34.3 bn; $1,870 per head (1988)

chronology
1786 Britain established control.
1826 Became a British colony.
1963 Federation of Malaysia formed, including Malaya, Singapore, Sabah (N Borneo), and Sarawak (NW Borneo).
1965 Secession of Singapore from federation.
1969 Anti-Chinese riots in Kuala Lumpur.
1971 Launch of *bumiputra* ethnic-Malay-oriented economic policy.
1981 Election of Dr Mahathir bin Mohamad as prime minister.
1982 Mahathir bin Mohamad re-elected.
1986 Mahathir bin Mohamad re-elected.
1987 Arrest of over 100 opposition activists, including DAP leader, as Malay-Chinese relations deteriorated.
1988 Split in ruling UMNO party over Mahathir's leadership style; new UMNO formed.
1989 Semangat'46 set up by former members of UMNO including ex-premier Tunku Abdul Rahman.
1990 Mahathir bin Mohamad re-elected.
1991 New economic-growth programme launched.
1993 Mahathir bin Mohamad re-elected UMNO Baru president.

Maldives

Republic of (*Divehi Jumhuriya*)

area 298 sq km/115 sq mi
capital Malé
towns Seenu
physical comprises 1,196 coral islands, grouped into 12 clusters of atolls, largely flat, none bigger than 13 sq km/5 sq mi, average elevation 1.8 m/6 ft; 203 are inhabited
environment the threat of rising sea level has been heightened by the frequency of flooding in recent years

features tourism developed since 1972
head of state and government Maumoon Abdul Gayoom from 1978
political system authoritarian nationalism
political parties none; candidates elected on the basis of personal influence and clan loyalties
exports coconuts, copra, bonito (fish related to tuna), garments
currency rufiya
population (1992) 230,000; growth rate 3.7% p.a.
life expectancy men 60, women 63 (1989)
languages Divehi (Sinhalese dialect), English
religion Sunni Muslim
literacy 36% (1989)
GNP $69 million (1987); $410 per head (1988)

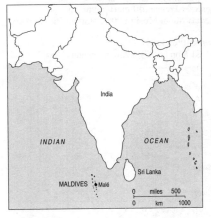

chronology
1887 Became a British protectorate.
1953 Long a sultanate, the Maldive Islands became a republic within the Commonwealth.
1954 Sultan restored.
1965 Achieved full independence outside the Commonwealth.
1968 Sultan deposed; republic reinstated with Ibrahim Nasir as president.
1978 Nasir retired; replaced by Maumoon Abdul Gayoom.
1982 Rejoined the Commonwealth.
1983 Gayoom re-elected.
1985 Became a founder member of South Asian Association for Regional Cooperation (SAARC).
1988 Gayoom re-elected. Coup attempt by mercenaries, thought to have the backing of former president Nasir, was foiled by Indian paratroops.
1993 Gayoom re-elected

Mali

Republic of (*République du Mali*)

area 1,240,142 sq km/478,695 sq mi
capital Bamako
towns Mopti, Kayes, Ségou, Timbuktu
physical landlocked state with river Niger and savanna in S; part of the Sahara in N; hills in NE; Senegal River and its branches irrigate the SW
environment a rising population coupled with recent droughts has affected marginal agriculture. Once in surplus, Mali has had to import grain every year since 1965

features ancient town of Timbuktu; railway to Dakar is the only outlet to the sea
head of state Alpha Oumar Konare from 1992
head of government Abdoulaye Sekou Sow from 1993
political system emergent democratic republic
political parties Alliance for Democracy in Mali (ADEMA), centrist; National Committee for Democratic Initiative (CNID), centre-left; Sudanese Union–African Democratic Rally (US–RDA), Sudanese nationalist
exports raw cotton and cotton products, peanuts, livestock, fish
currency franc CFA
population (1992) 8,464,000; growth rate 2.9% p.a.
life expectancy men 44, women 47 (1989)
languages French (official), Bambara
religions Sunni Muslim 90%, animist 9%, Christian 1%
literacy 10% (1989)
GNP $1.6 bn (1987); $230 per head (1988)

chronology
1895 Came under French rule.
1959 With Senegal, formed the Federation of Mali.
1960 Became the independent Republic of Mali, with Modibo Keita as president.
1968 Keita replaced in an army coup by Moussa Traoré.
1974 New constitution made Mali a one-party state.
1976 New national party, the Malian People's Democratic Union, announced.
1983 Agreement between Mali and Guinea for eventual political and economic integration signed.
1985 Conflict with Burkina Faso lasted five days; mediated by International Court of Justice.
1991 Demonstrations against one-party rule. Moussa Traoré ousted in a coup led by Lt-Col Amadou Toumani Toure. New multiparty constitution agreed, subject to referendum.
1992 Referendum endorsed new democratic constitution. Alliance for Democracy in Mali (ADEMA) won multiparty elections; Alpha Oumar Konare elected president.
1993 Abdoulaye Sekou Sow appointed prime minister.

Malta

Republic of (*Repubblika Ta'Malta*)

area 320 sq km/124 sq mi
capital and port Valletta
towns Rabat; port of Marsaxlokk

physical includes islands of Gozo 67 sq km/26 sq mi and Comino 2.5 sq km/1 sq mi
features occupies strategic location in central Mediterranean; large commercial dock facilities
head of state Vincent Tabone from 1989
head of government Edward Fenech Adami from 1987
political system liberal democracy
political parties Malta Labour Party (MLP), moderate, left of centre; Nationalist Party, Christian, centrist, pro-European
exports vegetables, knitwear, handmade lace, plastics, electronic equipment
currency Maltese lira
population (1990 est) 373,000; growth rate 0.7% p.a.
life expectancy men 72, women 77 (1987)
languages Maltese, English
religion Roman Catholic 98%
literacy 90% (1988)
GNP $1.6 bn; $4,750 per head (1988)

chronology
1814 Annexed to Britain by the Treaty of Paris.
1947 Achieved self-government.
1955 Dom Mintoff of the Malta Labour Party (MLP) became prime minister.
1956 Referendum approved MLP's proposal for integration with the UK. Proposal opposed by the Nationalist Party.
1958 MLP rejected the British integration proposal.
1962 Nationalists elected, with Borg Olivier as prime minister.
1964 Independence achieved from Britain, within the Commonwealth. Ten-year defence and economic-aid treaty with UK signed.
1971 Mintoff re-elected. 1964 treaty declared invalid and negotiations began for leasing the NATO base in Malta.
1972 Seven-year NATO agreement signed.
1974 Became a republic.
1979 British military base closed.
1984 Mintoff retired and was replaced by Mifsud Bonnici as prime minister and MLP leader.
1987 Edward Fenech Adami (Nationalist) elected prime minister.
1989 Vincent Tabone elected president. USA–USSR summit held offshore.
1990 Formal application made for EC membership.
1992 Nationalist Party returned to power in general election.

Marshall Islands

area 180 sq km/69 sq mi
capital Dalap-Uliga-Darrit (on Majuro atoll)
physical comprises the Radak (13 islands) and Ralik (11 islands) chains in the W Pacific
features include two atolls used for US atom-bomb tests 1946–63, Eniwetok and Bikini, where radioactivity will last for 100 years; and Kwajalein atoll (the largest) which has a US intercontinental missile range
head of state and government Amata Kabua from 1991
political system liberal democracy
political parties no organized party system
products copra, phosphates, fish; tourism is important
currency US dollar
population (1990) 31,600
language English (official)
religions Christian, mainly Roman Catholic, and local faiths
GNP $512 million; $16,516 per head (1990)

chronology
1855 Occupied by Germany.
1914 Occupied by Japan.
1920–45 Administered by Japan under United Nations mandate.
1946–63 Eniwetok and Bikini atolls used for US atom-bomb tests; islanders later demanded rehabilitation and compensation for the damage.
1947 Became part of the UN Pacific Islands Trust Territory, administered by the USA.
1986 Compact of free association with USA granted islands self-government, with USA retaining military control and taking tribute.
1990 UN trust status terminated.
1991 Independence agreed; UN membership granted.

Mauritania

Islamic Republic of (*République Islamique de Mauritanie*)

area 1,030,700 sq km/397,850 sq mi
capital Nouakchott
towns port of Nouadhibou, Kaédi, Zouérate
physical valley of river Senegal in S; remainder arid and flat
features part of the Sahara Desert; dusty sirocco wind blows in March
head of state and government Maaouia Ould Sid Ahmed Taya from 1984
political system emergent democratic republic
political parties Democratic and Social Republican Party (PRDS), centre-left, militarist; Union of Democratic Forces (UFD), centre-left; Rally for Democracy and National Unity (RDUN), centrist; Mauritian Renewal Party (PMR), centrist; Umma, Islamic fundamentalist; Socialist and Democratic Popular Front Union (UDSP), left of centre
exports iron ore, fish, gypsum
currency ouguiya
population (1992) 2,108,000 (Arab-Berber 30%, black African 30%, Haratine – descendants of black slaves, who remained slaves until 1980–30%); growth rate 3% p.a.
life expectancy men 43, women 48 (1989)
languages French (official), Hasaniya Arabic, black African languages
religion Sunni Muslim 99%
literacy 17% (1987)
GNP $843 million; $480 per head (1988)

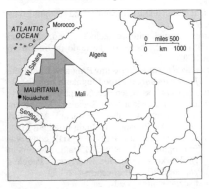

chronology
1903 Became a French protectorate.
1960 Independence achieved from France, with Moktar Ould Daddah as president.
1975 Western Sahara ceded by Spain. Mauritania occupied the southern area and Morocco the north. Polisario Front formed in Sahara to resist the occupation by Mauritania and Morocco.
1978 Daddah deposed in bloodless coup; replaced by Mohamed Khouna Ould Haidalla. Peace agreed with Polisario Front.
1981 Diplomatic relations with Morocco broken.
1984 Haidalla overthrown by Maaouia Ould Sid Ahmed Taya. Polisario regime formally recognized.
1985 Relations with Morocco restored.
1989 Violent clashes between Mauritanians and Senegalese. Arab-dominated government expelled thousands of Africans into N Senegal; governments had earlier agreed to repatriate each other's citizens (about 250,000).
1991 Amnesty for political prisoners. Multiparty elections promised. Calls for resignation of President Taya.
1992 First multiparty elections won by ruling PRDS. Diplomatic relations with Senegal resumed.

Mauritius
Republic of

area 1,865 sq km/720 sq mi; the island of Rodrigues is part of Mauritius; there are several small island dependencies
capital Port Louis
towns Beau Bassin-Rose Hill, Curepipe, Quatre Bornes
physical mountainous, volcanic island surrounded by coral reefs
features unusual wildlife includes flying fox and ostrich; it was the home of the dodo (extinct from about 1680)
interim head of state Veerasamy Ringadoo from 1992
head of government Aneerood Jugnauth from 1982
political system liberal democratic republic
political parties Mauritius Socialist Movement (MSM), moderate socialist-republican; Mauritius Labour Party (MLP), centrist, Hindu-oriented; Mauritius Social Democratic Party (PMSD), conservative, Francophile; Mauritius Militant Movement (MMM), Marxist-republican; Rodriguais People's Organization (OPR), left of centre
exports sugar, knitted goods, tea
currency Mauritius rupee
population (1992) 1,081,000, 68% of Indian origin; growth rate 1.5% p.a.
life expectancy men 64, women 71 (1989)
languages English (official), French, creole, Indian languages
religions Hindu 51%, Christian 30%, Muslim 17%
literacy 94% (1989)
GNP $1.4 bn (1987); $1,810 per head (1988)

chronology
1814 Annexed to Britain by the Treaty of Paris.
1968 Independence achieved from Britain within the Commonwealth, with Seewoosagur Ramgoolam as prime minister.
1982 Aneerood Jugnauth became prime minister.
1983 Jugnauth formed a new party, the Mauritius Socialist Movement. Ramgoolam appointed governor general. Jugnauth formed a new coalition government.
1985 Ramgoolam died; succeeded by Veersamy Ringadoo.
1987 Jugnauth's coalition re-elected.
1990 Attempt to create a republic failed.
1991 Jugnauth's ruling MSM–MMM–OPR coalition won general election; pledge to secure republican status by 1992.

1992 Mauritius became a republic while remaining a member of the Commonwealth. Ringadoo became interim president.

Mexico
United States of (*Estados Unidos Mexicanos*)
area 1,958,201 sq km/756,198 sq mi
capital Mexico City
towns Guadalajara, Monterrey; port Veracruz
physical partly arid central highlands; Sierra Madre mountain ranges E and W; tropical coastal plains
environment during the 1980s, smog levels in Mexico City exceeded World Health Organization standards on more than 300 days of the year. Air is polluted by 130,000 factories and 2.5 million vehicles
features Rio Grande; 3,218 km/2,000 mi frontier with USA; resorts Acapulco, Cancun, Mexicali, Tijuana; Baja California, Yucatán peninsula; volcanoes, including Popocatépetl; pre-Columbian archaeological sites
head of state and government Carlos Salinas de Gortari from 1988
political system federal democratic republic
political parties Institutional Revolutionary Party (PRI), moderate, left-wing; National Action Party (PAN), moderate Christian socialist
exports silver, gold, lead, uranium, oil, natural gas, handicrafts, fish, shellfish, fruits and vegetables, cotton, machinery
currency peso
population (1992) 84,439,000 (mixed descent 60%, Indian 30%, Spanish descent 10%); 50% under 20 years of age; growth rate 2.6% p.a.
life expectancy men 67, women 73
languages Spanish (official) 92%, Nahuatl, Maya, Mixtec
religion Roman Catholic 97%
literacy men 92%, women 88% (1989)
GNP $126 bn (1987); $2,082 per head

chronology
1821 Independence achieved from Spain.
1846–48 Mexico at war with USA; loss of territory.
1848 Maya Indian revolt suppressed.
1864–67 Maximilian of Austria was emperor of Mexico.
1917 New constitution introduced, designed to establish permanent democracy.

1983–84 Financial crisis.

1985 Institutional Revolutionary Party (PRI) returned to power. Earthquake in Mexico City.

1986 International Monetary Fund (IMF) loan agreement signed to keep the country solvent until at least 1988.

1988 PRI candidate Carlos Salinas de Gortari elected president. Debt reduction accords negotiated with USA.

1991 PRI won general election. President Salinas promised constitutional reforms.

1992 Public outrage following Guadalajara gas-explosion disaster.

Micronesia

Federated States of (FSM)

area 700 sq km/270 sq mi

capital Kolonia in Pohnpei state

towns Moen, in Chuuk state; Lelu, in Kosrae state; Colonia, in Yap state

physical an archipelago in the W Pacific

features equatorial, volcanic island chain, with extensive coral, limestone, and lava shores

head of state and government Bailey Olter from 1991

political system democratic federal state

political parties no formally organized political parties

products copra, fish products, tourism

currency US dollar

population (1985) 91,440

languages English (official) and local languages

religion Christianity

chronology

16th century Colonized by Spain.

1885 Purchased from Spain by Germany.

1914 Occupied by Japan.

1920 Administered by Japan under League of Nations mandate.

1944 Occupied by USA.

1947 Became part of the UN Pacific Islands Trust Territory, administered by the USA.

1982 Compact of Free Association signed with USA.

1990 UN trust status terminated. Independent state established, with USA responsible for defence and foreign affairs.

1991 First independent president elected. Entered into UN membership.

Moldova

Republic of

area 33,700 sq km/13,012 sq mi

capital Chişinău (Kishinev)

towns Tiraspol, Beltsy, Bendery

physical hilly land lying largely between the rivers Prut and Dniester; northern Moldova comprises the level plain of the Beltsy Steppe and uplands; the climate is warm and moderately continental

features Black Earth region

head of state Mircea Snegur from 1989

head of government Andre Sangheli from 1992

political system emergent democracy

political parties Moldavian Popular Front (MRF), Romanian nationalist; Gagauz-Khalky People's Movement (GKPM), Gagauz separatist

products wine, tobacco, canned goods

population (1992) 4,394,000 (Moldovan 64% Ukrainian 14%, Russian 13%, Gagauzi 4%, Bulgarian 2%)

language Moldavian, allied to Romanian

religion Russian Orthodox

chronology

1940 Bessarabia in the E became part of the Soviet Union whereas the W part remained in Romania.

1941 Bessarabia taken over by Romania–Germany.

1944 Red army reconquered Bessarabia.

1946–47 Widespread famine.

1988 A popular front, the Democratic Movement for Perestroika, campaigned for accelerated political reform.

1989 Jan–Feb: nationalist demonstrations in Chişinău. May: Moldavian Popular Front established. July: former Communist Party deputy leader Mircea Snegur became head of state. Aug: Moldavian language granted official status, triggering clashes between ethnic Russians and Moldavians. Nov: Gagauz-Khalky People's Movement formed to campaign for Gagauz autonomy.

1990 Feb: Popular Front polled strongly in supreme soviet elections. June: economic and political sovereignty declared; renamed Republic of Moldova. Oct: Gagauzi held unauthorized elections to independent parliament; state of emergency declared after interethnic clashes. Trans-Dniester region declared its sovereignty. Nov: state of emergency declared in Trans-Dniester region after interethnic killings.

1991 March: Moldova boycotted the USSR's constitutional referendum. Aug: independence declared after abortive anti-Gorbachev coup; Communist Party outlawed. Dec: Moldova joined new Commonwealth of Independent States.

1992 Admitted into United Nations and the Con- ference on Security and Cooperation in Europe; diplomatic recognition granted by USA. Possible union with Romania discussed. Trans-Dniester region fighting intensified; Russian peacekeeping force reportedly deployed after talks between Moldova and Russia. Andrei Sangheli became premier.

1993 Ceasefire, in Gagauz and Trans-Dniester regions, holding.

Monaco

Principality of

area 1.95 sq km/0.75 sq mi
capital Monaco-Ville
towns Monte Carlo, La Condamine; heliport Fontvieille
physical steep and rugged; surrounded landwards by French territory; being expanded by filling in the sea
features aquarium and oceanographic centre; Monte Carlo film festival, motor races, and casinos; world's second smallest state
head of state Prince Rainier III from 1949
head of government Jean Ausseil from 1986
political system constitutional monarchy under French protectorate
political parties National and Democratic Union (UND); Democratic Union Movement; Monaco Action; Monégasque Socialist Party
exports some light industry; economy dependent on tourism and gambling
currency French franc
population (1989) 29,000; growth rate –0.5% p.a.
languages French (official), English, Italian
religion Roman Catholic 95%
literacy 99% (1985)

chronology
1861 Became an independent state under French protection.
1918 France given a veto over succession to the throne.
1949 Prince Rainier III ascended the throne.
1956 Prince Rainier married US actress Grace Kelly.
1958 Birth of male heir, Prince Albert.
1959 Constitution of 1911 suspended.
1962 New constitution adopted.

Mongolia

State of (*Outer Mongolia* until 1924; *People's Republic of Mongolia* until 1991)

area 1,565,000 sq km/604,480 sq mi
capital Ulaanbaatar
towns Darhan, Choybalsan
physical high plateau with desert and steppe (grasslands)
features Altai Mountains in SW; salt lakes; part of Gobi Desert in SE
head of state Punsalmaagiyn Ochirbat from 1990
head of government Puntsagiyn Jasray from 1992
political system emergent democracy
political parties Mongolian People's Revolutionary Party (MPRP), reform-communist; Mongolian Democratic Party (MDP), main opposition party; Mongolian Democratic Union
exports meat and hides, minerals, wool, livestock, grain, cement, timber
currency tugrik
population (1992) 2,182,000; growth rate 2.8% p.a.
life expectancy men 63, women 67 (1989)
languages Khalkha Mongolian (official), Chinese, Russian, and Turkic languages
religion officially none (Tibetan Buddhist Lamaism suppressed 1930s)
literacy 89% (1985)
GNP $3.6 bn; $1,820 per head (1986)

chronology
1911 Outer Mongolia gained autonomy from China.
1915 Chinese sovereignty reasserted.
1921 Chinese rule overthrown with Soviet help.
1924 People's Republic proclaimed.
1946 China recognized Mongolia's independence.
1966 20-year friendship, cooperation, and mutual-assistance pact signed with USSR. Relations with China deteriorated.
1984 Yumjaagiyn Tsedenbal, effective leader, deposed and replaced by Jambyn Batmonh.
1987 Soviet troops reduced; Mongolia's external contacts broadened.
1989 Further Soviet troop reductions.
1990 Democratization campaign launched by Mongolian Democratic Union. Punsalmaagiyn Ochirbat's MPRP elected in free multiparty elections. Mongolian script readopted.

1991 Massive privatization programme launched as part of move towards a market economy. The word 'Republic' dropped from country's name. GDP declined by 10%.
1992 Jan: New constitution introduced. Economic situation worsened; GDP again declined by 10%. Puntsagiyn Jasray appointed as the new prime minister.
1993 Punsalmaagiyn Ochirbat won first direct presidential election.

Morocco

Kingdom of (*al-Mamlaka al-Maghrebia*)

area 458,730 sq km/177,070 sq mi (excluding Western Sahara)
capital Rabat
towns Marrakesh, Fez, Meknès; ports Casablanca, Tangier, Agadir
physical mountain ranges NE–SW; fertile coastal plains in W
features Atlas Mountains; the towns Ceuta (from 1580) and Melilla (from 1492) are held by Spain; tunnel crossing the Strait of Gibraltar to Spain proposed 1985
head of state Hassan II from 1961
head of government Mohamed Lawrani from 1992
political system constitutional monarchy
political parties Constitutional Union (UC), rightwing; National Rally of Independents (RNI), royalist; Popular Movement (MP), moderate socialist; Istiqlal, nationalist, right of centre; Socialist Union of Popular Forces (USFP), progressive socialist; National Democratic Party (PND), moderate, nationalist
exports dates, figs, cork, wood pulp, canned fish, phosphates
currency dirham (DH)
population (1992) 26,239,000; growth rate 2.5% p.a.
life expectancy men 62, women 65 (1989)
languages Arabic (official) 75%, Berber 25%, French, Spanish
religion Sunni Muslim 99%
literacy men 45%, women 22% (1985 est)
GNP $18.7 bn; $750 per head (1988)

chronology
1912 Morocco divided into French and Spanish protectorates.

1956 Independence achieved as the Sultanate of Morocco.
1957 Sultan restyled king of Morocco.
1961 Hassan II came to the throne.
1969 Former Spanish province of Ifni returned to Morocco.
1972 Major revision of the constitution.
1975 Western Sahara ceded by Spain to Morocco and Mauritania.
1976 Guerrilla war in Western Sahara with the Polisario Front. Sahrawi Arab Democratic Republic (SADR) established in Algiers. Diplomatic relations between Morocco and Algeria broken.
1979 Mauritania signed a peace treaty with Polisario.
1983 Peace formula for Western Sahara proposed by the Organization of African Unity (OAU); Morocco agreed but refused to deal directly with Polisario.
1984 Hassan signed an agreement for cooperation and mutual defence with Libya.
1987 Cease-fire agreed with Polisario, but fighting continued.
1988 Diplomatic relations with Algeria restored.
1989 Diplomatic relations with Syria restored.
1992 Mohamed Lawrani appointed prime minister; new constitution approved in referendum.
1993 Peace accord with Israel.

Mozambique

People's Republic of (*República Popular de Moçambique*)

area 799,380 sq km/308,561 sq mi
capital and chief port Maputo
towns Beira, Nampula
physical mostly flat tropical lowland; mountains in W
features rivers Zambezi, Limpopo; 'Beira Corridor' rail, road, and pipeline link with Zimbabwe
head of state and government Joaquim Alberto Chissano from 1986
political system emergent democratic republic
political parties National Front for the Liberation of Mozambique (Frelimo), Marxist-Leninist; Renamo, or Mozambique National Resistance (MNR), former rebel movement
exports prawns, cashews, sugar, cotton, tea, petroleum products, copra

currency metical (replaced escudo 1980)
population (1992) 14,842,000 (mainly indigenous Bantu peoples; Portuguese 50,000); growth rate 2.8% p.a.; nearly 1 million refugees in Malawi
life expectancy men 45, women 48 (1989)
languages Portuguese (official), 16 African languages
religions animist 60%, Roman Catholic 18%, Muslim 16%
literacy men 55%, women 22% (1985 est)
GDP $4.7 bn; $319 per head (1987)

chronology
1505 Mozambique became a Portuguese colony.
1962 Frelimo (liberation front) established.
1975 Independence achieved from Portugal as a socialist republic, with Samora Machel as president and Frelimo as the sole legal party.
1977 Renamo resistance group formed.
1983 Re-establishment of good relations with Western powers.
1984 Nkomati accord of nonaggression signed with South Africa.
1986 Machel killed in air crash; succeeded by Joaquim Chissano.
1988 Tanzania announced withdrawal of its troops. South Africa provided training for Mozambican forces.
1989 Frelimo offered to abandon Marxist-Leninism; Chissano re-elected. Renamo continued attacks on government facilities and civilians.
1990 One-party rule officially ended. Partial ceasefire agreed.
1991 Peace talks resumed in Rome, delaying democratic process. Attempted antigovernment coup thwarted.
1992 Peace accord signed, but fighting continued.

Myanmar

Union of (*Thammada Myanmar Naingngandaw*) (formerly *Burma*, until 1989)

area 676,577 sq km/261,228 sq mi
capital (and chief port) Yangon (formerly Rangoon)
towns Mandalay, Moulmein, Pegu
physical over half is rainforest; rivers Irrawaddy and Chindwin in central lowlands ringed by mountains in N, W, and E

environment landslides and flooding during the rainy season (June–Sept) are becoming more frequent as a result of deforestation
features ruined cities of Pagan and Mingun
head of state and government General Khin Nyunt from 1993.
political system military republic
political parties National Unity Party (NUP), military-socialist ruling party; National League for Democracy (NLD), pluralist opposition grouping
exports rice, rubber, jute, teak, jade, rubies, sapphires
currency kyat
population (1992) 43,466,000; growth rate 1.9% p.a. (includes Shan, Karen, Ráljome, Chinese, and Indian minorities)
life expectancy men 53, women 56 (1989)
language Burmese
religions Hinayana Buddhist 85%, animist, Christian
literacy 66% (1989)
GNP $9.3 bn (1988); $210 per head (1989)

chronology
1886 United as province of British India.
1937 Became crown colony in the British Commonwealth.
1942–45 Occupied by Japan.
1948 Independence achieved from Britain. Left the Commonwealth.
1962 General Ne Win assumed power in army coup.
1973–74 Adopted presidential-style 'civilian' constitution.
1975 Opposition National Democratic Front formed.
1986 Several thousand supporters of opposition leader Suu Kyi arrested.
1988 Government resigned after violent demonstrations. General Saw Maung seized power in military coup Sept; over 1,000 killed.
1989 Martial law declared; thousands arrested including advocates of democracy and human rights. Country renamed Myanmar and capital Yangon.
1990 Landslide victory for NLD in general election was ignored by military junta; opposition leader Aung San Suu Kyi placed under house arrest. Breakaway opposition group formed 'parallel government' on rebel-held territory.
1991 Martial law and human-rights abuses continued. Military offensives continued. Suu Kyi awarded Nobel Prize for Peace but was not released.
1992 Jan–April: Pogrom against Muslim community in Arakan province, W Myanmar, carried out with army backing. April: Saw Maung replaced by Than Shwe. Several political prisoners liberated. Sept: martial law lifted, but restrictions on political freedom remained.
1993 Constitutional convention agreed on a more liberal constitution. Suu Kyi still being held. General Khin Nyunt heading ruling junta, the State Law and Order Restoration Council

Namibia

Republic of (formerly *South West Africa*)

area 824,300 sq km/318,262 sq mi
capital Windhoek
towns Swakopmund, Rehoboth, Rundu
physical mainly desert

features Namib and Kalahari deserts; Orange River; Caprivi Strip links Namibia to Zambezi River; includes the enclave of Walvis Bay (area 1,120 sq km/ 432 sq mi)
head of state Sam Nujoma from 1990
head of government Hage Geingob from 1990
political system democratic republic
political parties South-West Africa People's Organization (SWAPO), socialist Ovambo-oriented; Democratic Turnhalle Alliance (DTA), moderate, multiracial coalition; United Democratic Front (UDF), disaffected ex-SWAPO members; National Christian Action (ACN), white conservative
exports diamonds, uranium, copper, lead, zinc
currency Namibian dollar
population (1992) 1,512,000 (black African 85%, European 6%)
life expectancy blacks 40, whites 69
languages Afrikaans (spoken by 60% of white population), German, English (all official), several indigenous languages
religions 51% Lutheran, 19% Roman Catholic, 6% Dutch Reformed Church, 6% Anglican
literacy whites 100%, nonwhites 16%
GNP $1.6 bn; $1,300 per head (1988)

chronology
1884 German and British colonies established.
1915 German colony seized by South Africa.
1920 Administered by South Africa, under League of Nations mandate, as British South Africa.
1946 Full incorporation in South Africa refused by United Nations (UN).
1958 South-West Africa People's Organization (SWAPO) set up to seek racial equality and full independence.
1966 South Africa's apartheid laws extended to the country.
1968 Redesignated Namibia by UN.
1978 UN Security Council Resolution 435 for the granting of full sovereignty accepted by South Africa and then rescinded.
1988 Peace talks between South Africa, Angola, and Cuba led to agreement on full independence for Namibia.
1989 Unexpected incursion by SWAPO guerrillas from Angola into Namibia threatened agreed inde-

pendence. Transitional constitution created by elected representatives; SWAPO dominant party.
1990 Liberal multiparty 'independence' constitution adopted; independence achieved. Sam Nujoma elected president.
1991 Agreement on joint administration of disputed port of Walvis Bay reached with South Africa, pending final settlement of dispute.
1992 Agreement on establishment of Walvis Bay Joint Administrative Body.
1993 South Africa relinquished claim to Walvis Bay sovereignty. Namibian dollar launched with South African rand parity.

Nauru

Republic of (*Naoero*)

area 21 sq km/8 sq mi
capital (seat of government) Yaren District
physical tropical island country in SW Pacific; plateau encircled by coral cliffs and sandy beaches
features lies just S of equator; one of three phosphate rock islands in the Pacific
head of state and government Bernard Dowiyogo from 1989
political system liberal democracy
political party Democratic Party of Nauru (DPN), opposition to government
exports phosphates
currency Australian dollar
population (1990 est) 8,100 (mainly Polynesian; Chinese 8%, European 8%); growth rate 1.7% p.a.
languages Nauruan (official), English
religions Protestant 66%, Roman Catholic 33%
literacy 99% (1988)
GNP $160 million (1986); $9,091 per head (1985)

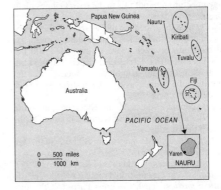

chronology
1888 Annexed by Germany.
1920 Administered by Australia, New Zealand, and UK until independence, except 1942–45, when it was occupied by Japan.
1968 Independence achieved from Australia, New Zealand, and UK with 'special member' Commonwealth status. Hammer DeRoburt elected president.
1976 Bernard Dowiyogo elected president.
1978 DeRoburt re-elected.
1986 DeRoburt briefly replaced as president by Kennan Adeang.
1987 DeRoburt re-elected; Adeang established the Democratic Party of Nauru.

1989 DeRoburt replaced by Kensas Aroi, who was later succeeded by Dowiyogo.
1992 Dowiyogo re-elected.
1993 Nauru issued lawsuit against Australian firm of solicitors for the recovery of $14 million of the island's trust fund. A claim against Australia for compensation for 60 years of environmental destruction was in progress at the International Court of Justice.

Nepal

Kingdom of (*Nepal Adhirajya*)

area 147,181 sq km/56,850 sq mi
capital Katmandu
towns Pátan, Moráng, Bhádgáon
physical descends from the Himalayan mountain range in N through foothills to the river Ganges plain in S
environment described as the world's highest rubbish dump, Nepal attracts 270,000 tourists, trekkers, and mountaineers each year. An estimated 500 kg/1,100 lb of rubbish is left by each expedition trekking or climbing in the Himalayas. Since 1952 the foothills of the Himalayas have been stripped of 40% of their forest cover
features Mount Everest, Mount Kangchenjunga; the only Hindu kingdom in the world; Lumbini, birthplace of the Buddha
head of state King Birendra Bir Bikram Shah Dev from 1972
head of government Girija Prasad Koirala from 1991
political system constitutional monarchy
political parties Nepali Congress Party (NCP), left-of-centre; United Nepal Communist Party (UNCP), Marxist-Leninist-Maoist; United Liberation Torch-bearers; Democratic Front, radical republican
exports jute, rice, timber, oilseed
currency Nepalese rupee
population (1992) 19,795,000 (mainly known by name of predominant clan, the Gurkhas; the Sherpas are a Buddhist minority of NE Nepal); growth rate 2.3% p.a.
life expectancy men 50, women 49 (1989)
language Nepali (official); 20 dialects spoken
religions Hindu 90%; Buddhist, Muslim, Christian
literacy men 39%, women 12% (1985 est)
GNP $3.1 bn (1988); $160 per head (1986)

chronology
1768 Nepal emerged as unified kingdom.
1815–16 Anglo-Nepali 'Gurkha War'; Nepal became a British-dependent buffer state.
1846–1951 Ruled by the Rana family.
1923 Independence achieved from Britain.
1951 Monarchy restored.
1959 Constitution created elected legislature.
1960–61 Parliament dissolved by king; political parties banned.
1980 Constitutional referendum held following popular agitation.
1981 Direct elections held to national assembly.
1983 Overthrow of monarch-supported prime minister.
1986 New assembly elections returned a majority opposed to *panchayat* system of partyless government.
1988 Strict curbs placed on opposition activity; over 100 supporters of banned opposition party arrested; censorship imposed.
1989 Border blockade imposed by India in treaty dispute.
1990 *Panchayat* system collapsed after mass prodemocracy demonstrations; new constitution introduced; elections set for May 1991.
1991 Nepali Congress Party, led by Girija Prasad Koirala, won the general election.
1992 Communists led anti-government demonstrations in Katmandu and Pátan.

Netherlands

Kingdom of the (*Koninkrijk der Nederlanden*), popularly referred to as *Holland*

area 41,863 sq km/16,169 sq mi
capital Amsterdam
towns The Hague (seat of government), Utrecht, Eindhoven, Maastricht; chief port Rotterdam
physical flat coastal lowland; rivers Rhine, Scheldt, Maas; Frisian Islands
territories Aruba, Netherlands Antilles (Caribbean)
environment the country lies at the mouths of three of Europe's most polluted rivers, the Maas, Rhine, and Scheldt. Dutch farmers contribute to this pollution by using the world's highest quantities of nitrogen-based fertilizer per hectare/acre per year

features polders (reclaimed land) make up over 40% of the land area; dyke (*Afsluitdijk*) 32 km/20 mi long 1932 has turned the former Zuider Zee inlet into the freshwater IJsselmeer; Delta Project series of dams 1986 forms sea defence in Zeeland delta of the Maas, Scheldt, and Rhine
head of state Queen Beatrix Wilhelmina Armgard from 1980
head of government Ruud Lubbers from 1989
political system constitutional monarchy
political parties Christian Democratic Appeal (CDA), Christian, right of centre; Labour Party (PvdA), moderate, left of centre; People's Party for Freedom and Democracy (VVD), free-enterprise, centrist
exports dairy products, flower bulbs, vegetables, petrochemicals, electronics
currency guilder
population (1992) 15,163,000 (including 300,000 of Dutch-Indonesian origin absorbed 1949–64 from former colonial possessions); growth rate 0.4% p.a.
life expectancy men 74, women 81 (1989)
language Dutch
religions Roman Catholic 40%, Protestant 31%
literacy 99% (1989)
GNP $320.4 bn (1992)

chronology
1940–45 Occupied by Germany during World War II.
1947 Joined Benelux customs union.
1948 Queen Juliana succeeded Queen Wilhelmina to the throne.
1949 Became a founding member of North Atlantic Treaty Organization (NATO).
1953 Dykes breached by storm; nearly 2,000 people and tens of thousands of cattle died in flood.
1958 Joined European Economic Community.
1980 Queen Juliana abdicated in favour of her daughter Beatrix.
1981 Opposition to cruise missiles averted their being sited on Dutch soil.
1989 Prime Minister Ruud Lubbers resigned; new Lubbers-led coalition elected.
1992 Maastricht Treaty on European political and monetary union ratified.

New Zealand

Dominion of

area 268,680 sq km/103,777 sq mi
capital and port Wellington
towns Hamilton, Palmerston North, Christchurch, Dunedin; port Auckland
physical comprises North Island, South Island, Stewart Island, Chatham Islands, and minor islands; mainly mountainous
overseas territories Tokelau (three atolls transferred 1926 from former Gilbert and Ellice Islands colony); Niue Island (one of the Cook Islands, separately administered from 1903: chief town Alafi); Cook Islands are internally self-governing but share common citizenship with New Zealand; Ross Dependency in Antarctica
features Ruapehu on North Island, 2,797 m/9,180 ft, highest of three active volcanoes; geysers and hot springs of the Rotorua district; Lake Taupo (616 sq km/238 sq mi), source of Waikato River; Kaingaroa state forest. On South Island are the Southern Alps and Canterbury Plains

head of state Elizabeth II from 1952 represented by governor general (Catherine Tizard from 1990)
head of government Jim Bolger from 1990
political system constitutional monarchy
political parties Labour Party, moderate, left of centre; New Zealand National Party, free enterprise, centre-right; Alliance Party, left of centre, ecologists
exports lamb, beef, wool, leather, dairy products, processed foods, kiwi fruit, seeds and breeding stock, timber, paper, pulp, light aircraft
currency New Zealand dollar
population (1992) 3,481,000 (European, mostly British, 87%; Polynesian, mostly Maori, 12%); growth rate 0.9% p.a.
life expectancy men 72, women 78 (1989)
languages English (official), Maori
religions Protestant 50%, Roman Catholic 15%
literacy 99% (1989)
GNP $40.3 bn (1992)

chronology
1840 New Zealand became a British colony.
1907 Created a dominion of the British Empire.
1931 Granted independence from Britain.
1947 Independence within the Commonwealth confirmed by the New Zealand parliament.
1972 National Party government replaced by Labour Party, with Norman Kirk as prime minister.
1974 Kirk died; replaced by Wallace Rowling.
1975 National Party returned, with Robert Muldoon as prime minister.
1984 Labour Party returned under David Lange.
1985 Non-nuclear military policy created disagreements with France and the USA.
1987 National Party declared support for the Labour government's non-nuclear policy. Lange re-elected. New Zealand officially classified as a 'friendly' rather than 'allied' country by the USA because of its non-nuclear military policy.
1988 Free-trade agreement with Australia signed.
1989 Lange resigned over economic differences with finance minister (he cited health reasons); replaced by Geoffrey Palmer.
1990 Palmer replaced by Mike Moore. Labour Party defeated by National Party in general election; Jim Bolger became prime minister.
1991 Formation of amalgamated Alliance Party set to challenge two-party system.
1992 Ban on visits by US warships lifted. Referendum aproved change in voting system from 1996.

1993 National Party won general election with majority of one seat.

Nicaragua

Republic of (*República de Nicaragua*)

area 127,849 sq km/49,363 sq mi
capital Managua
towns León, Granada; chief ports Corinto, Puerto Cabezas, El Bluff
physical narrow Pacific coastal plain separated from broad Atlantic coastal plain by volcanic mountains and lakes Managua and Nicaragua
features largest state of Central America and most thinly populated; Mosquito Coast, Fonseca Bay, Corn Islands
head of state and government Violeta Barrios de Chamorro from 1990
political system emergent democracy
political parties Sandinista National Liberation Front (FSLN), Marxist-Leninist; Democratic Conservative Party (PCD), centrist; National Opposition Union (UNO), loose, US-backed coalition
exports coffee, cotton, sugar, bananas, meat
currency cordoba
population (1992) 4,131,000 (mestizo 70%, Spanish descent 15%, Indian or black 10%); growth rate 3.3% p.a.
life expectancy men 61, women 63 (1989)
languages Spanish (official), Indian, English
religion Roman Catholic 95%
literacy 66% (1986)
GNP $2.1 bn; $610 per head (1988)

chronology
1838 Independence achieved from Spain.
1926–1933 Occupied by US marines.
1936 General Anastasio Somoza elected president; start of near-dictatorial rule by Somoza family.
1962 Sandinista National Liberation Front (FSLN) formed to fight Somoza regime.
1979 Somoza government ousted by FSLN.
1982 Subversive activity against the government by right-wing Contra guerrillas promoted by the USA. State of emergency declared.
1984 The USA mined Nicaraguan harbours.
1985 Denunciation of Sandinista government by US president Reagan. FSLN won assembly elections.

1987 Central American peace agreement cosigned by Nicaraguan leaders.
1988 Peace agreement failed. Nicaragua held talks with Contra rebel leaders. Hurricane left 180,000 people homeless.
1989 Demobilization of rebels and release of former Somozan supporters; cease-fire ended.
1990 FSLN defeated by UNO, a US-backed coalition; Violeta Barrios de Chamorro elected president. Antigovernment riots.
1991 First presidential state visit to USA for over fifty years.
1992 June: US aid suspended because of concern over role of Sandinista in Nicaraguan government. Sept: around 16,000 made homeless by earthquake.

Niger

Republic of (*République du Niger*)

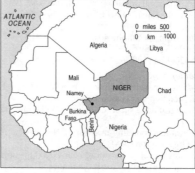

area 1,186,408 sq km/457,953 sq mi
capital Niamey
towns Zinder, Maradi, Tahoua
physical desert plains between hills in N and savanna in S; river Niger in SW, Lake Chad in SE
features part of the Sahara Desert and subject to Sahel droughts
head of state Mahamane Ousmane from 1993
head of government Mahamdou Issaoufou from 1993
political system military republic
political parties Alliance for the Forces of Change (AFC), moderate left of centre; National Movement for a Development Society (MNSD), right of centre
exports peanuts, livestock, gum arabic, uranium
currency franc CFA
population (1992) 8,281,000; growth rate 2.8% p.a.
life expectancy men 48, women 50 (1989)
languages French (official), Hausa, Djerma, and other minority languages
religions Sunni Muslim 85%, animist 15%
literacy men 19%, women 9% (1985 est)
GNP $2.2 bn; $310 per head (1987)

chronology
1960 Achieved full independence from France; Hamani Diori elected president.
1974 Diori ousted in army coup led by Seyni Kountché.
1977 Cooperation agreement signed with France.
1987 Kountché died; replaced by Col Ali Saibu.
1989 Ali Saibu elected president without oppostion.
1990 Multiparty politics promised.
1991 Saibu stripped of executive powers; transitional government formed.

1992 Transitional government collapsed. Referendum endorsed the adoption of multiparty politics.
1993 Mamahame Ousmane elected president in multiparty elections; Mahamdou Issaufou appointed prime minister.

Nigeria
Federal Republic of

area 923,773 sq km/356,576 sq mi
capital Abuja
towns Ibadan, Ogbomosho, Kano; ports Lagos, Port Harcourt, Warri, Calabar
physical arid savanna in N; tropical rainforest in S, with mangrove swamps along the coast; river Niger forms wide delta; mountains in SE
environment toxic waste from northern industrialized countries has been dumped in Nigeria
features harmattan (dry wind from the Sahara); rich artistic heritage, for example, Benin bronzes
head of state and government General Sani Abacha from 1993
political system military republic pending promised elections
political parties Social Democratic Party (SDP), left of centre; National Republican Convention (NRC), right of centre
exports petroleum (largest oil resources in Africa), cocoa, peanuts, palm oil (Africa's largest producer), cotton, rubber, tin
currency naira
population (1992) 89,666,000 (Yoruba in W, Ibo in E, and Hausa-Fulani in N); growth rate 3.3% p.a.
life expectancy men 47, women 49 (1989)
languages English (official), Hausa, Ibo, Yoruba
media all radio and television stations and almost 50% of all publishing owned by the federal government or the Nigerian states
religions Sunni Muslim 50% (in N), Christian 40% (in S), local religions 10%
literacy men 54%, women 31% (1985 est)
GNP $78 bn (1987); $790 per head (1984)

chronology
1914 N Nigeria and S Nigeria united to become Britain's largest African colony.
1954 Nigeria became a federation.
1960 Independence achieved from Britain within the Commonwealth.
1963 Became a republic, with Nnamdi Azikiwe as president.

1966 Military coup, followed by a counter-coup led by General Yakubu Gowon. Slaughter of many members of the Ibo tribe in north.
1967 Conflict over oil revenues led to declaration of an independent Ibo state of Biafra and outbreak of civil war.
1970 Surrender of Biafra and end of civil war.
1975 Gowon ousted in military coup; second coup put General Olusegun Obasanjo in power.
1979 Shehu Shagari became civilian president.
1983 Shagari's government overthrown in coup by Maj-General Muhammadu Buhari.
1985 Buhari replaced in a bloodless coup led by Maj-General Ibrahim Babangida.
1989 Two new political parties approved. Babangida promised a return to pluralist politics; date set for 1992.
1991 Nine new states created. Babangida confirmed his commitment to democratic rule for 1992.
1992 Multiparty elections won by Babangida's SDP.
1993 Results of presidential elections suspended by national commission, following complaints of ballot rigging. SDP agreed to work with NRC to form an interim government but Babangida postponed talks. Aug: ernest Shonekan appointed interim prime minister. Nov: General Sani Abacha took over as prime minister, restoring military rule and dissolving political parties.

Norway
Kingdom of (*Kongeriket Norge*)

area 387,000 sq km/149,421 sq mi (includes Svalbard and Jan Mayen)
capital Oslo
towns Bergen, Trondheim, Stavanger
physical mountainous with fertile valleys and deeply indented coast; forests cover 25%; extends N of Arctic Circle
territories dependencies in the Arctic (Svalbard and Jan Mayen) and in Antarctica (Bouvet and Peter I Island, and Queen Maud Land)
environment an estimated 80% of the lakes and streams in the southern half of the country have been severely acidified by acid rain
features fjords, including Hardanger and Sogne, longest 185 km/115 mi, deepest 1,245 m/4,086 ft; glaciers in north; midnight sun and northern lights
head of state Harald V from 1991
head of government Gro Harlem Brundtland from 1990

political system constitutional monarchy
political parties Norwegian Labour Party (DNA), moderate left of centre; Conservative Party, progressive, right of centre; Christian People's Party (KrF), Christian, centre-left; Centre Party (SP), left of centre, rural-oriented
exports petrochemicals from North Sea oil and gas, paper, wood pulp, furniture, iron ore and other minerals, high-tech goods, sports goods, fish
currency krone
population (1992) 4,283,000; growth rate 0.3% p.a.
life expectancy men 73, women 80 (1989)
languages Norwegian (official); there are Saami-(Lapp) and Finnish-speaking minorities
religion Evangelical Lutheran (endowed by state) 94%
literacy 100% (1989)
GNP $113.1 bn (1992)

chronology
1814 Became independent from Denmark; ceded to Sweden.
1905 Links with Sweden ended; full independence achieved.
1940–45 Occupied by Germany.
1949 Joined North Atlantic Treaty Organization (NATO).
1952 Joined Nordic Council.
1957 King Haakon VII succeeded by his son Olaf V.
1960 Joined European Free Trade Association (EFTA).
1972 Accepted into membership of European Economic Community; application withdrawn after a referendum.
1988 Gro Harlem Brundtland awarded Third World Prize.
1989 Jan P Syse became prime minister.
1990 Brundtland returned to power.
1991 King Olaf V died; succeeded by his son Harald V.
1992 Defied whaling ban to resume whaling industry. Brundtland relinquished leadership of the Labour Party. Formal application made for EC membership.
1993 Brundtland re-elected. Growing opposition to EC membership.

Oman

Sultanate of (*Saltanat `Uman*)

area 272,000 sq km/105,000 sq mi
capital Muscat
towns Salalah, Nizwa
physical mountains to N and S of a high arid plateau; fertile coastal strip
features Jebel Akhdar highlands; Kuria Muria islands; Masirah Island is used in aerial reconnaissance of the Arabian Sea and Indian Ocean; exclave on Musandam Peninsula controlling Strait of Hormuz
head of state and government Qaboos bin Said from 1970
political system absolute monarchy
political parties none
exports oil, dates, silverware, copper
currency rial Omani
population (1992) 1,640,000; growth rate 3.0% p.a.
life expectancy men 55, women 58 (1989)
languages Arabic (official), English, Urdu, other Indian languages

religions Ibadhi Muslim 75%, Sunni Muslim, Shi'ite Muslim, Hindu
literacy 20% (1989)
GNP $7.5 bn (1987); $5,070 per head (1988)

chronology
1951 The Sultanate of Muscat and Oman achieved full independence from Britain. Treaty of Friendship with Britain signed.
1970 After 38 years' rule, Sultan Said bin Taimur replaced in coup by his son Qaboos bin Said. Name changed to Sultanate of Oman.
1975 Left-wing rebels in south defeated.
1982 Memorandum of Understanding with UK signed, providing for regular consultation on international issues.
1985 Diplomatic ties established with USSR.
1991 Sent troops to Operation Desert Storm, as part of coalition opposing Iraq's occupation of Kuwait.

Pakistan

Islamic Republic of

area 796,100 sq km/307,295 sq mi; one-third of Kashmir under Pakistani control
capital Islamabad
towns Karachi, Lahore, Rawalpindi, Peshawar
physical fertile Indus plain in E, Baluchistan plateau in W, mountains in N and NW
environment about 68% of irrigated land is waterlogged or suffering from salinization
features the 'five rivers' (Indus, Jhelum, Chenab, Ravi, and Sutlej) feed the world's largest irrigation system; Tarbela (world's largest earthfill dam); K2 mountain; Khyber Pass; sites of the Indus Valley civilization
head of state Farooq Leghari from 1993
head of government Benazir Bhutto from 1993
political system emergent democracy
political parties Pakistan People's Party (PPP), moderate, Islamic, socialist; Islamic Democratic Alliance (IDA), including the Pakistan Muslim League (PML), Islamic conservative; Mohajir National Movement (MQM), Sind-based *mohajir* (Muslims previously living in India) settlers
exports cotton textiles, rice, leather, carpets
currency Pakistan rupee
population (1992) 130,129,000 (Punjabi 66%, Sindhi 13%); growth rate 3.1% p.a.

life expectancy men 54, women 55 (1989)
languages Urdu and English (official); Punjabi, Sindhi, Pashto, Baluchi, other local dialects
religions Sunni Muslim 75%, Shi'ite Muslim 20%, Hindu 4%
literacy men 40%, women 19% (1985 est)
GDP $39 bn (1988); $360 per head (1984)

chronology
1947 Independence achieved from Britain, Pakistan formed following partition of British India.
1956 Proclaimed a republic.
1958 Military rule imposed by General Ayub Khan.
1969 Power transferred to General Yahya Khan.
1971 Secession of East Pakistan (Bangladesh). After civil war, power transferred to Zulfiqar Ali Bhutto.
1977 Bhutto overthrown in military coup by General Zia ul-Haq; martial law imposed.
1979 Bhutto executed.
1981 Opposition Movement for the Restoration of Democracy formed. Islamization process pushed forward.
1985 Nonparty elections held, amended constitution adopted, martial law and ban on political parties lifted.
1986 Agitation for free elections launched by Benazir Bhutto.
1988 Zia introduced Islamic legal code, the Shari'a. He was killed in a military plane crash in Aug. Benazir Bhutto elected prime minister Nov.
1989 Pakistan rejoined the Commonwealth.
1990 Army mobilized in support of Muslim separatists in Indian Kashmir. Bhutto dismissed on charges of incompetence and corruption. Islamic Democratic Alliance (IDA), led by Nawaz Sharif, won Oct general election.
1991 Shari'a bill enacted; privatization and economic deregulation programme launched.
1992 Sept: Floods devastated north of country. Oct: Pakistan elected to UN Security Council 1993–95.
1993 Oct: Benazir Bhutto elected prime minister. Farooq Leghari elected president, promising to restore full parliamentary political system.

Panama

Republic of (*República de Panamá*)

area 77,100 sq km/29,768 sq mi
capital Panamá (Panama City)

towns Cristóbal, Balboa, Colón, David
physical coastal plains and mountainous interior; tropical rainforest in E and NW; Pearl Islands in Gulf of Panama
features Panama Canal; Barro Colorado Island in Gatún Lake (reservoir supplying the canal), a tropical forest reserve since 1923; Smithsonian Tropical Research Institute
head of state and government Guillermo Endara from 1989
political system emergent democratic republic
political parties Democratic Revolutionary Party (PRD), right-wing; Labour Party (PALA), right of centre; Panamanian Republican Party (PPR), right-wing; Nationalist Liberal Republican Movement (MOLIRENA), left of centre; Authentic Panamanian Party (PPA), centrist; Christian Democratic Party (PDC), centre-left
exports bananas, petroleum products, copper, shrimps, sugar
currency balboa
population (1992) 2,515,000 (mestizo, or mixed race, 70%; West Indian 14%; European descent 10%; Indian (Cuna, Choco, Guayami) 6%); growth rate 2.2% p.a.
life expectancy men 71, women 75 (1989)
languages Spanish (official), English
religions Roman Catholic 93%, Protestant 6%
literacy 87% (1989)
GNP $4.2 bn (1988); $1,970 per head (1984)

chronology
1821 Achieved independence from Spain; joined confederacy of Gran Colombia.
1903 Full independence achieved on separation from Colombia.
1974 Agreement to negotiate full transfer of the Panama Canal from the USA to Panama.
1977 USA–Panama treaties transferred the canal to Panama, effective from 1990, with the USA guaranteeing its protection and an annual payment.
1984 Nicolás Ardito Barletta elected president.
1985 Barletta resigned; replaced by Eric Arturo del Valle.
1987 General Noriega (head of the National Guard and effective ruler) resisted calls for his removal, despite suspension of US military and economic aid.
1988 Del Valle replaced by Manuel Solis Palma. Noriega, charged with drug smuggling by the USA, declared a state of emergency.

1989 Opposition won election; Noriega declared results invalid; Francisco Rodríguez sworn in as president. Coup attempt against Noriega failed; Noriega declared head of government by assembly. 'State of war' with the USA announced. US invasion deposed Noriega; Guillermo Endara installed as president. Noriega sought asylum in Vatican embassy; later surrendered and taken to US for trial.
1991 Attempted antigovernment coup foiled. Army abolished.
1992 Noriega found guilty of drug offences. Referendum voted down overwhelmingly government's constitutional changes, including abolition of a standing army.

Papua New Guinea

area 462,840 sq km/178,656 sq mi
capital Port Moresby (on E New Guinea)
towns Lae, Rabaul, Madang
physical mountainous; includes tropical islands of New Ireland, New Britain, and Bougainville; Admiralty Islands, D'Entrecasteaux Islands, and Louisiade Archipelago
features one of world's largest swamps on SW coast; world's largest butterfly, orchids; Sepik River
head of state Elizabeth II, represented by governor general
head of government Paias Wingti from 1992
political system liberal democracy
political parties Papua New Guinea Party (Pangu Pati: PP), urban- and coastal-oriented nationalist; People's Democratic Movement (PDM), 1985 breakaway from the PP; National Party (NP), highlands-based; Melanesian Alliance (MA), Bougainville-based autonomy; People's Progress Party (PPP), conservative
exports copra, coconut oil, palm oil, tea, copper, gold, coffee
currency kina
population (1992) 3,834,000 (Papuans, Melanesians, Negritos, various minorities); growth rate 2.6% p.a.
life expectancy men 53, women 54 (1987)
languages English (official); pidgin English, 715 local languages
religions Protestant 63%, Roman Catholic 31%, local faiths
literacy men 55%, women 36% (1985 est)
GNP $2.5 bn; $730 per head (1987)

chronology
1883 Annexed by Queensland; became the Australian Territory of Papua.
1884 NE New Guinea annexed by Germany; SE claimed by Britain.
1914 NE New Guinea occupied by Australia.
1921–42 Held as a League of Nations mandate.
1942–45 Occupied by Japan.
1975 Independence achieved from Australia, within the Commonwealth, with Michael Somare as prime minister.
1980 Julius Chan became prime minister.
1982 Somare returned to power.
1985 Somare challenged by Paias Wingti, the deputy prime minister, who later formed a five-party coalition government.
1988 Wingti defeated on no-confidence vote and replaced by Rabbie Namaliu, who established a six-party coalition government.
1989 State of emergency imposed on Bougainville in response to separatist violence.
1991 Peace accord signed with Bougainville secessionists. Economic boom as gold production doubled. Wiwa Korowi elected as new governor general. Deputy Prime Minister Ted Diro resigned, having been found guilty of corruption.
1992 April: killings by outlawed Bougainville secessionists reported. July: Wingti elected premier.

Paraguay

Republic of (*República del Paraguay*)

area 406,752 sq km/157,006 sq mi
capital Asunción
towns Puerto Presidente Stroessner, Pedro Juan Caballero; port Concepción
physical low marshy plain and marshlands; divided by Paraguay River; Paraná River forms SE boundary
features Itaipú dam on border with Brazil; Gran Chaco plain with huge swamps
head of state and government Juan Carlos Wasmosy from 1993
political system emergent democratic republic
political parties National Republican Association (Colorado Party), right of centre; Liberal Party (PL), right of centre; Radical Liberal Party (PLR), centrist

exports cotton, soya beans, timber, vegetable oil, maté
currency guaraní
population (1992) 4,519,000 (95% mixed Guarani Indian–Spanish descent); growth rate 3.0% p.a.
life expectancy men 67, women 72 (1989)
languages Spanish 6% (official), Guarani 90%
religion Roman Catholic 97%
literacy men 91%, women 85% (1985 est)
GNP $7.4 bn; $1,000 per head (1987)

chronology
1811 Independence achieved from Spain.
1865–70 War with Argentina, Brazil, and Uruguay; less than half the population survived and much territory lost.
1932–35 Territory won from Bolivia during the Chaco War.
1940–48 Presidency of General Higinio Morínigo.
1948–54 Political instability; six different presidents.
1954 General Alfredo Stroessner seized power.
1989 Stroessner ousted in coup led by General Andrés Rodríguez. Rodríguez elected president; Colorado Party won the congressional elections.
1991 Colorado Party successful in assembly elections.
1993 Free multi-party elections won by Colorado Party and Juan Carlos Wasmosy won presidential elections.

Peru

Republic of (*República del Perú*)

area 1,285,200 sq km/496,216 sq mi
capital Lima, including port of Callao
towns Arequipa, Iquitos, Chiclayo, Trujillo
physical Andes mountains NW–SE cover 27% of Peru, separating Amazon river-basin jungle in NE from coastal plain in W; desert along coast N–S
environment an estimated 38% of the 8,000 sq km/3,100 sq mi of coastal lands under irrigation are either waterlogged or suffering from saline water. Only half the population has access to clean drinking water
features Lake Titicaca; Atacama Desert; Nazca lines, monuments of Machu Picchu, Chan Chan, Charín de Huantar

head of state and government Alberto Fujimori from 1990
political system democratic republic
political parties American Popular Revolutionary Alliance (APRA), moderate, left-wing; United Left (IU), left-wing; Change 90, centrist
exports coca, coffee, alpaca, llama and vicuña wool, fish meal, lead (largest producer in South America), copper, iron, oil
currency new sol
population (1992) 22,454,000 (Indian, mainly Quechua and Aymara, 46%; mixed Spanish–Indian descent 43%); growth rate 2.6% p.a.
life expectancy men 61, women 66
languages Spanish 68%, Quechua 27% (both official), Aymara 3%
religion Roman Catholic 90%
literacy men 91%, women 78% (1985 est)
GNP $19.6 bn (1988); $940 per head (1984)

chronology
1824 Independence achieved from Spain.
1849–74 Some 80,000–100,000 Chinese labourers arrived in Peru to fill menial jobs such as collecting guano.
1902 Boundary dispute with Bolivia settled.
1927 Boundary dispute with Colombia settled.
1942 Boundary dispute with Ecuador settled.
1948 Army coup, led by General Manuel Odría, installed a military government.
1963 Return to civilian rule, with Fernando Belaúnde Terry as president.
1968 Return of military government in a bloodless coup by General Juan Velasco Alvarado.
1975 Velasco replaced, in a bloodless coup, by General Morales Bermúdez.
1980 Return to civilian rule, with Fernando Belaúnde as president. Sendero Luminoso ('Shining Path') Maoist guerrilla group formed.
1981 Boundary dispute with Ecuador renewed.
1985 Belaúnde succeeded by Social Democrat Alan García Pérez.
1987 President García delayed the nationalization of Peru's banks after a vigorous campaign against the proposal.
1988 García pressured to seek help from the International Monetary Fund (IMF). Sendero Luminoso increased campaign of violence.
1989 Writer Mario Vargas Llosa entered presidential race; his Democratic Front won municipal elections Nov.
1990 Alberto Fujimori defeated Vargas Llosa in presidential elections. Assassination attempt on president failed.
1992 Two coup attempts against the government failed. USA suspended humanitarian aid. Sendero Luminoso leader Abimael Guzman Reynoso was arrested and sentenced to life imprisonment after a show trial. Single-chamber legislature replaced two-chamber system.
1993 National congress voted to allow Fujimori to seek re-election in 1995.

Philippines

Republic of the (*Republika ng Pilipinas*)
area 300,000 sq km/115,800 sq mi
capital Manila (on Luzon)

towns Quezon City (Luzon), Zamboanga (Mindanao); ports Cebu, Davao (on Mindanao), and Iloilo
physical comprises over 7,000 islands; volcanic mountain ranges traverse main chain N–S; 50% still forested. The largest islands are Luzon 108,172 sq km/ 41,754 sq mi and Mindanao 94,227 sq km/36,372 sq mi; others include Samar, Negros, Palawan, Panay, Mindoro, Leyte, Cebu, and the Sulu group
environment cleared for timber, tannin, and the creation of fish ponds, the mangrove forest was reduced from 5,000 sq km/1,930 sq mi to 380 sq km/146 sq mi between 1920 and 1988
features Luzon, site of Clark Field, US air base used as a logistical base in Vietnam War; Subic Bay, US naval base; Pinatubo volcano (1,759 m/5,770 ft); Mindanao has active volcano Apo (2,954 m/9,690 ft) and mountainous rainforest
head of state and government Fidel Ramos from 1992
political system emergent democracy
political parties People's Power, including the PDP–Laban Party and the Liberal Party, centrist pro-Aquino; Nationalist Party, Union for National Action (UNA), and Grand Alliance for Democracy (GAD), conservative opposition groupings; Mindanao Alliance, island-based decentralist body
exports sugar, copra (world's largest producer) and coconut oil, timber, copper concentrates, electronics, clothing
currency peso
population (1992) 63,609,000 (93% Malaysian); growth rate 2.4% p.a.
life expectancy men 63, women 69 (1989)
languages Tagalog (Filipino, official); English and Spanish
religions Roman Catholic 84%, Protestant 9%, Muslim 5%
literacy 88% (1989)
GNP $38.2 bn; $667 per head (1988)

chronology
1542 Named the Philippines (Filipinas) by Spanish explorers.
1565 Conquered by Spain.
1898 Ceded to the USA after Spanish–American War.
1935 Granted internal self-government.
1942–45 Occupied by Japan.
1946 Independence achieved from USA.

1965 Ferdinand Marcos elected president.
1983 Opposition leader Benigno Aquino murdered by military guard.
1986 Marcos overthrown by Corazon Aquino's People's Power movement.
1987 'Freedom constitution' adopted, giving Aquino mandate to rule until June 1992; People's Power won majority in congressional elections. Attempted right-wing coup suppressed. Communist guerrillas active. Government in rightward swing.
1988 Land Reform Act gave favourable compensation to holders of large estates.
1989 Referendum on southern autonomy failed; Marcos died in exile; Aquino refused his burial in Philippines. Sixth coup attempt suppressed with US aid; Aquino declared state of emergency.
1990 Seventh coup attempt survived by President Aquino.
1991 June: eruption of Mount Pinatubo, hundreds killed. USA agreed to give up Clark Field airbase but keep Subic Bay naval base for ten more years. Sept: Philippines Senate voted to urge withdrawal of all US forces. US renewal of Subic Bay lease rejected. Nov: Imelda Marcos returned.
1992 Fidel Ramos elected to replace Aquino.

Poland

Republic of (*Polska Rzeczpospolita*)

area 127,886 sq km/49,325 sq mi
capital Warsaw
towns Łódź, Kraków, Wrocław, Poznań, Katowice, Bydgoszcz, Lublin; ports Gdańsk, Szczecin, Gdynia
physical part of the great plain of Europe; Vistula, Oder, and Neisse rivers; Sudeten, Tatra, and Carpathian mountains on S frontier
environment atmospheric pollution derived from coal (producing 90% of the country's electricity), toxic waste from industry, and lack of sewage treatment have resulted in the designation of 27 ecologically endangered areas. Half the country's lakes have been seriously contaminated and three-quarters of its drinking water does not meet official health standards
features last wild European bison (only in protected herds)
head of state Lech Wałęsa from 1990
head of government Waldemar Pawlak from 1993

political system emergent democratic republic
political parties Democratic Union, centrist, ex-Solidarity; Democratic Left Alliance, ex-communist; Centre Alliance, right of centre, Wałesa-linked; Social Democratic Party of the Polish Republic, 1990 successor to Polish United Workers' Party (PUWP), social democratic; Union of Social Democrats, radical breakaway from PUWP formed 1990; Solidarność (Solidarity) Parliamentary Club (OKP), anticommunist coalition
exports coal, softwood timber, chemicals, machinery, ships, vehicles, meat, copper (Europe's largest producer)
currency zloty
population (1992) 38,429,000; growth rate 0.6% p.a.
life expectancy men 66, women 74 (1989)
languages Polish (official), German
media broadcasters required by law to 'respect Christian values'
religion Roman Catholic 95%
literacy 98% (1989)
GNP $276 billion (1988); $2,000 per head (1986)

chronology
1918 Poland revived as independent republic.
1939 German invasion and occupation.
1944 Germans driven out by Soviet forces.
1945 Polish boundaries redrawn at Potsdam Conference.
1947 Communist people's republic proclaimed.
1956 Poznań riots. Wladyslaw Gomułka installed as Polish United Workers' Party (PUWP) leader.
1970 Gomułka replaced by Edward Gierek after Gdańsk riots.
1980 Solidarity emerged as a free trade union following Gdańsk disturbances.
1981 Martial law imposed by General Wojciech Jaruzelski.
1983 Martial law ended.
1984 Amnesty for political prisoners.
1985 Zbigniew Messner became prime minister.
1987 Referendum on economic reform rejected.
1988 Solidarity-led strikes and demonstrations called off after pay increases. Messner resigned; replaced by the reformist Mieczysław F Rakowski.
1989 Solidarity relegalized. April: new 'socialist pluralist' constitution formed. June: widespread success for Solidarity in assembly elections, the first open elections in 40 years. July: Jaruzelski elected president. Sept: 'Grand coalition', first non-Communist government since World War II formed; economic restructuring undertaken on free-market lines; W Europe and US create $1 billion aid package.
1990 Jan: PUWP dissolved; replaced by Social Democratic Party and breakaway Union of Social Democrats. Lech Wałesa elected president; Dec: prime minister Mazowiecki resigned.
1991 Oct: Multiparty general election produced inconclusive result. Five-party centre-right coalition formed under Jan Olszewski. Treaty signed agreeing to complete withdrawal of Soviet troops.
1992 June: Olszewski ousted on vote of no confidence; succeeded by Waldemar Pawlak. July: Hanna Suchocka replaced Pawlak.
1993 14% of workforce (2.6 million) unemployed. Suchocka lost vote of confidence. Sept: general election; Pawlak appointed prime minister.

Portugal

Republic of (*República Portuguesa*)

area 92,000 sq km/35,521 sq mi (including the Azores and Madeira)
capital Lisbon
towns Coimbra; ports Pôrto, Setúbal
physical mountainous in N, plains in S
features rivers Minho, Douro, Tagus (Tejo), Guadiana; Serra da Estrêla mountains
head of state Mario Alberto Nobre Lopes Soares from 1986
head of government Aníbal Cavaco Silva from 1985
political system democratic republic
political parties Social Democratic Party (PSD), moderate left of centre; Socialist Party (PS), progressive socialist; Democratic Renewal Party (PRD), centre-left; Democratic Social Centre Party (CDS), moderate left of centre
exports wine, olive oil, resin, cork, sardines, textiles, clothing, pottery, pulpwood
currency escudo
population (1992) 9,844,000; growth rate 0.5% p.a.
life expectancy men 71, women 78 (1989)
language Portuguese
religion Roman Catholic 97%
literacy men 89%, women 80% (1985)
GNP $83.9 bn (1992)

chronology
1928–68 Military dictatorship under António de Oliveira Salazar.
1968 Salazar succeeded by Marcello Caetano.
1974 Caetano removed in military coup led by General António Ribeiro de Spínola. Spínola replaced by General Francisco da Costa Gomes.
1975 African colonies became independent.
1976 New constitution, providing for return to civilian rule, adopted. Minority government appointed, led by Socialist Party leader Mario Soares.
1978 Soares resigned.
1980 Francisco Balsemão formed centre-party coalition after two years of political instability.
1982 Draft of new constitution approved, reducing powers of presidency.
1983 Centre-left coalition government formed.
1985 Aníbal Cavaco Silva became prime minister.
1986 Mario Soares elected first civilian president in 60 years. Portugal joined European Community.
1988 Portugal joined Western European Union.

1989 Constitution amended to allow major state enterprises to be denationalized.

1991 Mario Soares re-elected president; Social Democrat (PSD) majority slightly reduced in assembly elections.

Qatar

State of (*Dawlat Qatar*)

area 11,400 sq km/4,402 sq mi
capital and chief port Doha
town Dukhan, centre of oil production
physical mostly flat desert with salt flats in S
features negligible rain and surface water; only 3% is fertile, but irrigation allows self-sufficiency in fruit and vegetables; extensive oil discoveries since World War II
head of state and government Sheik Khalifa bin Hamad al-Thani from 1972
political system absolute monarchy
political parties none
exports oil, natural gas, petrochemicals, fertilizers, iron, steel
currency riyal
population (1992) 520,000 (half in Doha; Arab 40%, Indian 18%, Pakistani 18%); growth rate 3.7% p.a.
life expectancy men 68, women 72 (1989)
languages Arabic (official), English
religion Sunni Muslim 95%
literacy 60% (1987)
GNP $5.9 bn (1983); $35,000 per head

chronology
1916 Qatar became a British protectorate.
1970 Constitution adopted, confirming the emirate as an absolute monarchy.
1971 Independence achieved from Britain.
1972 Emir Sheik Ahmad replaced in bloodless coup by his cousin, Crown Prince Sheik Khalifa.
1991 Forces joined UN coalition in Gulf War against Iraq.

Romania

area 237,500 sq km/91,699 sq mi
capital Bucharest
towns Braşov, Timişoara, Cluj-Napoca, Iaşi; ports Galaţi, Constanta, Brăila
physical mountains surrounding a plateau, with river plains S and E

environment although sulphur-dioxide levels are low, only 20% of the country's rivers can provide drinkable water
features Carpathian Mountains, Transylvanian Alps; river Danube; Black Sea coast; mineral springs
head of state Ion Iliescu from 1989
head of government Nicolai Vacaroiu from 1992
political system emergent democratic republic
political parties National Salvation Front (NSF), reform socialist; Civic Alliance (CA), right of centre; Convention for Democracy, umbrella organization for right-of-centre National Liberal Party (NLP) and ethnic-Hungarian Magyar Democratic Union (UDM)
exports petroleum products and oilfield equipment, electrical goods, cars, cereals
currency leu
population (1992) 23,332,000 (Romanians 89%, Hungarians 7.9%, Germans 1.6%); growth rate 0.5% p.a.
life expectancy men 67, women 73 (1989)
languages Romanian (official), Hungarian, German
media television is state-run; there are an estimated 900 newspapers and magazines, but only the progovernment papers have adequate distribution and printing facilities
religions Romanian Orthodox 80%, Roman Catholic 6%
literacy 98% (1988)
GNP $151 bn (1988); $6,400 per head

chronology
1944 Pro-Nazi Antonescu government overthrown.
1945 Communist-dominated government appointed.
1947 Boundaries redrawn. King Michael abdicated and People's Republic proclaimed.
1949 New Soviet-style constitution adopted. Joined Comecon.
1952 Second new Soviet-style constitution.
1955 Romania joined Warsaw Pact.
1958 Soviet occupation forces removed.
1965 New constitution adopted.
1974 Ceauşescu created president.
1985–86 Winters of austerity and power cuts.
1987 Workers demonstrated against austerity programme.
1988–89 Relations with Hungary deteriorated over 'systematization programme'.
1989 Announcement that all foreign debt paid off. Razing of villages and building of monuments to

Ceaușescu. Communist orthodoxy reaffirmed; demonstrations violently suppressed; massacre in Timisoara. Army joined uprising; heavy fighting; bloody overthrow of Ceaușescu regime in 'Christmas Revolution'; Ceaușescu and wife tried and executed; estimated 10,000 dead in civil warfare. Power assumed by new National Salvation Front, headed by Ion Iliescu.

1990 Securitate secret police replaced by new Romanian Intelligence Service; religious practices resumed; mounting strikes and protests against effects of market economy.

1991 April: treaty on cooperation and good neighbourliness signed with USSR. Aug: privatization law passed. Sept: prime minister Petre Roman resigned following riots; succeeded by Theodor Stolojan heading a new cross-party coalition government. Dec: new constitution endorsed by referendum.

1992 Iliescu re-elected president; Nicolai Vacaroiu appointed prime minister.

Russian Federation

formerly (until 1991) Russian Soviet Federal Socialist Republic (RSFSR)

area 17,075,500 sq km/6,591,100 sq mi
capital Moscow
towns St Petersburg (Leningrad), Nizhny-Novgorod (Gorky), Rostov-on-Don, Samara (Kuibyshev), Tver (Kalinin), Volgograd, Vyatka (Kirov), Ekaterinburg (Sverdlovsk)
physical fertile Black Earth district; extensive forests; the Ural Mountains with large mineral resources
features the heavily industrialized area around Moscow; Siberia; includes 16 autonomous republics (capitals in brackets): Bashkir (Ufa); Buryat (Ulan-Ude); Checheno-Ingush (Grozny); Chuvash (Cheboksary); Dagestan (Makhachkala); Kabardino-Balkar (Nalchik); Kalmyk (Elista); Karelia (Petrozavodsk); Komi (Syktyvkar); Mari (Yoshkar-Ola); Mordovia (Saransk); Vladikavkaz (formerly Ordzhonikidze); Tatarstan (Kazan); Tuva (Kizyl); Udmurt (Izhevsk); Yakut (Yakutsk)
head of state Boris Yeltsin from 1990/91
head of government Viktor Chernomyrdin from 1992
political system emergent democracy
political parties Russia's Choice, pro-Yeltsin reformist; Party of Russia, Unity of Accord, moderate reformist; Yabloko bloc, radical, free-market; Russian Communist Party, left-wing, conservative; Agrarian party, centrist; Liberal Democratic Party, far-right, neo-Fascist.

products iron ore, coal, oil, gold, platinum, and other minerals, agricultural produce
currency rouble
population (1992) 149,469,000 (82% Russian, Tatar 4%, Ukrainian 3%, Chuvash 1%)
language Great Russian
religion traditionally Russian Orthodox

chronology
1945 Became a founding member of United Nations (UN).
1988 Aug: Democratic Union formed in Moscow as political party opposed to totalitarianism. Oct: Russian-language demonstrations in Leningrad, tsarist flag raised.
1989 March: Boris Yeltsin elected to USSR Congress of People's Deputies. Sept: conservative-nationalist Russian United Workers' Front established in Sverdlovsk.
1990 May: anticommunist May Day protests in Red Square, Moscow; Yeltsin narrowly elected RSFSR president by Russian parliament. June: economic and political sovereignty declared; Ivan Silaev became Russian prime minister. Aug: Tatarstan declared sovereignty. Dec: rationing introduced in some cities; private land ownership allowed.
1991 June: Yeltsin directly elected president under a liberal-radical banner. July: Yeltsin issued a decree to remove Communist Party cells from workplaces; sovereignty of the Baltic republics recognized by the republic. Aug: Yeltsin stood out against abortive anti-Gorbachev coup, emerging as key power-broker within Soviet Union; national guard established and pre-revolutionary flag restored. Sept: Silaev resigned as Russian premier. Nov: Yeltsin named prime minister; Soviet and Russian Communist Parties banned; Yeltsin's goverment gained control of Russia's economic assets and armed forces. Oct: Checheno-Ingush declared its independence. Dec: Yeltsin negotiated formation of new confederal Commonwealth of Independent States; Russia admitted into UN; independence recognized by USA and European Community.
1992 Jan: admitted into Conference on Security and Cooperation in Europe; assumed former USSR's permanent seat on UN Security Council; prices freed. Feb: demonstrations in Moscow and other cities as living standards plummeted. June: Yeltsin–Bush summit meeting. March: 18 out of 20 republics signed treaty agreeing to remain within loose Russian Federation; Tatarstan and Checheno-Ingush refused to sign. Dec: Victor Chernomyrdin elected prime minister; new constitution agreed in referendum. START II arms-reduction agreement signed with USA.
1993 Power struggle between Yeltsin and Congress of People's Deputies. Referendum gave vote of confidence in Yeltsin's presidency but did not support constitutional change. Sept: Yeltsin dissolved Supreme Soviet. Attempted coup by conservative opponents led to their arrest. Dec: new constitution approved.

Rwanda

Republic of (*Republika y'u Rwanda*)
area 26,338 sq km/10,173 sq mi
capital Kigali

towns Butare, Ruhengeri
physical high savanna and hills, with volcanic mountains in NW
features part of lake Kivu; highest peak Mount Karisimbi 4,507 m/14,792 ft; Kagera River (whose headwaters are the source of the Nile) and National Park
head of state Maj-Gen Juvenal Habyarimana from 1973
head of government Agathe Uwilingiyimana from 1993
political system one-party military republic
political party National Revolutionary Movement for Development (MRND), nationalist, socialist
exports coffee, tea, pyrethrum
currency franc
population (1992) 7,347,000 (Hutu 90%, Tutsi 9%, Twa 1%); growth rate 3.3% p.a.
life expectancy men 49, women 53 (1989)
languages Kinyarwanda, French (official); Kiswahili
religions Roman Catholic 54%, animist 23%, Protestant 12%, Muslim 9%
literacy men 50% (1989)
GNP $2.3 bn (1987); $323 per head (1986)

chronology
1916 Belgian troops occupied Rwanda; League of Nations mandated Rwanda and Burundi to Belgium as Territory of Ruanda-Urundi.
1959 Interethnic warfare between Hutu and Tutsi.
1962 Independence from Belgium achieved, with Grégoire Kayibanda as president.
1972 Renewal of interethnic fighting.
1973 Kayibanda ousted in a military coup led by Maj-Gen Juvenal Habyarimana.
1978 New constitution approved; Rwanda remained a military-controlled state.
1980 Civilian rule adopted.
1988 Refugees from Burundi massacres streamed into Rwanda.
1990 Government attacked by Rwandan Patriotic Front (FPR), a Tutsi military-political organization based in Uganda.
1992 Peace accord with FPR.
1993 Power-sharing agreement with government repudiated by FPR. Peace accord formally signed. July: Agathe Uwilingiyimana became first female prime minister.

St Christopher (St Kitts)–Nevis

Federation of

area 269 sq km/104 sq mi (St Christopher 176 sq km/68 sq mi, Nevis 93 sq km/36 sq mi)

capital Basseterre (on St Christopher)
towns Charlestown (largest on Nevis)
physical both islands are volcanic
features fertile plains on coast; black beaches
head of state Elizabeth II from 1983 represented by governor general
head of government Kennedy Simmonds from 1980
political system federal constitutional monarchy
political parties People's Action Movement (PAM), centre-right; Nevis Reformation Party (NRP), Nevis-separatist; Labour Party, moderate left of centre
exports sugar, molasses, electronics, clothing
currency Eastern Caribbean dollar
population (1992) 43,100; growth rate 0.2% p.a.
life expectancy men 69, women 72
language English
media no daily newspaper; two weekly papers, published by the governing and opposition party respectively – both receive advertising support from the government
religions Anglican 36%, Methodist 32%, other Protestant 8%, Roman Catholic 10% (1985 est)
literacy 90% (1987)
GNP $40 million (1983); $870 per head

chronology
1871–1956 Part of the Leeward Islands Federation.
1958–62 Part of the Federation of the West Indies.
1967 St Christopher, Nevis, and Anguilla achieved internal self-government, within the British Commonwealth, with Robert Bradshaw, Labour Party leader, as prime minister.
1971 Anguilla returned to being a British dependency.
1978 Bradshaw died; succeeded by Paul Southwell.
1979 Southwell died; succeeded by Lee L Moore.
1980 Coalition government led by Kennedy Simmonds.
1983 Full independence achieved within the Commonwealth.
1984 Coalition government re-elected.
1989 Prime Minister Simmonds won a third successive term.

St Lucia

area 617 sq km/238 sq mi
capital Castries
towns Vieux-Fort, Soufrière

physical mountainous island with fertile valleys; mainly tropical forest
features volcanic peaks; Gros and Petit Pitons
head of state Elizabeth II from 1979, represented by governor general
head of government John Compton from 1982
political system constitutional monarchy
political parties United Workers' Party (UWP), moderate left of centre; St Lucia Labour Party (SLP), moderate left of centre; Progressive Labour Party (PLP), moderate left of centre
exports coconut oil, bananas, cocoa, copra
currency Eastern Caribbean dollar
population (1992) 135,000; growth rate 2.8% p.a.
life expectancy men 68, women 73 (1989)
languages English; French patois
media two independent biweekly newspapers
religion Roman Catholic 90%
literacy 78% (1989)
GNP $166 million; $1,370 per head (1987)

chronology
1814 Became a British crown colony following Treaty of Paris.
1967 Acquired internal self-government as a West Indies associated state.
1979 Independence achieved from Britain within the Commonwealth. John Compton, leader of the United Workers' Party (UWP), became prime minister. Allan Louisy, leader of the St Lucia Labour Party (SLP), replaced Compton as prime minister.
1981 Louisy resigned; replaced by Winston Cenac.
1982 Compton returned to power at the head of a UWP government.
1987 Compton re-elected with reduced majority.
1991 Integration with Windward Islands proposed.
1992 UWP won general election.

St Vincent and the Grenadines

area 388 sq km/150 sq mi, including islets of the Northern Grenadines 43 sq km/17 sq mi
capital Kingstown
towns Georgetown, Chateaubelair
physical volcanic mountains, thickly forested
features Mustique, one of the Grenadines, a holiday resort; Soufrière volcano
head of state Elizabeth II from 1979, represented by governor general

head of government James Mitchell from 1984
political system constitutional monarchy
political parties New Democratic Party (NDP), moderate, left of centre; St Vincent Labour Party (SVLP), moderate, left of centre
exports bananas, taros, sweet potatoes, arrowroot, copra
currency Eastern Caribbean dollar
population (1992) 109,000; growth rate –4% p.a.
life expectancy men 69, women 74 (1989)
languages English; French patois
media government-owned radio station; two privately owned weekly newspapers, subject to government pressure
religions Anglican 47%, Methodist 28%, Roman Catholic 13%
literacy 85% (1989)
GNP $188 million; $1,070 per head (1987)

chronology
1783 Became a British crown colony.
1958–62 Part of the West Indies Federation.
1969 Achieved internal self-government.
1979 Achieved full independence from Britain, within the Commonwealth, with Milton Cato as prime minister.
1984 James Mitchell replaced Cato as prime minister.
1989 Mitchell decisively re-elected.
1991 Integration with Windward Islands proposed.

Samoa, Western

Independent State of (*Samoa i Sisifo*)

area 2,830 sq km/1,093 sq mi
capital Apia (on Upolu island)
physical comprises South Pacific islands of Savai'i and Upolu, with two smaller tropical islands and islets; mountain ranges on main islands
features lava flows on Savai'i
head of state King Malietoa Tanumafili II from 1962
head of government Tofilau Eti Alesana from 1988
political system liberal democracy
political parties Human Rights Protection Party (HRPP), led by Tofilau Eti Alesana; the Va'ai Kolone Group (VKG); Christian Democratic Party (CDP), led by Tupua Tamasese Efi. All 'parties' are personality-based groupings
exports coconut oil, copra, cocoa, fruit juice, cigarettes, timber

currency talà
population (1992) 160,000; growth rate 1.1% p.a.
life expectancy men 64, women 69 (1989)
languages English, Samoan (official)
religions Protestant 70%, Roman Catholic 20%
literacy 90% (1989)
GNP $110 million (1987); $520 per head

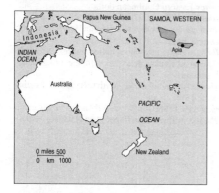

chronology
1899–1914 German protectorate.
1920–61 Administered by New Zealand.
1959 Local government elected.
1961 Referendum favoured independence.
1962 Independence achieved within the Commonwealth, with Fiame Mata Afa Mulinu'u as prime minister.
1975 Mata Afa died.
1976 Tupuola Taisi Efi became first nonroyal prime minister.
1982 Va'ai Kolone became prime minister; replaced by Tupuola Efi. Assembly failed to approve budget; Tupuola Efi resigned; replaced by Tofilau Eti Alesana.
1985 Tofilau Eti resigned; head of state invited Va'ai Kolone to lead the government.
1988 Elections produced a hung parliament, with first Tupuola Efi as prime minister and then Tofilau Eti Alesana.
1990 Universal adult suffrage introduced.
1991 Tofilau Eti Alesana re-elected. Fiame Naome became first woman in cabinet.

San Marino

Republic of (*Repubblica di San Marino*)

area 61 sq km/24 sq mi
capital San Marino
towns Serravalle (industrial centre)
physical on the slope of Mount Titano
features surrounded by Italian territory; one of the world's smallest states
heads of state and government two captains regent, elected for a six-month period
political system direct democracy
political parties San Marino Christian Democrat Party (PDCS), right of centre; Democratic Progressive Party (PDP), Socialist Unity Party (PSU), and Socialist Party (PSS), all three left of centre
exports wine, ceramics, paint, chemicals, building stone
currency Italian lira

population (1992) 23,600; growth rate 0.1% p.a.
life expectancy men 70, women 77
language Italian
religion Roman Catholic 95%
literacy 97% (1987)

chronology
1862 Treaty with Italy signed; independence recognized under Italy's protection.
1947–86 Governed by a series of left-wing and centre-left coalitions.
1986 Formation of Communist and Christian Democrat 'grand coalition'.
1992 Joined the United Nations.

São Tomé e Príncipe

Democratic Republic of

area 1,000 sq km/386 sq mi
capital São Tomé
towns Santo Antonio, Santa Cruz
physical comprises two main islands and several smaller ones, all volcanic; thickly forested and fertile
head of state and government Miguel Trovoada from 1991
political system emergent democratic republic
political parties Movement for the Liberation of São Tomé e Príncipe (MLSTP), nationalist socialist; Democratic Convergence Party–Reflection Group (PCD–EM), centre-left
exports cocoa, copra, coffee, palm oil and kernels
currency dobra
population (1992) 126,000; growth rate 2.5% p.a.
life expectancy men 62, women 62

languages Portuguese (official), Fang (Bantu)
religions Roman Catholic 80%, animist
literacy men 73%, women 42% (1981)
GNP $32 million (1987); $384 per head (1986)

chronology
1471 Discovered by Portuguese.
1522–1973 A province of Portugal.
1973 Achieved internal self-government.
1975 Independence achieved from Portugal, with Manuel Pinto da Costa as president.
1984 Formally declared a nonaligned state.
1987 Constitution amended.
1988 Unsuccessful coup attempt against da Costa.
1990 New constitution approved.
1991 First multiparty elections held; Miguel Trovoada replaced Pinto da Costa.

Saudi Arabia

Kingdom of (*al-Mamlaka al-'Arabiya as-Sa'udiya*)

area 2,200,518 sq km/849,400 sq mi
capital Riyadh
towns Mecca, Medina, Taif; ports Jidda, Dammam
physical desert, sloping to the Persian Gulf from a height of 2,750 m/9,000 ft in the W
environment oil pollution caused by the Gulf War 1990–91 has affected 460 km/285 mi of the Saudi coastline, threatening desalination plants and damaging the wildlife of saltmarshes, mangrove forest, and mudflats
features Nafud Desert in N and the Rub'al Khali (Empty Quarter) in S, area 650,000 sq km/250,000 sq mi; with a ban on women drivers, there are an estimated 300,000 chauffeurs
head of state and government King Fahd Ibn Abdul Aziz from 1982
political system absolute monarchy
political parties none
exports oil, petroleum products
currency rial
population (1992) 15,267,000 (16% nomadic); growth rate 3.1% p.a.
life expectancy men 64, women 67 (1989)
language Arabic
religion Sunni Muslim; there is a Shi'ite minority
literacy men 34%, women 12% (1980 est)
GNP $70 bn (1988); $6,170 per head (1988)

chronology
1926-32 Territories of Nejd and Hejaz united and kingdom established.
1953 King Ibn Saud died and was succeeded by his eldest son, Saud.
1964 King Saud forced to abdicate; succeeded by his brother, Faisal.
1975 King Faisal assassinated; succeeded by his half-brother, Khalid.
1982 King Khalid died; succeeded by his brother, Crown Prince Fahd.
1987 Rioting by Iranian pilgrims caused 400 deaths in Mecca; diplomatic relations with Iran severed.
1990 Iraqi troops invaded and annexed Kuwait and massed on Saudi Arabian border. King Fahd called for help from US and UK forces.
1991 King Fahd provided military and financial assistance in Gulf War. Calls from religious leaders for 'consultative assembly' to assist in government of kingdom. Saudi Arabia attended Middle East peace conference.
1992 Formation of a 'consultative council' seen as possible move towards representative government.

Senegal

Republic of (*République du Sénégal*)

area 196,200 sq km/75,753 sq mi
capital (and chief port) Dakar
towns Thiès, Kaolack
physical plains rising to hills in SE; swamp and tropical forest in SW
features river Senegal; the Gambia forms an enclave within Senegal
head of state Abdou Diouf from 1981
head of government Habib Thiam from 1993
political system emergent socialist democratic republic
political parties Senegalese Socialist Party (PS), democratic socialist; Senegalese Democratic Party (PDS), left of centre
exports peanuts, cotton, fish, phosphates
currency franc CFA
population (1992) 7,691,000; growth rate 3.1% p.a.
life expectancy men 51, women 54 (1989)
languages French (official); African dialects are spoken
religions Muslim 80%, Roman Catholic 10%, animist
literacy men 37%, women 19% (1985 est)
GNP $2 bn (1987); $380 per head (1984)

chronology
1659 Became a French colony.
1854–65 Interior occupied by French.
1902 Became a territory of French West Africa.
1959 Formed the Federation of Mali with French Sudan.
1960 Independence achieved from France, but withdrew from the federation. Léopold Sédar Senghor, leader of the Senegalese Progressive Union (UPS), became president.
1966 UPS declared the only legal party.
1974 Pluralist system re-established.
1976 UPS reconstituted as Senegalese Socialist Party (PS). Prime Minister Abdou Diouf nominated as Senghor's successor.
1980 Senghor resigned; succeeded by Diouf. Troops sent to defend Gambia.
1981 Military help again sent to Gambia.
1982 Confederation of Senegambia came into effect.
1983 Diouf re-elected. Post of prime minister abolished.
1988 Diouf decisively re-elected.
1989 Violent clashes between Senegalese and Mauritanians in Dakar and Nouakchott killed more than 450 people; over 50,000 people repatriated from both countries. Senegambia federation abandoned.
1991 Constitutional changes outlined.
1992 Diplomatic links with Mauritania re-established.
1993 Diouf re-elected. Habib Thiam appointed prime minister.

Seychelles
Republic of

area 453 sq km/175 sq mi
capital Victoria (on Mahé island)
towns Cascade, Port Glaud, Misere
physical comprises two distinct island groups, one concentrated, the other widely scattered, totalling over 100 islands and islets
features Aldabra atoll, containing world's largest tropical lagoon; the unique 'double coconut' (*coco de mer*); tourism is important
head of state and government France-Albert René from 1977
political system one-party socialist republic
political party Seychelles People's Progressive Front (SPPF), nationalist socialist
exports copra, cinnamon

currency Seychelles rupee
population (1992) 71,000; growth rate 2.2% p.a.
life expectancy 66 years (1988)
languages creole (Asian, African, European mixture) 95%, English, French (all official)
religion Roman Catholic 90%
literacy 80% (1989)
GNP $175 million; $2,600 per head (1987)

chronology
1744 Became a French colony.
1794 Captured by British.
1814 Ceded by France to Britain; incorporated as a dependency of Mauritius.
1903 Became a separate British colony.
1975 Internal self-government agreed.
1976 Independence achieved from Britain as a republic within the Commonwealth, with James Mancham as president.
1977 France-Albert René ousted Mancham in an armed coup and took over presidency.
1979 New constitution adopted; Seychelles People's Progressive Front (SPPF) sole legal party.
1981 Attempted coup by South African mercenaries thwarted.
1984 René re-elected.
1987 Coup attempt foiled.
1989 René re-elected.
1991 Multiparty politics promised.
1992 Mancham returned from exile. Constitutional commission elected; constitutional reform received insufficient support in referendum.
1993 René defeated Mancham in multi-party presidential elections. New constitution adopted.

Sierra Leone
Republic of

area 71,740 sq km/27,710 sq mi
capital Freetown
towns Koidu, Bo, Kenema, Makeni
physical mountains in E; hills and forest; coastal mangrove swamps
features hot and humid climate (3,500 mm/138 in rainfall p.a.)
head of state and government military council headed by Capt Valentine Strasser from 1992
political system transitional
political parties All People's Congress (APC), moderate socialist; United Front of Political Movements (UNIFORM), centre-left

exports palm kernels, cocoa, coffee, ginger, diamonds, bauxite, rutile
currency leone
population (1992) 4,373,000; growth rate 2.5% p.a.
life expectancy men 41, women 47 (1989)
languages English (official), local languages
media no daily newspapers; 13 weekly papers, of
which 11 are independent but only one achieves sales
of over 5,000 copies
religions animist 52%, Muslim 39%, Protestant 6%,
Roman Catholic 2% (1980 est)
literacy men 38%, women 21% (1985 est)
GNP $965 million (1987); $320 per head (1984)
chronology
1808 Became a British colony.
1896 Hinterland declared a British protectorate.
1961 Independence achieved from Britain within the
Commonwealth, with Milton Margai, leader of Sierra
Leone People's Party (SLPP), as prime minister.
1964 Milton succeeded by his half-brother, Albert
Margai.
1967 Election results disputed by army, who set up a
National Reformation Council and forced the governor general to leave.
1968 Army revolt made Siaka Stevens, leader of the
All People's Congress (APC), prime minister.
1971 New constitution adopted, making Sierra Leone
a republic, with Stevens as president.
1978 APC declared only legal party. Stevens sworn
in for another seven-year term.
1985 Stevens retired; succeeded by Maj-Gen Joseph
Momoh.
1989 Attempted coup against President Momoh
foiled.
1991 Referendum endorsed multiparty politics.
1992 Military take-over; President Momoh fled.
National Provisional Ruling Council (NPRC) established under Capt Valentine Strasser.

Singapore

Republic of

area 622 sq km/240 sq mi
capital Singapore City
towns Jurong, Changi
physical comprises Singapore Island, low and flat,
and 57 small islands

features Singapore Island is joined to the mainland
by causeway across Strait of Johore; temperature
range 21°–34°C/69°–93°F
head of state Ong Teng Cheong from 1993
head of government Goh Chok Tong from 1990
political system liberal democracy with strict limits
on dissent
political parties People's Action Party (PAP), conservative; Workers' Party (WP), socialist; Singapore
Democratic Party (SDP), liberal pluralist
exports electronics, petroleum products, rubber,
machinery, vehicles
currency Singapore dollar
population (1992) 2,792,000 (Chinese 75%, Malay
14%, Tamil 7%); growth rate 1.2% p.a.
life expectancy men 71, women 77 (1989)
languages Malay (national tongue), Chinese, Tamil,
English (all official)
religions Buddhist, Taoist, Muslim, Hindu, Christian
literacy men 93%, women 79% (1985 est)
GDP $19.9 bn (1987); $7,616 per head

chronology
1819 Singapore leased to British East India Company.
1858 Placed under crown rule.
1942 Invaded and occupied by Japan.
1945 Japanese removed by British forces.
1959 Independence achieved from Britain; Lee Kuan
Yew became prime minister.
1963 Joined new Federation of Malaysia.
1965 Left federation to become an independent
republic.
1984 Opposition made advances in parliamentary
elections.
1986 Opposition leader convicted of perjury and prohibited from standing for election.
1988 Ruling conservative party elected to all but one
of available assembly seats; increasingly authoritarian rule.
1990 Lee Kuan Yew resigned as prime minister;
replaced by Goh Chok Tong.
1991 PAP and Goh Chok Tong re-elected.
1992 Lee Kuan Yew surrendered PAP leadership to
Goh Chok Tong.
1993 Ong Teng Cheong elected president.

Slovak Republic

(*Slovenská Republika*)

area 49,035 sq km/18,940 sq mi
capital Bratislava
towns Košice, Nitra, Prešov, Banská Bystrica
physical W range of the Carpathian Mountains
including Tatra and Beskids in N; Danube plain in S;
numerous lakes and mineral springs
features fine beech and oak forests with bears and
wild boar
head of state Michal Kovak from 1993
head of government Vladimir Meciar from 1993
political system emergent democracy
political parties Civic Democratic Union (CDU),
centre-left; Movement for a Democratic Slovakia
(HZDS), centre-left, nationalist; Christian Democratic Movement (KDH), right of centre; Slovak
National Party, nationalist; Party of the Democratic
Left, left-wing, ex-communist; Coexistence and Hungarian Christian Democratic Movement, both representing Hungarian minority

exports iron ore, copper, mercury, magnesite, armaments, chemicals, textiles, machinery
currency new currency based on koruna
population (1991) 5,268,900 (with Hungarian and other minorities); growth rate 0.4% p.a.
life expectancy men 68, women 75
languages Slovak (official)
religions Roman Catholic (over 50%), Lutheran, Reformist, Orthodox
literacy 100%
GDP $10,000 million (1990); $1,887 per head

chronology
1918 Independence achieved from Austro-Hungarian Empire; Slovaks joined Czechs in forming Czechoslovakia as independent nation.
1948 Communists assumed power in Czechoslovakia.
1968 Slovak Socialist Republic created under new federal constitution.
1989 Prodemocracy demonstrations in Bratislava; new political parties formed, including Slovak-based People Against Violence (PAV); Communist Party stripped of powers. Dec: new government formed, including former dissidents; political parties legalized; Václav Havel appointed president.
1991 Evidence of increasing Slovak separatism. March: PAV splinter group formed under Slovak premier Vladimir Meciar. April: Meciar dismissed, replaced by Jan Carnogursky; pro-Meciar rallies held in Bratislava.
1992 March: PAV renamed Civic Democratic Union (CDU). June: Havel resigned following Slovak gains in assembly elections. Aug: agreement on creation of separate Czech and Slovak states.
1993 Jan: Slovak Republic became sovereign state, with Meciar, leader of the MFDS, as prime minister. Feb: Michal Kovak became president. June: Slovakia gained membership of Council of Europe.

Slovenia

Republic of

area 20,251 sq km/7,817 sq mi
capital Ljubljana
towns Maribor, Kranj, Celji; chief port: Koper
physical mountainous; Sava and Drava rivers

head of state Milan Kucan from 1990
head of government Janez Drnovsek from 1992
political system emergent democracy
political parties Christian Democratic Party, right of centre; People's Party, right of centre; Liberal Democratic Party, left of centre; Democratic Party, left of centre
products grain, sugarbeet, livestock, timber, cotton and woollen textiles, steel, vehicles
currency tolar
population (1992) 1,985,000 (Slovene 91%, Croat 3%, Serb 2%)
languages Slovene, resembling Serbo-Croat, written in Roman characters
religion Roman Catholic

chronology
1918 United with Serbia and Croatia.
1929 The kingdom of Serbs, Croats, and Slovenes took the name of Yugoslavia.
1945 Became a constituent republic of Yugoslav Socialist Federal Republic.
mid-1980s The Slovenian Communist Party liberalized itself and agreed to free elections. Yugoslav counterintelligence (KOV) began repression.
1989 Jan: Social Democratic Alliance of Slovenia launched as first political organization independent of Communist Party. Sept: constitution changed to allow secession from federation.
1990 April: nationalist DEMOS coalition secured victory in first multiparty parliamentary elections; Milan Kucan became president. July: sovereignty declared. Dec: independence overwhelmingly approved in referendum.
1991 June: independence declared; 100 killed after federal army intervened; cease-fire brokered by European Community (EC). July: cease-fire agreed between federal troops and nationalists. Oct: withdrawal of Yugoslav army completed. Dec: DEMOS coalition dissolved.
1992 Jan: EC recognized Slovenia's independence. April: Janez Drnovsek appointed prime minister; independence recognized by USA. May: admitted into United Nations and Conference on Security and Cooperation in Europe. Dec: Liberal Democrats and Christian Democrats won assembly elections; Kucan re-elected president.
1993 Drnovsek re-elected prime minister.

Solomon Islands

area 27,600 sq km/10,656 sq mi
capital Honiara (on Guadalcanal)
towns Gizo, Yandina
physical comprises all but the northernmost islands (which belong to Papua New Guinea) of a Melanesian archipelago stretching nearly 1,500 km/900 mi. The largest is Guadalcanal (area 6,500 sq km/2,510 sq mi); others are Malaita, San Cristobal, New Georgia, Santa Isabel, Choiseul; mainly mountainous and forested
features rivers ideal for hydroelectric power
head of state Elizabeth II represented by governor general
head of government Francis Billy Hilly from 1993
political system constitutional monarchy
political parties People's Alliance Party (PAP), centre-left; Solomon Islands United Party (SIUPA), right of centre
exports fish products, palm oil, copra, cocoa, timber
currency Solomon Island dollar
population (1992) 339,000 (Melanesian 95%, Polynesian 4%); growth rate 3.9% p.a.
life expectancy men 66, women 71
languages English (official); there are some 120 Melanesian dialects
religions Anglican 34%, Roman Catholic 19%, South Sea Evangelical 17%
literacy 60% (1989)
GNP $141 million; $420 per head (1987)

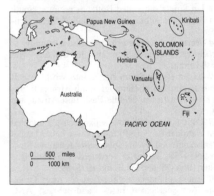

chronology
1893 Solomon Islands placed under British protection.
1978 Independence achieved from Britain within the Commonwealth, with Peter Kenilorea as prime minister.
1981 Solomon Mamaloni of the People's Progressive Party (PPP) replaced Kenilorea as prime minister.
1984 Kenilorea returned to power, heading a coalition government.
1986 Kenilorea resigned after allegations of corruption; replaced by his deputy, Ezekiel Alebua.
1988 Kenilorea elected deputy prime minister. Joined Vanuatu and Papua New Guinea to form the Spearhead Group, aiming to preserve Melanesian cultural traditions and secure independence for the French territory of New Caledonia.

1989 Solomon Mamaloni, now leader of the People's Action Party (PAP), elected prime minister; formed PAP-dominated coalition.
1990 Mamaloni resigned as PAP party leader, but continued as head of a government of national unity.
1993 Francis Billy Hilly, an independent politician, elected prime minister.

Somalia

Somali Democratic Republic
(*Jamhuriyadda Dimugradiga Somaliya*)

area 637,700 sq km/246,220 sq mi
capital Mogadishu
towns Hargeisa, Kismayu, port Berbera
physical mainly flat, with hills in N
environment destruction of trees for fuel and by grazing livestock has led to an increase in desert area
features occupies a strategic location on the Horn of Africa
head of state and government Ali Mahdi Mohammed from 1991
political system one-party socialist republic
political party Somali Revolutionary Socialist Party (SRSP), nationalist, socialist
exports livestock, skins, hides, bananas, fruit
currency Somali shilling
population (1992) 7,872,000 (including 350,000 refugees in Ethiopia and 50,000 in Djibouti); growth rate 3.1% p.a.
life expectancy men 53, women 53 (1989)
languages Somali, Arabic (both official), Italian, English
religion Sunni Muslim 99%
literacy 40% (1986)
GNP $1.5 bn; $290 per head (1987)

chronology
1884–87 British protectorate of Somaliland established.
1889 Italian protectorate of Somalia established.
1960 Independence achieved from Italy and Britain.
1963 Border dispute with Kenya; diplomatic relations broken with Britain.
1968 Diplomatic relations with Britain restored.
1969 Army coup led by Maj-Gen Mohamed Siad Barre; constitution suspended, Supreme Revolutionary Council set up; name changed to Somali Democratic Republic.
1978 Defeated in eight-month war with Ethiopia. Armed insurrection began in north.

1979 New constitution for socialist one-party state adopted.

1982 Antigovernment Somali National Movement formed. Oppressive countermeasures by government.

1987 Barre re-elected president.

1989 Dissatisfaction with government and increased guerrilla activity in north.

1990 Civil war intensified. Constitutional reforms promised.

1991 Mogadishu captured by rebels; Barre fled; Ali Mahdi Mohammed named president; free elections promised. Secession of NE Somalia, as the Somaliland Republic, announced. Cease-fire signed, but later collapsed. Thousands of casualties as a result of heavy fighting in capital.

1992 Relief efforts to ward off impending famine severely hindered by unstable political situation; relief convoys hijacked by 'warlords'. Dec: UN peacekeeping troops, mainly US Marines, sent in to protect relief operations; dominant warlords agreed truce.

1993 March: leaders of armed factions agreed to federal system of government, based on 18 autonomous regions. June: US-led UN forces destroyed headquarters of warlord Gen Mohammad Farah Aidid, following killing of Pakistani peacekeeping troops. US announced withdrawal of its troops in 1994.

South Africa

Republic of (*Republiek van Suid-Afrika*)

area 1,223,181 sq km/472,148 sq mi (includes Walvis Bay and independent black homelands)

capital and port Cape Town (legislative), Pretoria (administrative), Bloemfontein (judicial)

towns Johannesburg; ports Durban, Port Elizabeth, East London

physical southern end of large plateau, fringed by mountains and lowland coastal margin

territories Marion Island and Prince Edward Island in the Antarctic

features Drakensberg Mountains, Table Mountain; Limpopo and Orange rivers; the Veld and the Karoo; part of Kalahari Desert; Kruger National Park

head of state and government Nelson Mandela from 1994

political system liberal democracy

political parties African National Congress (ANC), left of centre; National Party (NP), right of centre; Inkatha Freedom Party (IFP), centrist, multiracial (formerly Zulu nationalist); Freedom Front (FF), right wing; Democratic Party (DP), moderate, centre left, multiracial; Pan-Africanist Congress (PAC), black, left wing; African Christian Democratic Party (ACDP), Christian, right of centre

currency rand

population (1992) 32,063,000 (77% black Africa, 12% white (of European desacent): 9% mixed, 2% Asian); growth rate 2.2% (1990–95)

life expectancy whites 71, Asians 67, blacks 58

languages Afrikaans and English (both official), Bantu

religions Dutch Reformed Church and other Christian denominations, Hindu, Muslim

literacy 81% (1995 est)

GNP $81 bn; $1,890 per head (1987)

chronology

1910 Cape Colony, Natal, Transvaal, and Orange Free State formed Union of South Africa, with Louis Botha as prime minister.

1912 Gen Barry Hertzog founded (Boer) Nationalist Party; ANC formed to campaign for rights of black majority.

1914 Boer revolt in Orange Free State suppressed; South African troops fought for British Empire in World War I.

1919 Jan Smuts succeeded Botha as premier; South West Africa (Namibia) became South African mandate.

1924 Hertzog became prime minister, aiming to sharpen racial segregation and loosen ties with British Empire.

1939–45 Smuts led South Africa into World War II despite neutralism of Hertzog; South African troops fought with Allies in Middle East, East Africa, and Italy.

1948 Policy of apartheid ('separateness') adopted when National Party (NP) took power under Daniel Malan; continued by his successors Johannes Strijdom 1954–58, Hendrik Verwoerd 1958–66, B J Vorster 1966–78, and P J Botha 1978–89.

1950 Entire population classified by race; Group Areas Act segregated blacks and whites; ANC responded with campaign of civil disobedience.

1960 70 black demonstrators killed at Sharpville; ANC banned.

1961 South Africa left Commonwealth and became republic.

1964 ANC leader Nelson Mandela sentenced to life imprisonment.

1967 Terrorism Act introduced indefinite detention without trial.

1970s Over 3 million people forcibly resettled in black 'homelands'.

1976 Over 600 killed in clashes between black protesters and security forces in Soweto.

1984 New constitution gave segregated representation to coloureds and Asians, but continued to exclude blacks.

1985 Growth of violence in black townships led to proclamation of state of emergency.

1986 USA and Commonwealth imposed limited economic sanctions against South Africa.

1989 F W de Klerk succeeded P W Botha as president; public facilities desegregated; many ANC activists released.

1990 Ban on ANC lifted; Mandela released; talks began between government and ANC; daily average of 35 murders; Namibia became independent.

1991 De Klerk repealed remaining apartheid laws; sanctions lifted; severe fighting between ANC and Zulu Inkatha movement.

1993 Interim majority rule constitution adopted; de Klerk and Mandela agreed to form government of national unity after free elections.

1994 ANC victory in first nonracial elections; Mandela became president; Commonwealth membership restored.

1996 De Klerk withdrew NP from coalition after new constitution failed to provide for power-sharing after 1999.

1997 New constitution signed by President Mandela. F W de Klerk announced his retirement from politics. Thabo Mbeki succeeded Mandela as ANC president.

Spain

(España)

area 504,750 sq km/194,960 sq mi
capital Madrid
towns Zaragoza, Seville, Murcia, Córdoba; ports Barcelona, Valencia, Cartagena, Málaga, Cádiz, Vigo, Santander, Bilbao
physical central plateau with mountain ranges; lowlands in S
territories Balearic and Canary Islands; in N Africa: Ceuta, Melilla, Alhucemas, Chafarinas Is, Peñón de Vélez
features rivers Ebro, Douro, Tagus, Guadiana, Guadalquivir; Iberian Plateau (Meseta); Pyrenees, Cantabrian Mountains, Andalusian Mountains, Sierra Nevada
head of state King Juan Carlos I from 1975
head of government Felipe González Márquez from 1982
political system constitutional monarchy
political parties Socialist Workers' Party (PSOE),

democratic socialist; Popular Alliance (AP), centre-right; Christian Democrats (DC), centrist; Liberal Party (PL), left of centre
exports citrus fruits, grapes, pomegranates, vegetables, wine, sherry, olive oil, canned fruit and fish, iron ore, cork, vehicles, textiles, petroleum products, leather goods, ceramics
currency peseta
population (1992) 39,085,000; growth rate 0.2% p.a.
life expectancy men 74, women 80 (1989)
languages Spanish (Castilian, official), Basque, Catalan, Galician, Valencian, Majorcan
religion Roman Catholic 99%
literacy 97% (1989)
GNP $573.7 bn (1992)

chronology
1936–39 Civil war; General Francisco Franco became head of state and government; fascist party Falange declared only legal political organization.

1947 General Franco announced restoration of the monarchy after his death, with Prince Juan Carlos as his successor.

1975 Franco died; succeeded as head of state by King Juan Carlos I.

1978 New constitution adopted with Adolfo Suárez, leader of the Democratic Centre Party, as prime minister.

1981 Suárez resigned; succeeded by Leopoldo Calvo Sotelo. Attempted military coup thwarted.

1982 Socialist Workers' Party (PSOE), led by Felipe González, won a sweeping electoral victory. Basque separatist organization (ETA) stepped up its guerrilla campaign.

1985 ETA's campaign spread to holiday resorts.

1986 Referendum confirmed NATO membership. Spain joined the European Economic Community.

1988 Spain joined the Western European Union.

1989 PSOE lost seats to hold only parity after general election. Talks between government and ETA collapsed and truce ended.

1992 ETA's 'armed struggle' resumed. European Community's Maastricht Treaty ratified.

1993 Allegations of corruption within PSOE. González narrowly won general election and formed a new minority government, including independents in his cabinet.

Sri Lanka

Democratic Socialist Republic of (*Prajathanrika Samajawadi Janarajaya Sri Lanka*) (until 1972 *Ceylon*)

area 65,600 sq km/25,328 sq mi
capital (and chief port) Colombo
towns Kandy; ports Jaffna, Galle, Negombo, Trincomalee
physical flat in N and around the coast; hills and mountains in S and central interior
features Adam's Peak (2,243 m/7,538 ft); ruined cities of Anuradhapura, Polonnaruwa
head of state Dingiri Banda Wijetunga from 1993
head of government Ranil Wickremasinghe from 1993
political system liberal democratic republic

political parties United National Party (UNP), right of centre; Sri Lanka Freedom Party (SLFP), left of centre; Democratic United National Front (DUNF), centre-left; Tamil United Liberation Front (TULF), Tamil autonomy; Eelam People's Revolutionary Liberation Front (EPLRF), Indian-backed Tamil-secessionist 'Tamil Tigers'
exports tea, rubber, coconut products, graphite, sapphires, rubies, other gemstones
currency Sri Lanka rupee
population (1992) 17,464,000 (Sinhalese 74%, Tamils 17%, Moors 7%); growth rate 1.8% p.a.
life expectancy men 67, women 72 (1989)
languages Sinhala, Tamil, English
religions Buddhist 69%, Hindu 15%, Muslim 8%, Christian 7%
literacy 87% (1988)
GNP $7.2 bn; $400 per head (1988)

chronology
1802 Ceylon became a British colony.
1948 Ceylon achieved independence from Britain within the Commonwealth.
1956 Sinhala established as the official language.
1959 Prime Minister Solomon Bandaranaike assassinated.
1972 Socialist Republic of Sri Lanka proclaimed.
1978 Presidential constitution adopted by new government headed by Junius Jayawardene of the UNP.
1983 Tamil guerrilla violence escalated; state of emergency imposed.
1987 President Jayawardene and Indian prime minister Rajiv Gandhi signed Colombo Accord. Violence continued despite cease-fire policed by Indian troops.
1988 Left-wing guerrillas campaigned against Indo-Sri Lankan peace pact. Prime Minister Ranasinghe Premadasa elected president.
1989 Premadasa became president; D B Wijetunga, prime minister. Leaders of the TULF and the banned Sinhala extremist People's Liberation Front (JVP) assassinated.
1990 Indian peacekeeping force withdrawn. Violence continued.
1991 March: defence minister Ranjan Wijeratne assassinated; Sri Lankan army killed 2,552 Tamil Tigers at Elephant Pass. Oct: impeachment motion against President Premadasa failed. Dec: new party,

the Democratic United National Front (DUNF), formed by former members of the UNP.
1992 35 Tamil civilians massacred by Sinhalese soldiers.
1993 DUNF leader assassinated; DUNF and SLFP leaders held the government responsible. President Premadasa assassinated; succeeded by Prime Minister Wijetunga. Ranil Wickremasinghe became prime minister.

Sudan

Democratic Republic of (*Jamhuryat es-Sudan*)

area 2,505,800 sq km/967,489 sq mi
capital Khartoum
towns Omdurman, Juba, Wadi Medani, al-Obeid, Kassala, Atbara, al-Qadarif, Kosti; chief port Port Sudan
physical fertile valley of river Nile separates Libyan Desert in W from high rocky Nubian Desert in E
environment the building of the Jonglei Canal to supply water to N Sudan and Egypt threatens the grasslands of S Sudan
features Sudd swamp; largest country in Africa
head of state General Omar Hassan Ahmed el-Bashir from 1989
head of government Sadiq al-Mahdi from 1993
political system military republic
political parties New National Umma Party (NNUP), Islamic, nationalist; Democratic Unionist Party (DUP), moderate, nationalist; National Islamic Front, Islamic, nationalist
exports cotton, gum arabic, sesame seed, peanuts, sorghum
currency Sudanese pound
population (1992) 29,971,000; growth rate 2.9% p.a.
life expectancy men 51, women 55 (1989)
languages Arabic 51% (official), local languages
religions Sunni Muslim 73%, animist 18%, Christian 9% (in south)
literacy 30% (1986)
GNP $8.5 bn (1988); $330 per head (1988)

chronology
1820 Sudan ruled by Egypt.
1885 Revolt led to capture of Khartoum by self-proclaimed Mahdi.
1896-98 Anglo-Egyptian offensive led by Lord Kitchener subdued revolt.
1899 Sudan administered as an Anglo-Egyptian condominium.

1955 Civil war between Muslim north and non-Muslim south broke out.

1956 Sudan achieved independence from Britain and Egypt as a republic.

1958 Military coup replaced civilian government with Supreme Council of the Armed Forces.

1964 Civilian rule reinstated.

1969 Coup led by Col Gaafar Mohammed Nimeri established Revolutionary Command Council (RCC); name changed to Democratic Republic of Sudan.

1970 Union with Egypt agreed in principle.

1971 New constitution adopted; Nimeri confirmed as president; Sudanese Socialist Union (SSU) declared only legal party.

1972 Proposed Federation of Arab Republics, comprising Sudan, Egypt, and Syria, abandoned. Addis Ababa conference proposed autonomy for southern provinces.

1974 National assembly established.

1983 Nimeri re-elected. Shari'a (Islamic law) introduced.

1985 Nimeri deposed in a bloodless coup led by General Swar al-Dahab; transitional military council set up. State of emergency declared.

1986 More than 40 political parties fought general election; coalition government formed.

1987 Virtual civil war with Sudan People's Liberation Army (SPLA).

1988 Al-Mahdi formed a new coalition. Another flare-up of civil war between north and south created tens of thousands of refugees. Floods made 1.5 million people homeless. Peace pact signed with SPLA.

1989 Sadiq al-Mahdi overthrown in coup led by General Omar Hassan Ahmed el-Bashir.

1990 Civil war continued with new SPLA offensive.

1991 Federal system introduced, with division of country into nine states.

1993 March: SPLA leaders John Garang and Riek Machar announced unilateral cease-fire in ten years' war with government in Khartoum. April: peace talks began between government and two factions of the SPLA. Oct: civilian government headed by Sadiq al-Mahdi replaced military Revolutionary Command Council (RCC); army retained ultimate control.

Surinam

Republic of (*Republiek Suriname*)

area 163,820 sq km/63,243 sq mi

capital Paramaribo

towns Nieuw Nickerie, Brokopondo, Nieuw Amsterdam

physical hilly and forested, with flat and narrow coastal plain

features Suriname River

head of state and government Ronald Venetiaan from 1991

political system emergent democratic republic

political parties Party for National Unity and Solidarity (KTPI)*, Indonesian, left of centre; Surinam National Party (NPS)*, Creole, left of centre; Progressive Reform Party (VHP)*, Indian, left of centre; New Front for Democracy (NF)* members of Front for Democracy and Development (FDD)

exports alumina, aluminium, bauxite, rice, timber

currency Surinam guilder

population (1990 est) 408,000 (Hindu 37%, Creole 31%, Javanese 15%); growth rate 1.1% p.a.

life expectancy men 66, women 71 (1989)

languages Dutch (official), Sranan (creole), English, others

religions Christian 30%, Hindu 27%, Muslim 20%

literacy 65% (1989)

GNP $1.1 bn (1987); $2,920 per head (1985)

chronology

1667 Became a Dutch colony.

1954 Achieved internal self-government as Dutch Guiana.

1975 Independence achieved from the Netherlands, with Dr Johan Ferrier as president and Henck Arron as prime minister; 40% of the population emigrated to the Netherlands.

1980 Arron's government overthrown in army coup; Ferrier refused to recognize military regime; appointed Dr Henk Chin A Sen to lead civilian administration. Army replaced Ferrier with Dr Chin A Sen.

1982 Army, led by Lt Col Desi Bouterse, seized power, setting up a Revolutionary People's Front.

1985 Ban on political activities lifted.

1986 Antigovernment rebels brought economic chaos to Surinam.

1987 New constitution approved.

1988 Ramsewak Shankar elected president.

1989 Bouterse rejected peace accord reached by President Shankar with guerrilla insurgents, vowed to continue fighting.

1990 Shankar deposed in army coup.

1991 Johan Kraag became interim president. New Front for Democracy won assembly majority. Ronald Venetiaan elected president.

1992 Peace accord with guerrilla groups.

Swaziland

Kingdom of (*Umbuso weSwatini*)

area 17,400 sq km/6,716 sq mi

capital Mbabane

towns Manzini, Big Bend

physical central valley; mountains in W (Highveld); plateau in E (Lowveld and Lubombo plateau)

features landlocked enclave between South Africa and Mozambique

head of state King Mswati III from 1986

head of government Andreas Fukudzi (interim) from 1993

political system near-absolute monarchy
political party Imbokodvo National Movement (INM), nationalist monarchist
exports sugar, canned fruit, wood pulp, asbestos
currency lilangeni
population (1992) 826,000; growth rate 3% p.a. *life expectancy* men 47, women 54 (1989)
languages Swazi 90%, English (both official)
religions Christian 57%, animist
literacy men 70%, women 66% (1985 est)
GNP $539 million; $750 per head (1987)

chronology
1903 Swaziland became a special High Commission territory.
1967 Achieved internal self-government.
1968 Independence achieved from Britain, within the Commonwealth, as the Kingdom of Swaziland, with King Sobhuza II as head of state.
1973 The king suspended the constitution and assumed absolute powers.
1978 New constitution adopted.
1982 King Sobhuza died; his place was taken by one of his wives, Dzeliwe, until his son, Prince Makhosetive, reached the age of 21.
1983 Queen Dzeliwe ousted by another wife, Ntombi.
1984 After royal power struggle, it was announced that the crown prince would become king at 18.
1986 Crown prince formally invested as King Mswati III.
1987 Power struggle developed between advisory council Liqoqo and Queen Ntombi over accession of king. Mswati dissolved parliament; new government elected with Sotsha Dlamini as prime minister.
1991 Calls for democratic reform.
1992 Mswati dissolved parliament, assuming 'executive powers'.
1993 General election. Andreas Fukudzi appointed interim prime minister.

Sweden

Kingdom of (*Konungariket Sverige*)

area 450,000 sq km/173,745 sq mi
capital Stockholm
towns Göteborg, Malmö, Uppsala, Norrköping, Västerås

physical mountains in W; plains in S; thickly forested; more than 20,000 islands off the Stockholm coast
environment of the country's 90,000 lakes, 20,000 are affected by acid rain; 4,000 are so severely acidified that no fish are thought to survive in them
features lakes, including Vänern, Vättern, Mälaren, Hjälmaren; islands of Öland and Gotland; wild elk
head of state King Carl XVI Gustaf from 1973
head of government Carl Bildt from 1991
political system constitutional monarchy
political parties Social Democratic Labour party (SAP), moderate, left of centre; Moderate Party, right of centre; Liberal Party, centre-left; Centre Party, centrist; Christian Democratic Party, Christian, centrist; Left (Communist) Party, European, Marxist; Green, ecological
exports aircraft, vehicles, ballbearings, drills, missiles, electronics, petrochemicals, textiles, furnishings, ornamental glass, paper, iron and steel
currency krona
population (1992) 8,673,000 (including 17,000 Saami [Lapps] and 1.2 million immigrants from Turkey, Yugoslavia, Greece, Iran, Finland and other Nordic countries); growth rate 0.1% p.a.
life expectancy men 74, women 81 (1989)
languages Swedish; there are Finnish- and Saami-speaking minorities
religion Lutheran (official) 95%
literacy 99% (1989)
GNP $245.8 bn (1992)

chronology
12th century United as an independent nation.
1397–1520 Under Danish rule.
1914–45 Neutral in both world wars.
1951–76 Social Democratic Labour Party (SAP) in power.
1969 Olof Palme became SAP leader and prime minister.
1971 Constitution amended, creating a single-chamber Riksdag, the governing body.
1975 Monarch's last constitutional powers removed.
1976 Thorbjörn Fälldin, leader of the Centre Party, became prime minister, heading centre-right coalition.
1982 SAP, led by Palme, returned to power.
1985 SAP formed minority government, with Communist support.
1986 Olof Palme murdered. Ingvar Carlsson became prime minister and SAP party leader.

1988 SAP re-elected with reduced majority; Green Party gained representation in Riksdag.
1990 SAP government resigned.
1991 Formal application for European Community (EC) membership submitted. Election defeat for SAP; Carlsson resigned. Coalition government formed; Carl Bildt became new prime minister.
1992 Cross-party collaboration to solve economic problems.

Switzerland

Swiss Confederation (German *Schweiz*, French *Suisse*, Romansch *Svizzera*)

area 41,300 sq km/15,946 sq mi
capital Bern
towns Zürich, Geneva, Lausanne; river port Basel (on the Rhine)
physical most mountainous country in Europe (Alps and Jura mountains); highest peak Dufourspitze 4,634 m/15,203 ft in Apennines
environment an estimated 43% of coniferous trees, particularly in the central Alpine region, have been killed by acid rain, 90% of which comes from other countries. Over 50% of bird species are classified as threatened
features winter sports area of the upper valley of the river Inn (Engadine); lakes Maggiore, Lucerne, Geneva, Constance
head of state and government Adolf Ogi from 1993
government federal democratic republic
political parties Radical Democratic Party (FDP), radical, centre-left; Social Democratic Party (SPS), moderate, left of centre; Christian Democratic Party (PDC), Christian, moderate, centrist; People's Party (SVP), centre-left; Liberal Party (PLS), federalist, centre-left; Green Party, ecological
exports electrical goods, chemicals, pharmaceuticals, watches, precision instruments, confectionery
currency Swiss franc
population (1992) 6,911,000; growth rate 0.2% p.a.
life expectancy men 74, women 82 (1989)
languages German 65%, French 18%, Italian 12%, Romansch 1% (all official)
religions Roman Catholic 50%, Protestant 48%
literacy 99% (1989)
GNP $240.5 bn (1992)

chronology
1648 Became independent of the Holy Roman Empire.
1798–1815 Helvetic Republic established by French revolutionary armies.
1847 Civil war resulted in greater centralization.
1874 Principle of the referendum introduced.
1971 Women given the vote in federal elections.
1984 First female cabinet minister appointed.
1986 Referendum rejected proposal for membership of United Nations.
1989 Referendum supported abolition of citizen army and military service requirements.
1991 18-year-olds allowed to vote for first time in national elections. Four-party coalition remained in power.
1992 René Felber elected president with Adolf Ogi as vice president. Closer ties with European Community rejected in national referendum.
1993 Ogi replaced Felber as head of state.

Syria

Syrian Arab Republic (*al- Jamhuriya al-Arabya as-Suriya*)

area 185,200 sq km/71,506 sq mi
capital Damascus
towns Aleppo, Homs, Hama; chief port Latakia
physical mountains alternate with fertile plains and desert areas; Euphrates River
features Mount Hermon, Golan Heights; crusader castles (including Krak des Chevaliers); Phoenician city sites (Ugarit), ruins of ancient Palmyra
head of state and government Hafez al-Assad from 1971
political system socialist republic
political parties National Progressive Front (NPF), pro-Arab, socialist; Communist Action Party, socialist
exports cotton, cereals, oil, phosphates, tobacco
currency Syrian pound
population (1992) 12,471,000; growth rate 3.5% p.a.
life expectancy men 67, women 69 (1989)
languages Arabic 89% (official), Kurdish 6%, Armenian 3%
religions Sunni Muslim 74%; ruling minority Alawite, and other Islamic sects 16%; Christian 10%
literacy men 76%, women 43% (1985 est)
GNP $17 bn (1986); $702 per head

chronology
1946 Achieved full independence from France.
1958 Merged with Egypt to form the United Arab Republic (UAR).
1961 UAR disintegrated.
1967 Six-Day War resulted in the loss of territory to Israel.
1970–71 Syria supported Palestinian guerrillas against Jordanian troops.
1971 Following a bloodless coup, Hafez al-Assad became president.
1973 Israel consolidated its control of the Golan Heights after the Yom Kippur War.
1976 Substantial numbers of troops committed to the civil war in Lebanon.
1978 Assad re-elected.
1981–82 Further military engagements in Lebanon.
1982 Islamic militant uprising suppressed; 5,000 dead.
1984 Presidents Assad and Gemayel approved plans for government of national unity in Lebanon.
1985 Assad secured the release of 39 US hostages held in an aircraft hijacked by extremist Shi'ite group, Hezbollah. Assad re-elected.
1987 Improved relations with USA and attempts to secure the release of Western hostages in Lebanon.
1989 Diplomatic relations with Morocco restored. Continued fighting in Lebanon; Syrian forces reinforced in Lebanon; diplomatic relations with Egypt restored.
1990 Diplomatic relations with Britain restored.
1991 Syria fought against Iraq in Gulf War. President Assad agreed to US Middle East peace plan. Assad re-elected president.
1993 Syria joined Iraq and other Arab countries in boycotting UN treaty outlawing production and use of chemical weapons.

Taiwan

Republic of China (*Chung Hua Min Kuo*)

area 36,179 sq km/13,965 sq mi
capital Taipei
towns ports Kaohsiung, Keelung
physical island (formerly Formosa) off People's Republic of China; mountainous, with lowlands in W
environment industrialization has taken its toll: an estimated 30% of the annual rice crop is dangerously contaminated with mercury, cadmium, and other heavy metals

features Penghu (Pescadores), Jinmen (Quemoy), Mazu (Matsu) islands
head of state Lee Teng-hui from 1988
head of government Lien Chan from 1993
political system emergent democracy
political parties Nationalist Party of China (Kuomintang: KMT), anticommunist, Chinese nationalist; Democratic Progressive Party (DPP), centrist-pluralist, pro-self-determination grouping; Workers' Party (Kuntang), left of centre
exports textiles, steel, plastics, electronics, foodstuffs
currency New Taiwan dollar
population (1992) 20,727,000 (Taiwanese 84%, mainlanders 14%); growth rate 1.4% p.a.
life expectancy 70 men, 75 women (1986)
languages Mandarin Chinese (official); Taiwan, Hakka dialects
religions officially atheist; Taoist, Confucian, Buddhist, Christian
literacy 90% (1988)
GNP $119.1 bn; $6,200 per head (1988)

chronology
1683 Taiwan (Formosa) annexed by China.
1895 Ceded to Japan.
1945 Recovered by China.
1949 Flight of Nationalist government to Taiwan after Chinese communist revolution.
1954 US–Taiwanese mutual defence treaty.
1971 Expulsion from United Nations.
1972 Commencement of legislature elections.
1975 President Chiang Kai-shek died; replaced as Kuomintang leader by his son, Chiang Ching-kuo.
1979 USA severed diplomatic relations and annulled 1954 security pact.
1986 Democratic Progressive Party (DPP) formed as opposition to the nationalist Kuomintang.
1987 Martial law lifted; opposition parties legalized; press restrictions lifted.
1988 President Chiang Ching-kuo died; replaced by Taiwanese-born Lee Teng-hui.
1989 Kuomintang won assembly elections.
1990 Formal move towards normalization of relations with China. Hau Pei-tsun became prime minister.
1991 President Lee Teng-hui declared end to state of civil war with China. Constitution amended. Kuomintang won landslide victory in assembly elections.
1992 Diplomatic relations with South Korea broken. Dec: in first fully democratic elections Kuomintang lost support to DPP but still secured a majority of seats.
1993 Lien Chan appointed prime minister.

Tajikistan

Republic of

area 143,100 sq km/55,251 sq mi
capital Dushanbe
towns Khodzhent (formerly Leninabad), Kurgan-Tyube, Kulyab
physical mountainous, more than half of its territory lying above 3,000 m/10,000 ft; huge mountain glaciers, which are the source of many rapid rivers
features Pik Kommunizma (Communism Peak); health resorts and mineral springs
head of state Akbasho Iskandrov from 1992
head of government to be appointed

political system emergent democracy
political parties Socialist (formerly Communist) Party of Tajikistan (SPT); Democratic Party; Islamic Revival Party
products fruit, cereals, cotton, cattle, sheep, silks, carpets, coal, lead, zinc, chemicals, oil, gas
population (1992) 5,568,000 (Tajik 63%, Uzbek 24%, Russian 8%, Tatar 1%, Kyrgyz 1%, Ukrainian 1%)
language Tajik, similar to Farsi (Persian)
religion Sunni Muslim

chronology
1921 Part of Turkestan Soviet Socialist Autonomous Republic.
1929 Became a constituent republic of USSR.
1990 Ethnic Tajik-Armenian conflict in Dushanbe resulted in rioting against Communist Party of Tajikistan (TCP); state of emergency and curfew imposed.
1991 Jan: curfew lifted in Dushanbe. March: maintenance of Soviet Union endorsed in referendum. Aug: President Makhkamov forced to resign after failed anti-Gorbachev coup; TCP broke links with Moscow. Sept: declared independence; Rakhman Nabiyev elected president; TCP renamed Socialist Party of Tajikistan; state of emergency declared. Dec: joined new Commonwealth of Independent States.
1992 Jan: admitted into Conference for Security and Cooperation in Europe. Nabiyev temporarily ousted; state of emergency lifted. Feb: joined the Muslim Economic Cooperation Organization. March: admitted into United Nations; US diplomatic recognition achieved. May: coalition government formed. Sept: Nabiyev forced to resign; replaced by Akbasho Iskandrov; Abdumalik Abulajanov became prime minister.
1993 Civil war between the forces of the country's communist former rulers and Islamic and prodemocracy groups continued to rage. Dec: Abulajanov resigned as prime minister.

Tanzania

United Republic of (*Jamhuri ya Muungano wa Tanzania*)

area 945,000 sq km/364,865 sq mi
capital Dodoma (since 1983)
towns Zanzibar Town, Mwanza; chief port and former capital Dar es Salaam

physical central plateau; lakes in N and W; coastal plains; lakes Victoria, Tanganyika, and Niasa
environment the black rhino faces extinction as a result of poaching
features comprises islands of Zanzibar and Pemba; Mount Kilimanjaro, 5,895 m/19,340 ft, the highest peak in Africa; Serengeti National Park, Olduvai Gorge; Ngorongoro Crater, 14.5 km/9 mi across, 762 m/2,500 ft deep
head of state and government Ali Hassan Mwinyi from 1985
political system one-party socialist republic
political party Revolutionary Party of Tanzania (CCM), African, socialist
exports coffee, cotton, sisal, cloves, tea, tobacco, cashew nuts, diamonds
currency Tanzanian shilling
population (1992) 25,809,000; growth rate 3.5% p.a.
life expectancy men 49, women 54 (1989)
languages Kiswahili, English (both official)
religions Muslim 35%, Christian 35%, traditional 30%
literacy 85% (1987)
GNP $4.9 bn; $258 per head (1987)

chronology
16th–17th centuries Zanzibar under Portuguese control.
1890–1963 Zanzibar became a British protectorate.
1920–46 Tanganyika administered as a British League of Nations mandate.
1946–62 Tanganyika came under United Nations (UN) trusteeship.
1961 Tanganyika achieved independence from Britain, within the Commonwealth, with Julius Nyerere as prime minister.
1962 Tanganyika became a republic with Nyerere as president.
1964 Tanganyika and Zanzibar became the United Republic of Tanzania with Nyerere as president.
1967 East African Community (EAC) formed. Nyerere comitted himself to building a socialist state (the Arusha Declaration).
1977 Revolutionary Party of Tanzania (CCM) proclaimed the only legal party. EAC dissolved.
1978 Ugandan forces repulsed after crossing into Tanzania.

1979 Tanzanian troops sent to Uganda to help over-throw the president, Idi Amin.
1985 Nyerere retired from presidency but stayed on as CCM leader; Ali Hassan Mwinyi became president.
1990 Nyerere surrendered CCM leadership; replaced by President Mwinyi.
1992 CCM agreed to abolish one-party rule. East African cooperation pact with Kenya and Uganda to be re- established.

Thailand

Kingdom of (*Prathet Thai* or *Muang-Thai*)

area 513,115 sq km/198,108 sq mi
capital and chief port Bangkok
towns Chiangmai, Nakhon Sawan river port
physical mountainous, semi-arid plateau in NE, fertile central region, tropical isthmus in S
environment tropical rainforest was reduced to 18% of the land area 1988 (from 93% in 1961); logging was banned by the government 1988
features rivers Chao Phraya, Mekong, Salween; ancient ruins of Sukhothai and Ayurrhaya
head of state King Bhumibol Adulyadej from 1946
head of government Chuan Leekpai from 1992
political system military-controlled emergent democracy
political parties New Aspiration Party; Samakkhi Tham (Justice and Unity) Party, right of centre, air-force-linked; Palang Dharma, anti-corruption; Social Action Party (Kij Sangkhom), right of centre; Thai Nation (Chart Thai), conservative, pro-business; Liberal Democratic Party
exports rice, textiles, rubber, tin, rubies, sapphires, maize, tapioca
currency baht
population (1992) 56,801,000 (Thai 75%, Chinese 14%); growth rate 2% p.a.
life expectancy men 62, women 68 (1989)
languages Thai and Chinese (both official); regional dialects
religions Buddhist 95%, Muslim 4%
literacy 89% (1988)
GNP $52 bn (1988); $771 per head (1988)

chronology
1782 Siam absolutist dynasty commenced.

1896 Anglo-French agreement recognized Siam as independent buffer state.
1932 Constitutional monarchy established.
1939 Name of Thailand adopted.
1941-44 Japanese occupation.
1947 Military seized power in coup.
1972 Withdrawal of Thai troops from South Vietnam.
1973 Military government overthrown.
1976 Military reassumed control.
1980 General Prem Tinsulanonda assumed power.
1983 Civilian government formed; martial law maintained.
1988 Prime Minister Prem resigned; replaced by Chatichai Choonhavan.
1989 Thai pirates continued to murder, pillage, and kidnap Vietnamese 'boat people' at sea.
1991 Military seized power in coup. Interim civilian government formed under Anand Panyarachun. 50,000 demonstrated against new military-oriented constitution.
1992 General election produced five-party coalition; the subsequent appointment of General Suchinda Kraprayoon as premier provoked widespread riots, and Suchinda fled the country after army shooting of 100 demonstrators. New coalition government led by Chuan Leekpai.

Togo

Republic of (*République Togolaise*)

area 56,800 sq km/21,930 sq mi
capital Lomé
towns Sokodé, Kpalimé
physical two savanna plains, divided by range of hills NE–SW; coastal lagoons and marsh
environment the homes of thousands of people in Keto were destroyed by coastal erosion as a result of the building of the Volta dam
features Mono Tableland, Oti Plateau, Oti River
head of state Etienne Gnassingbé Eyadéma from 1967
head of government Jospeh Kokou Koffigoh from 1991
political system emergent democracy
political parties Rally of the Togolese People (RPT), centrist nationalist; Alliance of Togolese Democrats (ADT), left of centre; Togolese Movement for Democracy (MDT), left of centre; Co-ordination of New Forces, left of centre, broad coalition
exports phosphates, cocoa, coffee, coconuts
currency franc CFA
population (1992) 3,701,000; growth rate 3% p.a.

life expectancy men 53, women 57 (1989)
languages French (official), Ewe, Kabre
religions animist 46%, Catholic 28%, Muslim 17%, Protestant 9%
literacy men 53%, women 28% (1985 est)
GNP $1.3 bn (1987); $240 per head (1985)

chronology
1885–1914 Togoland was a German protectorate until captured by Anglo-French forces.
1922 Divided between Britain and France under League of Nations mandate.
1946 Continued under United Nations trusteeship.
1956 British Togoland integrated with Ghana.
1960 French Togoland achieved independence from France as the Republic of Togo with Sylvanus Olympio as head of state.
1963 Olympio killed in a military coup. Nicolas Grunitzky became president.
1967 Grunitzky replaced by Lt-Gen Etienne Gnassingbé Eyadéma in bloodless coup.
1973 Assembly of Togolese People (RPT) formed as sole legal political party.
1975 EEC Lomé convention signed in Lomé, establishing trade links with developing countries.
1979 Eyadéma returned in election. Further EEC Lomé convention signed.
1986 Attempted coup failed.
1991 Eyadéma legalized opposition parties. National conference elected Joseph Kokou Koffigoh head of interim government; troops loyal to Eyadéma failed to reinstate him.
1992 Overwhelming referendum support for multiparty politics.
1993 Feb: all-party talks to avoid civil war began in France but were suspended after disagreements among participants. July/August: President Eyadéma won multi-party election.

Tonga

Kingdom of (*Pule'anga Fakatu'i 'o Tonga*) or *Friendly Islands*

area 750 sq km/290 sq mi
capital Nuku'alofa (on Tongatapu island)
towns Pangai, Neiafu
physical three groups of islands in SW Pacific, mostly coral formations, but actively volcanic in W
features of 170 islands in the Tonga group, 36 are inhabited
head of state King Taufa'ahau Tupou IV from 1965

head of government Baron Vaea from 1991
political system constitutional monarchy
political parties none
currency Tongan dollar or pa'anga
population (1992) 97,300; growth rate 2.4% p.a.
life expectancy men 69, women 74 (1989)
languages Tongan (official), English
religions Wesleyan 47%, Roman Catholic 14%, Free Church of Tonga 14%, Mormon 9%, Church of Tonga 9%
literacy 93% (1988)
GNP $65 million (1987); $430 per head

chronology
1831 Tongan dynasty founded by Prince Taufa'ahau Tupou.
1900 Became a British protectorate.
1965 Queen Salote died; succeeded by her son, King Taufa'ahau Tupou IV.
1970 Independence achieved from Britain within the Commonwealth.
1990 Three prodemocracy candidates elected. Calls for reform of absolutist power.

Trinidad and Tobago

Republic of

area Trinidad 4,828 sq km/1,864 sq mi and Tobago 300 sq km/116 sq mi
capital Port-of-Spain
towns San Fernando, Arima, Scarborough (Tobago)
physical comprises two main islands and some smaller ones; coastal swamps and hills E–W
features Pitch Lake, a self-renewing source of asphalt used by 16th-century explorer Walter Raleigh to repair his ships
head of state Noor Hassanali from 1987
head of government Patrick Manning from 1991
political system democratic republic
political parties National Alliance for Reconstruction (NAR), nationalist, left of centre; People's National Movement (PNM), nationalist, moderate, centrist; National Development Party (NDP), centre-left
exports oil, petroleum products, chemicals, sugar, cocoa
currency Trinidad and Tobago dollar
population (1992) 1,261,000 (African descent 40%, Indian 40%, European 16%, Chinese and others 2%), 1.2 million on Trinidad; growth rate 1.6% p.a.

life expectancy men 68, women 72 (1989)
languages English (official), Hindi, French, Spanish
media freedom of press guaranteed by constitution
and upheld by government; there are two independent
morning newspapers and several weekly tabloids
religions Roman Catholic 32%, Protestant 29%,
Hindu 25%, Muslim 6%
literacy 97% (1988)
GNP $4.5 bn; $3,731 per head (1987)

chronology
1888 Trinidad and Tobago united as a British colony.
1956 People's National Movement (PNM) founded.
1959 Achieved internal self-government, with PNM
leader Eric Williams as chief minister.
1962 Independence achieved from Britain, within the
Commonwealth, with Williams as prime minister.
1976 Became a republic, with Ellis Clarke as president and Williams as prime minister.
1981 Williams died and was succeeded by George
Chambers, with Arthur Robinson as opposition
leader.
1986 National Alliance for Reconstruction (NAR),
headed by Arthur Robinson, won general election.
1987 Noor Hassanali became president.
1990 Attempted antigovernment coup defeated.
1991 General election saw victory for PNM, with
Patrick Manning as prime minister.

Tunisia

Tunisian Republic (*al-Jumhuriya at-Tunisiya*)

area 164,150 sq km/63,378 sq mi
capital and chief port Tunis
towns ports Sfax, Sousse, Bizerta
physical arable and forested land in N graduates
towards desert in S
features fertile island of Jerba, linked to mainland by
causeway (identified with island of lotus-eaters);
Shott el Jerid salt lakes; holy city of Kairouan, ruins
of Carthage
head of state and government Zine el-Abidine Ben
Ali from 1987
political system emergent democratic republic
political party Constitutional Democratic Rally
(RCD), nationalist, moderate, socialist
exports oil, phosphates, chemicals, textiles, food,
olive oil
currency dinar

population (1992) 8,413,000; growth rate 2% p.a.
life expectancy men 68, women 71 (1989)
languages Arabic (official), French
media publications must be authorized; the offence
of defamation is used to protect members of the government from criticism
religion Sunni Muslim 95%; Jewish, Christian
literacy men 68%, women 41% (1985 est)
GNP $9.6 bn (1987); $1,163 per head (1986)

chronology
1883 Became a French protectorate.
1955 Granted internal self-government.
1956 Independence achieved from France as a
monarchy, with Habib Bourguiba as prime minister.
1957 Became a republic with Bourguiba as president.
1975 Bourguiba made president for life.
1985 Diplomatic relations with Libya severed.
1987 Bourguiba removed Prime Minister Rashed
Sfar and appointed Zine el-Abidine Ben Ali. Ben Ali
declared Bourguiba incompetent and seized power.
1988 Constitutional changes towards democracy
announced. Diplomatic relations with Libya restored.
1989 Government party, RDC, won all assembly
seats in general election.
1991 Opposition to US actions during the Gulf War.
Crackdown on religious fundamentalists.

Turkey

Republic of (*Türkiye Cumhuriyeti*)

area 779,500 sq km/300,965 sq mi
capital Ankara
towns ports Istanbul and Izmir
physical central plateau surrounded by mountains
environment only 0.3% of the country is protected by
national parks and reserves compared with a global
average of 7% per country
features Bosporus and Dardanelles; Mount Ararat;
Taurus Mountains in SW (highest peak Kaldi Dağ,
3,734 m/12,255 ft); sources of rivers Euphrates and
Tigris in E; archaeological sites include Çatal Hüyük,
Ephesus, and Troy; rock villages of Cappadocia; historic towns (Antioch, Iskenderun, Tarsus)
head of state Suleyman Demirel from 1993
head of government Tansu Ciller from 1993
political system democratic republic
political parties Motherland Party (ANAP), Islamic,
nationalist, right of centre; Social Democratic Pop-

ulist Party (SDPP), moderate, left of centre; True Path Party (TPP), centre-right
exports cotton, yarn, hazelnuts, citrus, tobacco, dried fruit, chromium ores
currency Turkish lira
population (1992) 58,584,000 (Turkish 85%, Kurdish 12%); growth rate 2.1% p.a.
life expectancy men 63, women 66 (1989)
languages Turkish (official), Kurdish, Arabic
religion Sunni Muslim 98%
literacy men 86%, women 62% (1985)
GNP $112.5 bn (1992)

chronology
1919–22 Turkish War of Independence provoked by Greek occupation of Izmir. Mustafa Kemal (Atatürk), leader of nationalist congress, defeated Italian, French, and Greek forces.
1923 Treaty of Lausanne established Turkey as independent republic under Kemal. Westernization began.
1950 First free elections; Adnan Menderes became prime minister.
1960 Menderes executed after military coup by General Cemal Gürsel.
1965 Suleyman Demirel became prime minister.
1971 Army forced Demirel to resign.
1973 Civilian rule returned under Bulent Ecevit.
1974 Turkish troops sent to protect Turkish community in Cyprus.
1975 Demirel returned to head of a right-wing coalition.
1978 Ecevit returned, as head of coalition, in the face of economic difficulties and factional violence.
1979 Demeril returned. Violence grew.
1980 Army took over, and Bulent Ulusu became prime minister. Harsh repression of political activists attracted international criticism.
1982 New constitution adopted.
1983 Ban on political activity lifted. Turgut Özal became prime minister.
1987 Özal maintained majority in general election.
1988 Improved relations and talks with Greece.
1989 Turgut Özal elected president; Yildirim Akbulut became prime minister. Application to join European Community (EC) rejected.
1991 Mesut Yilmaz became prime minister. Turkey sided with UN coalition against Iraq in Gulf War. Conflict with Kurdish minority continued. Coalition government formed under Suleyman Demirel after inconclusive election result.
1992 Earthquake claimed thousands of lives.
1993 Özal died and was succeeded by Demirel. Tansu Ciller became first female prime minister.

Turkmenistan

Republic of

area 488,100 sq km/188,406 sq mi
capital Ashkhabad
towns Chardzhov, Mary (Merv), Nebit-Dag, Krasnovodsk
physical some 90% of land is desert including the Kara Kum 'Black Sands' desert (area 310,800 sq km/120,000 sq mi)
features on the edge of the Kara Kum desert is the Altyn Depe, 'golden hill', site of a ruined city with a ziggurat, or stepped pyramid; river Amu Darya; rich

deposits of petroleum, natural gas, sulphur, and other industrial raw materials
head of state Saparmurad Niyazov from 1991
head of government Sakhat Muradov from 1992
political system socialist pluralist
products silk, karakul, sheep, astrakhan fur, carpets, chemicals, rich deposits of petroleum, natural gas, sulphur, and other industrial raw materials
population (1992) 3,859,000 (Turkmen 72%, Russian 10%, Uzbek 9%, Kazakh 3%, Ukrainian 1%)
language West Turkic, closely related to Turkish
religion Sunni Muslim

chronology
1921 Part of Turkestan Soviet Socialist Autonomous Republic.
1925 Became a constituent republic of USSR.
1990 Aug: economic and political sovereignty declared.
1991 Jan: Communist Party leader Sakhat Niyazov became state president. March: endorsed maintenance of the Union in USSR referendum. Aug: Niyazov initially supported attempted anti-Gorbachev coup. Oct: independence declared. Dec: joined new Commonwealth of Independent States.
1992 Jan: admitted into Conference for Security and Cooperation in Europe. Feb: joined the Muslim Economic Cooperation Organization. March: admitted into United Nations; US diplomatic recognition achieved. May: new constitution adopted. Nov–Dec: 60-member assembly popularly elected with Sakhat Muradov as prime minister.

Tuvalu

South West Pacific State of (formerly *Ellice Islands*)

area 25 sq km/9.5 sq mi
capital Funafuti
physical nine low coral atolls forming a chain of 579 km/650 mi in the SW Pacific
features maximum height above sea level 6 m/20 ft; coconut palms are main vegetation
head of state Elizabeth II from 1978, represented by governor general
head of government Bikenibeu Paeniu from 1989
political system liberal democracy

political parties none; members are elected to parliament as independents
exports copra, handicrafts, stamps
currency Australian dollar
population (1992) 9,500 (Polynesian 96%); growth rate 3.4% p.a.
life expectancy 60 men, 63 women (1989)
languages Tuvaluan, English
religion Christian (Protestant)
literacy 96% (1985)
GDP (1983) $711 per head

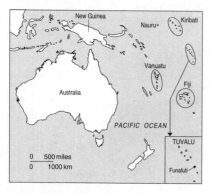

chronology
1892 Became a British protectorate forming part of the Gilbert and Ellice Islands group.
1916 The islands acquired colonial status.
1975 The Ellice Islands were separated from the Gilbert Islands.
1978 Independence achieved from Britain, within the Commonwealth, with Toaripi Lauti as prime minister; reverted to former name Tuvalu.
1981 Dr Tomasi Puapua replaced Lauti as premier.
1986 Islanders rejected proposal for republican status.
1989 Bikenibeu Paeniu elected new prime minister.

Uganda

Republic of

area 236,600 sq km/91,351 sq mi
capital Kampala
towns Jinja, M'Bale, Entebbe, Masaka
physical plateau with mountains in W; forest and grassland; arid in NE
features Ruwenzori Range (Mount Margherita, 5,110 m/16,765 ft); national parks with wildlife (chimpanzees, crocodiles, Nile perch to 70 kg/160 lb); Owen Falls on White Nile where it leaves Lake Victoria; Lake Albert in W
head of state Kabuka Ronald Muwenda Mutebi from 1993
head of government Yoweri Museveni from 1986
political system emergent democratic republic
political parties National Resistance Movement (NRM), left of centre; Democratic Party (DP), centre-left; Conservative Party (CP), centre-right; Uganda People's Congress (UPC), left of centre; Uganda Freedom Movement (UFM), left of centre
exports coffee, cotton, tea, copper
currency Uganda new shilling
population (1992) 17,194,000 (largely the Baganda, after whom the country is named; also Langi and

Acholi, some surviving Pygmies); growth rate 3.3% p.a.
life expectancy men 49, women 51 (1989)
languages English (official), Kiswahili, Luganda, and other African languages
religions Roman Catholic 33%, Protestant 33%, Muslim 16%, animist
literacy men 70%, women 45% (1985 est)
GNP $3.6 bn (1987); $220 per head

chronology
1962 Independence achieved from Britain, within the Commonwealth, with Milton Obote as prime minister.
1963 Proclaimed a federal republic with King Mutesa II as president.
1966 King Mutesa ousted in coup led by Obote, who ended the federal status and became executive president.
1969 All opposition parties banned after assassination attempt on Obote.
1971 Obote overthrown in army coup led by Maj-Gen Idi Amin Dada; ruthlessly dictatorial regime established; nearly 49,000 Ugandan Asians expelled; over 300,000 opponents of regime killed.
1978 Amin forced to leave country by opponents backed by Tanzanian troops. Provisional government set up with Yusuf Lule as president. Lule replaced by Godfrey Binaisa.
1978–79 Fighting broke out against Tanzanian troops.
1980 Binaisa overthrown by army. Elections held and Milton Obote returned to power.
1985 After opposition by National Resistance Army (NRA), and indiscipline in army, Obote ousted by Brig Tito Okello; power-sharing agreement entered into with NRA leader Yoweri Museveni.
1986 Agreement ended; Museveni became president, heading broad-based coalition government.
1992 Announcement made that East African cooperation pact with Kenya and Tanzania would be revived.
1993 King of Baganda reinstated as formal monarch.

Ukraine

area 603,700 sq km/233,089 sq mi
capital Kiev
towns Kharkov, Donetsk, Odessa, Dnepropetrovsk, Lugansk (Voroshilovgrad), Lviv (Lvov), Mariupol (Zhdanov), Krivoi Rog, Zaporozhye
physical Russian plain; Carpathian and Crimean Mountains; rivers: Dnieper (with the Dnieper dam 1932), Donetz, Bug

features Askaniya-Nova Nature Reserve (established 1921); health spas with mineral springs
head of state Leonid Kravchuk from 1990
head of government Leonid Kravchuk from 1993
political system emergent democracy
political party Ukrainian People's Movement (Rukh), umbrella nationalist grouping, with three leaders
products grain, coal, oil, various minerals
currency grivna
population (1992) 52,135,000 (Ukrainian 73%, Russian 22%, Byelorussian 1%, Russian-speaking Jews 1% – some 1.5 million have emigrated to the USA, 750,000 to Canada)
language Ukrainian (Slavonic)
famous people Ivan Kotlyarevsky and Taras Shevchenko
religions traditionally Ukrainian Orthodox; also Ukrainian Catholic

chronology
1918 Independent People's Republic proclaimed.
1920 Conquered by Soviet Red Army.
1921 Poland alloted charge of W Ukraine.
1932–33 Famine caused the deaths of more than 7.5 million people.
1939 W Ukraine occupied by Red Army.
1941–44 Under Nazi control; Jews massacred at Babi Yar; more than 5 million Ukrainians and Ukrainian Jews deported and exterminated.
1944 Soviet control re-established.
1945 Became a founder member of the United Nations.
1946 Ukrainian Uniate Church proscribed and forcibly merged with Russian Orthodox Church.
1986 April: Chernobyl nuclear disaster.
1989 Ukrainian People's Movement (Rukh) established. Ban on Ukrainian Uniate Church lifted.
1990 July: voted to proclaim sovereignty; former Communist Party (CP) leader Leonid Kravchuk indirectly elected president; sovereignty declared.
1991 Aug: demonstrations against the abortive anti-Gorbachev coup; independence declared, pending referendum; CP activities suspended. Oct: voted to create independent army. Dec: Kravchuk popularly elected president; independence overwhelmingly endorsed in referendum; joined new Commonwealth of Independent States; independence acknowledged by USA and European Community.
1992 Jan: admitted into Conference on Security and Cooperation in Europe (CSCE); pipeline deal with Iran to end dependence on Russian oil; prices freed. Feb: prices 'temporarily' re-regulated. March: agreed

tactical arms shipments to Russia suspended. May: Crimean sovereignty declared, but subsequently rescinded. Aug: joint control of Black Sea fleet agreed with Russia. Oct: Leonid Kuchma became prime minister.
1993 Sept: President Kravchuk eliminated post of prime minister. START-1 nuclear arms reduction treaty ratified.

United Arab Emirates

(UAE) (*Ittihad al-Imarat al-Arabiyah*) federation of the emirates of Abu Dhabi, Ajman, Dubai, Fujairah, Ras al Khaimah, Sharjah, Umm al Qaiwain

total area 83,657 sq km/32,292 sq mi
capital Abu Dhabi
towns (chief port) Dubai
physical desert and flat coastal plain; mountains in E
features linked by dependence on oil revenues
head of state and of government Sheik Sultan Zayed bin al-Nahayan of Abu Dhabi from 1971
political system absolutism
political parties none
exports oil, natural gas, fish, dates
currency UAE dirham
population (1992) 1,989,000 (10% nomadic); growth rate 6.1% p.a.
life expectancy men 68, women 72 (1989)
languages Arabic (official), Farsi, Hindi, Urdu, English
religions Muslim 96%, Christian, Hindu
literacy 68% (1989)
GNP $22 bn (1987); $11,900 per head

chronology
1952 Trucial Council established.
1971 Federation of Arab Emirates formed; later dissolved. Six Trucial States formed United Arab Emirates, with ruler of Abu Dhabi, Sheik Zayed, as president.
1972 The seventh state, Ras al Khaimah, joined the federation.
1976 Sheik Zayed threatened to relinquish presidency unless progress towards centralization became more rapid.
1985 Diplomatic and economic links with USSR and China established.
1987 Diplomatic relations with Egypt restored.
1990–91 Iraqi invasion of Kuwait opposed; UAE fights with UN coalition.

1991 Bank of Commerce and Credit International (BCCI), controlled by Abu Dhabi's ruler, collapsed.

United Kingdom
of Great Britain and Northern Ireland (UK)

area 244,100 sq km/94,247 sq mi
capital London
towns Birmingham, Glasgow, Leeds, Sheffield, Liverpool, Manchester, Edinburgh, Bradford, Bristol, Belfast, Newcastle-upon-Tyne, Cardiff
physical became separated from European continent about 6000 BC; rolling landscape, increasingly mountainous towards the N, with Grampian Mountains in Scotland, Pennines in N England, Cambrian Mountains in Wales; rivers include Thames, Severn, and Spey
territories Anguilla, Bermuda, British Antarctic Territory, British Indian Ocean Territory, British Virgin Islands, Cayman Islands, Falkland Islands, Gibraltar, Montserrat, Pitcairn Islands, St Helena and Dependencies (Ascension, Tristan da Cunha), Turks and Caicos Islands
environment an estimated 67% (the highest percentage in Europe) of forests have been damaged by acid rain
features milder climate than N Europe because of Gulf Stream; considerable rainfall. Nowhere more than 120 km/74.5 mi from sea; indented coastline, various small islands
head of state Elizabeth II from 1952
head of government Tony Blair from 1997
political system liberal democracy
political parties Conservative and Unionist Party, right of centre; Labour Party, moderate left of centre; Social and Liberal Democrats, centre-left; Scottish National Party (SNP), Scottish nationalist; Plaid Cymru (Welsh Nationalist Party), Welsh nationalist; Official Ulster Unionist Party (OUP), Northern Ireland moderate right of centre; Democratic Unionist Party (DUP), Northern Ireland, right of centre; Social Democratic Labour Party (SDLP), Northern Ireland, moderate left of centre; Ulster People's Unionist Party (UPUP), Northern Ireland, militant right of centre; Sinn Féin, Northern Ireland, pro-united Ireland; Green Party, ecological
exports cereals, rape, sugar beet, potatoes, meat and meat products, poultry, dairy products, electronic and telecommunications equipment, engineering equipment and scientific instruments, oil and gas, petrochemicals, pharmaceuticals, fertilizers, film and television programmes, aircraft
currency pound sterling
population (1996 est) 58,144,000 (81.5% English, 9.6% Scottish, 1.9% Welsh, 2.4% Irish, 2% West Indian, Asian, and African); growth rate 0.3% (1990–95)
religion Christian (55% Protestant, 10% Roman Catholic); Muslim, Jewish, Hindu, Sikh
life expectancy men 72, women 78 (1989)
languages English, Welsh, Gaelic
literacy 99% (1995 est)
GNP $1,040.5 bn (1992)

chronology
1707 Act of Union between England and Scotland created United Kingdom of Great Britain, governed by a single parliament.

1721–42 Cabinet government developed under Robert Walpole, in effect the first prime minister.
1745 'The Forty-Five': rebellion of Scottish Highlanders in support of Jacobite pretender to throne; defeated 1746.
c. 1760–1850 Industrial Revolution: Britain became the first industrial nation in the world.
1775–83 American Revolution: Britain lost 13 American colonies; empire continued to expand in Canada, India, and Australia.
1793–1815 Britain at war with revolutionary France, except for 1802–03.
1800 Act of Union created United Kingdom of Great Britain and Ireland, governed by a single parliament; effective 1801.
1832 Great Reform Act extended franchise; further extensions 1867, 1884, 1918, and 1928.
1846 Repeal of Corn Laws reflected shift of power from landowners to industrialists.
1870 Home Rule Party formed to campaign for restoration of separate Irish parliament.
1880–90s Rapid expansion of British Empire in Africa.
1906–14 Liberal governments introduced social reforms and curbed power of House of Lords.
1914–18 United Kingdom played leading part in World War I; British Empire expanded in Middle East.
1919–21 Anglo-Irish war ended with secession of S Ireland as Irish Free State; Ulster remained within United Kingdom of Great Britain and Northern Ireland with some powers devolved to Northern Irish parliament.
1924 First Labour government led by Ramsay MacDonald.
1926 General Strike arose from coal dispute. Equality of status recognized between United Kingdom and Dominions of British Commonwealth.
1931 National Government coalition formed to face economic crisis; unemployment reached 3 million.
1939–45 United Kingdom played a leading part in World War II.
1945 First Scottish Nationalist MP elected; first Welsh Nationalist MP 1966.
1945–51 Labour government of Clement Attlee created welfare state and nationalized major industries.

1947–71 Decolonization brought about end of British Empire.

1969 Start of Troubles in Northern Ireland; Northern Irish Parliament suspended 1972.

1973 UK joined European Economic Community.

1979 Referenda failed to approve devolution of power to Scottish and Welsh assemblies.

1979–90 Conservative government of Margaret Thatcher pursued radical free-market economic policies.

1982 Unemployment over 3 million. Falklands War.

1991 British troops took part in US-led war against Iraq under United Nations umbrella. Severe economic recession and unemployment.

1993 Peace proposal for Northern Ireland, the Downing Street Declaration, issued jointly with Irish government.

1994 Irish Republican Army and Protestant paramilitary declared cease-fire in Northern Ireland.

1996 IRA renewed bombing campaign in London. Conservative Party's majority in House of Commons reduced to one seat.

1997 Labour Party won landslide victory in general election; Tony Blair became prime minister. Blair launched new Anglo-Irish peace initiative; IRA declared a cease-fire. Princess Diana killed in car crash. Meeting between Blair and Sinn Féin leader Gerry Adams; all-party peace talks began in Northern Ireland.

United States of America

area 9,368,900 sq km/3,618,770 sq mi

capital Washington DC

towns New York, Los Angeles, Chicago, Philadelphia, Detroit, San Francisco, Washington, Dallas, San Diego, San Antonio, Houston, Boston, Baltimore, Phoenix, Indianapolis, Memphis, Honolulu, San José

physical topography and vegetation from tropical (Hawaii) to arctic (Alaska); mountain ranges parallel with E and W coasts; the Rocky Mountains separate rivers emptying into the Pacific from those flowing into the Gulf of Mexico; Great Lakes in N; rivers include Hudson, Mississippi, Missouri, Colorado, Columbia, Snake, Rio Grande, Ohio

environment the USA produces the world's largest quantity of municipal waste per person (850 kg/ 1,900 lb)

features see individual states

territories the commonwealths of Puerto Rico and Northern Marianas; the federated states of Micronesia; Guam, the US Virgin Islands, American Samoa, Wake Island, Midway Islands, Marshall Islands, Belau, and Johnston and Sand Islands

head of state and government Bill Clinton from 1993

political system liberal democracy

political parties Democratic Party, liberal centre; Republican Party, centre-right

currency US dollar

population (1992) 255,414,000 (white 80%, black 12%, Asian/Pacific islander 3%, American Indian, Inuit, and Aleut 1%, Hispanic [included in above percentages] 9%); growth rate 0.9% p.a.

life expectancy men 72, women 79 (1989)

languages English, Spanish

religions Christian 86.5% (Roman Catholic 26%, Baptist 19%, Methodist 8%, Lutheran 5%), Jewish 1.8%, Muslim 0.5%, Buddhist and Hindu less than 0.5%

literacy 99% (1989)

GNP $5,880.7 bn (1990)

chronology

1776 Declaration of Independence.

1787 US constitution drawn up.

1789 Washington elected as first president.

1803 Louisiana Purchase.

1812–14 War with England, arising from commercial disputes caused by Britain's struggle with Napoleon.

1819 Florida purchased from Spain.

1836 The battle of the Alamo, Texas, won by Mexico.

1841 First wagon train left Missouri for California.

1846 Mormons, under Brigham Young, founded Salt Lake City, Utah.

1846–48 Mexican War resulted in cession to USA of Arizona, California, part of Colorado and Wyoming, Nevada, New Mexico, Texas, and Utah.

1848–49 California gold rush.

1860 Lincoln elected president.

1861–65 Civil War between North and South.

1865 Slavery abolished. Lincoln assassinated.

1867 Alaska bought from Russia.

1890 Battle of Wounded Knee, the last major battle between American Indians and US troops.

1898 War with Spain ended with the Spanish cession of Philippines, Puerto Rico, and Guam; it was agreed that Cuba be independent. Hawaii annexed.

1917–18 USA entered World War I.

1919–1921 Wilson's 14 Points became base for League of Nations.

1920 Women achieved the vote.

1924 American Indians made citizens by Congress.

1929 Wall Street stock-market crash.

1933 F D Roosevelt's New Deal to alleviate the Depression put into force.

1941–45 The Japanese attack on Pearl Harbor Dec 1941 precipitated US entry into World War II.

1945 USA ended war in the Pacific by dropping atom bombs on Hiroshima and Nagasaki, Japan.

1950–53 US involvement in Korean War. McCarthy anticommunist investigations (HUAC) became a 'witch hunt'.

1954 Civil Rights legislation began with segregation ended in public schools.

1957 Civil Rights bill on voting.

1958 First US satellite in orbit.

1961 Abortive CIA-backed invasion of Cuba at the Bay of Pigs.

1963 President Kennedy assassinated; L B Johnson assumed the presidency.

1964–68 'Great Society' civil-rights and welfare measures in the Omnibus Civil Rights bill.

1964–75 US involvement in Vietnam War.

1965 US intervention in Dominican Republic.

1969 US astronaut Neil Armstrong was the first human on the Moon.

1973 OPEC oil embargo almost crippled US industry and consumers. Inflation began.

1973–74 Watergate scandal began in effort to re-elect Richard Nixon and ended just before impeachment; Nixon resigned as president; replaced by Gerald Ford, who 'pardoned' Nixon.

1975 Final US withdrawal from Vietnam.

1979 US–Chinese diplomatic relations normalized.

1979–80 Iranian hostage crisis; relieved by Reagan concessions and released on his inauguration day Jan 1981.

1981 Space shuttle mission was successful.

1983 US invasion of Grenada.

1986 'Irangate' scandal over secret US government arms sales to Iran, with proceeds to antigovernment Contra guerrillas in Nicaragua.

1987 Reagan and Gorbachev (for USSR) signed intermediate-range nuclear forces treaty. Wall Street stock-market crash caused by programme trading.

1988 USA became world's largest debtor nation, owing $532 billion. George Bush elected president.

1989 Bush met Gorbachev at Malta, end to Cold War declared; large cuts announced for US military; USA invaded Panama; Noriega taken into custody.

1990 Bush and Gorbachev met again. Nelson Mandela freed in South Africa, toured USA. US troops sent to Middle East following Iraq's invasion of Kuwait.

1991 Jan–Feb: US-led assault drove Iraq from Kuwait in Gulf War. US support was given to the USSR during the dissolution of communism and the recognition of independence of the Baltic republics. July: Strategic Arms Reduction Treaty (START) signed at US–Soviet summit in Moscow. Nov: Bush co-hosted Middle East peace conference in Spain.

1992 Bush's popularity slumped as economic recession continued. Widespread riots in Los Angeles. Nov: Bill Clinton won presidential elections for the Democrats; independent candidate Ross Perot won nearly 20% of votes.

1993 Jan: Clinton inaugurated. He delayed executive order to suspend ban on homosexuals in the armed forces. Feb: medium-term economic plan passed by Congress to cut federal budget deficit. July: air strike on Baghdad, Iraq. Nov: North American Free Trade Agreement (NAFTA), between USA, Canada, and Mexico, approved by Congress.

Uruguay

Oriental Republic of (*República Oriental del Uruguay*)

area 176,200 sq km/68,031 sq mi

capital Montevideo

towns Salto, Paysandú

physical grassy plains (pampas) and low hills

features rivers Negro, Uruguay, Río de la Plata

head of state and government Luis Lacalle Herrera from 1989

political system democratic republic

political parties Colorado Party (PC), progressive, centre-left; National (Blanco) Party (PN), traditionalist, right of centre; Amplio Front (FA), moderate, left-wing

exports meat and meat products, leather, wool, textiles

currency nuevo peso

population (1992) 3,130,000 (Spanish, Italian; mestizo, mulatto, black); growth rate 0.7% p.a.

life expectancy men 68, women 75 (1989)

language Spanish

media the Ministry of Defence controls broadcasting licences; press heavily dependent on official advertising. Four national and two Montevideo daily papers, combined circulation 500,000 copies per week (1993); all proprietors associated with political parties

religion Roman Catholic 66%

literacy 96% (1984)

GNP $7.5 bn; $2,470 per head (1988)

chronology

1825 Independence declared from Brazil.

1836 Civil war.

1930 First constitution adopted.

1966 Blanco party in power, with Jorge Pacheco Areco as president.

1972 Colorado Party returned, with Juan Maria Bordaberry Arocena as president.

1976 Bordaberry deposed by army; Dr Méndez Manfredini became president.

1984 Violent antigovernment protests after ten years of repressive rule.

1985 Agreement reached between the army and political leaders for return to constitutional government.

Colorado Party won general election; Dr Julio Maria Sanguinetti became president.
1986 Government of national accord established under President Sanguinetti's leadership.
1989 Luis Lacalle Herrera elected president.

Uzbekistan
Republic of

area 447,400 sq km/172,741 sq mi
capital Tashkent
towns Samarkand, Bukhara, Namangan
physical oases in the deserts; rivers: Amu Darya, Syr Darya; Fergana Valley; rich in mineral deposits
features more than 20 hydroelectric plants; three natural gas pipelines
head of state Islam Karimov from 1990
head of government Abdul Hashim Mutalov from 1991
political system socialist pluralist
political parties National Democratic (formerly Communist) Party, reform-socialist; Democratic Party, tolerated opposition
products rice, dried fruit, vines (all grown by irrigation); cotton, silk
population (1992) 21,363,000 (Uzbek 71%, Russian 8%, Tajik 5%, Kazakh 4%)
language Uzbek, a Turkic language
religion Sunni Muslim

chronology
1921 Part of Turkestan Soviet Socialist Autonomous Republic.
1925 Became constituent republic of the USSR.
1944 Some 160,000 Meskhetian Turks forcibly transported from their native Georgia to Uzbekistan by Stalin.
1989 Tashlak, Yaipan, and Ferghana were the scenes of riots in which Meskhetian Turks were attacked; 70 killed and 850 wounded.
1990 June: economic and political sovereignty declared; former Uzbek Communist Party (UCP) leader Islam Karimov became president.
1991 March: Uzbek supported 'renewed federation' in USSR referendum. Aug: anti-Gorbachev coup in Moscow initially accepted by President Karimov; later, Karimov resigned from Soviet Communist

Party (CPSU) Politburo; UCP broke with CPSU; pro-democracy rallies dispersed by militia; independence declared. Dec: joined new Commonwealth of Independent States.
1992 Jan: admitted into Conference on Security and Cooperation in Europe; violent food riots in Tashkent. March: joined the United Nations; US diplomatic recognition achieved.

Vanuatu
Republic of (*Ripablik Blong Vanuatu*)
area 14,800 sq km/5,714 sq mi
capital Vila (on Efate)
towns Luganville (on Espíritu Santo)
physical comprises around 70 islands, including Espíritu Santo, Malekula, and Efate; densely forested, mountainous
features three active volcanoes
head of state Fred Timakata from 1989
head of government Maxime Carlot from 1991
political system democratic republic
political parties Union of Moderate Parties (UMP), Francophone centrist; Vanuatu National United Party (VNUP), formed by Walter Lini; Vanua'aku Pati (VP), Anglophone centrist; Melanesian Progressive Party (MPP), Melanesian centrist; Fren Melanesian Party
exports copra, fish, coffee, cocoa
currency vatu
population (1992) 154,000 (90% Melanesian); growth rate 3.3% p.a.
life expectancy men 67, women 71 (1989)
languages Bislama 82%, English, French (all official)
literacy 53%
religions Presbyterian 40%, Roman Catholic 16%, Anglican 14%, animist 15%
GDP $125 million (1987); $927 per head

chronology
1906 Islands jointly administered by France and Britain.
1975 Representative assembly established.
1978 Government of national unity formed, with Father Gerard Leymang as chief minister.
1980 Revolt on the island of Espíritu Santo delayed independence but it was achieved within the Commonwealth, with George Kalkoa (adopted name Sokomanu) as president and Father Walter Lini as prime minister.

1988 Dismissal of Lini by Sokomanu led to Sokomanu's arrest for treason. Lini reinstated.
1989 Sokomanu sentenced to six years' imprisonment; succeeded as president by Fred Timakata.
1991 Lini voted out by party members; replaced by Donald Kalpokas. General election produced UMP–VNUP coalition under Maxime Carlot.

Vatican City State
(*Stato della Città del Vaticano*)

area 0.4 sq km/109 acres
physical forms an enclave in the heart of Rome, Italy
features Vatican Palace, official residence of the pope; basilica and square of St Peter's; churches in and near Rome, the pope's summer villa at Castel Gandolfo; the world's smallest state
head of state and government John Paul II from 1978
political system absolute Catholicism
currency Vatican City lira; Italian lira
population (1985) 1,000
languages Latin (official), Italian
religion Roman Catholic
chronology
1929 Lateran Treaty recognized sovereignty of the pope.
1947 New Italian constitution confirmed the sovereignty of the Vatican City State.
1978 John Paul II became the first non-Italian pope for more than 400 years.
1985 New concordat signed under which Roman Catholicism ceased to be Italy's state religion.

Venezuela
Republic of (*República de Venezuela*)

area 912,100 sq km/352,162 sq mi
capital Caracas
towns Barquisimeto, Valencia; port Maracaibo
physical Andes Mountains and Lake Maracaibo in NW; central plains (llanos); delta of river Orinoco in E; Guiana Highlands in SE
features Angel Falls, world's highest waterfall
head of state and of government Rafael Caldera from 1993

government federal democratic republic
political parties Democratic Action Party (AD), moderate left of centre; Social Christian Party (COPEI), Christian centre-right; Movement towards Socialism (MAS), left of centre
exports coffee, timber, oil, aluminium, iron ore, petrochemicals
currency bolívar
population (1992) 20,184,000 (mestizos 70%, white (Spanish, Portuguese, Italian) 20%, black 9%, Amerindian 2%); growth rate 2.8% p.a.
life expectancy men 67, women 73 (1989)
religions Roman Catholic 96%, Protestant 2%
languages Spanish (official), Indian languages 2%
literacy 88% (1989)
GNP $47.3 bn (1988); $2,629 per head (1985)

chronology
1961 New constitution adopted, with Rómulo Betancourt as president.
1964 Dr Raúl Leoni became president.
1969 Dr Rafael Caldera became president.
1974 Carlos Andrés Pérez became president.
1979 Dr Luis Herrera became president.
1984 Dr Jaime Lusinchi became president; social pact established between government, trade unions, and business; national debt rescheduled.
1987 Widespread social unrest triggered by inflation; student demonstrators shot by police.
1988 Carlos Andrés Pérez elected president. Payments suspended on foreign debts (increase due to drop in oil prices).
1989 Economic austerity programme enforced by $4.3 billion loan from International Monetary Fund. Price increases triggered riots; 300 people killed. Feb: martial law declared. May: General strike. Elections boycotted by opposition groups.
1991 Protests against austerity programme continued.
1992 Attempted anti-government coups failed. Pérez promised constitutional changes.
1993 Pérez resigned, accused of corruption; Ramon José Velasquez succeeded him as interim head of state pending elections. Dec: former president Rafael Caldera re-elected.

Vietnam

Socialist Republic of (*Công Hòa Xã Hôi Chu Nghĩa Viêt Nam*)

area 329,600 sq km/127,259 sq mi
capital Hanoi
towns ports Ho Chi Minh City (formerly Saigon), Da Nang, Haiphong
physical Red River and Mekong deltas, centre of cultivation and population; tropical rainforest; mountainous in N and NW
environment during the Vietnam War an estimated 2.2 million hectares/5.4 million acres of forest were destroyed. The country's National Conservation Strategy is trying to replant 500 million trees each year
features Karst hills of Halong Bay, Cham Towers
head of state Le Duc Anh from 1992
head of government Vo Van Kiet from 1991
political system communism
political party Communist Party
exports rice, rubber, coal, iron, apatite
currency dong
population (1992) 69,052,000 (750,000 refugees, majority ethnic Chinese left 1975–79, some settled in SW China, others fled by sea – the 'boat people' – to Hong Kong and elsewhere); growth rate 2.4% p.a.
life expectancy men 62, women 66 (1989)
languages Vietnamese (official), French, English, Khmer, Chinese, local languages
media independent newspapers prohibited by law 1989; central government approval is required for appointment of editors
religions Buddhist, Taoist, Confucian, Christian
literacy 78% (1989)
GNP $12.6 bn; $180 per head (1987)

chronology
1945 Japanese removed from Vietnam at end of World War II.
1946 Commencement of Vietminh war against French.
1954 France defeated at Dien Bien Phu. Vietnam divided along 17th parallel.
1964 US troops entered Vietnam War.
1973 Paris cease-fire agreement.
1975 Saigon captured by North Vietnam.
1976 Socialist Republic of Vietnam proclaimed.

1978 Admission into Comecon. Vietnamese invasion of Cambodia.
1979 Sino-Vietnamese border war.
1986 Retirement of 'old guard' leaders.
1987–88 Over 10,000 political prisoners released.
1988–89 Troop withdrawals from Cambodia continued.
1989 'Boat people' leaving Vietnam murdered and robbed at sea by Thai pirates. Troop withdrawal from Cambodia completed. Hong Kong forcibly repatriated some Vietnamese refugees.
1991 Vo Van Kiet replaced Do Muoi as prime minister. Cambodia peace agreement signed. Relations with China normalized.
1992 Sept: Le Duc Anh elected president. Dec: relations with South Korea normalized; USA eased 30-year-old trade embargo.

Yemen

Republic of (*al Jamhuriya al Yamaniya*)

area 531,900 sq km/205,367 sq mi
capital San'a
towns Ta'iz; and chief port Aden
physical hot moist coastal plain, rising to plateau and desert
features once known as *Arabia felix* because of its fertility, includes islands of Perim (in strait of Bab-el-Mandeb, at S entrance to Red Sea), Socotra, and Kamaran
head of state Ali Abdullah Saleh from 1990
head of government Haydar Abu Bakr al-Attas from 1993
political system emergent democratic republic
political parties Yemen Socialist Party (YSP), Democratic Unionist Party, National Democratic Front, Yemen Reform Group, General People's Congress
exports cotton, coffee, grapes, vegetables
currency rial
population (1992) 12,147,000; growth rate 2.7% p.a.
life expectancy men 47, women 50
language Arabic
religions Sunni Muslim 63%, Shi'ite Muslim 37%
literacy men 20%, women 3% (1985 est)
GNP $4.9 bn (1983); $520 per head

chronology
1918 Yemen became independent.
1962 North Yemen declared the Yemen Arab Republic (YAR), with Abdullah al-Sallal as presi-

dent. Civil war broke out between royalists and republicans.

1967 Civil war ended with the republicans victorious. Sallal deposed and replaced by Republican Council. The People's Republic of South Yemen was formed.

1970 People's Republic of South Yemen renamed People's Democratic Republic of Yemen.

1971–72 War between South Yemen and the YAR; union agreement signed but not kept.

1974 Ibrahim al-Hamadi seized power in North Yemen and Military Command Council set up.

1977 Hamadi assassinated and replaced by Ahmed ibn Hussein al-Ghashmi.

1978 Constituent people's assembly appointed in North Yemen and Military Command Council dissolved. Ghashmi killed by envoy from South Yemen; succeeded by Ali Abdullah Saleh. War broke out again between the two Yemens. South Yemen president deposed and Yemen Socialist Party (YSP) formed.

1979 Cease-fire agreed with commitment to future union.

1983 Saleh elected president of North Yemen for a further five-year term.

1984 Joint committee on foreign policy for the two Yemens met in Aden.

1985 Ali Nasser re-elected secretary general of the YSP in South Yemen; removed his opponents. Three bureau members killed.

1986 Civil war in South Yemen; Ali Nasser dismissed. New administration under Haydar Abu Bakr al-Attas.

1988 President Saleh re-elected in North Yemen.

1989 Draft constitution for single Yemen state published.

1990 Border between two Yemens opened; countries formally united 22 May as Republic of Yemen.

1991 New constitution approved.

1992 Anti-government riots.

1993 General People's Congress won most seats in general elections but no overall majority; coalition government formed, led by Haydar Abu Bakr al-Attas. Five-man presidential council formed.

Yugoslavia

area 88,400 sq km/34,100 sq mi
capital Belgrade
towns Kraljevo, Leskovac, Pristina, Novi Sad, Titograd
head of state Zoran Lilic from 1993
head of government Radoje Kontic from 1993
political system socialist pluralist republic
political parties Socialist Party of Serbia, ex-communist; Serbian Renaissance Movement, pro-monarchist; Democratic Party, Serbia-based, liberal, free market; Montenegro League of Communists; Democratic Coalition of Muslims; Alliance of Reform Forces, Montenegro-based; Internal Macedonian Revolutionary Organization–Democratic Party for Macedonian National Unity (VMRO–DMPNE), Macedonian nationalist; Macedonian League of Communists
exports machinery, electrical goods, chemicals, clothing, tobacco
currency dinar
population (1992) 10,394,000 (Serb 53%, Albanian 15%, Macedonian 11%, Montenegrin 5%, Muslim 3%, Croat 2%)

life expectancy men 69, women 75 (1989)
languages Serbian variant of Serbo-Croatian, Macedonian, Slovenian
religion Eastern Orthodox 41% (Serbs), Roman Catholic 12% (Croats), Muslim 3%
literacy 90% (1989)
GNP $154.1 bn; $6,540 per head (1988)

chronology

1918 Creation of Kingdom of the Serbs, Croats, and Slovenes.

1929 Name of Yugoslavia adopted.

1941 Invaded by Germany.

1945 Yugoslav Federal Republic formed under leadership of Tito; communist constitution introduced.

1948 Split with USSR.

1953 Self-management principle enshrined in constitution.

1961 Nonaligned movement formed under Yugoslavia's leadership.

1974 New constitution adopted.

1980 Tito died; collective leadership assumed power.

1987 Threatened use of army to curb unrest.

1988 Economic difficulties: 1,800 strikes, 250% inflation, 20% unemployment. Ethnic unrest in Montenegro and Vojvodina; party reshuffled and government resigned.

1989 Reformist Croatian Ante Marković became prime minister. 29 died in ethnic riots in Kosovo province, protesting against Serbian attempt to end autonomous status of Kosovo and Vojvodina; state of emergency imposed. May: inflation rose to 490%; tensions with ethnic Albanians rose.

1990 Multiparty systems established in Serbia and Croatia.

1991 June: Slovenia and Croatia declared independence, resulting in clashes between federal and republican armies; Slovenia accepted European Community (EC)-sponsored peace pact. Fighting continued in Croatia; repeated calls for cease-fires failed. Dec: President Stipe Mesic and Prime Minister Ante Marković resigned.

1992 Jan: EC-brokered cease-fire established in Croatia; EC and USA recognized Slovenia's and Croatia's independence. Bosnia-Herzegovina and Macedonia declared independence. April: Bosnia-Herzegovina recognized as independent by EC and USA amid

increasing ethnic hostility. New Federal Republic of Yugoslavia (FRY) proclaimed by Serbia and Montenegro but not recognized externally. UN membership suspended. Ethnic Albanians proclaimed new 'Republic of Kosovo' but it was not recognized.
1993 Zoran Lilic became president. Radoje Kontic became prime minister. Macedonia recognized as independent. Yugoslav economy severely damaged by international sanctions.

Zaire (now Democratic Republic of Congo)
Republic of (*République du Zaïre*)

area 2,344,900 sq km/905,366 sq mi
capital Kinshasa
towns Lubumbashi, Kananga, Kisangani; ports Matadi, Boma
physical Zaïre River basin has tropical rainforest and savanna; mountains in E and W
features lakes Tanganyika, Mobutu Sese Seko, Edward; Ruwenzori mountains
head of state and government Laurent Kabila from 1997
political system transitional
political parties Popular Movement of the Revolution (MPR), African socialist; Sacred Union, moderate, centrist; numerous new parties registered 1991
exports coffee, copper, cobalt (80% of world output), industrial diamonds, palm oil
currency zaïre
population (1992) 41,151,000; growth rate 2.9% p.a.
life expectancy men 51, women 54 (1989)
languages French (official), Swahili, Lingala, other African languages; over 300 dialects
religions Roman Catholic, Protestant, Kimbanguist, also half a million Muslims
literacy men 84%, women 61% (1995 est)
GNP $5 bn (1987); $127 per head

chronology
1908 Congo Free State annexed to Belgium.
1960 Independence achieved as Republic of the Congo. Civil war broke out between central government and Katanga province.
1963 Katanga secessionist war ended.
1967 New constitution adopted.

1971 Country renamed Republic of Zaire, with Mobutu as president.
1972 Mobutu's Popular Movement of the Revolution (MPR) became only legal political party. Katanga province renamed Shaba.
1974 Foreign-owned businesses and plantations seized by Mobutu and given to his political allies.
1977 Original owners of confiscated properties invited back. Zairean guerrillas invaded Shaba province from Angola, but were repulsed by Moroccan, French, and Belgian paratroopers.
1980s International creditors forced series of austerity programmes, after level of foreign indebtedness had mounted with collapse in world copper prices.
1991 After antigovernment riots, Mobutu agreed to end ban on multiparty politics and share power with opposition; Etienne Tshisekedi appointed premier, but soon dismissed.
1992 Tshisekedi reinstated against Mobutu's wishes after renewed rioting.
1993 Rival pro- and anti-Mobutu governments created.
1994 Kengo Wa Dondo elected prime minister by interim parliament, with Mobutu's agreement. Mass influx of Rwandan refugees.
1995 Continuing secessionist activity in Shaba and Kasai provinces and interethnic warfare in Kivu, adjoining Rwanda in E.
1996 Zaire on brink of war with Rwanda after Rwandan support of Hutu killings by Tutsis in Zaire. Massive Hutu refugee crisis narrowly averted as thousands allowed to return to Rwanda.
1997 Mobutu ousted by rebel forces of Laurent Kabila, who declared himself president and renamed Zaire the Democratic Republic of Congo. Fighting between rival army factions.

Zambia
Republic of

area 752,600 sq km/290,579 sq mi
capital Lusaka
towns Kitwe, Ndola, Kabwe, Chipata, Livingstone, Kasama
physical forested plateau cut through by rivers

features Zambezi River, Victoria Falls, Kariba Dam
head of state and government Frederick Chiluba
from 1991
political system socialist pluralist republic
political parties United National Independence Party
(UNIP), African socialist; Movement for Multiparty
Democracy (MMD), moderate, left of centre; National
Democratic Alliance (Nada), moderate, centrist
exports copper, cobalt, zinc, emeralds, tobacco, lead
currency kwacha
population (1992) 8,303,000; growth rate 3.3% p.a.
life expectancy men 54, women 57 (1989)
language English (official); Bantu dialects
religions Christian 66%, animist, Hindu, Muslim
literacy 54% (1988)
GNP $2.1 bn (1987); $304 per head (1986)
chronology
1899–1924 As Northern Rhodesia, under administration of the British South Africa Company.
1924 Became a British protectorate.
1964 Independence achieved from Britain, within the
Commonwealth, as the Republic of Zambia with
Kenneth Kaunda as president.
1972 United National Independence Party (UNIP)
declared the only legal party.
1976 Support for the Patriotic Front in Rhodesia
declared.
1980 Unsuccessful coup against President Kaunda.
1985 Kaunda elected chair of the African Front Line
States.
1987 Kaunda elected chair of the Organization of
African Unity (OAU).
1988 Kaunda re-elected unopposed for sixth term.
1990 Multiparty system announced for 1991.
1991 Movement for Multiparty Democracy won
landslide election victory; Frederick Chiluba became
president.
1992 Food and water shortages caused by severe
drought.

Zimbabwe

Republic of

area 390,300 sq km/150,695 sq mi
capital Harare
towns Bulawayo, Gweru, Kwekwe, Mutare, Hwange
physical high plateau with central high veld and
mountains in E; rivers Zambezi, Limpopo
features Hwange National Park, part of Kalahari
Desert; ruins of Great Zimbabwe
head of state and government Robert Mugabe from
1987
political system effectively one-party socialist republic
political party Zimbabwe African National Union–
Patriotic Front (ZANU–PF), African socialist; Forum
Party, moderate centrist
exports tobacco, asbestos, cotton, coffee, gold, silver,
copper
currency Zimbabwe dollar
population (1992) 9,871,000 (Shona 80%, Ndbele
19%; about 100,000 whites); growth rate 3.5% p.a.
life expectancy men 59, women 63 (1989)
languages English (official), Shona, Sindebele
religions Christian, Muslim, Hindu, animist
literacy men 81%, women 67% (1985 est)
GNP $5.5 bn (1988); $275 per head (1986)

chronology
1889–1923 As Southern Rhodesia, under administration of British South Africa Company.
1923 Became a self-governing British colony.
1961 Zimbabwe African People's Union (ZAPU)
formed, with Joshua Nkomo as leader.
1962 ZAPU declared illegal.
1963 Zimbabwe African National Union (ZANU)
formed, with Robert Mugabe as secretary general.
1964 Ian Smith became prime minister. ZANU
banned. Nkomo and Mugabe imprisoned.
1965 Smith declared unilateral independence.
1966–68 Abortive talks between Smith and UK
prime minister Harold Wilson.
1974 Nkomo and Mugabe released.
1979 Smith produced new constitution and established a government with Bishop Abel Muzorewa as
prime minister. New government denounced by Nkomo
and Mugabe. Conference in London agreed independence arrangements (Lancaster House Agreement).
1980 Independence achieved from Britain, with
Robert Mugabe as prime minister and Rev Canaan
Banana as president.
1981 Rift between Mugabe and Nkomo.
1982 Nkomo dismissed from the cabinet.
1984 ZANU–PF party congress agreed to create a
one-party state in future.
1985 Relations between Mugabe and Nkomo
improved. Troops sent to Matabeleland to suppress
rumoured insurrection; 5,000 civilians killed.
1986 Joint ZANU–PF rally held amid plans for
merger.
1987 White-roll seats in the assembly were abolished. President Banana retired; Mugabe combined
posts of head of state and prime minister with the title
executive president.
1988 Nkomo returned to the cabinet and was
appointed vice president.
1989 Opposition party, the Zimbabwe Unity Movement, formed by Edgar Tekere; draft constitution
drawn up, renouncing Marxism–Leninism; ZANU
and ZAPU formally merged.
1990 ZANU–PF re-elected. State of emergency
ended. Opposition to creation of one-party state.
1992 United Front formed to oppose ZANU–PF.
Mugabe declared dire drought and famine situation a
national disaster

World's 100 largest countries by area

Country	Area sq km	sq mi	Country	Area sq km	sq mi
Russian Federation	17,075,500	6,592,883	Turkmenistan	488,100	188,456
Canada	9,970,610	3,849,671	Cameroon	475,440	183,568
USA	9,638,900	3,721,597	Papua New Guinea	462,840	178,703
China	9,596,960	3,705,404	Morocco	458,730	177,117
Brazil	8,511,965	3,286,486	Sweden	450,000	173,746
Australia	7,682,300	2,966,150	Uzbekistan	447,400	172,742
India	3,166,829	1,222,719	Iraq	434,924	167,925
Argentina	2,780,092	1,073,399	Paraguay	406,752	157,048
Kazakhstan	2,717,300	1,049,155	Zimbabwe	390,300	150,696
Sudan	2,505,800	967,494	Norway	387,000	149,421
Algeria	2,381,741	919,595	Japan	377,535	145,767
Zaire	2,344,900	905,370	Germany	357,041	137,854
Saudi Arabia	2,200,518	849,624	Congo	342,000	132,047
Mexico	1,958,201	756,065	Finland	338,145	130,558
Indonesia	1,919,443	741,101	Malaysia	329,759	127,321
Libya	1,759,540	679,362	Vietnam	329,600	127,259
Iran	1,648,000	636,296	Ivory Coast	322,463	124,504
Mongolia	1,565,000	604,249	Italy	301,300	116,332
Peru	1,285,200	496,218	Philippines	300,000	115,831
Chad	1,284,000	495,755	Burkina Faso	274,122	105,839
Angola	1,246,700	481,353	Oman	272,000	105,020
Mali	1,240,142	478,821	Ecuador	270,670	104,506
South Africa	1,223,181	472,272	New Zealand	268,680	103,738
Ethiopia	1,221,900	471,778	Gabon	267,667	103,347
Niger	1,186,408	458,074	Guinea	245,857	94,926
Colombia	1,141,748	440,831	United Kingdom	244,100	94,247
Bolivia	1,098,581	424,164	Ghana	238,305	92,010
Mauritania	1,030,700	397,955	Romania	237,500	91,699
Egypt	1,001,450	386,662	Laos	236,790	91,425
Tanzania	945,000	364,866	Uganda	236,600	91,352
Nigeria	923,773	356,670	Guyana	214,969	83,000
Venezuela	912,000	352,125	Belarus	207,600	80,155
Namibia	824,300	318,264	Kyrgyzstan	198,500	76,641
Mozambique	799,380	308,642	Senegal	196,200	75,753
Pakistan	796,100	307,376	Syria	185,200	71,506
Turkey	779,500	300,966	Cambodia	181,035	69,898
Chile	756,950	292,260	Uruguay	176,200	68,031
Zambia	752,600	290,580	Tunisia	164,150	63,379
Myanmar	676,577	261,228	Surinam	163,820	63,251
Afghanistan	652,090	251,773	Nepal	147,181	56,827
Somalia	637,700	246,217	Bangladesh	144,000	55,599
Central African			Tajikistan	143,100	55,251
Republic	622,436	240,324	Greece	131,957	50,949
Ukraine	603,700	233,090	Poland	127,886	49,377
Madagascar	587,041	226,658	Nicaragua	127,849	49,363
Kenya	582,600	224,943	Korea, North	120,538	46,540
Botswana	582,000	224,711	Malawi	118,000	45,560
France	543,965	210,026	Benin	112,622	43,484
Yemen	531,900	205,368	Honduras	112,100	43,282
Thailand	513,115	198,115	Liberia	111,370	43,000
Spain	504,750	194,885			

World's countries ranked by population size

1993	Population ('000s)	2025	Population ('000s)
1 China	1,178,526	1 China	1,546,301
2 India	897,443	2 India	1,379,556
3 United States	258,328	3 United States	334,716
4 Indonesia	187,638	4 Indonesia	278,170
5 Brazil	151,989	5 Pakistan	275,108
6 Russia	149,001	6 Nigeria	246,030
7 Japan	124,767	7 Bangladesh	211,224
8 Pakistan	122,398	8 Brazil	205,250
9 Bangladesh	113,882	9 Iran	161,913
10 Nigeria	95,060	10 Russia	152,280
11 Mexico	89,998	11 Ethiopia	140,800
12 Germany	81,064	12 Mexico	137,483
13 Vietnam	71,788	13 Japan	125,806
14 Philippines	64,648	14 Vietnam	107,225
15 Iran	62,847	15 Egypt	104,607
16 Turkey	60,705	16 Zaire	104,530
17 Egypt	58,292	17 Philippines	100,845
18 United Kingdom	58,030	18 Turkey	98,744
19 Italy	57,837	19 Thailand	76,403
20 France	57,678	20 Germany	73,201

Source: Population Reference Bureau

The world's largest cities, 200 BC—2000 (population in millions)

Top five	200 BC	Top five	AD 100	Top five	AD 622
Pataliputra (India)	0.35	Rome (Italy)	0.65	Constantinople (Turkey)	0.50
Alexandria (Egypt)	0.30	Loyang (China)	0.50	Changan (China)	0.45
Seleucia (Syria)	0.30	Alexandria (Egypt)	0.40	Loyang (China)	0.40
Changan (China)	0.25	Seleucia (Persia)	0.30	Ctesiphon (Persia)	0.25
Loyang (China)	0.20	Changan (China)	0.25	Alexandria (Egypt)	0.20

Top five	1000	Top five	1400	Top five	1600
Cordoba (Spain)	0.45	Nanjing (China)	0.47	Beijing (China)	0.71
Constantinople (Turkey)	0.45	Cairo (Egypt)	0.45	Constantinople (Turkey)	0.70
Kaifeng (China)	0.40	Vijayanagar (India)	0.35	Agra (India)	0.50
Xian (China)	0.30	Hangzhou (China)	0.33	Cairo (Egypt)	0.40
Kyoto (Japan)	0.20	Beijing (China)	0.32	Osaka (Japan)	0.40

Top five	1800	Top five	1900	Top five	1950
Beijing (China)	1.10	London (UK)	6.48	New York (USA)	12.30
London (UK)	0.95	New York (USA)	4.24	London (UK)	8.86
Guangzhou (China)	0.80	Paris (France)	3.33	Tokyo (Japan)	7.55
Constantinople (Turkey)	0.57	Berlin (Germany)	2.42	Paris (France)	5.90
Paris (France)	0.55	Chicago (USA)	1.72	Shanghai (China)	5.41

Top ten	1985	Top ten 2000	(projected)
Tokyo-Yokohama (Japan)	25.43	Tokyo-Yokohama (Japan)	29.97
Mexico City (Mexico)	16.90	Mexico City (Mexico)	27.87
São Paulo (Brazil)	14.91	São Paulo (Brazil)	25.35
New York (USA)	14.60	Seoul (South Korea)	21.98
Seoul (South Korea)	13.67	Bombay (India)	15.36
Osaka-Kobe-Kyoto (Japan)	13.56	New York (USA)	14.65
Buenos Aires (Argentina)	10.75	Osaka-Kobe-Kyoto (Japan)	14.33
Calcutta (India)	10.46	Tehran (Iran)	14.25
Bombay (India)	10.14	Rio de Janeiro (Brazil)	14.17
Rio de Janeiro (Brazil)	10.12	Calcutta (India)	14.09

Urban population growth, 1990–2000

	1990		*2000*		*1990–2000*
	Urban population	Urban population/ total population	Urban population	Urban population/ total population	Growth
	millions	%	millions	%	millions
World	2,282.4	43	2,962.1	48	679.7
Developing countries	1,401.4	34	1,993.7	40	592.3
Africa	205.5	32	322.1	38	116.6
Algeria	12.9	52	19.5	60	6.6
Ivory Coast	4.9	40	8.0	47	3.1
Egypt	23.0	44	30.0	46	7.0
Kenya	5.7	24	11.1	32	5.4
Nigeria	38.2	35	63.9	43	25.7
Zaire	10.5	28	15.8	31	5.3
Latin America	315.5	72	400.6	77	71.1
Bolivia	3.7	51	5.2	58	1.5
Brazil	112.1	75	140.8	82	28.7
Mexico	61.3	73	79.7	78	18.4
Peru	15.0	70	19.6	75	4.6
Asia	974.3	31	1,370.0	37	395.7
Bangladesh	18.7	16	33.1	23	14.4
China	302.2	26	451.7	35	149.5
India	216.1	26	290.9	29	74.8
Indonesia	53.1	29	79.5	37	26.4
Pakistan	37.8	32	58.6	38	20.8
Philippines	26.7	43	37.2	49	10.5
Thailand	12.1	22	17.7	29	5.6
Developed countries	880.9	73	968.4	76	87.5
Australia	14.6	85	16.8	86	2.2
United States	188.1	75	213.3	78	25.2
Europe	373.4	73	401.4	77	28.0
Japan	95.3	77	101.1	79	5.8

Source: World Urbanisation Prospects 1992, United Nations, New York, 1993

Worldwide population growth

Figures are for population growth rates as a percentage per annum.

Brunei	12.00	Cameroon	2.70	Chile	1.60
United Arab Emirates	6.10	Lesotho	2.70	Gabon	1.60
Kuwait	5.50	Yemen	2.70	Trinidad and Tobago	1.60
Bahrain	4.40	Congo	2.60	Argentina	1.50
Kenya	4.20	Costa Rica	2.60	Australia	1.50
Solomon Islands	3.90	Mexico	2.60	Mauritius	1.50
Maldives	3.70	Papua New Guinea	2.60	Korea, South	1.40
Qatar	3.70	Peru	2.60	Liechtenstein	1.40
Iraq	3.60	Angola	2.50	Taiwan	1.40
Jordan	3.60	Belize	2.50	Antigua and Barbuda	1.30
Botswana	3.50	Ethiopia	2.50	Dominica	1.30
Syria	3.50	Korea, North	2.50	China	1.20
Tanzania	3.50	Morocco	2.50	Cyprus	1.20
Zimbabwe	3.50	São Tomé Principe	2.50	Singapore	1.20
Djibouti	3.40	Sierra Leone	2.50	Canada	1.10
Tuvalu	3.40	South Africa	2.50	Samoa, Western	1.10
Ivory Coast	3.30	Burkina Faso	2.40	Surinam	1.10
Malawi	3.30	Egypt	2.40	New Zealand	0.90
Nicaragua	3.30	Guinea-Bissau	2.40	United States of America	0.90
Nigeria	3.30	Philippines	2.40	Iceland	0.80
Rwanda	3.30	Tonga	2.40	Malta	0.70
Uganda	3.30	Vietnam	2.40	Uruguay	0.70
Vanuatu	3.30	Central African Republic	2.30	Afghanistan	0.60
Zambia	3.30	Chad	2.30	Cuba	0.60
Ghana	3.20	Dominican Republic	2.30	Poland	0.60
Iran	3.20	Guinea	2.30	Barbados	0.50
Madagascar	3.20	Nepal	2.30	Finland	0.50
Comoros	3.10	Brazil	2.20	Japan	0.50
Honduras	3.10	Cambodia	2.20	Portugal	0.50
Libya	3.10	Colombia	2.20	Romania	0.50
Pakistan	3.10	Equatorial Guinea	2.20	Czech Republic	0.40
Saudi Arabia	3.10	Jamaica	2.20	Netherlands	0.40
Senegal	3.10	Laos	2.20	Slovakia	0.40
Somalia	3.10	Panama	2.20	France	0.30
Algeria	3.00	Seychelles	2.20	Greece	0.30
Benin	3.00	Bangladesh	2.17	Norway	0.30
Liberia	3.00	Fiji	2.10	Hungary	0.20
Mauritania	3.00	Turkey	2.10	Spain	0.20
Oman	3.00	Bhutan	2.00	St Christopher-Nevis	0.20
Paraguay	3.00	Guyana	2.00	Switzerland	0.20
Swaziland	3.00	India	2.00	Austria	0.10
Togo	3.00	Indonesia	2.00	Belgium	0.10
Ecuador	2.90	Malaysia	2.00	Bulgaria	0.10
El Salvador	2.90	Thailand	2.00	Ireland	0.10
Mali	2.90	Tunisia	2.00	Italy	0.10
Sudan	2.90	Albania	1.90	San Marino	0.10
Zaire	2.90	Cape Verde	1.90	Sweden	0.10
Burundi	2.80	Gambia	1.90	United Kingdom	0.10
Guatemala	2.80	Myanmar	1.90	Denmark	0.00
Mongolia	2.80	Bahamas	1.80	Luxembourg	0.00
Mozambique	2.80	Israel	1.80	Lebanon	-0.10
Niger	2.80	Sri Lanka	1.80	Grenada	-0.20
St Lucia	2.80	Haiti	1.70	Monaco	-0.50
Venezuela	2.80	Kiribati	1.70	Germany	-0.70
Bolivia	2.70	Nauru	1.70	St Vincent and the Grenadines	-4.00

World literacy rates

Figures are percentages of the population of each country. Where separate figures are given for male and female literacy, the ranking is based on a simple average of the two.

	Men	Women	Average		Men	Women	Average
Andorra	100	100	100	Grenada	85	85	85
Czech Republic	100	100	100	St Vincent and the Grenadines	85	85	85
Iceland	100	100	100	Portugal	89	80	85
Luxembourg	100	100	100	Botswana	84	84	84
Norway	100	100	100	Ecuador	85	80	83
Slovakia	100	100	100	Fiji	88	77	83
Australia	99	99	99	Jamaica	82	82	82
Canada	99	99	99	Dominica	80	80	80
Cyprus	99	99	99	Malaysia	80	80	80
Denmark	99	99	99	Seychelles	80	80	80
Finland	99	99	99	Brazil	79	76	78
France	99	99	99	Dominican Republic	78	77	78
Germany	99	99	99	Albania	75	75	75
Hungary	99	99	99	Lebanon	75	75	75
Japan	99	99	99	Bolivia	84	65	75
Korea, North	99	99	99	China	82	66	74
Monaco	99	99	99	Indonesia	83	65	74
Nauru	99	99	99	Turkey	86	62	74
Netherlands	99	99	99	Zimbabwe	81	67	74
New Zealand	99	99	99	Bahrain	79	64	72
Sweden	99	99	99	Jordan	71	71	71
Switzerland	99	99	99	Kuwait	71	71	71
United Kingdom	99	99	99	Swaziland	70	66	68
USA	99	99	99	United Arab Emirates	68	68	68
Austria	98	98	98	Congo	79	55	67
Belgium	98	98	98	Myanmar	66	66	66
Bulgaria	98	98	98	Nicaragua	66	66	66
Poland	98	98	98	Surinam	65	65	65
Romania	98	98	98	Zaire	79	45	62
Italy	97	97	97	Gabon	70	53	62
San Marino	97	97	97	Honduras	61	58	60
Spain	97	97	97	Qatar	60	60	60
Trinidad and Tobago	97	97	97	Solomon Islands	60	60	60
Argentina	96	95	96	Syria	76	43	60
Cuba	96	95	96	Cambodia	78	39	59
Uruguay	96	96	96	São Tomé e Principe	73	42	58
Bahamas	95	95	95	Uganda	70	45	58
Brunei	95	95	95	Cameroon	68	45	57
Chile	94	94	94	Equatorial Guinea	55	55	55
Costa Rica	94	93	94	Guatemala	63	47	55
Belize	93	93	93	Tunisia	68	41	55
Greece	96	89	93	Ghana	64	43	54
Korea, South	92	92	92	Madagascar	53	53	53
Antigua and Barbuda	90	90	90	Vanuatu	53	53	53
Kiribati	90	90	90	Iran	62	39	51
Malta	90	90	90	Algeria	63	37	50
Mexico	92	88	90	Cape Verde	61	39	50
Samoa, Western	90	90	90	Iraq	68	32	50
St Christopher-Nevis	90	90	90	Kenya	50	50	50
Taiwan	90	90	90	Rwanda	50	50	50
Yugoslavia (former)	90	90	90	Papua New Guinea	55	36	46
Mongolia	89	89	89	Egypt	59	30	45
Thailand	89	89	89	India	57	29	43
Colombia	89	87	88	Nigeria	54	31	43
Paraguay	91	85	88	Central African Republic	53	29	41
Philippines	88	88	88	Togo	53	28	41
Venezuela	88	88	88	Somalia	40	40	40
Panama	87	87	87	Mozambique	55	22	39
Peru	91	78	85	Haiti	40	35	38
Singapore	93	79	86	Maldives	36	36	36

World literacy rates *(cont.)*

	Men	Women	Average		Men	Women	Average
Burundi	43	26	35	Nepal	39	12	26
Ivory Coast	35	35	35	Malawi	25	25	25
Liberia	47	23	35	Afghanistan	39	8	24
Morocco	45	22	34	Saudi Arabia	34	12	23
Bangladesh	43	22	33	Angola	20	20	20
Guinea-Bissau	46	17	32	Djibouti	20	20	20
Sudan	30	30	30	Oman	20	20	20
Pakistan	40	19	30	Mauritania	17	17	17
Sierra Leone	38	21	30	Comoros	15	15	15
Guinea	40	17	29	Burkina Faso	21	6	14
Senegal	37	19	28	Yemen	20	3	12
Benin	37	16	27	Mali	10	10	10
Chad	40	11	26	Bhutan	5	5	5
Gambia	36	15	26				

World life expectancy

Figures are ages of the population of each country. Where separate figures are given for male and female life expectancy, the ranking is based on a simple average of the two.

Nation	Men	Women	Average	Nation	Men	Women	Average
Liechtenstein	78	83	81	Slovakia	68	75	72
Japan	76	82	79	Bulgaria	69	74	72
Switzerland	74	82	78	St Vincent and the Grenadines	69	74	72
Australia	75	80	78	Albania	69	73	71
Netherlands	74	81	78	Germany	68	74	71
Sweden	74	81	78	St Lucia	68	73	71
Iceland	74	80	77	St Christopher-Nevis	69	72	71
Spain	74	80	77	Hungary	67	74	71
Italy	73	80	77	United Arab Emirates	68	72	70
Jamaica	75	78	77	Qatar	68	72	70
Norway	73	80	77	Venezuela	67	73	70
Canada	72	79	76	Mexico	67	73	70
USA	72	79	76	Korea, North	67	73	70
Belgium	72	78	75	Trinidad and Tobago	68	72	70
Denmark	72	78	75	Antigua and Barbuda	70	70	70
France	71	79	75	Poland	66	74	70
New Zealand	72	78	75	Romania	67	73	70
United Kingdom	72	78	75	Paraguay	67	72	70
Israel	73	76	75	Tunisia	68	71	70
Luxembourg	71	78	75	Sri Lanka	67	72	70
Malta	72	77	75	Argentina	66	73	70
Portugal	71	78	75	Korea, South	66	73	70
Brunei	74	74	74	Bahrain	67	71	69
Kuwait	72	76	74	Jordan	67	71	69
Singapore	71	77	74	Vanuatu	67	71	69
Cyprus	72	76	74	Fiji	67	71	69
Finland	70	78	74	Grenada	69	69	69
Greece	72	76	74	Solomon Islands	66	71	69
Costa Rica	71	76	74	Guyana	66	71	69
Cuba	72	75	74	Chile	64	73	69
San Marino	70	77	74	Surinam	66	71	69
Austria	70	77	74	Syria	67	69	68
Panama	71	75	73	China	67	69	68
Ireland	70	76	73	Malaysia	65	70	68
Taiwan	70	75	73	Mauritius	64	71	68
Barbados	70	75	73	Lebanon	65	70	68
Yugoslavia (former)	69	75	72	Libya	64	69	67
Tonga	69	74	72	Samoa, Western	64	69	67
Uruguay	68	75	72	Philippines	63	69	66
Czech Republic	68	75	72	Seychelles	66	66	66

World life expectancy (cont.)

Nation	Men	Women	Average	Nation	Men	Women	Average
Saudi Arabia	64	67	66	Senegal	51	54	53
Mongolia	63	67	65	Zaire	51	54	53
Thailand	62	68	65	Bolivia	51	54	53
El Salvador	63	66	65	Haiti	51	54	53
Turkey	63	66	65	Ghana	50	54	52
Ecuador	62	66	64	Tanzania	49	54	52
Vietnam	62	66	64	Madagascar	50	53	52
Peru	61	66	64	Rwanda	49	53	51
Morocco	62	65	64	Cameroon	49	53	51
Colombia	61	66	64	Bangladesh	50	52	51
Brazil	61	66	64	Swaziland	47	54	51
Dominican Republic	61	65	63	Djibouti	50	50	50
Iraq	62	63	63	Uganda	49	51	50
Nicaragua	61	63	62	Comoros	48	52	50
São Tomé e Principe	62	62	62	Nepal	50	49	50
Maldives	60	63	62	Laos	48	51	50
Tuvalu	60	63	62	Niger	48	50	49
Kenya	59	63	61	Gabon	47	51	49
Zimbabwe	59	63	61	Yemen	47	50	49
Algeria	59	62	61	Nigeria	47	49	48
Lesotho	59	62	61	Malawi	46	50	48
Honduras	58	62	60	Burundi	45	48	47
Belize	60	60	60	Mozambique	45	48	47
Botswana	59	59	59	Congo	45	48	47
Guatemala	57	61	59	Equatorial Guinea	44	48	46
Cape Verde	57	61	59	Mauritania	43	48	46
Egypt	57	60	59	Mali	44	47	46
Dominica	57	59	58	Burkina Faso	44	47	46
Iran	57	57	57	Benin	42	46	44
Oman	55	58	57	Sierra Leone	41	47	44
Zambia	54	57	56	Chad	42	45	44
India	56	55	56	Cambodia	42	45	44
Togo	53	57	55	Bhutan	44	43	44
Pakistan	54	55	55	Central African Republic	41	45	43
Liberia	53	56	55	Angola	40	44	42
Myanmar	53	56	55	Guinea-Bissau	42	42	42
Ivory Coast	52	55	54	Gambia	42	42	42
Papua New Guinea	53	54	54	Afghanistan	43	41	42
Indonesia	52	55	54	Guinea	39	42	41
Somalia	53	53	53	Ethiopia	38	38	38
Sudan	51	55	53				

Human development index, 1993

Overall top-ranked countries

1. Japan
2. Canada
3. Norway
4. Switzerland
5. Sweden
6. United States
7. Australia
8. France
9. Netherlands
10. Britain
11. Iceland
12. Germany
13. Denmark
14. Finland
15. Austria
16. Belgium
17. New Zealand
18. Luxembourg
19. Israel

Top developing nations (overall ranking)

1. Barbados (20)
2. Hong Kong (24)
3. Cyprus (27)
4. Uruguay (30)
5. Trinidad and Tobago (31)
6. Bahamas (32)
7. S Korea (33)
8. Chile (36)
9. Costa Rica (42)
10. Singapore (43)
11. Brunei (44)
12. Argentina (46)
13. Venezuela (50)
14. Dominica (51)
15. Kuwait (52)
16. Mexico (53)
17. Qatar (55)
18. Mauritius (56)
19. Malaysia (57)
20. Bahrain (58)
21. Grenada (59)
22. Antigua and Barbuda (60)

The index is based on income and quality of life, a factor that measures life expectancy, literacy, ability to take part in society's institutions and real purchasing power. The above rankings are included in the UN Development Programme's fourth annual report on human development. According to the report, 90 percent of the world's population have no control over institutions affecting their lives, and the gap between rich and poor is continuing to widen across the globe.
Source: UNDP

States of the USA

State	Nickname(s)	Abbreviation(s)
Alabama	Heart of Dixie/Camellia State	AL, Ala
Alaska	Mainland State/The Last Frontier	AK, Alas
Arizona	Grand Canyon State/Apache State	AZ, Ariz
Arkansas	Wonder State/Bear State/Land of Opportunity	AR, Ark
California	Golden State	CA, Cal, Calif
Colorado	Centennial State	CO, Colo
Connecticut	Constitution State/Nutmeg State	CT, Conn
Delaware	First State/Diamond State	DE/Del
Florida	Sunshine State/Everglade State	FL, Fla
Georgia	Empire State of the South/Peach State	GA, Ga
Hawaii	Aloha State	HI
Idaho	Gem State	ID, Id, Ida
Illinois	Inland Empire/Prairie State/Land of Lincoln	IL, Ill
Indiana	Hoosier State	IN, In, Ind
Iowa	Hawkeye State/Corn State	IA, Ia
Kansas	Sunflower State/Jayhawker State	KS, Kans
Kentucky	Bluegrass State	KY, Ky
Louisiana	Pelican State/Sugar State/Creole State	LA, La
Maine	Pine Tree State	ME, Me
Maryland	Old Line State/Free State	MD, Md
Massachusetts	Bay State/Old Colony	MA, Mass
Michigan	Great Lake State/Wolverine State	MI, Mich
Minnesota	North Star State/Gopher State	MN, Minn
Mississippi	Magnolia State	MS, Miss
Missouri	Show Me State/Bullion State	MO, Mo
Montana	Treasure State/Big Sky Country	MT, Mont
Nebraska	Cornhusker State/Beef State	NE, Neb, Nebr
Nevada	Sagebrush State/Silver State/Battleborn State	NV, Nev
New Hampshire	Granite State	NH
New Jersey	Garden State	NJ
New Mexico	Land of Enchantment/Sunshine State	NM, N Mex
New York	Empire State	NY
North Carolina	Tar Heel State/Old North State	NC
North Dakota	Sioux State/Flickertail State	ND, N Dak
Ohio	Buckeye State	OH, O
Oklahoma	Sooner State	OK, Okla
Oregon	Beaver State/Sunset State	OR, Oreg
Pennsylvania	Keystone State	PA, Pa, Penn, Penna
Rhode Island	Little Rhody/Ocean State/Plantation State	RI
South Carolina	Palmetto State	SC
South Dakota	Coyote State/Sunshine State	SD, S Dak
Tennessee	Volunteer State	TN, Tenn
Texas	Lone Star State	TX, Tex
Utah	Beehive State/Mormon State	UT, Ut
Vermont	Green Mountain State	VT, Vt
Virginia	Old Dominion State/Mother of Presidents	VA, Va
Washington	Evergreen State/Chinook State	WA, Wash, Wa
West Virginia	Mountain State/Panhandle State	WV, W Va
Wisconsin	Badger State/America's Dairyland	WI, Wis, Wisc
Wyoming	Equality State	WY, Wyo
District of Columbia	(Federal District)	DC

Capital	Area sq km/sq mi	Population (1991)	Joined the Union
Montgomery	134,700/51,994	4,089,000	1819
Juneau	1,531,100/591,005	570,000	1959
Phoenix	294,100/113,523	3,750,000	1912
Little Rock	137,800/53,191	2,372,000	1836
Sacramento	411,100/158,685	30,380,000	1850
Denver	269,700/104,104	3,377,000	1876
Hartford	13,000/5,018	3,291,000	1788
Dover	5,300/2,046	680,000	1787
Tallahassee	152,000/58,672	13,277,000	1845
Atlanta	152,600/58,904	6,623,000	1788
Honolulu	16,800/6,485	1,135,000	1959
Boise	216,500/83,569	1,039,000	1890
Springfield	146,100/56,395	11,543,000	1818
Indianapolis	93,700/36,168	5,610,000	1816
Des Moines	145,800/56,279	2,795,000	1846
Topeka	213,200/82,295	2,495,000	1861
Frankfort	104,700/40,414	3,713,000	1792
Baton Rouge	135,900/52,457	4,252,000	1792
Augusta	86,200/33,273	1,235,000	1820
Annapolis	31,600/12,198	4,860,000	1788
Boston	21,500/8,299	5,996,000	1788
Lansing	151,600/58,518	9,368,000	1837
St Paul	218,700/84,418	4,432,000	1858
Jackson	123,600/47,710	2,592,000	1817
Jefferson City	180,600/69,712	5,158,000	1821
Helena	381,200/14,143	808,000	1889
Lincoln	200,400/77,354	1,593,000	1867
Carson City	286,400/110,550	1,284,000	1864
Concord	24,000/9,264	1,105,000	1788
Trenton	20,200/7,797	7,760,000	1787
Santa Fé	315,000/121,590	1,548,000	1912
Albany	127,200/49,099	18,058,000	1788
Raleigh	136,400/52,650	6,737,000	1789
Bismarck	183,100/70,677	635,000	1889
Columbus	107,100/41,341	10,939,000	1803
Oklahoma City	181,100/69,905	3,175,000	1907
Salem	251,500/97,079	2,922,000	1859
Harrisburg	117,400/45,316	11,961,000	1787
Providence	3,100/1,197	1,004,000	1790
Columbia	80,600/31,112	3,560,000	1788
Pierre	199,800/77,123	703,000	1889
Nashville	109,200/42,151	4,953,000	1796
Austin	691,200/266,803	17,349,000	1845
Salt Lake City	219,900/84,881	1,770,000	1896
Montpelier	24,900/9,611	567,000	1791
Richmond	105,600/40,762	6,286,000	1788
Olympia	176,700/68,206	5,018,000	1889
Charleston	62,900/24,279	1,801,000	1863
Madison	145,500/56,163	4,955,000	1848
Cheyenne	253,400/97,812	460,000	1890
Washington	180/69	598,000	Established by Act of Congress 1790–91

National holidays[1]

	Jan	Feb	March	April	May	June	July	Aug
Afghanistan				27	1			19
Albania	1, 11				1			
Algeria	1				1	19	5	
Andorra	1, 6	19			1	24		15
Angola	1	4			1			
Argentina	1				1, 25	10, 20	9	17
Australia	1			25				
Austria	1, 6				1			15
Bahamas	1						10	
Bahrain	1							
Bangladesh		21	26		1		1	
Barbados	1							
Belgium	1				1		21	15
Belize	1		9		1, 24			
Benin	1, 16			1	1			
Bhutan					2	2	21	
Bolivia	1				1			6
Botswana	1, 2							
Brazil	1			21	1			
Brunei	1	23			31		15	
Bulgaria	1				1, 24			
Burkina Faso	1, 3				1			4, 15
Burundi	1				1		1	15
Cameroon	1	11			1, 20			15
Canada	1						1	
Cape Verde	1, 20		8		1	1		
Central African Republic	1		29		1	1		13, 15
Chad	1				1, 25	7		11
Chile	1				1, 21	29		15
China	1				1			
Colombia	1, 6				1	29	20	7, 15
Congo	1		18		1		31	13–15
Costa Rica	1		19	11	1	29	25	2, 15
Côte d'Ivoire	1				1			15
Cuba	1				1		25	
Cyprus	1, 6		25		1			
Czechoslovakia	1, 2				1, 9			
Denmark	1					5		
Djibouti	1				1	27		
Dominica	1				1			
Dominican Republic	1, 6, 21, 26	27			1			16
Ecuador	1				1	30	24	10
Egypt	7			25	1	18	1, 23	
El Salvador	1				1	29, 30		
England and Wales	1							
Equatorial Guinea	1				1	5		3
Ethiopia	7, 19		2	6	1			
Fiji	1							
Finland	1				1			
France	1				1, 8		14	14, 15
Gabon	1		12		1			17
Gambia	1	1, 18			1			15
German Federal Republic	1				1	17		

[1] Chart excludes ex-USSR republics and Baltic states.

Sept	Oct	Nov	Dec	Variable[2]
				Ad (3), Ar, As, ER(3), NY (Hindu), PB, R
		28,29		
		1		Ad, As, ER, NY (Muslim), PB
8		1, 4	8, 25, 26	A, CC, EM, GF, WM
17		11	10, 25	
	12		8, 25, 31	GF, HT
			25, 26	EM, GF, HS
	26	1	8, 24, 25, 26	A, CC, EM, WM
			25, 26	
			16	Ad(3), As(2), ER(3), NY (Muslim), PB
		7	16, 25, 31	Ad(3), ER(3), NY (Bengali), PB, etc
		30	25, 26	EM, GF, WM, Kadooment (Aug), May Hol, United Nations (Oct)
		1, 11	25	A, EM, WM; May, Aug, Nov BH; regional hol (July/Sept)
10, 21	12	19	25, 26	EM, GF, HS
	26	30	25, 31	Ad, ER
		11–13	17	
		1	25	C(2), CC, GF
30			25, 26	A, EM, GF, HS; President's Day (July); PH July, Oct
7	12	2, 15	25	C(2), CC, GF, HS, HT
			25	Ad, ER(2), GF, NY (Chinese, Muslim), PB, R, Mi'raj (March–April), Koran (May)
9		7		
		1	25	A, Ad, EM, ER, PB, WM
18		1	25	A
			25	A, Ad, ER, GF
		11	25, 26	EM, GF, Labour (Sept), Thanksgiving (Oct), Victoria (May)
12			24, 25	GF
1		1	1, 25	A, EM, WM
		1, 28	25	Ad, EM, ER, PB
11, 18, 19	12	1	8, 25, 31	GF, HS
	1			Spring Fest (4) (Jan/Feb)
	12	1, 15	8, 25, 30, 31	A, CC, GF, HT, St Joseph (March), Sacred Heart (June)
		1	25, 31	
15	12		8, 25	CC, GF, HS, HT
		1	24, 25, 31	A, Ad, EM, ER, GF, WM
	10			
	28, 29		25, 26	Ad, EM, ER, GF, HS, PB
			24, 25, 26, 31	EM
			24, 25, 26	A, EM, GF, HT, WM, General Prayer (April/May)
			25	Ad(2), ER(2), NY (Muslim), PB, Mi'raj (March/April)
		3, 4	25, 26	C(2), EM, GF, WM, Aug Monday
24			25	CC, GF
	9, 12	2, 3	6, 25, 31	C(2), GF, HT
	6			Ad(2), Ar, ER(2), NY (Muslim), PB, Ps, ES (E Orth), Sham El-Nessim (April/May)
15	12	2, 5	24, 25, 30, 31	GF, HT, AW, San Salvador (4)
				EM, GF; BH Early May, Late May, Aug
	12		10, 25	CC, GF, Constitution (Aug)
12, 27				Ad, ER, NY (Ethiopian, Sept), PB, Ethiopian GF and Easter
	12		25, 26	D, EM, GF, HS, PB, Aug BH, Queen's b'day (June), Pr Charles' b'day (Nov)
	31	1	6, 24, 25, 26, 31	A, EM, GF, Midsummer Eve and Day (June), Twelfthtide (Jan), Whit (May/June)
	31	1, 11	24, 25, 31	A, EM, GF, HS, WM, Ascension Eve, Whit Hol Eve, Law of 20 Dec 1906, Law of 23 Dec 1904
		1	25	Ad, EM, ER, WM
			25	Ad, As, ER(2), GF, PB
			24, 25, 26	A, EM, GF, WM, Day of Penance (Nov)

[2] For abbreviation key see end of chart. Numbers in brackets refer to number of days devoted to the holiday.

National holidays *(cont.)*

	Jan	Feb	March	April	May	June	July	Aug	Sept
Ghana	1		6		1	4	1		
Greece	1, 6		25		1			15	
Grenada	1, 2	7			1			3, 4	
Guatemala	1				1	30	1		15
Guinea	1			3	1			15	
Guyana	1	23			1			1	
Haiti	1, 2			14	1			15	
Honduras	1			14	1				15
Hungary	1			4	1			20	
Iceland	1				1	17			
India	1, 26				1	30		15	
Indonesia	1							17	
Iran		11	20, 21	1, 2		5			
Iraq	1, 6	8	21		1		14, 17		
Ireland	1		17						
Israel	1				14				
Italy	1, 6			25				14, 15	
Jamaica	1				23			5	
Japan	1, 2, 3, 15	11	21	29	3, 5				15, 23
Jordan	1				1, 25	10		11	
Kenya	1				1	1			
Korea, South	1, 2, 3		1, 10	5	5	6	17	15	
Kuwait	1	25, 26, 27							
Lebanon	1	9			1			15	
Lesotho	1		12, 21		2				
Liberia	1	11	15	12	14		26	24	
Libya			2, 8, 28			11	23		1
Liechtenstein	1, 6	2	19		1			15	
Luxembourg	1				1	23		15	
Madagascar	1		29		1	26		15	
Malawi	1		3		14	6			
Malaysia	1				1	3		31	
Maldives	1						26, 27		
Mali	1, 20				1, 25				22
Malta	1		31		1			15	
Mauritania	1				1, 25	10			
Mauritius	1, 2		12		1				
Mexico	1	5	21		1, 5				1, 16
Monaco	1, 27				1, 8	14		15	3
Mongolia	1, 2		8		1		10, 11, 12		
Morocco	1		3		1, 23		9	14	
Mozambique	1	3		7	1	25			7, 25
Myanmar	4	12	2, 27	1	1		19		
Nauru	1, 31				17		1		
Nepal	11	19							
Netherlands	1			30	5				
New Zealand	1, 2	6		25					
Nicaragua	1				1		19		14, 15
Niger	1			15	1			3	
Nigeria	1				1				
Northern Ireland	1		17						
Norway	1				1, 17				
Oman									

Oct	Nov	Dec	Variable
		25, 26, 31	EM, GF, HS
28		25, 26	GF, EM, WM, Mon in Lent
25		25, 26	CC, EM, GF, WM
12, 20	1	24, 25, 31	GF, HS, HT
2	1	25	Ad, EM, ER, PB
		25, 26	Ad, D, EM, GF, PB, Phagwah (March), Caribbean (July)
17, 24	1, 2, 18	5, 25	A, C, CC, GF
3, 12, 21		25, 31	GF, HT
	7	25, 26	EM
		25, 26	A, EM, GF, HT, WM, First Day of Summer, Aug Hol Mon
2		25, 31	NY (Parsi, Aug)
		25	A, AD, ER(2), GF, NY (Icaka, March; Muslim), PB, Ascension of Prophet (March/April), Waisak (May)
			Ad, As, ER, PB, Prophet's Mission (April), Birth of 12th Imam (April/May) Martyrdom of Imam Ali (May), Death of Imam Jaffar Sadegh (June/July), Birth of Imam Reza (July), Eid-E-Ghadir (Aug), Death of Prophet and Martyrdom of Imam Hassan (Oct/Nov) Ad(4), As, ER(3), NY (Muslim), PB
		25, 26	EM, GF, Aug Hol, Oct Hol, Christmas Hol
			NY (Jewish, Sept/Oct), Purim (March), First Day of Passover (April), Last Day of Passover (April), Pentecost (May/June), Fast of Av (July/Aug), Day of Atonement (Oct), Feast of Tabernacles (Oct)(2)
	1	8, 25, 26	EM
20		25, 26	AW, EM, GF
10	3	23	
	14	25	Ad(4), R, ER(4), NY (Muslim), PB
20		12, 25, 26	EM, GF, ER(3) 26 GF, HS, EM, Youth (Aug)
1, 3, 9		25	NY (Chinese, Jan/Feb), Lord Buddha's Birthday (May), Moon Fest (Sept/Oct)
			Ad(3), ER(3), NY (Muslim), PB, Ascension of Prophet (March/April), Standing on Mt Ararat (Aug)
	1, 22	25	Ad(3), As, EM, GF, ER(3), NY (Muslim), PB
4		25, 26	A, EM, GF, Family (July), National Sports (Oct)
	29	25	Decoration (March), National Fast and Prayer (April), Thanksgiving (Nov)
7			Ad(4), ER(3), PB
	1	8, 24, 25, 26, 31	A, C, CC, EM, GF, WM
	1, 2	25, 26, 31	A, EM, WM, Shrove Mon
	1	25 , 30	A, EM, GF, WM
17		22, 25, 26	EM, GF, HS
		25	Ad, D, ER(2), NY (Chinese, Jan/Feb; Muslim), PB, Wesak
	11, 12		Ad(4), ER(3), NY (Muslim), PB, R(2), Huravee (Feb), Martyrs (April), National (Oct/Nov)(2)
	19	25	Ad, ER, PB, Prophet's Baptism (Nov)
		13, 25	GF
	28		Ad, ER, NY (Muslim), PB
	1	25	Ad, D, ER, PB, Chinese Spring Fest (Feb)
12	2, 20	12, 25, 31	HT, GF
	1, 11, 19	8, 25	EM, WM
	7		
	6, 18		Ad(2), ER(2), NY (Muslim), PB
		25	
1		25	NY (Burmese), Thingyan (April)(4), End Buddhist Lent, full moon days
27		25, 26	EM, GF, Easter Tue
	8	16, 29	NY (Sinhala/Tamil, April), Maha Shivarata (Feb/March)
		25, 26	A, EM, GF, WM
		25, 26	EM, GF, Queen's b'day (June), Labour (Oct)
		8, 25	GF, HT
		18, 25	Ad, ER, PB
1		25, 26	Ad(2), EM, ER(2), GF, PB
		25, 26, 29	BH early May, late May, July, Aug
		25, 26	A, EM, GF, HT, WM
	18, 19	31	Ad(5), ER(4), NY (Muslim), PB, Lailat al-Miraj (March/April)

National holidays *(cont.)*

	Jan	Feb	March	April	May	June	July	Aug	Sept
Pakistan		23			1		1	14	6, 11
Panama	1, 9				1				
Papua New Guinea	1							15	16
Paraguay	1	3	1		1, 14, 15	12		15, 25	29
Peru	1				1	29, 30	28	30	
Philippines	1				1	12	4		
Poland	1				1		22		
Portugal	1			25	1	10		15	
Qatar									3
Romania	1, 2				1, 2			23	
Rwanda	1, 28				1		1, 5	1, 15	25
St Christopher and Nevis	1								19
St Lucia	1, 2	22			1				
St Vincent and the Grenadines	1, 22								
São Tomé e Principe	1	3			1		12		6, 30
Saudi Arabia									23
Scotland	1, 2								
Senegal	1	1		4	1			15	
Seychelles	1, 2				1	5, 29		15	
Sierra Leone	1			19					
Singapore	1				1			9	
Solomon Islands	1						7		
Somalia	1				1	26	1		
South Africa	1			6	31				
Spain	1, 6		19		1			15	
Sri Lanka	14	4			1, 22	30			
Sudan	1		3	6					
Suriname	1	25			1		1		
Swaziland	1			25			22		6
Sweden	1, 6				1				
Switzerland	1							1, 15	
Syria	1		8	17	1, 6		23		1
Taiwan	1, 2, 3		29	5			1		28
Tanzania	1, 12	5			1		7		
Thailand	1			6, 13	1, 5		1	12	
Togo	1, 13, 24			24, 27	1			15	
Tonga	1			25	5	4	4		
Trinidad and Tobago	1					19		1, 31	24
Tunisia	1, 18		20	9	1	1, 2	25	3, 13	3
Turkey	1			23	19			30	
Uganda	1			1	1				
United Arab Emirates	1							6	
USA	1, 21						4		
Uruguay	1			19	1, 18	19	18	25	
Vanuatu	1		5		1		30	15	
Venezuela	1, 6		19	19	1	24, 29	5, 24	15	
Western Samoa	1, 2			25	1, 2, 3				
Yemen Arab Republic					1				26
Yemen People's Democratic Republic	1		8		1	22			26
Yugoslavia	1, 2				1, 2		4		
Zaire	1, 4				1, 20	24, 30		1	
Zambia	1				1, 25				
Zimbabwe	1			18, 19	1, 25			11, 12	

Oct	Nov	Dec	Variable
	9	25, 31	Ad(3), As(2), ER(3), PB, R
11, 12	3, 4, 28	8, 25	C(2), GF
		25, 26	EM, GF, HS, Queen's b'day (June), Remembrance (July)
12	1	8, 25, 31	CC, GF, HT
8	1	8, 25, 31	GF, HT
	1, 30	25, 30, 31	GF, HT
	1	25, 26	CC, EM
5	1	1, 8, 24, 25	C, CC, GF
		31	Ad(4), ER(4)
26	1	25	A, EM, WM
		25, 26, 31	EM, GF, WM, Labour (May), Queen's b'day (June), Aug Mon
		13, 25, 26	C, CC, EM, GF, WM, Emancipation (Aug), Thanksgiving (Oct)
27		25, 26	C (July), EM, GF, WM, Labour (May), Caricom (July), Emancipation (Aug)
		21, 25	
		25, 26	Ad(7), ER(4)
	1	25	GF, Early May, Late May, Summer BH (Aug)
			Ad , EM, ER, NY (Muslim), PB, WM
	1	8, 25	CC, GF, HS
		25, 26	Ad, EM, ER, GF, PB
		25	Ad, D, ER, GF, NY (Chinese, Jan/Feb)(2), Vesak
		25, 26	EM, GF, HS, WM, Queen's b'day (June)
21, 22			Ad(2), ER(2), PB
10		16, 25, 26	A, GF, Family (March/April)
12	1	6, 8, 25	CC, GF, HS, HT
		25, 31	Ad, D, ER, GF, NY (Sinhala, Tamil, April), PB, Maha Sivarathri (Feb/March), Full Moon (monthly)
		25	Ad(5), ER(5), NY (Muslim), PB, Sham al-Naseem (April/May)
	25	25, 26	EM, ER, GF, Holi (March)
24		25, 26	A, EM, GF, Commonwealth (March)
	1	24, 25, 26, 31	A, EM, GF, WM, Midsummer Eve and Day (June)
	1	24, 25, 26	A, CC, EM, GF, WM
6		25	Ad(3), ER(4), ES, NY (Muslim), PB
10, 25, 31	12	25	NY (Chinese, Jan/Feb), Dragon Boat Fest (June), Mid-Autumn Fest (Sept/Oct)
		9, 25	Ad, EM, ER(2), GF, PB
23		5, 10, 31	ER, Makha Bucha (Feb), Visakha Bucha (May), Buddhist Lent (July)
	1	25	A, Ad, ER
	4	4, 25, 26	EM, GF
		25, 26	CC, EM, GF, WM
15			Ad(2), ER(2), NY (Muslim), PB
29			Ad(4), ER(3)
9		25, 26	EM, ER, GF, HS
		2, 3	Ad(3), ER(4), NY (Muslim), PB, Mi'raj (March/April)
	11	25	Washington's b'day (Feb), Memorial (May), Labor (Sept), Discoverers' (Oct), Thanksgiving (Nov)
12	2	25	C(2), GF, HT, Mon- Wed of Holy Week
		25, 26	A, EM, GF, Constitution (Oct), Unity (Nov)
12	1	8, 25	A, C(2), CC, GF, HT
12		25, 26	EM, GF, HS
			Ad(5), ER(4), NY (Muslim), PB
14		30	Ad(3), ER(2), NY (Muslim), PB
	29, 30, 31		People's Uprising (July)
14, 27	17, 24	25	
24		25	GF, HS, Youth (March), Heroes (July), Unity (July), Farmers (Aug)
		25, 26	EM, GF

Abbreviations used for variable holidays are as follows:

A	Ascension Thursday	As	Ashora
Ad	Eid-ul-Adha	AW	Ash Wednesday
Ar	Arafa	BH	Bank holiday
		C	Carnival (before Christian Lent, unless specified)

CC   Corpus Christi
D   Diwali, Deepavali
Abbreviations *(cont.)*
EM   Easter Monday
ER   End of Ramadan

Estimated populations of indigenous peoples, selected countries

Country	Share of population[1] (million)	National population (percent)
Papua New Guinea	3.0	77
Bolivia	5.6	70
Guatemala	4.6	47
Peru	9.0	40
Ecuador	3.8	38
Myanmar	14.0	33
Laos	1.3	30
Mexico	10.9	12
New Zealand	0.4	12
Chile	1.2	9
Philippines	6.0	9
India	63.0	7
Malaysia	0.8	4
Canada	0.9	4
Australia	0.4	2
Brazil	1.5	1
Bangladesh	1.2	1
Thailand	0.5	1
USA	2.0	1
ex-USSR	1.4	1

[1] Generally excludes those of mixed ancestry

Source: Worldwatch Institute, 1992

Areas legally controlled by indigenous peoples, selected countries

Country	Area legally controlled[1] ('000 sq km)	Share of national territory (percent)
Papua New Guinea	449	97
Fiji	15	83
Ecuador	190	41
Nicaragua	59	40
Sweden	137	31
Venezuela	234	26
Colombia	260	23
Canada	2,222	22
Australia	895	12
Panama	15	20
Mexico	160	8
Brazil	573	7
New Zealand	16	6
USA	365	4
Costa Rica	2	4

[1] Figures are in most cases liberal. They include area over which, in principle, indigenous peoples have exclusive rights to use land and water bodies. Does not imply recognized indigenous ownership (many states retain ownership of indigenous reserves), or rights to minerals of petroleum (which states often retain). Does not necessarily imply effective state backing and full enforcement of rights. Some indigenous rights to use resources are limited (for example, Sweden recognizes indigenous peoples' rights only to graze reindeer). figures generally exclude private, individually owned farms of indigenous peoples, as in Andean countries and Mexico.

Source: Worldwatch Institute, 1992

Ethnic Groups and Languages

Abkhazi member of a Muslim minority in Georgia. Abkhazia was a Georgian kingdom from the 4th century, and converted from Christianity to Islam in the 17th century. By the 1980s some 17% of the population were Muslims and two-thirds were of Georgian origin.

Afrikaans language an official language (with English) of the Republic of South Africa and Namibia. Spoken mainly by the Afrikaners – descendants of Dutch and other 17th-century colonists – it is a variety of the Dutch language, modified by circumstance and the influence of German, French, and other immigrant as well as local languages. It became a standardized written language about 1875.

Afro-Asiatic languages or *Hamito-Semitic languages* family of languages spoken throughout the world. There are two main branches, the *Hamitic* languages of N Africa and the *Semitic* languages originating in Syria, Mesopotamia, Palestine, and Arabia, but now found from Morocco in the west to the Persian Gulf in the east.

Ainu member of the aboriginal people of Japan, who were driven north in the 4th century AD by ancestors of the Japanese. The Ainu number about 25,000 (1986), inhabiting Japanese and Russian territory on Sakhalin, Hokkaido, and the Kuril Islands. Their language has no written form, and is unrelated to any other.

Algonquin member of the Algonquian-speaking hunting and fishing people formerly living around the Ottawa River in E Canada. Many now live on reservations in NE USA, E Ontario, and W Québec; others have chosen to live among the general populations of Canada and the USA.

Amhara member of an ethnic group comprising approximately 25% of the population of Ethiopia; 13 million (1987). The Amhara are traditionally farmers. They speak Amharic, a language of the Semitic branch of the Afro-Asiatic family. Most are members of the Ethiopian Christian Church.

Annamese member of the majority ethnic group in Vietnam, comprising 90% of the population. The Annamese language is distinct from Vietnamese, though it has been influenced by Chinese and has loan words from Khmer. Their religion combines elements of Buddhism, Confucianism, and Taoism, as well as ancestor worship.

Arab any of a Semitic people native to the Arabian peninsula, but now settled throughout North Africa and the nations of the Middle East. Arabic is the main Semitic language of the Afro-Asiatic family of W Asia and N Africa, originating among the Arabs of the Arabian peninsula. It is spoken by about 120 million people (1991). Arabic script is written from right to left.

Armenian member of the largest ethnic group inhabiting Armenia. There are Armenian minorities in Azerbaijan, as well as in Turkey and Iran. Christianity was introduced to the ancient Armenian kingdom in the 3rd century. There are 4–5 million speakers of Armenian, which belongs to the Indo-European family of languages.

Ashanti or *Asante* member of a people of central Ghana, west of Lake Volta. The Ashanti speak Akan (or Twi), which belongs to the Kwa branch of the Niger-Congo family of languages.

Australian Aborigine any of the 500 groups of indigenous inhabitants of the continent of Australia, who migrated to this region from S Asia about 40,000 years ago. They were hunters and gatherers, living throughout the continent in small kin-based groups before European settlement. Several hundred different languages developed, the most important being Aranda (Arunta), spoken in central Australia, and Murngin, spoken in Arnhem Land. There are about 227,645 Aborigines in Australia, making up about 1.5% of the country's population of 16 million.

Aymara member of an American Indian people of Bolivia and Peru, builders of a great culture, who were conquered first by the Incas and then by the Spaniards. Today 1.4 million Aymara farm and herd llamas and alpacas in the highlands; their language, belonging to the Andean-Equatorial language family, survives and their Roman Catholicism incorporates elements of their old beliefs.

Azerbaijani or *Azeri* native of the Azerbaijan region of Iran (population 5,500,000) or of the Republic of Azerbaijan (formerly a Soviet republic) (population 7,145,600). Azerbaijani is a Turkic language belonging to the Altaic family. Of the total population of Azerbaijanis, 70% are Shi'ite Muslims and 30% Sunni Muslims.

Bashkir member of the majority ethnic group of the autonomous republic of Bashkir in Russia. The Bashkirs have been Muslims since the 13th century. The Bashkir language belongs to the Turkic branch of the Altaic family, and has about 1 million speakers.

Basque member of a people inhabiting the Basque Country of central N Spain and the extreme SW of France. The Basques are a pre-Indo-European people who largely maintained their independence until the 19th century. Their language (*Euskara*), spoken by some half a million people, is unrelated to any other language. The Basque separatist movement ETA (*Euskadi ta Askatasuna*, 'Basque Nation and Liberty') and the French organization Iparretarrak ('ETA fighters from the North Side') have engaged in guerrilla activity from 1968 in an attempt to secure a united Basque state.

Belarusian or *Byelorussian* or *Belorussian* 'White Russian' native of Belarus. Belarusian, a Balto-Slavonic language belonging to the Indo-European family, is spoken by about 10 million people, including some in Poland. It is written in the Cyrillic script. Belarusian literature dates from the 11th century AD.

Bengali person of Bengali culture from Bangladesh or India (W Bengal, Tripura). There are 80–150 million speakers of Bengali, an Indo-Iranian language belonging to the Indo-European family. It is the official language of Bangladesh and of the state of Bengal, and is also used by emigrant Bangladeshi and Bengali communities in such countries as the UK and the USA. Bengalis in Bangladesh are predominantly Muslim, whereas those in India are mainly Hindu.

Bhil member of a semi-nomadic people of Dravidian origin, living in NW India and numbering about 4 million. They are hunter-gatherers and also practise shifting cultivation. The Bhili language belongs to the Indo-European family, as does Gujarati, which is also spoken by the Bhil. Their religion is Hinduism.

Bihari member of a N Indian people, also living in Bangladesh, Nepal, and Pakistan, and numbering over 40 million. The Bihari are mainly Muslim. The Bihari language is related to Hindi and has several widely varying dialects. It belongs to the Indic branch of the Indo-European family. Many Bihari were massacred during the formation of Bangladesh, which they opposed.

Burmen member of the largest ethnic group in Myanmar (formerly Burma). The Burmans, speakers of a Sino-Tibetan language, migrated from the hills of Tibet, settling in the areas around Mandalay by the 11th century AD.

Bushman former name for the Kung, San, and other hunter-gatherer groups (for example, the Gikwe, Heikom, and Sekhoin) living in and around the Kalahari Desert in southern Africa. They number approximately 50,000 and speak San and other languages of the Khoisan family. They are characteristically small-statured and brown-skinned.

Celtic languages branch of the Indo-European family, divided into two groups: the *Brythonic* or *P-Celtic* (Welsh, Cornish, Breton, and Gaulish) and the *Goidelic* or *Q-Celtic* (Irish, Scottish, and Manx Gaelic). Celtic languages once stretched from the Black Sea to Britain, but have been in decline for centuries, limited to the so-called 'Celtic fringe' of western Europe.

Chinese native to or an inhabitant of China or Taiwan, or a person of Chinese descent. The Chinese comprise more than 25% of the world's population, and the Chinese language (Mandarin) is the largest member of the Sino-Tibetan family. Chinese traditions are ancient, many going back to at least 3000 BC. They include a range of philosophies and religions, including Confucianism, Taoism, and Buddhism. Descendants of Chinese migrants are found throughout SE Asia, the Pacific, Australia, North and South America, and Europe.

Chuang member of the largest minority group in China, numbering about 15 million. They live in S China, where they cultivate rice fields. Their religion includes elements of ancestor worship. The Chuang language belongs to the Tai family.

Chuvash member of the majority ethnic group inhabiting the autonomous republic of Chuvash, Russia. The Chuvash have lived in the middle Volga region since the 8th century. Their language belongs to the Altaic family, although whether it is a member of the Turkic branch or constitutes a branch on its own is not certain.

Copt descendant of those ancient Egyptians who adopted Christianity in the 1st century and refused to convert to Islam after the Arab conquest. They now form a small minority (about 5%) of Egypt's population. *Coptic* is a member of the Hamito-Semitic language family. It is descended from the language of the ancient Egyptians and is the ritual language of the Coptic Christian church. It is written in the Greek alphabet with some additional characters derived from demotic script.

creole language any pidgin language that has ceased to be simply a trade jargon in ports and markets and has become the mother tongue of a particular community. Many creoles have developed into distinct languages with literatures of their own; for example, Jamaican Creole, Haitian Creole, Krio in Sierra Leone, and Tok Pisin, now the official language of Papua New Guinea.

Croat member of the majority ethnic group in Croatia. Their language is generally considered to be identical to that of the Serbs, hence Serbo-Croatian. The Croats are mainly Roman Catholics.

Dariganga member of a Mongolian people numbering only 30,000. Their language is a dialect of Khalka, the official language of Mongolia. In the past, the Dariganga were nomads, and lived by breeding camels for use in the Chinese imperial army. With the rise of the communist regime in China they supported the new Mongolian state, and have become sedentary livestock farmers.

Dinka Nilotic minority group in S Sudan. Primarily cattle herders, the Dinka inhabit the lands around the river system that flows into the White Nile. Their language belongs to the Nilo-Saharan family. The Dinka's animist beliefs conflict with those of Islam, the official state religion; this has caused clashes between the Dinka and the Sudanese army. The Dinka number around 1–2 million.

Dogon member of the W African Dogon culture from E Mali and NW Burkina Faso. The Dogon number approximately 250,000 and their language belongs to the Voltaic (Gur) branch of the Niger-Congo family.

Dongxiang ethnic group living in NW China, numbering around 279,000 (1992). The Dongxiang farm in oases in the desert region of Gansu. They are Muslims, in spite of pressure from the state. Their language belongs to the Altaic family.

Estonian member of the largest ethnic group in Estonia. There are 1 million speakers of the Estonian language, a member of the Finno-Ugric branch of the Uralic family. Most live in Estonia.

Ewe member of a group of people inhabiting Ghana and Togo, and numbering about 2.5 million (1991). The Ewe live by fishing and farming, and practise an animist religion. Their language belongs to the Kwa branch of the Niger-Congo family.

Fang member of a W African people living in the rainforests of Cameroon, Equatorial Guinea, and NW Gabon, numbering about 2.5 million. The Fang language belongs to the Bantu branch of the Niger-Congo family.

Farsi or *Persian* language belonging to the Indo-Iranian branch of the Indo-European family, and the official language of Iran (formerly Persia). It is also spoken in Afghanistan, Iraq, and Tajikistan. It is written in Arabic script, from right to left.

Finno-Ugric group or family of more than 20 languages spoken by some 22 million people in scattered communities from Norway in the west to Siberia in the east and to the Carpathian mountains in the south. Members of the family include Finnish, Saami, and Hungarian.

Fon member of a people living mainly in Benin, and also in Nigeria, numbering about 2.5 million. The Fon language belongs to the Kwa branch of the Niger-Congo family. The Fon founded a kingdom which became powerful in the 18th and 19th centuries through the slave trade, and the region became known as the Slave Coast.

Fulani member of a W African culture from the southern Sahara and Sahel. Traditionally nomadic pastoralists and traders, Fulani groups are found in Senegal, Guinea, Mali, Burkina Faso, Niger, Nigeria, Chad, and Cameroon. The Fulani language is divided into four dialects and belongs to the W Atlantic branch of the Niger-Congo family; it has more than 10 million speakers.

Galla or *Oromo* nomadic pastoralists inhabiting S Ethiopia and NW Kenya. Galla is an Afro-Asiatic language, and is spoken by about 12 million people.

Ganda member of the Baganda people, the majority ethnic group in Uganda; the Baganda also live in Kenya. Until the 19th century they formed an independent kingdom, the largest in E Africa. Their language, Luganda, belongs to the Niger-Congo language family and has about 3 million speakers.

Georgian or *Grazinian* member of any of a number of related groups which make up the largest ethnic group in Georgia and the surrounding area. There are 3–4 million speakers of Georgian, a member of the Caucasian language family.

Germanic languages branch of the Indo-European language family, divided into *East Germanic* (Gothic, now extinct), *North Germanic* (Danish, Faroese, Icelandic, Norwegian, Swedish), and *West Germanic* (Afrikaans, Dutch, English, Flemish, Frisian, German, Yiddish).

Gond member of a heterogenous people of central India, about half of whom speak unwritten languages belonging to the Dravidian family. The rest speak Indo-European languages. There are over 4 million Gonds, most of whom live in Madhya Pradesh, E Maharashtra, and N Andra Pradesh, although some live in Orissa. Gond beliefs embrace Hinduism as well as a range of more ancient gods and spirits, and the society has a clan structure. Agriculture and livestock are the basis of their economy.

Guaraní member of a South American Indian people who formerly inhabited the area that is now Paraguay, S Brazil, and Bolivia. The Guaraní live mainly in reserves; few retain the traditional ways of hunting in the tropical forest, cultivation, and ritual warfare. About 1 million speak Guaraní, a member of the Tupian language group.

Gujarati inhabitant of Gujarat on the NW coast of India. The Gujaratis number approximately 30 million and speak their own Indo-European language, Gujarati, which has a long literary tradition. They are predominantly Hindu (90%), with Muslim (8%) and Jain (2%) minorities.

Hamito-Semitic languages former name for the Afro-Asiatic languages.

Han member of the majority ethnic group in China, numbering about 990 million. The Hans speak a wide variety of dialects of the same monosyllabic language, a member of the Sino-Tibetan family. Their religion combines Buddhism, Taoism, Confucianism, and ancestor worship.

Hausa member of an agricultural Muslim people of NW Nigeria, numbering 9 million. The Hausa language belongs to the Chadic subfamily of the Afro-Asiatic language group. It is used as a trade language throughout W Africa.

Hindi language member of the Indo-Iranian branch of the Indo-European language family, the official language of the Republic of India, although resisted as such by the Dravidian-speaking states of the south. Hindi proper is used by some 30% of Indians, in such northern states as Uttar Pradesh and Madhya Pradesh. Hindi has close historical and cultural links with Sanskrit, the classical language of Hinduism, and is written (from left to right) in Devanagari script.

Hmong member of a SE Asian highland people. They are predominantly hill farmers, rearing pigs and cultivating rice and grain, and many are involved in growing the opium poppy. Estimates of the size of the Hmong population vary between 1.5 million and 5 million, the greatest number being in China. Although traditional beliefs remain important, many have adopted Christianity. Their language belongs to the Sino-Tibetan family. The names *Meo* or *Miao*, sometimes used to refer to the Hmong, are considered derogatory.

Hui member of one of the largest minority ethnic groups in China, numbering about 25 million. Members of the Hui live all over China, but are concentrated in the northern central region. They have been Muslims since the 10th century, for which they have suffered persecution both before and since the communist revolution.

Hutu member of the majority ethnic group of both Burundi and Rwanda, numbering around 9.5 million. The Hutu tend to live as peasant farmers, while the ruling minority, the Tutsi, are town dwellers. There is a long history of violent conflict between the two groups. The Hutu language belongs to the Bantu branch of the Niger-Congo family.

Iban or *Sea Dyak* member of a Dyak people of central Borneo. Approximately 250,000 Iban live in the interior uplands of Sarawak, while another 10,000 live in the border area of W Kalimantan. Traditionally the Iban live in long houses divided into separate family units, and practise shifting cultivation. Their languages belong to the Austronesian family.

Ibo or *Igbo* member of the W African Ibo culture group occupying SE Nigeria and numbering about 18 million. Primarily cultivators, they inhabit the richly forested tableland, bounded by the river Niger to the west and the river Cross to the east. They are divided into five main groups, and their languages belong to the Kwa branch of the Niger-Congo family.

Ifugao member of an indigenous people of N Luzon in the Philippines, numbering approximately 70,000. In addition to practising shifting cultivation on highland slopes, they build elaborate terraced rice fields. Their language belongs to the Austronesian family.

Indian languages traditionally, the languages of the subcontinent of India; since 1947, the languages of the Republic of India. These number some 200, depending on whether a variety is classified as a language or a dialect. They fall into five main groups, the two most widespread of which are the Indo-European languages (mainly in the north) and the Dravidian languages (mainly in the south).

Indo-European languages family of languages that includes some of the world's major classical languages (Sanskrit and Pali in India, Zend Avestan in Iran, Greek and Latin in Europe), as well as several of the most widely spoken languages (English worldwide; Spanish in Iberia, Latin America, and elsewhere; and the Hindi group of languages in N India). Indo-European languages were once located only along a geographical band from India through Iran into NW Asia, E Europe, the northern Mediterranean lands, N and W Europe and the British Isles.

Inuit people inhabiting the Arctic coasts of North America, the E islands of the Canadian Arctic, and the ice-free coasts of Greenland. *Inuktitut*, their language, has about 60,000 speakers; it belongs to the Eskimo-Aleut group. The Inuit object to the name Eskimos ('eaters of raw meat') given them by the Algonquin Indians.

Jat member of an ethnic group living in Pakistan and N India, and numbering about 11 million; they are the largest group in N India. The Jat are predominantly farmers. They speak Punjabi, a language belonging to the Iranian branch of the Indo-European family. They are thought to be related to the Romany people.

Javanese member of the largest ethnic group in the Republic of Indonesia. There are more than 50 million speakers of Javanese, which belongs to the western branch of the Austronesian family. Although the Javanese have a Hindu-Buddhist heritage, they are today predominantly Muslim, practising a branch of Islam known as *Islam Jawa*, which contains many Sufi features.

Kannada or *Kanarese* language spoken in S India, the official state language of Karnataka; also spoken in Tamil Nadu and Maharashtra. There are over 20 million speakers of Kannada, which belongs to the Dravidian family. Written records in Kannada date from the 5th century AD.

Karen member of a group of SE Asian peoples, numbering 1.9 million. They live in E Myanmar (formerly Burma), Thailand, and the Irrawaddy delta. Their language belongs to the Thai division of the Sino-Tibetan family. In 1984 the Burmese government began a large-scale military campaign against the Karen National Liberation Army (KNLA), the armed wing of the Karen National Union (KNU).

Kazakh or *Kazak* member of a pastoral Kyrgyz people of Kazakhstan. Kazakhs also live in China (Xinjiang, Gansu, and Qinghai), Mongolia, and Afghanistan. There are 5–7 million speakers of Kazakh, a Turkic language belonging to the Altaic family. They are predominantly Sunni Muslim, although pre-Islamic customs have survived.

Khmer or *Kmer* member of the largest ethnic group in Cambodia, numbering about 7 million. Khmer minorities also live in E Thailand and S Vietnam. They practise Theravāda Buddhism and trace descent through both male and female lines. The Khmer lan-

guage belongs to the Mon-Khmer family of Austro-Asiatic languages.

Khoikhoi (formerly *Hottentot*) member of a people living in Namibia and the Cape Province of South Africa, and numbering about 30,000. Their language is related to San (spoken by the Kung) and belongs to the Khoisan family. Like the Kung, the Khoikhoi once inhabited a wider area, but were driven into the Kalahari Desert by invading Bantu peoples and Dutch colonists in the 18th century. They live as nomadic hunter-gatherers, in family groups, and have animist beliefs.

Khoisan the smallest group of languages in Africa. It includes fewer than 50 languages, spoken mainly by the people of the Kalahari Desert (including the Khoikhoi and Kung). Two languages from this group are spoken in Tanzania. The Khoisan languages are known for their click consonants (clicking sounds made with the tongue, which function as consonants).

Kikuyu member of Kenya's dominant ethnic group, numbering about 3 million. The Kikuyu are primarily cultivators, although many are highly educated and have entered the professions. Their language belongs to the Bantu branch of the Niger-Congo family.

Kirghiz member of a pastoral people numbering approximately 1.5 million. They inhabit the central Asian region bounded by the Hindu Kush, the Himalayas, and the Tian Shan mountains. The Kirghiz are Sunni Muslims, and their Turkic language belongs to the Altaic family.

Kung (formerly *Bushman*) member of a small group of hunter-gatherer peoples of the NE Kalahari, southern Africa, still living to some extent nomadically. Their language belongs to the Khoisan family.

Kurd member of the Kurdish culture, living mostly in the Taurus and Sagros mountains of W Iran and N Iraq in the region called Kurdistan. Although divided among more powerful states, the Kurds have nationalist aspirations; there are some 8 million in Turkey (where they suffer from discriminatory legislation), 5 million in Iran, 4 million in Iraq, 500,000 in Syria, and 500,000 in Azerbaijan, Armenia, and Georgia. Several million live elsewhere in Europe. Some 2 million Kurds became refugees from Iraq between 1984 and 1991. The Kurdish languages (Kurmanji, Sorani Kurdish, Guraní, and Zaza) are members of the Indo-Iranian branch of the Indo-European family, and the Kurds are a non-Arab, non-Turkic ethnic group. The Kurds are predominantly Sunni Muslims, although there are some Shi'ites in Iran.

Lahnda language spoken by 15–20 million people in Pakistan and N India. It is closely related to Punjabi and Romany, and belongs to the Indo-Iranian branch of the Indo-European language family.

Latvian (or *Lett*) member of the majority ethnic group living in Latvia. The region has been Christian since the 13th century. The Latvian language is also known as *Lettish*; with Lithuanian, it is one of the two surviving members of the Baltic branch of the Indo-European family.

Lithuanian member of the majority ethnic group living in Lithuania, comprising 80% of the population. The Lithuanian language belongs to the Baltic branch of the Indo-European family and is closely related to Latvian. It acquired a written form in the 16th century, using the Latin alphabet, and is currently spoken by about 3–4 million people.

Makua member of a people living to the north of the Zambezi River in Mozambique. With the Lomwe people they make up the country's largest ethnic group. The Makua are mainly farmers, living in villages ruled by chiefs. The Makua language belongs to the Niger-Congo family, and has about 5 million speakers.

Malagasy inhabitant of or native to Madagascar. The Malagasy language has about 9 million speakers; it belongs to the Austronesian family.

Malayalam southern Indian language, the official language of the state of Kerala. Malayalam is closely related to Tamil, also a member of the Dravidian language family; it is spoken by about 20 million people. Written records in Malayalam date from the 9th century AD.

Maori member of the indigenous Polynesian people of New Zealand, numbering 294,200 (1986), about 10% of the total population. Their language, Maori, belongs to the eastern branch of the Austronesian family. Only one-third use the Maori language today, but in recent years there has been increased Maori consciousness.

Maratha or *Mahratta* member of a people living mainly in Maharashtra, W India. There are about 40 million speakers of Marathi, a language belonging to the Indo-European family. The Maratha are mostly farmers, and practise Hinduism. In the 17th and 18th centuries the Maratha formed a powerful military confederacy in rivalry with the Mogul emperors.

Masai member of an E African people whose territory is divided between Tanzania and Kenya, and who number about 250,000. They were originally warriors and nomads, breeding humped zebu cattle, but some have adopted a more settled life. Their cooperation is being sought by the Kenyan authorities to help in wildlife conservation. They speak a Nilotic language belonging to the Nilo-Saharan family.

Mende member of a W African people living in the rainforests of central east Sierra Leone and W Liberia. They number approximately 1 million. The Mende are farmers as well as hunter-gatherers, and each of their villages is led by a chief and a group of elders. The Mende language belongs to the Niger-Congo family.

Moldavian member of the majority ethnic group living in Moldova, comprising almost two-thirds of the population; also, an inhabitant of the Romanian province of Moldavia. The Moldavian language is a dialect of Romanian, and belongs to the Romance group of the Indo-European family.

Mon (or *Talaing*) member of a minority ethnic group living in Myanmar (Burma) and Thailand. The Mon established kingdoms in the area as early as the 7th century. Much of their culture was absorbed by the Khmer and Thai invaders who conquered them. The Mon language belongs to the Mon-Khmer branch of the Austro-Asiatic family. They are Buddhists, but also retain older animist beliefs.

Mordvin Finnish people inhabiting the middle Volga Valley in W Asia. They are known to have lived in the region since the 1st century AD. There are 1 million speakers of Mordvin scattered throughout W Russia, about one-third of whom live in the Mordvinian republic. Mordvin is a Finno-Ugric language belonging to the Uralic family.

Mossi member of the majority ethnic group living in Burkina Faso. Their social structure, based on a monarchy and aristocracy, was established in the 11th century. The Mossi have been prominent traders, using cowrie shells as currency. There are about 4 million speakers of Mossi, a language belonging to the Gur branch of the Niger-Congo family.

Munda member of any one of several groups living in NE and central India, numbering about 5 million (1983). Their most widely spoken languages are Santali and Mundari, languages of the Munda group, an isolated branch of the Austro-Asiatic family. The Mundas were formerly nomadic hunter-gatherers, but now practise shifting cultivation. They are Hindus, but retain animist beliefs.

Naga member of any of the various peoples who inhabit the highland region near the India–Myanmar (Burma) border; they number approximately 800,000. These peoples do not possess a common name; some of the main groups are Ao, Konyak, Sangtam, Lhota, Sema, Rengma, Chang, and Angami. They live by farming, hunting, and fishing. Their languages belong to the Sino-Tibetan family.

Nahuatl member of any of a group of Mesoamerican Indian peoples (Mexico and Central America), of which the best-known group were the Aztecs. The Nahuatl are the largest ethnic group in Mexico, and their languages, which belong to the Uto-Aztecan (Aztec-Tanoan) family, are spoken by over 1 million people today.

Natchez member of a North American Indian people of the Mississippi area, one of the Mound-builder group of peoples. They had a highly developed caste system unusual in North America, headed by a ruler priest (the 'Great Sun'). Members of the highest caste always married members of the lowest caste. The system lasted until French settlers colonized the area 1731. Only a few Natchez now survive in Oklahoma. Their Muskogean language is extinct.

Navajo or *Navaho* (Tena *Navahu* 'large planted field') member of a North American Indian people related to the Apache, and numbering about 200,000, mostly in Arizona. They speak an Athabaskan language, belonging to the Na-Dené family. The Navajo were traditionally cultivators; many now herd sheep and earn an income from tourism, making and selling rugs, blankets, and silver and turquoise jewellery. The Navajo refer to themselves as *Dineh*, 'people'.

Niger-Congo languages the largest group of languages in Africa. It includes about 1,000 languages and covers a vast area south of the Sahara desert, from the west coast to the east, and down the east coast as far as South Africa. It is divided into groups and subgroups; the most widely spoken Niger-Congo languages are Swahili (spoken on the east coast), the members of the Bantu group (southern Africa), and Yoruba (Nigeria).

Nuba member of a minority ethnic group living in S Sudan, numbering about 1 million (1991). They speak related dialects of Nubian, which belongs to the Chari-Nile family. Forced Islamization threatens their cultural identity, and thousands were killed in the Sudan civil war.

Nyanja member of a central African people living mainly in Malawi, and numbering about 400,000 (1984). The Nyanja are predominantly farmers, living in villages under a hereditary monarchy. They speak a Bantu language belonging to the Niger-Congo family.

Oriya member of the majority ethnic group living in the Indian state of Orissa. Oriya is Orissa's official language; it belongs to the Eastern group of the Indo-Iranian branch of the Indo-European family.

Oromo member of any of a group of E African peoples, especially of S Ethiopia, who speak an Afro-Asiatic language.

Palikur member of a South American Indian people living in N Brazil and numbering about 1 million (1980). Formerly a warlike people, they occupied a vast area between the Amazon and Orinoco rivers.

Pathan member of a people of NW Pakistan and Afghanistan, numbering about 14 million (1984). The majority are Sunni Muslims. The Pathans comprise distinct groups, some living as nomads with herds of goats and camels, while others are farmers. The Pakistani Pathans are now claiming independence, with the Afghani Pathans, in their own state of Pakhtoonistan, although this has not yet been recognized. The Pathans speak Pashto, a member of the Indo-Iranian branch of the Indo-European family.

pidgin language any of various trade jargons, contact languages, or lingua francas arising in ports and markets where people of different linguistic backgrounds meet for commercial and other purposes. Usually a pidgin language is a rough blend of the vocabulary of one (often dominant) language with the syntax or grammar of one or more other (often dependent) groups. Pidgin English in various parts of the world, *français petit negre*, and Bazaar Hindi or Hindustani are examples of pidgins that have served long-term purposes to the extent of being acquired by children as one of their everyday languages. At this point they become creole languages.

Potiguara member of a group of South American Indians living in NW Brazil, and numbering about 1 million (1983). Their language belongs to the Tupi-Guaraní family. Their religion is centred around a shaman, who mediates between the people and the spirit world.

Punjabi member of the majority ethnic group living in the Punjab. Approximately 37 million live in the Pakistan half of Punjab while another 14 million live on the Indian side of the border. In addition to Sikhs there are Rajputs in Punjab, some of whom have adopted Islam. The Punjabi language belongs to the Indo-Iranian branch of the Indo-European family. It is considered by some to be a variety of Hindi, by others to be a distinct language.

Pygmy (sometimes *Negrillo*) member of any of several groups of small-statured, dark-skinned peoples of the rainforests of equatorial Africa. They were probably the aboriginal inhabitants of the region, before the arrival of farming peoples from elsewhere. They live nomadically in small groups, as hunter-gatherers; they also trade with other, settled people in the area.

Quechua or *Quichua* or *Kechua* member of the largest group of South American Indians. The Quechua live in the Andean region. Their ancestors included the Inca, who established the Quechua language in the region. Quechua is the second official language of Peru and is widely spoken as a lingua franca in Ecuador, Bolivia, Columbia, Argentina, and Chile; it belongs to the Andean-Equatorial family.

Romance languages branch of Indo-European languages descended from the Latin of the Roman Empire ('popular' or 'vulgar' as opposed to 'classical' Latin). The present-day Romance languages with national status are French, Italian, Portuguese, Romanian, and Spanish.

Romany member of a nomadic people, also called *Gypsy* (a corruption of 'Egyptian', since they were erroneously thought to come from Egypt). They are now believed to have originated in NW India, and live throughout the world. The Romany language, spoken in several different dialects, belongs to the Indic branch of the Indo-European family.

Russian member of the majority ethnic group living in Russia. Russians are also often the largest minority in neighbouring republics. The Russian language is a member of the East Slavonic branch of the Indo-European language family and was the official language of the USSR, with 130–150 million speakers. It is written in the Cyrillic alphabet. The ancestors of the Russians migrated from central Europe between the 6th and 8th centuries AD.

Saami (or *Lapp*) member of a group of herding people living in N Scandinavia and the Kola Peninsula, and numbering about 46,000 (1983). Some are nomadic, others lead a more settled way of life. They live by herding reindeer, hunting, fishing, and producing handicrafts. Their language belongs to the Finno-Ugric family. Their religion is basically animist, but incorporates elements of Christianity.

Serb member of Yugoslavia's largest ethnic group, found mainly in Serbia, but also in the neighbouring independent republics of Bosnia-Herzegovina and Croatia. Their language is generally recognized to be the same as Croat and hence known as Serbo-Croatian. The Serbs are predominantly Greek Orthodox Christians.

Serbo-Croatian (or *Serbo-Croat*) the most widely spoken language in Yugoslavia, with more than 17 million speakers. It is a member of the South Slavonic branch of the Indo-European family. The different dialects of Serbo-Croatian tend to be written by the Serbs in the Cyrillic script, and by the Croats in the Latin script.

Shona member of a Bantu-speaking people of southern Africa, comprising approximately 80% of the population of Zimbabwe. They also occupy the land between the Save and Pungure rivers in Mozambique, and smaller groups are found in South Africa, Botswana, and Zambia. The Shona are mainly farmers, living in scattered villages. The Shona language belongs to the Niger-Congo family.

Sindhi member of the majority ethnic group living in the Pakistani province of Sind. The Sindhi language is spoken by about 15 million people.

Sinhalese member of the majority ethnic group of Sri Lanka (70% of the population). Sinhalese is the official language of Sri Lanka; it belongs to the Indo-Iranian branch of the Indo-European family, and is written in a script derived from the Indian Pali form. The Sinhalese are Buddhists.

Sino-Tibetan languages group of languages spoken in SE Asia. This group covers a large area, and includes Chinese and Burmese, both of which have numerous dialects. Some classifications include the Tai group of languages (including Thai and Lao) in the Sino-Tibetan family.

Slav member of an Indo-European people in central and E Europe, the Balkans, and parts of N Asia, speaking closely related Slavonic languages. The ancestors of the Slavs are believed to have included the Sarmatians and Scythians. Moving west from Central Asia, they settled in E and SE Europe during the 2nd and 3rd millennia BC.

Slavonic languages or *Slavic languages* branch of the Indo-European language family spoken in central and E Europe, the Balkans, and parts of N Asia. The family comprises the *southern group* (Slovene, Serbo-Croatian, Macedonian, and Bulgarian); the *western group* (Czech and Slovak, Sorbian in Germany, and Polish and its related dialects); and the *eastern group* (Russian, Ukrainian, and Belarusian).

Slovene member of the Slavonic people of Slovenia and parts of the Austrian Alpine provinces of Styria and Carinthia. There are 1.5–2 million speakers of Slovene, a language belonging to the South Slavonic branch of the Indo-European family. The Slovenes use the Roman alphabet and the majority belong to the Roman Catholic Church.

Sotho member of a large ethnic group in southern Africa, numbering about 7 million (1987) and living mainly in Botswana, Lesotho, and South Africa. The Sotho are predominantly farmers, living in small village groups. They speak a variety of closely related languages belonging to the Bantu branch of the Niger-Congo family. With English, Sotho is the official language of Lesotho.

Sundanese member of the second largest ethnic group in the Republic of Indonesia. There are more than 20 million speakers of Sundanese, a member of the western branch of the Austronesian family. Like their neighbours, the Javanese, the Sundanese are predominantly Muslim.

Swahili language belonging to the Bantu branch of the Niger-Congo family, widely used in east and central Africa. Swahili originated on the E African coast as a *lingua franca* used among traders, and contains many Arabic loan words. It is an official language in Kenya and Tanzania. The name Swahili is also used for a member of an African people using the language, especially someone living in Zanzibar and adjoining coastal areas of Kenya and Tanzania. The Swahili are not an isolated group, but are part of a mixed coastal society engaged in fishing and trading.

Tagalog member of the majority ethnic group living around Manila on the island of Luzon, in the Philippines, and numbering about 10 million (1988). The Tagalog live by fishing and trading. In its standardized form, known as Pilipino, Tagalog is the official language of the Philippines, and belongs to the Western branch of the Austronesian family. The Tagalogs' religion is a mixture of animism, Christianity, and Islam.

Tajik or *Tadzhik* member of the majority ethnic group living in Tajikistan. Tajiks also live in Afghanistan and parts of Pakistan and W China. The Tajiki language belongs to the West Iranian subbranch of the Indo-European family, and is similar to Farsi; it is written in the Cyrillic script, however. The majority of the Tajik people are Sunni Muslims; there is a Shi'ite minority in Afghanistan.

Tamil member of the majority ethnic group living in the Indian state of Tamil Nadu (formerly Madras). Tamils also live in S India, N Sri Lanka, Malaysia, Singapore, and South Africa, totalling 35–55 million worldwide. Tamil belongs to the Dravidian family of languages; written records in Tamil date from the 3rd century BC. The 3 million Tamils in Sri Lanka are predominantly Hindu, although some are Muslims, unlike the Sinhalese majority, who are mainly Buddhist. The *Tamil Tigers*, most prominent of the various Tamil groupings, are attempting to create a separate homeland in N Sri Lanka through both political and military means.

Tatar or *Tartar* member of a Turkic people, the descendants of the mixed Mongol and Turkic followers of Genghis Khan, called the Golden Horde because of the wealth they gained by plunder. The vast Tatar state was conquered by Russia 1552. The Tatars now live mainly in the Russian autonomous republic of Tatarstan, W Siberia, Turkmenistan, and Uzbekistan (where they were deported from the Crimea 1944). There are over 5 million speakers of the Tatar language, which belongs to the Turkic branch of the Altaic family. The Tatar people are mainly Muslim, although some have converted to the Orthodox Church.

Telugu language spoken in SE India. It is the official language of Andhra Pradesh, and is also spoken in Malaysia, giving a total number of speakers of around 50 million. Written records in Telugu date from the 7th century AD. Telugu belongs to the Dravidian family.

Thai member of the majority ethnic group living in Thailand and N Myanmar (Burma). Thai peoples also live in SW China, Laos, and N Vietnam. They speak Thai languages, all of which belong to the Sino-Tibetan language family. There are over 60 million speakers (1991), the majority of whom live in Thailand. Most Thais are Buddhists, but the traditional belief in spirits, *phi*, remains.

Tibetan member of a Mongolian people inhabiting Tibet, who practise Lamaism, a form of Mahāyāna Buddhism, introduced in the 7th century. Until Tibet's annexation by China 1959, it was a theocratic state. The Tibetans claim to be victims of 'cultural genocide' as result of Chinese immigration and economic colonization, and refugee communities have formed in India and Nepal. The Tibetan language belongs to the Sino-Tibetan language family.

Tigré people of N Ethiopia. The Tigré language is spoken by about 2.5 million people; it belongs to the SE Semitic branch of the Afro-Asiatic family. *Tigrinya* is a closely related language spoken slightly to the south.

Tswana member of the majority ethnic group living in Botswana. The Tswana are divided into four sub-groups: the Bakwena, the Bamangwato, the Bang-waketse, and the Batawana. Traditionally they are rural-dwelling farmers, though many now leave their homes to work as migrant labourers in South African industries. The Tswana language belongs to the Bantu branch of the Niger-Congo family.

Tuareg Arabic name given to nomadic stockbreeders from west and central Sahara and Sahel (Algeria, Libya, Mali, Niger, and Burkina Faso). The eight Tuareg groups refer to themselves by their own names. Their language, *Tamashek*, belongs to the Berber branch of the Afro-Asiatic family and is spoken by 500,000–850,000 people. It is written in a noncursive script known as *tifinagh*, derived from ancient Numidian.

Turkoman or *Turkman* member of the majority ethnic group in Turkmenistan. They live to the E of the Caspian Sea, around the Kara Kum desert, and along the borders of Afghanistan and Iran. Traditionally the Turkomen were tent-dwelling pastoral nomads, though the majority are now sedentary farmers. Their language belongs to the Turkic branch of the Altaic family. They are predominantly Sunni Muslims.

Tutsi member of a minority ethnic group living in Rwanda and Burundi. Although fewer in number, they have traditionally been politically dominant over the Hutu majority and the Twa (or Pygmies). The Tutsi are traditionally farmers; they also hold virtually all positions of importance in Burundi's government and army. They have carried out massacres in response to Hutu rebellions, notably in 1972 and 1988. In Rwanda the balance of power is more even.

Twa member of an ethnic group comprising 1% of the populations of Burundi and Rwanda. The Twa are the aboriginal inhabitants of the region. They are a pygmoid people, and live as nomadic hunter-gatherers in the forests.

Uigur member of a Turkic people living in NW China and Kazakhstan; they form about 80% of the population of the Chinese province of Xinjiang Uigur. There are about 5 million speakers of Uigur, a language belonging to the Turkic branch of the Altaic family; it is the official language of the province. The Uigur are known to have lived in the region since the 3rd century AD, and converted to Islam in the 14th century.

Ukrainian member of the majority ethnic group living in Ukraine; there are minorities in Siberian Russia, Kazakhstan, Poland, the Slovak Republic, and Romania. There are 40–45 million speakers of Ukrainian, a member of the East Slavonic branch of the Indo-European family, closely related to Russian. Ukrainian-speaking communities are also found in Canada and the USA.

Urdu language member of the Indo-Iranian branch of the Indo-European language family, related to Hindi and written not in Devanagari but in Arabic script. Urdu is strongly influenced by Farsi (Persian) and Arabic. It is the official language of Pakistan and is used by Muslims in India.

Uzbek member of the majority ethnic group (almost 70%) living in Uzbekistan; minorities live in Turkmenistan, Tajikistan, Kazakhstan, and Afghanistan. There are 10–14 million speakers of the Uzbek language, which belongs to the Turkic branch of the Altaic family. Uzbeks are predominantly Sunni Muslims.

Vedda member of the aboriginal peoples of Sri Lanka, who occupied the island before the arrival of the Aryans c. 550 BC. Formerly cave-dwelling hunter-gatherers, they have now almost died out or merged with the rest of the population. They speak a Sinhalese language, belonging to the Indo-European family.

Wolof member of the majority ethnic group living in Senegal. There is also a Wolof minority in Gambia. There are about 2 million speakers of Wolof, a language belonging to the Niger-Congo family. The Wolof are Muslims. The remnants of a three-tiered social structure comprising aristocracy, artisans, and slaves can still be seen.

Xhosa member of a Bantu people of southern Africa, living mainly in the Black National State of Transkei. Traditionally, the Xhosa were farmers and pastoralists, with a social structure based on a monarchy. Many are now town-dwellers, and provide much of the labour in South African mines and factories. Their Bantu language belongs to the Niger-Congo family.

Yanamamo or *Yanomamo* (plural *Yanamami*) member of a semi-nomadic South American Indian people, numbering approximately 15,000, who live in S Venezuela and N Brazil. The Yanamamo language belongs to the Macro-Chibcha family. In Nov 1991 Brazil granted the Yanamami possession of their original land, 58,395 km/36,293 sq mi on its northern border.

Yao member of a people living in S China, N Vietnam, N Laos, Thailand, and Myanmar (Burma), and numbering about 4 million (1984). The Yao language may belong to either the Sino-Tibetan or the Thai language family. The Yao incorporate elements of ancestor worship in their animist religion. Most are hill-dwelling farmers.

Yi member of a people living in S China; there are also Yi populations in Laos, Thailand, and Vietnam, totalling about 5.5 million (1987). The Yi are farmers, producing both crops and livestock. Their language belongs to the Sino-Tibetan family; their religion is animist.

Yoruba member of the majority ethnic group living in SW Nigeria; there is a Yoruba minority in E Benin. They number approximately 20 million in all, and their language belongs to the Kwa branch of the Niger-Congo family. The Yoruba established powerful city states in the 15th century.

Zulu member of a group of southern African peoples mainly from Natal, South Africa. Their present homeland, KwaZulu, represents the nucleus of the once extensive and militaristic Zulu kingdom. Today many Zulus work in the industrial centres around Johannesburg and Durban. The Zulu language, closely related to Xhosa, belongs to the Bantu branch of the Niger-Congo family.

INDEX

Aalto, Alvar 224
Abacha, General Sami 633
abacus 168
Abbott, Berenice 311
abbreviations 279–87
Abdul-Salam-al-Mujali 609
aberration of starlight 43
Abkhazi 689
Aborigine, Australian 689
 aboriginal religion 403
abortion 334
abortion pill 334, 354
Abraham 407, 413
abscissa 168
absolute dating 21
absolute majority 397
absolute monarchy 392
absolute war 478
absolute zero 182
absolutism 392
absorption spectroscopy 65
Abstract Expressionism 240
Absurd, Theatre of the 315
Abu Bakr 413
Abú Nuwás, Hasan ibn Háni 257
abyssal zone 96
abzyme 166
Academy Awards (Oscars) 249–50
a cappella 293
accelerator mass spectrometry (AMS) 21
accessory 373
accomplice 373
acetylenes see alkyne
Achilles tendon 336
acid 65
acid rain 107, 119
acid rock music 304
acne 346
acoustics 182, 293
acquired immune deficiency syndrome (AIDS) 346
acquittal 373
acronyms 279–87
act of God 373
action, legal 373
Action Aid 372
activation analysis 65
activation energy 65
Act of Parliament 373
acupressure 356
acupuncture 354
acute rheumatism 349
Adam, Robert 224
Adam, William 224
Adami, Edward Fenech 622
Adams, Ansel 311
Adams, John Couch 49
Adamson, Robert 311
adaptation 149
added value 202
adder, in electronics 85
additional member voting system 397
additive 141
Adenauer, Konrad 530

adenoids 336
adenosine triphosphate (ATP) 53, 164
Adi Granth 413
adjective 267
adjournment 373
admiral 473
adobe 111
adoption 373
adrenal gland 336
adult education 330
adultery 373
Adventist 409
adverb 267
adverse variance 202
advertising, restrictions, European television 391
Advertising Standards Authority (ASA) 385
advocate 373
Aegean civilizations, art of 229
aerial 196
aerial archaeology 21
aerial photography 21
aerial reconnaissance 21
aerobic 154
aerogel 65
aeroplane 461
 flight chronology 462
aerosol 68, 119
Aeschylus 319
Afewerki, Issaias 589
affidavit 373
affirmative action 394
Afghanistan 557
Africa 547
 historical time charts 506–28, 547
 religions 403
 traditional dance 251
African Development Bank (ADB) 215
Afrikaans language 689
Afro-Asiatic languages 689
ageing 151
agoraphobia 341
Agostini, Giacomo 445
agricultural revolution 143
agriculture 143–8
 chronology 147–8
 organic farming 124
 overproduction 143
agrochemical 144
agronomy 144
Aho, Esko 592
aid, development 210
AIDS see acquired immune deficiency syndrome
Ainu 689
airborne early warning (AEW) system 498
aircraft carrier 463, 478, 486
air force 473
air pollution 119
airship 462
air transport 461–3
 distances between major cities 470–1

airway bill 203
Airy, George Biddell 49
Akayev, Askar 613
Akihito, Emperor of Japan 608
Akmadzic, Mile 570
Alamein, El, Battles of 479
Albania 557
 revolution 505
albedo 43
Albee, Edward 319
Albert, King of Belgium 566
Alberti, Leon Battista 224
alcohol 62
alcoholism and alcohol dependence 342, 346
aldehyde 63
Aldrin, Edwin 49
Alesana, Tofilau Eti 643
Alexander technique 354
Alexeev, Vasiliy 445
Alfonsín Foulkes, Raúl Ricardo 530
algae 161
algebra 168
Algeria 558
Algol 40
Algonquin 689
Algonquin Radio Observatory 47
Ali 413
Ali, Muhammad 445
Ali, Zine el-Abidine Ben 660
alibi 373
alien 373
alimentary canal 160, 337
alimony 373
aliphatic compound 63
Aliyev, Geidar 563
alkali 65
alkane 63
alkene 63
alkyne 63, 64
allele 152
Allen, Woody 243
Allende Gossens, Salvador 504, 530
allergen 334
allergy 334
Alley, Alvin 256
alliance 394
Allied Mobile Force (AMF) 473
Allies, the 473
alluvial deposit 96
Alma-Tadema, Sir Lawrence 237
Alpha Centauri 40
alpha share 202
Alston, Richard 256
Altdorfer, Albrecht 233
alternate angles 168
alternation of generations 152
alternative medicine 354–9
alternative vote 397
altitude 168
Altman, Robert 243
alto 293
Alzheimer's disease 346
Amazon Pact 360
ambassador 394

American ballet 251
American War of Independence 502
Americas 553–6
　historical time charts 483–29, 553, 555
Ames Research Center 29
Amhara 689
Amin (Dada), Idi 530
amino acid 53, 64, 164
ammonia 56
amnesty 373
Amnesty International 372
amniocentesis 334
amortization 202
Ampère, André Marie 191
amphibian 158
amplifier 85, 196
Amritsar 414
amylase 164
amyotrophic lateral sclerosis 350
anabolic steroid 353
anabolism 55
anaemia 346
anaerobic 154
anaesthetic 353
Analects 411
analgesic 353
analogue signal 86, 182
analogue-to-digital converter (ADC) 86
analytical chemistry 53
analytical geometry 171
anarchism 392
Anaximander 49
Andean Group 360
Andersen, Hans Christian 257
Andorra 558
Andre, Carl 240
Andrea del Sarto 233
Andreotti, Giulio 530
Andromeda galaxy 40
angina pectoris 346
angiosperm 161
angle 168
angling 424
Anglo-Australian Telescope 35
Angola 559
animals 155–61
　classification 156
　collective nouns 160
　lifespans and gestation periods 155
　speeds 161
Annamese 689
annelid 157
anno Domini (AD) 403
annual accounts 202
annual general meeting (AGM) 202
annual percentage rate (APR) 202
anorexia 341
Anouilh, Jean 319
Antall, Jozsef 530
Antarctica 548
　Antarctic exploration 548
Antarctic Circle 96
Antarctic Treaty 360
antenna 196
anthem 293
anthropology 21
　cultural (or social) 22
antiballistic missile (ABM) 477

antibiotic 353
antibody 337
anticline 94, 96
antidepressant 353
Antigua and Barbuda 560
anti-inflammatory 353
antiknock 119
antimatter 189
antiseptic 353
antiviral 353
Antonello da Messina 233
Antonioni, Michelangelo 243
anxiety 342
Anyaoko, Emeka 370
aorta 337
Aouita, Said 445
apartheid 394
aperture 308
apex 168
aphelion 43
apogee 43
Apollo asteroid 34
Apollo project 29
Apollo-Soyuz test project 29
apoplexy 353
apostrophe 267
appeal 373
appendicitis 346
applied kinesiology 355
Aptidon, Hassan Gouled 585
aquaculture 144
aqua fortis 60
aqua regia 56
aquifer 96
Aquino, Corazon 530
Arab 689
Arab Common Market 215
Arabic language 272
Arabic numerals 168
Arab-Israeli Wars 479
Arab League 360
Arab Maghreb Union (AMU) 360
Arab Monetary Fund (AMF) 215
arachnid 157
Arafat, Yassir 530
arbitrageur 202
arbitration 374
Arbus, Diane 311
arc 168
arch 222
Archaean 90
archaebacteria 163
archaeobotany 27
archaeology 21–8
　chronology 24–6
　historical 23
archaeomagnetic dating 21
Archaeozoic 90
archaeozoology 21
Archaic art 230
archery 424
Archigram 224
Archimedes 178
archipelago 96
architectural orders 226
architecture 221–8
　biographies 224–8
　history 221–2
　terms 222–4
arc minute 43
arc second 43

Arctic 549
　Arctic exploration 549
Arctic Circle 96
Ardennes offensive 480
area, in mathematics 168
　common areas 168
Arecibo 47
Argentina 560
aria 293
Ariane 29
Ariel 29
Ariosto, Ludovico 257
Aristarchus of Samos 49
Aristophanes 320
arithmetic 168
arithmetic and logic unit (ALU) 77
Armani, Giorgio 327
armed forces ranks 489
Armenia 561
Armenian 689
Armistice Day 473
armour 473
armoured personnel carrier 486
arms control 394
arms trade 473, 488
Armstrong, Louis 300
Armstrong, Neil Alden 49
army 473
Arnhem, Battle of 479
aromatherapy 355
aromatic compound 64
Arp, Hans 239
Arras, Battle of 479
arrest 374
Arrhenius, Svante August 72
arson 374
art 229–42
　15th and 16th centuries 233, 235
　17th century 235–6
　18th century 236–7
　19th century 237–8
　20th century 238–40
　ancient 229
　classical 229–30
　eastern 241–2
　Italian Renaissance 232–3
　major western artists 234
　medieval 231
　patronage 231
　prehistoric 229
Artaud, Antonin 320
artefact 21
artery 337
artesian well 96
arthritis 346
arthropod 157
article, in grammar 268
articles of association 202
artificial insemination (AI) 144
artificial intelligence (AI) 77
artificial selection 149
artillery 473, 475
Art Nouveau 222
Arutyunyan, Gagik 561
ASA, in photography 308
Asante 688
ASCII (American standard code for information interchange) 81
asexual reproduction 150
Ashanti 689
Ashe, Arthur 446

Ashikaga period 242
Ashton, Frederick 256
Asia 550
    historical time charts 506–28, 551
Asian Development Bank (ADB) 215
Asian and Pacific Council (ASPAC) 360
Asia-Pacific Economic Cooperation
        Conference (APEC) 360
Asoka 413
aspirin 353
Assas, Hafez al- 530, 655
assault 374
assault ship 486
assay 65
assemblage 21
asset 202
asset stripping 202
Assisted Places Scheme 330
Association of South East Asian
        Nations (ASEAN) 360
associative operation 168
asterisk 268
asteroid 34
asthenosphere 94
asthma 346
astrological diagnosis 355
astrometry 43
astronaut 29, 49–52
astronautics 29
Astronomers Royal 50
astronomical unit 43
astronomy 29–52
    biographies 49–52
    chronology 45
    technical terms 43–7
astrophotography 44
Asturias, Miguel Angel 257
Asuka period 242
Atget, Eugène 311
atherosclerosis 346
athletics 424
Atlantic, Battle of the 479
atmosphere 101–4
atoll 98
atom 65
atom bomb 476
atomic absorption spectrometry 21
atomic number 65
atomic orbital 65
atomic weight 464
atonality 293
ATP see adenosine triphosphate
atrium 222
Attas, Haydar Abu Bakr al- 669
Attlee, Clement 530
Attorney General 374
attribute, in archaeology 21
Atwood, Margaret 257
audit 202
auger 21
Augustine, Saint 413
aura diagnosis 355
aurora (australis; borealis) 34
Ausseil, Jean 626
Austen, Jane 257
Australasia, historical time chart
        506–28
Australia 562
    prime ministers 544
Australia Telescope 47
Austria 562

Austria-Hungary
    emperors 498
authoritarianism 392
autochrome 308
autogenics 355
autoimmunity 346
autonomy 394
autoradiography 166
autos sacramentales 315
autotroph 154
avant-garde dance 251
Avedon, Richard 311
AWACS 473
Axel Springer 384
axis 168
Ayckbourn, Alan 320
Aylwin, Patricio 578
Aymara 689
Azerbaijan 563
Azerbaijani 689
Azeri 688
Azlan Muhibuddin Shah, Rajah 620
AZT see zidovudine
Aztec emperors 495

Baade, Walter 49
Babangida, Ibrahim 530
Baccalauréat 330
Bach, Johann Sebastian 296
Bach flower healing 355
bacillus 163
back pain 346
Bacon, Francis 2241
bacteria 163
bacteriophage 166
bad debt 202
badlands 96
badminton 425
Bad painters 241
BAFTA see British Academy of Film
        and Television Arts Awards
bagatelle 293
Baha'i 409
Bahamas 564
Bahrain 564
bail 374
bailey 222
Bailey, David 311
Baily's beads 34
Balaguer, Joaquín Ricardo 586
balance of nature 116
balance of payments 210
balance sheet 202
Balanchine, George 256
Baldwin, James 257
Balla, Giacomo 239
Balladur, Edouard 530, 592
Ballen, Sixto Duran 587
Ballesteros, Severiano 446
ballet 251–3
ballistic missile 487
balloon 462
ballot 394
Balzac, Honoré de 257
Banda, Hastings Kamusu 620
Bandaranaike, Sirimavo 530
Bangladesh 565
bank 210
Bank of England 215
Bank for International Settlements
        (BIS) 215

bankruptcy 202
Bannister, Roger 468
baptism 410
bar 293
Bar, the 381
Barbados 565
barbershop 293
baritone 293
Barker, Howard 320
Barlach, Ernst 240
bar mitzvah 410
Barnard's star 40
barometer 101
Baroque architecture 221
Baroque art 235
barrier island 98
barrier lake 98
barrister 374
Barry, Charles 224
Bartók, Béla 296
baryon 189
basal metabolic rate (BMR) 154
base
    in chemistry 67
    in mathematics 169
baseball 426
base lending rate 202
Baselitz, Georg 241
base pair 164
Bashir, General Omar Hassan Ahmed
        el- 652
Bashkir 689
Bashō 257
BASIC computer language 85
basilica 222
basketball 426
Basque 689
bass 293
Bastille 502
Bataan 480
Bates eyesight training 355
bathing-water standards 130–1
bathyal zone 101
battalion 473
battleship 473, 478
baud 196
Baudelaire, Charles Pierre 257
Bauhaus 239
Bausch, Pina 256
bauxite 56
Baylis, Lilian 320
bayonet 486
BBC see British Broadcasting Corpora-
        tion
BCE/CE 403
beach 101
    recommended beaches 130–1
Beach Boys, the 300
bear, on stock exchange 202
bearing 168
Beatles, the 300
beat music 300
Beaton, Cecil 311
Beatrix Wilhelmina Armgard, Queen of
        the Netherlands 631
Beaufort scale 101
bebop 300
Beckenbauer, Franz 446
Becker, Boris 446
Beckett, Samuel 320
bed, in earth science 94

Bedie, Henri Konan 607
beer 133
Beethoven, Ludwig van 296
Begin, Menachem 531
behaviour therapy 342
Belarus 566
    revolution 505
Belarussian 689
bel canto 293
Belgium 567
Belize 567
Bellini, Giovanni 233
Bellow, Saul 257
belly dancing 253
Belorussian 688
Benares 415
Ben Bella, Ahmed 531
Benelux 360
Bengali 689
Ben-Gurion, David 531
Benin 568
Berg, Alban 296
Bergman, Ingmar 243
Bergman, Ingrid 247
Berisha, Sali 557
Berkoff, Steven 320
Berlage, Hendrikus 224
Berlin Film Festival 248
Berlioz, Hector 296
Bernini, Giovanni Lorenzo 224, 235
Bernoulli family 178
Berov, Lyuben 572
Berry, Chuck 300
Bertelsmann 384
Berzelius, Jöns Jakob 72
Bessel, Friedrich Wilhelm 50
Best, George 446
beta-blocker 353
Beta Persei 40
beta share 202
Bhagwan 409
bhangra 300
Bhil 689
Bhumibol Adulyadej, King of Thailand
    658
Bhutan 568
Bhutto, Benazir 531, 634
Bhutto, Zulfikar Ali 531
Bible 411, 412
bicycle 464
bigamy 374
big-band jazz 300
Big Bang
    in astronomy 40
    in economics 210
Bihari 690
Bildt, Carl 654
bill of exchange 202
billiards 426
bill of lading 203
Billy Hilly, Francis 649
binary fission 150
binary number system 81, 82
binary star 40
binary weapon 486
binomial 169
biochemic tissue salts therapy 355
biochemistry 53–6
    chronology 54
biodegradable 119
biodiversity 116, 150

bioenergetics 355
biofeedback 355
biofuel 105
biological anthropology 27
biological oxygen demand 116
biological warfare 473
biology
    chronology 151
    evolutionary 149–50
    molecular 165
    see also life sciences
biome 116
biosensor 166
biosphere 116
biosynthesis 154
biotechnology 166
bird 158
Bird, Vere C 560
Birendra Bir Bikram Shah Dev, King of
    Nepal 630
Birindwa, Faustin 671
birth 152
birth rites 410
birthstones 19
biscuit 133
bistable circuit 86
Biswas, Abdur Rahman 565
bit 81
bit pad 80
Biya, Paul 575
black hole 40
blackmail 374
Blake, William 237, 257
Blanco, Serge 446
blasphemy 374
blindness 347
blockade 394
blood 337
    poisoning 347
    pressure 334
blue chip 203
blue-green algae 163
blues, in music 300
boarding school 330
bobsleighing 427
Boccaccio, Giovanni 257
Boccioni, Umberto 239
Bode, Johann Elert 50
Bodhidharma 413
Body art 240
Bohr, Niels Henrik David 191
boiling point 67
Bokassa, Jean-Bédel 531
Bolger, Jim Brendan 531, 631
Bolivia 569
Böll, Heinrich 257
Bologna, Giovanni 233
bomb 474
bond
    in chemistry 67
    in economics 203
Bond, Edward 320
bone 160, 337
    human body, bones of 338
bone marrow 337
Bongo, Omar 593
Bonnard, Pierre 238
boogie-woogie 300
Booker Prize winners 266
Boole, George 178
boot, in computing 81

Border, Alan 446
Borg, Bjorn 446
Borges, Jorge Luis 257
Boross, Peter 600
Borromini, Francesco 224
borstal institution 381
Bosch, Hieronymous 233
bosing 21
Bosnia-Herzegovina 570
boson 189
Botha, P.W. 531
Botham, Ian 447
Botswana 570
Botticelli, Sandro 232
Boucher, François 236
Boucicault, Dionysus Larner 320
Boumédienne, Houari 531
Bourdelle, Emile-Antoine 240
Bourguiba, Habib ben Ali 531
Bourke-White, Margaret 311
Boutros-Ghali, Boutros 364, 531
bovine spongiform encephalopathy
    (BSE) 144
Bowie, David 300
bowls 427
boxing 427
Boycott, Geoffrey 447
Boyle, Robert 191
Bradley, James 50
Bradley, Omar Nelson 480
Bradman, Donald George 447
Brady, Matthew B 311
Brahe, Tycho 50
Brahms, Johannes 296
brain 160, 337
Braithwaite, Nicholas 597
Bramante, Donato 224
Branagh, Kenneth 320
Brancusi, Constantin 240
brand 203
brand leader 203
Brandt, Bill 311
Brandt, Willy 531
Braque, Georges 238
Brassaï 312
Brazauskas, Algirdas 618
Brazil 571
bread 133
breakeven point 203
Breathalyzer 374
Brecht, Bertolt 320
Breton, André 239
Breuer, Marcel 224
Brezhnev, Leonid Ilyich 531
brick 111
bridge 111
    highest railway bridges 112
    longest bridges, by span 112
    world's most remarkable 111
bridge odds 181
brief, legal 374
brigade 474
Bristow, Eric 447
Britain, Battle of 480
British Academy of Film and Televi-
    sion Arts (BAFTA) Awards
    248
British ballet 251
British Broadcasting Corporation
    (BBC) 384
British Commonwealth 370–2

Britten, Benjamin 296
Broadcasting Complaints Commission 385
Broadcasting Standards Council 385
Broglie, Louis de 191
broker 203
bronchitis 347
bronchus 337
Brontë, Anne 258
Brontë, Charlotte 258
Brontë, Emily Jane 258
Brontë, Patrick Branwell 258
Bronzino, Agnolo 233
Brook, Peter 320
Brown, Barbara 355
Brown, James 300
brown dwarf 40
Bruckner, (Joseph) Anton 296
Bruegel, Pieter the Elder 233
Brundtland, Gro Harlem 531, 633
Brunei 572
Brunelleschi, Filippo 224, 232
Brutalism 222
Bryant, David 447
bryophyte 161
BSkyB (British Sky Broadcasting) 384
Büchner, Georg 320
buckminsterfullerene 64
buckyball 49
Buddha 411, 413
Buddhism 403, 411
    Buddhist art 241, 242
    festivals 415, 419
budding 150
Budge, Donald 447
budget 203
buffer 81
buffer mixture 67
building and construction 111–17
    world's tallest buildings and struc-
        tures 114
Bulgaria 572
Bulge, Battle of the 480
bulghur wheat 133
bulimia 90
bull, on stock exchange 203
Buñuel, Luis 243
burden of proof 374
burglary 374
Burkina Faso 573
burlesque 315
Burlington, Richard Boyle 224
Burmen 690
Burns, Robert 258
Burundi 573
bus, in computing 77
Bush, George 531
Bushman 690
business plan 203
business terms 202–9
Buthelezi, Chief Gatsha 531
butoh dance 253
butter 133
Butterfield, William 224
buttress 222
Byelorussia see Belarus
Byrds, the 300
Byron, George Gordon 258
byte 81
Byzantine architecture 221
Byzantine art 231

cabaret 315
cabinet 394
Cable News Network 384
cable television 196
CAD see computer-aided design
cadence 293
cadenza 293
Caesarean section 334
Cajun 300
cake 133
calculus 169
Calder, Alexander 240
caldera 96
Caldera, Rafael 668
Caldéron, Rafael 582
calendars 11–17
call, in economics 203
Callaghan, James 532
Callejas, Rafael Leonardo 600
Callisto 35
calotype 308
calypso 300
CAM see computer-aided manufacturing
Cambodia 574
Cambrian 90
camcorder 201
camera 308
camera obscura 308
Cameron, Julia Margaret 312
Cameroon 575
Camoëns (Camões), Lús Vaz de 258
Campaign for Nuclear Disarmament
    (CND) 372
Campbell, Kim 532
Campese, David 448
Campin, Robert 233
Camus, Albert 258
Canada 575
    prime ministers 545
Canadian Broadcasting Corporation
    (CBC) 384
Canaletto, Antonio 236
canals 111, 113
    longest ship canals 113
cancer 347
candidiasis 352
Cannes Film Festival 248
canning 141
Cannizzaro, Stanislao 72
Cannon, Annie Jump 50
canoeing 427
canon 293
Canova, Antonio 236
cantata 293
cantilever 222
Cantor, Georg 178
Cao Chan (T'sao Chan) 258
Capa, Robert 312
capacitor 86
capacity, in economics 203
Cape Canaveral 29
Cape Verde 576
capital 210
    employed 203
    expenditure 203
    flight 203
Capital Cities/ABC 384
capital punishment 374
Caporetto 480
Capra, Frank 243
capriccio 293

car 464
    chronology 465
Caravaggio, Michelangelo Merisi da
    235
carbohydrate 53
carbolic acid 64
carbon 56
carbon cycle 116
carbon dating 27
carbon dioxide 119
Carboniferous 90
carbon monoxide 119
carbon tetrachloride 65
carboxyl group 64
carboxylic acid 64
cardiac asthma 346
Cardin, Pierre 327
cardinal number 169
care order 375
Caribbean Community and Common
    Market (CARICOM) 360
Carl XVI Gustaf, King of Sweden 654
Carlot, Maxime 667
Carné, Marcel 243
carnivore 154
Carnot, Sadi 191
Carracci, Annibale 235
carrier warfare 474
Carroll, Lewis 258
carrying capacity 116
Carson, Willie 448
cartel 203
Carter, Jimmy 532
Cartier-Bresson, Henri 312
caryatid 222
cash crop 144
cash flow 203
Caslavska, Vera 448
Cassini, Giovanni Domenico 50
Cassini, space probe 29
Cassini division 50
Cassino 480
Casson, Hugh 224
Castagno, Andrea del 232
castle 222
Castro Ruz, Fidel 504, 532, 583
catabolism 55
catalyst 67
catalytic converter 119
cataract 347
cathedral 222
cathode 86
cattle 144
Cauchy, Augustin Louis 178
Cavaco Silva, Anibal 532
Cavendish, Henry 191
CD-I see compact-disc interactive
CD-ROM see compact-disc read-only
    memory
Ceausescu, Nicolae 532
celestial mechanics 44
celestial sphere 44
cell 163
Cellini, Benvenuto 233
cellular phone 196
Celtic art 229, 237
Celtic languages 690
cement 111
Central African Republic 577
Central American Common Market
    (CACM) 215

Central Command 474
central processing unit (CPU) 77
centre of gravity 182
centre of mass 182
centrifuge 67
Cepheid variable 40
cereal 144
   breakfast 133
cerebellum 160
cerebral cortex 160
cerebrovascular accident 352
cerebrum 160
Ceres 35
CERN 360
certiorari 377
Cervantes Saavedra, Miguel de 258
cervical smear 334
Cézanne, Paul 238
CFC see chlorofluorocarbon
Chad 577
Chadli, Benjedid 532
Chadwick, James 193
Chagall, Marc 240
chain reaction 67, 182
chamber music 293
Chambers, William 224
Chamorro, Violeta Barrios de 632
Chandrasekhar, Subrahmanyan 50
Chandrasekhar limit 50
Channel tunnel 114
   chronology 115
Chaplin, Charlie 243
Chardin, Jean-Baptiste Siméon 236
charge-coupled device (CCD) 44
Charles, Eugenia 586
Charles, Ray 301
Charlton, Bobby 448
château 222
Chaucer, Geoffrey 258
cheese 133
Chekhov, Anton Pavlovich 320
chemical elements see elements
chemical equation 67
chemical equilibrium 67
chemical oxygen demand (COD) 116
chemical warfare 474
chemistry 53–76
   biographies 72–6
   chronology 66–7
   Nobel Prize winners 74–5
chemosynthesis 154
chemotherapy 334
Chernomyrdin, Viktor 641
Chiang Kai-shek 503
chickenpox 347
child abuse 375
Chile 578
   Chilean Revolution 504
Chiluba, Frederick 671
China 579
   art 241
   calendar 13
   Chinese Revolution 503
   Communist Party leaders 546
   dynasties 241, 494
   festivals 415
   prime ministers 546
   religions 410, 411
Chinese 690
chip, in computing 82, 86
Chirac, Jacques 532

Chiron 35
chiropractic 355
Chissano, Joaquim Alberto 532, 627
chlorination 67
chlorofluorocarbon (CFC) 116, 120
chlorophyll 163
chloroplast 163
chocolate 134
Chopin, Frédéric 296
chord, in mathematics 169
choreographers 256
Chretien, Jean 575
Christian art, early 231
Christianity 404, 411
   feasts and festivals 415, 418
   patron saints 420
   rites 410, 411
   saints' days 421–3
Christie, Linford 448
Christo 240
chromatography 68
chromosome 152
chromosphere 35
chronic fatigue syndrome 350
Chuang 690
church 222
Churchill, Caryl 320
Chuvash 690
Chyngyshev, Tursunbek 613
Ciampi, Carlo Azeglio 606
Cibachrome 308
cider 133
Ciller, Tansu 660
cine camera 308
cinema 243–50
   awards 248–50
   chronology 245
   film directors 243–50
circle 169
circulating asset 204
circulatory system 160
circumcision 410
circumference 169
circus 315
cirrhosis 347
CIS see Commonwealth of Independent
   States
CITES see Convention on International
   Trade in Endangered Species
Citizens Advice Bureau (CAB) 381
citizens' band (CB) 196
citizenship 394
citric acid cycle 43, 55
city technology college (CTC) 330
civil defence 474
civil disobedience 375
civil law 375
civil service 398
civil war 478
civil wars and related battles 485–6
cladding 112
cladistics 149
Clapton, Eric 301
Clark, Jim 448
class, in mathematics 167
Classical architecture 221
Classical art 229–31
class struggle 393
Clausewitz, Karl von 480
claustrophobia 342
clef 293

Clemente, Francesco 241
Clerides, Glafkos 584
client-server architecture 82
climate 116
clinical ecology 355
clinical psychology 342
Clinton, Bill 532, 665
cloister 222
clone 166
clothes and fashion 327–9
cloud 101, 102
Clouet, François 233
Clouet, Jean 233
CLT 385
CND see Campaign for Nuclear Disarmament
CNN see Cable News Network
coalition 394
Coates, Nigel 224
coaxial cable 197
Cobb, Tyrus Raymond 448
coccus 163
cocoa 134
coda 293
codeine 353
codon 164
Coe, Sebastian 448
coeducation 330
coefficient 169
coffee 134
cognitive archaeology 22
cognitive therapy 342
coil 335
COIN (counter insurgency) 474
Coleman, Ornette 301
collective bargaining 210
collective farm 144
collectivism 392
college of higher education 330
colligative property 68
colloid 68
Collor de Mello, Fernando 532
Colombia 579
Colombo Plan 216
colon 268
colonialism 501–2
colonization 116
colonnade 222
coloratura 293
Colossus of Rhodes 490
colour therapy 355
Coltrane, John 301
Columbia Broadcasting System (CBS)
   384
column 222
Comaneci, Nadia 449
combined cycle generation 105
combined heat and power generation
   105
combined pill 354
combine harvester 144
Comecon (Council for Mutual Economic Assistance) 216
comedy 315
comet 35
comma 268
commando 474
commedia dell'arte 315
Comme des Garçons 327
commissioner for oaths 375
committal proceedings 375

commodity 203
commodity markets 203
Common Agricultural Policy (CAP) 144, 364
common law 375
Common Market 363
Commonwealth, British 370–2
Commonwealth Games, sites of 460
Commonwealth of Independent States (CIS) 360
Commune of Paris 503
communications satellite 29, 197
communism 392
community 117
community architecture 223
community charge 216
commutative operation 169
Comoros 580
compact-disc interactive (CD-I) 80
compact-disc read-only memory (CD-ROM) 77, 80
company 203
company, army 474
company stock 203
Compaoré, Blaise 573
comparative advantage 210
competition 149
compiler 77
complement, in mathematics 169
complementary metal-oxide semiconductor (CMOS) 86
composers 296–9
Composite order 225
compost 120
compound 68
comprehensive school 330
Compton, John 643
compulsory purchase 375
computer 77–85
    chronology 78
    game 78
    generation 77
    graphics 78
    hardware 80–1, 83
    memory 77, 80
    menu 77
    personal 77
    programming languages 77, 84
    simulation 79
    terms 81–5
    uses for, generally 77–80
computer-aided design (CAD) 77
computer-aided manufacturing (CAM) 78
computer-assisted learning (CAL) 77
computerized axial tomography (CAT) 22
concave 169
concentric circle 169
Conceptualism 240
concerto 293
concrete 112
condenser 86
conductive education 330
cone 169
confederation 395
conferences, international 478–9
Conference on Security and Co-operation in Europe (CSCE) 360
configuration 68

confirmation 410
Confucianism 405, 411
Confucius 404, 413
Congo 581
Congreve, William 321
congruent 169
conic section 169
conjunction
    in astronomy 44
    in grammar 268
Connolly, Maureen 449
Connors, Jimmy 449
Conrad, Joseph 258
Conran, Jasper 327
conscription 474
consent, age of 375
conservation 116–30
    architectural 223
    definition 120
conservatism 392
Constable, John 237
constant 169
constants, fundamental 593
constellations 40,41
constitution 394
Constructivism 239
consumer 203
    protection of 375
    sovereignty 203
consumer durable 203
consumption 352
consumption, in economics 210
contact improvisation 253
Conté, Lansana 598
contemporary art 240
contempt of court 375
context, in archaeology 22
continent 94, 547–55
continental drift 90
continental island 98
continental shelf 378
contraceptive 334
contract archaeology 2
contract of employment 375
contralto 293
contributory negligence 378
Convention on International Trade in Endangered Species (CITES) 127
convergent evolution 149
converse 169
conversion tables 2
convertible loan stock 203
convex 171
convulsion 334
cooking methods 140
Cooper, Samuel 236
coordinated universal time (UTC) 32
coordinate geometry 171
Copernicus, Nicolaus 50
Coppola, Francis Ford 243
Copt 690
copyright 375
coral island 98
coral reef biological diversity 116
core, in archaeology 22
core, earth's 94
Corinthian order 223
Coriolis effect 101
cornea 337
Corneille, Pierre 321
corona 35

coroner 375
Corot, Jean-Baptiste Camille 237
corporal punishment 375
corporate strategy 203
corps 475
cortex 336
corticosteroid 353
cosine 171
cosmic background radiation 40
cosmid 166
cosmology 44
Cosmos 29
Costa Rica 581
cost-benefit analysis 204
Costello, Elvis 301
cost of living 210
cost of sales 204
cost-push inflation 210
cot death 347
council 394
Council of the Entente 361
Council of Europe 361
Council of Ministers (EC) 363
Council for the Protection of Rural England (CPRE) 127
counterpoint 293
Countryside Council for Wales 127
country and western music 301
county court 381, 382
coup d'état 394
Courbet, Gustave 237
Courrèges, André 327
Court, Margaret 449
Court of Appeal 381, 382
court martial 375
court order 130
Court of Protection 381
courts, law 388
covalent bond 68
Coward, Noel 321
cracking, in chemistry 68
Cranach, Lucas the Elder 233
cranium 337
Cranko, John 256
crater 35, 96
crater lake 98
craton 94
Craxi, Bettino 532
cream 134
credit 210
creditor 204
creole language 690
crescent 35
Cretaceous 90
cricket 428
Criminal Injuries Compensation Board 381
Criminal Investigation Department (CID) 381
criminal law 375
Cristiani, Alfredo 588
critical mass 182
critical path analysis 204
Croat 690
Croatia 582
crop rotation 144
Crosby, Bing 301
cross-dating 22
crowding out 210
crown court 381, 382
Crown Prosecution Service 381

crude oil 107
Cruelty, Theatre of 315
cruise missile 487
crust, in earth science 94
crustacean 157
Cruyff, Johann 449
Crvenkovski, Branko 619
cryogenics 182
crystal therapy 355
Cuba 583
    Cuban Revolution 504
cube 171
Cubism 238
cuboid 171
cultural anthropology 22
cultural resource management (CRM)
    22
cumulative preference shares 204
Cunningham, Imogen 312
Cunningham, Merce 256
cupping 355
Curie, Marie 72, 191
Curie, Pierre 72, 191
curing 141
curling 429
currency 210
    exchange rates 211, 219–20
current 101
current asset 204
current liability 204
current ratio 204
curriculum 330
curtain wall 225
curve, in mathematics 171
custody 376
Cuyp, Aelbert 236
cybernetics 171
cycling 429
cycloid 171
cyclone 101
    worst recorded cyclones 103
cylinder 171
Cyprus 583
cystic fibrosis 347
cystitis 347
cytochrome 164
cytoplasm 163
Czechoslovakia, Velvet Revolution 505
Czech Republic 584

Dada 239
Daguerre, Louis 312
daguerrotype 308
dairying 145
Dalai Lama 532
Dali, Salvador 239
Dalton, John 72
dam 113
    world's highest dams 113
damages, legal 376
dance 251–6
    choreographers 256
    chronology 254–5
Dante Alighieri 258
Danton, Georges Jacques 503
Danube Commission 361
Dariganga 690
Darío, Rubén 258
Dark Ages, art of the 231
dark matter 40
darts 429

data 82
    communications 197
    compression 82, 197
database 79
dating
    archaeology 22
    geological 90
Daumier, Honoré 237
David, Jacques-Louis 236
David Dunlap Observatory 47
Davis, Miles 301
Davis, Steve 449
Davy, Humphry 72
dawn raid 204
daycare 330
days of the week, name derivations 19
D-day 480
DDT 120
deafness 347
Dean, Christopher 459
death 152
death penalty 374
death rites 411
debenture 204
debt 204
    international debt crisis 210
Debussy, (Achille) Claude 296
Deby, Idriss 577
deception 475
de Chirico, Giorgio 239
decibels 5
decimal fraction 171
declaration 377
declination 44
decomposer 154
decomposition 68
Deconstruction 222
decree absolute 376
decree nisi 376
dedicated computer 82
deed 376
deed poll 376
deep freezing 141
deer farming 145
defamation 376
defence (in law) 376
defendant 376
deferred share 204
deficit financing 211
de Filippo, Eduardo 321
Defoe, Daniel 258
deforestation 120, 537
    tropical 120
Degas, Edgar 238
de Gaulle, Charles 480
degree, in mathematics 171
Dehaene, Jean-Luc 566
dehydration 143
Deimos 35
de Klerk, F W 532, 650
Delacroix, Eugène 237
Delaunay, Robert 239
Delors, Jacques 533
delta 96
Delta Force 475
Delta rocket 29
delusion 342
demand-pull inflation 211
dementia 348
DeMille, Agnes George 256
De Mille, Cecil B(lount) 243

Demirel, Suleyman 533, 660
democracy 392
Dempsey, Jack 449
dendrochronology 22
Denktas, Rauf 584
Denmark 585
denominator 171
density 182
Den Xiaping 533
deoxyribonucleic acid (DNA) 53, 164,
    165, 166, 167
    fingerprinting 167
    recombinant 55
depreciation 204
depression 342
Derain, André 238
deregulation 211
dermatitis 348
dermatology 334
dermatosis 348
dervish dance 253
Descartes, René 179
desert 96
    largest deserts 97
desertification 121
Desert Shield, Operation 480
Desert Storm, Operation 480
de Sica, Vittorio 244
designer drugs 345
designers, fashion 327–9
desktop publishing (DTP) 79
destroyer 475
détente 394
detergent 68
determinant 172
de la Tour, Georges 235
devaluation 211
developing, in photography 308
developing nations, top 678
Devonian 90
dextrose 55
diabetes 348
diagenesis 94
dialectical materialism 393
dialysis 334
diamond ring effect 17
diarrhoea 348
diatonic 293
dice chances 181
Dickens, Charles 258
dictatorship 394
dietetics 355
differentiation 172
diffraction 182
diffusion 22, 68
digital 86, 182, 197
digital data transmission 197
digital sampling 197
digital television 197
digital-to-analogue converter 86
digitizer 80
Di Maggio, Joe 450
Dinka 690
dinosaur 96
diode 86
Diouf, Abdou 533, 645
dioxin 121
diploid 152
diplomacy 394
dipole 68
Dirac, Paul Adrien Maurice 192

direct democracy 392
directed number 172
director 204
Director of Public Prosecutions (DPP) 376
directory, in computing 82
Dire Straits 301
disaccharide 44, 53
disarmament 475
disc, computer 77, 80
disco music 301
diseases 342–51
diseconomies of scale 204
disinvestment 211
Disney, Walt 244
disorders, psychological 339–42
dissident 395
dissociation 68
distance learning 331
distillation 68
distributive operation 172
diversification 204
dividend 204
diving 429
division, military 475
divorce 376
Dixieland jazz 301
Djibouti 585
Djohar, Said Mohammad 580
DNA see deoxyribonucleic acid
dodecahedron 172
Dogon 690
Doisneau, Robert 312
Dolce, Domenico 327
Dolce e Gabbana 327
doldrums 101
Domagk, Gerhard 72
Domenichino 235
Dominica 586
Dominican Republic 586
Dominion Astrophysical Observatory 47
Donatello 232
Donellan, Declan 321
Dongxiang 690
Dönitz, Karl 480
Donne, John 259
Doors, the 301
Doric order 225
DOS (disc operating system) 82
Dos Passos, John 259
Dostoievsky, Fyodor Mikhailovich 259
double star 40
Dowiyogo, Bernard 629
Dow Jones 385
Dow Jones Index 211
Down's syndrome 348
dowsing 22
DRAM (dynamic random-access memory) 86
Dreamtime 403
Dreyer, Carl Theodor 244
drink 133–43
Drnovsek, Janez 648
drought 102
drugs
  dependence on 342
  medical 353–4
  misuse of 348
Dubček, Alexander 533
Duccio 231

Duchamp, Marcel 239
dune 96
Dunkirk 480
Dunlop, J B 490
Duras, Marguerite 259
Dürer, Albrecht 233
Duvalier, Franáois 533
Duvalier, Jean-Claude 533
Dvořák, Antonin (Leopold) 296
dye-transfer print 308
Dylan, Bob 301
dynamics 182
dyslexia 342

ear 337
early warning system 475
earnings 204
Earth, the 35
  development of 90–3
  interior of 94–7
  surface of 96–101
Earth art 240
earthquakes 94
earth science 90–106
  chronology 92
easement 376
Eastern art 241–2
Eastern European Mutual Assistance Pact 363
East Germany, Revolution 505
EC see European Community
ecclesiastical law 376
echinoderm 157
eclipse 36, 37
eclipsing binary 40
ecliptic 44
ecology 117
Economic Commission for Africa (ECA) 369
Economic Commission for Europe (ECE) 369
Economic Commission for Latin America (ECLA) 369
Economic Commission for Western Asia (ECWA) 370
Economic Community of Central African States (CEEAC) 361
Economic Community of West African States (ECOWAS) 361
Economic Cooperation Organization (ECO) 361
economic growth 211
economics 210–21
  Nobel Prize winners 218
  terms 210–15
Economic and Social Commission for Asia and the Pacific (ESCAP) 369
Economic and Social Committee (EC) 365
Economic and Social Council (UN) 365
economies of scale 204
ecosystem 117
Ecuador 587
eczema 348
Edberg, Stefan 450
Eddington, Arthur Stanley 50
Edo period 242
education 330–3
Edwards, Gareth 450
Edwards Air Force Base 29

EEPROM (electrically erasable programmable read-only memory) 86
Effelsberg, radio telescope 47
efficiency 182
EFTPOS (electronic funds transfer at point of sale) 204
egalitarianism 392
egg 134
Eggleston, William 312
Egypt 587
  ancient Egypt, chronology 490
  ancient Egyptian art 229
Ehrlich, Paul 83
eidophor 197
Einstein, Albert 192
Eisenhower, Dwight David 533
Eisenstein, Sergei Mikhailovich 244
elasticity 182
elastomer 68
electric current 182
electricity 105–10, 182
electroconvulsive therapy (ECT) 342
electrocrystal diagnosis 355
electrodynamics 183
electrolysis, in archaeology 22
electromagnetic waves 183
electron 69, 86, 189
  microscope 166
  spin resonance (ESR) 22
  tube 84
electronegativity 69
electronic mail (E-mail) 79, 197
electronics 85–9
  chronology 87
  digital 197
electrophoresis 69
electroporation 166
electroshock therapy 342
electrovalent bond 58
elements 57–8
  discovery of 60–1
  periodic table 62–3, 70
  transuranic 59, 62
Eleven Plus examination 331
Elgar, Edward 296
El Greco 233
Eliot, George 259
Eliot, T S 259
Elizabeth II, Queen of Great Britain 370
Ellington, Duke 302
ellipse 172
elongation 44
El Salvador 588
elution 69
E-mail see electronic mail
embryo 152
emperors
  Aztec 495
  Chinese 494
  Habsburg 498
  Holy Roman 494
  Inca 495
  Indian 495
  Japanese 496–7
  Ottoman 493
  Roman 493
empires 501–2
empirical formula 69
employment law 376
EMS see European Monetary System
emulator 82

emulsion 68, 69
Encke's comet 36
encore 293
endangered species 121–2
Endara, Guillermo 635
endogenous endocrinotherapy 355
endometriosis 348
endoscopy 334
endothermic reaction 69
end-use certificate 204
Energiya, space rocket 29
energy 105–10, 183
    conservation 121
    UK production and consumption 108
    worldwide demands 109
energy of reaction 69
engine 183
England
    art in 233, 236, 237
    sovereigns of 500
English bond 111
English legal system 376
English Nature 127
English sovereigns 500
enhanced radiation weapon 486
enthalpy of reaction 69
entropy 183
E numbers 142
environmental archaeology 22
Environmentally Sensitive Area (ESA)
    127
Environmental Protection Agency
    (EPA) 128
environment and conservation 116–32
    environmental groups and initiatives
    127–31
    ways to reduce damage to the envi-
    ronment 128
enzyme 54, 164
    restriction 167
eolith 22
epicentre 94
epicycloid 172
epilepsy 348
epoch 90
Epstein, Jacob 240
equal opportunities 204, 376
equation 172
equator 96
Equatorial Guinea 589
equestrianism 409
equilateral 172
equilibrium 183
equinox 44
equity 204, 376
era 90
Eratosthenes 179
Eritrea 589
ERM *see* Exchange Rate Mechanism
Eros, asteroid 36
erosion 97
Ershad, Hussain Mohammad 533
erythrocyte 340
escape velocity 44
escrow 376
Esquivel, Manuel 568
ester 64
Estes, Richard 240
Estonia 590
    Revolution 505
Estonian 690

estuary 102
ethanoic acid 64
ether 64
Ethiopia 590
ethnic cleansing 395
ethnic groups and languages 689–696
ethnoarchaeology 23
ethnography 23
ethnology 23
Etruscan art 230
étude 293
Euclid 179
eukaryote 163
eukaryotic cell 155
Euler, Leonhard 179
Euripides 321
Eurobond 205
Europa, moon 36
Europe 551
    historical time charts 483–29, 552
European Atomic Energy Commission
    (EURATOM) 363, 364
European Bank for Reconstruction and
    Development (EBRD) 216
European Broadcasting Union (EBU)
    384
European Charter of Social Rights 363
European Coal and Steel Community
    (ECSC) 363, 364
European Commission 364
    presidents 364
European Common Market 363
European Community (EC) 363–5
    aims 363
    budget 364
    Committee of Permanent Represen-
    tatives 365
    Common Agricultural Policy (CAP)
    144, 364
    Council of Ministers 364–5
    Economic and Social Committee 365
    European Monetary System (EMS)
    216, 364
    Exchange Rate Mechanism (ERM)
    216
    legislation 387
    Maastricht Treaty 363
    members 363
European Court of Human Rights 381
European Court of Justice 364, 381
European Economic Community (EEC)
    363, 364
European Free Trade Association
    (EFTA) 361
European Investment Bank (EIB) 364
European Monetary System (EMS)
    216, 364
European Parliament 365
European Southern Observatory 47
European Space Agency (ESA) 29, 361
eutrophication 98, 121
Evans, Walker 312
Evert, Chris 450
evolution 149
evolutionary biology 149–50
Ewe 690
excavation, archaeological 23
Exchange Rate Mechanism (ERM) 216
exchange-rate policy 211
exchange rates 211, 219–20
excise duty 211

exclamation mark 268
exclusion principle 188
executive director 205
executor 376
exobiology 44
exosphere 102
exothermic reaction 69
experience curve 205
experimental archaeology 23
expert system 79
Explorer 29
explosive 475
exponent, in mathematics 172
exponential 172
export 211
exposure meter 308
Expressionism 239
external economies of scale 205
extinction 121–2, 149
extradition 376
Eyadéma, Etienne Gnassingbé 658
Eyck, Aldo van 224
eye 337
Eyre, Richard 321

facsimile transmission 197
factor, in mathematics 172
factorial 172
factoring 205
factory farming 145
Fahd Ibn Abdul Aziz, King of Saudi
    Arabia 533, 645
Faldo, Nick 450
Falklands War 480
Fallopian tube 337
fallout 475
fallow 145
Fang 690
Faraday, Michael 73, 192
farce 315
Farhi, Nicole 327
Farrell, Terry 225
Farsi 690
fascism 392
fashion 327–9
fasting 356
fat 54
fat-soluble 44
fatty acid 64
Faulkner, William 259
fault 94
faunal dating 23
Fauvism 238
favourable variance 205
fax 197
feature 23
federalism 395
Federal Reserve System 216
Fellini, Frederico 244
fencing 409
Fenton, Roger 312
Fermat, Pierre de 179
Fermi, Enrico 192
fermion 189
Ferrari, Enzo 450
ferrite 56
fertilization 152
fertilizer 145
fetus 152
Feydeau, Georges 321
Feynman, Richard P 192

Fibonacci, Leonardo 179
fibre, dietary 134
fibre crop 145
field
  in agriculture 145
  in physics 183
Fielding, Henry 259
field marshal 475
Fields medalists 178
field particle 183
field survey 23
Fiji 591
film
  cinematic see cinema
  photographic 308
filter 86
finale 293
Financial Times Index (FT Index) 205, 211
financial year 205
Fininvest 384
Finland 591
Finnbogadóttir, Vigdís 601
Finney, Tom 450
Finno-Ugric language group 690
fiord 97
Fiorentino, Rosso 233
Firdawsi, Mansûr Abu'l Qâsim 259
firearm 475
firewood 122
first past the post 397
fiscal policy 212
Fischer, Emil Hermann 73
fish 134, 158
  classification 159
  overfishing 124
fish farming see aquaculture
fission-track dating 23
Fitzgerald, Ella 302
Fitzgerald, F Scott 259
fixed cost 205
fixed hard disc 80
fjord 97
flamenco 253
Flamsteed, John 50
flatworm 158
Flaubert, Gustave 259
Flemish bond 111
flight, chronology 462
flip-flop 86
floating asset 204
flood plain 97
floods, worst recorded 103
floppy disc 80
Florence 232
flour 134
flower 163
fluorescence microscopy 166
f-number 308
Fo, Dario 321
foam 68
focus 310
fog 102
fold, in earth science 94
folk dance 253
Fon 691
food and drink 133–43
  cooking methods 140
Food and Agriculture Organization (FAO) 366
food chain 154

food poisoning 348
food technology 141–3
foot-and-mouth disease 145
football
  American 431
  association 431
  Australian rules 432
  Gaelic 432
forage crop 145
force 183
forces, fundamental 189
Ford, John (film director) 244
Ford, John (poet and dramatist) 321
Fordism 205
foreclosure 376
foreign words and phrases 271–5, 287–92
forest, deforestation 120
forgery 376
formula 69
fossil fuels 105, 122
Foster, Norman 225
Foucault, Jean Bernard Léon 192
Fouquet, Jean 233
Fra Angelico 232
fractal 172
fraction 172
fractional distillation 69
fractionation 69
Fragonard, Jean-Honoré 236
France 592
  art in 233, 235, 236, 237
  French Revolution 502
  kings 498
  Paris Commune 503
franchise 205
Franck, César Auguste 297
Franco, Francisco 533
Franco, Itamar 533, 571
Francome, John 450
fraud 377
free-enterprise economy 212
freehold 377
free-market economy 212
free radical 69
freeze-drying 143
freezing point 69
frequency 183
fresco painting 231
fret 293
Frick, Mario 617
friction 183
Friedrich, Caspar David 237
Friel, Brian 321
Friends of the Earth (FoE) 128
frigate 475
fringe theatre 315
front 102
frost 102
fruit 134
fruit juice 135
f-stop see f-number
Fuchs, Klaus 480
fuel-air explosive 486
fugue 293
Fujimori, Alberto 533, 637
Fukudzi, Andreas 653
Fulani 691
Fuller, Buckminster 225
Fuller, John Frederick Charles 480
fullerene 49

full stop 408
function
  in computing 82
  in mathematics 172
functional group 64
fundamental constant 183
fungicide 125, 146
funk dance music 302
further education college 331
Fuseli, Henry 237
future, in economics 205
futures market 205
Futurism 239
fuzzy logic 82

G7 see Group of Seven
Gabbana, Stefano 327
Gabo, Naum 239
Gabon 593
Gabor, Dennis 192
Gaddhafi, Moamer al 536
Gaelic 273
Gagarin, Yuri 50
Gaia hypothesis 122
gain 86
Gainsborough, Thomas 236
galaxies 40–3
Galileo Galilei 192
Galileo, spacecraft 29
Galla 691
gall bladder 337
Galle, Johann Gottfried 50
Galliano, John 327
Gallipoli 480
gallium arsenide 56
gallstone 334
Galois, Evariste 179
Galtieri, Leopoldo 480
Gambia 593
game farming 145
gamelan 293
gamete 152
Gance, Abel 244
Ganda 691
Gandhi, Indira 533
Gandhi, Mohandas Karamchand (Mahatma) 534
Gandhi, Rajiv 534
Ganilau, Ratu Sir Penaia 591
Gannett 385
Ganymede, moon 36
García Márquez, Gabriel 259
Garcia Lorca, Federico see Lorca, Federico Garcia
garden city 223
gargoyle 223
Gascoigne, Paul 451
gas exchange 154
gastroenteritis 348
GATT see General Agreement on Tariffs and Trade
Gaudí, Antonio 225
Gaudier-Brzeska, Henri 240
gauge boson 189
Gauguin, Paul 238
Gaultier, Jean-Paul 327
Gauss, Karl Friedrich 179
Gavaskar, Sunil Manohar 451
Gayoom, Maumoon Abdul 621
gearing, financial 205
Gehry, Frank 225

Geingob, Hage Gottfried 534, 629
gel 68
Gell-Mann, Murray 192
Gemara 407
Gemini project 29
gene 152
  bank 166
  therapy 167
general 475
General Agreement on Tariffs and
  Trade (GATT) 216, 366
General Certificate of Secondary Education (GCSE) 331
Genet, Jean 321
genetics
  genetic code 165
  genetic engineering 167
  genetic fingerprinting 167
Geneva Convention 377
Genocide Convention 377
genome 152
genotype 152
genre pictures 236
geochemistry 94
geodesic dome 223
geological time 90
  chart 91
geometry 173
geophysics 94
Georgetown, Declaration of 478
Georgia 594
Georgian 691
geostationary orbit 44
geosynchronous orbit 44
geothermal energy 105
geriatrics 334
Géricault, Theodore 237
Germanic languages 691
German measles 348
Germany 594
  art in 233, 237
germination 152
Gershwin, George 302
Gershwin, Ira 302
Gerson therapy 356
gestation 153
gestation periods, animals 155
geyser 94
Ghana 595
Ghazzali, al- 413
Ghiberti, Lorenzo 232
Ghirlandaio, Domenico del 232
Giacometti, Alberto 240
Gibbs, James 225
Gibbs, Josiah Williard 73
Gide, André 259
gigabyte 82
Gilbert, Cass 225
Gillespie, Dizzy 302
gilt-edged securities 212
Giorgione 233
Giotto 231
Giotto, space probe 29
Girondins 503
Giscard d'Estaing, Valéry 534
glacial lake 98
glacier 97
glandular fever 348
Glashow, Sheldon Lee 192
glasnost 395, 505
glaucoma 348

Glenn, John Herschel 50
Gligorov, Kiro 619
global warming 122
globular cluster 41
glucose 55
gluon 189
GmbH 205
Gobind Singh 413
Godard, Jean-Luc 244
Goddard Space Flight Center 29
Gödel, Kurt 179
Godmanis, Ivars 614
Goethe, Johann Wolfgang von 259, 321
Gogol, Nikolai 260
Goh Chok Tong 534, 647
gold 56
golden share 205
Goldoni, Carlo 321
golf 433
Göncz, Arpád 600
Gond 691
Gondwana 90
Gondwanaland 90
González Márquez, Felipe 534
Gonzalez, Julio 240
Gooch, Graham 451
Goodman, Benny 302
Gorbachev, Mikhail Sergeyevich 534
Gorbunov, Anatolijs 614
Gortari, Carlos Salinas de 624
gospel music 302
Gothic style 221, 231
gout 348
government departments (UK) 397–400
Gower, David 451
Goya y Lucientes, Francisco de 236
Grace, W G 451
Graf, Steffi 451
Graham, Martha 256
grammar 267–71
grammar school 331
grand unified theory (GUT) 184
grant-maintained school 331
grape-sugar 55
graphical user interface (GUI) 81, 82
graphics, computer 78
graphics tablet 80
Grass, Günter 260
grassland 99
gravitational lensing 44
graviton 189
gravity 44, 184
Grazinian 690
Greece 596
  ancient Greece, chronology 491
  ancient Greek art 229
Green, Lucinda 451
green audit 122
green belt 223
Greene, Graham 260
greenhouse effect 102, 122
greenmail 205
Green Party 129
Greenpeace 129
green revolution 143, 145
Greenwich Mean Time (GMT) 44
Gregorian calendar 11, 14
Gregorian chant 293
Grenada 597
Gretzky, Wayne 451
greyhound racing 433

grey market 205
grid system 23
Grieg, Edvard 297
grievous bodily harm (GBH) 377
Griffith, D W 244
Griffith-Joyner, Delorez Florence 452
Grignard, François Auguste-Victor 73
Grimshaw, Nicholas 225
Gropius, Walter 225
gross 205
gross national product (GNP) 212
gross profit 205
Grotesque 230
Grotowski, Jerzy 322
ground water 97
group, in mathematics 173
Group of Eight 361
Group of Rio 361
Group of Seven (G7) 361
Grünewald, Mathias 233
grunge music 302
Grupo Andino 360
Guaraní 691
Guardi, Francesco 236
Guatemala 597
guerrilla 475
guerrilla war 478
Guevara, Ernesto 'Che' 504
Guinea 598
Guinea-Bissau 598
Gujarati 691
Gulf Cooperation Council (GCC) 361
Gulf War (1991) 481
Gurkha 475
Guru Gobind Singh 408
Guru Granth Sahib 408, 413
Guseinov, Suret 563
Guthrie, Tyrone 322
Guthrie, Woody 302
Guyana 599
gymnastics 433
gymnosperm 161
gynaecology 334
Gypsy 401
gyre 102

Haber, Fritz 73
habitat 117
Habsburg, House of 498
Habyarimana, Maj-Gen Juvenal 642
Hachette 384
hacking 83
Hadlee, Richard John 452
hadron 189
haematology 334
haemophilia 348
haemorrhoids 349
Hâfiz, Sham al-Din Muhammad 260
Haggadah 407
ha-ha 223
Hahnemann, Samuel 356
hail 102
hair 337
hair analysis 356
Haiti 599
Hale, George Ellery 50
half-life 184
Hall, Peter 322
Halley, Edmond 50
Halley's comet 37
halogen 58

halon 123
Hals, Frans 236
Hamilton, Richard 240
Hamito-Semitic languages 691
Hamnett, Katharine 327
Han 691
handball 434
Handel, Georg Frederic 297
Han dynasty art 241
Hanging Gardens of Babylon 490
Hanley, Ellery 452
Hans Adam II, Prince of Liechtenstein 617
Hanson, Duane 240
haploid 152, 153
Harald V, King of Norway 633
hardcore rock music 302
hard disc 77, 80
Hardy, Thomas 260
Hare, David 322
Hariri, Rafik al- 615
harmonics 294
Harrier 486
harrow 145
Hassan II, King of Morocco 627
Hassanali, Noor 659
Haughey, Charles 534
Hausa 691
Haussmann, Georges Eugène 225
Havel, Václav 534, 584
Hawke, Bob 534
Hawking, Stephen 192
Hawkins, Coleman 302
Hawks, Howard 244
Hawksmoor, Nicholas 225
Haworth, Norman 73
hay 147
Haydn, Franz Joseph 297
hay fever 349
HD-MAC 194
health 334–59
   education 331
   screening 336
   see also medicine
hearsay evidence 377
Hearst, William Randolph 144
heart 337
heart attack 349
heartburn 349
heat 184
   pump 105
   storage 105
Heath, Edward 534
heavy metal 302
Hebrew 272
hedgerow 117
Heian period 242
Heine, Heinrich 260
Heinrich Bauer 385
Heisenberg, Werner Carl 192
Hekmatyar, Gulbuddin 534, 557
helicopter 463
heliopause 20
heliosphere 37
helix 173
Hellenistic art 230
Helmont, Jean Baptiste van 73
Helsinki Conference 478
Hemingway, Ernest 260
Hendrix, Jimi 302
Hendry, Stephen 452

Henry Doubleday Research Association 129
hepatitis 349
herb 135
herbalism 356
herbicide 127, 145
herbivore 154
hermaphrodite 153
hernia 349
herpes 349
Herrera, Luis Lacalle 666
Hersant 385
Herschel, John Frederick William 50
Herschel, William 50
Hertz, Heinrich 192
Hertzsprung-Russell diagram 44
heterotroph 155
heterotype 155
heterozygous 153
Hewish, Antony 51
hexadecimal number system 83
Hick, Graeme 452
Higgs particle 189
high commissioner 395
High Court of Justice 382
High Court of Justiciary 382
higher education 331
high seas 378
High Tech architecture 222
Hilbert, David 179
Hill, David Octavius 312
Hill, Graham 452
Hilliard, Nicholas 233
Hīnayāna Buddhism 403
Hindi language 691
Hinds, Sam 599
Hindu art 241
Hindu calendar 14
Hinduism 405, 411
   festivals 416, 419
   rites 410
Hine, Lewis 312
hip-hop 302
Hipparchus 51
Hipparcos, satellite 29
Hiroshima 481
historical archaeology 23
history 490–529
   time chart 506–29
Hitchcock, Alfred 246
HIV see human immunodeficiency virus
Hmong 691
hoard 23
Hobbs, Jack 452
Ho Chi Minh 534
hockey 434
   ice 435
Hodgkin, Dorothy Crowfoot 73
Hofmann, August Wilhelm von 73
Hogarth, William 237
Holbein, Hans 233
Holiday, Billie 302
holidays, national 682–7
holistic medicine 356
Holly, Buddy 302
Holocene 91
Holy Roman emperors 494
Homer 260
Home Service Force (HSF) 475
homicide 377

homoeopathy 356
homologous series 64
homozygous 153
Honduras 600
Honecker, Erich 534
honey 135
Hooch, Pieter de 236
Hooke, Robert 192
Hooke's law 194
Horace 260
hormone 337
hormone-replacement therapy (HRT) 335
horse racing 434
horticulture 145
Hosking, Eric 312
Hosokawa, Morihiro 608
hospice 335
hot-air balloon 462
Hottentot 691
Houphouët-Boigny, Félix 534
House of Commons 395
House of Habsburg 641
House of Lords 382, 395
house music 302
hovercraft 466
Howard, Ebenezer 225
Howe, Gordie 452
Hoxha, Enver 535
Hoyle, Frederick 51
Hrawi, Elias 615
Hubble, Edwin Powell 51
Hubble's constant 45
Hubble's law 45
Hubble Space Telescope (HST) 30
Hugo, Victor 260
Hui 691
human body 336–41
human development index 679
human immunodeficiency virus (HIV) 346
humanism, in art 233
human-resource management 205
human-rights groups 372
Human Rights Watch 372
human species, origins of 149
Hungary 600
   Revolution 505
Hun Sen 535
hunting of selected species 132
hurling 435
hurricane 102
Hussain, Ahmed 604
Hussein al-Tikriti, Saddam 535, 604
Hussein ibn Talai, King of Jordan 535, 609
Huston, Anjelica 246
Huston, John 246
Huston, Walter 246
Hutton, Len 453
Hutu 691
Huxley, Aldous 260
hybrid offences 379
hydrocarbon 53, 64
hydrochloric acid 58
hydrodynamics 184
hydroelectric power (HEP) 106
hydrofoil boat 466
hydrogen 59
hydrogenation 143
hydrogen bomb 476

hydrological cycle 108
hydrophobia 351
hydroponics 145
hydrostatics 184
hydrotherapy 356
hyperactivity 342
hyperbola 173
hyperinflation 212
hyperon 189
hypertension 349
hypertext 79
hyphen 268
hypnosis 342
hypnotherapy 356
hypo 310
hypotenuse 173
hypothermia 349
hysterectomy 335
hysteria 342

Iapetus Ocean 91
Iban 691
Ibo 691
Ibrahim, Halidi Abderamane 580
Ibsen, Henrik 322
Icarus, asteroid 37
ice ages 91
ice cream 135
ice hockey 435
Iceland 601
I Ching 411
icosahedron 173
Ifugao 691
Igbo 690
Iliescu, Ion 535, 640
illegitimacy 377
image compression 83
immiscible 69
immunization 335
immunoglobulin 55
imperialism 393
imperial units 1
import 212
import control 212
impotence 349
Impressionism 237
imprisonment, cost of 138
impromptu 294
Inca emperors 495
incendiary bomb 486
inclination, in astronomy 46
incomes policy 212
income tax 212
incontinence 349
incubation time 144
indemnity 377
indentures 379
independent school 331
Independent Television Commission (ITC) 384
indeterminacy principle 193
index of a number 172
India 602
   art 241
   emperors 495
   Indian languages 691
   Indian Mutiny 503
   prime ministers 545
indicator 69
indictable offences 379
indie music 302

indigenous populations 688
   areas legally controlled by 688
indirect cost 205
indirect tax 205
individualism 393
Indo-European languages 692
Indonesia 602
Industrial Revolution 502
industrial tribunal 205
inertia 184
infection 349
inferior planet 37
infinity 173
inflammation 335
inflation 212
inflation accounting 206
inflection 269
influenza 349
information technology (IT) 79
Ingraham, Hubert 564
Ingres, Jean-Auguste Dominique 237
initiation rites 410
injunction 377
Inns of Court 382
inorganic chemistry 56–62
   definition 53
inquest 377
insect 158
   classification 157
insecticide 145
insider dealing 206
insider trading 206
insolvency 206
insulation 123
insulin 353
integer 173
integrated circuit (IC) 83, 86
Integrated Services Digital Network (ISDN) 197
integration 173
Intelsat 30
interactive video (IV) 198
Inter-American Development Bank (IADB) 216
intercontinental ballistic missile (ICBM) 475, 476
interest 212
interface 83
interference 184
intermediate nuclear forces (INF) 478
Intermediate Nuclear Forces (INF) Treaty 478
intermediate vector boson 193
intermezzo 294
internal-combustion engine 465
internal economies of scale 206
internal waters 378
International Atomic Energy Agency (IAEA) 366
International Bank for Reconstruction and Development (IRBD) 366
International Civil Aviation Organization (ICAO) 366
International Court of Justice 366, 382
International Date Line 98
International Development Association (IDA) 221, 366
International Finance Corporation (IFC) 366
International Fund for Agricultural Development (IFAD) 366

International Labour Organization (ILO) 366
International Law 377
International Maritime Organization (IMO) 367
International Monetary Fund (IMF) 217, 367
international organizations 360–72
International Telecommunication Union (ITU) 367
International Union for Conservation of Nature (IUCN) 129
International Whaling Commission (IWC) 117
interplanetary matter 37
Interpol 382
interstellar molecules 41
intestacy 377
intrauterine device (IUD) 335
intrusion 95
Inuit 692
Inuktitut 691
inventory 206
invertebrates 155–8
investment 206
investment trust 206
invisible trade 212
in vitro fertilization (IVF) 335
Io, moon 36
ion 69
Ionesco, Eugène 322
ion exchange 69
ionic bond 70
Ionic order 223
ionization therapy 356
Iqbāl, Muhammad 260
Iran 603
   Iranian Revolution 505
Iraq 604
IRAS (Infrared Astronomy Satellite) 30
Ireland, Republic of 604
iridology 356
iris, of eye 337
Iron Age 23
irradiation 143
irrigation 145
Isa bin Sulman al-Khalifa, Sheik 564
ISDN see Integrated Services Digital Network
Ishiguro, Kazuo 260
Iskandrov, Akbasho 656
Islam 405–6, 412
   festivals 416
   Islamic architecture 221
   Islamic calendar 11, 14
   Islamic law 406
   rites 410, 411
Islamic Conference Organization (ICO) 361
island 98
   major islands 97
islets of Langerhans 89
ISO, in photography 310
isobar 103
isoenzyme 41
isomer 64
isotope 70
isotopic analysis 24
Isozaki, Arata 225
isozyme 41, 55
Israel 605

Issaufou, Mahamdou 632
issued capital 206
Italy 606
   art in 232–3, 235, 236
   kings 498
Ivory Coast 607
Ivy League 331
Iwo Jima 481
Izetbegović, Alija 570

Jackson, Betty 327
Jackson, Michael 303
Jacobins 503
Jagan, Cheddi 599
Jainism 406–7, 412
Jamaica 607
James, Henry 260
Janáček, Leoš 297
Jansky, Karl Guthe 51
Japan 608
   emperors 496–7
   Japanese art 242
   prime ministers 545
Japanese language 273
Jaruzelski, Wojciech 535
Jasray, Puntsagiyn 626
Jat 692
jaundice 349
Javanese 692
Jawara, Dawda K 593
Jayawardene, Junius Richard 535
jazz 299–307
   chronology 303
jazz dance 253
Jean, Grand Duke of Luxembourg
   618
Jehovah's Witness 409
Jellicoe, Geoffrey 225
jellyfish 158
Jencks, Charles 225
Jennings, Humphrey 246
Jerusalem 415
Jesus 413
jetfoil 466
jet propulsion 463
Jet Propulsion Laboratory 30
jet stream 103
Jews see Judaism
Jiang Jie Shi 503
Jiang Zemin 535, 579
job enrichment 206
Jodrell Bank 47
John Paul II, Pope 668
Johns, Jasper 240
Johnson, Jack 453
Johnson, Lyndon Baines 535
Johnson, Philip 225
Johnson, Samuel 260
Johnson Space Center 31
joint 338
joint venture 206
Jōmon period 242
Jones, Bobby 453
Jones, Inigo 225
Jonson, Ben 322
Jordan 609
Josephson, Brian 192
Joule, James Prescott 192
Joyce, James 260
joystick, computer 80
Juan Carlos I, King of Spain 651

Judaism 407, 412
   fasts and festivals 12, 416
   Jewish calendar 12, 14
   rites 410, 411
judge 377
judicial review 377
judiciary 395
judo 435
Jugnauth, Aneerood 624
jump jet 486
junk bond 206
Jupiter 37
jurisprudence 377
jury 377
justice 140
just-in-time (JIT) 206
Jutland, Battle of 481
juvenile court 382
juvenile offender 377

Kádár, János 535
kaaba 437
Kabua, Amata 623
kabuki 315
Kafi, Ali 558
Kafka, Franz 260
Kahn, Louis 225
Kalidasa 260
Kamakura period 242
Kami-no-Michi 407
Kamiya, Joseph 355
Kanarese 691
Kandinsky, Wassily 239
Kang Song San 611
Kannada 692
Kantor, Tadeusz 322
Karadzic, Radovan 535
Karamanlis, Constantine 596
Karan, Donna 327
karaoke 303
Karen 692
Karimov, Islam 667
Karsh, Yousuf 312
karyotype 153
Kaunda, Kenneth 535
Kawakubo, Rei 235
Kazakh 692
Kazakhstan 609
Kazan, Elia 322
Keating, Paul 535, 562
Keats, John 261
Kebich, Vyacheslav 566
Kechua 693
Keck Telescope 47
Keifer, Anslem 241
Kekulé von Stradonitz, Fredrich August
   73
Kelvin, William Thomson 192
kelvin scale 194
Kendall, Edward 73
Kendrew, John 73
Kennedy, John F. 536
Kennedy Space Center 31
Kenya 610
Kenyatta, Jomo 536
Kenzo Takada 327
Kepler, Johannes 51
Kerouac, Jack 261
Kertész, André 312
ketone 64
key 294

keyboard, computer 80
key-results analysis 206
Khaddhafi, Moamer al- 536, 616
Khalifa bin Hamad al-Thani, Sheik 640
Khamenei, Seyed Ali 603
Khan, Imran 453
Khan, Jahangir 453
Khasbulatov, Rusian 536
Khe Sanh 481
Khmer 692
Khoikhoi 692
Khoisan 692
Khomeini, Ayatollah Ruhollah 536
Khrushchev, Nikita Sergeyevich 536
Khwarizma, Muhammad ibn Musac al-
   179
kidney 339
Kikuyu 692
kilobyte (K or KB) 83
Kim Il Sung 536, 611
Kim Young Sam 536, 612
kindergarten 332
kinetics and kinetic theory 182, 184
King, Billie Jean 453
King, Martin Luther 536
King's Counsel 377, 379
kings and queens
   English 500
   French 498
   Italian 498
   Scottish 499
   Spanish 498
Kinigi, Sylvie 574
Kipling, Rudyard 261
Kirchner, Ernst Ludwig 239
Kirghiz 692
Kiribati 610
Kitt Peak National Observatory 47
Klammer, Franz 453
Klaus, Václav 584
Klee, Paul 240
Klein, Calvin 327
Klein, Roland 328
Klestil, Thomas 563
Kmer 691
Kobarid 481
Koffigoh, Joseph Kokou 658
Kofun period 242
Kohl, Helmut 536, 595
Koirala, Girija Prasad 630
Koivisto, Mauno 536, 592
Kolingba, André 577
Konare, Alpha Oumar 622
Kontic, Radoje 670
Koran 406, 412
Korbut, Olga 453
Korea, North 611
Korea, South 612
Kornberg, Arthur 73
Kourou 31
Kovak, Michal 647
Kravchuk, Leonid 536, 663
Krebs cycle 55
Kristiansen, Ingrid 453
K-T boundary 91
Kubrick, Stanley 246
Kucan, Milan 648
Kuhn, Richard 73
Kuiper belt 37
Kung 692

K'ung Tzu 413
Kurd 692
Kurosawa, Akira 246
Kuwait 612
Kuyon, Bismark 616
Kyrgyzstan 613

Laar, Mart 590
Lacroix, Christian 328
lacrosse 436
La Fontaine, Jean de 261
Lafontaine, Oskar 261
Lagerfeld, Karl 328
lagoon 103
Lagrange, Joseph Louis 179
Lagrangian points 37
Lahnda 692
laissez faire 212
lake 98
    major lakes 98
Lamaism 403
Lamarckism 149
Land, Erwin Herbert 312
Land art 240
Land Registry, HM 382
Landsat 31
Landsbergis, Vytautas 536
landscape archaeology 24
landslide 98
Lang, Fritz 246
lang, k d 303
Lange, David 536
Lange, Dorothea 312
Langmuir, Irving 73
languages
    common roots 271
    English grammar and usage 267–270
    main language groups 275
    word-borrowings from foreign
        271–5
Laos 613
Lao Tzu 413
Lao Zi 408, 413
Laplace, Pierre Simon, Marquis de 51
Lapp 693
laptop computer 83, 84
larceny 377
lard 135
large numbers 180
large-scale integration (LSI) 87
largest cities 674
largest countries
    by area 673
    by population 674
larva 153
laryngitis 349
Las Campanas Observatory 47
Lasdun, Denys 226
laser 184
    guidance system 474
Latin American Economic System
        (LAES) 362
Latin American Integration Association
        (ALADI) 362
latitude 98
Latter-day Saints, Church of Jesus
        Christ of 409
Latvia 614
    Revolution 505
Latvian 692
Latynina, Larissa Semyonovna 454

Lauda, Niki 454
Laurasia 91
Lauren, Ralph 328
lava 95
Laver, Rodney George 454
Lavoisier, Antoine Laurent 73
law 375–83
Law Commission 382
law courts 382
law lords 378
Lawrani, Mohamed 627
Lawrence, D H 261
Lawrence, Ernest O 192
L-dopa 353
leaching 123
lead 123
leaders of the modern world 619–34
leaf 163
Lean, David 246
learning curve 206
leasehold 378
Leavitt, Henrietta Swan 51
Lebanon 614
Lebrun, Charles 235
Le Corbusier 226
Ledoux, Claude-Nicolas 226
Le Duc Anh 669
Lee Hoi Chang 612
Leekpai, Chuan 658
Lee Kuan Yew 537
Lee Teng-hui 656
left wing 395
legacy 378
legal action 375
legal aid 378
legal institutions 386–9
legal terms 124–35
Leghari, Farooq 634
Le Gray, Gustave 312
legume 145
Leibniz, Gottfried Wilhelm 179
Leibovitz, Annie 313
Leighton, Frederic, Lord 237
Lely, Peter 236
Lemaître, Georges Edouard 51
Lenin, Vladimir Ilich Ulyanov 504
Lennon, John 303
lens
    of eye 337
    in optics 184
Leonard, Sugar Ray 454
Leonardo da Vinci 232
Leon Carpio, Ramiro de 597
Leonov, Aleksei Arkhipovich 51
Leopardi, Giacomo 261
lepton 189
Lesotho 615
Lethaby, William Richard 226
Letsie III, King of Lesotho 615
Lett 691
letters patent 379
Lettish 691
leukaemia 350
lever 184
leveraged buyout 206
Leverrier, Urbain Jean Joseph 51
Levi, Primo 261
Lewis, Carl 454
Lewis, Lennox 454
Lewis, Sinclair 261
ley 146

Lhasa 156
libel 378
liberal democracy 392
liberalism 393
Liberia 616
libretto 294
Libya 616
licensing laws 378
Li Chi 411
Lichtenstein, Roy 240
Lick Observatory 47
Liddell Hart, Basil 481
Liebig, Justus, Baron von 73
Liechtenstein 617
lied 294
lien 378
Lien Chan 656
life cycle 151–4
life expectancy 678–9
life sciences 149–67
light 184
light-emitting plastics 613
lightning 103
light pen 80
light year 46
Lilic, Zoran 670
Lillee, Dennis 454
Limbourg brothers 232
limited company 206
limited liability 206
limited vote system 397
limited war 478
linear equation 173
Lineker, Gary 454
Li Peng 537, 579
lipid 55, 64
Li Po 261
liqueur 135
liquidation 206
Lissitsky, El 239
Lissouba, Pascal 581
listed building 223
Lister, Joseph 103
Liszt, Franz 297
literacy 331
literacy rates 677–8
literature 257–67
    awards 265–7
lithification 94
lithosphere 95
Lithuania 617
    Revolution 505
Lithuanian 692
litmus 70
Littlewood, Joan 322
liver 339
loan 206
Lobachevsky, Nikolai Ivanovich 179
lobby 395
local area network (LAN) 83
local government 395
Local Group 41
lockjaw 352
locus 173
logarithm 173
logic circuit 87
logic gate 87
Lomé Convention 362
London, Jack 261
London International Financial Futures
        Exchange (LIFFE) 217

lone pair 70
Long, Richard 240
longitude 98
Lopez, Nancy 455
Lorca, Federico García 261, 322
Lord Advocate 378
Lord Chancellor 378
Lorenz, Ludwig Valentine 179
Lorenzetti, Ambrogio 231
Lorrain, Claude 235
loss 206
loudspeaker 198
Louis, Joe 455
Lovell, Bernard 51
Lowell, Percival 51
Lowell Observatory 47
low-intensity conflict 478
Lu, annals of 411
Lubbers, Rudolph Franz Marie (Ruud) 537, 631
Lubovitch, Lar 256
Luftwaffe 475
luminescence 185
luminosity 46
Lumumba, Patrice 537
lunar eclipse 36, 37
lung 340
Luther, Martin 414
Lutyens, Edwin Landseer 226
Luxembourg 618
lymph node 340
Lysippus 230

Maastricht Treaty 363
McBride, Willie John 455
McCullin, Donald 313
Mcdonald Observatory 48
Macedonia 619
McEnroe, John 455
McGrath, John 322
Machado de Assis, Joaquim Maria 257
Machel, Samora 537
machine code, computer 77
machine gun 487
Macintosh computer 83
Mackintosh, Charles Rennie 226
Macmillan, Harold 537
MacMillan, Kenneth 256
macro 83
macrobiotics 135
Madagascar 619
mad cow disease 144
Madonna 303
madrigal 294
Magellan, space probe 31
Magellanic Clouds 41
magic square 173
magistrate 378
magistrates' court 382
magma 95
magnetic disc 77, 80
magnetic storm 103
magnetism 185
magnetometer 24
magnetosphere 37
magnet school 331
magnet therapy 356
magnitude 46
Magritte, René 239
Mahābhārata 412
Mahavira 414

Mahāyāna Buddhism 403, 404
Mahdi, Sadiq al- 652
Mahler, Gustav 297
Mahomet 414
Mahratta 692
Maimonides 414
mainframe computer 77
maintenance payment 378
Major, John 537, 664
Makarios III 537
Maksi, Alexander 557
Makua 693
Malagasy 693
malaria 350
Malawi 620
Malayalam 692
Malaysia 620
Maldives 621
Malek, Redha 558
Malevich, Kasimir 239
Mali 621
Malietoa Tanumafili II, King of Western Samoa 643
malnutrition 335
malpractice 378
Malta 622
Malval, Robert 599
Mamet, David 322
mammal 160
   classification 158
mammography 335
management accounting 206
management buyout 206
management information system 206
managing director 206
Mandaba, Jean-Luc 577
mandamus 377
mandate 395
Mandela, Nelson 537
Mandelbrot, Benoit B 180
Manet, Edouard 237
mangrove 117
manic depression 342
manifesto 395
Manley, Michael 537
Mann, Thomas 261
Mannerism 232
Manning, Patrick 659
manoeuvre 476
Man Ray 313
Mansell, Nigel 455
manslaughter 378
Mantegna, Andrea 233
mantle 95
Mantle, Mickey 455
Manzoni, Alessandro 261
Maoism 393
Maori 693
Mao Zedong (Mao Tse-Tung) 503, 537
Mapplethorpe, Robert 313
Maradona, Diego 455
Marat, Jean Paul 503
Maratha 693
Marc, Franc 239
Marciano, Rocky 455
Marcos, Ferdinand 537
mare 37
margarine 135
Margiela, Martin 328
Margrethe II, Queen of Denmark 585
Mariner spacecraft 31

Marines 476
Marinetti, Filippo 239
maritime law 378
market 213
   capitalization 206
   economy 213
   forces 213
   segment 207
   share 207
marketing mix 207
market maker 207
Markov, Andrei 180
Marley, Bob 303
Marlowe, Christopher 322
Marne, Battles of the 481
Márquez, Felipe González 651
marriage rites 410–11
Mars 37
Marshall Islands 623
Marshall Space Flight Center 31
Mars Observer, space probe 31
marsupial 160
Martens, Wilfried 537
Marti i Alanis, Joan 558
martial law 378
Martin, Archer John Porter 73
Martini, Simone 232
Marxism 393
Masaccio 232
Masai 693
Masire, Quett Ketamile Joni 538, 570
masonry 113
masque 317
mass 185
mass action, law of 70
mass extinction 91
Massine, Léonide 256
Masson, André 239
material culture 24
mathematics 168–81
   awards 178
   biographies 178–81
   chronology 170–1
   terms 168–77
Matisse, Henri 238
matrix
   archaeological 24
   mathematical 173
Matthews, Stanley 456
Matura, Mustapha 322
Mauna Kea 48
Maupassant, Guy de 261
Mauritania 623
Mauritius 624
maximum 173
Mbasogo, Teodoro Obiang Nguema 589
M-discontinuity 95
ME see myalgic encephalitis
mean 174
meander 98
measles 350
measures 1–8
meat 135
Mecca 415
mechanics 185
mechanized infantry combat vehicle 487
Meciar, Vladimir 538, 647
media 384–91
   conglomerates 384–5
   international news agencies 386–7

newspaper circulations 388–91
UK watchdogs 385
medicine 334–59
    alternative therapies 354–9
    chronology of Western medicine 341
    diseases and disorders 346–53
    drug types 353–4
    medical terms 334–46
    Nobel Prize winners 357–8
Medieval art 231
Medina 415
Mediterranean climate 103
medium range ballistic missile (MRBM) 476
medulla 336
medulla oblongata 160
megabyte 83
megavitamin therapy 356
Meier, Richard 226
Meiji period 242
meiosis 153
Meir, Golda 538
Meiselas, Susan 313
melanoma 350
Méliès, Georges 246
melodrama 317
melody 294
Melville, Herman 261
Memlinc, Hans 233
memorandum of association 207
memory, computer 77, 80
Mende 693
Mendeleyev, Dmitri Ivanovich 73
Mendelsohn, Erich 226
Mendelssohn, Felix 297
Menem, Carlos 538, 561
Mengistu, Haile Mariam 538
meningitis 350
mental handicap 342
menu, computer 83
Mercalli scale 95
mercenary 476
Merckx, Eddie 456
Mercosur 362
mercury 123
Mercury (planet) 37
merger 207
Meri, Lennart 590
meridian 98
Mesolithic 24
meson 189
mesosphere 103
Mesozoic 91
Messiaen, Olivier 297
Messier, Charles 51
metabolism 55
metal 59
metal detector 25
metallographic examination 25
metamorphism 95
metamorphosis 153
metazoan 155
meteor 37
meteorite 36, 37
meteorology 103
methanogenic bacteria 163
methylated spirit 70
metre, in music 294
metric conversion tables 2
metric units 1

Mexico 624
Meyerhold, Vsevolod 322
mezzanine 223
mezzo-soprano 294
Miandad, Javed 456
Michelangelo 232
Michelson, Albert Abraham 192
Michelson-Morley experiment 192
microbe 164
microcomputer 77
Micronesia 625
microorganism 164
microphone 198
microprocessor 77, 87
microwear analysis 26
middle C 294
Middle East, time chart 506–28
Mies van der Rohe, Ludwig 226
mifepristone 354
migraine 350
military
    equipment 486–9
    leaders 479–86
    ranks 489
    terms 473–8
militia 395
milk 135
milking machine 146
Milky Way 41
Miller, Arthur 323
Miller, Glenn 303
Millet, Jean-François 237
mills 110
Mills Cross 48
Milosevic, Slobodan 538
Milton, John 261
mime 317
minaret 223
mine 487
minerals, trace 137
mineral water 135
minesweeper 476
Ming dynasty 241, 494
Mingus, Charles 303
minicomputer 77
Minimalism 240
minimum 173
minipill 354
ministerial gradings (UK) 397
ministries (UK government) 397–400
Minoan civilization 229
minor, in law 378
minority interest 207
Minority Rights Group 372
minuet 294
Mir, space station 31
Mira 42
miracle play 311, 312
Miró, Joan 239
mirror 185
miserere 223
misericord 223
Mishima, Yukio 262
Mishna 407
missile systems and technology 487
Missoni, Ottavio 328
Missoni, Rosia 328
Mitchell, James 643
Mitchell, Peter 73
mitochondria 165
mitosis 153

Mitterrand, François 538, 592
mixed-ability teaching 331
mixture, chemical 70
Miyake, Issey 328
Miyazawa, Kiichi 538
Mnouchkine, Ariane 323
mobile phone 193
mobilization 476
Möbius, August Ferdinand 180
Mobutu, Sese Seko Kuku Ngbeandu Wa Zu Banga 538
modem (modulator/demodulator) 81
modern dance 253
Modernism 222
Modigliani, Amedeo 240
Modotti, Tina 313
modular course 331
modulation
    in music 294
    in telecommunications 198
module 113
modulus 164
Mogul art 242
Mohamad, Mahathir bin 538, 620
Mohammed see Muhammad
Mohammed, Ali Mahdi 649
Moholy-Nagy, Laszlo 313
Mohorovičič discontinuity 95
Moi, Daniel arap 538, 610
Mokhehle, Ntsu 616
Moldavia, Revolution 505
Moldavian 693
Moldova 625
molecular biology 165
molecular clock 167
molecular formula 69
molecule 70
Molière (Jean-Baptiste Poquelin) 323
mollusc 158
    classification 158
Momoyama period 242
Mon 693
Monaco 626
Mondrian, Piet 239
Monet, Claude 238
monetarism 213
monetary policy 213
money 213
money supply 213
Mongolia 626
monitor, in computing 81
Monk, Thelonius 303
monoculture 146
monomer 65
Monopolies and Mergers Commission (MMC) 217
monopoly 213
monorail 463
monosaccharide 53, 55
monotreme 160
Monoyama period 242
monsoon 103
Montaigne, Michel Eyquem de 262
Montana, Claude 328
Montana, Joe 456
Monteiro, Mascarenhas 576
Monteverdi, Claudio 297
Montgomery, Bernard Law 481
months, name derivations 19
Montréal Protocol 129
moon 38

Moon, the 36, 38
  lunar eclipse 36, 37
Moonies 409
Moon probe 31
Moore, Bobby 456
Moore, Charles 226
Moore, Henry 240
moraine 98
morality play 317
Mordvin 693
Moreau, Gustave 238
Mormon 409
Morocco 627
morphing, in computing 83
Morris, William 237
Morrison, Van 303
mortar bomb 487
mosaic 230
Moses 407, 414
Mossi 693
motorbike 466
motorcycle 466
  racing 436
motoring law 378
motor neuron disease 350
motor racing 437
mountain 98
  highest mountains 99
Mount Palomar 48
Mount Wilson 48
Mounyar, Fuidel 577
mouse, computer 81
movement, in music 294
moving coil speaker 198
Mozambique 627
Mozart, Leopold 297
Mozart, Wolfgang Amadeus 297
MS see multiple sclerosis
MS-DOS (Microsoft Disc Operating
  System) 84
Mswati III, King of Swaziland 653
Mubarak, Hosni 538, 588
Muda Hassanal Bolkiah Mu'izzaddin
  Waddaulah, Sultan of Brunei
  572
mufti 406
Mugabe, Robert 538, 672
Mugler, Thierry 328
Muhammad 406, 414
Muir, Jean 328
Muldoon, Robert David 538
Mullard Radio Astronomy Observatory
  48
Müller, Heiner 323
Mulrony, Brian 538
multicultural education 331
multimedia 79
multinational corporation 207
Multiple Mirror Telescope 48
multiple sclerosis (MS) 350
multiplexing 198
multiplier 213
multiprogramming 84
multitasking 84
mumps 350
Munch, Edvard 238
Munda 693
Munkácsi, Martin 313
muon 189
Muradov, Sakhat 661
murder 378

Murdoch, Rupert 392
Murillo, Bartolomé Esteban 235
Muromachi period 242
muscle 160, 340
muscular dystrophy 350
Museveni, Yoweri Kaguta 539, 662
mushroom 137
music 293–307
  biographies 296–307
  musical expressions 289
  popular music and jazz 300–307
  terms 293–6, 299
musical 318
  comedy 318
musical instruments digital interface
  (MIDI) 77, 83
music hall 318
music therapy 356
Musil, Robert 262
Muslims see Islam
Mussorgsky, Modest Petrovich 297
mustard 137
Mutalov, Abdul Hashim 667
mutation 149
Mutebi, Kabuka Ronald Muwenda
  662
Muybridge, Eadweard 313
Mwinyi, Ali Hassan 657
myalgic encephalitis (ME) 350
Myanmar 628
Mycenean civilization 229
mystery play 318

Nabis, The 238
Nabokov, Vladimir 262
Nadar 313
nadir 46
NAFTA see North American Free
  Trade Agreement
Naga 693
Nahuatl 693
Naipaul, V S 262
Naipaul, Shivadhar 262
Najibullah, Ahmadzai 539
Nakasone, Yasuhiro 539
Namath, Joe 456
Namibia 628
Namuth, Hans 313
Nanak 408, 414
napalm 487
Napier, John 180
Nara period 242
Narasimha Rao, P V 539, 602
NASA see National Aeronautics and
  Space Administration
Nash, John 226
Nash, Paul 240
Nasser, Gamal Abdel 539
Natanyahu, Binjamin 539
Natchez 693
National Aeronautics and Space
  Administration (NASA) 31
National Broadcasting Company
  (NBC) 384
national curriculum 331
national debt 213
National Guard 395
national holidays 682–7
national insurance 207
nationalism 393
nationalization 395

national park 117
  major national parks 128
National Rivers Authority 129
National Trust 129
national vocational qualification
  (NVQ) 332
NATO see North Atlantic Treaty Organization
Natural Environment Research Council
  (NERC) 129
natural gas 106
natural selection 149
Nature Conservancy Council (NCC) 129
nature reserve 117
naturopathy 356
Nauru 629
Navajo (Navaho) 693
naval battles 483
Navratilova, Martina 456
navy 476
Nazarbayev, Nursultan 539, 609
nebula 42
negative/positive image 310
negligence, in law 378
Negrillo 401
Nehru, Jawaharlal 539
neighbourhood watch 378
nematode 158
Neo-Classical architecture 222
neo-Darwinism 149
Neo-Expressionism 241
neo-fascism 393
Neo-Gothic architecture 222
Neolithic 26
neo-nazism 393
Neo-Plasticism 239
Nepal 630
Neptune 38
Nerette, Joseph 599
Nernst, Walther Hermann 75
Neruda, Pablo 262
nerve 340
Nervi, Pier Luigi 226
nervous breakdown 342
nervous system 161
net 207
net assets 207
netball 437
net current assets 207
Netherlands 630
net worth 207
neural network 84
neurosis 342
Neutra, Richard Joseph 226
neutralization 70
neutral solution 70
neutrino 189
neutron 70, 189
neutron bomb 476
neutron star 42
New Age music 303
New Archaeology 27
newly industrialized country (NIC) 213
News International/News Corporation
  385
newspapers and their circulations
  388–91
New Technology Telescope 48
New Testament 411, 412
Newton, Isaac 181, 193
Newton's laws of motion 185

New Wave music 303
New Zealand 631
  prime ministers 545
Nicaragua 632
  Nicaraguan Revolution 505
niche, in ecology 117
Nicklaus, Jack 456
Nielsen, Carl 297
Niemeyer, Oscar 226
Niger 632
Niger-Congo languages 693
Nigeria 633
Nightingale, Florence 334
Nijinsky, Vaslav 256
nitrate 123
nitric acid 60
nitrogen 60
nitrogen cycle 155
Nixon, Richard 539
Niyazov, Saparmurad 661
Nkomo, Joshua 539
Nkrumah, Kwame 539
Nobel, Alfred Bernhard 75
Nobel Prize winners
  chemistry 74–5
  economics 218
  literature 265
  peace 401–2
  physics 194–5
  physiology or medicine 357–8
nocturne 294
nonexecutive director 207
nonmetal 60
Nō (Noh) 318
nonrenewable resource 117
nonvoting share 207
Noriega, Manuel 539
Norman art 231
North America 553
  historical time charts 483–29, 553
  indigenous religions 407
North American Free Trade Agreement
    (NAFTA) 362
North Atlantic Cooperation Council
    362, 476
North Atlantic Treaty Organization
    (NATO) 362, 476
North Star 42
Norway 633
notebook, computer 84
noun 269
nova 42
Nuba 694
nuclear
  accidents 107
  energy 106
  fission 106, 185
  fusion 106, 185
  reactor 106, 107
  safety 123
  unilateral nuclear disarmament 397
  warfare 476
  waste 123
nuclear, biological and chemical war-
    fare (NBC) 476
nucleic acid 55
nucleotide 55, 165
nucleus
  in biology 164
  in physics 189
Nujoma, Sam 539, 629

number 174
number theory 174
numerator 174
nursery school 332
nursing 335
nut 125
nutation 46
nutrients
  loss during cooking 140
  recommended daily amounts 138
nutrition 335
Nyanja 693
Nyerere, Julius 540
Nyunt, General Khin 628

oath 378
obelisk 223
Obote, Milton 540
obscenity law 378
observatories 47–9
  definition 48
obsession 342
obstetrics 335
O'Casey, Sean 323
occultation 38
ocean 101–4
  oceans and seas, listed 104
  ridge 103
  trench 103
Oceania 558
oceanography 117
Ochirbat, Punsalmaagiyn 626
Ochoa, Severo 76
octahedron 174
Oddsson, Davíd 601
Odets, Clifford 323
oesophagus 340
Ogi, Adolf 655
Ohm, Georg Simon 193
oil 107
  crop 146
  spills 124
oil of vitriol 46
oil, cooking 137
Okinawa 481
Olbers, Heinrich 51
Olbers' paradox 42
Olbrich, Joseph Maria 226
Old Bailey 382
Oldfield, Bruce 328
Oldfield, Harry 355
Old Testament 411, 412
olefins see alkene
oligopoly 214
Olivier, Laurence 323
Olter, Bailey 625
Olympia, Statue of Zeus at 490
Olympic Games, sites of summer 460
Oman 634
Omicron Ceti 42
omnivore 155
oncology 335
onco-mouse 167
O'Neill, Eugene 323
Ong Teng Cheong 647
Oort, Jan Hendrik 51
Oort cloud 38, 51
ooze 103
Op art 240
OPEC see Organization of Petroleum
    Exporting Countries

Open College 332
Open University 332
opera 294, 295
operating system (OS) 84
operational amplifier (op-amp) 87
operetta 294, 318
operon 165
ophthalmology 335
Ophuls, Marcel 246
Ophuls, Max 246
opposition, in astronomy 46
optical disc 80
optical fibre 198
optics 185
opting out, schools 332
option 207
optoelectronics 88
opus 294
oratorio 294
orbit 46
orchestration 294
orders, architectural 223
ordinal number 174
ordinary share 207
ordinate 174
Ordovician 91
organic chemistry 62–5
  definition 53
organic farming 124, 146
Organisation Commune Africaine et
    Mauricienne (OCAM) 362
Organisation Européenne pour la
    Recherche Nucléaire 360
Organización de Estados Centroameri-
    canos (OECDA) 362
Organization of African Unity (OAU)
    362
Organization of American States
    (OAS) 362
Organization of Arab Petroleum
    Exporting Countries (OAPEC)
    362
Organization of Central American
    States (ODECA) 362
Organization for Economic Coopera-
    tion and Development (OECD)
    217, 362
Organization of Petroleum Exporting
    Countries (OPEC) 217, 362
orienteering 437
origin, in geometry 174
Orion nebula 27
Oriya 694
Oromo 694
Orphism 239
Ortega Saavedra, Daniel 540
orthochromatic 310
Orthodox Church 404
orthopaedics 335
Orton, Joe 323
Orwell, George 262
Osborne, John 323
Oscars see Academy Awards
oscillating universe 42
oscillator 88, 199
osteoarthritis 346, 350
osteopathy 356
osteoporosis 350
Ostrovsky, Alexander 323
Ostwald, Wilhelm 76
otitis 351

Ottoman emperors 493
Ousmane, Mahamane 632
ovary 340
overfishing 124
overhead 203, 205, 207
overture 294
Ovid 262
oviduct 337
ovum 153
Owens, Jesse 456
Oxfam 372
oxidation 70
oxygen 60
oxytocin 354
Özal, Turgut 540
Ozbek, Rifat 328
ozone 61, 124
    depleter 124
    gound-level 124
    hole 124
Ozu, Yasujiro 246

pacemaker 335
packaging 125
paediatrics 335
Paeniu, Bikenibeu 661
pageant 318
pain 335
Pakistan 634
palaeobotany 27
Palaeolithic 27
palaeomagnetism 93
palaeontology 27, 93
Palaeozoic 93
Palestrina, Giovanni Perluigi da 297
Palikur 694
Palladio, Andrea 226
Palme, Olof 540
Palmer, Arnold 457
palynology 27
Panama 635
panchromatic film 310
pancreas 340
panel painting 231
Pangaea 93
Panthalassa 93
pantheon 223
pantomime 318
Paolozzi, Eduardo 240
Papandreou, Andreas 540, 596
paper sizes
    international 9
    metric book publishing 9
pap test 83
Papua New Guinea 636
parabola 174
paracetamol 354
paraffin 64, 70
Paraguay 636
parallax 46
parallel lines 174
parallelogram 174
parallel planes 174
paralysis agitans 351
paranoia 342
paraplegia 335
parathyroid 340
parent-teacher association (PTA) 332
Paris, treaties of 478
Paris Commune 503
Parker, Charlie 304

Parkes 48
Parkinson, Norman 313
Parkinson's disease 351
parliament 395
parole 379
parsec 46
Parsees 409
parthenogenesis 150
participle 269
part of speech 269
party, in law 379
party list system 397
Pascal, Blaise 180
Pasolini, Pier Paolo 246
Passchendaele 481
pasta 137
Pasternak, Boris Leonidovich 262
pasteurization 143
pastry 138
patent 207, 379
Pathan 694
pathenogenesis 559
Patriot missile 487
patron saints 420
Patterson, P J 608
Patton, George 481
Paul, Saint 414
Pauli, Wolfgang 193
Pauling, Linus Carl 76
Pawlak, Waldemar 638
Paxton, Joseph 226
Pay-As-You-Earn (PAYE) 207
Paz, Octavio 262
Paz, Victor 540
PC see computer, personal
Peace Prize, Nobel, winners 401–2
Pearl Harbor, Battle of 481
Pearson 385
peat 99
pediatrics 335
pediment 223
pedology 101
Pei, Ieoh Ming 226
Pelé 457
pelvic girdle 340
pelvis 340
penal institutions 386–9
penicillin 354
penis 340
Penn, Irving 313
People's Republic of China see China
pepper 138
peptide 55, 165
p/e ratio 208
percentage 174
perestroika 395, 505
Pérez de Cuéllar, Javier 365, 540
performance art 240
performance-related pay 207
perigee 46
perihelion 46
perimeter 174
period, in grammar 269
periodic table of the elements 62–3, 70
periscope 487
peristyle 223
perjury 379
Perkin, William Henry 76
permafrost 99
permanent revolution 394
Permian 93

permutation 174
Perón, Juan 540
perpendicular 175
perpetual calendar 14–17
Perrault, Charles 262
Perrier 124
Persian art 229
Persian language 689
personnel management 205
perspective 232
pertussis 352
Peru 637
Perutz, Max 76
perverting the course of justice 379
Pessoa, Fernando 262
pesticide 125, 146
Petrarch (Petrarca), Francesco 262
petrol, unleaded 526
petroleum 107
petrology 95
Phanerozoic 93
Pharos of Alexandria 490
pharynx 340
phase 46
phenol 64
phenotype 153
Philippines 637
phobia 342, 343–4
Phobos 38
phosphate 61
phosphate analysis 27
photogram 310
photography 308–14
    biographies 311–14
    chronology 309–10
    terms 308–11
photolysis 71
photon 189
Photo Realism 240
photosphere 38
photosynthesis 155
Phoumsavan, Nouhak 613
pH scale 70, 71
phthisis 352
phylogeny 149
physical anthropology 27
physical chemistry 53
physics 182–95
    biographies 191–3
    chronology 186–7
    Nobel Prize winners 194–5
    particle 189–191
    terms 182–8
physiotherapy 335
piano nobile 223
Piazzi, Giuseppe 51
Picasso, Pablo 238, 239
picketing 379
pickling 143
pidgin language 694
Piero della Francesca 232
Pietro da Cortona 235
pig 146
Piggott, Lester 457
piggy-back export scheme 207
piles 349
pilgrimage 414
pill, the 354
Pinochet, Augusto 540
Pinter, Harold 323
Pioneer space probes 31

Pirandello, Luigi 323
Piranesi, Giovanni Battista 227, 236
Pisano, Giovanni and Nicola 231
Piscator, Erwin 323
Pissarro, Camille 238
pixel 85
placebo 354
plain 99
plaintiff 379
Planchon, Roger 324
Planck, Max 193
planetarium 48
planetary nebula 42
planetary satellites 39
planets 38
plants 161–3
    classification 162
Plaskett's Star 42
plastic 64
plateau 99
plate tectonics 93
Platini, Michel 457
platoon 477
playwrights 319–26
Plesetsk 31
plotter 81
plough 146
pluralism 393
Pluto 38
plutonium 61
pneumonia 351
p-n junction diode 88
poaching 379
Poe, Edgar Allan 262
Poets Laureate 267
Poincaré, Jules Henri 181
point 409
pointillism 238
point-of-sale system 79
poison 335
poison pill 208
poker hands 181
Poland 638
    Revolution 505
Polaris 42
Polaroid camera 310
polder 99
pole 99
Pole Star 42
police 379
Police Complaints Authority 382
polio 351
poliomyelitis 351
political ideologies 392–4
political terms 394–7
political thinkers 400
Pollaiuolo 232
pollen 153
pollen analysis 27
Pollock, Jackson 240
poll tax 214
polluter-pays principle 125
pollution 119–27
polo 438
    water 444
Pol Pot 540
polychlorinated biphenyl (PCB) 70
polygon 175
polyhedron 175
Polykleitos 230
polymer 65

polysaccharide 53, 55
polytechnic 332
polyunsaturate 65
Pontormo 233
Pop art 240
Pope, Alexander 262
popes, dates of 414
popular music 300–7
    UK best-selling singles 306
population
    countries ranked by 674
    indigenous populations 688
    urban population growth 675
    world life expectancy 678
    world literacy rates 677
    world population growth 676
port, in computing 77
Porter, Cole 304
Porter, Edwin Stanton 246
Porter, George 76
portico 223
Portugal 639
possessive individualism 393
Post-Impressionism 238
Post-Modernism 222
postnatal depression 342
postviral fatigue syndrome 350
potassium-argon dating 27
potato 139
potential, electric 185
Potiguara 693
poultry 146
Pound, Ezra 262
Poussin, Nicolas 235
Powell, Cecil Frank 193
Powell, Michael 246
power 185
power of attorney 379
Praxiteles 230
Precambrian 93
precedent 379
precession 46
precipitation 71, 93
prefabricated building 113
preference share 208
Preferential Trade Area for Eastern and
        Southern African States (PTA)
        362
pregnancy 153
prehistoric art 237
prehistory 27
prelude 294
prematurity 335
premedication 354
premenstrual tension (PMT) 351
premier 396
premium price 208
preparatory school 332
preposition 269
Pre-Raphaelites 237
president 395
presidents
    South Africa 546
    USSR 520, 546
    USA 520
Presley, Elvis 304
press
    international news agencies 386–7
    newspaper circulations 388–91
Press Complaints Commission (PCC)
    385

pressure 185
prestressed concrete 113
price/earnings ratio 208
price elasticity of demand 208
pricing strategy 208
Priestley, Joseph 76
primary education 332
primary fuels, production and con-
        sumption 111
Primaticcio, Francesco 235
prime minister 396
prime ministers
    Australia 544
    Canada 545
    China 546
    India 545
    Japan 545
    New Zealand 545
    South Africa 546
    UK 543
prime number 175
prime rate 208
Prince 304
printer, computer 81
prism 175
prison 382
prisoner of war (POW) 477
privacy legislation 146
private school 332
privatization 214, 396
Prix Goncourt winners 267
probability 175
probate 379
probation 379
procedure, in computing 785
procurator fiscal 379
productivity 396
profit 208
profit and loss account 208
profit-sharing 208, 214
programming, computer 77
programming languages 77, 84
progression 175
progressive education 332
prohibition 377
prokaryote 164
Prokofiev, Sergey 297
PROLOG computer language 79
prominence 38
pronoun 269
proofreading marks 276–7
propaganda 396
proper motion 46
prophylaxis 335
proportion 175
proportional representation 397
prosecution 379
Prost, Alain 457
prostate gland 340
protein 55, 165
protein engineering 167
Proterozoic 93
Protestantism 404
protist 164
Proto-Atlantic 91
protohistory 27
proton 71, 190
proton number 51
Proton rocket 31
protozoa 164
Proust, Marcel 262

provost 379
Proxima Centauri 42
proxy 379
psionic medicine 356
psoriasis 351
psychedelic rock music 304
psychiatry 344
psychic healing 359
psychoanalysis 344
psychological disorders 341–6
psychology 344
    chronology 345
psychosis 344
psychosomatic 335
psychotherapy 344
psychotic disorder 344
pteridophyte 161
Ptolemy 51
puberty 153
Public Broadcasting System (PBS)
    384
public inquiry 379
public relations (PR) 208
public school 332
public-sector borrowing requirement
    (PSBR) 214
public-sector debt repayment (PSDR)
    214
Puccini, Giacomo 297
puerperal fever 351
puffing 143
Pugin, Augustus Welby Northmore 227
Pulitzer Prize winners 266–7
pulsar 42
pulse 139
pulse-code modulation (PCM) 199
pulsed high frequency (PHF) 356
punctuated equilibrium model 149
punctuation 270
Punjabi 694
punk rock 298
pupa 154
pupil, of eye 337
puppet theatre 318
Purcell, Henry 297
purge 396
Pushkin, Aleksandr 263
put option 208
Pygmy 694
pylon 113
Pynchon, Thomas 263
pyramid 175, 223
Pyramids of Egypt 490
Pythagoras 181
Pythagoras' theorem 175

Qaddhafi, Moamer al 536
Qatar 640
Qing dynasty 241, 494
quadratic equation 176
qualitative analysis 53
quality circle 208
quality control 208
Quant, Mary 328
quantitative analysis 53
quantity theory of money 214
quantum
    mechanics 185
    theory 185
quantum chromodynamics (QCD) 190
quantum electrodynamics (QED) 190

quark 190
quarter session 379
quasar 42
Quaternary 93
Quechua 694
queens see kings and queens
Queen's Counsel 377, 379
question mark 270
Quichua 693
quicksilver 123
Quran see Koran

Rabbani, Burhanuddin 557
Rabelais, François 263
rabies 351
Rabin, Yitzhak 540, 605
Rabuka, Col Sitiveni 591
Rachmaninov, Sergei 298
Racine, Jean 324
radian 176
radiation 185
radio 199
    networks 384
radioactivity 71, 185
radiocarbon dating 27
radio galaxy 43
radioisotope 185
radionics 356
Radio Telefis Eireann (RTE) 384
radio telescope 48
radiotherapy 336
radon 125
Rafsanjani, Ali Akbar Hoshemi 603
Rafsanjani, Hojatoleslam Ali Akbar
    Hashemi 540
ragga 304
ragtime 304
raï 304
rail transport 463
    chronology 464
    highest railway bridges 112
    longest railway tunnels 114
    worst railway disasters 472
rain 104
rainbow coalition 396
rainforest 117
    tropical deforestation 120
Rainier III, Prince of Monaco 626
Rajneesh meditation 409
Rāmāyana 411
Ramos, Fidel 540, 638
Ramsay, William 76
Ranariddh, Prince Norodom 574
random access memory (RAM) 80
rangefinder 310
Raoult, François 76
rape 379
Raphael (Raffaello Sanzio) 232
Rapid Reaction Force (RRF) 477
rap music 305
Rarotonga Treaty 363
Rasmussen, Poul Nyrup 585
Rastafarianism 409
rate of reaction 71
rate of return 208
ratio 176
Raueny, Francisque 619
Ravel, Maurice 298
Rawlings, Jerry 595
Ray, Satyajit 247
RCS Editori 385

reaction 71
reactivity series 71
read-only memory (ROM) 80
Reagan, Ronald 540
Realism in art 237
recall, in politics 396
receiver 208, 379
receiver, radio 199
recession 214
reciprocal 176
reconnaissance 477
rectangle 176
recycling 125
Red Army 477
red blood cell 340
Red Crescent 372
Red Cross, The 372
Red or Dead 328
red dwarf 43
redeemable preference share 208
red giant 43
Redon, Odilon 238
redox reaction 71
red shift 46
Redstone rocket 31
reduced instruction set computer
    (RISC) 85
reduction 71
redundancy rights 379
Reed, Carol 247
Reed/Elsevier 384
Reed, Lou 305
referendum 396
reflection 187
reflex camera 310
reflexology 356
refraction 187
refrigeration 141, 143
refugee 396
reggae 305
regiment 477
Reichian therapy 356
Reinhardt, Max 324
relative atomic mass 71
relative dating 27
relativity, theory of 187
relaxation therapy 356
relief organizations 372
religion
    festivals 415–19
    holy places 414–15
    major faiths, followers of 403
    movements 409–10
    patron saints 420
    religious books 411–13
    religious figures 413–14
    religious traditions 403–9
    rites of passage 410–11
    saints' days 421–3
remand 379
remanent magnetization 96
Rembrandt van Rijn 235
remedial education 332
remission 336
remix 305
remotely piloted vehicle (RPV) 487
remote sensing 27
removable hard disc 80
Renaissance architecture 221
René, France-Albert 646
renewable resource 108, 118

Renger-Patzsch, Albert 313
Reni, Guido 235
Renoir, Jean 247
Renoir, Pierre-Auguste 238
repellent 71
replication 154
reply, right of 379
reprieve 380
reproduction (biology) 150
reptile 160
requiem 294
rescue archaeology 27
research and development (R&D) 208
reserve currency 214
resistance 187
resistivity survey 27
resonance 187
respiration 55, 145
restriction enzyme 167
resuscitation 336
retail price index (RPI) 214
retina 337
retrovirus 336
reuse 125
revaluation 213
revenge tragedy 314
revenue 208
reverse takeover 208
revolution, permanent 394
revolutions 502–5
    of 1848 503
    of 1989 505
revue 318
Reynolds, Albert 541, 605
Reynolds, Joshua 236
rhapsody 294
rheumatic fever 351
rheumatoid arthritis 346
Rhodes, Wilfred 457
rhombus 176
rhythm 294
rhythm and blues 305
rib 340
Riba Reig, Oscar 558
Ribera, José 235
ribonucleic acid (RNA) 56, 166
ribosome 166
rice 139
Richards, Gordon 457
Richards, Viv 458
Richardson, Samuel 263
Richmond, John 328
Richter scale 95
Riemann, Georg Friedrich Bernhard 181
Rietveld, Gerrit 239
rifle 487
rift valley 100
right-angled triangle 176
right ascension 46
rights issue 208
right wing 396
Rigil Kent 24
Riley, Bridget 240
Rilke, Rainer Maria 263
Rimbaud, Arthur 263
Rimsky-Korsakov, Nikolay Andreyevich 298
Ringadoo, Veerasamy 624
risk capital 209
river 100

major rivers 100
RNA see ribonucleic acid
road transport 464–6
    car chronology 465
    countries that drive on the left 466
    European cities, distances between 468–9
    UK towns, distances between 468–9
Robbins, Jerome 256
Robespierre, Maximilien 503
Robinson, Mary 541, 605
Robinson, Smokey 305
Rocard, Michel 541
rocket 31, 463
rock and roll 305
Rococo architecture 221
Rococo art 236
Rodchenko, Alexander 313
Rodin, Auguste 238
Rodnina, Irina 458
Rogers, Richard 227
Rolfing 356
Rolling Stones, the 305
Roman Catholicism 404
Romance languages 694
Roman empire
    art 230
    chronology 492
    emperors 493
Romanesque architecture 221
Romanesque art 231
Romania 640
    Christmas Revolution 505
Roman numerals 176, 181
Romano, Giulio 232
Romantic art 237
Romantic ballet 251
Romany 694
Rommel, Erwin 481
rondo 294
root 151
root crop 146
roots, in language 271
roots music 306
ROSAT satellite 31
Rossellini, Isabella 247
Rossellini, Roberto 247
Rossetti, Dante Gabriel 237
Rossini, Gioachino 298
Rosso, Giovanni Battista 233
Roth, Christian Francis 70
Rothko, Mark 240
Rouault, Georges 238
roughage 134
Rousseau, Jean-Jacques 263
Rousseau, Theodore 237
rowing 438
Royal Air Force 477
Royal British Legion 477
Royal Greenwich Observatory 49
Royal Marines 477
RU-486 see mifepristone
rubella 348, 351
Rubens, Peter Paul 235
rubeola 347
Rubik, Erno 181
rugby league 438
rugby union 438
Ruisdael, Jacob van 236
rule of law 380
rupture 349

Russia
    Russian Revolution 503
    tsars 499
Russian 694
Russian ballet 251
Russian Federation 641
Russian language 274
Russo-Japanese War 481
Ruth, Babe 458
Rutherford, Ernest 193
Rwanda 641
Ryle, Martin 51

Saami 694
Saarinen, Eero 227
Saarinen, Eliel 227
Sabah, Jabir al-Ahmad al-Jabir al- 612
Sadat, Anwar 541
Said, Qaboos bin 634
St Christopher (St Kitts) Nevis 642
Saint-Denis, Michel 324
Saint-Laurent, Yves 328
St Lucia 642
Saint-Saëns, Charles Camille 298
St Vincent and the Grenadines 643
saints
    patron 420
    saints' days 421–3
Salam, Abdus 193
Salazar, Antonio de Oliveira 541
Saleh, Ali Abdullah 669
sales promotion 209
Salinas de Gortiari, Carlos 541
Salinger, J D 263
Saloth Sar 540
salsa 305
salt 71, 139
SALT see Strategic Arms Limitation Talks
saltation 149
salvage archaeology 27
Salyut space station 31
Samoa, Western 643
Sanchez de Lozado, Gonzalo 569
sanction 396
sand 100
Sander, August 313
Sandiford, Erskine Lloyd 565
Sangheli, Andre 625
San Marino 644
Sanskrit 274
Sant'Elia, Antonio 227
Santer, Jacques 618
Santos, José Eduardo dos 559
São Tomé e Príncipe 644
Sarney, José 541
Sartre, Jean-Paul 263
satellite 31, 38
    communications 29, 196
    direct broadcast 197
    planetary 39
satellite town 223
saturated compound 65
Saturn 39
Saturn rocket 31
sauce 139
Saudi Arabia 645
Save the Children Fund 372
savings 214
Sawchuk, Terry 458

Say's law 214
scabies 351
scalar quantity 176
scale, in music 294
Scalfaro, Oscar Luigi 606
scarp and dip 100
Scheele, Karl Wilhelm 76
scherzo 294
Schiaparelli, Giovanni Virginio 51
Schiller, Johann Christoph Friedrich
 von 324
Schinkel, Karl Friedrich 227
schizophrenia 344
Schlüter, Poul Holmskov 541
Schmidt, Helmut 541
Schmidt Telescope 49
Schmitt-Rotluff, Karl 239
Schnabel, Julian 241
Schoenberg, Arnold 298
School of Fontainebleau 235
Schrödinger, Erwin 193
Schubert, Franz 298
Schuessler, W H 355
Schultz, Johannes 355
Schumann, Robert 298
Schwarzkopf, H Norman 482
sciatica 351
Scientology 409
Scopas 230
Scorsese, Martin 247
Scotland, Kings and Queens of 499
Scots law 380
Scott, George Gilbert 227
Scott, Walter 263
Scottish Natural Heritage 129
scrambling circuit 199
scrapie 146
screen, computer 81
screening 336
scrip issue 209
Scudamore, Peter 458
Scud missile 487
scythe 146
Seaborg, Glenn Theodore 76
Sea Dayak 690
seafloor spreading 93
seas and oceans 105
sea transport 466–7
 chronology 467
secondary education 332
Secretariat (UN) 365
Securities and Exchange Commission
 (SEC) 217
Securities and Investment Board 217
Security Council (UN) 365
sediment 100
seed 154
seed drill 146
Seignoret, Clarence 586
Seles, Monica 458
self-sufficiency 214
semicircle 168
semicolon 270
semiconductor 88, 188
semi-variable cost 205
Semtex 487
Senegal 645
senile dementia 344, 348
Senna, Ayrton 458
septicaemia 351
sequencing 167

sequestrator 209
Serb 694
Serbo-Croatian 694
serenade 294
seriation 27
Serlio, Sebastiano 227
services, armed 477
set, in mathematics 176
settlement out of court 380
Seurat, Georges 238
Sevastopol 482
Seventh Day Adventist 409
Seven Wonders of the World 490
Severini, Gino 239
sewage disposal 125
sexual reproduction 150
Seychelles 646
Seyfert galaxy 43
Shakespeare, William 263, 324
 plays 324
Shamir, Yitzhak 541
Shankara 414
Shapley, Harlow 52
shareholder 209
Shari'a 406
Sharma, Shankar Dayal 602
Shaw, George Bernard 324
Shaw, Richard Norman 227
sheep 148
Shelley, Percy Bysshe 263
shellfish 139
Shepard, Alan Bartlett 52
Shepard, Sam 324
Sheridan, Richard Brinsley 325
sheriff 380
Shevardnadze, Edvard 541, 594
Shiah Muslims 406
shiatsu 356
Shi Ching 411
shield, in earth science 94
Shi'ite Muslims 406
Shilton, Peter 458
shingles 351
Shinto 407–8
shinty 439
ship 466–7
ship canals 113
shock 351
Shockley, William 193
Shoemaker, Willie 458
Shona 694
short takeoff and landing (STOL) craft
 461
Shostakovich, Dmitry 298
Showa period 242
show trial 380
Shushkevich, Stanislav 541, 566
shuttle diplomacy 396
sial 96
Sibelius, Jean 298
sick building syndrome 223
sickle-cell disease 351
Siddhanta 412
sidereal period 46
Siding Spring Mountain 49
Sierra Leone 646
signal-to-noise ratio 199
significant figures 176
sign language, English and American
 278
Sigua, Tengiz 594

Sihanouk, Norodom 541, 574
Sikhism 408, 413
 festivals 416–17
 rites 410, 411
silage 148
silicon 61
silicon chip 83, 86
Silva, Anibal Cavaco 639
silver 61
sima 96
Simmonds, Kennedy 642
Simon, (Marvin) Neil 325
Simon, Paul 305
simple plurality 397
simulation 79
simultaneous equation 176
Sinai 482
Sinan 227
Sinatra, Frank 305
Sindhi 695
sine 177
Singapore 647
Singer, Isaac Bashevis 263
Single European Act (1986) 129
single-lens reflex (SLR) 304
single-sideband transmission 199
single transferable vote 397
singularity, in astronomy 46
Sinhalese 695
Sino-Japanese Wars 483
Sino-Tibetan languages 695
sinusitis 351
Siphandon, General Khamtay 614
SI prefixes 5, 182
Siskind, Aaron 313
Sisley, Alfred 238
site 28
site catchment analysis (SCA) 28
site exploration territory (SET) 28
site of special scientific interest (SSSI)
 129
SI units 4–5, 188
Six-Day War 479
skating 439
skeleton 161
skiing 440
 water 444
skull 340
Skylab, space station 31
skyscraper 223
slander 380
slash and burn 125
Slav 695
Slavonic languages 695
Slezevicius, Adolfas 618
Slovak Republic 647
Slovene 695
Slovenia 648
SLR, in photography 310
slump 214
slurry 125
Sluter, Claus 233
small arms 475, 487
smart weapons 488
Smetana, Bedrich 298
Smirke, Robert 227
Smith, David 240
Smith, Ian 541
Smith, Paul 328
Smiths, the 305
Smithson, Alison 227

Smithson, Peter 227
smoking, food 143
Snegur, Mircea 625
snooker 440
Soane, John 227
Soares, Mario Alberto Nobre Lopes 541, 639
Sobers, Gary 459
soca 305
soccer 450
social anthropology 22
social costs and benefits 214
social democracy 392
socialism 393
Soddy, Frederick 76
sodium chloride 126
softball 440
soft drink 134
software 85
Soglo, Nicéphore 568
soil 100
    erosion 126
Soil Association 129
Sōka Gakkai 404
sol 68
solar
    eclipse 36, 37
    energy 108
    flare 39
    wind 39
Solar System 34–40
    definition 39
solicitor 380
solid-state circuit 88
Solomon Islands 649
solstice 46
solute 71
solution 68, 71
solvency 209
solvent 72
Solzhenitsyn, Alexander 263
Somalia 649
sonata 294
sondage 28
Sondheim, Stephen 305
Song dynasty 241
Sophocles 325
soprano 294
Sotho 695
soul music 305
sound 188
sound therapy 359
South Africa 650
    presidents 546
    prime ministers 546
South African Astronomical Observatory 49
South African Development Coordination Conference (SADCC) 361
South America 555
    historical time charts 483–29, 555
    indigenous religions 408
South Asian Association for Regional Cooperation 363
Southeast Asia Treaty Organization (SEATO) 363
Southern African Development Coordination Conference (SADCC) 363
South Pacific Bureau for Economic Cooperation (SPEC) 363
South Pacific Commission (SPC) 363

South Pacific Forum (SPF) 363
sovereigns see emperors; kings and queens; tsars
sovereignty 396
Soviet Army 477
Sow, Abdoulaye Sekou 622
Soyinka, Wole 263
Soyuz 32
space adaptation syndrome 32
space exploration 29–34
    space flight chronology 30
    space probe chronology 32
    main launches 33
space-frame 113
Spacelab, space station 32
space probe 32
space shuttle 32
space sickness 32
space station 33
space suit 34
Spain 651
    art in 233, 235, 236
    rulers 498
spastic 336
Special Air Service (SAS) 477
special education 332
species 150
speckle interferometry 46
Spector, Phil 305
spectrographic analysis 28
spectroscopy 188
spectrum 188
speech recognition 79
speed
    of animals 149
    in mathematics 177
Speer, Albert 227
spelling errors, common 270
Spenser, Edmund 263
sperm 154
spermatozoon 154
spermicide 336
sphere 177
spice 139
spicules, solar 23
Spielberg, Steven 247
spin 191
spina bifida 351
spinal cord 340
spirit 139
spiritual healing 359
Spitz, Mark Andrew 459
spore 154
sport
    biographies 445–59
    Commonwealth Games, sites of 460
    events and records 424–45
    Olympic Games, sites of summer 460
spreadsheet 79, 209
Springsteen, Bruce 305
Sputnik 34
square root 177
squash, in sport 441
Sri Lanka 651
stadium rock 305
stag, in business 209
stagflation 215
stakeholder 209
stalactite 100
stalagmite 100
Stalingrad 483

standard deviation 177
standard model 191
Standard and Poor's Stock Price Index 209
standard temperature and pressure (STP) 72
Stanislavsky, Konstantin Sergeivich 325
star cluster 43
starlight, aberration of 29
stars 40–3
    brightest stars 42
START see Strategic Arms Reduction Talks
Star Wars 477
state 396
statement, in education 332
states of matter 188
static random-access memory (SRAM) 88
statics 188
statistics 177
steady-state theory 43
stealth technology 488
steel band 306
Steen, Jan 236
Steichen, Edward 313
Stein, Peter 325
Steinbeck, John 264
Stendhal 264
step-trenching 28
sterilization 336
Sternberg, Josef von 247
Sterne, Laurence 264
steroid 56, 354
sterol 56
Stevenson, Robert Louis 264
Stewart, Jackie 459
Stieglitz, Alfred 314
still-life painting 236
Stirling, James 227
stock 139
stock exchange 215
Stockhausen, Karlheinz 298
stocks and shares 209
stomach 340
Stone Age 28
Stoppard, Tom 325
Storey, Helen 328
Strand, Paul 314
Strasberg, Lee 325
Strasser, Capt Valentine 646
Strategic Arms Limitation Talks (SALT) 479
Strategic Arms Reduction Talks (START) 479
Strategic Defense Initiative (SDI) 477
strategy, military 478
stratigraphy 28, 93
Strauss, Johann 298
Strauss, Richard 298
Stravinsky, Igor 298
streaming 332
strength of acids and bases 72
stress 344
stress and strain, of materials 188
Strindberg, August 325
Stroessner, Alfredo 541
Stroheim, Erich von 247
stroke 352
stromatolite 93

structural formula 69
Struve, Friedrich Georg Wilhelm 52
Stubbs, George 236
student finance 332
Sturges, Preston 247
sublimation 72
sub-machine gun 487
submarine 467, 478
submarine launched ballistic missile
    (SLBM) 477
subpoena 380
subscription certificate 209
subsistence farming 148
substrate 56
Su Ching 411
sucrose 56, 139
Sudan 652
sudden infant death syndrome (SIDS)
    347
Sufism 426
sugar 56, 139
Suharto, Raden 542
Suharto, T N J 602
suite 294
Sukarno, Achmed 542
Sullivan, Louis Henry 227
sulphur 61
sulphuric acid 61
Sumerian art 229
summary offences 379
summit 396
summit conference 396
summons 380
Sumner, James 76
Sun, the 39
    see also solar
Sundanese 695
Sunni Muslims 406
sunspot 39
Sun Yat-sen 503
Sun Zhong Shan 503
supercomputer 77
superheterodyne receiver 196
superior planet 39
supernova 43
superphosphate 62
Super Realism 240
superstring theory 191
supersymmetry 191
supply curve 209
suprarenal gland 336
Suprematism 239
Supreme Headquarters Allied Powers
    Europe (SHAPE) 477
Supremes, the 306
surface tension 188
surfactant 72
surfing 441
Surinam 653
Surrealism 239
Survival International 372
sustained-yield cropping 126
Svedberg, Theodor 76
Swahili 695
Swaziland 653
Sweden 654
sweetener, artificial 139
sweets 140
Swift, Jonathan 264
swimming 441
swing music 306

Switzerland 655
SWOT analysis 209
Symbolism 238
symphonic poem 296
symphony 296
syncline 94, 100
syncopation 306
Synge, J M 325
synodic period 47
syphilis 352
Syria 655
System X 199
Szent-Görgyi, Albert 76

table tennis 442
Tabone, Vincent 622
tactical air-to-surface missile (TASM)
    488
tactics, military 478
Tadzhik 694
Tagalog 695
tagging, electronic 380
Tagore, Rabindranath 264
Taiwan 656
Tajik 695
Tajikistan 656
takeover 209
Talbot, William Henry Fox 314
tallest structures 229
Talmud 407, 412
Tamashek 695
Tambo, Oliver 542
Tamil 695
Tamil Tigers 695
Tang dynasty 241
Tange, Kenzo 227
tangent 177
tank 477
Tanzania 657
Taoism 408, 411
Tao Te Ching 411
tap dancing 254
Tarkovsky, Andrei 247
Tatar 695
Tati, Jacques 247
Tatlin, Vladimir 239
tau 191
Taufa'ahau Tupou IV, King 659
tautomerism 72
tax-exempt special savings account
    (TESSA) 209
Taya, Maaouia Ould Sid Ahmed 623
TB see tuberculosis
Tchaikovsky, Pyotr Il'yich 298
tea 140
teacher training 333
Teannaki, Teatao 611
tectonic lake 98
tectonics 93
tektite 39
telecommunications 196–201
    chronology 198
telefax 197
telephone 199
    cellular 196
    tapping 380
telephoto lens 311
telescopes and observatories 47–9
teletext 199
television 199–201
    chronology 200

digital 197
    high-definition (HDTV) 197
    networks 384
telpher 490
Telstar, satellite 34
Telugu 695
temperature 188
temperature scales 3
Temple of Artemis 490
tempo 296
tenant farming 148
Teng Hsiao-ping 533
tennis, lawn 442
Tennyson, Alfred 264
tenor 296
tension, in physics 188
Tereshchenko, Sergey 609
Tereshkova, Valentina Vladimirovna 52
Ter-Petrossian, Levon 561
terrestrial planets 22
Territorial Army 395, 475, 478
territorial waters 378
terrorism 396
Terry, John Quinlan 227
Tertiary 93
tertiary college 333
testis 340
tetanus 352
tetrachloromethane 65
tetrahedron 177
Thackeray, William Makepeace 264
Thai 695
Thailand 658
Thales 181
thanatology 359
Thant, U 542
Tharp, Twyla 256
Thatcher, Margaret 542
Thatcherism 393
thaumatrope 311
theatre 315–26
    awards 319
    biographies 319–26
    chronology 316–17
    genres 315–19
theatre-in-the-round 319
theft 380
theocracy 393
Theravāda Buddhism 403
thermionics 88
thermodynamics 188
thermoluminescence 28
Thiam, Habib 645
thin-section analysis 28
Third Age 333
Thompson, Daley 459
Thomson, J J 193
Three Age System 28
threshing 148
throat 340
thrombosis 352
thrush 352
thunderstorm 104
thyristor 88
thyroid 340
Tibetan 695
tidal power station 108
tides 103
Tiepolo, Giovanni Battista 236
Tigré 696
Tigrinya 695

Timakata, Fred 667
timbre 296
Time-Warner 385
time zones and relative times 10
Tinguely, Jean 240
Tintoretto, Jacopo 233
Tipitaka 411
Tirpitz, Alfred von 483
Tiselius, Arne 76
Titan, moon 39
Titan rocket 34
Titian 233
Tito (Josip Broz) 542
Todd, Alexander, Baron Todd 76
Togo 658
Tokugawa period 242
Tol Saut 540
Tolstoy, Leo Nikolaievich 264
Tombaugh, Clyde (William) 52
Tomb of Mausolus 490
tomography 336
tonality 296
Tonga 659
tongue 340
Tonkin Gulf Incident 483
topography 100
topology 177
topsoil 148
Torah 407, 412
tornado 104
torpedo 488
tort 380
Torvill, Jayne 459
totalitarianism 393
total war 478
touch screen 81
Toulouse-Lautrec, Henri de 238
town planning 224
toxic shock syndrome 352
toxin 335
trace element analysis 28
trace minerals 130
trachea 340
tractor 148
trade cycle 215
trademark 203
trade union 396
trade wind 104
trading account 209
tragedy 319
trampolining 443
tramway 463
transcendental meditation 409
transcription 166
transfer orbit 47
transfusion 336
transgenic organism 167
transistor 88
transistor-transistor logic (TTL) 84
transit, in astronomy 47
translation, in cells 166
transparency 311
transplant 336
transport 461–72
transputer 88
transuranic (transuranium) elements
    59, 62
trapezium 177
trauma 336
travel sickness 352
treason 380

treasure trove 380
Treasury bill 215
treaties, peace 478–9
trespass 380
trial 380
triangle 177
Triassic 93
tribunal 380
tricarboxylic acid cycle 55
trigonometry 177
Trinidad and Tobago 659
triode 88
Tripitaka 411
triple bond 72
trolleybus 490
tropical deforestation 111
tropical diseases 352
tropics 100
tropopause 104
troposphere 104
Trotsky, Leon 504
Trotskyism 393
Trovoada, Miguel 644
Trudeau, Pierre 542
Truffaut, François 247
Trujillo, Cesar Gaviria 580
Truman, Harry 542
trust 381
Trusteeship Council (UN) 365
truth table 87
tsars of Russia 499
tsunami 104
Tswana 696
Tuareg 696
tuberculosis (TB) 352
Tudjman, Franjo 582
tumour 336
Tunisia 660
tunnel 113
    Channel 114, 115
    longest railway tunnels 114
turbine 108
Turgenev, Ivan 264
Turing, Alan Mathison 181
Turkey 660
Turkish language 274
Turkmenistan 661
Turkoman 696
Turner, Joseph Mallord William 237
turnover 209
Tuscan order 225
Tutsi 696
Tutu, Desmond 542
Tuvalu 661
Twa 696
Twain, Mark 264
twin-lens reflex (TLR) camera 311
typhoon 103
typology 28
tyre 490
Tyson, Mike 459
Tzara, Tristan 239

U-2 489
U-boat 489
Uccello, Paolo 232
Uganda 662
Uigur 696
Ukraine 662
    Revolution 505
Ukrainian 696

Ulbricht, Walter 542
ultraheat treatment (UHT) of food 143
ultrasonography 336
ultrasound 188, 336
Ulysses, space probe 34
uncertainty principle 191
uncommitted logic array (ULA) 88
underwater reconnaissance 28
unemployment 215
Unification Church (Moonies) 409
unilateralism 397
Union of Socialist Soviet Republics
    (USSR), leaders of 546
Unitarianism 409
United Arab Emirates (UAE) 663
United Kingdom Infrared Telescope
    (UKIRT) 49
United Kingdom (UK) 664
    central government 397–400
    prime ministers 543
    sovereigns 499–500
United Nations (UN) 365–70
    Centre for Human Settlements
        (UNCHS) 367
    charter 365
    Children's Emergency Fund
        (UNICEF) 365, 367
    Conference on Trade and Develop-
        ment (UNCTAD) 367
    Development Programme (UNDP)
        367, 369
    Disaster Relief Coordinator
        (UNDRO) 367
    Economic and Social Council 366
    Educational, Scientific and Cultural
        Organisation (UNESCO) 367
    Environmental Programme (UNEP)
        367
    Food and Agriculture Organization
        (FAO) 366
    Fund for Population Activities
        (UNFPA) 367
    General Assembly 365
    High Commissioner for Refugees
        (UNHCR) 367
    Institute for Training and Research
        (UNITAR) 367
    International Court of Justice 366
    members 368–9
    peacekeeping operations 370
    Research Institute for Social Devel-
        opment (UNRISD) 367
    Secretariat 366
    Secretary Generals 366
    Security Council 365
    Special Fund 365
    Trusteeship Council 366
United Newspapers 385
United States of America (USA) 665
    presidents 520
    states 680–1
United States Naval Observatory 49
unit trust 209
universal indicator 72
Universal Postal Union (UPU) 367
universal time (UT) 47
Universe, the 40–3
university 333
Unix 85
unleaded petrol 126
unlisted securities market (USM) 215

Unrepresented Nations' and Peoples' Organization (UNPO) 363
unsaturated compound 65
uranium 62
Uranus 39
urban guerrilla 475
urban population growth 675
urban renewal 224
Urdu language 696
urea 56
Urey, Harold Clayton 76
Uruguay 666
user interface 85
usewear analysis 8
uterus 341
Uwilingiyimana 642
Uzbek 696
Uzbekistan 667

Vacaroiu, Nicolai 640
vaccine 336
Vaea, Baron 659
vagina 341
valency 72
Valentic, Nikica 582
Valentino, Mario 328
value added 202
value-added tax (VAT) 205
valve 89
Van Allen, James 52
Vanbrugh, John 227
van der Goes, Hugo 233
van Doesburg, Theo 239
van Dyck, Anthony 236
Vane, John 76
van Eyck, Jan 233
van Gogh, Vincent 238
Vanguard 34
Vanuatu 667
Varanasi 415
Varèse, Edgard 299
variable 178
variable star 43
variance 178
variation, life sciences 150
varicella 347
varicose veins 352
varicosis 352
Vasarely, Victor 240
Vasari, Giorgio 233
vase painting, Greek 230
Vatican City State 668
vault 224
vector quantity 178
Veda 405, 411
Vedda 696
Vega, Lope Felix de 325
vegetable 140
Velasquez, Diego Rodriguez de Silva 235
velocity 178
Velvet Underground, the 306
Venetiaan, Ronald 653
Venezuela 668
Venice Film Festival 248
Venn diagram 178
venture capital 209
Venturi, Robert 227
Venus 39
verb 270
Verdi, Giuseppe 299

verdict 381
Verdun, Battle of 483
Verlaine, Paul 264
Vermeer, Jan 236
Veronese 233
Verrocchio, Andrea del 232
Versace, Gianni 329
Versailles, Treaty of 479
vertebrates 158–61
vertex 178
vertical takeoff and landing craft (VTOL) 461, 486, 489
Very Large Array (VLA) 49
very large-scale integration (VLSI) 89
veto 397
vibrato 296
video game 78
video technology 196–201
    camera 201
    disc 201
    interactive video 198
    tape recorder (VTR) 201
videotext 201
Viega, Carlos 576
Vieira, João Bernardo 598
Vietnam 669
Vietnamese 147
Vietnam War 483
viewdata 201
viewer protection 392
Vigo, Jean 247
Viking probes 34
Villon, François 264
vinegar 140
Virgil 264
viroids 153
virtual memory 85
virtual reality 79
virus 164
virus, computer 85
Visconti, Luchino 247
viscosity 188
visible trade 215
Visnews 384
visual display unit (VDU) 81
visualization 359
vitalistic medicine 359
vitamin 56, 136
Vitruvius 227
Vivaldi, Antonio 299
Vlaminck, Maurice de 238
vocational education 333
voice input 79
Vokshod, spacecraft 34
volcanic island 98
volcano 96
    major eruptions 96
Volgograd 483
volleyball 443
Volta, Alessandro 193
voltage amplifier 89
Voltaire, François-Marie Arouet 264
volume 178
Voluntary Service Overseas (VSO) 372
vomiting 352
Von Neumann, John 181
Vostok, spacecraft 34
vote 397
Vo Van Kiet 669
Voyager probes 34

Voysey, Charles Francis Annesley 227
Vranitzky, Franz 542, 563
Vuillard, Edouard 238

Wagner, Otto 227
Wagner, Richard 299
Wajda, Andrzej 248
Waldheim, Kurt 542
Waldsterben 126
Walesa, Lech 542, 638
Walker, Alice 264
Wangchuk, Jigme Singye 568
war 478
ward of court 381
warfare 473–89
    civil wars 485–6
    notable naval battles 483
warfarin 354
Warhol, Andy 240
wars 479–86
Warsaw Pact 363
warship 478
War on Want 372
Wasmosy, Juan Carlos 636
waste and waste disposal 126
water 62, 118
    mill 110
    pollution 127
    scarcity 118
waterfall 100
    major waterfalls 101
Waterhouse, Alfred 228
water polo 444
water skiing 444
water-soluble 44
water table 100
waterways 115
Watt, James 193
Watteau, Jean-Antoine 236
wave, in physics 188
wave power 110
Wayang Kulit 318
weakon 191
weapons 486–9
weathering 101
Webb, Philip (Speakman) 228
Webster, John 325
wedding anniversaries 19
Wedekind, Frank 325
weedkiller 127
weight 188
weightlessness 34
weightlifting 444
Weinberg, Steven 193
Weizman, Ezer 605
Weizsäcker, Richard von 594
welfare state 397
Welles, Orson 248
Welsh language 274
Western European Union (WEU) 363
Weston, Edward 314
Westwood, Vivienne 329
wetland 118
whaling 127
Wharton, Edith 264
what you see is what you get (WYSIWYG) 85
white dwarf 43
white knight 209
Whitman, Walter 265
whooping cough 352

Wickremasinghe, Ranil 651
wide-angle lens 311
wide area network 85
Wiener, Norbert 181
Wilde, Oscar 325
Wilder, Thornton 325
wilderness 118
wildlife trade 126, 127
will 381
Williams, Tennessee 325
Wilson, Harold 542
Wilson, Robert 326
WIMP 82
wind 104
windmill 110
window, in computing 85
windpipe 340
wind turbine 110
wine 140
    fortified 141
Wingti, Paias 636
withdrawal 478
witness 381
Witt, Katarina 459
Wöhler, Friedrich 76
Wolof 696
women's services 478
Woolcott, Marion Post 314
Woolf, Virginia 265
Woosnam, Ian 459
word, in computing 85
word processing 79
Wordsworth, William 265
work, in physics 188
work experience 333
working capital 209
working capital ratio 204
workstation 80
World Bank 217, 366
World Conservation Monitoring Centre
    129
World Council of Churches (WCC) 363
World Food Council (WFC) 367
World Food Programme (WFP) 367
World Health Organisation (WHO) 367

World Intellectual Property Organisa-
    tion (WIPO) 367
world leaders 530–43
World Meteorological Organisation
    (WMO) 369
world music 306
World War I 483
    chronology 482
World War II 484
    chronology 484
World Wide Fund for Nature (WWF)
    129
Worldwide Television News 384
Wren, Sir Christopher 228
wrestling 444
Wright, Frank Lloyd 228
Wright, Joseph 236
writ 381
Writers to the Signet 383

Xhosa 696
X-ray 336
    diffraction analysis 28
    fluorescence spectrometry (XRF) 28

yachting 445
Yalta Conference 479
Yamamoto, Yohji 329
Yanamamo 696
Yao 696
Yayoi period 242
yeast artificial chromosome (YAC) 167
Yeats, William Butler 265
Yeltsin, Boris 542, 641
Yemen 669
Yerkes Observatory 49
Yhombi-Opango, Jacques-Joachim 581
Yi 696
yield 209
yoghurt 141
Yom Kippur War 479
Yoruba 696
Young, Neil 307
young offender institution 381, 383
Youth Training Scheme 333

Ypres 484
Yugoslavia 670
    Revolution 505

Zabanga, Mobutu Sese Seko Kuku
    Ngbendu wa 671
Zafy, Albert 619
Zaire 671
Zambia 671
Zarathustra 409, 414
Zayed bin al-Nahayan, Sheik Sultan of
    Abu Dhabi 663
Zelenchukskaya 49
Zenawi, Meles 590
Zen Buddhism 403, 404
Zendavesta 409
zenith 47
zero-based budgeting 209
Zhao Ziyang 543
Zhelev, Zhelyu 543, 572
Zhivkov, Todor 543
Zhukov, Georgi Konstantinovich 486
Zia, Begum Khaleda 565
Zia ul-Haq, Mohammad 543
zidovudine (AZT) 354
Ziegler, Karl 76
Zimbabwe 672
zodiac 47
    signs of 20
zodiacal light 40
zoetrope 311
Zola, Emile Edouard Charles Antoine
    266
zone system, in photography 311
zone therapy 359
zooarchaeology 407
zoology 155
zoom lens 311
Zoroaster 409, 414
Zoroastrianism 409
Z particle 191
Zulu 696
Zurbarán, Francisco 235
zwitterion 72
zydeco 307